122.00

D0894581

FOR REFERENCE

Do Not Take

From This Room

Contemporary Authors®

Explore your options!
Gale databases offered in
a variety of formats

DISKETTE/MAGNETIC TAPE

Many Gale databases are available
on diskette or magnetic tape, allowing systemwide access to your
most-used information sources
through existing computer systems.
Data can be delivered on a variety
of mediums (DOS formatted
diskette, 9-track tape, 8mm data
tape) and in industry-standard
formats (comma-delimited, tagged,
fixed-field). Retrieval software is
also available with many of Gale's
databases that allows you to search,
display, print and download the data

ONLINE

For your convenience, many Gale
databases are available through
popular online services, including
DIALOG, NEXIS (Mead Data
Central), Data-Star, Orbit, Questel,
OCLC, I/Plus and HRIN.

CD-ROM

A variety of Gale titles is available
on CD-ROM, offering maximum flex-
ibility and powerful search software.

The information in this Gale
publication is also available in some
or all of the formats described here.
Your Customer Service Representative
will be happy to fill you in.

For information, call

GALE

Gale Research Inc.
1 - 8 0 0 - 8 7 7 - G A L E

ISSN 0275-7176

Contemporary Authors®

A Bio-Bibliographical Guide to Current Writers in Fiction, General Nonfiction, Poetry, Journalism, Drama, Motion Pictures, Television, and Other Fields

KATHLEEN J. EDGAR
Editor

David M. Galens
Scot Peacock
Associate Editors

volume **146**

 **Gale Research Inc.**

An International Thomson Publishing Company

I(T)P

NEW YORK • LONDON • BONN • BOSTON • DETROIT • MADRID
MELBOURNE • MEXICO CITY • PARIS • SINGAPORE • TOKYO
TORONTO • WASHINGTON • ALBANY NY • BELMONT CA • CINCINNATI OH

STAFF

Kathleen J. Edgar, *Editor, Original Volumes*

Pamela W. Aue, David M. Galens, Thomas Ligotti, Scot Peacock, Lynn M. Spampinato, Brandon Trenz,
Associate Editors

Carol A. Brennan, Mary Gillis, Nancy Godinez, Josh Henkin, Jeanne M. Lesinski, Michelle M. Motowski,
Les Stone, Arlene True, and Elizabeth Wenning, *Sketchwriters*

Joann Cerrito and Terrie M. Rooney, *Contributing Editors*

Roger Matuz, *Managing Editor*

Victoria B. Cariappa, *Research Manager*

Andrew Guy Malonis and Barbara McNeil, *Research Specialists*

Frank Vincent Castronova, Eva Marie Felts, and Norma Sawaya,
Research Associates

Amy Terese Steel and Amy Beth Wieczorek,
Research Assistants

∞ ™ This book is printed on acid-free paper that meets the minimum requirements
of American National Standard for Information Sciences-
Permanence Paper for Printed Library Materials, ANSI Z39.48-1984.

Library of Congress Catalog Card Number 62-52046
ISBN 0-8103-5696-1
ISSN 0010-7468

Printed in the United States of America

I(T)P™ Gale Research Inc., an International Thomson Publishing Company.
ITP logo is a trademark under license.

10 9 8 7 6 5 4 3 2 1

Contents

Indexing note: All *Contemporary Authors* entries are indexed in
the *Contemporary Authors* cumulative index, which is published
separately and distributed with even-numbered *Contemporary
Authors* original volumes and odd-numbered *Contemporary
Authors New Revision Series* volumes.

**As always, the most recent *Contemporary Authors* cumulative
index continues to be the user's guide to the location of an
individual author's listing.**

Contemporary Authors
was named an
"Outstanding
Reference Source" *by*
the American Library
Association Reference
and Adult Services
Division after its 1962
inception.
In 1985 it was listed by
the same organization
as one of the
twenty-five most
distinguished reference
titles published in the
past twenty-five years.

Preface

Contemporary Authors (*CA*) provides information on approximately 100,000 writers in a wide range of media, including:

- Current writers of fiction, nonfiction, poetry, and drama whose works have been issued by commercial publishers, risk publishers, or university presses (authors whose books have been published only by known vanity or author-subsidized firms are ordinarily not included)

- Prominent print and broadcast journalists, editors, photojournalists, syndicated cartoonists, screenwriters, television scriptwriters, and other media people

- Authors who write in languages other than English, provided their works have been published in the United States or translated into English

- Literary greats of the early twentieth century whose works are popular in today's high school and college curriculums and continue to elicit critical attention

A *CA* listing entails no charge or obligation. Authors are included on the basis of the above criteria and their interest to *CA* users. Sources of potential listees include trade periodicals, publisher's catalogs, librarians, and other users.

How to Get the Most out of *CA*: Use the Index

The key to locating an author's most recent entry is the *CA* cumulative index, which is published separately and distributed with even-numbered original volumes and odd-numbered revision volumes. It provides access to *all* entries in *CA* and *Contemporary Authors New Revision Series* (*CANR*). Always consult the latest index to find an author's most recent entry.

For the convenience of users, the *CA* cumulative index also includes references to all entries in these Gale literary series: *Authors and Artists for Young Adults, Authors in the News, Bestsellers, Black Literature Criticism, Black Writers, Children's Literature Review, Concise Dictionary of American Literary Biography, Concise Dictionary of British Literary Biography, Contemporary Authors Autobiography Series, Contemporary Authors Bibliographical Series, Contemporary Literary Criticism, Dictionary of Literary Biography, Dictionary of Literary Biography Documentary Series, Dictionary of Literary Biography Yearbook, DISCovering Authors, Drama Criticism, Hispanic Literature Criticism, Hispanic Writers, Junior DISCovering Authors, Major Authors and Illustrators for Children and Young Adults, Major 20th-Century Writers, Native North American Literature, Poetry Criticism, Short Story Criticism, Something about the Author, Something about the Author Autobiography Series, Twentieth-Century Literary Criticism, World Literature Criticism,* and *Yesterday's Authors of Books for Children.*

A Sample Index Entry:

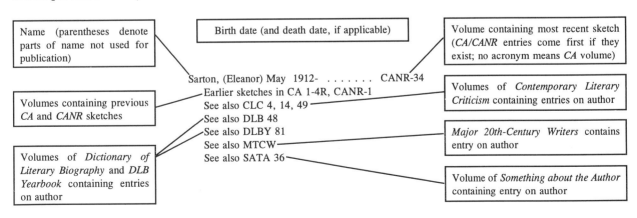

vii

How Are Entries Compiled?

The editors make every effort to secure new information directly from the authors; listees' responses to our questionnaires and query letters provide most of the information featured in *CA*. For deceased writers, or those who fail to reply to requests for data, we consult other reliable biographical sources, such as those indexed in Gale's *Biography and Genealogy Master Index*, and bibliographical sources, including *National Union Catalog, LC MARC*, and *British National Bibliography*. Further details come from published interviews, feature stories, and book reviews, and often the authors' publishers supply material.

An asterisk (∗) at the end of a sketch indicates that the listing has been compiled from secondary sources believed to be reliable but has not been personally verified for this edition by the author sketched.

What Kinds of Information Does an Entry Provide?

Sketches in *CA* contain the following biographical and bibliographical information:

- **Entry heading:** the most complete form of author's name, plus any pseudonyms or name variations used for writing

- **Personal information:** author's date and place of birth, family data, educational background, political and religious affiliations, and hobbies and leisure interests

- **Addresses:** author's home, office, or agent's addresses as available

- **Career summary:** name of employer, position, and dates held for each career post; resume of other vocational achievements; military service

- **Membership information:** professional, civic, and other association memberships and any official posts held

- **Awards and honors:** military and civic citations, major prizes and nominations, fellowships, grants, and honorary degrees

- **Writings:** a comprehensive, chronological list of titles, publishers, dates of original publication and revised editions, and production information for plays, television scripts, and screenplays

- **Adaptations:** a list of films, plays, and other media which have been adapted from the author's work

- **Work in progress:** current or planned projects, with dates of completion and/or publication, and expected publisher, when known

- **Sidelights:** a biographical portrait of the author's development; information about the critical reception of the author's works; revealing comments, often by the author, on personal interests, aspirations, motivations, and thoughts on writing

- **Biographical and critical sources:** a list of books and periodicals in which additional information on an author's life and/or writings appears

Obituary Notices in *CA* provide date and place of birth as well as death information about authors whose full-length sketches appeared in the series before their deaths. These entries also summarize the authors' careers and writings and list other sources of biographical and death information.

Related Titles in the *CA* Series

Contemporary Authors Autobiography Series complements *CA* original and revised volumes with specially commissioned autobiographical essays by important current authors, illustrated with personal photographs they provide. Common topics include their motivations for writing, the people and experiences that shaped their careers, the rewards they derive from their work, and their impressions of the current literary scene.

Contemporary Authors Bibliographical Series surveys writings by and about important American authors since World War II. Each volume concentrates on a specific genre and features approximately ten writers; entries list works written by and about the author and contain a bibliographical essay discussing the merits and deficiencies of major critical and scholarly studies in detail.

Available in Electronic Formats

CD-ROM. Full-text bio-bibliographic entries from the entire *CA* series, covering approximately 100,000 writers, are available on CD-ROM through lease and purchase plans. The disc combines entries from the *CA, CANR,* and *Contemporary Authors Permanent Series* (*CAP*) print series to provide the most recent author listing. It can be searched by name, title, subject/genre, personal data, and by using boolean logic. The disc will be updated every six months. For more information, call 1-800-877-GALE.

Online. The *Contemporary Authors* database will be made available online to libraries and their patrons through various online public access catalog (OPAC) vendors. Currently, *CA* is offered through Dynix, Innovative Interfaces, Inc., and The Library Corporation. More OPAC vendor offerings will follow soon.

Magnetic Tape. *CA* is available for licensing on magnetic tape in a fielded format. Either the complete database or a custom selection of entries may be ordered. The database will be available for internal data processing and nonpublishing purposes only. For more information, call 1-800-877-GALE.

Suggestions Are Welcome

The editors welcome comments and suggestions from users on any aspects of the *CA* series. If readers would like to recommend authors whose entries should appear in future volumes of the series, they are cordially invited to write: The Editors, *Contemporary Authors,* 835 Penobscot Bldg., Detroit, MI 48226-4094; call toll-free at 1-800-347-GALE; or fax to 1-313-961-6599.

CA Numbering System and Volume Update Chart

Occasionally questions arise about the *CA* numbering system and which volumes, if any, can be discarded. Despite numbers like "29-32R," "97-100" and "146," the entire *CA* print series consists of only 119 physical volumes with the publication of *CA* Volume 146. The following charts note changes in the numbering system and cover design, and indicate which volumes are essential for the most complete, up-to-date coverage.

CA First Revision	• 1-4R through 41-44R (11 books) *Cover:* Brown with black and gold trim. There will be no further First Revision volumes because revised entries are now being handled exclusively through the more efficient *New Revision Series* mentioned below.
CA Original Volumes	• 45-48 through 97-100 (14 books) *Cover:* Brown with black and gold trim. • 101 through 146 (46 books) *Cover:* Blue and black with orange bands. The same as previous *CA* original volumes but with a new, simplified numbering system and new cover design.
CA Permanent Series	• *CAP*-1 and *CAP*-2 (2 books) *Cover:* Brown with red and gold trim. There will be no further *Permanent Series* volumes because revised entries are now being handled exclusively through the more efficient *New Revision Series* mentioned below.
CA New Revision Series	• *CANR*-1 through *CANR*-46 (46 books) *Cover:* Blue and black with green bands. Includes only sketches requiring extensive changes; **sketches are taken from any previously published *CA, CAP,* or *CANR* volume**.

If You Have:	You May Discard:
CA First Revision Volumes 1-4R through 41-44R **and** *CA Permanent Series* Volumes 1 and 2	*CA* Original Volumes 1, 2, 3, 4 Volumes 5-6 through 41-44
CA Original Volumes 45-48 through 97-100 **and** 101 through 146	**NONE:** These volumes will not be superseded by corresponding revised volumes. Individual entries from these and all other volumes appearing in the left column of this chart may be revised and included in the various volumes of the *New Revision Series*.
CA New Revision Series Volumes *CANR*-1 through *CANR*-46	**NONE:** The *New Revision Series* does not replace any single volume of *CA*. Instead, volumes of *CANR* include entries from many previous *CA* series volumes. All *New Revision Series* volumes must be retained for full coverage.

A Sampling of Authors and Media People
Featured in This Volume

Charles Bennett
A playwright/screenwriter whose career has spanned most of the twentieth century, Bennett is best known as the scriptwriter of such Alfred Hitchcock films as *The Man Who Knew Too Much, The Thirty-Nine Steps,* and *Sabotage.*

John Berendt
In the nonfiction bestseller *Midnight in the Garden of Good and Evil,* Berendt recounts the story of a respected antiques dealer who was tried four times for the same murder.

Juan Butler
Butler's autobiographical novels, including *Cabbagetown Diary: A Documentary* and *Canadian Healing Oil,* reflect the social and personal darkness of a life shaped by an environment of violence and poverty.

Ray Davies
Rock musician Davies, author of such hit songs as "You Really Got Me" and "Lola" for his group the Kinks, paints an idiosyncratic portrait of himself in *X-Ray.*

Don Hewitt
Hewitt is best known as the Emmy Award-winning founding producer of television's acclaimed investigative journalism series *60 Minutes.* In his memoir, *Minute by Minute,* he recounts his four decades with CBS News.

Pagan Kennedy
Author of short stories and cultural histories, Kennedy is known as the "'zine Queen." In *Platforms: A Microwaved Cultural Chronicle of the 1970s,* she interprets meaning behind the fads of a pivotal decade in American culture.

Wilma Mankiller
Mankiller is the first woman Principal Chief of the Cherokee nation. Her autobiography, *Mankiller: A Chief and Her People,* details her experiences as tribal leader and provides a history of the Cherokee people.

Paul McCartney
A popular musician considered the most successful composer of all time, McCartney is also the author of the screenplay for the film *Give My Regards to Broadstreet.*

Anchee Min
Min is the author of *Red Azalea,* a critically acclaimed account of her experiences in the Maoist Cultural Revolution in China between 1966 and 1976. The book won the Carl Sandberg Literary Award in 1993.

Andrew Motion
Motion is one of the most celebrated poets of the late twentieth century. He is also the author of the biography *Philip Larkin: A Writer's Life,* which garnered significant critical praise.

Dale Peck
Peck's first novel, *Martin and John,* was acclaimed for its narrative complexity and unflinching portrayal of homosexuality and AIDS.

Mark Ribowsky
Ribowsky is best known for his biographies of famous sports and music industry personalities, including football coach Al Davis, baseball player Satchel Paige, and music producer Phil Spector.

Sandra Scofield
Scofield's 1991 novel, *Beyond Deserving,* received a 1992 American Book Award and was named one of the *New York Times Book Review*'s "Notable Books of the Year."

Lee Server
Server has received critical attention for his works on cultural history, including the books *Over My Dead Body: The Sensational Age of the American Paperback* and *Danger Is My Business.*

Frances Sherwood
Vindication, Sherwood's controversial 1993 novel based on the life of seminal feminist writer Mary Wollstonecraft, has sparked both acclaim and argument over her fictional use of facts.

Naomi Shihab Nye
Informed by her Palestinian American background, Nye's poetry has earned numerous honors--including three Pushcart Prizes--and is praised for its fresh perspective on ordinary events, people, and objects.

James Stewart
Stewart won a Pulitzer Prize for his *Wall Street Journal* coverage of the 1987 stock market crash and is also the author of the well-received 1991 book *Den of Thieves.*

Tad Williams
Fantasy fiction author/illustrator Williams garnered critical attention for his 1985 novel *Tailchaser's Song,* and has since produced several acclaimed novels, including 1994's *Caliban's Hour.*

Contemporary Authors ®

ABLE, Mark
  See KROOTH, Richard

*   *   *

ADDERSON, Caroline   1963-

PERSONAL: Born September 9, 1963, in Edmonton, Alberta, Canada; daughter of James Neil (an engineer) and Bernice (Goodfellow) Adderson. *Education:* University of British Columbia, B.Ed, 1986. *Religion:* Quaker.

ADDRESSES: Home—Vancouver, British Columbia, Canada. *Office*—Vancouver Community College, Vancouver, British Columbia, Canada. *Contact*—The Porcupine's Quill, 68 Main St., Erin, Ontario N0B 1T0, Canada.

CAREER: Vancouver Community College, Vancouver, British Columbia, Canada, instructor; writer. Received residencies at Banff School of Fine Arts, 1987 and 1991, Tyrone Guthrie Centre for Artists (Canada-Ireland Artist Exchange Program), 1989 and 1992, and Leighton Artist Colony, 1993. Has staged readings, including at the Springrites New Play Festival, 1991.

AWARDS, HONORS: Put It in Words National Fiction Competition award, Canada Commissioner of National Languages, 1986, for "Waiting for Claudine"; Canada Council grants, 1987, 1989, and 1992; third prizes, Canadian Broadcasting Corporation (CBC) Literary Competition, 1988, for "The Chmarnyk," and 1991, for "The Hanging Gardens of Babylon"; Governor-General's Literary Award for Fiction nomination, 1993, and Ethel Wilson Fiction Prize, 1994, both for *Bad Imaginings.*

WRITINGS:

Bad Imaginings (short stories), Porcupine's Quill, 1993.

Contributor to anthologies, including *The Journey Prize Anthology,* Volume 5, McClelland and Stewart, 1993, and *Out of Place,* Coteau Books, 1991; contributor to periodicals, including *Quarry, The Mahalat Review, Canadian Fiction Magazine,* and *Saturday Night;* work has been broadcast on the radio, including the short story "Bestiary," on *Ambience,* CBC, 1987, and the five-part drama *Fire of Stones* on *Morningside,* CBC, 1989.

SCREENPLAYS

Tokyo Cowboy, Big Space Productions, 1993.

Also author of the screenplay *Animal Passions,* 1993.

SIDELIGHTS: Caroline Adderson, a Canadian author, won national acclaim with her first published volume, the short-story collection *Bad Imaginings.* Adderson's storytelling technique involves describing rather offbeat subjects with straightforward narration, and her characters are often social outsiders. Among the ten stories in *Bad Imaginings* is a prize-winning tale titled "The Chmarnyk," which relates the escapades of a budding rainmaker during a drought in 1929 Alberta. Other tales, set in the present, are linked to the historical stories by "a quirky, sometimes harsh authorial intelligence that illuminates odd corners of identity and doubt," commented Lesley Krueger in the Toronto *Globe and Mail.* The critic went on to praise *Bad Imaginings* as a "singular book, deep and mature" and affirmed that the volume "stays with a reader long after it has been closed."

BIOGRAPHICAL/CRITICAL SOURCES:

PERIODICALS

Globe and Mail (Toronto), November 13, 1993, pp. C3, C9.

*   *   *

AFKHAMI, Mahnaz 1941-

PERSONAL: Born January 18, 1941, in Kerman, Iran; daughter of Majid and Ferdows (Naficy) Ebrahimi; married Gholam R. Afkhami (a scholar), 1959; children: Babak. *Education:* University of Colorado, M.A. and doctoral study. *Religion:* Muslim.

ADDRESSES: Home—3101 Cummings Lane, Chevy Chase, MD 20815. *Office*—4343 Montgomery Ave., Bethesda, MD 20814. *Agent*—Edite Kroll, Edite Kroll Literary Agency, 12 Grayhurst Park, Portland, ME 04102.

CAREER: Abstracts of English Studies, Boulder, CO, assistant editor, 1965-66; University of Colorado, Colorado Springs, lecturer, 1966-67; National University of Iran, Teheran, assistant professor of English, 1967-68, department head, 1968-70; Women's Organization of Iran, secretary general, 1970-79; consultant on women and development, 1979-81; Foundation for Iranian Studies, executive director and publisher of *Iran Nameh,* 1981—. Oral History of Iran Archives, founder, 1982, director, 1982—; Sisterhood Is Global Institute, vice-president, 1989-92, executive director, 1992—; Human Rights Watch, member of advisory committee on women, 1991—. Women's Organization of Iran, chairperson of board of trustees of School of Social Work, 1973-79; National Blood Transfusion Organization of Iran, founding member, 1974; Government of Iran, member of High Council for Welfare, 1974-79, and High Council for Family Planning, 1975-79, minister of state for women's affairs and prime minister's deputy for South Teheran Urban Development and Welfare Project, both 1976-78; Sixth National Development Plan of Iran, chairperson of Quality of Life Planning Committee, 1977; Organization for Exceptional Children, member of board of directors and chairperson of executive committee, 1977-79. International Council of Women, head of Iranian delegations, 1972-75; United Nations General Assem-

bly, adviser to Iranian delegation, later organizer of a panel on global feminism, 1993. Member of board of trustees, Kerman University, 1976-79, and Farah University for Women, 1977-79.

MEMBER: Middle East Studies Association, Association of Women in Development.

WRITINGS:

(With Charlotte Albright) *Iran: A Pre-Collegiate Handbook,* Foundation for Iranian Studies, 1992.
Women in Exile, University Press of Virginia, 1994.
(Editor with Erika Friedl) *In the Eye of the Storm: Women in Post-Revolutionary Iran,* Syracuse University Press, 1994.
(Editor and author of introduction) *Women and the Law in Iran, 1967-1978* (in Persian), Foundation for Iranian Studies, 1994.

Also editor, with Goli Emami, of *Readings in Feminist Theory: An Anthology* (in Persian), 1995. Work represented in anthologies, including *Sisterhood Is Global: The International Women's Movement Anthology,* edited by Robin Morgan, 1984; *Women, Culture, and Society: A Reader,* Kendall/Hunt, 1994; and *Women in Iran From Medieval Times to the Islamic Republic,* edited by Guity Nashat, 1994. Contributor to periodicals, including *Ms.*

*   *   *

AGICH, George J. 1947-

PERSONAL: Born May 27, 1947, in Rochester, PA; son of Charles and Mary Agich; married Mary Kate Fredriksen; children: Nicholas Carl. *Education:* Duquesne University, B.A. (cum laude), 1969; University of Texas at Austin, M.A., 1971, Ph.D., 1976.

ADDRESSES: Home—1509 Earthwind Dr., Springfield, IL 62704. *Office*—Department of Medical Humanities, School of Medicine, Southern Illinois University, Springfield, IL 62794-9230.

CAREER: University of Texas Medical Branch at Galveston, research fellow in medical humanities, 1975-76; Southern Illinois University, Springfield, assistant professor, 1976-81, associate professor, 1981-88, professor of medical humanities and psychiatry, 1988—, director of Ethics and Philosophy of Medicine Program, 1976-86, and Medical Ethics Program, 1990—. Memorial Medical Center, member of allied health professional staff and director of Ethics

Consultation Service, 1991—. Sangamon State University, adjunct professor of philosophy, 1978—; Cambridge University, visiting scholar in history and philosophy of science, 1982-83; Southern Illinois University, Carbondale, associate professor, 1981-88; Wayne State University, Paul E. Ruble Memorial Lecturer, 1987; lecturer at colleges and universities in the United States and abroad. Springfield Committee for Research Involving Human Subjects, vice-chairperson, 1979-86; Joint Commission on Accreditation of Health Care Organizations, member of external standards development work group, 1993—. Greater Springfield Interfaith Association, member of Committee on Ethical Dilemmas in Long Term Care, 1987-88; Friends of Lincoln Library, member of board of directors, 1991—; consultant to Planned Parenthood of Springfield.

MEMBER: International Association of Bioethics (chairperson of Network on Bioethics Education), North American Kant Society, European Society for Philosophy of Medicine and Health Care, American Philosophical Association, American Society of Law and Medicine, Association for the Advancement of Philosophy and Psychiatry (founding fellow; member of executive council, 1989—; vice-president, 1991-94; president, 1994—), Association for Faculty in Medical Humanities (member of executive committee, 1986-87; chairperson, 1991-92), Society for Bioethics Consultation, Society for Health and Human Values (chairperson of Task Force on International Activities, 1994), Society for Phenomenology and Existential Philosophy, Hastings Center, Kennedy Institute of Ethics.

AWARDS, HONORS: Fellow of Institute on Human Values in Medicine, Society for Health and Human Values, 1976, and National Endowment for the Humanities, 1984; Nellie Westerman Prize for Research in Ethics, American Federation for Clinical Research, 1985; grants from Institute on Human Values in Medicine, 1976, Illinois Humanities Council, 1981, University of Texas Health Science Center, 1985, Retirement Research Foundation, 1987, and Central Research Council, 1992.

WRITINGS:

(Editor and contributor) *Responsibility in Health Care,* D. Reidel (Dordrecht), 1982.
(Editor with Charles E. Begley, and contributor) *The Price of Health,* D. Reidel (Dordrecht), 1986.
Autonomy and Long-Term Care, Oxford University Press, 1993.

Work represented in books, including *Ethics and Sports Medicine,* edited by Richard M. Zaner, Hu-

man Kinetic Publishers, 1994; *Alzheimer Disease: Therapeutic Strategies,* edited by Ezio Giacobini and Robert E. Becker, Birkhauser Boston, 1994; and *Death: Biology, Science, and Bioethics,* edited by David Thomasma and Thomasine Kushner, Cambridge University Press, 1994. Contributor of about seventy articles and reviews to scholarly journals. Associate editor, *Bulletin of the Society for Health and Human Values,* 1985-91; member of editorial board, *Philosophy, Psychiatry, and Psychology,* 1993—.

WORK IN PROGRESS: Justifying Clinical Ethics; The Myth of Autonomy in Medical Ethics.

*   *   *

AKARLI, Engin Deniz   1945-

PERSONAL: Born September 26, 1945; son of Ahmet (a technician) and Muazzez (a homemaker; maiden name, Temeltas) Akarli; married Tuna Kermen (an instructor and translator), 1974; children: Aysecan (daughter). *Education:* Robert's College, Istanbul, Turkey, B.A., 1968; University of Wisconsin—Madison, M.A. (history), 1972; Princeton University, M.A. (Near Eastern history), 1973, Ph.D., 1976. *Politics:* Liberal. *Religion:* Islamic. *Avocational interests:* Tennis, jogging, bicycling, reading novels and poetry.

ADDRESSES: Home—745 Westwood Dr., No. 3-W, Clayton, MO 63105. *Office*—Department of History, Washington University, Campus Box 1062, St. Louis, MO 63130.

CAREER: Princeton University, Princeton, NJ, lecturer in Near Eastern studies, 1975-76; Bosphorus University, Istanbul, Turkey, began as assistant professor, became associate professor of history, 1976-83; Yarmouk University, Irbid, Jordan, associate professor of history, 1983-89; Washington University, St. Louis, MO, associate professor of history, 1989—. Institute of Advanced Studies, Berlin, Germany, fellow, 1985-86. Yurt Publications, member of board of editors, 1980-83; Turkish Peace Committee, member of publications committee, 1977-81; Social and Economic History Foundation (Istanbul), member; consultant to Adam Publications. *Military service:* Turkish Army Reserve, 1976.

MEMBER: American Historical Association, Middle East Studies Association, Law and Society Association.

AWARDS, HONORS: Best History Book Award, Missouri Historical Society, 1993, for *The Long Peace: Ottoman Lebanon, 1861-1920;* Fulbright fellowship.

WRITINGS:

(Editor with Gabriel Ben-Dor, and contributor) *Political Participation in Turkey,* Bosphorus University Press (Istanbul), 1974.
Political Testaments of Ali and Fuad (in Turkish), Bosphorus University Press, 1977.
Documents on Jordan (monograph; bilingual in English and Arabic), University of Jordan (Amman), 1989.
The Long Peace: Ottoman Lebanon, 1861-1920, University of California Press, 1993.

Contributor to periodicals.

WORK IN PROGRESS: Ruling a Doomed Empire: The Reign of Sultan Abdulhamid II, 1876-1909; The Uses of Law: Dispute Settlement Among Istanbul Artisans, 1750-1850.

SIDELIGHTS: Engin Deniz Akarli told *CA:* "A part of us is involved in our writings, I believe. In *The Long Peace* I explain in detail the scholarly reasons and objectives that guided me in writing the book. Why I was personally attracted to Lebanon for research, however, is not that explicit.

"My interest in Lebanon is related to my aversion of chauvinistic behavior and wars, particularly civil wars which pit neighbor against neighbor. My father is a Turkish Cypriot, with a Greek grandmother and many other Greek relatives. My parents used to live in Adlanja, a village in southern Cyprus. In 1964 the small Turkish community of Adlanja was forced to abandon its property and flee. My parents went to Turkey. After the Turkish occupation of northern Cyprus in 1974, they went back to the island to live, not in our own village, but in an abandoned Greek house in Magosa. They were only poorly recompensed for what they had lost and suffered, and that was at the expense of another family's suffering. Who were the winners?

"As a member of the Turkish peace movement, I worked for the restoration of peace and the establishment of conditions for normal relations between the two communities on the island. When there was a military coup in Turkey in 1981, the peace movement was suppressed, along with many other organizations that were supposedly undermining national integrity. Simultaneously, the military regime demanded the teaching of history, even at the university level, according to the official nationalist ideology. I took a stance against such policies, keeping in mind the example of Lebanon, which was being torn apart by a civil war at the time. On the basis of sound initial evidence, I thought the war in Lebanon resulted, not from 'ancient sectarian hatreds,' but from a rather recent cultivation of such hatreds, partly by means of distorted perspectives on history. I had won a Fulbright fellowship to write a book around this theme. The military regime forbade me to use that fellowship, revoked my permission to work in the archives, and gave me the choice of being expelled from my tenured position at Bosphorus University in Istanbul or resigning by my own will. It wasn't much of a choice.

"I resigned and left Turkey. I worked in Jordan for five years, where I saw the gradual deterioration of the relations between Jordanians and Palestinians. I worked in Berlin for one year, where I observed the chauvinistic reaction of certain groups of Germans against foreigners and also the concerned efforts of the German government and liberal intellectuals to curtail that trend. These experiences colored my approach to Lebanese history and my attraction to it in order to set the historical record right, to document the dialogue and close relationships between communities, which are only normal, but are so readily overlooked and forgotten at moments of militant confrontation."

*   *   *

ALBERTSON, Susan
See WOJCIECHOWSKI, Susan

*   *   *

ALBRECHT, Steve   1963-

PERSONAL: Born February 22, 1963, in Baltimore, MD; son of Karl G. (a writer) and Eileen D. (Hodes) Albrecht; married May 9, 1992; wife's name, Leslie A. (a police officer); children: Carly, Matthew Rice. *Education:* University of San Diego, B.A., 1984. *Avocational interests:* Physical fitness, martial arts.

ADDRESSES: Office—Albrecht Training and Development, 2065 Arnold Way, Suite 103B, Alpine, CA 91901. *Agent*—Oriole Literary Agency, 2065 Arnold Way, Suite 103B, Alpine, CA 91901.

CAREER: Police officer in San Diego, CA, 1984-85; Albrecht Training and Development, Alpine, CA, writer and seminar leader, 1985—. San Diego Police Reserve, officer.

MEMBER: American Society of Training and Development, Authors Guild, Mystery Writers of America, Sisters in Crime, California Reserve Peace Officers Association.

WRITINGS:

(With Karl Albrecht) *The Creative Corporation,* Dow Jones-Irwin, 1987.

(With John Morrison) *Contact and Cover,* C.C Thomas, 1990.

Streetwork, Paladin Press, 1992.

One-Strike Stopping Power, Paladin Press, 1992.

The Paralegal's Desk Reference, Prentice-Hall, 1993.

(With Albrecht) *Added Value Negotiating,* Irwin, 1993.

(With Michael Mantell) *Ticking Bombs,* Irwin, 1994.

Service, Service, Service!, Bob Adams, 1994.

(With John Clemens) *Timeless Leaders,* Bob Adams, 1995.

Corporate Self-Defense, AMACOM, 1995.

Film scripts include *White Fire, Red Horse Down,* and the television pilot *Decoy Cops;* videotapes include *Ticking Bombs, Police Moments of Truth,* and *Contact and Cover;* author of scripts for audio tapes. Author of "Streetwork," a monthly column in *Informant,* 1986—.

*   *   *

ALEXANDER, Jeb   1899-1965
(A pseudonym)

PERSONAL: Born October 17, 1899, in Atlanta, GA; died following a stroke, 1965, in Washington, DC. *Education:* Attended Washington and Lee University, 1918-22; graduated from George Washington University, 1927. *Politics:* Liberal Democrat. *Avocational interests:* Film and theater, traveling, nature, and collecting.

CAREER: U.S. Dept. of Agriculture, Washington, DC, editor, until retirement in the early 1960s.

WRITINGS:

Jeb and Dash: A Diary of Gay Life, 1918-1945, edited by Ina D. Russell, Faber and Faber, 1994.

SIDELIGHTS: Jeb Alexander worked as an editor for the U.S. Department of Agriculture in Washington, D.C., for most of his life, but during this time he also kept an extensive diary that recorded not only historical events in Washington and his ambition of being a writer but also his existence as a closeted gay man. When he died in 1965, he left these diaries—which amounted to fifty volumes—to his niece, Ina D. Russell. In the late 1980s Russell began editing them for publication, a task that required nearly eighteen months of full-time work. It was Russell who created the Jeb Alexander pseudonym, and who also came up with one for the man her uncle had most loved during his lifetime, C. C. Dasham—the "Dash" of the title. Reviewing *Jeb and Dash* in the *Village Voice,* James Hannaham commented: "As they record the life of a pre-Stonewall gay Washingtonian, Alexander's diaries fill in the anthropological gaps of those tortured and desperate years with articulate, perceptive prose and make his life story a window into gay history." However, Alice Echols, writing in *The Nation,* contends that the diaries are more compelling in their honest revelations of Alexander's personal struggle to reconcile himself to his sexual orientation and in their depiction of his feelings of frustration, anxiety, and jealousy. Echols notes: "I think Jeb's story is less 'a diary of gay life' than 'a diary of a gay life'."

BIOGRAPHICAL/CRITICAL SOURCES:

BOOKS

Alexander, Jeb, *Jeb and Dash: A Diary of Gay Life, 1918-1945,* edited by Ina D. Russell, Faber and Faber, 1994.

PERIODICALS

The Nation, July 4, 1994, pp. 25-27.
Publishers Weekly, October 11, 1993, pp. 24-25.
Village Voice, November 23, 1993, p. 93.

OTHER

Additional information provided by Ina D. Russell, September 30, 1994.

*   *   *

ALLEN, E. John B.   1933-

PERSONAL: Born May 13, 1933, in England; son of Bedford (in Royal Air Force) and Rosetta (Machell) Allen; married Heide Gelbert (a ski instructor); children: Peter, Ariane Allen Shuffleton, Jacqueline Allen Downing. *Education:* Sir George Williams University (now Concordia University), B.A., 1965; Brigham Young University, M.A., 1966, Ph.D., 1969. *Politics:* Democrat.

ADDRESSES: Home—Buffalo Rd., Rumney, NH 03266. *Office*—Rounds 314, Plymouth State College, Plymouth, NH 03264.

CAREER: Plymouth State College, Plymouth, NH, began as assistant professor, became professor of history, 1968—. New England Ski Museum, member; consultant for the documentary films *Legends of American Skiing,* broadcast by Public Broadcasting System, 1984, and *Spirit of the Mountains,* 1993. *Military service:* British Army, Parachute Regiment, 1951-53; became second lieutenant.

MEMBER: International Society for the History of Physical Education and Sport, North American Society for Sport History, British Society for Sports History.

AWARDS, HONORS: Grant from Deutsche Akademische Austauschdientz; book award from International Skiing History Association, for *From Skisport to Skiing.*

WRITINGS:

Post and Courier Service in the Diplomacy of Early Modern Europe, Nijhoff, 1972.
Reflections of Berlin, privately printed (Berlin, NH), 1984.
Teaching and Technique: A History of Professional Ski Instruction, PSIA Educational Foundation, 1987, 2nd edition, 1987.
From Skisport to Skiing: One Hundred Years of an American Sport, 1840-1940, University of Massachusetts Press (Amherst, MA), 1993.

Work represented in books, including *Sports in Massachusetts: Historical Essays,* edited by Ronald Story, Institute of Massachusetts Studies, 1991. Contributor of articles and reviews to periodicals, including *Historical New Hampshire, Postal History Journal, Journal of American Culture, Oral History Review, Quest,* and *Canadian Journal of the History of Sport.*

WORK IN PROGRESS: Research on the European and international history of skiing.

*   *   *

ALOFSIN, Anthony 1949-

PERSONAL: Born in Memphis, TN; married Patricia Tierney (a researcher), June 5, 1993. *Education:* Harvard University, A.B. (magna cum laude), 1971, M.Arch. (with distinction), 1981; Columbia University, M.Phil., 1983, Ph.D., 1987.

ADDRESSES: *Home*—110 West 33rd St., Austin, TX 78705. *Office*—School of Architecture, Goldsmith Hall, University of Texas at Austin, Austin, TX 78712.

CAREER: University of Texas at Austin, associate professor of architecture, 1987—, adjunct professor of art history, 1988—, Sid W. Richardson Centennial fellow in architecture, 1987—. Architect and exhibition curator. Lecturer at colleges and universities in the United States and abroad.

AWARDS, HONORS: International Architecture Book Award, American Institute of Architects, 1993, for *Frank Lloyd Wright: The Lost Years, 1910-1922.*

WRITINGS:

(Editor and author of introduction) *Frank Lloyd Wright: An Index to the Taliesin Correspondence,* Garland Publishing, 1988.
Frank Lloyd Wright: The Lost Years, 1910-1922, University of Chicago Press, 1993.
An Arrival of Modernism: Architecture, Landscape Architecture, and City Planning at Harvard, 1894-1952, Southern Illinois University Press, in press.

Work represented in books, including *The History of History in American Schools of Architecture, 1865-1975,* Princeton Architectural Press, 1990. Contributor of articles and reviews to art and architecture journals.

WORK IN PROGRESS: Chief curator for "A Tense Alliance," an international exhibition on Central European architecture, 1848-1928, completion expected in 1998.

BIOGRAPHICAL/CRITICAL SOURCES:

PERIODICALS

Globe and Mail (Toronto), February 26, 1994.
Journal of Architectural Education, winter, 1990, p. 54.
Journal of the Society of Architectural Historians, volume 48, number 3, 1989, p. 200.
London Review of Books, April 7, 1994.
New York Review of Books, January 13, 1994, p. 28.
New York Times Book Review, February 20, 1994, p. 20.
Times Literary Supplement, May 16, 1994, p. 16.
Urban Explorer, April, 1994, p. 9.
Wilson Quarterly, spring, 1994, p. 36.

*   *   *

ALTSCHUL, Aaron Mayer 1914-1994

OBITUARY NOTICE—See index for *CA* sketch: Born March 13, 1914, in Chicago, IL; died of a brain tumor, July 4, 1994, in Arlington, VA. Scientist, educator, and author. Altschul's area of specialty was global food resources and inequities in food consumption. After receiving a Ph.D. from the University of Chicago in 1937, he worked as a government research scientist for over two decades, eventually becoming special assistant to the United States Secretary of Agriculture in 1966. Altschul also served as a consultant to the United Nations and the Israeli government. In 1971 he joined the faculty of community and family medicine at Georgetown University, becoming head of the department of nutrition in 1975. In 1976 Altschul founded the school's Diet Management and Eating Disorders Program, and retired in 1983 as professor emeritus. The scientist was the recipient of an impressive number of awards during his career, including those from the U.S. Department of Agriculture, American Chemical Society, and the Society for Experimental Biology and Medicine. In his many books and magazine articles, Altschul stressed the importance of developing alternate sources of protein and a better distribution network to help eradicate famine in poorly-developed economies. His first published work was 1958's *Processed Plant Protein Foodstuffs,* which he edited; he was also the author of *World Protein Resources* (1966) and, more recently, *Weight Control: A Guide for Counselors and Therapists* (1987). He also edited a multi-volume series entitled *New Protein Foods,* a work on which he partially collaborated with H. L. Wilcke.

OBITUARIES AND OTHER SOURCES:

BOOKS

Who's Who in America, 47th edition, Marquis, 1992.

PERIODICALS

Washington Post, July 7, 1994, p. B7.

* * *

AMES, Mildred 1919-1994

OBITUARY NOTICE—See index for *CA* sketch: Born November 2, 1919, in Bridgeport, CT; died after a respiratory illness, July 20, 1994. Author. Ames penned short stories as a child, but in her adult life worked in a variety of jobs—including millinery salesperson, telephone operator, and secretary. It was not until she was well into her fifties that *Shadows of Summers Past,* her first book, appeared in print. Her fiction for children and young adults was characterized by uplifting tales of relationships and personal growth, often moved along by elements of suspense, science fiction, or animal rights. Ames wrote over a dozen other books for young readers, including *Is There Life on a*

Plastic Planet?, Nicky and the Joyous Noise, and *The Silver Link, the Silken Tie. What Are Friends For?* and a science-fiction novel for young readers, *Anna to the Infinite Power,* were adapted for television.

OBITUARIES AND OTHER SOURCES:

BOOKS

Something About the Author, Volume 22, Gale, 1981.

PERIODICALS

Society for Children's Book Writers and Illustrators Bulletin, October/November, 1994.

* * *

AMOS, William (David) 1933-

PERSONAL: Born December 16, 1933, in Ipswich, England; son of William (a motor engineer) and Margery (Lambert) Amos; married Judith Morley, March 16, 1957; children: Jolyon Luke, Silas Seth. *Education:* Attended Oakham School, 1947-50.

ADDRESSES: Home—Hacket Forge, Little Langdale, Ambleside, Cumbria LA22 9NU, England.

CAREER: Liverpool Daily Post, daily columnist, 1963-70; *Lancashire Life,* editor, 1970-86; Whitethorn Press, director, 1974-85, editor in chief, 1982-86; Hotel Publishing International, editor in chief, 1986-89; *Warwickshire & Worcestershire Life,* editor, 1989-91; freelance editor, 1991—. *Military service:* British Army, 1952-54, served in Germany, Egypt, and Libya.

WRITINGS:

Literary Liverpool, Scouse Press, 1971.
(Editor) *Just Sithabod: Dialect Verse from "Lancashire Life,"* Whitethorn Press, 1975.
(Editor) *Steam-up in Lancashire: Railwayana from "Lancashire Life,"* Whitethorn Press, 1976.
(Editor) *Cheyp at T'Price: Dialect Verse from "Lancashire Life,"* Whitethorn Press, 1978.
The Originals: Who's Really Who in Fiction, Cape, 1985, published in North America as *The Originals: An A-Z of Fiction's Real-Life Characters,* Little, Brown, 1986.
Derbyshire, Countryside Books, 1995.
Tales of Old Lancashire, Countryside Books, in press.

WORK IN PROGRESS: An update of *The Originals,* confined to twentieth-century English-language fiction.

SIDELIGHTS: In *The Originals* William Amos identifies or speculates about the models for nearly 3,000 literary characters. Amos told *CA:* "I am a collector of unconsidered trifles, believing that literature's footnotes are often more illuminating than the text they accompany. This interest was in part the inspiration of *The Originals.*"

Anthony Burgess in the *Times Literary Supplement* pointed out the pros and cons of a work such as *The Originals.* While Burgess often found the anecdotes interesting, he questioned the value of discovering the sources for authors' characters. "The only trouble with the kind of work that Amos has done is that it encourages us to forget—what too many novel-readers are only too willing to forget—that fiction is frequently a triumph of the imagination, and that the raw material which feeds it is of rather minor importance. It often happens too that the real-life personages on whom the novelist finds it convenient to draw are of no great interest to anyone except himself." *Washington Post* reviewer Jonathan Yardley noted the British perspective of Amos's work, but, calling Amos the "all-time champion" trivia sleuth, he confessed, "'The Originals' is appealing not because anything in it really matters, but because it is simply fun. . . . For literary trivia mavens, 'The Originals' is a gold mine."

BIOGRAPHICAL/CRITICAL SOURCES:

PERIODICALS

Los Angeles Times Book Review, May 11, 1986, p. 14.
New York Times Book Review, May 4, 1986, p. 3.
Times (London), December 19, 1985.
Times Literary Supplement, November, 29, 1985, p. 1349.
Washington Post, June 4, 1986.

*   *   *

ANDERSON, Edward F. 1932-

PERSONAL: Born June 17, 1932, in Covina, CA; son of Edward W. (a teacher and rancher) and Dorothy (a homemaker; maiden name, Kaiser) Anderson; married Adele Bowman (a homemaker), March 31, 1956; children: Clark E., Adrienne Anderson Fioretti, Duc D., Erica R., Stephen P., Monica T., Bruce K. *Education:* Pomona College, B.A., 1954; Claremont Graduate School, M.A., 1959, Ph.D., 1961. *Politics:* "Moderate Republican." *Religion:* Presbyterian. *Avocational interests:* Photography.

ADDRESSES: Home—17001 South 30th Pl., Phoenix, AZ 85048. *Office*—Desert Botanic Garden, 1201 North Galvin Parkway, Phoenix, AZ 85008.

CAREER: Pomona College, Claremont, CA, instructor in botany, 1961-62; Whitman College, Walla Walla, WA, professor of biology, 1962-92; Desert Botanical Garden, Phoenix, AZ, senior research botanist, 1992—. *Military service:* U.S. Army, 1955-57; became captain.

MEMBER: International Organization for Succulent Plant Study, Society for Economic Botany, Rotary International, Planned Parenthood, Linnean Society of London, Symphony Society.

WRITINGS:

Peyote: The Divine Cactus, University of Arizona Press, 1980.
Plants and People of the Golden Triangle: Ethnobotany of the Hill Tribes of Northern Thailand, Dioscorides Press (Portland, OR), 1993.
(With S. Arias M. and N. P. Taylor) *Threatened Cacti of Mexico,* Royal Botanic Garden (Kew, England), 1994.

WORK IN PROGRESS: Revising *Peyote: The Divine Cactus;* research on the ethnobotany of the cacti.

*   *   *

ANDERSON, Lindsay (Gordon) 1923-1994

OBITUARY NOTICE—See index for *CA* sketch: Full name, Lindsay Gordon Anderson; born April 17, 1923, in Bangalore, India; died of a heart attack, August 30, 1994, in the South of France. Director and writer for stage, film, and television. Anderson won an Academy Award for best short subject documentary in 1954 for *Thursday's Children,* which he wrote and directed. He is best known for his feature films, including *If. . .,* which won the 1968 Golden Palm Award from the Cannes Film Festival. In addition to his awards as a film director, Anderson received an Antoinette Perry Award nomination as well as a New York Drama Critics Award nomination as best director for the play *Home* in 1971. After studying at both Cheltenham and Wadham Colleges at Oxford University, Anderson went on to found—with Karel Reisz in 1947—*Sequence,* a film magazine for which he also served as editor. In 1956, Anderson founded the Free Cinema Group with the National Film Theatre. Throughout the 1960s and

1970s he served in numerous capacities in the film and theatre industry, including serving on the board of directors for the British Film Institute and as artistic director for London's Royal Court Theatre. Among Anderson's other feature films are *This Sporting Life, O Lucky Man!*, and *The Whales of August*, which was released in 1987 and starred Hollywood legends Lillian Gish and Bette Davis. Anderson's credits as television director include several episodes of the series *Robin Hood*, and HBO mini-series *Glory! Glory!*. In addition to wri-ting numerous documentaries, Anderson has auth-ored several nonfiction works, including *Making a Film: The Story of "Secret People"*, *If. . .: A Story, O Lucky Man!*, and a biography, *About John Ford*, depicting the film director he most admired.

OBITUARIES AND OTHER SOURCES:

BOOKS

Who's Who, 144th edition, St. Martin's, 1992.

PERIODICALS

Los Angeles Times, September 2, 1994, p. A22.
Times (London), September 1, 1994, p. 23.
Washington Post, September 2, 1994, p. C6; September 3, 1994, p. B6.

*   *   *

ANUNOBI, Fredoline O.   1956-

PERSONAL: Born September 14, 1956; son of Chief Amaeze Simon (in business) and Geradine U. (a homemaker) Anunobi; married; wife's name, Eucharia U. (a pharmacist); children: Ijeoma C., Uchenna F. *Education:* Alabama A & M University, B.A., 1983, M.S., 1984; Atlanta University, M.A., Ph.D., 1990.

ADDRESSES: Home—8200 Palm St., Apt. 118, New Orleans, LA 70118. *Office*—Department of Political Science, Xavier University of Louisiana, 7325 Palmetto St., New Orleans, LA 70125.

CAREER: Alabama A & M University, Normal, instructor in economics, 1984-85; Morris Brown College, Atlanta, GA, teaching assistant in economics, 1987-88; Selma University, Selma, AL, assistant professor of political science, head of Division of Business Administration and Social Sciences, and director of Third World studies, 1988-92; Xavier University of Louisiana, New Orleans, assistant professor of political science, 1992—.

MEMBER: American Economic Association, American Political Science Association, National Conference of Black Political Scientists, Southern Political Science Association.

AWARDS, HONORS: Grants from International Paper Co. for Center for Third World Studies and Development, 1989-92, and from U.S. Department of Education, 1993-95; Nissian fellow at Howard University, 1992, and University of California, Los Angeles, 1993; award from Students in Free Enterprise, 1992-93, 1993-94.

WRITINGS:

The Implications of Conditionality: The International Monetary Fund and Africa, University Press of America, 1992.
International Dimensions of African Political Economy: Trends, Challenges, and Realities, University Press of America, 1994.

Work represented in anthologies, including *The State of Black America, 1995*, National Urban League. Contributor to political science and African studies journals and newspapers.

WORK IN PROGRESS: Editing *International Political Economy: Competition, Conflict, and Cooperation*.

SIDELIGHTS: Fredoline O. Anunobi told *CA:* "The accelerated inflation and large payments imbalances that have plagued the world economy in recent years have created new challenges for economic policy. Institutions such as the International Monetary Fund and World Bank have found themselves operating in a global environment markedly different from that for which they were originally designed, and developing countries have found their aspirations threatened by large increases in their payment deficits. There have been wide disagreements about the most suitable policy responses by developing countries, and about the appropriateness of the stabilization programs favored by the International Monetary Fund.

"Despite the increasing attention that has been focused on this controversy, remarkably little work has been performed to determine systematically whether Fund-supported politics actually aggravate economic problems, or whether the relationship between the two phenomena is indeed merely coincidental. The work that has been done suggests that they do.

"My study *The Implications of Conditionality: The International Monetary Fund and Africa,* examines the Fund-supported adjustment programs and the Third World's economic problem in a systematic fashion, using Africa as a case study. The book critically examines whether the introduction of the Fund-supported adjustment programs do significantly aggravate Third World economic problems. It also provides a detailed examination of the impact of Fund-supported adjustment programs on African economic development. This is one of the first in-depth analyses of International Monetary Fund-Africa relations."

*   *   *

APPLEBY, Louis 1955-

PERSONAL: Born February 27, 1955, in Middlesbrough, England; son of James and Doris (Cooper) Appleby; married Juliet Haselden (a press officer), September 9, 1992; children: Michelle, Matthew. *Education:* University of Edinburgh, M.B., Ch.B., M.R.C.P., M.R.C.Psych., 1980.

ADDRESSES: Home—15 Danesmoor Rd., Didsbury, Manchester, England.

CAREER: Victoria University of Manchester, Manchester, England, senior lecturer in psychiatry, 1991—. Physician and psychiatrist.

MEMBER: Royal College of Physicians, Royal College of Psychiatrists.

WRITINGS:

A Medical Tour through the Whole Island of Great Britain, Faber, 1994.

WORK IN PROGRESS: Research for a sequel to *A Medical Tour through the Whole Island of Great Britain.*

*   *   *

ARON, Michael 1946-

PERSONAL: Born May 14, 1946, in Philadelphia, PA; son of David H. L. (an actor and businessperson) and Joan (a writer and homemaker; maiden name, Tobias) Aron; married, wife's name, Carolyn B. (an arts administrator), August 20, 1976; children: Leah,

Nina, Alexa. *Education:* Harvard University, B.A., 1968; Princeton University, M.P.A., 1970. *Avocational interests:* Soccer.

ADDRESSES: Home—289 Western Way, Princeton, NJ 08540. *Office*—*NJN News,* New Jersey Network, CN777, Trenton, NJ 08625-0777.

CAREER: Harper's, New York City, associate editor, 1975-76; *Rolling Stone,* New York City, associate editor, 1977; *New Jersey Monthly,* Princeton, editor, 1978-82; New Jersey Network, Trenton, senior political correspondent, 1982—.

AWARDS, HONORS: Mid-Atlantic Emmy Award, 1987.

WRITINGS:

Governor's Race: A TV Reporter's Chronicle of the 1993 Florio/Whitman Campaign, Rutgers University Press, 1993.

Media columnist, *New Jersey Reporter,* 1991—.

*   *   *

ASHALL, Frank 1957-

PERSONAL: Born October 10, 1957, in Bradford, Yorkshire, England; son of Frank (a weaver) and Kitty (a weaver; maiden name, Berry) Ashall; married Alison Goate (a scientist), July 10, 1987; children: Juliet. *Education:* Oxford University, B.A., 1980, D.Phil., 1982; medical student at St. Louis University, 1994—. *Politics:* "Democrat/Liberal."

ADDRESSES: Home—1177 Claytonia Terr., Richmond Heights, MO 63117. *Office*—School of Medicine, St. Louis University, South Grand Blvd., St. Louis, MO 63104.

CAREER: Eleanor Roosevelt Institute for Cancer Research, Denver, CO, postdoctoral researcher, 1982-85; University of London, London, England, postdoctoral researcher at London School of Hygiene and Tropical Medicine, 1985-89, senior research fellow at Imperial College of Science and Technology, 1989-92; Washington University, St. Louis, MO, assistant professor, 1992-94.

MEMBER: American Medical Student Association, American Association of Family Practitioners, Physicians for Human Rights.

WRITINGS:

Remarkable Discoveries!, Cambridge University Press, 1994.
(Editor with A. M. Goate) *Plaques and Tangles in Alzheimer's Disease,* Academic Press, 1995.

Contributor of more than thirty articles to academic journals.

SIDELIGHTS: Frank Ashall told *CA:* "I was educated at Oxford University, where I obtained a bachelor's degree in biochemistry and a doctorate in cancer research. In 1991, after spending ten years in scientific research, I was offered a media fellowship in the United Kingdom, and I worked for several months as a science reporter for the newspaper *The Independent.* While at the newspaper, I realized how little I knew about areas of science outside my own specialty. This strengthened my conviction that scientists have a duty to communicate their subjects to the public.

"My experience as a science reporter led me to write my book about scientific discoveries. I firmly believe that science needs to be written for everyone, not merely for other scientists or for people with a particular interest in science. The gap between academic science and public knowledge is already wide, and scientists must try to narrow the gap. Fundamental science needs to be communicated for numerous reasons. The beauty of nature is for all to enjoy. People need to understand the good that science can bring to humanity. World leaders, whose knowledge of basic science is often pitifully deficient, need to be informed of the value of science to their societies.

"Having worked on tropical diseases for seven years, I am aware of many of the global problems associated with the inadequate and unfair distribution of science and medical technology. The high rates of childhood illness and deaths that result from preventable diseases or poor sanitation in the developing world can be addressed if science, medicine, and technology are viewed as global imperatives. I hope to continue to write on science and medicine for the layperson, and on global medical and scientific issues."

*   *   *

ASPER, Kathrin 1941-

PERSONAL: Born March 12, 1941, in Zurich, Switzer-land; daughter of Herbert (in business) and Marian (maiden name, Weckherlin; present surname, Irminger) Bruggisser; married Hans K. Asper (an engineer), July 9, 1965; children: Martin. *Education:* University of Zurich, Ph.D., 1967; C. G. Jung Institute, Zurich, Diploma in Analytical Psychology, 1977. *Religion:* Protestant.

ADDRESSES: Home—Plattenstrasse 98, CH-8706 Meilen, Switzerland.

CAREER: Private practice of psychoanalysis and psychotherapy, 1978—. C. G. Jung Institute, lecturer, supervisor, and member of Curatorium. Lecturer and seminar leader in Europe, Canada, and the United States; also worked as a teacher, including a year in Paris.

MEMBER: International Association for Analytical Psychology, Swiss Society for Analytical Psychology, Swiss Society of Psychotherapists.

WRITINGS:

Verlassenheit und Selbstentfremdung, 1987, translation published as *The Abandoned Child Within: On Losing and Regaining Self-Worth,* Fromm International, 1993.
Von der Kindheit zum Kind in uns, 1988, translation published as *The Inner Child in Dreams,* Shambhala, 1992.

Untranslated works include *Kindtraeume, Muttertraeume, Vatertraeume* (with Renee Nell and Helmut Hark), 1991; *Schritte im Labyrinth: Tagebuch einer Psychotherapeutin,* 1992; and *Fenster im Alltag: Psychologisches Skizenbuch,* 1994. Contributor to psychology journals.

WORK IN PROGRESS: Research on therapeutic approaches to trauma and homosexuality.

SIDELIGHTS: Kathrin Asper told *CA:* "I spent my childhood and youth in Kusnacht, the village that now harbors the C. G. Jung Institute. After my father died in a Japanese concentration camp in Manila in 1944, my mother married a widower with two sons and made two families into a new and happy one. I trained as a high school teacher, studying languages, literature, and pedagogy. Then I worked in various schools; for example, I spent one year in Paris, teaching German at the Lycee Fenelon. I was relatively young when I met my husband, who is interested in psychology, but whose main field of study lies in research on alternative energies.

"In the early 1970s I began to study Jungian psychology. After receiving my diploma in 1977, I established a private practice in Meilen, a suburb of Zurich. I also give lectures at the C. G. Jung Institute, where my natural taste for pedagogy has led me into the training and supervision of candidates. I also enjoy writing and sometimes need to do this in order to get energy for my work as a psychotherapist.

"Apart from my interest in fairy tales, symbols, and theoretical and therapeutic problems, the emphasis of my work is on narcissism and narcissistic disorders, trying to understand them from a Jungian perspective. My other main interest is childhood and the role it plays in the analysis of adults. At present, these interests have led me to the psychology of trauma and the psychology of homosexuals. Both traumatization and homosexuality deeply affect a person's identity."

*   *   *

ATTENBOROUGH, John   1908-1994

OBITUARY NOTICE—See index for *CA* sketch: Born December 30, 1908, in Bromley, England; died May 11, 1994. Publisher and author. Attenborough was a managing editor for many years at one of Britain's venerable publishing firms, Hodder & Stoughton. Attenborough joined the company that had been founded by relatives on his mother's side after receiving a degree from Trinity College, Oxford, in 1930. His career was interrupted by World War II, however, and he was knighted for his service in the Royal Army. He returned to Hodder & Stoughton at the war's end; soon afterward the reins of the business were handed over to him and his cousin, Paul Hodder-Williams. Hodder-Williams oversaw the firm's finances, while Attenborough made editorial and marketing decisions that benefitted the company well. In 1972 he was made a commander of the British Empire for his work for the Book Development Council. He retired from the publishing side of the business in 1973, then used his experiences in writing *A Living Memory: Hodder & Stoughton, 1868-1974.* The history of the company received positive reviews and a letter that Attenborough received from a reader inspired his second book, the novel *One Man's Inheritance.* He penned three other works of fiction, including *The Day of Small Things,* published in 1994, only months before his death.

OBITUARIES AND OTHER SOURCES:

PERIODICALS

Times (London), May 12, 1994, p. 19.

AUSTERLITZ, Robert Paul   1923-1994

OBITUARY NOTICE—See index for *CA* sketch: Born December 13, 1923, in Bucharest, Romania; emigrated to the United States, 1938; became U.S. citizen, 1946; died of cancer, September 9, 1994, in the Bronx, NY. Linguist, educator and author. Austerlitz's field of interest was in the structure and development of Uralic languages such as Finnish and Hungarian. After earning degrees from the New School for Social Research and Columbia University, he joined Columbia's faculty in 1958. Aus-terlitz was made professor of linguistics and Uralic studies seven years later and then served as chair of the department until 1968; he also held a number of visiting professorships at universities around the world, traveled extensively for his research into languages, and served as a consultant to the Smith-sonian Institution. Austerlitz was knighted by the Finnish government in 1958 for his academic achievements, and throughout his career was an active member of numerous professional organizations. In 1990 he served as president of the Linguistic Society of America. His published works include *Ob-Ugric Metrics: The Metrical Structure of Ostyak and Vogul Folk-Poetry, Finnish Reader and Glossary,* and *The Scope of American Linguistics,* which he edited.

OBITUARIES AND OTHER SOURCES:

BOOKS

Who's Who in America, 46th edition, Marquis, 1990, p. 124.

PERIODICALS

New York Times, September 18, 1994, p. 54.

*   *   *

AYER, Eleanor H.   1947-

PERSONAL: Born September 6, 1947, in Burlington, VT; daughter of William H. (a plumbing and heating contractor) and Shirley T. (an elementary school teacher; maiden name, Thomas) Hubbard; married John Ayer (a publisher); children: Madison, William. *Education:* Newhouse School of Journalism, Syracuse University, B.S., 1969, M.S., 1970.

ADDRESSES: Office—P.O. Box 177, 541 Oak St., Frederick, CO 80530.

CAREER: Laubach Literacy Foundation, Syracuse, NY, associate editor for *News for You,* 1967-69; Laubach Literacy Foundation, Syracuse, associate editor for New Readers Press, 1969-70; *Jackson Hole Guide,* Jackson, WY, assistant editor, 1971; Jende-Hagan (book distribution and publishing company), Frederick, CO, cofounder, editor, and marketing manager, 1972—; Pruett Publishing Company, Boulder, CO, production/promotion coordinator, 1972; Shields Publishing Company, Fort Collins, CO, production/promotion coordinator, 1973-74; Renaissance House Publishing Company, Frederick, CO, editor and marketing manager, 1984—. Founder and writer for *The American Traveler* (travel guides), 1987—; free-lance writer.

MEMBER: Society of Children's Book Writers and Illustrators, Rocky Mountain Book Publishers Association, Mountains and Plains Booksellers Association, Colorado Authors' League.

AWARDS, HONORS: Top Hand Award for young adult nonfiction, Colorado Authors' League, 1991, for *Teen Marriage;* Notable Children's Trade Book in the field of social studies, Children's Book Council and the National Council for Social Studies, 1992, for *Margaret Bourke-White;* Top Hand Award for specialty writing, Colorado Authors' League, 1992, for *Southwest Traveler: The Anasazi: A Guide to Ancient Southwest Indians,* Top Hand Award for booklength nonfiction for young adults, Colorado Authors' League, 1992, for *The Value of Determination.*

WRITINGS:

Green Light on the Tipple, Platte 'N Press, 1978.

"COLORADO CHRONICLES" SERIES

Famous Colorado Men, Platte 'N Press, 1980.
Famous Colorado Women, Platte 'N Press, 1981.
Indians of Colorado, illustrated by Jane Kline, Renaissance House, 1981.
Hispanic Colorado, illustrated by Kline, Renaissance House, 1982.
Colorado Wildlife, Platte 'N Press, 1983.
(Editor) *Colorado Businesses,* Renaissance House, 1984.
(Editor) Suzanne Thumhart, *Colorado Wonders,* illustrated by Kline, Renaissance House, 1986.
Colorado Chronicles Index, illustrated by Kline, Renaissance House, 1986.

"TRAVEL GUIDES" SERIES

Colorado Traveler—Hall of Fame: A Gallery of the Rich and Famous, Renaissance House, 1987.
Colorado Traveler—Birds, Renaissance House, 1987.
Colorado Traveler—Parks and Monuments, Renaissance House, 1987.

Colorado Traveler—Wildflowers: A Guide to Colorado's Unique Varieties, Renaissance House, 1987.
Colorado Traveler—Skiing, Renaissance House, 1987.
Colorado Traveler—Discover Colorado, Renaissance House, 1988.
Arizona Traveler: Birds of Arizona—A Guide to Unique Varieties, Renaissance House, 1988.
Arizona Traveler: Discover Arizona—The Grand Canyon State, Renaissance House, 1988.
Arizona Traveler: Arizona Wildflowers, Renaissance House, 1989.
Arizona Traveler: Indians of Arizona, Renaissance House, 1990.
Southwest Traveler: A Guide to the Anasazi and Other Ancient Southwest Indians, Renaissance House, 1991.
California Traveler Earthquake Country: Traveling California's Fault Lines, Renaissance House, 1992.
California Traveler National Parks and Monuments: A Scenic Guide, Renaissance House, 1992.

Also editor of volumes in the Colorado, Arizona, California, and Southwest Traveler series.

NONFICTION FOR YOUNG ADULTS

Teen Marriage, Rosen Publishing Group, 1990.
Germany, Rourke, 1990.
The Value of Determination, Rosen Publishing Group, 1991.
Berlin, New Discovery Books/Macmillan, 1992.
Boris Yeltsin: Man of the People (biography), Dillon Press/Macmillan, 1992.
Margaret Bourke-White: Photographing the World (biography), Dillon Press/Macmillan, 1992.
Our Flag, Millbrook Press, 1992.
Our National Monuments, Millbrook Press, 1992.
The Anasazi, Walker and Company, 1993.
Everything You Need to Know about Teen Fatherhood, Rosen Publishing Group, 1993.
Teen Suicide: Is It Too Painful to Grow Up?, Twenty-first Century Books/Holt, 1993.
Our Great Rivers and Waterways, Millbrook Press, 1994.

Also author of revised editions of *Drug Abuse,* Rosen Publishing Group, 1991; *Sexual Abuse,* Rosen Publishing Group, 1992; *Family Violence,* Rosen Publishing Group, 1993.

WORK IN PROGRESS: Ruth Bader Ginsburg, and *The Holocaust Museum: America Keeps the Memory Alive* are under contract for Dillon Press (Macmillan), and *Depression* is under contract for Rosen Publishing Group. Ayer has completed manuscripts for

Parallel Journey for Atheneum/Macmillan, and *Stress* for the Rosen Publishing Group. All are expected to be published in 1994.

SIDELIGHTS: Eleanor H. Ayer is the author of numerous books. She has written travel guides and nonfiction works for young adults. She is also the author of the "Colorado Chronicles" series, which depicts various historical elements of the state.

BIOGRAPHICAL/CRITICAL SOURCES:

PERIODICALS

Booklist, June 15, 1992, p. 1818; December 1, 1992.
Kirkus Reviews, January 1, 1993.
School Library Journal, October, 1992, p. 124; March, 1993, p. 205.
Voice of Youth Advocate, December, 1992, p. 298.

B

BAHLKE, Valerie Worth 1933-1994
(Valerie Worth)

OBITUARY NOTICE—See index for *CA* sketch: Born October 29, 1933, in Philadelphia, PA; died of cancer, July 31, 1994, in Clinton, NY. Poet and novelist. Bahlke was an author who wrote prose and poetry under her maiden name, Valerie Worth. After graduating from Swarthmore College in 1955, she married and began raising a family in Clinton, NY. Through a writers' group in her community, Worth met Natalie Babbitt, who encouraged her to send some of her poetry to an editor at Farrar, Straus, & Giroux. Her first published titles—*The Crone's Book of Words* and *Small Poems*—appeared in the early 1970s. The latter work, illustrated by Babbitt, was followed by three similar volumes that were collectively published in 1987 as *All the Small Poems*. In these books, which earned Worth praise from critics, she penned free-form verses that appealed to a child's natural curiosity about the world. *New York Times Book Review* critic Doris Orgel noted that Worth's verse "looks at everyday creatures and objects . . . and lights up their extraordinary aspects with a brilliance not to be missed."

Another book of verse, *At Christmastime,* was joined by Worth's novels for children and young adults, *Curlicues: The Fortunes of Two Pug Dogs, Gypsy Gold,* and *Fox Hill.* Her work also appeared in several anthologies and periodicals, and for her contributions to children's literature she received the 1991 Award for Excellence in Poetry for Children from the National Council of Teachers of English. Before her passing Worth had finished two other volumes of poetry for young readers scheduled to appear in 1995 and 1996.

OBITUARIES AND OTHER SOURCES:

BOOKS

Children's Literature Review, Volume 21, Gale, 1990.
Something About the Author, Volume 70, Gale, 1993.

PERIODICALS

New York Times, August 3, 1994, p. D18.
Publishers Weekly, August 22, 1994, p. 27.
Washington Post, August 5, 1994, p. D4.

*   *   *

BAHN, Paul (Gerard) 1953-

PERSONAL: Born July 29, 1953, in Hull, England; son of Charles Edward and Emilia (a schoolteacher; maiden name, Gobbers) Bahn. *Education:* Gonville and Caius College, Cambridge, B.A., 1974, M.A., 1978, Ph.D., 1979. *Avocational interests:* Music, cinema, genealogy.

ADDRESSES: Home—Hull, England. *Agent*—Watson, Little Ltd., 12 Egbert St., London NW1 8LJ, England.

CAREER: University of Liverpool, Liverpool, England, postdoctoral research fellow in archaeology, 1979-82; University of London, London, England, V. Canada Blanch research fellow in archaeology, 1982-83; J. Paul Getty research fellow in the history of art and humanities, 1985-86; freelance writer, translator, and broadcaster, 1986—. Easter Island Foundation, vice-president.

MEMBER: Prehistoric Society, Society of Antiquaries

(fellow), Rock Art Association of America, Australian Rock Art Research Association (vice-president, 1992-96), Societe Prehistorique Francaise, Rock Art Association of South Africa.

WRITINGS:

Pyrenean Prehistory, Aris & Phillips (Westminster), 1984.
(With Jacquetta Hawkes) *The Shell Guide to British Archaeology,* M. Joseph (London), 1986.
(With Glyn Daniel) *Ancient Places: The Prehistoric and Celtic Sites of Britain,* Constable, 1987.
(With Jean Vertut) *Images of the Ice Age,* Facts on File (New York), 1988.
The Bluffer's Guide to Archaeology, Ravette (Horsham), 1989.
(With Colin Renfrew) *Archaeology: Theories, Methods, and Practice,* Thames & Hudson, 1991.
(With John Flenley) *Easter Island, Earth Island,* Thames & Hudson, 1992.
(Editor and contributor) *The Collins Dictionary of Archaeology,* HarperCollins, 1992, American Bibliographical Center-Clio Press, 1993.
(With Adrian Lister) *Mammoths,* Macmillan, 1994.
(Editor and contributor) *The Cambridge Illustrated History of Archaeology,* Cambridge University Press, in press.
The Cambridge Illustrated History of Prehistoric Art, Cambridge University Press, in press.

Contributing editor, *Archaeology.*

TRANSLATOR

Paul Courbin, *What Is Archaeology?,* University of Chicago Press (Chicago), 1988.
Marina Rodna, *The Bluffer's Guide to Modern Art,* Ravette (Horsham), 1990.
Serge Gruzinski, *The Aztecs: Rise and Fall of an Empire,* Abrams, 1992.
Maurice Krafft, *Volcanoes: Fire from the Earth,* Abrams, 1993.
Carmen Bernand, *The Incas,* Abrams, 1994.

*   *   *

BAILYN, Lotte   1930-

PERSONAL: Born July 17, 1930, in Vienna, Austria; daughter of Paul F. (a professor) and Marie Jamoda (a professor; maiden name, Albu) Lazarsfeld; married Bernard Bailyn (a professor), 1952; children: Charles, John. *Education:* Swarthmore College, B.A. (with high honors), 1951; Harvard University, M.A., 1953, Ph.D., 1956.

ADDRESSES: Home—170 Clifton St., Belmont, MA 02178. *Office*—Sloan School of Management, Massachusetts Institute of Technology, E52-585, Cambridge, MA 02139. *Agent*—Palmer & Dodge Agency, 1 Beacon St., Boston, MA 02108.

CAREER: Harvard University, Cambridge, MA, postdoctoral research associate in education, 1956-57; Massachusetts Institute of Technology, Cambridge, instructor in economics and social science, 1957-58; Harvard University, research associate, 1958-64, lecturer in social relations, 1963-67; Massachusetts Institute of Technology, research associate, 1969-70, lecturer, 1970-71, senior lecturer, 1971-72, associate professor, 1972-80, professor, 1980-91, T. Wilson Professor of Management, 1991—. University of London, Imperial College of Science and Technology, visiting scholar in social and economic studies, 1982, academic visitor at Management School, 1991; Rockefeller Foundation Study and Conference Center (Bellagio, Italy), scholar in residence, 1983; University of Auckland, visiting university fellow in management studies, 1984; Cambridge University, visiting scholar at New Hall, 1986-87.

MEMBER: Academy of Management, American Psychological Association (fellow), American Psychological Society (charter fellow), American Sociological Association, Phi Beta Kappa, Sigma Xi.

WRITINGS:

Mass Media and Children: A Study of Exposure Habits and Cognitive Effects (monograph), American Psychological Association, 1959.
(With E. H. Schein) *Living with Technology: Issues at Mid-Career,* MIT Press, 1980.
(With M. B. Arthur, D. J. Levinson, and H. A. Shepard) *Working with Careers,* Center for Research in Career Development, Columbia University, 1984.
Breaking the Mold: Women, Men, and Time in the New Corporate World, Free Press (New York, NY), 1993.

Work represented in books, including *Transforming Organizations,* edited by T. Kochan and M. Useem, Oxford University Press, 1992; *Career Development in the 1990s: Theory and Practice,* edited by D. H. Montross and C. J. Shinkman, C. C. Thomas, 1992; and *Men, Work, and Family,* edited by J. C. Hood, Sage Publications, 1993. Contributor to periodicals, including *New Technology, Work, and Employment, Human Resource Management, Journal of Occupational Behaviour, Annals of the New York Academy of Sciences, Journal of Conflict Resolution* and

Daedalus. Editor, *Journal of Social Issues,* 1962.

WORK IN PROGRESS: Research on the organizational constraints on individuals, families, and communities.

* * *

BALDASSARRI, Mario 1946-

PERSONAL: Born September 10, 1946, in Macerata, Italy; son of Zelido and Lucia (Vigiano) Baldassarri; divorced; children: Pierfrancesco, Marta, Pierluca. *Education:* University of Ancona, D.Econ., 1969; Massachusetts Institute of Technology, Ph.D., 1978. *Politics:* "Liberal—center." *Religion:* Roman Catholic.

ADDRESSES: Home—Via G. Pezzana 110, Rome, Italy. *Office*—Department of Economics, University of Rome, Via del Castro Laurenziano 9, Rome, Italy.

CAREER: Catholic University of Milan, Milan, Italy, associate professor of economics, 1974-79; University of Bologna, Bologna, Italy, professor of economics, 1980-89; University of Rome, Rome, Italy, professor of economics, 1989—. ENI, member of board of directors; member of Italian Ministry of the Treasury and Ministry of the Budget. Television commentator.

MEMBER: International Economic Association, European Economic Association, American Economic Association.

WRITINGS:

Saggi di programmazione economica, ITL, 1977.
Spesa pubblica, inflazione, crescita, Il Mulino, 1978.
The Italian Economy: Heaven or Hell, Macmillan, 1990.
World Savings, Inflation, and Growth, Macmillan, 1992.
The Italian Economy: A New Miracle, Macmillan, 1993.

Co-editor of the book *Eastern Europe's Transition to a Market Economy,* St. Martin's. Contributor to magazines and newspapers. Editor, *Rivista di Politica Economica.*

WORK IN PROGRESS: Research on human capital, savings, and endogenous growth.

SIDELIGHTS: Mario Baldassarri told *CA:* "I was born in 1946, in a small, country village in Italy which, despite its size, housed one of the oldest European universities, founded in 1284. I was raised in a good, traditional family and, at university, I met with very intelligent teachers. Two days after graduation, I left Ancona to discover the world. I spent three years in Milan, three in Turin, four in Boston, ten in Bologna, and six in Rome. I was lucky to be awarded scholarships and fellowships for graduate study.

"My luck also convinced me of the importance of human capital. My net worth, after twenty-five years of work, is not remarkable, but I did make huge investments in the human capital of my children. I hope to be lucky enough, once again, to see the results."

* * *

BANERJEE, Asit 1940-

PERSONAL: Born December 24, 1940, in Dacca, India (now Bangladesh); son of Atul Chandra and Prativa Banerjee; married Bela (a librarian), February 22, 1966; children: Maitree Banerjee Kanjilal. *Education:* Presidency College, Calcutta, graduated, 1959; University of Calcutta, post-graduate degree in physics, 1961, Ph.D., 1970. *Religion:* Hindu. *Avocational interests:* Music, literature.

ADDRESSES: Home—G1, Cluster IX, Purbachal, Salt Lake, Calcutta 700091, India. *Office*—Department of Physics, Jadavpur University, Calcutta 700032, India.

CAREER: Jadavpur University, Calcutta, India, lecturer, 1964-78, reader, 1978-86, professor of physics, 1986—, and coordinator of Relativity and Cosmology Research Centre. Institut Henri Poincare, postdoctoral fellow, 1971-72; Federal University of Rio de Janeiro, visiting professor, 1979-81; Inter-University Centre for Astronomy and Astrophysics (Pune), senior associate.

MEMBER: Indian Association for General Relativity and Gravitation (member of executive committee).

WRITINGS:

(Co-author) *General Relativity, Astrophysics, and Cosmology,* Springer-Verlag, 1992.

Contributor of nearly eighty articles to scientific journals.

WORK IN PROGRESS: Research on general relativity and cosmology.

SIDELIGHTS: Asit Banerjee told *CA:* "I have been working in the field of relativity and cosmology since 1966. About ten years back, a workshop on general relativity and cosmology was organized in Calcutta for young researchers in that field. That was the beginning of my book. My co-authors and I felt encouraged to combine three topics—general relativity, astrophysics, and cosmology—into a single volume as a general introduction to the subject. We hope this will enable students and researchers to proceed with more detailed treatises in the future. I would like to write more books on physics, mainly for the benefit of students at the graduate level."

* * *

BANGERT, Sharon 1951-

PERSONAL: Born January 8, 1951, in St. Louis, MO; daughter of Bill (a real estate developer, athlete, and singer) and Rosemary (a singer; maiden name, Ryan) Bangert; married Terry Corcoran (an artist), December 13, 1992. *Education:* Washington University, St. Louis, MO, B.A., 1980, M.F.A., 1983. *Avocational interests:* Music, art, the environment.

ADDRESSES: Home—Greenhall Lodge, Tinahely, County Wicklow, Ireland.

CAREER: Writer. Coolattin Woods Action Committee, secretary, 1992-94.

WRITINGS:

TRANSLATOR FROM FRENCH

Isabelle Eberhardt, *In the Shadow of Islam* (travel book), P. Owen, 1993.
Eberhardt, *Prisoner of Dunes* (travel book), P. Owen, 1994.

WORK IN PROGRESS: A novel.

* * *

BARAM, Amatzia 1938-

PERSONAL: Born in 1938, in Kibbutz Kfar Menachem, Israel; son of Mayrim and Rose Baram; married Bonnie Belkin, 1993. *Education:* Hebrew University of Jerusalem, B.A., 1975, M.A., 1977, Ph.D., 1986.

ADDRESSES: Home—50 Pinsker St., Neveh Shaanan, Haifa, Israel. *Office*—Department of Modern History of the Middle East, University of Haifa, Haifa, Israel.

CAREER: Science teacher at the high school in Kibbutz Kfar Menachem, Israel, 1968-73; Hebrew University of Jerusalem, Jerusalem, Israel, tutor, 1976-80; University of Haifa, Haifa, Israel, lecturer, became senior lecturer in modern history of the Middle East, 1982—, and deputy director of Jewish-Arab Center and Gustav Heinemann Institute for Middle Eastern Studies, 1992-93. Hebrew University of Jerusalem, research fellow in advanced studies, 1986-87; Oxford University, senior associate member of St. Antony's College, 1988, 1990; Smithsonian Institution, fellow at Woodrow Wilson International Center for Scholars, 1989, 1993-94. Member of the Israeli prime minister's advisory team on Middle Eastern affairs, 1984-88. Analyst for U.S. television and radio news programs; guest on television and radio programs in England, Europe, and Japan.

WRITINGS:

Culture, History, and Ideology in the Formation of Ba'thist Iraq, 1968-1989, St. Martin's, 1991.
(Editor, with Barry Rubin)*Iraq's Road to War,* St. Martin's Press, 1994.

Work represented in books, including *Islamic Fundamentalism and the Gulf War,* edited by James Piscatori, American Academy of Arts and Sciences, 1991; *The Politics of Change in the Middle East,* edited by Robert Satloff, Westview, 1993; and *International Perspective of the Gulf War, 1990-91,* edited by Alex Danchev and Dan Koehane, St. Martin's, 1994. Contributor to Middle East studies journals.

WORK IN PROGRESS: Iraq of the Ba'th 1968-1994: Domestic Strife and Foreign Conflicts.

* * *

BARBER, E(lizabeth) J. W(ayland) 1940-

PERSONAL: Born December 2, 1940, in Pasadena, CA; daughter of J. Harold (an engineering science professor) and Virginia (a historical researcher and author) Wayland; married Paul Barber (an author, scholar, and small business owner/operator), June 14, 1965. *Education:* Bryn Mawr College, B.A. (magna cum laude), 1962; received M.A. and Ph.D. (1968) from Yale University.

ADDRESSES: Home—Pasadena, CA. *Office*—Language Department, Occidental College, 1600 Campus Dr., Los Angeles, CA 90041.

CAREER: Chinese Linguistics Project, Princeton University, Princeton, NJ, research associate, 1968-69; Occidental College, Los Angeles, CA, 1970—, became professor of linguistics and archaeology. Consultant to Asia Foundation on Chinese machine translation project, 1974; lecturer for the Archaeological Institute of America, 1974-76, 1983-84, and 1993-94.

MEMBER: Southern California Society of Archaeological Institute of America (vice-president, 1989-92; president, 1992-95), Archaeological Institute of America, Linguistic Society of America, Textile Society of America (board member, 1988-94), Centre International d'Etudes des Textiles Anciens.

AWARDS, HONORS: National Endowment for the Humanities (NEH) Education Grant for linguistics, 1972-74; John Simon Guggenheim Memorial Foundation Fellowship for archaeology of textiles, 1979-80; Wenner-Gren Foundation for Anthropological Research fellowship for archaeology of textiles, 1984; Getty Foundation grant/award in art history, 1989; Millia P. Davenport Book Award (first prize), 1992, for *Prehistoric Textiles;* Graham L. Sterling Faculty Achievement Award, Occidental College, 1993; Charles Breasted book prize in ancient history, 1994, for *Prehistoric Textiles;* Los Angeles Times Book Prize in history, finalist, 1994, for *Women's Work.*

WRITINGS:

Archaeological Decipherment, Princeton University Press, 1974.
Prehistoric Textiles: The Development of Cloth in the Neolithic and Bronze Ages, Princeton University Press, 1991.
Women's Work—The First 20,000 Years, Norton, 1994.

Contributor to books, including *Goddess and Polis: The Panathenaic Festival in Ancient Athens,* edited by Jenifer Neils, Princeton University Press, 1992; and *Critical Essays in Homer,* edited by K. Atchity, G. K. Hall (Boston, MA), 1987. Contributor to periodicals, including *Diachronica, Journal of Indo-European Studies,* and *American Journal of Archeology.*

WORK IN PROGRESS: Articles on early history of costume; research into the development of mythology as function of human cognitive and linguistic processes, research into history of European costume and of European dance, and research into the Bronze Age diaspora of the Indo-Europeans.

SIDELIGHTS: E. J. W. Barber told *CA:* "My lifelong love of archaeology, which took me over at age twelve, is antedated only by my love of dancing, which took hold at age five. Since then I have dived deeply (successively) into studying the Minoans, ancient Greek, linguistics, Russian, and choreography. Recently all these interests have begun to converge.

"Growing up at Caltech, I absorbed the thought patterns of scientists from my father and his colleagues, a trait that has had lasting effects on my work. But I also absorbed their humanistic interests—music, dance, the visual arts, and especially language. 'If you can't explain it clearly to people, what's the point of making the discovery?' I often heard my father say. Himself a polyglot, he encouraged my sister and me to learn to write English clearly, concisely, and interestingly and to learn other languages. We both now have Ph.D.s in linguistics and have done some joint research.

"My interests in languages and archaeology have always been closely tied, and I constantly explore new ways that linguistics can help archaeology. (For example, my undergraduate and Ph.D. theses, my first book, and several articles deal with the problems of undeciphered scripts.) Convergence of my 'professional' and 'personal' interests began with my work on ancient textiles, which was greatly facilitated by a knowledge of traditional European folk costumes and crafts that I had acquired in conjunction with folkdancing (as well as from my mother). This project, which I originally thought would take a month, turned out to be so rich that it took seventeen years and travel to fourteen countries, and ended in two books. Convergence became even more striking when I began researching the origins of dances and costumes referred to in an archaic Russian folk tale, preparatory to choreographing it for a dance troupe. The trail led deep into the archaeology of the Stone Age of East Europe and occupied me for three years. With *Women's Work,* thanks to help from my husband, Paul Barber, and my editor at Norton, Edwin Barber (no relation), I have also discovered the pleasure that my father predicted so long ago, of writing up my discoveries in such a way that readers at large could share in the fun of the chase."

BIOGRAPHICAL/CRITICAL SOURCES:

PERIODICALS

Antiquity, March, 1992, pp. 271-272.
Archaeology, spring, 1992, pp. 2-11.
New York Times Book Review, July 10, 1994, pp. 12-13.
Science, May 15, 1992, pp. 1065-1066.
Scientific American, September, 1994, pp. 108-109.

*   *   *

BARKER, Raffaella   1964-

PERSONAL: Born November 24, 1964, in London, England; daughter of George (a poet) and Elspeth (a writer) Barker. *Education:* Attended girls' secondary school in Norwich, England. *Religion:* "Renegade Catholic." *Avocational interests:* Horseback riding, buying items from auctions, reading, talking on the telephone.

ADDRESSES: Agent—Alexandra Pringle, Toby Eady Associates, 9 Orme Ct., London W.2, England.

CAREER: Free-lance writer, 1988—. Worked as a features writer for *Harpers and Queen.*

MEMBER: London Library, Groucho Club.

WRITINGS:

Come and Tell Me Some Lies (novel), Hamish Hamilton, 1994, Penguin, 1995.

Contributing editor, *Harpers and Queen.*

WORK IN PROGRESS: Do Not Forsake Me, a novel, publication expected in 1996.

SIDELIGHTS: Raffaella Barker told *CA:* "I began my writing career by accident. I had no skills whatsoever, not even typing, but was fortunate to get my first job as a journalist when I was twenty-one years old. Once I learned to type, the scope of my writing increased. I wrote my first novel as my way of coming to terms with the death of my father in 1991. My next book is about the nature of trust.

"My writing is not particularly influenced by anyone, although I admire the work of Michael Ondaatje, Tolstoy, Edith Wharton, Candia McWilliam, and many others. I find it best not to read any of them when I am writing. My working habits are undisciplined—four hours one day and none the next. I advise aspiring writers to be aware of the solitary nature of writing, and

to have an unstoppable urge to say whatever it is they are trying to communicate. You can't lie, and you should beware of adjectives."

*   *   *

BARKER, Rocky
See BARKER, Roland

*   *   *

BARKER, Roland   1953-
(Rocky Barker)

PERSONAL: Born September 10, 1953, in Galesburg, IL; son of Gordon (a furniture dealer) and Alberta (an accountant; maiden name, Reihm) Barker; married Tina Nelson (an office manager), April 7, 1979; children: Daniel, David, Nicole. *Education:* Northland College, B.A., 1975. *Politics:* Independent. *Religion:* United Church of Christ. *Avocational interests:* Fishing, hiking, hunting, skiing, hockey.

ADDRESSES: Home and office—1020 11th St., Idaho Falls, ID 83404.

CAREER: Washburn Times, Washburn, WI, reporter, 1975-77; *Daily Press,* Ashland, WI, reporter, 1977-80; *Daily News,* Rhinelander, WI, reporter and managing editor, 1980-85; *Post Register,* Idaho Falls, ID, reporter and editor, 1985-94. *Wisconsin Sportsman,* Northwest field editor, 1976-80; *High Country News,* Idaho correspondent, 1987-88. University of Maryland at College Park, fellow of Knight School of Specialized Journalism.

MEMBER: Society of Environmental Journalists, Idaho Press Club (member of board of directors, 1988-91).

AWARDS, HONORS: Two Pulitzer Prize nominations; three Blethen Awards from Pacific Northwest Newspaper Association; award from Idaho Steelhead and Salmon Unlimited, 1991; finalist for the Edward J. Meeman Award for environmental journalism, for series of reports on the Endangered Species Act; state and regional journalism awards.

WRITINGS:

(Under name Rocky Barker) *Saving All the Parts: Reconciling Economics and the Endangered Species Act,* Island Press (Washington, DC), 1993.

Contributor to periodicals, including *Outside, Fin and Feathers, Wisconsin Natural Resources,* and *Buzzworm.*

WORK IN PROGRESS: "The Next West," a chapter to be included in a collection of essays; research on fires in Yellowstone National Park, wolves in the West, biodiversity in Hawaii, and Russia's wild East.

SIDELIGHTS: Roland Barker told *CA:* "Journalists are taught to write objectively, or at least to have objectivity as a goal. A separate set of journalism ethics has been developed to help journalists reach that goal and to keep themselves outsiders—flies on the wall—to the events and institutions we cover. I reject the erection of these false Chinese walls between the writer and his subjects. The ethics I follow are the same ethics I follow in life: basically, respect of human dignity and of the entire life community. The balance I use is the knowledge that, no matter how comprehensively I have researched a subject, I may not understand the real truth. I may be wrong, so I have a responsibility to show my readers plausible alternative realities to those I present.

"I am a columnist and correspondent-at-large for the Idaho Falls *Post Register.* I led the newspaper's team of reporters and editors in its examination of the Endangered Species Act and its effects on the Pacific Northwest and the Northern Rockies. The series was a finalist for the Edward J. Meeman Award for environmental journalism.

"I also was the lead reporter for the *Post Register's* award-winning coverage of the Yellowstone fires in 1988, as well as the paper's nationally recognized coverage of nuclear waste problems at the Idaho National Engineering Laboratory. I have covered environmental issues ranging from mining in Wisconsin, acid rain in Canada, and rain forest protection in Hawaii to budding environmentalism in the former Soviet Union."

*   *   *

BARNES, Annie S.   1932-

PERSONAL: Born April 15, 1932, in Red Level, AL; daughter of Adam (a sharecropper) and Annie S. (a sharecropper; maiden name, Howell) Shaw; married Bennie M. Barnes (a college professor), June 9, 1963; children: Trina Miranda Barnes Jones. *Education:* Shaw University, B.A., 1953; Atlanta University, M.A., 1955; attended New York University, summers, 1957-58; University of Virginia, Ph.D., 1971.

Politics: Democrat. *Religion:* Baptist.

ADDRESSES: Home—1029 Dulcie Ave., Virginia Beach, VA 23455. *Office*—Department of Sociology, Norfolk State University, 2401 Corprew Ave., Norfolk, VA 23504-3907.

CAREER: High school teacher of American history and government, 1954-65; Hampton Institute, Hampton, VA, instructor in sociology, 1965-68; Norfolk State University, Norfolk, VA, associate professor, 1971-76, professor of anthropology and sociology, 1976—. Tidewater Assembly on Family Life, member of Task Force on Human Sexuality, 1979-81; lecturer at colleges and universities, including Old Dominion University; workshop leader; guest on television and radio programs.

MEMBER: National Council of Anthropology and Education, American Anthropological Association (fellow; member of executive committee, General Anthropology Division, 1984-86; member of board of directors, 1992-94), Association of Black Anthropologists (president, 1992-93), American Ethnological Association (fellow), Southern Anthropological Association, Virginia Social Science Association (life member; member of executive board, 1980-81; vice president, 1982; president, 1983-84).

AWARDS, HONORS: Grant from Eastern Virginia International Studies Consortium (for West Africa), 1975; grant from National Science Foundation, 1976; Service Award, District Organization of the Veterans of Foreign Wars, 1979; grant from Minority Institutions Science Improvement Program, 1980; Virginia Social Science Association, Sociology Honors Award, 1981, Distinguished Service Award, 1986; elected one of thirteen Virginia Outstanding Faculty Members, Virginia State Council of Higher Education, 1988; Martin Luther King, Jr. Certificate, Norfolk chapter of Links, Inc., 1993.

WRITINGS:

The Black Middle Class Family: A Study of Black Subsociety, Neighborhood, and Home in Interaction, Wyndham Hall Press, 1985.
(Editor) *Social Science Research Skills Handbook,* Wyndham Hall Press, 1985.
Black Women: Interpersonal Relationships in Profile, Wyndham Hall Press, 1986.
Single Parents in Black America: A Study in Culture and Legitimacy, Wyndham Hall Press, 1987.
Retention of African-American Males in High School, with video cassette, University Press of America, 1992.

Research Skills in the Social Sciences, Kendall/ Hunt, 1993.

Work represented in books, including *Dimensions for Growing Up,* edited by Georgeanna Seegar Jones, Norfolk Planning Council, 1983; *Contemporary Black Marriages and Family Life,* edited by Constance E. Obudho, Greenwood Press, 1983; and *African-Americans in the American South,* edited by Hans Baer and Yvonne Jones, University of Georgia Press, 1992. Contributor to sociology and anthropology journals.

WORK IN PROGRESS: A Portrait of Racism since Desegregation; Please Come Home College Daddy to Mama and Me, a study of unwed college students who are fathers; research on the exclusion of African American enlisted males from the military judicial system, with a publication expected to result.

*   *   *

BARNHARDT, Deanna
See KAWATSKI, Deanna

*   *   *

BARTOSZEWSKI, Wladyslaw T(eofil) 1955-

PERSONAL: Surname pronounced "Bartoshevsky"; born October 22, 1955, in Warsaw, Poland; British citizen; son of Wladyslaw Bartoszewski (a historian and diplomat) and Antonina Bartoszewska (a medical doctor; maiden name, Mijal). *Education:* University of Warsaw, M.A., 1980; University of Cambridge, Ph.D., 1984. *Religion:* Roman Catholic.

ADDRESSES: Home—15 Queen's Gate Pl., London SW7 5NX, England. *Office*—Central Europe Trust, 197 Knightsbridge, London SW7 1RB, England.

CAREER: Catholic University of Lublin, Lublin, Poland, assistant in Department of History and Culture, 1980; Max Weinreich Center for Advanced Jewish Studies, YIVO Institute for Jewish Research and Columbia University, New York City, research fellow, 1982-83; Hebrew University of Jerusalem, Jerusalem, Israel, visiting fellow in Department of Anthropology and Sociology, 1984-85; University of Cambridge, Cambridge, England, visiting lecturer in Department of Social Anthropology, 1985; St. Antony's College, Oxford, England, research fellow, 1985-89, senior associate member, 1989-90; Institute of Polish-Jewish Studies, Oxford, secretary, 1985-92, director, 1985—; Sarah Lawrence College

Year Abroad Programme at Wadham College, Oxford, tutor in modern history and politics, 1986-90; London School of Economics and Political Science, London, England, research assistant in Department of International History, 1987-91; historical adviser in the War Crime Enquiry, Home Office, London, 1988-89; Oxford Year Abroad at Lady Margaret Hall, Oxford, tutor in modern history and politics, 1988-90; Institute of Russian, Soviet, and East European Studies, University of Oxford, Oxford, senior associate, 1988-90; University of London, London, tutor in Jewish history, 1989-90; University of Warwick, lecturer in Department of History, 1989-91; British and European Studies Group, London, lecturer in East European history, 1990; COBA-M.I.D., London, associate, 1990-91; Central Europe Trust, London, manager, 1991-93, senior manager, 1993-94, director, CIS, 1994—. Lecturer on Israel, Radio Free Europe/Radio Liberty, 1986.

MEMBER: American Anthropological Association, Association of Social Anthropologists of the Commonwealth, Hawks Club (Cambridge), Royal Anthropological Institute (fellow), Societe Historique et Litteraire Polonaise, Traditional Cosmology Society, United Oxford and Cambridge University Club.

AWARDS, HONORS: De Brzezie Lanckoronski Foundation, 1982; "ORS Awards Scheme," Committee of Vice Chancellors and Principals of the Universities of the U.K., 1982-84; Pilsudski Institute of America for Research in the Modern History of Poland, 1982; Memorial Foundation for Jewish Culture scholarship, 1983, fellowship, 1985.

WRITINGS:

(Editor) Samuel Willenberg, *Surviving Treblinka,* Basil Blackwell (Oxford), 1989.
The Convent at Auschwitz, Bowerdean Press (London), 1990, George Braziller (New York), 1991.
(Editor, with A. Polonsky) *The Jews of Warsaw,* Basil Blackwell (Oxford), 1991.
(Editor) Salomon W. Slowes, *The Road to Katyn: A Soldier's Story,* Basil Blackwell (Oxford), 1992.

Contributor to books, including *Poland, Trade and Investment Opportunities,* Caversham Press (London), 1991; *Hostages of Modernization: Studies on Modern Antisemitism 1870-1933/39 (Austria - Hungary - Poland - Russia),* edited by Herbert A. Strauss, Walter de Gruyter (New York), 1993; and *The International Review for Chief Executive Officers: International Edition, Russia and the New Republics (Part I),* Sterling Publications (London), 1994.

Contributor of articles and reviews to scholarly

publications, including *Teksty, JASO,* and *Jewish Quarterly. POLIN: A Journal of Polish-Jewish Studies* (Oxford, England), book review editor, 1985-87, associate editor, 1987-93, member of editorial board, 1993—.

WORK IN PROGRESS: Research into Polish-German relations in modern history.

SIDELIGHTS: Wladyslaw T. Bartoszewski told *CA:* "Writing was an extension of my academic career and a natural activity in my family, as my father is an author of over twenty books. (Family home had a strong influence over my career.) I have been drawn to inter-ethnic topics (relations between different ethnic/national groups) since very little was written at the time (late 1970s) in Poland on such issues, and Jewish topics were virtually taboo subjects due to communist censorship. Following in the footsteps of my father, I have always been interested in breaking the barriers and prejudices between different and historically sometime hostile nations (e.g. Poles/Jews/Germans/Ukrainians)."

BIOGRAPHICAL/CRITICAL SOURCES:

PERIODICALS

New York Times Book Review, July 28, 1991, p. 21.
Times Literary Supplement, December 21, 1990, p. 1379.

*   *   *

BATCHELOR, R. E.   1934-

PERSONAL: Born July 15, 1934, in Southampton, England; son of E. W. and L. Batchelor; married, wife's name Patricia Anne (an inspector of schools), August 11, 1962; children: Jennifer, Helen, Roland, Patrick. *Education:* University of Southampton, B.A., M.A., Certificate of Education, 1960; University of Nottingham, Ph.D., 1966. *Politics:* Liberal. *Avocational interests:* Windsurfing.

ADDRESSES: Home—20 Moor Lane, Bramcote, Nottingham NG9 3FH, England. *Office*—Department of French, University of Nottingham, Nottingham NG7 2RD, England.

CAREER: University of Besancon, Besancon, France, teacher of English, 1957-59; English teacher in San Sebastian, Spain, 1959-60; University of Nottingham, Nottingham, England, teacher of French and Spanish, 1961—. Teacher and researcher at European universities, including University of Paris, University of Salamanca, and University of Valencia.

WRITINGS:

Unamuno, Novelist: A European Perspective, Dolphin Book Co. (Oxford), 1972.
(With M. Offord) *Using French: A Guide to Contemporary Usage,* Cambridge University Press, 1982, 2nd edition, 1993.
(With C. Pountain) *Using Spanish: A Guide to Contemporary Usage,* Cambridge University Press, 1992.
(With M. Offord) *Using French Synonyms,* Cambridge University Press, 1993.
Using Spanish Synonyms, Cambridge University Press, 1994.

Contributor to European studies journals.

WORK IN PROGRESS: Using English Synonyms, a book for Japanese students, with Kyoko Iimura and Ryuichi Iimura, for Yutaka Kubota (Tokyo); *Using French: The Language of the Media and Communications,* with M. Saadi.

SIDELIGHTS: R. E. Batchelor told *CA:* "Although I teach in a department of French, I do not regard myself as limited to the study or the teaching of French, or indeed to publications related to France. I have always promoted a wider view of the world; hence, my publications related to Spain and the Spanish language, and a whole series of articles on European literature, ranging from Dostoyevsky to Nietzsche to Camus and Unamuno. Having spent a number of years in France and Spain, and having taught French and Spanish in the language of the country over a period of many years, I am entirely fluent in those languages. I have naturally advocated teaching foreign languages in the target language.

"My language books offer a deep penetration into French and Spanish, while the books on synonyms do not merely consist of arid lists. They highlight the differences and similarities between synonyms, and encourage students to use the languages in an articulate and essentially creative manner.

"I do not believe the English language or English culture takes priority over other languages and cultures. The study of foreign languages and cultures is a method of combatting the obscurantist attitudes, whether ethnic, political, or religious, that have blighted the history of humanity."

*   *   *

BEAUD, Michel   1935-

PERSONAL: Born May 30, 1935, in Chambery,

France; son of Antoine (a civil servant) and Augusta (Denat) Beaud; married Dominique Calliope Constantinides (in business), 1958. *Education:* Institut d'Etudes Politiques, Licence en Droit, 1956, Doctorat Sciences Economiques, 1964, Agregation, 1966. *Avocational interests:* Equity, sustainability, and the search for humanist perspectives.

ADDRESSES: Home—15 rue La Tour d'Auvergne, 75009 Paris, France. *Office*—Department of Political Economy, University of Paris VII, 2 Place Jussieu, 75005 Paris, France.

CAREER: University of Lille, Lille, France, assistant professor, 1965-66, associate professor of economics, 1966-69; University of Paris VIII, Paris, France, associate professor, 1969-70, professor of economics, 1970-91, and department head; University of Paris VII, Paris, professor of economics, 1991—, and department head. GIS Economie Mondiale, Tiers-Monde, Developpement (GEMDEV), cofounder, 1983, chairperson, 1983-90, member of executive committee, 1990-93, honorary chairperson, 1993—; Vezelay Group, co-founder, 1988; French Ministry of the Environment, vice-chairperson of ECLAT Commission on climate and atmospheric changes, 1989-93; French National Center for Scientific Research, member of scientific committee for environment, society, and long-term development, 1990-93. *Military service:* French Army, 1960-62; became sub-lieutenant.

MEMBER: Association Francaise de Science economique.

AWARDS, HONORS: Prix de These, 1964.

WRITINGS:

Histoire du capitalisme, Le Seuil (Paris), 1981, translation published as *A History of Capitalism, 1500-1980,* Monthly Review Press (New York), 1983.
Le Socialisme a l'epreuve de l'histoire, Le Seuil (Paris), 1982, translation published as *Socialism in the Crucible of History,* Humanities (New Jersey), 1993.
(With Gilles Dostaler) *Le Pensee economique depuis Keynes,* Le Seuil (Paris), 1993, translation published as *Economic Thought Since Keynes,* Edward Elgar (London), 1994.

Contributor to books, including *The Role of the State in Development Processes,* edited by Claude Auroi, Frank Cass, 1992. Contributor to periodicals. Coeditor, *European Journal of Development Research,* 1991. Author of monthly review of economic journals in *Le Monde,* 1986-92.

UNTRANSLATED WORKS

(With P. Danjou and J. David) *Une multinationale francaise: Pechiney Ugine Kuhlmann,* Le Seuil (Paris), 1975.
(With P. Allard, B. Bellon, and others) *Dictionnaire des groupes industriels et financiers en France,* Le Seuil (Paris), 1978.
(Editor with G. de Bernis and Jean Masini), *La France et le Tiers-Monde,* PUG (Grenoble), 1979.
La Politique economique de la gauche, Syros (Paris), Volume I: *Le mirage de la croissance,* 1983, Volume II: *Le grand ecart,* 1985.
L'Art de la these: Comment rediger une these de doctorat . . . ou tout autre travail universitaire, La Decouverte (Paris), 1985.
Le Systeme national/mondial hierarchise: Une nouvelle lecture du capitalisme mondial, La Decouverte (Paris), 1987.
L'Economie mondiale dans les annees 1980, La Decouverte (Paris), 1989.
(With Rodrigo Alvayay and Gustavo Marin) *El Socialismo en el umbral del Siglo XXI,* Editorial Melguiades (Santiago), 1990.
(Author of preface) Lester R. Brown, Christopher Flavin and Sandra Postel, *Le defi planetaire: Pour une economie, ecologique et durable,* Sang de la terre (Paris), 1992.
(Editor with Larbi Bouguerra and wife, Calliope Beaud) *L'Etat de l'environnement dans le monde,* La Decouverte (Paris), 1993.

Contributor to periodicals.

WORK IN PROGRESS: Research on economic problems and economic thought at the end of the century.

SIDELIGHTS: Michel Beaud told *CA:* "I became an economist with the hope that economics could help us to solve some problems of the post-war world. I have become more and more impressed by the gap between 'modern economics' and the rise of economic and social problems in the world—poverty, inequality, social exclusions, etc. I am also greatly influenced by the contrast between the accumulation of technical, scientific, industrial, and financial means and the incapability of our societies to satisfy the basic needs of poor populations, safeguard the main environmental balances, and avoid the sins of new forms of barbarism. In short, I am worried about the contrast between economic means and the lack of meaning and value that characterizes our world. After having tried to understand our world—and become more and more anxious—I am convinced that the answers have to be reached mainly in the ethnic dimension and in a humanist justification."

BEAULIEU, Victor-Levy   1945-

PERSONAL: Born September 2, 1945, in Saint-Paul-de-la-Croix, Quebec, Canada; son of Edmond and Leonie (Belanger) Beaulieu; married Francine Cantin; children: Julie, Melanie. *Education:* Attended the University of Montreal.

ADDRESSES: Home—Montreal, Quebec.

CAREER: Editor and writer.

AWARDS, HONORS: Hachette-Larousse Prize, 1967; Grand Prix de la Ville de Montreal, 1972, for *Les Grands-Peres;* Governor General's Literary Award, 1975, for *Don Quichotte de la Demanche;* Berand-Molson Prize, 1981, for *Satan Belhumeur;* Prix Canada-Belgique, 1981, for *Monsieur Melville.*

WRITINGS:

Memoires d'outre-tonneau, Editions Esterel (Montreal), 1968.
Race de monde! Editions du Jour (Montreal), 1969.
La Nuitte de Malcomm Hudd, Editions du Jour, 1969.
Jos Conaissant, Editions du Jour, 1970, revised edition, VLB (Montreal), 1978, translation by Ray Chamberlain, Exile (Toronto), 1982.
Quand les ecrivains quebecois jouent le jeu, Editions du Jour, 1970.
Pour saluer Victor Hugo, Editions du Jour, 1971.
Les Grands-Peres, Editions du Jour, 1972, revised edition, VLB, 1979, published as *The Grandfathers: A Novel,* translation by Marc Plourde, Harvest House (Montreal), 1975.
Jack Kerouac, Essai-poulet Editions du Jour, 1973, published as *Jack Kerouac: A Chicken-Essay,* translation by Sheila Fischman, Coach House Press (Toronto), 1975.
Oh Miami, Miami, Miami, Editions du Jour, 1973.
Don Quichotte de la demanche, Editions de l'Aurore (Montreal), 1974, published as *Don Quixote in Nighttown,* translation by Fischman, Porcepic (Erin, ON), 1978.
Manuel de la petite litterature du Quebec, Editions de l'Aurore, 1974.
En attendant Trudot (play), Editions de l'Aurore, 1974.
Blanche forcee: Recit, VLB, 1976.
Ma Corriveau suivi de La sorcellerie en finale sexuee: Theatre, VLB, 1976.
N'evoque plus que le desenchantement de ta tenebre, mon si pauvre Abel: Lamentation, VLB, 1976.
Sagamo Job J, VLB, 1977.
Monsieur Zero, VLB, 1977.

Monsieur Melville, 3 volumes, VLB, 1978, translation by Chamberlain, Coach House Press, 1984.
La tete de Monsieur Ferron, VLB, 1979.
Una, VLB, 1980.
Satan Belhumeur, VLB, 1981, translation by Chamberlain, Exile, 1983.
Moi Pierre Leroy, prophete, martyr et un peu fele du chaudron: Plagiarie, VLB, 1982.
Discours de Samm, VLB, 1983.
Entre la saintete et le terrorisme (essays), VLB, 1984.
Steven Le Herault, Stanke (Montreal), 1985, translation by Chamberlain, Exile, 1986.
Chroniques polissonnes d'un telephage enrage (essays), Stanke, 1986.

Also author of theatrical play *Ceremonial pour l'assassinat d'un ministre,* 1978.

SIDELIGHTS: Victor-Levy Beaulieu is considered one of Quebec's foremost proponents and practitioners of experimental literature. Beaulieu identifies with another literary French Canadian, Jack Kerouac, for the autobiographical inspiration of his novels, as well as with nineteenth-century French author Victor Hugo, for the vastness of his oeuvre. As an editor at several avant-garde publishing houses and journals, Beaulieu has fostered innovative, and often nationalistic, literature in Quebec since 1970. Of his own writings, Eva-Marie Kroller wrote in *Dictionary of Literary Biography (DLB):* "Beaulieu's work as a novelist is inseparable from his life; with other Quebecois authors, he shares a fascination with autobiography as a narcissistic mirror and means of self-scrutiny."

Several of Beaulieu's novels are considered part of an ongoing series focusing on the Beauchemin family, entitled "La Vraie Saga des Beauchemin." His first two publications, *Memoires d'outre-tonneau* and *Race du monde!,* introduce the main characters and themes in the series, though as the work has progressed the author has modified his goals for the series and revised some of the volumes accordingly. Other novels in this series include *Jos Connaissant, Les Grands-peres, Don Quichotte de la demanche, Satan Belhumeur,* and *Steven Le Herault.* The Beauchemin family also figures largely in Beaulieu's other main series of connected novels, collectively entitled "Les Voyageries." This series is comprised of *Blanche forcee, N'evoque plus que le desenchantement de ta tenebre, mon si pauvre Abel, Sagamo Job J, Monsieur Melville, Una,* and *Discours de Samm.* As in *Blanche forcee,* which centers on a man equally obsessed by his affair with an unstable woman and his research for a television documentary on whales, these experimental narratives often feature extended interior monologues and explorations of the role of the writer in revealing the workings of the unconscious.

Several of Beaulieu's novels have been translated into English. Of the works in the series entitled "La Vraie Saga des Beauchemin," *Les Grand-peres* has appeared in English as *The Grandfathers. Choice* described this work as depicting "a very sordid image of the world." The elderly man at the center of the novel reminisces about his past aided by a series of odors, including pig's blood, manure, urine, and sweat, recalling the tasks he performed on the farm that had been his home. Of this character *Choice* concluded: "He and his wife, when the reader meets them, are nothing more than decaying, suffering flesh, whose memories include few moments that one would normally call tender or human." A subsequent book in this series, *Don Quichotte de la Demanche,* translated into English as *Don Quixote in Nighttown,* won Canada's most prestigious literary prize, the Governor General's Award, in 1974. In a laudatory review article in the *Canadian Forum,* Joseph Pivato remarked that beyond the allusion to the classic Spanish novel *Don Quixote de la Mancha,* Beaulieu's title exhibits his characteristic dedication to puns, *demanche* meaning *Sunday* but also carrying connotations of mental and physical instability.

Abel Beauchemin, a character who appears in several of Beaulieu's novels, is the main character in *Don Quixote in Nighttown.* A novelist, Beauchemin "shows a passionate concern for the problems of the literary artist. . . . Life experience is used, people are exploited, all for the greater glory of art," according to Pivato. In addition, Pivato found that despite Beauchemin's similarity to the typical hero of Quebecois literature, which he characterizes as "the angry, alienated, underdog," the political element in Beaulieu's novel remains implicit rather than overt, thus lending the novel to a broader interpretation. As Pivato put it: "Abel Beauchemin is not just the type of the Quebec novelist, representing *la condition quebecoise,* but a character in *la condition humaine.*" The *Canadian Forum* reviewer concluded: "The politics of Quebec are transcended, or at least distilled into an artistic creation. In this respect the novel seems to anticipate the international perspective that may emerge in the literary works of the new Quebec." Cedric May of the *Times Literary Supplement* commented: "This crippled Don Quixote is far from myopic. He identifies the intangible threats to the sanity and self-realization of his people and tilts at them with

a desperate glee which is touchingly heroic."

Beaulieu has also written several nonfiction works, including *Manuel de la petite litterature du Quebec* and *Entre la saintete et le terrorisme,* which analyze Quebec cultural history and literature. The *Times Literary Supplement*'s May described the former title as "a curious anthology, a museum of publications which the literary historian systematically ignores: the sermons, the temperance tracts, the lives of local saints and martyrs, the parish monographs, the improving real-life stories which [Beaulieu] sees as indicative of a diminished existence, sacrificially borne in the cause of national survival." *Jack Kerouac: Essai-poulet,* translated as *Jack Kerouac: A Chicken-Essay,* is a biography of the cult American author of French-Canadian ancestry. May remarked: "Beaulieu recognizes in Kerouac a blocked creative imagination which betrays his Canadian origins." Echoing the autobiographical concern that critics find at the center of Beaulieu's novels, *Jack Kerouac* intersperses discussion of the subject with information about occurrences in the author's life as he wrote the book. May concluded of this effort: "Justifiably, he feels that the tribute will be the more honest, the more unashamedly he displays his *parti pris.* His habits of work and his attitudes he offers as his credentials."

Beaulieu's avoidance of realism in his novels has drawn comparisons to such Latin American magic realists as Gabriel Garcia Marquez. In addition, "Beaulieu's professional versatility and the volume of his work have made him somewhat of a living myth on the Quebec literary scene," according to Kroller in *DLB.* Beaulieu even draws on his own past for his inspiration, recognizing in it concealed elements that he himself cannot understand. May declared in the *Times Literary Supplement* that "Beaulieu's considerable merit lies in the fact that he is not defeated by the forces of incoherence he recognizes within himself."

BIOGRAPHICAL/CRITICAL SOURCES:

BOOKS

Dictionary of Literary Biography, Volume 53: *Canadian Writers since 1960,* Gale, 1986.

PERIODICALS

Canadian Forum, June-July, 1978, pp. 39-40.
Choice, January, 1976, pp. 1451-52.
Times Literary Supplement, May 14, 1976, p. 578.
World Literature Today, summer, 1979, p. 471.*

BECKER, Charles M(axwell)   1954-

PERSONAL: Born October 31, 1954, in Staten Island, NY; son of Edward Joshua and Joanna Hazel (Maxwell) Becker; married Mary Winn Chrestenson (a mathematics teacher), June 4, 1977; children: Stephen R., Andrew L. *Education:* Grinnell College, B.A. (with honors), 1976; Princeton University, M.A., 1979, Ph.D., 1981. *Avocational interests:* Bicycling, mountain climbing, coaching Little League baseball.

ADDRESSES: Home—2851 LaGrange Circle, Boulder, CO 80303. *Office*—Economics Institute, 1030 13th St., Boulder, CO 80302; and Institute of Behavioral Science, Campus Box 484, University of Colorado, Boulder, CO 80309.

CAREER: Vanderbilt University, Nashville, TN, assistant professor of economics, 1981-86; Economics Institute, Boulder, CO, deputy director of academic program, 1987-89, president, 1990—. University of Colorado, Boulder, adjunct associate professor and research associate in population processes, Institute of Behavioral Science, both 1987—; University of Colorado at Denver, member of advisory council of Center for International Business Education and Research, 1993—. TEMOK (African business and investment opportunities consulting firm), member of advisory board, 1987—; Social Science Research Council/American Council of Learned Societies, member of Joint Committee on African Studies, 1988-93, and Subcommittee on African Agriculture, 1989-92; consultant to World Bank.

MEMBER: Regional Science Association International, American Economic Association, Population Association of America, African Studies Association, Southern Economic Association, Southern Regional Science Association, Western Economic Association, Phi Beta Kappa.

WRITINGS:

(With Edwin S. Mills) *Studies in Indian Urban Development,* Oxford University Press, 1986.
(With Trevor Bell, Haider Ali Khan, and Patricia Pollard) *The Impact of Sanctions on South Africa,* Part I: *The Economy,* Investor Responsibility Research Center, 1990.
(With Edwin S. Mills and Jeffrey G. Williamson) *Indian Urbanization and Economic Development,* Johns Hopkins University Press, 1992.
(With Andrew Hamer and Andrew Morrison) *Beyond Urban Bias: African Cities in an Age of Structural Adjustment,* Heinemann & James Currey, 1994.

Business section columnist, *Rocky Mountain News,* 1994—. Contributor to economic and international studies journals. Member of editorial board, *World Development* and *Global Economic Review,* both 1994—.

BIOGRAPHICAL/CRITICAL SOURCES:

PERIODICALS

Economic Development and Cultural Change, February, 1994.
Journal of Economic Literature, September, 1993.

*   *   *

BEISSINGER, Steven R.   1953-

PERSONAL: Born January 12, 1953; married Whendee L. Silver. *Education:* Miami University, Oxford, OH, B.A., 1974, M.S., 1978; University of Michigan, Ph.D., 1984.

ADDRESSES: Office—School of Forestry and Environmental Sciences, Yale University, 205 Prospect St., New Haven, CT 06511.

CAREER: National Institute for Urban Wildlife, Columbia, MD, field biologist, 1978; Florida Game and Fresh Water Fish Commission, contract biologist, 1979; University of Michigan, Ann Arbor, lecturer in ecology and environmental science, 1984-85; University of Florida, Gainesville, adjunct assistant professor of wildlife science, 1986-88; Yale University, New Haven, CT, assistant professor, 1988-91, associate professor of ecology and conservation biology, 1991—. Lecturer at colleges and universities, including Universidad de Cordoba and University of Puerto Rico, 1994. U.S. National Park Service, staff member of International Seminar on National Parks and Equivalent Reserves, 1984; U.S. Fish and Wildlife Service, population biologist, 1993—; Smithsonian Institution, research associate, 1985—; International Union for the Conservation of Nature, member of Species Survival Commission for Parrots.

MEMBER: International Society for Behavioral Ecology, American Ornithologists Union (fellow), Association for Parrot Conservation (founding member; member of board of directors, 1993—), Organization of Tropical Studies (member of board of directors, 1992—), Society for Conservation Biology, American Association for the Advancement of Science, Ecological Society of America, Society of American Naturalists, Cooper Ornithological Society, Wilson Ornithological Society.

AWARDS, HONORS: National Science Foundation, fellowship, 1986-88, grants, 1992 and 1994; grants from U.S. Army Corps of Engineers and South Florida Water Management District, 1986-88, National Geographic Society, 1989-91, 1994, Lincoln Park Zoological Society, 1990, International Council for Bird Preservation, 1991, and Remington Arms Manufacturing Co., 1992-94.

WRITINGS:

(Editor with N. F. R. Snyder, and contributor) *New World Parrots in Crisis: Solutions from Conservation Biology,* Smithsonian Institution Press (Washington, DC), 1992.

Contributor to books, including *Handbook of North American Birds,* Volume IV, edited by R. S. Palmer, Yale University Press, 1988. Contributor of articles and reviews to scientific journals and popular magazines, including *American Naturalist, Journal of Field Ornithology, Condor,* and *American Birds.* Member of editorial board, *Current Ornithology,* 1994—.

WORK IN PROGRESS: Conservation Biology: From Theory to Practice, with P. B. Stacey, A. E. Lugo, and T. W. Clark, for Oxford University Press.

* * *

BENNAHUM, Judith Chazin   1937-

PERSONAL: Born April 8, 1937, in New York, NY; daughter of Maurice (a professor of Romance languages) and Mary (a high school English teacher; maiden name, Berry) Chazin; married David Alexander Bennahum (a physician); children: Nina, Rachel, Aaron. *Education:* Brandeis University, B.A. (magna cum laude), 1958; studied ballet at School of Performing Arts, New York City. *Politics:* "Generally liberal." *Religion:* Jewish.

ADDRESSES: Home—1707 Notre Dame NE, Albuquerque, NM 87106. *Office*—Department of Theater and Dance, University of New Mexico, Albuquerque, NM 87131.

CAREER: Professional ballet dancer, 1954-64; choreographer; University of New Mexico, Albuquerque, head of Dance Program, 1987-92, professor of theater and dance, 1988—. Santa Fe Opera, teacher of body movement; worked as a ballet dancer with Robert Joffrey, George Balanchine, and Antony Tudor at the Metropolitan Opera Ballet Company; danced on Broadway with Agnes de Mille.

WRITINGS:

Dance in the Shadow of the Guillotine, Southern Illinois University Press, 1988.
The Ballets of Antony Tudor: Studies in Psyche and Satire, Oxford University Press, 1994.

Contributor of about twenty articles and reviews to scholarly journals.

SIDELIGHTS: Judith Chazin Bennahum told *CA:* "I began writing when I went back to school, after working for years as a ballet dancer. I loved French poetry, so I did my graduate work in French. It took a long time. I finally chose a dissertation subject that concerned ballet during the French Revolution. Basically my work is quite scholarly and academic. I was shocked that my book on Antony Tudor sold as well as it did. I do not expect that many people will want to read what I write.

"I work extremely hard physically, as I still teach ballet and other forms of dance. That means I am tired, and the only time I can write is during the summer or early in the mornings when the house is quiet. I wrote both my books because the academic dance field is still very young, perhaps only fifty years old, and no books on these two subjects had been published before. I have been influenced by dance writers such as Selma Jeanne Cohen and Marie-Francoise Christout.

"At present, I am working on a study of the evolution of women dancers' costumes at the time of the French Revolution, leading into the Romantic Ballet in Paris. I will also study changes in the way people viewed the woman's body, changes in attitudes toward men and women dancing together and holding one another, and so on. It will be a very interesting study."

* * *

BENNETT, Charles   1899-

PERSONAL: Born August 2, 1899, in Shoreham-on-Sea, Sussex, England; son of Charles and Lilian (Langrishe) Bennett; married Faith Margaret Riddick (an actress; marriage ended); married second wife, Betty (deceased); children: (second marriage) John.

ADDRESSES: Agent—Renaissance Agency, 8523 Sunset Blvd., Los Angeles, CA 90069.

CAREER: Playwright and screenwriter. Actor in stage productions, including *The Miracle,* 1911, *A*

Midsummer Night's Dream, 1927, and *Cyrano de Bergerac,* 1927; toured with the Compton Comedy Company, 1920, the Lena Ashwell Players, 1922, and the Ben Greet Players, 1925. Director of the films *Madness of the Heart,* 1949, and *No Escape,* 1953. *Military service:* served in British Army during World War I; writer for British Ministry of Information during World War II.

WRITINGS:

PLAYS

The Return, produced in London, England, at the Everyman Theatre, 1927.
Midnight, produced in Nottingham, England in 1928, produced in London at the Comedy Theatre as *The Last Hour,* 1928.
Blackmail, produced in London at the Globe Theatre, 1928.
After Midnight (one-act), produced in London at the Rudolph Steiner Hall, 1929.
The Danger Line, produced in London in 1930.
Sensation, produced in London at the Lyceum Theatre, 1931.
Big Business, produced in London in 1932.
Page from a Diary, produced in London at the Garrick Theatre, 1936.

SCREENPLAYS

(With Alfred Hitchcock and Benn W. Levy) *Blackmail* (adapted from Bennett's play), British International, 1929.
The Last Hour, Universal, 1930.
(With Billie Bristow) *Deadlock,* George King, 1931.
(With Bristow) *Number Please,* George King, 1931.
(With Bristow) *Two-way Street,* Nettlefold, 1931.
Partners Please, Producers Distributing, 1932.
(With D. B. Wyndham Lewis and A. R. Rawlinson) *The Man Who Knew Too Much,* Gaumont-British, 1934.
(With Robert Edmunds and Bryan E. Wallace) *The Clairvoyant,* Gainsborough-British, 1934.
(With Alma Reville) *The Thirty-Nine Steps* (adapted from John Buchan's novel), Gamount-British, 1935.
(With Sidney Gilliatt and Noel Langley) *King of the Damned,* Gaumont-British, 1935.
Sabotage (adapted from Joseph Conrad's novel *The Secret Agent*), Gaumont-British, 1936, released in the United States as *The Woman Alone.*
Secret Agent (adapted from a play by Campbell Dixon and from W. Somerset Maugham's stories "Triton" and "The Hairless Mexican"), Gaumont-British, 1936.
(With Rawlinson, Michael Hogan, Roland Pertwee,

and Ralph Spence) *King Solomon's Mines* (adapted from H. Rider Haggard's novel), Gainsborough, 1937.
(With Edwin Greenwood and Anthony Armstrong) *The Girl Was Young* (also released as *Young and Innocent*), Gaumont-British, 1938.
(With Paul Osborn) *The Young in Heart,* David O. Selznick, 1938.
(With Leon Gordon and Jacques Deval) *Balalaika* (based on the operetta by Eric Maschwitz, George Ponford, and Bernard Gruen), Metro-Goldwyn-Mayer (MGM), 1939.
(With Joan Harrison, James Hilton, and Robert Benchley) *Foreign Correspondent,* United Artists (UA), 1940.
(With Ernest Vajda) *They Dare Not Love,* Columbia, 1941.
(With Ellis St. Joseph) *Joan of Paris,* Twentieth Century-Fox, 1942.
(With Jesse L. Lasky, Jr., and Alan LeMay) *Reap the Wild Wind* (adapted from a story by Thelma Strabel), Paramount, 1942.
(With others) *Forever and a Day,* R.K.O., 1943.
(With LeMay) *The Story of Dr. Wassell,* Paramount, 1944.
Ivy, Universal, 1947.
(With Lasky and Frederic Frank) *Unconquered,* Paramount, 1947.
The Sign of the Ram, Columbia, 1948.
Black Magic, Edward Small, 1949.
(And director) *Madness of the Heart* (adapted from Flora Sandstrom's novel), Two Cities, 1950.
Where Danger Lives, R.K.O., 1950.
(With Edward Chodorov and Jerry Davis) *Kind Lady,* MGM, 1951.
The Green Glove, UA, 1952.
(And director) *No Escape,* UA, 1953.
(With Horace McCoy and W. R. Burnett) *Dangerous Mission,* R.K.O., 1954.
(With Hal E. Chester) *Night of the Demon* (adapted from Montague R. James's story "Casting the Runes"), Columbia, 1957, abridged version released in the United States as *Curse of the Demon.*
(With Irwin Allen) *The Story of Mankind,* Warner Bros., 1957.
(With Allen and Irving Wallace) *The Big Circus,* Allied Artists, 1959.
(With Allen) *The Lost World* (adapted from Arthur Conan Doyle's novel), Twentieth Century-Fox, 1960.
(With Allen) *Voyage to the Bottom of the Sea,* Twentieth Century-Fox, 1961.
(With Allen and Al Gail) *Five Weeks in a Balloon,* Twentieth Century-Fox, 1962.
(With Louis M. Heyward) *War Gods of the Deep*

(based on a poem by Edgar Allen Poe; also released as *The City under the Sea*), American International, 1965.

OTHER

Author of the teleplays "Secret of the Loch," "Escape from Venice," "The Heat Monster," "The Deadly Dolls," and "The Terrible Leprechaun" for the series *Voyage to the Bottom of the Sea*, ABC, 1964-68; author of the teleplay "Terror-Go-Round" for *The Land of the Giants*, ABC, 1968. Author of teleplays for *Schlitz Playhouse* and *Cavalcade of America*, and *The Wild, Wild West*.

Contributor to periodicals, including *Screen Writer*.

WORK IN PROGRESS: Collaborating with Stuart Birnbaum on an adaptation of director Alfred Hitchcock's 1929 thriller *Blackmail*, which was, in turn, adapted from Bennett's play; an autobiography.

SIDELIGHTS: Charles Bennett, who has written scripts for the stage, motion picture screen, and television, is particularly noted for his screenplays to such cinematic thrillers as *The Man Who Knew Too Much, The Thirty-Nine Steps,* and *Sabotage*. These films, as well as others, were the fruit of Bennett's collaboration with acclaimed director Alfred Hitchcock during the 1930s. "A screenwriter back when Hollywood emphasized stories rather than high concepts, Bennett is increasingly recognized as a leading 'constructionist' of the golden era—and as one of Hitchcock's important collaborators," informed Pat H. Broeske in the *Los Angeles Times*. Bennett's work during the 1940s, 1950s, and 1960s include collaborations with the film directors Cecil B. De Mille and Irwin Allen.

Bennett began his career as a playwright, and by the late 1920s he had seen several of his plays produced in London. *Blackmail,* produced in 1928, is a mystery wherein a woman, having killed her assailant, finds herself targeted for blackmail. Hitchcock obtained the film rights to Bennett's play and filmed it for release in 1929 as England's first movie featuring sound dialogue. Bennett was credited as one of the film's writers, but he has claimed that he actually did no work on it. Nonetheless, *Blackmail* marks the first of many suspense movies to which Bennett and Hitchcock are both credited.

In the early 1930s Bennett wrote regularly for both the stage and the film screen. He teamed again with Hitchcock for *The Man Who Knew Too Much*, a thriller in which a vacationing family in St. Moritz run afoul of killers plotting a political assassination to occur in London. Like *Blackmail, The Man Who Knew Too Much* proved successful with the film-going public; a critic in the *New York Times* commended the movie for its "fascinating staccato violence," noting that it is "an interesting example of technical ingenuity as well as an absorbing melodrama."

Bennett and Hitchcock followed *The Man Who Knew Too Much* with *The Thirty-Nine Steps,* an adaptation of John Buchan's novel about a Canadian who becomes involved with scheming spies in London. The film proved still another success for Bennett and Hitchcock—in the *New York Times,* Andre Sennwald commented that "by comparison with the sinister delicacy and urbane understatement of *The Thirty-Nine Steps,* the best of our melodramas seem crude and brawling." Their next joint venture, *Secret Agent*—a thriller in which two English spies pose as a married couple while trailing an enemy agent into Switzerland—was received with less enthusiasm. A *New York Times* critic stated, "It is a defect of the screen narrative that all the spies seem to be continually engaged in melodramatic shadow boxing." The reviewer continued, "The authors . . . never really make out a case for the necessity of spying and never convince you that there is anything in Geneva worth spying on."

Sabotage, another Bennett and Hitchcock collaboration, is the story of an American woman who suspects her husband of using his London moviehouse as a meeting place for foreign espionage agents. This drama of domestic tension and suspicion is still ranked by critics as one of Hitchcock's most impressive works from the 1930s. In the *Dictionary of Literary Biography,* Kevin Mace affirms that "*Sabotage* is more than just a spy thriller; it is also a moral fable that asks its audience to side with both the helpless young wife and her charming, basically honest husband whose politics eventually lead to tragedy and death."

By the early 1940s both Bennett and Hitchcock were working in the American film industry, although Bennett also served with the British Ministry of Information during World War II. Bennett and Hitchcock collaborated in 1940 on *Foreign Correspondent,* a charged adventure-thriller about an American journalist who uncovers an assassination plot in Europe. While investigating the story, the journalist falls in love with the daughter of a vehement pacifist, who is eventually exposed as the principal behind the assassination plot.

Foreign Correspondent proved immensely successful, but it marked the final collaboration between Bennett and Hitchcock. Bennett later explained his parting with Hitchcock by telling the *Los Angeles Times:* "It is no great mystery. . . . We both became successful. I was busy—and so was he." Bennett subsequently worked with director Cecil B. De Mille, for whom he supplied the scripts for such films as *Reap the Wild Wind,* an epic set in the nineteenth century, and *Unconquered,* an account of the conflict between American settlers and Native Americans.

Throughout the remainder of the 1940s, and into the 1950s, Bennett continued to write the scripts for film thrillers. He also undertook the direction of his script for the conventional drama *Madness of the Heart,* in which a blind bride must contend with an envious neighbor. A *New York Times* reviewer complimented the film for delivering "with sympathy and feeling a poignant story"—however, the review was mixed, as the critic stated that "the artful restraint evidenced in the writing and direction by Charles Bennett throughout most the of the film's ninety-one minutes is completely and jarringly absent in a mendacious, melodramatic climax." Bennett directed only one other film, *No Escape,* wherein a husband and wife are suspected of murder and thus decide to apprehend the actual killer.

Among Bennett's work from the late 1950s is *Night of the Demon* (also known, in abbreviated form, as *Curse of the Demon*), director Jacques Tourneur's critically acclaimed horror film in which an American arrives in London to disprove a satanist, only to learn that the satanist actually possesses supernatural powers. Among this film's many enthusiasts is Danny Peary, who hailed it in *Cult Movies 2* as "the best horror movie of the science fiction-dominated fifties, the most intriguing film ever made with a witchcraft theme."

Bennett's career slowed towards the end of the 1950s. He teamed with director Irwin Allen, who later become known as the producer of such disaster films as *The Poseidon Adventure* and *The Towering Inferno.* With Allen, Bennett wrote the screenplays for such science-fiction films as *The Lost World,* derived from Arthur Conan Doyle's novel, and *Voyage to the Bottom of the Sea.* His final screenwriting credit is *War Gods of the Deep,* a science-fiction film released in 1965. He subsequently wrote for the television shows *Voyage to the Bottom of the Sea,* which was inspired by the earlier Bennett-Allen film, and *Land of the Giants.*

In 1990, more than twenty years since his last pro-

duced writings, Bennett disclosed that he is planning, with Stuart Birnbaum, a re-make of *Blackmail.* Birnbaum, discussing Bennett to the *Los Angeles Times,* described the screenwriter as "a window to the past—to that other world of cinema we hold so dear."

BIOGRAPHICAL/CRITICAL SOURCES:

BOOKS

Dictionary of Literary Biography, Volume 44: *American Screenwriters, Second Series,* Gale, 1986.
Peary, Danny, *Cult Movies 2,* Dell, 1983, pp. 108-110.
Spoto, Donald, *The Art of Alfred Hitchcock: Fifty Years of His Motion Pictures,* Hopkinson & Blake, 1976.
Taylor, John Russell, *Hitch: The Life and Times of Alfred Hitchcock,* Pantheon, 1978.

PERIODICALS

Chicago Tribune, November 9, 1986.
Los Angeles Times, September 30, 1990.
New York Times, March 23, 1935; September 14, 1935; July 13, 1936; February 27, 1937; July 3, 1937; February 11, 1938; November 4, 1938; October 12, 1950.*

*   *   *

BENSON, Charles S(cott)   1922-1994

OBITUARY NOTICE—See index for *CA* sketch: Born May 20, 1922, in Atlanta, GA; died after a heart attack, July 2, 1994, in Carlsbad, CA. Economist, educator, and author. Benson's career was devoted to the study of fiscal and funding problems in public school systems. After earning degrees from Princeton and Columbia universities, Benson taught at Bowdoin College and Harvard University before joining the faculty of the University of California, Berkeley, in 1964. There he became a professor of education in 1968, and in 1988 director of a seven-school consortium, the National Center for Research in Vocational Education, located at the university. He retired in the early 1990s after serving as an associate dean from 1986 to 1989. Benson was often called upon as a consultant to various state, federal, and foreign agencies interested in educational reform. In 1987 he was honored with a distinguished service award from the American Educational Finance Association, an organization for which he had once served as president. In his numerous writings, he explored the problems of public education in the United States—funding, fiscal responsibility, labor issues, and preparing students for the future—and offered solutions based on his research. Benson authored several books, including *The Economics of Public Education, Planning for Educational Reform: Financial and Social Alternatives,* and *Education Finance and Organization: Research Perspectives for the Future,* and was a contributor to or coauthor of many others.

OBITUARIES AND OTHER SOURCES:

BOOKS

Who's Who in America, 47th edition, Marquis, 1992.

PERIODICALS

New York Times, July 8, 1994, p. A19.

*   *   *

BENTLEY, Gerald Eades   1901-1994

OBITUARY NOTICE—See index for *CA* sketch: Born September 15, 1901, in Brazil, IN; died July 25, 1994, in Hightown, NJ. Scholar, educator, and author. Bentley was an authority on seventeenth-century English drama, a subject he explored in his doctoral dissertation for the University of London. He taught at a number of institutions before joining the faculty of the University of Chicago in 1929; he was made professor of English in 1943. Two years later he obtained a similar position at Princeton University and remained there for the rest of his academic career, becoming the Murray Professor of English in 1950. Before Bentley retired from the university in the mid-1970s, he served as head of its English department and rare-book librarian. As a scholar, his area of expertise was in the plays of William Shakespeare and other playwrights of the era, and over the course of his long career Bentley authored, edited, and contributed to numerous books on the subject. His major opus was the seven-volume *Jacobean and Caroline Stage,* an exhaustive work published between 1941 and 1968 and described by the London *Times* as "an unmatched scholarly source book for all study of the playwrights and stage of the early seventeenth century." He was also a coauthor of the fourth volume of *The Revels History of Drama in English* (1981), penned *The Profession of Player in Shakespeare's Time* (1984), and served as editor of *William Shakespeare: His World, His Work, His Influence* (1985). He also left a legacy to his grandchildren in the form of an unpublished, five-volume memoir about his rural childhood in Indiana.

OBITUARIES AND OTHER SOURCES:

BOOKS

Who's Who in America, 47th edition, Marquis, 1992, p. 253.

PERIODICALS

Times (London), September 8, 1994, p. 19.

*   *   *

BENTLEY, Nancy   1946-

PERSONAL: Born September 11, 1946, in East Orange, NJ; daughter of George E. (an instrument technician) and Antoinette Dorothy (a telephone company supervisor; maiden name, Grobosky) Bentley; married John Turner Atkinson (a computer systems analyst) November 17, 1990. *Education:* Lake Erie College, B.A., 1968; University of Hawaii, M.Ed., 1974; University of Denver, M.A.L.S., 1981; attended Stanford University Publishing Course, 1983. *Politics:* Democrat. *Religion:* Catholic, Unitarian Universalist. *Avocational interests:* singing, hiking, skiing, bird-watching.

ADDRESSES: Home—1220 West High Point Ln., Colorado Springs, CO 80904.

CAREER: Dancer-Fitzgerald-Sample, San Francisco, CA, production department assistant, 1968-70; San Mateo Educational Resources Center, San Mateo, CA, educational research assistant, 1972-74; Colorado Springs School District, Colorado Springs, CO, media specialist, 1974-78, teacher, 1979—.

MEMBER: Society of Children's Book Writers and Illustrators (former president, Rocky Mountain Region), Colorado Mountain Club, Common Cause.

AWARDS, HONORS: The Making of a Storybook: Mary Calhoun—Storyteller was shown at Chicago International Children's Film Festival, 1991; Junior Literary Guild Selection, 1992, for *I've Got Your Nose!;* Chautauqua Writer's Conference grant.

WRITINGS:

I've Got Your Nose!, Doubleday, 1991.
(With Donna Guthrie) *The Young Author's Do-it-Yourself Book: How to Write, Illustrate, and Produce Your Own Book,* Millbrook Press, 1994.

"BUSY BODY BOARD BOOK" SERIES; ILLUSTRATED BY KATY ARNSTEEN

Let's Go, Feet!, Price, Stern, 1987.
Do This, Hands!, Price, Stern, 1987.
Listen to This, Ears!, Price, Stern, 1987.
What's on Top, Head?, Price, Stern, 1987.

OTHER

(Script writer) *I've Got Your Nose!* (videotape), Chip Taylor Communications, 1992.

Also author of script for videotape *The Making of a Storybook: Mary Calhoun—Storyteller,* 1991. Contributor to *Colorado Fever,* 1983-85.

SIDELIGHTS: Nancy Bentley commented: "Before I ever thought of becoming a writer I was a reader. I read so much in high school, locked away in my bedroom, perched on my favorite overstuffed chair, that my mother worried about me. I read partially to escape my loud and freewheeling family and partially to enter a lifelong journey into other worlds.

"I love books—I love reading them, sharing them with children, writing them! *I've Got Your Nose!* was written out of a childhood memory of one of my many uncles leaning down to 'steal my nose' with his fingers. The idea of losing or changing one's nose seemed utterly fascinating—then as well as now. *The Making of a Storybook: Mary Calhoun—Storyteller* was created for children, teachers, and librarians to see Mary up close and to explain how books and stories are created. *The Young Author's Do-it-Yourself Book: How to Write, Illustrate, and Produce Your Own Book* was written in an effort to explain the publishing process to children and help them publish their own works."

*   *   *

BERENBAUM, Michael   1945-

PERSONAL: Born July 31, 1945, in Newark, NJ; son of Saul (a retail merchant) and Rhea (Kass) Berenbaum; divorced; children: Ilana Beth, Lev. *Education:* Attended Jewish Theological Seminary, 1963-67, and Hebrew University, 1965-66; Queens College, A.B., 1967; attended Boston University, 1967-69; Florida State University, Ph.D., 1975. *Politics:* Democrat. *Religion:* Jewish.

ADDRESSES: Home—Chevy Chase, MD. *Office—* 100 Raoul Wallenberg Place SW, Washington, DC 20024. *Agent*—Ronald Goldfarb, 918 16th St. NW, Washington, DC 20005.

CAREER: Colby-Sawyer College, New London, NH, instructor in philosophy and religion, 1969-71; Wesleyan University, Middletown, CT, university Jewish chaplain and adjunct assistant professor of religion, 1973-80; Zachor: The Holocaust Resource Center, New York City, associate director, 1978; President's Commission on the Holocaust, Washington, DC, deputy director, 1979-80; Jewish Community Council of Greater Washington, Washington, DC, executive director, 1980-83; George Washington University, Washington, DC, associate professorial lecturer in religion, 1981-83; United States Holocaust Memorial Museum, Washington, DC, research fellow, 1987-88, project director, 1988-93; U.S. Holocaust Research Institute, Washington, director, 1993—. Georgetown University, Hyman Goldman Professor of Theology (adjunct), 1983—; University of Maryland, visiting professor of Hebrew studies, 1983; Religious Action Center, senior scholar, 1986-88; American University, adjunct professor of Judaic studies, 1987; United States Holocaust Memorial Museum, research fellow, 1987-88; Gannett Center for Media Studies, Columbia University, associate, 1987—.

MEMBER: American Academy of Religion, Association of Jewish Studies.

AWARDS, HONORS: Charles E. Merrill fellow, department of religion, Florida State University, 1972-73; George Wise fellow, Tel Aviv University, 1974; Underwood fellow, Danforth Foundation, 1976-77; fellow of Society for Values in Higher Education, 1977; Ezra Styles fellow, Yale University, 1979; Silver Angel Award for outstanding program in religious broadcasting on television, Religion and the Media, 1981, for "Religion and the White House" broadcast on WRC-TV, January 28, 1981; Simon Rockower Memorial Award in Jewish Journalism for Distinguished Editorial Writing, American Jewish Press Association, 1986; Simon Rockower Memorial Award in Jewish Journalism for Distinguished Coverage of the Arts, American Jewish Press Association, 1987.

WRITINGS:

The Vision of the Void: Theological Reflections on the Works of Elie Wiesel, Wesleyan University Press, 1979, reprinted as *Elie Wiesel: God, the Holocaust, and the Children of Israel,* Behrman House, 1994.
(Editor) *From Holocaust to New Life,* American Gathering of Jewish Holocaust Survivors, 1985.
(Editor with John Roth) *Holocaust: Religious and Philosophical Implications,* Paragon Books, 1989.

After Tragedy and Triumph: Modern Jewish Thought and the American Experience, Cambridge University Press, 1990.

(Editor) *A Mosaic of Victims: Non-Jews Persecuted and Murdered by the Nazis,* New York University Press, 1990.

The World Must Know: A History of the Holocaust, Little, Brown, 1993.

(Editor with Israel Gutman) *Anatomy of the Auschwitz Death Camp,* University of Indiana Press, 1994.

(Editor with Bettery Rogers Rubenstein) *Reflections on the Thought of Richard L. Rubenstein: Triage, the Holocaust, and Faith,* Hedgehog Press, 1994.

A Holocaust Reader, HarperCollins, 1995.

Author of *Who Rules New York? Willie, Mickey, or the Duke?,* in press. Member of editorial boards of *Tikkun* and *Journal of Holocaust and Genocide Studies;* contributing editor to *Sh'ma;* opinion-page editor of the *Washington Jewish Week,* 1983-86, and acting editor, 1985.

*   *   *

BERENDT, John (Lawrence)   1939-

PERSONAL: Born December 5, 1939, in Syracuse, NY; son of Ralph Sidney and Carol (Deschere) Berendt. *Education:* Harvard University, A.B., 1961.

ADDRESSES: Home and office—20 West 76th St., No. 2B, New York, NY 10023. *Agent*—Suzanne Gluck, International Creative Management, 40 West 57th St., New York, NY 10019.

CAREER: Esquire, New York City, associate editor, 1961-69; *Holiday,* New York City, senior staff editor, 1969; worked in New York City as associate producer for the *David Frost Show,* 1969-71, and for the *Dick Cavett Show,* 1973-75; *New York,* New York City, editor, 1977-79; writer.

WRITINGS:

Midnight in the Garden of Good and Evil: A Savannah Story (nonfiction), Random House, 1993.

Author of column in *Esquire,* 1979—. Contributor to periodicals.

SIDELIGHTS: John Berendt, a journalist who has served as an editor with both *Esquire* and *New York* magazines, is the author of *Midnight in the Garden of Good and Evil: A Savannah Story.* An account of life in Savannah, Georgia, as observed by Berendt in the 1980s, the book provides portraits of Savannah's more colorful citizens, notably the transvestite performer Lady Chablis and various members of the storytelling Married Woman's Card Club. In addition, *Midnight in the Garden of Good and Evil* reports on the murder case in which Jim Williams, a respected antiques dealer, was accused of the murder of his youthful companion, Danny Hansford. Berendt, who has also worked in television as an associate producer for the *David Frost Show* and the *Dick Cavett Show,* lived part-time in Savannah for eight years prior to writing the volume.

The details of the Hansford killing and the four ensuing murder trials occupy the second half of *Midnight in the Garden of Good and Evil.* Williams, who was eventually acquitted, died in 1990 with the distinction of being the only Georgian to be tried by the state four times for the same murder. "In recounting the tale of Williams's trials, [Berendt] frequently veers off and includes overheard conversations, funny vignettes and bits of historical and architectural data—a method that a lesser observer might have botched but that works wonderfully here," commented Glenna Whitley in the *New York Times Book Review.* One of Williams's strategies to fight off a conviction is to employ Minerva, a voodoo priestess. As Jean Hanff Korelitz remarked in the *Times Literary Supplement,* "When Minerva's roots and spells fail to stop Williams's subsequent trials, he none the less puts her on a kind of retainer, and has her called to appear as a defence witness to put curses on the D.A., the judge, and the jury . . . the results are uncertain, but Williams is philosophical: 'She'll never cost me fraction of what I've had to pay my lawyers.'"

Midnight in the Garden of Good and Evil has been appraised by critics as a quirky, fascinating work. A reviewer in *Publishers Weekly* commended Berendt for his "smart, sympathetic observations," while in *Newsweek,* Malcolm Jones, Jr., noted that the author "has fashioned a Baedeker to Savannah that, while it flirts with condescension, is always contagiously affectionate. Few cities have been introduced more seductively." Whitley, who in the *New York Times Book Review* described the book as "a peculiar combination of true crime and travelogue," stated that "Berendt's writing is elegant and wickedly funny." In the *Times Literary Supplement,* Korelitz summed up *Midnight in the Garden of Good and Evil* as "a strange but satisfying brew."

BIOGRAPHICAL/CRITICAL SOURCES:

PERIODICALS

Library Journal, January, 1994, p. 139.
Los Angeles Times, December 30, 1993, p. E4.
Los Angeles Times Book Review, January 23, 1994,
    p. 6.
Newsweek, February 28, 1994, p. 62.
New York Times Book Review, March 20, 1994, p.
    12.
Publishers Weekly, December 13, 1993, p. 58.
Times Literary Supplement, July 29, 1994, p. 7.
Washington Post, February 24, 1994, p. C1.
Washington Post Book World, February 6, 1994,
    p. 3.

*   *   *

BERGER, Anna Maria Busse

PERSONAL: Born in Hamburg, Germany; daughter of Joseph (an anthropologist and theologian) and Erika (a teacher) Busse; married Karol Berger (a professor); children: Anna Katharina Berger Nestaas, Susanna. *Education:* Earned degree from University of Trondheim, 1974; Boston University, 1986.

ADDRESSES: Home—2741 Forest Ave., Berkeley, CA 94705. *Office*—Department of Music, University of California, Davis, CA 95616.

CAREER: University of California, Davis, professor of music, 1989—.

WRITINGS:

Mensuration and Proportion Signs: Origins and Evolution, Oxford University Press, 1993.

*   *   *

BERIO, Luciano 1925-

PERSONAL: Born October 24, 1925, in Imperia, Oneglia, Italy; son of Ernesto Filippo (a musician) and Ada (Dal Fiume) Berio; married Cathy Berberian, October 1, 1950 (divorced, 1964); married Susan Oyama, 1964 (divorced, 1971); married Talia Pecker, 1977; children: (first marriage) Christina Luisa; (second marriage) Marina, Stefano; (third marriage) Daniel, Jonathan. *Education:* Conservatorio Giuseppe Verdi, graduated, 1951.

ADDRESSES: Home—Il Colombaio, Radicondoli, Siena, Italy.

CAREER: Studio de Fonologia Musicale, RAI Broadcasting, Milan, Italy, founder and co-director, 1955-60; Juilliard School of Music, New York City, professor of composition, 1965-71; IRCAM, Paris, France, director of electro-acoustic section, 1974-80; Tempo Reale, Florence, Italy, founder and director, beginning 1987; composer and writer. Artistic director, Israel Chamber Orchestra, 1975, Accademia Filarmonica Romana, 1976, Orchestra Regionale Toscana, 1982, and Maggio Musicale Florentio, 1984; instructor at such institutions as Mills College and Harvard University.

AWARDS, HONORS: Honorary degree from City University, London, 1980; various music awards.

WRITINGS:

(With Rossana Dalmonte and Balint Andras Varga)
    Two Interviews, translated into English and edited by David Osmond-Smith, Marion Boyars,
    1984.
Remembering the Future, Harvard University Press
    (Cambridge), 1994.
Collected Writings, Einaudi (Torino, Italy), 1995.

Compositions include: *Pastorale,* 1937; *Toccata,* 1939; *Preludio a una festa marina,* 1944; *Divertimento,* 1946, revised 1985; *O bone Jesu,* 1946; *Tre canzoni popolari,* 1947; *Tre pezzi,* 1947; *Petite Suite pour piano,* 1948; *Tre liriche greche,* 1948; *Magnificat,* 1949; *Due pezzi,* 1951, revised 1966; *El mar la mar,* 1952; *Mimusique No. 2,* 1952-55; *Allez Hop,* 1952-59; *Chamber Music,* 1953; *Cinque variazioni,* 1953, revised 1966; *Mimusique No.1,* 1953; *Variazioni,* 1953-54; *Nones,* 1954; *Quartetto,* 1955-56; *Perspectives,* 1957; *Serenata,* 1957; *Allelujah II,* 1957-58; *Sequenza I,* 1958; *Thema (Omaggio a Joyce),* 1958; *Tempi concertati,* 1958-59; *Differences,* 1959; *Epifanie,* 1959-62; *Circles,* 1960; *Momenti,* 1960; *Visage,* 1960-61; *Passaggio,* 1961-62; *Sequenza II,* 1963; *Sincronie,* 1963-64; *Folk Songs,* 1964; *Chemins I,* 1965; *Laborintus II,* 1965; *Rounds,* 1965; *Sequenza III,* 1965; *Sequenza IV,* 1965; *Gesti,* 1966; *Sequenza V,* 1966; *Chemins II,* 1967; *Sequenza VI,* 1967; *Chemins III,* 1968; *Questo vuol dire che,* 1968-69; *Sinfonia,* 1968-69; *Sequenza VII,* 1969; *Opera,* 1969-70, revised, 1977; *Memory,* 1970; *Bewegung,* 1971; *Concerto,* 1972-73; *Still,* 1973; *A-Ronne,* 1974-75; *Chemins IV,* 1975; *Coro,* 1975-76; *Ritorno degli snovidenia,* 1976-77; *Sequenza VIII,* 1976-77; *La vera storia,* 1977-81; *Un re in ascolto,* 1979-84; *Sequenza IX,* 1980; *Accordo,* 1980-81; *Sequenza X,* 1984; *Voci,* 1984; *Requies,* 1985; *Formazioni,* 1985-87; *Ricorrenze,* 1985-87; *Sequenza XI,* 1987-88; *Canticum novissimi testamenti,* 1988; *Ofanim,* 1988;

Concerto II (Echoing Curves), 1988-89; *Calmo,* 1989; *Festum,* 1989; *Rendering,* 1989; *Continuo,* 1989; and *Notturno (quartetto III),* 1990-91.

SIDELIGHTS: Luciano Berio rose to prominence in the 1950s as one of the most influential avant-garde composers in Europe. In 1985, in collaboration with interviewers Rossana Dalmonte and Balint Andras Varga, Berio published *Two Interviews,* in which he discusses contemporary music and provides insights and reflections on his own works.

BIOGRAPHICAL/CRITICAL SOURCES:

BOOKS

Berio, Luciano, Rossana Dalmonte, and Balint Andras Varga, *Two Interviews,* translated into English and edited by David Osmond-Smith, Marion Boyars, 1984.
Osmond-Smith, David, *Berio,* Oxford University Press, 1991.

PERIODICALS

Connoisseur, October, 1990, p. 76.
Los Angeles Times Book Review, June 30, 1985, p. 4.
New York Times Book Review, May 19, 1985, p. 23.
Times Literary Supplement, February 15, 1985, p. 161.

* * *

BERKUS, Clara Widess   1909-

PERSONAL: Born December 27, 1909, in Providence, RI; daughter of Calmon Max and Marion Beatrice (Wolk) Widess; married Harry J. Berkus, 1932; children: Barry Alan, David William. *Education:* Attended University of California at Los Angeles, 1927-28, and University of California at Berkeley, 1929; University of Southern California, B.A., 1930. *Avocational interests:* "Walking with friends and taking courses that open fresh areas of thought."

CAREER: Writer.

MEMBER: Society of Children's Book Writers and Illustrators, Monday Writers, Lena Passman Book Club, Pasadena Area Liberal Arts Center, Hadassah, Orton Dyslexia Society.

WRITINGS:

Charlsie's Chuckle, Woodbine Press, 1992.

WORK IN PROGRESS: A Boy and a Horse Named Dakota, the story of the struggle of a boy with dyslexia to achieve his personal goal; *The Humpty, Dumpy, Grumpy, Day;* and *The Most Wonderful Things.*

SIDELIGHTS: "I began writing at an early age and received my first rejection slip at age nine," Clara Berkus commented. "At UCLA, I was a member of Tri-C and the local honorary journalism society, [and I was] society editor and a writer for the *Daily Bruin.* I studied playwriting at UCLA and at USC and later with George Abbot's play doctor, Martha Sheridan Stanton. . . . I published skits, short stories, articles, chiefly for children." During the 1960s, Berkus became active in grass roots politics and wrote publicity for candidates.

Berkus's first published book for children is *Charlsie's Chuckle,* a story about a boy with Down syndrome who charms his town with his laugh. *School Library Journal* critic Constance A. Mellon wrote that Berkus's "conversational approach" in *Charlsie's Chuckle* "effectively introduces Down syndrome without dwelling on potentially baffling points."

BIOGRAPHICAL/CRITICAL SOURCES:

PERIODICALS

School Library Journal, March, 1993, p. 170.

* * *

BERLAN, Kathryn Hook   1946-

PERSONAL: Born November 30, 1946, in Franklin County, OH; daughter of Robert Earl (owner of a hamburger and ice-cream shop) and Norma Jean (a porcelain artist; maiden name, Speaks) Hook; married Ronald George Berlan (an insurance underwriter) May 12, 1972; children: Michael David, Andrew Brian. *Education:* Ohio State University, B.S., 1969, additional studies, 1970-71; John Carroll University, M.Ed., 1993. *Religion:* Catholic. *Avocational interests:* Children, nature, trees, hiking, reading, collecting, drawing, painting, building, gardening, horses.

ADDRESSES: Home—5034 Hartley Dr., Lyndhurst, OH 44124.

CAREER: Hamilton Local Schools, Columbus, OH, third-grade teacher, 1969-70; Newark City Schools, Newark, OH, sixth-grade and elementary art teacher, 1971-77; Licking Valley Local Schools,

Newark, second- and third-grade teacher, 1978-85. Freelance creator of workshops and teacher in-service projects, Cleveland, OH; Cleveland City Schools, creator and facilitator of classroom publishing project, 1991—. Owner and founder, ImagiBooks. Has given presentations for libraries and P.T.A. groups on writing with children.

MEMBER: International Reading Association, Society of Children's Book Writers and Illustrators.

WRITINGS:

Andrew's Amazing Monsters, Macmillan, 1993.

WORK IN PROGRESS: Tent Wars; Morning Glorious.

SIDELIGHTS: Kathryn Hook Berlan commented that she "loved to daydream and create stories" in her mind as she was growing up in Ohio, but she did not consider herself to be a writer. Instead, she "loved drawing and painting," and was "especially adept at three-dimensional art, and loved to experiment with new materials." Berlan also explained that she was "an avid reader. . . . Through reading I could step into other worlds, make new friends of the characters that readers would love and miss at the book's end, but I still considered myself an artist, not a writer."

It was not until Berlan had been teaching school for some time that she began to seriously think about children's books. With her sons, Michael and Drew, and the young children she taught, she read children's books and "explored making books and imitating styles of famous illustrators such as Leo Leonni." Later, Berlan began to teach bookmaking. "Whole language teaching and young authors' conferences were the big buzz words in the Cleveland educational community," she commented. Berlan began to teach "freelance workshops to teachers and students in the suburban schools" of Cleveland. "In my first workshop I saw that rare light a teacher sometimes sees in a child's eyes when something is happening in the classroom that really excites him; only I saw it in most of the students' eyes. I knew that this is what I wanted to do."

Berlan has since "taught thousands of children and many teachers how to create their own original books." She teaches classroom publishing at several elementary schools in Cleveland, and works with children—grades four through six—as they write newspapers and newsletters as well as create books. "There is magic in creating a three-dimensional book. It's like a sculpture. It clears away the assembly line fog of writing assignments and brings back the age of craftsmanship where the craftsman creates the product from start to finish. There is a feeling of ownership and pride that can't be beat."

*　　*　　*

BERRIDGE, G. R. 1947-

PERSONAL: Born June 8, 1947, in Scunthorpe, Lincolnshire, England; son of Charles Raymond (an instrument engineer) and Dorothy Harriet (Jones) Berridge; married Sheila Mary Harper (a teacher), February 8, 1969; children: Catherine Jane, William James. *Education:* University of Durham, B.A., 1968, Ph.D., 1978; University of Sussex, M.A., 1969. *Politics:* Social Democrat.

ADDRESSES: Home—17 Morland Ave., Leicester LE2 2PF, England. *Office*—Department of Politics, University of Leicester, Leicester LE1 7RH, England.

CAREER: Metropolitan Police College, Ashford, England, assistant lecturer, 1969-71; teacher at a secondary school in Farnsborough, England, 1975-78; University of Leicester, Leicester, England, lecturer, 1978-89, reader, 1989-93, professor of politics, 1993—.

MEMBER: Royal Institute of International Affairs, British International Studies Association, Political Studies Association, Commonwealth Trust.

WRITINGS:

Economic Power in Anglo-South African Diplomacy: Simontown, Sharpeville, and After, Macmillan, 1981.
(Editor with A. Jennings, and contributor) *Diplomacy at the UN,* Macmillan, 1985.
The Politics of the South Africa Run: European Shipping and Pretoria, Clarendon Press, 1987.
International Politics: States, Power, and Conflict since 1945, Harvester Press, 1987, 2nd edition, 1992.
Return to the UN: United Nations Diplomacy in Regional Conflicts, Macmillan, 1991.
South Africa, the Colonial Powers, and "African Defence": The Rise and Fall of the White Entente, 1948-60, St. Martin's, 1992.
(With Derek Heater) *An Introduction to International Relations,* Harvester Press, 1993.
Talking to the Enemy: How States without "Diplomatic Relations" Communicate, Macmillan, 1994.

Work represented in anthologies, including *Superpower Competition and Crisis Prevention in the Third World,* edited by R. Allison and P. Williams, Cambridge University Press (New York), 1989; *British Foreign Policy, 1945-56,* edited by M. Dockrill and J. Young, Macmillan (New York), 1989; and *International Relations and Pan-Europe,* Lit Verlag (Hamburg), 1993. Contributor to political science and international studies journals. Editor, *Leicester Discussion Papers in Politics,* 1992-93.

WORK IN PROGRESS: Diplomacy: Theory and Practice, for Harvester Press.

SIDELIGHTS: G. R. Berridge told *CA:* "I try to write about international politics with a clarity of which George Orwell would have approved. Temperamentally hostile to fashionable approaches, I am also inclined to emphasize (perhaps to overemphasize) its unchanging features. I am now writing mostly about diplomacy because I am fed up with reading about war. I am also concerned at the widespread misunderstanding of the subtleties of the diplomat's job and the political attacks to which, as a result, it is perennially exposed."

*   *   *

BESSINGER, Jess B(alsor), Jr.   1921-1994

OBITUARY NOTICE—See index for *CA* sketch: Born September 25, 1921, in Detroit, MI; died of a heart attack, June 23, 1994, in Middletown, RI. Medieval scholar, educator, and author. Bessinger was considered an authority on one of the earliest extant examples of English-language literature, the epic poem "Beowulf." He earned advanced degrees from Harvard University before joining the faculty of Brown University in 1952, spent several years teaching at the University of Toronto, and returned to the United States as a professor of English with New York University in 1964; Bessinger remained there until his retirement in 1992. Besides books on "Beowulf"—*A Concordance to Beowulf* (1969) and, with Robert F. Yeager, *Approaches to the Teaching of Beowulf* (1983)—Bessinger wrote *A Concordance to the Anglo-Saxon Poetic Records* (1978) and numerous professional articles. In the late 1960s Bessinger cofounded and edited the *Old English Newsletter,* and for a number of years was involved with spoken-word recordings of English literature classics for Caedmon Records. He had also served as the general editor of the *Harvard Old English* series since 1965.

OBITUARIES AND OTHER SOURCES:

BOOKS

Who's Who in America, 47th edition, Marquis, 1992, p. 280.

PERIODICALS

New York Times, June 28, 1994, p. A15.

*   *   *

BISHOP, Courtney
See RUEMMLER, John D(avid)

*   *   *

BLACK, Donald   1941-

PERSONAL: Born June 14, 1941, in Mount Vernon, NY; son of Herman and Anne (maiden name, Czemka; also spelled Chamka) Black. *Education:* Indiana University—Bloomington, B.A., 1963; University of Michigan, M.A., 1965, Ph.D., 1968; postdoctoral study at Yale University, 1968-70.

ADDRESSES: Home—P.O. Box 5749, Charlottesville, VA 22905. *Office*—Department of Sociology, Cabell Hall, University of Virginia, Charlottesville, VA 22903.

CAREER: Yale University, New Haven, CT, assistant professor of sociology and lecturer in law, 1970-74, associate professor of sociology, 1974-79; Harvard University, Cambridge, MA, research associate and lecturer in law, 1979-85; University of Virginia, Charlottesville, professor of sociology, 1985-88, University Professor of the Social Sciences, 1988—.

AWARDS, HONORS: Theory Prize and Distinguished Book Award, both American Sociological Association, both 1994, for *The Social Structure of Right and Wrong.*

WRITINGS:

(Editor with M. Mileski) *The Social Organization of Law,* Academic Press, 1973.
The Behavior of Law, Academic Press, 1976.
The Manners and Customs of the Police, Academic Press, 1980.
(Editor) *Toward a General Theory of Social Control,* two volumes, Academic Press, 1984.
Sociological Justice, Oxford University Press, 1989.
The Social Structure of Right and Wrong, Academic Press, 1993.

WORK IN PROGRESS: Research toward a general theory of conflict.

*   *   *

BLACKMORE, Susan (Jane) 1951-

PERSONAL: Born July 29, 1951, in London, England; daughter of Roy Clifford (a printer) and Edith Joanne (Leech) Blackmore; married Tom Troscianko (a university lecturer), September 17, 1977 (separated, 1990); children: Emily Tamarisk, Jolyon Tomasz. *Education:* St. Hilda's College, Oxford, B.A., 1973; University of Surrey, M.Sc., 1974, Ph.D., 1980. *Religion:* None.

ADDRESSES: Home—31 Berkeley Rd., Bishopston, Bristol BS7 8HF, England. *Office*—Department of Psychology, St. Matthias College, University of the West of England, Bristol BS16 2JP, England. *Agent*—Sheila Watson, 12 Egbert St., London NW1 8LJ, England.

CAREER: University of Surrey, Surrey, England, associate lecturer in parapsychology, 1975-80; University of Utrecht, Utrecht, Netherlands, temporary research fellow at Parapsychology Laboratory, 1980; University of Bristol, Bristol, England, visiting research fellow at Brain and Perception Laboratory, 1980-88, tutor in behavioral sciences, 1989-90, lecturer in psychology, 1990-91; University of the West of England, Bristol, senior lecturer in psychology, 1992—. Committee for the Scientific Investigation of Claims of the Paranormal, fellow and member of executive committee. North East London Polytechnic, lecturer, 1974-78; Thames Polytechnic, lecturer, 1977-78; University of Bath, lecturer, 1990-91; visiting lecturer at Universities of Edinburgh, Leicester, Liverpool, Newcastle-upon-Tyne, Wales, and Freiburg. Anglia Television, resident parapsychologist for the series *The Magic and Mystery Show,* 1993, and *Something Strange;* British Broadcasting Corp., presenter of the programs *Antenna,* 1986, *Open Forum,* 1987, *You're Not What You Think,* 1991, *Out of This World,* 1994, and *Horizon: Alien Abductions;* BBC-Radio 4, presenter of the radio series *All in the Mind,* 1989-91; frequent guest on radio and television programs.

MEMBER: International Association for Near Death Studies, Society for Psychical Research, British Psychological Society, UK Skeptics (fellow).

AWARDS, HONORS: Winner of New Scientist Sheldrake Competition, 1982; Alexander Imich Essay Prize, 1991; Distinguished Skeptics Award (Berkeley, CA), 1991.

WRITINGS:

Parapsychology and Out-of-the-Body Experiences, Transpersonal Books, 1978.
Beyond the Body: An Investigation of Out-of-the-Body Experiences, Heinemann, 1982, new edition, Academy Chicago, 1992.
The Adventures of a Parapsychologist, Prometheus Books (Buffalo, NY), 1986.
Dying to Live: Near-Death Experiences, Prometheus Books, 1993.

Work represented in books, including *Not Necessarily the New Age: Critical Essays,* edited by R. Basil, Prometheus Books, 1988; *The Hundredth Monkey and Other Paradigms of the Paranormal,* edited by K. Frazier, Prometheus Books, 1991; and *Reincarnation: Fact or Fable?,* edited by A. S. Berger and J. Berger, Aquarian, 1991. Contributor of more than a hundred-thirty articles and reviews to periodicals. Editor, *Society for Psychical Research Newsletter,* 1981-85 and 1986-91; correspondence editor, *Journal of the Society for Psychical Research,* 1982-85.

WORK IN PROGRESS: Research on imagery (especially viewpoints in memory and dreams), out-of-body and near-death experiences, parapsychology, origins of belief in the paranormal, and the Barnum Effect, perceptions of astrology and divination.

SIDELIGHTS: Susan Blackmore told *CA:* "It all started at Oxford when, as a student of physiology and psychology, I had some utterly inexplicable experiences. Leaving my body, seeing auras, and seeming to understand the mysteries of the universe simply did not fit into the science I was learning. Perhaps this was what drove me to a long-lasting determination to try to understand the stranger capacities of the human mind.

"At first I assumed they were paranormal and threw myself into the science of parapsychology. I researched and wrote about telepathy, ghosts, reincarnation, and precognition, but this was completely unsatisfying. The theories went against everything that science had to tell us. In addition, after many years of research, I could find no evidence that paranormal phenomena really exist.

"Yet the experiences certainly did. Gradually I began to find scientific explanations for them. For example, I am now convinced that all the phenomena of near-death (the tunnels and lights, visions and insights) can be understood in terms of what happens in the dying brain.

"This makes me deeply unpopular. In my writing

and media work, I am constantly up against people who 'know' that God exists, that there is life after death, that they have an everlasting soul, and that they've been here before. I am accused of being anti-spiritual and a hardened skeptic.

"Yes, I am a skeptic, prepared to question every idea and every claim. That does not mean I am anti-spiritual; it means that my idea of mysticism is completely opposed to the New Age platitudes that pass for spirituality. True spirituality is much tougher than this, and I think it resides in seeing some awful truths: that we are just biological organisms and our precious 'selves' are pure invention. Science tell us this, but so did the Buddha and countless mystics.

"If I want to do anything in my writing now, it is to bring together these twin insights: the one acquired by the empirical method and centuries of research, the other by disciplined meditation and self-examination. This means I really live the insights, whether I am playing with my children, digging the garden, doing another television show, or setting up an experiment. If my writing in the future can reflect this coming together of science and spirituality, then I shall be well pleased, whether or not I am rejected as a wicked debunker."

* * *

BLAKEMORE, Harold   1930-1991

PERSONAL: Born June 13, 1930, in Mexborough, Yorkshire, England; died February, 1991; son of Ernest Edward (a miner) and Harriett (a homemaker; maiden name, Scott) Blakemore; married Miriam Bucknell (a homemaker) December 23, 1955; children: Christopher Scott, Alison Ruth. *Education:* University of London, B.A. (with honors), 1951, Ph.D., 1955. *Politics:* Social Democrat. *Religion:* "Not quite sure; Methodist by upbringing."

ADDRESSES: Home—43 Fitzjohn Ave., Barnet, Hertfordshire EN5 2HN, England. *Office*—Institute of Latin American Studies, 31 Tavistock Sq., London WC1H 9HA, England.

CAREER: Mexborough Grammar School, Yorkshire, England, assistant master, 1955; University of Sheffield, England, assistant to director of extramural studies, 1955-57, staff tutor of history and international affairs, 1957-60; University of London, London, England, education officer in School of Oriental and African Studies, 1960-65, secretary at Institute of Latin American Studies, 1965—, reader in Latin American history, 1974—. Secretary to

Latin American Publications Fund, London, 1969—; chair, Anglo-Argentine-Chilean-Mexican Scholarships Boards of British Council, 1970; member of Latin American Trade Advisory Group, 1972—; member of selection committee for Ford Foundation foreign area fellowships program, 1972-75; consultant on Latin America to Lloyds Bank International, 1974—, and Control Risks Ltd., 1980—; secretary-general to European Council for Social Science Research on Latin America, 1975-83; chair of national committee and president of 44th International Congress of Americanists, 1982; member of working group on European-Latin American Relations of EEC Foreign Affairs Commission, 1984—.

MEMBER: Chilean Academy of History (corresponding member), Anglo-Chilean Society of the United Kingdom, Royal Historical Society (fellow, 1967—), European Association of Latin American Historians, Society for Latin American Studies, South Atlantic Council.

AWARDS, HONORS: Darby Studentship in history, 1951, from University of London; fellow, Royal Historical Society, 1967; fellow, Institute of Development Studies, University of Sussex, 1972; fellow, Catholic University of Chile, 1978.

WRITINGS:

Latin America, Oxford University Press (New York), 1966, 4th edition, 1973.
(Editor with Clifford T. Smith) *Latin America: Geographical Perspectives,* Methuen (London), 1972, 2nd revised edition, 1983.
British Nitrates and Chilean Politics, 1886-96: Balmaceda and North, Athlone Press (London), 1974.
(Editor) *Latin America: Essays on Continuity,* BBC, 1974.
(Editor with Simon Collier and Thomas E. Skidmore) *The Cambridge Encyclopedia of Latin American and the Caribbean,* Cambridge University Press (New York), 1985, 2nd edition, 1992.
(Compiler) *Chile,* Clio Press (Santa Barbara, CA), 1988.
From the Pacific to La Paz: The Antofagasta (Chili) and Bolivia Railway Company, 1888-1988, Lester Crook Academic (London), 1990.
(Editor with others) *South America, Central America, and the Caribbean, 1986,* Europa (New York), 1986.

Also author of *South American Economic Handbook,* 1987. Founding coeditor, *Journal of Latin American Studies,* Cambridge University Press (London),

1969—; member of editorial advisory board, *Historian, Estudios Sociales, Latin American International Affairs Series, Annuario de Estudios, Hispanoamericanos,* and *Nueva Historica.* Contributor to books, including *Since 1945: Aspects of Contemporary World History,* edited by J. L. Henderson, Methuen, 1966; *Revolution in the Middle East & Other Case Studies,* edited by P. J. Vatikiotis, Allen & Unwin, 1972; *The Making of the Modern World,* edited by D. Johnson, Benn, 1971; *Encyclopaedia of Latin American History,* edited by Helen Delpar, McGraw, Hill, 1975; and *Educational Aid and National Development,* edited by Dame Nancy Parkinson, Macmillan, 1976. Also contributor of articles to periodicals, including *Hispanic American Historical Review, Pacific Historical Review, History Today, Year Book of World Affairs, Latin American Research Review,* and *Bank of London & South America Review.* Reviewer of books for periodicals, including *Times Literary Supplement, British Book News,* and *International Affairs.* Many of Blakemore's works have been printed in Spanish.

SIDELIGHTS: Harold Blakemore has devoted his life to the study of Latin American history and is a prolific writer of books and articles documenting the rapid growth, struggles, and contributions of Latin American countries.

Many of Blakemore's writings focus on the ever-changing landscape of Latin American countries, contrasting the busy metropolitan areas and high-tech communication centers with the primitive aboriginal dwellings, dirt roads, and old-fashioned farm implements. Because the population of Latin America is among the fastest growing in the world, Latin American countries face housing shortages, high unemployment rates, and the need to incorporate industry into their largely agrarian economy. One of Blakemore's studies, *Latin America: Geographical Perspectives,* which he edited with Clifford T. Smith, is a comprehensive collection of essays depicting life in various regions of Latin America. A *Times Literary Supplement* reviewer of *Latin America* noted: "Agrarian reform and programmes of regional development need to be brought into closer harmony, but the obstacles—financial, social, technological, and environmental are enormous. The present authors do not, for the most part, attempt to formulate solutions to these and other problems. They do, however, succeed very well in their main task of uncovering the antecedents and assessing the strength of present trends."

Another of Blakemore's exhaustive volumes of history is *The Cambridge Encyclopedia of Latin America and the Caribbean,* which he edited with Simon Collier and Thomas E. Skidmore. Reviewer E. Bradford Burns, a history professor and author of his own book on Latin American history, faulted Blakemore's book on the people, politics and culture of Latin America for being "as long on facts as it is short on interpretation. The paucity of interpretation robs the facts of their meaning and dulls the drama. Consequently, a rather lifeless Latin America lies in these pages." Still, Burns concluded, "'The Cambridge Encyclopedia of Latin America and the Caribbean' merits commendation for its factual contributions and its experiment with a different format."

Times Literary Supplement critic Edward Best, however, found *The Cambridge Encyclopedia of Latin America and the Caribbean* "an impressive achievement. It is an admirably broad but detailed presentation of the region's evolution and current profile, an attractive and informative book of considerable value to the interested general reader." While suggesting that Blakemore's book is not a replacement for a general encyclopedia or yearbook, which give precise statistics, Best deemed *The Cambridge Encyclopedia of Latin America* "a very valuable means to help understand the issues facing Latin America and the Caribbean, to see all dimensions of this continent's past and present, and to appreciate the nature of both its enormous problems and its enormous potential."

BIOGRAPHICAL/CRITICAL SOURCES:

PERIODICALS

Library Journal, April 1, 1986, p. 144.
Los Angeles Times Book Review, October 13, 1985, p. 6.
Times Literary Supplement, June 9, 1972, p. 656; May 3, 1974, p. 472; May 16, 1986, p. 522.

[Sketch reviewed by wife, Miriam Blakemore.]

*   *   *

BLAKESLEY, Christopher L.   1945-

PERSONAL: Born February 28, 1945, in California; son of Leonal Alvin and Alice Moselle (Ralphs) Blakesley; married Susan Elian, August 19, 1968; children: Chantalle, Angelique, Christopher II. *Education:* University of Utah, B.A. (magna cum laude), 1969, M.A., 1970, J.D., 1973; Fletcher School of International Law and Diplomacy, Tufts University, M.A., 1970; Columbia University, LL.M., J.S.D., 1985. *Avocational interests:* Running, reading, writing, public speaking.

ADDRESSES: Home—235 West Woodstone Ct., Baton Rouge, LA 70808. *Office*—Paul M. Hebert Law Center, Louisiana State University, Baton Rouge, LA 70803-1000.

CAREER: U.S. Department of State (Office of the Legal Adviser), Washington, DC, attorney and adviser, 1973-75; Louisiana State University, Baton Rouge, began as assistant professor, became associate professor of law, 1976-80; University of the Pacific, Sacramento, CA, professor of law, 1980-87; Louisiana State University, professor, 1987—, J. Y. Sanders Professor of Law, 1991—. Lecturer in Hungary, Austria, and France.

MEMBER: Association International de Droit Penal (member of board of directors, 1994), American Society of Comparative Law (member of board of directors), American Society of International Law, American Bar Association, Utah Bar Association, Bar Association of Washington, DC, Phi Kappa Phi, Coif.

AWARDS, HONORS: Jervey fellow, 1975-77.

WRITINGS:

(With Wardle and Parker) *Treatise: Family Law in the United States,* four volumes, Callaghan and Co., 1988.
Terrorism, Drugs, International Law, and the Protection of Human Liberty, Transnational Publishers, 1992.
Louisiana Family Law, Butterworth, 1994.
(With Oliver, Firmage, Scott, and Williams) *The International Legal System,* 4th edition, Foundation Press, 1995.

Work represented in anthologies, including *Doing Business Abroad: Identifying and Avoiding Criminal Liability,* Butterworth, 1991, 2nd edition, 1994; *Introduction to the Law of the United States,* Kluwer, 1992; and *Principles and Procedures for a New Transnational Criminal Law,* Max-Planck Institute for Foreign and International Criminal Law (Freiburg), 1992. Contributor of more than a hundred articles and reviews to professional journals in the United States and abroad. Member of board of editors, *Revue International de Droit Penal,* 1992—.

WORK IN PROGRESS: International Criminal Law: A Coursebook, with Ruth Wedgwood, Irwin Cotler, and others; *Family Autonomy: A Critical Analysis of the Critical Analysts,* with Collin Mangrum; *Human Rights and Extradition,* with Otto Lagodny; *Comparative Criminal Law and Procedure,* with George W. Pugh; research on terrorism and other areas of international criminal law.

SIDELIGHTS: Christopher L. Blakesley told *CA:* "I have written coursebooks, treatises, and hundreds of articles on international criminal law, comparative criminal law, and family law. I focus on the moral and legal conundra implicated in matters of terrorism, war crimes, and even family law."

BIOGRAPHICAL/CRITICAL SOURCES:

PERIODICALS

Criminal Law Forum, Volume IV, number 1, 1993, p. 187.
Studies in Conflict and Terrorism, Volume XVI, number 234, 1994.

*   *   *

BLEDSOE, Timothy   1953-

PERSONAL: Born June 18, 1953, in Lake Village, AR; son of Billie H. (in amusement industry) and Daisy (a homemaker; maiden name, Morrison) Bledsoe; married Mary Herring (a university professor), August, 1989; children: Daisy Caroline. *Education:* Louisiana State University, B.A.; University of Arkansas, M.A.; University of Nebraska, Ph.D. *Politics:* Democrat. *Religion:* None.

ADDRESSES: Home—936 Lincoln, Grosse Pointe, MI 48230. *Office*—Department of Political Science, Wayne State University, Detroit, MI 48202.

CAREER: University of South Carolina at Columbia, assistant professor of political science, 1984-89; Wayne State University, Detroit, MI, associate professor of political science, 1989—.

MEMBER: American Political Science Association, Midwest Political Science Association.

WRITINGS:

Urban Reform and Its Consequences, University of Chicago Press, 1988.

Author of the book *Careers in City Politics,* University of Pittsburgh Press.

WORK IN PROGRESS: A study of contextual influences on racist attitudes in an urban setting.

SIDELIGHTS: Timothy Bledsoe told *CA:* "My work in progress examines the attitudes and experiences of blacks and whites in neighborhoods of different racial mix, in both a predominantly black central city and predominantly white suburbs."

BLOCH, Robert (Albert)   1917-1994
(Tarleton Fiske, Will Folke, Nathan
Hindin, E. K. Jarvis, Wilson Kane, John
Sheldon, Collier Young)

OBITUARY NOTICE—See index for CA sketch: Born April 5, 1917, in Chicago, IL; died of cancer, September 23, 1994, in Los Angeles, CA. Writer. Bloch, a prolific spinner of horror, mystery, and fantasy tales, is the author of the 1959 novel *Psycho,* which filmmaker Alfred Hitchcock adapted into the suspense movie of the same name. Based on Bloch's research into the life of an actual Wisconsin serial killer, *Psycho* became the work the author has been most closely associated with; later in his career, however, Bloch expressed concern about the graphic violence routinely depicted in modern film and television productions that *Psycho* had helped spawn. Bloch began his career in the 1930s creating lurid stories for such pulp magazines as *Weird Tales.* For a time he worked as a copywriter in advertising, but moved to California in the 1950s to work in the film and television industry. He also penned hundreds of short stories under a variety of pseudonyms, among them the tale of the Victorian-era English murderer Jack the Ripper that was produced on radio and television numerous times. Bloch's television writing credits include episodes of *Alfred Hitchcock Presents, Star Trek,* and *Night Gallery*; his screenwriting work was seen in the films *Strait-Jacket, The Psychopath, The House That Dripped Blood,* and *Twilight Zone—The Movie.* He was also the author of over twenty novels, such as *The Scarf* (1947), *Firebug* (1961), *It's All in Your Mind* (1971), *American Gothic* (1974), and *Strange Eons* (1979); his later books include *Midnight Pleasures* (1987), *Fear and Trembling* (1989), *Psycho House* (1990), and *The Jekyll Legacy* (1990). Bloch and his immense contribution to the genre were honored in 1991 with the Bram Stoker Award from the Horror Writers of America.

OBITUARIES AND OTHER SOURCES:

BOOKS

Contemporary Theatre, Film, and Television, Volume 2, Gale, 1986.
Who's Who in America, 47th edition, Marquis, 1992.

PERIODICALS

Chicago Tribune, September 25, 1994, sec. 2., p. 6.
New York Times, September 25, 1994, p. 48.
Times (London), September 26, 1994, p. 21.
Washington Post, September 25, 1994, p, B6.

BLOODSTEIN, Oliver   1920-

PERSONAL: Born December 2, 1920, in Bronx, NY; son of Morris (a sign painter) and Clara (a homemaker) Bloodstein; married, wife's name Annette, September 7, 1941; children: Judith Bloodstein Blackstone, Daniel. *Education:* College of the City of New York (now City College of the City University of New York), B.A., 1941; University of Iowa, M.A., 1942, Ph.D., 1948. *Politics:* Independent. *Religion:* "None; ethnic identity, Jewish."

ADDRESSES: Home—135 Willow St., Brooklyn, NY 11201. *Office*—Department of Speech, Brooklyn College of the City University of New York, 2900 Bedford Ave., Brooklyn, NY 11210.

CAREER: Brooklyn College of the City University of New York, Brooklyn, NY, professor of speech pathology, 1948—, director of Speech and Hearing Center, 1985—. City University of New York, member of doctoral faculty. *Military service:* U.S. Army, 1943-45; became technical sergeant.

MEMBER: American Speech-Language-Hearing Association (fellow), Correspondence Chess League of America (expert).

AWARDS, HONORS: Award from American Speech-Language-Hearing Association, 1989.

WRITINGS:

A Handbook on Stuttering, National Easter Seal Society, 1969, 5th edition, Singular Publishing Group, 1995.
Speech Pathology: An Introduction, Houghton, 1979, 2nd edition, 1984.
Stuttering: The Search for a Cause and Cure, Allyn & Bacon, 1993.

SIDELIGHTS: Oliver Bloodstein told *CA:* "I am a speech pathologist, not a writer. One of the great pleasures of my career, however, has been the joyful effort of putting words together to create something compelling out of a research report or textbook. My ambition in writing *Stuttering* was to communicate the fascination of one of the unsolved problems of speech pathology to the educated reader."

*   *   *

BLUM, Howard   1948-

PERSONAL: Born in 1948.

ADDRESSES: Agent—Lynn Nesbit, Janklow &

Nesbit Associates, 598 Madison Ave., New York, NY 10022.

CAREER: Former journalist for the *New York Times* and the *Village Voice;* author of fiction and nonfiction.

AWARDS, HONORS: Two Pulitzer Prize nominations.

WRITINGS:

Wanted! The Search for Nazis in America, Quadrangle/New York Times Book Company (New York), 1977.
Wishful Thinking (novel), Atheneum (New York), 1985.
I Pledge Allegiance—The True Story of the Walkers: An American Spy Family, Simon and Schuster (New York), 1987.
Out There: The Government's Secret Quest for Extraterrestrials, Simon and Schuster (New York), 1990.
Gangland: How the FBI Broke the Mob, Simon and Schuster (New York), 1993.

ADAPTATIONS: I Pledge Allegiance—The True Story of the Walkers: An American Spy Family was adapted as a mini-series by the Columbia Broadcasting System (CBS-TV).

SIDELIGHTS: Howard Blum is an author of both fiction and nonfiction works, including several books on high profile subjects such as Nazis, spies, and extraterrestrials. In his first publication, 1977's *Wanted! The Search for Nazis in America,* Blum describes how a group of former Nazis emigrated to the United States after World War II and were protected from extradition by various government agencies. Of the fifty-nine such people the author found, four form the focus of his expose. Blum's book was widely reviewed, and some critics noted that despite flaws as an author, Blum had chosen a subject of intrinsic interest. In a comment that echoed the reviews of other critics, C. Michael Curtis wrote in the *Atlantic:* "The plot sounds tailor-made for a thriller, and the book is written with precisely that sense of structure and characterization." Richard F. Shepard in *New York Times,* added: "Even an uninformed reader might raise an eyebrow at some of the dramatic narration, were it not that this is such a fascinating story that one is glued to it, sharing its emotions." Robert Jay Lifton, a *New York Times Book Review* contributor, concluded: "Blum has written a very important book, to which he brings a compelling blend of investigative skill and moral passion."

For his 1985 publication, *Wishful Thinking,* Blum turned to fiction with a roman a clef based on his experiences as a journalist for the *Village Voice.* In the novel, Russ Lewis, a young college professor, submits a piece to a new magazine called *City,* in the process becoming friends with the owner, Max Fox, and Lewis is soon a regular contributor. Then Fox sells the magazine, and Lewis finds himself seduced into working for the paper's new management. Some reviewers faulted Blum's lack of technical skills as a novelist, others, such as Daniel Stern in the *New York Times Book Review,* observed that "it is the broad strokes that sketch men of ambition against a backdrop of 'real' events—a characteristic of journalists when they turn to fiction—that lends this romantic first novel its energy."

In his 1987 publication, *I Pledge Allegiance—The True Story of the Walkers,* "Blum has made an almost novelistic drama of John A. Walker Jr.'s decision to betray his country and sell military secrets to the Soviet Union," according to *New York Times* contributor Christopher Lehmann-Haupt. The author traces his subject's career in the Navy, including the start of his life as a spy, how he convinced his family to become active accomplices, through to his capture by the Federal Bureau of Investigation.

In Blum's next investigative effort, *Out There: The Government's Secret Quest for Extraterrestrials,* the author examines the U.S. government's attempts to conceal its interest in Unidentified Flying Objects (UFOs), again using techniques reviewers identified as novelistic. Richard Severo of the *New York Times* observed that the book "contains excellent science reporting and lucid explanations of the nature of research." Blum reconstructs aspects of his story in the first person, as though he had himself witnessed the events he relates. While acknowledging the technique as a questionable journalistic liberty, Severo praised Blum's storytelling ability. *New York Times Book Review* critic John A. Adam further praised Blum's inclusion of facts on cosmology and the history of the government's investigations into the existence of UFOs.

Continuing the theme of investigative reporting and disclosure, Blum's next work, *Gangland: How the FBI Broke the Mob,* details the case which the United States government built over the course of five years against mafia boss John Gotti, eventually sending him to jail. A *Publishers Weekly* critic hailed the work as a "suspenseful and superbly written expose."

BIOGRAPHICAL/CRITICAL SOURCES:

PERIODICALS

Atlantic, March, 1977, p. 115.
Newsweek, February 21, 1977, pp. 86-87.
New York Times, February 16, 1977; October 8, 1987; October 19, 1990.
New York Times Book Review, January 16, 1977; July 28, 1985, p. 8; September 9, 1990, pp. 7-8.
Publishers Weekly, September 20, 1993, p. 52.
Village Voice, October 1, 1985, p. 54.*

*   *   *

BOAZ, Noel T(homas) 1952-

PERSONAL: Born February 8, 1952, in Martinsville, VA; son of T. Noel (in business) and Elena More (a social worker; maiden name, Taylor; present surname, Robertson) Boaz; married Dorothy Dechant (marriage ended); married Meleisa McDonell (a podiatrist); children: Lydia Elena, Peter Vernon, Alex-ander McDonell. *Education:* University of Virginia, B.A. (with distinction), 1973; University of California, Berkeley, M.A., 1974, Ph.D., 1977.

ADDRESSES: Home—19470 Dusty Loop, Bend, OR 97701. *Office*—International Institute for Human Evolutionary Research, Central Oregon University Center, 2600 Northwest College Way, Bend, OR 97701.

CAREER: University of California, Los Angeles, lecturer in anthropology, 1977-78; New York University, New York City, assistant professor of anthropology, 1978-83; Virginia Museum of Natural History, Martinsville, director and curator, 1983-90; International Institute for Human Evolutionary Research, Bend, OR, research professor of anthropology and director of the institute, 1990—. Field work includes direction of International Sahabi Research Project in Libya, Senliki Research Expedition in Zaire, and Western Rift Research Expedition in Uganda. Virginia Museum of Natural History Foundation, president, 1984-89; International Foundation for Human Evolutionary Research, president, 1990—.

MEMBER: American Association of Physical Anthropologists, American Anthropological Association, Explorers Club (fellow).

AWARDS, HONORS: Rolex Award honorable mention, 1981.

WRITINGS:

(Editor with A. E. Arnanti, A. Gaziry, and others) *Neogene Paleontology and the Geology of Sahabi, Libya,* Alan Liss (New York), 1987.
(Editor) *The Evolution of Environments and Hominidae in the African Western Rift Valley,* Virginia Museum of Natural History (Martinsville), 1990.
Quarry: Closing in on the Missing Link, Free Press (New York), 1993.

WORK IN PROGRESS: Eco Homo, an ecological history of the human species; *Mystery at Dragon Bone Hill,* based on research on Beijing Man; paleoanthropological research on the earliest records of hominids.

SIDELIGHTS: Noel T. Boaz told *CA:* "I am an anthropologist who writes professional papers and monographs on subjects relating to early hominid evolution, paleoecology, and biological anthropology. I have been doing research and publishing the results for about twenty years.

"In 1993 I published my first book intended for a general audience, *Quarry: Closing in on the Missing Link.* I did this for several reasons. I believe that I have learned something in the last twenty years or so about why we are the way we are and how we got that way. Almost everyone is an anthropologist at some level: people have their own classification of the human species into types and 'races'; they have their own (usually intensely felt) ideas about their own origins, and they feel that they know better than anyone else how their minds and bodies work. So, it is not necessarily an easy task to attempt to tell people about themselves. Many times, however, our closely held folk beliefs about who we are and where we came from are wrong, and these misconceptions can have significant effects on how we deal with the rest of the world. In *Quarry* I attempted to tell something of how biological anthropologists go about their work, using a semi-autobiographical vehicle for this. It was my hope that, by understanding the methods, one might become more convinced of the conclusions.

"I direct a new research institute, the International Institute for Human Evolutionary Research, which has recently moved from Washington, DC, to Oregon to take advantage of a unique interdisciplinary collaboration with the public institutions of higher learning in the state. We do research on human biology, paleoanthropology and human origins, molecular evolution, and the interaction of the environment and human adaptation. Writing for general audiences plays an important role in my position because a critical component of research is communication. If a tree falls in a forest and no one hears the event, it might as well not have happened, at least from a human perspective. So it is with research.

"I believe that much of what anthropologists do, particularly biological anthropologists, is of clear relevance to a wide range of human concerns and problems. Yet very little of an evolutionary perspective has made it into most discussions of public issues. Part of my mission as a writer is to help correct this situation. There is a widely held misconception that creationism and evolutionism are diametrically opposed polarities when it comes to looking at our origins, and this confusion has clouded the wider acceptance of our biological evolution. But creationism is not science, and evolutionism is not theology, and the twain will never meet. Because they are different, they are both compatible. It is time to move past this phantom barrier to more effective public education in science. A good national public school program in human biology could do wonders for such wide-ranging practical problems as teenage pregnancy, drug and alcohol abuse, and obesity, for example. People do not, in general, change their behavior because they are told to. They must understand their biology and gain a grasp of how their bodies work and have worked over the past millions of years.

"I am currently working on a book that deals with the dynamics of human evolution and the environment. Most people accept that climate and the environment exert tremendous effects on human life today, but they are unaware of the even greater effects that climate change had on the evolutionary career of our species. With our greatly expanded view of past climates, we can now assess much more fully the correlation of climatic changes and human evolution. With this perspective of immense time depth to our adaptations, we can better understand our modern adaptations."

*   *   *

BOEGEHOLD, Alan L(indley)   1927-

PERSONAL: Born March 21, 1927, in Detroit, MI; son of Alfred L. (a metallurgist) and Katherine (a homemaker; maiden name, Yager) Boegehold; married Julie Elizabeth Marshall (a homemaker), April 3, 1954; children: Lindley, Alan M. Jones, David M., Alison Hiraga. *Education:* University of Michigan, A.B., 1950; Harvard University, A.M., 1954,

Ph.D., 1958; attended American School of Classical Studies at Athens, 1955-57.

ADDRESSES: Home—241 Transit St., Providence, RI 02906. *Office*—Department of Classics, Brown University, Providence, RI 02912.

CAREER: University of Illinois at Urbana/Champaign, began as instructor, became assistant professor of classics, 1957-60; Brown University, Providence, RI, began as assistant professor, became professor of classics, 1960—, department head, 1966-71, director of Ancient Studies Program, 1985-91, and director of summer sessions at American School of Classical Studies at Athens. Harvard University, visiting lecturer, 1967; American School of Classical Studies at Athens, visiting professor, 1968-69, research fellow, 1974-75, research fellow at Agora Excavations, 1980-81, senior associate member, 1983-84 and 1990-91; Yale University, visiting professor, 1971; University of California, Berkeley, visiting professor, 1978; guest lecturer at colleges and universities, including University of Glasgow, Georgetown University, Middlebury College, Ohio State University, Smith College, Boston University, and University of Texas at Austin.

WRITINGS:

(Editor with A. C. Scafuro) *Athenian Identity and Civic Ideology,* Johns Hopkins University Press (Baltimore, MD), 1993.

Author of revision, *Ancient History* by Charles A. Robinson, Jr., 2nd edition, 1967; co-editor, *Studies Presented to Sterling Dow,* [Durham, NC], 1984; editor and contributor, *Lawcourts at Athens: Sites, Buildings, Equipment, Procedure, and Testimonia,* 1995. Contributor to books, including *Hunger in History: Food Shortage, Poverty, and Deprivation,* edited by L. F. Newman, W. Crossgrove, and others, Basil Blackwell, 1990. Contributor of about eighty articles, translations, and reviews to archaeology and classical studies journals.

*   *   *

BOELTS, Maribeth   1964-

PERSONAL: Born January 19, 1964, in Waterloo, IA; daughter of Gerald Clifford (a machinist) and Dorothy Angela (a registered nurse; maiden name, Shimek) Condon; married Darwin Dale Boelts (a firefighter), August 1, 1983; children: Adam, Hannah. *Education:* University of Northern Iowa, B.A., 1987; Hawkeye Institute of Technology, emergency medical technician certification, 1988. *Politics:* Democrat. *Religion:* Christian Reformed. *Avocational interests:* Reading, exercise, spending time with husband and children.

ADDRESSES: Home—3710 Veralta Dr., Cedar Falls, IA 50613.

CAREER: St. John/St. Nicholas School, Evansdale, IA, preschool teacher, 1988-91; substitute teacher, 1991—; *Waterloo Courier,* Waterloo, IA, freelance feature writer, 1992—. Has held many church-related positions.

MEMBER: Society of Children's Book Writers and Illustrators, National Writer's Union, National League of American PEN Women.

WRITINGS:

With My Mom, with My Dad, Pacific Press, 1992.
Kids to the Rescue!: First Aid Techniques for Kids, Parenting Press, 1992.
Tornado, Paulist Press, 1993.
Dry Days, Wet Nights, A. Whitman, 1994.
Grace and Joe, A. Whitman, 1994.
The Lulla-Book, A. Whitman, 1994.
Summer's End, Houghton, in press.

WORK IN PROGRESS: "I usually try to have two or three stories on file to work on at any given time—with a backlog of ideas."

SIDELIGHTS: Maribeth Boelts explained her decision to write children's books: "I grew up in a family of readers, spending long hours at the Waterloo Public Library, filling my backpack every Saturday with Beverly Cleary, Laura Ingalls Wilder, and *Boy's Life* magazine (much more exciting, I thought, than anything out for girls at the time.) The writing joined the reading when I was in first grade, and from that [first] poem on, I was hooked on words. I continued to write through high school and into college, but as a twenty-year-old married college student with a newborn baby, pursuing an actual writing career seemed like a frivolous dream. I needed a job, and because I liked kids and had always liked school, teaching seemed a reasonable choice. After three years of teaching, however, I realized that the writing, like an impatient child, wouldn't wait. I quit my job, taking with me a file folder of ideas from the children I taught and the two young children I had at home. I wrote a few really bad children's stories, received a lot of rejections, did some more research, spent hours reading children's books, and then wrote some more. Eventually, I got

some good news from a publisher, and that was all I needed for fuel.

"Currently, I try to write daily, mostly for children, but I also do freelance feature writing for our local newspaper. Substitute teaching helps me with ideas and is something I also enjoy. I feel that as long as there are children around me, our own, or the others I am privileged to meet, there will be stories to write."

*   *   *

BOSTON, Bruce 1943-

PERSONAL: Born July 16, 1943, in Chicago, IL; son of John Edmond (a laborer) and Lillian Rose (a homemaker) Boston. *Education:* University of California, Berkeley, B.A. (with honors), 1965, M.A., 1967.

ADDRESSES: Home—Berkeley, CA. *Office*—P.O. Box 6398, Albany, CA 94706.

CAREER: Freelance writer, book designer, and text programmer. John F. Kennedy University, associate professor of creative writing, 1980-84; also worked as bibliographer, research assistant, copy editor, editor, technical writer, COBOL programmer, movie projectionist, retail clerk, furniture mover, gardener, and book buyer. Science Fiction Writers of America, chairperson of Nebula Awards Jury, 1987.

MEMBER: Science Fiction Writers of America, Science Fiction Poetry Association.

AWARDS, HONORS: Milford science fiction fellow, 1973; fiction fellow, Yaddo Colony, 1974; Pushcart Prize for fiction, 1976; Rhysling Awards, best short poem of the year, science fiction category, 1985, 1988, 1993, best long poem of the year, 1989; Odyssey Science Fiction Poetry Award, 1988; SPWAO Awards, best small press poet, 1988, 1989; readers' poll Fiction Awards, *Z Miscellaneous,* 1988, and *Aboriginal Science Fiction,* 1989; Reader's Choice Awards, poetry, *Isaac Asimov's Science Fiction,* 1989, 1994; winner, Best Soft Science Fiction Contest, Soft Science Fiction Writers Association, 1994.

WRITINGS:

Jackbird (stories), Berkeley Poets Workshop and Press, 1976, reprinted, Borgo Press, 1991.
She Comes When You're Leaving (stories), Berkeley Poets Workshop and Press, 1982.
All the Clocks Are Melting (poems; collages by Andrew Joron), Velocities, 1984.

Alchemical Texts (poetry and collages), Ocean View Books, 1985.

Nuclear Futures (poems; collages by Robert Frazier), Velocities, 1987.

A Bruce Boston Omnibus (includes *Jackbird, She Comes When You're Leaving, All the Clocks Are Melting, Alchemical Texts,* and *Nuclear Futures*), Ocean View Books, 1987.

Time (poems; collages by Robert Frazier), Titan Press, 1988.

The Nightmare Collector (poems; illustrations by Gregorio Montejo), 2 AM Publications, 1988.

Skin Trades (stories; illustrations by Allen Koszowski), Chris Drumm Books, 1988.

Musings (poetry broadside), Eldritch Emu Press, 1988.

Faces of the Beast (poems; illustrated by Allen Koszowski), Starmont House, 1990.

The New Bruce Boston Omnibus (includes *Jackbird, She Comes When You're Leaving, Nuclear Futures, Time,* and *The Nightmare Collector*), Ocean View Books, 1990.

After Magic (novelette; illustrated by Lari Davidson), Eotu Group, 1990.

Hypertales and Metafictions (stories; collages by t. winter-damon), with audio tape, Chris Drumm Books, 1990.

Short Circuits (prose poems and stories; collages by t. winter-damon), Ocean View Books, 1991.

All the Clocks Are Melting (stories), Pulphouse, 1991.

Houses and Other Stories, Talisman, 1991.

Cybertexts (poems; illustrated by Alan Giana), Talisman, 1992.

(With Robert Frazier) *Chronicles of the Mutant Rain Forest* (poems), Horror's Head Press, 1992.

Accursed Wives (poems), Night Visions, 1993.

Night Eyes (stories), Chris Drumm Books, 1993.

The Last Existentialist (poetry broadside), Chris Drumm Books, 1993.

Specula: Selected Uncollected Poems, 1968-1993, Talisman, 1993.

Stained Glass Rain (novel), Ocean View Books, 1993.

Sensuous Debris: Selected Poems, 1970-1994 (illustrated by Thomas Wiloch), Dark Regions, 1994.

Work represented in anthologies, including *Alien Pregnant by Elvis,* DAW Books; *Angels!,* Ace Books; and *Pushcart Prize Anthology,* Avon. Contributor to periodicals, including *Amazing Stories, Cavalier, Portland Review, Twilight Zone, Weird Tales,* and *Science Fiction Age.*

SIDELIGHTS: Bruce Boston told *CA:* "My earliest memories include Golden Books and the poems of Robert Louis Stevenson, read to me as bedtime stories by my parents. My first library card, at about the age of seven, led me to science books for children, usually about astronomy, and to the Walter Farley 'Black Stallion' novels. About the same time, I developed a mania for comic books, particularly the 'Classic Illustrated' comics, and would sometimes spend an entire day reading and rereading them.

"I must have been about nine when I discovered science fiction and coincidentally decided that I wanted to be a writer. I think the first science fiction novel I read was Heinlein's *Red Planet.* I was hooked immediately, and within a few years I had devoured nearly all of the science fiction and fantasy my local library had to offer, was buying paperbacks and science fiction periodicals at the local newsstand, and had joined the Science Fiction Book Club. Some of my favorite writers from this period were Asimov, Clarke, Merrit, Robert E. Howard, Poe, Van Vogt, Eric Frank Russell, Heinlein, Burroughs, Charles Eric Maine, and, of course, the king of space opera, E. E. Doc Smith. The two books that impressed me most, continue to impress me to this day, and influenced me most in the direction of science fiction were Alfred Bester's *The Stars My Destination* and *The Demolished Man.*

"In 1957 Sputnik went into orbit, America decided it was losing the space race and, all across the country, public schools began singling out those they considered the brighter students and segregating them into special classes. At my high school these were called More Capable Learner (MCL) classes, and they led me away from science fiction for a number of years to literature, the kind with a capital 'L'. Probably my most significant influences in this area have been Dostoevsky, Hesse, Melville, Henry Miller, Lawrence Durrell, Gunter Grass, Kerouac, and Nabokov; in terms of poets Ezra Pound, T. S. Eliot, Dylan Thomas, and Alan Ginsberg are the names that first come to mind.

"At the height of the turbulent sixties, I attended the University of California, Berkeley, where I was active in political protest and psychedelic exploration. A long-time resident of the San Francisco Bay Area, I have hitchhiked extensively in the United States, and I lived briefly in New York, Oregon, and Mexico.

"Thus, my influences have been eclectic, and to this day I continue to read and write eclectically. I am primarily known as a science fiction-fantasy poet because this is the portion of my work that has received the widest reader response. In fact, I've published as many books of fiction as poetry. I would describe myself as a writer of both traditional and speculative fiction and poetry. If I have anything that could be called a *magnum opus,* it would be my novel *Stained Glass Rain,* which is mostly mainstream with some speculative elements.

"When I sit down to write, I tend for the most part to follow my imagination and creative impulses, rather than the dictates of the marketplace. In common parlance, I suppose this classifies me as an artist, as well as a writer. The result has been considerable critical success, much less in the way of financial success. I continue to make most of my living from free-lance book design and text programming, usually computer books.

"Some of the writers I've been most interested in and excited about in recent years include Mervyn Peake, Steve Erickson, Cynthia Ozick, Angela Carter, Jim Thompson, and Barrington Bayley."

*   *   *

BOUCHELLE, Joan Hoiness 1928-

PERSONAL: Born April 20, 1928, in Brooklyn, NY; daughter of Niels (an audio engineer) and Johanne (a homemaker; maiden name, Torgesen) Hoiness; married McLemore Bouchelle (a surgeon), March 31, 1951; children: Karen Pearce McLemore, Thadeus, Ethel. *Education:* Attended Vassar College, 1947-48; Columbia Presbyterian School of Nursing, B.S., 1951; California State University, Fullerton, M.A., 1978. *Politics:* Republican. *Religion:* Lutheran.

ADDRESSES: Home and office—28398 Buena Vista, Mission Viejo, CA 92692.

CAREER: Writer. Choir director at Grace Lutheran Church, Anaheim, CA, 1961-82.

MEMBER: Children's Home Society, Medical Association Auxiliary, Martin Luther Heartbeats, Anaheim Assistance League (past vice president).

WRITINGS:

(Editor) *With Tennyson at the Keyboard: A Victorian Songbook,* Garland, 1985.

SIDELIGHTS: Joan Hoiness Bouchelle is the editor of *With Tennyson at the Keyboard: A Victorian*

Songbook, which she described to *CA* as "a look at a selection of English poet laureate Alfred Tennyson's shorter poems and some of the music written for them by his contemporaries." The book provides both the text of Tennyson's poems and their musical settings by such composers as Hubert Parry and Edward Lear. In the *Times Literary Supplement,* Arthur Jacobs noted that "the songs by Lear . . . are known to have had the approval of Tennyson himself, despite his general suspicion of musical treatment."

Bouchelle told *CA: "With Tennyson at the Keyboard: A Victorian Songbook* is an inter-disciplinary effort combining music and poetry. My purpose in writing it was to determine, in a purely subjective manner, whether the music enhanced, helped interpret, or betrayed the poet Tennyson's work."

BIOGRAPHICAL/CRITICAL SOURCES:

PERIODICALS

Los Angeles Times Book Review, April 21, 1985, p. 2.
Times Literary Supplement, September 6, 1985, p. 971.

*   *   *

BOUCHER, Bruce (Ambler) 1948-

PERSONAL: Born November 5, 1948, in Birmingham, AL; son of John Walter (a teacher) and Louise Ambler (a bookkeeper; maiden name, Kean) Boucher; married Gillian Moore (divorced, 1981); married Isabel Ruth Carlise (a journalist), February 13, 1982; children: Venetia, Miranda. *Education:* Harvard University, A.B. (magna cum laude), 1970; Oxford University, B.A., 1972, M.A., 1977; University of London, M.A., 1974, Ph.D., 1987. *Religion:* Episcopalian.

ADDRESSES: Home—London, England. *Office*—Department of the History of Art, University College, University of London, London WC1E 6BT, England.

CAREER: University of London, London, England, lecturer, 1976-92, reader in art history, 1992—.

MEMBER: International Association of Art Critics (corresponding member), Ateneo Veneto.

AWARDS, HONORS: Salimbeni Prize for Italian Art History, 1992.

WRITINGS:

The Sculpture of Jacopo Sansavino, Yale University Press, 1991.

(Editor) *Piero di Cosimo de'Medici: Art in the Service of the Medici,* Akademie Verlag (Berlin), 1993.

Andrea Palladio: The Architect in His Time, Abbeville Press (New York, NY), 1994.

WORK IN PROGRESS: Italian Baroque Sculpture, for Thames & Hudson; *Death in Venice: Tombs and Social Hierarchy in Renaissance Venice;* research on sculpture in theory and practice from the sixteenth century to the end of the eighteenth century.

*   *   *

BOUCHER, Philip P. 1944-

PERSONAL: Born July 22, 1944, in Hartford, CT; son of Albert (a machinist) and Loretta (a nurse; maiden name, Poulin) Boucher; married Mary Alice Henderson (a teacher), March 31, 1989; children: Andrew Philip, Thomas Alexander. *Education:* University of Hartford, B.A., 1966; University of Connecticut, M.A., 1967, Ph.D., 1974.

ADDRESSES: Office—History Department, RH 401, University of Alabama in Huntsville, Huntsville, AL 35899.

CAREER: Instructor in Charlotte, NC, 1973-74; University of Alabama, Huntsville, assistant professor, 1974-80, associate professor, 1980-89, professor, 1989—.

WRITINGS:

Shaping of the French Colonial Empire, Garland, 1985.

Les Nouvelles Frances, John Carter Brown Library, 1989.

Also author of *Cannibal Encounters* for Johns Hopkins University Press (Baltimore, MD).

WORK IN PROGRESS: A book on France and the Caribbean before 1789, expected completion, 2000.

*   *   *

BOUQUET, Mary (Rose) 1955-

PERSONAL: Born March 2, 1955, in England; daughter of Michael Rome (a historian) and Joyce Lilian (Sandercock) Bouquet; married Henk de Haan (a university lecturer), 1988; children: Hendrik John Michael Rome. *Education:* Cambridge University, B.A., 1977, M.A. and Ph.D., 1981. *Avocational interests:* Art, music.

ADDRESSES: Home—Wageningen, Netherlands. *Agent*—Andrew B. Durnell, 43 High St., Tunbridge Wells, Kent TN1 1XL, England.

CAREER: University of Lisbon, Lisbon, Portugal, lecturer, 1983-87; National Museum of Ethnology, Lisbon, exhibition developer, 1986-88; University of Amsterdam, Amsterdam, Netherlands, lecturer, 1989; National Museum of Natural History, Leiden, Netherlands, exhibition developer, 1992-93.

MEMBER: Royal Anthropological Institute (fellow), Association of Social Anthropologists.

WRITINGS:

Reclaiming English Kinship, Manchester University Press, 1993.

Author of exhibition catalogues.

WORK IN PROGRESS: Research for a film about the American anthropologist David M. Schneider, with Anna Grimshaw; genealogical research.

SIDELIGHTS: Mary Bouquet told *CA:* "I grew up in rural Devon in the 1950s and 1960s, went to Cambridge to study anthropology in the 1970s, lived and worked in Lisbon in the 1980s, and moved to the Netherlands in the 1990s. This rather peripatetic trajectory has nurtured my love of the English language and my need to write in it, wherever I am. My understanding of the English has been at one or more removes for most of my life. This was certainly central to the writing of *Reclaiming English Kinship,* which was completed in the Netherlands after leaving Portugal. In addition to writing in English, I am also interested in narration through space—in using objects and images from museum and archival collections, in addition to texts."

*   *   *

BOWEN, Roger W. 1947-

PERSONAL: Born March 12, 1947, in Indianapolis, IN; son of Eugene S. and Eloise (Wilson) Bowen; married Barbara H., December 22, 1968; children: Jessica Sarah, Anna Ashley. *Education:* Wabash College, B.A., 1969; University of Michigan, M.A., 1970; University of British Columbia, Ph.D., 1977.

ADDRESSES: Office—Vice President for Academic Affairs, Hollins College, P.O. Box 9706, Roanoke, VA 24020.

CAREER: Colby College, Waterville, ME, assistant professor, 1978-82, associate professor, 1982-87; Hollins College, Roanoke, VA, vice president for academic affairs, 1992—. St. Mary's University, Halifax, Nova Scotia, Canada, visiting professor, 1978; Japan Institute of Harvard University, associate in research, 1980—.

WRITINGS:

Rebellion and Democracy in Meiji Japan: A Study of Commoners in the Popular Rights Movement, University of California Press, 1980.

(Editor) *E. H. Norman: His Life and Scholarship,* University of Toronto Press, 1984.

Innocence Is Not Enough: The Life and Death of Herbert Norman, Douglas & McIntyre, 1986, M. E. Sharpe, 1988.

WORK IN PROGRESS: Writing a book on postwar Japanese democracy.

SIDELIGHTS: American academic Roger W. Bowen is noted for his research into the life and mysterious death of Canadian diplomat E. H. Norman, an alleged Communist and spy who committed suicide in Cairo, Egypt, in 1957. Norman's career in the Canadian foreign service as well as his writings on Japan brought him acclaim until Cold War fever in the early 1950s tarnished his reputation. Bowen's first volume on the subject, *E. H. Norman: His Life and Scholarship,* a work he edited, is a collection of essays by historians and diplomats that brings perspective to the diplomat's life and ideas. Bowen is also the author of a full-scale biography entitled *Innocence Is Not Enough: The Life and Death of Herbert Norman,* published in 1988. This second work delves deeper into the investigation of Norman by the U.S. government at the height of anti-Communist fervor and discusses Norman's subsequent suicide.

The 1984 work *E. H. Norman: His Life and Scholarship,* which grew out of an earlier conference Bowen organized on Norman's life, includes selections of Norman's own writings. The essays by others reflect upon Norman's personality, scholarship, and diplomatic career. One piece traces Norman's upbringing in Japan by rural Canadian missionary parents and his broadminded view of other cultures, an essential trait for a career in the foreign service. Other essays chronicle Norman's political develop-

ment at Cambridge, England, in the 1930s, where he joined the Communist Party. The essays also cover Norman's academic pursuits and his work in helping establish the postwar Japanese state.

In his research on the subject, Bowen obtained documents under the U.S. Freedom of Information Act to trace the scandal that beset Norman after World War II. By then a high-ranking Canadian diplomat, Norman came under investigation by the Royal Canadian Mounted Police (RCMP) as a suspected Communist and spy. He was cleared of any wrongdoing in the matter, and Bowen's exploration of the FBI files and State Department records revealed no clear connection with spying for the Soviet Union nor any other government. *E. H. Norman: His Life and Scholarship* also includes four essays by Norman himself.

Bowen's first volume on the life of E. H. Norman received praise from reviewers for its fresh insights into the mystery surrounding the diplomat's career. While Bernard Ostry in the *Times Literary Supplement* suggested the book leaves some "unanswered simple questions," he concluded that "a strong impression of Norman emerges from this work of collective defence."

Bowen's full-scale biography of Norman, *Innocence Is Not Enough,* delves further into Norman's career and the implications that he was a spy. The book delves into the investigations of Norman by both the RCMP and American Communist hunters. Bowen explains that in 1951, Norman's name was brought forth by the U.S. Senate Subcommittee on International Security and he was denounced as a Communist. Norman's ally in the matter was future Canadian prime minister Lester Pearson, who publicly supported him. Bowen explains how Pearson later named Norman ambassador to Egypt, where in 1956 a conflict developed over the Suez Canal. World tensions ran high, as Soviet forces occupied the waterway and a third world war seemed imminent. Norman was a key player in helping to resolve the crisis, but, as Bowen details, more investigations by the Senate Subcommittee again threatened Norman's career. The diplomat ultimately committed suicide.

Both of Bowen's works on Norman present the idea that because of his grounding in eastern philosophy, the diplomat saw suicide as a preferable alternative to dishonor, rather than as an admission of guilt. Canadian scholar Charles Taylor, reviewing *Innocence Is Not Enough* for the *Globe and Mail,* described Bowen's examination of Norman's career and ideology as "thorough and convincing." Taylor went on to laud the biography for offering "a wealth of new information and speculation."

BIOGRAPHICAL/CRITICAL SOURCES:

PERIODICALS

Globe and Mail, July 14, 1984; November 8, 1986.
Times Literary Supplement, December 21, 1984, p. 1470.

*   *   *

BOWSER, Benjamin P(aul) 1946-

PERSONAL: Born August 20, 1946, in New York, NY; son of Benjamin J. and Nathalia (Earle) Bowser; married Deborah Whittle, September 19, 1992; children: Paul I. *Education:* Franklin and Marshall College, B.A., 1969; Cornell University, Ph.D., 1976.

ADDRESSES: Home—305 Mendocino Way, Redwood City, CA 94065. *Office*—Department of Sociology and Social Services, California State University, 25800 Carlos Bee Blvd., Hayward, CA 94542.

CAREER: Cornell University, Ithaca, NY, assistant dean of Graduate School, 1975-82; Western Interstate Commission for Higher Education, director of Minority Education Office, 1982-83; University of Santa Clara, Santa Clara, CA, director of Office of Black Student Affairs, 1983-85; Stanford University, Stanford, CA, assistant to the director of information technology services, 1985-87; California State University, Hayward, associate professor of sociology and social services, 1987—. Indiana University of Pennsylvania, visiting research scholar, 1984; University of California, San Francisco, associate research scientist, Treatment Research Unit, Substance Abuse Services, 1990-91; Bayview Hunter's Point Community Foundation, director of multi-cultural inquiry and research on AIDS, 1990-91; National Research Council/National Academy of Science Committee on Drug Prevention Research, member, 1990-91. Our Developing World, Inc., member of advisory board, 1984—; Bayshore Employment Service, Inc., member of board of directors, 1986—; Dr. Martin Luther King, Jr. Center for Social Change of Santa Clara Valley, member of board of directors, 1986-89.

MEMBER: American Sociological Association, Association of Black Sociologists, Peninsula Association of Black Personnel Administrators.

AWARDS, HONORS: Grants from Rockefeller Foundation, 1976-81, Social Science Research Council,

1977, National Institute of Mental Health, 1979-81, 1988, and 1991, National Science Foundation, 1988-89, U.S. Centers for Disease Control, 1990-91, 1992-93, and 1993—, Robert Wood Johnson Foundation, 1991-93, and National Institutes of Health, 1992—; award from Santa Clara Valley Urban League, 1987; Field faculty fellow, California Field Poll Institute, 1992-93.

WRITINGS:

(Editor with E. Mann and M. Oling) *Census Data with Maps for Small Areas of New York City, 1910-1960,* Research Publications (Woodbury, CT), 1981.
(Editor with R. Hunt) *Impacts of Racism on White Americans,* Sage Publications, 1981, second edition, 1995.
(Editor) *Black Male Adolescents: Parenting and Education in Community Context,* University Press of America, 1991.
(With G. Auletta and T. Jones) *Dealing with Diversity in the University,* Sage Publications, 1993.
(Editor with T. Jones and G. Auletta) *Toward the Multicultural University,* Praeger, 1995.
(Editor) *Racism and Anti-Racism in World Perspective,* Sage, 1995.

Contributor to books, including *The American Black Male: His Present Status and His Future,* edited by Richard Majors and J. Gordon, Nelson-Hall, 1993; *Researching Sensitive Topics,* edited by Claire Renzetti and R. Lee, Sage Publications, 1993; and *AIDS Prevention and Services: Community-Based Research,* edited by Johannes P. Van Vugt, Bergin & Garvey, 1994. U.S. associate editor, "Sage Race Relations Abstracts," Race Relations Institute (London), 1981—. Contributor to academic journals.

*   *   *

BOYD, Steven R(ay) 1946-

PERSONAL: Born July 6, 1946, in Hampton, IA; son of Orris E. (a service station operator) and Phyllis Faye (a homemaker; maiden name, Dubberke) Boyd; married Sandra Lee Douglas (a computer company representative), June 9, 1968; children: Melissa Stephanie, Melinda Suzanne. *Education:* Claremont McKenna College, B.A., 1968; University of Wisconsin—Madison, M.A., 1970, Ph.D., 1974. *Politics:* Democrat. *Religion:* Unitarian Universalist.

ADDRESSES: Home—12918 Kings Forest, San Antonio, TX 78230. *Office*—Division of Behavioral and

Cultural Sciences, University of Texas at San Antonio, San Antonio, TX 78249.

CAREER: St. Olaf College, Northfield, MN, instructor, 1974-75; University of Texas at San Antonio, assistant professor, 1975-81, associate professor, 1981-94, professor of history, 1994—. Member of advisory board, Center for the Study of the Constitution, Dickinson College, 1980—; member of program committee, Society for Historians of the Early American Republic, 1983-84; Friends of San Antonio Public Library, member of board of trustees, 1990-91, treasurer, 1991-93.

MEMBER: Organization of American Historians, Society for Historians of the Early Republic.

AWARDS, HONORS: Fellow of Project 87, Brookings Institution, 1983; Beveridge Travel grant, American Historical Association, 1984; National Endowment for the Humanities Constitutional Studies research fellowship, 1985; grant, National Council of Social Studies, 1991, for conducting collaborative inservice workshops on the Bill of Rights; travel grant, Law School Admissions Council, 1992.

WRITINGS:

The Politics of Opposition: Antifederalists and the Acceptance of the Constitution, [New York], 1979.
(Editor) *The Whiskey Rebellion: Past and Present Perspectives,* Greenwood Press (Westport), 1985.
The Constitution in State Politics: From the Calling of the Constitutional Convention to the Calling of the First Federal Elections, [New York], 1990.
(Editor) *Alternative Constitutions for the United States: A Documentary History,* Greenwood Press, 1992.

Contributor to books, including *The Human Dimensions of Nation Making: Essays in Colonial and Revolutionary History,* edited by James K. Martin, 1976; *American Political Trials,* edited by Michael Belknap, Greenwood Press, 1981; *Dictionary of Political Trials in History,* edited by Ron Christenson, 1991; and *The American Nation, 1775-1820: A Twelve Volume Anthology of Outstanding Articles,* edited by Peter S. Onuf, 1991. Contributor of articles to periodicals, including *Social Education, Reviews in American History, Journal of the Early Republic, San Antonio Express,* and *San Antonio Light.*

WORK IN PROGRESS: A study of the use of the item veto in Texas from 1940 to 1990 with Pat Thompson.

*   *   *

BRACKMAN, Barbara   1945-

PERSONAL: Born July 6, 1945, in New York, NY; daughter of Benjamin H. (an accountant) and Cecelia (a homemaker; maiden name, McNally) Brackman; married James H. Holmes, 1981 (divorced, 1992). *Education:* University of Kansas, B.A., 1967, M.S., 1974. *Politics:* Democrat.

ADDRESSES: Office—3115 West 6th, No. C-237, Lawrence, KS 66049.

CAREER: Educator in special education, University of Kansas and University of Illinois, 1970-85; freelance writer, 1976—. Also freelance consultant and museum curator for facilities such as the Spencer Museum of Art, Kansas Museum of History, and the Knoxville Museum of Art.

WRITINGS:

Clues in the Calico: A Guide to Identifying and Dating Antique Quilts, EPM, 1989.
Encyclopedia of Applique, EPM, 1993.
Encyclopedia of Pieced Quilts, American Quilters Society, 1993.
(Editor) *Kansas Quilts and Quilters,* University Press of Kansas (Lawrence, KS), 1993.
(With M. Waldvogel) *Patchwork Souvenirs,* Rutledge Hill Press, 1993.

WORK IN PROGRESS: Grassroots Art on the Central Plains, University Press of Kansas, 1996; research into cowboy boot history and women's history.

*   *   *

BRAINARD, Cecilia Manguerra   1947-

PERSONAL: Born November 21, 1947, in Cebu, Philippines; naturalized U.S. citizen, 1972; daughter of Mariano Flores (a civil engineer) and Concepcion (a realtor and businessperson; maiden name, Cuenco) Manguerra; married Lauren Robson Brainard (a lawyer), 1969; children: Christopher, Alexander, Andrew. *Education:* Maryknoll College, Quezon City, Philippines, B.A., 1968; graduate study at University of California, Los Angeles, 1969, 1971. *Religion:* Roman Catholic.

ADDRESSES: Home—Santa Monica, CA. *Office*—P.O. Box 5099, Santa Monica, CA 90409. *Agent*—Betsy Amster Literary Enterprises, 2151 Kenilworth Ave., Los Angeles, CA 90039.

CAREER: Communications specialist, ranging from documentary scriptwriting to public relations work, 1969-81; freelance writer, 1981—. University of California Extension, Los Angeles, instructor in writing program, 1989—; Santa Monica College, instructor, 1991—. Philippine American Literary House, partner, 1994—; workshop presenter; public speaker.

MEMBER: International P.E.N. (member of board of directors of P.E.N. Center U.S.A. West, 1990-93), Philippine American Women Writers and Artists (founding member; past member of board of directors), Filipino American Press Club of Los Angeles (member of board of directors, 1993—).

AWARDS, HONORS: Fortner Prize, 1985, for the story "The Balete Tree"; Recognition Award, National Citizen Movement for Free Elections (Philippines), 1987; fellow of California Arts Council, 1989-90; grant from City of Los Angeles, 1990-91; Special Recognition Award, Los Angeles Board of Education, 1991; fellow, Brody Arts Fund, 1991; Literature Award, Filipino Women's Network, 1992.

WRITINGS:

Woman With Horns and Other Stories, New Day/Cellar Book Shop, 1988.
The Philippine Woman in America, New Day/Cellar Bookshop, 1991.
Song of Yvonne, New Day/Cellar Bookshop, 1991, published as *When the Rainbow Goddess Wept,* Dutton, 1994.
(Editor) *Seven Stories From Seven Sisters: A Collection of Philippine Folktales,* Philippine American Women Writers and Artists, 1992.
(Editor) *Fiction by Filipinos in America,* New Day/Cellar Bookshop, 1993.
(Co-editor and contributor) *Asian Folktales,* Philippine American Women Writers and Artists, in press.

Work represented in anthologies, including *Making Waves: An Anthology of Writings by and About Asian American Women,* Beacon Press, 1989; *The Perimeter of Light: Writing about the Vietnam War,* New Rivers Press, 1992; and *Forbidden Fruit,* Anvil Publishing, 1992. Contributor of more than two hundred articles and stories to periodicals, including *Multicultural Review, Amerasia Journal, Mindscapes,*

Outlook, Bamboo Ridge Journal, and *Focus Philippines.* Fiction co-editor, *West/Word Journal,* 1992; editor of women's section and culture section, *Los Angeles Filipino Bulletin,* 1992; member of editorial board, *Center,* 1992.

WORK IN PROGRESS: Fiction, both long and short.

SIDELIGHTS: Cecilia Manguerra Brainard told *CA:* "I like to write stories about Filipinos, whether they are in the Philippines or other places. Growing up, I read a lot of materials that were basically Eurocentric. I like to imagine and recreate places in the Philippines and present historical events from my own point of view. I like to give voice to Filipinos in America, to the women in particular, who are at a greater disadvantage."

*   *   *

BRASCHI, Giannina 1953-

PERSONAL: Born February 5, 1953, in San Juan, PR; daughter of Euripides (an athlete) and Edmee (a real estate broker; maiden name, Firpi) Braschi. *Education:* State University of New York at Stony Brook, Ph.D. (summa cum laude), 1980.

ADDRESSES: Home—350 West 50th St., Apt. 9G, New York, NY 10019. *Office*—c/o Jonathan Brent, Senior Editor, Yale University Press, 92A Yale Station, New Haven, CT 06520.

CAREER: Writer. Gives bilingual readings from her works.

MEMBER: International P.E.N., Modern Language Association, Academy of American Poets, Poetry Society of America, Phi Sigma Iota.

AWARDS, HONORS: Instituto de Puerto Rico en Nueva York, 1979; grants from Danforth Foundation, 1978-80, Ford Foundation, 1978-80, Instituto de Cooperacion Iberoamericana, Madrid, Spain, 1980, Rutgers University (Minority Faculty), 1983, and Painted Bride Art Center, 1989-90; award from Columbia University Translation Center, 1994, for *Empire of Dreams*; NEA grant, 1995, for poetry.

WRITINGS:

Asalto al Tiempo (poems), Ambitos Literario (Barcelona), 1981.
La Poesia de Becquer (criticism), Costa Amic (Mexico City), 1982.

La Comedia Profana (poems), Anthropos Editorial del Hombre (Barcelona), 1985.

Libro de Payasos y Bufones (poems), Giorgio Upiglio (Milan), 1987.

El Imperio de los Suenos (poems and a novella), Anthropos Editorial del Hombre (Barcelona), 1988, translation from Spanish by Tess O'Dwyer published as *Empire of Dreams,* Yale University Press, 1994.

WORK IN PROGRESS: Yo-Yo Boing, "bilingual dialogues about the creative process."

SIDELIGHTS: Giannina Braschi told *CA:* "Born into a well-to-do family in San Juan, Puerto Rico, in 1956, I lived briefly in Madrid, Rome, Paris, and London before settling in New York City in 1975. I found the city's violence, velocity, and aura of instability awesome and threatening; yet, its raw energy and diversity fascinated me. New York is a place where there are no illusions of stability and safety; it is a place that is constantly under reconstruction; and, therefore, it is a place to re-invent oneself. I vowed to myself, as many immigrants do, to make this city mine, and that is what I have done in *Empire of Dreams.* I wanted to create a poetic city, in which many languages would be spoken, in which the tempo of the verses would be as fast and as unpredictable as the subways, in which the idea of continuous self-reconstruction would prevail.

"My collected works, *Empire of Dreams,* is a testimony of my love affair with New York City, of my social, political, and linguistic relationships to the place that has acted as a magnet for foreigners for so many years. Written in three stages and styles, this trilogy transforms the city streets into the site of liberation for its marginal citizens, who struggle through internal and external trials in order to experience the center of political power and personal identity. 'Part I: Assault on Time' spies upon the mysteries of a new world, in which the language feels as foreign as the cityscape. 'Part II: Profane Comedy' appropriates stylistic conventions from plays, songs, and commercials, as it pays homage to mass media, performance, and street spectacles. Anonymous characters such as clowns, buffoons, and fortune tellers violently protest their marginal situation, as shepherds invade, conquer, and colonize New York City with their own language, song, and dance. 'Part III: The Intimate Diary of Solitude' further challenges the boundaries of genre by adopting literary techniques from diary, tabloids, gossip, videos, autobiography, musical, and manifesto. Here the marginal citizens find alternative ways of appropriating authority. Swapping names, ages, nationalities and genders, the characters continually reconstruct their identities through role playing and, thereby, create their own places in this city of displacement.

"I am currently completing *Yo-Yo Boing,* which is composed of bilingual dialogues about being 'alive and kicking' at the turn of the twenty-first century. Meditating on creative processes and the artist's role in the new century, these dialogues (between two prominent New York writers) delve into erotic bantering, intense conflict, and sheer violence. As a counter-current, a chorus of anonymous immigrants and minorities vehemently 'strategize and philosophize' about their future roles inside and outside the American mainstream. With rapid tempos and humorous gusto, the scenes cross-cut throughout public and private spaces of the city, from the Upper East Side *soiree* to the Lower East Side *tertulia,* from the Greek diner booth to the subway platform, from the movie theater line to the unemployment line, from the public bathroom to the private bathroom, and from the bathroom to the bedroom."

*   *   *

BRENNEMAN, Helen Good   1925-1994

OBITUARY NOTICE—See index for *CA* sketch: Born November 26, 1925, in Harrisonburg, VA; died January 13, 1994. Religious activist and writer. Brenneman was the author of numerous inspirational books for those in difficult circumstances. An active Mennonite, she and her minister husband served as relief workers in Germany after World War II. Her first book, *Meditations for the New Mother: A Devotional Book for the New Mother During the First Month Following the Birth of Her Baby,* was published in 1953 and appeared in a revised edition in 1985. Brenneman also wrote a novel, *But Not Forsaken,* and *My Comforters,* a book of devotional messages she wished to impart to readers after she was diagnosed with multiple sclerosis in 1963. A freelance writer, Brenneman's articles often appeared in *Christian Living* and other religious magazines. She was also the author of *Marriage: Agony and Ecstasy, Cope: Handibook for the Handicapped,* and *Morning Joy: Meditations for Those Who Have Suffered Loss.*

OBITUARIES AND OTHER SOURCES:

BOOKS

Writers Directory 1994-1996, St. James Press, 1993.

[Date of death provided by husband, Virgil John Brenneman, September, 1994.]

* * *

BREWER, Gay 1965-

PERSONAL: Born April 3, 1965, in Louisville, KY; son of Harvey (an independent builder) and Gail (MacDonald) Brewer. *Education:* University of Louisville, B.A., 1985; Ohio State University, M.A., 1988, Ph.D., 1992. *Politics:* Unaffiliated. *Religion:* Unaffiliated.

ADDRESSES: Home—Murfreesboro, TN. *Office*—Middle Tennessee State University, Department of English, P.O. Box 70, Murfreesboro, TN 37132.

CAREER: Indian Hills College, Ottumwa, IA, instructor, 1992-93; Middle Tennessee State University, Murfreesboro, TN, assistant professor of English, 1993—. Director of plays.

WRITINGS:

CRITICISM

A Detective in Distress: Philip Marlowe's Domestic Dream (monograph), Brownstone (Madison, IN), 1989.
David Mamet and Film: Illusion/Disillusion in a Wounded Land, McFarland (Jefferson, NC), 1993.
Laughing Like Hell: The Harrowing Satires of Jim Thompson, Borgo Press, 1994.

POETRY CHAPBOOKS

Book Lover, Mulberry Press (Wichita, KS), 1991.
Zocalo, Bogg (Arlington, VA), 1991.
The Woman and the White Dog, Bootleg Press (Uniondale, NY), 1994.

PLAYS

Undertakings, Aran Press (Louisville, KY), 1993.
JFK, Rudolph, and A Life with Fear in It, produced by Contemporary American Theatre Company, Columbus, OH, June 7-16, 1992.

Author of annotated bibliography, *David Mamet: A Casebook,* edited by Leslie Kane, Garland Press, 1991. Editor of the literary review *Poems & Plays.* Contributor of articles, book reviews, plays, poetry, and fiction to *American Drama, The Mystery Fancier, Literature/Film Quarterly, And Review, Illinois Writers Review, Cornfield Review, Dominion Review, New Poets Review, Wormwood Review, New York Quarterly, RE*

Arts & Letters, Ambergris, Thinker, Oasis, Stage Whisper: A Playscript Series, and the *Kentucky Poetry Review.*

WORK IN PROGRESS: Red Canary, a novel.

SIDELIGHTS: Gay Brewer told *CA:* "I say what Pascal said: 'The last act is bloody, however fine the rest of the play. They throw earth over your head, and it is finished forever.'"

* * *

BRIDE, Nadja
See NOBISSO, Josephine

* * *

BROCKINGTON, J(ohn) L(eonard) 1940-

PERSONAL: Born December 5, 1940, in Oxford, England; son of L. H. (a university teacher and minister) and F. E. (Woodward) Brockington; married Mary Fairweather (a researcher), August 2, 1966; children: Anne, Michael. *Education:* Corpus Christi College, Oxford, B.A. (with honors), 1963, M.A., 1966, Ph.D., 1968.

ADDRESSES: Office—Department of Sanskrit, University of Edinburgh, 7 Buccleuch Pl., Edinburgh EH8 9LW, Scotland.

CAREER: University of Edinburgh, Edinburgh, Scotland, assistant lecturer, 1965-67, lecturer, 1967-82, senior lecturer, 1982-89, reader in Sanskrit, 1989—, director of studies, 1969-75, department head, 1975—. Guest lecturer, Cambridge University, 1979, Utkal University, 1981 and 1994, Sri Jagannatha Sanskrit University, 1981 and 1994, University of Calcutta, 1981, University of Zagreb, 1987, London School of Oriental and African Studies, London, 1993, and Jadavpur University, 1993.

MEMBER: Traditional Cosmology Society.

WRITINGS:

The Sacred Thread: Hinduism in Its Continuity and Diversity, Edinburgh University Press, 1981.
Righteous Rama: The Evolution of an Epic, Oxford University Press (Delhi), 1985.
Hinduism and Christianity, Macmillan (London), 1992.
(Compiler with P. Flamm, Heinrich von Stietencron, and others) *Epic and Puranic Bibliography: Up to 1985,* Purana Research Publications (Tuebingen), 1992.

Contributor to books, including *The Impeachment of Warren Hastings: Papers from a Bicentenary Commemoration,* edited by Geoffrey Carnall and Colin Nicholson, Edinburgh University Press, 1989; *The Penguin Encyclopedia of Classical Civilizations,* edited by Arthur Cotterell, Penguin, 1993; and *World Mythology,* edited by Roy Willis, Simon & Schuster, 1993. Contributor of more than thirty-five articles to learned journals. Member of editorial board, *Indologica Taurinensia, Jagannath Jyotih,* and *Cosmos.*

WORK IN PROGRESS: *A Catalogue of the Chandra Shum Shere Collection in the Bodleian Library,* Part II: *Epics and Puranas,* for Clarendon Press; editing the commentary of Varadaraja, for the Oriental Institute, Baroda, India.

SIDELIGHTS: J. L. Brockington told *CA:* "My research so far has been concerned mainly with the Ramayana, the Puranas, and the development of Vaisnavism. I collaborated for several years with the Tuebingen Purana Project of the Seminar fuer Indologie und vergleichende Religionswissenschaft at the University of Tuebingen. In 1984 I was invited by the Sahitya Akademi in New Delhi to participate in the critical inventory of Ramayana studies throughout the world, by compiling information on holdings of manuscripts and other materials relating to any version of the Ramayana located in Britain.

"I am continuing my studies on textual problems of the Ramayana, and I am also widening my epic research, with studies on the Ramayana tradition in India and the rest of Asia, and with an edition of Varadaraja's commentary."

*   *   *

BROOKS, Jeremy 1926-1994 (Clive Meikle)

OBITUARY NOTICE—See index for *CA* sketch: Born December 17, 1926, in Southampton, England; died June 27, 1994, in Llanfrothen, Wales. Novelist, playwright, theater manager, and reviewer. Throughout his career, Brooks divided his time between his own writings and a variety of other literary activities. After beginning as a stage designer and scene painter in 1949, he worked as a magazine writer, literary agent, and reviewer. From 1962 he was also affiliated with the Royal Shakespeare Company, serving first as literary manager and later as play advisor. In addition to writing plays and novels, which include *The Water Carnival* (1957), *Jampot*

Smith (1960), *Smith, as Hero* (1965), and—more recently—*Doing the Voices* (1985), Brooks translated and adapted numerous Russian plays for the stage and screen. He also wrote under the pseudonym Clive Meikle.

OBITUARIES AND OTHER SOURCES:

BOOKS

The Writers Directory: 1992-1994, St. James Press, 1991.

PERIODICALS

New York Times, July 4, 1994, p. 26.

*   *   *

BROWN, James (Joe, Jr.) 1928(?)-

PERSONAL: Born May 3, 1928 (some sources say June 17, 1928, or 1934, or May 3, 1933), in Barnwell, SC (some sources say Pulaski, TN, or Augusta, GA); son of Joe (a sap supplier for turpentine manufacturers) and Susie (Behlings) Brown; married Velma Warren (divorced, 1968); married second wife, Deirdre, 1968 (divorced); married Adrienne Lois Rodriguez (a hair stylist and makeup artist), September, 1984; children: (first marriage) Teddy (deceased), Larry, Deanna, Terry, Daryl, Venisha, Yamma. *Education:* Attended school in Augusta, GA.

ADDRESSES: *Home*—Beech Island, SC. *Agent*—Brothers Management Associates, 141 Dunbar Ave., Fords, NJ 08863.

CAREER: Singer, musician, and songwriter, performing in the James Brown Revue, Cremona Trio, Gospel Starlighters, Swanees, Flames, Famous Flames, James Brown and the Famous Flames, and JB's; performed for U.S. troops in Vietnam, 1968; performed at presidential inauguration celebration for Richard Nixon, 1968; appeared in films, including *The T.A.M.I. Show,* 1965, *Ski Party,* 1965, *The Blues Brothers,* 1980, *Dr. Detroit,* 1983, and *Rocky IV,* 1985; appeared in television programs, including *Where the Action Is, The Ed Sullivan Show, Solid Gold,* 1981, *Watch Me Move!,* 1987, and *Amen,* 1991; appeared in videotaped productions, including *Shindig!,* 1992. Fair Deal Productions, cofounder, 1963; owner of radio stations in Knoxville, TN, Baltimore, MD, Atlanta, GA, and Augusta, GA; owner and president of J. B. Broadcasting, Ltd., 1968—, and James Brown Network, 1968—; chair of the board of James Brown Productions, James Brown Entertainment; owner of restaurant chains and seventeen publishing companies. Also worked odd jobs; worked as a boxer and semi-professional baseball player, c. 1953-55.

AWARDS, HONORS: Grammy Award for best rhythm and blues recording, National Academy of Recording Arts and Sciences, 1965, for "Papa's Got a Brand New Bag," and for best rhythm and blues male vocal performance, 1986, for "Living in America"; best male pop vocalist, *Cash Box,* 1968; Humanitarian Award, Music and Performing Arts Lodge of B'nai B'rith, 1969; inducted into Rock and Roll Hall of Fame, 1986; Award of Merit for lifetime achievement, American Music Awards, 1992; forty-four gold record awards from Recording Industry Association of America.

WRITINGS:

(With Bruce Tucker) *James Brown: The Godfather of Soul,* Macmillan (New York), 1986, revised, new introduction by Tucker, epilogue by Dave Marsh, Thunder's Mouth Press (New York), 1990.

Also composer and lyricist on recordings, including *The James Brown Show Live at the Apollo,* Solid Smoke, 1963; *Sex Machine,* King, 1970; *Super Bad,* King, 1970; *Sho Is Funky down Here,* King, 1971; *Hot Pants,* Polydor, 1971; *Revolution of the Mind,* Polydor, 1971; *Soul Classics,* Polydor, 1972; *There It Is,* Polydor, 1972; *Get on the Good Foot,* Polydor, 1972; *Black Caesar,* Polydor, 1973; *Slaughter's Big Rip-off,* Polydor, 1973; *Soul Classics Volume II,* Polydor, 1973; *The Payback,* Polydor, 1973; *Hell,* Polydor, 1974; *Reality,* Polydor, 1974; *Sex Machine Today,* Polydor, 1975; *Everybody's Doin' the Hustle and Dead on the Double Bump,* Polydor, 1975; *Hot,* Polydor, 1975; *Get up Offa That Thing,* Polydor, 1976; *Bodyheat,* Polydor, 1976; *Mutha's Nature,* Polydor, 1977; *Jam/1980's,* Polydor, 1978; *Take a Look at Those Cakes,* Polydor, 1978; *The Original Disco Man,* Polydor, 1979; *Gravity,* CBS, 1986; *Cool Yule,* 1987; *I'm Real,* CBS, 1988; *The CD of JB,* 1988; *The CD of JB II,* 1988; *Through the Storm,* 1989; *Roots of a Revolution,* 1989; *Messing with the Blues,* PolyGram, 1990; *Star Time,* four volumes, PolyGram, 1991; *Love Over-Due,* 1991; *The Gospel According to James Brown and Reverend Al Sharpton,* 1991; *Pimps, Players, and Private Eyes,* 1992; and *Love Power Peace: Live at the Olympia, Paris, 1971,* 1992; composer or co-composer of songs, including "Please Please Please," "Try Me," "Prisoner of Love," "(Do the) Mashed Potato," "Think," "Out of Sight," "Papa's Got a Brand New Bag," "I Got You (I Feel Good),"

"Don't Be a Drop-Out," "Cold Sweat," "I Don't Want Nobody to Give Me Nothin'," "Say It Loud, I'm Black and I'm Proud," "Hot Pants," "Make It Funky," "Unity" (with Afrika Bambaataa), "Living in America," "I Want You So Bad," "The Popcorn," and "Sex Machine."

SIDELIGHTS: Known as the "Godfather of Soul" and "the hardest-working man in show business," James Brown was one of the first artists to be inducted into the Rock and Roll Hall of Fame. Intense rhythms and powerful emotion fill his music, which grew out of the poverty and potent gospel preaching he experienced as a child, and flamboyant showmanship has long been his stage trademark. His musical talents, seemingly boundless energy, a considerable ego, and obsessive discipline enabled Brown to leave behind a life of odd jobs and petty crime to become one of popular music's most influential performers. His achievements have included two Grammy awards and dozens of Gold Record awards. Brown has been credited with creating or influencing musical forms including soul, funk, rock and roll, disco, and rap. In 1986 he published a book chronicling his decades in popular music, *James Brown: The Godfather of Soul,* which he wrote with Bruce Tucker.

In his book Brown recalls a life touched by both poverty and riches. He grew up in shacks and was sometimes sent home from school because he lacked appropriate clothing, but years later, at the peak of his popularity, he could boast of owning businesses, limousines, and a jet. Music was an important constant in Brown's life, leading him from his aunt's brothel to a sprawling estate of his own. He taught himself to play an old pump organ as a boy, and at thirteen he had his own small band. When he was jailed as a teenager for breaking into cars, he formed a gospel quartet in the reformatory. The adult Brown fused passion born of hardship with dynamic, original music, rousing black pride with its boldness and attracting racially mixed audiences. A hard-driving life had its pitfalls, however; the U.S. Government at one point claimed he owed millions of dollars in back taxes, and police wrangled with him over allegations of wife-beating and possession of illegal drugs.

Telling his story, Brown is "arrogant and humble, fascinating and believable," asserted Val Wilmer in a *New Statesman* review. He is frank about the money he lost in bad record contracts and managers that indulged in payola, a promotional practice that often involves paying disc jockeys to play an artist's records. He presents his view of his tax situation, laying responsibility on the shoulders of a justice system that held him in the reformatory instead of allowing him to finish his education. He does not, to some reviewers' disappointment, address his more recent problems with the law, an omission that led Bob Allen in the *Washington Post Book World* to add "often stubbornly unrevealing" to his appraisal of the book, which he also called "engrossing." V. R. Peterson of *People* found Brown's book "surprisingly perceptive." The critic noted that in telling his life story Brown also evokes the larger story of black America, casting himself as "a kind of cultural godfather." Peterson admitted that the singer's egotism shows in such claims, but concedes that in light of Brown's contributions to black life and the popularization of black music, "it's hard to argue with him."

BIOGRAPHICAL/CRITICAL SOURCES:

BOOKS

Brown, James, and Bruce Tucker, *James Brown: The Godfather of Soul,* Macmillan, 1986, revised, Thunder's Mouth Press, 1990.
Contemporary Musicians, Volume 2, Gale, 1990, pp. 35-37.
Rose, Cynthia, *Living in America: The Soul Saga of James Brown,* Serpent's Tail, 1991.

PERIODICALS

Atlanta Constitution, April 10, 1988, section A, p. 1; December 12, 1988, section B, p. 1; December 15, 1988, section A, p. 1; December 16, 1988, section A, p. 17; December 15, 1989, section F, p. 1.
Boston Globe, April 20, 1989, p. 81.
Chicago Tribune, November 20, 1986, section 5, p. 3.
Down Beat, September, 1980, pp. 23-27.
Interview, December, 1990.
Los Angeles Times, March 11, 1986, section 6, p. 1; October 19, 1986, section C, p. 64; February 9, 1989, section 6, p. 1; April 20, 1990, section F, p. 1; September 24, 1990, section F, p. 1.
Nation, June 3, 1991, pp. 748-52.
New Statesman, September 18, 1987.
Newsweek, June 24, 1991, p. 68.
New York, June 3, 1991, p. 24.
New York Times, December 16, 1988, p. A28; May 3, 1990, p. C17.
People, December 8, 1986; April 25, 1988, p. 139; April 15, 1991, p. 42.
Rolling Stone, April 1, 1982, pp. 26-29, 52; November 17, 1988, p. 42; January 26, 1989, p. 13; April 6, 1989, pp. 36, 39-41, 44, 91-92; August 23, 1990.

Time, February 20, 1989, p. 40.
Washington Post, February 23, 1989, section D, p. 3; September 28, 1990, section C, p. 1.
Washington Post Book World, September 9, 1990.

OTHER

James Brown: The Man, the Music and the Message (television documentary), syndicated, 1991.*

* * *

BROYLES, Michael 1939-

PERSONAL: Born August 29, 1939, in Houston, TX; son of William Kingsley and Margaret L. (Connally) Broyles; married Nina Fedoroff (a scientist), June 16, 1990; children: Peggi Broyles Bloomquist, Tracy K. *Education:* Austin College, B.A., 1961; University of Texas at Austin, M.M., 1964, Ph.D., 1967.

ADDRESSES: Home—2398 Shagbank Ct., State College, PA 16803. *Office*—School of Music, Pennsylvania State University, State College, PA 16802.

CAREER: University of Maryland, Baltimore County, Catonsville, assistant professor, 1967-71, associate professor, 1971-87, professor of music, 1987-93, presidential research professor, 1993-94, director of honors program in music, 1980-94; Pennsylvania State University, State College, distinguished professor of music and professor of American history, 1994—. Johns Hopkins University, lecturer, 1990—; John F. Kennedy Center for the Performing Arts, lecturer, 1994; American Antiquarian Society, research associate, 1990.

MEMBER: American Musicological Society (chairperson of Capital chapter, 1983-85), American Society for Eighteenth-Century Studies, Organization of American Historians.

AWARDS, HONORS: National Endowment for the Humanities, grant, 1977, fellowship, 1984, senior fellowship, 1989-90; fellow of Newbery Library, 1993.

WRITINGS:

The Emergence and Evolution of Beethoven's Heroic Style, Excelsior Music Publishing, 1987.
A Yankee Musician in Europe: The 1837 Journals of Lowell Mason, UMI Research Press, 1990.
Music of the Highest Class: Elitism and Populism in Antebellum Boston, Yale University Press, 1992.

Work represented in anthologies, including *The Orchestra: Origins and Transformations,* edited by Joan Peyser, Scribner, 1986. Music critic, *Baltimore Sun,* 1977—. Contributor of articles and reviews to music journals.

WORK IN PROGRESS: A study of vernacular dance music in nineteenth-century America, with particular emphasis on the waltz as social metaphor; a study of Charles Ives and American cultural traditions, including political movements, Puritanism, and the 'maverick tradition'—that of the eccentric, isolated artist, which has been prominent in the history of the arts in America.

*   *   *

BUCHWALD, Ann   1920-1994

OBITUARY NOTICE—See index for *CA* sketch: Born April 18, 1920, in Warren, PA; died of lung cancer, July 3, 1994, in Washington, DC. Publicist, literary agent, and writer. Buchwald, the wife of columnist Art Buchwald, began her career as a fashion coordinator for the Nieman-Marcus department store in Dallas. She later traveled to Paris, where she worked as the publicity director for the noted couturier Pierre Balmain and established her own public relations firm. It was also in Paris that she met Art Buchwald; the couple were married in 1952 and remained in Paris until 1962, when they relocated to Washington, D.C. During the 1970s and 1980s, Buchwald worked as a literary agent and was briefly affiliated with Irving Lazar, one of the most prominent literary and talent agents in Hollywood. In 1980, Buchwald published a memoir of her years in Paris titled *Seems Like Yesterday.* She was also the coauthor, with Marjabelle Young Stewart, of the books *White Gloves and Party Manners, Stand Up, Shake Hands, Say How Do You Do,* and *What to Do When and Why.*

OBITUARIES AND OTHER SOURCES:

BOOKS

Buchwald, Ann, *Seems Like Yesterday,* Putnam, 1980.
Who's Who in America, 46th edition, Marquis, 1990.

PERIODICALS

Chicago Tribune, July 5, 1994, p. 5.
New York Times, July 5, 1994, p. D14.
Washington Post, July 5, 1994, p. B4.

BULL, Barry L.   1947-

PERSONAL: Born August 29, 1947, in Billings, MT; son of Arthur C. (in small business) and Marjorie (a bookkeeper; maiden name, Grenier) Bull; married Irene Ruderman (a teacher), December 16, 1971; children: Alan G., Ethan S. *Education:* Yale University, B.A., 1969; University of Virginia, M.A., 1970; University of Idaho, M.A.T., 1972; Cornell University, Ph.D., 1979.

ADDRESSES: Home—2505 Rechter Rd., Bloomington, IN 47401. *Office*—Education Building, Indiana University—Bloomington, Bloomington, IN 47405.

CAREER: Wellesley College, Wellesley, MA, assistant professor of education, 1979-84; University of Hawaii at Manoa, Honolulu, began as assistant professor, became associate professor of education, 1986-89; University of Minnesota—Twin Cities, Minneapolis, associate professor of education, 1989-90; Indiana University—Bloomington, associate professor of education, 1990—. Indiana Education Policy Center, co-director, 1992—.

MEMBER: International Network of Philosophers of Education, Philosophy of Education Society, American Educational Research Association.

AWARDS, HONORS: Fellow in modern society and values, American Council of Learned Societies.

WRITINGS:

(With Royal Fruehling and Virgie Chatterby) *The Ethics of Multicultural and Bilingual Education,* Teachers College Press, 1992.
Education in Indiana: An Overview, Indiana Education Policy Center, 1994.

WORK IN PROGRESS: Research on the moral justification of systemic education reform.

*   *   *

BURNETT, Alan   1932-

PERSONAL: Born April 2, 1932, in New Zealand; married Robin McMeekan (a lawyer), January 30, 1960; children: Genevieve. *Education:* Victoria University of Wellington, B.A.; Oxford University, M.A.

ADDRESSES: Home and office—13 Coles Place, Torrens, Canberra, Australian Capital Territory 2607.

CAREER: Worked for New Zealand Foreign Service, 1956-69; Australian National University, Canberra, senior research fellow, 1970-92; author.

WRITINGS:

The Western Pacific: The Challenge of Sustainable Growth, Edward Elgar, 1992.

WORK IN PROGRESS: Research on China and its neighbors.

* * *

BURNS, Grant (Francis)   1947-

PERSONAL: Born June 18, 1947, in Owosso, MI; son of Francis (an engineer) and Marie (a teacher; maiden name, Olsen) Burns; married Stephanie Winston Voight, February 4, 1972; children: Andrea, Steven. *Education:* Michigan State University, B.A., 1969; University of Michigan, M.A., 1973, M.L.S., 1976. *Politics:* Independent. *Religion:* "In doubt." *Avocational interests:* Reading, furniture building, piano.

ADDRESSES: Office—University of Michigan—Flint Library, Flint, MI 48502.

CAREER: University of Michigan—Flint, Flint, MI, reference librarian, 1977-92, head librarian of public services, 1992—. Coalition for Innovative Housing and Jobs, member of board of directors.

AWARDS, HONORS: The Atomic Papers was named an "Outstanding Academic Book" by *Choice* magazine, 1985.

WRITINGS:

The Atomic Papers, Scarecrow, 1984.
The Sports Pages, Scarecrow, 1987.
Affordable Housing, McFarland, 1989.
The Nuclear Present, Scarecrow, 1992.

Editor of *New Pages: News and Reviews of the Progressive Book Trade,* 1980-89. Contributor of articles to professional journals.

WORK IN PROGRESS: A novel entitled *Dear Landlord;* a bibliography which includes an analysis of the portrayal of librarians in American fiction.

SIDELIGHTS: Grant Burns told *CA:* "I have been a writer since realizing in the sixth grade that I could amuse people with words on paper. It was an amazing discovery that I haven't yet learned to handle.

I hope to get a grip on it in time either to save the world or at least provide it with some comic relief as it goes to hell.

"The conflict between the comic and the grave is one that I trace to my grandfathers. One was a humorless Swedish clergyman for whom only the serious was sufficient. The other was an agnostic Irishman who regarded life, so far as I could tell, as a kind of low-rent burlesque production.

"I hope that time is patient enough to let me sort out this problem, toward either salvation or laughter. (I'm not sure, actually, that one isn't the same as the other.)"

BIOGRAPHICAL/CRITICAL SOURCES:

PERIODICALS

Booklist, May 1, 1993.
Bulletin of the Atomic Scientists, December, 1984, p. 27.

* * *

BUSER, Pierre   1921-

PERSONAL: Born August 19, 1921, in Strasbourg, France; son of Albert and Elisabeth (Schenckel) Buser; married Arlette Rougeul (a physician), April 7, 1962; children: Bernard, Edith, Myriam. *Education:* Attended Ecole Normale Superieure, 1941-44; University of Paris, Ph.D., 1953.

ADDRESSES: Home—62 Boulevard Arago, 75013, Paris, France. *Office*—University of Paris, 9 Quai St. Bernard, 75005, Paris, France. *Agent*—Heimann Co., 293 Rue Le courbe, 75015, Paris, France.

CAREER: University of Paris, Paris, France, assistant professor, 1944-50, associate professor, 1950-55, professor of neurosciences, 1955-91, professor emeritus, 1991—. *Military service:* French army, 1945, achieved rank of lieutenant.

MEMBER: French Academy of Sciences.

AWARDS, HONORS: Swiss Academy of Medicine, 1961; International Fyssen Prize, 1986.

WRITINGS:

Neurophysiologie, Hermann (Paris), 1975.
Psychophysiologie, Hermann, 1982.
(With Michel Imbert) *Audition,* Hermann, 1987, translation by Roy H. Kay, MIT Press, 1992.

(With Imbert) *Vision,* Hermann, 1987, translation by Kay, MIT Press, 1992.
Neurobiologie, Hermann, 1993.

WORK IN PROGRESS: Regulations autonomes, for Hermann, 1994; research for *Studies in Neurobiological Mechanisms of Behavior* and specialized publications in this field.

*   *   *

BUTLER, Juan (Antonio)   1942-1981

PERSONAL: Born July 4, 1942, in London, England; immigrated to Canada, 1942; committed suicide, June 2, 1981; son of an insurance clerk; married in 1974 (marriage ended).

CAREER: Worked variously as a shoe salesperson, warehouse laborer, translator, insurance clerk, bartender, and cashier in a socialist bookstore.

AWARDS, HONORS: Received grants from the Canada Council and the Ontario Arts Council, mid-1970s.

WRITINGS:

Cabbagetown Diary: A Documentary, PMA (Toronto), 1970.
The Garbageman, PMA, 1972.
Canadian Healing Oil, PMA, 1974.

"The Happy Gang Rides Again" appeared in *Northern Journey.*

SIDELIGHTS: The three novels of Juan Butler "are impassioned indictments of a squalid world that robs man of dignity," asserted *Oxford Companion to Canadian Literature* writer David Staines. Born in London, Butler immigrated to Toronto with his family shortly after his birth in 1942; he dropped out of school as a teenager and later alternated time in Europe with job stints that ranged from insurance firm clerk to warehouse laborer to shoe salesperson. In the late 1960s Butler lived in an infamous working-class neighborhood of Toronto known as Cabbagetown and began keeping a journal of his observations and impressions of the rough and poverty-stricken area. After three months of note-taking, he assembled his chronicle into the 1970 novel *Cabbagetown Diary: A Documentary.* Michael, its protagonist, shares certain traits with the author; an immigrant to Canada and a denizen of Cabbagetown eking out a living as a bartender, he manifests the effects of his life of privation. Explaining his rejection of a

woman he has impregnated, he states simply, "Somebody had to show her how to make out in this world." Wayne Grady, in an essay on Butler for the *Dictionary of Literary Biography,* termed *Cabbagetown Diary* "a highly charged delineation of the mind-numbing effects of poverty" and "a powerful and compelling book." Grady also remarked, "It is not inappropriate that *Cabbagetown Diary* has been placed on reading lists for university sociology courses, for it is more social documentary than novel, an attempt to portray the effects of environment rather than to explore solutions to the poverty and violence."

Butler's second novel, *The Garbageman,* is similarly autobiographical. The 1972 work, completed in just six weeks, chronicles a period in the life of another troubled young male protagonist, Fred Miller. Miller rejects a budding career in his father's insurance business (as did Butler) to travel to Europe. He winds up in a psychiatric hospital back in Canada, however, and believes he may have committed two murders during the course of his travels. Much of the book is given over to recounting the gory particulars of each of the deeds. Butler sent *The Garbageman* to English writer Colin Wilson, who wrote back that he "found it very interesting although (as you probably expected) a bit revolting." Wilson urged Butler to move away from simple gratuitous violence in his writing and suggested that his opportunity to be heard might be better spent addressing the sociological issues that are the root of violence.

Butler's third novel, *Canadian Healing Oil,* appeared in 1974, after the writer had been awarded grants from Canadian arts agencies to travel to Puerto Rico and the Virgin Islands. He incorporated some of his experiences there into the surrealistic plot of this final literary effort. John, another confused male protagonist (employed in a bookstore, as Butler once was), becomes enamored of an exotic female customer; on her bed he dreams of a journey to the Caribbean, but then awakes and either dreams again of his sojourn or actually embarks upon it. When he arrives, somebody gives him a bottle of the "Canadian Healing Oil" that is to be applied "solely for the moment when you come face to face with your . . . destiny." Many elements in *Canadian Healing Oil* speak of Butler's own troubled introspection and identity crisis. John (Juan) wanders through both San Juan, Puerto Rico, and the island of St. John; St. John the Baptist also appears at various points in the narrative, as does Jean de Brebeuf, a Catholic missionary killed by Iroquois in 1649. This "artist-as-martyr theme became a sad prophecy of Butler's final years," noted Staines in the *Oxford Companion to Canadian Literature,* "when his psychological suffering offered him no peace."

No further work of Butler's was published, and he was found dead in a psychiatric clinic in 1981, having hanged himself. In the *Dictionary of Literary Biography* essay, Grady praised the trio of books the writer left behind that "speak eloquently and convincingly of Butler's futile search for meaning in a universe he perceived as violent and illogical."

BIOGRAPHICAL/CRITICAL SOURCES:

BOOKS

Butler, Juan, *Cabbagetown Diary: A Documentary,* PMA (Toronto), 1970.
Butler, *Canadian Healing Oil,* PMA, 1974.
Dictionary of Literary Biography, Volume 53: *Canadian Writers since 1960,* Gale, 1986.
Oxford Companion to Canadian Literature, Oxford University Press, 1983.*

*   *   *

BUTLER, Pierce A.   1952-

PERSONAL: Born in 1952, in Waterford, Ireland; immigrated to the United States, 1979; married; wife's name, Susan (a writer). *Education:* National University of Ireland, Cork, B.E., 1973, M.Eng.Sc., 1976; Harvard University, Ed.M., 1980; Northeastern University, C.A.G.S., 1983.

ADDRESSES: Home—24 Harris St., Waltham, MA 02154.

CAREER: National University of Ireland, Cork, assistant lecturer in engineering design, 1976-79; Harvard University, Cambridge, MA, instructor in creative writing, 1983; University of Massachusetts, Boston, lecturer in English, 1982-83; Bentley College, Waltham, MA, adjunct assistant professor of communication, 1983-84; Babson College, Wellesley, MA, preceptor in English, 1984-88; Bentley College, writer in residence, 1988—. Gives readings from his works.

MEMBER: Irish American Cultural Institute, and American Commission for Irish Studies.

WRITINGS:

A Malady (novel), Co-Op Books (Dublin), 1982.
Sean O'Faolain: A Study of the Short Fiction, Twayne, 1993.

Work represented in anthologies, including *The Next Parish Over: A Collection of Irish American Writing,* New Rivers Press, 1993. Contributor to periodicals, including *American Way* and *San Jose Studies.*

WORK IN PROGRESS: A novel.

SIDELIGHTS: Pierce A. Butler told *CA:* "Most of my stories are set in Ireland. I am interested in the stories people tell each other and in what these stories inadvertently reveal. There is a long tradition of storytelling in Ireland and, though many of these stories seem to be tall and fantastic tales, there is something in the telling that goes beyond entertainment or diversion. The Irish are renowned for being great talkers, but I think that, at bottom, we are a very private and reserved race. We use stories, not only to entertain and divert, but also to communicate emotions that are too highly charged to be put directly into words. The rituals of storytelling, which everyone instinctively understands, allow us to do this without embarrassment. I keep my ears open when people are telling stories and try to get down on paper what might otherwise be lost.

"From the time I was a year old until I was fourteen, I spent my summers on Valentia Island, off the southwest coast of Ireland, with my aunt and uncle. Valentia is still a source of inspiration in my work, as is the literature of the Blasket Islands, the autobiographical writings of Tomas O'Crohan, Maurice O'Sullivan, Peig Sawyers, and Micheal O'Guiheen, which describe a culture and a way of life that has all but disappeared. I am interested in the old days in the West of Ireland, in the folk tradition, and in the stories of the mythological cycles.

"How can we reconcile ourselves to the passing of the old ways? How can we preserve somthing of what former generations held dear? How can an Irishman living in the United States maintain contact with that which has formed him? These are some of the questions I have dramatized in my work in progress, a novel set in Ireland and the United States."

*   *   *

BYNUM, Victoria E.   1947-

PERSONAL: Born November 21, 1947, in Lancaster, CA; daughter of Oma Stanley (an Air Force officer) and Margaret (a homemaker; maiden name, Huckenpoehler) Bynum; married Burton E. Pierce, August 22, 1964 (divorced, December 2, 1980); married

Gregg Andrews (a history professor), March 10, 1990; children: (first marriage) Randy James, Erika Lynn. *Education:* California State University, B.A., 1978; University of California, San Diego, M.A., 1979, Ph.D., 1987.

ADDRESSES: Home—819-A Hazelton St., San Marcos, TX 78666. *Office*—Southwest Texas State University, Department of History, San Marcos, TX 78666.

CAREER: Southwest Texas State University, San Marcos, associate professor of history, 1986—.

AWARDS, HONORS: Best First Book Prize, Phi Alpha Theta History Society, for *Unruly Women: The Politics of Social and Sexual Control in the Old South.*

WRITINGS:

Unruly Women: The Politics of Social and Sexual Control in the Old South, University of North Carolina Press, 1992.

The Jones County Uprising and Its Aftermath: Civil War, Reconstruction, and Redemption in Piney Woods, Mississippi, University of North Carolina Press, in press.

C

CAINE, Michael 1933-

PERSONAL: Born Maurice Micklewhite, March 14, 1933, in London, England; son of Maurice (a porter) and Ellen Frances Marie Micklewhite; married Patricia Haines, 1954 (divorced); married Shakira Baksh (an actress), 1973; children: (first marriage) Dominique, Natasha. *Avocational interests:* Collecting unusual facts, collecting art.

ADDRESSES: Home—Wallingford near Oxford, Oxfordshire, England. *Agent*—Dennis Sellinger, International Creative Management, 76 Oxford House, London W1R 1RB, England; and Jerry Pam, 8500 Wilshire Boulevard, Suite 801, Beverly Hills, CA 90211.

CAREER: Screen, television, and stage actor. Westminster Repertory, Horsham, Sussex, England, assistant stage manager, 1953; Lowestoft Repertory, actor, 1953-55; Theatre Workshop, London, actor, 1955. Appeared in more than 100 British television dramas, 1957-63. Appeared in more than 70 motion pictures, including *Zulu* (1964), *The Ipcress File* (1965), *Alfie* (1966), *The Wrong Box* (1966), *Gambit* (1967), *Woman Times Seven* (1967), *The Magus* (1968), *Sleuth* (1973), *The Romantic Englishwoman* (1974), *The Man Who Would Be King* (1974), *A Bridge Too Far* (1976), *California Suite* (1978), *Deathtrap* (1982), *Educating Rita* (1983), *Hannah and Her Sisters* (1986), *Mona Lisa* (1986), *Jaws: The Revenge* (1987), *The Fourth Protocol* (1987; also co-executive producer), *Dirty Rotten Scoundrels* (1988), and *Noises Off* (1991). Appeared in several television miniseries, including *Jack the Ripper* (1988) and *Jekyll and Hyde* (1990).

AWARDS, HONORS: Academy Award for best supporting actor, 1987, for *Hannah and Her Sisters*.

WRITINGS:

Not Many People Know That!: Michael Caine's Almanac of Amazing Information, illustrated by John Jensen, Robson Books (London), 1984, published in United States as *Michael Caine's Almanac of Amazing Information,* St. Martin's, 1986.

Not Many People Know It's 1988!, Robson, 1987.

Michael Caine's Moving Picture Show (film trivia), St. Martin's, 1988.

Acting in Film: An Actor's Take on Moviemaking, edited by Maria Aitken, Applause Theatre Book Publishers (New York City), 1990.

What's It All About? (autobiography), Turtle Bay Books, 1992.

ADAPTATIONS: Acting in Film: An Actor's Take on Moviemaking was also released as a videotape.

SIDELIGHTS: When *Chicago Tribune* interviewer Cynn van Matre asked movie star Michael Caine why he decided to write his autobiography after being the subject of at least seven biographies, Caine replied, "When I first became an actor in the theater, people would hear my working-class accent and ask me how I remembered all the lines, as though I were some kind of moron. All the biographies about me, even the nice ones, have been patronizing and condescending, and it annoyed the hell out of me. So I wrote this." "This" is Caine's critically praised bestseller, *What's It All About?*, which took its title from the theme song of his first major hit movie, *Alfie.* Caine's reply was true to his reputation for honesty and his faithfulness to his working-class Cockney roots.

The son of an impoverished porter in London's Billingsgate fish market, Caine, under his given name Maurice Micklewhite, was enthralled by

American movies as a child, and took his professional name from the Humphrey Bogart film *The Caine Mutiny;* later, he expressed great delight at being given a role originally intended for Bogart in John Huston's film *The Man Who Would Be King.* As he recalled in *What's It All About?,* Caine, after being cast for the role, "rambled along the great boulevards [of Paris] . . . no longer dreaming the impossible dream but *living it.*" In between his boyhood dreams and his middle-aged success came years of struggle to learn the craft of acting, as well as a first marriage that failed because, as Caine appraised, "I was too young and immature to take the triple burden of grinding poverty and personal and professional failure."

Critics were impressed both by Caine's forthright presentation of his difficult early years and by his decision to write the book himself without the aid of a ghostwriter. Jonathan Yardley, in the *Washington Post Book World,* objected to excessive name-dropping in the later parts of the book, which dealt with Caine's years of celebrity, but said, "The best part of *What's It All About?* is the first couple of hundred pages. A hard but ultimately fruitful apprenticeship is the stuff of show-business drama and legend; Michael Caine herein lays his claim to a share of both." Christopher Lehmann-Haupt, in the *New York Times,* opined that Caine had a chip on his shoulder, and complained both about Caine's alleged anti-feminism and about a lack of depth in Caine's depictions of the "angry young man" character type in British theater and film in the 1960s. Diane Jacobs of the *New York Times Book Review,* however, stated that, "In his own words, at least, [Caine] comes across as a blunt, fun-loving, loyal, nice guy." Jacobs, sounding a note similar to Yardley's, wrote that Caine was "at his best when recounting sustained tales," such as those about his military experiences or his love-at-first-sight romance with Indian actress Shakira Baksh, who became his second wife. An especially poignant story, noted by van Matre, was Caine's belated discovery of an illegitimate, epileptic half-brother who, misdiagnosed as insane, spent 67 years in a British mental institution until his death.

What's It All About? was not Caine's first book; he had actually begun writing books reflecting his love of trivia and film in the early 1980s. His *Not Many People Know . . .* books deal with general trivia, while *Michael Caine's Moving Picture Show* deals specifically with cinematic facts, presenting some biographical information about Caine as well. The British periodical *Books* noted approvingly that Caine gave the royalties from his *Not Many*

People Know . . . books to charity.

In 1990 Caine issued *Acting in Film: An Actor's Take on Moviemaking.* The book is a transcription, edited by Maria Aitken, of a British Broadcasting Corporation (BBC) Program in which Caine talked to young actors about the craft of screen acting. He carefully differentiated this craft from that of stage acting, and that of acting in American movies (which he called "moving pictures") from British films (which he called "talking pictures.") Film critic Stanley Kauffmann, in the *New Republic,* called Caine "one of the best of present-day film actors" and applauded him for presenting practical tips and advice on technique. "Caine's spectrum isn't wide, but everything he says is sensible and much of it is resonant," Kauffmann wrote. Allen Barra, reviewing the book for the *New York Times Book Review,* said that "no one is more qualified [than Caine] to discuss the craft and business of film acting," and praised the actor-author for emphasizing practical craft rather than art.

BIOGRAPHICAL/CRITICAL SOURCES:

BOOKS

Caine, Michael, *Acting in Film: An Actor's Take on Moviemaking,* Applause Theatre Book Publishers, 1990.
Caine, Michael, *What's It All About?,* Turtle Bay Books, 1992.

PERIODICALS

Booklist, June 15, 1989, p. 1767.
Books, November, 1987, p. 88.
Chicago Tribune, December 21, 1992, sec. 5, pp. 1, 5.
Los Angeles Times Book Review, April 6, 1986, p. 8.
New Republic, June 25, 1990, pp. 26-27.
New York Times, December 14, 1992, p. C15.
New York Times Book Review, May 27, 1990, p. 14; January 10, 1993, p. 9.
Washington Post Book World, January 12, 1986, p. 13; April 22, 1990, p. 17; December 13, 1992, p. 3.*

*   *   *

CAIRNS, Scott   1954-

PERSONAL: Born November 19, 1954, in Tacoma, WA; son of Bud Clifford Eugene Cairns (a teacher) and Irene Elizabeth Cairns Laursen (an accountant; maiden name, Stubbs); married Barbara Lunke (divorced, June 1982); married Marcia Vanderlip (a journalist), March 12, 1983; children: Elizabeth Vanderlip, Benjamin Vanderlip. *Education:* Western Washington University, B.A., 1977; Hollins College, M.A., 1979; Bowling Green State University, M.F.A., 1981; University of Utah, Ph.D., 1990. *Politics:* Progressive Democrat. *Religion:* Presbyterian. *Avocational interests:* Metaphorical theology.

ADDRESSES: Home—Virginia Beach, VA. *Office*—English Department, Old Dominion University, Norfolk, VA 23529.

CAREER: Kansas State University, Manhattan, instructor, 1981-84; University of Utah, Salt Lake City, teaching fellow, 1984-87; Westminster College, Salt Lake City, assistant professor, 1987-90; University of North Texas, Denton, assistant professor, 1990-94; Old Dominion University, Norfolk, VA, associate professor, 1994—. Director of creative writing, University of North Texas, 1990-94, and Old Dominion University, 1994—. Elder, Presbyterian Church, U.S.A., 1987—.

MEMBER: Associated Writing Programs, PEN, Modern Language Association.

WRITINGS:

The Theology of Doubt, Cleveland State University Poetry Center, 1985.
The Translation of Babel, University of Georgia Press (Athens, GA), 1990.
Figures for the Ghost, University of Georgia Press, 1994.

WORK IN PROGRESS: Which Tribe? Which River?, a collection of poems. Also research into the Kabbalah, gnostic and other, non-canonical gospels, Midrashim, and other revisionary sacred texts.

SIDELIGHTS: Scott Cairns told *CA:* "As the poet W. H. Auden put it in 'Archaeology': 'Knowledge may have its purposes, but guessing is always more fun than knowing.' I spend most of my 'writing time' reading English translations of ancient texts, more often than not *sacred* texts. And while I suppose that much of the time I am reading in order to know something, what I savor most about these texts are those moments when their rhetorics fail, when their coherences are compromised, when incommensurate and appalling *wrongness* disrupts the narrative. That's when I start guessing, and this guesswork becomes my next poem.

"Even so, it would be misleading to imply that *making poems* is all I want out of the practice. What I actually want, what I have always wanted, is—

forgive the audacity—to see God. In those moments when the god-talk fails to convince, one is able to suspect something of the enormity which will not be confined to likely stories."

*   *   *

CALLANDER, Don 1930-

PERSONAL: Surname is pronounced like "calendar"; born March 23, 1930, in Minneapolis, MN; son of Raymond Alexander (a pharmacist) and Myrna (Nash) Callander; married Mary Omohundro, June, 1952 (marriage ended, December, 1970); married Margaret Millikan (a promotion director), December 23, 1972; children: Miles Bruce, Neal Matthew, Carol Ann, Alan Brian. *Education:* Attended George Washington University and University of Minnesota—Twin Cities.   *Religion:* Methodist. *Avocational interests:* Photography, printing, design, woodworking.

ADDRESSES: Home and office—560 South Longview Pl., Longwood, FL 32779.

CAREER: George Washington University, Washington, DC, member of public relations staff; *Washington Post,* Washington, DC, began as copy boy, became reporter; American Automobile Association, staff writer, editor, photographer, and graphic designer in Falls Church, VA, and Heathrow, FL, 1961-91; freelance writer, 1991—. *Military service:* U.S. Navy, 1947-51; U.S. Naval Reserve, 1952-72.

MEMBER: National Writers Union, Society of American Travel Writers.

WRITINGS:

Pyromancer (novel), Ace Books, 1991.
Aquamancer (novel), Ace Books, 1992.
Geomancer (novel), Ace Books, 1993.

Associate editor, *American Motorist,* 1964-80.

WORK IN PROGRESS: Five fantasies: *Dragon Companion, Dragon Rescue, Aeromancer, Dragon Tempest,* and *Marbleheart Sea Otter.*

SIDELIGHTS: Don Callander told *CA:* "I have been a writer of news, books, travel, and general topics since I joined the headquarters staff of the American Automobile Association (AAA) in the early 1960s. Upon my retirement from AAA, I fulfilled my life's ambition to publish fiction novels, many of which were written over years in my spare time.

"I have always been an avid reader, especially of science fiction and fantasy, ranging from the L. Frank Baum 'Oz' books through J. R. R. Tolkien's *Lord of the Rings*.

"I am the father of four, the grandfather of two, step-grandfather of four, and step-great-grandfather of two. I live in Florida because my position with AAA required the move and, once here, I stayed because Florida is an enjoyable, pleasant place to live and work. Today my household consists of my wife, Margaret, and our wire-haired terrier, Eleanor of Acquitaine of Thistlefield (Nora for short), and my Macintosh QUADRA, an important member of our family."

*   *   *

CAMERON, M(alcolm) L(aurence)   1918-

PERSONAL: Born October 23, 1918, in Orangedale, Nova Scotia, Canada; son of Duncan Alexander (a farmer) and Ellen Sophia (a schoolteacher; maiden name, MacPhail) Cameron; married Anne Hibbard Goss Watts (a householder), July 1, 1952; children: Peter D. W., Janet R. Cameron Sneed, Susan E. *Education:* Dalhousie University, B.Sc. (with honors), 1950, M.Sc., 1951; Cambridge University, Ph.D., 1953. *Religion:* United Church of Canada. *Avocational interests:* Photography, gardening, crochet, baking (especially bread).

ADDRESSES: Home and office—6306 Jubilee Rd., Halifax, Nova Scotia, Canada B3H 2G7.

CAREER: University of New Brunswick, Fredericton, New Brunswick, Canada, research associate, 1953-55; University of Saskatchewan, Saskatoon, Saskatchewan, Canada, began as assistant professor, became associate professor of biology, 1955-65; Dalhousie University, Halifax, Nova Scotia, Canada, began as assistant professor, became professor, 1965-79, Campbell Professor of Biology, 1979-84. *Military service:* Canadian Dental Corps, 1942-46; became quartermaster sergeant.

MEMBER: International Society of Anglo-Saxonists, Nova Scotia Institute of Science (president, 1969-70).

WRITINGS:

Anglo-Saxon Medicine, Cambridge University Press (Cambridge, England), 1993.

Contributor to scholarly journals.

WORK IN PROGRESS: Editing old-English leechbooks, completion expected after 1996.

SIDELIGHTS: M. L. Cameron told *CA:* "I have always been interested in the history of science, particularly the history of medicine. I taught biology for thirty years, and this gave me a measure of insight into the current publications on historical subjects. It also made me aware of the narrow outlooks of their authors, particularly the implication that most science before the nineteenth century was superstition and nonsense. This seemed, to me, to be prejudice inimical to a proper appreciation of the accomplishments of our ancestors. So, when I contemplated a vocation to pursue in retirement, I thought of the history of medicine. I spent a pleasant sabbatical year examining the subject at Cambridge University and the British Library, and concluded that there was a place for a reassessment of the medical practices of the Anglo-Saxons.

"I have published several papers on the medical works of the Anglo-Saxons, and I gathered this material, with additions, into my book, *Anglo-Saxon Medicine.* When I began to publish in the field, there was, so far as I know, only one researcher, C. H. Talbot, who was devoting sympathetic understanding to these medical works. Inspired by his work, [a number of us are now] writing in the field and exchanging ideas through membership in the International Society of Anglo-Saxonists. Our aim is to present Anglo-Saxon medical science in a sympathetic manner, rather than implying that its whole outlook was based on magic and superstition.

"I am a most untidy writer who works in a welter of loose papers and notes. Because this seems to work for me, I do nothing to tidy it up. I spend a few hours every day, usually in the morning, at my word processor. Most of what goes into it never comes out as a finished product, but the effort to put ideas into understandable prose serves to focus my ideas and make them available for later use.

"I wish there were more young researchers in the field of the history of medieval medicine and science. The preparation for such work is difficult: one must have a working knowledge of the language in which the texts are written (in my case, Old English), and in the languages in which much of their inspiration lies (in the case of Anglo-Saxon medicine, classical and medieval Latin and Greek). It is also useful to have some knowledge of biological and biochemical principles (even better to know something of modern medicine), although this is not an essential requirement. One can always call on friends for help and advice. The fun of the research is worth the preparation in language-learning.

"My hobby is bread-baking. I hope one day to publish a book on the subject."

*   *   *

CAMPBELL, David   1961-

PERSONAL: Born August 15, 1961, in Australia; immigrated to the United States; married Kate Manzo. *Education:* University of Melbourne, B.A. (with first class honors), 1985; Australian National University, Ph.D., 1990.

ADDRESSES: Office—Graduate Program in Foreign Affairs, Australian National University, Canberra, Australian Capital Territory 0200.

CAREER: Principal private secretary to Australian senator D. L. Chipp, 1981-85; Johns Hopkins University, Baltimore, MD, assistant professor of political science, 1989-94; Australian National University, Canberra, senior lecturer and director of studies, Graduate Program in Foreign Affairs, 1994—.

MEMBER: International Studies Association, American Political Science Association.

AWARDS, HONORS: Lilly Foundation teaching fellow, 1991-92.

WRITINGS:

The Social Basis of Australian and New Zealand Security Policy, Peace Research Centre (Canberra), 1989.
Writing Security: United States Foreign Policy and the Politics of Identity, University of Minnesota Press, 1992.
(Editor with Michael Dillon, and contributor) *The Political Subject of Violence,* Manchester University Press, 1993.
Politics without Principle: Sovereignty, Ethics, and the Narratives of the Gulf War, Lynne Reinner, 1993.

Contributor to books, including *Citizenship: East and West,* edited by Andre Liebich and Daniel Warner, Kegan Paul International, 1994; *The Return of Culture and Identity in International Relations Theory,* edited by Yosef Lapid and Friedrich Kratochwil, Lynne Reinner, in press; and *Territorial Identities and Global Flows,* edited by Michael J. Shapiro and Hayward Alker, University of Minnesota Press, in press. Contributor to academic jour-

nals. Coeditor of the series "Borderlines," University of Minnesota Press, 1993—.

WORK IN PROGRESS: Prosaics of Order: Transversal Politics in the Anarchical World; research on responsiblity, sovereignty, and humanitarianism; research on globalization, culture, and identity; research on the representation of world politics.

*   *   *

CAMPBELL, Tracy (A.)   1962-

PERSONAL: Born April 4, 1962, in Lexington, KY; son of Alexander B. and Anna B. Campbell; married Leslie Crawford (a social worker), August 21, 1984; children: Alexander. *Education:* University of Kentucky, B.A., 1984; Duke University, M.A., 1985, Ph.D., 1988. *Politics:* "A democrat, with lower-case 'd'."

ADDRESSES: Home—P.O. Box 1208, Mars Hill, NC, 28754. *Office*—Department of History, Mars Hill College, Mars Hill, NC 28754.

CAREER: Union College, Barbourville, KY, assistant professor of history and director of Appalachian Semester Program, 1989-91; Mars Hill College, Mars Hill, NC, assistant professor of history, 1991—.

MEMBER: Phi Beta Kappa.

AWARDS, HONORS: Carstensen Prize from Agricultural History Society, 1992, for the article "The Limits of Agrarian Action"; Mellon Appalachian fellow, University of Kentucky, 1994-95.

WRITINGS:

The Politics of Despair: Power and Resistance in the Tobacco Wars, University Press of Kentucky, 1993.

Contributor to history journals.

WORK IN PROGRESS: A biography of Edward Fretwell Prichard, Jr., 1915-1984.

*   *   *

CANETTI, Elias   1905-1994

OBITUARY NOTICE—See index for *CA* sketch: Born July 25, 1905, in Ruse, Bulgaria; died August 14, 1994, in Zurich, Switzerland. Cultural historian and author. Elias Canetti's literary reputation, which earned him the 1981 Nobel Prize in Literature, is based largely on two works, his 1935 novel *Die Blendung* (*Auto-da-fe*) and his 1960 sociological study of group behavior, *Masse und Macht* (*Crowds and Power*). Concerned with the coercive and brutalizing power of human beings when organized in groups, Canetti sought in both works to explore the roots of this terrifying behavior and to document its effects. Commentators frequently note the biographical origin of Canetti's concerns: born in Bulgaria to parents of Jewish descent, Canetti spent much of his youth in Vienna, where he witnessed the disintegration of western European governments and the resulting rise of fascism. Trained as a chemist, Canetti nevertheless determined to become a writer, and in 1935 he published *Auto-da-fe,* the story of a sensitive scholar who is driven to madness and suicide by three brutish characters. The book was widely interpreted as a criticism of fascism and was banned in Germany by the Nazi government. After fleeing Austria in 1938, Canetti devoted more than two decades to the creation of his next major work, *Crowds and Power,* which, according to Bruce Cook of the *Washington Post Book World,* "astonished the intellectual world—not just with its scholarship, some of it from the most recondite sources, but also with its insights." Always a somewhat reclusive writer, Canetti went into complete seclusion after winning the Nobel Prize. At the same time, he began work on a multi-volume autobiography, describing his own intellectual growth as well as his friendships with such notable figures as writers Bertolt Brecht and Isaac Babel and German Expressionist artist George Grosz. Canetti was also the author of a number of plays, several essay collections, a travel book, and a highly regarded study of Franz Kafka titled *Der Andere Prozess* (*Kafka's Other Trial*).

OBITUARIES AND OTHER SOURCES:

BOOKS

Contemporary Literary Criticism, Volume 75, Gale, 1993.

PERIODICALS

Chicago Tribune, August 20, 1994, sec. 2, p. 17.
Los Angeles Times, August 19, 1994, p. A20.
New York Times, August 19, 1994, p. A25.
Times (London), August 19, 1994, p. 19.
Washington Post Book World, September 26, 1983.

*   *   *

CANFIELD, Sandra (Kay Patterson) 1944-

PERSONAL: Born November 21, 1944, in Longview, TX; daughter of Ira James (an oil field worker) and Ruby Belle (a nurse's aide; maiden name, Looney) Patterson; married Charles Keast Canfield, Jr. (a project manager), May 29, 1965. *Education:* Attended Centenary College of Louisiana, Northwestern State University, Natchitoches, LA, and Louisiana State University. *Avocational interests:* Reading, keeping a journal.

*ADDRESSES: Home—*2052 Pepper Ridge Dr., Shreveport, LA 71115. *Agent—*Maria Carvainis, Maria Carvainis Agency, 235 West End Ave., New York, NY 10023.

CAREER: Writer.

MEMBER: Romance Writers of America.

WRITINGS:

The Loving, HarperCollins, 1992.
Dark Journey, Bantam, 1994.

Author of other romances.

WORK IN PROGRESS: Night Moves, a contemporary romantic suspense novel, for Bantam.

SIDELIGHTS: Sandra Canfield told *CA:* "I began writing about fifteen years ago and, after a successful career in category romance, moved into larger books. The first crossover book was *The Loving.* Both that book and *Dark Journey* have a number of things in common: an investigation of the human spirit (for instance, its ability to rise above adversity), a look at the dark underbelly of human beings (I've always been more interested in what makes one cry than what makes one laugh), a study of the complexity of human nature, and the redemptive power of love.

"In particular, I write of the deep romantic feelings that can exist between man and woman, feelings that set us human beings apart from all other animals. As a counterbalance to my struggling characters, I always guarantee a happy ending. My work has been called moving and emotional, and I can ask for no greater accolade. I also like to think that my work is substantive. For example, in *Dark Journey,* I investigate the subject of infidelity: what constitutes infidelity and what are its moral and ethical implications. In *The Loving,* a time-travel novel, I look at physical abuse. In the book I am currently writing, I consider the close connection between love and hate."

CAPIE, Forrest H(unter) 1940-

PERSONAL: Born December 1, 1940, in Glasgow, Scotland; son of Daniel Forrest and Isabella Ferguson (Doughty) Capie; married Dianna Dix (a marketing executive), February 11, 1967. *Education:* University of Auckland, B.A., 1967; University of London, M.Sc., 1969, Ph.D., 1972. *Politics:* "Manchester Liberal." *Religion:* Protestant.

ADDRESSES: Home—2 Fitzroy Rd., Primrose Hill, London NW1 8TX, England. *Office*—Department of Banking and Finance, Business School, Barbican Centre, City University, London EC2Y, England.

CAREER: University of Warwick, Coventry, England, lecturer in economics, 1972-74; University of Leeds, Leeds, England, lecturer in economic studies, 1974-79; City University, London, England, visiting lecturer, 1978-79, lecturer, 1979-82, senior lecturer, 1982-83, reader, 1983-86, professor of economic history, 1986—, head of Department of Banking and Finance, 1988—. University of Aix-Marseille, visiting professor, 1978-79; University of London, London School of Economics and Political Science, visiting professor, 1991-92; lecturer at universities around the world, including Oxford University, University of Quebec, University of Kiel, University of Rochester, University of Illinois at Urbana-Champaign, University of Madrid, University of Copenhagen, and Harvard University. University of London, associate of Centre for Metropolitan History, 1986—; Rutgers University, member of advisory board, Centre for Financial History; Institute of Economic Affairs, member of Teachers Advisory Council, 1990—.

MEMBER: Royal Society of Arts (fellow), Economic History Society (member of council, 1986-90 and 1992—), Economic History Association, Cliometrics Society, Royal Economic Society, Association of Business Historians, Western Economics Association, Leeds Literary and Philosophical Society.

AWARDS, HONORS: Grants from British Social Science Research Council, 1976, 1980, 1982, and 1983, and Manpower Services Commission, 1977; British Academy overseas fellow, National Bureau of Economic Research, New York City, 1978; grants from Bank of England, 1987 and 1993, British Council (for Brazil), 1989, Economic and Social Research Council, 1990, and Wincott Foundation, 1990; Sasakawa Foundation fellow in Japan, 1990.

WRITINGS:

(With M. Collins) *The British Economy between the Wars,* Manchester University Press, 1983.
Depression and Protectionism: Britain between the Wars, Allen & Unwin, 1983.
(With A. Webber) *A Monetary History of the United Kingdom, 1870-1982: Data Sources and Methods,* Allen & Unwin, 1985.
(Editor with G. E. Wood, and contributor) *Financial Crises and the World Banking System,* Macmillan, 1986.
(Editor with G. E. Wood) *Monetary Economics in the 1980s: Some Themes from Henry Thornton,* Macmillan, 1989.
(Editor) *A Directory of Economic Institutions,* Macmillan, 1990.
(Editor with G. E. Wood, and co-author of introduction) *Unregulated Banking: Chaos or Order,* Macmillan, 1991.
(Editor and contributor) *Major Inflations in History,* Edward Elgar, 1991.
(Editor and contributor) *Protectionism in the World Economy,* Edward Elgar, 1992.
(With M. Collins) *Did the Banks Fail British Industry?,* IEA, 1992.
(Editor with M. Bordo, and contributor) *Monetary Regimes in Transition,* Cambridge University Press, 1993.
(Editor and contributor) *A History of Banking,* ten volumes, Pickering & Chatto, 1993.
Commercial Policy in the Modern World Economy, Manchester University Press, 1994.

Coeditor of a series on monetary and financial history, Cambridge University Press, 1988—; editor of a series on macroeconomic and financial history, Edward Elgar, 1989-94. Work represented in books, including *Money and Power,* edited by Moggridge and Cottrell, Macmillan, 1988; *New Perspectives on the Late-Victorian Economy,* edited by Foreman-Peck, Cambridge University Press, 1991; and *An Economic History of Britain,* edited by Floud and McCloskey, Cambridge University Press, 1993. Contributor of about a hundred articles and reviews to economic and finance journals. *Economic History Review,* book review editor, 1986-90, editor, 1992—.

* * *

CARLESS, Jennifer 1960-

PERSONAL: Born July 23, 1960, in Santa Cruz, CA; daughter of Christopher John and Penelope Susan (a medical transcriber; maiden name, Ermen) Carless.

Education: University of the Pacific, B.A., 1981; Monterey Institute of International Studies, M.A., 1983. _Politics:_ Liberal Democrat. _Religion:_ "Personal spiritual beliefs."

ADDRESSES: Home—P.O. Box 7616, Santa Cruz, CA 95061-7616.

CAREER: Manager of research support for a consulting firm that specialized in strategic political and defense analyses, Monterey, CA, 1983-85; manager of European agents for a U.S. online information service, London, England, 1986-87; freelance technical writer of software users manuals, London, 1987-88; office manager and attorney's assistant for a law firm specializing in business litigation, contract law, and creditor bankruptcy work, Santa Cruz, CA, 1992—.

MEMBER: Authors Guild.

WRITINGS:

Taking out the Trash: A No-Nonsense Guide to Recycling, Island Press (Washington, DC), 1992.
Renewable Energy: A Concise Guide to Green Alternatives, Walker and Co. (New York), 1993.

Member of editorial board, Amnesty International's _Policy Forum,_ 1992-94.

WORK IN PROGRESS: "A historical novel, set in eighteenth-century California, dealing with the Native American struggle to preserve this culture in the face of the developing mission system."

SIDELIGHTS: Jennifer Carless told _CA:_ "At the outset, my strongest motivation to write was the desire to work for myself, not to have to answer to anyone else. I also craved satisfying and challenging work. From my past educational and work experience, I was very comfortable with research and organization, so I tended naturally toward nonfiction. At the time I was most interested in, and concerned about, environmental issues. This led to my first two books.

"For a variety of reasons (I couldn't come up with a good environmental topic with a positive focus; I wanted a break from contractual deadlines; I wanted to explore my interest in California Indian history, and try to express myself in fiction), I am now trying something 'completely different.' My current work is much more challenging (I'm not so comfortable with fiction!), and I'm learning a lot."

CARTMILL, Matt 1943-

PERSONAL: Born January 4, 1943, in Los Angeles, CA; son of Cleve Eugene (a writer) and Jeanne R. (a homemaker; maiden name, Irvine; later surname, Klein) Cartmill; married Kaye Brown (an editor), May 29, 1971; children: Erica A. _Education:_ Pomona College, B.A., 1964; University of Chicago, M.A., Ph.D., 1970. _Avocational interests:_ Animation, shape-note singing.

ADDRESSES: Office—Department of Biological Anthropology, Medical Center, Duke University, Durham, NC 27710.

CAREER: Duke University, Durham, NC, professor of biological anthropology and anatomy, 1969—.

MEMBER: International Primatological Society, American Association of Physical Anthropologists, Sigma Xi.

AWARDS, HONORS: Grant from National Institutes of Health, 1975-80; Guggenheim fellow, 1985; W. W. Howells Prize, 1994.

WRITINGS:

Human Structure, Harvard University Press, 1987.
A View to a Death in the Morning: Hunting and Nature through History, Harvard University Press, 1993.

*   *   *

CARWARDINE, Richard J(ohn) 1947-

PERSONAL: Born January 12, 1947, in Cardiff, Wales; son of John Francis (a schoolmaster) and Beryl (a homemaker; maiden name, Jones) Carwardine; married Linda Margaret Kirk (a university teacher and historian), May 17, 1975. _Education:_ Corpus Christi College, Oxford, B.A., 1968; attended University of California, Berkeley, 1969-70; Queen's College, Oxford, D.Phil., 1975. _Religion:_ Church of England.

ADDRESSES: Home—14 Park Lane, Sheffield S10 2DW, England. _Office_—Department of History, University of Sheffield, Sheffield S10 2TN, England.

CAREER: University of Sheffield, Sheffield, England, lecturer, 1971-90, senior lecturer, 1990-94, professor of history, 1994—. Syracuse University, visiting professor, 1974-75; University of North Carolina at Chapel Hill, research fellow, 1989.

Sheffield Hallam Liberal Democrats, chairperson, 1992-94.

MEMBER: Royal Historical Society (fellow), British Association for American Studies, Organization of American Historians, Society for the History of the Early Republic, Ecclesiastical History Society.

AWARDS, HONORS: Fulbright fellow in North Carolina, 1989; fellow of American Council of Learned Societies, 1989.

WRITINGS:

Transatlantic Revivalism: Popular Evangelicalism in Britain and America, 1790-1865, Greenwood Press, 1978.
Evangelicals and Politics in Antebellum America, Yale University Press, 1993.

WORK IN PROGRESS: Research on Abraham Lincoln and on religion and the U.S. Civil War.

*   *   *

CASALE, Anne L. 1930-

PERSONAL: Born July 15, 1930, in Perth Amboy, NJ; daughter of Amadeo (a sculptor and chef) and Rose (a homemaker; maiden name, Guarnieri) Lovi; married John V. Casale (in retail sales); children: Joanne Casale Murphy, Amy Casale Savage. *Education:* Berkeley School of Business, earned business degree; attended Culinary Institute of America. *Politics:* Republican. *Religion:* Roman Catholic.

ADDRESSES: Home and office—369 Mountain Blvd., Watchung, NJ 07060. *Agent*—Amy Berkower, Writers House, 21 West 26th St., New York, NY 10010.

CAREER: Annie's Kitchen (cooking school), director, 1978-84; culinary educator at schools, including Peter Kump's School of Culinary Arts, Adventures in Cooking (Wayne, NJ), and Cook 'n' Tell (Colts Neck, NJ). International Association of Culinary Professionals, certified culinary professional; consultant to retail stores and cooking schools.

MEMBER: New York Association of Cooking Teachers (member of board of directors, 1982-90; president, 1985-86).

WRITINGS:

Italian Family Cooking: Like Mama Used to Make, Fawcett Columbine, 1984.

The Long Life Cookbook: Delectable Recipes for Two, Ballantine, 1986.
Lean Italian Cooking, Fawcett Columbine, 1994.

WORK IN PROGRESS: Lean Italian Meatless.

*   *   *

CASSUTT, Michael (Joseph) 1954-

PERSONAL: Born April 13, 1954, in Owatonna, MN; son of Florian Francis (a baseball player, coach, and teacher) and Joyce (a teacher; maiden name, Williams) Cassutt; married Cynthia Stratton (a magazine editor), August 19, 1978; children: Ryan Spencer, Alexandra Lee. *Education:* University of Arizona, B.A., 1975. *Politics:* Democrat. *Religion:* Roman Catholic.

ADDRESSES: Home—12241 Hillslope St., Studio City, CA 91604-3604. *Agent*—(literary) Richard Curtis Assoc., 171 East 74th St., New York, NY 10021; (television/film) Creative Artists Agency, 9830 Wilshire Blvd., Beverly Hills, CA 90212-1825.

CAREER: KHYT Radio, Tucson, AZ, disc jockey and operations manager, 1975-78; CBS Television, Los Angeles, CA, held various positions including children's programming executive, 1979-85; freelance writer and television producer, 1985—.

MEMBER: Science Fiction and Fantasy Writers of America (vice president, 1988-89), Writers Guild of America—West, Academy of Television Arts and Sciences.

AWARDS, HONORS: Nancy B. Reynolds Award, Center for Population Options, 1989, for "First Love Trilogy" episode of television series *TV 101.*

WRITINGS:

TELEPLAYS

Love, Sidney, NBC, 1982.
Gloria, CBS, 1982.
It's Not Easy, ABC, 1983.
Alice, CBS, 1983-84.
Dungeons and Dragons, CBS, 1985.
Rocky Road, (syndicated), 1985.
Misfits of Science, NBC, 1985.
The Twilight Zone, CBS, 1985-87.
Centurions, (syndicated), 1986.
Simon and Simon, CBS, 1986.
The Wizard, CBS, 1987.
Max Headroom, ABC, 1987-88.

Beauty and the Beast, CBS, 1988.
TV 101, CBS, 1988-89.
CBS Storybreak, CBS, 1989.
WIOU, CBS, 1990.
Eerie, Indiana, NBC, 1992.
Sirens, ABC, 1993.
Sea Quest, NBC, 1993.

OTHER

The Star Country (science fiction), Doubleday, 1986.
Who's Who in Space: The First Twenty-five Years (reference), G. K. Hall, 1987, 2nd edition published as *Who's Who in Space: The International Space Year,* 1993.
(Author of introduction) Valentin Lebedev, *Diary of a Cosmonaut: Two Hundred Eleven Days in Space,* PhytoResource Research, 1988.
Dragon Season (fantasy), Tor Books, 1991.
(Editor with Andrew Greeley and Martin H. Greenberg) *Sacred Visions* (science fiction anthology), Tor Books, 1991.
(With Donald K. "Deke" Slayton) *Deke! U.S. Manned Space: Mercury to the Shuttle,* Forge, 1994.

Author of screenplay for the film *Dungeonmaster II: Mestema's Challenge,* Empire Films. Contributor of short stories to periodicals, including *Magazine of Fantasy and Science Fiction, Isaac Asimov's SF Magazine, Mike Shayne Mystery Magazine,* and *Amazing Science Fiction;* contributor of short stories to anthologies; contributor of nonfiction articles to periodicals, including *Science Fiction Review, McGill's Guide to Space Science, Spaceflight, Orbiter, Omni, L-5 News, Future Life, Starlog,* and *Space World.*

WORK IN PROGRESS: Mount Thunder, a novel.

SIDELIGHTS: "For years I've been pursuing three parallel writing careers," Michael Cassutt commented, "prose fiction, especially science fiction and fantasy; nonfiction, most of it on the subject of space flight; and TV scriptwriting.

"A number of well-meaning friends have suggested I'd be further along in any one of these fields if I dropped the other two, but I'm reluctant to do that, even though it makes for awkward moments at social occasions. How do I introduce myself? Am I a science fiction writer or an aerospace historian or a television scriptwriter? In weak moments I tailor the answer to suit the situation.

"Anyway, there's a hidden benefit to this apparent lack of commitment: whenever I get tired of one type of project, I can turn to something completely different. This means I rarely appear to be blocked, though under oath I would have to admit I'm stuck as often as any other writer.

"More seriously, I'd also point out that I became interested in space flight in the mid-1960s, just as it was changing from science fiction into reality. For me the truest sort of SF, even though I've rarely written it, is about exploring other worlds. And I owe my television career in part to SF, since my first two staff positions were on *The Twilight Zone* and *Max Headroom.* So there's really no inconsistency, is there?"

Michael Cassutt's first novel, *The Star Country,* is set in the year 2038, in a world where the United States has broken up into smaller nation-states and the Soviet Union and China have destroyed each other. When representatives of an alien nation arrive on Earth to deliver the Genesis File, a package of advanced knowledge and technology, they have difficulty finding any person or nation worthy of receiving it. Then a young Iowa farmer rescues one of the aliens after he crashes near the commune on which the man lives. A *Kirkus Reviews* critic claimed *The Star Country* possessed a "brisk, reasonably gripping narrative." Bill Collins in *Fantasy Review,* however, noted several flaws in the book's plot but concluded: "If one doesn't read too critically, the time passes pleasantly." Gerald Jonas of the *New York Times Book Review,* on the other hand, commended the "generosity of vision" that inspired the author to spend as much time with his humble characters as he does with his elite ones and called *The Star Country* "a pleasantly small-scale book about world-shaking events."

Cassutt's next project, *Who's Who in Space: The First Twenty-five Years,* is a comprehensive reference book on astronauts and others involved in space travel. The book features short biographies, photographs, and appendices detailing all spaceflights, with information on crew members, launch and landing dates, and accomplishments. *Booklist* praised Cassutt's biographies as "objective and very readable," and recommended the book as "the first source to include information on all astronauts from all nations."

Cassutt returned to novel writing with the publication of *Dragon Season,* a fantasy tale about Rick Walsh, an Air Force lieutenant who returns from overseas duty to discover he is the father of a baby boy whose mother is missing. Rick's search for her leads him to a parallel world ruled by a god named Griffon and populated with dragon-like creatures and buildings that grow. Patricia S. Franz of *Kliatt* liked the fast-paced adventure story, and concluded: "Cassutt tells a story that most fantasy/SF readers will enjoy."

BIOGRAPHICAL/CRITICAL SOURCES:

PERIODICALS

Booklist, June 15, 1987, p. 1584.
Fantasy Review, October, 1986, p. 22.
Kirkus Reviews, July 1, 1986, p. 976.
Kliatt, April, 1992, p. 12.
New York Times Book Review, September 21, 1986.
Publishers Weekly, June 20, 1986, p. 94.
Voice of Youth Advocates, June, 1992, p. 108.

* * *

CAZDEN, Courtney B(orden) 1925-

PERSONAL: Born November 30, 1925, in Chicago, IL; daughter of John and Courtney (Letts) Borden; married Norman Cazden (divorced, 1971); children: Elizabeth, Joanna. *Education:* Radcliffe College, B.A., 1946; University of Illinois, M.Ed., 1953; Harvard University, Ed.D., 1965. *Religion:* Quaker.

ADDRESSES: Office—Harvard Graduate School of Education, Longfellow Hall 205, Cambridge, MA 02138.

CAREER: Elementary school teacher in various public schools, 1947-49, 1954-61, and 1974-75; Harvard University, Cambridge, MA, assistant professor, 1965-68, associate professor, 1968-71, professor, 1971—. Visiting professor, University of New Mexico, 1980, University of Alaska, 1982, University of Auckland, 1983, and Bread Loaf School of English, 1986—. Chair of board of trustees for Center of Applied Linguistics, 1981-85.

MEMBER: American Educational Research Association, American Association of Applied Linguistics, National Education Association, Council on Anthropology and Education.

AWARDS, HONORS: Center of Advanced Study in Behavioral Sciences fellow, 1978-79; Fulbright research fellow, New Zealand, 1987; Alumna Recognition award, Radcliffe College, 1988.

WRITINGS:

Environmental Assistance to the Child's Acquisition of Grammar, Harvard University Press, 1965.

Child Language and Education, Holt, 1972.
(Editor with Vera P. John and Dell Hymes) *Functions of Language in the Classroom,* Teachers College Press, 1972.
(Editor) *Language in Early Childhood Education,* National Association for the Education of Young Children, 1972.
Classroom Discourse: The Language of Teaching and Learning, Heinemann, 1988.
(Coauthor) *Whole Language Plus,* Teachers College Press, 1992.

Contributor of articles to periodicals, including *Journal of Special Education* and *Merrill-Rolmer Quarterly.*

* * *

CHALKER, Sylvia

PERSONAL: Maiden name Burls-Hunt; born in London, England. *Education:* Cambridge University, M.A.; also attended University of London.

ADDRESSES: Agent—c/o Oxford University Press, 200 Madison Ave., New York, NY 10016.

CAREER: Worked as a journalist, public relations representative, and teacher of English as a foreign language.

WRITINGS:

Going It Alone, Macmillan, 1978.
Let's See Great Britain, Macmillan, 1979.
Advanced English Course: Study Programmes, Linguaphone Institute, 1979.
Police!, Longman Malaysia, 1981.
Fire!, Longman Malaysia, 1981.
Current English Grammar, Macmillan, 1984.
Intermediate Grammar Workbooks, Volume I-III, Longman, 1987.
Fast Forward 3 Resource Book, Oxford University Press, 1988, abridged edition (with Marion Geddes), 1990.
English Grammar Word by Word, Thomas Nelson, 1991.
A Student's English Grammar Workbook, Longman, 1992.
(With Edmund Weiner) *The Oxford Dictionary of English Grammar,* Oxford University Press, 1994.
The Little Oxford Dictionary of English Grammar, Oxford University Press, in press.

Contributor to books, including *How to Write and Speak Better,* Reader's Digest Association, 1991;

The Oxford Companion to the English Language, Oxford University Press, 1992; and *Grammar and the Language Teacher,* Prentice-Hall International, 1994. Contributor of articles and reviews to periodicals. Book review editor, *EFL Gazette.*

SIDELIGHTS: Sylvia Chalker told *CA:* "I began my career of teaching English as a foreign language in London, where I taught foreign students. I later spent two years teaching with the British Council in Singapore, from 1979 to 1981. I have run courses or lectured, particularly on grammar, in India, the Philippines, Austria, the Canaries, France, Italy, Switzerland, and, of course, Britain.

"I am fascinated by how language works. I believe that grammar should be seen as a system of meaning, not a set of arbitrary rules. I enjoy new and evolving grammar, but I dislike femspeak and other P.C. forms of language abuse."

*   *   *

CHAMBERLAIN, Lorna M(arie)   1945-

PERSONAL: Born July 30, 1945, in Saint John, New Brunswick, Canada; daughter of George Austin and Victoria (Penney) Chamberlain; married Rod John Preece (a professor), July 10, 1994. *Education:* York University, B.A. (with honors), 1970; University of Toronto, B.Ed., 1972; University of Windsor, M.Ed., 1983. *Avocational interests:* Animal protection, animal rights issues, clogging.

ADDRESSES: Home—279 Vidal St. North, Sarnia, Ontario, Canada N7T 5Y5. *Office*—Sarnia General Hospital, 220 North Mitton St., Sarnia, Ontario, Canada N7T 6H6.

CAREER: Whitby Psychiatric Hospital, Whitby, Ontario, Canada, psychometrist, 1971; Addiction Research Foundation, Sarnia, Ontario, community consultant, 1972-80; Sarnia General Hospital, Sarnia, associate director, 1980-92, director of addiction services, 1992—. Lambton District Health Council Substance Abuse Subcommittee member, 1980—, Lambton Drug Awareness Action Committee member, 1983—, chair of professional resources committee, 1989—; Sarnia and District Society for the Prevention of Cruelty to Animals (SPCA), secretary, 1984-86, vice-president, 1986-89, president, 1989-93, past president, 1993-94; Ontario Society for the Prevention of Cruelty to Animals, executive committee, 1989—, vice chairperson, 1990-94; Lambton County Coordinating Council for Children and Youth member, 1989—; Canadian Federation of Humane Societies, member of executive committee, 1991-93; Ontario Addictions Coordinating Group member, 1993—.

AWARDS, HONORS: Community Achievement Award, Addiction Research Foundation, 1991, for dedication to improve and enhance addiction treatment programs in Lambton County, Ontario.

WRITINGS:

(With husband, Rod Preece) *Animal Welfare and Human Values,* Wilfrid Laurier University Press (Waterloo, Ontario, Canada), 1993.

SIDELIGHTS: Lorna M. Chamberlain told *CA:* "Through our involvement in the humane movement in Ontario, my husband, Dr. Rod Preece, and I became exasperated and quite horrified to learn of the many atrocities committed by humankind toward our fellow sentient beings. Fueled by innumerable disturbing new awarenesses along with a desire to enlighten others, we began researching then writing about some of the most contentious issues in animal welfare disputes. Our philosophy, depicted in *Animal Welfare and Human Values,* is one that embraces the principles of common sense and compromise as the surest paths to the goal of animal welfare. It is our view that justice is best approximated by holding in balance the inexorably and unequally competing interests of all living creatures. Our work has convinced us that, in the final analysis, solutions to animal welfare issues can only be found in the refinement of human sensibilities."

*   *   *

CHAUDHURI, Amit   1962-

PERSONAL: Born May 15, 1962, in Calcutta, India; son of Nages Chandra (a retired corporate executive) and Bijoya (a homemaker and singer; maiden name, Nandi Majumdar) Chaudhuri; married Rinka Khastgir, December 12, 1991. *Education:* University College, London, B.A. (with honors), 1986; attended Balliol College, Oxford, D.Phil., 1993. *Religion:* Hindu. *Avocational interests:* North Indian classical music (vocal).

ADDRESSES: Home—6 Sunny Park, Flat 10, 8th Fl., Calcutta, India 700019. *Agent*—Derek Johns, A. P. Watt Ltd., 20 John Street, London W1, England.

CAREER: Writer. Wolfson College, Oxford, creative arts fellow, 1992-95.

AWARDS, HONORS: Betty Trask Award, Society of

Authors, 1991, for *A Strange and Sublime Address;* K. Blundell Trust award, 1993, for writing a second novel; Commonwealth Writers' Prize for Best First Book (Eurasia), for *A Strange and Sublime Address;* Encore Prize, Society of Authors, 1994, for *Afternoon Raag;* Arts Council writing award.

WRITINGS:

A Strange and Sublime Address, Heinemann (London), 1991.
Afternoon Raag, Heinemann, 1993.

Contributor to periodicals, including *London Review of Books, Times Literary Supplement,* and *London Magazine;* contributor to anthologies, including *Oxford Companion to Twentieth Century Poetry.*

WORK IN PROGRESS: A third novel set in Calcutta.

SIDELIGHTS: Amit Chaudhuri, who was born in Calcutta, India, raised in Bombay, and received university education in England, has impressed critics with his ability to write with affection about his native land. *A Strange and Sublime Address,* a work which met with critical acclaim and won Chaudhuri the Betty Trask Award (regularly bestowed to first-time novelists under the age of thirty-five), is comprised of a novella and short stories. The 35,000-word novella tells of Sandeep, a ten-year-old boy living a lonely life in Bombay, who visits his uncle for the holidays in Calcutta. Although Chaudhuri reportedly denies that the novella is narrowly autobiographical, *Times of India* reviewer Mandira Sen observed that it does bear the imprint of the author's own life. "As a child, growing up in Bombay, [Chaudhuri] too visited relatives in Calcutta," Sen commented. However, the critic pointed out that Chaudhuri is primarily "interested in interweaving what he perceives as culture and place, to put it together, rather the way a painting is." Throughout *A Strange and Sublime Address,* Chaudhuri's lyrical prose bears the imprint of the visual arts. As reported in *Times of India,* Chaudhuri acknowledges that painting has shaped his work. The author has been especially influenced by Indian folk art, which he believes has retained certain aspects of cultural integrity that colonialism sought to abolish.

Sensibility itself is at the heart of Chaudhuri's novella. *A Strange and Sublime Address* evokes Sandeep's childhood, painting a panoramic picture of everyday life within his large family. "The days drift into each other, the children play ceaselessly, are caught, oiled, and bathed by one of the aunts.

Mealtimes are leisurely affairs, each moment spent savouring the sensual delights of food," remarked Kaveri Ponnapa in *Times of India.* The reviewer went on to comment that this accumulated detail, expressed in Chaudhuri's imagistic prose, conjures the "enigmatic city" of Calcutta. In *Vogue,* John Lanchester noted that the "most original, most dramatic, and most impressive feature" of the novella is "that nothing whatsoever happen[s] in it—nothing *at all.* . . . The evocation of the routine . . . strikes me still as an extraordinary thing to have brought off." The stories in *A Strange and Sublime Address,* which were considered "slight" by Mark Wormald in *Times Literary Supplement,* impressed Ponnapa in *Times of India.* The critic found the tales "seamless, atmospheric, and rich in imagery" and stated that Chaudhuri "excels in transfixing a single, evanescent incident."

According to critics, *Afternoon Raag,* Chaudhuri's second novel, is filled with rich, textured language and devoid of conventional plot. Here Chaudhuri's narrator, an Indian man attending Oxford University, tries unsuccessfully to strike up a relationship with two female students. The book conveys such sentiments as a longing for home and a distinct sensitivity to detail. In *Afternoon Raag,* Chaudhuri describes "the abidingness of an English interior" and a foreign student's attachment to a room as "one's first friend . . . a relationship that is natural and unthinking, its air and light what one shares with one's thoughts." Like Amitav Ghosh and Sunetra Gupta, two of Chaudhuri's Indian literary contemporaries, Chaudhuri demonstrates—in the words of Aamer Hussein of the *Times Literary Supplement*—"an untainted pride in his culture and an unambiguous attitude to the hazards and vagaries of the migrant's situation."

BIOGRAPHICAL/CRITICAL SOURCES:

BOOKS

Chaudhuri, Amit, *Afternoon Raag,* Heinemann, 1993.

PERIODICALS

Guardian (London), June 29, 1993.
London Review of Books, August 19, 1993.
Observer (London), June 13, 1993, p. 62.
Times (London), August 22, 1993.
Times Literary Supplement, August 23, 1991, p. 21; June 18, 1993, p. 23.
Times of India, September 23, 1991.
Vogue, July, 1991.

CHEYETTE, Bryan (Henry) 1959-

PERSONAL: Born January 15, 1959, in Leicester, England; son of Jack Keith (a company director) and Sonia (a company director; maiden name, Woolfson) Cheyette. *Education:* University of Sheffield, Ph.D., 1986.

ADDRESSES: Office—School of English, Queen Mary and Westfield College, University of London, Mile End Rd., London E1 4NS, England.

CAREER: Spiro Institute, London, England, adult education lecturer, 1983-85; Hebrew University of Jerusalem, Jerusalem, Israel, research fellow, 1985-86; University of Leeds, Leeds, England, Montague Burton research fellow, 1986-89, British Academy fellow, 1989-92; University of London, Queen Mary and Westfield College, London, lecturer in English, 1992—, executive member of Centre for European Studies. Guest on television and radio programs.

AWARDS, HONORS: Grant from British Academy, 1989-92; overseas travel grants from University of Leeds, 1986, 1988, and 1991, British Academy, 1990, and S. H. Burton Trust, 1993.

WRITINGS:

Constructions of "The Jew" in English Literature and Society Racial Representations, 1875-1945, Cambridge University Press, 1993.
(Editor) *Between "Race" and Culture: Representations of "The Jew" in English and American Literature,* Stanford University Press, 1995.

Contributor to books, including *The Making of Modern Anglo-Jewry,* edited by David Cesarini, Basil Blackwell, 1990; *The Politics of Marginality,* edited by T. Kushner and K. Lunn, Frank Cass, 1990; and *Distinguishing Factors: British and American Literature in the Twentieth Century,* edited by Ann Massa and Alistair Stead, Longman, 1994. Contributor of articles and reviews to literature journals and newspapers. Literary editor, *Jewish Quarterly;* member of editorial board, *Patterns of Prejudice.*

WORK IN PROGRESS: Editing *Tono-Bungay,* by H. G. Wells, publication by Oxford University Press expected in 1996; editing *Modernity, Culture, and "The Jew,"* University of California Press, 1996; *The Hidden Tradition: A Critical History of British-Jewish Literature,* 1996.

SIDELIGHTS: Bryan Cheyette told *CA:* "Like most intellectuals, I have two completely irreconcilable sides to my work. On the one hand, I am a literary editor and review fiction and criticism regularly for newspapers and weeklies. In these short pieces, I attempt to empathize as much as possible with individual authors and, by getting under their skin, give a good account of their writing. I hope that my longer publications also demonstrate this empathetic quality.

"In these longer works, however, such as my book *Constructions of 'The Jew' in English Literature and Society,* I am much less of a neutral critic. Instead, I wish to show the extent to which European literature is saturated with the race-thinking that is most often thought to be outside civilized culture. By showing that such race-thinking is right at the heart of the English literary tradition, for example, I do not wish to belittle individual authors who were clearly a product of a particular (if unpleasant) history. The target in my longer works is my fellow literary critics who well know the consequences of race-thinking in this bloody century, but still choose to ignore instances of it in their favored authors. Such silences, I believe, can only enable racism and anti-semitism to continue in the twentieth century. Unlike those 'politically correct' academics who want to banish any literary text deemed racist from the seminar room, I strongly believe that such texts should be freely discussed. Only then can the tenacity of race-thinking be understood, along with its closeness to the literary imagination. Only then can we all help to end such thinking wherever possible."

* * *

CHILDRESS, Alice 1920-1994

OBITUARY NOTICE—See index for *CA* sketch: Born October 12, 1920 (one source cites 1916), in Charleston, SC; died of cancer, August 14, 1994, in Queens, NY. Actress, playwright, and novelist. Childress was known for her frank treatment of the problems faced by African-Americans in contemporary American society, and, as a result, her works were often the center of controversy. After beginning her career as an actress with the American Negro Theatre in New York City, Childress turned to playwrighting in the 1940s; in 1949 she directed and starred in the American Negro Theatre production of her one-act play *Florence.* She subsequently wrote a number of plays, and in 1973 she published her first novel, the story of a young African-American drug addict titled *A Hero Ain't Nothin' but a Sandwich,* which was widely praised for its power and realism but later banned as obscene by a Long

Island school district. Later, when her play about interracial marriage, *Wedding Band,* was adapted for television, a number of stations refused to carry the broadcast. Undeterred by such censure, Childress continued to write about her concerns throughout her lifetime, and her works received numerous honors and awards. Her other writings include a play about black actors titled *Trouble in Mind,* the novels *A Short Walk* and *Rainbow Jordan,* several musical dramas, and screenplays for *Wedding Band* and *A Hero Ain't Nothin' but a Sandwich.*

OBITUARIES AND OTHER SOURCES:

BOOKS

Black Literature Criticism, Gale, 1992.
Who's Who in America, 47th edition, Marquis, 1992.

PERIODICALS

Chicago Tribune, August 21, 1994, sec. 2, p. 8.
Los Angeles Times, August 19, 1994, p. A20.
New York Times, August 19, 1994, p. A24.
Washington Post, August 19, 1994, p. B4.

*   *   *

CHILDS, Michael J. 1956-

PERSONAL: Born November 24, 1956, in Barrie, Ontario, Canada. *Education:* Carleton University, B.A. (with honors), 1980; McGill University, M.A., 1982, Ph.D., 1987.

ADDRESSES: Office—Department of History, Bishop's University, Lennoxville, Quebec, Canada, J1M 1Z7.

CAREER: University of Lethbridge, Lethbridge, Alberta, Canada, assistant professor of history, 1987-88; Bishop's University, Lennoxville, Quebec, Canada, assistant professor, 1988-92, associate professor of history, 1992—.

MEMBER: North American Conference on British Studies.

WRITINGS:

Labour's Apprentices, McGill-Queen's University Press, 1992.

Coeditor, *Journal of History and Politics,* 1991—.

WORK IN PROGRESS: Northampton in the Great War.

CHOATE, Pat 1941(?)-

PERSONAL: Born c. 1941. *Education:* Received Ph.D. from University of Oklahoma.

ADDRESSES: Home—4100 Cathedral Ave. N.W., Washington, DC 20002. *Office*—201 Massachusetts Ave. N.E., Suite C7, Washington, DC 20002.

CAREER: Worked as regional administrator for Economic Development Administration in a Commerce Department, 1965-73; associated with Department of Economic and Community Development, TN, 1973-75; Economic Development Administration, Washington, DC, director of Office of Economic Research, beginning 1975; associated with Office of Management and Budget, Washington, DC; associated with Academy for Contemporary Problems; TRW Inc., Cleveland, OH, vice president for policy analysis, 1981-90; currently associated with Manufacturing Policy Project, Washington, DC, 1992—. Frequent guest on television news and talk shows.

WRITINGS:

As Time Goes By: The Costs and Consequences of Delay, Academy of Contemporary Problems, 1980.
(With Gail Garfield Schwartz) *Being Number One: Rebuilding the U.S. Economy,* Free Press, 1980.
(With Susan M. Walter) *America in Ruins: Beyond the Public Works Pork Barrel,* Columbia Scholastic Press, 1981.
(With Walter) *America in Ruins: The Decaying Infrastructure,* Duke University Press, 1981.
(With Walter) *Thinking Strategically: A Primer for Public Leaders,* Columbia Scholastic Press, 1984.
(With J. K. Linger) *The High-Flex Society: Shaping America's Economic Future,* Knopf, 1986.
Agents of Influence, Knopf, 1990, also published as *Agents of Influence: How Japan's Lobbyists in the United States Manipulate America's Political and Economic System,* Touchstone Books, 1990.
(With T. Boone Pickens and Christopher Burke) *The Second Pearl Harbor: Say No to Japan,* National Press Books, 1991.
(With Ross Perot) *Save Your Job, Save Our Country: Why NAFTA Must Be Stopped—Now!,* Hyperion, 1993.

Contributor of numerous articles to various periodicals including the *Chicago Tribune, New York Times,* and *Wall Street Journal. Agents of Influence* has been recorded on an audiocassette.

SIDELIGHTS: Pat Choate has become an important figure in the world of American political analysis and policymaking. His book *Agents of Influence,* an account of the power Japan wields in the American political system, created an uproar throughout the highest levels of government. Choate does not directly accuse the Japanese of unfair tactics in the book, but shows how the Japanese have learned to play the American political game in the United States. A common practice is the hiring of former American government officials, who have extensive contacts and experience, by Japanese government agencies to promote Japanese interests in the United States. Choate profiles specific politicians in a forty-one page index whom he alleges accepted Japanese money in exchange for lobbying Japanese interests. Choate also describes how Japan is trying to improve its image in the United States with the help of public relations firms. Japan pays for trips of American officials to Japan, funds programs such as Japanese studies in American schools, and presents speakers at different conferences and symposiums.

After graduating with a Ph.D. from the University of Oklahoma, Choate went to work for Governor Henry Bellmon of Oklahoma as an economic planner. Other posts within the nation's capital followed, and Choate developed a reputation for his innovative ideas on policy. In 1981, TRW, a manufacturer of auto parts and defense equipment, asked Choate to join its staff as a senior analyst who was familiar with Washington, D.C., and could predict events within government that might affect TRW business.

In 1986, Choate teamed with J. K. Linger to write *The High-Flex Society: Shaping America's Economic Future,* which helped spawn a number of congressional bills. *The High-Flex Society* outlines challenges to America's position as a world economic leader and presents steps the government needs to take in the future to remain competitive on a global scale.

Choate stayed with TRW as a vice president for policy analysis until 1990. He was fired after the release of *Agents of Influence,* allegedly because of a complaint received by the TRW chair from a former official of the Japanese trade ministry about Choate's book. Choate was labelled a "Japan-basher" and as a result lost some of his political allies in Washington, D.C.

Because of its controversial topic, *Agents of Influence* has received mixed reviews. "For a book that purports to be about 'our' problem, [Choate] throws a remarkable number of rotten tomatoes at 'them,'" assessed Christopher Lehmann-Haupt of the *New York Times.* "The book is worthy of wide debate," commented Jeffrey E. Garten of the *New York Times Book Review,* "and a firestorm it is sure to cause. But when the emotions die down, certain considerations, some of them highlighted by Mr. Choate, might be taken into account."

Choate started his own organization for interdisciplinary research, the Manufacturing Policy Project. He has also teamed up with businessperson and former presidential candidate Ross Perot as a policy advisor and helped Perot to write *Save Your Job, Save Our Country: Why NAFTA Must Be Stopped—Now!,* a criticism of the North American Free Trade Agreement.

BIOGRAPHICAL/CRITICAL SOURCES:

PERIODICALS

Los Angeles Times Book Review, October 28, 1990.
New Republic, September 20-27, 1993.
New York Times, May 3, 1987; September 27, 1990.
New York Times Book Review, October 7, 1990, pp. 9-10.
Publishers Weekly, August 8, 1986, p. 6.
Washington Post, November 15, 1993, p. B4.
Washington Post Book World, October 14, 1990.*

* * *

CHOUDHURY, Masudul Alam   1948- (Masud)

PERSONAL: Born January 1, 1948, in Calcutta, India; son of A. B. M. Sultanul Alam (a university professor) and Farkhunda Alam Chowdhury; married, December 31, 1978; wife's name, Nuzhat (a homemaker); children: Mufeedh, Nafay, Moaz, Naba. *Education:* University of Dhaka, B.Sc. (with honors); University of Islamabad, M.Phil., M.Sc.; University of Tor, M.A., Ph.D. *Religion:* Islamic. *Avocational interests:* Travel.

ADDRESSES: Home—58 Leeside Dr., Sydney, Nova Scotia, Canada, B1R 1S6. *Office*—Centre of Humanomics, University College of Cape Breton, Sydney, Nova Scotia, B1P 6L2, Canada.

CAREER: Saskatchewan Department of Labour, Regina, Saskatchewan, Canada, research economist, 1977-79; King Abdulaziz University, Jeddah, Saudi Arabia, assistant professor of economics, 1979-83; Islamic Development Bank, Jeddah, senior economist, 1983-85; University College of Cape Breton, Sydney, Nova Scotia, Canada, professor of economics, 1985—, and director of Centre of Humanomics. National University of Malaysia, visiting professor; Ontario Institute for Studies in Education, University of Toronto, visiting professor; lecturer at colleges and universities, including National University of Malaysia; Oxford University, St. Cross College, fellow of Oxford Centre for Islamic Studies.

MEMBER: Canadian Economic Association, Atlantic Canada Economic Association.

AWARDS, HONORS: Rockefeller scholar, Bellagio Study and Conference Centre.

WRITINGS:

(With U. A. Malik) *The Foundations of Islamic Political Economy,* St. Martin's, 1992.
The Unicity Precept and the Socio-Scientific Order, University Press of America, 1993.
The Principles of Islamic Political Economy, St. Martin's, 1993.
Comparative Development Studies, St. Martin's, 1993.
Theory and Practice of Islamic Development Cooperation, Statistical, Economic, and Social Research and Training Centre for Islamic Countries (Ankara, Turkey), 1993.
Epistemological Foundations of the Islamic Economic, Social, and Scientific Order, six volumes and a booklet, Statistical, Economy, and Social Research and Training Centre for Islamic Countries (Ankara), in press.

Some writings appear under the pseudonym Masud. Editor, *Humanomics;* special issue editor, *Managerial Finance,* 1995. Contributor to scholarly journals.

WORK IN PROGRESS: Editing *Alternative Perspectives of Third-World Development: The Case of Malaysia* for St. Martin's.

SIDELIGHTS: Masudul Alam Choudhury told *CA:* "My intensive research focus, publication, and academic involvement in recent times has been in the specific area of epistemology and methodology of interactive systems. Taking an approach polar to the neo-classical, monetarist, and Keynesian orthodoxy, I am developing an academic and institutionalist paradigm that examines the endogenous (systemic) role of ethics in socio-scientific epistemology. To promote this seriously policy-theoretic paradigm, I direct the Centre of Humanomics at the University College of Cape Breton."

CLAMPITT, Amy   1920-1994

OBITUARY NOTICE—See index for *CA* sketch: Born June 15, 1920, in New Providence, IA; died of ovarian cancer on September 10, 1994, in Lenox, MA. Editor and poet. Upon publication of her book of poems *The Kingfisher* in 1983, Clampitt became one of the most highly regarded poets in America. Born in rural Iowa and raised on a farm, she studied first at Grinnell College in Grinnell, Iowa, and later at Columbia University and the New School for Social Research in New York City. Throughout the 1940s and 1950s Clampitt held a variety of jobs and attempted unsuccessfully to write novels, and in the 1960s she turned her attention to poetry. In 1974 she published a small volume of poetry titled *Multitudes, Multitudes;* thereafter her work appeared frequently in the *New Yorker.* However, it was not until the publication of *The Kingfisher,* when Clampitt was sixty-three years old, that her work received significant attention, with critics praising in particular the allusive richness and syntactical sophistication of her verse. Clampitt's subsequent poetry collections *What the Light Was Like, Archaic Figure, Westward,* and *A Silence Opens,* have also garnered wide critical praise, and in 1992 she received a MacArthur Fellowship in recognition of her achievements.

OBITUARIES AND OTHER SOURCES:

BOOKS

Who's Who of American Women, 18th edition, Marquis, 1993.

PERIODICALS

Chicago Tribune, September 18, 1994, sec. 2, p. 6.
Los Angeles Times, September 13, 1994, p. A29.
New York Times, September 12, 1994, p. D10.
Times (London), September 20, 1994, p. 21.
Washington Post, September 13, 1994, p. B7.

*   *   *

CLAVELL, James (duMaresq)   1925-1994

OBITUARY NOTICE—See index for *CA* sketch: Born October 10, 1925, in Sydney, Australia; died of cancer, September 6, 1994, in Vevey, Switzerland. Producer, director, screenwriter, and novelist. Clavell was the author of enormously popular adventure novels, most notably *Shogun,* the story of a Western visitor to feudal seventeenth-century Japan, which sold millions of copies and served as the basis for one of the most successful television miniseries of all time. Born in Australia to English parents, Clavell was raised in England. In 1940, as the Second World War began, he joined the Royal Artillery; while serving in the Far East he was captured by the Japanese and imprisoned at Changi, a notoriously brutal facility where nearly 140,000 prisoners died. After being discharged from the military in 1946, Clavell developed an interest in the film industry, and in 1953 he relocated to the United States to further pursue his interests. He subsequently worked in a variety of capacities, writing screenplays for *The Fly, The Great Escape,* and *To Sir with Love,* as well as directing and producing films and television shows. Clavell published his first novel, *King Rat,* based on his experiences at Changi, in 1962; this was followed by the publication of *Tai-Pan: A Novel of Hong Kong* in 1966 and *Shogun* in 1975. Both *Tai-Pan* and *Shogun* were immediately successful, garnering praise for their minutely detailed, exotic settings and compelling plots while establishing Clavell as one of the most skilled and widely read creators of adventure fiction; this reputation was enhanced in 1980 by the broadcast of the *Shogun* miniseries, which attracted 120 million viewers. Clavell's subsequent novels, *Noble House: A Novel of Contemporary Hong Kong,* and *James Clavell's Whirlwind*—a novel about the dramatic events in Iran following the overthrow of the Shah in 1979—were also well-received, yet neither attained the level of popularity of *Shogun.*

OBITUARIES AND OTHER SOURCES:

BOOKS

The Writers Directory: 1992-1994, St. James Press, 1991.

PERIODICALS

New York Times, September 8, 1994, p. D19.
Times (London), September 9, 1994, p. 21.
Washington Post, September 8, 1994, p. D4.

*   *   *

CLEMO, Jack
  See CLEMO, Reginald John

*   *   *

CLEMO, Reginald John   1916-1994
  (Jack Clemo)

OBITUARY NOTICE—See index for *CA* sketch: Born March 11, 1916, in Goonamarris, England; died July 25, 1994, in Weymouth, England. Poet. Self-educated, and, from his late thirties, deaf and blind,

Clemo achieved acclaim for his highly personal mystical poetry. His early works reflect the influence of his strong Calvinist beliefs and the harshness of the landscape in his native Cornwall, while later poems, written after his marriage in 1968, display broader concerns and a less doctrinaire metaphysical approach. Among Clemo's writings are several poetry collections; two novels, *Wilding Graft* and *The Shadowed Bed;* a collection of theological essays titled *The Invading Gospel;* and two volumes of autobiography, *Confessions of a Rebel* and *The Marriage of A Rebel: A Mystical Erotic Quest.* His later works include *A Different Drummer,* published in 1986, and *Selected Poems,* published in 1988.

OBITUARIES AND OTHER SOURCES:

BOOKS

The Writers Directory: 1992-1994, St. James Press, 1991.

PERIODICALS

Times (London), July 26, 1994, p. 17.

*   *   *

CLEMONS, Walter, Jr.,   1929-1994

OBITUARY NOTICE—See index for *CA* sketch: Born November 14, 1929 in Houston, TX; died from complications of diabetes, July 6, 1994, in Long Island City, NY. Critic and author. Clemons was best known for his work as a reviewer for *Newsweek* and the *New York Times.* After earning his bachelor's degree in English with highest honors at Princeton University and studying at Oxford University as a Rhodes scholar, he became a freelance writer. In 1959 he published a volume titled *The Poison Tree and Other Stories.* Later, Clemons worked as an editor for McGraw-Hill, and from 1968 to 1971 he served as editor of the *New York Times Book Review.*

OBITUARIES AND OTHER SOURCES:

BOOKS

Who's Who in America, 47th edition, Marquis, 1992.

PERIODICALS

Chicago Tribune, July 10, 1994, sec. 2, p. 6.
New York Times, July 7, 1994, p. D19.
Washington Post, July 10, 1994, p. B7.

CLOUSER, Roy A.   1937-

PERSONAL: Born December 20, 1937, in Philadelphia, PA; son of Roy F. (in sales) and Aida (a homemaker; maiden name, Tomasulo) Clouser; married Anita Briguglio (an administrative assistant), May 4, 1985; children: John, Ruth Clouser Iorio, Philip; stepchildren: Geoffrey Young, Evan Young. Education: Gordon College, B.A. (summa cum laude), 1961; Reformed Episcopal Seminary, B.D. (summa cum laude), 1962; graduate study at Harvard University, 1961-62; University of Pennsylvania, M.A., 1965, Ph.D., 1972; attended Free University of Amsterdam, 1967 and 1971.

ADDRESSES: Home—204 Bradley Ave., Haddonfield, NJ 08033. Office—Department of Philosophy and Religion, Trenton State College, P.O. Box 4700, Trenton, NJ 08650-4700.

CAREER: Rutgers University, New Brunswick, NJ, instructor in symbolic logic, 1965-66; La Salle College, Philadelphia, PA, instructor in philosophy, 1966-68; Trenton State College, Trenton, NJ, professor of philosophy and religion, 1968—, department head, 1979-82 and 1985-86; writer. Staley Distinguished Christian Scholar Lecture Foundation, fellow. Assistant pastor of a Lutheran church in Haddonfield, NJ. Singer with Haddonfield Symphony Chorale and Pennsylvania Ballet Chorus; trombonist for Haddonfield Symphony and Haddonfield Brass Quintette.

MEMBER: American Philosophical Association, Society of Christian Philosophers, American Academy of Religion, American Scientific Affiliation (member of New York and New Jersey regional council, 1992—), Association for Public Justice (member of board of directors, 1991—), Association for Calvinist Philosophy (Netherlands).

AWARDS, HONORS: Grants from Institute for Advanced Christian Studies, 1975, and Andreas Foundation, 1983.

WRITINGS:

The Myth of Religious Neutrality: An Essay on the Hidden Role of Religious Belief in Theories, University of Notre Dame Press, 1991.

Contributor to books, including Rationality in the Calvinian Tradition, edited by Hart, Vander Hoeven, and Wolterstorff, University Press of America, 1983. Contributor of articles and reviews to academic journals. Member of editorial board, Journal for Christian Scholarship, 1988.

WORK IN PROGRESS: Religious Experience and Belief in God.

SIDELIGHTS: Roy A. Clouser told CA: "The central claim of The Myth of Religious Neutrality: An Essay on the Hidden Role of Religious Belief in Theories is that all abstract theories—both philosophical and scientific—are unavoidably controlled by some religious belief. This claim is explained to mean that religious belief cannot fail to function as a presupposition to theories, internally regulating them so that the contents of theories differ relative to the content of the religious belief they presuppose.

"This position is based on the work of the contemporary Dutch Calvinist philosopher Herman Dooyeweerd. My exposition includes a reformulation and defense of his critique of theory-making, and of his program for theorizing with belief in God as the internal controlling presupposition for theories in philosophy and the sciences. This program is contrasted to the prevailing approach which sees the relation of faith to theories largely as a matter of merely externally harmonizing them."

Clouser added: "My work in progress is about the epistemic status of belief in God, and I side with the 'non-evidentialists' in the current debate on this topic. The book begins with an examination of the phenomenon of religious experience and finds the common core of all its types to be that of direct, non-inferential truth recognition. This is followed by a phenomenological analysis of the experience of knowing something self-evidently. Some current definitions of self-evidency are examined or corrected in the light of the analysis. Once corrected, however, it becomes clear that the core of both religious experience and the experience of self-evidency are the same, so that the claims of each have the same epistemic warrant. The appeal to self-evidency is then defended as unavoidable (contrary to pragmatist claims), reliable though not infallible, and as the only ground for many important beliefs, including the belief in God."

*   *   *

COATES, Charles (K.)   1929-

PERSONAL: Born December 13, 1929, in Orange, NJ; son of Charles B. (a journalist and public relations consultant) and Rose (an editor and homemaker; maiden name, Kudner) Coates; married Elinor Lindsay (a writer and technical editor), September 6, 1958; children: Lindsay Coates Patterson, Charles W., Elinor Coates-Gersing. Education: University of Virginia, B.A., 1951; graduate study at New York University, 1951-52; attended University of Madrid, 1954-55. *Politics:* Democrat. *Religion:* Episcopalian.

ADDRESSES: Home—P.O. Box 1378, Tijeras, NM 87059. *Office*—Department of Communication and Journalism, University of New Mexico, Albuquerque, NM 87131.

CAREER: Nashville Tennesseean, Nashville, TN, reporter and editor, 1956-61; National Broadcasting Company (NBC), New York City, writer, editor, and producer of *NBC News,* 1961-72, 1975, 1980, and 1981, including work for *The Huntley-Brinkley Report;* University of New Mexico, Albuquerque, associate professor, 1972—.

MEMBER: Radio Television News Directors Association.

AWARDS, HONORS: Shared Emmy Award, 1969, for producing a segment of *The Huntley-Brinkley Report*'s 1968-69 coverage of hunger in the United States.

WRITINGS:

The Professional's TV News Handbook, Bonus Books (Chicago), 1994.

WORK IN PROGRESS: What Reporters (and Journalism Students) Need to Know (tentative title).

SIDELIGHTS: Charles Coates told *CA:* "I have spent most of my adult life in journalism. It is important to me, and that is why I wrote my book. It would be sheer vanity, however, to claim many virtues for a simple 'how-to' book for students, fledgling broadcast journalists, and (with luck) a few general readers. Still, if this volume can be said to have an underlying message, it is that technology and 'hype' are leading broadcast journalism into trouble. Too many practitioners are obsessed with what technology enables them to do. They are confusing flashy television with journalism and forgetting the common-sense notion that absolutely nothing is more important than carefully chosen words, fundamental fairness, and straightforward presentation."

* * *

COHEN, Judith Love 1933-

PERSONAL: Born August 16, 1933, in Brooklyn, NY; daughter of Maurice Bernard (a soft drink manufacturer) and Sarah (a homemaker; maiden name, Roisman) Cohen; married Bernard Siegel (divorced, 1965); married Thomas W. Black, January 20, 1965 (divorced, 1980); married David Katz (a teacher), February 20, 1981; children: (first marriage) Neil G., Howard K., Constance Rachel; (second marriage) T. Jack. *Education:* Attended Brooklyn College, 1950-52; University of Southern California, B.S., 1957, M.S., 1962; University of California, Los Angeles, M.E., 1982. *Politics:* Conservative. *Religion:* Jewish.

ADDRESSES: Office—c/o Cascade Pass, 10734 Jefferson Blvd., No. 235, Culver City, CA 90230.

CAREER: TRW-Aerospace, Redondo Beach, CA, project manager, 1959-90; Command Systems Group-Aerospace, Torrance, CA, project manager, 1990-92; freelance consulting engineer, 1993—; writer.

MEMBER: Society of Women Engineers (chair of Los Angeles section), Los Angeles Technical Societies Council (secretary), Tau Beta Pi, Eta Kappa Nu.

AWARDS, HONORS: Outstanding Engineer award, Institute for the Advancement of Engineering, 1977; certificate of recognition, National Aeronautics and Space Administration (NASA), 1991, for contributions made to the Hubble Space Telescope Program.

WRITINGS:

A Passover to Remember (play), first produced at Act One Stage, Los Angeles, CA, 1985.
You Can Be a Woman Engineer, Cascade Pass, 1991.
(With Margot Siegel) *You Can Be a Woman Architect,* Cascade Pass, 1992.
(With Flo McAlary) *You Can Be a Woman Marine Biologist,* illustrated by David A. Katz, Cascade Pass, 1992.
(With Betsy Bryan) *You Can Be a Woman Egyptologist,* illustrated by Katz, Cascade Pass, 1993.
(With Diane Gabriel) *You Can Be a Woman Paleontologist,* illustrated by Katz, Cascade Pass, 1993.
(With Valerie Thompson) *You Can Be a Woman Zoologist,* illustrated by Katz, Cascade Pass, 1993.

Also contributor of a monthly column to *Engineer of California* magazine, 1977—. Many of Cohen's books are available in Spanish.

WORK IN PROGRESS: Life after Aerospace; Starting Your Own Business; What Makes a Good Marriage;

(with Sharon Franks) *You Can Be an Oceanographer.*

BIOGRAPHICAL/CRITICAL SOURCES:

PERIODICALS

Science Books and Films, May, 1992.

* * *

COHEN, Richard M(artin) 1941-

PERSONAL: Born February 6, 1941, in New York, NY; son of Harry Louis and Pearl (Rosenberg) Cohen; married Barbara Stubbs, May 3, 1969; children: Alexander Prescott. *Education:* New York University, B.S. 1967; Columbia University, M.S., 1968.

ADDRESSES: Home—2617 Woodley Place NW, Washington, DC 20008. *Office—Washington Post,* 1150 15th St. NW, Washington, DC 20071.

CAREER: United Press International, reporter, 1967-68; *Washington Post,* Washington, DC, general assignment reporter, 1968-76, syndicated columnist, 1976—; author.

WRITINGS:

(With Jules Witcover) *A Heartbeat Away: The Investigation and Resignation of Vice President Spiro T. Agnew,* Viking, 1974.

SIDELIGHTS: In 1973 *Washington Post* reporter Richard M. Cohen was assigned to cover a breaking story on corruption charges against then-vice president Spiro T. Agnew. At the time, the White House beat was a hotbed of intrigue for journalists—Republican Richard M. Nixon had just taken the oath for his second consecutive presidential term, yet several of his top aides were being investigated regarding a break-in months before at Democratic headquarters at the Washington Watergate Hotel. Over the course of the next eighteen months, it became increasingly clear that the White House had obstructed justice in attempting to cover up the break-in; Nixon eventually resigned in August of 1974 as motions for an impeachment hearing against him were underway. In the midst of these scandals, it was discovered by the Maryland attorney general's office that vice president Agnew had taken kickbacks for years while an officeholder in that state, and that the bribery had continued when he entered the White House in 1969. Cohen's *Washington Post* coverage of this affair led to his collaboration with Jules Witcover on *A Heartbeat Away: The*

Investigation and Resignation of Vice President Spiro T. Agnew, a 1974 look at the second-in-command's very public fall from grace.

Cohen and Witcover—also a *Washington Post* reporter—examine the personal and political sides of Agnew and the ease with which the corruption began and then snowballed. They chronicle his rise—from an ambitious Maryland lawyer who initially became involved in local civic clubs in order to drum up business to a powerful Baltimore-area regional executive and then finally governor of Maryland. The Baltimore business community was rife with ardent supporters of the tough-talking and seemingly upright Republican. Agnew had long received lavish gifts and other perks from other conservatives who were glad to see him in office. Most of the 1973 corruption charges against Agnew stemmed from his stint as a Baltimore county executive, during which he asked for and received kickbacks from a plethora of firms. The companies, primarily engineering and architectural contractors, had won lucrative state jobs, then "kicked back" to Agnew usually five percent of the amount they had received from the state coffers for their work.

In *A Heartbeat Away,* Cohen and Witcover describe how Agnew grew increasingly reliant on the tax-free cash to supplement his income while his lifestyle escalated accordingly. The bribes continued when he took the governor's office and after Nixon's successful 1968 election that made Agnew vice president; unmarked envelopes filled with as much as $10,000 were hand-delivered to his office in the White House. *A Heartbeat Away* chronicles the investigation of the second-in-command and the trail of subpoenas, diaries, and deals that led to official charges against Agnew in August of 1973. The vice president denied any wrongdoing and unequivocally stated his refusal to resign. The authors analyze the initial official and public reactions to the scandal while also examining its wider implications. During this period, Nixon was under extreme stress due to the Watergate burglary investigation and it was feared that he might succumb to a heart attack or stroke—a disaster that would leave Agnew in charge. Top Republican and Democratic power-brokers in Washington were fearful of the shameful political ramifications if the nation's chief executive was under investigation for bribery. With this in mind, prosecutors managed to strike a deal favorable to all parties—Agnew pleaded *no lo contendre* or "no contest" to one count of tax evasion, paid a $10,000 fine, and resigned in October of 1973.

Cohen and Witcover construct a narrative that incorporates all the key players involved, including Attorney General Elliot Richardson and Walter Hoffmann, the United States District Court judge who sentenced Agnew. *A Heartbeat Away,* in its final chapter, analyzes the reasons for and consequences of the deal during this period in American politics. When Cohen and Witcover's book was published in the spring of 1974, Nixon was still in office and cynics assumed that the nation's leader would be let off the hook in a similarly lenient fashion for his wrongdoings. The tome joined a legion of books that year both by and about the main figures in the Washington scandals. *Washington Post Book World* reviewer Fred Graham contended that Cohen and Witcover's "narrative is fuller than the rules of evidence would have permitted legal proceedings to be" had Agnew actually gone to trial to fight the charges publicly. In a review of *A Heartbeat Away* for the *New York Times Book Review,* Theo Lippman, Jr. deemed it "a richly detailed and fascinating account of the familiar story," and one that "reads like a detective novel. It is so well researched and thorough I wonder if even the memoirs of the principals will provide much new of significance."

BIOGRAPHICAL/CRITICAL SOURCES:

PERIODICALS

New Republic, April 27, 1974, p. 23.
New Yorker, June 3, 1974, p. 110.
New York Times Book Review, June 23, 1974, p. 22; December 1, 1974, p. 78.
Washington Post Book World, April 28, 1974, p. 1; October 20, 1974, p. 4.*

*　　　*　　　*

COLE, Robert　1939-

PERSONAL: Born August 24, 1939, in Harper, KS; son of Charles Edgar (a farmer) and Olive Gertrude (a teacher; maiden name, Columber) Cole; married first wife, Glenda, August 9, 1963 (divorced); married Ilona Jappinen (a professor), September 14, 1990; children: Teresa Cole-Das. *Education:* University of Ottawa, B.A., 1961; Kansas State University, M.A., 1967; Claremont Graduate School, Ph.D., 1970. *Politics:* Liberal Democrat. *Religion:* Episcopalian. *Avocational interests:* Skiing, singing, cooking.

ADDRESSES: Home—999 Sumac Dr., Logan UT 84321. *Office*—Department of History, Utah State University, Logan, UT 84322-0710.

CAREER: Utah State University, Logan, professor of history, 1970—.

MEMBER: North American Conference on British Studies (past president).

WRITINGS:

(Editor) *The Dissenting Tradition,* Ohio University Press, 1975.
A Traveller's History of France, Windrush Press, 1988, 3rd edition, 1994.
Britain and the War of Words in Neutral Europe, 1939-45, Macmillan, 1990.
A. J. P. Taylor: The Traitor within the Gates, Macmillan, 1993.
A Traveller's History of Paris, Windrush Press, 1994.
Twentieth-Century Political and War Propaganda: An Annotated Bibliography, Scarecrow, 1995.

WORK IN PROGRESS: Research on Anglo-American propaganda in neutral Ireland, 1939-1945.

SIDELIGHTS: Robert Cole told *CA:* "Writing has many venues. Mine is historical, for the most part, including a short story 'Water Music,' a tongue-in-cheek version of the first performance of the G. F. Handel composition on a barge in the Thames. Otherwise, I have written serious history and popular history such as the travelers' histories. The serious works are the sort of archive-based monographs that professional historians write as part of their jobs. *France* and *Paris,* on the other hand, were a labor of love—general histories of one of my two favorite countries and cities, which required the integration of enormous amounts of detail into readable and interpretive summaries. *Paris* has been particularly well received, I am happy to say.

"Students are usually perplexed over how to write history. It seems so obvious when they read what a historian has written; how it is done is another matter. The answer is that students must find their own way. What they put on paper has to come from their own perceptions of what they have found and what it means—and, of course, they have to find their own styles. There is, as A. J. P. Taylor once put it, 'no reason why history can't be written so that someone wants to read it.' That is what I have tried to do in my work. If any single historical writer has been my mentor, at least in terms of style, it has been Taylor.

"I started out to be an artist; at least, I majored in art at university. Looking back at what survives of my early efforts, I do not expect the Guggenheim to come knocking at my door. In any case, I was much better at art history than at painting or drawing. Some of this came from my father, who seemed always to see things in the perspective of the passage of time, and who was also an avid reader. A Kansas farmer, he would sometimes arrive late in the fields because he could not tear himself away from a magazine article he had started over breakfast. I inherited his instincts in this regard, and that, together with a preference for historical novels over anything else and the enjoyment of expressing myself on paper, turned me into a professional historian. I have never regretted it for a moment."

*   *   *

COOK, Robert William Arthur   1931-1994
(Robin Cook, Derek Raymond)

OBITUARY NOTICE—See index for *CA* sketch: Born June 12, 1931, in London, England; died of cancer, July 30, 1994, in London, England. Mystery writer. After leaving school at the age of seventeen, Cook worked at a variety of jobs which sometimes involved illegal activities, and he used these experiences as the basis for his darkly satirical crime novels. Cook later began using the pseudonym Derek Raymond to distinguish himself from the popular American writer Robin Cook, author of the novel *Coma.* Among his early works, written under the name Robin Cook, are *The Crust on Its Uppers* and *The Legacy of the Stiff Upper Lip;* later works include *He Died with His Eyes Open* and *I Was Dora Suarez.*

OBITUARIES AND OTHER SOURCES:

BOOKS

The Writers Directory: 1992-1994, St. James Press, 1991.

PERIODICALS

Los Angeles Times, August 4, 1994, p. A16.
New York Times, August 3, 1994, p. D18.

*   *   *

COOK, Robin
See COOK, Robert William Arthur

*   *   *

COOPER, Jennifer Gough
See GOUGH-COOPER, Jennifer

COOPER, Lettice (Ulpha)   1897-1994

OBITUARY NOTICE—See index for *CA* sketch: Born September 3, 1897, in Eccles, England; died July 24, 1994, in Coltishall, England. Writer. Cooper first gained popularity as a novelist in 1925 with the publication of *The Lighted Room,* and her subsequent works of the 1920s and 1930s were well-received by critics and the public, praised for their stylistic simplicity and perceptive characterizations. Later, during the 1960s, she wrote a series of successful children's books, and in the 1980s her early works became the focus of renewed interest when they were reissued by her publisher. Cooper was also active in a variety of professional and social causes—she was a member of both PEN and the Writer's Action Group—and many of her works reflect her liberal political ideals. Her writings include the novels *National Provincial, Fenny, Snow and Roses,* and *Unusual Behavior,* as well as children's biographies of Queen Victoria, Florence Nightingale, and Edgar Allan Poe.

OBITUARIES AND OTHER SOURCES:

BOOKS

The Writers Directory: 1992-1994, St. James Press, 1991.

PERIODICALS

Times (London), July 26, 1994, p. 17.

*   *   *

COPENHAVER, John D., Jr.   1949-

PERSONAL: Born March 4, 1949, in Roanoke, VA; son of John D. (a lawyer) and Mary Glenn (a homemaker; maiden name, Stone) Copenhaver; married Marsha A. Childs (a nurse and licensed professional counselor); children: Thomas C. *Education:* Washington and Lee University, B.A., 1971; Fuller Theological Seminary, M.Div., 1977; Shalem Institute of Spiritual Formation, Certificate, 1982; Catholic University of America, M.A., 1982, Ph.D., 1986; postdoctoral study at University of Virginia, 1994-95. *Politics:* "Democrat/green/pacifist." *Religion:* "United Methodist/Quaker." *Avocational interests:* Running, hiking, photography.

ADDRESSES: Home—215 Laurel Hill Dr., Stephens City, VA 22655. *Office*—Department of Religion, Shenandoah University, 1460 University Dr., Winchester, VA 22601-1595.

CAREER: Kings Canyon National Park, student pastor, 1975; pastor of United Methodist churches in Virginia, 1977-80; Harrisonburg Area Wesley Foundation, campus minister for four colleges, including James Madison University, 1981-83; pastor of United Methodist church in Salem, VA, 1983-87; Shenandoah University, Winchester, VA, chaplain, 1987-89, assistant professor, 1987-92, associate professor of religion, 1992—, head of Department of Religion and Philosophy, 1989. Shenandoah Peace Coalition, cofounder, 1978, coordinator, 1978—. *Military service:* U.S. Army Reserve; became lieutenant.

MEMBER: Spiritual Directors International, American Academy of Religion, Society for the Study of Christian Spirituality, Association for Religion and Intellectual Life, Disciplined Order of Christ, Fellowship of Reconciliation, Methodists United for Peace and Justice (member of national board of directors, 1989-92), Theta Alpha Kappa (member of board of directors, 1992-94), Torch Club.

AWARDS, HONORS: Coolidge fellow, Association for Religion and Intellectual Life, 1990; Exemplary Teaching Award, Board of Higher Education of the United Methodist Church, 1992; Mellon Appalachian fellow, University of Kentucky, 1994-95; grant from Elizabeth Ann Bogert Fund for the Study and Practice of Christian Mysticism.

WRITINGS:

Prayerful Responsibility: Prayer and Social Responsibility in the Religious Thought of Douglas Steere, University Press of America, 1992.

Contributor to periodicals.

WORK IN PROGRESS: The Human Spirit and Spirituality, a book that seeks to explore the interface between psychology and spirituality, and theological anthropology as it is applied to the emerging academic discipline of Christian spirituality.

SIDELIGHTS: John D. Copenhaver, Jr. told *CA:* "As one who has embraced the Christian contemplative tradition, I write and do research as a response to divine grace. Writing is becoming an increasingly important part of my Christian vocation. This presents a problem, however, because writing is extremely laborious for me. I remember numerous occasions when I spent several hours working on a single sentence in my doctoral dissertation. In contrast, I read that Thomas Merton's fingers flew over the keyboard and that he sustained this pace for long periods. When I finish a sentence, I feel it is time for a coffee break!

"I am writing this as I begin a sabbatical to work on the most ambitious writing project of my career. I hope to find a way of writing that expresses the grace and clarity I find in the reality of God and that also deepens my awareness of the presence of God. If so, I believe my work will be doubly useful.

"My life has been shaped by my experiences in the late sixties and early seventies. Along with my contemporaries in college, I was fascinated by the exotic spirituality of the Eastern religions, especially Hinduism, Buddhism, and Taoism. After an extended time of reading and exploration in these traditions, I still felt spiritually empty. Returning to the Christian tradition, which I had rejected just a few years before, I experienced a conversion that reoriented my entire life. Nevertheless, I found little in conventional congregational life that responded to my deep spiritual hunger. It wasn't until I discovered the Christian contemplative tradition that I found my home.

"I sense that part of my vocation is to explore this tradition and make it more accessible to Christians (especially Protestants) in the United States. Too often, I find my contemporaries turning to the East as if it was the sole source for spiritual wisdom. In many cases, they are completely ignorant of the Christian contemplative tradition. Through my teaching and writing, I seek to acquaint others with these rich spiritual resources.

"While embracing contemplative Christianity, I don't want a spirituality divorced from the pressing social issues of our time. As a pacifist, I found the classical Quaker approach attractive. I wrote my doctoral dissertation on the integration of prayer and social responsibility in the religious thought of Douglas Steere, one of the leading Quaker thinkers of this century and a pioneer in ecumenical spirituality. In both his life and thought, Steere found a way to unite prayer and social responsibility that was mutually enriching and mutually clarifying. In a more liturgical fashion, I seek this same integration in my life and thought.

"My current project is titled *The Human Spirit and Spirituality.* In it I will seek to recover a neglected (and at one time rejected) aspect of Christian theological anthropology. The apostle Paul adopted the three-dimensional wholistic anthropology of the Hebrew tradition. The human person was a unity of body, soul, and spirit. In the early church's fight with Gnostic dualism, it abandoned spirit as an essential dimension of the human being because, in dualism, spirit mediated between the realms of matter and soul. This rejection may have served the church in its battle with Gnosticism, but it impoverished the later Christian tradition. Once the discipline of psychology had taken over the psyche, there was little left for religion in the human person. In my project, I will seek to recover the biblical meaning of human spirit, demonstrate that this understanding has been recovered by several twentieth-century theologians (Niebuhr, Tillich, and Rahner), enrich this recovery by drawing on the feminist emphasis on an embodied spirituality, and explore the implications of a renewed understanding of human spirit.

"I hope this work will assist the emerging academic discipline of Christian spirituality in its articulation of its method and purpose. More importantly, I hope it well help those who read it to recover an appreciation of the spiritual dimension of their beings."

*   *   *

CORBIN, Alain   1936-

PERSONAL: Born January 12, 1936, in Courtomer, France; son of Antoine (a physician) and Colette (Brune) Corbin; married Annie Lagorce (a professor), September 9, 1963; children: Philippe, Benoit. *Education:* University of Caen, B.A., M.A., 1959, Ph.D., 1968, Ph.D., 1973.

ADDRESSES: Home—3 rue Chapon, Paris, France 75003. *Office*—Universite Paris I, Pantheon-Sorbonne, 17 rue de la Sorbonne, Paris, France 75005.

CAREER: University of Limoges, assistant lecturer, 1968-69; University of Tours, senior lecturer, 1969-72, assistant professor, 1973-85, professor of history, 1985-86; Universite Paris I, Pantheon-Sorbonne, professor of history, 1987—; Institut Universitaire de France, professor of history, 1992.

MEMBER: Societe d'Histoire de la Revolution de 1848 et des Revolutions du XIX siecle (president).

WRITINGS:

The Foul and the Fragrant: Odor and the French Social Imagination, translation by Miriam L. Kochan with Roy Porter and Christopher Prendergast, Harvard University Press, 1986.

(With Michelle Perrot) *A History of Private Life,* Volume 4: *From the Fires of Revolution to the Great War,* edited by G. Duby, Harvard University Press, 1990.

Le Village des Cannibales, Aubier, 1990, translation by Arthur Goldhammer published as *The Village of Cannibals: Rage and Murder in France, 1870,* Polity Press, 1991.

Women for Hire: Prostitution and Sexuality in France after 1850, translation by Alan Sheridan, Harvard University Press, 1992.

WORK IN PROGRESS: Research on a cultural history of time.

SIDELIGHTS: Alain Corbin, a history professor at the Sorbonne in Paris, has focused attention on several topics not often given scholarly scrutiny, notably the social histories of odors and of prostitution in nineteenth-century France published respectively as *The Foul and the Fragrant: Odor and the French Social Imagination* and *Women for Hire: Prostitution and Sexuality in France after 1850.*

Corbin posits in *The Foul and the Fragrant* that in the period between 1760 and 1880, the French—especially the middle class—became increasingly interested in the sense of smell. According to Corbin, this new concern with odors and fragrances led to greater sanitary efforts, social stratification based on perceptions of odors, and the increased use of perfumes and disinfectants in the bourgeoisie household, among other effects. *The Foul and the Fragrant* was the subject of mixed reviews. Marjorie Williams, writing for the *Washington Post Book World,* called the book an "unapologetically rigorous work," remarking that the subject was "explored with elegance and erudition." Tony Judt, a reviewer for the *Times Literary Supplement,* noted the author's "copious research and wide learning. . . . The book abounds with interesting observations," he remarked; on the other hand, Judt faulted what he called Corbin's "shoddy reasoning," maintaining that "nowhere does Corbin ever construct an argument, a reason for believing that his examples and conclusion bear any relation to one another." Despite these perceived faults, Judt labeled *The Foul and the Fragrant* "an original and suggestive piece of writing." Joan W. Scott of the *New York Times Book Review* highly praised the work: "It is not only serious, but interesting and important; one of those studies that profoundly alter both our understanding of social life and of history."

Women for Hire is a detailed study, based on much archival work, of the politics and economics of prostitution, and the sexual desires of French men, from 1850 to the mid-twentieth century. James F. McMillan of the *Times Literary Supplement* called it a "pioneering work" and "a challenging and provocative book which remains the essential study in its field." Though McMillan went on to warn that Corbin is "not always convincing on his primary theme of male sexual privation and men's changing demands," he nevertheless concluded: "To contest some of his conclusions, however, is in no way to challenge the status of *Women for Hire:* Corbin amply demonstrates the centrality of prostitution to the social history of modern France."

Corbin drew on his knowledge of French cultural, political, and social history to produce *The Village of Cannibals,* published between *The Foul and the Fragrant* and *Women for Hire* in 1991. The book is a study of the torture and mob killing by peasants of a young noble at a cattle fair in central France in 1870. "Corbin did not discover this episode," noted Patrice Higonnet in the *Times Literary Supplement,* "but its bizarre specificity gives to this book an unusual immediacy and sharpness. His pages on the history of the Dordogne, its geography and economy, have a ring of keen authenticity." In the words of Robert Tombs of the *Times Literary Supplement,* Corbin "achieves here a brilliant *tour de force,* a model of history as practiced in France in the 1990s, with its stress on cultural representations: symbol, ritual, gesture, rumour, myth."

BIOGRAPHICAL/CRITICAL SOURCES:

PERIODICALS

Globe and Mail (Toronto), July 2, 1988.
New York Times Book Review, November 2, 1986, pp. 11-12; July 16, 1992, pp. 31-34.
Times Literary Supplement, April 24, 1987, p. 430; September 28-October 4, 1990, p. 1029; December 7-13, 1990, p. 1317; October 16, 1992, p. 11.
Washington Post Book World, January 11, 1987, p. 10.

*   *   *

CORBIN, Jane 1954-

PERSONAL: Born July 16, 1954, in Exeter, Devon, England; daughter of Aubrey and Olive Corbin; married John Maples (a politician), 1987; children: Tom, Rose. *Education:* King's College, London, B.A. (with honors). *Religion:* Church of England.

ADDRESSES: Office—British Broadcasting Corp.,

201 Wood Ln., London W12, England. *Agent*—Bill Hamilton, A. M. Heath and Co. Ltd., 79 St. Martin's Ln., London WC2N 4AA, England.

CAREER: ITN-TV, foreign correspondent for *Channel 4 News,* c. 1983-88; British Broadcasting Corp., London, England, current affairs and investigative journalist for BBC-TV, senior foreign correspondent for the television program *Panorama,* c. 1988—, presenter of the live debate program *Behind the Headlines,* c. 1991—. Also worked for Thames Television and Granada Television.

AWARDS, HONORS: Rainier Award from Monte Carlo Television Festival, 1990, for film *The Poisoned Land, the Dying Sea;* Emmy Award nomination, best investigative journalist, American Academy of Television Arts and Sciences, 1992, for the news story "Saddam's Secret Arms Ring"; four awards for television journalism from Royal Television Society, including an award in 1994 for the story "The Norway Channel"; shortlisted for Louis Gelber Award, a Canadian prize for nonfiction.

WRITINGS:

The Norway Channel, Grove/Atlantic, 1994.

Contributor to periodicals in England and abroad.

SIDELIGHTS: Jane Corbin told *CA:* "For the past several years I have been the senior correspondent for *Panorama,* the BBC-TV prime-time flagship current affairs program. I have covered events in the former Soviet Union and Eastern Europe, including the fall of the Berlin Wall, an award-winning program on the legacy left by Chernobyl, and the environmental disaster of the Aral Sea. I also made a program examining the Red Army's role in the bloody quashing of rebellion in Azerbaijan and other outposts of the Soviet Empire.

"I was the first journalist in 1988 to travel widely inside Cambodia to report on the political and social trauma of the country a decade after Year Zero. I have also reported from South America and from the United States.

"During my time at *Panorama,* I have specialized in Middle East affairs. At the end of the Gulf War, I entered Kuwait with the first Allied troops and reported the first documentary from there just five days after liberation. Between 1989 and 1993 I made a series of four investigative programs on Iraq's project to develop weapons of mass destruction. This included 'Project Babylon: Saddam's Supergun' and an investigation into the Iraqi nuclear program, which proved remarkably accurate in the light of discoveries by the United Nations weapons teams.

"In 1993 I traveled to Iran to report on clandestine chemical, nuclear, and biological weapons programs and to look at the Islamic revolution fifteen years after Khomeni ousted the Shah. In September I achieved a world exclusive with the inside story of 'The Norway Channel,' which revealed how a small group of Norwegians, Israelis, and Palestinians had negotiated a secret Middle East peace accord.

"Much of my work has been shown in the United States, mainly on PBS-TV, on *Frontline* or *The MacNeil, Lehrer Report,* but also on ABC-TV's *Nightline.* My programs have also been broadcast on Australian, Canadian, and European broadcasting networks and in Japan. My work is regularly shown in Africa, the Far and Middle East on the BBC's World Service Television."

*   *   *

CORNELL, George W.   1920-1994

OBITUARY NOTICE—See index for *CA* sketch: Born July 21, 1994, in Weatherford, OK; died August 10, 1994, in Manhattan, NY. Reporter. Cornell was one of the most prominent American religion reporters. After graduating from the University of Oklahoma, he took a job with the Associated Press in New York, and beginning in 1951 he wrote a weekly feature titled "Religion Today," which was the first column on that subject to appear regularly in newspapers. Cornell was also the author of several book-length studies of religion, including *They Knew Jesus, The Way and Its Ways,* and *The Catholic Church in Transition.*

OBITUARIES AND OTHER SOURCES:

BOOKS

Who's Who in America, 47th edition, Marquis, 1992.

PERIODICALS

Chicago Tribune, August 14, 1994, sec. 2, p. 8.
Washington Post, August 12, 1994, p. B6.

*   *   *

COSGROVE, Denis (Edmund)   1948-

PERSONAL: Born May 3, 1948, in Liverpool, England; son of Peter (a bank employee) and Gwen (Mackrill) Cosgrove; married second wife, Carmen Mills (an acupuncturist), 1989; children: Emily, Isla. *Education:* St. Catherine's College, Oxford, B.A. (with honors), 1969, D.Phil., 1976; University of Toronto, M.A., 1970.

ADDRESSES: Home—70 Priory Park Rd., London NW6, England. *Office*—Department of Geography, Royal Holloway College, University of London, Egham, Surrey TW20 0EX, England.

CAREER: Oxford Polytechnic, Oxford, England, lecturer, 1972-75, senior lecturer, 1975-79, principal lecturer in geography, 1979-80; Loughborough University of Technology, Loughborough, England, lecturer, 1980-84, senior lecturer, 1984-88, reader in cultural geography, 1988-93; University of London, Royal Holloway College, London, England, professor of human geography, 1994—. Landscape Research Group Ltd., director, 1980-87. University of Toronto, visiting assistant professor, 1977-78; University of London, visiting lecturer, 1985-87; University of Texas at Austin, visiting associate professor, 1988-89; Cambridge University, visiting lecturer, 1992; University of Oregon, visiting professor, 1993. Council for National Academic Awards, member of Combined Studies Board, 1978-84, and Interfaculty Studies Board, 1980-86; Economic and Social Research Council, member of working party on post-graduate training guidelines for geography, 1990.

MEMBER: Institute of British Geographers (member of council, 1986-89), Association of American Geographers.

AWARDS, HONORS: Gladys Krieble Delmar fellow in the history and culture of Venice, 1981 and 1983; grants from British Academy, 1983, Nature-Environment Research Programme, 1985, and Royal Society, 1987 and 1988; Back Medal, Royal Geographical Society, 1988; grants from Landscape Research Group, 1989, Nuffield Foundation, 1990-91, and Commission of the European Communities.

WRITINGS:

Social Formation and Symbolic Landscape, Croom Helm (London), 1984.
(Editor with S. J. Daniels, and contributor) *The Iconography of Landscape: Essays on the Symbolic Representation, Design, and Use of Past Environments,* Cambridge University Press (Cambridge), 1988.
(Editor with G. E. Petts, and contributor) *Water, Engineering, and Landscape: Water Control*

and Landscape Transformation in the Modern Period, Belhaven Press (London), 1990.

The Palladian Landscape: Geographical Change and Its Cultural Representations in Sixteenth-Century Italy, Pennsylvania State University Press, 1993.

Contributor to books, including *Horizons in Human Geography,* edited by D. Gregory and R. Walford, Macmillan, 1989; *The Power of Place,* edited by J. Agnew and J. Duncan, Unwin & Hyman, 1989; and *Place, Culture, and Representation,* edited by J. Duncan and D. Ley, Routledge & Kegan Paul, 1993. Contributor of more than forty articles and reviews to geography and education journals. Founding co-editor, *Ecumene: A Geographical Journal of Environment, Culture, and Meaning,* 1993—.

WORK IN PROGRESS: Images of the Globe.

*   *   *

COTMAN, John Walton   1954-

PERSONAL: Born March 2, 1954, in Springfield, MA; son of John Daniel, Jr. (a chemist) and Barbara May (a hospital unit clerk; maiden name, Walton) Cotman; married Julia Ann Misplon (a microbiologist), May 22, 1993. *Education:* Attended University of Washington, Seattle, 1972-73; University of Colorado, Boulder, B.A. (with distinction), 1977; graduate study at Yale University, 1978-79; Boston University, M.A., 1987, Ph.D., 1992. *Politics:* Independent. *Religion:* None. *Avocational interests:* Hiking, fishing, photography.

ADDRESSES: Home—11903 Parklawn Place, No. 201, Rockville, MD 20852-5213. *Office*—Department of Political Science, Howard University, P.O. Box 849, Washington, DC 20059.

CAREER: Howard University, Washington, DC, instructor, 1990-91, assistant professor of political science, 1991—. American University, visiting assistant research professor, School of International Service, 1994—.

MEMBER: International Political Science Association, American Political Science Association, Caribbean Studies Association, Center for Cuban Studies, Latin American Studies Association, TransAfrica, Middle Atlantic Council of Latin American Studies, New England Council of Latin American Studies, Phi Beta Kappa.

AWARDS, HONORS: Fulbright grant for Grenada,

1988-89; fellow, Ford Foundation, 1994-95.

WRITINGS:

Birmingham, JFK, and the Civil Rights Act of 1963: Implications for Elite Theory, Peter Lang, 1989.
The Gorrion Tree: Cuba and the Grenada Revolution, Peter Lang, 1993.

Contributor to books, including *Cuba: New Ties to a New World,* edited by Donna Rich Kaplowitz, Lynne Rienner, 1993. Contributor to political science and Caribbean studies journals. Co-editor, *Forward Ever,* 1984-86; associate editor, *Government and Politics Newsletter,* 1992-94.

WORK IN PROGRESS: Research on Cuba-CARICOM relations since 1983.

*   *   *

COUSINEAU, Phil   1952-

PERSONAL: Born November 26, 1952, in Columbia, SC; son of Stanley (in public relations) and Rosemary (a florist; maiden name, La Chance) Cousineau. *Education:* University of Detroit, B.A. (cum laude), 1974.

ADDRESSES: Home—337 10th Ave., No. 5, San Francisco, CA 94118. *Agent*—Tim Seldes, Russell and Volkening, Inc., 50 West 29th St., New York, NY 10001.

CAREER: Writer, film director, film producer, and script consultant. Seminar leader/guest lecturer at the following institutions: American Film Institute, 1983-85; Mill Valley Film Festival, 1985; Film Arts Foundation, 1986; San Francisco State University, 1986—; University of London, 1987; Confluence, Paris, France, 1987; New York Open Center, 1988—; Empty Gate Zen Center, 1989; Center for Energetic Studies, 1989-90; Pasadena Asian Art Museum, 1989; San Francisco Jung Institute, 1989; University of California, Berkeley Extension, 1989-92; Interface, Boston, 1989—; University of California, Los Angeles, 1989—; Oasis Institute, Chicago, 1990; Seabourn Cruise Lines, 1990—; Festival Mythos, Philadelphia, 1991; California Institute of Integral Studies, 1992; and Long Beach State University, 1993—. Writer-in-residence, Shakespeare and Co. Bookstore, 1987. Co-director of film, *The Peyote Road,* 1993.

MEMBER: Film Arts Foundation, California Institute of Integral Studies, San Francisco Film Society, San Francisco Film Festival.

AWARDS, HONORS: National Educational Film and Video Festival Silver Apple Award, 1987, for *The Hero's Journey: The World of Joseph Campbell;* Academy Award nomination and San Francisco Jury Prize, 1990, for *Forever Activists: Stories from the Veterans of the Abraham Lincoln Brigade;* Best Video, American Indian Film Festival, Silver Telly Award, and National Educational Film Festival Gold Apple, 1991, all for *Wiping the Tears of Seven Generations;* Fallot Literary Award, National Association of Independent Publishers, for *Deadlines: A Rhapsody on a Theme of Famous Last Words,* 1992; Quality Paperback Book Club selection, *The Soul of the World,* 1993; Best Documentary, Great Plains Film Festival, Bronze Telly Award, Chicago Film Festival Silver Award, and Mill Valley Film Festival, 1993, all for *The Peyote Road;* fellow, California Institute of Integral Studies.

WRITINGS:

SCREENPLAYS

(Coauthor) *The 1932 Ford V8,* Silverado Productions, 1986.

(Coauthor) *The Presence of the Goddess,* Balcorman Films, 1987.

(Coauthor) *Eritrea: A Portrait of the Eritrean People,* Mill Valley Film Festival, Leningrad Film Festival, 1989.

(Coauthor and associate producer) *The Hero's Journey: The World of Joseph Campbell,* Mythology Ltd., 1987, published by Harper, 1990.

(Coauthor) *Forever Activists: Stories from the Veterans of the Abraham Lincoln Brigade,* Montell Films, 1990.

(Coauthor) *Wiping the Tears of Seven Generations,* Kifaru Productions, 1991.

The Peyote Road, Kifaru Productions, 1993.

Design Outlaws: On the Ecological Frontier (also see below), Knossus Project, 1994.

OTHER

(Editor and author of introduction) *The Hero's Journey: Joseph Campbell on His Life and Work,* Harper & Row, 1990.

Deadlines: A Rhapsody on a Theme of Famous Last Words, Sisyphus Press, 1991.

(With John Densmore; and editor) *Riders on the Storm: My Life with Jim Morrison,* Delacorte Press, 1991.

(Editor and author of introduction) *The Soul of the World: A Modern Book of Hours,* photographs by Eric Lawton, HarperSan Francisco, 1993.

(Editor and contributor) *Soul: Archaeology of the Spirit—Readings from Socrates to Ray Charles,* HarperSan Francisco, 1994.

(And editor) *Design Outlaws: On the Ecological Frontier,* Knossus Project, 1994.

Burning the Midnight Oil, Harper Collins, 1995.

The Book of Roads, Sisyphus Press, 1995.

Contributor to *Peace Prayers,* Harper, 1991; *To Be a Man: In Search of the Deep Masculine,* by Keith Thompson, J. P. Tarcher, 1991; and *Uses of Comparative Mythology,* Garland Press, 1992. Contributor of articles, reviews, and poetry to the *Los Angeles Times, Hungry Mind Review, Paris Magazine,* the *San Francisco Chronicle,* the *Oakland Tribune,* the *San Francisco Examiner, Wingspan,* the *Hollywood Scriptwriter, New Age Journal, Poetry U.S.A.,* National Arts Society Anthology, the *Plowman,* and *Cups Cafe Journal.*

WORK IN PROGRESS: Prayers at 3 A.M.; The Red Road to Sobriety (screenplay), for Kifaru Films.

SIDELIGHTS: Phil Cousineau told *CA:* "Since I began my professional career with a series of lectures and seminars at the American Film Institute in the early 1980s (with talks entitled 'Myth, Dreams, and the Movies'), I've been fascinated by synthesizing the classical wisdom traditions with popular culture and modern street realities."

BIOGRAPHICAL/CRITICAL SOURCES:

PERIODICALS

Publishers Weekly, April 13, 1990, p. 50.

*   *   *

COX, Gordon   1942-

PERSONAL: Born March 30, 1942, in Cwmcarn, Wales; married; wife's name, Sheila (an adult placement officer); children: Eustacia, Brendan. *Education:* Attended Royal Academy of Music, 1960-64; Memorial University of Newfoundland, M.A., 1976; University of Reading, Ph.D., 1991. *Religion:* Anglican. *Avocational interests:* Playing the organ, walking.

ADDRESSES: Home—18 New Road, Reading RG1 5JD, England.

CAREER: School teacher, 1964-80; University of Reading, Reading, England, lecturer in education, 1980—.

MEMBER: International Society for Music Education.

WRITINGS:

Folk Music in a Newfoundland Outport, National Museums of Canada (Ottawa), 1980.

A History of Music Education in England, 1872-1928, Scolar Press (Aldershot, England), 1993.

Contributor of articles on music education to academic journals, including *Lore and Language* and *Folk Music Journal.*

WORK IN PROGRESS: Life Histories of Music Teachers, a book, and *An Oral History of Music Education in England, 1872-1928,* a book.

SIDELIGHTS: Gordon Cox told *CA:* "My research focuses upon the functions of music making in communities, and the history of music education. My aim is to write a contemporary social history of music education through the perspectives of music teachers themselves."

*   *   *

CRABTREE, Adam   1938-

PERSONAL: Born December 30, 1938, in Bertha, MN; son of Glenn (a farmer) and Angeline (a teacher; maiden name, Delsing) Crabtree; married Joanne Hindley-Smith (a psychotherapist), March 6, 1976; children: Edward, Andrew. *Education:* St. John's University, Collegeville, MN, B.A., 1960; studied at St. John's Abbey and Seminary, 1964; University of Toronto, M.A., 1967; Open International University of Contemporary Medicine, Ph.D., 1993.

ADDRESSES: Home—Richmond Hill, Ontario, Canada. *Office*—316 Dupont St., Toronto, Ontario, Canada M5R 1V9.

CAREER: Psychotherapist in private practice, 1966—. Centre for Training in Psychotherapy, Toronto, Ontario, Canada, cofounder, 1986, training psychotherapist and lecturer, 1986—; founder and director of Willow Workshops; cofounder of Stress Analysis Consultants. Open International University, clinical teacher, 1993—; lecturer at St. John's University, Humber College, and McMaster University. Narrator of radio documentary series *The Enchanted Boundary,* CBC-Radio; *The Splitting of the Mind,* CBC-Radio; *Mysteries of the Mind,* CJRT-Radio; and *In Sickness and in Health,* CJRT-Radio; guest on radio and television programs throughout Canada. Former Benedictine monk and Roman Catholic priest.

MEMBER: International Society for the Study of Dissociation, Ontario Society of Psychotherapists (clinical member).

WRITINGS:

Multiple Man: Explorations in Possession and Multiple Personality, Holt, 1985.

Animal Magnetism, Early Hypnotism, and Psychical Research from 1766 to 1925: An Annotated Bibliography, Kraus International, 1988.

From Mesmer to Freud: Magnetic Sleep and the Roots of Psychological Healing, Kraus International, 1993.

Author of radio documentary series *The Enchanted Boundary,* CBC-Radio; *The Splitting of the Mind,* CBC-Radio; *Mysteries of the Mind,* CJRT-Radio; and *In Sickness and in Health,* CJRT-Radio. Work represented in anthologies, including *Split Minds/Split Brains,* edited by Jacques Quen, New York University Press, 1986; and *Handbook of the History of Psychiatry,* edited by John Gach and Edwin Wallace, Yale University Press. Contributor to psychology journals.

WORK IN PROGRESS: Entranced: Trances in Everyday Life; revising *Multiple Man.*

SIDELIGHTS: Adam Crabtree told *CA:* "In the 1960s I became a Benedictine monk and was ordained as a Roman Catholic priest. When I came to Toronto from Minnesota in 1965, I became involved with a group who formed a psychotherapeutic community. Although I came to Toronto to study philosophy, I put aside my academic work for some years to work as a psychotherapist. In 1980 I took up my academic pursuits again, concentrating on the history of hypnosis and psychology, and related areas such as parapsychology and dissociation.

"My first book was about multiple personality, possession, and other dissociative phenomena. There has been a continuous thread of interest running through my work and studies; it has to do with striving to understand the human psyche and how it functions in life. In particular, I want to make use of the windows into the internal workings of the psyche provided by the more unusual dissociative phenomena, such as multiple personality and possession.

"It was a peculiar thing for me to discover that I, who hated history with a passion in school, found myself relentlessly pursuing the history of these phenomena and the evolution of thinking in connection with them. That led to my annotated bibliography and eventually to *From Mesmer to Freud*. My next task is to try to make sense of the often contradictory ideas about the nature of trance."

* * *

CRAWFORD, T. Hugh 1956-

PERSONAL: Born August 31, 1956, in Woodstock, VA; son of William Burdette (a doctor) and Florence Marian (a nurse; maiden name, Nelson) Crawford; married Maria Brown Gregory, May 23, 1981; children: Thomas Nelson, Charles Gregory. *Education:* Virginia Military Institute, B.A., 1978; Claremont Graduate School, M.A., 1979; Duke University, Ph.D., 1988.

ADDRESSES: Office—Department of English, Virginia Military Institute, Lexington, VA 24450.

CAREER: Virginia Military Institute, Lexington, associate professor of English.

WRITINGS:

Modernism, Medicine, and William Carlos Williams, University of Oklahoma Press, 1993.

WORK IN PROGRESS: Rethinking Agency: Melville, Foucault, Latour.

* * *

CRAWLEY, Alan 1887-1975

PERSONAL: Born August 23, 1887, in Cobourg, Ontario, Canada; died July 28, 1975, in Cordova Bay, British Columbia, Canada; son of Charles James (a banker) and Maude (Buck) Crawley; married Jean Horn, 1915; children: David, Michael.

CAREER: Affiliated with Machray, Sharpe (a law firm and later an investment banking concern), Winnipeg, Manitoba, Canada, as a clerk, 1905 (admitted to the bar, 1911), and as an attorney, 1911-18; founding member of Community Players of Winnipeg, a community theater group, 1915-25; founding partner in law firm, 1918-33; editor and author.

WRITINGS:

Editor of the poetry journal *Contemporary Verse: A Canadian Quarterly,* 1941-52.

Crawley's correspondence is housed at Queen's University, Kingston, Ontario, and at the University of Toronto.

SIDELIGHTS: Alan Crawley is credited with furthering the early careers of a number of Canadian poets during his twelve-year editorship of the influential journal *Contemporary Verse: A Canadian Quarterly*. Crawley, born in 1887, lived in several provinces across Canada over the course of his life, and a good part of his adult years were spent as a lawyer in Winnipeg. In 1933, then in his forties, Crawley retired from the profession when an infection robbed him of his eyesight. With his wife, Jean, and their two children he relocated to Victoria, British Columbia.

Crawley's newfound hours of enforced leisure became increasingly taken up with literary matters, long a passion of his. His wife often read aloud to him, and he learned Braille to further increase his knowledge of contemporary writers. At a lecture on American poetry, Crawley became acquainted with a number of writers then active in the burgeoning literary scene in British Columbia. He soon became a regular fixture among the group, lecturing and giving readings in the area, and known as an enthusiastic supporter of modernism. The poets and other writers associated with this literary direction were interested in breaking away from some of the constraints and traditions that had kept Canadian poetry a few steps behind its British and American counterparts. When a group of like-minded western Canadian writers decided to start a literary journal, they invited Crawley to become its editor, and *Contemporary Verse: A Canadian Quarterly* was born.

The first issue appeared in 1941 and, from the start, Crawley tried to avoid the ideological infighting common to many forward-thinking artistic currents during this era. As editor he asserted in a manifesto statement that "the aims of CONTEMPORARY VERSE are simple and direct and seem worthy and worthwhile. These aims are to entice and stimulate the writing and reading of poetry and to provide means for its publication free from restraint of politics, prejudices and placations, and to keep open its pages to poetry that is sincere in theme and treatment and technique." Crawley, who tackled the business and editorial side of the publication with the help of the eyes of his wife and assistant editors, made the fourteen-page quarterly a respectable success early on. A section on *Contemporary Verse* in the *Oxford Companion to Canadian Literature* pointed out that the journal "played an important role at a time when there were few literary magazines in Canada. Crawley sought to maintain a high standard of writing, while keeping his pages open to poets of many inclinations."

Acclaimed Canadian writers such as Doris Ferne, Earle Birney, Dorothy Livesay, and P. K. Page were regular contributors to *Contemporary Verse*. Additionally—despite the difficulties his blindness sometimes presented—Crawley eagerly corresponded with less-established poets and offered encouragement and construction criticism. "A poem isn't a picture," he was quoted as saying in the *Dictionary of Literary Biography*. "It's a statement of an idea. . . . Make your language like your speech. Be brief, clearcut." The initial work of many outstanding Canadian poets, including Phyllis Webb, Malcolm Lowry, and Raymond Souster, debuted in *Contemporary Verse*. A dozen exciting years had wrought numerous changes upon the Canadian literary scene, however, and newer journals, centered in Toronto and other eastern cities, eventually took away some of the import and influence of *Contemporary Verse*. In 1952, after thirty-nine issues, the journal ceased publication. Crawley's stewardship of the journal was the subject of Joan McCullagh's 1976 book *Alan Crawley and "Contemporary Verse,"* a tome that appeared a year after his death at the age of eighty-seven. In an essay for the *Dictionary of Literary Biography*, W. H. New described Crawley as "a champion of the Canadian voice, and of its relevance to literary modernism . . . [and] one of the leading forces that reshaped Canadian poetry in the 1940s."

BIOGRAPHICAL/CRITICAL SOURCES:

BOOKS

Dictionary of Literary Biography, Volume 68: *Canadian Writers, 1920-1959,* Gale, 1988.
McCullagh, Joan, *Alan Crawley and "Contemporary Verse,"* University of British Columbia, 1976.
Oxford Companion to Canadian Literature, Oxford University Press, 1983.

PERIODICALS

Canadian Literature, winter, 1964, p. 33; autumn, 1967, p. 63; summer, 1969, p. 89.
Tamarack Review, spring, 1957, p. 55.*

*   *   *

CROMER, Alan (Herbert) 1935-

PERSONAL: Born August 15, 1935, in Chicago, IL; son of Abraham Bertram (in business) and Helen (in business; maiden name, Cohn) Cromer; married Marjorie Scheckman (died June 3, 1975); married Janet McIsaac (a psychotherapist), January 18, 1987. *Education:* University of Wisconsin—Madison, B.S., 1954; Cornell University, Ph.D., 1960. *Avocational interests:* Kayaking, walking, bicycling, travel.

ADDRESSES: Home—303 Lamartine St., Jamaica Plain, MA 02130. *Office*—Department of Physics, Northeastern University, Boston, MA 02115. *Agent*—Mark Joly, Scott Meredith Literary Agency, Inc., 845 Third Ave., New York, NY 10022.

CAREER: Harvard University, Cambridge, MA, research fellow, 1959-61; Northeastern University, Boston, MA, assistant professor, 1961-65, associate professor, 1965-70, professor of physics, 1970—. EduTech, Inc., founder, 1980, president, 1980-86.

MEMBER: American Association of Physics Teachers, American Association for the Advancement of Science, National Science Teachers Association, Phi Beta Kappa, Sigma Xi, Phi Kappa Phi.

WRITINGS:

(With Eugene Saletan) *Theoretical Mechanics,* Wiley, 1970.
Physics for the Life Sciences, 2nd edition, McGraw, 1977.
Physics in Science and Industry, McGraw, 1980.
Computer-Simulated Physics Experiments, with software, EduTech, 1980.
AstroLab, with software, EduTech, 1980.
Experiments in Physics, 3rd edition, Kendall/Hunt, 1984.
Uncommon Sense: The Heretical Nature of Science, Oxford University Press, 1993.
(With Christos Zahopoulos) *Sourcebook of Demonstrations, Activities, and Experiments* (laboratory manual), RonJon Publishing, 1994.
Experiments in Introductory Physics (laboratory manual), RonJon Publishing, 1994.

Contributor to books, including *Thinking Science for Education: The Case of Physics,* Pergamon, 1995. Contributor to magazines and newspapers, including *Education Week, Physics Teacher,* and *Skeptical Inquirer.*

WORK IN PROGRESS: Connected Knowledge: Science, Philosophy, and Education, a defense of science against its postmodern critics; working with Project Science Education Through Experiments and Demonstrations (SEED) and Project Retirees Enhancing Science Education Through Experiments and Demonstrations (RE-SEED) to assist middle school science teachers integrate mathematics and experimentation into their teaching of physical science.

SIDELIGHTS: Alan Cromer told *CA:* "I have been in love with science ever since my pediatrician first carried me into the laboratory next to his examining room. It was a magical place, with shelves of brown bottles, assorted glassware on a high, black table, and a bunsen burner, with which he bent and shaped the glass. I loved Doctor Moore and his laboratory, and I wanted to be a doctor like him, until a medical emergency dramatically demonstrated to me the difference between science and medicine.

"I was in bed, playing with a rubber safety button on my pajamas, when it came off in my hand. I realized at once that, by bending the button, I could easily stick it way up my nose. I didn't realize that it wouldn't be so easy to get it out. After a call to Doctor Moore, a terrified child was driven rapidly to downtown Chicago, where a security guard opened a deserted office building. There was Doctor Moore, friendly and cheerful, to remove the button. 'Here,' he said, 'take it in case you want to put it up your nose again.' All I could think was that, when I grew up, I didn't want to be called out in the middle of the night to take a button out of some stupid kid's nose!

"Science was a self-indulgent pleasure for me, and I pursued it with microscope and chemistry set at home. In school, my interests turned to theoretical physics. My first book was a graduate textbook in mechanics. The experience of writing it taught me that I loved writing and hated collaborating.

"The transition from textbook writer to trade book writer was very difficult. I had recently remarried and had no further ambition than to teach my courses and stay out of trouble. In this mood, I began to write for my own pleasure. Gradually I began to find my voice and the special insights I had to bring to some issues of science and education. From classroom teaching at an average university, I learned that ideas obvious to me (for instance, the limitations imposed by the natural order) are not part of the world view of average students. Perhaps from their religious upbringing, or from watching too much *Star Trek,* these people generally believe that anything is possible. Their difficulty in understanding physics was the starting point for my own insights into just how peculiar science is. The result was the book *Uncommon Sense: The Heretical Nature of Science.*

"During the writing of *Uncommon Sense,* I started a collaboration with colleagues on a middle-school science teacher enhancement program called Project SEED. I was paid to develop for teachers the kinds of experiments I enjoyed so much as a child. The work also enhanced my own knowledge of the educational system in the United States, giving me a last chapter for my book and a segue into the next one, *Connected Knowledge: Science, Philosophy, and Education.*

"*Connected Knowledge* goes more deeply into the structure of science, using simple middle-school science experiments as its examples. It is critical of postmodernism, which is having an alarming influence on our battered educational system. As I complained in *Uncommon Sense* about the poor science background of science teachers, I complain in *Connected Knowledge* about the poor philosophical roots of our education system. This carries me out of the elementary laboratory, into the world of quantum mechanics and sociology, as I try to define the boundary between science and storytelling."

*   *   *

CROSBIE, Lynn   1963-

PERSONAL: Born August 7, 1963, in Montreal, Quebec, Canada; daughter of Douglas James (a chartered accountant) and Heather (an accountant) Crosbie; common-law wife of Tony Burgess (a writer). *Education:* Attended Dawson College; York University, B.A., 1986, M.A., 1987; University of Toronto, Ph.D., 1995. *Politics:* "Left/feminist." *Religion:* "Non-denominational revisionist Christian." *Avocational interests:* Art, music, celebrities, love, science.

ADDRESSES: Home—Toronto, Ontario, Canada. *Office*—Coach House Press, 50 Prince Arthur Ave., Suite 107, Toronto, Ontario, Canada M5R 1B5.

CAREER: York University, Downsview, Ontario, Canada, director of a course on Canadian women writers, 1990-92, instructor, 1993-94; Coach House Press, Toronto, Ontario, director and editor, 1993—. Gives readings from her works.

AWARDS, HONORS: Canada Council grant.

WRITINGS:

True Confessions (poems), Pink Dog Press, 1988.
The Honeymoon Killers (poems), Lowlife, 1990.
Miss Pamela's Mercy (poems), Coach House Press, 1992.

(Editor) *The Girl Wants To* (anthology), Coach House Press, 1993.

VillainElle (poems), Coach House Press, 1994.

Author of "Pop Tart," a column in *This*, 1994—. Contributor of articles and poems to magazines, including *Fuse, What, Fireweed, Books in Canada, Tessera,* and *Alphabet City.*

WORK IN PROGRESS: Pearl, a volume of poems; research on themes in the poetry of Anne Sexton; research on infamous men.

SIDELIGHTS: Lynn Crosbie told *CA:* "I began writing when I was a teenage art student. At that time, I interfaced my poems with drawings and paintings. I have always been fascinated by pop culture, and my early poems were based on film and television.

"I began publishing and reading my work in the late 1980s and I compiled a series of dramatic monologues, *Miss Pamela's Mercy,* about famous and infamous women, including the Marchesa Casati, Farrah Fawcett, and Myra Hindley, the Monster of the Moors. Many of the poems in *Miss Pamela* are derived from tabloid and magazine stories, from visual images, and from the (imagined) lives of celebrities or sub-celebrities.

"*VillainElle* is also a collection of dramatic monologues, written from a female perspective with female speakers. These poems draw from a variety of sources, including the film *Saturday Night Fever, Titus Andronicus,* and Alice Cooper. These poems use more fictional narrators, as many of the narratives are explorations of moments, of incidents of desire and longing, and they are usually set in a disconcerting psycho/sexual context (for example, 'Nancy Drew's Theatre of Blood' is about female autoerotic hanging). My work with this collection led me to compile and edit *The Girl Wants To,* an anthology of women's representations of sex and the body. The dedication illustrates my participation within, and debt to, the challenging and critical work female artists are currently producing, with regard to the frank delineation of our bodies, desires, and sexual imaginations.

"My work has been very well received, but it seems unlikely I will ever be accepted in the mainstream— one reviewer recently sniffed, 'How could *anyone* create a poem from *Saturday Night Fever?*'. My work as a feminist, academic, and pop junkie informs my creative and prose work. My essays tend to focus on pop figures, from a third-wave feminist perspective, one that I associate with the eradication of dogma, binary thinking, and exclusion.

"I love too many writers to list and, while I don't suffer from anxiety of influence, it is hard to locate a small selection of influences. Underground female cartoonists, films, trashy novels, diverse writers have influenced me. Tabloids, celebrity biographies, the love of brutish men, the memories of my twenties (a period of mad and blissful chaos) and Kensington Market at night make me want to write. Feminist criticism also inspires me, and assures me that my project, to continue exploring my own and other women's experiences from a female perspective, is valuable and integral. The conflation of high and low culture in my work is also strategically important. The mind of the artist, as Eliot observed, 'is constantly amalgamating disparate experience.'"

*   *   *

CROWDER, George 1956-

PERSONAL: Born February 27, 1956, in Wellington, New Zealand. *Education:* Victoria University of Wellington, LL.B. (with honors), 1977, B.A. (with honors), 1981; Oxford University, D.Phil., 1988.

ADDRESSES: Home—Brooklyn, NY. *Office*—Department of Political Science, Bernard M. Baruch College of the City University of New York, 17 Lexington Ave., Box 333, New York, NY 10010.

CAREER: Department of Justice, Wellington, New Zealand, legal adviser, 1978-80; Oxford University, Oxford, England, tutor in political theory, 1985-90; California State University, Fullerton, lecturer in political science, 1991; Vytantas Magnus University, Kaunas, Lithuania, lecturer in political theory, 1992-93; Bernard M. Baruch College of the City University of New York, New York City, assistant professor of political science, 1993—. Hunter College of the City University of New York, assistant professor, 1993—.

MEMBER: American Philosophical Association, American Political Science Association.

AWARDS, HONORS: Commonwealth scholar, 1982-85.

WRITINGS:

Classical Anarchism: The Political Thought of Godwin, Proudhon, Bakunin, and Kropotkin, Oxford University Press (New York, NY), 1991.

CROWLEY, David 1966-

PERSONAL: Born May 29, 1966, in London, England. *Education:* Attended Brighton Polytechnic, 1984-87, and Royal College of Art, London, 1988-90.

ADDRESSES: Office—University of Brighton, 11 Pavilion Parade, Brighton BN2 1RA, England.

CAREER: University of Brighton, Brighton, England, lecturer, 1991—. University of Staffordshire, lecturer. Consultant to Fitzroy Dearborn's *Encyclopedia of Interior Design.*

MEMBER: Design History Society.

WRITINGS:

Victorian Style, Quintet, 1990.
National Style and Nation-State: Design in Poland from the Vernacular Revival to the International Style, Manchester University Press, 1992.

WORK IN PROGRESS: A book on the history of graphic design, with Paul Jobling; research on the late-nineteenth-century vernacular revival in architecture and applied arts in Central Europe.

*   *   *

CROWLEY-MILLING, Michael C. 1917-

PERSONAL: Born May 7, 1917, in Rhyl, North Wales; son of Thomas William (a lawyer) and Gillian (Chinnery) Crowley-Milling; married Gee Dickson, 1957. *Education:* St. John's College, Cambridge, B.A. (with honors), 1938, M.A., 1943. *Politics:* Conservative. *Religion:* "None." *Avocational interests:* Sailing, vintage cars.

ADDRESSES: Home—142 The Green, Worsley M28 2PA, England.

CAREER: Metropolitan Vickers Electrical Co. Ltd., Manchester, England, research engineer, 1938-66; Daresbury Nuclear Physics Laboratory, near Warrington, England, member of directorate, 1966-71; European Organization for Nuclear Research, Geneva, Switzerland, group leader to the director for the accelerator program, 1971-83. Holder of thirty British and foreign patents; consultant to laboratories in Europe and the United States.

MEMBER: Institute of Electrical Engineers (fellow).

AWARDS, HONORS: Companion, Order of St. Michael and St. George; Glazebrook Medal, Institute of Physics, 1981.

WRITINGS:

(Editor) *Accelerator Control Systems,* North-Holland Publishing, 1986.
(Editor) *Accelerator and Experimental Physics Control Systems,* North-Holland Publishing, 1990.
John Bertram Adams, Engineer Extraordinary: A Tribute, Gordon & Breach, (Langhorne, PA), 1993.

Contributor of more than forty articles to scientific journals.

WORK IN PROGRESS: An autobiography; a history of Alfa Romeo racing cars.

*   *   *

CUSHING, Peter (Wilton) 1913-1994

OBITUARY NOTICE—See index for *CA* sketch: Born May 26, 1913, in Kenley, England; died of cancer, August 11, 1994, in Canterbury, England. Actor and author. Cushing was best known for his roles in a series of horror films produced by the prolific Hammer studio, including *The Curse of Frankenstein, The Horror of Dracula, The Evil of Frankenstein, Dr. Terror's House of Horrors,* and *Tales from the Crypt.* After studying at the Guildhall School of Music and Drama, Cushing made his stage debut in 1935 and later joined Sir Laurence Olivier's Old Vic repertory company. In 1948 he played the role of Osric in Olivier's acclaimed film version of *Hamlet* and subsequently appeared in a number of other films and on television before beginning his affiliation with Hammer in 1957. Thereafter Cushing became—with Christopher Lee and Vincent Price—one of Hammer's central players, creating convincingly sinister characters and earning praise for his polished acting style. Cushing also wrote two books about his life, *Peter Cushing: An Autobiography* and *Past Forgetting: A Memoir of the Hammer Years.*

OBITUARIES AND OTHER SOURCES:

BOOKS

Who's Who in the World, 12th edition, Marquis, 1993.

PERIODICALS

Chicago Tribune, August 12, 1994, sec. 3, p. 12.
Los Angeles Times, August 12, 1994, p. A26.

New York Times, August 12, 1994, p. A21.
Times (London), August 12, 1994, p. 17.
Washington Post, August 12, 1994, p. B6.

*   *   *

CUTHBERT, Neil   1951-

PERSONAL: Born May 5, 1951, in Montclair, NJ; son of Herman Girvin and Ruth Janet (McNeilly) Cuthbert; married Wende Dasteel (an actress), September 6, 1980. *Education:* Rutgers University, B.A., 1973, M.F.A., 1978.

ADDRESSES: Home—New York, NY. *Agent*—c/o George Lane, William Morris Agency, 1350 Avenue of the Americas, New York, NY 10019.

CAREER: Rutgers University, New Brunswick, NJ, playwright-in-residence, 1976-c. 1979; Ensemble Studio Theater, New York City, literary manager, 1979-81; full-time writer, 1981—.

MEMBER: Dramatists Guild, Writers Guild-East.

AWARDS, HONORS: American College Theatre Festival Award for best new play, 1974, for *The Soft Touch.*

WRITINGS:

STAGE PLAYS

The Soft Touch, produced at Rutgers University, then American College Theatre Festival, Washington, DC, both 1973.
Snapping People, produced at Rutgers University, 1975.
Buddy Pals, produced at Ensemble Studio Theatre, New York City, 1978.
First Thirty, produced at Ensemble Studio Theatre, 1979.
The Perfect Stranger, produced at Ensemble Studio Theatre, 1980.
The Smash, produced at Ensemble Studio Theatre, 1981.
Strange Behavior, produced at Ensemble Studio Theatre, then Upstairs at Greene Street, New York City, 1984.
The Deep End, produced at Judith Anderson Theater, 1987.

Also author of *The Home Planet.*

SCREENPLAYS

Saucer!, Film Writers Co., 1982.

Pluto Nash, Martin Bregman Productions and Universal, 1983.

TELEPLAYS

"Cora," episode for *St. Elsewhere,* NBC, 1982.
Washingtoons (pilot), Showtime, 1984.
The Recovery Room (pilot), CBS, 1985.

Also author of pilot for *When in Rome,* CBS.

SIDELIGHTS: Although Neil Cuthbert has made brief forays into the realm of television and movie screenwriting, his name is best known Off-Broadway in New York City and at New Jersey's Rutgers University. During his association with Rutgers, he was playwright-in-residence and earlier saw his award-winning play, *The Soft Touch,* first produced. His Off-Broadway work has included being the literary manager of the Ensemble Studio Theatre, where several of his plays were produced. He also acquired a reputation for writing that combines off-the-wall comedy with serious themes of love, loneliness, and the need to escape life's tedium.

His first and perhaps best-known play is *The Soft Touch,* a farce about a young man who is obsessed with pornography. The story is set in his rundown one-room apartment, where he is attacked by an assortment of characters, including his landlord, a homemaker who turns into a sexual predator, and a schizophrenic. The play won the 1974 American College Theatre Festival Award for best new play and was nearly produced on Broadway by actor Alan Arkin. "It's a play about isolation, violence, madness and sex," Cuthbert said in the *New York Times,* "and to make it more tolerable we make it a farce." In this respect, critics note, *The Soft Touch* bears much in common with the author's later plays.

Buddy Pals, for instance, features three seventeen-year-old boys who meet on Friday nights, one night restoring their childhood friendship by recreating games from their past. *New York Times* theater critic Mel Gussow enjoyed the play's "exuberant" comedy. In contrast, he found *First Thirty,* a one-act play that tries to span thirty years of contemporary life in a half hour, "mannered." However, the critic felt the work is saved by some "enlivening moments," such as a scene in which a disappointed writer burns his manuscripts in a trash can and a bum asks him, "'Burning your novels, huh?'" Gussow enjoyed the "irrepressible, sometimes contagious, humor" of Cuthbert's *Perfect Stranger,* the tale of a suicidal homemaker who enjoys a morning-long dalliance with her water-meter reader. The play tries to make a serious statement about loneliness and escape through romantic love, but, according to Gussow, it is "undercut by an overabundance of . . . antics."

New York theater critics became the target of Cuthbert's satire in *The Smash,* a one-act, backstage play-within-a-play about a dreadful Off-Broadway theater company and the attempts that are made on the life of Bax Raving, an equally lousy critic. *Strange Behavior* is a comedy revue comprising twenty-six sketches, including a burlesque of Cleopatra and a running joke about a suburban man who uses his backyard pool to ensnare guests. *The Deep End,* another one-act, is a satire about a wealthy cocaine-addicted New York couple and an ice-cream vendor.

BIOGRAPHICAL/CRITICAL SOURCES:

BOOKS

Contemporary Theatre, Film, and Television, Volume 6, Gale, 1989.
National Playwrights Directory, 1982, p. 68.

PERIODICALS

New York Times, January 28, 1977; June 15, 1979; February 5, 1980, p. C6; June 10, 1981; March 18, 1984; January 9, 1987; January 15, 1987.*

D

DANNER, Mark (David) 1958-

PERSONAL: Born November 10, 1958, in Utica, NY; son of Robert (a dentist) and Rosalyn (a teacher) Danner. *Education:* Harvard University, A.B. (magna cum laude), 1980.

*ADDRESSES: Home—*New York, NY. *Office—New Yorker,* 20 West 43rd St., New York, NY 10036. *Agent—*Kathy Robbins, Robbins Group, 405 Park Ave., New York, NY 10023.

CAREER: New York Review of Books, New York City, editorial assistant, 1981-84; *Harper's,* New York City, senior editor, 1984-86; *New York Times Magazine,* New York City, story editor, 1986-90; *New Yorker,* New York City, staff writer, 1990—. American Broadcasting Co., writer and producer for the ABC-TV program *Peter Jennings Reports.* New York University, fellow of New York Institute for the Humanities. Guest on television programs, including *The Charlie Rose Show, The MacNeil-Lehrer NewsHour,* and *World News Now.*

MEMBER: Council on Foreign Relations.

AWARDS, HONORS: National Magazine Award, reporting, 1990, for the three-part series "A Reporter at Large: Beyond the Mountains"; award from Overseas Press Club of America, 1994, for the article "The Truth of El Mozote"; Latin American Studies Award, 1994.

WRITINGS:

The Massacre at El Mozote: A Parable of the Cold War, Vintage, 1994.
Beyond the Mountains: The Legacy of Duvalier, Knopf, 1995.

Television news documentaries include the specials *House on Fire: America's Haitian Crisis* and *While America Watched: The Bosnia Tragedy,* both ABC-TV, 1994. Contributor to books, including *Europe and America: Between Drift and New Order,* edited by Frye and Weidenfeld, Council on Foreign Relations, 1993. Contributor to periodicals, including *Aperture.*

*   *   *

DATTEL, Eugene R.   1944-

PERSONAL: Born March 31, 1944, in Greenwood, MS; son of I. E. (a farmer and merchant) and E. (a homemaker) Dattel. *Education:* Yale University, B.A., 1966; Vanderbilt University, J.D. *Politics:* "Pragmatic." *Avocational interests:* Hiking, biking, reading, tennis, jogging, theater, music, daydreaming, travel.

*ADDRESSES: Office—*120 West 45th St., Suite 2600, New York, NY 10036. *Agent—*Jane Gelfman, Gelfman Schneider Literary Agents, 250 West 57th St., New York, NY 10107.

CAREER: Salomon Brothers, managing director, 1969-87; Morgan Stanley, managing director, 1987-88.

WRITINGS:

The Sun That Never Rose, Probus Publishing, 1994.

*   *   *

DAVEY, Jocelyn
See RAPHAEL, Chaim

DAVID, Paul T(heodore)   1906-1994

OBITUARY NOTICE—See index for *CA* sketch: Born August 12, 1906, in Brockton, MA; died of cancer, September 7, 1994, in Charlottesville, VA. Economist, government official, educator, and author. Long a member of policymaking circles in the nation's capitol, David began his career in 1931 as a research fellow with the Brookings Institution and later worked as an assistant government economist. In 1933 he joined the fledgling staff of the Tennessee Valley Authority's Washington, D.C., office. Over the next few decades David held posts with various sectors of the government, including the American Youth Commission, the Bureau of the Budget, and the International Civil Aviation Organization in Quebec, Canada. He returned to the Brookings Institution for a ten year stint in 1950 and in 1960 became a professor of government and foreign affairs at the University of Virginia. Between 1990 and 1992 he served as a consultant to the Miller Center Committee on the Selection Process of the Vice President. David authored a number of books, research papers, and government documents during the course of his career. For the Brookings Institution he wrote *The Economics of Air Mail Transportation, The Changing Party Pattern,* and *The Presidential Election and Transition, 1980-1981.* He was a collaborator with Malcom Moos and Ralph M. Goldman on a five-volume study on delegates to the 1952 Republican National Convention entitled *Presidential Nominating Politics in 1952.* David was also the author of *Party Strength in the United States, 1872-1970* as well as *Proportional Representation in Presidential Nominating Politics* with James W. Ceaser, a study that was influential in a United States Supreme Court decision on legislative apportionment.

OBITUARIES AND OTHER SOURCES:

BOOKS

Who's Who in America, 47th edition, Marquis, 1992, pp. 791-92.

PERIODICALS

Washington Post, September 14, 1994, p. D9.

*   *   *

DAVIES, Ray(mond Douglas)   1944-

PERSONAL: Surname is pronounced "Davis"; born June 21, 1944, in London, England; son of a gardener and a homemaker; married Rasa Dictpatris, c.

1964 (divorced, 1973); married Yvonne Gunner (a teacher), 1976 (divorced, c. 1980); married Pat Crosbie (a ballet dancer); children: (first marriage) Louisa, one other daughter; (with singer Chrissie Hynde) Natalie. *Education:* Attended art school, early 1960s.

ADDRESSES: Agent—c/o Sony Music, 550 Madison Ave., New York, NY 10022.

CAREER: Songwriter, singer, and guitarist. Played during the early 1960s with the Dave Hunt Band; member of the Ravens, 1963, band name changed to the Kinks, 1964—. With the Kinks, founded Konk Records, 1974. Director of the film *Return to Waterloo,* 1985.

WRITINGS:

Return to Waterloo (screenplay), New Line Cinema, 1985.
A Song for Marty, Rudi Publishing, 1992.
X-Ray: The Unauthorised Autobiography, Viking, 1994.

Davies's songs have been recorded and released by Reprise, RCA, Arista, MCA, and Columbia Records; song titles include "You Really Got Me," "All Day and All of the Night," "Tired of Waiting for You," "Well-Respected Man," "Dedicated Flower of Fashion," "Lola," "Big Sky," "Set Me Free," and "Waterloo Sunset"; album titles include *You Really Got Me,* 1964, *Kinks-Size,* 1965, *The Kinks Are the Village Green Preservation Society,* 1969, *Arthur (or the Decline and Fall of the British Empire),* 1969, *Lola versus Powerman and the Moneygoround,* 1970, *Schoolboys in Disgrace,* 1975, *Sleepwalker,* 1977, *UK Jive,* 1990, and *Phobia,* 1993. Also composer of movie and television soundtracks, including *Percy* and *Return to Waterloo.*

SIDELIGHTS: Rock musician Ray Davies, whose songwriting talent strongly contributed to the success of the Kinks during the 1960s, is the composer of such hit songs as "You Really Got Me" and "Lola." Versatility and wit are two qualities often attributed to Davies's songs; as *Rolling Stone* contributor Jim Miller noted in 1974, there were "two periods of Kinks creativity, one marked by crude energy, raw nerve and powerful rock ('All Day and All of the Night'), the other by accomplished artiness, social commentary and wistful vignettes ('Waterloo Sunset')." Despite constant tension within the Kinks—notably between Ray and his brother and bandmate Dave—the group has continued to record critically-acclaimed music for three decades. Besides writing songs for more than forty albums, Davies has authored the screenplay (and music) for the film *Return to Waterloo,* as well as the memoir *X-Ray: The Unauthorised Autobiography.*

Davies's career as a rock musician and songwriter began when he was a London teenager, playing rhythm and blues in local bars with his brother Dave. At age nineteen, he dropped out of art school to join the Ravens, a rock band that in 1964 became the Kinks. When the song "You Really Got Me" was released that year, the band's reputation crossed the Atlantic, and the group began to build a following in the United States as part of the "British Invasion." Soon, Davies emerged as the group's featured artist, writing songs that continue to receive as much attention for the artistry of their lyrics as for their musical qualities.

In *Crawdaddy,* John Swenson affirmed that "Davies is arguably the finest songwriter England has produced." Swenson pointed out that John Lennon and Paul McCartney of the Beatles, Mick Jagger and Keith Richards of the Rolling Stones, and Pete Townsend of the Who have penned "more standards" than any other rock composers, including Davies—however, Davies and Townsend are the only songwriters who "have been able to completely articulate a unique point of view which evolves in direct relation to their on-going attempt to understand themselves and the world they live in." Swenson added, "Davies refined his cameos and determinedly became a social and political critic in the manner of the nineteenth century neo-Romantics, [George Bernard] Shaw and [Oscar] Wilde." Examples of Davies's critical tendencies can be found in many of the Kinks's early songs satirizing society and fashion. The target of "Well-Respected Man," for example, is the prototypical conservative, while "Dedicated Flower of Fashion" skewers the dandified Carnaby Street scene of mid-1960s London, and "Lola" was one of the first hit songs to deal openly with transvestism. By the late 1960s and 1970s, however, Davies's vision had taken a more nostalgic turn. In so-called concept albums (albums whose songs all reflect a similar theme) such as *The Kinks Are the Village Green Preservation Society* and *Arthur (or the Decline and Fall of the British Empire)*—the latter written as the soundtrack for an English television musical—the songs lament the decline of British morals and traditional values. In mood they become what the *Illustrated Encyclopedia of Rock* called a "continuous evocation of the passing of time, a sepia photograph of old England."

This vision of British society informs the film *Return to Waterloo,* Davies's 1985 screenplay which *New York Times* critic Janet Maslin called "assured" and "energetic." Originally written for television, the fifty-eight-minute musical is the story of an unnamed train traveler who never speaks. The film, accompanied by a soundtrack featuring Davies's songs, records the traveler's romantic fantasies. More importantly, it reflects what Maslin called "suburban malaise"—the passiveness of a British middle class that seems indifferent to its own decline. The title ironically calls attention to a more glorious past, when a largely British force in 1815 defeated Napoleon at the battle of Waterloo.

In 1994 Davies completed his autobiography, *X-Ray,* which uses a fictional narrator reporting from the year 2004 as a device to distance the author from his own life. This narrative framework, commented Robert Potts in the *Times Literary Supplement,* allows "Davies to recount his life at one remove, usefully casting doubt on his own pronouncements and establishing what he appears to see as his defining characteristic: a quirky, quintessentially English individuality." To be an individual is a dangerous pursuit in 2004, and it is the book's conceit that the narrator is employed by a shadowy authoritarian agency known as "the Corporation," which is highly critical of Davies's outlook and lifestyle. "The level of self-conscious paranoia built into the structure of the book is nothing compared to the conspiracy theories that Davies floats," observed Robert Sandall in the London *Times.* The reviewer then referred to Davies's early musical career when, according to *X-Ray,* the Kinks were beset by "incompetent managers and greedy song publishers" as well as "a hostile music press."

Davies details his life as a womanizing rock star in *X-Ray,* recalling encounters with fellow celebrities such as Rolling Stone vocalist Mick Jagger. "There is a good crop of anecdotes about the Beatles, the Rolling Stones and the rest," informed Sandall in the London *Times.* Potts, writing in the *Times Literary Supplement,* found the memoir "a brave, convincing account," explaining that "the idiosyncratic and not unsophisticated structure of the book itself bears out Davies's picture of himself as an utterly individual talent."

BIOGRAPHICAL/CRITICAL SOURCES:

BOOKS

Contemporary Musicians, Volume 5, Gale, 1991.
Illustrated Encyclopedia of Rock, revised edition, Harmony Books, 1978.

PERIODICALS

Crawdaddy, July, 1975, pp. 65-66.
Detroit Free Press, December 7, 1984, pp. 1C, 8C.
Musician, June, 1993, p. 7.
New York Times, May 17, 1985.
People, July 6, 1987, p. 86.
Pulse!, May, 1993, pp. 39-43.
Rolling Stone, March 29, 1973, p. 56; May 13, 1993, p. 24.
Times (London), September 11, 1994, sec. 7, p. 5.
Times Literary Supplement, September 23, 1994, p. 32.*

*   *   *

DAVIES, Stan Gebler   1943-1994

OBITUARY NOTICE—See index for *CA* sketch: Born July 16, 1943, near Dublin, Ireland; died of a heart attack, June 23, 1994. Journalist and author. Davies began his career as a writer in the early 1960s with stints at various London newspapers, including the *Evening Standard* and *Independent.* He was also a theater critic and a contributor to periodicals such as *Spectator* and *Punch.* As a journalist the nationalist tendencies inside Great Britain were of especial interest to Davies, and he was once subpoenaed to testify in court about a secret militia in Wales he had encountered when writing an article. One of his first published books was *James Joyce: A Portrait of the Artist,* a look at the famed Irish literary writer with anecdotes about his personal life. Irish by birth as well as a practicing Catholic, Davies nevertheless supported the British rule in Ireland and in 1987 ran for election "at the risk of his life" in his district, according to the *Times* of London. He received 134 votes. The following year he was diagnosed with cancer but survived to write about it. Davies also authored *Chichester 10,* with Zsuzsi Roboz, and *The Kaufmann Snatch,* with Robin Moore.

OBITUARIES AND OTHER SOURCES:

PERIODICALS

Times (London), June 25, 1994, p. 19.

*   *   *

DAVIS, Donald   1944-

PERSONAL: Born June 1, 1944, in Waynesville, NC; son of Joseph (a banker) and Lucille (a teacher; maiden name, Walker) Davis; married Merle Smith (a teacher), April 16, 1992; children: Douglas, Patrick, Kelly, Jonathan. *Education:* Davidson College, B.A., 1966; Duke University, M.Div., 1969. *Politics:* Democrat. *Religion:* Methodist.

ADDRESSES: Home and office—P.O. Box 397, Ocracoke Island, NC 27960. *Agent*—Liz Parkhurst, August House Inc., P.O. Box 3223, Little Rock, AR 72203.

CAREER: Western North Carolina, United Methodist minister, 1967-88; nationwide storyteller, 1967—. Featured storyteller at Smithsonian Institute, the World's Fair, festivals, and concerts. National Association for the Preservation and Perpetuation of Storytelling, chairperson, 1983-88. Producer of books and tapes of his works; teacher of workshops and storytelling courses; guest host for the National Public Radio program *Good Evening.*

MEMBER: National Storytelling Association.

AWARDS, HONORS: Honorary doctorate of Humane Letters from LaGrange College, 1994.

WRITINGS:

My Lucky Day, Johnson (Chicago), 1983.
Listening for the Crack of Dawn, August House (Little Rock, AR), 1990.
Barking at a Fox-Fur Coat, August House, 1991.
Jack Always Seeks His Fortune, August House, 1992.
Telling Your Own Stories, August House, 1993.
Thirteen Miles from Suncrest, August House, 1994.

Also author of *My Uncle Frank Used to Say. . . .* Contributor of articles and fiction to *Publishers Weekly, Time, Mother Earth News, Parenting, Teacher,* and the *Utne Reader.*

RECORDED STORIES

Storytelling Festival, 2 vols., NAPPS, 1983.
Listening for the Crack of Dawn, August House, 1991.
Rainy Weather, August House, 1992.
Jack's First Job, August House, 1992.
Uncle Frank Invents the Electron Microphone, August House, 1992.
Party People, August House, 1993.
Miss Daisy, August House, 1993.
Christmas at Grandma's, August House, 1994.
The Southern Bells, August House, 1994.
Walking through Sulphur Springs, August House, 1995.
Jack and the Animals, August House, 1995.

Also author of recorded story collection *American*

Storytelling Series, Volume 8: "The Crack of Dawn" and "Twelve Huntsmen," published by H. W. Wilson in the 1980s.

WORK IN PROGRESS: A movie script based on *Listening for the Crack of Dawn.*

*   *   *

DAVIS, Joel   1948-

PERSONAL: Born October 11, 1948, in Ventura, CA; son of Gerald H. (a newspaper printer) and Antonia Davis; married Marie Celestre, August 30, 1975 (divorced, 1988); married Judy Lewis (a psychotherapist), March 20, 1993; stepchildren: Kirsten Nash, Greg Zagelow. *Education:* Studied for the priesthood; California Lutheran University, B.A., 1970; University of Oregon, M.L.S., 1975. *Politics:* Democrat. *Religion:* "Christian-pagan." *Avocational interests:* Science fiction, bicycling, walking.

ADDRESSES: Home—1201 West 12th Ave., Spokane, WA 99204-3907. *Agent*—Scott Meredith Literary Agency, 845 Third Ave., New York, NY 10022.

CAREER: Worked for B. Dalton Bookseller, Los Angeles, CA, the county library in Ventura, CA, and Spokane County Library, Spokane, WA; *Spokane Community Press,* Spokane, reporter; freelance science writer, 1979—. Teacher at University of Washington, Seattle, and Evergreen State College; lecturer and workshop leader; consultant to organizations and state agencies.

MEMBER: Authors Guild, National Association of Science Writers, Science Fiction and Fantasy Writers of America, Environmental Education Association of Washington, Friends of the Washington State Library (founding member; past president).

AWARDS, HONORS: Forum Award, print media category, U.S. Council for Energy Awareness, 1988, for the magazine article "Nuclear Reactions."

WRITINGS:

Endorphins: New Waves in Brain Chemistry, Doubleday, 1984.
Flyby: The Interplanetary Odyssey of Voyager 2, Atheneum, 1987.
(With Robert L. Forward) *Mirror Matter: Pioneering Antimatter Physics,* Wiley, 1988.
Defending the Body: Unraveling the Mysteries of Immunology, Atheneum, 1989.

Mapping the Code: The Human Genome Project and the Choices of Modern Science, Wiley, 1990.
Journey to the Center of Our Galaxy: A Voyage in Space and Time, Contemporary Books, 1991.
Mother Tongue: How Humans Create Language, Birch Lane Press, 1994.

Contributor to books, including *Project Solar Sail,* edited by Arthur C. Clarke, Penguin, 1990. Contributor of more than a hundred-fifty articles to popular magazines in the United States, England, and Australia, including *Astronomy, Family Weekly, OMNI, Popular Mechanics, Parade,* and *Science Digest.* Editor, *EEAW Newsletter;* past co-editor, *SFWA Publicity Newsletter.*

WORK IN PROGRESS: Seeing Things Invisible: Science, Vision, and the Nature of Reality, on science, philosophy, and the way we perceive reality.

SIDELIGHTS: Joel Davis told *CA:* "I consider writing popular science books a form of teaching. We live in a culture whose two most important driving forces are science and technology, yet most of us are woefully ignorant about both. Today, more and more political, social, and ethical decisions center on scientific and technological issues. We cannot hope to make informed, democratic decisions about these issues without having at least a basic understanding of them. My hope is that my books and magazine articles contribute to the greater scientific and technological education of the 'polis.'

"Writing and literature have always been important to me. My father was a newspaper printer and, along with my mother, he instilled in me a love and respect for the written word. I discovered libraries, science fiction, and the books of Isaac Asimov at an early age. All three have been strong influences since childhood. I knew that I probably didn't have the 'right stuff' to become a scientist, but I also knew that I loved reading about science and scientists. When I made the decision to start freelance writing, I chose to write about science. If I have had any hero or model for my work, it's been Isaac Asimov. Other writers of popular science who are influences include Paul Davies, John Gribbin, John McPhee, Richard Restak, and Fred Alan Wolf.

"Science fiction and science are not the only genres I read and enjoy, though. I discovered modern American poetry and poets when I was in college—cummings, Eliot, Pound, and Williams, followed later by the West Coast poets like Ferlinghetti, Corso, and Snyder, and even later by people like Marge Piercy, Adrienne Rich, and Diane Wakoski.

Their poems have inspired me and nourished my soul. Whenever I'm in San Francisco, I make a conscious pilgrimage to the City Lights Bookstore, home of Lawrence Ferlinghetti and Mecca to the Beats.

"Whenever I'm in southern California, I try to stop by at California Lutheran University and walk the campus once again. Without the wonderful influence of professors like Lyle Murley and Jack Ledbedder, I never would have delved deeply into the richness of modern poetry, discovered the joy of Chaucer, or been exposed to the fascinating mysteries of linguistics."

*   *   *

DAVIS, Linda W.   1945-

PERSONAL: Born February 20, 1945, in Cedar Rapids, IA; daughter of Leslie E. and Eleanor D. Wiles; married Lawrence C. Davis (a biochemist), July 22, 1967; children: Colin C., Steven L. *Education:* Swarthmore College, B.A., 1967; Kansas State University, M.S., 1988. *Religion:* Lutheran.

ADDRESSES: Home—3419 Womack, Manhattan, KS 66502. *Office*—Division of Biology, Kansas State University, Ackert Hall, Manhattan, KS 66506.

CAREER: Kansas State University, Manhattan, KS, instructor, 1988—.

WRITINGS:

Weed Seeds of the Great Plains, University Press of Kansas (Lawrence, KS), 1993.

WORK IN PROGRESS: Research into plant distributions and the databasing of plant information.

*   *   *

DAVIS, Richard A. (Jr.)   1937-

PERSONAL: Born September 11, 1937, in Joliet, IL; son of Richard A. (a manager of a lumber company) and Gertrude (a secretary; maiden name, Johannsen) Davis; married Mary Ann Chilen (an educator), January 26, 1962; children: Laurie Elizabeth Davis Booker, Lee Andrew. *Education:* Beloit College, B.S., 1959; University of Texas at Austin, M.A., 1961; University of Illinois at Urbana-Champaign, Ph.D., 1964.

ADDRESSES: Home—2613 Wilson Cir., Lutz, FL

33549. *Office*—Department of Geology, University of South Florida, Tampa, FL 33620.

CAREER: Affiliated with the department of geology at Western Michigan University, Kalamazoo, MI, 1965-73; affiliated with department of geology at University of South Florida, Tampa, 1973—.

WRITINGS:

Principles of Oceanography, Addison-Wesley (Reading, MA), 1972, 2nd edition, 1981.
Deposition of Systems, Prentice-Hall (Englewood Cliffs, NJ), 1983, 2nd edition, 1992.
Oceanography, W. C. Brown (Dubuque), 1987, 2nd edition, 1991.
The Evolving Coast, Scientific American Books, 1994.

*   *   *

DAWE, R(oger) D(avid)   1934-

PERSONAL: Born in 1934, in Bristol, England; son of Charles Vivian (a university reader) and Louisa (a homemaker; maiden name, Butler) Dawe; married Kerstin Marianne Wallner (a homemaker), 1960; children: Simon Roger Frederick, Susanna Louise. *Education:* Attended Gonville and Caius College, Cambridge, 1953-57; received Ph.D., 1960; received Litt.D., 1974. *Politics:* None. *Religion:* None.

ADDRESSES: Home—Cambridge, England. *Office*—Trinity College, Cambridge University, Cambridge CB2 1TQ, England.

CAREER: Cambridge University, Cambridge, England, research fellow of Caius College, 1957-63, teaching fellow at Trinity College, beginning in 1963; author and editor.

WRITINGS:

Collation and Investigation of the Manuscripts of Aeschylus, Cambridge University Press, 1964.
A Repertory of Conjectures on Aeschylus, E. J. Brill, 1965.
Studies on the Text of Sophocles, E. J. Brill, Volumes I-II, 1973, Volume III, 1978.
(Editor) *Sophocles,* B. G. Teubner, Volume I, 1975, 3rd edition, 1995, Volume II, 1979, 3rd edition, in press.
(Editor) Sophocles, *Oedipus Rex,* Cambridge University Press, 1982, 4th edition, 1988.
(Translator and editor) Homer, *The Odyssey: Translation and Analysis,* Book Guild, 1993.

DAWSON, Giles E(dwin)   1903-1994

OBITUARY NOTICE—See index for *CA* sketch: Born March 4, 1903, in Columbus, OH; died after a stroke, August 26, 1994, in Washington, DC. Professor, librarian, editor, and author. Dawson taught English in North Dakota and Ohio in the late 1920s and early 1930s before relocating to the Washington, D.C. area in 1932. He worked for many years at the Folger Shakespeare Library, first as reference librarian and then as books and manuscripts curator, before retiring in 1967. He became a professor of English at Catholic University, where he had been a faculty member for several decades. Dawson retired again in 1972 but in the early 1980s became a volunteer rare book librarian at Washington National Cathedral. His first published work was 1929's *The Seven Champions of Christendom,* which he edited; Dawson also wrote *Life of William Shakespeare* and *Plays and Players in Kent: 1450-1642,* in addition to editing the *Shakespeare Quarterly* from 1950 to 1972.

OBITUARIES AND OTHER SOURCES:

BOOKS

Who's Who in America, 41st edition, Marquis, 1980.

PERIODICALS

Washington Post, August 29, 1994, p. D4.

*   *   *

DEANS, Sis Boulos   1955-

PERSONAL: Born November 4, 1955, in Portland, ME; daughter of James (an electrician) and Velma (a nurse; maiden name, Pellitier) Boulos; married John Deans (a farrier), October 7, 1978; children: Jessica Emily, Rachel Marie, Emma Lee. *Education:* University of Maine, Orono, A.S. (animal medical technology), 1976; received degree from Maine Medical Center School of Surgical Technology, 1985. *Politics:* Democrat. *Religion:* Roman Catholic. *Avocational interests:* Camping, photography, sports.

ADDRESSES: Home—260 Gray Rd., Gorham, ME 04038.

CAREER: Mercy Hospital, Portland, ME, surgical technician, 1985—. Has worked variously as a lifeguard, a waitress, a writing instructor, and nine years as an animal medical technician for veterinarians.

MEMBER: Association of Surgical Technologists, Maine Writers and Publishers Alliance.

AWARDS, HONORS: The Legend of Blazing Bear was a Maine Writers and Publishers Alliance bestselling children's book for 1992.

WRITINGS:

Chick-a-dee-dee-dee: A Very Special Bird, illustrated by Nantz Comyns, Gannett Books, 1987.
Emily Bee and the Kingdom of Flowers, illustrated by Comyns, Gannett Books, 1988.
The Legend of Blazing Bear, illustrated by Comyns, Windswept House Publishers, 1992.

Also author of adult short fiction, poetry, and plays, published in periodicals, including *Tableau, New England Sampler,* and *Portland Review of the Arts.*

WORK IN PROGRESS: Brick Walls, a young adult novel; *Summer of the Gang,* a book for middle readers; *Jessica's Christmas Pageant* and *Olivia's Operation,* both children's books.

SIDELIGHTS: Sis Boulos Deans shares a farm in Maine with her husband, their three daughters, two horses, two dogs, a cat, a rabbit, and three chickens. "My husband and children share my love for camping, and vacations for us usually involve sleeping in a tent," Deans commented. "My girls swim competitively, and are also active in other sports, church, and school activities, so I'm usually en route to a pool or a ball field.

"Besides being a wife, mother, and writer, I work three days and a night on call in the operating room as a surgical technician. My specialty is orthopedics; my favorite cases are total knee and hip replacements. People usually ask how I manage to balance such a hectic life and still write. My answer: 'I write when normal people are sleeping.' Which is true—it's the only time our house is quiet.

"For me, writing is like breathing—something that comes naturally and is a necessity of life. Since childhood, I've been motivated by a creative desire to capture with words the world around me. Dialogue is one of my favorite vehicles, and humor is usually in the driver's seat." In addition to children's books, Deans has written plays and stories for adults. "I didn't start writing children's books until my eldest daughter was four," she commented. "After seeing one of my short stories published in a magazine that she was too young to read, she said, 'Momma, you write for everyone but me.'

My guilt kicked in, and I immediately called Nantz Comyns, a good friend and an artist I'd known since college. 'Nantz,' I said, 'I'm going to write a kids' book and you're going to illustrate it.'"

Since then, Deans and Comyns have worked on three books together. Their third book, *The Legend of Blazing Bear,* was the Maine Writers and Publishers Alliance bestselling children's book for 1992. In the book, an Abenaki father gently teaches his son through storytelling, emphasizing Abenaki culture and customs. Jeanette K. Cakouros in the *Maine Sunday Telegram* declares that *Blazing Bear* is "more than a storybook," noting that the book also contains a glossary of American Indian words and terms, a chart of Maine's Kennebec and Abenaki Indians, a map showing the locations and place names of the tribes, and a bibliography for further reading. Cakouros also praises the book's colorful artwork. "Nantz and I have an excellent working relationship," Deans explains, "and our successful collaborations have been, and continue to be, rewarding and fun."

BIOGRAPHICAL/CRITICAL SOURCES:

PERIODICALS

Maine Sunday Telegram, September 20, 1992.
School Library Journal, February, 1993, p. 92.

* * *

DeBLIEU, Jan   1955-

PERSONAL: Born January 6, 1955; daughter of Ivan K., Jr. (a chemical engineer) and Helen (a homemaker; maiden name, Snider) DeBlieu; married Jeffrey Burton Smith (an administrator of the Nature Conservancy), June 19, 1982; children: Reid. *Education:* University of Delaware, B.A., 1976.

ADDRESSES: Agent—Elizabeth Grossman, Sterling Lord Literistic, 1 Madison Ave., New York, NY 10010.

CAREER: News-Journal, Wilmington, DE, staff reporter, 1974-78; *Register-Guard,* Eugene, OR, 1978-80; freelance author and journalist (specializing in natural history and ecology), 1980—; *Newsweek,* Atlanta, GA, correspondent and contributor, 1982-85; *Emory Magazine,* Emory University, Atlanta, GA, staff writer, 1983-85.

AWARDS, HONORS: Meant to Be Wild: The Struggle to Save Endangered Animals through Captive Breeding was chosen by *Library Journal* as one of the three best books on natural history published during 1991.

WRITINGS:

Hatteras Journal, Fulcrum Press, 1987.
Meant to Be Wild: The Struggle to Save Endangered Animals through Captive Breeding, Fulcrum Press, 1991.

Contributor of articles to periodicals, including *New York Times Magazine, Smithsonian, Southern Living,* and *Orion.*

WORK IN PROGRESS: A nonfiction book of essays about the natural and cultural history of the wind.

SIDELIGHTS: Jan DeBlieu told *CA:* "I began my writing career as a general interest journalist, working for newspapers in my hometown of Wilmington, Delaware, and in Eugene, Oregon. From 1981 to 1984 I was a freelance magazine journalist in Atlanta, Georgia, writing for a variety of publications, including *Newsweek,* the *Atlanta Constitution*'s Sunday magazine, and the award-winning alumni magazine published by Emory University.

"During the early 1980s I became increasingly interested in writing about nature and ecology. I was influenced during this period by a number of classic nature works, especially Annie Dillard's *Pilgrim at Tinker Creek* and the writings of Barry Lopez. In 1985 I moved to the Outer Banks of North Carolina, settling into a rickety house in the Cape Hatteras hamlet of Rodanthe. I spent the next year and a half exploring the barrier island beaches, marshes, and waters. My first book, *Hatteras Journal,* published in 1987, is a first-person account of my island experiences. *Hatteras Journal* is both a natural history and a cultural portrayal of the people of the Outer Banks.

"My work on *Hatteras Journal* made me acutely aware of how greatly humans influence the natural world, even in the most pristine settings. In 1987 I became intrigued with a proposal to return the rare red wolf to the marshes of the Alligator River, a national wildlife refuge just west of the Outer Banks. Once a common denizen of Southern forests, the red wolf was all but extinct. Only eighty-five animals survived, all in captivity. I began working as a volunteer for the release program, all the while exploring the philosophical questions that surround captive breeding. I spent time living in the bush and caring for the wolves as they grew acclimated to the site. Then, after the release, I worked alongside biologists radio-tracking the animals and charting their progress as they learned their way in the woods. My efforts are chronicled in *Meant to Be Wild: The Struggle to Save Endangered Animals through Captive Breeding.* This second book includes accounts of my experiences not only with the red wolf but with biologists who are working to save the California condor, the Florida panther, the Puerto Rican parrot, and other rare species. It explores in detail the question of whether the wild spirit of animals can be preserved in captivity."

*   *   *

DEE, Ed(ward J., Jr.)   1940-

PERSONAL: Born February 3, 1940, in Yonkers, NY; son of Edward J., Sr. (a highway toll collector) and Ethel (a waiter and teletype operator; maiden name, Lawton) Dee; married Nancy Lee Hazzard, October 1, 1962; children: Brenda Sue Dee Crawford, Patricia Ann Dee Flanagan. *Education:* Rockland Community College, A.A.S., 1974; Fordham University, B.A., 1976, law student, 1977-78; Arizona State University, M.F.A., 1992. *Politics:* Independent. *Religion:* Roman Catholic.

ADDRESSES: Home—69 Henlopen Gardens, Lewes, DE 19958. *Agent*—Gail Hochman, Brandt & Brandt, 1501 Broadway, New York, NY 10036.

CAREER: New York Police Department, New York City, police officer, 1962-82, retiring as lieutenant; writer. *Military service:* U.S. Army, 1958-60; U.S. Army Reserve, 1960-64.

MEMBER: Mystery Writers of America, Superior Officers Association for Retirees.

WRITINGS:

14 Peck Slip, Warner Books (New York, NY), 1994.

WORK IN PROGRESS: Bronx Angel, a sequel to *14 Peck Slip.*

SIDELIGHTS: Ed Dee told *CA:* "After retiring from the New York Police Department, I wanted to write about the department in a way that no one had done before. After receiving my M.F.A. in creative writing, I submitted my first book. *Bronx Angel* is a sequel. I intend to use the same characters in a series of books that, I hope, get to the heart of the experience of being a cop in a city like New York. I hope they get at the *truth.*"

De FERRARI, Gabriella   1941-

PERSONAL: Born June 3, 1941, in Tacna, Peru; immigrated to the United States, 1959; naturalized American citizen, 1964; daughter of Armando and Delia (Brignole) De Ferrari; married Raymond Learsy (in business); children: Nathaniel Jeppson, Gabriella Jeppson. *Education:* St. Louis University, B.A., 1963; graduate study at Georgetown University, 1963-64; Tufts University, Fletcher School of Law and Diplomacy, M.A., 1966; Harvard University, M.A., 1981.

ADDRESSES: Home—55 Hudson St., New York, NY 10013. *Office*—10 Jay St., New York, NY 10013. *Agent*—Lynn Nesbit, Janklow & Nesbit Associates, 598 Madison Ave., New York, NY 10022.

CAREER: Institute of Contemporary Art, Boston, MA, director, 1975-77; Harvard University, Cambridge, MA, acting curator of the Busch Reisinger Museum, 1978-79, assistant director of curatorial affairs for the Fogg Art Museum, 1979-82; freelance writer and editor. UCLA Art Council, member of board of directors and chair of exhibition committee, 1985-86; New School for Social Research, Vera List Center for Art and Politics, chair, 1988—; Colby College Museum of Art, chair of board of governors, 1989—; Harvard University Art Museums, chair of committee of Contemporary Collections, 1992—, and member of visiting committee, 1994—; Museum of Modern Art, member of drawing committee, 1993—.

AWARDS, HONORS: A Cloud on Sand was named one of the ten best books of 1990 by *Entertainment Weekly.*

WRITINGS:

A Cloud on Sand, Knopf (New York), 1990.
Gringa Latina, Houghton-Mifflin (Boston), 1995.

Contributor to periodicals, including *Mirabella, Connoisseur, Vanity Fair, Boston Review,* and *Travel and Leisure. A Cloud on Sand* has been published in Italy, Germany, France, Japan, and Denmark.

SIDELIGHTS: In her first novel, *A Cloud on Sand,* Gabriella De Ferrari depicts the lives of a mother and daughter against a backdrop that shifts from the Italian Riviera of the 1920s and 1930s to South America during World War II. "Against these rich, dense backgrounds, her characters grow in strength and vitality," commented Elaine Kendall in the *Los Angeles Times,* "welcoming us into a mysterious, vanished world."

In the beginning of *A Cloud on Sand,* Dora, as a young woman living in a small Italian village, meets and marries an Italian businessperson who has made his fortune in Argentina. When Dora refuses to live with him in Buenos Aires, he builds her a villa in her native village. There she regularly entertains her lovers, occasionally plays the loving wife to her visiting husband, and halfheartedly raises her son and daughter. The daughter, Antonia, eventually escapes her mother's neglect by marrying her own Italian businessperson and accompanying him to a country on the Pacific coast of South America. As Merle Rubin noted in the *Christian Science Monitor,* De Ferrari's novel "is, to some extent, a story about the challenge and disorientation of moving from the Old World to the New; and, to an even greater extent, the story of a domineering mother and a daughter who manages to break free from her powerful influence."

The strength of *A Cloud on Sand* is, according to several reviewers, De Ferrari's development of characters and her description of the settings in which they find themselves. "The story is so familiar that, in the hands of a less talented writer, it would be merely a cliche," wrote Linda Simon in *Commonweal.* "But Gabriella De Ferrari . . . has created characters of rare charm and set them in a richly detailed context. *A Cloud on Sand* is an impressive debut." Kendall asserted that "there is a lushness here, a sense of hyper-reality and an expansiveness of character that contrasts strongly with our contemporary home-grown pragmatism." Susie Campbell, in the *Listener,* also noted these strengths, but contrasted them with what she considered De Ferrari's main weakness. "Sometimes, particularly near the beginning," Campbell pointed out, "the narrative falters, as if De Ferrari loses confidence in her ability to control all the elements of the story." She continued, "As a writer, De Ferrari is not yet as skilled at constructing narrative as she is at characterising people and places."

Many critics asserted that ultimately it is the characters that remain with the reader. "For all of Antonia's underlying strength and 'hidden asymmetry,' for all the 'glowing coals' ready to burst into flame," remarked Simon in *Commonweal,* "Antonia seems far less complex, far less mysterious than her mother. . . . [Dora] stands as the single tragic figure in this novel, and the one who, throughout, commands our attention." Rubin contended in the *Christian Science Monitor* that "De Ferrari's novel shows an eye for the idiosyncrasies of characters and the oddities of fate, as well as a subtle understanding of the patterns in people's lives and the surprising

turns that cannot be reduced to a pattern." *Entertainment Weekly* reviewer L. S. Klepp suggested that *A Cloud on Sand* "can't be described as promising. It's far too good to be promising." Klepp went on to say that De Ferrari's book is "a classically assured, quietly enthralling masterpiece."

BIOGRAPHICAL/CRITICAL SOURCES:

BOOKS

Contemporary Literary Criticism, Volume 65, Gale, 1991.

PERIODICALS

Atlanta Journal and Constitution, July 15, 1990, p. N8.
Christian Science Monitor, April 30, 1990, p. 13.
Commonweal, June 1, 1990, pp. 362-63.
Entertainment Weekly, April 27, 1990.
Listener, September 27, 1990, pp. 32-33.
Los Angeles Times, March 30, 1990.
New York Times Book Review, June 24, 1990, p. 21.

*   *   *

DELAMAIDE, Darrell (George) 1949-

PERSONAL: Born September 25, 1949, in Pittsburg, KS; son of Bill (an accountant) and Lillian (a telephone company employee; maiden name, Lanham) Delamaide. *Education:* St. Louis University, A.B. (magna cum laude), 1971; Columbia University, Master of International Affairs, 1975. *Avocational interests:* Cooking, traveling, sports, and culture.

ADDRESSES: Home—10 passage Turquetil, Paris, France 75011. *Office*—June Hall, 19 College Cross, London N1 1PT, England.

CAREER: A.P.-Dow Jones News Agency, New York and Germany, reporter, 1975-78; correspondent for *Barron's* and other publications, 1978-80; *International Herald Tribune,* Paris, France, copy editor, 1980-81; *Institutional Investor,* New York City, European bureau chief based in Paris, France, 1981—.

MEMBER: Authors Guild.

AWARDS, HONORS: Fulbright scholarship to University of Munich, Germany, 1971-72.

WRITINGS:

Debt Shock: The Full Story of the World Credit Crisis, Doubleday (New York), 1984.

SIDELIGHTS: In August 1982, the Mexican government announced to the world that Mexico could no longer make payments on its national debt. This announcement staggered Mexico's creditors—European and American banks—and triggered what became known as the "world banking crisis." In his book *Debt Shock: The Full Story of the World Credit Crisis,* Darrell Delamaide takes on the difficult challenge of explaining this financial debacle to the general reader. *Debt Shock* provides an analysis of how the world got into the crisis, and how it might get out of it.

The banking crisis arose, Delamaide explains, from the oil crisis of the 1970s. Between 1973 and 1979, the price of oil increased dramatically. The oil-producing nations of the Middle East suddenly found themselves rich and deposited their new wealth in foreign banks. What the banks chose to do with this money was unprecedented: they loaned huge amounts to the world's poorer nations, who were in need of cash. Countries such as Mexico, Brazil, Zaire, and Egypt accepted loans on which they could barely pay the interest, much less repay the principal.

Several factors made these loans extraordinary, beyond their sheer size. First, banks had not customarily loaned money to sovereign nations due to the difficulty of seizing assets in case of default. Second, most bank loans are made based on a careful assessment of the borrower's ability to repay, yet the banks asked for no such safeguards from the Third World countries who received these loans. Eager to reap huge profits, which they did at first, the bankers rewrote the rules of their profession. They loaned billions of dollars to nations which showed little evidence of the ability to repay them.

Delamaide writes that the bankers themselves were aware of the fragility of the credit structure they had created, but continued to make loans nonetheless. When Mexico defaulted on its loan payments, the lending spree was exposed for the reckless adventure it was. The banks, realizing that their billions would never be repaid, turned to their governments and the International Monetary Fund to bail them out.

Delamaide's book is critical in its portrayal of the bankers whose decisions brought on the crisis. Ann Crittenden wrote in the *New York Times Book Review:* "*Debt Shock* places much of the burden of responsibility for the debt debacle squarely on the shoulders of the international bankers, whom Mr. Delamaide sees as well-tailored hucksters who flew around the world selling money without any thought of the consequences." Those consequences hit hard the debtor nations, where the hardships of debt led to considerable economic damage—and in some cases to bread riots and fighting in the streets. However, Crittenden also noted that "*Debt Shock* says too little about the responsibility of the regulators and borrowers." Reviewing the book in the *Los Angeles Times Book Review,* Tom Groenfeldt commended Delamaide's "fine explanation of international debt" but noted that the final chapters, in which Delamaide looks into the future of international banking, are less effective.

BIOGRAPHICAL/CRITICAL SOURCES:

PERIODICALS

Globe and Mail (Toronto), August 25, 1984.
Los Angeles Times Book Review, August 12, 1984, p. 2.
Nation, June 30, 1984, p. 806.
New York Times, July 7, 1984, p. 12.
New York Times Book Review, July 8, 1984, p. 6.
Times Literary Supplement, November 30, 1984, p. 1371.*

*   *   *

deLEON, Peter   1943-

PERSONAL: Born August 21, 1943, in Santa Ana, CA; son of Salvador and Phyllis (Gird) deLeon; married Sheryl Rene Keppler, September 8, 1976 (deceased); married Linda Margaret Butler (a professor), August 16, 1988. *Education:* University of California, Los Angeles, B.A., 1965, M.A., 1966; Rand Graduate Institute, Ph.D., 1978. *Politics:* Liberal. *Religion:* Christian. *Avocational interests:* Tennis, skiing.

ADDRESSES: Home—14310 West Fifth Ave., Golden, CO 80401. *Office*—Graduate School of Public Affairs, University of Colorado at Denver, 1445 Market St., Suite 350, Denver, CO 80217-3664.

CAREER: University of Colorado at Denver, professor of public affairs, 1985—, director of Office of International Education, 1994—. Also worked for Rand Corp. as a senior researcher. Invited lecturer in China and Mexico; consultant to European Center for Social Welfare, Swedish Colloquium for Advanced Study in the Social Sciences, and Science Center, Berlin, Germany.

AWARDS, HONORS: Grants from Ford Foundation, Alfred J. Sloan Foundation, German Marshall Fund,

Russell Sage Foundation, Asia Foundation, and Swedish Bicentennial Fund.

WRITINGS:

(Coauthor) *The Prosecution of Adult Felony Defendants in Los Angeles County,* Lexington Books, 1976.

The Development and Diffusion of the Nuclear Power Reactor: A Comparative Analysis, Ballinger, 1979.

(With Garry D. Brewer) *The Foundations of Policy Analysis,* Dorsey, 1983.

(With Helga Nowotny and Bjorn Wittrock) *Choosing Futures: Evaluating the Secretariat for Futures Studies,* Council for the Planning and Coordination of Research (Stockholm), 1985.

The Altered Strategic Environment: Towards the Year 2000, Heath, 1987.

Advice and Consent: The Development of the Policy Sciences, Russell Sage Foundation, 1988.

Thinking about Political Corruption, M. E. Sharpe (Armonk, NY), 1993.

Democracy and the Policy Sciences, State University of New York Press, in press.

Work represented in books, including *The Policy Cycle,* edited by May and Wildavsky, Sage Publications, 1978; *The Politics of Program Evaluation,* edited by Dennis Palumbo, Sage Publications, 1987; and *Policy Analysis: Concepts and Methods,* edited by D. Brinkerhoff and M. Ingle, JAI Press, 1995. Contributor to policy and administration journals. Past editor, *Policy Sciences.*

SIDELIGHTS: Peter deLeon told *CA:* "I have specialized in policy research, on issues of technology development, assessment, and utilization, with substantive expertise on national security and energy gained as a senior researcher at the Rand Corporation. I have also written extensively on public policy processes, especially program implementation, evaluation, policy termination, and comparative public policy.

"I have tried to write books in both the theory and practice of public policy; hence, the swings between topical books on such subjects as commercial nuclear reactors, nuclear strategy, and political corruption, and the more theory-oriented books on policy analysis and the policy sciences. Having just finished a topical book, *Thinking about Political Corruption,* I am now starting on a more theoretical topic, *Democracy and the Policy Sciences* (my shot at political theory).

"As my book titles indicate, I have deliberately opted for the broader, rather than an intensive, perspective. The reason is simple: I'd prefer learning vastly new areas to keep the exercise interesting. The primary themes recur, however; namely, a continuing concern for policy questions, especially the way they are framed and then implemented. The two streams thus reinforce, feed upon, and support one another.

"When I am not doing my professor gig, I lately find myself doing an administrator's thing. Last year I was asked to become the university's director of the Office of International Education. The challenges are fundamentally distinct from those of research, so I am enjoying myself more than one should normally admit.

"The rest of my life is hab-drab stuff: married, no children, a wife I love, a house I'm comfortable in. Barring the possible reinstatement of the Eisenhower years (an event whose odds increased with the November, 1994 elections) I have no serious quarrels with the powers that be, excepting, of course, the strike by major league baseball. I spend a lot of my time, therefore, trying to explain why things are, rather than how they should be. Maybe the latter will become a theme for my 'n'th book!"

*　　*　　*

DELGADO, Hector L.   1949-

PERSONAL: Born March 2, 1949, in Ponce, PR; son of Jose E. (a career soldier) and Cecilia (a factory worker; maiden name, Guindin) Delgado; married Miriam Lopez (an attorney), August 20, 1983; children: Andres Martin. *Education:* Temple University, B.A., 1971; Rutgers University, Ed.M., 1975; University of Michigan, M.A., 1985, Ph.D., 1990.

ADDRESSES: Home—Pasadena, CA. *Office*—Department of Sociology, University of Arizona, Tucson, AZ 85721.

CAREER: Rutgers University, Camden Campus, Camden, NJ, assistant director of admissions services and coordinator of Latino student recruitment, 1971-73, vice-chairperson of academic foundations department and coordinator of Hispanic affairs, 1978-80; Princeton University, Princeton, NJ, assistant dean of student affairs, 1980-83; University of Michigan, Ann Arbor, instructor in sociology and Latino studies, 1984-86; Occidental College, Los Angeles, CA, assistant professor of sociology and anthropology, 1988-92; University of Arizona, Tucson, assistant professor of sociology and assistant research social scientist at Mexican-American Studies and Research Center, 1993—.

MEMBER: American Sociological Association, American Academy of Political and Social Science, Pacific Sociological Association.

WRITINGS:

New Immigrants, Old Unions: Organizing Undocumented Workers in Los Angeles, Temple University Press (Philadelphia, PA), 1993.

Contributor to books, including *Strategies for Improving Race Relations: The Anglo-American Experience,* edited by John W. Shaw, Peter G. Nordie, and Richard M. Shapiro, Manchester University Press, 1987; and *The Changing Role of Mexican Labor in the U.S. Economy: Sectoral Perspectives,* edited by Wayne Cornelius, Center for U.S.-Mexico Studies, University of California, San Diego, in press. Contributor of articles and reviews to sociology journals.

WORK IN PROGRESS: Research on the immigration debate in southern California.

*   *   *

DELO, David Michael   1938-

PERSONAL: Born June 24, 1938, in Galesburg, IL; son of David Marlon (a college president) and Elsie Muriel (Crooker) Delo; married, wife's name, Anne P. (divorced); married Iloilo Marguerita de la Cerda Jones (a financial analyst and archaeologist), June 18, 1989. *Education:* Attended Colgate University, 1956-58; Antioch College, B.A., 1962; New York University, M.A., 1985. *Politics:* None. *Religion:* None. *Avocational interests:* Photography, sketching, backpacking, solar house design.

ADDRESSES: Home—Westcliffe, CO.

CAREER: American Geological Institute, Washington, DC, associate project director, 1967-69; Levi Strauss and Co., San Francisco, CA, systems analyst and vice-president of customer service, 1970-80; freelance writer and scholar, 1980—. Northwestern University, manager of development communications for university library, 1988-90. *Military service:* U.S. Army, Intelligence, special agent, 1962-66.

WRITINGS:

Peddlers and Post Traders: The Army Sutler on the Frontier, University of Utah Press, 1992.

The Right Touch (novel), Salt Lake Publishing, 1994.

Coauthor of *Board of Directors Guide and Development Manual,* a guide for not-for-profit organizations, 1993. Contributor to magazines, including *True West, Army, Golden Years, Journal of Geological Education, Wind River Mountaineer,* and *New York.*

WORK IN PROGRESS: Building on the Past: The Archaeology of the Central Illinois Expressway; Stay in Touch, a novel, completion expected in 1996; *Self-Seeking Men,* a historical novel of the creation of Yellowstone National Park, completion expected in 1997.

SIDELIGHTS: David Michael Delo told *CA:* "I am not a writer; I am a creative, well-organized child. I write, but I do equally well as a photographer, artist, or solar home designer. I began writing at age forty-two, after I discovered I needed to rely on a profession that was not location-specific. I completed the master's program in journalism at New York University and sold my first article to *New York* magazine in 1981.

"Soon thereafter, while owning and managing a Wyoming guest ranch, I became curious about the history of the area. I began to concentrate on western history and became the local historian. I tried fiction for four years, but my first published book was the first history of military post traders, known as sutlers. I wrote the book as a journalist, for a broad audience, rather than as a historian or scholar, but the book nonetheless was rated as graduate-level reading. Pity.

"Nonfiction writing is highly satisfying because it is mentally strenuous. It requires the integration of more skills than most other creative activities, and it demands incredible patience and tenacity. To write nonfiction well, one must know how to research and organize volumes of materials, and also gain immense satisfaction from those activities.

"Fiction, on the other hand, offers a great, free flow of thought and emotion. It seems much easier to write fiction but, without the same understanding of and attention to word choice, structure, and what I call 'flow,' the product will be poor.

"Historical biographies and historical novels are both history books and novels. They require, therefore, a rigorous blend of organization and creative flow. This is the arena in which I hope to succeed.

For money and a change of pace, I occasionally write a good page-turner."

*   *   *

DEL VECCHIO, Deborah   1950-

PERSONAL: Born December 17, 1950, in New York, NY; daughter of Raymond Edward and Edna (a homemaker; maiden name, Gardella) Bennett; married Carl A. Del Vecchio (a corporate legal manager), April 22, 1978. *Education:* High school graduate. *Religion:* Roman Catholic.

ADDRESSES: Home—Westwood, NJ.

CAREER: Worked for New York Telephone Co., 1968-77, and New Jersey Bell Telephone Co., 1977-89; writer.

MEMBER: American Peter Cushing Club (president, 1972-80), Beverly Garland Club (vice president).

WRITINGS:

(With Tom Johnson) *Peter Cushing: The Gentle Man of Horror and His Ninety-One Films,* McFarland (Jefferson, NC), 1992.
(With Johnson) *Hammer Film Productions,* McFarland, 1995.

Contributor to periodicals, including *Fangoria, Scarlet Street,* and *Midnight Marquee.*

WORK IN PROGRESS: New Age Vampires, 1960-1993, publication by Borgo Press expected in 1997.

SIDELIGHTS: Deborah Del Vecchio told *CA:* "Because I am a fledgling writer myself, I am much too green to offer any wit or wisdom to aspiring authors. I am living proof, however, that *anyone* who has the burning need to see his or her name on a book cover or byline can succeed. If you truly want this to happen, never give up on your dream. Fate will take care of the rest."

*   *   *

DENNARD, Deborah   1953-

PERSONAL: Born October 8, 1953, in Houston, TX; daughter of Margaret (Kelly) Ward; married Robert Marion Dennard (an engineer), December 22, 1973. *Education:* Texas A & M University, B.A., 1976. *Religion:* Methodist. *Avocational interests:* Community theater, dogs, music, bird watching, tap dancing, travel.

ADDRESSES: Agent—c/o Cobblehill Books, 375 Hudson St., New York, NY 10014.

CAREER: Fort Worth Zoo, Fort Worth, TX, zoo educator, 1976-92; writer.

MEMBER: Society of Children's Book Writers and Illustrators.

WRITINGS:

How Wise Is an Owl?, illustrated by Michelle Neavill, Carolrhoda, 1993.
Do Cats Have Nine Lives?, illustrated by Jackie Ubanovic, Carolrhoda, 1993.
Can Elephants Drink through Their Noses?, illustrated by Terry Boles, Carolrhoda, 1993.
Travis and the Better Mousetrap, Cobblehill Books, in press.

WORK IN PROGRESS: "I am always doing research for at least ten projects at once. All (or most) of my projects are animal or nature oriented. Some are serious, some are frivolous, all are fun."

SIDELIGHTS: Deborah Dennard commented: "As a newly published author, still in a state of shock over my first three books, I feel that the greatest motivation behind my writing is a desire to excite children, and hopefully to inspire in them a lifelong interest in reading, animals, and nature. I am available as a visiting author, an activity which I greatly enjoy, and hope to continue publishing both my nonfiction and fiction works in the future. What could be more exciting than to see your name on the cover of a book?"

*   *   *

de VALLBONA, Rima
See VALLBONA, Rima-Gretel Rothe

*   *   *

DICKEY, Christopher   1951-
(H. D. P.)

PERSONAL: Born August 31, 1951, in Nashville, TN; son of James (a writer) and Maxine (Syerson) Dickey; married Susan Tuckerman, November 29, 1969 (divorced, December, 1979); married Carol Salvatore, March 22, 1980; children: James B. T. *Education:* University of Virginia, B.A., 1972; Boston University, M.S., 1974.

ADDRESSES: Office—Newsweek, 251 West 57th St.,

New York, NY 10019. *Agent*—Theron Raines, 71 Park Ave., New York, NY 10016.

CAREER: Washington Post, Washington, DC, editor, reporter, foreign correspondent, 1974-86; *Newsweek,* New York City, became Cairo Bureau Chief, then Paris Bureau Chief, 1986-93, Middle East Regional Editor, 1993—.

MEMBER: Council on Foreign Relations.

AWARDS, HONORS: Interamerican Press Association Award for Reporting on Latin America, 1980; Overseas Press Club Award for Magazine Article, 1983.

WRITINGS:

With the Contras: A Reporter in the Wilds of Nicaragua, Simon & Schuster (New York), 1986, updated with a preface, Touchstone, 1987.
Expats: Travels in Arabia, from Tripoli to Teheran, Atlantic Monthly Press (New York), 1990.

Contributor to *Central America: Anatomy of a Conflict,* Tergamon, 1983. Columnist for *Rolling Stone* under the pseudonym H. D. P., 1983. Also contributor to periodicals, including *Foreign Affairs, New Republic, Vanity Fair,* and *New York Review of Books.*

WORK IN PROGRESS: A nonfiction book dealing with the Middle East; a novel about espionage and crime.

SIDELIGHTS: In his nonfiction writings, Christopher Dickey combines the keen insight of a journalist with a novelist's sense of drama and personality. This approach has produced two well-received and distinctive books. Written in 1986, with the United States deeply involved in the war between Nicaragua's Sandinista government and the so-called Contra rebels, Dickey's *With the Contras: A Reporter in the Wilds of Nicaragua* sheds a harsh, revealing light on that conflict. His 1990 book, *Expats: Travels in Arabia, from Tripoli to Teheran* presents portraits of Westerners living and working in Libya, Egypt, Saudi Arabia, Iran, and elsewhere in the Middle East.

"It is one of Dickey's strengths that he is just, honest and respectful about almost all the characters who appear in his testimony of what it was like to be in the middle of a nightmare," wrote Robert Cox in the *Washington Post Book World* of *With the Contras.* Dickey begins his tale by charting the history of the Contras, the counter-revolutionary army that attempted to overthrow the leftist Sandinista government after the Sandinistas ousted Nicaraguan dictator Anastasio Somoza Debayle in 1979. The Contra army had its origins in the remnants of the disposed Somoza's brutal National Guard. As the conflict between the guerrilla and government forces escalated and the Sandinista regime grew more repressive, the Contras were joined by other members of Nicaraguan society, ranging from peasants to politicians, who had grown disillusioned with Sandinista rule. Dickey notes that the United States became involved with the Contras—covertly at first—supplying arms and military training, mainly through agents of the Central Intelligence Agency (CIA). He further describes the men and women who took positions of leadership within the guerrilla force, bearing names such as "Suicida" and "El Muerto" (meaning "The Dead One"). He also notes the confusion, fighting and killing within the factions. Andrew Nikiforuk of the Toronto *Globe and Mail* commended "Dickey's lucid portrait of Nicaragua's 'freedom fighters.'"

Dickey's book, however, is not one-sided in its view of the war. Rod Nordland, writing in *Newsweek,* noted that Dickey "is no special pleader for the Sandinistas. He documents some of the Sandinista injustices that turned many onetime supporters into what President Reagan chooses to call 'freedom fighters.' But his book quickly disabuses us of any sympathy with the anti-Sandinista cause. Hoodlums, assassins, even known terrorists parade through its pages." *New York Times Book Review* contributor Abraham Brumberg declared that Dickey portrays the Contra leaders as "men addicted to violence" whose "brutality is indiscriminate."

"*With the Contras* easily rates as one of the better books about Nicaragua's revolution and its aftermath," judged Nikiforuk. "Dickey writes elegantly . . . and he lays out the complicated web of a counter-revolution with the ease of a mapmaker." A few critics did remark, however, on Dickey's style as being more suited to fiction. Cox suggested that "perhaps because the material is so incredible, he has woven a book of nonfiction as if it were a novel." Brumberg objected to the presentation as "in the vein of a grade-B thriller, replete with . . . abrupt and bewildering cuts from one incident to another; lurid passages; far-fetched similes and metaphors." Christopher Lehmann-Haupt of the *New York Times* also said that while *With the Contras* "seems a little like fiction," it is nevertheless, "a vivid if horrifying report on recent events in Central America."

In his second book, Dickey takes his reporter's eye

and his novelist's flair thousands of miles away from Central America, to the deserts of Arabia. *Expats: Travels in Arabia, from Tripoli to Teheran* is Dickey's exploration of how Westerners interact with the Arab world. He presents a wide cast of characters, including aging explorers, famine-relief workers, secretaries, and oil-tanker crews. Most of Dickey's "expats" have come to the Middle East for the money: they could never earn so much and live so well doing the same jobs at home. "The expats crowd into compounds, count their money, drink themselves silly and leaf through out-of-date and censored magazines from America," explained Robert Irwin in *Washington Post Book World.* "There are exceptions, but mostly their lives seem shallow and depressing, though well paid."

The tales and anecdotes of the expats unite the book, with the Arab world serving as "more backdrop than subject," stated *Los Angeles Times Book Review* contributor David Rieff. The critic further commented, "Interestingly, *Expats* is almost entirely free of theorizing about the Middle East." Robert Fox, writing in the *Times Literary Supplement,* also commended the "interviews and encounters" which "sometimes provide [Dickey] with impressions at second hand, but they are vivid impressions and often illuminating." "Moving across the Middle East, Mr. Dickey constructs a richly hued collage of foreigners enmeshed in the Arab world," surmised Sandra Mackey in the *New York Times Book Review.*

BIOGRAPHICAL/CRITICAL SOURCES:

PERIODICALS

Chicago Tribune Book World, April 6, 1986, p. 43.
Globe and Mail (Toronto), April 5, 1986.
Los Angeles Times Book Review, June 24, 1990, pp. 3, 12.
Nation, February 15, 1986, p. 181.
Newsweek, February 17, 1986, p. 71.
New Yorker, February 17, 1986, p. 103; September 3, 1990, p. 108.
New York Review of Books, April 10, 1986, p. 3.
New York Times, January 20, 1986, p. 17.
New York Times Book Review, January 26, 1986, pp. 3, 39; May 24, 1987, p. 20; June 24, 1990, p. 14.
Times Literary Supplement, September 7-13, 1990, p. 938; December 27, 1991, p. 24.
Washington Post Book World, January 26, 1986, p. 5; June 14, 1987, p. 12; June 17, 1990, pp. 6, 8.

DICKMAN, Thomas   1955-

PERSONAL: Born June 27, 1955, in Salt Lake City, UT; married Anny Lefebvre, October 17, 1981; children: Elizabeth, Samuel. *Education:* Attended Reed College, 1974-76; University of Utah, B.A., 1985, M.S.W., 1990. *Politics:* "Left."

ADDRESSES: Home—1784 South 800 E., Salt Lake City, UT 84105.

CAREER: Writer. Licensed clinical social worker.

WRITINGS:

(Translator with wife, Anny Lefebvre) Michael Beaud, *A History of Capitalism, 1500-1980,* Monthly Review Press, 1983.

Translator of the book *Socialism in the Crucible of History,* Humanities. Author of the unpublished novel *Inside the Millenium.*

WORK IN PROGRESS: Fused, a novel, completion expected in 2000.

*   *   *

DIETERICH, Michele M.   1962-

PERSONAL: Born June 8, 1962, in Ohio; daughter of Don (an engineer) and Barbara (an artist; maiden name, Sigler) Dieterich. *Education:* Boston University, B.S. (magna cum laude), 1984.

ADDRESSES: Home and office—P.O. Box 7273, Bozeman, MT 58715.

CAREER: Artist and writer. Freelance commercial artist in Newport Beach, CA; *Mountain Biker International,* London, England, itinerant correspondent; *Happenings Magazine,* Bozeman, MT, staff writer and art critic. Contributing photographer to *Mountain Biker International.* Member of Gallatin County Search and Rescue.

WRITINGS:

Skiing, photographs by Bob Allen, Wayland Publishers, 1991.

Also contributor to *Mountain City Biking, Bicycle Guide,* and *Happenings Magazine.* Contributor of photographs to *Mountain Biking,* by Allen, Wayland Publishing, 1991.

WORK IN PROGRESS: A children's book about experiencing art; traveling in Guatemala and Peru to research a novel about shamanism.

SIDELIGHTS: Michele M. Dieterich commented: "I recently finished a short book about skiing for children between the ages of ten and thirteen. I had wondered if the idea was a bit redundant until I wandered through a variety of libraries in England and the United States in search of something—anything—about snow sports written for children. The few books I discovered were concise, well written, and informative, but they were written for adults in reference to children or written in a manner that forgets children are aware, intelligent individuals with a unique understanding of the world, especially those in the age group that my book targets.

"It was a pleasure to write directly to children and to encourage children to read by touching upon a subject most enjoyable to them. I believe that just writing for children on an intelligent level can and will encourage them to read. And why not broach subjects of all kinds to children, who are most receptive to new ideas and who are like sponges for knowledge? It is my theory that children are listless about reading because vibrant, provocative subjects are often unavailable to them. When I was young, I was a voracious reader bored by what I found in the children's section of the library. I often ventured into the adult areas, picking up everything I could find that looked intriguing, getting a bit lost by technical language but being fascinated by the topics.

"Since my interests in writing follow from my life choices, I have mostly written about skiing, mountain biking, art, and travel. I would love to write about both art and travel for children in an experiential format. For example, art as a subject would not be a list of famous artists and paintings and museums but how to experience and relate to art. What it means to enjoy a painting or sculpture on all levels, I believe, would be reiterating something children already feel when they see art. While children can and should be the most receptive to art, they are unsure of the significance of their reactions. It is tough to rarely be taken seriously.

"Different cultures and places on this planet could be related to children so well in an adventure format. I believe that the best way to reach children about something they are completely removed from is to tell it in the form of a mystical but reality-filled story of travel. I would really like to introduce alien cultures and religions to children through the people and places [I've] experienced.

"Meanwhile I am skiing, rock climbing, ice climbing, telemarking, biking, running, and hiking in Bozeman, Montana. On the scribe side of things, I am currently writing a series on local artists for a regional arts magazine and, of course, writing proposals."

*   *   *

DILLER, Harriett 1953-

PERSONAL: Born August 9, 1953, in Lancaster, SC; daughter of Neal (an office services manager) and Betty (a college professor; maiden name, Hovis) Hodges; married Jeffrey Diller (a member of the clergy), August 21, 1976; children: Adam, Michael. *Education:* Davidson College, B.A., 1975. *Politics:* Democrat. *Religion:* United Church of Christ. *Avocational interests:* Bicycling, reading, watching baseball and football.

ADDRESSES: Home and office—590 East King St., Chambersburg, PA 17201.

CAREER: Freelance writer, 1979—.

WRITINGS:

Celebrations That Matter, Augsburg, 1990.
Grandaddy's Highway, illustrated by Henri Sorensen, Boyds Mills, 1993.
The Waiting Day, Green Tiger Press, 1994.

SIDELIGHTS: Harriett Diller commented: "I'm often asked how I chose to write for children, and I give a different answer each time. The truth is, I really don't know. Or maybe the truth is, there are so many reasons that I could give a different one to everybody who ever asks and never run out of sincere answers.

"I'm always intimidated by the kind of writer who is called a natural storyteller, because I'm not a natural storyteller at all. I would rather hide in a closet than tell a story. Or listen to other people tell stories. I consider myself to be more of a collage artist than a storyteller. I take what I hear, see, feel, read, and think, and try to form them into a story."

In Diller's 1993 book, *Grandaddy's Highway,* young Maggie and her grandfather imagine their way across the country in a pretend truck, traveling west through Pittsburgh, Chicago, the West, and finally to the Pacific Ocean. A *Publishers Weekly* critic praised Diller's tale as a "warm intergenerational story [that] offers a subtle geography lesson in the form of a loosely structured fantasy." And *School*

Library Journal contributor Sharron McElmeel noted that Henri Sorensen's accompanying illustrations "have a dreamy element that highlights the fantasy."

BIOGRAPHICAL/CRITICAL SOURCES:

PERIODICALS

Children's Book Review Service, April, 1993, p. 103.
Kirkus Reviews, March 15, 1993, p. 369.
Publishers Weekly, February 1, 1993, p. 95.
School Library Journal, May, 1993, p. 83.

*   *   *

DIZDAREVIC, Zlatko   1948-

PERSONAL: Born January 22, 1948, in Belgrade, Yugoslavia (now Serbia); son of Mustafa (an officer) and Sefika (Dzanovic) Dizdarevic; married Biljana Zagorac (a psychology professor), November 28, 1978; children: Ognjen, Drazen. *Education:* Sarajevo University, faculty of law, 1973.

ADDRESSES: Office—Skerlica 18, 71000 Sarajevo. *Agent*—c/o Oslobodjenje Sarajevo, Dz Bivedica 185, Sarajevo, BIH 71000.

CAREER: Journalist in Sarajevo, 1973-92. *Military service:* Yugoslav National Army, captain, 1976-77.

MEMBER: Union of Journalists in Bosnia-Herzegovina, Intellectual Circle 99.

AWARDS, HONORS: Award from Reporters without Borders, Paris, 1992; Bruno Kreisky Award for Human Rights, Vienna, 1993.

WRITINGS:

A Time of Decision: Israeli-Palestinian Relations, Oslobodjenje, 1989.
Sarajevo: A War Journal, Fromm (New York), 1993.
Sarajevo Portraits, Spengler (Paris), 1994.

WORK IN PROGRESS: Black and Red Fascism, a book on contemporary fascism in Europe.

*   *   *

DOANE, Janice (L.)   1950-

PERSONAL: Born August 10, 1950, in Louisville, KY; daughter of Ivan G. (a personnel director) and Mary Martha (a teacher; maiden name, Rice) Doane; married James Anthony Mott (a systems engineer), August 18, 1979; children: Sara Doane, Alex Doane. *Education:* State University of New York at Buffalo, B.A. (cum laude), 1972, Ph.D., 1981; University of Wisconsin—Madison, M.A., 1974.

ADDRESSES: Home—8160 Phaeton Dr., Oakland, CA 94605. *Office*—Department of English, St. Mary's College of California, Moraga, CA 94575.

CAREER: State University of New York College at Buffalo, instructor in English, 1980-83; St. Mary's College of California, Moraga, assistant professor, 1984-89, associate professor of English, 1989—, department head, 1993—. Instructor at Canisius College, 1980-82, and Medaille College, 1981.

MEMBER: Phi Beta Kappa.

AWARDS, HONORS: Fellow of Pembroke Center for Women, Brown University, 1983-84.

WRITINGS:

Silence and Narrative: The Early Novels of Gertrude Stein, Greenwood Press (Westport, CT), 1986.
(With Devon Hodges) *Nostalgia and Sexual Difference: The Resistance to Contemporary Feminism,* Methuen (New York), 1987.
(With Hodges) *From Klein to Kristeva: Psychoanalytic Feminism and the Search for the "Good Enough" Mother,* University of Michigan Press (Ann Arbor), 1992.

Contributor to books, including *Gender Studies: New Directions in Feminist Criticism,* edited by Judith Spector, Bowling Green State University Press, 1986; and *Modernity and Mass Culture,* edited by James Naremore and Patrick Brantlinger, Indiana University Press, 1991. Contributor to literature journals.

WORK IN PROGRESS: Feminism, Memory, and Narrative, with Devon Hodges, a study of authors for whom "the history of our social lives is powerfully imbricated in the structure of our personal identities."

SIDELIGHTS: Janice Doane told *CA:* "After briefly considering a career in journalism, I elected instead to pursue my love and fascination for literature. I was particularly interested in the State University of New York at Buffalo for its fine offerings in literary theory, especially the program in psychology and literature, the only such program at the time. I pursued a minor in psychology and literature, while focusing on contemporary critical theory and modernist literature.

"As I began my dissertation on Gertrude Stein, I became convinced that Stein's position as a woman writer had profoundly influenced her stylistic departures from nineteenth-century literature. This intellectual discovery drew me into a more active communal effort with other women in the English literature graduate program. With them I initiated courses on feminist critical theory, and I began writing with a fellow graduate student, Devon Hodges, who has since become my co-author on a number of projects.

"Although I often claim that it is 'theoretically' appropriate for feminists to write together, more simply it is also a joy to work with someone with whom I feel theoretically and temperamentally aligned. Our partnership has enabled us to remain productive through job searches, heavy teaching loads, and family demands.

"In 1983 I was awarded a postdoctoral fellowship at the Pembroke Center for Women at Brown University. This fellowship not only put me in contact with many exciting feminist scholars, but also enabled me to accomplish an enormous amount of research and writing for my second book, *Nostalgia and Sexual Difference.*

"The primary focus of my career has been feminist critical theory, but my interest has carried me beyond my academic specialty in American literature into research and writing on psychoanalysis, sociology, history, the media, and popular culture."

*   *   *

DODDS, Bill 1952-

PERSONAL: Born July 24, 1952, in Des Moines, IA; son of John J. (a lawyer) and Margaret (a homemaker; maiden name, Farrell) Dodds; married Monica Faudree (a social worker), March 23, 1974; children: Tom, Carrie, Andy. *Education:* Attended St. Thomas Seminary, 1970-72; University of Washington, B.A., 1974. *Religion:* Roman Catholic.

ADDRESSES: Agent—c/o Boyds Mills Press, 910 Church St., Honesdale, PA 18431.

CAREER: Catholic Youth Organization, Seattle, WA, retreat leader, 1974-76; King County Advocates for Retarded Citizens, Seattle, WA, recreation center assistant director, 1976-78; *The Progress,* Seattle, WA, reporter and editor, 1978-88.

Freelance writer of fiction and nonfiction for adults and children, 1988—. Volunteer for Special Olympics, Catholic Worker Family Kitchen, Knights of Columbus.

MEMBER: Catholic Press Association.

AWARDS, HONORS: International Three-Day Writing Contest award, 1990; twenty-five regional, state, and national writing and editing awards from the Catholic Press Association, the Society of Professional Journalists, and the Washington Press Association.

WRITINGS:

JUVENILE

The Hidden Fortune, Liguori Publications, 1991.
My Sister Annie, Boyds Mills Press, 1993.
Bedtime Parables, Our Sunday Visitor, 1993.

OTHER

(Coauthor) *Speaking Out, Fighting Back: Personal Experiences of Women Who Survived Childhood Sexual Abuse in the Home,* Madrona Publications, 1985.
The Parents' Guide to Dirty Tricks (humor), Meadowbrook, 1989, reprinted as *How to Outsmart Your Kids: The Parents' Guide to Dirty Tricks,* 1993.
How to Be a Catholic Mother (humor), Meadowbrook, 1990.
Dads, Catholic Style (humor/inspirational/spirituality), Servant Publications, 1990.
How to Survive Your 40th Birthday (humor), Meadowbrook, 1990.
O Father: A Murder Mystery, Pulp, 1991.
How I Flunked Penmanship and Other Tales of Growing up Catholic, Servant Publications, 1991.

Also contributor to *Keeping Your Kids Catholic,* Servant Publications, 1989, and *Kids Pick the Funniest Poems,* Meadowbrook, 1991. Author of weekly family humor column, "Dad Knows Best," 1983-88, syndicated nationally in Catholic papers, 1983-85; coauthor (with wife, Monica) of Catholic News Service monthly advice column and family advice column for *Columbia Magazine;* also columnist for and contributor to periodicals including *Columbia Magazine, Our Sunday Visitor, New Covenant, Catholic Digest, Liguorian, National Catholic Reporter, St. Anthony Messenger, Salt, U.S. Catholic,* and *Woman's World.*

SIDELIGHTS: Bill Dodds commented: "I love writing (and reading) because I had five very special teachers: two in grade school, one in high school, and two in college. They not only taught me the basics, they encouraged me to develop the talent they saw in me.

"I didn't like to read when I was young. I have one brother and three sisters, and I was the only one in my family who never received a certificate for reading ten books during summer vacation. I'm not sure I read even one. It wasn't until I was in high school (a boarding school) that I began to read for fun.

"Almost all my books have humor in them, the kind that doesn't make fun of anyone in a mean way. I really like making people laugh, especially kids."

BIOGRAPHICAL/CRITICAL SOURCES:

PERIODICALS

Booklist, February 15, 1993, p. 1059; March 1, 1993, p. 1229.
Children's Book Review Service, March, 1993, p. 92.
Quill and Quire, July, 1991, p. 50.
School Library Journal, February, 1993, p. 92.

*   *   *

DOLINAR, Stephen J.   1926-

PERSONAL: Born November 15, 1926, in Kansas City, KS; son of Stephen E. and Anna Dolinar; married Dorothy Schleicher, September 4, 1948; children: Stephen M., Dorothy Anne Dolinar Gragg. *Education:* Kansas City Junior College, A.A., 1948; University of Missouri—Kansas City, B.A., 1950, J.D., 1953. *Politics:* Democrat. *Religion:* Roman Catholic.

ADDRESSES: Home—3 N.R. 47th St., Kansas City, MO 64116.

CAREER: Trial attorney in Kansas City, MO, 1953-88. *Military service:* U.S. Army, paratrooper, 1944-46; served in the Philippines; became sergeant; received Philippine Liberation Medal.

MEMBER: Kansas Bar Association.

WRITINGS:

Stratagem Rex, Branden Publishing, 1976.
The Tree, Winston-Derek, 1993.

WORK IN PROGRESS: Mitzie's Reply, a suspense novel; *Cano Chase,* a western novel.

*   *   *

DONALDSON, Joan   1953-

PERSONAL: Born May 24, 1953, in Mount Clemens, MI; daughter of James (an engineer) and Ruth (a homemaker and artist; maiden name, Schnoor) Donaldson; married John Van Voorhees (a farmer), October 18, 1975; children: (adopted) Mateo, Carlos. *Education:* Hope College, B.A., 1975. *Religion:* Anabaptist (Mennonite). *Avocational interests:* Traditional music and dance, Spencerian script, knitting lace, gardening.

ADDRESSES: Home—Pleasant Hill Farm, Route 4, Fennville, MI 49408. *Agent*—Colleen Mohyde, Doe Coover Agency, 58 Sagamore Ave., Medford, MA 02155.

CAREER: Organic fruit farmer, 1975—. Hope College, Hope, MI, teaching associate of dance, 1981-84. Michigan Literacy Tutor, folk dance instructor with Community Education, and musician for church services, 1982-87. Quiltmaker, creating commissioned pieces of folk art.

MEMBER: Comhaltas Ceoltoirr Eireann (traditional music and dance association of Ireland), Bread for the World, Michigan Organic Growers, Lacy Knitters.

AWARDS, HONORS: Allegan County Homemaker of the Year, 1986; Michigan State Fair Homemaker of the Year, 1987.

WRITINGS:

The Real Pretend, illustrated by Tasha Tudor, Checkerboard Press, 1992.
Great American Quilts 1994, Oxmoor House, 1994.

Contributor of articles to *Practical Homeschooling.*

WORK IN PROGRESS: A biography of Platt Rogers Spencer, master penman; a book about international adoption called *Forever Family.*

SIDELIGHTS: Joan Donaldson commented: "The values of simplicity, self-reliance and community, as seen from a Christian viewpoint, have shaped and governed the goals of my life.

"I approach my writing from the perspective of an organic farmer, homemaker, and folk artist. As a writer, I draw on the experiences and lessons learned from those roles. Writing and telling stories has been a part of my life since I was six years old. I still have a book of collected stories and poems I wrote, illustrated, and bound when I was ten. Now when I am dismayed over my children's spelling (whom I homeschool), I turn to my youthful writings to recall my own spelling mistakes.

"Pencil and paper are where stories begin for me. Having many jobs to fill each day, I snatch time for writing whenever time arises. But a blessing of manual labor is that ideas can flourish in your mind even if your hands are busy packing fruit or quilting. Recently I discovered a dear writer friend, and together we critique and encourage each other as writers and homemakers. I feel this sharing is important, and when speaking to 'young authors' groups I advise them to seek out someone who is willing to read their works a dozen times.

"As a child I read constantly, and, in my early dreams about being an author, I knew I wanted to give back a little of what I had claimed as a young reader. Now I hope to present a glimpse into my own 'far from the madding crowd' lifestyle. I would like to give children a sense of simpler values, the delights of nurturing, and the joys to be found in community. With these thoughts in mind I pray about my stories and begin to write."

*   *   *

DORROS, Arthur (M.) 1950-

PERSONAL: Surname is pronounced "doh-*rohs*"; born May 19, 1950, in Washington, DC; son of Sidney Dorros (an educator) and Dorothy Louise Dorros (a nurse); married Sandra Marulanda (a teacher, translator, and editor), May, 1986; children: Alex. *Education:* University of Wisconsin, B.A., 1972; Pacific Oaks College, postgraduate studies and teaching certification, 1979. *Avocational interests:* Filmmaking, building, carpentry, horticulture, hiking in Central and South America, Asia, and Spanish language and literature.

ADDRESSES: Agent—Ruth Cohen, Inc., P.O. Box 7626, Menlo Park, CA 94025.

CAREER: Writer and illustrator, 1979—. Worked variously as a builder, carpenter, drafter, photographer, horticultural worker, and dockhand; teacher in elementary and junior high schools and adult education in Seattle, WA, and New York City for six years; artist in residence for more than a dozen New York City public schools, running programs in creative writing, bookmaking, and video; University of Washington, former teacher of courses on writing in the classroom; consultant in libraries and schools; director of Children's Writing Workshop, presenting seminars and workshops on writing to students, teachers, and administrators in schools, libraries, and at conferences internationally.

MEMBER: Authors Guild, Authors League of America.

AWARDS, HONORS: Reading Rainbow Book selection, 1986, for *Alligator Shoes,* 1989, for *Ant Cities,* and 1993, for *Abuela; Ant Cities, Feel the Wind,* and *Rain Forest Secrets* were selected as Outstanding Science Books by the National Science Teachers Association Children's Book Council, 1987, 1989, and 1990 respectively; *Tonight Is Carnaval* was named to *Booklist*'s Best of Year list, 1991; *Abuela* was named an American Library Association notable book and a *Horn Book* 20 Best, both 1991; Parent's Choice, 1991, for *Abuela;* Notable Book in Field of Social Studies, 1991, for *Tonight Is Carnaval;* 25 Best of the Year, *Boston Globe,* 1991, for *Abuela;* Book of Distinction, *Hungry Mind Review,* 1991, for *Abuela;* American Book Association Pick of Lists citation, 1992, for *This Is My House;* Books for Children List, Children's Literature Center in the Library of Congress, 1992, for *Abuela* and *Tonight Is Carnaval.*

WRITINGS:

JUVENILE

Abuela, illustrated by Elisa Kleven, Dutton, 1991.
Tonight Is Carnaval, Dutton, 1991, translated into Spanish by wife, Sandra Marulanda Dorros, as *Por Fin Es Carnaval,* illustrated by Club de Madres Virgenes del Carmen, Dutton, 1991.

SELF-ILLUSTRATED; JUVENILE

Pretzels, Greenwillow, 1981.
Alligator Shoes, Dutton, 1982.
Yum Yum (board book for toddlers), Harper, 1987.
Splash Splash (board book for toddlers), Harper, 1987.
Ant Cities (nonfiction), Harper, 1987.
Feel the Wind (nonfiction), Harper, 1989.
Rain Forest Secrets (nonfiction), Scholastic, 1990.
Me and My Shadow (nonfiction), Scholastic, 1990.
Follow the Water from Brook to Ocean (nonfiction), HarperCollins, 1991.
This Is My House (nonfiction), Scholastic, 1992.
Animal Tracks (nonfiction), Scholastic, 1992.

Radio Man/Don Radio, Spanish translation by S. M. Dorros, HarperCollins, 1993.
Elephant Families (nonfiction), HarperCollins, 1994.

Also illustrator of children's books *Charlie's House, What Makes Day and Night,* and *Magic Secrets.*

OTHER

Scriptwriter and photographer for filmstrips, including "Teaching Reading, a Search for the Right Combination," released by the National School Public Relations Association, and "Sharing a Lifetime of Learning," released by the National Education Association. Author and director of *Portrait of a Neighborhood* and other videos. Contributor of articles and illustrations published in periodicals and purchased by Dodd-Mead Publishers and *USA Today.*

WORK IN PROGRESS: *A Tree Is Growing,* for Scholastic, 1995; *Isla,* for Dutton, 1995.

SIDELIGHTS: As Arthur Dorros wrote in a profile for Scholastic Books, he "never imagined that" he "would be making books someday" when he was a child growing up in Washington, D.C. Nevertheless, the award-winning children's author loved to read and draw and was enthralled with animals. His family and friends fostered his latent talent. "First there was my grandfather, who would occasionally send me letters, all with the same drawing of a bird on them," he wrote in his profile. "Then there was the ninety-year-old neighbor who made sculptures out of tree roots he found, and my mother who kept a set of oil pastels in a drawer and would provide . . . art supplies or a bottle of tempera paint at the drop of a hat. And my father was a great storyteller."

Despite this environment, Dorros did not pursue drawing through elementary and junior high school. Dorros remembers that he grew frustrated with his attempts to draw, and he "quit drawing in the fifth grade." He did not begin to draw again until he reached high school and had to draw amoebas and animals in biology class. He has been drawing ever since. Dorros makes a point of encouraging children to persist in their endeavors despite frustration. When he gives bookmaking seminars and workshops in schools internationally, he tells children that they should continue to create even if they make mistakes. Jeff Green of the *Oakland Press* reported that Dorros told a group of children: "I wasn't born an author. I had to learn, just like you guys. You have to keep on trying and don't let anyone make you stop."

Dorros himself began to create picture books at the age of twenty-nine, after exchanging stories with children who wandered close to watch him remodel houses. "I found I really enjoyed swapping stories, and my interest in making pictures had continued," he explained in his Scholastic Books profile. His first book, *Pretzels,* provides a whimsical account of the invention of the pretzel. The silly crew members of the *Bungle* let the anchor chain rust away, and the ship's cook, I Fryem Fine, replaces it with biscuit dough. When the salt encrusted, dough anchor chain is no longer needed, the cook shapes it into a twisted biscuit. First Mate Pretzel loves the cook's invention so much that it is named after him. Two other tales, "The Jungle" and "A New Land," are also included in this account of the *Bungle* crew's adventures. With Dorros' "knack for writing straight-faced nonsense" and the book's "droll" pictures, concluded a commentator for *Kirkus Reviews, Pretzels* is "mighty companionable." A reviewer for the *Bulletin of the Center for Children's Books* wrote that the "ineptitude of the characters" and "humor in the writing style" may be enjoyed by children. A reviewer for *School Library Journal* decided that the stories have a "refreshing, slightly off-the-wall feel. . . . Kids will enjoy the absurdities."

Dorros' next published work, *Alligator Shoes,* was inspired by his earliest childhood memory: sitting on an alligator's tail. In *Alligator Shoes,* an alligator fascinated with footwear visits a shoe store. Locked in after closing time, he tries on pair after pair, and finally falls asleep. When he wakes up in the morning, he hears a woman say that she would like a pair of alligator shoes. Realizing that not having shoes is better than becoming shoes, the alligator flees. *Alligator Shoes* was eventually selected as a Reading Rainbow book.

The publication of *Ant Cities* in 1987 marked Dorros' debut as a writer of children's nonfiction. In *Ant Cities,* Dorros uses text and cartoon-like illustrations to explain ants and their various activities, from processing food to caring for eggs. Instructions for building an ant farm are also provided. A reviewer for the *Bulletin of the Center for Children's Books* characterized the illustrations as "inviting and informative." Ellen Loughran, writing for *School Library Journal,* noted that the book would be a "useful addition to the science section." *Ant Cities* was selected as an Outstanding Science Book of 1987 by the National Science Teachers Association Children's Book Council. *Feel the Wind,* published in 1989, and *Rain Forest Secrets,* released in 1990, also earned this distinction, and his other picture books about science—*Me and My Shadow, Follow the Water from Brook to Ocean,* and *Animal Tracks*—have also been well received.

Dorros, who spent a year living in South America and speaks Spanish, made a much-needed contribution to children's literature in the United States with the publication of *Abuela* and *Tonight Is Carnaval,* which was translated by his wife, Sandra Marulanda Dorros, and released in Spanish as *Por Fin Es Carnaval.* Both volumes were published by Dutton in 1991. In *Abuela,* Rosalba imagines that she and her Abuela (grandmother) fly together over New York City. While the text is primarily English, Spanish words are interspersed throughout the story. Readers may infer meaning from the text or look up these words in the glossary provided. Elisa Kleven's vivid illustrations complement the text and the resulting book is, according to Molly Ivins, "just joyful." In a review for *New York Times Book Review* Ivins asserted that *Abuela* "is a book to set any young child dreaming." Kate McClelland, writing in *School Library Journal,* concluded that the "innovative fantasy" will enrich "intellectually curious children who are intrigued by the exploration of another language."

In *Tonight Is Carnaval,* a young boy tells of his community's preparation for *carnaval.* The tapestries, or *arpilleras,* sewn by Club de Madres Virgen del Carmen of Lima, Peru, illustrate the beauty and excitement of the cultural event Dorros describes. A reviewer for *Horn Book* described the book as "brilliant, beautiful . . . affirmative and valuable." Both *Abuela* and *Tonight Is Carnaval* have won several awards, including selection to the Books for Children List recommended by the Children's Literature Center in the Library of Congress.

Dorros also wrote *Radio Man/Don Radio,* and his wife provided the Spanish translation. The story centers on friends Diego and David, children who are members of migrant farm worker families. Diego, who constantly listens to the radio, has earned the nickname of "Radio Man" from David. The boys lose touch with one another when Diego's family begins a journey to Washington state, where they intend to work in the apple orchards. Diego, however, finds a way to contact David through the radio. Reviewer Janice Del Negro noted in *Booklist* that the illustrations provided by Dorros provide "a solid sense of place and reflect the strong family ties and efforts at community Dorros conveys in his story."

The nonfiction book *This Is My House* conveys the respect and admiration for other cultures communicated by *Abuela, Tonight Is Carnaval, Radio Man/ Don Radio.* In this book, Dorros describes twenty-two houses around the world and discusses the climate in which they are built, the people whom they shelter, and their construction. These dwellings range from stone houses in Bolivia, to the car in which an otherwise homeless family in the United States lives. The phrase, "This is my house" is included on every page in the language of the people who occupy each house. Mary Lou Budd, writing for the *School Library Journal,* praised this "engaging" book by noting that there is "unlimited value in the succinct, interesting text and pictures" and that the watercolors are "bright" and "pleasing."

BIOGRAPHICAL/CRITICAL SOURCES:

PERIODICALS

Booklist, January 15, 1994.
Bulletin of the Center for Children's Books, January, 1982; March, 1987.
Horn Book, May, 1991, p. 360.
Junior Bookshelf, February, 1990, p. 25.
Kirkus Reviews, November 1, 1981; August 15, 1990, p. 1167.
New York Times Book Review, December 8, 1991, p. 26.
Oakland Press, April 18, 1991.
Publishers Weekly, August 14, 1987, p. 100; November 15, 1991, p. 71; August 3, 1992, p. 70.
School Library Journal, December, 1981, p. 74; August, 1987, pp. 66-67; May, 1990, p. 96; September, 1991, p. 245; October, 1991, pp. 90-94; September, 1992, p. 215-16.

OTHER

Arthur Dorros (publicity profile), Scholastic Books, c. 1992.

*   *   *

DOWD, John David   1945-

PERSONAL: Born March 12, 1945, in Dargaville, New Zealand; son of Daniel H. H. (a dentist) and Audrey Belle Judd (a dental technician) Dowd; married Beatrice Thiboutot (an editor and translator), June 19, 1976; children: Dylan Xavier, Olympia Hardy. *Education:* Attended Auckland University. *Avocational interests:* Gardening, scuba diving, sea kayaking.

ADDRESSES: Home—Box 91323, West Vancouver, British Columbia, Canada V7V 3N9.

CAREER: Freelance photographer and writer, 1970-80; commercial scuba diver in the North Sea, United Kingdom, and Scotland, 1976-77; Ecomarine Ocean Kayak Center, British Columbia, Canada, owner and manager, 1980-90; *Sea Kayaker Magazine,* Seattle, WA, owner and editor, 1984-89. Writer for children, 1990—. Adventure tour operator, South America, 1971-72; led kayak expedition in Caribbean, 1977-78. Outward Bound Instructor in United Kingdom, New Zealand, and Canada. Former president and founding member of Trade Association of Sea Kayaking (TASK), Seattle, WA.

MEMBER: Society of Children's Book Writers and Illustrators.

WRITINGS:

JUVENILE

Ring of Tall Trees, Alaska Northwest, 1992.
Abalone Summer, Alaska Northwest, 1993.

OTHER

Sea Kayaking: A Manual for Long-Distance Touring, University of Washington Press, 1981.

WORK IN PROGRESS: Hogsty Reef, Elk in the Fields, The Butterfly (all complete manuscripts); *Flight from the Generals;* and *Rare and Endangered.*

SIDELIGHTS: John David Dowd commented: "In 1990 I reassessed my priorities and discovered that when I matched them with a time allotment, the lists matched almost perfectly—if one was inverted. At the time I was president of three companies and a trade association. My wife averaged twelve hours a day editing a magazine, and we hired people to help care for our children. As a result of our reassessment, we sold all business interests, and I have spent the past three years writing children's books and 'doing things' with my family. In particular, we traveled more together, visiting Japan, Bali, New Zealand, Fiji, the U.K., and France. This year, we drove across the U.S.A. and Canada.

"I left university in Auckland in 1965, then spent the next fifteen years travelling the world, systematically seeking adventure. I hitchhiked South America, Europe, North Africa, and the Mid-East to India. I kayaked South Chile (Punta Arenas to Puerto Montt), Indonesia, and the Caribbean. I dived on the North Sea oil rigs and worked as a freelance photographer in London, as well as an Outward Bound school instructor around the world.

"I had decided to write at an early age, so I kept logbooks throughout my travels and considered myself to be 'loading' up with writable adventures and experiences. It had not occurred to me to write children's books until, living in Vancouver, B.C., I became a father and discovered that I enjoyed telling my kids stories. All my books to date are based upon adventures from my past. Because I write from personal experience, research is limited to checking details. My kids' stuff tends to involve the resolution of problems through action, with a minimum amount of introspection. This has been my experience with children. For me, writing is fun—another adventure—and when it stops being that way, I'll do something else."

BIOGRAPHICAL/CRITICAL SOURCES:

PERIODICALS

Booklist, April 1, 1989, p. 1340.
Kliatt, winter, 1982, p. 71.
Library Journal, January, 1981, p. 1942.
Quill and Quire, September, 1992, p. 76.
School Library Journal, January, 1993, pp. 97-98.

*   *   *

DOWNING, David C(laude)   1951-

PERSONAL: Born January 31, 1951, in New York, NY; son of James W. (an executive) and Murena M. (a homemaker) Downing; married, August 17, 1974, wife's name, Crystal. *Education:* Westmont College, B.A., 1973; University of California, Los Angeles, M.A., 1975, Ph.D., 1977.

ADDRESSES: Home—608 Antler Dr., Lewisberry, PA 17339.

CAREER: Westmont College, Santa Barbara, CA, assistant professor, 1977-83, associate professor, 1983-89, professor of English, 1989-94.

AWARDS, HONORS: Teacher of the Year, Westmont College, 1980 and 1990; book of the year, Mythopoeic Society, 1993, for *Planets in Peril;* academic book of the year, American Library Association, 1993, for *Planets in Peril.*

WRITINGS:

What You Know Might Not Be So, Baker Books, 1987.
Imagine Yourself a Perfect Speller, National Textbook, 1990.
Planets in Peril: A Critical Study of C. S. Lewis's

Ransom Trilogy, University of Massachusetts Press (Amherst, MA), 1992.

WORK IN PROGRESS: Cross Purposes, a novel; *The Trials of Salem,* a study of literary interpretations of the Salem witch trials.

SIDELIGHTS: David C. Downing told *CA:* "My writing comes out of my college teaching. My books on Bible misinterpretations, on a mnemonic approach to spelling, and on C. S. Lewis's Ransom trilogy all come out of classroom experiences in which I felt the need to create my own text. Even my forthcoming novel, *Cross Purposes,* is set on a college campus and deals with issues many students and faculty have wrestled with."

*   *   *

DRAWE, D. Lynn   1942-

PERSONAL: Born November 3, 1942, in Mercedes, TX; son of Dale U. (a rancher) and Doris (a homemaker; maiden name, Garrison) Drawe; married Kathleen Kious (a teacher), August 24, 1964; children: Kimberly Anne, Pamela Lynn. *Education:* Texas College of Arts and Industries (now Texas A & M University, Kingsville), B.S., 1964; Texas Tech University, M.S., 1967; Utah State University, Ph.D., 1971. *Politics:* "Independent Conservative." *Religion:* Methodist. *Avocational interests:* Hunting, fishing, skiing, physical fitness.

ADDRESSES: Office—Welder Wildlife Foundation, P.O. Box 1400, Sinton, TX 78387.

CAREER: Texas A & M University, Kingsville, assistant professor of agriculture, 1970-74; Welder Wildlife Foundation, Sinton, TX, assistant director, 1974—. Private rancher; consultant on rangeland ecology and ecosystem management.

MEMBER: Society for Range Management (second vice president of Texas Section, 1995-96), Wildlife Society (president-elect of Texas Chapter, 1994), Sinton Rotary Club (president, 1989).

AWARDS, HONORS: Outstanding Achievement Award, Society for Range Management (SRM), 1993; honored for Outstanding Contribution to Range Management, Texas section of SRM, 1994.

WRITINGS:

(With Jim Everitt) *Trees, Shrubs, and Cacti of South Texas,* Texas Tech University Press, 1993.

Also author of *Grasses of the Texas Gulf Coastal Prairies and Marshes.* Contributor of more than seventy articles to scientific journals.

WORK IN PROGRESS: Flowering Plants of South Texas, completion expected in 1996; revising *Grasses of the Texas Gulf Coastal Prairies and Marshes,* 1996; revising *Trees, Shrubs, and Cacti of South Texas,* 1997.

SIDELIGHTS: D. Lynn Drawe told *CA:* "I was born and raised on a cattle ranch in deep South Texas, and this made me aware of the 'monte' or chaparral at an early age. Chaparral is a rich mixture of more than two hundred species of thorny, many-stemmed woody plants, many of which provide food and cover for the wildlife in the area. When I was young, my father taught me the value of these plants to livestock and wildlife. My acquaintances in the Texas ranchland included oldtimers who had grown up on the land and knew the value of these plants from their own experiences or from their parents. It was both an opportunity and a challenge to learn scientific and common names for a small number of the species present in the Coastal Bend region of South Texas for my first advanced degree. Subsequently, in my continuing professional experience, I have learned most of the plants of South Texas. Writing *Trees, Shrubs, and Cacti of South Texas* with Jim Everitt allowed us both to impart some of this knowledge to others."

*   *   *

DREWES, Athena A.   1948-

PERSONAL: Born September 23, 1948, in Bronx, NY; daughter of Charles John (a manager) and Mariko (an artist; maiden name, Atheneas) Drewes; married James Richard Bridges (a school psychologist and Unitarian-Universalist minister), May 11, 1975; children: Scott Richard, Seth Andrew. *Education:* City College of the City University of New York, B.A., 1973; New York University, M.A., 1977; Pace University, M.S., 1990, Psy.D., 1992. *Politics:* Democrat. *Religion:* Unitarian-Universalist. *Avocational interests:* Embroidery, needlework, science fiction, music, reading, Star Trek.

ADDRESSES: Home—4 Capitol Dr., Washingtonville, NY 10992. *Office*—Astor Home for Children, 36 Mill St., Rhinebeck, NY 12575.

CAREER: Mimonides Hospital, research assistant in Division of Parapsychology and Psychophysics, 1969-75; Jewish Board of Family and Children's

Services, New York City, play therapist and psychometrician at Child Development Center, 1974-82; Child Study Center, Goshen, NY, play therapist and psychometrician, 1986-91; Astor Home for Children, Rhinebeck, NY, clinical coordinator, 1992—. Stoneride Homeowners Association, president, 1979-82; member of board of directors of Blooming Grove day care center, 1981-88. Guest on radio talk shows.

MEMBER: Parapsychology Association, American Orthopsychiatric Association (fellow), American Psychology Association, National Association of School Psychologists, Association of Play Therapists, Unitarian-Universalist Society of Orange County (president, 1994-95), Psi Chi.

WRITINGS:

(With Sally A. Drucker) *Parapsychological Research with Children: An Annotated Bibliography* (foreword by John Palmer), Scarecrow, 1991.

Contributor to psychology journals and newspapers. Editor, *Psi News,* 1970-73.

WORK IN PROGRESS: A book on children and extra-sensory perception.

SIDELIGHTS: Athena A. Drewes told *CA:* "At age ten I had a dream (after an argument with my mother) that my family was in a car accident. I 'saw' my brother sitting in a wheelchair, but I knew he was not injured. I watched as my mother was wheeled into a hospital on a stretcher, a type I had never seen. One week later my dream became a reality. It distressed and excited me. How could a dream tell of the future? Did I make the accident happen? What are dreams? These questions led me on a lifetime journey to discover the field of dreams through psychology, extra-sensory perception, and parapsychology.

"Ultimately I received my doctorate in psychology, and I have been working with emotionally disturbed children for the past seventeen years in a variety of mental health settings. In 1969 I stumbled upon a parapsychology research laboratory that happened to be conducting research on dream and extra-sensory perception. I stayed the night, helped with an experiment, and remained there as a research assistant for six years. While conducting my own research on children and extra-sensory perception, it became clear to me that there were no comprehensive books or articles reviewing the research available on these topics. My own book is an attempt to

make a resource available to professionals and lay researchers.

"I believe we all have extra-sensory perception or psychic abilities. Using these skills is like playing the piano: some are gifted geniuses, others plod along hitting the wrong notes. Some of us may deny or suppress our psychic abilities, only becoming aware of them at a moment of stress or crisis. Others work at their skills and develop them. Children, I feel, are more in tune with their psychic skills but, as they mature, enter school, and become socialized by our society, they begin to suppress and deny their abilities. I hope that my book will help keep alive our interest in children and extra-sensory perception."

BIOGRAPHICAL/CRITICAL SOURCES:

PERIODICALS

Choice, July, 1992.

*   *   *

DREZ, Ronald J(oseph)   1940-

PERSONAL: Born March 2, 1940, in New Orleans, LA; son of J. Roger Drez and Aline Raynaud Drez; married Judith LaCour (an interior designer), June 13, 1964; children: Ronald Jr., Kevin, Diane Barnett, Craig. *Education:* Tulane University, B.B.A., 1962; University of New Orleans, M.A., 1985. *Religion:* Catholic.

ADDRESSES: Home and office—8516 Fordham Ct., New Orleans, LA 70127.

CAREER: Bonded Carbon and Ribbon Co., Inc., New Orleans, LA, salesperson, 1969-72; Dockside Elevators, New Orleans, operations manager, 1973-82; Delta Transload, New Orleans, general manager, 1982-86; self-employed, 1987—. University of New Orleans Metro College Eisenhower Center, assistant director, 1987—. *Military service:* U.S. Marine Corps, 1962-69; served in Vietnam; became captain; received two Bronze Stars and the Vietnamese Cross of Gallantry.

AWARDS, HONORS: Outstanding, Young Men of America, 1968; George Wendell Award for outstanding thesis, University of New Orleans, 1985.

WRITINGS:

Voices of D-Day, Louisiana State University Press, 1994.

WORK IN PROGRESS: Midnight in a Flaming Town, a novel about boat people, intrigue, and lost treasures; research about military action at Khe Sanh and in the Persian Gulf War.

SIDELIGHTS: Ronald J. Drez told *CA:* "As the assistant director of the Eisenhower Center at the University of New Orleans, I began research into the invasion of Normandy with the idea to preserve the oral histories and thoughts of the veterans who had fought in that climactic battle of World War II. Over the next eight years I interviewed hundreds of veterans, encouraging hundreds of others to make their own oral histories to submit to the Eisenhower Center so that by the end of 1992, we possessed some 1400 memoirs or oral histories.

"After much editing, *Voices of D-Day* emerged as a work in which the men who fought at Normandy told the story of the invasion of June 6, 1944. The guiding person who influenced the creation of *Voices* was Dr. Stephen Ambrose, the noted historian and biographer of General Dwight Eisenhower."

*　　*　　*

DRIEDGER, Leo

PERSONAL: Born in Saskatoon, Saskatchewan, Canada; son of Cornelius (a farmer) and Maria (a homemaker; maiden name, Pauls; present surname, Buhler) Driedger; married Darlene Koehn (an office manager), June 1, 1956; children: Diane, Dale. *Education:* University of Chicago, M.A., 1955; Michigan State University, Ph.D., 1964.

ADDRESSES: Home—83 Rutgers Bay, Winnipeg, Manitoba, Canada R3T 3C9. *Office*—Department of Sociology, University of Manitoba, Winnipeg, Manitoba, Canada R3T 2N2.

CAREER: University of Manitoba, Winnipeg, professor of ethnic relations, urban sociology, and sociology of religion, 1966—. Elizabethtown College, fellow at Young Center for the Study of Anabaptist and Pietist Groups, 1991.

WRITINGS:

(With Neena Chappell) *Aging and Ethnicity,* Butterworth (Toronto), 1987.
Ethnic Canada, Copp, Clark, Pitman (Toronto), 1987.
Mennonite Identity in Conflict, Edwin Mellen, 1988.
The Ethnic Factor, McGraw (Toronto), 1989.

Mennonites in Winnipeg, Kindred Press (Winnipeg), 1990.
(With Halli and Trovato) *Ethnic Demography,* Carleton University Press, 1990.
The Urban Factor, Oxford University Press (Toronto), 1991.
(With Howard Kauffman) *The Mennonite Mosaic: Identity and Modernization,* Herald Press, 1991.
(With Donald Kraybill) *Mennonite Peacemaking: From Quietism to Activism,* Herald Press, 1994.

Contributor to sociology journals.

*　　*　　*

DRISCOLL, James P.   1946-

PERSONAL: Born in 1946, in Neosho, MO; son of Patrick and Phyllis Driscoll. *Education:* Whitman College, B.A., 1966; attended Duke University; University of Wisconsin—Madison, Ph.D., 1972.

ADDRESSES: Office—69 Central Ave., San Francisco, CA 94117.

CAREER: Writer.

WRITINGS:

Identity in Shakespearean Drama, Bucknell University Press, 1983.
The Unfolding God of Jung and Milton, University Press of Kentucky, 1992.

Medical satirist, with columns in *Wall Street Journal* and *Los Angeles Times.* Author of articles on cancer, AIDS, and other topics.

*　　*　　*

DUNCOMBE, Frances (Riker)   1900-1994

OBITUARY NOTICE—See index for *CA* sketch: Born July 11, 1900, in Bernardsville, NJ; died after a long illness, June 27, 1994, in Briarcliff Manor, NY. Community activist and children's author. Duncombe was educated at Bryn Mawr College and the New York School of Fine and Applied Arts before she married and began raising a family. A longtime resident of the suburban New York county of Westchester, she was active in civic affairs there. She belonged to the Katonah Women's Civic Club and the Bedford Historical Society, and in 1975 bestowed 48 acres of land to the Mount Holly Nature Preserve. Her first two books, *Hoo De Witt* and *High Hurdles,* were published in 1941, followed by several more over the next few decades, including

Eemi, the Story of a Clown, The Quetzal Feather, and *Summer of the Burning.* Duncombe was also a contributor to a local history of her area called *Katonah: A History of a New York Village and Its People.*

OBITUARIES AND OTHER SOURCES:

PERIODICALS

New York Times, July 7, 1994, p. D19.

* * *

DURHAM, Jerry D. 1946-

PERSONAL: Born April 15, 1946, in Grassey, MO; son of Benton (a farmer) and Audrey (a homemaker; present surname, Kretzer) Durham; married Kathleen Deltmeyer (a dentist), December 26, 1969. *Education:* Attended School (now College) of the Ozarks; Southeast Missouri State College (now University), B.S.Ed., 1968; Bradley University, M.A., 1973; St. Louis University, B.S.N., M.S.N., Ph.D., 1978; University of Illinois at Chicago Circle, M.S., 1984.

ADDRESSES: Home—518 Locherbie Circle S., Indianapolis, IN 46202. *Office*—Illinois School of Nursing, Indiana University—Indianapolis, 1111 Middle Dr., Indianapolis, IN 46202.

CAREER: Worked as staff nurse, nurse supervisor, and private practitioner; Illinois Wesleyan University, Bloomington, director of School of Nursing; Indiana University—Indianapolis, professor of nursing and executive associate dean, 1990—. *Military service:* U.S. Army, 1969-72.

MEMBER: American Academy of Nursing, American Nurses Association, Association of Nurses in AIDS Care, National League for Nursing, Midwest Alliance in Nursing, Sigma Theta Tau.

AWARDS, HONORS: Fellow, National Endowment for the Humanities, 1984 and 1988; Book of the Year Awards, *American Journal of Nursing,* 1987, and 1993, for *Women, Children, and HIV/AIDS.*

WRITINGS:

(With Felissa Cohen) *The Person with AIDS,* Springer Publishing (New York, NY), 1986, revised edition, 1991.
(With Cohen) *The Nurse Psychotherapist,* Springer Publishing, 1986.
(Editor with Cohen) *Women, Children, and HIV/AIDS,* Springer Publishing, 1993.

(With Cohen) *Tuberculosis: A Sourcebook for Nursing,* Springer Publishing, 1995.

Contributor to professional journals.

WORK IN PROGRESS: HIV Infection in Health Professionals, with Felissa Cohen, completion expected in 1997.

SIDELIGHTS: Jerry D. Durham told *CA:* "I was born in rural southeast Missouri. My future career as an author and academician seemed unlikely. As the youngest of seven children, I moved with my family to central Illinois, where I lived and worked on a farm for most of my formative years. I returned to Missouri with my family when I was sixteen and graduated from a tiny, rural high school where most of the students did not attend college. I had read extensively, however, and excelled in English. This led me to believe that I could be the first member of my family to attend college. I left home with the vague goal of a career as a high school teacher. My studies were interrupted by the Vietnam war. Following wartime service, I completed a master's degree in English, but found that no teaching positions were available. This led me to a career in nursing."

* * *

DUVALL, Robert (Selden) 1931-

PERSONAL: Born January 5, 1931, in San Diego, CA; son of William Howard Duvall (a naval officer); married Barbara Benjamin, 1964 (divorced); married Gail Youngs, 1982 (divorced, 1986); married Sharon Brophy, May 1, 1991. *Education:* Principia College, B.A., c. 1955; studied acting with Sanford Meisner at the Neighborhood Playhouse. *Avocational interests:* Ornithology, tennis, spectator sports.

ADDRESSES: Agent—c/o William Morris Agency, 151 El Camino Dr., Beverly Hills, CA 90212.

CAREER: Actor, singer, director, and writer. Actor in motion pictures, including *To Kill a Mockingbird,* 1963; *The Chase,* 1965; *True Grit,* 1969; *The Rain People,* 1969; *M*A*S*H,* 1970; *THX-1138,* 1971; *The Godfather,* 1972; *Tomorrow,* 1972; *The Godfather, Part II,* 1974; *Network,* 1976; *Apocalypse Now,* 1979; *The Great Santini,* 1980; *True Confessions,* 1981; *Tender Mercies,* 1983; *Colors,* 1988; *The Handmaid's Tale,* 1990; *Rambling Rose,* 1991; *Newsies,* 1992; and *Falling Down,* 1993. Actor in television productions, including *Ike,* 1979;

Lonesome Dove, 1989; and *Stalin,* 1992. Actor in stage productions, including *Call Me by My Rightful Name,* 1961; *A View from the Bridge,* 1965; and *American Buffalo,* 1977. *Military service:* U.S. Army during Korean War.

AWARDS, HONORS: Obie Award, *Village Voice,* 1965, for *A View from the Bridge;* best supporting actor award, New York Film Critics Circle, and Academy Award nomination for best supporting actor, Academy of Motion Picture Arts and Sciences, both 1972, for *The Godfather;* best supporting artist award, British Academy of Film and Television Arts, and Academy Award nomination for best supporting actor, both 1979, and Golden Globe for best supporting actor, Hollywood Foreign Press Association, all for *Apocalypse Now;* best actor award, Montreal Film Festival, and Academy Award nomination for best actor, both 1980, for *The Great Santini;* Golden Globe for best dramatic actor and Academy Award for best actor, both 1983, for *Tender Mercies;* Golden Globe for best actor in a miniseries or television film, 1990, for *Lonesome Dove.*

WRITINGS:

SCREENPLAYS, AND DIRECTOR

Angelo, My Love, Cinecom, 1983.

OTHER

Directed and wrote the script for *We're Not the Jet Set,* a documentary, 1975; and contributed songs to the motion picture *Tender Mercies,* 1982.

SIDELIGHTS: Robert Duvall is an acclaimed American actor who has also distinguished himself as a filmmaker. He began his acting career in the mid-1950s after graduating from Principia College and serving in the U.S. Army. Following two years of study at the Neighborhood Playhouse in New York City, Duvall played the lead in a single performance of Arthur Miller's *A View from the Bridge,* a drama about a dock worker in love with his niece. Through his work in that production, Duvall gained significant attention. He subsequently played various roles in the television series *The Naked City,* and in the next several years he made appearances in such shows as *The Defenders, Kraft Suspense Theatre,* and *The FBI.* But he also remained active on the stage, showing considerable skill in both dramatic and comedic parts.

In 1963 Duvall made his film debut in *To Kill a Mockingbird,* an adaptation of Harper Lee's popular novel about racial injustice in the 1930s South. In that film Duvall won praise for his portrayal of an unjustly feared, but nonetheless truly unnerving, recluse. Another triumph came in a 1965 Off-Broadway production of *A View from the Bridge,* where Duvall again showed impressively in the lead. During the next year he received still further acclaim in a Broadway production of *Wait until Dark,* in which he played the leader of a group of criminals determined to retrieve heroin placed in a blind woman's apartment.

Throughout the remainder of the 1960s Duvall served as a supporting player in a broad range of films. He played a bank worker harried by both his employer and his unfaithful wife in *The Chase,* which also featured Marlon Brando, Jane Fonda, Robert Redford, and Angie Dickinson; he depicted a zealous police officer in *The Detective,* which showcased the acting talents of Frank Sinatra; and he took the role of an outlaw in director Henry Hathaway's western *True Grit.* Of greater distinction, perhaps, was Duvall's portrayal of an aggressive, but ultimately sensitive police officer in director Francis Ford Coppola's *The Rain People,* a 1969 drama about an edgy woman and her encounters with both Duvall's character and actor James Caan as a somewhat dimwitted drifter. Duvall was also lauded for his role in another Coppola production, *The Godfather.* In this gangster epic, which also featured Brando, Caan, and Al Pacino, Duvall played the no-nonsense attorney and adopted son of a powerful Mafia figure. The role brought Duvall his first Academy Award nomination.

In the 1970s Duvall continued to garner praise for his varied film roles. He played a disturbingly disciplined army major, who eventually goes mad, in director Robert Altman's Korean War comedy *M*A*S*H,* then teamed with director George Lucas on *THX-1138,* a science-fiction drama set in a future where love and sex are considered criminal offenses. And in *Tomorrow,* adapted by screenwriter Horton Foote from a story by William Faulkner, Duvall further distinguished himself in the lead as a kindly Southerner who tends a pregnant woman and then, upon her death, provides for the infant, only to have the child removed from his care.

Duvall again worked with Coppola for *The Godfather, Part II,* which also reunited him with much of the earlier film's cast. With this feature, a highly successful sequel to the earlier epic, Duvall was again singled out for particular praise. He continued to excel in films such as writer Paddy Chayefsky's comedy *Network,* in which Duvall played an unsympathetic executive, and Coppola's Vietnam drama *Apocalypse Now,* in which he played a zealous Air

Cavalry commander. For this latter performance he was again nominated for an Academy Award.

By the 1980s Duvall was increasingly distinguishing himself in lead roles. He received an Academy Award nomination for best actor for his performance as an uncompromising, intimidating family man and military pilot in *The Great Santini*—"I've done my share of soldiers," he later conceded to *People Weekly*—and he won the Academy Award for best actor for his role as a grizzled country-western singer in *Tender Mercies*. *Chicago Tribune* reviewer Gene Siskel, in his assessment of *Tender Mercies*, ranked Duvall "among the half-dozen best American movie actors" and hailed him as "an American original."

While Duvall reaped accolades for his film performances, he also found time to explore other sides of filmmaking. In the mid-1970s he directed *We're Not the Jet Set*, a documentary he authored about a farming family in Nebraska. In 1983 he also wrote and directed *Angelo, My Love*, an off-beat feature about the gypsy community in New York City. The *New York Times*'s Vincent Canby wrote that the film "is fiction . . . though the dialogue was often improvised by the gypsy actors, most of whom play themselves." Much of the motion picture concerns the theft of pre-adolescent Angelo's ring by a villainous fellow gypsy. This theft, as Canby noted, "provides the film with a plot of sorts." But the picture also follows Angelo on his daily adventures as he hustles pedestrians and cavorts with others in the gypsy community. *Time*'s Richard Corliss noted the film's "wonderful performances" and hailed Duvall's "critical, compassionate, intelligent eye." *Newsweek*'s David Ansen deemed *Angelo, My Love* "funny, charming, unnerving," while *Nation*'s Robert Hatch reported that "the rollicking energy of [Duvall's] gypsy world feels authentic, and the movie is a refreshment."

In 1989 Duvall returned to television for *Lonesome Dove*, an ambitious mini-series derived from Larry McMurtry's novel about the Old West. Here Duvall played Gus McRae, a former Texas Ranger who teams with others to conduct a cattle drive from Texas to Montana. For this performance, Duvall won a Golden Globe.

Throughout his career, Duvall has been acknowledged as a dedicated actor who aims at realism in his performances. "Moviemakers talk about a higher level of reality," he told *Newsweek*. "But I don't think anything's bigger than life. I mean, life is so rich, I don't think you should tamper with it."

BIOGRAPHICAL/CRITICAL SOURCES:

PERIODICALS

Chicago Tribune, March 4, 1983; July 1, 1983.
Films in Review, May, 1983, pp. 272-85.
Los Angeles Times, January 31, 1989.
Nation, June 4, 1983, p. 714.
New Republic, May 30, 1983, p. 25.
Newsweek, September 18, 1972, pp. 99-100; May 9, 1983, p. 82; April 23, 1984, pp. 79-80.
New York, October 12, 1981, p. 98; March 7, 1983, pp. 20-21.
New York Times, April 23, 1972; October 25, 1981; April 27, 1983.
People Weekly, April 23, 1984, pp. 76-82.
Rolling Stone, April 28, 1983.
Time, May 30, 1983, p. 765.
Washington Post, May 20, 1983.*

* * *

DYER, Joyce 1947-

PERSONAL: Born July 20, 1947, in Akron, OH; daughter of Thomas William (a supervisor at a rubber factory) and Edna Annabelle (a board of education clerk; maiden name, Haberkost) Coyne; married Daniel Osborn Dyer (a teacher and writer), December 20, 1969; children: Stephen Osborn. *Education:* Wittenberg University, B.A., 1969; Kent State University, Ph.D., 1977. *Politics:* Democrat.

ADDRESSES: Home—60 East Pioneer Trail, Aurora, OH 44202. *Office*—Hinsdale Hall, Hiram College, Hiram, OH 44234.

CAREER: Teacher at a private school in Hudson, OH, 1979-90; Hiram College, Hiram, OH, associate professor of English and director of writing, 1990—.

MEMBER: Modern Language Association of America, National Council of Teachers of English, Popular Culture Association, Society for the Study of Midwestern Literature, National Alzheimer's Association, Hudson Library and Historical Society, Friends of the Center for Appalachian Studies (Boone, NC), Friends of the Hiram College Library.

AWARDS, HONORS: National Endowment for the Humanities, fellow, 1987 and 1988, grant, 1990-91; Gerstacker-Gund grants, 1993 and 1994; Paul E. Martin Award, 1993; *The Awakening* was named one of the best academic books of the year by *Choice*, 1993.

WRITINGS:

The Awakening: A Novel of Beginnings (nonfiction), Twayne (New York, NY), 1993.

Contributor of more than a hundred articles to scholarly journals and popular magazines, including *Southern Literary Journal* and *Seventeen.*

WORK IN PROGRESS: Tanglewood (tentative title), a work of literary nonfiction about life in an Alzheimer's unit; a book on Appalachian women writers; other works of literary nonfiction.

SIDELIGHTS: Joyce Dyer told *CA:* "My roots are Appalachian. For a long while, when I was growing up under the brow of a rubber factory in Akron, Ohio, I fought hard not to admit that fact. Only after I left home did I gain enough perspective to see that my life, growing up in South Akron, growing up with a huge bronze statue of Harvey S. Firestone nearly in my back yard, was not only amazing and odd, but worth writing about.

"Writing my way to the center of that experience has taken many circuitous routes, but they have all been important. They have all permitted me to bore closer to the center of mystery I know is there—the mystery of family history, of American vision gone wrong, of class arrogance, of brave and frugal and adoring parents, of aunts who ironed to the twelve-o'clock 'Hymn for the Day' on the radio, of people on the fringe, of genes. I often try to rescue people or peoples on the margins: Kate Chopin, Dawn Powell, Mary Lee Settle, Appalachian artists. I do the little I can to ward off damaging or uninformed jeers—remembering jeers from my own past—and lift these writers up.

"Recently, my writing excursions have taken me closer to the center I always pursue, but probably will never quite find. Through literary nonfiction, my favorite form, I recorded life in an Alzheimer's unit, the home of my mother Annabelle for the past four years. It was a mystical and radiant experience, unlike any writing experience I've known before. It began with an invitation to write from two mute swans that suddenly appeared in the pond that borders my mother's unit. It ended, months later, in a manuscript that I'd like to say I wrote for my mother, but I know is really a gift from her to me. I was merely her scrivener.

"I will continue to write criticism and literary nonfiction side by side, for they are mutually dependent. We cannot lift ourselves up without lifting others along the way. Our own arms and pens grow stronger from the weight of others in our embrace."

*　　*　　*

DZUNG WONG, Baoswan 1949-

PERSONAL: Born September 27, 1949, in Baden, Switzerland; daughter of Lang Shuen (an engineer) and Dzaofang (a homemaker; maiden name, Feng) Dzung; married Shiufai Jimmy Wong (a sales engineer), July 25, 1981; children: Wingdzi. *Education:* Swiss Federal Institute of Technology, Diploma, 1973; University of California, Berkeley, M.A., 1979, Ph.D., 1981.

ADDRESSES: Home—Wegaecherstrasse 3, 5417 Untersiggenthal, Switzerland.

CAREER: Christ-Koenig Kolleg, Nuolen, Switzerland, instructor, 1973-76; Kantonsschule, Wettingen, Switzerland, instructor, 1982-86; Antares Consulting, Nussbaumen, Switzerland, software engineer, 1987-88; Oekreal Schools of Business, instructor, 1988-94. Kantonsschule, instructor, 1991—.

MEMBER: Swiss Mathematical Society, American Mathematical Society.

WRITINGS:

(Translator) *Group Theoretical Methods and Their Applications,* Birkhaueser (New York, NY), 1992.

WORK IN PROGRESS: A book of problems in calculus and analysis.

E-F

EGAN, Catherine 1943-

PERSONAL: Born March 3, 1943, in Saskatoon, Saskatchewan, Canada; daughter of William Arthur (a teacher) and Dorothy A. (a social worker; maiden name, Borland) Doyle. *Education:* Slade School of Fine Art, London, Diploma in Fine Art; University of Saskatchewan, B.A.; Concordia University, Montreal, Quebec, M.A.; also attended New York University and Ryerson Polytechnical University.

ADDRESSES: Home—1 Washington Square Village, No. 4K, New York, NY 10012.

CAREER: University of Regina, Regina, Saskatchewan, lecturer in art, 1965-68; Pennsylvania State University, University Park, audio-visual materials specialist, 1969-77, assistant director of audio-visual services, 1977-87, director of Penn State Brazilian Film Festival, 1980-88; New York University, New York City, director of Avery Fisher Center for Music and Media, 1987-94, project director and principal investigator for Media Alternatives Project, 1990-94 (MAP). Consortium of College and University Media Centers, past president; Pennsylvania Council on the Arts, member of media advisory panel, 1982-86. Co-producer of the documentary *Cover All Bases,* 1990; executive producer of the documentary *The Rebel Girl: Elizabeth Gurley Flynn,* 1993. Birmingham International Educational Film and Video Festival, member of national advisory board, 1985-87; judge of Jornada de Cinema, Salvador, Brazil, 1987, and Sinking Creek Film Festival, 1988; American Film and Video Festival, chairperson of Grierson Award Panel, 1990; New View Videoconference, panelist, 1990. Artist, with paintings and collages represented in shows and at 41 Union Square Open Studios.

MEMBER: American Film and Video Association (past president).

AWARDS, HONORS: Blue Ribbon, American Film and Video Festival, 1990, for *Cover All Bases.*

WRITINGS:

(Illustrator) Stanley Freiberg, *The Baskets of Baghdad: Poems of the Middle East,* Crest, 1972.
(Coauthor) *Mediating History: The MAP Guide to Independent Video by and About African American, Asian American, Latino, and Native American People,* New York University Press, 1992.

Contributor to professional journals. Contributing editor, *Sightlines,* 1978-86; founder and editor, *Perspectives on Film,* 1986-90.

* * *

ELIAS, Victor J. 1937-

PERSONAL: Born July 21, 1937, in Tucuman, Argentina; son of Julio (a trader) and Bahilla (a homemaker; maiden name, Assaf) Elias; married Ana M. Ganum (a professor of piano), May 21, 1966; children: Ana Georgina, Cecelia Alexandra, Julio Jorge. *Education:* University of Chicago, Ph.D., 1969; National University of Tucuman, D.E.S., 1972. *Politics:* Democrat. *Religion:* Orthodox Catholic.

ADDRESSES: Home—Balcarce 740, 4000 Tucuman, Argentina. *Office*—Casilla de Correo 209, 4000 Tucuman, Argentina.

CAREER: National University of Tucuman, Tucuman, Argentina, professor of econometrics, 1965-88, director of the magister of economics, 1988—.

WRITINGS:

Government Expenditures on Agriculture and Agricultural Growth in Latin American Countries, International Food Policy Research Institute, 1985.

Sources of Growth: A Study of Seven Latin American Economies, ICS Press (San Francisco), 1992.

WORK IN PROGRESS: Lectures on Economic Growth, completion expected in 1996; research on sources of growth and regional economic convergence in Latin America.

* * *

ELIOT, Nathan
See KRAMER, Edward (E.)

* * *

ELLIS, Trey 1962-
(Tom Ricostranza)

PERSONAL: Born in 1962, in Washington, DC; son of a psychiatrist and a psychologist. *Education:* Attended Stanford University.

ADDRESSES: Home—Santa Monica, CA. *Agent*—c/o Publicity Department, Simon & Schuster, 1230 Avenue of the Americas, New York, NY 10020.

CAREER: Writer.

MEMBER: Writer's Guild of America, West.

WRITINGS:

Platitudes, Vintage Books (St. Paul, MN), 1988.

Home Repairs, Simon & Schuster (New York), 1993.

(As Tom Ricostranza) *The Inkwell* (screenplay), Buena Vista, 1994.

Also author of teleplays *Cosmic Slop* and *Tuskegee,* both for Home Box Office (HBO). Contributor to periodicals, including *Interview* and *Playboy.*

WORK IN PROGRESS: A screenplay based on *Home Repairs.*

SIDELIGHTS: In his novels, Trey Ellis challenges common stereotypic images of black men. "Unfortunately," as he told V. R. Peterson in a *People* interview, "there are people who still try to pigeonhole black men and see us only as Africa, as a problem, or as something to be pitied or feared." Instead of street-wise, inner-city toughs, Ellis writes about young middle-class African Americans. His charac-

ters are men and women with educational and career opportunities who pursue middle-class interests and struggle with middle-class fears.

In his first book, *Platitudes,* Ellis explores both middle-class black America and more stereotypic images of African Americans through a novel-within-a-novel approach. One of Ellis's characters is black writer Dewayne Wellington, who is himself writing a novel about Earle Tyner, a sixteen-year-old middle-class black man seeking success at life and sex. Earle is a computer enthusiast who hopes to attract the interest of Dorothy LaMont, a sort of "valley girl" from Harlem. In Wellington's story of these black teenagers, "there is a welcome absence of sociological talk about being in a difficult racial and class position, and much good writing about how it feels to be there," according to Eric Lott in the *Nation.* "Ellis also coaxes a bemused interiority out of Dorothy's Valley-girl jargon, the kind of feat most young novelists are still reaching for."

Ellis's *Platitudes* also takes the black literary establishment to task. "It addresses a conflict percolating in the black literary community that concerns perceived disparities in the reception of black male and female authors," noted Maurice J. Bennett in the *Washington Post Book World.* "For some, the publishing and critical attention awarded a galaxy of prominent women—Toni Morrison, Alice Walker, and Gloria Naylor—has been accompanied by the slighting of their black male colleagues." In order to raise these issues, Ellis afflicts Wellington with a case of writer's block. Wellington seeks assistance through a letter to the public and finds himself on the receiving end of a barrage of criticism from Isshee Ayam, an outspoken award-winning black feminist novelist. Ayam offers another version of Wellington's story which moves Earle to a rural community in the South where the young man lives with a group of strong, proud black women.

Ellis's novel becomes a battle between Wellington and Ayam to tell Earle's story. "Wellington is full of 'reckless eyeballing' and self-admiration; Ayam is an ardent womanist whose faith in 'living by the word' lights her way to the bank," commented Marcellus Blount in the *Village Voice.* "Inevitably, these opposites attract. Their story lines merge. Our two novelists fall in love." In the reconciliation of these two battling novelists, Ellis sees a way for male and female, experimental and realist black writers to come together. "Trey Ellis's first novel will go down as a young writer's call for a truce in the black literary world," asserted Lott.

The sum of the two stories about Earle and Dorothy and the battle between the two novelists in *Platitudes* is "a mutant assemblage of love story, postmodern narrative techniques and postliberation political intentions whose effect is something like crossing Spike Lee with Gilbert Sorrentino," according to Lott. "Mr. Ellis is most successful when he's being irreverent about sacred subjects, social and political, American and un-American," concluded Doris Jean Austin in the *New York Times Book Review*. "There are more than a few laugh-out-loud and shake-your-head-at-the-awful-truth scenes in this insightful first novel—if you only can persevere."

Home Repairs, Ellis's second novel, "takes the form of a diary," noted a *New Yorker* reviewer, "in which Austin McMillan—a brainy African American kid who's trying to grow up as fast as possible—records his thoughts with a funky, necessity-is-the-mother-of-invention flair." Austin goes from an unpopular teenager to the handyman star of a cable television show called "Home Repairs." This novel "satirizes fame and campus life as well as sexual shenanigans," wrote V. R. Peterson in *People*.

In the opinion of *New York Times Book Review* contributor Elizabeth Gaffney, "despite its intimate account of a privileged young black man's life, particularly his sex life, Trey Ellis's second novel . . . manages *not* to be tantalizing." Veronica Chambers offered a similar view in the *Los Angeles Times Book Review*: "Unfortunately, the novel loses steam toward the end. Although Austin's post-college career as a cable TV host for a home repair show . . . is entertaining, his sexual pursuits become decreasingly so." Peterson observed that "[b]eneath the humor, [Ellis] shows that while Austin is always clearly a black man, he is never less than a man."

The Inkwell, Ellis's semiautobiographical screenplay set at Inkwell Beach on Martha's Vineyard, focuses on Drew Tate, a shy 16-year-old boy who learns about life and love while vacationing with his parents during the summer of 1976. After spending more than two years writing *The Inkwell,* Ellis was disappointed to learn that he would not be allowed to direct the filming of his script, and that young director Matty Rich (*Straight out of Brooklyn*) would be hired for the project. In an interview with Maria Ricapito for an article in *Entertainment Weekly,* Ellis asserted that Rich had commented that *The Inkwell* "wasn't black enough," but Ellis stated that he thought that Rich believed that the script "wasn't stereotypically black enough." Ellis faulted Rich for infusing *The Inkwell* with "silly class war-

fare" humor, complaining that after Rich's input the film was "more like *What's Happening! The Movie.*"

Critics echoed Ellis's sentiments concerning *The Inkwell. Entertainment Weekly* contributor Lisa Schwarzbaum asserted that "the 22-year-old Rich's inexperience gets the better of him. . . . *The Inkwell* is just ungainly and amateurish. Characters and conflicts are never fully developed; moods swing from broad parody to sticky emotionalism." A reviewer for *People* magazine remarked: "This should be a sensitive coming-of-age story; instead, you keep expecting Jimmie Walker to jump on screen and bray, 'DY-NO-MITE!'" To illustrate his dissatisfaction with *The Inkwell* and to distance himself from the project, Ellis used the pseudonym Tom Ricostranza in the film's credits. He told Ricapito: "So much of [*The Inkwell* is now] about black dysfunction. . . . We black people want to see ourselves going to school, going to work, kissing each other. The black middle class are not very different from the white, meaning that they try to send their kids to school and make their house payments. They're still as black as any gang-banger or welfare mother."

BIOGRAPHICAL/CRITICAL SOURCES:

BOOKS

Contemporary Literary Criticism, Volume 55, Gale, 1989.

PERIODICALS

Entertainment Weekly, April 29, 1994, pp. 19-20; May 6, 1994, pp. 47-8.
Los Angeles Times Book Review, July 25, 1993, p. 4.
Nation, December 19, 1988, pp. 691-92.
New York Review of Books, November 4, 1993, p. 33.
New York Times Book Review, February 19, 1989, p. 20; July 18, 1993, p. 16.
New Yorker, September 6, 1993, p. 117.
People, August 2, 1993, p. 26; May 9, 1994, p. 20.
Village Voice, November 29, 1988, p. 66.
Washington Post Book World, October 9, 1988, p. 9.

*   *   *

ELLWOOD, Sheelagh (Margaret)   1949-

PERSONAL: Born February 21, 1949, in Whitehaven, Cumberland, England; daughter of Frank (a bank manager) and Janet (Pow) Ellwood. *Education:* University of Essex, B.A. (with honors),

1973; University of Reading, M.A., 1975; Queen Mary College, London, Ph.D., 1983.

ADDRESSES: Office—Foreign and Commonwealth Office (Gibraltar), King Charles St., London SW1A 2AH, England.

CAREER: Freelance writer in Madrid, Spain, 1975-88; Foreign and Commonwealth Office, London, England, principal research officer for Iberia, 1988-94, assistant to the deputy general of Gibraltar, 1994—.

WRITINGS:

Prietas las filas, Editorial Critica (Barcelona, Spain), 1983.
Spanish Fascism in the Franco Era, Macmillan (London, England), 1987.
The Spanish Civil War, Basil Blackwell (Oxford, England), 1991.
Profiles in Power: Franco, Longman (London, England), 1994.

Contributor to books, including *Neo-Fascism in Europe,* edited by L. Cheles and others, Longman, 1991.

*   *   *

EMMET, Olivia (Lily) 1933-

PERSONAL: Born March 20, 1933, in New York, NY; daughter of William Temple Emmet and Lily Cushing; married Anthony West (a writer), December, 1952; children: Sophia West, Adam West. *Education:* Attended Harvard University, 1950-53. *Politics:* Liberal. *Religion:* "No formal religion."

ADDRESSES: Home and office—2 Jane St., Apt. 3C, New York, NY 10014.

CAREER: Translator and writer.

WRITINGS:

TRANSLATIONS

Guy Sajer, *The Forgotten Soldier,* Harper, 1970.
Jean Starobinski, *Words upon Words,* Yale University Press, 1979.
Max Gallo, *The Night of Long Knives: Hitler and the S.A.,* HarperCollins, 1984.
Pierre Daix, *Picasso: Life and Art,* HarperCollins, 1993.
Pierre Bofill, *Espaces d'une Vie,* HarperCollins, 1994.

OTHER

Contributor of articles and translations to periodicals, including *Harper's Bazaar, Vogue,* and *New York Review of Books.*

*   *   *

ENER, Guener 1935-

PERSONAL: Born May 24, 1935, in Turkey; daughter of Fahri (a military officer) and Zehra (a homemaker) Ener. *Education:* Academy of Fine Arts, Istanbul, diploma, 1958; Mimar Sinan University, Diploma, 1973; certificate from Cambridge University. *Politics:* "Humanist." *Religion:* Muslim. *Avocational interests:* Gardening, protection of animals.

ADDRESSES: Home—Akyol sok. Taskin, Ap. 16/2, 80060 Cihangir, Istanbul, Turkey. *Office*—ICBS/IBIS, Skindergade 3B, Copenhagen K, Denmark.

CAREER: Translator for a state bank in Ankara, Turkey, 1967; Yuekselis College, Ankara, teacher of painting, 1968-69; Cem Yayinevi, Istanbul, Turkey, illustrator of book covers, 1972-78; freelance painter, 1978—. Presenter of tales for children on a radio program in Helsinki, Finland, 1985.

MEMBER: International P.E.N., Danish Writers Union, Turkish Artists Union (member of executive committee, 1971-73), Turkish Writers Syndicate.

AWARDS, HONORS: Grand Prix, Academy Concourt, 1971, 1972, and 1973.

WRITINGS:

Tired of September (stories), Yanki Yayinevi, 1969.
Blue of the Broken Glass (stories), Soyut Dergisi, 1972.
The Bald-Headed Girl (children's stories), Cem Yayinevi, 1990.
(Translator) *Sister Shako and Kolo the Goat,* Lothrop (New York, NY), 1994.

Contributor to art magazines and newspapers.

WORK IN PROGRESS: Children's stories.

SIDELIGHTS: Guener Ener told *CA:* "I come from a family of artists. My grandfather and great-grandfather were the chief masters of the Ottoman Palace. My father, a general by profession, was also a very good painter. My older two sisters are well-known painters. Painting was usual, ordinary for our family, so I had a great impulse to do something different, unexpected, such as write stories or learn a foreign language. I managed to combine translation, literature, and painting. Painting is my main occupation and the natural, instinctive way to make a living and a reputation for myself. There are, however, things that go beyond the limits of colors, shades, and lines. Then I write."

*   *   *

ENER, Guner
   See ENER, Guener

*   *   *

ENGEL, Matthew (Lewis) 1951-

PERSONAL: Born June 11, 1951, in Northampton, England; son of Max David (a lawyer) and Betty Ruth (a homemaker; maiden name, Lesser) Engel; married Hilary Davies (a publisher), October 27, 1990; children: Laurence Gabriel. *Education:* Victoria University of Manchester, B.A. (with honors), 1972.

ADDRESSES: Home—The Oaks, Newton St. Margarets, Herefordshire HR2 0YN, England. *Office—Guardian,* 119 Farringdon Rd., London EC1R 3ER, England. *Agent*—Vivien Green, Sheil and Associates, 43 Doughty St., London WC1N 2LF, England.

CAREER: Northampton Chronicle and Echo, Northampton, England, journalist, 1972-75; Reuters News Agency, journalist, 1977-79; *Guardian,* London, England, feature writer, 1979—, cricket correspondent, 1982-87, sports columnist and occasional political, foreign, and war correspondent, 1987—.

AWARDS, HONORS: Named sports journalist of the year by *What the Papers Say,* 1985, and by British Press Awards, 1991.

WRITINGS:

Ashes '85, Pelham Books, 1986.
The Guardian Book of Cricket, Pavilion Books, 1986.

Editor, *Sportspages Almanac,* Simon & Schuster, 1989-91, and *Wisden Cricketers' Almanack,* Gollancz, 1992—.

WORK IN PROGRESS: A History of the British Press.

*   *   *

ERLBACH, Arlene 1948-

PERSONAL: Born October 8, 1948, in Cleveland,

OH; daughter of Morris (in sales) and Lillian (Fried) Faverman; married Herb Erlbach (a computer trainer and consultant), November 27, 1977; children: Matthew. *Education:* Kent State University, B.S., 1971; Northeastern Illinois University, Chicago, M.S., 1989. *Politics:* Liberal. *Religion:* "Jewish (non-practicing)." *Avocational interests:* Animals.

ADDRESSES: Home and office—5829 Capulina Ave., Morton Grove, IL 60053. *Agent*—Lettie Lee, The Ann Elmo Agency, Inc., 60 East 42nd St., New York, NY 10165.

CAREER: Writer. Schoolteacher in Illinois.

MEMBER: Society of Children's Book Writers and Illustrators, Romance Writers of America, The Young Adult Network, Children's Reading Round Table.

AWARDS, HONORS: Golden Medallion for best young adult novel, Romance Writers of America, 1987, for *Does Your Nose Get in the Way, Too?*

WRITINGS:

Does Your Nose Get in the Way, Too?, Crosswinds, 1987.
Guys, Dating, and Other Disasters, Crosswinds, 1987.
Drop out Blues, Crosswinds, 1988.
Hurricanes (nonfiction), Children's Press, 1993.
Peanut Butter (nonfiction), Lerner Publications, 1994.

WORK IN PROGRESS: The Best Friend Book; research on the welfare system, children's rights, and background for a biography of Florence Kelley.

SIDELIGHTS: "I've always loved to write and make up stories," Arlene Erlbach commented. "When I was in grade school I'd make up stories about children while I lay in bed." It was not until much later, however, that Erlbach paid attention to the praise her writing had earned from teachers and professors and submitted a novel for publication.

The book, *Does Your Nose Get in the Way, Too?,* follows a teenage girl, Henny Zimmerman, through the trials of Highland High School, where her lack of inclusion in fashionable cliques has created a personal crisis for her. Henny thinks cosmetic surgery to reduce the size of her nose will solve her problems, but her father refuses to permit her to have the operation. Despite her nose, which she finally realizes isn't bad at all, Henny establishes a romantic relationship which relieves her anxiety.

In a *Voice of Youth Advocates* review of *Does Your Nose Get in the Way, Too?*, Joan Wilson complemented Erlbach's "genuine sympathy for the heroine." But Joyce Adams Burner took a contrary point of view in a *School Library Journal* review, calling the "characters stereotyped and run of the mill." Burner went on to express serious concern about the message of the book, speculating that it might convince certain teens to succumb to peer pressure.

Henny also appears in Erlbach's second book, *Guys, Dating, and Other Disasters,* in which a school assignment dealing with marriage runs a parallel course with the impending marriage of Henny's widowed father. Erlbach's third book, *Drop out Blues,* is about two cousins who drop out of school and move in together. Commenting on her inspirations for writing, Erlbach related: "I get ideas from my childhood, my son's experiences, the news and kids at the school where I teach. In addition to being an author, I teach elementary school. I am in charge of my school's Young Authors' Program. It gives me great joy to encourage children in reading and writing."

BIOGRAPHICAL/CRITICAL SOURCES:

PERIODICALS

School Library Journal, September, 1987, p. 195; October, 1987, pp. 149-50.
Voice of Youth Advocates, October, 1987, pp. 200-201; December, 1987, p. 234; June, 1988, p. 85.

*   *   *

ESTERHAMMER, Angela 1961-

PERSONAL: Born November 20, 1961, in Toronto, Ontario, Canada; daughter of Hermann (an office worker and independent scholar) and Marianne (a music teacher; maiden name, Schittich) Esterhammer; married John Kozub (a computer programmer), February 20, 1989. *Education:* University of Toronto, B.A. (with high honors), 1983; attended University of Tuebingen, 1983-84; Princeton University, Ph.D., 1989. *Religion:* Protestant.

ADDRESSES: Office—Department of English, University of Western Ontario, London, Ontario, Canada N6A 3K7.

CAREER: University of Western Ontario, London, assistant professor, 1989-94, associate professor of English and modern languages, 1994—.

MEMBER: North American Society for the Study of Romanticism, Modern Language Association of America, Canadian Comparative Literature Association, Association of Canadian College and University Teachers of English, Wordsworth-Coleridge Association, Blake Society, Christianity and Literature Study Group.

AWARDS, HONORS: Fellow of German Academic Exchange Service, 1983; Protege Award from Toronto Arts Awards Foundation, 1988; grants from Social Science and Humanities Research Council of Canada, 1989, 1992, 1992-95; John Charles Polanyi Prize from Government of Ontario, 1990.

WRITINGS:

Creating States: Studies in the Performance Language of John Milton and William Blake, University of Toronto Press, 1994.
(Translator and author of introduction) R. M. Rilke, *Two Stories of Prague,* University Press of New England, 1994.

Work represented in anthologies, including *Re-Membering Milton: Essays on the Texts and Traditions,* Methuen, 1987; and *New Essays: Women Novelists of the Romantic Period,* edited by Laura Dabundo, Contemporary Research Press, 1994. Contributor of articles, translations, and reviews to literature journals.

SIDELIGHTS: Angela Esterhammer told *CA:* "While I have been fascinated by the art of literary translation for a long time, *Two Stories of Prague* is my first published translation of a literary work. I felt it was a translation that was needed to balance and complement the many English versions of Rilke's poetic work. Rilke's stories also have personal resonances for me, because they reflect his intense involvement in the culture that my mother's family shares, and because I undertook the project as a young writer of about the age that Rilke was when he first wrote the stories. My current work is mainly critical, concerned with Romanticism and the philosophy of language, and I do some translation of scholarly articles. I continue, however, to be interested in literary translation, if I can find the right project and the time in which to do it."

*   *   *

EVANS, Calvin (Donald) 1931-

PERSONAL: Born March 23, 1931, in Northern Arm, Newfoundland, Canada; son of Donald Manuel (a laborer and equestrian) and Mary Jane (a home-maker; maiden name, Lidstone) Evans; married Goldie Helen Locke (a homemaker), December 26, 1952; children: Joanne, Jane Evans Meiser, Brian (deceased), Larry. *Education:* Dalhousie University, B.A., 1952; Atlantic School of Theology, B.D., 1955, M.Div., 1974; University of Toronto, B.L.S., 1967, Th.M., 1969. *Politics:* "Depends on issues and candidates." *Religion:* United Church of Canada. *Avocational interests:* Newfoundland history.

ADDRESSES: Home-Apt. 905, 1260 Ave Docteur Penfield, Montreal, Quebec, Canada H3G 1B6. *Office*—University Libraries, McGill University, 3459 McTavish St., Montreal, Quebec, Canada H3A 1Y1.

CAREER: Halifax Citadel Museum, Halifax, Nova Scotia, Canada, secretary, 1954; minister of United Church of Canada in Saskatchewan, Newfoundland, Ontario, and Nova Scotia, Canada, 1955-66; Memorial University of Newfoundland, St. John's, Newfoundland, Canada, cataloger, 1967-68, head of Periodicals Division at university library, 1968-73; University of Guelph, Guelph, Ontario, Canada, head of humanities and social sciences at university library, 1973-79; University of Alberta, Edmonton, Alberta, Canada, assistant librarian for public services, 1979-83, assistant librarian for planning and personnel, 1983-84; McGill University, Montreal, Quebec, Canada, area librarian at Humanities and Social Sciences Library, 1984-93, branch services coordinator, 1993—.

MEMBER: Canadian Association of College and University Libraries (member of board of directors, 1979; member of executive committee, 1979-82; president, 1980-81), Canadian Association of University Teachers (chairperson of Committee on Professional Librarians, 1976-79), Canadian Library Association, Association of College and Research Libraries, Special Libraries Association, Bibliographical Society of Canada, American Library Association.

WRITINGS:

For Love of a Woman: The Evans Family and a Perspective on Shipbuilding in Newfoundland, Harry Cuff Publications (St. John's), 1992.
Soren Kierkegaard Bibliographies: Remnants, 1944-1980, and the Multimedia, 1925-1991, McGill University Libraries (Montreal), 1993.

Contributor to library journals.

WORK IN PROGRESS: Women Shipowners and Boatowners of the Atlantic Provinces, 1654-1984, completion expected in 1995; *Master Shipbuilders of Newfoundland,* 1996.

SIDELIGHTS: Calvin Evans told *CA:* "I have had a somewhat checkered career to date. I was a minister of the United Church of Canada for eleven years. Experiencing a crisis of faith in the mid-1960s, I left the church and the ministry. A recovery of faith in the late 1970s brought me back into the church and, in 1982, I was restored to the ministry, but now serve only on a part-time basis. For years I 'credited' Kierkegaard with getting me out of the church, particularly after reading and pondering his 'Attack Upon Christendom' but, strangely, after I returned to the faith it was in the writings of Kierkegaard that I found the greatest beauty, strength, and comfort. That is typical of the strange ambivalence of Kierkegaard.

"I have not traveled widely, except that I have moved around a lot in Canada and visit the United States regularly. In a unique travel experience, I visited L'Anse aux Meadows (the only known Viking settlement in North America) in Newfoundland in 1990, and two months later I was in Oslo, Norway, at the Viking Ships Museum. The trip served to form a strange continuum between the old world and the new. On that same trip, I spent several days in Copenhagen and attempted to find every site and every archival collection related to Soren Kierkegaard.

"My family research resulted from a remarkable conversation I had in 1955 with the last of the great shipbuilders in my family, Robert Evans. He recited from memory, and in chronological order, the names of practically every ship built by the Evanses, including those that had been built ten years before he was born. The notes from that conversation languished in a desk drawer until the television series *Roots* aired in 1978. Rather than write a straightforward family history, I decided to set the family in the historic context (roughly 1840 to 1940) and to emphasize our shipbuilding activity during this period. The title of *For Love of a Woman* refers to the fact that my ancestor, Edward Evans of Cardiff, Wales, while on a British fishery protection vessel, deserted his ship and settled in Newfoundland for a woman.

"For my current research project, I have compiled data on about two-thousand women of the four Atlantic provinces of Canada who were involved in some aspect of the shipowning industry. I hope that my writing may serve to dispel some of the myths of the passive woman of the past, and assess the contributions of women to the economy of an earlier period. That project will be followed by a book on the master shipbuilders of Newfoundland. There may then be other books on Newfoundland, and possibly a book of children's stories (to satisfy the demands of my grandchildren), and I may even attempt a book on the Christian faith."

* * *

EVIOTA, Elizabeth Uy 1946-

PERSONAL: Born February 21, 1946, in the Philippines; daughter of Colman E. and Maria (Uy) Eviota. *Education:* Maryknoll College, Manila, Philippines, A.B., 1966; New School for Social Research, M.A., 1969; Rutgers University, Ph.D., 1985.

ADDRESSES: Home—Quezon City, Philippines. *Office*—Department of Sociology and Anthropology, Ateneo de Manila University, P.O. Box 154, Manila, Philippines.

CAREER: Institute of Philippine Culture, Quezon City, project director, 1976-79; UNICEF, New York City, research associate in Family Welfare, People's Participation, and Women in Development Division, 1980-81; Ateneo de Manila University, Manila, Philippines, instructor in sociology and anthropology, 1985—, coordinator of Gender Studies Committee, 1989—. University of Sussex, visiting fellow at Institute of Development Studies, 1990; consultant to Canadian International Development Agency, Asian Development Bank, and Economic Development Institute of the World Bank.

AWARDS, HONORS: Fellow of Rockefeller Foundation, 1990.

WRITINGS:

Philippine Women and Development: An Annotated Bibliography, Institute of Philippine Culture (Quezon City), 1978.
The Political Economy of Gender: Women and the Sexual Division of Labor in the Philippines, Zed Books (London), 1992.

Work represented in anthologies, including *Women and Development: Perspectives From South and Southeast Asia,* Dacca University Press (Dacca, Bangladesh), 1979; *Women in the Cities of Asia: Female Migration and Urban Adaptation,* Westview (Colorado), 1983; and *Women's Work,* edited by E. Leacock and H. Safa, Bergin & Garvey (Massachusetts), 1986. Contributor to sociology journals. Editor, *Philippine Sociological Review,* 1976-78.

WORK IN PROGRESS: Research on sexual politics in the Philippines.

EZELL, Margaret J. M. 1955-

PERSONAL: Born July 2, 1955, in Oklahoma City, OK; daughter of John S. (a professor of history) and Jean (a mathematician; maiden name, McLean) Ezell; married Juergen Mainzer (an international equestrian judge), May 19, 1994. *Education:* Wellesley College, B.A. (with honors), 1977; attended Cambridge University, 1977-81.

ADDRESSES: Home—Hearne, TX. *Office*—Department of English, Texas A&M University, College Station, TX 77843.

CAREER: Texas A&M University, College Station, professor of English, 1982—, and fellow of Interdisciplinary Group for History Literary Studies. Folger Shakespeare Library and Institute, visiting lecturer, 1991.

MEMBER: Modern Language Association of America, American Society for Eighteenth-Century Studies.

AWARDS, HONORS: Grant from National Endowment for the Humanities, 1988—.

WRITINGS:

The Patriarch's Wife: Literary Evidence and the History of the Family, University of North Carolina Press, 1987.
Writing Women's Literary History, Johns Hopkins University Press (Baltimore, MD), 1993.
(Editor) *The Poetry and Prose of Mary, Lady Chudleigh,* Oxford University Press, 1993.
(Editor with Katherine O'Brien O'Keeffe) *Cultural Artifacts and the Production of Meaning: The Page, the Body, and the Image,* University of Michigan Press, 1994.

Contributor to magazines and newspapers. Editor of *BachNotes,* newsletter of Brazos Association for Classical Horsemanship, 1991—; special issue editor, *South Central Review,* 1994.

WORK IN PROGRESS: The Oxford English Literary History Series, Volume V, publication by Oxford University Press expected in 2000.

* * *

FAIGLEY, Lester 1947-

PERSONAL: Born April 6, 1947, in Charleston, WV; son of V. V. and Madeline R. Faigley; married Linda Jurney, 1969; children: Garth, Ian. *Education:* North Carolina State University, B.A., 1969;

Miami University, Oxford, OH, M.A., 1972; University of Washington, Seattle, Ph.D., 1976.

ADDRESSES: Home—300 Battle Bend Blvd., Austin, TX 78745. *Office*—Division of Rhetoric and Composition, University of Texas at Austin, Austin, TX 78712.

CAREER: University of Texas at Austin, professor of English and director of Division of Rhetoric and Composition, 1979—. National University of Singapore, senior fellow, 1986-87; Pennsylvania State University, visiting professor, 1990; Oxford University, visiting professor at Brasenose College, 1992.

MEMBER: Conference on College Composition and Communication (chairperson, 1996).

AWARDS, HONORS: Mina P. Shaughnessy Award, outstanding research publication in the field of teaching language and literature, Modern Language Association of America, 1992, and Outstanding Book Award, Conference on College Composition and Communication, 1994, both for *Fragments of Rationality.*

WRITINGS:

(With Stephen White) *Evaluating College Writing Programs,* Southern Illinois University Press, 1983.
(With Roger Cherry, David Jolliffe, and Anna Skinner) *Assessing Writers' Knowledge and Processes of Composing,* Ablex Publishing, 1985.
Fragments of Rationality, University of Pittsburgh Press, 1992.

Member of editorial board, *Issues in Writing, Pre/Text, Rhetoric Society Quarterly,* and *Computers and Composition.*

*   *   *

FALZEDER, Ernst 1955-

PERSONAL: Born February 17, 1955, in Linz, Austria; son of Hans (a bookbinder) and Else (Rohraver) Falzeder; married Gertrude Haderlapp (a psychologist), 1980 (divorced, 1991); children: Florian Falzeder, Evi Erhart. *Education:* Earned "maturity certificate" (equivalent to B.A.), 1973; University of Salzburg, Ph.D., 1985; Salzburg Study Group for Psychoanalysis, postgraduate training, 1985—.

ADDRESSES: Home—Kajetanerplatz 3, A-5020 Salzburg, Austria; ch. 16 de la Gradelle, CH-1224 Chene-Bougeries, Switzerland.

CAREER: Austrian Society for Sexological Research, founding and board member, 1979; University of Salzburg, Psychological Institute, assistant, 1979-85, lecturer, 1985—, assistant professor, 1986-87; Verein Lebenshilfe, Salzburg, work with mentally and physically disabled children, 1983; Lebensberatung (Counseling Center), Salzburg, psychotherapist, 1985; University of Innsbruck, Psychological and Pedagogical Institutes, lecturer, 1985—; community improvement program, Salzburg, psychologist, 1986-87; Verein Beratung und Unterbringung Unterkunftsloser (program to aid the homeless), 1988-89; writer.

AWARDS, HONORS: Gustav Hans Graber Prize from the International Society for Pre- and Perinatal Psychology, 1986; research fellowships from the Institutions Universitaires de Psychiatrie de Genève, 1989-92, and the Fondation Louis Jeantet, 1992—.

WRITINGS:

Die "Sprachverwirrung" und die "Grundstorung:" Die Untersuchungen S. Ferenczis und Michael Balints uber Entstehung und Auswirkungen fruher Objektbeziehungen, Salzberger Sozialisationsstudien (Salzburg), 1986.
(Editor with Alfred Papst, and contributor) *Wie Psychoanalyse wirksam wird-Sepp Schindler zum 65. Gerburtstag,* [Salzburg], 1987.
(Editor with Eva Brabant and Patrizia Giampieri Deutsch) *Sigmund Freud-Sandor Ferenczi, Correspondance, Tome I, 1908-1914,* Calmann-Levy (Paris), 1992; also published as *Sigmund Freud-Sandor Ferenczi, Lettere, Vol. 1,* Cortina (Milan, Italy), 1993, and *Sigmund Freud-Sandor Ferenczi, Briefwechsel, Band I/2 (1912-1914),* Boehlau (Vienna, Austria), 1994; English translation published as *The Correspondence of Sigmund Freud and Sandor Ferenczi: Volume 1, 1908-1914,* Harvard University Press, 1994.
(Editor with Andre Haynal and contributor) *100 Years of Psychoanalysis,* International Universities Press (New York), 1994.

Psychoanalyse (professional journal), member of editorial board, 1985—. Contributor of numerous articles in German to professional books and periodicals dealing with the psychology. Falzeder's works have been published in German, English, French, and Italian.

WORK IN PROGRESS: (Editor with Eva Brabant) *Sigmund Freud/Sandor Ferenczi: Correspondence, Volumes II and III,* (editor) *The Complete Correspondence between Sigmund Freud and Karl Abraham,*

Karnac Books, and (editor with Peter Heller) *Selected Letters of Anna Freud,* International Universities Press.

SIDELIGHTS: Ernst Falzeder told *CA:* "For the last eight years, I have been teaching psychoanalytic theory at the Austrian universities of Salzburg and Innsbruck, and my training as a psychoanalyst is in an advanced stage. I have concurrently dedicated my work of the past six years to historical research, both as a research fellow in the Balint Archives (Geneva, Switzerland) and as coeditor of Freud's most important professional correspondence, that with Sandor Ferenczi. In addition, I have recently been appointed editor of the complete correspondence between Freud and Karl Abraham; and I will, together with Professor Peter Heller (Buffalo, NY), edit a selection of Anna Freud's letters.

"On previous occasions I had the opportunity to do research in the Freud Archives of the Library of Congress, leading, among other things, to the discovery of an important draft of one of Freud's major works ('Mourning and Melancholia') and to that of a hitherto unknown female patient of his who is one of the most important patients in the history of psychoanalysis. In a recent publication I showed, inter alia, how her treatment had monumental consequences for psychoanalytic technique and theory. Previous work done by myself has resulted in constituting a private archive, in accumulating rare Freudiana and psychoanalytica, and in my transcribing of some 4,000 unpublished letters by Freud.

"Among my other contributions are texts on the personal and scientific exchanges between Freud and important persons of his intellectual environment, Ferenczi, Alfred Adler, and Otto Rank in particular; and on locating the origins and developments of certain theoretical and technical notions, such as early object relations, transference and countertransference, and empathy. As the transmission of theory, knowledge, and tradition in psychoanalysis is significantly done by the psychoanalytic encounter itself, I have also drawn up a 'family tree' of psychoanalysis until about World War II."

*   *   *

FARIS, Clay
See NAFF, Clayton

*   *   *

FARR, Jory 1952-

PERSONAL: Born April 9, 1952, in New York, NY; son of Marshall (a psychologist) and Beatrice (an educational psychologist) Farr; children: Zachary Jason. *Education:* University of California, Santa Cruz, B.A., 1975; Northwestern University, M.A., 1981. *Politics:* "Liberal to radical." *Religion:* Jewish.

ADDRESSES: Home—1655 North Michigan Ave., Pasadena, CA 91104. *Agent*—Ken Sherman, 9507 Santa Monica Blvd., Suite 211, Beverly Hills, CA 90210.

CAREER: Press-Enterprise, Riverside, CA, popular culture critic and columnist, c. 1987—.

WRITINGS:

Moguls and Madmen: The Pursuit of Power in Popular Music, Simon & Schuster (New York, NY), 1994.

WORK IN PROGRESS: A book exploring "gender, sex, mythology, and art."

SIDELIGHTS: Jory Farr told *CA:* "As a writer, I am interested in storytelling, psychology, mythology, culture, and, of course, nature. Indigenous cultures fascinate me, because I feel they frequently hold the knowledge crucial to our survival as a species. Issues of race continue to motivate me. I feel the racial chasm in this country, between 'whites' and 'browns' and 'blacks,' is primed to devour us all. The violence of youth and the absence of elders is ripping this country apart. Unless we do something about it, as a people, life will become an endless cycle of fear and retribution, sorrow and disaster."

*   *   *

FARRELL, Warren (Thomas) 1943-

PERSONAL: Born June 26, 1943, in New York, NY; son of Thomas E. (an accountant) and Muriel Lee (a librarian) Farrell; married Ursie Fairbairn (senior vice president), 1966 (divorced, 1977). *Education:* Montclair State College, B.A., 1965; University of California at Los Angeles, M.A., 1966; New York University, Ph.D., 1974. *Politics:* Independent. *Religion:* Spiritual—no affiliation. *Avocational interests:* Tennis, running, reading, films—"I love discussing and reviewing films."

ADDRESSES: Home and Office—103 North Highway 101, Box 220, Encinitas, CA 92024. *Agent*—Ellen Levine, Ellen Levine Literary Agency, 15 East 26th St., No. 1801, New York, NY 10010.

CAREER: Author. Lecturer and consultant on gender, male-female relationships, and men's issues,

1969—. National Organization for Women (NOW), member of board of directors; board member of the Children's Rights Council and the National Coalition of Free Men.

AWARDS, HONORS: National awards from the National Coalition of Free Men, and Men's Rights, Inc., both 1986, both for *Why Men Are the Way They Are;* awards from National Congress for Men and Children, and Men's Rights, Inc., both 1993, both for *The Myth of Male Power;* Family Hero Award, Pennsylvania Family Rights Coalition, 1994; award of recognition from California Association of Marriage and Family Therapists, Santa Barbara.

WRITINGS:

The Liberated Man, Random House (New York), 1975.
Why Men Are the Way They Are, McGraw-Hill (New
    York), 1986.
*The Myth of Male Power: Why Men Are the Dispos-
    able Sex—Fated for War, Programmed for Work,
    Divorced from Emotion,* Simon & Schuster (New
    York), 1993.

WORK IN PROGRESS: Seven Great Myths about Men, publication expected in 1995-96.

SIDELIGHTS: Warren Farrell told *CA:* "Perhaps my writing career unconsciously began at about age 12—during the McCarthy era—with being labeled 'Pinko' for refusing to divide the world into Americans good/communists bad. Fortunately, when I was 14 and 15, my family moved to Europe, and I discovered that the questions that generated ostracism in the U.S. generated respect in Europe. It was an impressionable age at which to have my questioning process rewarded.

"When the civil rights, gay movements, and women's movements surfaced, I was again astonished at the inability of people to hear the best intent of the aggrieved groups. I got deeply enough involved in the women's movement to become the only man in the United States ever elected three times to the Board of Directors of the National Organization for Women (NOW) in New York City. This led to my writing my first book, *The Liberated Man,* in which I tried to articulate to men the value of independent women.

"Slowly, though, I began seeing the feminist leadership dividing the world into 'women good/men bad.' This led to *Why Men Are the Way They Are,* which was an attempt to take the most common questions

women asked about men (e.g., 'Why are men such jerks?') and answer these from men's perspective. Men had become, in essence, the latest misunderstood group.

"As it became a definition of 'liberal' to care more about saving whales than saving males, I began to see the legal system becoming a substitute husband—doing more, for example, to protect women in the work place from dirty jokes than to protect men in the work place from faulty rafters. This led to my asking myself whether men really had the power if they felt the *obligation* to earn more money that someone else spent while they died earlier. Questions like these led to six years of research, fifty pages of footnotes, and *The Myth of Male Power: Why Men Are the Disposable Sex— Fated for War, Programmed for Work, Divorced from Emotion.*"

Farrell was called the "Gloria Steinem of Men's Liberation," by *Washington Post* reviewer Don Oldenburg. Generally, critics note that Farrell's writings deal with "gender liberation." A founding member of the National Organization for Changing Men and the National Congress of Men, Farrell currently serves on numerous boards. Oldenburg noted that Farrell's writing reframes "'the balance of sexual power and politics in the contemporary world' in his [1986] book *Why Men Are the Way They Are.*" Farrell told the *Washington Post:* "I'm asking women and men, before they blame the other sex, to listen to the other sex's experience of the world—both their power experiences and powerless experiences. Too often people are arguing from their own self-interests."

Perhaps Farrell's most controversial observations in the gender discussion are captured in *The Myth of Male Power. Washington Post Book World* contributor Camille Paglia (herself a prominent figure in gender studies) called *The Myth of Male Power* "a bombshell. . . . It attacks the unexamined assumptions of feminist discourse with shocking candor and forces us to see our everyday world from a fresh perspective. . . . The Myth of Male Power* is the kind of original, abrasive, heretical text that is desperately needed to restore fairness and balance the present ideology-sodden curriculum of women's studies courses."

All men have a common bond in their "wound of disposability," according to Farrell. *Business Week* reviewer Bruce Nussbaum noted that Farrell examines the paradox of male aggression: "Farrell demonstrates male powerlessness by pointing to the violence done to males in school sports (which he terms male child abuse), the selling of men's time and bodies to support wife and family (prostitution of males), and the draft (enslaving men in the military). Farrell concludes that 'the wound that unifies all men is the wound of their disposability . . . as soldiers, workers, dads.'"

BIOGRAPHICAL/CRITICAL SOURCES:

PERIODICALS

Business Week, September 13, 1993, pp. 14-15.
Maclean's, February 1, 1988, p. 58.
New Statesman and Society, March 4, 1994, p. 38.
People, June 15, 1987, p. 49.
Time, March 7, 1994, p. 6.
Washington Post, October 17, 1986.
Washington Post Book World, July 25, 1993, p. 1.

*   *   *

FEATHER, Leonard G(eoffrey)   1914-1994

OBITUARY NOTICE—See index for *CA* sketch: Born September 13, 1914, in London, England; immigrated to the United States, 1935; naturalized U.S. citizen, 1948; died of pneumonia, September 22, 1994, in Encino, CA. Musician, composer, and critic. Considered a central figure in jazz music, Feather took up the piano and clarinet at an early age and later arranged music. After attending University College in London, he immersed himself in that city's thriving jazz scene. In addition to composing and performing, Feather also began writing about jazz, and published his first article in 1933. That same year he relocated to New York, where he continued to produce both criticism and music. As a composer, one of his more popular tunes was "How Blue Can You Get," a song recorded by both Louis Jordan and B. B. King. Many of the famous names in jazz, including Lionel Hampton and Count Basie, recorded songs composed by Feather. He produced the debut albums of Dinah Washington and Sarah Vaughan and worked as a press agent for the legendary Duke Ellington. Feather's first book, 1949's *Inside Bebop,* was described by the *Chicago Tribune* as "one of the first and more important books on [jazz] style." In the late 1950s he relocated to the Los Angeles area and continued to compose, arrange, and write; he also lectured at several universities. His articles on jazz for publications such as *Metronome, Playboy, Down Beat,* and *Esquire* helped earn Feather the first Grammy awarded for journalism in 1964. He also authored several other books, including *Laughter from the Hip, The Passion for Jazz,* and *The Jazz Years: Earwitness to an Era.* Feather's most important

book, by many accounts, was the *Encyclopedia of Jazz,* first published in 1955 and revised periodically. He was completing its latest edition, *The Oxford Encyclopedia of Jazz,* with Ira Gitler shortly before his death.

OBITUARIES AND OTHER SOURCES:

BOOKS

Writers Directory, St. James Press, 1992, p. 306.

PERIODICALS

Chicago Tribune, September 24, 1994, sec. 2, p. 17.
Los Angeles Times, September 23, 1994, p. A34.
Washington Post, September 24, 1994, p. C6.

*   *   *

FEDERSPIEL, J(uerg) F.   1931-

PERSONAL: Born June 28, 1931, in Kempthal, near Winterthur, Switzerland. *Education:* Attended Rudolf Steiner School, Basel.

ADDRESSES: Office—c/o Gotham Art and Literary Agency, Inc., 25 Tudor City Pl., Suite 1504, New York, NY 10017.

CAREER: Novelist, essayist, poet, playwright, and short-story writer. Journalist and film critic for Swiss and German newspapers.

AWARDS, HONORS: Prizes from the cities of Basel and Zurich, Switzerland; Schiller Prize (Switzerland); Georg Mackensen Prize for best German short story; C. F. Meyer Prize.

WRITINGS:

Orangen und Tode: Erzahlungen (title means "Oranges and Deaths"), Piper, 1961.
Massaker im Mond: Roman (title means "Massacre on the Moon"), Piper, 1963.
Der Mann, der Glueck brachte: Erzahlungen (title means "The Man with a Lucky Star"), Piper, 1966.
Orangen vor ihrem Fenster: Erzahlungen, Verlag Volk und Welt, 1977.
Die beste Stadt fuer Blinde und andere Berichte (title means "The Best City for the Blind and Other Reports"), Suhrkamp, 1980.
Die Ballade von der Typhoid Mary, Suhrkamp, 1982, published as *The Ballad of Typhoid Mary,* translated by Joel Agee, Dutton (New York), 1983.
Wahn und Muell: Berichte und Gedichte (title means "Illusions and Garbage"), Limmat, 1983.

An Earthquake in My Family: Stories, translated by Eveline L. Kanes, Dutton (New York), 1986.

Kilroy: Stimmen in der Subway (title means "Voices from the Subway"), Im Waldgut, 1988.

Geographie der Lust: Roman, Suhrkamp, 1989, published as *Laura's Skin,* translated by Breon Mitchell, Fromm International, 1991.

Eine Halbtagsstelle in Pompeji: Erzahlungen, Suhrkamp, 1993.

Also author of *Museum des Hasses: Tage in Manhattan* (title means "Museum of Hatred: Days in Manhattan"), 1969, a novel; *Die Maerchentante* (title means "The Fairytale Teller"), 1971; *Traume aus Plastic* (title means "Dreams of Plastic"), 1972, a collection of essays on literature, art, and film; *Paratuga kehrt zurueck* (title means "Paratuga's Return"), 1973; *Bruederlichkeit* (title means "Brotherhood"), 1979, a play; and *Die Liebe ist eine Himmelsmacht* (title means "Love Is a Heavenly Power"), 1985, a collection of short stories. Also contributor to *Begegnungen mit vier Zurcher Autoren: Jurg Federspiel, Hugo Loetscher, Adolf Muschg, Hans Schumacher,* GS-Verlag, 1986. Several of Federspiel's stories have been translated and published in magazines.

SIDELIGHTS: J. F. Federspiel is a prolific Swiss writer whose German-language works were first introduced in English translation in the United States in the 1980s. Federspiel's prose works, including numerous short stories and several novels, are characterized by an extravagance of emotion that manifests itself in stereotyped, grotesque, or mythological characters, blackly humorous and unrealistic plots, and other unconventional narrative devices.

Many critics have noted the strong visual elements in Federspiel's fiction. In *Der Mann, der Glueck brachte: Erzahlungen,* Federspiel resolves the question of how to document one's own existence at a time in which fact and fiction have become irrevocably confused by taking photographs of his characters. And in one of the stories in *Die beste Stadt fuer Blinde und andere Berichte,* a group of blind beggars lead the reader on an Odyssey-like tour of New York City. This latter work also collects two anti-war stories, of which Robert Schwarz claimed in *World Literature Today:* "These statements belong, not counting full-bodied novels, to the best anti-war literature in recent years. They are gripping without being sentimental, convincing without being didactic."

Also reviewed by the English-language press is *Paratuga kehrt zurueck,* a surreal, episodic adventure narrated by Paratuga, a character critics described as a grotesque collection of moral and physical aberrations. A reviewer in the *Times Literary Supplement* remarked, "Paratuga's role is, primarily, to attend, and occasionally induce, catastrophes in human affairs, and he has a sixth sense for discovering their actual or potential whereabouts." The critic concluded: "*Paratuga kehrt zurueck* is an uncomfortable, rather shocking, and thoroughly fascinating narrative exercise. One hopes there will be much more to come."

Federspiel's books began appearing in English translation in the 1980s, beginning with *Die Ballade von der Typhoid Mary,* published in the United States as *The Ballad of Typhoid Mary.* In this novel, the author extrapolates on the few known details about the historical Maria Anna Caduff, who infected numerous people with the contagious virus around the turn of the twentieth century. In Federspiel's rendition, Maria, who often went by the name Mary Mallon, is an immigrant to the United States whose parents and siblings died of typhoid on the journey from Switzerland. The teenage Mary is adopted by a lecherous doctor, whom she repays by cooking for him, thus beginning her career of feckless death-dealing. Throughout most of her life, until she is apprehended by the New York Department of Health, Mary makes her living as a cook, moving on to the next location whenever her employers show signs of coming down with typhoid. The story is narrated by a dying man, the grandson of one of the doctors who helped track down Typhoid Mary.

"Mr. Federspiel writes with poetic terseness. . . . Perhaps because to say more about so black a life would be to hiss at Creation, Mr. Federspiel says less, and cleverly. He is a passionate ironist," commented John Calvin Batchelor in the *New York Times Book Review.* Other critics commented on the irony in this widely reviewed novel, and the author's effective use of such distancing devices as second and third-person narrators to convey the fabulous aspect of the story. Richard Eder concluded his *Los Angeles Times Book Review* critique of *The Ballad of Typhoid Mary:* "There is a bleakness to the writing, and the arbitrary quality of any parable. This is a chilly work, and perhaps too much so to be quiet real. But it is a chill we catch." E. S. Turner, writing in the *Times Literary Supplement,* complained that, rather than a "witty moral fable" as advertised on the book jacket, Federspiel merely offers a chronicle of Mary's sexual escapades: "It is as if someone has set out to write a life of the Elephant Man and, finding the facts scarce, had decided to give him a sleazy sex life." Many critics, however, tended to echo M. Burkhard, who declared in *World Literature Today* that "Federspiel . . . transforms his material, which could easily qualify as a horror story, into a complex human drama."

The Ballad of Typhoid Mary was followed by *An Earthquake in My Family: Stories,* a collection of Federspiel's short stories garnered from earlier collections published only in German. The collection features Federspiel's anti-war stories along with some narrated by the macabre and humorous Paratuga and others. Although a critic in *Kirkus Review* concluded: "The subject matter here is uniformedly grim, the plots obscure; and the characters, a down-in-the-mouth lot, oddly predictable in their alienation," the work was generally well-received. Novelist and *New York Times Book Review* contributor Angela Carter allowed that "Some of the stories in *An Earthquake in My Family* are not so brilliant, but J. F. Federspiel is a very fine writer indeed." And a *Publishers Weekly* reviewer concluded, "These stories . . . are uniformly surehanded, quirky, driven by an idiosyncratic imagination, in tones ranging from dank to dark to bleakly comic."

Federspiel's next work, *Geographie der Lust: Roman,* appeared in English translation in 1991 as *Laura's Skin* to wide praise for the author's comic and ironic talents. *Laura's Skin* begins with Primo Antonio Robusti, a wealthy, middle-aged eccentric whose latest obsession is Laura, a nineteen-year-old with a beautiful backside. Robusti orders Laura's behind tattooed with a map of the world by a famous artist, and both he and the artist die shortly after sexual encounters with her. Laura goes on to travel the world, exhibiting the work of art imprinted on her body for large sums of money to everyone from art aficionados to members of the Japanese mafia, until she falls in love with a blind Irishman. More than one reviewer, such as *Library Journal* contributor Grove Koger, dubbed the result a "hodge-podge," though reviewer Robert Schwarz, again writing in the *World Literature Today,* allowed that despite Federspiel's extravagance, "the book is thoroughly entertaining." Anthony Vivis concluded his *Times Literary Supplement* review with the accolade: "Federspiel has created a rumbustiously Rabelaisian tale. His energy and humour are infectious, and his ironic vision is as sharp as a tattooist's needle."

Often surreal rather than realistic, Federspiel's books in English translation have been enthusiastically received by reviewers who appreciate the author's postmodern fables, and criticized by others as overdone. Angela Carter has commented: "[Feder-spiel] is the poet of anxiety and obsession, touched by Surrealism, crackling with black humor, but these strengths can be grounded by a leaden whimsy and dissipate themselves in perverse eccentricity." Nonetheless, Federspiel is widely respected as a leading voice in postmodern European literature.

BIOGRAPHICAL/CRITICAL SOURCES:

BOOKS

Contemporary Literary Criticism, Volume 42, Gale, 1987.
World Authors, 1980-1985, H. W. Wilson, 1991, pp. 277-79.

PERIODICALS

Best Sellers, April, 1984, p. 5.
Booklist, April 1, 1986, p. 1116.
Kirkus Review, February 1, 1986, p. 145.
Library Journal, April 1, 1991, p. 149.
Los Angeles Times Book Review, December 18, 1983, pp. 1, 8.
New York Times Book Review, February 12, 1984, p. 11; April 6, 1986; May 5, 1991, sec. 7, p. 20.
Publishers Weekly, February 14, 1986, p. 69.
Times Literary Supplement, February 8, 1974, p. 125; October 12, 1984; January 12, 1990.
Voice Literary Supplement, February, 1984.
World Literature Today, summer, 1981, p. 460; summer, 1983, p. 455; spring, 1990, p. 299.
Yale Review, January, 1985, pp. x, xiii.*

*   *   *

FEIKEMA, Feike
See MANFRED, Frederick (Feikema)

*   *   *

FELDMAN, Gayle   1951-

PERSONAL: Born September 7, 1951, in Philadelphia, PA; daughter of Joseph (a commercial artist) and Bernice (a homemaker; maiden name, Borkofsky) Feldman; married David Reid (a lawyer), 1976; children: Benjamin. *Education:* University of Pennsylvania, B.A., 1973; Cambridge University, M.A., 1975. *Avocational interests:* Chinese language, literature, and culture, reading, opera, bicycling.

ADDRESSES: Home—New York City. *Office—Publishers Weekly,* 249 West 17th St., New York, NY 10011. *Agent*—Molly Friedrich, Aaron M. Priest Literary Agency, Inc., 708 Third Ave., New York, NY 10017.

CAREER: Publishers Weekly, New York City, book news editor, 1989—.

MEMBER: Authors Guild, Women's Media Group.

WRITINGS:

You Don't Have to Be Your Mother, Norton (New York), 1994.

SIDELIGHTS: Gayle Feldman told *CA:* "*You Don't Have to Be Your Mother* is a memoir about my mother, myself, the birth of my son, and breast cancer. My mother died of breast cancer when she was in her fifties, near the age I am now. I was diagnosed with breast cancer in the eighth month of a first, much-desired pregnancy. I felt compelled to write this book as a record for my family, and to help other women and their families who are living with breast cancer or with its legacy."

*   *   *

FELINTO (Barbosa de Lima), Marilene 1957-

PERSONAL: Born December 5, 1957, in Recife, Brazil; daughter of Mariano Felinto and Alaide (a nurse; maiden name, Barbosa) de Lima. *Education:* University of Sao Paulo, B.A., 1981. *Politics:* Sao Paulo Worker's Party. *Religion:* None.

ADDRESSES: Home—Av. Afonso Mariano Fagundes 472/32, 04054-000 Sao Paulo, Brazil. *Office*—Secret. Admins., Al. Barao de Limeira 425, 01290-001 Sao Paulo, Brazil. *Agent*—Ray-Guede Mertin, Friedrichstrasse 1, 61348 Bad Hamburg, Germany.

CAREER: College of Journalism, Sao Paulo, Brazil, assistant professor of Portuguese language, 1983-87; *Folha de Sao Paulo,* Sao Paulo, journalist, 1989—. University of California, Berkeley, visiting writer, 1992; translator from English into Portuguese; Haus der Kulturen der Welt (Berlin), visiting lecturer, 1994.

AWARDS, HONORS: Prize from Brazilian Union of Writers, best unpublished novel, 1982, and *Jabuti* (Brazil's major literature award), best young writer category, 1983, both for *The Women of Tijucopapo;* scholar of Sao Paulo's Goethe Institute, 1994.

WRITINGS:

As Mulheres de Tijucopapa (novel), Editora 34 (Rio de Janeiro), 1982, 2nd edition, 1992, translation by Irene Mathews published as *The Women of Tijucopapo,* University of Nebraska Press (Lincoln, NE), 1994.

Author of the novel *Natural History,* published in 1995. Some writings have been translated into German.

UNTRANSLATED WORKS

Outros Herois e Este Graciliano (nonfiction), Editora Brasiliense (Sao Paulo), 1983.
O Lago Encantado de Grongonzo (novel), Editora Imago (Rio de Janeiro), 1987, 2nd edition, 1991.
Postcard (stories), Editora Iluminuras (Sao Paulo), 1992.

Work represented in anthologies.

WORK IN PROGRESS: Research on the Brazilian hinterland (*sertao*) and the Amazonas.

SIDELIGHTS: Marilene Felinto told *CA:* "I began writing fiction when I was around thirteen years old. My family and I had then just moved from Recife, my home town in the northeast, to Sao Paulo in the southeast. This was the year 1968, a time when poor immigrants from the Brazilian hinterland in the northeast went south in search of better work opportunities. That was the case with my father. Moving was a very traumatic change for me (the south part of the country is very different in climate, food, and habits in general), and I found it very difficult to adapt myself to a new life. I had, therefore, a very closed, lonely adolescence, during which I only read and wrote, hardly having the normal social relations people are accustomed to having during this period of their lives.

"At that time I never thought of being or becoming a writer, but the desire was there without my realizing it. I developed the habit of writing letters to friends and relatives in Recife, to the point that I became the official correspondent of the family. From letters I went to poems, and from there to short stories and novels.

"Later, already influenced by my studies of literature at the university, I decided to write fiction professionally. My work is mostly influenced by the literature of the Brazilian writers Guimaraes Rosa, Graciliano Ramos, and Clarice Lispector. Among the foreign influences, the American and British ones (especially D. H. Lawrence and Thomas Hardy) are the greatest.

"Writing fiction is my only means to try to restore something that seems definitely lost in my life—my home town, my childhood, or something deeper and not as clear as that."

FERRIS, John (Stephen) 1937-

PERSONAL: Born December 26, 1937, in Crookham, Hampshire, England; son of Charles (a bus driver) and Dorothy (a cleaning person; maiden name, Purbrick) Ferris; married first wife, Mary, March 30, 1963 (divorced, 1985); married Carol Gibson Norman (a teacher), July 25, 1992; children: (first marriage) Nathan, Anna. *Education:* London School of Economics and Political Science, London, Diploma in Social Administration (with distinction), 1971, M.A., 1972, M.Sc., 1973. *Politics:* "Green/radical." *Avocational interests:* Reading, cycling, travel.

ADDRESSES: Home—90 Denison St., Beeston, Nottingham NG9 1DQ, England; and 707 Mulberry St., Williamsport, PA 17701. *Office*—School of Social Studies, University of Nottingham, University Park, Nottingham NG7 2RD, England; and Department of Political Science, Lycoming College, Williamsport, PA 17701.

CAREER: British Home Office, London, England, administrative officer, 1963-69; University of Nottingham, Nottingham, England, lecturer in social studies, 1972—. Visiting research scholar or research associate, University of Bielefeld, 1988, University of Bremen, 1989, and Czech Academy of Sciences, 1992. Holloway Tenants Cooperative, coordinator and community worker, 1972-73. *Military service:* British Army, 1955-58; served in the Middle East.

MEMBER: British Social Policy Association, British Sociological Association, National Council for the Care and Rehabilitation of Offenders (member of executive committee), Second Base Housing Association (chairperson, 1986—).

WRITINGS:

Participation in Urban Planning: The Barnsbury Case, Bell (London), 1973.
(Editor with D. Whynes and P. T. Bean, and contributor) *The Defence of Welfare,* Tavistock Publications (London), 1986.
(Editor with Robert Page) *Social Policy in Transition: Anglo-German Perspectives,* Gower (Brookfield, VT), 1992.
(Editor) *Realism in Green Politics,* Manchester University Press (Dover, NH), 1993.

Work represented in anthologies, including *Current Issues in Planning,* edited by Sylvia Trench and Taner Oc, Gower, 1990; *The Politics of Nature,* edited by A. Dobson and P. Lucardie, Routledge & Kegan Paul, 1993; and *Nineteenth-Century Cities in Europe,* edited by P. Kratochvil, Central European University Press, 1994. Contributor to periodicals, including *New Statesman and Nation, Youth and Policy,* and *Environmental Politics.*

WORK IN PROGRESS: Research on cities and environmental sustainability.

*   *   *

FIELDS, L. Marc 1955-

PERSONAL: Born September 9, 1955, in Champaign-Urbana, IL; son of Armond (a market researcher and writer) and Rona M. (a psychologist) Fields; married Nancy R. Spencer (an educator), December 30, 1985. *Education:* Princeton University, B.A. (summa cum laude), 1977; New York University, M.F.A., 1984. *Politics:* "Secular humanist." *Avocational interests:* Theater, history, music.

ADDRESSES: Home—Hightstown, NJ. *Agent*—Oscar Collier Associates, 2000 Flat Run Rd., Seaman, OH 45679.

CAREER: Freelance writer for film and television, 1984—; New School for Social Research, New York City, instructor in media studies, 1987-89; New York University, New York City, assistant professor, 1989-93, associate chair in film and television graduate study program, 1992-93.

MEMBER: Phi Beta Kappa Society, Association of Independent Video and Film.

AWARDS, HONORS: Mobil Award semi-finalist, 1984; Cine Eagle, 1991.

WRITINGS:

(With Armond Fields) *From the Bowery to Broadway: Lew Fields and the Roots of American Popular Theater* (biography/history), Oxford University Press (New York, NY), 1993.

Also the author and director of the short film *Confessions of a Practical Man,* 1982. Contributor to periodicals, including *Artforum, Arts Magazine,* and *The Forward.*

WORK IN PROGRESS: The Bowery: A Social History, book and documentary film; *The Rise of American Popular Entertainment,* a documentary series about the history of show business.

FINCH, A. R. C.
  See FINCH, Annie (Ridley Crane)

*   *   *

FINCH, Annie (Ridley Crane)   1956-
  (A. R. C. Finch)

PERSONAL: Born October 31, 1956, in New Rochelle, NY; daughter of Henry Leroy, Jr. (a professor of philosophy) and Margaret Evelyn (a doll artist; maiden name, Rockwell) Finch; married Glen Brand, December 6, 1985; children: Julian Hughan. *Education:* Attended Simon's Rock Early College, 1973-74; Yale University, B.A. (magna cum laude and Distinction in English), 1979; University of Houston, M.F.A., 1986; Stanford University, Ph.D., 1991. *Politics:* "Feminist, environmentalist." *Religion:* "Quaker, Unitarian Universalist." *Avocational interests:* Baking, yoga, painting, camping, mythology, psychology, languages, children's literature.

ADDRESSES: Home—Cincinnati, OH. *Office*—Department of English, Miami University, Oxford, OH 45056.

CAREER: Natural History, editorial assistant, 1981-82; *Sequoia,* general editor and poetry editor, 1987-91; New College of San Francisco, San Francisco, CA, lecturer in poetry writing, 1991-92; University of Northern Iowa, Cedar Falls, poet-in-residence and assistant professor of English, 1992-95; Miami University, Oxford, OH, assistant professor of English, 1995--. Gives poetry workshops and readings from her works. Magic Theatre, San Francisco, CA, assistant to literary manager, 1989-90; theatrical director, producer, and actress.

MEMBER: Emily Dickinson International Society (charter member), Academy of American Poets, Poetry Society of America, Associated Writing Programs, Poets and Writers, Modern Language Association of America, Elizabethan Club of Yale University.

AWARDS, HONORS: Chauncey Brewster Tinker Prize, Yale University, 1979; graduate fellow, Stanford Humanities Center, 1989-90; Editor's Choice Award from *MacGuffin,* 1990; Mabelle McLeod Lewis fellow, 1990-91; Ina Coolbrith Circle, award for free verse, 1991; Orbis/Rhyme Award, William Wordsworth Award, and John Masefield Award from World Order of Narrative and Formalist Poets, 1992; Sparrow Sonnet Prize, 1993; Nicholas Roerich fellow, Wesleyan Writers Conference, 1993; Pushcart Prize nomination for poetry, 1994; finalist, National Poetry Series, 1994, for *No Snake.*

WRITINGS:

The Encyclopedia of Scotland (poem), produced by Fiction Music Ensemble, Hampshire College, Amherst, MA, 1982, published by Caribou Press, 1982.
The Mermaid Tragedy (play), performed in a staged reading at University of Houston, Houston, TX, 1986.
The Moon and the Snake (play), performed at Mama Bear's Bookstore, Oakland, CA, 1989.
Life by the Ocean (play), performed at Poets Theatre Festival at Theater Artaud, San Francisco, CA, 1990.
The Ghost of Meter: Culture and Prosody in American Free Verse, University of Michigan Press (Ann Arbor, MI), 1993.
(Editor and contributor) *A Formal Feeling Comes: Poems in Form by Contemporary Women,* Story Line Press, 1994.
The Furious Sun in Her Mane (song cycle), performed at Greenwich Music School in New York, 1994.
Catching the Mermother (poems), Aralia Press, 1995.
(Editor) *Revisioning the Traditions of Poetry: New Essays on Form and Narrative* (essays), Story Line Press, in press.

Some work appears under the name A. R. C. Finch. Work represented in anthologies, including *Walking between the Stars: A Far-Reaching Anthology,* edited by Francesca Dubie, Third Road, 1990; *An Introduction to Poetry,* edited by X. J. Kennedy, 8th edition, by Dana Gioia, HarperCollins, 1993; *A Contemporary American Anthology: The Unitarian Universalist Poets,* edited by Jennifer Bosveldt, Pudding House, 1994; and *New Formalist Poetry,* edited by David Mason and Mark Jarman, Story Line Press, 1995. Contributor to books, including *Meter in English: A Symposium,* edited by David Baker, University of Arkansas Press, in press; and *Essays in Honor of Maxine Kumin,* edited by Emily Grosholz, University of New England Press, in press.

Also author of essays, including "The Poetess in the World" for *Legacy,* "In Defense of Meter" for *Hellas,* and "The Sonnet Transfigured" for *How(ever),.* Contributor of poems, articles, and reviews to periodicals, including *Paris Review, Agni Review, Puerto del Sol, Poetry Flash, North American Review, San Francisco Chronicle, Women's Review of Books, Black Ice, Formalist,* and *Sparrow.*

WORK IN PROGRESS: No Snake, poems; "Marie Moving: A Narrative Poem in Nine Parts"; "Calendar," a series of poems for use in rituals and celebrations throughout the year; research for a study of the "sentimental" women's tradition of poetry in the United States, to be written in poetry and prose.

SIDELIGHTS: Annie Finch told *CA:* "Poetry has been the focus of my inner and outer life since I was about nine years old, when my first poem was published. Yet for many years I have felt the need to carve a place for my own poetry through critical writing and editorial work. I found no ready acceptance for my particular poetic blend of passion, music, and female sensibility. Through my critical studies of the female poetic tradition and the complexities of metrical interaction, as well as through editing projects that have expanded the definition of formal poetry to include chants, blues, and experimental poems, I feel I have finally been able to create a literary context in which my own poetry can make sense.

"I am fortunate to have had exceptional teachers from the earliest training in philosophy by my father and poetry by my mother (whose book of poems written from 1936 to 1995 I am currently editing) through John Hollander and Penelope Laurans at Yale, to Ntozake Shange and Diane Middlebrook, my mentors in graduate school. Yet for much of my life I have been self-taught, simply because I found myself in places where other people were not. I have come to accept and to even enjoy this condition, since it liberates much of my energy from nonessentials and directs it where I want it to go, toward the blood, guts, and health of poetry, which are based right now, as far as I am concerned, on a return to the originally mesmerizing structures of the art.

"At a time when formalism is widely associated with reactionary conservatism, I am proud to have acted as a bridge-builder to broaden the definition of form and to demonstrate the value of form to poets who might not have felt comfortable with it otherwise. To me, poetic form, with its unverbal, physical power, is radically important in reconnecting us with our human roots and rediscovering our intimacy with nature. I see it as a key element in the health and survival of our race through a more balanced relationship with the patterns of the cosmos. It is no coincidence that I am currently using arcane metrical patterns to write a series of poems in celebration of the earth's seasons for use by a group of non-poets in 'deep ecology' rituals. I have always wanted my poetry to be useful, and I have found that rhythmic formal poetry is of great value in celebrating, commemorating, and cementing the bonds of community."

BIOGRAPHICAL/CRITICAL SOURCES:

BOOKS

McPhillips, Robert, *New Formalism,* Twayne, in press.
New Princeton Encyclopedia of Poetry and Poetics, edited by Alex Preminger and T. V. Brogan, 1993, p. 406.
Cummings, Alison, *The Gender on Paper: Women in American Poetry Movements, 1975-1995,* Dissertation University of Madison (WI), 1995, pp. 162-210.

PERIODICALS

Anglia, 1995.
Contemporary Literature, summer, 1992, pp. 396-413.
Des Moines Register, January 15, 1995.
Eclectic Literary Forum, winter, 1994, pp. 45-48.
Edge City Review, vol. 1, no. 3, 1995, pp. 23-27, 37-46.
Eugene Weekly (Eugene, OR), December 1, 1994, p. 11.
Harvard Review, October, 1994.
Library Journal, June 1, 1994.
Publishers Weekly, May 30, 1994.
Sparrow, fall, 1994, pp. 52-56.
Style, spring, 1994, pp. 125-127.
Yale Review, January, 1995, pp. 121-141.

*   *   *

FINCH, Ron(ald Barry) Thorne
See THORNE-FINCH, Ron(ald Barry)

*   *   *

FINE, Richard   1951-

PERSONAL: Born September 24, 1951, in Audubon, NJ; son of Roy S. Fine (a business executive) and Ruth (Klosterman) Fine; married Sara Ferguson (a librarian), 1983; children: Mary, Alice. *Education:* Brown University, A.B. (with honors), 1973; University of Pennsylvania, A.M., 1975, Ph.D., 1979. *Politics:* "Unregenerate liberal." *Religion:* Unitarian. *Avocational interests:* "Raising my children, travel."

ADDRESSES: Home—612 W. Twenty-fifth St., Richmond, VA 23225. *Office*—Department of English, Box 842005, Virginia Commonwealth University, Richmond, VA 23284-2005.

CAREER: Virginia Commonwealth University, Richmond, VA, assistant professor, 1979-86, associate professor of English, 1986—, chair of English department, 1994—. Universite de Caen, Caen, France, Fulbright junior lecturer in American studies and American literature, 1981-82, visiting full professor at Institut d'Anglais, 1987-88. Publications director, Sabot School, Richmond. Manuscript reader for *American Quarterly,* 1986-88, and for University of Texas Press, 1992—.

MEMBER: American Studies Association, South Atlantic Modern Language Association, Association Francaise d'Etudes Americaines, Society for the History of Authorship, Reading, and Publishing, Society for Critical Exchange, Phi Beta Kappa.

AWARDS, HONORS: Recipient of National Endowment for the Humanities Fellowship for College Teachers and Independent Scholars, 1988-89; Ford Foundation Grant for Multicultural Studies, 1990-92.

WRITINGS:

Hollywood and the Profession of Authorship, 1928-1940, UMI Research Press (Ann Arbor, MI), 1985; reprinted with new preface as *West of Eden: Hollywood and the Profession of Authorship,* Smithsonian Institution Press (Washington, DC), 1993.
James M. Cain and the American Authors' Authority, University of Texas Press (Austin), 1992.

Contributor to reference works, including *Dictionary of Literary Biography,* volume 6, edited by James Kibler, Gale (Detroit), 1980; *Dictionary of Literary Biography: 1981 Yearbook,* edited by Karen L. Rood, Jean W. Ross, and Richard Ziegfield, Gale, 1982; *Magill's Critical Survey of Long Fiction,* edited by Frank Magill, Salem Press (La Canada, CA), 1983; *Research Guide to Biography and Criticism: Literature,* edited by Walton Beacham, Research Publishing (Washington, DC), 1985; and *Bibliography of United States Literature,* edited by Matthew J. Bruccoli, Manly (Columbia, SC), 1991. Contributor to professional journals, including *Literature/Film Quarterly, American Studies, English Exchange,* and *Richmond Quarterly.*

WORK IN PROGRESS: A comparative history of American, British, and French authorship (expected completion, 1996); a book on journalist A. J. Liebling and France.

SIDELIGHTS: Richard Fine told *CA:* "I do not consider myself a professional writer as such, but rather as an academic who happens to write books, and who happens to write books about the profession of authorship. My own books have explored the difficulties that professional American writers have encountered in an increasingly complex and often hostile literary marketplace. Throughout this century, I have argued, many American writers have clung with admirable if ineffective tenacity to the nineteenth-century conception of the writer as a 'gentleman-amateur,' invested with ownership of and control over his or her work, long after changes in the marketplace had made such a definition functionally obsolete. The result has been that writers have been increasingly a marginalized economic and, by extension, cultural voice, an effect I find at once troubling and regrettable.

"At present, I am at work on two major projects which extend the investigations I began in these two books—one is a comparative study of authorship in the United States, Britain, and France, and the other an analysis of how changes in copyright statute and case law have affected the contemporary American literary marketplace. I have also pursued a side project for several years—a study of the American journalist A. J. Liebling—which I hope to complete in the near future. In all of my own writing, I am most concerned with the cultural context in which literature is produced, and the institutional forces which affect its production."

*   *   *

FINLAY, Richard J(ason)   1962-

PERSONAL: Born April 17, 1962, in Falkirk, Scotland; son of Robert and Ealanor (Thomson) Finlay; married, January 26, 1993; wife's name, Jacqueline. *Education:* University of Stirling, B.A. (with honors), 1984; University of Edinburgh, Ph.D., 1990. *Politics:* Scottish National Party.

ADDRESSES: Home—39 Chisholm Ave., Causewayhead, Stirling, Scotland. *Office*—Department of History, University of Strathclyde, Glasgow, Scotland.

CAREER: University of Strathclyde, Glasgow, Scotland, lecturer in history.

WRITINGS:

Independent and Free: Scottish Politics and the Origins of the Scottish National Party, 1918-1945, John Donald (Edinburgh, Scotland), 1993.
A Partnership for Good: Scottish Politics and the Union, 1880-1992, John Donald, 1995.
(Editor with Dauvit Broon and Michael Lynch) *Scottish National Identity through the Ages,* Canongate Academic, 1995.

(Editor with Tom Devine) *Scotland in the Twentieth Century,* Edinburgh University Press, in press.

Contributor to books, including *Scotland and the British Empire: Studies in Imperialism,* edited by J. M. MacKenzie, Manchester University Press, 1995; and *A History of the Conservative Party from the Late Nineteenth Century to the Present Day,* edited by M. Francis, S. Nicholas, and I. Zweiniger-Bargielowska, University of Wales Press, 1995. Contributor to history journals.

*   *   *

FINN, Margot C.   1960-

PERSONAL: Born January 29, 1960, in Baltimore, MD; daughter of Rolphe Baxter (a psychiatrist) and Margaret Mary (a psychiatric nurse; maiden name, Wright) Finn. *Education:* Syracuse University, B.S., 1980; Columbia University, M.A., 1982, M.Phil., 1983, Ph.D., 1987.

ADDRESSES: Office—Department of History, Emory University, Atlanta, GA 30320.

CAREER: Emory University, Atlanta, GA, assistant professor, 1989-94, associate professor of history, 1994—.

WRITINGS:

After Chartism, Cambridge University Press (Cambridge, England), 1993.

WORK IN PROGRESS: The Culture of Credit: Social, Cultural, and Legal Aspects of Debt in England, c. 1760-1914, completion expected in 1998.

*   *   *

FISKE, Tarleton
See Bloch, Robert (Albert)

*   *   *

FLATH, Carol Apollonio   1955-

PERSONAL: Born February 12, 1955, in Bath, ME; daughter of Carleton and Elizabeth Lovejoy Apollonio; married July, 1982; children: two. *Education:* Attended Middlebury College, summer, 1976; Ohio University, B.A. (summa cum laude), 1977; attended Indiana University—Bloomington, 1977; University of North Carolina at Chapel Hill, M.A., 1980, Ph.D., 1987; attended International Christian University, Tokyo, Japan, 1983-84.

ADDRESSES: Home—6901 Valley Lake Drive, Raleigh, NC 27612.

CAREER: Duke University, Durham, NC, instructor, 1980-83, lecturer, 1985-89, assistant professor of the practice of Slavics, 1989—. University of Virginia, instructor, 1982; North Carolina State University, lecturer in Japanese, 1987-88; U.S. Department of State, conference interpreter of Russian (arms control negotiations), START treaty, 1989—.

MEMBER: American Association of Teachers of Slavic and East European Languages (chapter president, 1989-90), American Association for the Advancement of Slavic Studies, American Literary Translators Association, Southern Conference on Slavic Studies, Carolina Association of Translators and Interpreters.

AWARDS, HONORS: Exchange program for teachers of Russian in Moscow, U.S.S.R., International Research and Exchanges Board, 1981, 1988; fellow of North Carolina Japan Center, 1983; Prize for the Translation of Japanese Literature, Japan-United States Friendship Commission, 1988, for two novellas in *The Phoenix Tree and Other Stories;* grant from Southern Research and Exchanges Board, 1989; fellow of Russian Research Center at Harvard University, summers, 1989-90; ACTR grant for work on Russian interpreting in Moscow, 1990.

WRITINGS:

(With E. Andrews, J. Van Tuyl, E. Maksimova, and I. Dolgova) *S mesta v kar'er: Leaping into Russian; A Systematic Introduction to Contemporary Russian Grammar,* Focus, 1993.

Contributor to periodicals.

TRANSLATOR FROM JAPANESE

Satoko Kizaki, *The Phoenix Tree and Other Stories,* Kodansha, 1990.
Satoko Kizaki, *The Sunken Temple* (novel), Kodansha, 1993.

TRANSLATOR FROM RUSSIAN

T. Lakesen, V. Garros, and N. Korbanevshaya, editors, *Intimacy and Terror: Soviet Diaries of the 1930s,* New Press, 1995.

Contributor of translations to periodicals, including *Canadian-American Slavic Studies.*

WORK IN PROGRESS: Research on Dostoevsky, Chekhov, the literature of childhood, problems of translation and interpreting, nineteenth-century Russian prose fiction, modern Japanese literature, language teaching, modern Russian culture, and the media.

* * *

FLAYHART, William Henry (III)   1944-

PERSONAL: Born July 12, 1944, in Williamsport, PA; son of William Henry II (an office engineer) and Naomi (a registered nurse; maiden name, Laux) Flayhart; married Deborah Ann Smith (a gourmet chef), June 4, 1977; children: Thomas William, Catherine Ann, Jennifer Nicole. *Education:* Lycoming College, B.A. (with honors), 1966; University of Virginia, M.A., 1968, Ph.D., 1971. *Religion:* Presbyterian. *Avocational interests:* Cruising, travel.

ADDRESSES: Office—Department of History and Political Science, Delaware State University, Dover, DE 19904. *Agent*—Eleanor Wood, Spectrum Literary Agency, 111 Eighth Ave., Suite 1501, New York, NY 10011.

CAREER: Delaware State University, Dover, assistant professor, 1970-72, associate professor, 1972-74, professor of history, 1974—, department head, 1993—. University of Leiden, visiting professor, 1994-95; Netherlands Maritime Museum, visiting lecturer. Cunard Line, senior scholar in residence, 1964—. Delaware Historical Records Advisory Board, member, 1986-94; Friends of Old Dover, president, 1989-93, vice-president, 1993-94; Preservation Delaware, member of board of directors, 1993-94.

MEMBER: International Commission for Maritime History, North American Society for Oceanic History, Consortium on Revolutionary Europe, CNRO, Kiwanis Club of Dover (senior member; president, 1977-78).

AWARDS, HONORS: Gold Medal, Steamship Historical Society of America, 1973.

WRITINGS:

(With John H. Shaum, Jr.) *Majesty at Sea: The Four-Stackers,* Patrick Stephens, 1981, 2nd edition, 1995.
(With R. W. Warwick) *QE2,* Norton, 1985.
Counterpoint to Trafalgar: The Anglo-Russian Invasion of Naples, 1805-1806, University of South Carolina Press (Columbia, SC), 1992.
The American Line, Norton, 1995.

WORK IN PROGRESS: Research on the Netherlands Merchant Marine in World War II.

SIDELIGHTS: William Henry Flayhart told *CA:* "The field of maritime and naval history occupies my interests and research time because I grew up in rural Pennsylvania, and the travel advertisements in various magazines spelled adventure to me. Ship brochures and schedules led me to postcards, and that led me to a desire to know more about every vessel I encountered. The lure of the sea and ships has been very great in my life, and was transformed from an avocation into a vocation."

* * *

FLEMING, Robert E.   1936-

PERSONAL: Born December 18, 1936, in Shullsburg, WI; son of Francis A. (a tool company department head) and Rose (a homemaker; maiden name, Mayer) Fleming; married Esther Bogusch (a college teacher), February 7, 1959; children: Kathleen. *Education:* Northern Illinois University, B.A., 1959, M.A., 1964; University of Illinois at Urbana-Champaign, Ph.D., 1967. *Politics:* Republican. *Religion:* Roman Catholic.

ADDRESSES: Home—Albuquerque, NM. *Office*—Department of English, Humanities 217, University of New Mexico, Albuquerque, NM 87131.

CAREER: Teacher at a junior high school in Rockford, IL, 1959-60, and a high school, Rockford, 1960-64; University of New Mexico, Albuquerque, assistant professor, 1967-71, associate professor, 1971-76, professor of English, 1976—, associate dean, College of Arts and Sciences, 1988—. National Endowment for the Humanities-New Mexico Humanities Council, lecturer, 1978, 1980, 1985; lecturer at Gorky Institute, Moscow State University, and Kuban State University, 1993. Ernest Hemingway Foundation, member of board of directors, 1993—. *Military service:* U.S. Marine Corps, 1957-63.

MEMBER: Modern Language Association of America, Sinclair Lewis Society (member of board of directors, 1992-94), Rocky Mountain Modern Language Association, Western Literature Association.

AWARDS, HONORS: Grant from National Endowment for the Humanities, 1972.

WRITINGS:

Willard Motley, Twayne, 1978.
James Weldon Johnson and Arma Wendell Bontemps: A Reference Guide, G. K. Hall, 1978.

Sinclair Lewis: A Reference Guide, G. K. Hall, 1980.
Charles F. Lummis, Boise State University, 1981.
James Weldon Johnson, Twayne, 1987.
The Face in the Mirror: Hemingway's Writers, University of Alabama Press, 1994.

Contributor of more than a hundred articles and reviews to academic journals. Associate editor, *Minority Voices,* 1979-83, and *American Poetry,* 1983-86; coeditor, *American Literary Realism,* 1986—.

WORK IN PROGRESS: Continuing research on Ernest Hemingway and Sinclair Lewis.

SIDELIGHTS: Robert E. Fleming told *CA:* "I try to emulate Hemingway by working early in the morning. I also find that problems in my writing get solved on a subconscious level when I'm walking the dog or taking long drives."

*   *   *

FOLEY, Denise (M.)   1950-

PERSONAL: Born June 28, 1950, in Abington, PA; daughter of Thomas J. (an electrical engineer) and Grace (a secretary; maiden name, Heary) Foley; married Edward J. Rogan (a writer), July 21, 1984; children: Patrick Michael Rogan. *Education:* Temple University, B.S. (cum laude), 1972.

ADDRESSES: Home and office—528 Kingston Rd., Oreland, PA 19075. *Agent*—Connie Clausen, 250 East 87th St., Apt. 16 H, New York, NY 10128.

CAREER: Bucks County Courier Times, Levittown, PA, reporter and columnist, 1977-83; *Prevention* (magazine), Emmaus, PA, senior editor, 1983-86; *Children* (magazine), Emmaus, managing editor, 1986-89; freelance writer, 1989—; Temple University, Philadelphia, PA, instructor in writing, 1990—.

AWARDS, HONORS: Distinguished Achievement Award, Educational Press Association of America, 1991; Silver National Health Information Award, Health Information Resource Center, 1994.

WRITINGS:

(With Eileen Nechas) *What Do I Do Now?,* Fireside Press, 1992.
(With Nechas) *The Women's Encyclopedia of Health and Emotional Healing,* Rodale Press, 1993.
(With Nechas, Dena Salmon, and Susan Perry) *The Doctors' Book of Home Remedies for Children,* Rodale Press, 1994.

(With Nechas) *Unequal Treatment: What You Don't Know about How Women Are Mistreated by the Medical Community,* Simon & Schuster (New York, NY), 1994.

Contributor to periodicals, including *Healthy Woman, McCalls, Parenting, Sesame Street Parent's Guide, Teacher, Woman's Day,* and *Working Mother.*

*   *   *

FOLKE, Will
See Bloch, Robert (Albert)

*   *   *

FONAGY, Peter   1952-

PERSONAL: Born August 14, 1952. *Education:* University of London, B.Sc. (with first class honors), 1974, Ph.D., 1980; British Psychological Society, Diploma in Clinical Psychology, 1980.

ADDRESSES: Office—Psychoanalysis Unit, Philips House, University College, University of London, Gower St., London WC1E 6BT, England.

CAREER: University of London, London, England, lecturer, 1977-87, senior lecturer, 1988-92, Freud Memorial Professor of Psychoanalysis, 1992—, founding member of Centre for Health in Society, and director of Psychoanalysis Unit. Anna Freud Centre, coordinator of research, 1989—. Royal Free Hospital, probationer clinical psychologist, 1976-78, honorary senior clinical psychologist and lecturer, 1981-85; North East Thames Regional Authority, probationer clinical psychologist, 1977-80; London Clinic of Psychoanalysis, staff member, 1982-85; private practice of psychoanalysis, 1986—; consultant to Council of Europe, National Institute of Mental Health of the United States, and University of Haifa. Joint Seminar on Contemporary British Art, initiator.

MEMBER: International Psychoanalytic Association (member of executive council, 1989—), World Association of Infant Mental Health (member of executive council, 1992—), British Psychological Society (fellow; chartered psychologist), British Psychoanalytical Society (chairperson of Contemporary Freudian Group, 1988-91, and member of board of directors and executive council, 1992—); British Institute of Psychoanalysis, Experimental Psychology Society, Association of Child Psychiatry, Psychology, and Allied Disciplines, Society for Psychotherapy Research, Psychoanalysts for the

Prevention of Nuclear War (past member of executive committee), American Psychological Association (affiliate member).

AWARDS, HONORS: Grants from Psychoanalytic Research and Development Fund, 1984-87, Anna Freud Foundation, 1985-88, MacArthur Foundation, 1988, 1989, 1992, Nuffield Foundation, 1988, Edith Ludowyk-Gyomroi Charitable Trust, 1989-90, 1993, New Land Foundation, 1989-90, Child Psychotherapy Trust, 1990, Lord Ashdown Trust, 1990-93, Kohler Foundation, 1991, 1993-94, and International Psychoanalytic Association, 1994-98.

WRITINGS:

(With A. Higgitt) *Personality Theory and Clinical Practice,* Methuen, 1985.

(With Higgitt and M. Lader) *The Natural History of Tolerance to the Benzodiazepines,* Psychological Monographs, 1988.

(Editor with J. Sandler and E. Person, and coauthor of introduction) *Freud's "On Narcissism: An Introduction,"* Yale University Press, 1991.

(Editor with E. Spector Person and A. Hagelin) *On Freud's "Observations on Transference-Love,"* Yale University Press, 1993.

(Editor with A. Cooper and R. Wallerstein) *The Theory of Psychoanalytic Practice,* Routledge & Kegan Paul, 1994.

Work represented in anthologies, including *Psychological Treatment in Disease and Illness,* edited by M. Hodes and S. Moorey, Gaskell Press, 1993; *The Imaginative Body: Psychodynamic Psychotherapy in Health Care,* edited by A. Erskine and D. Judd, Whurr Publications, 1994; and *Attachment Research: The State of the Art,* edited by S. Goldberg and J. Kerr, Analytic Press (New York City), 1994. Coeditor of the "Contemporary Freud" series, Yale University Press. Contributor of more than sixty articles to professional journals. Member of editorial board, *British Journal of Medical Psychology, International Journal of Psychoanalysis, International Review of Psychoanalysis, Psychoanalytic Psychotherapy, Revue Internationale de Psychopathologie, Devenir, Psychoanalytic Books, Kinder, Journal of Child Psychotherapy,* and *Clinical Psychology and Psychotherapy.*

SIDELIGHTS: Peter Fonagy told *CA:* "Throughout my academic career, I have had a dual interest in psychoanalytic clinical work and clinical theory, on the one hand, and the relationship of psychoanalysis to allied disciplines on the other. My clinical work has led me to develop an interest in borderline phenomena and the characteristic thought processes observable in the clinical context in the patients who exhibit these phenomena. I have a longstanding concern about the nature of psychoanalytic concepts and, specifically, about the relationship of theoretical understanding and clinical practice.

"The focus of my applied interest is the extension of psychoanalytic ideas into the domain of other academic disciplines, particularly the natural sciences. It is my firm conviction that the psychoanalytic situation yields vital information concerning the nature of human thought and personality, without which our model of mind is incomplete. Unfortunately, psychoanalysis, unlike more traditional academic disciplines, has had insufficient academic resources to insure the integration of its findings into relevant disciplines. Many prior attempts at integration were based on outdated theory and were insufficiently informed by direct clinical experience. In my position as research coordinator at the Anna Freud Centre, I have drawn up a comprehensive long-term research plan which is currently in the process of implementation. The two foci of this program are studies of the outcome of psychodynamic interventions and developmental psychopathology.

"My early research has covered the area of individual differences in personality and psychopathology, with the overall aim of combining psychoanalytic with experimental (biological) approaches. One example of this is my work on the etiology of psychosomatic disorders, particularly poorly controlled diabetes in children. A funded longitudinal study of brittle diabetic children has been completed. More recently, I have completed the first phase of a major longitudinal study of the influence of parental childhood experiences upon infant emotional development.

"The evaluation of the effectiveness of psychoanalytically oriented approaches in the treatment of children and adults is my current focus of concern, and the development of a statistical tool for studying the association of symptoms with the content of psychoanalytic treatment is an important product of this work."

*   *   *

FONSECA, James W(illiam)   1947-

PERSONAL: Born October 13, 1947, in Fall River, MA; son of James A. (in sales) and Elizabeth (a clerk; maiden name, Armstrong) Fonseca; married Elaine Hart (a teacher), November 20, 1972; children: James E. *Education:* Bridgewater State College, (cum laude), 1969; Clark University, Ph.D., 1975.

ADDRESSES: Home—8576 Yoder St., Manassas, VA 22110. *Office*—Department of Geography, George Mason University, Fairfax, VA 22030.

CAREER: George Mason University, Fairfax, VA, associate professor of geography, 1973—, acting dean of Graduate School, 1988-90, director of Prince William Institute, 1992—, and director of individualized studies. Prince William Symphony Orchestra, member of board of directors; member of Manassas City Business Council and Prince William-Greater Manassas Chamber of Commerce.

MEMBER: Association of American Geographers, National Council for Geographic Education, Manassas Area Writers Roundtable.

WRITINGS:

The Urban Rank-Size Hierarchy (monograph), Institute for Mathematical Geography (Ann Arbor, MI), 1989.
(With Alice C. Andrews) *The Atlas of American Higher Education,* New York University Press, 1993.
(With Andrews) *The Atlas of American Society,* New York University Press, 1995.

Editor, *Virginia Geographer,* 1980-87. Contributor to geography journals.

WORK IN PROGRESS: The Geography of Virginia, publication by Johns Hopkins University Press expected in 1996; *Bridges,* a novel, completion expected in 1996.

*   *   *

FORD, Jerome W. 1949-
(Jerry Ford)

PERSONAL: Born November 30, 1949, in Pipestone, MN; son of L. Eldon Ford (a farmer) and Opal Marie Yackley Ford Barron (a homemaker and painter); married Martha Patricia Bates (an administrative assistant), April 26, 1975; children: Maggie, Louis. *Education:* Northern Arizona University, B.S., 1979. *Politics:* Independent. *Religion:* Presbyterian.

ADDRESSES: Agent—c/o Publicity Director, Lerner Publications Co., 241 First Ave. N., Minneapolis, MN 55401.

CAREER: Scottsdale Progress, Scottsdale, AZ, sports reporter, 1971-77; *Arizona Daily Sun,* Flagstaff, AZ, sports reporter, 1977-79; *Logan Herald & Journal,* Logan, Utah, entertainment/news reporter, 1979-84; *Decatur Herald Review,* Decatur, IL, news editor, 1984-88; *Holland Sentinel,* Holland, MI, managing editor, 1988-90.

WRITINGS:

(Under name Jerry Ford) *The Grand Slam Collection: Have Fun Collecting Baseball Cards,* Lerner Publications, 1993.

SIDELIGHTS: Jerome W. Ford commented: "When I was sixteen, I decided I wanted to be a writer. I learned writing in the newspaper business. Now I am working on a variety of projects which are competing for my attention, time, and energy. Writing is probably the toughest thing to do and do well. But when you get a key segment right, so that it fits into a story, it is very satisfactory. What is really a kick, however, is to get a book published and have it start selling."

BIOGRAPHICAL/CRITICAL SOURCES:

PERIODICALS

Horn Book Guide, fall, 1992, p. 319.
School Library Journal, December, 1992, p. 118.

*   *   *

FORD, Jerry
See FORD, Jerome W.

*   *   *

FORRESTER, Michael A. 1953-

PERSONAL: Born March 21, 1953, in Glasgow, Scotland; son of John (a teacher) and Moira (a teacher; maiden name, Martin) Forrester. *Education:* Attended St. Aloysius College, 1960-69; University of Strathclyde, B.A. (with honors), 1983, Ph.D., 1986.

ADDRESSES: Home—Canterbury, Kent, England. *Office*—Department of Psychology, University of Kent, Canterbury CT2 7LZ, England.

CAREER: Loughborough University, Leicestershire, England, research associate, 1986-87; University of Kent, Canterbury, England, lecturer, 1987—.

MEMBER: British Society for Research into Learning Mathematics.

WRITINGS:

The Development of Young Children's Social-Cognitive Skills, Lawrence Erlbaum (Hillsdale, NJ), 1992.

WORK IN PROGRESS: A book on language entitled *Thinking, Talk, and Text,* for Sage Publications, with an expected completion date of 1995.

SIDELIGHTS: In the first section of his 1992 book, *The Development of Young Children's Social-Cognitive Skills,* Michael A. Forrester presents the history of research and theory on the development of social cognition (the ability to participate in conversation) in children, citing and analyzing the research and ideas of such noted psychologists as George Herbert Mead and Jean Piaget. After presenting this overview, Forrester goes on to present his own theory, which is comprised of five "essential components involved in the study of children's early developing social-cognitive skills," drawn from and based upon a variety of theories and schools of thought. The final section of *The Development of Young Children's Social-Cognitive Skills* contains several case studies in which Forrester illustrates his theories in action and then extrapolates meaning from them.

BIOGRAPHICAL/CRITICAL SOURCES:

PERIODICALS

Journal of Child Language, 1993, pp. 725-27.
Times Educational Supplement, 1992.

*   *   *

FOWLER, Earlene   1954-

PERSONAL: Born August 23, 1954, in Lynwood, CA; daughter of Earl J. (a sheet metal machinist) and Mary (a homemaker and secretary; maiden name, Webb) Worley; married Allen W. Fowler (a process engineer), September 8, 1973. *Politics:* Democrat. *Religion:* Baptist.

ADDRESSES: Home—Fountain Valley, CA. *Agent*—Deborah Schneider Gelfman, Schneider Literary Agents, Inc., 250 West 57th St., Suite 2515, New York, NY 10107.

MEMBER: Sisters in Crime, Mystery Writers of America, Flying Geese Quilt Guild.

WRITINGS:

A Fool's Puzzle, Berkley Publishing (New York, NY), 1994.
Irish Chain, Berkley Publishing, 1995.

WORK IN PROGRESS: Kansas Troubles.

SIDELIGHTS: Earlene Fowler told *CA:* "I have read mysteries all my life, but when I started writing in my late twenties, for some reason, it didn't occur to me to write a mystery. I also read a lot of literary fiction, especially stories, so that seemed to be the area that attracted me. I attempted to write mystery short stories, but could never get the hang of a plot-oriented story, so I continued writing character-oriented stories with no publishing success.

"I think, looking back now, that I felt short stories were an emotionally easier way to start writing. I discovered, after writing my first novel, that committing to a character for twenty-five or thirty pages is not nearly as exhausting or terrifying as staying with him or her for four hundred. I suppose it's like the difference between dating and being married. With short stories, I always had that thrill of a new character or situation to keep me interested. When I get to the halfway point in a novel, I'm often ready to commit mass 'charactericide' on everyone. Like being in a long marriage, however, writing a novel brought me a deeper satisfaction than any of my short stories. In the stories, I always had a point to make, and I think that is really why anyone writes a short story. In a novel, if it is going well, the characters live and become a part of your life permanently.

"When I decided to write a mystery, I promised myself one thing. I was going to put everything in it that I liked; otherwise, it would bore me. I firmly believe if the writing bores the writer, it's certainly going to bore the reader. Though I was born and raised in a primarily Latino community in southern California, I was very influenced by farm women my whole life. Both my grandmothers were raised on farms, as were my mother and my mother-in-law. The decision to name my books after quilt patterns was natural, because my Arkansas grandmother and great-grandmother were both avid quilters, and my Kansas grandmother was a talented needlewoman. Folk art and crafts are a strong part of my personal history and would naturally find their way into my writing. The western influence comes from my father. He was born in Colorado and spent most of his young years wandering the west with his parents, who were migrant workers. My books are a combination of the wild west and the crazy south and a little 'anything goes' California thrown in. Hopefully, they aren't boring."

*   *   *

FOXWORTH, Thomas G(ordon)   1937-1994

OBITUARY NOTICE—See index for *CA* sketch: Born

November 11, 1937, in Rahway (some sources say Summit), NJ; died of cancer, September 26, 1994, in Woodbridge, VA. Aviator and writer. Foxworth was the son of a pilot and attended Princeton University before serving in the United States Navy as a flier. He began his career as a commercial pilot with Pan American Airlines in 1965, and joined United Airlines in 1986. Before he retired in 1994, he was a senior captain for the airline's fleet of Boeing 767 jets. Foxworth received the Scroll of Merit from the International Federation of Airline Pilot Associations in 1975. He was the author of numerous articles on air travel and aviation history for publications such as *Newsweek, USA Today,* and *Professional Pilot. The Speed Seekers,* Foxworth's first book and a chronicle of air racing in the 1920s, won the Strebig Award for best aviation writing from the Aviation/Space Writers' Association in 1976. He also wrote a novel, *Passengers,* with Michael Laurence.

OBITUARIES AND OTHER SOURCES:

BOOKS

International Authors and Writers Who's Who, 11th edition, International Biographical Centre, 1989, p. 290.

PERIODICALS

Washington Post, September 28, 1994, p. B6.

*   *   *

FRASER, George (C.)   1945-

PERSONAL: Born May 1, 1945, in Brooklyn, NY; son of Walter Frederick (a taxi driver) and Ida Mae (a homemaker) Fraser; married Nora Jean Spencer (a secretary), September 7, 1973; children: George C. II, Scott Spencer. *Education:* Attended New York University and Dartmouth College. *Politics:* Independent. *Religion:* Baptist.

ADDRESSES: Home—31201 Ainsworth Dr., Pepper Pike, OH 44124. *Office*—SuccessSource, Inc., 1949 East 105th St., Cleveland, OH 44106.

CAREER: Procter & Gamble, Cincinnati, OH, unit marketing manager, 1972-84; United Way Services, Cleveland, OH, director of marketing and communications, 1984-87; Ford Motor Co., Dearborn, MI, minority dealership development program trainee, 1987-89; SuccessSource, Inc., Cleveland, president and publisher, 1988—. Member of board of trustees,

Ohio Building Authority, Greater Cleveland Growth Association, and National Business League; Cleveland Museum of Art, member of corporate council. Past member of board of trustees, John Carroll University, Black Professionals Association Foundation, Cleveland Convention and Visitors Bureau, Cleveland Scholarship Program, Center for Human Services, Clean-Land Ohio, Cleveland 500 Foundation, Greater Cleveland Roundtable, Great Lakes Theater Festival, Goodwill Industries, and Karamu House Theater; past member of board of directors, Operation Alert and Ohio Junior Olympics. Guest on more than a hundred television and radio talk shows.

MEMBER: National Association for the Advancement of Colored People (past member of board of trustees of Cleveland chapter).

AWARDS, HONORS: Named Most Eligible Bachelor by *Ebony,* 1971; Manager of the Year Award, Procter & Gamble, 1974, 1975, 1980, 1981; elected to Leadership Cleveland, 1982-83; named National Volunteer of the Year, United Negro College Fund, 1982, 1983; Community Service Commendation, Ohio Senate and House of Representatives, 1985; named Role Model of the Year, Teen Father Program, 1988; first place award for community events, *Northern Ohio Live,* 1989; Communicator of the Year Award, National Association of Black Journalists and Black Media Workers of Cleveland, 1990; named Minority Business Advocate of the Year, City of Cleveland, 1991; Communication Excellence to Black Audiences (CEBA) Award, World Institute of Black Communications, 1991, for *SuccessGuide;* named Black Professional of the Year, Black Professionals Association of Cleveland, 1992; George C. Fraser Day was declared by the City of Cleveland, 1992; named Black Achiever of the Year, Voices of Cleveland, 1992.

WRITINGS:

Success Runs in Our Race: The Complete Guide to Effective Networking in the African American Community, Morrow, 1994.

Creator and publisher, *SuccessGuide.*

BIOGRAPHICAL/CRITICAL SOURCES:

PERIODICALS

Black Enterprise, July, 1994.
Clubdate, November, 1983.
In-Flight, May, 1991.
UPSCALE, August, 1992.

FREUND, Thatcher   1955-

PERSONAL: Born September 13, 1955, in Austin, TX; son of Warren S., Jr. (a stockbroker) and Karen (a homemaker; maiden name, Thatcher) Freund; married Laura Underkuffler (a professor of law), July 31, 1993. Education: Stanford University, B.A., 1978; Columbia University, M.S., 1984. Politics: Democrat.

ADDRESSES: Home—Chapel Hill, NC. Agent—Liz Darhansoff, Darhansoff & Verrill, 1220 Park Ave., New York, NY 10128.

CAREER: Substitute teacher at public schools in Cambridge, MA, 1979; Howard, Prim, San Francisco, CA, paralegal, 1979-82; New England Monthly, Northampton, MA, staff writer, 1986-89. Also worked as ice cream server and waiter.

WRITINGS:

Objects of Desire: The Lives of Antiques and Those Who Pursue Them, Pantheon (New York), 1994.

*   *   *

FRIEDLAND, Martin L(awrence)   1932-

PERSONAL: Born September 21, 1932, in Canada; son of Jack and Mina Friedland; married Judith Pless (a professor), June 19, 1958; children: Tom, Jenny, Nancy. Education: University of Toronto, B.Comm., 1955, LL.B., 1958; Cambridge University, Ph.D., 1967.

ADDRESSES: Office—Faculty of Law, University of Toronto, 78 Queen's Park, Toronto, Ontario, Canada M5S 2C5.

CAREER: Osgoode Hall Law School, Toronto, Ontario, Canada, began as assistant professor, became associate professor of law, 1961-65; University of Toronto, Toronto, associate professor, 1965-68, professor of law, 1968—, university professor, 1985—, dean of law faculty, 1972-79; writer. Visiting professor at Hebrew University of Jerusalem and Tel Aviv University, both 1979; Cambridge University, visiting fellow of Clare Hall and Institute of Criminology, 1980; Centre of Criminology, member, 1984—; Massey College, senior fellow, 1985—; Canadian Institute for Advanced Research, fellow, 1986—. Law Reform Commission of Canada, member, 1971-72; Ontario Task Force on Inflation Protection for Employment Pension Plans, chairperson, 1987-88; Ontario Securities Commission, member,

1989-91. Associated with Canadian Attorney-General's Committee on Securities Regulation (Kimber Committee), 1965, Minister of Reform Institutions' Planning Committee on Regional Detention Centres, 1967, Ouimet Committee on Corrections, 1969, Solicitor-General's Task Force on Gun Control, 1975, Royal Commission on the Royal Canadian Mounted Police (McDonald Commission), 1978, and Criminal Code Review, 1980—.

AWARDS, HONORS: Appointed Queen's Counsel, 1975; award for nonfiction, Crime Writers of Canada, and finalist for nonfiction award, British Crime Writers, both 1984, for The Trials of Israel Lipski; award from Canadian Association of Law Teachers and Law Reform Commission of Canada, 1985; finalist for nonfiction award, Crime Writers of Canada, 1986, for The Case of Valentine Shortis; David W. Mundell Medal, 1990; officer, Order of Canada, 1990; Ramon John Hnatyshyn Award and G. Arthur Martin Criminal Law Award, both 1994.

WRITINGS:

Detention before Trial, University of Toronto Press, 1965.
Double Jeopardy, Clarendon Press, 1969.
Courts and Trials: A Multidisciplinary Approach, University of Toronto Press, 1975.
Access to the Law, Carswell/Methuen, 1975.
National Security: The Legal Dimensions, Canadian Government Publishing Centre, 1980.
The Trials of Israel Lipski: A True Story of a Victorian Murder in the East End of London, Macmillan, 1984, Beaufort Books (New York City), 1985.
A Century of Criminal Justice: Perspectives on the Development of Canadian Law, Carswell, 1984.
The Case of Valentine Shortis: A True Story of Crime and Politics in Canada, University of Toronto Press, 1986.
Sanctions and Rewards in the Legal System: A Multidisciplinary Approach, University of Toronto Press, 1989.
Securing Compliance: Seven Case Studies, University of Toronto Press, 1990.
(With Michael Trebilcock and Kent Roach) Regulating Traffic Safety, University of Toronto Press, 1990.
Rough Justice: Essays on Crime in Literature, University of Toronto Press, 1991.
(With Roach) Cases and Materials on Criminal Law and Procedure, 7th edition, Emond-Montgomery, 1994.
The Death of Old Man Rice: A True Story of Criminal Justice in America, New York University Press, 1994.

WORK IN PROGRESS: Collaborating in research comparing the administration of criminal justice from police to corrections in Niagara, Ontario, and Niagara, NY; research on judicial independence and accountability, for Canadian Judicial Council.

* * *

FUNT, Allen 1914-

PERSONAL: Born September 16, 1914, in New York, NY; married, first wife's name, Evelyn (divorced); married, second wife's name, Marilyn (divorced); children: Peter, Patricia, John, Juliet, William. *Education:* Cornell University, B.A., 1934.

ADDRESSES: Office—P.O. Box 827, Monterey, CA 93942.

CAREER: Candid Microphone, host, producer, director, American Broadcasting Company (ABC), 1948-49, Columbia Broadcasting System (CBS), 1949-51, name changed to *Candid Camera,* ABC, 1951-56, CBS, 1957-67, syndicated as *The New Candid Camera,* 1974-80. Also host and executive producer of numerous television specials, including *The Candid Camera Special,* National Broadcasting Company (NBC), 1981; *Candid Camera Looks at the Difference between Men and Women,* NBC, 1983; and *Candid Camera: The First 40 Years,* CBS, 1987. Performer on *The Jerry Lewis Show,* NBC, 1960; writer for television, radio and film. *Military service:* U.S. Army, served during World War II; became second lieutenant.

WRITINGS:

Eavesdropper at Large, Vanguard, 1952.
Candid Kids, Bernard Geis, 1963.
Candidly Allen Funt: A Million Smiles Later, Barricade Books (Fort Lee, NJ), 1994.

Contributor to radio programs, including *Truth or Consequences,* films, including *What Do You Say to a Naked Lady?,* 1970, and *Money Talks,* 1972, and

television specials, including *Candid Camera . . . Funny Money, Candid Camera Comedy Shopping Spree, Candid Camera . . . Getting Physical,* and *Candid Camera . . . Smile, You're on Vacation!,* all 1990.

SIDELIGHTS: Allen Funt is best known as the host and creator of *Candid Camera,* a television show that specialized in playing practical jokes on unsuspecting members of the American public. After using a hidden camera to film his subjects's "candid" responses to various bizarre situations, Funt would reveal the ruse with his trademark slogan: "Smile! You're on *Candid Camera*!" *Candid Camera,* which began in 1947 as a radio program entitled *Candid Microphone,* has appeared on three major television networks, and has been imitated world-wide. The show has also been adapted as *What Do You Say to a Naked Lady?,* a full-length feature film run in movie theaters in the early 1970s, reproduced on videocassette, adapted for such cable television networks as Home Box Office (HBO), and has become an area of study for several college psychology programs. *Candid Camera* was the first television program to appear on the ABC network in 1948, and was featured regularly by Jack Paar and Garry Moore during the 1950s. It became a successful series during the 1960s and enjoyed great popularity in syndication during the 1970s. As they did throughout the 1980s, *Candid Camera* specials continue to appear frequently on network television.

In his 1994 memoir, *Candidly, Allen Funt: A Million Smiles Later,* Funt traces his rise to fame, beginning with his childhood in Brooklyn, New York. He recounts his association with such notable entertainers as Woody Allen and Charles Grodin, who worked on *Candid Camera* during its early years, and Johnny Carson and Eddie Albert, who purportedly failed their auditions for the show. Funt also delineates his experiences with an airplane hijacking, a multi-million-dollar embezzlement scheme, and Laugh Therapy, a program he founded to help brighten the lives of critically ill people.

G

GALLARDO, Evelyn 1948-

PERSONAL: Surname is pronounced "guy-*are*-doe"; born October 10, 1948, in Los Angeles, CA; daughter of Carlos (a construction supervisor) and Molly (a homemaker; maiden name, Subia) Gallardo; married David Leon Root (a consultant), January 2, 1992; children: Dawn Andrea. *Education:* Attended University of California, Los Angeles. *Politics:* Democrat.

ADDRESSES: Home and office—2208 The Strand, B, Manhattan Beach, CA 90266. *Agent*—Susan Cohen, Writers House, Inc., 21 West 26th St., New York, NY 10010.

CAREER: Writer and photographer, 1988—. Educational Travel Services, instructor, 1989—.

MEMBER: Young International People Protecting the Environments of the Earth (advisory board member), International Primate Protection League (West Coast/USA representative), Orangutan Foundation International, National Wildlife Federation, Society of Children's Book Writers and Illustrators, South Bay Area Reading Council.

AWARDS, HONORS: Outstanding Support for Antipoaching Patrol, Digit Fund, 1989; Magazine Merit Honor Certificate, Society of Children's Book Writers and Illustrators, 1990.

WRITINGS:

Among the Orangutans: The Birute Galdikas Story, Chronicle Books, 1993.

Also contributing author to *Endangered Wildlife,* GINN Publishing, 1993. Contributor to numerous magazines, including *International Primate Protection League News, Ranger Rick Magazine, EarthWhile, Mini-World Magazine,* and *The Easy Reader.* Gallardo's photographs have appeared on the cover of *Jane Goodall's Animal World: Gorillas,* in books, including *The Dark Romance of Dian Fossey* and numerous McGraw Hill college textbooks, and in magazines and newspapers, including *Science Magazine, Animal Magazine, Zoolife, Earthwatch, Owl Magazine, Terre Sauvage, GEO,* and the *Los Angeles Times.*

WORK IN PROGRESS: Farewell Orphan Ape, a story about a former pet orangutan; *The Fossey Files,* the story of Gallardo's involvement with Dr. Dian Fossey, publication expected in 1995.

SIDELIGHTS: Evelyn Gallardo commented: "I'm a Los Angeles-born Mexican-American writer whose fascination for great apes stems from childhood. I fell in love with King Kong at the age of three, which launched my lifelong devotion to primates.

"Nature photography and travel are my passions. I've photographed gorillas in Africa and orangutans in Borneo. In 1975, I spent nine months in South America and hitched cargo boats up the Amazon river. I've also been to Nepal, India, Costa Rica, Japan, Thailand, China, Singapore, and Mexico.

"After working with orangutans for Birute Galdikas in Borneo in 1984 and 1987, I discovered her desire to involve children in her efforts to save the apes from extinction. I wrote *Among the Orangutans* to give kids a candid look at the life of a field scientist and the mysterious apes she studies and to spur children's imaginations to seek creative ways to help orangutans survive."

BIOGRAPHICAL/CRITICAL SOURCES:

PERIODICALS

Los Angeles Times, July 16, 1987; May 27, 1988, pp. 8, 15; July 29, 1988, p. 2.
News-Pilot, December 19, 1988.
Publishers Weekly, March 22, 1993.
South Pasadena Review (Pasadena, CA), February 25, 1987.

* * *

GAMMER, Moshe 1950-

PERSONAL: Born September 24, 1950, in Russia; immigrated to Israel, 1960; son of David and Bella (Goldenber) Gammer; married Ruth Frankl (a librarian), June 17, 1994. *Education:* Tel Aviv University, B.A., 1977, graduate study, 1977-82; London School of Economics and Political Science, London, Ph.D., 1989.

ADDRESSES: Home—17 Weizman St., Petach Tiqwa 49556, Israel. *Office*—Department of Middle Eastern and African History, Tel Aviv University, 69978 Tel Aviv, Israel.

CAREER: Tel Aviv University, Tel Aviv, Israel, external teacher, 1989-93, postdoctoral fellow at Cummings Center for Russian and East European Studies, 1990-92, visiting lecturer, 1993, visiting senior lecturer in Middle Eastern and African history, 1994—, Dayan fellow, Dayan Center for Middle Eastern and African Studies, 1990-91; writer. Open University, Tel Aviv, tutor, 1989-90, 1991-1993; Bar Ilan University, visiting lecturer, 1990-91. *Military service:* ZAHAL, 1969-72.

MEMBER: European Society for Caucasian Studies, Israel Oriental Society, Society for the Study of Central Asia, Society for the Study of Caucasia (United States), Association for Central Asian Studies (United States).

AWARDS, HONORS: Fellow, Committee of Planning and Budgeting, Israel Council on Higher Education, 1990-92.

WRITINGS:

(Editor) *The Political Negotiations between Israel and Egypt, September, 1978-March, 1979: Main Documents* (in Hebrew), Shiloah Center (Tel Aviv), 1979.
(Editor) *The Normalization of Relations between Israel and Egypt, April, 1979-October, 1980: Main Documents* (in Hebrew), Shiloah Center (Tel Aviv), 1981.
(Editor) *The Autonomy Negotiations, April, 1979-October, 1980: Main Documents* (in Hebrew), Shiloah Center, 1981.
Muslim Resistance to the Tsar: Shamil and the Conquest of Chechnia and Daghestan, Frank Cass, 1993.

Work represented in anthologies, including *Arab Relations in the Middle East: The Road to Realignment,* edited by Colin Legum and Haim Shaked, Holmes & Meier, 1979; *The North Caucasus Barrier: The Russian Advance towards the Muslim World,* edited by Marie Benningsen-Broxup, C. Hurst (London), 1992; and *Muslim Eurasia: Tradition and Change,* Frank Cass, 1995. Contributor of articles and reviews to scholarly journals. Member of editorial board, *Central Asian Survey,* 1991—.

WORK IN PROGRESS: Research on France and the revolt in Syria, 1925-27, anti-Russian and Soviet revolts in the northern Caucasus, the "deportation" and restoration of the Chechens, Ingush, Balkars, and Karachays, and the historiography of the Khazars.

* * *

GARNER, John S. 1945-

PERSONAL: Born March 10, 1945, in Denton, TX; son of Lloyd (an educator) and Juanita (a homemaker; maiden name, Welch) Garner; married Susan Kampbell (an educator); children: Patrick, Maria. *Education:* Oklahoma State University, B.Arch., 1969; University of Illinois at Urbana-Champaign, M.Arch., 1970; Boston University, Ph.D., 1974. *Avocational interests:* Travel.

ADDRESSES: Home—502 East Sunnyside Court, Urbana, IL 61801. *Office*—School of Architecture, University of Illinois at Urbana-Champaign, Urbana, IL 61820.

CAREER: Texas A&M University, Denton, assistant professor, 1974-77, associate professor of architecture, 1977-81; University of Illinois at Urbana-Champaign, Urbana, associate professor, 1981-87, professor of architecture, 1987—. Consultant in architectural history and preservation. *Military service:* U.S. Army, 1962-64.

MEMBER: Society of Architectural Historians, Society of American City and Regional Planning Historians, National Trust for Historic Preservation.

AWARDS, HONORS: Fulbright grant for France.

WRITINGS:

The Model Company Town, University of Massachusetts Press, 1984.
The Midwest in American Architecture, University of Illinois Press, 1991.
(Editor) *The Company Town,* Oxford University Press, 1992.

WORK IN PROGRESS: Building for War: The Planning and Architecture of U.S. Military Bases, 1917-1945.

SIDELIGHTS: John S. Garner told *CA:* "The history of technology and its representation in architecture and city planning has long fascinated me. During my life, I've witnessed America transform itself from a highly industrialized, product-oriented society to a post-industrial consumer and service society."

*　　*　　*

GARRETT, Susan   1931-

PERSONAL: Born April 10, 1931, in Philadelphia, PA; daughter of Anthony H. and Alice Benedict (a photographer; maiden name, Dunn) Jackson; married George Garrett (a writer), June 14, 1952; children: William, George G., Alice. *Education:* Attended Mary Washington College, 1947-49; University of Pittsburgh, B.A., 1951; Bernard M. Baruch College of the City University of New York, M.B.A., 1977. *Politics:* Democrat. *Religion:* Episcopalian.

ADDRESSES: Home—1845 Wayside Pl., Charlottesville, VA 22903. *Agent*—Jane Gelfman, Gelfman-Schneider, 250 West 57th St., No. 2515, New York, NY 10107.

CAREER: York Hospital, York, ME, administrator, 1978-82; University of Michigan, Ann Arbor, associate administrator at Medical School, 1983-84; Martha Jefferson Hospital, Charlottesville, VA, vice-president, 1984-87; Hospice of the Piedmont, president, 1988-90. Coalition for Mentally Disabled Citizens of Virginia, co-chairperson, 1989-92.

WRITINGS:

Taking Care of Our Own, Dutton (New York, NY), 1994.

WORK IN PROGRESS: A book on Rural Elder Outreach, a Virginia health care project; research on mental health and rural issues.

SIDELIGHTS: Susan Garrett told *CA:* "My interest is in reporting on and interpreting health care issues for the general reader, and in bringing some clarity to the complexity of current health care."

*　　*　　*

GATI, Charles   1934-

PERSONAL: Born September 14, 1934, in Budapest, Hungary; immigrated to the United States, 1957; naturalized citizen, 1962; married Toby T. (a vice president of UNA/USA), April 28, 1974; children: Tom, Steve, Sue, Daniel, Adrienne. *Education:* Indiana University, A.B. and A.M., 1961, Russian area certificate, 1962, Ph.D., 1965. *Politics:* "Domestic: left-of-center; foreign: right-of-center."

ADDRESSES: Home—4935 Loughboro Rd. NW, Washington, DC 20016-3456. *Office*—Department of Political Science, Union College, Schenectady, NY 12308.

CAREER: Union College, Schenectady, NY, instructor in political science, 1963-65, assistant professor, 1965-68, associate professor, 1969-74, professor, 1974—, founder and director of program in comparative communist studies, 1970-71 and 1972-74, chair of political science department, 1975-78; Columbia University, New York City, senior research scholar at Research Institute on International Change, 1971-72, 1977-78, and 1979—, visiting lecturer, 1972, visiting associate professor, 1972-74, visiting professor at Harriman Institute for Advanced Study of the Soviet Union, 1975-86, director of East Europe Project, Research Institute on International Change, 1984-85.

Visiting professor, University of Kansas, 1968-69, and Yale University, 1975; International Research and Exchanges Board, member of program committee and board, 1980-83; consultant to the National Security Council, 1980, Ford Foundation, 1980, Rockefeller Foundation, 1981-82, United States Department of State, 1982, Radio Free Europe, 1984-85, Board of International Broadcasting, 1988, and to INTERINVEST, among others. Lecturer to various groups, including the Council on Foreign Relations, the Wilson Center, the Foreign Service Institute, and the U.S. State Department Executive Seminar; organizer and chair of various academic conferences.

MEMBER: Council on Foreign Relations, American Association for the Advancement of Slavic Studies (board member, 1984-89), American Political Science Association.

AWARDS, HONORS: Outstanding Faculty Member of the Year Award, Union College, 1971; first recipient of Marshall Shulman Prize for Outstanding Book on Soviet Foreign Policy, American Association for the Advancement of Slavic Studies and Harriman Institute of Columbia University, 1987, for *Hungary and the Soviet Bloc;* Fulbright/Hays Award, 1977; Union College Faculty Research grants, 1964, 1965, 1970, and 1977; numerous grants and fellowships from National Council for Soviet and East European Research, the Ford Foundation, and the International Research and Exchanges Board, among others.

WRITINGS:

(With wife, Toby Gati) *The Debate over Detente,* Foreign Policy Association Headline Series, 1977.
Hungary and the Soviet Bloc, Duke University Press, 1986.
The Bloc That Failed: Soviet-East European Relations in Transition, Indiana University Press, 1990.

Contributor to numerous books, including *The Soviet Union since Stalin,* edited by S. Cohen, A. Rabinowitch, and R. Sharlet, Indiana University Press, 1980; *Soviet Foreign Policy in a Changing World,* edited by Robbin F. Laird and Erik P. Hoffman, Aldine, 1986; and *The Future of the New Soviet Empire,* edited by Henry S. Rowen and Charles Wolf, Jr., St. Martin's, 1988. Also contributor to periodicals, including *Foreign Affairs, Problems of Communism, Foreign Policy, World Politics, East European Quarterly, New York Times, Washington Post,* and *Current History.*

EDITOR AND CONTRIBUTOR

The Politics of Modernization in Eastern Europe: Testing the Soviet Model, Praeger, 1974.
Caging the Bear: Containment and the Cold War, Bobbs-Merrill, 1974.
The International Politics of Eastern Europe, Praeger, 1976.
(With Jan F. Triska) *Blue-Collar Workers in Eastern Europe,* Allen & Unwin, 1981.

SIDELIGHTS: Charles Gati is an accomplished scholar whose expertise lies in the former Soviet Union and Eastern Europe. He has written, edited, or contributed to numerous works on the politics of the region, and is a sought-after lecturer and advisor to both corporate and public institutions. Gati, a native of Hungary, immigrated to the United States in the late 1950s and received undergraduate and graduate degrees from Indiana University, one of the nation's premier schools of Russian and East European studies. He has held academic positions at Union College in New York in addition to an appointment at Columbia University as a research scholar.

One of Gati's works in the field of Eastern European politics is the 1981 volume *Blue-Collar Workers in Eastern Europe,* edited with Jan F. Triska. This collection of essays, originally presented at a conference, appeared as world attention focused on the Solidarity labor union movement in Poland. Strikes by workers led first to a declaration of martial law by the Soviet-backed Polish government, but later to some democratic reforms that helped usher in a new era for the entire region, culminating with the fall of Germany's Berlin Wall in 1989.

As the title of *Blue-Collar Workers* denotes, its subject matter concerns the role of proletarian forces in the individual countries of Eastern Europe as well as their overall affect on the Soviet Bloc. Gati and Triska solicited chapters from various experts on the diverse nature of blue-collar workers among the individual nations. One of the strongest themes asserted throughout the essays is the notion of an unspoken "contract" between workers and the state that many scholars believe held the Bloc together over the decades. The volume discusses this implicit contract by which workers were guaranteed job security, a multitude of state-provided benefits, access to a decent standard of living, moderate demands on productivity, and a pension upon leaving the workforce. In return for these benefits, the workers were expected to remain relatively docile and not agitate against the regime. Archie Brown, reviewing *Blue-Collar Workers* for the *Times Literary Supplement,* remarked that "Triska and Gati have picked a strong team of contributors and no other book comes close to providing so much information and thoughtful reflection as this on the social, economic and political position of manual workers in Eastern Europe." Brown further noted that this is "a theme which is likely to retain its pressing interest and relevance in the years ahead."

Gati's 1986 book, *Hungary and the Soviet Bloc,* received critical attention for using a fresh approach to tackle a familiar subject in the area of Eastern European studies. This collection of the author's essays recounts the politics and history of the nation that straddles Eastern and Western Europe and examines its postwar relationships with both the Soviet Union and its neighbors. *Hungary and the Soviet Bloc* briefly describes some salient points of Hungarian history leading up to World War II and provides insight about postwar Soviet plans for the country. Part of the work delineates the 1956 revolution that the Soviet Union crushed, putting an end to Hungary's hopes of becoming a part of the Western European political, economic, and cultural sphere.

As Gati narrates, Soviet troops remained on Hungarian soil in the aftermath of World War II while political operatives sought to ensconce a firmly pro-Soviet communist regime. A coalition government ruled for a decade and western powers encouraged a democratic regime, but noncommunist factions lacked cohesiveness and an uprising in the fall of 1956 sealed Hungary's fate. During that period, workers and students demonstrated in the streets for democracy until Russian troops, on orders from Soviet premier Nikita Khrushchev, invaded and put an end to the insurrection. Gati portrays the leaders on both sides of the 1956 struggle, drawing upon the 500,000-word memoirs of Zoltan Vas, a significant player in the Hungarian communist movement. The author also chronicles the Soviet-controlled actions that attempted to solidify a socialist state after World War II. Many Hungarians died in the struggle and the crushing of the revolt made it clear to the world that the Soviets were extremely intolerant of any noncommunist governmental system among the countries of the Bloc.

Hungary and the Soviet Bloc also provides an analysis of the democratic forces within the country and theorizes why they were doomed to fail. Additionally, Gati examines the Hungarians' hope of western intervention and the motives behind the lack of such action. In the aftermath of the revolt, the country did indeed embark upon the socialist road, but took a different path from its neighbors under head of state Janos Kadar. For the next three decades Hungary was viewed with envy by its fellow Bloc members for its relatively high standard of living, benign attitudes toward dissenters, and state-sponsored economic reform that included a modicum of free enterprise. Gati theorizes that these relaxed attitudes are evidence that Moscow has not always been able to retain as much control over the countries of the Soviet Bloc as it would have liked, and that in permitting some experimentation in Hungary it bought off more serious unrest.

Gati's mid-1980s assertions proved correct a few short years later as Hungary's neighbors took to the streets, inducing a dramatic end to Eastern European communism. Critical reaction to *Hungary and the Soviet Bloc* was favorable. A. James McAdams,

reviewing the work for the *New York Times Book Review,* described it as "an elegantly written collection," and asserted, "what makes Mr. Gati's account so noteworthy is . . . that he gives us a new way of looking at familiar events." *Washington Post Book World* contributor Timothy Foote lauded the work as a "judicious and often graceful study," likening the portrayals of the leaders involved in the 1956 uprising as "the stuff of high human drama."

During the late 1980s Gati had been at work on another book, tentatively titled *The Soviet Bloc at Century's End,* and expected to complete it in 1989. The chain of events that led to the fall of the Berlin Wall in 1989 and the subsequent ouster of communist regimes in the Soviet Bloc nations, however, altered the tenor of the work. Gati's next effort was instead the 1990 volume *The Bloc That Failed: Soviet-East European Relations in Transition.* The book examines the changes the Soviet Bloc has undergone since its rise to power under Soviet premiers Josef Stalin and Nikita Khrushchev, who both retained a tight hold on the economic and political direction of Eastern Europe. The end of the era culminated in the more relaxed attitude of late 1980s leader Mikhail Gorbachev, who allowed Czechoslovakia, East Germany, and Poland to disembark from the communist ship without a struggle.

The Bloc That Failed also predicts the future course of Eastern European politics, forecasting that a return to communism is unlikely and that inhabitants will most likely overcome the obstacles on the road to free-market capitalism and democracy. Murray Polner, critiquing the work for the *New York Times Book Review,* praised *The Bloc That Failed* as "lucid and stimulating."

Gati told *CA:* "I'm a workaholic. When I take time out from work, I wonder why I work so hard. My best guess is that I compensate for being a terrible high-school student; as a junior, I failed six of the seven courses I took, a record in the one-hundred-year history of my high school. Another possibility is that as an immigrant, I still try to prove myself. To find out for sure, I'll be a psychoanalyst in my next life. Stay tuned."

BIOGRAPHICAL/CRITICAL SOURCES:

PERIODICALS

New York Times Book Review, December 14, 1986, p. 34; June 24, 1990, p. 12.
Times Literary Supplement, October 8, 1982, p. 1111.
Washington Post Book World, December 21, 1986, pp. 3, 14.

GEORGE, David (John) 1948-

PERSONAL: Born October 6, 1948, in Rhondda, Wales; married Maria Antonia Babi i Vila; children: Elisenda Rhiannon, Carys Zenia, Mair Alba. *Education:* University of Wales, University College, Cardiff, B.A. (with honors), 1966, Ph.D., 1974.

ADDRESSES: Office—Department of Hispanic Studies, University College of Swansea, Singleton Park, Swansea SA2 8PP, Wales.

CAREER: University of Wales, University College of Swansea, lecturer in Spanish, 1972—.

WRITINGS:

(Editor with Derek Gagen) *La guerra civil espanola: Arte y violencia,* Universidad de Murcia, 1990.
Spain and 1992 (computer disk), Information Education, 1991.
(Editor with C. J. Gossip, and contributor) *Studies in the Commedia Dell'arte,* University of Wales Press, 1993.
From Pierrot to Harlequin: Valle-Inclan, Lorca, and the Commedia Dell'arte in Hispanic Literature, 1890-1935, Edwin Mellen, 1994.
(Coeditor and contributor) *Contemporary Catalan Drama,* Anglo Catalan Society, 1994.

Work represented in anthologies, including *Lorca, Poet and Playwright,* edited by Robert Havard, University of Wales Press, 1992; and *History of the Theatre: Sources and Documents,* Cambridge University Press, 1994. Contributor of articles and reviews to Hispanic studies journals.

*   *   *

GERSTLER, Amy 1956-

PERSONAL: Born October 24, 1956, in San Diego, CA. *Education:* Received B.A. from Pitzer College.

ADDRESSES: Home—Los Angeles, CA. *Office*—c/o Viking Penguin, 375 Hudson St., New York, NY 10014.

CAREER: Poet, fiction writer, and journalist.

AWARDS, HONORS: National Book Critics Circle Award, 1991, for *Bitter Angel.*

WRITINGS:

Yonder (poems), Little Caesar Press, 1981.
Christy's Alpine Inn (poems), Sherwood Press, 1982.
White Marriage/Recovery (poems), Illuminati (Los Angeles), 1984.
Early Heaven (poems), Ouija Madness Press, 1984.
Martine's Mouth (fiction), Illuminati, 1985.
The True Bride (poems), Lapis Press (Santa Monica, CA), 1986.
Primitive Man (fiction), Hanuman Books (New York), 1987.
(With Alexis Smith) *Past Lives* (artists book), Santa Monica Museum of Art (Santa Monica, CA), 1989.
Bitter Angel (poems), North Point Press (San Francisco, CA), 1990.
Nerve Storm (poems), Viking-Penguin (New York), 1993.

Contributor of articles to periodicals, including *Art Forum* and *Los Angeles Times.*

SIDELIGHTS: Known for witty, complex poetry that reflects such themes as redemption, suffering, and survival, Amy Gerstler won the 1991 National Book Critics Circle Award for the collection *Bitter Angel.* Though Gerstler has penned several poetry volumes, including *Yonder, Early Heaven, Christy's Alpine Inn,* and 1993's *Nerve Storm,* she is best known for *Bitter Angel,* which garnered significant critical acclaim. Gerstler has also received praise for *White Marriage/Recovery,* which *Los Angeles Times Book Review* contributor Jonathan Kirsch deemed "an odd but utterly beguiling bit of small-press ephemera." The critic called the writing "spare, almost encoded, but richly evocative."

In *Bitter Angel* Gerstler introduces a variety of narrators, including a saint, ghost, clairvoyant, father, child, and lover. Her characters are often outsiders who, according to *Publishers Weekly,* "share a kind of grace" because of their disenfranchisement. Gerstler also evokes the surreal, supernatural, and ironic using various poetic forms and vernacular speech. Sexuality is another of Gerstler's themes, as Eileen Myles observed in the *Voice Literary Supplement:* "Actually, it's not sex she's talking about but desire, even lust, which cohabits with unlikely traits: modesty, a longing for disembodiment, death, disintegration, and a queer reverence for sainthood and suffering."

Gerstler speaks of a saintlike character in "Shrine": She is "stumbling and stupid. Now that's my kind / of saint. . . . The more neurotic, unattractive / and accident prone, the better." Addressing an anxious lover in "Doubt," the poet writes: "It's a fat cactus / desert travelers tap / for a mucuslike lubricant / that protects their skins. / It's the psyche's dry lakebed / from which moans of pleasure / bubble up in gaseous form / and crack the sunbaked mud." And in "Rising Up," the deceased narrator declares: "You can't come after me. / My traits escaped in a blaze. / I ditched my dripping limbs / at the mouth of a splendid cave—."

Bitter Angel was enthusiastically received by reviewers, who often noted Gerstler's originality. A *Publishers Weekly* critic commented that "Gerstler balances classical allusion with bold experimentation in voice, form and content." The result is a "tension" that lends an "urgent, honest edge" to her work. According to Myles, Gerstler's "poetry is extremely rich. But not cluttered and not loud." The reviewer continued, observing that "the supernatural, the sexy mundane, the out-of-sight are simply her materials, employed as they might be in a piece of religious art."

"In Gerstler," wrote David Shapiro in *American Poetry Review,* "we see how effective a quiet ruminative and contemplative poem can be. . . . On the other hand, Gerstler has a series of complex, humorous prose poems which can be as immediate and imagistic as a germ: 'A few germs float up the baby's nose while the mother reads, making the infant sneeze.'" According to *American Book Review* contributor Sarah Gorham, the poems in *Bitter Angel* "strip down all basic assumptions about beauty and truth and holiness, and begin a struggle for redemption from the gutter. . . . Because of this, the drive for ascension in Gerstler's work becomes that much more valiant, and comic." And Michael Dirda, writing in *Washington Post Book World,* noted that although some of the poet's juxtapositions appeared "improbable," "all objections are overruled by Gerstler's sheer acrobatic brilliance."

Gerstler followed *Bitter Angel* with *Nerve Storm,* where she "continues her intense, and often savage, pursuit of redemption," according to *Publishers Weekly.* Pat Monaghan, writing in *Booklist,* called Gerstler's realm one "of hallucinatory moments in normal, even crass, circumstances." In one poem, a cow announces that "Prior to this promotion / I was the town drunk." Although disappointed with some of the poems in *Nerve Storm,* a *Publishers Weekly* reviewer noted that Gerstler's "best poems are relentless, soul-searching, surreal and wonderfully inexplicable."

BIOGRAPHICAL/CRITICAL SOURCES:

BOOKS

Gerstler, Amy, *Bitter Angel,* North Point Press, 1990.

Gerstler, *Nerve Storm,* Viking-Penguin, 1993.

PERIODICALS

American Book Review, January-March, 1991, pp. 27, 29.
American Poetry Review, January-February, 1991, pp. 37-47.
Booklist, October 1, 1993.
Los Angeles Times Book Review, April 8, 1984, p. 6.
New York Times, December 14, 1990.
Publishers Weekly, December 22, 1989, pp. 4-5; October 18, 1993, p. 69.
Voice Literary Supplement, February, 1990, pp. 7-8.
Washington Post Book World, March 3, 1991, pp. 6-7.

*　　*　　*

GIBSON, William M(erriam)   1912-1987

OBITUARY NOTICE—See index for *CA* sketch: Born January 16, 1912, in Wilmette, IL; died January 22, 1987. Educator and author. Gibson earned degrees from Princeton University and the University of Chicago; while still in graduate school he began his teaching career at the latter institution in 1937. He later taught English at Williams College in the 1940s before joining the faculty of New York University in 1949. He edited two books on Mark Twain—*Selected Mark Twain-Howells Letters, 1872-1910,* in collaboration with Frederick Anderson and Henry Nash Smith, and *Mark Twain's "Mysterious Stranger" Manuscripts.* He left New York University in 1973 for a position at the University of Wisconsin at Madison, where he remained as a professor of English until 1981. Gibson authored two other works during his tenure there—*The Art of Mark Twain* and *Theodore Roosevelt among the Humorists: W. D. Howells, Mark Twain, and Mr. Dooley.*

OBITUARIES AND OTHER SOURCES:

Date of death provided by Barbara C. Gibson, April 27, 1994.

BOOKS

Who Was Who in America with World Notables, Volume 9: *1985-1989,* Marquis, 1989.

*　　*　　*

GILL, Walter   1937-
(Brother Wali Hakeem)

PERSONAL: Born in 1937, in Greenville, MS; son of Robert Lewis and Rubye Cordelia Harris; married

Frances Nichols; children: Valerie, Michelle, Stacy, Danell, Daren. *Education:* Morgan State College, B.A., 1960; Syracuse University, Ph.D., 1977.

ADDRESSES: Home—P.O. Box 4618, Baltimore, MD 21212. *Office*—School of Education, Millersville University, Millersville, PA 17551-0302.

CAREER: Junior high school art and social studies teacher, 1962-72; case worker, 1992-94; Millersville University, Millersville, PA, assistant professor of education, 1994—. Producer of educational films; actor in community theater productions; movie extra; newspaper columnist.

WRITINGS:

Issues in African American Education, Winston-Derek, 1991.

Contributor of more than a hundred articles to periodicals, sometimes under the name Brother Wali Hakeem.

WORK IN PROGRESS: The Urban Chameleon, an autobiography; and *Models, Methods and Media.*

*   *   *

GLICK, William H. 1952-

PERSONAL: Born in 1952, in Harbor Beach, MI; son of William H. and Joanne R. Glick; married Rhonda G. Rush; children: Aaron, Devin. *Education:* University of Michigan, A.B., 1975; University of California, Berkeley, Ph.D., 1981.

ADDRESSES: Office—Department of Management, University of Texas at Austin, Austin, TX 78712.

CAREER: University of Texas at Austin, assistant professor, 1981-87, associate professor of management, 1987—.

MEMBER: Academy of Management, American Psychological Society, American Sociological Association, Institute for Management Science, American Society for Quality Control.

AWARDS, HONORS: Best Competitive Paper award, Organization Behavior Division, Academy of Management, 1983, for "Job Characteristics and Job Responses: Cause and Effect or Common Methods Variance?"; grants from International Business Machines Co., 1984-94, and Army Research Institute, 1985-90; Ascendent Scholar Award, Southern Management Association, 1987; grant from National Science Foundation, 1988-89; best Article Award, *Academy of Management Journal,* 1993.

WRITINGS:

(Editor, with G. P. Huber, and contributor) *Organizational Change and Redesign: Ideas and Insights for Improving Performance,* Oxford University Press, 1993.

Contributor to books, including *Productivity in Organizations: New Perspectives from Industrial and Organizational Psychology,* edited by J. P. Campbell and R. J. Campbell, Jossey-Bass, 1988. Contributor of more than twenty articles and reviews to management journals. Associate guest editor, *Organization Science,* 1991; member of editorial board, *Academy of Management Journal,* 1984-90, *Academy of Management Review,* 1990—, and *Journal of Management,* 1992—; member of special issue editorial board, *Communication Research.*

*   *   *

GOODMAN, James 1956-

PERSONAL: Born November 21, 1956; son of Burton S. (a travel agent) and Rachel Jeanne (an attorney; maiden name, Lehr) Goodman; married Jennifer McFeely (a clinical social worker), June 1, 1986; children: M. Samuel, M. Jackson. *Education:* Hobart College, B.A., 1979; attended Columbia University, 1980-81; New York University, M.A., 1983; Princeton University, Ph.D., 1990. *Politics:* Liberal.

ADDRESSES: Home—Cambridge, MA. *Office*—Department of History, 201 Robinson Hall, Harvard University, Cambridge, MA 02138.

CAREER: New York City Commission on Human Rights, New York City, assistant director of public relations, 1980-81; Daniel J. Edelman Public Relations, Inc., New York City, account executive, 1981-82; Harvard University, Cambridge, MA, assistant professor of history and social studies, 1990—. Holy Roman Repertory Company, historical consultant.

MEMBER: Phi Beta Kappa.

AWARDS, HONORS: Grant from American Council of Learned Societies, 1990.

WRITINGS:

Stories of Scottsboro, Pantheon (New York, NY), 1994.

Contributor of articles and reviews to periodicals, including *Newsday*.

WORK IN PROGRESS: A book about the memory and legacy of Robert F. Kennedy.

SIDELIGHTS: James Goodman told *CA:* "I began my graduate studies in creative writing and finished (at least for the time being) in history, so it should not be surprising that I am a historian who thinks that history ought to be creative writing about the past. The great challenge is to imagine and create literary forms that do justice to the richness, complexity, power, and drama of the past and the complicated stories we tell ourselves about it. I write nonfiction narrative, but each day I learn about the past, and about how to write history, from those who write novels, short stories, essays, poems, and plays.

"In politics, I am to the left of most American liberals, but, in hard times for liberals, I am happy to be known as one. Of course, politics in the present is one thing, in history and literature another."

*   *   *

GOODMAN, John   1952-

PERSONAL: Born September 19, 1952, in Petersburg, VA; son of John and Elizabeth (Jones) Goodman. *Education:* Columbia University, B.A., 1974; New York University, M.A., 1981, Ph.D., 1991.

ADDRESSES: Home and office—114 South Portland Ave., No. 4B, Brooklyn, NY 11217.

CAREER: Translator from French to English. Art historian. Lecturer at Columbia University and New York University.

AWARDS, HONORS: Fellow, J. Paul Getty Foundation, 1991-92.

WRITINGS:

TRANSLATOR

Jean-Marie Perouse de Montclos, *Versailles,* Abbeville, 1991.
Industrial Design: Reflection of a Century, Flammarion (Paris), 1993.
Alain Gruber, editor, *The Decorative Arts in Europe,* Volume I: *Renaissance and Mannerism,* Abbeville, 1994.
Hubert Damisch, *The Origin of Perspective,* MIT Press, 1994.

Damisch, *The Judgment of Paris,* University of Chicago Press, in press.
Diderot on Art, Volume I: *The Salon of 1765,* Volume II: *The Salon of 1767,* Yale University Press, in press.

Contributor of articles and reviews to art journals.

WORK IN PROGRESS: Altar against Altar: Cultural Activism and Artistic Practice in Pre-Revolutionary Paris, completion expected in 1996; *The Worm in the Apple: The Gender Politics of European Neoclassicism,* 1997; research on Gabriel de Saint-Aubin and the world of the marginal artist in eighteenth-century Paris; a critical edition of letters and documents by or relating to Jacques-Louis David and his students; research on Theodore Gericault and Paul Cezanne.

*   *   *

GOODMAN, Susan   1951-

PERSONAL: Born March 20, 1951, in Boston, MA; daughter of Ralph (in business) and Rhoda (an artist; maiden name, Cohen) Rudnick; married Gregory Goodman (divorced, 1991). *Education:* University of New Hampshire, B.A., 1972, M.Ed., 1974, M.A., 1987, Ph.D., 1989.

ADDRESSES: Home—105 Bent Lane, Newark, DE 19711. *Office*—Department of English, University of Delaware, Newark, DE 19711.

CAREER: Public school teacher, 1972-83, including English teacher, high school reading specialist, and coordinator of English as a second language; California State University, Fresno, professor of English, 1990-94; University of Delaware, Newark, professor of English, 1994—.

MEMBER: Modern Language Association of America, American Library Association, Edith Wharton Society, Ellen Glasgow Society.

AWARDS, HONORS: Fellow of Virginia Humanities Foundation, 1994.

WRITINGS:

Edith Wharton's Women: Friends and Rivals, University Press of New England, 1990.
Edith Wharton's Inner Circle, University of Texas Press (Austin, TX), 1994.
(Editor with Daniel Ryot) *Femmes de Conscience: Aspects du Feminisme Americain, 1848-1875,* Sorbonne Press, 1994.

WORK IN PROGRESS: A biographical and critical study of Ellen Glasgow.

SIDELIGHTS: Susan Goodman told *CA:* "My work has focused on the lives and works of women writers, primarily Edith Wharton and Ellen Glasgow. In trying to relate another's past, I have looked at those intersections between fact and imagination, knowing that what I offer is itself a kind of embroidery, a piecing together of separate appliques. Commenting on history, I cannot wholly escape making it. Living as we all do, in both real and fictive worlds, both inside and outside history, I echo Alain Besancon in arguing that historical research, indeed all writing, is a form of introspection, *la recherche de soi-meme.* The relationship between writer and subject is an exchange that evolves in its various stages. How much so is illustrated by a dream I had at the beginning of my research on Edith Wharton. She had invited me for a motor-flight, after which I elatedly skipped down a hill, secure in the knowledge that she liked me. Since then, I have read a letter she wrote to her sister-in-law, stating that women scholars would be better off staying home and having babies. Although the dream illustrates the danger of filtering another's story through one's own, it also gave me permission to explore Wharton's life.

"Writing the life of someone who must, in large part, remain unknown raises questions about the construction of identity and the nature of biography itself. In *The Woman Within,* Ellen Glasgow asks a question that haunts all writers: 'How can one tell where memory ends and imagination begins?' This question has particular significance for a biographer. The 'truth' of biography, like that of autobiography, is necessarily evolving. It grows from a process of amendment and revision. If we accept that any writer tells, as Glasgow believed of herself, his or her own disguised story, then the biographer is also an autobiographer, whose personal narrative develops within, alongside, or in opposition to that of the subject. Leon Edel describes the biographer's dilemma as twofold: 'he must apprise the life of another by becoming that other person; and he must be scrupulously careful that in the process the other person is not refashioned in his image.' The relationship—subtle, intimate, and ambivalent—is complicated by any number of factors. A biographer may choose a subject who seems a soulmate in need of rescue, or who represents the values of a secretly envied class or a bygone era. In other cases, a biographer may be motivated by a kind of self-righteous, usually termed 'moral' wrath. Perhaps the nearest approach to another's life is through the divination of an inexplicable presence, whether a verbal mood or an emotional aura."

* * *

GOODWIN, Richard N(aradhof) 1931-

PERSONAL: Born December 7, 1931, in Boston, MA; son of Joseph C. (an engineer) and Belle (Fisher) Goodwin; married Sandra Leverant, June 15, 1958 (died, 1972); married Doris Kearns (a professor of government and author), December 14, 1975; children: (first marriage) Richard Joseph, (second marriage) Michael. *Education:* Tufts University, B.A. (summa cum laude), 1953; Harvard Law School (summa cum laude), 1958. *Avocational interests:* Modern American literature—especially Faulkner—photography, playing touch football.

ADDRESSES: Office—P.O. Box 166, Kingfield, ME 04947.

CAREER: Attorney, government official, and political speechwriter. Law clerk for U.S. Supreme Court Justice Felix Frankfurter, 1958-59; member of U.S. House of Representatives subcommittee on legislative oversight, 1959; speechwriter for John F. Kennedy, 1959-60; member of President's Task Force on Latin American Affairs, 1960-61; assistant special counsel to the president, 1961; deputy assistant secretary of state for inter-American affairs, 1961-63; secretary-general for International Peace Corps Secretariat, 1963-64; special assistant to the president, 1964-65; Wesleyan University, Center for Advanced Studies, fellow, 1965-67; Massachusetts Institute of Technology, visiting professor of public affairs, 1968; writer. Also served as speechwriter for Eugene McCarthy, Robert Kennedy, and Edmund Muskie in their presidential campaigns.

WRITINGS:

The Sower's Seed: A Tribute to Adlai Stevenson, New American Library, 1965.
Triumph or Tragedy: Reflections on Vietnam, Random House, 1966.
The American Condition, Doubleday, 1974.
Remembering America: A Voice from the Sixties (memoir), Little, Brown, 1988.
Two Men of Florence (play), read at the Actors Studio, New York City, 1988.
Promises to Keep: A Call for a New American Revolution, Times Books, 1992.

Contributing editor to *Rolling Stone* magazine. Contributor of political pieces to the *New Yorker.*

SIDELIGHTS: Richard N. Goodwin graduated first in his class at both Tufts University and Harvard Law School and took for his first job a position as law clerk to U.S. Supreme Court Justice Felix Frankfurter. His subsequent work on a subcommittee for the U.S. House of Representatives, charged with investigating rigged television quiz shows and radio payola, brought him to the attention of Senator John F. Kennedy, whose speechwriting staff Goodwin joined in 1959, less than two years after he graduated from law school. Following Kennedy's successful bid for the presidency, Goodwin became the chief executive's specialist on Latin America and was appointed deputy assistant secretary of state for inter-American affairs. He was also one of the founders of the Alliance for Progress, a program intended to relieve economic hardship in Latin American countries. Goodwin later developed a domestic program, known as the Great Society, for Kennedy's successor, Lyndon B. Johnson. Growing disenchantment with President Johnson's handling of the war in Vietnam led Goodwin to leave government service in 1965. His return to political life in 1968 was shortlived as he wrote speeches for Eugene McCarthy, Robert Kennedy, and then Edmund Muskie in their unsuccessful bids for the presidency (Kennedy's efforts as a candidate were cut short by an assassin).

After leaving the Johnson Administration Goodwin wrote *Triumph or Tragedy: Reflections on Vietnam,* based on a lengthy article published in the *New Yorker* magazine. The volume offers an insider's view of how American politicians became mired in what is commonly referred to as the Vietnam debacle. Critical reaction to the short monograph was mixed. While a critic for the *Saturday Review* described the issues Goodwin "tackles" in *Triumph or Tragedy* as "maddeningly complex," a contributor to the *New York Times Book Review* dubbed Goodwin's work "a readable little essay." Other reviewers blamed Goodwin's residual loyalties to the Johnson Administration for the author's contradictory positions on such pivotal issues as culpability and future directions with regard to the ongoing conflict in Vietnam. While Hans J. Morgenthau of the *New York Review of Books* noted that at times Goodwin argues "with considerable skill and eloquence," internal contradictions result in "an extraordinarily strange book." Bernard B. Fall of the *Saturday Review* admitted that the author's assertions regarding how best to end the conflict in Vietnam "are by now only of historical value. Events have totally outstripped them on every count." The critic suggested that this affirms the value of Goodwin's revelations about behind-the-scenes oc-

currences in the Kennedy and Johnson administrations.

By the early 1970s, Goodwin had become disillusioned with politics in the United States and his next publication, *The American Condition,* expresses the belief that American society is suffering a "pathology" brought on, in part, by the proliferation of bureaucracies. A number of reviewers focused on Goodwin's speculations on the nature of freedom, his belief that the United States has become an increasingly oppressive society, and his lack of faith that this process can be, or will be, reversed. "Richard Goodwin offers no heroic call for a new exertion of the will or program for a 'rebirth of the nation.' His understanding is far more realistic and his analysis too careful and honest for that kind of conclusion," summarized Joseph Duffey of the *Washington Post Book World.* Richard Todd of the *Atlantic* remarked: "Goodwin stakes out a large territory for himself, little less than the history of Western thought." Walter Clemons of *Newsweek* found *The American Condition* "an ambitious, richly idiosyncratic essay."

In the 1980s, Goodwin added a memoir, *Remembering America: A Voice from the Sixties,* to his growing body of work. Centered on his years as a speechwriter for presidents Kennedy and Johnson, the book offers "a cautionary parable on the pitfalls of hero worship and the seductions of high office," according to *New York Times Book Review* critic Jim Miller. Some reviewers compared the volume's relative optimism regarding the country's chances of returning to the best of what the decade of the 1960s stands for to the bleakness of Goodwin's predictions in *The American Condition.* Critic Alan Brinkley of the *New York Times Book Review,* however, faulted the author of "this impassioned memoir" for failing to supplement his memories of the policies and politics of the 1960s with the scholarly reassessments of the period that have appeared since then. Other reviewers remarked, both positively and negatively, that Goodwin's skills as a speechwriter are clearly in evidence in the prose of *Remembering America.* J. Anthony Lukas of *Washington Post Book World* stated that while "the rhetoric that soars from a podium sometimes looks a bit stagey in cold type," he ultimately concluded: "At his best, Dick Goodwin still proves able to touch a nation." *Chicago Tribune* critic William J. Drummond prophesied: "*Remembering America: A Voice from the Sixties* should win its author a lasting place in American political theory."

Critics also remarked on the controversial conclusions that Goodwin draws in his book regarding the mental health of Lyndon Baines Johnson while he was president of the United States. In their reviews of *Remembering America,* Drummond and others responded primarily to Goodwin's statements that Johnson suffered from paranoid fits during his tenure in office, and that his irrational behavior resulting from those fits had wide-ranging effects. Critical reaction to Goodwin's accusations that Johnson was mentally unstable ranged from those who refused to take them seriously, as, for example, *Time*'s Tamar Jacoby, who wrote: "surely history's judgment of Lyndon B. Johnson cannot rest on the worried musings of a young aide," to Hugh Sidey, also of *Time,* who praised Goodwin for daring to "probe a dim corner of Washington history," and averred, "Goodwin . . . cannot be dismissed."

Goodwin has also written *Promises to Keep: A Call for a New American Revolution,* which outlines the author's diagnosis of the major problems suffered by contemporary American society, and his proposals for social, economic, and political solutions to these ills. Critics disagreed about the fundamental soundness of Goodwin's ideas for reform, but Alex Raksin of the *Los Angeles Times Book Review* noted that an early version of the book had fallen into the hands of former governor of California Jerry Brown, who incorporated some of its ideas into the platform of his 1992 bid for the presidency. While *Publishers Weekly* concluded: "this succinct essay sets forth visionary, if seemingly impractical, plan to revitalize our ailing economy," reviewer Raksin asserted that the more subtle of Goodwin's ideas "warrant serious consideration."

Goodwin's rise to power in American politics came quickly and at an early age. Within a decade, the political idealism nurtured during the Kennedy era would be destroyed by the continuing war in Vietnam. In words that echo other reviewers, Susan Jenks of *Biography News* described Goodwin as "a gifted wordsmith with far-reaching intellectual talents who helped to shape policies and attitudes in the governing process." Even critics such as Sheldon S. Wolin of the *New York Review of Books,* who called Goodwin's treatise *The American Condition* "a soulful lament masquerading as searching criticism," paid the author the compliment of discussing his writing in terms set forth by Machiavelli, Plato, and de Tocqueville. Throughout his writing career, he has been best known as, in the words of *Washington Post* writer Jim Naughton, "an adviser and speech writer for our last generation of charismatic liberal leaders."

BIOGRAPHICAL/CRITICAL SOURCES:

BOOKS

Goodwin, Richard, *Remembering America: A Voice from the Sixties,* Little, Brown, 1988.
Lichtenstein, Nelson, editor, *Political Profiles: The Kennedy Years,* Facts on File, 1976, pp. 187-88.
Lichtenstein, editor, *Political Profiles: The Johnson Years,* Facts on File, 1976, pp. 227-28.

PERIODICALS

Atlantic, March, 1974, pp. 90-92.
Biography News, May, 1974, p. 524.
Chicago Tribune, October 9, 1988, sec. 14, p. 5.
Los Angeles Times, September 14, 1988.
Los Angeles Times Book Review, September 25, 1988, pp. 1, 11; September 27, 1992.
Newsweek, May 20, 1974, p. 108; September 5, 1988, p. 70.
New York Review of Books, June 23, 1966, pp. 12-14; May 2, 1974, pp. 10-12.
New York Times Book Review, August 21, 1966, pp. 22, 24; May 12, 1974; September 4, 1988, pp. 7-8.
Publishers Weekly, July 1, 1988, pp. 41-43; July 29, 1988, p. 213; August 17, 1992, p. 484.
Saturday Review, July 30, 1966, p. 39; October 8, 1966, pp. 102-3;
Time, September 5, 1988, p. 22.
Washington Post, September 6, 1988.
Washington Post Book World, April 7, 1974, pp. 1-2; August 21, 1988, pp. 1-2; October 1, 1989.*

—Sketch by Mary Gillis

*   *   *

GORDON, Robert Ellis   1954-

PERSONAL: Born May 25, 1954, in Boston, MA; son of Mark (in sales) and Joan (a teacher; maiden name, Strumph) Gordon. *Education:* Harvard College, B.A. (cum laude), 1977; Iowa Writers Workshop, M.F.A., 1979.

ADDRESSES: Home—P.O. Box 20129, Seattle, WA 98102.

CAREER: Washington State Prison Writers Project, director.

AWARDS, HONORS: James Michener Creative Writing fellow, 1983-84; Artist Trust Grant, 1992; King County Arts Commission Publication Award for Fiction, 1993, for *When Bobby Kennedy Was a Moving Man.*

WRITINGS:

When Bobby Kennedy Was a Moving Man, Black Heron Press (Seattle), 1993.

Contributor of short stories to periodicals, including *Fiction, Ploughshares, Other Voices,* and the *Seattle Review.*

WORK IN PROGRESS: Between Worlds, "a nonfiction account of my experiences teaching in the prisons."

SIDELIGHTS: In Robert Ellis Gordon's 1993 novel, *When Bobby Kennedy Was a Moving Man,* Robert F. Kennedy is reincarnated as a moving man. Endowed by the gods who returned him to the earth with such magical powers as the ability to levitate furniture and the power to read people's thoughts, Kennedy defies the gods' orders and seeks out the gangster he believes murdered his brother, former U.S. president John F. Kennedy. Bobby is incarcerated, and is severely punished for sins he committed in his former life as well as for the sins he has committed in his present life before the gods forgive him and he is allowed to ascend to heaven. *Publishers Weekly* praised the book's combination of "messianic novel and Kennedy tell-all," *Kirkus Reviews* dubbed it "the yarn to end all Kennedy yarns," and in the *New York Times Book Review,* Scott Veale observed that *When Bobby Kennedy Was a Moving Man* is somewhat sympathetic toward its "flawed but fascinating protagonist."

In her review in the *Philadelphia Inquirer,* Madeline Crowley commented: "[The novel] dissects a human heart, shadowed by evil, rent by corruption and yet brilliantly lit by a heartfelt passion for social justice. As fiction, it plays fast and loose with facts, but it is scrupulous in its refusal to simplify the fine and the malign facets of Bobby Kennedy's character."

Robert Ellis Gordon told *CA:* "When I stumbled into prison teaching in 1988 (I was afraid of teaching in prison, but the job was offered and I needed the money) I discovered a second passion, right up there with writing. Clearly, my incarcerated students have problems with boundaries. Indeed, they have, on occasion, destroyed lives through their impulsiveness and rage. Still, when this same absence of inhibition is put in the service of story, the results can be penetrating, dazzling, profoundly moving in a way that 100 well-crafted stories in *Atlantic Monthly* will never be. My students teach me a lot about the literary perils of risk-aversion, about how to reach for the stories that matter. When

I hear about critics or professors of literature proclaiming the death of literature, I think that these people are simply looking in the wrong places. Stories will live so long as the human race lives. We are a storytelling species, and that is all there is to it.

"I am a terribly slow writer, and I do not know what to do about that except to proceed, slowly, sentence by sentence, year by year. I pay as little attention as possible to the folks (there are so many of them!) who believe it is a writer's job to write about the world as they wish to see it. I can't even write about the world as *I* wish to see it. A writer's job, I believe, is to be as true to his or her own vision as possible; to bring all the craft (and then some) at his or her disposal to bear upon the vision, and to hope, over time, that the vision and the craft will evolve. Time, not current intellectual fashion, will determine if a story has staying power, if it is one that matters."

BIOGRAPHICAL/CRITICAL SOURCES:

PERIODICALS

Kirkus Reviews, August 1, 1993.
New York Times Book Review, November 28, 1993, p. 26.
Philadelphia Inquirer, January 9, 1994.
Publishers Weekly, August 30, 1993, p. 90.

*   *   *

GORRELL, Lorraine

PERSONAL: Born in Baltimore, MD; daughter of Wilson (an engineer) and Clara (a homemaker; maiden name, Horstman) Gorrell; married Wilburn Wendell Newcomb (a director of grants); children: Rachel. *Education:* Received B.A. from Hood College and M.Mus. and M.A. from Yale University.

ADDRESSES: Office—Department of Music, Winthrop University, Rock Hill, SC 29733.

CAREER: Winthrop University, Rock Hill, SC, professor of music, 1973—. Professional singer (mezzo soprano); performs recitals. Recorded as soloist, *Experiences Anonymes,* Volume IX: *The Fourteenth Century.*

WRITINGS:

The Nineteenth-Century German Lied, Amadeus Press, 1993.

Contributor to music journals.

WORK IN PROGRESS: Research on Viennese song composers of the early twentieth century.

* * *

GOUGH-COOPER, Jennifer 1942-

PERSONAL: Born May 28, 1942, in Farningham, Kent, England; daughter of Walter Henry (a house builder) and Vivien Margaret (Gordon) Gough-Cooper. *Education:* Studied portrait photography with Dorothy Wilding and Walter Bird, 1960-61; attended Camberwell School of Art, 1963-64, and Hornsey College of Art, 1964-67.

ADDRESSES: Home—Le Ver a Val, 76190 Hautot-le-Vatois, France.

CAREER: Writer.

WRITINGS:

(With Jacques Caumont) *Marcel Duchamp,* MIT Press, 1993.

* * *

GRAMBS, David (Lawrence) 1938-

PERSONAL: Born August 6, 1938, in Paterson, NJ; son of George Lorenzo (an Episcopal cleric) and Myrtle Jane (a homemaker; maiden name, Wood) Grambs. *Education:* Haverford College, A.B., 1959. *Avocational interests:* Jazz piano, running, swimming, scuba diving.

ADDRESSES: Office—22 West Ninetieth St., New York, NY 10024. *Agent*—Jim Trupin, JET Literary Associates, 124 East Eighty-Fourth St., New York, NY 10028.

CAREER: Stratemeyer Syndicate (publisher), juvenile fiction editor and author of "Hardy Boys" series mysteries, 1963-65; American Heritage Publishing Company, senior editor of *American Heritage Dictionary,* 1967-69; Funk & Wagnalls, Inc., senior editor and writer of *New Encyclopedia,* 1969-71; Charles Scribner's Sons, associate editor of *The Dictionary of Scientific Biography,* 1971-73; Penthouse International, Inc., copyeditor of *Penthouse,* 1976-83; Random House, Inc., staff editor of *Random House Dictionary of the English Language,* 1983-1987; freelance editor and writer. *Military service:* U.S. Army, 1959-61; served in West Germany.

WRITINGS:

(Translator) *Cathedrals of Europe,* Crowell, 1976.
Words about Words, McGraw-Hill, 1984, published in England as *Literary Companion Dictionary,* later revised as *The Random House Dictionary for Writers and Readers,* Random House, 1990.
Dimboxes, Epopts, and Other Quidams: Words to Describe Life's Indescribable People, Workman Publishing, 1986.
(Editor) Theodore Bernstein, *Bernstein's Reverse Dictionary,* 2nd edition, Times Books (New York, NY), 1988.
Death by Spelling, Harper, 1989, later published in hardcover as *The Ultimate Spelling Quiz Book,* Wings, 1992.
The Describer's Dictionary, Norton, 1993.
Did I Say Something Wrong?, NAL/Dutton/Penguin, 1993.
The Endangered English Dictionary, Norton, 1994.
Just Ask Mr. Wordwizard, Dell, 1995

Contributor to books, including *Fodor's Caribbean '90; Psychology: An Introduction,* edited by Charles G. Morris, for Prentice-Hall; and *The Renaissance Rediscovery of Linear Perspective,* for Basic Books. Also contributor to *Penthouse* and *Today's Jogger.*

* * *

GRAY, Alfred 1939-

PERSONAL: Born October 22, 1939; son of Alfred and Eloise (Evans) Gray; married Mary Wheat (a mathematician), August, 1964.

ADDRESSES: Home—6807 Connecticut Ave., Chevy Chase, MD 20811. *Office*—Department of Mathematics, University of Maryland at College Park, College Park, MD 20742.

CAREER: Mathematician.

WRITINGS:

Tubes, Addison-Wesley, 1992.
Modern Differential Geometry of Curves and Surfaces, CRC Press, 1993.

WORK IN PROGRESS: A film and computer software to accompany *Modern Differential Geometry of Curves and Surfaces.*

* * *

GRAYSON, Donald K. 1945-

PERSONAL: Born April 10, 1945. *Education:* State

University of New York at Buffalo, B.A., 1966; University of Oregon, M.A., 1969, Ph.D., 1973.

ADDRESSES: Office—Department of Anthropology, University of Washington, Seattle, WA 98195.

CAREER: University of Oregon, Eugene, instructor in anthropology, 1969-71; Kirkland College, Clinton, NY, assistant professor of anthropology, 1971-74; Bureau of Land Management, Oregon State Office, Portland, state office archaeologist, 1974-75; University of Washington, Seattle, assistant professor, 1975-78, associate professor, 1978-83, professor of anthropology, 1983—, adjunct faculty at Quaternary Sciences Center, 1975—, adjunct assistant curator of environmental archaeology at Thomas Burke Memorial Museum, 1977-78, adjunct associate curator, 1978-83, adjunct curator, 1983—, acting curator of archaeology, 1988-89. New York University, visiting associate professor, 1981. American Museum of Natural History, research associate in anthropology, 1979—; National Science Foundation, member of Archaeology Panel, 1985-87; Desert Research Institute, member of National Scientific Advisory Board, 1989-90; conducted extensive archaeological and biological field work in the northwestern United States; also worked in France.

MEMBER: International Council for Archaeozoology (member of international council, 1986—), American Society for Conservation Archaeology (vice-president, 1977-78; president, 1978-79), American Society of Mammalogists, Society for American Archaeology (executive officer, 1979-81), Society for Conservation Biology, Arizona Archaeological Society, Idaho Archaeological Society, Nevada Archaeological Society, Utah Archaeological Society.

AWARDS, HONORS: Best Book of the Year Award, American Library Association, 1984, for *The Establishment of Human Antiquity;* Fryxell Award, Society for American Archaeology, 1986; Distinguished Alumni Award, University of Oregon, 1990; grants from Mellon Foundation, 1973, American Philosophical Society, 1976, National Science Foundation, 1977-93, American Museum of Natural History, 1977-78, 1979-81, Mr. Bingham's Trust for Charity Research, 1982-83, U.S. Forest Service, 1983-84, L. S. B. Leakey Foundation, 1990-92, and U.S. Department of Defense, 1993-96.

WRITINGS:

A Bibliography of the Literature on North American Climates of the Past 13,000 Years, Garland

Publishing (New York City), 1975.
(Editor with P. D. Sheets, and contributor) *Volcanic Activity and Human Ecology,* Academic Press (New York City), 1979.
The Establishment of Human Antiquity, Academic Press, 1983.
Quantitative Zooarchaeology: Topics in the Analysis of Archaeological Faunas, Academic Press, 1984.
The Deserts' Past: A Natural Prehistory of the Great Basin, Smithsonian Institution Press (Washington, DC), 1993.

Work represented in anthologies, including *American Archaeology: Past and Future,* edited by D. J. Meltzer, D. D. Fowler, and J. A. Sabloff, Smithsonian Institution Press, 1986; *The Concept and Measure of Diversity in Archaeology,* edited by R. D. Leonard and G. T. Jones, Cambridge University Press, 1989; and *A Natural History of the Colorado Plateau and Great Basin,* edited by K. T. Harper, L. St. Clair, and others, University Press of Colorado, 1994. Contributor of about a hundred articles and reviews to scholarly journals. Editor, *Studies in Archaeological Science,* 1982-85; *Quaternary Research,* associate editor, 1983-93, member of editorial board, 1994—; member of editorial board, *Advances in Archaeological Method and Theory,* 1983—, *Advances in Archaeological and Museum Science,* 1989—, *Journal of World Prehistory,* 1991—, *Journal of Archaeological Science,* 1991—, and *Biodiversity Letters,* 1992—.

WORK IN PROGRESS: Research on the history of archaeology, North American prehistory, the European paleolithic age, method and theory in archaeology, statistical methods in archaeological and paleontological research, quaternary paleoecology, and vertebrate faunal analysis.

SIDELIGHTS: Donald K. Grayson told *CA:* "Archaeologists tend to share many experiences in common, above and beyond the fact that numbers of us work in areas so remote that few people even know they exist. One of those shared experiences is the response we get when someone finds out that we are archaeologists: 'Gee, that's what I always wanted to be.' Of course, people say that without thinking about the other common shared experiences: no bathrooms, rare showers, shelter often no more substantial than a tent, and water that can lay you up for weeks, if there is water at all.

"On the other hand, they are right. If you are interested in the human past, can take the rigors of field work, and can get through a modern archaeology graduate program, then archaeology is a great career. In fact, if I weren't an archaeologist, and I met someone who was, the first thing I'd say would be, 'Gee, that's what I always wanted to be.'

"If you combine that background and those interests with a love of writing, then writing about things archaeological—the things that excite you intellectually and that few other people know about—then writing archaeological books is just plain fun. I've written three, not counting scientific monographs and edited volumes, and I look forward to writing the next one, whatever it might me.

"Since my academic work is heavily quantitative, I have no fear of computers. Without them, I couldn't do the research I do. Even so, I long ago discovered the truth about writing. Computers not only don't know anything, they are incapable of creating anything; they have little metal parts inside, but no words. Pens, on the other hand, are quite different. They contain articles and books, all mushed up in the form of ink. The trick to writing is to find the pen that already contains what you are going to write. Once you find that pen, all you have to do is push it around to make the words come out. The wrong pen, and the words either won't come out or they will come out all wrong. When I start writing something substantial, my first step is to find the right pen. I know when I have found it because I can feel the words inside, wanting to get out onto the page. There is clearly some synergy involved here."

*　　*　　*

GREENSLADE, Roy　1946-

PERSONAL: Born December 31, 1946, in London, England; son of Ernest Frederick William (a clerk) and Joan Olive (an accountant; maiden name, Stocking) Greenslade; married Noreen Anna McElhone Taylor (a journalist), 1984; children: one stepson, one stepdaughter. *Education:* Sussex University, B.A. (with honors), 1979. *Avocational interests:* Squash, tennis.

ADDRESSES: Home—Kensington, England.

CAREER: Barking Advertiser, London, England, trainee journalist, 1962-66; *Lancashire Evening Telegraph,* Lancashire, England, sub-editor, 1966-67; *Daily Mail,* London, England, sub-editor, 1967-69; *Sun,* London, sub-editor, 1969-71; *Daily Star,* London, sub-editor, 1979-80 and 1981; *Daily Express,* London, sub-editor, 1980-81; *Sun,* assistant editor, 1981-87; *Sunday Times,* London, managing

editor, 1987-90; *Daily Mirror,* London, editor, 1991; freelance writer.

WRITINGS:

Goodbye to the Working Class, Boyars, 1975.
Maxwell: The Rise and Fall of Robert Maxwell and His Empire, Birch Lane, 1992.

WORK IN PROGRESS: A novel titled *Delirium of the Grave;* coediting *The Penguin Book of Columnists.*

SIDELIGHTS: Roy Greenslade has long worked for various British newspapers, including the London *Daily Express* and *Sunday Times.* His own writings include *Goodbye to the Working Class,* which describes educational conditions in 1960s Great Britain, and *Maxwell: The Rise and Fall of Robert Maxwell and His Empire,* which concerns the life of controversial newspaper magnate Robert Maxwell, who drowned mysteriously in the early 1990s. Greenslade was editor at Maxwell's London *Daily Mirror* in 1991 but resigned due to dissatisfaction with Maxwell's tampering with editorial policy. In *Maxwell,* Greenslade portrays the notorious publisher as a pompous, duplicitous opportunist. A *Publishers Weekly* reviewer called the book "juicy [and] relentlessly unflattering."

Greenslade told *CA:* "I now commentate on the media, a poacher turned gamekeeper. Only after giving up full-time staff positions on newspapers did I realize what wrong I had been doing for years."

BIOGRAPHICAL/CRITICAL SOURCES:

PERIODICALS

Listener, July 15, 1976.
Publishers Weekly, July 20, 1992, p. 242.

*　　*　　*

GREHAN, Ida　1916-

PERSONAL: Born January 3, 1916, in Dublin, Ireland; daughter of Thomas (a newspaper manager) and Elizabeth (a homemaker; maiden name, McKeever) Grehan; married J. Dover (a military police officer), August 30, 1947 (died January 12, 1981); children: Michael Grehan. *Politics:* None. *Religion:* Christian.

ADDRESSES: Home—Milk Wood, Sandycove Ave. E., County Dublin, Ireland.

CAREER: Freelance writer. Broadcaster for local radio programs in Nigeria.

WRITINGS:

Irish Family Histories, Roberts Rinehart (Boulder, CO), 1992, revised edition, 1995.

Author of the book *Waterford, an Irish Art: The History of Waterford Crystal. Irish Times,* feature writer and columnist, beginning in 1963. Contributor to periodicals in Malaysia, England, and Ireland, including *Cara* and *Books Ireland.*

SIDELIGHTS: Ida Grehan told *CA:* "I began freelancing feature articles for a variety of Irish publications and for Radio Eireann. Because of family commitments, I could not leave Ireland during the war, but afterward I went to Malaysia. There I married a British Army officer and freelanced for radio and newspapers there and in the United Kingdom and Ireland. After that, I broadcast a weekly diary for a local radio station in Nigeria for eleven years, and worked as a 'stringer' for the London *Times* and *Telegraph.* Returning to Dublin in 1963, I reviewed books and worked for the *Irish Times.* I freelanced for Irish journals and wrote for a number of tourist magazines.

"I had always been interested in the history of Irish names. Following a family from its origins reveals history unbiased by nationality or religion—as far as that is possible. In the 1970s I was commissioned to write a history of Waterford crystal. I toured the United States to promote the book and found people avid for their family histories. At home I began to research and write comprehensive histories of Irish names. In 1992 Roberts Rinehart published my illustrated history of eighty families."

*   *   *

GRENHAM, John   1954-

PERSONAL: Born September 21, 1954, in Athlone, Ireland; son of Sean (an engineer) and Brege (a homemaker; maiden name, Roche) Grenham; married Breda Kearney (a homemaker), August 30, 1986; children: Doireann, Eoin. *Education:* National University of Ireland, University College, Dublin, B.A., M.A., 1976. *Politics:* "Wooly liberal." *Religion:* None.

ADDRESSES: Home—30 Cremore Crescent, Glasnevin, Dublin 11, Ireland. *Office*—2 Kildare St., Dublin 2, Ireland.

CAREER: National University of Ireland, University College, Dublin, tutor, 1981-85; professional gene-

alogist, 1985-90; Irish Genealogical Project, Dublin, project manager, 1990—.

AWARDS, HONORS: Hennessy Literary Award, 1985; shortlisted for Kavanagh Poetry Competition, 1985, 1986 and 1988.

WRITINGS:

Daedalus: Introductions, Daedalus (Dublin), 1990.
The Cloverdale Anthology of Irish Poetry, Cloverdale, 1991.
Tracing Your Irish Ancestors, Gill & Macmillan (Dublin), 1992, Genealogical Publishing (Baltimore, MD), 1993.
Clans and Families of Ireland, Gill & Macmillan, 1993.

*   *   *

GRIGGS, Barbara
See VAN DER ZEE, Barbara (Blanche)

*   *   *

GUERNSEY, Thomas F.   1951-

PERSONAL: Born November 3, 1951, in Battle Creek, MI; son of Richard L. and Ruth F. Guernsey; married Kathe Klare, June 22, 1974; children: Alison, Adam. *Education:* University of Michigan, B.A. (with distinction), 1973; Wayne State University, J.D. (cum laude), 1976; Temple University, LL.M., 1980.

ADDRESSES: Home—12110 Diamond Hill Dr., Midlothian, VA 23113. *Office*—School of Law, University of Richmond, Richmond, VA 23173.

CAREER: Admitted to the Bars of Virginia, New Hampshire, Supreme Court of the United States, United States Court of Appeals for the Fourth Circuit, United States District Courts, Eastern District of Virginia, Eastern District of Pennsylvania, and District of New Hampshire. Vermont Law School, South Royalton, instructor in law, 1976-78; Temple University, Philadelphia, PA, Abraham L. Freedman fellow and lecturer in law, and assistant general counsel for Temple Legal Aid Office, all 1978-80; University of Richmond, Richmond, VA, assistant professor, 1980-83, associate professor, 1983-86, professor of law, 1986—, associate dean for academic affairs, 1992—. Attorney specializing in disability law, 1985—. Offender Aid and Restoration of Richmond, member of board of directors and chairperson of mediation committee, 1984-87, vice president, 1985-87; Virginia State Bar, member of board of directors of section on legal education and co-chairperson of law school committee, both 1993—; lecturer at schools, including University of Virginia, and at workshops; consultant to National Conference of Bar Examiners, Virginia Department for Rights of the Disabled, and Virginia Housing Development Authority.

MEMBER: American Bar Association.

WRITINGS:

(With Bacigal) *Admissibility of Evidence in Virginia,* with supplements, Harrison Co., 1990.

Problems and Simulations in Evidence, with instructor's manual, Anderson Publishing, 1991.

(With Lawrence A. Dubin) *Trial Practice,* Anderson Publishing, 1991.

Virginia Evidence, with supplements, Harrison Co., 1992.

(With wife, Kathe Klare) *Special Education Law,* Carolina Academic Press, 1993.

(With Klare) *Negotiations for Health Care Materials Managers: A Systematic Approach,* American Hospital Association, 1993.

(With Harbaugh and Zwier) *Negotiate for Success!* (interactive computer program), McGraw, 1994.

Contributor of articles and reviews to law journals. Member of editorial board, *Journal of Child and Family Studies,* 1991—.

WORK IN PROGRESS: Procedural Violations and Substantive Relief under IDEA.

*   *   *

GUTHRIE, Randolph H.   1934-

PERSONAL: Born December 8, 1934, in New York, NY; son of Randolph H., Sr., and Mable (Welton) Guthrie; married Beatrice Holden (an executive director), March 20, 1965; children: Randolph H. III, Michael Phipps, Philip Holden. *Education:* Princeton University, A.B., 1957; Harvard University, M.D., 1961. *Religion:* Episcopalian. *Avocational interests:* Skiing, whitewater rafting, fishing, reading.

ADDRESSES: Home and office—15 East Seventy-fourth St., New York, NY 10021.

CAREER: New York Hospital, New York City, intern, 1961-62, resident, 1962-63 and 1969-71; St. Luke's Hospital, New York City, resident, 1963-66; Memorial Sloan-Kettering Cancer Center, chief of plastic surgery, 1971-77; New York Downtown Hospital, New York City, chief of plastic surgery, 1981—. New York Hospital, attending surgeon, 1988—; Cornell University, clinical professor of surgery, 1988—. Diplomate, American Board of Plastic and Reconstructive Surgery and American Board of Surgery; New York State Supreme Court, plastic surgery representative on Malpractice Panel, 1971—. Acacia Foundation, president; Save Venice, Inc., president and chief executive officer; American-Italian Foundation for Cancer Research, director. Guest on television and radio programs. *Military service:* U.S. Army, Medical Corps, assistant chief of surgery in Heidelberg, Germany, 1966-69; became major.

MEMBER: American College of Surgeons (fellow), American Society of Plastic and Reconstructive Surgeons, Royal Society of Medicine, Harvard Medical Society of New York.

AWARDS, HONORS: First prize for research, National Plastic Surgery Chief Resident's Competition, 1971.

WRITINGS:

(With G. Schwartz) *Reconstructive and Aesthetic Mammoplasty,* Saunders, 1989.

(With D. Podolsky) *The Truth about Breast Implants,* Wiley, 1994.

Contributor of about fifty articles to medical journals.

H

H. D. P.
See DICKEY, Christopher

*   *   *

HAARSAGER, Sandra (L.)   1946-
(Sandra Watkinson)

PERSONAL: Born September 17, 1946, in West Plains, MO; daughter of Victor Everett (a laborer) and Melba Louise (a seamstress and copyeditor; maiden name, Rowlett) Smith; married James Barry Watkinson, June 15, 1969 (marriage ended October 15, 1975); married Dennis Lee Haarsager (a television and radio manager), January 1, 1977; children: Jennie Ella, Anna Lynn, Andrew Lee. *Education:* College of Idaho, B.A., 1968; Boise State University, M.P.A., 1982; Washington State University, Ph.D., 1990. *Politics:* Independent. *Religion:* Unitarian-Universalist.

ADDRESSES: Home—1171 Border Ln., Moscow, ID 83843-8741. *Office*—School of Communication, University of Idaho, Moscow, ID 83843-1072.

CAREER: Times-News, Twin Falls, ID, general assignment reporter and special editions editor, summers, 1965-67, then 1968-69; *Idaho Statesman,* Boise, reporter and editor, 1972-75; Idaho Department of Education, Boise, public information specialist and administrative assistant to the state superintendent, 1975-78; University of Idaho, Moscow, director of information services, 1979-83; *Idahoan/ Daily News,* Moscow, reporter and editor, 1983-85; News-Review Publishing Co., Moscow, general manager, 1985-88; University of Idaho, instructor, 1988-89, assistant professor, 1989-94, associate professor of communication and coordinator of American studies program, 1994—. Boise Hotline, member of board of directors, 1974-75; Idaho Law Enforcement Planning Commission, liaison to Juvenile Justice Council, 1976-78; Moscow Chamber of Commerce, member of board of directors, 1982-83; member of Pullman Chamber of Commerce and Lewiston Chamber of Commerce, 1987-88. Washington Idaho Symphony Chorus, member, 1981-84, 1990-93.

MEMBER: Society for the History of Technology, American Journalism Historians Association, American/Popular Culture Association, American Studies Association, Association for Education in Journalism and Mass Communication (head of Professional Freedom and Responsibility Committee, 1990-91), Council for the Advancement and Support of Education (member of board of directors, Northwest Region, 1981-82), Rocky Mountain American Studies Association, Northwest Communications Association, Northern Pacific Popular Culture Association, Pacific Northwest American Studies Association, Idaho Press Club (member of board of directors, 1986-87), Idaho Parent-Teacher Association (life member), University of Idaho Alumni Association (member of board of directors, 1992-95), Phi Kappa Phi.

AWARDS, HONORS: Idaho Press Club Awards, best in-depth reporting, 1974, and best feature writing, 1975; Council for the Advancement and Support of Education, Excellence in Broadcast Media Awards, 1979, 1980, and Excellence in Public Information Award, 1981; Education Media Award, Idaho Association of School Administrators, 1984, for columns and editorials on education; grants from John Calhoun Smith Fund, 1991-94.

WRITINGS:

Student Rights and Responsibilities: A Handbook for

Schools and Students (monograph), Idaho Department of Education, 1978.
Bertha Knight Landes of Seattle: Big City Mayor, University of Oklahoma Press (Norman), 1994.
"Organized Womanhood": Women's Clubs and Cultural Politics in the Pacific Northwest, 1875-1915, University of Oklahoma Press, 1995.

Work represented in anthologies, including *Mass Media and Culture,* edited by Jan Whitt, Allyn & Bacon, 1995. Author of "Local Comment," a biweekly column, *Idahoan/Daily News,* 1985—. Editor (under name Sandra Watkinson), *Idaho Reports,* 1975-77. Contributor of articles and reviews to periodicals, until 1977 under the name Sandra Watkinson.

WORK IN PROGRESS: Rainbows in the Water: The Story of Trout Ranching in Idaho's Hagerman Valley; The Conquest of Science and Technology: The Transformation of the Nobel Prizes into a Contest of National Excellence; Cruising: Crossing Alaska's 54th Parallel at Middle Age; research on the water crisis along the Snake River; research for a distance education handbook.

SIDELIGHTS: Sandra Haarsager told *CA:* "After I left college, I sought a job that would pay me, if not for writing the Great American Novel, at least for writing. I found that job at my hometown newspaper and began a career with words and journalism that has taken me through voracious professional assignments and into a place where I can write books.

"The journalistic training and experience, especially in the power of observation and the skills for conducting interviews, have stood me in good stead for writing nonfiction. I also use that journalistic mindset, that innate curiosity about how the world works and a drive to explain it as much to myself as to readers, as a touchstone for what might make interesting reading. I set artificial deadlines and hear the ghosts of editors past when I sit down to write. My subsequent academic training in American studies heightened my research skills and cultural perspective, and my work as a newspaper columnist personalized my writing.

"Unlike some writers, I love the process of research. I have colleagues who cannot understand how I can go from a political biography to writing about trout ranching, but I found them both interesting topics worthy of study.

"As I move into the uncharted territory of middle age, I find myself increasingly attached to the Pacific Northwest and Idaho, a region of the country

that, at least until recently, has been largely a void on the country's cultural map. I feel a strong sense of place, and my current projects reflect that orientation and the conflicts swirling around the region's natural resources, public lands, and ways of life. I hope to create a greater understanding of both the history and culture of the region through the books I write."

*   *   *

HAAS, Carol 1949-

PERSONAL: Born November 8, 1949, in Allentown, PA; daughter of John (a retail manager) and Margaret Brandmeir; married Ken Haas (an advertising executive), October 16, 1974; children: Adam, Jake. *Education:* Moravian College, B.A., 1972; attended University of North Carolina at Chapel Hill, 1975; Woodrow Wilson College of Law, J.D., 1984.

ADDRESSES: Office—2849 Henderson Mill Rd., Atlanta, GA 30341.

CAREER: Private practice of law in Atlanta, GA, 1984—. Georgia State Bar, member, 1984—.

MEMBER: Georgia Writers.

AWARDS, HONORS: Georgi Award from Writers Foundation of America, 1993, for *Your Driving and the Law.*

WRITINGS:

Your Driving and the Law, Horizon Publishing, 1991.
In the World of Policitics, Barron's, 1991.
Engel v. Vitale, Enslow Publications, 1994.
The Consumer Reports Law Book, Consumer Reports Books (Yonkers, NY), 1994.

Columnist, *Atlanta Business Chronicle.*

WORK IN PROGRESS: The Fifty-Plus Guide to the Law, for Consumer Reports Books, completion expected in 1996; *A Case for Winning* (tentative title), a book on becoming a business success, with Jim Simmons.

*   *   *

HABER, Karen 1955-

PERSONAL: Born January 7, 1955, in Bronxville, NY; daughter of David Haber and Edythe Cohen Marinoff; married Robert Silverberg (a writer), February 14, 1987. *Education:* Cedar Crest College, B.A., 1976. *Avocational interests:* Antiques, music, theater, gardening, and crafts.

ADDRESSES: Home—P.O. Box 13160, Station E, Oakland, CA 94661. *Agent*—Chris Lott, Ralph Vicinanza Ltd., 111 Eighth Ave., Suite 1501, New York, NY 10011.

CAREER: Writer, editor, and journalist.

MEMBER: Science Fiction and Fantasy Writers of America, Friends of Ethnic Art (board member, 1992—).

WRITINGS:

(With husband, Robert Silverberg) *The Mutant Season,* Bantam/Spectra, 1990.
Thieves' Carnival (novella), Tor Books, 1990.
The Mutant Prime, Bantam/Spectra, 1991.
Mutant Star, Bantam/Spectra, 1992.
Mutant Legacy, Bantam/Spectra, 1993.

Coeditor with Silverberg of *Universe,* an anthology of original science fiction stories published by Bantam Doubleday Dell. Also author of numerous short stories and articles which have appeared in *Isaac Asimov's Science Fiction Magazine, Magazine of Fantasy and Science Fiction, Full Spectrum, Fires of the Past, Women of Darkness,* and *Journeys to the Twilight Zone,* as well as other journals and anthologies.

SIDELIGHTS: "I think that love of reading inevitably leads to writing," Karen Haber commented. "That was certainly the case for me: I was an early reader, drawn to books, magazines, and even the backs of cereal boxes. A trip to the library with my parents was a marvelous treat: I could roam the stacks, pulling out any books I fancied, and actually bring them home with me. By the time I was in grade school, I was writing my own little stories and had composed two books by the age of sixteen—now safely buried.

"After college, I pursued journalism because I enjoyed the people, the diversity, and the stimulation. What I didn't enjoy were the hours and low pay. Eventually, I was lured by fiction, and I found the field rewarding both artistically and in terms of compensation. (I like to have things both ways, however, and I still dally with a couple of articles a year, primarily on art-related topics.) I find writing to be an intriguing, slow-motion form of communication, peculiar for the quasi-intimate relationship it creates between reader and writer.

"Science fiction and fantasy keep the imagination fresh and vital. Dealing with what might be is so often more interesting than writing about what is: a broadening exercise for both reader and writer—one hopes."

*   *   *

HADDOCK, Lisa (Robyn) 1960-

PERSONAL: Born November 9, 1960, in Tulsa, OK; daughter of Benjamin (a factory foreman) and Elizabeth Anne (a legal secretary; maiden name, Foley) Haddock; partner of Lisa Ann Bell (a chef), beginning February 9, 1985. *Education:* University of Tulsa, B.A. (with honors), 1983, M.A., 1986; graduate study at Southern Illinois University—Edwardsville, 1983. *Politics:* "Progressive/liberal."

ADDRESSES: Home—Suffern, NY. *Office*—The *Record,* 150 River St., Hackensack, NJ 07601.

CAREER: University of Tulsa, Tulsa, OK, news editor and managing editor of *Collegian,* 1981-82, editor in chief, 1982-83; *St. Louis Globe-Democrat,* St. Louis, MO, clerk, 1984; substitute teacher at public schools in Tulsa, 1985; *Tulsa World,* Tulsa, copy editor, 1986-89; *The Record,* Hackensack, NJ, copy editor and layout editor, 1989—. Neighbor Newspapers, intern, 1982.

WRITINGS:

Edited Out (novel), Naiad Press (Tallahassee, FL), 1994.
Final Cut (novel), Naiad Press, 1995.

SIDELIGHTS: Lisa Haddock told *CA:* "My goal is to provide an entertaining, thought-provoking read for lesbian and gay readers."

*   *   *

HAINES, Richard W. 1957-

PERSONAL: Born August 24, 1957, in Westchester, NY; son of Richard D. (a music teacher) and Lesia (a music teacher) Haines. *Education:* New York University, B.F.A., 1979. *Politics:* Republican. *Religion:* "None."

ADDRESSES: Home—Apt. 4R, Dove Court, Croton on Hudson, NY 10520. *Office*—New Wave Film Distribution, Inc., 360 South Broadway, Suite 4, Yonkers, NY 10705.

CAREER: Independent film producer, director, distributor, and screenwriter. New Wave Film Distribution, Inc., Yonkers, NY, president, 1983—; staff writer for *The Perfect Vision* magazine, 1992-93. Film archivist, restoring *Carnival of Souls,* 1990. Film editor of *Stuck on You,* 1984; *The First Turn On,* 1986; and *Toxic Avenger,* 1988.

WRITINGS:

BOOKS

Technicolor Movies: The History of Dye Transfer Printing, McFarland and Co. (Jefferson, NC), 1993.

SCREENPLAYS; ALSO COPRODUCER AND DIRECTOR

Splatter University, New Wave, 1984.
Class of Nuke Em High, New Wave, 1986.
(And distributor) *Space Avenger,* New Wave, 1991.
(And distributor) *Head Games,* New Wave, 1993.
(And distributor) *Run for Cover in 3-D,* New Wave, 1995.

Also author and narrator of *The Archival Film Disc,* released by Motocade Entertainment, 1994.

*   *   *

HAINS, Harriet
See WATSON, Carol

*   *   *

HAIZLIP, Shirlee Taylor   1937-

PERSONAL: Born September 3, 1937, in Stratford, CT; daughter of Julian Augustus (a minister and teacher) and Margaret (Morris) Taylor; married Harold C. Haizlip (an educator); children: Deirdre, Melissa. *Education:* Wellesley College, B.A., 1959; Harvard University, M.A., 1966. *Politics:* Liberal Democrat. *Religion:* Baptist.

ADDRESSES: Home and office—1754 North Serrano Ave., Los Angeles, CA 90027. *Agent*—Faith Childs Literary Agency, 275 West Ninety-sixth St., New York, NY 10025.

CAREER: WBNB-TV, St. Thomas, U.S. Virgin Islands, general manager, 1975-81; WNET-TV, New York City, director of corporate communications, 1981-86; National Center for Film and Video Preservation, Los Angeles, CA, executive director, 1989-93. Tufts University, teaching fellow; Allergy Center (Boston, MA), editorial director. Registrar of Voters of New Haven, CT, campaign director, 1989.

MEMBER: P.E.N. West (member of board of directors), Women in Film.

AWARDS, HONORS: D.H.L. from University of New Haven, 1994.

WRITINGS:

The Sweeter the Juice, Simon & Schuster (New York, NY), 1994.

Work represented in anthologies. Contributor to *American Heritage.*

WORK IN PROGRESS: When the Lions Tell Their Stories; Tales of a Southern Family.

SIDELIGHTS: Shirlee Taylor Haizlip told *CA:* "My goal is to add more stories and insights about African Americans to our nation's literary treasure. It is necessary to fill many historical, sociological, and literary gaps with contributions that have been muted, distorted, avoided, and muffled from the beginning of this century's history."

*   *   *

HAKEEM, Brother Wali
See GILL, Walter

*   *   *

HALLIE, Philip P(aul)   1922-1994

OBITUARY NOTICE—See index for *CA* sketch: Born May 4, 1922, in Chicago, IL; died of cardiac arrest, August 7, 1994, in Middletown, CT. Educator and author. Hallie earned degrees from Grinnell College, Harvard University, and Oxford University before embarking on a career in academia. He taught philosophy at Nashville's Vanderbilt University from 1953 to 1964, then took a position with Wesleyan University in Connecticut. He remained there until his retirement in 1988 as the William Griffin Professor of Philosophy and Humanities. Hallie wrote a number of books on contemplative subjects, including *Scepticism, Man, and God, The Scar of Montaigne,* and *The Paradox of Cruelty,* but is perhaps best remembered for his 1979 tome *Lest Innocent Blood Be Shed: The Story of the Village of Le Chambon and How Goodness Happened There.* For several years Hallie researched the community in France, where residents banded together during World War II to keep over 2,500 Jews from being captured and sent to concentration camps by Nazi occupiers and collaborators. *Lest Innocent Blood Be Shed* was termed by *Harper's* writer Terrence Des

Pres "one of the rarest of books, the kind that can change the way we live."

OBITUARIES AND OTHER SOURCES:

BOOKS

Who's Who in America, 43rd edition, Marquis, 1984.

PERIODICALS

Chicago Tribune, August 10, 1994, sec. 1, p. 10.

* * *

HAMID, Ahmad A. 1948-

PERSONAL: Born October 10, 1948, in Egypt; son of Ahmad and Wagdia (Tantawi) Hamid; married Nevan El-Khorazaty; children: Shadi, Sherif. *Education:* Ain-Shams University, B.Sc., 1971, M.Sc., 1974; McMaster University, Ph.D., 1978. *Religion:* Moslem.

ADDRESSES: Home—209 Drakes Drum Dr., Bryn Mawr, PA 19010. *Office*—Department of Civil and Architectural Engineering, Drexel University, Philadelphia, PA 19104.

CAREER: University of Oklahoma, Norman, assistant professor, 1979-81; Drexel University, Philadelphia, PA, professor of civil engineering, 1982—. Consultant in structural engineering.

MEMBER: American Concrete Institute, American Society of Civil Engineers, American Society for Testing and Materials, Masonry Society.

WRITINGS:

(Coauthor) *Masonry Structures,* Prentice-Hall, 1994.

* * *

HAMM, Diane Johnston 1949-

PERSONAL: Born November 10, 1949, in Portland, OR; daughter of Harold David (a rancher, logger, and real estate agent) and Claire (a nurse; maiden name, Trueworthy) Johnston; married Jeffrey Hamm (a transportation director), December 29, 1971; children: Nathan, Jesse, Valarie. *Education:* Attended Beloit College, 1968-70; Montana State University, B.A., 1971; University of Washington, M.Ed., 1979. *Avocational interests:* Carpentry, drawing, reading, travel.

ADDRESSES: Office—525 Benton St., Port Townsend, WA 98368.

CAREER: Freelance writer, 1971—. Barranquilla, Colombia, teacher and community extension worker, 1973-75; Community School, Seattle, WA, workshop counselor, 1981-83; has also taught in Mexico and Spain. Health clinic, volunteer counselor, 1990—.

MEMBER: Society of Children's Book Writers and Illustrators.

AWARDS, HONORS: Outstanding Juvenile Fiction—Western Heritage Wrangler Award, National Cowboy Hall of Fame, 1990, and Reluctant Reader Choice, American Library Association, 1991, both for *Bunkhouse Journal;* Alternate Book of the Month Selection, 1992, for *Rockabye Farm.*

WRITINGS:

FOR CHILDREN

Grandma Drives a Motor Bed, illustrated by Charles Robinson, A. Whitman, 1987.
How Many Feet in the Bed, illustrated by Kate Salley Palmer, Simon & Schuster, 1991.
Laney's Lost Momma, illustrated by Sally G. Ward, A. Whitman, 1991.
Rockabye Farm, illustrated by Rick Brown, Simon & Schuster, 1992.

FOR YOUNG ADULTS

Bunkhouse Journal, Scribner's, 1990.
Second Family, Scribner's, 1992.

WORK IN PROGRESS: Two self-illustrated children's books, *Sleep Tight, Blue Ram* and *Let's Have a Picnic;* and *Borderline,* a novel for young adults,

SIDELIGHTS: "I grew up in rural Western Montana with three brothers and a sister in a television-free home," Diane Johnston Hamm commented in discussing the development of her writing skills. "As a young person I was a prolific letter and journal writer, and I discovered as I grew older that it was easier for me to express myself in writing than it was in person. . . . Writing allows me to explore what is important to me. When a manuscript is accepted, my observations go public."

Hamm's first book, *Grandma Drives a Motor Bed,* describes the observations of a curious little boy who visits his bedridden grandmother and joins friends, family, and professionals in caring for her.

Reviewing the book for *School Library Journal,* Virginia Opocensky describes it as a "realistic story of age and infirmity" filled with "gentle understanding and steadfast love," while a reviewer for the *Bulletin of the Center for Children's Books* suggests that it should be useful to children attempting to understand "their own experience of gerontological problems." *How Many Feet in the Bed* is a counting book for young children. In this "warm and cozy" book, as a reviewer for the *Children's Book Review Service* describes it, a mother, father, baby, and two children lounge in the bed on Sunday morning, and the little girl counts ten feet until, one by one, the family members leave the bed to begin the day.

Laney's Lost Momma is for somewhat older children. When Laney's mother disappears in the department store, both Laney and her mother remember Momma's warnings that Laney should never leave a store without her. After a frantic search, Laney asks a salesman for help, and Laney and her mother are reunited. Deborah Abbott, writing for *Booklist,* assures readers that "Hamm handles the traumatic experience adroitly, including the emotional jitters of both mother and child." *Rockabye Farm,* another book for young children, will, according to a *Publishers Weekly* critic, "surely soothe youngsters." The farmer in this bedtime story rocks his baby to sleep and then his dog, chicken, cow, and horse as well. After all this work, the farmer sits in a chair and rocks himself to sleep. "With its low-key humor and lullaby cadence, the book is as warm and reassuring as a hug," Marge Loch-Wouters writes in the *School Library Journal.*

Hamm was inspired to write her first book for young adults after reading the published letters of a pioneer woman. In *Bunkhouse Journal,* a novel set around the year 1910, sixteen-year-old Sandy Mannix has run away from his alcoholic father in Denver. His journal entries record his life on a ranch and his attempts to deal with the anger and guilt he feels towards his father. Through the relationships he develops on the ranch, including a blossoming romance, he begins to forge a new life for himself and makes the decision to depart for college. Gladys Hardcastle writes in *Voice of Youth Advocates* that readers should find Sandy to be an engaging and realistic character: "The writing style and vocabulary of a 16 year old are exceptionally well represented and highly believable, as well as beautifully expressed." Martha V. Parravano praises Hamm's "sense of people, time and place" in *Horn Book,* and a reviewer for *Publishers Weekly* concludes that "Hamm's novel offers many rewards."

In *Second Family,* a "realistic and touching novel," according to Kay Weisman in *Booklist,* "Hamm portrays the themes of loneliness and adjusting to new life situations." When Catherine Donovue, a divorcee, and her twelve-year-old son, Rodney, move in to live with lonely Mr. Torkleson, a widower, all three have difficulties adjusting to each other and to their new life situations. Eventually, despite Catherine's attempts to busy herself with graduate school and Rodney's shoplifting scheme, the three learn to respect each other and communicate more effectively. Maria B. Salvadore, writing in *School Library Journal,* comments that "this contemporary, realistic novel moves swiftly to a credible, satisfying conclusion."

Hamm's books for children and young adults encompass a wide variety of characters and situations. Explaining her ability to create realistic and engaging works, Hamm commented: "I am more a 'muser' than a storyteller. I always start by wondering—wondering about a situation or a character trait. Story line develops from there." Hamm, who has lived in Mexico, Colombia, and Spain, and now lives in Washington state with her husband and children, has been writing since the 1970s and is developing her talent for drawing. "It suits my style to be at one time wayfarer, researcher, philosopher, and guide," she remarked. "I trust that I will never write a story that does not leave both me and the reader feeling strengthened and hopeful."

BIOGRAPHICAL/CRITICAL SOURCES:

PERIODICALS

Booklist, December 15, 1987, p. 707; March 15, 1991, p. 1481; July, 1991, p. 2050; January 1, 1992, p. 834; November 1, 1992, p. 513.

Bulletin of the Center for Children's Books, December, 1987, p. 65.

Children's Book Review Service, September, 1991, p. 2.

Horn Book, November, 1990, p. 748.

Publishers Weekly, August 31, 1990, p. 69; June 22, 1992, p. 60.

School Library Journal, January, 1988, pp. 65-66; December, 1990, p. 102; October, 1991, p. 95; December, 1991, p. 92; July, 1992, p. 59; January, 1993, p. 106.

Voice of Youth Advocates, December, 1990, p. 282.

*   *   *

HANLON, Gregory 1953-

PERSONAL: Born August 29, 1953, in Toronto,

Ontario, Canada; son of Thomas (a factory worker and foreman) and Joyce (Tassie) Hanlon; married Anne Lesimple (an instructor in French), October 24, 1981; children: Ariane. *Education:* Universite de Bordeaux, *licence,* 1977, *doctorat,* 1983; University of Toronto, M.A., 1978. *Politics:* "Small 'l' liberal: undogmatic (antidogmatic!)." *Religion:* "None (born Roman Catholic)."

ADDRESSES: Home—5539 Columbus Pl., Halifax, Nova Scotia, Canada B3K 2G7. *Office*—Department of History, Dalhousie University, Halifax, Nova Scotia, Canada B3H 2J5.

CAREER: York University, Toronto, Ontario, Canada, part-time history teacher, 1983-88; University of California, Berkeley, visiting assistant professor of history, 1988-89; Dalhousie University, Halifax, Nova Scotia, Canada, associate professor of history, 1989—. Universite de Laval, adjunct professor, 1993.

MEMBER: Society for Academic Freedom and Scholarship.

AWARDS, HONORS: Brewer Prize from American Association of Church History, 1992, for *Community and Confession in Seventeenth-Century France;* research grants.

WRITINGS:

L'Univers des gens de bien: Culture et comportements des elites urbaines en Aquitaine au 17e siecle, Presses Universitaires de Bordeaux, 1989.
Community and Confession in Seventeenth-Century France: Catholic and Protestant Coexistence in Aquitaine, University of Pennsylvania Press, 1993.

Contributor to periodicals.

WORK IN PROGRESS: The Decline of the Italian Military Tradition, 1560-1800; The Origins of Modern Italy, 1560-1800, completion expected in 1996; *Authority and Deference on Baroque Tuscany, c. 1570 - c. 1740.*

SIDELIGHTS: Gregory Hanlon told *CA:* "History has been my dominant passion and the center of my life since the moment I understood the concept of it, at the age of six or seven. I was shaped unconsciously thereafter by my agnostic and left-leaning father, who, despite being an inarticulate proletarian, knew a great deal about many things. My parents were willing to finance my formative years in

university in France. It was clearly a gamble, but in France I discovered (quite by accident) those trends and questions in cultural history that were taking the world by storm. My professors had all been trained in economic and demographical history; they were number-crunchers who nevertheless were operating the transition from great impersonal forces in history to those of human goals and actions. What I never doubted was the importance of evidence, as much of it, and as varied, as possible.

"Early modern Europe is the field where I apply my curiosity to problems of human behavior and motivation. I have no clear idea yet of the final implications of what I'm trying to say. I work most often on problems relating to the divergence between ideals and beliefs (which are articulate), on the one hand, and behavior (which is usually not), on the other. We frequently assume that the first *cause* (or incite or motivate, etc.) the second, but my explorations in social psychology lead me to doubt this. My books and articles have almost all dealt with this theme. My thesis staked out the problems of behavior in the baroque period. My second book explored the existence of tolerance in the complete absence of any accepted justification for it, and the processes of social integration leading to the absorption of the tolerated minority. It also led me into problems of the purpose of institutions and sanctioned ideological structures and systems, which I am exploring in my ongoing research into authority and deference. This work is guided and prodded by social psychologists like Serge Moscovici, Jean-Pierre Deconchy, and the sociology of Raymond Boudon.

"My work differs from that of most North American scholars exploring social and cultural history in Europe, and the difference lies in the subordination of theory to archival spade work. This is the single most important piece of advice I could give to any aspiring historian. Most European societies generated enormous quantities of records, of many different kinds. The range of potentially interesting sources is considerable—but they require the knowledge of the handwriting, familiarity with the jurisdictions, and recognition of their purpose; all sources contain hidden shortcomings. The traps in the documentation can often be overcome by turning to several different kinds of sources and consulting each in sufficient quantity to derive a sense of the normal and the possible. Only then should one resort to social theory to help explain the data. If the data do not match the theory, the theory must be jettisoned.

"As I become conversant with the aims and products of North American graduate schools, I am increasingly struck by how little practical training future historians receive, and how little methodological sophistication is expected of them. This partly has practical reasons, for serious research takes time and trouble, and costs money. The danger, however, is that historians can be buffeted back and forth by the prevailing winds of social history, lacking a heavy anchor in the banality of facts."

*   *   *

HANSEN, Debra Gold   1953-

PERSONAL: Born September 16, 1953, in Orange, CA; daughter of James M. (a financial analyst) and Jean (a homemaker) Gold; married Arthur A. Hansen (a historian), June 25, 1977. *Education:* California State University, Fullerton, B.A. (with high honors), 1975, M.A., 1979; University of California, Los Angeles, M.L.S., 1983; University of California, Irvine, Ph.D., 1988. *Avocational interests:* Quilting, gardening, hiking.

ADDRESSES: Home—Yorba Linda, CA. *Office*—California State University, P.O. Box 1450, Fullerton, CA 92634.

CAREER: Claremont Colleges, Claremont, CA, history bibliographer and reference librarian at Honnold Library, 1984-89; Anaheim Public Library, Anaheim, CA, archivist, 1989-90; San Jose State University, San Jose, CA, assistant professor of library and information science, 1989—. Pomona College, assistant coordinator of bibliographic instruction, 1988-89; California State University, Fullerton, instructor, 1990. California State Archives, editor of California State Legislature Oral History Project, 1991-93.

MEMBER: Organization of American Historians, Radical Historians, Oral History Association, American Library Association, Society of California Archivists.

AWARDS, HONORS: Grant from American Philosophical Society, 1994.

WRITINGS:

Strained Sisterhood: Gender and Class in the Boston Female Anti-Slavery Society, University of Massachusetts Press, 1993.

Work represented in anthologies, including *Post-suburban California: The Transformation of Orange County since World War II,* edited by Rob Kling, Spencer Olin, and Mark Poster, University of California Press, 1991; and *The Abolitionist Sisterhood: Antislavery and Women's Political Culture,* edited by Jean Fagan Yellin and John Van Horne, Cornell University Press, 1994. Contributor of articles and reviews to history and library journals. Newsletter editor, American Society of Indexers, 1980-82; associate editor, *Oral History Review,* 1980-87; resources editor, *Journal of Orange County Studies,* 1988-92.

WORK IN PROGRESS: Research on the feminization of librarianship, 1880-1920.

SIDELIGHTS: Debra Gold Hansen told *CA:* "While employed as a librarian during my graduate school years, I became intrigued by the experience of working in a profession dominated by women. I was equally intrigued, if not dismayed, by the persistence of the bun-toting, shushing librarian portrayed in the popular media, though rarely did I encounter such a librarian on the job. As a consequence, I now have begun research into the feminization of librarianship to discover why and how an occupation becomes feminized and determine the consequences for both the woman worker and the profession itself."

*   *   *

HARGROVE, Erwin C.   1930-

PERSONAL: Born October 11, 1930, in St. Joseph, MO; son of Erwin C. and Gladys (France) Hargrove; married; three children. *Education:* Yale University, B.A., 1953, Ph.D., 1963.

ADDRESSES: Home—662 Timber Lane, Nashville, TN 37215. *Office*—Department of Political Science, Vanderbilt University, Nashville, TN 37235.

CAREER: Brown University, Providence, RI, member of faculty, 1960-76, professor of political science and department chairperson, 1971-73; Urban Institute, Washington, DC, senior fellow, 1973-75; Vanderbilt University, Nashville, TN, professor of political science, 1976—, director of Institute for Policy Studies, 1976-85, department chairperson, 1992-94.

AWARDS, HONORS: Richard Neustadt award, Presidential Research Group of the American Political Science Association, 1988, for *Jimmy Carter as President: Leadership and the Politics of the Public Good;* Jeffrey Nordhaus award, College of Arts and

Sciences, Vanderbilt University, 1988, and Madison Sarratt award, Vanderbilt University, 1990, both for excellence in undergraduate teaching; Vanderbilt University Alumni Education Award, 1994.

WRITINGS:

Presidential Leadership: Personality and Political Style, Macmillan, 1966.

Professional Roles in Society and Government: The English Case, Sage Publications, 1972.

The Power of the Modern Presidency, foreword by Harold D. Lasswell, Temple University Press, 1974.

The Missing Link: The Study of the Implementation of Social Policy, Urban Institute, 1975.

(With Roy Hoopes) *The Presidency: A Question of Power,* Educational Associates, 1975.

The Search for Implementation Theory, Institute for Public Policy Studies, 1981.

Regulation and Schools: The Implementation of Equal Education for Handicapped Children, Institute for Public Policy Studies, 1982.

(Editor with Paul K. Conkin) *Tennessee Valley Authority: Fifty Years of Grass-Roots Bureaucracy,* University of Illinois Press, 1983.

(With Michael Nelson) *Presidents, Politics, and Policy,* Johns Hopkins University Press, 1984.

(Editor with Samuel A. Morley) *The President and the Council of Economic Advisors: Interviews with the C.E.A. Chairmen,* Westview Press, 1984.

(Editor with Jameson W. Doig) *Leadership and Innovation: A Biographical Perspective on Entrepreneurs in Government,* Johns Hopkins University Press, 1987.

Jimmy Carter as President: Leadership and the Politics of the Public Good, Louisiana State University Press, 1988.

(Editor with John C. Glidewell) *Impossible Jobs in Public Management,* University Press of Kansas, 1990.

Prisoners of Myth: Leadership of the Tennessee Valley Authority, 1933-1990, Princeton University Press, 1994.

SIDELIGHTS: A professor of political science at Vanderbilt University, Erwin C. Hargrove is the author of several volumes on twentieth-century American politics. His first published work was *Presidential Leadership: Personality and Political Style,* which appeared in 1966. Later Hargrove achieved prominence with further studies on various facets of the presidency and government policy. These works include *The Power of the Modern Presidency,* published in 1974, and *The Presidency: A Question of Power,* a 1975 book written with Roy Hoopes.

In 1981 Hargrove, through Vanderbilt University's Institute for Public Policy Studies, was involved in a symposium marking the fiftieth anniversary of the Tennessee Valley Authority (TVA). The essays presented there were published in the 1983 volume *Tennessee Valley Authority: Fifty Years of Grass-Roots Bureaucracy,* a book Hargrove edited with Paul K. Conkin. The TVA originated in the 1930s as part of a vast social welfare program and is perhaps best known for its success in harnessing the power of the area's rivers. The TVA's system of dams and hydroelectric plants brought electricity and running water to millions of people in Appalachia. At the time, this was one of the poorest sections of the country and its rural inhabitants had benefited little from the advances of the twentieth century.

During its first five decades the TVA became a major regional development agency with great influence in the South. The essays in Hargrove and Conkin's book analyze both the effectiveness of the TVA's original goals and its ongoing administrative problems. The conference participants and contributors to *Tennessee Valley Authority* are economists, political scientists, and historians, and most of the essays concentrate on the bureaucratic personality of the agency rather than its overall social impact. The work is divided into four sections that examine the history of the TVA, its leadership, certain legal issues, and its overall political legacy. Conkin contributed an essay that explores the restrictions placed on the TVA from its inception, contradicting its image as a bastion of decentralized progressivism.

William R. Childs, writing in *South Atlantic Quarterly,* remarked that "the reader will discover some important insights among the jargon-laden social science essays" in Hargrove and Conkin's *Tennessee Valley Authority. Political Science Quarterly* contributor John T. Tierney termed the book "a comprehensive and balanced portrait of America's most famous regional development agency" and "a valuable contribution to the literature on government agencies."

One of Hargrove's studies of the American presidency is entitled *Presidents, Politics, and Policy.* This work, written with Michael Nelson, appeared in 1984 and examines the executive branch of the United States government and its relationship to the rest of the country's political infrastructure. To explore these issues, the authors analyze several aspects of each twentieth-century presidential administration. These factors center around the leadership qualities of men such as Franklin D. Roosevelt and

John F. Kennedy and the manner in which they were able, or unable, to implement their individual and partisan political agendas. Hargrove and Nelson analyze shifts in policy and effectiveness and critique the merits and shortcomings of the presidency itself.

Included in *Presidents, Politics, and Policy* are chapters examining other elements related to the executive branch, such as its constitutional powers. I. M. Destler, writing in *Political Science Quarterly,* commended this last facet of Hargrove and Nelson's book, noting that "since the analysis everywhere is of high quality, this eclecticism adds breadth and insight." *Virginia Quarterly Review* contributor James Deakin asserted that *Presidents, Politics, and Policy* "reeks of common sense." Deakin admitted that Hargrove and Nelson's thesis "is not as glamorous as some other theories of the presidency, but it covers more ground and therefore explains more."

Hargrove is also the author of several other volumes on the subject of the presidency, including 1984's *The President and the Council of Economic Advisors: Interviews with the C.E.A. Chairmen,* edited with Samuel A. Morley, and 1988's *Jimmy Carter as President: Leadership and the Politics of the Public Good.*

BIOGRAPHICAL/CRITICAL SOURCES:

PERIODICALS

Political Science Quarterly, fall, 1984; winter, 1985-86.
South Atlantic Quarterly, summer, 1985, pp. 336-37.
Virginia Quarterly Review, autumn, 1985.

*   *   *

HARKABI, Yehoshafat   1921-1994

OBITUARY NOTICE—See index for *CA* sketch: Born September 21, 1921, in Haifa, Israel; died of cancer, August 26, 1994, in Jerusalem, Israel. Intelligence expert, educator, and writer. Harkabi fought in Israel's 1948 war for independence, then acted as a negotiator for Israel with its neighboring countries. Educated at Hebrew University and Harvard University, he served as head of military intelligence for Israel until 1959, later taking a position with the Ministry of Defense. For much of his career Harkabi espoused a moderate approach toward the strained relationship between Israel and Palestine, advocating a compromise that was not achieved until 1993. In 1968 he left the Israeli government to become

professor of international relations and Middle Eastern Studies at his alma mater, Hebrew University of Jerusalem. There he rose to chair of the department and director of the Leonard Davis Institute for International Relations. He also taught at Israeli National Defense College. Harkabi wrote a number of books that sought to clarify the emotional and divisive conflict between Israel and its Arab neighbors, including *Arab Attitudes to Israel, The Palestinian Covenant and Its Meaning,* and *Israel's Fateful Hour.* At the time of his death his last book, *War and Strategy,* was being translated for English publication.

OBITUARIES AND OTHER SOURCES:

BOOKS

Who's Who in the World, 5th edition, Marquis, 1980.

PERIODICALS

New York Times, August 27, 1994, p. 10.

*   *   *

HARRIS, James F.   1941-

PERSONAL: Born June 30, 1941, in Nashville, TN; son of James F. (in sales) and Martha (a schoolteacher; maiden name, Elder) Harris; married Peggy Young, June, 1994; children: James F. III. *Education:* University of Georgia, B.A., 1962; Vanderbilt University, Ph.D., 1966. *Avocational interests:* Fishing.

ADDRESSES: Home—3721 Salt Pan Lane, White Marsh, VA 23183. *Office*—Department of Philosophy, College of William and Mary, Williamsburg, VA 23187.

CAREER: Transylvania University, Lexington, KY, assistant professor of philosophy, 1966-67; University of Georgia, Athens, assistant professor of history, 1967-73; College of William and Mary, Williamsburg, VA, Haserot Professor of Philosophy, 1974—. Virginia Living Museum, volunteer, 1991—.

MEMBER: American Philosophical Association, Southern Society for Philosophy and Psychology (president, 1992-93), Phi Beta Kappa.

AWARDS, HONORS: Fellow of American Council of Learned Societies.

WRITINGS:

Analyticity, Quadrangle, 1970.
Against Relativism, Open Court (Chicago, IL), 1992.
Single Malt Whiskies of Scotland, Open Court, 1992.
Philosophy at 33 1/3 RPM: Themes of Classic Rock Music, Open Court, 1993.
American Classic Whiskies, Open Court, 1995.
Relativism: For and Against, Open Court, in press.

*   *   *

HARRIS, Ruth Elwin 1935-

PERSONAL: Born June 22, 1935, in Bristol, England; daughter of Herbert Elwin (a surgeon) and Rowena (a children's nurse; maiden name, Clarkson) Harris; married Christopher John Lincoln Bowes (an accountant), July 25, 1964; children: Jonathan, Jennifer, Richard.

ADDRESSES: Contact—c/o Random House, 20 Vauxhall Bridge Rd., London SW1V 2SA, England.

CAREER: Author.

MEMBER: Society of Authors.

AWARDS, HONORS: Shortlist, *Observer* Teenage Fiction Award, 1986, for *The Silent Shore.*

WRITINGS:

"QUANTOCKS QUARTET" NOVEL SERIES

The Silent Shore, Julia MacRae Books (London), 1986.
The Beckoning Hills, Julia MacRae Books, 1987.
The Dividing Sea, Julia MacRae Books, 1989.
Beyond the Orchid House, Julia MacRae Books, 1994.

OTHER

Billie: The Nevill Letters, 1914-1916, Julia MacRae Books, 1991.

Author of articles and short stories; also author of broadcasts for the British Broadcasting, Corporation (BBC).

SIDELIGHTS: Ruth Elwin Harris is the author of a series of historical novels that features the four orphaned Purcell sisters and is set during the early 1900s. In the first volume, *The Silent Shore,* the author covers the years 1910 to 1920 by focusing on the youngest sister, Sarah, who has a crush on Gabriel Mackenzie, the son of their next-door neighbor and guardian. Sarah is contrasted with Frances, the oldest Purcell sister and, in a family of talented artists, the most accomplished and ambitious. The romance between Gabriel and Frances is portrayed through Sarah's eyes. Sarah initially judges her sister harshly for Frances's decision not to give up her career in order to marry Gabriel before he leaves for the war. Brian Alderson of the London *Times* saw in *The Silent Shore* and the promise of subsequent volumes, "what may be the *Little Women* of our times." Although Miranda Seymour of the *Times Literary Supplement* warned the author against "an occasional tendency to let virtuous thoughts get the better of her writing," she also averred: "*The Silent Shore* is, in the best sense of that usually derogatory term, an old-fashioned book, a good read with a strong moral underpinning."

The second installment in the series, *The Beckoning Hills,* was equally well-received. Covering the same time period through the eyes of Frances Purcell, Harris provides a more adult view of the years directly preceding the First World War and of the challenges and changes wrought by the war itself. Although the duplication of scenes and dialogue between these first two volumes in the series was deemed a weakness by *Times Literary Supplement* contributor Deborah White, the critic also noted that the book highlights Harris's strengths as a novelist: "Ruth Elwin Harris identifies totally with her characters, her style is direct and unaffected, and her plot development rapid." White judged that, particularly if Harris allows her characters to grow beyond the 1910-20 period defined in the first volume, future works in the series are equally likely to "enthrall teenage readers."

Ruth Elwin Harris told *CA:* "I am working on a group of novels about four sisters, of which *The Silent Shore* is the first, portraying in turn each of the four Purcell sisters. Opening in 1910, shortly before the death of King Edward VII, and set in the West Country of England, London, France during World War One, Ireland, and India, the series explores family relationships and the differing effects of genius and talent on such relationships; while in the background the fabric of society with its ideals and illusions is beginning to crumble and, with the Troubles in Ireland, the British Empire to disintegrate.

"I use my novels to explore, consciously (and sometimes subconsciously), situations and subjects that interest me—relationships, for instance, particularly sibling relationships. I am also fascinated by the differences between talent and genius, and the effect of genius on those close to it. Latterly, I have become interested in the long term effect of being orphaned early in life, and I may well explore this in an extension of the Quantocks Quartet."

Billie: The Nevill Letters, 1914-1916 is Harris's only nonfiction book and is based on the letters of the Nevill family. The letters are housed in the Imperial War Museum in London and were, in large part, authored by Captain Wilfred Percy Nevill, a British Army officer in World War I, who achieved fame during his short life by providing footballs for his men to kick across no man's land in the attack on the first day of the Battle of the Somme.

Harris completed her Quantocks Quartet series in 1994, with the publication of *Beyond the Orchid House,* which concludes the tale of the Purcell family.

BIOGRAPHICAL/CRITICAL SOURCES:

PERIODICALS

Times (London), July 3, 1986.
Times Literary Supplement, April 25, 1986, p. 458; February 19, 1988, p. 200.

*   *   *

HARRIS, Wayne T. (Sr.) 1954-

PERSONAL: Born June 9, 1954; son of Arthur and Frances Olivia (a homemaker; maiden name, Morton) Harris; married Deidra LaVaun Jones (a corporate trust officer), August 5, 1978; children: Wayne T., Jr., Jonathan Quincy, Kristal Faith. *Education:* Birmingham Baptist Bible College, B.A., B.Th., 1977; Alabama Christian School of Religion, M.A., 1977; Southern Baptist Bible Seminary, D.D., 1978; Trinity Theological Seminary, Ph.D., 1992.

ADDRESSES: Office—Mount Olive Missionary Baptist Church, 1003 West 16th St., Indianapolis, IN 46202.

CAREER: Mount Olive Missionary Baptist Church, Indianapolis, IN, senior pastor. Mount Olive Critical Care Center and Shelter, founder and administrator; IUPUI Center on Philanthropy, charter associate. Candidate for mayor of Indianapolis, 1990.

MEMBER: Baptist Ministers Alliance, Concerned Clergy.

AWARDS, HONORS: Ashorne-Sanders Award for

community service; Excellence Award from Operation PUSH.

WRITINGS:

Biblical Authority on Controversial Issues, Winston-Derek (Nashville, TN), 1992.
Umph, Umph, Umph . . . , First Quality Publishers, 1993.

Other books include *All Is Not Well in Naptown,* Sirrah Publishers; *Church Talk I and II: The Ephesian Letter,* Mount Olive Press; and *A Perspective from a Black Man to Black Men,* 1994.

SIDELIGHTS: Wayne T. Harris told *CA:* "I love the Lord. I love people, and I write out of a sense of urgency and need to address spiritual and social ills."

*   *   *

HARRISON, Joan (Mary) 1909-1994

OBITUARY NOTICE—See index for *CA* sketch: Born June 20, 1909 (one source cites 1911), in Guildford, Surrey, England; died August 11, 1994, in London, England. Producer and screenwriter. Harrison, who began her film career in 1933 as a secretary to noted British director Alfred Hitchcock, became one of the first women to write and produce feature films in Hollywood. Moving quickly beyond the scope of secretarial work, Harrison learned every aspect of filmmaking during eight years under Hitchcock's tutelage, collaborating with him on such well-known and highly acclaimed screenplays as *Foreign Correspondent, Suspicion,* and *Saboteur.* During the 1940s, Harrison wrote screenplays and produced films for Metro-Goldwyn-Mayer and Universal, one of the few women to do so within the old Hollywood studio system. She produced eight films, including the 1944 film noir, *Phantom Lady, Nocturne* (1946), *Ride the Pink Horse* (1947), *Once More, My Darling* (1949), and *Circle of Danger* (1950). Her work was considered subtle, intelligent, and stylish, distinguished by strong women characters, elegance in sets and costuming, and a preference for well-photographed, suspenseful action over graphic displays of violence. From 1953 to 1964, she once again worked with Hitchcock, as producer of his television series, *Alfred Hitchcock Presents* and *The Alfred Hitchcock Hour.* Among her writing credits are her own 1944 film, *Dark Waters,* and numerous Hitchcock collaborations, including *Jamaica Inn* and *Rebecca,* which won the 1940 Academy Award for best picture.

OBITUARIES AND OTHER SOURCES:

BOOKS

International Dictionary of Films and Filmmakers, Volume 4: *Writers and Production Artists,* St. James Press, 1987.

PERIODICALS

New York Times, August 25, 1994, p. D19.

*   *   *

HART, Lynda 1953-

PERSONAL: Born August 23, 1953, in Memphis, TN; daughter of Harold (a journalist) and Billie (a sales manager; maiden name, Luther) Hart. *Education:* Memphis State University, B.A., 1976; Tulane University, M.A., 1977, Ph.D., 1984.

ADDRESSES: Home—2 Washington Square Village, #1A, New York, NY 10012. *Office*—3440 Walnut, 119 Bennett Hall, University of Pennsylvania, Philadelphia, PA 19104.

CAREER: Xavier University, Cincinnati, OH, assistant professor of English and director of women's studies, 1984-88; University of Pennsylvania, Philadelphia, PA, associate professor of English and theater, 1988—.

MEMBER: Modern Language Association, Association for Theater in Higher Education.

WRITINGS:

Sam Shepard's Metaphorical Stages, Greenwood Press (Westport, CT), 1987.
(Editor) *Making a Spectacle: Feminist Essays on Contemporary Women's Theatre,* University of Michigan Press (Ann Arbor), 1989.
(Editor with Peggy Phelan) *Acting Out: Feminist Performance,* University of Michigan Press (Ann Arbor), 1993.
Fatal Women: Lesbian Sexuality and the Mark of Aggression, Princeton University Press (Princeton, NJ), 1994.

WORK IN PROGRESS: Between the Body and the Flesh, a book about erotic practices between women in the context of debates over censorship and pornography, to be published by Columbia University Press.

SIDELIGHTS: Lynda Hart told *CA:* "My writing has always been about performances. Beginning with *Making a Spectacle,* I began to move away from the rigid boundaries of academic disciplines. *Acting Out* and *Fatal Women* push even harder at these limits.

"The feminist slogan of the '70s—'The personal is political'—is still resisted in academic discourse. In part, I write to overcome that resistance."

*   *   *

HASSALL, William Owen 1912-1994

OBITUARY NOTICE—See index for *CA* sketch: Born August 4, 1912, in York, England; died July 19, 1994, in England. Librarian, medievalist, and author. During his career at Oxford University's Bodleian Library, Hassall developed a rare microfilm collection of medieval illuminated manuscripts designed to provide scholars with hard-to-find illustrations of medieval life. Hassall's worked at Oxford University, from 1938 to 1980, and as librarian to the Earls of Leicester, from 1937 to 1983. He served in World War II. In 1942, Hassall joined the Royal Artillery of the British army. He was soon transferred to the Ministry of Economic Warfare, where he served as a researcher, gathering and disseminating intelligence information for the Allies. He traveled to Germany after the war to re-establish contact with university libraries throughout Germany. While there he also gathered examples of Nazi war propaganda for historical records. In addition to the management of medieval manuscripts and local historical documents which characterized his primary career, Hassall was an examiner in history for the Oxford Institutes of Education and for several other universities. He authored books about history for both scholarly and general interest readership. Among his publications are *They Saw It Happen: An Anthology of Eye-witnesses' Accounts for Events in British History, 55 B.C.-A.D. 1485, Treasures from the Bodleian,* and *History through Surnames.* The latter resulted in a radio series featuring research and information about listeners' names. His final collaboration, *Lordship and Landscape in Norfolk 1250-1350,* was published in 1994, prior to his death.

OBITUARIES AND OTHER SOURCES:

BOOKS

Who's Who, 146th edition, St. Martin's, 1994, p. 846.

PERIODICALS

Times (London), July 29, 1994, p. 21.

HASTORF, Christine Ann   1950-

PERSONAL: Born December 7, 1950, in Hanover, NH. *Education:* Stanford University, B.A., 1972; University of California, Los Angeles, M.A., 1977, Ph.D., 1983.

ADDRESSES: Office—Department of Anthropology, University of California, Berkeley, CA 94720.

CAREER: U.S. Geological Survey, Division of Western Regional Geology, Menlo Park, CA, archaeologist, 1977-79, 1980-82; University of Minnesota—Twin Cities, Minneapolis, assistant professor, 1983-90, associate professor of anthropology, 1990-93, director of Archaeobotany Laboratory, 1983-93; University of California, Berkeley, associate professor of anthropology, 1994—. Guest lecturer at University of Wisconsin—Madison, St. Thomas College, State Universities of New York, Columbia University, Stanford University, Universities of Southampton, Sheffield, and London, University of Iowa, Hamline University, and Northern Illinois University. Conducted extensive field work in the Peruvian Andes, including the Upper Mantaro and Pancan; adviser to field teams in Bolivia and Denmark.

AWARDS, HONORS: Fulbright grant, 1979-80; grants from National Science Foundation, 1982—, McMillan Travel Fund, University of Minnesota, 1983-86, Dow Chemical Co., 1985-86, Control Data Corp., 1986-87, McKnight Foundation, 1987-90, Winton Conference Fund, 1990, and Stahl Foundation, 1994; fellow, Center for Advanced Study in the Behavioral Sciences, Palo Alto, CA, 1986-87.

WRITINGS:

(Editor with V. Popper, and contributor) *Current Paleoethnobotany: Analytical Methods and Cultural Interpretation of Archaeological Plant Remains,* University of Chicago Press (Chicago, IL), 1988.
(Editor with M. W. Conkey, and contributor) *The Uses of Style in Archaeology,* Cambridge University Press, 1990, 2nd edition, 1993.
Agriculture and the Onset of Political Inequality before the Inka, Cambridge University Press, 1993.
(Editor with S. Johannessen, and contributor) *Corn and Culture in the Prehistoric New World,* Westview (Boulder, CO), 1994.

Work represented in anthologies, including *The Evolution of Political Systems,* edited by S. Upham, Cambridge University Press, 1990; *Engendering Archaeology: Women and Prehistory,* edited by J. Gero and M. Conkey, Basil Blackwell, 1991; and *Inka Storage Systems,* edited by T. LeVine, University of Oklahoma Press, 1992. Contributor of about forty articles and reviews to professional journals, including *American Antiquity, Nature,* and *Science.*

WORK IN PROGRESS: Research on the Andean region of South America, the archaeology of political complexity and social theory, prehistoric agricultural systems, paleoethnobotany and food in culture, and social relations.

*   *   *

HATFIELD, Phyllis   1944-

PERSONAL: Born August 12, 1944, in Akron, OH; daughter of Albert L. (a certified public accountant) and Janet (a homemaker; maiden name, Abramson) Schultz; married James Barrie Hatfield (divorced, 1971). *Education:* Attended Simmons College, 1962-64. *Politics:* Democratic Socialists of America. *Religion:* Jewish. *Avocational interests:* Piano, chamber music, hiking.

ADDRESSES: Home and office—906 Thirty-Third Ave. South, Seattle, WA 98144. *Agent*—Arthur Orrmont, 340 East Fifty-Second St., New York, NY 10022.

CAREER: Founder of word processing business, 1980; became freelance book editor.

MEMBER: American Civil Liberties Union, Jewish Peace Lobby, Women's Funding Alliance.

WRITINGS:

Pencil Me In: A Memoir of Stanley Olson, Andre Deutsch (London, England), 1994.

SIDELIGHTS: Phyllis Hatfield provided the following commentary to *CA,* based on excerpts from a reading she gave at Elliott Bay Book Company in Seattle, Washington: "My publisher described Stanley Olson on the dust jacket as 'scholar, writer, biographer, dandy, aesthete, gourmet and impeccable host.' A friend of mine, after reading *Pencil Me In,* described him as 'an exasperating, fascinating, lovable, talented gustatorian.' He was all those things and more—so many that for most of my adult life I found him indescribable. I'd fall mute when friends asked me to tell about the character I'd just visited in London, or the man who'd just sent me a letter that I simply *had* to read aloud to them. I think I had to write this book in order to describe him to myself, so that I could then describe him to my friends.

"It was very difficult. People who make their living in the way I do have a hard time writing books. Perfectionism is something of a curse to writers, while a boon to editors (up to a point), and a perfectionist editor like me trying to write about a perfectionist writer like Stanley spells trouble. My difficulties were complicated by the fact that my interview subjects and future readers happened to be many of the British writers I had most admired for years—people like Sybille Bedford and Frances Partridge, Michael Holroyd and Victoria Glendinning, Angelica Garnett and Henrietta Garnett (both of them nieces of Virginia Woolf and writers in their own right).

"As I immersed myself in Stanley's letters and diaries written during the times when he had writer's block and fell into depression, I got writer's block and fell into depression. He believed —and I agree with him—that writing well is so difficult that making a career of it seems a form of masochism. 'I am certain,' he said, 'that writing anything is like having the builders in: comprehensive torture hotly followed by disbelief that one ever voluntarily endured such pain. It seems nothing less than a miracle if the paint stays up on the wall. I remember actually thinking that all the words would fall off the paper once I lifted up the typescript. Self-inflicted lunacy, if you ask me.'

"But fortunately, it's all turned out well for me. My book has been splendidly received in England (reviews in *Times Literary Supplement, Spectator,* and the [London] *Times*), and I had the time of my life when I went to launch it there at the end of May [1994] at a party at Claridge's, Stanley's favorite posh hotel."

*   *   *

HAY, Denys   1915-1994

OBITUARY NOTICE—See index for *CA* sketch: Born August 29, 1915, in Newcastle upon Tyne, England; died June 14, 1994, in Edinburgh, Scotland. Historian, educator, and author. A Renaissance scholar known for his innovative work in medieval Italian history, Hay was affiliated with Edinburgh University from 1945 to 1980. One of the first British scholars to seriously examine medieval Italian history within the wider context of the European Renaissance, Hay also served as professor of History at the European University Institute in Badia Fie-

solana, Italy from 1980 to 1982, and lectured at universities in Europe and the United States, including Trinity College in Cambridge, Glasgow University, Cornell University, and the University of Virginia. His work was influenced by a belief that history, as a field of academics, should be more closely affiliated with literature and philosophy than with the social sciences. Through his lectures and books, including *Europe: The Emergence of an Idea, The Italian Renaissance in Its Historical Background, The Italian Church in the Fifteen Century, Italy in the Age of the Renaissance,* and *Renaissance Essays,* Hay argued that the cultural achievements of the European Renaissance can only be fully understood within the context of political, economic, and social history. In 1980, Hay was awarded Italy's Order of Merit. He received an honorary doctorate from Tours University in 1982.

OBITUARIES AND OTHER SOURCES:

BOOKS

Who's Who, 146th edition, St. Martin's, 1994.

PERIODICALS

Times (London), June 28, 1994, p. 23.

*   *   *

HAYNES, Jonathan   1952-

PERSONAL: Born December 4, 1952, in Bethlehem, PA; son of Thomas and Jane Haynes. *Education:* McGill University, B.A. (with first class honors), 1974; Yale University, M.A., 1976, Ph.D., 1980.

ADDRESSES: Office—71 Barrow St., #18, New York, NY 10014.

CAREER: American University in Cairo, Cairo, Egypt, visiting assistant professor of English and director of freshman writing program, 1980-82; Tufts University, Medford, MA, visiting assistant professor of English, 1982-83; Albion College, Albion, MI, assistant professor of English, 1983-85; Bennington College, Bennington, VT, professor of English, 1985-94; New York University, English Department, visiting scholar, 1994—.

AWARDS, HONORS: Grants from American Council of Learned Societies, 1984, 1988; Fulbright scholar, University of Nigeria, Nsukka, 1991-92, and Ahmadu Bello University, 1992-93.

WRITINGS:

The Humanist As Traveler: George Sandys's "Relation of a Journey Begun An. Dom. 1610", Associated University Presses, 1986.
The Social Relations of Jonson's Theater, Cambridge University Press (New York), 1992.

Work represented in anthologies, including *Modern Critical Views: Ben Jonson,* edited by Harold Bloom, Chelsea House, 1987. Contributor of articles and reviews to periodicals.

*   *   *

HAYWARD, Philip 1956-

PERSONAL: Born June 1, 1956, in London, England; son of Roy Arthur (in business) and Ruth Joy (a teacher; maiden name, Gibson) Hayward; married Rebecca Dawn Coyle (an academic), August 1, 1991; children: Rosa Siobhan Miranda. *Education:* University of Wales, University College, Cardiff, B.A. (with honors), 1978; Institute of Education, London, Post Graduate Certificate of Education, 1985; Macquarie University, Ph.D., 1993. *Politics:* Socialist. *Religion:* Atheist. *Avocational interests:* Gardening, playing the guitar.

ADDRESSES: Home—55 Britannia St., Umina, New South Wales 2257, Australia. *Office*—School of English and Linguistics, Macquarie University, Sydney, New South Wales 2109, Australia.

CAREER: West Surrey College of Art, Farnham, England, lecturer in media studies, 1988-90; Macquarie University, Sydney, Australia, senior lecturer in mass communications, 1991—. University of London, new technologies projects officer, 1989-90.

MEMBER: International Association for the Study of Popular Music (member of Australian executive committee), Society for Education in Film and Television (member of executive committee, 1984-88).

WRITINGS:

(Editor) *Picture This: Media Representations of Modern Art,* John Libbey (London, England), 1988.
(Editor) *Culture, Technology, and Creativity,* John Libbey (London, England), 1991.
(Editor) *From Pop to Punk to Postmodernism,* Allen & Unwin (Sydney, Australia), 1992.
(Editor with Tana Wollen) *Future Visions: New Technologies of the Screen,* BFI Publishing (London, England), 1993.

Author (with wife, Rebecca Coyle) of the book *3-D Images: Australian Holography,* Power Press. Editor, *Perfect Beat: Pacific Journal of Research into Contemporary Music and Popular Culture,* 1992—.

WORK IN PROGRESS: Music Video in the Western Pacific; research on musical exchanges between Australia and Papua New Guinea.

SIDELIGHTS: Philip Hayward told *CA:* "My principal interests are new visual technologies and popular music. I have always tried to explore and illuminate under-researched areas, and I work collaboratively with colleagues. I am now dedicated exclusively to research on issues related to the Australia-Pacific region."

*   *   *

HEADLEY, Victor 1960-

PERSONAL: Born November 25, 1960, in Kingston, Jamaica. *Education:* Attended boys' secondary school in Kingston. *Politics:* "Black consciousness." *Religion:* Rastafarian.

ADDRESSES: Agent—c/o X Press, 55 Broadway Marker, London E8 4PH, England.

CAREER: Writer.

WRITINGS:

Yardie, X Press (London), 1992, Grove/Atlantic (New York), 1993.
Excess, X Press, 1993.
Yush!, X Press, 1994.

WORK IN PROGRESS: A history of black Britain since 600 B.C.; an inner-city love story.

*   *   *

HEDIN, Robert (Alexander) 1949-

PERSONAL: Born February 9, 1949, in Red Wing, MN; son of Raymond F. (a physician) and Elizabeth Lydia Hedin; married Carolyn A. Sweasy (a private investor), August 3, 1971; children: Alexander, Benjamin. *Education:* Luther College, B.A., 1971; University of Alaska, M.F.A., 1973. *Politics:* Democrat. *Religion:* "None."

ADDRESSES: Home—P.O. Box 59, Frontenac, MN 55026.

CAREER: Sheldon Jackson College, Sitka, AK, instructor in English, 1972-73; University of Alaska, Anchorage, visiting instructor in creative writing, 1976-77; Ecole Nationale d'Administration, Paris, France, teacher of English as a second language, 1978; University of Alaska, Fairbanks, visiting assistant professor of English, 1979-80; Wake Forest University, Winston-Salem, NC, poet in residence, 1980-92; Loft, Minneapolis, MN, instructor, 1993—. University of Minnesota—Minneapolis, adjunct professor, 1993—; Anderson Center of Interdisciplinary Studies, member of board of directors. Director of Midnight Sun Writers Symposium, 1980, Mary Arden Poetry Festival, 1982-92, and Conference on Poetic Thought and Translation, 1988; writing teacher at numerous writers' conferences, including Marshall Fest: Celebration of Rural Writers and Writing, 1992; judge of poetry contests and literary awards; gives readings from his works.

MEMBER: International PEN, Poetry Society of America, Academy of American Poets, National Writers Union, Loft, Red Wing Arts Association (member of board of directors).

AWARDS, HONORS: William Stafford Award, Washington Poetry Association, 1973; Branford P. Millar Memorial Prize in Poetry, *Portland Review,* 1976; fellow of National Endowment for the Arts, 1977, 1985, and 1994; John Atherton fellow in poetry, Bread Loaf Writers Conference, 1979; New York Poetry in Public Places Award, New York State Arts Council, 1980; fellow of Yaddo Foundation, 1981, 1983, and 1987; Alaska state humanities grant, 1983; Blumenthal Writers and Readers Awards, 1987 and 1992; poetry prize, *Nebraska Review,* 1988; fellow of North Carolina Arts Council, 1989; Pushcart Prize nominations, 1989 and 1991; winner of State Street Press book competition, 1994; poetry fellow, Minnesota State Arts Board, 1994.

WRITINGS:

POEMS

Snow Country, Copper Canyon Press, 1975.
At the Home-Altar, Copper Canyon Press, 1979.
County O, Copper Canyon Press, 1984.
Tornadoes, Ion Books, 1990.

Author of broadsides and pamphlets. Work represented in anthologies, including *Anthology of Magazine Verse and Yearbook of American Poetry,* edited by Alan Pater, Monitor Book, 1981, 1986, 1988, and 1991; *Environment: Essence and Issue,* edited by Jim Villani, Pig Iron, 1993; and *Writers' Fellowship: North Carolina Poets and Writers,* edited by Alan Brilliant, Unicorn Press, 1994. Contributor of

poems to periodicals in England, Canada, and the United States, including *Poetry Now, Malahat Review, Prism International, Raven, Alaska Quarterly Review,* and *Greenfield Review.*

EDITOR OF ANTHOLOGIES

(With David Stark) *In the Dreamlight: Twenty-One Alaskan Writers,* Copper Canyon Press, 1984.
(With Gary Holthaus) *Alaska: Reflections on Land and Spirit,* University of Arizona Press (Tucson, AZ), 1989.
(With Holthaus) *The Great Land: Reflections on Alaska,* University of Arizona Press, 1994.

OTHER

(Translator) *In Lands Where Light Has Another Color: Poems of Rolf Jacobsen* (chapbook), Mid-American Review Translation Series, 1990.
(Translator) *Night Music: Poems of Rolf Jacobsen,* State Street Press, 1994.

Work represented in anthologies, including *The Poetry of Philip Levine,* edited by Christopher Buckley, University of Michigan Press, 1990. Contributor of articles, translations from Swedish and Norwegian prose, and reviews to magazines.

BIOGRAPHICAL/CRITICAL SOURCES:

BOOKS

Haines, John, *Living Off the Country: Essays on Poetry and Place,* University of Michigan Press, 1981.
Haines, *You and I and the World,* Graywolf, 1994.

PERIODICALS

Permafrost, spring, 1980.

*   *   *

HEFFERNAN, Nancy Coffey   1936-

PERSONAL: Born in 1936.

ADDRESSES: Agent—c/o University Press of New England, 23 South Main St., Hanover, NH 03755.

CAREER: Writer.

WRITINGS:

WITH ANN PAGE STECKER

New Hampshire: Crosscurrents in Its Development, Thompson & Rutter, 1986.

Sisters of Fortune: Being the True Story of How Three Motherless Sisters Saved Their Home in New England and Raised Their Younger Brother While Their Father Went Fortune Hunting in the California Gold Rush, University Press of New England, 1993.

OTHER

(With Louis Judson) *What's In a Name?: The Heroes and Heroines Baby Name Book,* Prima Publications and Communications, 1990.

SIDELIGHTS: Writer Nancy Coffey Heffernan collaborated with Ann Page Stecker on *Sisters of Fortune: Being the True Story of How Three Motherless Sisters Saved Their Home in New England and Raised Their Younger Brother While Their Father Went Fortune Hunting in the California Gold Rush.* Primarily a compilation of letters dating from the mid-nineteenth century, the volume relates the struggle of the Wilson sisters—Lizzie, Annie, and Charlotte—to maintain a household and raise their younger brother, Jamie, by themselves. The story is told through the correspondence the sisters regularly sent to their father, James Wilson, a widowed general and ex-congressman who left the family to search for gold in California. Wilson was gone for eleven years, leaving his daughters, whose ages at the time of his departure ranged from thirteen to twenty-four, to fend for themselves. The Wilson daughters "present themselves in their letters as loving, dutiful daughters . . . attempting with pluck but with increasingly limited resources to survive the disastrous financial situation in which he left them," observed Walter Satterthwait in the *New York Times Book Review.* The critic then pointed out that the daughters' perception of their father as "loving" in return was flawed: He "clearly was not a loving father, he did *not* want to come rushing back."

Satterthwait hailed *Sisters of Fortune* as "an extraordinary account of . . . survival" and complimented Heffernan and Stecker for producing "a remarkable documentary history." Reviewer Carolynne Myall in *Library Journal* also praised the pair for their skill at editing the letters and for providing "well-integrated connective material," efforts which served "to create a compelling domestic narrative." Heffernan also teamed with Stecker on *New Hampshire: Crosscurrents in Its Development,* and collaborated with Louis Judson on *What's In a Name?: The Heroes and Heroines Baby Name Book.* For further information on Ann Page Stecker, see her entry in this volume.

BIOGRAPHICAL/CRITICAL SOURCES:

PERIODICALS

Library Journal, November 15, 1993, p. 87.
New York Times Book Review, December 19, 1993, p. 7.
Publishers Weekly, October 4, 1993, p. 71.*

* * *

HELM, Levon 1940-

PERSONAL: Born Mark Lavon Helm, May 26, 1940, in Marvel, AR; father, a cotton farmer; children: Amy.

Home—Springdale, AR. *Agent*—David Vigliano Agency Ltd., 240 Ashland Ave., Santa Monica, CA 90405.

CAREER: Musician, singer, actor, and writer. Rock musician (with Rick Danko, Garth Hudson, Richard Manuel, and Robbie Robertson) in the Hawks (backup group for rockabilly performer Ronnie Hawkins), then as Levon and the Hawks, the Canadian Squires, and the Crackers, renamed the Band, 1967-76, 1993—. Actor in various films, including *Coal Miner's Daughter* and *The Right Stuff,* and on television, 1978—.

WRITINGS:

(With Stephen Davis) *This Wheel's on Fire: Levon Helm and the Story of the Band,* Morrow (New York), 1993.

SIDELIGHTS: Levon Helm gained prominence as a musician with the Band, a popular and critically acclaimed rock group that formed in the 1960s. Helm had known from an early age that he wanted to be a musician, recalling in his memoir, *This Wheel's on Fire: Levon Helm and the Story of the Band,* that at the age of six he pretended to play guitar with a broom after seeing Bill Monroe and His Blue Grass Boys perform. When Helm was seventeen, he became a drummer in the backup band for a performer named Ronnie Hawkins. While touring in Canada, the band attracted the devotion of a fifteen-year-old musician named Robbie Robertson, who was eventually invited to join the group. Robertson and Helm became friends, and formed the nucleus around which the group of musicians who came to be known as the Band was formed. With Rick Danko, Garth Hudson, and Richard Manuel, Robertson and Helm performed with folk (and subsequently rock) musician Bob Dylan when he began experimenting with electronic music in the mid-

1960s, though Helm had a disagreement with Dylan and left the group during this period.

In 1967 the Band settled near Woodstock, New York, while Dylan recuperated from a motorcycle accident, and Helm rejoined them as a guitarist (he had been replaced on the drums) to record their first album, *Music from Big Pink,* an album named for the house in which the group rehearsed. The *Rolling Stone Illustrated History of Rock and Roll* called *Music from Big Pink* "a revolutionary album in many ways: The emphasis was on ensemble work rather than on the soloing that had previously dominated rock; the melodies, few of them blues based, were delivered by an ensemble that was almost orchestral in scope . . . the lyrics were elusive, like Dylan's, but with a distinctive and compelling cast." At this time the Band also recorded songs with Dylan that were eventually released in 1975 on a two-album set entitled *The Basement Tapes.* With the 1969 release of their second album, simply entitled *The Band,* the group became immensely popular, and though subsequent releases were not as favorably received, the Band had been assured a place in rock and roll history.

In 1976 the Band announced that they would no longer perform in concert together, and their final live performance, a five-hour, star-studded extravaganza, was filmed by director Martin Scorcese and released as *The Last Waltz* in 1978. In 1977 their final album was released, and the individual members pursued separate endeavors. Helm began appearing in feature films, most notably as Loretta Lynn's father in *Coal Miner's Daughter* and as a narrator/performer in the film adaptation of Tom Wolfe's book *The Right Stuff.*

In 1993 the Band regrouped—minus Richard Manuel, who died of an apparent suicide in 1986—to perform at the presidential inauguration of Arkansas-native Bill Clinton. A revamped version of the Band, minus Robertson, united to record an album, *Jericho,* that was released in 1994. That same year Helm published *This Wheel's on Fire,* which recounts his youth on a cotton farm in Arkansas, his early career with rockabilly bands in the late 1950s and early 1960s, his friendship, and eventual feud, with Robertson, the Band's long association with Bob Dylan, the eventual demise of the Band in the 1970s, and the death of Manuel. A reviewer in *Publishers Weekly* dubbed *This Wheel's on Fire* "plainspoken," noting that it "doesn't put its subjects on too high a pedestal." *Los Angeles Times Book Review* contributor John Schulian called *This Wheel's on Fire* "admirable." Dubbing Helm's mem-

oir "a lament," Schulian concluded that the book is "about the loss of something special, a loss you feel most deeply when you step back into the past."

BIOGRAPHICAL/CRITICAL SOURCES:

BOOKS

Contemporary Musicians, Volume 9, Gale, 1993.

PERIODICALS

Los Angeles Times Book Review, November 21, 1993, pp. 2, 5.
Publishers Weekly, October 4, 1993.
Rolling Stone, November 11, 1993, pp. 67-70.*

*   *   *

HELVARG, David   1951-

PERSONAL: Born April 10, 1951, in Flushing, NY; son of Max (an executive) and Eva (an art gallery owner; maiden name, Lee) Helvarg. *Education:* Attended Boston University, 1971; Goddard College, B.A., 1974. *Politics:* "Yes." *Religion:* "Sort of."

ADDRESSES: Home—Sausalito, CA. *Agent*—Joe Spigler, 154 West 57th St., Room 135, New York, NY 10019.

CAREER: Reporter in Northern Ireland, 1973; print reporter in San Diego, CA, 1974-79; print, radio, and television reporter in Central America, 1979-83; television news and documentary producer, 1983-93; writer and television producer, 1993—.

AWARDS, HONORS: Censored Story Award from University of California Project, 1978; San Diego Emmy Award, 1982, for investigative reporting, and 1985, for best documentary; investigative reporting award, Radio and Television News Directors Association of Northern California, 1986; American Academy of Television Arts and Sciences, Emmy Award nominations, outstanding background/analysis of a single current story, 1986, 1988, Emmy Award, community service, 1988, for *AIDS Lifeline;* television news award from John Muir Medical Film Festival, 1990; NIA Interpretive Media Award, 1991.

WRITINGS:

The War against the Greens, Sierra Books (San Francisco, CA), 1994.

Contributor to magazines and newspapers, including *Mother Jones, Penthouse, In These Times, Califor-*

nia, and *Columbia Journalism Review.* Editor, *San Diego Newsline,* 1974-79.

SIDELIGHTS: David Helvarg told *CA:* "As a reporter in Northern Ireland, I acquired my first combat reporting experience while covering the conflict between the British and the Irish Republican Army (IRA). I reported on the IRA car-bombing campaign and British undercover operations.

"In Central America, I covered the expanding U.S. role in the conflict there as a stringer for the Associated Press. Exclusive reports included combat coverage of the first town to fall to Sandinista rebels, the first delivery of U.S. gunships to El Salvador, the first visit to Contra camps in Honduras, and the last interview with Sister Ita Ford before her murder. I was arrested by the army, while reporting on a civilian massacre, and was deported from El Salvador in 1983.

"As a television news and documentary producer, I created programs focusing on the military, politics, health, and environmental issues, as well as immigration, technology, and the oceans. I used my reporting background to get a private investigator's license. I produced these works in the United States, Mexico, Bolivia, and Brazil."

* * *

**HENRY, Faith
  See LEVINE, Nancy D.**

* * *

HENRY, Gordon D., Jr.   1955-

PERSONAL: Born October 19, 1955, in Philadelphia, PA; son of Gordon D. Henry and Wilma (Vizenor) Henry; married Mary Anne Bezucha, June 16, 1979; children: Kehli Ardis, Mira Ann, Emily Rose. *Education:* University of Wisconsin-Parkside, B.S., 1980; Michigan State University, M.A., 1983; University of North Dakota, Ph.D., 1992. *Politics:* "Mostly unaffiliated." *Religion:* "Universalist—unaffiliated, traditional." *Avocational interests:* Music (guitar).

ADDRESSES: Home—14069 215th Ave., Big Rapids, MI 49307. *Office*—Department of English, 201 Morrill, Michigan State University, East Lansing, MI 48824.

CAREER: Ferris State University, Big Rapids, MI, assistant professor, 1988-92; Michigan State University, East Lansing, MI, assistant professor of English, 1993—. Lecturer, storyteller.

MEMBER: Wordcraft Writers Circle, North American Native Writers Circle.

AWARDS, HONORS: Thomas McGrath Poetry Award, University of North Dakota, 1985.

WRITINGS:

The Light People (novel) University of Oklahoma (Norman, OK), 1994.

Author of "Outside White Earth" for *Blue Cloud Quarterly,* 1985.

WORK IN PROGRESS: Aphorisms for Long Knives, a book of poetry; *The Golden Arrow,* a novel; research about Ojibwa culture and literature.

SIDELIGHTS: Gordon D. Henry, Jr., a member of the White Earth Chippewa tribe, drew critical praise with his first novel, *The Light People.* The work is comprised of multiple-genre, interconnected tales that tell the story of young Oskinaway's generation-spanning quest for knowledge of his Native American Anishinabe heritage. Raised by his grandparents on a reservation in Minnesota, Oskinaway enlists the help of tribal elders and a young medicine man in a search for his parents that becomes a wide-ranging exploration of past and present in Native American history and culture.

The Light People received favorable reviews as a first novel and an example of contemporary Native American fiction. In a *Booklist* profile of the volume, Whitney Scott called it a "tapestry of memories within memories, stories within stories, and myths within myths," while a *Publisher's Weekly* contributor characterized the book as a "gentle, comic piece" within whose pages poetry, prose, and drama are interwoven with factual narrative. The juxtaposition of literary forms in *The Light People* was lauded by some reviewers as a structural technique that reflects the perspective of the contemporary Native American whose heritage must accommodate both ancestral traditions and the structures imposed by western popular culture and politics.

Henry told *CA:* "My writing tends to work within mythic communities and constructs, most of which come out of oral traditions of the Anishinabe (Ojibwa), family history, reinvented personal history, and imagined analogues. My writing also tends toward multi-genre experimentation with multiple narrative voices and mythic elements of time and space. The poetry I write relies on imagery and subdued rhythmic diction, and my fiction works through various literary forms and genres to open up possibilities for storytelling. Thus my work, in particular my fiction, stems from a belief in the importance and the power of storytelling. That is, native oral traditions and lifeways have influenced my thinking, if not my writing style."

BIOGRAPHICAL/CRITICAL SOURCES:

PERIODICALS

Booklist, February 15, 1994.
Kirkus Reviews, January 1, 1994.
Library Journal, February 1, 1994.
Publisher's Weekly, January 10, 1994.

*　　*　　*

HENRY, William A(lfred) III　1950-1994

OBITUARY NOTICE—See index for *CA* sketch: Born January 24, 1950, in South Orange, NJ; died of a heart attack, May 28, 1994, in London (one source says Maidenhead), England. Journalist, drama critic, author, and educator. An award-winning reporter and arts critic, Henry was, at the time of his death, the drama critic for *Time* magazine. As a reporter for the *Boston Globe,* where he covered education, state politics, television, and the arts from 1971 to 1980, he was a corecipient of a 1975 Pulitzer prize for public service reporting. In 1980, Henry received a Pulitzer prize of his own for television criticism and moved to the *New York Daily News* as a columnist and critic at large. He joined the editorial staff of *Time* in 1981, and was appointed drama critic in 1985. In 1990, Henry received an award from the Overseas Press Club and an Emmy award for *Bob Fosse: Steam Heat,* a PBS *Great Performances* documentary he wrote. Henry also authored several books, including *Visions of America: How We Saw the 1984 Election, The Great One: The Life and Legend of Jackie Gleason, Jack Benny: The Radio and Television Years,* and the posthumously-published volume, *In Defense of Elitism.* A member of the faculty of Tufts University in 1979, Yale University in 1980, and New York University in 1986, Henry lectured at numerous schools and universities, including Harvard University, Massachusetts Institute of Technology, and Columbia University. He served as a Pulitzer prize drama judge for 1986-87, and as chair in 1989-90, 1991-92, and 1993-94. Henry was a founding member of the Television Critics Association and served as president of the New York Drama Critics Circle from 1991 until his death.

OBITUARIES AND OTHER SOURCES:

BOOKS

Who's Who in America, 48th edition, Marquis, 1994.

PERIODICALS

Chicago Tribune, June 29, 1994, sec. 1, p. 10; July 3, 1994, sec. 2, p. 6.
New York Times, May 29, 1994, p. D19.
Washington Post, June 29, 1994, B4.

*　　*　　*

HENSON, Lance　1944-

PERSONAL: Born in 1944 in Oklahoma; married Pat French (marriage ended). *Education:* Graduated from Oklahoma College of Liberal Arts (now University of Science and Arts of Oklahoma), Chickasha, OK; earned master's degree in creative writing at University of Tulsa, Tulsa, OK.

ADDRESSES: *Agent*—Jeanetta Calhoun, 2541 Northwest 36th St., Oklahoma City, OK 73112.

CAREER: Writer and educator. *Military service:* Served in the United States Marine Corps during the Vietnam war.

WRITINGS:

Keeper of Arrows, Renaissance Press, 1972.
Naming the Dark: Poems for the Cheyenne, Point Riders Press (Norman, OK), 1976.
Mistah, Strawberry Press, 1978.
Buffalo Marrow on Black, Full Count Press, 1979.
A Circling Remembrance, Blue Cloud Quarterly Press, 1982.
In a Dark Mist (chapbook), Cross-Cultural Communications (Merrick, NY), 1982.
Selected Poems, 1970-1983, Greenfield Review Press (Greenfield Center, NY), 1985.
Another Song for America, Point Riders Press (Norman, OK), 1987.
Another Distance: New and Selected Poems, Point Riders Press (Norman, OK), 1991.
A Motion of Sudden Aloneness, University of Arkansas Press, 1991.
Poems for a Master Beadworker, OMBA (Germany), 1991.

Contributor to numerous publications, including *Wooster Review* and *Nimrod.*

Henson's works have been translated into Dutch, Italian, and German.

SIDELIGHTS: Lance Henson is a poet of Cheyenne heritage whose work is deeply rooted in his ancestral background. His early collections include *Naming the Dark: Poems for the Cheyenne,* published in 1976, and a 1982 chapbook, *In a Dark Mist. Selected Poems, 1970-1983* appeared in 1985, its contents culled from his previously published selections in anthologies and poetry journals. Henson's style has been described as minimalist: his poems are typically short, terse, and filled with powerful imagery. Explaining his approach in an interview in Joseph Burchac's book *Survival This Way,* Henson noted: "We are born out of a perfect state to be here. . . . I think brevity is . . . one way to acknowledge and pay homage to the Great Silence we came out of." Henson's subject matter is also derived from his Native American background; *Selected Poems, 1970-1983,* for example, includes an exploration of the peyote ritual, which involves ingesting hallucinogens in order to attain communion with the spirit world. Critiquing the volume for *World Literature Today,* Robert L. Berner noted that Henson's poems "are the work of a poet who knows that language is the original magic."

Another Song for America, Henson's 1987 collection of verse, is buttressed by two poems that serve as critiques of the violence of the Native American experience at the hands of white civilization and the contemporary social and racial tensions of twentieth-century America. The first poem is taken from a death song of a Native American warrior killed in battle, while the closing piece is based on the incident at Kent State University in 1970, when antiwar protesters were killed by National Guard troops. Other selections return to Henson's Cheyenne heritage, such as "january song." In reviewing the volume for another issue of *World Literature Today,* Berner asserted that the poet's "great strength is his ability to create striking images which he relates to the history and wisdom of his Cheyenne forebears."

Another Distance: New and Selected Poems, published in 1991, contains sixty-three poems that are, for the most part, either no longer available in print or recently written; of the latter category, many were composed in Europe and manifest what Berner, in a *World Literature Today* review, called "the chilling awareness of exile." This volume also reflects Henson's concern for environmental issues. In his "walking at teutoburger wald," Henson describes the ancient forest now ravaged by acid rain as "a war zone." Berner notes that in this volume Henson seems to expand his view of the situation of the modern Native American, suggesting that "the old victories and defeats seem less important than

the present predicament—international, ecological, basic—of the entire race in a world which continues to be threatened by social stupidity."

BIOGRAPHICAL/CRITICAL SOURCES:

PERIODICALS

World Literature Today, summer, 1986, p. 506; spring, 1988, p. 320; summer, 1990, pp. 418-21; summer, 1992, p. 561.

BOOKS

Burchac, Joseph, *Survival This Way: Interviews with Native American Poets,* University of Arizona Press, 1987, pp. 105-17.*

*   *   *

HERMANS, Hubert J. M.   1937-

PERSONAL: Born October 9, 1937, in Maastricht, Netherlands; son of Mathias (a baker) and Jeannette M. (Spronck) Hermans; married Els C. Jansen (a psychotherapist), November 28, 1961; children: Matthieu, Desiree. *Education:* Catholic University of Nijmegen, M.A., 1965, D.Psych., 1967. *Religion:* Roman Catholic.

ADDRESSES: Home—Bosweg 18, Berg en Dal 6571 CD, Netherlands. *Office*—Department of Clinical Psychology and Personality, Catholic University of Nijmegen, P.O. Box 9104, 6500 HE Nijmegan, Netherlands; and Montessorilaan 3, 6525 HR Nijmegen, Netherlands.

CAREER: Asthma Center, Groesbeek, Netherlands, assistant psychologist and diagnostician, 1963-65; Catholic University of Nijmegen, Nijmegen, Netherlands, staff member at Psychology Laboratory, 1965-72, lecturer, 1972-80, professor of psychology, 1980—. Guest lecturer at Catholic University of Lublin and University of Ghent; guest professor at University of Louvain and Duquesne University. Chairperson of a foundation for valuation theory and self-confrontation; Han Fortmann Center for Human Growth, chairperson of advisory committee. *Military service:* Served in Dutch armed forces.

MEMBER: Dutch Organization of Psychologists, U.S. Society for Personology (international associate).

AWARDS, HONORS: Scholarship for research in the United States, Dutch Organization for Pure Research, 1968; fellow, Netherlands Institute for Advanced Studies in the Humanities and Social Sciences, 1976-77.

WRITINGS:

(With Harry Kempen) *The Dialogical Self: Meaning As Movement,* Academic Press, 1993.

(With wife Els Hermans-Jansen) *Self-Narratives: The Emergence of Meaning,* Guilford (New York, NY), 1995.

Contributor to periodicals, including *Contemporary Psychology.*

WORK IN PROGRESS: Research on valuation theory (self theory) and the self-confrontation method.

SIDELIGHTS: Hubert J. M. Hermans told *CA:* "I received my psychological training at the University of Nijmegen. My doctoral dissertation was on achievement motivation and the fear of failure. Building on this work, I constructed two original psychological tests for the assessment of these motives, the PMT for adults and the PMT-k for children. Since 1979 both tests have been in the top twenty of the most-used psychological tests in the Netherlands.

"In 1968 I received a scholarship to visit some universities and research institutes in the United States, including the Oregon Research Institute, Stanford University, and Harvard University. Inspired by these experiences, I changed my research interests and started to explore the field of personal valuation. This led to the development of valuation theory and the self-confrontation method. The theory and method were developed and applied in a diversity of practical settings in the 1970s and 1980s. Since 1985 they have been published in various European and American psychology journals."

*   *   *

HEWITT, Don (S.)   1922-

PERSONAL: Born December 14, 1922, in New York, NY; son of Ely S. (in advertising sales) and Frieda (Pike) Hewitt; married Mary Weaver (deceased); married second wife, Frankie (divorced); married Marilyn Berger (a television news correspondent), April 14, 1979; children: Jeffrey, Steven, Jill, Lisa. *Education:* Attended New York University, 1941, and Merchant Marine Academy. *Avocational interests:* Tennis, poker, Scrabble, watching professional football on television.

ADDRESSES: Home—New York, NY. *Office*—60 Minutes, CBS News, 51 West 52nd St., New York, NY 10019.

CAREER: New York Herald Tribune, New York City, head copyboy, 1942; war correspondent for *Stars and Stripes,* 1943; Associated Press, Memphis, TN, night editor, 1945; *Pelham Sun,* New York City, editor, 1946; Acme News Pictures, night telephoto editor, c. 1947; CBS News, New York City, began as associate director and became producer and director of *CBS TV News* (later renamed *Douglas Edwards with the News*), 1948-62, producer at Cape Canaveral, 1960-65, executive producer of *CBS Evening News with Walter Cronkite,* 1961-64, producer and director of various documentaries and special reports, 1965-68, executive producer of *60 Minutes,* 1968—, and *Who's Who,* 1977.

AWARDS, HONORS: Received seven Emmy Awards from Academy of Television Arts and Sciences; winner of George Polk Memorial Award; honored for distinguished service to journalism by University of Missouri; named broadcaster of the year by International Radio and Television Society, 1980; Paul White Memorial Award from Radio-Television News Directors Association, 1987; Alfred I. Dupont-Columbia University Award, 1988; gold medal from International Television and Radio Society, 1988; Peabody Award, 1989; named to Television Hall of Fame by Academy of Television Arts and Sciences, 1990; received honorary degree from Brandeis University, 1990.

WRITINGS:

Minute by Minute (nonfiction), Random, 1985.

SIDELIGHTS: Don Hewitt is a longtime CBS News producer, who is probably best known as the founding producer of *60 Minutes,* television's acclaimed investigative journalism series. Hewitt came to CBS News after working several years as a journalist, including stints as a war correspondent for the U.S. Army's *Stars and Stripes* and as an editor with the Associated Press in Memphis. Hired by CBS News in 1948, Hewitt began working as associate director of the network's *CBS TV News,* but by 1950 he was serving as both producer and director of the show, which was renamed *Douglas Edwards with the News.* Hewitt remained with CBS's television news for the next fourteen years, and during that period he pioneered technical innovations, particularly with regards to graphics. In addition, he conceived of the newsroom as the actual broadcasting studio, and he devised unconventional means of presenting news, including aerial views from planes.

During Hewitt's tenure at CBS, the network's evening news show, which became *CBS Evening News with Walter Cronkite* in the early 1960s, overcame its competitors in the ratings. Despite this success, Hewitt was dismissed from the program in 1964. For the next few years he concentrated on documentary productions, including *CBS Reports: Hunger in America,* which earned the network an Emmy Award.

In 1968 Hewitt convinced executives that an investigative news program would bring further success to the CBS network, and thus *60 Minutes* was developed. The show, which initially featured broadcasters Harry Reasoner and Mike Wallace, soon established itself as a provocative, compelling forum for reports on social and political developments. Notable among the subjects explored on *60 Minutes* in its early years were student unrest in Europe, black activism, drug addiction, child abuse, and war crimes.

For more than twenty years, *60 Minutes,* with its controversial topics, has maintained a strong hold on television viewers, and it often ranks among the medium's most watched shows. Indeed, E. J. Kahn, Jr., in a two-part *New Yorker* piece, described *60 Minutes* as "the most widely watched nonentertainment series in television history." Personalities such as Andy Rooney, Morley Safer, Barbara Walters, Ed Bradley, Dan Rather, and Diane Sawyer, have all contributed to the show's sustained success, but Hewitt is often accorded principal responsibility in that regard. "You take Don out," Dan Rather told Martha Smilgis of *People,* "and the whole thing collapses."

Hewitt insists that his achievement with *60 Minutes* is the result of his instincts, as opposed to his intellect. "I operate by my guts and fingertips," he told Kahn. He also observed, "I don't articulate very well, but I can take a producer and an editor into a screening room and *show* them what's wrong." Hewitt is also baffled by the show's consistent appeal with American television viewers. "I don't really have any idea why people watch us," he told Kahn in the *New Yorker* articles. And he added, "Maybe it's because they just think they ought to watch it."

Hewitt's book *Minute by Minute,* which appeared in 1985, provides what Toronto *Globe and Mail* reviewer Desmond Smith described as "a sanitized yet compulsively readable account of [Hewitt's] four decades inside CBS News." Smith, who hailed Hewitt as "the most accomplished camera director of his generation," found *Minute by Minute* "packed . . . with great pictures and amusing anecdotes." Similarly, Richard F. Shepard wrote in his *New York Times*

appraisal, "Mostly, Mr. Hewitt shoots the breeze, and a lot of it is downright amusing." For all his success, Hewitt seems unlikely to slow his pace or diminish his work load. "Relaxing," he told *People,* "tires me out."

BIOGRAPHICAL/CRITICAL SOURCES:

PERIODICALS

Globe and Mail (Toronto), August 9, 1986.
Journalism Quarterly, winter, 1987, p. 897.
New Yorker, July 19, 1982, pp. 40-61; July 26, 1982, pp. 38-55.
New York Times, December 25, 1985, p. 15.
New York Times Book Review, January 5, 1986, p. 17.
People, May 28, 1979, pp. 84-93.*

*   *   *

HIGGINS, Michael James   1946-

PERSONAL: Born January 17, 1946, in Bangor, ME; son of Frank F. and Beatrice (Daily) Higgins; married Cheleen Mahar (marriage ended); married Tanya Coen (an anthropologist), May 5, 1984; children: (first marriage) Tristan, Siobhan. *Education:* Colorado State College (now University of Northern Colorado), B.A., 1968; University of Illinois at Urbana-Champaign, Ph.D., 1974. *Politics:* "Radical leftist." *Religion:* None.

ADDRESSES: Home—Apt. Postal 742, Oaxaca, 68000 Oaxaca, Mexico.

CAREER: Anthropologist. University of Northern Colorado, Greeley, professor, 1974-94.

WRITINGS:

Oigame! Oigame! Westview, 1992.

Author of two books in Spanish.

WORK IN PROGRESS: Que Honda Oaxaca: Class, Gender, and Sexuality in Post-Modern Mexico, with wife Tanya Coen.

SIDELIGHTS: Michael James Higgins told *CA:* "As an anthropologist, I search for ways to place theory in the center of people's everyday lives."

*   *   *

HILL, Edmund   1923-

PERSONAL: Born July 23, 1923, in Huelva, Spain; son of Laurence Carr (a mining engineer) and Nan

(Ross) Hill. *Education:* Magdalen College, Oxford, B.A. (with honors), 1948, S.T.L., 1958. *Politics:* "Center Left." *Religion:* Roman Catholic.

*ADDRESSES: Home—*Blackfriars, Buckingham Rd., Cambridge CB3 0DD, England. *Agent—*Campbell, Thompson & McLaughlin Ltd., 23 Newington Green, London N16 9PG, England.

CAREER: Joined Ordo Praedicatorum (Order of Preachers; Dominicans; O.P.), 1948; Blackfriars, Oxford, England, teacher, 1956-66; teacher in Stettenbosch, South Africa, 1966-69; St. Peter's Seminary for Africans, Hammanskraal, South Africa, 1969-72; teacher in Swaziland, 1973-74; St. Augustine's Seminary, in Lesotho, teacher, 1974-90; Holy Spirit Seminary, Port Moresby, Papua New Guinea, teacher, 1991; St. Augustine's Seminary, teacher, 1992-94. *Military service:* British Army, 1944-46.

MEMBER: Catholic Theological Association of Southern Africa.

WRITINGS:

Nine Sermons of St. Augustine on the Psalms, DLT, 1958.
Summa Theologiae of St. Thomas, McGraw, 1964.
Being Human, Geoffrey Chapman, 1984.
The Mystery of the Trinity, Geoffrey Chapman, 1985.
Ministry and Authority in the Catholic Church, Geoffrey Chapman, 1988.
(Translator and author of notes) *The Sermons of St. Augustine,* Volumes I-VII, New City Press (Brooklyn, NY), 1990-93.
(Translator and author of introduction and notes) *The Trinity of St. Augustine,* New City Press, 1991.

Also author of *Prayer, Praise, and Politics: Selections on Psalms,* 1973.

WORK IN PROGRESS: Continuing the translation of the works of St. Augustine.

SIDELIGHTS: Edmund Hill told *CA:* "I became a Roman Catholic while serving in the British Army (never heard a shot fired in anger) in 1944. On demobilization in 1946, I finished my university studies, then joined the Order of Preachers. Since finishing my studies, I have spent all my life teaching theology, first in England, then in South Africa. While on a sabbatical year in England, I was declared a prohibited immigrant in South Africa, so I taught for a year at the university in Swaziland and later at a seminary in Lesotho.

"In theology and in 'ecclesiastical politics,' I was delighted by Vatican II, John XXIII being my leading modern hero. I am highly critical of the conservative, not to say reactionary, stance being taken by the Holy See, above all since John Paul II became pope. I have never been formally rebuked or questioned, however; English Catholic theology is hardly noticed in Rome."

*   *   *

HILLMAN, Libby 1919-

PERSONAL: Born July 7, 1919, in New York City; married Herbert E. Hillman, September 15, 1940; children: David, Donald, Betty. *Education:* Juilliard School, B.S. *Avocational interests:* Music.

*ADDRESSES: Home and office—*P.O. Box 135, Chase Hill Rd., Whitingham, VT 05361.

CAREER: Teacher of adult cooking classes at public schools, 1953-69, coordinator of cooking classes, 1969-81; Libby Hillman's Cooking School, New Hyde Park, NY, owner and director. Owner and director of a cooking school in Mount Snow, VT; gives benefit cooking classes for civic organizations. Member of Brattleboro Music Center and Marlboro Music Festival.

MEMBER: International Association of Culinary Professionals, International Association of Wine and Food, Les Dames d'Escoffier (charter member).

WRITINGS:

Lessons in Gourmet Cooking, Hearthside, 1963.
Menu and Cookbook for Entertaining, Hearthside, 1968.
New Lessons in Gourmet Cooking, Hearthside, 1971, reprinted as *Libby Hillman's Gourmet Cookbook.*
The Best From Libby Hillman's Kitchen, Countryman Press (Woodstock, VT), 1993.

Contributor to periodicals, including *Newsday.*

*   *   *

HILLYER, Barbara 1934-

PERSONAL: Born March 1, 1934, in Creston, IA; daughter of Murrell Newman (in educational media) and Wanda (a nurse; maiden name, Griswold) Hillyer; married Robert Murray Davis, December 27, 1958 (divorced, April, 1982); children: Megan Elizabeth, Jennifer Anne, John Murray. *Education:* Rockford College, B.A., 1956; Claremont Graduate

School, M.A., 1957; University of Wisconsin—Madison, Ph.D., 1962. *Politics:* "Feminist."

ADDRESSES: Home—736 Nancy Lynn Terr., Norman, OK 73069. *Office*—Department of Human Relations, University of Oklahoma, Norman, OK 73019.

CAREER: University of Oklahoma, Norman, assistant professor, 1976-82, associate professor of women's studies and human relations, 1982—, director of women's studies, 1976-88. Oklahoma Humanities Committee, chairperson of executive committee; Oklahoma Department of Human Services, member of affirmative action advisory board, 1985-90; Oklahoma governor's Commission on the Status of Women, member, 1987-90. United Ministry Center, member of board of directors, 1993-96.

MEMBER: National Women's Studies Association (NWSA; member of coordinating council), South Central Women's Studies Association (member of national council; copresident), Western Social Sciences Association, Phi Beta Kappa.

AWARDS, HONORS: Emily Toth Award, best single-author feminist book in American or popular culture, Women's Caucus of Popular Culture, American Culture Association, for *Feminism and Disability,* which was also selected by *Choice* as one of the best academic books published in 1993; University of Oklahoma Regents award for superior teaching.

WRITINGS:

Feminism and Disability, University of Oklahoma Press, 1993.

Member of editorial board, *NWSA Journal.*

WORK IN PROGRESS: Research on feminist theory, disability, and the recovery movement.

* * *

HINDIN, Nathan
  See Bloch, Robert (Albert)

* * *

HITZEROTH, Deborah L. 1961-

PERSONAL: Born June 13, 1961, in Missouri; daughter of Gary (an engineer) and Kathy (a nurse; maiden name, Boll) Hughes; married Ryan Hitzeroth (an engineer), June 11, 1988. *Education:* University of Missouri—Columbia, B.A., 1983; graduate study at San Diego State University.

ADDRESSES: Home—5800 Quantrell #304, Alexandria, VA 22312.

CAREER: Waco Tribune Herald, Waco, TX, reporter, 1983-86; American Association of Colleges of Podiatric Medicine, director of public affairs, 1988-89; American Airlines, customer service representative, 1992—.

AWARDS, HONORS: Recipient of awards for featuring writing.

WRITINGS:

Radar: The Silent Detector, Lucent Books, 1990.
(With sister, Sharon Heerboth) *Movies: The World on Film,* Lucent Books, 1991.
Telescopes: Searching the Heavens, Lucent Books, 1991.
(With Heerboth) *The Importance of Galileo Galilei,* Lucent Books, 1992.
(With sister, Sharon [Heerboth] Leon) *The Importance of Isaac Newton,* Lucent Books, 1992.
Guns: Tools of Destructive Force, Lucent Books, 1994.

Also contributor of articles to *Journal of Podiatric Medicine, Fort Worth Magazine,* and *Landscape News.*

SIDELIGHTS: Deborah L. Hitzeroth commented: "I grew up in a university town where the best known division was the department of journalism and the major industry was the media. With this type of background, I was convinced by third grade that I wanted to be 'a writer.' I spent the next twenty years trying to make my dream a reality. I'm currently working with educational books for junior high and high school students, but my next goal is to move into the field of fiction."

* * *

HODGSON, Geoffrey M. 1946-

PERSONAL: Born July 28, 1946, in Watford, England; son of Peter Kenneth (a headmaster) and Joan Sonia (a headmistress; maiden name, Whiteman) Hodgson; married Vinny Logan (a research nurse), July 26, 1980; children: Sarah Logan, James Thomas. *Education:* Victoria University of Manchester, B.Sc., 1968, M.A., 1974. *Politics:* Labour. *Religion:* Agnostic.

ADDRESSES: Home—Malting House, West Wickham, Cambridge CB1 6SD, England. *Office*—Judge Institute of Management Studies, Cambridge University, Mill Lane, Cambridge CB2 1RX, England. *Agent*—Tessa Sayle Agency, 11 Jubilee Pl., London SW3 3TE, England.

CAREER: University of Northumbria, Newcastle upon Tyne, England, professor of economics, 1990-92; Cambridge University, Cambridge, England, visiting lecturer in economics, 1992—. Consultant to Lifespan NHS Trust and Union of Communication Workers.

MEMBER: European Association for Evolutionary Political Economy (general secretary, 1989—), Royal Economic Society.

AWARDS, HONORS: Dehn Prize, University of Manchester, 1974.

WRITINGS:

Socialism and Parliamentary Democracy, Spokesman (Nottingham, England), 1977.
Labour at the Crossroads, Martin Robertson (Oxford, England), 1981.
Capitalism, Value, and Exploitation, Martin Robertson, 1982.
The Democratic Economy, Penguin (Harmondsworth, England), 1984.
Economics and Institutions, University of Pennsylvania Press (Philadelphia, PA), 1988.
After Marx and Sraffa: Essays in Political Economy, Macmillan (London), 1991.
(Editor with E. Screpanti) *Rethinking Economics,* Edward Elgar (Aldershot, England), 1991.
Economics and Evolution: Bringing Life Back Into Economics, University of Michigan Press (Ann Arbor, MI), 1993.
(Editor) *The Economics of Institutions,* Edward Elgar, 1993.
(Editor with W. Samuels and M. Tool) *The Elgar Companion to Institutional and Evolutionary Economics,* Edward Elgar, 1994.
(Editor) *Economics and Biology,* Edward Elgar, 1994.

Contributor of about forty articles to economic and future studies journals.

WORK IN PROGRESS: The Political Economy of Utopia, for Routledge & Kegan Paul; research on evolutionary and institutional economics.

SIDELIGHTS: Geoffrey M. Hodgson told *CA:* "I am concerned with making economics a useful, realistic, and practical science, so that it can once again contribute to the alleviation of problems such as poverty, famine, unemployment, and environmental destruction."

*   *   *

HOFFMAN, Jon T.   1955-

PERSONAL: Born September 23, 1955, in Fremont, OH; son of Thomas L. (a carpenter) and Doris Mae (Lau) Hoffman; married Mary H. Craddock (a graphic designer), September 4, 1988. *Education:* Miami University, Ohio, B.A. (cum laude), 1978; Ohio State University, M.A., 1988; Duke University Law School, J.D. (with honors), 1994.

ADDRESSES: Home—19 Birchcrest Ct., Durham, NC 27713.

CAREER: U.S. Marine Corps, infantry officer, 1981-92; U.S. Marine Corps Reserve (became major), historian, 1992—.

MEMBER: Society for Military History, International Commission on Military History, Marine Corps Historical Foundation.

AWARDS, HONORS: Marine Corps Association Essay Contest, second place, 1987 and 1989, first place, 1990; Naval Institute Marine Corps Essay Contest, second place, 1990; Naval Institute Burke Essay Contest, second place, 1990; Marine Corps Historical Foundation's Heinl Award, 1992, 1993, and 1994; Marine Corps Historical Foundation's Greene Book Award, 1994.

WRITINGS:

Once a Legend, Presidio Press (Novato, CA), 1994.
(Contributor) *The War of 1898,* Garland, 1994.
Shock Battalions, U.S. Marine Corps, 1995.

Contributor to periodicals, including *Marine Corps Gazette, Naval Institute Proceedings, Naval History,* and *Vermont History.*

WORK IN PROGRESS: Biography of Lt. Gen. Lewis Puller, USMC, published by Random House, 1996.

*   *   *

HOLMES, Leslie (Templeman)   1948-

PERSONAL: Born October 5, 1948, in London, England; son of Leslie (a manager) and Beryl Elsie (a singer; maiden name, Templeman) Holmes; married Susan Mary Bleasby, September 4, 1971 (divorced, October, 1989). *Education:* University of Hull, B.A. (with honors), 1971; University of Essex, M.A., 1974, Ph.D., 1979; also attended Free University of Berlin, Leningrad University, and Moscow State University. *Religion:* Methodist. *Avocational interests:* Jogging, weight training, off-road driving, bush walking, concerts.

ADDRESSES: Home—154 Smith St., Thornbury, Victoria 3071, Australia. *Office*—Department of Political Science, University of Melbourne, Parkville, Victoria 3052, Australia.

CAREER: University of Wales, Aberystwyth, lecturer in political science, 1976-78; University of Kent at Canterbury, Canterbury, England, began as lecturer, became senior lecturer in political science, 1978-83; University of Melbourne, Parkville, Australia, began as lecturer, became senior lecturer, 1983-88, professor of political science, 1988—, department head, 1988-93. Oxford University, senior associate member of St. Antony's College, 1987, 1993; Harvard University, visiting fellow at Russian Research Center, 1993. International Council for Central and East European Studies, Australian representative, 1990—; consultant to Australian radio and television networks.

MEMBER: International Association for Communist and Post-Communist Studies (member of executive committee), Australasian Political Studies Association (member of executive committee, 1990-93; president, 1991-92), Australasian Association for the Study of Socialist Countries, Australian Institute of International Affairs (member of council of Victoria branch, 1985—), Contemporary European Studies Association of Australia (member of executive committee).

AWARDS, HONORS: Grants from Australian Research Council, 1985-87, 1991-93.

WRITINGS:

The Policy Process in Communist States: Industrial Administration and Politics, Sage Publications (Beverly Hills, CA), 1981.
(Editor) *The Withering Away of the State?* Sage Publications, 1981.
Politics in the Communist World, Oxford University Press (New York), 1986.
The End of Communist Power: Anti-Corruption Campaigns and Legitimation Crisis, Oxford University Press, 1993.

Post-Communism, Polity Press, in press.

Work represented in anthologies, including *The Development of Civil Society in Communist Systems,* edited by R. F. Miller, Allen & Unwin, 1992; *The Road to Disillusion,* edited by R. Taras, M. E. Sharpe, 1992; and *From a One-Party State to Democracy,* edited by J. Frentzel-Zagorska, Rodopi, 1993. Contributor to political studies journals. East European editor, *British Journal of Communist Affairs,* 1981-83. Member of editorial board, *Australian Slavonic and East European Studies* and *Australian Journal of Political Science.*

WORK IN PROGRESS: Research on the development of the Russian Far East; research on corruption in post-communist states.

*   *   *

HOMAN, Sidney   1938-

PERSONAL: Born May 21, 1938, in Philadelphia, PA; son of Sidney Ramsden and May Elaine Homan; married Barbara Peter (marriage ended); married Norma Marjorie Schultz (a children's art program director), July 30, 1977; children: Christopher, Elizabeth, David, Daniel. *Education:* Princeton University, A.B., 1960; Harvard University, M.A., 1962, Ph.D., 1965. *Politics:* Democrat.

ADDRESSES: Home—1500 Northwest 36th Way, Gainesville, FL 32605. *Office*—Department of English, 4008 Turlington Hall, University of Florida, Gainesville, FL 32611.

CAREER: University of Illinois at Urbana-Champaign, assistant professor of English, 1965-69; Boston University, Boston, MA, associate professor of English, 1969-72; University of Florida, Gainesville, professor of English and theater, 1977—. Jilin University, visiting professor, 1986—. Theatrical director and actor; member of Theatre Strike Force theatrical company. Member of the national artistic board of the Orlando Shakespeare Festival.

WRITINGS:

Shakespeare's "More Than Words Can Witness," Bucknell University Press, 1981.
When the Theatre Turns to Itself, Bucknell University Press, 1982.
Beckett's Theatres, Bucknell University Press, 1983.
Shakespeare and the Triple Play, Bucknell University Press, 1986.

Shakespeare's Theatre of Presence, Bucknell University Press, 1987.

The Audience As Actor and Character, Bucknell University Press, 1989.

(Coeditor) *Shakespeare's Personality,* University of California Press, 1989.

Beckett's Television Plays, Bucknell University Press, 1992.

(Coauthor) *Pinter's Odd Man Out: Staging and Filming "Old Times,"* Bucknell University Press, 1993.

WORK IN PROGRESS: Stories from the Bone Marrow Unit: Growing up in Philly, a story collection.

SIDELIGHTS: Sidney Homan told *CA:* "My interests range from metadramatic to performance criticism, from the ways in which the 'triple play' can be executed from study to stage to classroom, to accounts of my own experience as an actor and director in professional, experimental, and university theaters. My prize-winning book *Beckett's Theatres* emerged from a production of *Waiting for Godot* that toured Florida's ten state prisons.

"On stage, I have directed works as wide-ranging as *The Comedy of Errors,* Bogosian's *Talk Radio,* Stoppard's *Dirty Linen/New-Found-Land,* Brecht's *Galileo,* Wasserstein's *Uncommon Women and Others,* and even a production of *The Merry Wives of Windsor* in the People's Republic of China. As an actor I have appeared in the plays of Beckett, Williams, Shakespeare, Pinter, Shaw, Stoppard, Churchill, and Wilde. In the style of *Saturday Night Live* and *In Living Color,* my company, Theatre Strike Force, engages in experimental, political, and improvisational theater.

"I have also directed a production of Pinter's *Old Times* for television, as well as television films of Beckett's five plays. Recently I directed a new comedy about high school coaches, *Boston Baked Bean,* which had performances in theaters, bars, and prisons. I am currently at work on *Number One Son,* a rock musical in the style of *Hair.*"

*   *   *

HORAN, Elizabeth (Rosa) 1956-

PERSONAL: Born July 6, 1956, in Boston, MA; daughter of Richard P. (a marine sergeant and billings clerk) and Harriet (a salesperson and social worker; maiden name, Clouter) Horan; married Paul Skilton (an information systems manager), June 19, 1980; children: Amalia Elizabeth. *Education:* At-tended Simon's Rock of Bard College, 1973-75; Barnard College, A.B. (magna cum laude), 1978; attended Universidad Catolica and Universidad de Chile, 1985-86; University of California, Santa Cruz, Ph.D., 1988. *Politics:* "Left." *Religion:* "Recovering Unitarian."

ADDRESSES: Home—Tempe, AZ. *Office*—Department of English, Arizona State University, Tempe, AZ 85287-0302.

CAREER: Cabrillo Community College, Aptos, CA, instructor in English, 1984; Tufts University, Medford, MA, lecturer, 1987-88, visiting assistant professor of English, 1989; Arizona State University, Tempe, assistant professor of English and women's studies and director of Comparative Literature Program, 1989—. Wheelock College, lecturer, 1987-88.

MEMBER: Modern Language Association of America, American Studies Association, Latin American Studies Association, Feministas Unidas.

AWARDS, HONORS: Fulbright fellow in Chile, 1985-86; grant from National Endowment for the Humanities, 1990; First Prize in International Concurso-Homenaje Gabriela Mistral, Organization of American States, 1990, for *Gabriela Mistral;* Rockefeller Regional Scholar Award, Southwest Institute for Research on Women, 1991.

WRITINGS:

(Translator and author of introduction) *Happiness: Stories by Marjorie Agosin,* White Pine Press, 1993.

Gabriela Mistral: An Artist and Her People, Organization of American States, 1994.

Imagining the Audience: Gabriela Mistral among Latin American Women, University of Texas Press, in press.

Work represented in anthologies, including *The Word and the Market: American Women in Publishing from Colonial Times to 1900,* edited by Susan Albertine, University of Tennessee Press, 1994; *A New Critical Reception of Gabriela Mistral,* edited by Ric McAllister and Sonia Riquelme, Edwin Mellen, 1994; and *Latin American Gay and Lesbian Literature: A Biographical and Critical Sourcebook,* edited by David W. Foster, Greenwood Press, 1994. Contributor of articles, poems, translations, and reviews to periodicals, including *Poet Lore, Quarry West, Chinquapin,* and *Dawn.*

WORK IN PROGRESS: Editing and translating a critical edition, *Selected Writings of Gabriela Mistral,* completion expected in 1996.

SIDELIGHTS: Elizabeth Horan told *CA:* "I have always been a writer, and I do not discriminate between modes or genres. The tougher question was always how to make ends meet, how to pay for school, how to persevere. I grew up ostensibly middle class, but actually in poverty, with schooling and health care through government programs, and always looking to travel. Someday, I will write about what it has meant for me, a seventh-generation New Englander, to leave for California, Latin America, and Arizona. In the meantime I read and teach and translate and write about these wonderful literatures."

*   *   *

HOWE, Christine J.   1948-

PERSONAL: Born November 21, 1948, in Birmingham, England; daughter of Walter Virgil (a businessperson) and Joyce Winifred (a homemaker; maiden name, Barmby) Howe; married William Robertson (a tax consultant), September 23, 1979; children: Miriam Emily, Jeremy Daniel. *Education:* Sussex University, B.A. (with honors), 1970; Cambridge University, Ph.D., 1974. *Politics:* "Left of centre."

ADDRESSES: Home—Auchendarroch, Balfron, G63 0RL, Scotland. *Office*—Centre for Research into Interactive Learning, 40 George St., Glasgow, G1 1QE, Scotland.

CAREER: Sussex University, Brighton, England, lecturer, 1974-76; Strathclyde University, Glasgow, Scotland, lecturer, 1976-90, senior lecturer, 1990—. Consultant to Craig Corporate Managements.

MEMBER: International Association for Study of Child Language, Association for Science Education, British Psychological Society.

AWARDS, HONORS: Emanuel Miller Prize (philosophy) from St. John's College, Cambridge University.

WRITINGS:

Acquiring Language in a Conversational Context, Academic, 1981.
Language Learning: A Special Case for Developmental Psychology, Lawrence-Earlbaum (Hillsdale, NJ), 1993.

Group and Interactive Learning, Computational Mechanics, 1994.

WORK IN PROGRESS: Writing *Theory and Concept in Children's Thinking: The Case of Everyday Physics;* researching early language, everyday physics, peer interaction, and learning.

*   *   *

HSUEH, Tien-tung   1939-

PERSONAL: Born February 11, 1939, in Taiwan; son of Fang-wen and Yuen-po (Huang) Hsueh; married Fei-ai Hou (a homemaker), February 2, 1965; children: Sara Li-ju, Paul Chih-chung, Frank Chih-cheng. *Education:* National Taiwan University, B.A., 1961, M.A., 1965; University of Colorado, Ph.D., 1969. *Politics:* None. *Religion:* Christian. *Avocational interests:* "Serious music."

ADDRESSES: Home—7A Block, 2 Ravana Garden, Shatin, New Territory, Hong Kong. *Office*—Department of Economics, Chinese University of Hong Kong, Shatin, New Territory, Hong Kong.

CAREER: Council for U.S. Aid, Taipei, Taiwan, member of research staff at Economic Research Center, 1962-63; National Taiwan University, Taipei, instructor, 1965-67, associate professor of economics, 1969-71; Chinese University of Hong Kong, Hong Kong, lecturer, 1971-80, senior lecturer, 1980-90, reader in economics, 1990—, head of department at United College, 1972-77, director of China's Reform and Development Programme at Hong Kong Institute of Asia-Pacific Studies, 1990—. Harvard University, research fellow at Harvard-Yenching Institute, 1977-78; Peking University, educational expert in economics, 1985-86; Nagoya University, visiting research fellow in economics, 1993; lecturer at institutions of higher learning, including Northeast University of Technology, Shenyang, 1983, Xiamen University, 1984, Peking University, 1985-86, Beijing Institute of Information and Control, Chinese Academy of Social Sciences, Xian Institute of Metallurgy and Construction Engineering, Nankai University, Huazhong University of Science and Technology, and Beijing Metallurgical Management Cadres Institute, all 1986, and Zhongshan University, 1994. Transportation Planning Board of Taiwan, head of Economic Section, 1970-71; consultant to World Bank, Asian Development Bank, and Asian Productivity Organization. United Kingdom Council for National Academic Awards, Hong Kong member, 1988. *Military service:* Statistical officer in a national air force, 1961-62; became second lieutenant.

MEMBER: American Economic Association.

AWARDS, HONORS: Fulbright fellow, 1967-68.

WRITINGS:

An Econometric Model for Taiwan Economic Development, China Committee for Publication Aid and Prize Awards (Taipei), 1971.

(Translator into Chinese, and author of notes) Paul A. Samuelson, *Foundations of Economic Analysis,* two volumes, Hsieh Chih Industrial Library Publishing (Taipei), 1974.

Modern Western Public Finance (in Chinese), Shanghai People's Publishing House (Shanghai), 1983.

National Economic Management (in Chinese), Shanghai Institute of International Economic Management (Shanghai), 1983.

(With Tun-oy Woo) *Trade between Hong Kong and China* (in Chinese), Foreign Economic Relations and Trade Publishing House (Beijing), 1984.

Quantitative Economics (in Chinese), Publishing House of Huazhong University of Science and Technology (Wuhan), 1986.

(Editor with Yu Jingyuan and Shi Ruohua, and contributor) *Studies on Economic Reforms and Development in the People's Republic of China* (in Chinese), Commercial Press (Beijing), 1990.

(With Tun-oy Woo) *The Economics of Industrial Development in the People's Republic of China,* Hong Kong Institute of Asia-Pacific Studies, Chinese University of Hong Kong, 1991.

(With Sung Yun-wing and Jingyuan) *Studies on Economic Reforms and Development in the People's Republic of China,* St. Martin's, 1993.

(Editor with Li Jingwen and Zheng Yuxin, and contributor) *Studies on China's Productivity Trend* (in Chinese), Social Sciences Literature Publishing House (Beijing), 1993.

(With Li Qiang and Liu Shucheng) *China's Provincial Statistics, 1949-1989,* Westview, 1993.

(Editor with Shucheng and Qiang, and contributor) *Studies on China's Regional Economic Development* (in Chinese), China's Statistics Publishing House (Beijing), 1994.

(Editor with Kai-yuen Tsui and Thomas G. Rawski, and contributor) *Productivity, Efficiency, and Reform in China's Economy,* Hong Kong Institute of Asia-Pacific Studies, Chinese University of Hong Kong, 1995.

Work represented in anthologies, including *Hong Kong: Economic, Social, and Political Studies in Development,* edited by T. B. Lin, R. L. Lee, and U. E. Simonis, M. E. Sharpe, 1979; and *Comparative Asian Economics,* edited by John Y. T. Kuark, JAI Press, 1995. Contributor of about a hundred articles and reviews to economic journals. Executive member of editorial board, *Twenty-First Century Bimonthly,* 1993—; member of editorial board, *Hong Kong Economic Papers,* 1978-82.

WORK IN PROGRESS: China's Regional Economic Development; China's National Income, 1952-1993.

SIDELIGHTS: Tien-tung Hsueh told *CA:* "I set up the Chinese Economic Research Programme at the Centre for Contemporary Asian Studies, Chinese University of Hong Kong, in 1986. This was the predecessor of China's Economic Reform and Development Programme at the Hong Kong Institute of Asia-Pacific Studies. The program is dedicated to tackling systematically the fundamental issues and relevant statistics of the Chinese economy in a consistent framework, by means of modern economic theory. The first joint project of this program, in cooperation with the Beijing Institute of Information and Control, resulted in the book *Studies on Economic Reforms and Development in the People's Republic of China.* The second project, conducted jointly with the Institute of Quantitative and Technical Economics, Chinese Academy of Social Sciences, and Department of Statistics on National Economic Balances, resulted in *China's Provincial Statistics, 1949-1989.*

"Apart from publishing seven books in the People's Republic of China, I was invited to give numerous lectures on various subjects of western economics, quantitative economics, public finance, economic development and planning, and project evaluation. Through these activities, I am determined to enable the program to play the role of a bridge to promote research activities between China, Hong Kong, and the rest of the world, and to make these Chinese economic studies available to students of the field all over the world."

*   *   *

HUMPHREYS, Margaret   1955-
(Margaret Warner)

PERSONAL: Born December 6, 1955, in New Orleans, LA; daughter of Kelton Brooks (a dentist) and Mary Ellen (a teacher; maiden name, Donnelly) Humphreys; married John Harley Warner, May, 1981 (divorced, September, 1986). *Education:* Attended St. Mary's College, 1972-73; University of Notre Dame, B.A., 1976; Harvard University, M.A., 1977, Ph.D., 1983, M.D., 1987. *Politics:* Liberal Democrat. *Avocational interests:* Hiking, backpacking, canoeing, gardening.

ADDRESSES: Home—Durham, NC. *Office*—Department of History, Box 90719, Duke University, Durham, NC 27710.

CAREER: Harvard University, Cambridge, MA, instructor, 1983-84, lecturer, 1986-93, Fae Kass Lecturer, 1987; Duke University, Durham, NC, assistant professor of history and medicine, and physician (internal medicine) at university medical center, both 1993—. Francis Wood Institute, editorial consultant, 1993—.

MEMBER: American Association for the History of Medicine, History of Science Society, Society of General Internal Medicine, American College of Physicians.

WRITINGS:

Yellow Fever and the South, Rutgers University Press, 1992.

Contributor to history journals, sometimes under the name Margaret Warner.

WORK IN PROGRESS: Research on the history of malaria in the twentieth-century American South; research on Civil War medicine.

SIDELIGHTS: Margaret Humphreys told *CA:* "My interest in southern history matured while I was a graduate student at Harvard, where the history of New England dominated the scholarly landscape. Hence, I had an underdog attitude from the start, in my striving to bring the best techniques of modern social history to bear on the South's medical past. There I also decided to attend medical school, for I felt that history was not quite an important enough life's occupation. At the other end of the medical training process, I acquired a better appreciation of both the limitations of medicine and the glorious value of history. Now I practice medicine 'on the side' while pursuing my primary passion of historical research."

*   *   *

HUNDERT, Gershon David   1946-

PERSONAL: Born December 8, 1946, in Toronto, Ontario, Canada. *Education:* Columbia University, B.A., 1969, Ph.D., 1978; Jewish Theological Seminary, B.Rel.Ed., 1969; Ohio State University, M.A., 1971.

ADDRESSES: Home—4838 Fulton, Montreal, Quebec, Canada H3W 1V3. *Office*—Department of Jewish Studies, McGill University, 3511 Peel St., Montreal, Quebec, Canada H3A 1W7; Department of History, McGill University, 855 Sherbrooke St. W., Montreal, Quebec, Canada H3A 2T7.

CAREER: McGill University, Montreal, Quebec, lecturer, 1975-78, assistant professor, 1978-84, associate professor, 1984-92, professor, 1992—, Montreal Jewish Community professor of Jewish studies, 1993—. Yale University, visiting associate professor, 1988. Association for Jewish Studies, on North American board of directors, 1986-88 and 1992-94; Polish Jewish Heritage Foundation of Canada, founding president and chair of the board, 1987—; World Union for Jewish Studies, member of council, 1993—. Consultant to a film project on Hasidism sponsored by the National Endowment for the Humanities, 1992.

MEMBER: American Association for the Advancement of Slavic Studies, American Historical Association, Economic History Association, Historical Society of Israel.

AWARDS, HONORS: Recipient of grants from McGill University, 1979, 1981, 1985, 1990, and 1991, Interuniversity Centre for European Studies (Montreal), 1981, Social Sciences and Humanities Research Council of Canada, 1981-82, 1987-89, and 1993-96, and Memorial Foundation for Jewish Culture, 1981-82 and 1990-91; Horace W. Goldsmith Fellow in Judaic Studies, Yale University, 1988; I. J. Segal Prize for the best book on a Jewish theme by a Canadian, 1992, for *The Jews in a Polish Private Town: The Case of Opatow in the Eighteenth Century;* Institute for Advanced Studies, Hebrew University (Jerusalem), fellow, 1993-94.

WRITINGS:

(With Gershon Bacon) *The Jews in Poland and Russia: Bibliographical Essays,* Indiana University Press, 1984.
(Editor with Ronald S. Aigen) *Community and the Individual Jew: Essays in Honor of Lavy M. Becker,* Reconstructionist Rabbinical College Press (Montreal), 1986.
(Editor) *Essential Papers on Hasidism: Origins to Present,* New York University Press, 1991.
The Jews in a Polish Private Town: The Case of Opatow in the Eighteenth Century, Johns Hopkins University Press, 1992.

Contributor of articles on Poland and Polish-Jewish history to professional journals. *Polin: Studies in Polish Jewry,* editor, 1992—.

HUTSON, Lorna   1958-

PERSONAL: Born November 27, 1958, in West Berlin, Germany; daughter of John Whiteford (a diplomat) and Doris (a teacher and homemaker; maiden name, Kemp) Hutson. *Education:* Somerville College, Oxford, B.A. (with first class honors), 1979, D.Phil., 1983. *Politics:* Labour. *Religion:* Agnostic.

ADDRESSES: Home—40 Magdalen Rd., Oxford OX4 1RB, England. *Office*—Department of English, Queen Mary and Westfield College, University of London, Mile End Rd., London E1 4NS, England.

CAREER: University of London, Queen Mary and Westfield College, London, England, lecturer in English, 1986—.

AWARDS, HONORS: Fellow at Folger Shakespeare Library and Huntington Library, 1995.

WRITINGS:

Thomas Nashe in Context, Oxford University Press, 1989.
The Usurer's Daughter: Male Friendship and Fictions of Women in Sixteenth-Century England, Routledge & Kegan Paul, 1994.

WORK IN PROGRESS: Economies of Uncertainty, a book on Shakespeare; research on concepts of rhetoric and temperance (discursivity and moral/physical conduct) in sixteenth- and seventeenth-century literature.

I-J

IACCINO, James F(rancis) 1955-
(Jim Iaccino)

PERSONAL: Born May 23, 1955, in Chicago, IL; son of Vincent Mitchell, Jr. (a chemist) and Victoria (a homemaker; maiden name, Marelli) Iaccino; married January, 1989; wife's name, Michele Diane (a homemaker); children: Jonathan James, Nicole Erin. *Education:* Rosary College, B.A. (summa cum laude), 1977; DePaul University, M.A., 1979, Ph.D., 1982. *Politics:* Conservative. *Religion:* Roman Catholic.

ADDRESSES: Home—54 Clarece Trail, Somonauk, IL 60552. *Office*—Department of Psychology, Illinois Benedictine College, 5700 College Rd., Lisle, IL 60532.

CAREER: DePaul University, Chicago, IL, instructor in psychology, 1978-80; Rosary College, River Forest, IL, instructor in psychology, 1980; Illinois Benedictine College, Lisle, assistant professor, 1981-84, associate professor, 1984-91, professor of psychology, 1991—, director of academic advising, 1987—, and experimental psychologist. Guest on local television programs; consultant to Peat-Marwick.

MEMBER: American Psychological Association, National Academic Advising Association, Midwestern Psychological Association, Illinois Psychological Association, Pi Gamma Mu, Psi Chi.

WRITINGS:

Left Brain-Right Brain Differences: Inquiries, Evidence, and New Approaches, Lawrence Erlbaum, 1993.
Psychological Reflections on Cinematic Terror: Jungian Archetypes in Horror Films, Praeger, 1994.
More Jungian Reflections in the Cinema: A Psycho- *logical Analysis of Science Fiction and Fantasy Archetypes,* Praeger, 1995.

Some writing appears under the name Jim Iaccino. Contributor of about thirty articles and reviews to psychology and education journals.

WORK IN PROGRESS: Research on brain assymetries in the processing of information between the genders as a function of attentional bias effects.

SIDELIGHTS: James F. Iaccino told *CA:* "While at Rosary College, I became interested in brain differences between the genders. My independent study consisted of feeding different verbal materials in the right and left ears of male and female subjects. The results of my study supported the hypothesis that males process sounds differently than females do. Men typically did better with their right ears, while women did equally well with either ear.

"Further research at DePaul University and Illinois Benedictine College tended to replicate these findings. I was fascinated by the gender variations and tried to relate them to basic brain differences. It would seem that females store information on both sides of their brain; hence, they would show no ear advantage. Males, on the other hand, have a left hemisphere more equipped to handle verbal items exclusively; therefore, their right ears should show a corresponding advantage.

"Although my research is hardly original, it does support the findings in the literature. At the very least, applications of my work can be derived to show how the genders process each other's conversations. It is intriguing to note the differences, for it would indicate that men and women are not the same, psychologically

212

and cognitively. Recently I conducted a workshop on this subject, with noteworthy speakers from other institutions. Theological, psychological, cognitive, and environmental arguments were made, with the resulting awareness that we have barely scratched the surface of this area.

"When I am not conducting brain research, I spend time with my rapidly expanding family. I keep busy with home improvement projects and, in my spare time, I read voraciously everything I can find on horror and science fiction, and I try to see as many films in these genres as possible.

"What started out as a relaxing hobby has turned into a scholarly pursuit. I have applied Carl Jung's list of archetypal images to the horror and science fiction genres with some success. One of the reasons audiences are fascinated by these stories is that common themes are transmitted over and over again. These stories have been transmitted since the beginning of history, to the point where they have been inbred into our collective unconscious. For example, the *Star Wars* films, though set in a futuristic period, are still classic fairy tales that involve white knights battling evil black knights and rescuing feisty princesses.

"No one has attempted to do a thorough analysis of the horror and science fiction/fantasy film genres from a Jungian archetypal perspective, so I decided to take a shot at this venture. The result has been an enjoyable one, as I found the correlations between archetypes and the films are quite striking. Through my books *Psychological Reflections on Cinematic Terror* and *More Jungian Reflections in the Cinema* I hope to show readers the real reasons why they are drawn to these films, and why such movies will continue to be a part of the ever-growing popular culture movement in the United States."

*   *   *

IACCINO, Jim
See IACCINO, James F(rancis)

*   *   *

IWAMATSU, Jun Atsushi   1908-1994
(Taro Yashima)

OBITUARY NOTICE—See index for *CA* sketch: Born September 21, 1908, in Kagoshima, Japan; immigrated to the U.S. in 1939; died June 30, 1994. Artist, illustrator, and author. Iwamatsu, an award-winning author and illustrator, began his writing career with the publication of *The New Sun,* an autobiography published in 1943.

When he was hired during World War II to work for the U.S. Army Office of War Information and the Office of Strategic Services, Iwamatsu adopted the pseudonym Taro Yashima, which he would use from the 1940s until his death. Iwamatsu is known for the delicate, impressionistic illustrations he created for such books as *Crow Boy, Umbrella,* and *Seashore Story.* Named a 1967 *New York Times* Choice of Best Illustrated Children's Books of the Year, *Seashore Story* was noted by critics for the sophistication of its abstract artwork. In addition to writing and illustrating his own books, Iwamatsu provided illustrations for stories by American authors Eleanor M. Jewett, Claude Robert Bulla, and June Behrens. He also collaborated with his wife, Tomoe Iwamatsu—whose pseudonym is Mitsu Yashima—on *Plenty to Watch* and *Momo's Kitten.* Iwamatsu was the director of the Yashima Art Institute in Los Angeles, where he taught methods and techniques for teaching art; his paintings are part of permanent collections of several museums, including the Phillips Memorial Museum in Washington, D.C.

OBITUARIES AND OTHER SOURCES:

BOOKS

Twentieth-Century Children's Writers, 3rd edition, St. James Press, 1989.

PERIODICALS

School Library Journal, October, 1994, p.24.

*   *   *

JACKSON, J(ames) R(obert) de J(ager) 1935-

PERSONAL: Born July 14, 1935, in St. Andrews, Scotland; son of Reginald Jackson (a university teacher) and Clara Marion Brooke; married Heather Joanna Murphy (a university teacher), 1969; children: Katherine, Elizabeth. *Education:* Queen's University (Canada), B.A., 1957, M.A., 1958; Princeton University, A.M., 1960, Ph.D., 1961; University of London, Ph.D., 1963.

ADDRESSES: Home—Toronto, Ontario, Canada. *Office*—Victoria College, Toronto, Ontario, Canada M5S 1K7.

CAREER: McMaster University, Hamilton, Ontario, Canada, assistant professor, 1963-64; University of Toronto, Toronto, Ontario, began as assistant professor, 1964, became university professor beginning in 1994.

AWARDS, HONORS: Royal Society of Canada fellow; Guggenheim fellow, 1972-73; Killam Research fellow, 1975-76 and 1982-84; Connaught senior fellow, 1985-86.

WRITINGS:

Method and Imagination in Coleridge's Criticism, Routledge/Harvard University Press, 1969.
(Editor) *Coleridge: The Critical Heritage,* 2 volumes, Routledge, 1970-1991.
Poetry of the Romantic Period, Routledge, 1980.
(Editor) S. T. Coleridge, *Logic* (part of "Collected Coleridge" series), Routledge/Princeton University Press, 1981.
Annals of English Verse, 1770-1835, Garland, 1985.
Historical Criticism and the Meaning of Texts, Routledge, 1989.
Romantic Poetry by Women: A Bibliography 1770-1835, Oxford University Press (New York, NY), 1993.

WORK IN PROGRESS: Editing (with H. J. Jackson) S. T. Coleridge's *Shorter Works and Fragments.*

*   *   *

JAKOBSON, Michael   1939-

PERSONAL: Born March 4, 1939, in Moscow, Russia; son of Lev and Alexandria; children: Leo. *Education:* University of Minnesota, received degree, 1979, Ph.D., 1988.

ADDRESSES: Home—2732 Kenwood Blvd., No. 204, Toledo, OH 43606. *Office*—Department of History, University of Toledo, Toledo, OH 43606.

CAREER: West Virginia University, Morgantown, assistant professor of history, 1989-91; University of Toledo, Toledo, OH, associate professor of history, 1991—.

WRITINGS:

Guide to the Boris I. Nicolaevsky Collection, Hoover Institution Press, 1989.
Origins of the GULAG: The Soviet Prison-Camp System, 1917-1934, University Press of Kentucky, 1992.

WORK IN PROGRESS: Soviet Prisoners' Songs as a Historical Source.

*   *   *

JAMES, Deana
See SIZER, Mona Young

JARVIS, E. K.
See Bloch, Robert (Albert)

*   *   *

JEANS, Peter D(ouglas)   1936-

PERSONAL: Born October 4, 1936, in Perth, Australia; son of Douglas James Tendron (a physician) and Evelyn Dorothy (Goodenough) Jeans; married Judith Elizabeth Taylor (a schoolteacher), 1966; children: Romony Kathleen, Simon Bourchier. *Education:* University of Western Australia, B.A. and Diploma in Education, 1962. *Politics:* "Strictly a-political." *Religion:* "Bush Baptist." *Avocational interests:* Sailing, metalwork and wood turning.

ADDRESSES: Home—36 Acanthus Rd., Willetton, Perth, Western Australia 6155. *Agent*—Christine Nagel, 7 Hartung St., Mundaring, Perth, Western Australia 6073.

CAREER: Department of Education of Western Australia, secondary schoolteacher, 1958—, including English teacher and department head, 1972-87.

MEMBER: State Schoolteachers Union of Western Australia.

WRITINGS:

My Word, St. George Books (Perth, Australia), 1993.
Ship to Shore: A Dictionary of Everyday Words and Phrases Derived from the Sea, American Bibliographical Center-Clio Press (Santa Barbara, CA), 1993.
The Long Road to London, Literary Mouse Press (Perth), 1995.

WORK IN PROGRESS: Two novels, including *The Mirror Man.*

SIDELIGHTS: Peter D. Jeans told *CA:* "My father, a medical doctor, went to war in 1940 and was killed in North Africa. I have powerful memories of the war years in Australia, and consequently I despise politicians as a sub-set of humanity.

"When I graduated from teacher's college in 1958, I worked in the tropical north of Western Australia. After graduation from the University of Western Australia, I spent seven years traveling the world. Part of these travels—a fifteen-month journey by motorcycle from Singapore to London, 1962-63—is recounted in my book *The Long Road to London.*

"I learned one powerful lesson from my travels: never complain. I eat everything put in front of me and am grateful for it. I cannot abide people who complain.

"I have two passions (apart from the English language, which is my profession): model steam engines and sailing. Model steaming tests my application of the laws of physics. Sailing tests my understanding of, and adaptability to, the laws of nature. I admire and revere the professional seamen, especially the seamen of old, the iron men in wooden ships, for their thorough mastery of 'conducting a ship at sea,' and for their utter humility in the face of the world's great oceans. No other profession tests a man as thoroughly as that of seafaring."

*   *   *

JENKINS, Dafydd 1911-

PERSONAL: Born March 1, 1911, in Hornsey, Middlesex, England; son of William J. (a bank official) and Elizabeth (Evans) Jenkins; married Gwyneth Elizabeth Owen, February 21, 1942 (marriage ended, August 17, 1962); children: Rhys Owen. *Education:* Sidney Sussex College, Cambridge, B.A., 1933, LL.B., 1934, M.A., 1937, LL.M., 1949, Litt.D., 1973. *Politics:* Plaid Gymru. *Religion:* Church in Wales.

ADDRESSES: Home—17 Min y Bryn, Aberystwyth SY23 1LZ, Wales.

CAREER: Called to the Bar at Gray's Inn, 1934; barrister, 1934-38; Welsh Language Petition, organizing secretary, 1938-39; agricultural worker and organizer, 1940-69; University of Wales, Aberystwyth, law teacher, 1962-75, professor of history and Welsh law, 1975-78.

AWARDS, HONORS: Honorary J.D., University of Wuerzburg, 1991.

WRITINGS:

Tan yn Llyn, Aberystwyth Press, 1937, 2nd edition, Plaid Gymru, 1975.
Thomas Johnes o'r Hafod, University of Wales Press, 1948.
Llyfr Colan, University of Wales Press, 1963.
Gyfraith Hywel, Gomer Press, 1970, 2nd edition, 1976.
Damisciniau Colan, Cymdeithas Lyfrau Cereligion, 1973.
(Editor) *Hywel Dda: The Law,* Gomer Press, 1986, 2nd edition published as *The Law of Hywel the Good,* 1990.

JOHNSON, Eric W(arner) 1918-1994

OBITUARY NOTICE—See index for *CA* sketch: Born March 22, 1918, in Philadelphia, PA; died of head injuries suffered after a fall, August 4, 1994, in Philadelphia, PA. Educator and author. A prolific writer of books for young people and adults, Johnson was a Quaker educator who began writing books as a means of providing his junior high school students with practical guidelines for improving their academic skills as well as dealing with the social concerns of adolescence. Two of his most popular books for teens include *Improve Your Own Spelling* and *Love and Sex in Plain Language.* As a junior high school principal, Johnson observed parents and teachers seeking straightforward information about the transition from childhood to adolescence; he also noted that these same groups were asking for practical assistance in relating to and nurturing young adults. These observations led to the publication of such volumes as *How to Live Through Junior High School* (1959), *The Family Book About Sexuality* (1981), and *Raising Children to Achieve* (1984). Johnson authored more than fifty volumes, including text books, teacher education materials, and two stories for younger readers, *The Stolen Ruler* (1970) and *Escape into the Zoo* (1971). Among his most recent books are *Humorous Stories about the Human Condition* and *Quaker Meeting: A Risky Business,* both published in 1991.

OBITUARIES AND OTHER SOURCES:

BOOKS

The Writers Directory: 1994-1996, St. James Press, 1993.

PERIODICALS

New York Times, August 9, 1994, p. B10.
Washington Post, August 10, 1994, p. B4.

*   *   *

JOHNSON, John L. 1945-

PERSONAL: Born June 10, 1945; married, wife's name Artimese L. (a nurse), June 12, 1971; children: Julian R. *Education:* St. Louis University, B.S., D.D. *Politics:* Democrat. *Religion:* Apostolic.

ADDRESSES: Home—8312 Pepperidge Dr., Berkeley, MO 63134.

CAREER: Former U.S. Postal Service worker. *Military service:* U.S. Maritime Service; received National Citation Medal.

WRITINGS:

Black Biblical Heritage, Winston-Derek (Nashville, TN), 1994.

Also author of *God's Kinship with Dark Colors.*

WORK IN PROGRESS: A book on tricks and games.

*   *   *

JOHNSTON, Julie   1941-

PERSONAL: Born January 21, 1941, in Smith Falls, Ontario, Canada; daughter of J. A. B. (a lawyer) and Sarah Mae (a homemaker; maiden name, Patterson) Dulmage; married Basil W. Johnston (an orthopedic surgeon), 1963; children: Leslie, Lauren, Andrea, Melissa. *Education:* University of Toronto, received degree, 1963; Trent University, B.A., 1984. *Avocational interests:* Old wooden boats, vegetable gardening, bicycling, hiking, travelling, reading, and stone masonry.

ADDRESSES: Home and office—463 Hunter St. W., Peterborough, Ontario K9H 2M7, Canada.

CAREER: Occupational therapist at a school for mentally handicapped children, Smith's Falls, Ontario, 1963-65; Rehabilitation Centre, Kingston, Ontario, occupational therapist, 1965-69. Peterborough Board of Education, Continuing Education Department, creative writing instructor, 1988-89.

MEMBER: Canadian Society of Children's Authors, Illustrators, and Performers (CANSCAIP), Canadian Children's Book Centre, The Writer's Union of Canada, Ottawa Independent Writers.

AWARDS, HONORS: Runner-up, *Chatelaine* Fiction Contest, 1979, for the short story "Canadian Content"; first prize, Solange Karsh Award, Birks Gold Medal, and cash prize, Canadian Playwriting Competition, Ottawa Little Theatre, 1979, for *There's Going to Be a Frost;* Kawartha Region Best Play award, 1980, for *There's Going to Be a Frost* and co-winner for best play, 1984, for *Lucid Intervals;* Canadian Library Association Young Adult Honour Book, 1993, shortlisting for Mister Christie's Book Award, 1993, National Chapter of Canada Independent Order Daughters of the Empire (IODE) Violet Downey Book Award, 1993, Governor General's Literary Award for children's literature, 1993, *School Library Journal* Best Book, 1994, New York Public Library's 1994 Books for the Teen Age list selection, Ontario Library Association Silver Birch Award nomination, 1994, and American Library Association notable book selection, all for *Hero of Lesser Causes.*

WRITINGS:

There's Going to Be a Frost (one-act play), first produced at the Sears Drama Festival, 1980.
Lucid Intervals (one-act play), first produced at the Sears Drama Festival, 1984.
Hero of Lesser Causes (young adult novel), Lester Publishing, 1992, Joy Street Books, 1993.
Adam and Eve and Pinch-Me (young adult novel), Little, Brown, 1994.

Contributor of the novella *The Window Seat* to *Women's Weekly Omnibus,* 1984, and the story "Mirrors" to the anthology *The Blue Jean Collection,* Thistledown Press, 1992. Contributor of fiction to periodicals, including *Women's Weekly Buzz, Chatelaine, Woman and Home,* and *Matrix;* contributor of nonfiction to periodicals, including *Wine Tidings, Homemakers, Doctor's Review,* and *Canadian Author and Bookman.* Johnston's work has been translated into French.

WORK IN PROGRESS: A screenplay based on *Hero of Lesser Causes* for Canadian producer Roy Krost, proposed production date 1994-95.

SIDELIGHTS: Julie Johnston won praise for her first novel for young adults, *Hero of Lesser Causes,* which reviewer Deborah Stevenson described in a *Bulletin of the Center for Children's Books* review as a "touching and funny story of sibling maturation." Set in Canada in 1946, the book begins as twelve-year-old Keely sees her brother Patrick paralyzed by polio after swimming in a public pool. Keely and her brother, just a year apart in age, are close friends, and Keely cannot imagine her life without him. Yet Patrick seems a different person as he becomes more and more bitter about his disease. Patrick's frustration and depression moves Keely to concoct wild plans to cheer and heal him. One of these plans is to find the fiance of Patrick's nurse, who is missing and presumed dead in World War II. Despite her efforts, Patrick's emotional condition grows increasingly serious. Finally, after an attempted suicide, Patrick begins to understand that his life is worth living, and he responds to Keely's optimism.

Hero of Lesser Causes was well received. A *Kirkus Review* writer noted that the book was "a fine first novel," while a *Publishers Weekly* reviewer found that the book "accelerates into a spectacular novel, balancing coming-of-age-angst with the grief from a sudden, devastating affliction." Cindy Darling Codell praised the book in *School Library Journal* as being "wonderfully simple, yet layered with meaning." Nancy Vasilakis, a reviewer for *Horn Book,* appreciated the "unique period details" which "create a strong sense of the place and the time without slowing down the action." *Hero of Lesser Causes* earned Johnston Canada's prestigious Governor General's Literary Award in 1993.

Explaining her approach to writing, Johnston commented: "Fiction is about developing characters who never existed but might have, and allowing them to do things that never happened but could have. It's making up the truth. What I enjoy most about writing fiction is burrowing so deeply into these characters that I am in tune with how they think, how they sound, and how they see the world. The only way I can do this is to explore every facet of myself and use bits for every character—good, bad, or ridiculous. Creating a character is like going on an archeological dig of the soul. Truth is what I'm digging for; the trick is in recognizing it. When I agonize over my own flaws and failures, or rejoice in chunks of good fortune, I find myself storing it all away in some closet in my mind to use as a hand-me-down for a future character. While I'm grubbing around under the surface of things I sometimes find the one true passion that rules a character's life."

BIOGRAPHICAL/CRITICAL SOURCES:

PERIODICALS

Booklist, July, 1993, p. 1966.
Bulletin of the Center for Children's Books, April, 1993, p. 254.
Children's Book News, spring, 1992, p. 17.
Emergency Librarian, March, 1993, p. 14.
Horn Book, August, 1993, p. 457.
Kirkus Review, May 15, 1993, p. 663.
Publishers Weekly, May 24, 1993, p. 89; July 12, 1993, p. 24.
Quill and Quire, April, 1992, p. 31.
School Library Journal, June, 1993, p. 107.
Toronto Star, December 22, 1992.

*   *   *

JONAS, Susan 1938-

PERSONAL: Born March 15, 1938, in Pittsburgh, PA; daughter of Leonard (in business) and Rosalyn (Sedler) Krieger; married Gerald Jonas, 1966 (divorced, 1976); children: Sarah, Phoebe. *Education:* Wellesley College, B.A., 1960. *Politics:* Democrat. *Religion:* Jewish.

ADDRESSES: Home and office—450 West End Ave., New York, NY 10024-5343. *Agent*—Wendy Weil, 232 Madison Ave., New York, NY 10016.

CAREER: Time, Inc., New York City, 1961-87, began as secretary for *Time,* became deputy picture editor, then picture editor of *Discover;* freelance writer. Women's Commission on Refugee Women and Children, member of board of directors, 1989—.

WRITINGS:

(With Marilyn Nissenson) *Cuff Links,* Abrams, 1991.
(With Nissenson) *The Ubiquitous Pig,* Abrams, 1992.
(With Nissenson) *Going, Going, Gone: Vanishing Americana,* Chronicle Books, 1994.
Snake-Charm, Abrams, 1995.

*   *   *

JONASDOTTIR, Anna G(udrun) 1942-

PERSONAL: Born December 2, 1942, in Akureyri, Iceland; Icelandic citizen; permanent resident of Sweden since 1969; daughter of Jonas Johannsson and Indiana Gisladottir; married Bo Jonsson (a political scientist), July 14, 1989; children: Bjarni Bjarnason, Anna Bjarnason, Sif Bjarnason. *Education:* University of Gothenburg, Ph.D., 1991; also attended the Universities of Orebro and Uppsala.

ADDRESSES: Office—Department of Social Science, Section of Politics, University of Orebro, Box 923, 701 30 Orebro, Sweden.

CAREER: Taught courses and lectured in sociology, politics, and women's studies, beginning in 1973; University of Orebro, Orebro, Sweden, senior lecturer in politics, 1986—; University of Gothenburg, Gothenburg, Sweden, affiliated with women's studies and political science departments.

AWARDS, HONORS: Fellowship from the Swedish Council for Research in the Humanities and the Social Sciences, 1992-98.

WRITINGS:

(Editor with Kathleen B. Jones), *The Political Interests of Gender,* Sage (London), 1988.
Why Women Are Oppressed, Temple University Press (Philadelphia, PA), 1994.

Why Women Are Oppressed has been translated into Spanish.

WORK IN PROGRESS: Co-editing *Nordic Feminist Thought* (tentative title), a cross-disciplinary collection of articles in English from the five Nordic countries; writing *Are Interests Still Interesting? On Gender Relations and Political Interests,* a book manuscript in English expected to be completed in 1996; editing a collection of essays in Swedish on gender and political interest.

JONES, Amelia 1961-

PERSONAL: Born July 14, 1961, in Durham, NC; daughter of Edward E. (a professor) and Virginia S. (a freelance editor) Jones; married Anthony Sherin (a film editor), March 7, 1987; children: Evan E. *Education:* Harvard University, B.A. (magna cum laude), 1983; University of Pennsylvania, M.A., 1987; University of California, Los Angeles, Ph.D., 1991. *Politics:* "Left/democrat." *Religion:* Atheist.

ADDRESSES: Home—1621 South Stanley Ave., Los Angeles, CA 90019. *Office*—Department of the History of Art, University of California, Riverside, CA 92521.

CAREER: University of California, Los Angeles, instructor in visual arts at Extension School, 1989; Art Center College of Design, Pasadena, CA, instructor and adviser, 1990-91; University of California, Riverside, assistant professor of contemporary art and theory and the history of photography, 1991—, resident fellow, Center for Ideas and Society, 1994; *Artscribe,* London, England, contributing editor in charge of West Coast coverage, 1991-92; University of Southern California, Los Angeles, instructor in art history, 1992. Curator of exhibitions at California Museum of Photography and Armand Hammer Museum of Art; public speaker, including lectures at Otis College of Art and Design, Cornell University, and University of London. Los Angeles Center for Photographic Studies, member of board of directors; member of California Museum of Photography, Riverside, Highways Performance Space, Los Angeles, and Los Angeles Contemporary Exhibitions.

MEMBER: International Association of Art Critics, College Art Association, Society for Photographic Education, Los Angeles Film Forum, National Organization for Women, Teachers for a Democratic Culture.

AWARDS, HONORS: Fellow of American Council of Learned Societies, 1994-95.

WRITINGS:

Postmodernism and the En-Gendering of Marcel Duchamp, Cambridge University Press (New York City), 1994.

Contributor to books, including *The Body Imaged,* edited by Kathleen Adler and Marcia Pointon, Cambridge University Press, 1993; *Beyond Walls and Wars: Art, Politics, and Multiculturalism,* edited by Kim Levin, Midmarch Arts Press, 1993; and *New Feminist Criticisms: Art/Identity/Action,* edited by Cassandra Langer, Joanna Frueh, and Arlene Raven,

HarperCollins, 1994. Contributor of articles and reviews to art and history journals.

WORK IN PROGRESS: Performing the Subject: Body Art, 1960-1995.

SIDELIGHTS: Amelia Jones told *CA:* "Initially inspired to write the great American novel, I realized in my early twenties that academic prose offered a more direct (and less frightening) path toward becoming a writer, and was better suited to my polemical writing style. After studying art history in college and graduate school, I became increasingly comfortable writing about contemporary art and culture.

"It seemed to me that I can do a great deal in this area, especially by diversifying my writing into a wide range of venues, in order to reach academics, the non-academic art world, and (ideally) the general public. In diverse publications I have enjoyed attacking subjects ranging from postfeminism, representations of women in Hollywood films, and feminist art from the 1970s to the construction of the French-turned-American avant-garde artist Marcel Duchamp as a father figure for U.S. postmodern art and the contemporary use of the artist's body in or *as* the work of art.

"My goal with all of these publications has been to open areas of accepted thought in contemporary culture to critical analysis and to disrupt traditional narratives of art history by insisting on the inclusion of women and artists of color. In my writing, as in my teaching, I encourage readers and students to take a critical distance from the information that bombards them in the contemporary world. I have been motivated by the importance of communicating the powerful relevance of art history (understood in this broad sense as the study of culture through historical and theoretical models) to everyone who lives in the imagery-saturated contemporary world. I try to convince readers and students that, by grasping the inevitably ideological ways in which visual culture is made to mean, they can become empowered in relation to these representations and can potentially find ways to intervene in, critique, or encourage various representations in progressive ways.

"I believe in writing as polemic, but also as a kind of seduction. While some may try to veil it, all writers have a point of view, and the best favor we can do our readers is to make that point of view as clear as possible. To this end, my favorite writers are philosophers whose main project has been the poeticizing of academic writing (bell hooks, Jacques Derrida, Luce Irigaray) and fiction writers—especially black women who have negotiated with passion and eloquence the commingling of oppressiveness and potentially liberatory magic in the English language—Alice Walker and Toni Morrison especially. Norman Rush is, for me, one of the great contemporary authors, in that he, too, writes in that ephemeral but fabulous space in which the gorgeousness of language, the complexity of intellectual and political ideas regarding race and gender, and profound emotional and sensual meanings intersect.

"My long-standing love of fiction has held me in good stead with my academic prose. Recently, I have enjoyed opening up this usually rather formulaic kind of writing to fictionalized and playful modes of expression. In doing so, I not only answer my own desire to merge my emotional, personal self with my academic, rational self, but also expose the illusion of objectivity thrown up by the mannered poses of academic prose. Looking at art and experiencing culture are always emotionally invested processes. For this, I have been called—sometimes derisively, sometimes in praise—a 'new art historian' and a 'poststructuralist feminist.'

"Writing is the process that has allowed me to exist. Without writing I would have nothing to say."

*   *   *

JONES, Dorothy   1948-

PERSONAL: Born May 19, 1948, in Columbia, SC; daughter of Thomas (a health care worker) and Georgia (a health care worker; maiden name, Dowdy) Bratton; married Robert Jones, Sr. (a truck driver), March 22, 1966; children: Robert, Jr., Camellia Iris Jones Mivens, Deborah D. Education: Columbia Hospital School of Nursing, L.P.N., 1970. Religion: Apostolic. Avocational interests: Singing, reading.

ADDRESSES: Home—Elgin, SC.

CAREER: Licensed practical nurse in Cola, SC, 1970-89. Teacher's assistant for the handicapped at local elementary school, 1986-87.

WRITINGS:

The Spiritual Enlightenment (poems), Winston-Derek, 1994.

Work represented in anthologies, including The World of Poetry Anthology, World of Poetry Press, 1991.

WORK IN PROGRESS: Another book of poems.

SIDELIGHTS: Dorothy Jones told CA: "I first began writing poetry in 1990, after retiring from nursing be-

cause of disabling health conditions. After many days of pain and depression, I gained a closer relationship to the Lord. I felt the need to express my gratitude and share experiences of mercy. Although I began writing as a form of therapy for myself, I also hope to reach the hearts and touch the lives of others by projecting positive attitudes toward life. I feel that inspirational poetry is needed now more than ever by a world longing for love, compassion, happiness, beauty, and tranquility. I want all of my poems to appeal to the heart, with a power that encourages and uplifts lives."

*   *   *

JONES, J. Gwynfor   1936-

PERSONAL: Born November 22, 1936, in Conwy Valley, North Wales; children: two sons, one daughter. Education: Attended University of Wales, University College, Cardiff, 1955-60, and University College of North Wales, Bangor, 1960-62. Religion: Presbyterian.

ADDRESSES: Home—1 Westminster Dr., Cyncoed, Cardiff CF2 6RD, Wales. Office—School of History and Archaeology, University College, University of Wales, Cardiff, Wales.

CAREER: University of Wales, University College, Cardiff, senior lecturer in Welsh history, 1975—.

WRITINGS:

Wales and the Tudor State, 1534-1605, University of Wales Press, 1989.
(Editor) The Memoirs of Sir John Wynn, Gomer Press, 1990.
Concepts of Order and Gentility in Wales, 1540-1640, Gomer Press, 1992.
Early Modern Wales, 1526-1640, Macmillan, 1994.

WORK IN PROGRESS: The Wynn Family of Gwydir; Caernarfonshire Quarter Sessions, 1560-1640; a book on "the black legend" and cognate themes in Welsh history, 1540-1640.

*   *   *

JONES, James Earl   1931-

PERSONAL: Born January 17, 1931, in Arkabutla, MS; son of Robert Earl (an actor) and Ruth (Williams) Jones; married Julienne Marie Hendricks (an actress; divorced); married Cecilia Hart (an actress), March 15, 1982; children: (second marriage) Flynn. Education: University of Michigan, B.A., 1953; received diploma from the American Theater Wing, 1957.

ADDRESSES: Office—c/o Bauman & Hiller, 5750 Wilshire Blvd., Suite 512, Los Angeles, CA 90036.

CAREER: Stage actor, appeared in productions of *Romeo and Juliet, A Midsummer Night's Dream, Moon on a Rainbow Shawl, The Great White Hope, Hamlet, The Cherry Orchard,* and *Fences.* Film actor, appeared in numerous features, including *Dr. Strangelove, The Great White Hope, Claudine, Gardens of Stone, Field of Dreams,* and *Matewan.* Television actor, appeared in movies, miniseries, specials, and series, including *East Side/West Side, Roots: The Next Generation, The Last Elephant, By Dawn's Early Light,* and *Gabriel's Fire.* Voice talent for various projects, including feature films, documentaries, and commercials. Appointed by President John F. Kennedy to Advisory Board of the National Council on the Arts, 1962. *Military service:* Served in U.S. Army; became first lieutenant.

MEMBER: Screen Actors Guild, Actors Equity, American Federation of Television and Radio Artists, National Council of the Arts.

AWARDS, HONORS: Obie Award, best actor, 1962, for New York Shakespeare Festival productions of *Clandestine on the Morning Line, The Apple,* and *Moon on a Rainbow Shawl; Theatre World* Award, most promising new actor, 1962, for *Moon on a Rainbow Shawl;* Emmy Award nomination, outstanding single performance by an actor in a leading role, and Golden Nymph Award, best performance by an actor, both 1963, both for *East Side/West Side;* Drama Desk Award, best performance, 1964, and Vernon Rice Award, 1965, both for *Othello;* Obie Award, best performance, 1965, for *Baal;* Antoinette Perry Award, best actor in a dramatic play, and Drama Desk Award, outstanding performance, both 1969, both for the play *The Great White Hope;* Drama Desk Award, outstanding performance, 1970, for *Les Blancs;* Academy Award nomination, best actor, 1970, and Golden Globe Award, new male star of the year, 1971, both for the film *The Great White Hope;* Drama Desk Awards, outstanding performances, 1973, for *Hamlet* and *The Cherry Orchard;* Image Award, best actor, National Association for the Advancement of Colored People (NAACP), and Golden Globe nomination, best actor in a musical or comedy, both 1974, both for *Claudine;* Golden Hugo Award, Chicago Film Festival, Golden Gate Award, San Francisco International Film Festival, and Gabriel Award, Mercy College, all 1975, all for *The Cay;* Grammy Award (with Orson Welles, Henry Fonda, and Helen Hayes), best spoken word or nonmusical recording, 1976, for *Great American Documents.*

Medal for Spoken Language, American Academy of Arts and Letters, 1981; Office of Black Ministries'

Toussaint Medallion, 1982; inducted into Theatre Hall of Fame, 1985; Antoinette Perry Award, Drama Desk Award, and Outer Critics Circle Award, all best actor, all 1987, all for *Fences;* Distinguished Performance Award, Drama League of New York, 1987; Emmy Award nomination, best performance in children's programming, 1987, for *Soldier Boys;* ACE Award, best actor in a dramatic series, c. 1989, for *Third and Oak: The Pool Hall;* ACE Award nomination, 1990, for *The Last Elephant;* Emmy Award nomination, 1990, for *By Dawn's Early Light;* Emmy Award, outstanding supporting actor, and ACE Award, best actor in a supporting role, both 1990, both for *Heatwave!;* Los Angeles Film Teachers Jean Renoir Award, 1990; Emmy Award, outstanding lead actor in a drama series, 1990, for *Gabriel's Fire;* Common Wealth Award for distinguished service in the dramatic arts, Bank of Delaware, 1991; People's Choice Award nomination, best new star, 1992; Golden Globe Award nomination, best actor, 1992; Hall of Fame Image Award for contributions to the arts, NAACP, 1992; best actor, NAACP, 1992, for *Gabriel's Fire;* National Medal of Arts for outstanding contributions to cultural life of the country, 1992; received honorary degrees from University of Michigan, 1970, Princeton University, 1980, Columbia College, 1982, and Yale University.

WRITINGS:

(With Penelope Niven) *Voices and Silences* (autobiography), Scribner (New York), 1993.

WORK IN PROGRESS: Cry the Beloved Country, a motion picture; *Under One Roof,* a television series on CBS, 1995.

SIDELIGHTS: Stage, film, and television actor James Earl Jones chronicles his award-winning career in the 1993 autobiography *Voices and Silences,* a collaborative effort between Jones and coauthor Penelope Niven. Although Jones is well-known to audiences for his deeply resonant, authoritative voice (he provided the voice for the villain Darth Vader in the popular *Star Wars* film trilogy), he reveals in *Voices and Silences* that he once suffered from a serious speech impediment. His stutter was in part due to a less-than-idyllic childhood: abandoned by his parents as a baby, Jones and his six siblings moved from rural Mississippi to Michigan, where they were reared by grandparents. At the age of eight the stutter had become so pronounced that Jones simply stopped talking. Remaining mute until the age of fourteen, he finished high school and won a scholarship to the University of Michigan. After graduating in 1953, Jones did a stint in the army and briefly considered the military as a career.

As Jones recalls in *Voices and Silences,* his estranged father had been an actor. Curious about his own performing abilities, Jones moved to New York City and stayed with his father while attending drama school; within a few years, he was working steadily in Broadway productions and winning acclaim from critics, directors, and theatergoers alike. His memoirs journey back to this era and the actor recounts many of the roles he interpreted, including several with the prestigious New York Shakespeare Festival.

In a *New York Times* interview Jones told Helen Dudar, "I love a role where I'm asked to play a common man who has no obvious reasons to call attention to himself. Lear is my favorite king because by the time the play opens, he's not really the king. He's a crazy old kid looking for salvation."

Jones's career branched out to include work in television dramas and then motion pictures; one of his first film roles was in the 1963 Cold War satire *Dr. Strangelove; or, How I Learned to Stop Worrying and Love the Bomb.* Over the years Jones has won numerous honors, including a Tony for his portrayal of a doomed prizefighter in 1969's *The Great White Hope,* a role he recreated for film the following year. The theater production of *The Great White Hope,* according to Dudar in the *New York Times,* "not only made [Jones] a star, it established him as America's premier black actor, a status yet to be challenged."

In *Voices and Silences,* Jones discusses his stage and screen performances, the controversies some of them have elicited, and his collaborations and friendships with other luminaries. To a lesser degree, the actor also talks about his two marriages and concludes the volume with an intimate reflection on middle-aged life. A reviewer in *Publishers Weekly,* who considered *Voices and Silences* "a compelling memoir," stated that Jones presents "lively and nuanced reflections on his great and sometimes controversial parts."

BIOGRAPHICAL/CRITICAL SOURCES:

BOOKS

Jones, James Earl and Penelope Niven, *Voices and Silences,* Scribner (New York), 1993.

PERIODICALS

Boston Globe, September 14, 1988, p. 33.
Christian Science Monitor, January 4, 1988, p. 23.
New York Times, March 22, 1987, sec. 2, p. 1.
Publishers Weekly, August 2, 1993, p. 72.

JONES, Margaret C.   1949-

PERSONAL: Born January 30, 1949; daughter of Frederick Jeffery (an air force officer) and Marjorie G. (a secretary; maiden name, Penseney) Jones; married Essam el Din Aref Fattouh (a university lecturer), February, 1978. *Education:* University of Wales, University College of North Wales, Bangor, B.A., 1970, M.A., 1973; Purdue University, Ph.D., 1989. *Politics:* "Militant Labour."

ADDRESSES: Home—14 Hawkesbury Rd., Fishponds, Bristol BS16 2AP, England. *Office*—Department of Humanities, University of the West of England, Bristol BS16 2JP, England.

CAREER: University of Alexandria, Alexandria, Egypt, teacher, 1972-76; Goucher College, Towson, MD, instructor, 1987-88; Central Washington University, Ellensburg, assistant professor, 1990-92; University of the West of England, Bristol, senior lecturer in humanities and coordinator of American studies, 1992-94.

MEMBER: British Association for American Studies, Modern Language Association of America, American Studies Association.

WRITINGS:

In Shadow (play), broadcast by Radio Telefis Eireann, 1982.
Prophets in Babylon: Five California Novelists in the 1930s, Peter Lang, 1992.
Heretics and Hellraisers: Women Contributors to "The Masses", 1911-1917, University of Texas Press, 1993.
(Editor) Elsie Clews Parsons, *The Journal of a Feminist,* Thoemmes Press, 1994.

WORK IN PROGRESS: Five African-American Women Writers, for British Association for American Studies; *Inventing Africa* (tentative title), a study of Afro-American cultural appropriations or representations of the cultures of Egypt and Ghana.

SIDELIGHTS: Margaret C. Jones told *CA:* "For me, writing is very much an extension of other kinds of political action. All my work of the past seven years or so has involved the questioning of received truths, of hegemonic ideas and images of the past. I undertake this questioning in several ways.

"*Prophets in Babylon,* for instance, examines utopian alternatives to capitalism, as proposed by five novelists in the context of the Depression era. I invite the reader to contemplate the possible alternatives put forward by

Sinclair, Steinbeck, and others, while examining the symbolic and fictional modes employed to criticize the status quo and to suggest alternatives to it.

"*Heretics and Hellraisers* likewise entails a revisionist approach to history. In this study of turn-of-the-century radical women writers and artists, I have two aims. One is to remind anyone studying United States radical movements of the interesting and crucial roles played by women writers and activists, such as Emma Goldman, Elsie Parsons, Elizabeth Flynn, and Mary Heaton Vorse. The other is to attempt to convince readers of the impoverishment inflicted on contemporary feminist movements by their estrangement from radical and working-class causes—causes which, after all, involve the majority of society's women. *Heretics and Hellraisers* calls for the recovery of this radically working-class-oriented legacy."

* * *

JONES, Norman (Leslie) 1951-

PERSONAL: Born April 27, 1951, in Twin Falls, ID; son of Leslie Raymond (a farmer) and Charlotte (a farm manager and homemaker; maiden name, Miller) Jones; married Carolyn Rhodes, June 21, 1975 (divorced June 21, 1990); married Lynn Langer Meeks (a professor), June 24, 1994. *Education:* Attended College of Southern Idaho, 1968-70; Idaho State University, B.A. (with honors), 1972; University of Colorado, Boulder, M.A. (summa cum laude), 1974; Clare College, Cambridge, Ph.D., 1978. *Politics:* "Rocky Mountain Democrat." *Religion:* Christian. *Avocational interests:* Travel, wild flowers, hiking, cooking, skiing.

ADDRESSES: Home—121 East 3700 S., Nibley, UT 84321. *Office*—Department of History, Utah State University, Logan, UT 84322-0710.

CAREER: Utah State University, Logan, instructor, 1977, assistant professor, 1978-81, associate professor, 1981-87, professor of history, 1987—, head of department, 1994—, head of Oxford University Exchange Program, 1989—, acting director of Liberal Arts and Sciences Program, 1993-94. Harvard University, Mellon faculty fellow, 1982-83; Cambridge University, visiting fellow of Clare College, 1992; guest speaker at colleges and universities, including Waikato University, Victoria University of Wellington, Otago University, University of Canterbury, Massey University, University of London, Arizona State University, University of Colorado, Yale University, and Concordia University, Montreal, Quebec; gives workshops and public lectures.

MEMBER: North American Conference on British Studies, Reformation Society of America, Sixteenth Century Studies Conference, American Association of Colleges, American Association for Higher Education, Royal Historical Society (associate), Rocky Mountain Medieval and Renaissance Association (member of council, 1986—), Western Conference on British Studies, Association for the Humanities in Idaho (member of board of directors), Phi Kappa Phi, Phi Alpha Theta.

AWARDS, HONORS: Archbishop Cranmer Prize in Ecclesiastical History from Cambridge University, 1979, and Whitefield Prize from Royal Historical Society, 1982, both for *Parliament and the Settlement of Religion;* fellow of the conference Inventing the West, Institute of the American West, Sun Valley, ID, 1982; grant from Utah Endowment for the Humanities, 1989; Charles Redd Prize from Utah Acadmey of Sciences, 1990; Fletcher Jones fellow, Huntington Library, 1991-92.

WRITINGS:

Faith by Statute: Parliament and the Settlement of Religion, 1559, Royal Historical Society (London), 1982.
God and the Moneylenders: Usury and Law in Early Modern England, Basil Blackwell (Oxford, England), 1989.
(Editor with David Dean, and contributor) *The Parliaments of Elizabethan England,* Basil Blackwell, 1993.
The Birth of the Elizabethan Age: England in the 1560s, Blackwell Scientific (Oxford), 1993.

Work represented in anthologies, including *The Political Context of Law,* edited by Richard Eales, 1987; *The Commonwealth of Tudor England,* edited by P. Fideler and T. Mayer, Routledge & Kegan Paul, 1992; and *Perspective As a Problem in the Art, History, and Literature of Early Modern England,* edited by Mark Lussier, Edwin Mellen, 1992. Contributor to scholarly journals. Co-editor of special issue, *Parliamentary History,* Volume VIII, number 2, 1989.

SIDELIGHTS: Norman Jones told *CA:* "I did not know I was a writer until somewhere in the middle of my third book. As a historian, I had conceived my task to be one of communicating the past, not writing. In order to communicate the truth about the past, one assembled the evidence, synthesized it, and expressed conclusions in the clearest language one could write. I believed an historian did not bother with the tricks of the literary trade, and had no truck with the sophistry of the literary critics. When I began writing *The Birth of the Elizabethan Age,* however, it dawned on me that, to succeed, the work had to be a tightly controlled fictive act. To bring the 1560s in England to life for the reader, I had to work like an impressionist painter, hinting at reality through the relation of light and color, rather than by mere description. As I became self-conscious about my composition process, I also began to enjoy writing history in a way I never had before. Clinging tightly to the evidence, and yet playing with the language to create the desired impression, I reconceptualized myself as a historian and as a writer.

"The intellectual question that underlies my work as a historian is the way in which ideologies relate to behaviors. I chose to study the Reformation because it was a time in which people explicitly changed religious ideology. I could trace the impact of their changing world views in their behaviors toward the economy, the poor, their families, and anything and everything else. My work in progress is an attempt to link these changes in ideology and behavior by examining inter-generational conflicts in the early modern period."

*   *   *

JONES, Pamela M. 1953-

PERSONAL: Born November 11, 1953, in Charleston, WV; daughter of Tilford (an attorney) and Margaret (a homemaker; maiden name, Lyon) Jones; married Kenneth Sprague Rothwell, Jr. (a professor of classics), 1989; children: Rosalind Springs. *Education:* Goucher College, B.A., 1975; George Washington University, M.A., 1978; Brown University, Ph.D., 1985.

ADDRESSES: Office—Department of Art, University of Massachusetts at Boston, 100 Morrissey Blvd., Boston, MA 02125-3393.

CAREER: National Museum of American Art, intern, 1977-78, cataloger of twentieth-century painting and sculpture, 1978-79; Franklin and Marshall College, Lancaster, PA, visiting assistant professor of art history, 1985-86; University of Maine at Orono, visiting assistant professor of art history, 1987-88; University of Massachusetts at Boston, assistant professor, 1988-94, associate professor of art history, 1994—. Brown University, guest lecturer, 1991.

AWARDS, HONORS: George Wittenborn Memorial Award, 1982; Kress Foundation fellowships for Italy, 1982-83, 1983-84; grant from Healey Endowment, 1989; fellow of National Endowment for the Humanities, 1990-91; faculty grant for Italy, University of Massachusetts at Boston, 1994.

WRITINGS:

Federico Borromeo and the Ambrosiana: Art, Patronage, and Reform in Seventeenth-Century Milan, Cambridge University Press, 1993.

Work represented in anthologies, including *Reframing the Renaissance: Studies in the Migration of Visual Culture,* edited by Claire J. Farago, University of Colorado Press, in press. Contributor of articles and reviews to art and history journals.

WORK IN PROGRESS: Genre, Audience, and Display in Italian Religious Art and Culture, 1560-1660, a comprehensive study of ecclesiastical art and theory from Giovanni Andrea Gilio to Giovanni Domenico Ottonelli, focusing on notions of appropriate audience and place/method of display of various media and genres of art; annotated translations of Federico Borromeo's *De pictura sacra* and *Musaeum Bibliothecae Ambrosianae,* originally published in Milan in 1624 and 1625.

BIOGRAPHICAL/CRITICAL SOURCES:

PERIODICALS

Church History, Volume 63, 1994, p. 106.
Sixteenth-Century Journal, Volume 25, number 2, 1994, p. 444.

*   *   *

JONES, Stuart 1933-

PERSONAL: Born March 29, 1933, in Manchester, England. *Education:* Degrees from Oxford University, 1955 and 1958, Victoria University of Manchester, 1962, and University of British Columbia, 1968. *Politics:* Conservative. *Religion:* Anglican.

ADDRESSES: Home—82 Sixth St., Parkhurst, Johannesburg, South Africa 2193. *Office*—Department of Economics, University of South Africa, Box 392, Pretoria, South Africa 0001.

CAREER: University of the Witwatersrand, Johannesburg, South Africa, began as lecturer, became senior lecturer in economic history and head of division, 1969-93; University of South Africa, Pretoria, professor of economics, 1993—.

MEMBER: Economic History Society of South Africa (president, 1986-88, 1994—).

WRITINGS:

(With Andre Muller) *The South African Economy, 1910-90,* St. Martin's, 1992.

EDITOR

Banking and Business in South Africa, Macmillan, 1988.

Financial Enterprise in South Africa Since 1950, Macmillan, 1992.

Economic Interpretations of Nineteenth-Century Imperialism, Economic History Society of Southern Africa, 1992.

Entrepreneurs of the Industrial Revolution, Economic History Society of Southern Africa, 1993.

Also editor of *South African Journal of Economic History,* 1986-94.

WORK IN PROGRESS: The Business of the Great Imperial Banks in South Africa, 1862-1961; editing *The South African Economy in the 1980s* and *Business Imperialism in Africa.*

* * *

JORDAN, David C. 1935-

PERSONAL: Born April 30, 1935, in Chicago, IL; son of Edwin Pratt (a physician) and Marjorie (Crichton) Jordan; married Anabella Guzman (a foundation executive), December 14, 1964; children: Stephen, Victoria, Anne. *Education:* Harvard University, A.B., 1957; University of Virginia, LL.B., 1960; University of Pennsylvania, Ph.D., 1964.

ADDRESSES: Office—Department of Government, Cabell 232, University of Virginia, Charlottesville, VA 22903.

CAREER: University of Virginia, Charlottesville, professor of government and foreign affairs, 1965—, department head, 1969-77. U.S. ambassador to Peru, 1984-86; New World Institute, president, 1993—.

MEMBER: American Political Science Association.

AWARDS, HONORS: Named Ambassador of the Year, *La Gente,* 1975; Order of Merit, Chilean Ministry of Education, 1990.

WRITINGS:

(With Arthur P. Whitaker) *Nationalism in Contemporary Latin America,* Free Press, 1966.
World Politics in Our Time, Heath, 1970.

Spain, the Monarchy, and the Atlantic Community (monograph), Institute for Policy Analysis, 1979.
(Editor and contributor) *A Strategy for Latin America in the Nineties* (monograph), Council for Inter-American Security, 1988.
Revolutionary Cuba and the End of the Cold War, University Press of America, 1993.
(Editor and contributor) *U.S. Latin American Policy for the Nineties* (monograph), New World Institute, 1994.

Member of editorial board, *Strategic Review* and *Comparative Strategy.*

WORK IN PROGRESS: Two books, tentatively titled *Strategic Theory* and *Democratic Crises.*

SIDELIGHTS: David C. Jordan told *CA:* "I am motivated to write more by the exploration of ideas and political problems than I am for literary or stylistic reasons. What drives me to analyze political issues is the challenge of understanding a period or turning point in a historical or national era. So, my writing is derived from my teaching and intellectual interest, rather than a need to write for the sake of writing.

"I am particularly interested in challenging vested opinions that are held despite all the contrary evidence to these conventions. For example, there have been apologists for various kinds of regimes which have been bolstered by claims to objective theoretical underpinnings. It is interesting to me to show how such opinions are both historically and intellectually flawed and held for reasons other than intellectual integrity. One of the most difficult problems for a scholar in these circumstances is to demonstrate how the passions get in the way of an intrinsic understanding."

* * *

JUDD, Naomi 1946-

PERSONAL: Born Diana Judd, January 11, 1946, in Ashland, KY; daughter of Glen (a gas station owner) and Pauline Oliver Rideout (a riverboat cook) Judd; married Michael Ciminella, c. 1963 (divorced, 1970); married Larry Winfield Strickland (a manager and producer), May 6, 1989; children: (first marriage) Wynonna, Ashley. *Education:* College of Marin, R.N., 1978. *Politics:* Republican. *Religion:* Pentecostal.

ADDRESSES: Office—P.O. Box 681828, Nashville, TN 37068.

CAREER: Worked as a model and secretary in Los Angeles, 1968-76, as a waitress in Marin County, CA,

c. late-1970s, and as a registered nurse in Nashville, TN, 1979-83; formed country music duo the Judds with daughter Wynonna in 1983; recorded albums for RCA Records, 1983-90, and on MCA Records, 1990-91, including *The Judds,* 1984, *Rockin' with the Rhythm,* 1985, *River of Time,* 1989, and *Love Can Build a Bridge;* toured the United States and Europe; retired from the music business, 1991. Spokesperson for American liver Foundation, 1991—.

AWARDS, HONORS: Horizon Award, Country Music Association, 1984, for best new act; Academy of Country Music awards for best vocal duet, 1984, 1985, 1986, 1987, 1988, 1989, 1990, and 1991; best vocal duo, TNN *Music City News* Country Awards, 1984, 1985, 1986, 1987, 1988, 1989, and 1990; *Rolling Stone* Magazine Music Award, 1985, for best country artist; Star of Tomorrow Award, TNN (the Nashville Network) *Music City News* Country Awards, 1985; Country Music Association Award, 1985, 1986, and 1987, for vocal group of the year; American Music Award, country favorite single, and American Music Awards Country Video Awards, favorite video single, both 1987, both for song "Grandpa"; Grammy Award, country—best vocal performance, duo or group, 1988, for "Give a Little Love," and five other Grammys; Country Music Association Award, 1988, 1989, and 1990, for vocal duo of the year.

WRITINGS:

(With Bud Schaetzle) *Love Can Build a Bridge,* Villard Books, 1992.

WORK IN PROGRESS: A mini-series based on *Love Can Build a Bridge,* for NBC, completion expected in 1995.

SIDELIGHTS: Country music superstar Naomi Judd's autobiography *Love Can Build a Bridge* topped the bestseller lists upon its release in 1992. Such success was taken in stride by the first-time author, who with her daughter Wynonna had soared to fame in the 1980s with their popular country music singing duo the Judds. Together they racked up Grammy and American Music Awards as well as nearly every honor bestowed by the country music industry for such popular albums as *Why Not Me* and *River of Time.* Yet *Love Can Build a Bridge,* also the name of a Judds album, tells of a rocky road to stardom and gives an intimate portrait of the family's unusual closeness even through difficult times. The work is told in Judd's conversational style and discusses the impoverished early years on the road to stardom, the ups and downs of the Judds' phenomenal success in the music business, as well as the author's spirituality, her battle with a chronic illness, and the difficulty of being a single mother to two head-strong young women (her other daughter is actress Ashley Judd, star of the acclaimed film *Ruby in Paradise*).

Cowritten with Bud Schaetzle, Judd's memoirs begin by recounting her early life in Kentucky, including the devastation wrought by her parents' unhappy marriage and the death of her teenaged brother from Hodgkin's disease. She married at seventeen, had Wynonna at eighteen, and moved to Los Angeles. The marriage ended after a few years and Judd worked as a secretary and a model to support her family, which now included Ashley.

In 1976 the family returned to Kentucky, where they lived in a small home without a television or telephone. Such bare-bones economics led to a burgeoning resourcefulness on the part of Wynonna and Ashley. They entertained themselves through a variety of creative pursuits, including a guitar with which Wynonna soon became obsessed. Naomi and Wynonna discovered they sang well together, and it was often only during these recreational times that mother and daughter managed to stop bickering. *Love Can Build a Bridge* relates yet another series of moves, this time back to California—where Judd earned a nursing degree—and finally to Nashville, Tennessee. It was there that Wynonna befriended a high-school classmate whose father was a country music record producer. After a car accident landed the young woman in the hospital, Naomi, working there as a nurse, also befriended her; this series of events led to a live audition with a record company which earned the Judds their first recording contract in 1983.

In her book, Judd describes the dramatic changes that country music stardom had upon her life and that of her daughters. The new lifestyle included months of obligatory touring in addition to songwriting and recording schedules that produced a bestselling album every year. The Judds earned an impressive array of Grammy and country-music industry awards during the late 1980s and early 1990s, but their career together came to an end in 1990 when Naomi was diagnosed with chronic active hepatitis, a liver disease that she most likely came in contact with while working as a nurse. The duo announced a series of farewell concerts that culminated in a final performance in Tennessee in December of 1991.

While Wynonna went on to a successful solo career, Judd began nursing herself back to health through a series of holistic treatments (she later became a popular speaker on the subject of mind and body healing). She also used this recuperative time to write her memoirs. This she did in longhand while sitting at her kitchen table, and the result was the 544-page *Love Can Build a Bridge*. The book landed on the *New York Times* bestseller list and its publicity tour brought Judd back into the public eye. Jack Hurst of the *Chicago Tribune* described the autobiography as "outrageous, breathless, voluble, fast-moving, funny, didactic, medically technical, sometimes religiously self-righteous and always mercilessly candid." *Boston Globe* writer Steve Morse praised *Love Can Build a Bridge* as "lucidly written" and a "book [that] reads like a primer for independent women."

BIOGRAPHICAL/CRITICAL SOURCES:

BOOKS

Contemporary Musicians, Volume 2, Gale, 1990.
Judd, Naomi, and Bud Schaetzle, *Love Can Build a Bridge,* Villard Books, 1992.

PERIODICALS

Boston Globe, November 29, 1993, p. 27.
Chicago Tribune, November 28, 1993, section 13, pp. 5, 20.
People, December 9, 1991, p. 114.

K

KAHN, Joan   1914-1994

OBITUARY NOTICE—See index for *CA* sketch: Born April 13, 1914, in New York, NY; died following a brief illness, October 11, 1994, in Manhattan, NY. Editor and author. A leading editor of mystery and suspense anthologies, Kahn was also the author of numerous volumes, including the children's books *Ladies and Gentlemen, Said the Ringmaster* (1938) and *Hi, Jock, Run around the Block* (1978), the novels *To Meet Miss Long* (1943) and *Open House* (1946), and a collection of short fiction entitled *Ready or Not: Here Come Fourteen Frightening Stories* (1987). In 1945, Kahn began a thirty-four-year career at Harper & Row as an editor of nonfiction art, history, theater, and travel books. Bringing to public attention the works of authors such as Dorothy L. Sayers, Patricia Highsmith, and Tony Hillerman, Kahn developed a reputation for excellence among readers and writers of suspense fiction. She later left Harper & Row to serve as an editor for Ticknor & Fields, Dutton, and St. Martin's Press, then retired in 1989. Honored twice by the Mystery Writers of America, Kahn recieved the 1985 Ellery Queen Award for lifetime service to the mystery industry and, upon retirement, an Edgar Allen Poe Award.

OBITUARIES AND OTHER SOURCES:

BOOKS

Authors of Books for Young People, 3rd edition, Scarecrow, 1990.

PERIODICALS

Chicago Tribune, October 16, 1994, sec. 2, p. 6.
New York Times, October 13, 1994, p. B15.

KALETA, Kenneth C.   1948-

PERSONAL: Born April 11, 1948, in Chicago, IL; son of Charles J. (a lawyer) and Wanda (a homemaker; maiden name, Wiercioch) Kaleta; married Jane Green (a travel agent), November, 1969. *Education:* Villanova University, B.A., 1967, M.A., 1975; New York University, Ph.D., 1986. *Politics:* Republican. *Religion:* Roman Catholic. *Avocational interests:* Seal-point Siamese cats, travel.

ADDRESSES: Home—1008 Front St., Glendora, NJ 08029. *Office*—Rowan College of New Jersey, 201 Mullica Hill Rd., Glassboro, NJ 08021.

CAREER: Rowan College of New Jersey, Glassboro, professor of film, 1977—.

MEMBER: U.S. Diving Association, University Film and Video Association.

WRITINGS:

Asphodel, Blackbird Press, 1989.
Occasional Papers, Glassboro College Press, 1993.
David Lynch, Twayne (New York, NY), 1993.

WORK IN PROGRESS: Next Generation Story Teller, on contemporary Anglo-Asian aesthetics.

SIDELIGHTS: Kenneth C. Kaleta told *CA:* "The power of film as an international language is evident to me. I investigate it daily in teaching my film courses. It is equally evident in my everyday filmgoing. I am particularly interested in the dynamics of literature and film. Writing and its place in filmmaking is fascinating, as is the influence of film on contemporary writing. F. Scott Fitzgerald, my favorite author, wrote about and for the movies. David Lynch, about whom I wrote my third book, is a screenwriter. I am now writing a book about author Hanif Kureishi. I was first drawn to his screenplays, and I am now investigating the breadth of his writing in short stories, novels, plays, essays, and television and film scripts."

*   *   *

KALLGREN, Beverly Hayes   1925-

PERSONAL: Born May 10, 1925, in Boston, MA; daughter of Philip R. (a business executive) and Mabel (an artist; maiden name, Long) Hayes; married Carl E. Kallgren (a hospital plant engineer), July 18, 1949; children: Carl Philip, Jennifer Kallgren McEachern. *Education:* Wheelock College, B.S., 1947; University of Hartford, M.A., 1965. *Politics:* Independent. *Religion:* "Protestant-Philosophy." *Avocational interests:* Music.

ADDRESSES: Home—49 Goodhouse Rd., Litchfield, CT 06759.

CAREER: Schoolteacher in Litchfield, CT, 1947-53, 1959-64; guidance counselor in New Milford, CT, 1965-84; writer.

MEMBER: General Federation of Women's Clubs, Litchfield Woman's Forum.

AWARDS, HONORS: First place award from poetry contest, General Federation of Women's Clubs of Connecticut, 1987.

WRITINGS:

(Editor with James L. Crouthamel) *"Dear Friend Anna": The Civil War Letters of a Common Soldier from Maine,* University of Maine Press, 1992.

Author of the poetry collection *Merry Christmas—And Then Some,* 1993, and an unpublished study *I Wish We Spoke the Same Language: An Alzheimer Case.* Contributor to local newspapers.

WORK IN PROGRESS: Editing the family letters of a Civil War veteran for *Abial and Anna,* a sequel to *"Dear Friend Anna";* research on the life of Americans in India during the late 1930s and early 1940s.

SIDELIGHTS: Beverly Hayes Kallgren told *CA:* "For years I worked with children and taught child development and parenting techniques. On retirement, I changed focus entirely and moved into the adult world. I had always enjoyed writing and research; the chance discovery of my great-grandfather's Civil War letters

seemed to set up the ideal vehicle for combining these interests. The Litchfield Hills provide a beautiful and quite lifestyle, with time for writing between frequent activities with grandchildren. The writing was such fun that I plan to pursue several other projects in the near future."

*   *   *

KANE, Wilson
See Bloch, Robert (Albert)

*   *   *

KAPLAN, Andrew   1960-

PERSONAL: Born April 26, 1960, in New York, NY; son of Jerome (an editor and writer) and Thelma (a career counselor; maiden name, Cornon) Kaplan. *Education:* Cornell University, B.A., 1982.

ADDRESSES: Home and office—25 Tudor City Pl., Apt. 1205, New York, NY 10017.

CAREER: Curriculum Concepts, New York City, editor and writer, 1982-85; freelance writer and editor, 1985—.

WRITINGS:

Careers for Sports Fans, Millbrook Press, 1991.
Careers for Computer Buffs, Millbrook Press, 1991.
Careers for Artistic Types, Millbrook Press, 1991.
Careers for Outdoor Types, Millbrook Press, 1991.
Careers for Number Lovers, Millbrook Press, 1991.
Careers for Wordsmiths, Millbrook Press, 1991.
War of the Raven, Avon, 1991.

WORK IN PROGRESS: Research on "career changers" and "oral histories of neighborhood residents."

SIDELIGHTS: Andrew Kaplan commented: "Glancing at the 'personal' section of this entry, you would see that my father is an editor and writer and my mother is a career counselor. At that point, you might look at my 'writings' section, which includes six books in which I profiled eighty-four people in different careers, and decide 'Kaplan's books represent the combined effects of his parents' influence. Case closed.' However, although the match seems almost perfect, I deny it. There's no connection whatsoever. In fact, the very drawing of that conclusion would only prove, one more time, that pop-psychology has overrun our culture and is leading us to misunderstand the events and people which we're analyzing. What's the real answer? No one knows for sure, least of all me. All I can tell you is that I've always liked stories, books, and movies, and talking to people and listening to their stories. Even if those stories are made up. Or, perhaps, especially if they're made up."

* * *

KAPLAN, Barbara Beigun 1943-

PERSONAL: Born August 7, 1943, in Chicago, IL; daughter of Jack L. (an accountant) and Mollie (a secretary; maiden name, Schulman) Beigun; married Howard Theodore Kaplan (a software engineer), June 20, 1965; children: Jeffrey Mark, Eric Michael, Brian Robert, Robyn Stacie. *Education:* University of Chicago, B.A., 1965, M.A., 1966; University of Maryland at College Park, Ph.D., 1979. *Avocational interests:* Gardening, crafts, reading.

ADDRESSES: Home—5 Triple Crown Ct., Gaithersburg, MD 20878. *Office*—University of Maryland at College Park, University at Adelphi Rd., College Park, MD 20742.

CAREER: University of Maryland at College Park, adjunct professor of history, 1981—, senior instructional designer at Center for Instructional Development and Evaluation, 1985-90, executive director of Program in Science, Technology, and Society Studies, 1988-91, coordinator of faculty development, 1993—. *Gaithersburg Gazette,* journalist, 1984; Applied Science Associates, Inc., instructional technologist, 1985-90.

MEMBER: History of Science Society, American Historical Society, American Association for the History of Medicine, National Association of Science, Technology, and Society, National Association of Women in Education, Association for Professional and Organizational Development in Higher Education, National University Continuing Education Association, British History of Science Society, Virginia Historical Society, Washington Society for the History of Medicine (president, 1984), Fox Hills Green Civic Association (president, 1984), Potomac Commons Garden Club (president, 1980), Phi Alpha Theta, Nu Pi Sigma.

WRITINGS:

Divulging Useful Truths in Physick: The Medical Agenda of Robert Boyle, Johns Hopkins University Press (Baltimore, MD), 1993.
Land and Heritage in the Virginia Tidewater: A History of King and Queen County, Byrd Press (Richmond, VA), 1993.

Work represented in anthologies. Contributor of articles and reviews to academic journals.

WORK IN PROGRESS: Rural Public Health in Virginia and Maryland, 1870-1925, completion expected in 1996; research on women writers of science books for children in nineteenth-century America; research on faculty strategies for teaching in the diverse classroom.

* * *

KAWAKAMI, Barbara Fusako 1921-

PERSONAL: Born August 24, 1921, in Kumamoto, Japan; naturalized citizen of the United States; daughter of Torasaku (a sugar-company clerk) and Matsu Saito (a homemaker) Oyama; married Douglas Yoshito Kawakami (a feed-store owner), February 1, 1944; children: Steven, Mrs. Fay Toyama, Gary. *Education:* University of Hawaii, Manoa, B.S., 1979, M.A., 1983.

ADDRESSES: Home—94-421 Alapoai St., Mililani, HI 96789. *Agent*—University of Hawaii Press, 2840 Kolowalu St., Honolulu, HI 96822.

CAREER: Professional dressmaker and designer, 1938-78; Leeward Community College, sewing instructor, 1975-78; University of Hawaii, Manoa, sewing instructor, 1978; Hawaii Public Television ARCHIVE Project, researcher, writer, associate producer, interviewer, translator, and costumer, 1985-89; Japanese American National Museum, Los Angeles, advisory council member, 1990—. Also served as historical consultant for *Picture Bride,* an English and Japanese language film production directed by Kayo Hatta for Thousand Cranes Filmwork, 1995 release scheduled.

AWARDS, HONORS: Myrle Clark Creative Writing Award with Special Distinction from the University of Hawaii at Manoa, 1986; Distinguished Alumni Award from Leeward Community College, University of Hawaii, 1990; Golden Poet Award, 1990, for *Immigrant Child's First Day in School;* World Poetry Publications Award, 1990; Pride in Waipahu Award, Waipahu Business Association, 1991; Silver Gavel Award from Toastmasters International, 1993; Outstanding Book in the History Division from the Association of Asian American Studies, 1994, for *Japanese Immigrant Clothing in Hawaii, 1885-1941.*

WRITINGS:

Japanese Immigrant Clothing in Hawaii, 1885-1941, University of Hawaii Press (Honolulu), 1993.

Contributing scriptwriter for the film *Everlasting Reflection (Ichimadin Washin Nayo),* a "docudrama depicting the lives of Okinawan picture brides," 1990.

Contributor of "Kasuri to Palaka: Journey through Clothing from Japanese Villages to Hawaiian Plantations, 1885-1941" to *Issei Pioneers: Hawaii and the Mainland, 1885-1924,* Japanese American National Museum lecture series. Contributor of poetry and fiction to the *Hawaii Herald* (Hawaii's Japanese American Journal).

SIDELIGHTS: In *Japanese Immigrant Clothing in Hawaii, 1885-1941,* Barbara Fusako Kawakami, who grew up on the Oahu sugar plantation in Waipahu, presents a history of issei (first-generation Japanese immigrants) plantation workers and their families through descriptions of the clothing made and worn by them as well as the circumstances under which they lived and worked. Kawakami began her career as a dressmaker in 1936, when she enrolled in sewing school shortly after completing the eighth grade. Kawakami enrolled in college at the age of fifty-three, and *Japanese Immigrant Clothing* began as a term paper she wrote for a course in East Asian costumes.

Based in part on information derived from interviews with issei and their families, *Japanese Immigrant Clothing* begins by summarizing the history of Japanese immigration to Hawaii, including the social and economic situation in Japan that compelled its citizens to leave. The book also presents a section dealing with Okinawan "picture brides," who were sent to Hawaii for arranged marriages, describing their wedding attire as well as the unique challenges they faced in adjusting to western culture. Kawakami delineates the sewing techniques used by Japanese women to create their own wardrobes as well as their families' wardrobes and illustrates how these women incorporated western clothing styles into their traditional mode of dress. Kawakami also examines the changes that took place in issei clothing styles as opportunities for employment and education increased from one generation of plantation workers to another.

Japanese Immigrant Clothing was praised by Suzanne De Atley, who stated in a review in *Piecework:* "Barbara F. Kawakami's book is more than a compendium of ethnic costume and details of fabrication. While her research began as a documentation project, she found in her interviews with issei . . . in Hawaii that details of clothing were intimately tied to many facets of immigrant life on the sugarcane and pineapple plantations. . . . Her perspective enriches the description of costume with an understanding of the conditions under which the clothing was made and used." In a review in the *Japan Times,* Beverly Findlay-Kaneko asserted: "Typical photographs of the early Hawaiian plantation landscape depict anonymous and seemingly identical straw-hatted figures toiling bent-

backed in row after row of ripening pineapple. In her enlightening study of Japanese immigrant clothing, Barbara Kawakami lifts the wide brims of Japanese plantation workers' hats and reveals a vibrant community of individuals with shared dreams and values." Harry Eagar, writing for the *Maui News,* declared: "It is perhaps unfortunate that this book is called simply *Japanese Immigrant Clothing,* because that does not tip the potential reader to the treasure trove of trivia about daily life and the simple but powerful human stories that Kawakami has assembled."

BIOGRAPHICAL/CRITICAL SOURCES:

PERIODICALS

Japan Times, February 8, 1994, p. 17.
Maui News, October 10, 1993, p. C5.
Piecework, March/April, 1994, p. 84.

*   *   *

KAWATSKI, Deanna   1951-
   (Deanna Barnhardt)

PERSONAL: Born April 11, 1951, in Salmon Arm, British Columbia, Canada; daughter of Allan Bertrand and Lorna May Barnhardt; married Jay Paul Kawatski (divorced); children: Natalia, Ben Kyle. *Education:* Attended Banff School of Fine Arts, 1975, and University of British Columbia. *Politics:* "Left and green." *Religion:* "I believe in a higher power." *Avocational interests:* Nature study, hiking, biking, gardening, reading.

ADDRESSES: Home and office—Site 16, Comp 2, R.R.1, Chase, British Columbia, Canada V0E 1M0.

CAREER: Freelance writer.

MEMBER: Periodical Writers Association of Canada.

WRITINGS:

(Under name Deanna Barnhardt) *Bird, Bubble, and Stream* (poems), Fiddlehead Press, 1980.
Wilderness Mother, Lyons & Burford (New York, NY), 1994.

Columnist, *Mother Earth News.* Contributor to periodicals, including *Harrowsmith, Canadian Gardening, Country Journal, Country Woman,* and *Outdoor Canada.*

WORK IN PROGRESS: Clara and Me (tentative title).

SIDELIGHTS: Deanna Kawatski told *CA:* "I believe that

I was born a writer. As a child, I lightened the burden of classroom tedium by spinning yarns in my head. I also wrote books of original poetry and bound them together with bits of ribbon. My love affair with words was confirmed in print when I was in my mid-twenties. I was living in London at the time and had two poems accepted by a British literary magazine. During the three years I spent abroad, I also became an avid journal keeper, and I now have twenty years' worth stockpiled.

"Even though I've had little in the way of higher education, the world has been my school, and I have experienced a rich array of lifestyles. For five years I lived largely in the city, where I wrote and studied modern dance. This was financed by short, intense bouts of tree planting in the rugged mountains of British Columbia.

"In 1979, I married and moved off to the wilds of northwestern British Columbia. It turned out to be an adventure like no other. In 1980 I published an article about my experiences as a lookout attendant on a remote fire tower—the job that took me north in the first place. In the midst of hand washing, home schooling, and surviving in the bush, I also managed to write and sell numerous feature articles to national magazines in Canada and the United States. There are further facets of my thirteen years in isolation that I wish to explore with words.

"The passion in my prose does not come without a purpose. I wish to wake people up to the beauty and vast value of the natural world. The planet is in peril, and my view of the future will brighten only when humanity changes its attitude toward nature, from one of exploitation to one of reverence."

* * *

KEEGAN, John E. 1943-

PERSONAL: Born April 29, 1943, in Spokane, WA; son of Edwin P. (a retailer and developer) and Betsy (Ross) Keegan; married, wife's name Macaela C. (a yoga and English teacher), June 29, 1991; children: Carla B., David B. *Education:* Gonzaga University, B.A., 1965; Harvard University, J.D., 1968. *Politics:* Independent. *Religion:* "Baptized Catholic."

ADDRESSES: Home—954 17th Ave. E., Seattle, WA 98112. *Office*—Davis Wright Tremaine, 2600 Century Sq., Seattle, WA 98101. *Agent*—Neil G. McCluskey, Westchester Literary Agency, 4728 D'Este Court, No. 203, Lake Worth, FL 33467.

CAREER: U.S. Department of Housing and Urban Development, Washington, DC, attorney, 1968-70;

private practice of law in Seattle, WA, 1970-72; Office of the Prosecuting Attorney of King County, Seattle, deputy prosecutor, 1972-79; private practice of law, Seattle, 1979—. Seattle-King County Economic Development Council, general counsel, 1989—. Member of Oregon Shakespeare Festival, KUOW Public Radio, and Southern Poverty Law Center.

MEMBER: Amnesty International, American Civil Liberties Union, Sierra Club, Harvard-Radcliffe Club.

WRITINGS:

Clearwater Summer, Carroll & Graf, 1994.

Contributor to law journals.

WORK IN PROGRESS: Novels.

SIDELIGHTS: John E. Keegan told *CA:* "At this stage in my career, I am practicing law full-time in a law firm with two-hundred-eighty lawyers, with offices in ten cities. I am only able to write for fifteen to twenty hours per week, a circumstance that I would like to change to honor my still unsatisfied appetite for writing. At this pace I can write a novel every two years, but my 'story folder' is already brimming with too much material to finish in my lifetime.

"I wish I had started serious writing sooner, but I also wonder if I would have had anything important to say. I am grateful for the urge to write. Next to raising kids or making a relationship work, writing has to be one of the most humbling and humanizing things a person can do. The act of writing (says David Hume) is the act of discovering what you believe."

BIOGRAPHICAL/CRITICAL SOURCES:

PERIODICALS

Bellingham Herald, March 13, 1994.
Library Journal, March 1, 1994.

* * *

KELEMEN, Julie 1959-

PERSONAL: Born September 17, 1959, in St. Louis, MO; daughter of Joseph (a professor of electrical engineering) and Marcella (a family counseling office administrator; maiden name, Voss) Kelemen; married Toby W. Paone (a union organizer), September 30, 1989. *Education:* Western Michigan University, B.A. (magna cum laude), 1981; Washington University, M.F.A. (writing), 1986. *Avocational interests:* Foreign languages, ethnic cooking, gardening, early television trivia and memorabilia, Africana, "hanging out with kids," computers, dogs.

ADDRESSES: Home and office—6408 South Kingshighway, St. Louis, MO 63109-3741.

CAREER: Central Institute for the Deaf, St. Louis, MO, technical writer/editor, 1986-87; Liguori Publications, Liguori, MO, associate editor, book and pamphlet department, 1987-90, associate editor, Parish Education Products, 1990-93. Adjunct English instructor at St. Louis Community College, St. Louis, and St. Charles County Community College, St. Peters, MO, 1993—.

MEMBER: Society of Children's Book Writers and Illustrators, St. Louis Writers' Guild (secretary, 1990-92; president, 1992-93).

AWARDS, HONORS: First prize, James Nash Memorial Writing Contest, St. Louis Writer's Guild, 1987, for the short story "Zero O'Clock."

WRITINGS:

Lent Is for Children, Liguori, 1987.
Advent Is for Children, Liguori, 1988.
Prayer Is for Children, Liguori, 1992.

WORK IN PROGRESS: "A book of stories that take place in Nigeria, where I lived as a child; I'm also trying to expand into trade children's publishing from the children's religious field where I've been for the past seven years."

SIDELIGHTS: "During the late sixties, I was in the second and third grades in Nigeria where my father taught college," Julie Kelemen remembered. "I went to school with mostly African children—Yorubas, Ibos, Hausas, Fulanis. These were fascinating, fun years of learning about West African culture.

"My family returned to the United States in 1968. On the news and in magazines I remember looking, aghast, at images of Martin Luther King after he'd been shot. Bobby Kennedy had just been shot. Race riots were erupting. Riot police came out in full force at the Democratic National Convention. The horror of these images sharply contrasted with the racial harmony I'd experienced in Nigeria. Returning to America was more of a culture shock than going to Nigeria. My sadness about this contrast remains with me today.

"I was both blessed, and cursed, with a harmonious, pleasant exposure to African culture at a young age. I say 'cursed' because I fear intercultural tolerance won't happen in the United States in my lifetime. Thus, I tend to involve myself in ventures (including writing) that promote intercultural understanding and harmony.

"I seriously began considering a writing career in Mrs. Groening's sixth grade class at St. Joseph's school in Kalamazoo, Michigan. One day, Mrs. Groening had us read aloud stories we'd written. When my turn came, I gulped and read my science fiction tale about earthlings visiting another planet and finding nice creatures, for a change. When I finished, there were a few seconds of insufferable silence. Then . . . the whole class burst into applause (they hadn't clapped for anyone else's story).

"Wish I'd saved the story. All I remember is a character named Barney and the last line: '. . . and they feasted on goodiak soup.'

"Three children's authors have influenced me more than any others—Shel Silverstein, Dr. Seuss, and Bernadette McCarver Snyder. They've perfected the art of exploring controversial or complicated elements of life without boring or offending their readers. They're true masters of silliness, and silliness is serious business in kids' writing! Viva la silly!

"To be a successful children's author, four things are necessary (in addition to the ability to write coherently). First, talk *with* (not at) children whenever you can. Take them seriously. Listen more than you talk. Second, be confident and take your desire to write for children seriously. Lots of folks won't want you to do it. They think it's frivolous. Stand firm. Repeat 'I am a writer' to yourself every day, then DO it. Third, have a vivid memory of, and respect for, your own childhood—knowing what it is to be a child. Fourth, maintain a childlike attitude and outlook, even if you're eighty. That means cultivating hope, wonder, and silliness when cynicism and worry try to crawl under the door. I have to work on that every day!"

*　　*　　*

KELLY, Deirdre M. 1959-

PERSONAL: Born March 18, 1959, in Medford, OR; daughter of Bernard and Sylvia (McCabe) Kelly; married David Beers, June 1, 1986. *Education:* Attended Sorbonne, University of Paris IV, 1979; University of Santa Clara, B.A. (summa cum laude), 1981; Fletcher School of Law and Diplomacy, Tufts University, M.A.L.D., 1983; Stanford University, Ph.D., 1991.

ADDRESSES: Home—1435 Nelson St., No. P-3, Vancouver, British Columbia V6G 2Z3, Canada. *Office*—Department of Social and Educational Studies,

University of British Columbia, 2125 Main Mall, Vancouver, British Columbia V6T 1Z2, Canada.

CAREER: High school music appreciation teacher in Santa Clara, CA, 1988-89; University of British Columbia, Vancouver, assistant professor of sociology of schooling, 1991—.

MEMBER: Phi Beta Kappa.

AWARDS, HONORS: Harry S. Truman public service scholarship, 1979-83; Inter-American Foundation masters fellowship, 1983-84; Stanford International Development Education Committee teaching fellowship, 1986-87; Spencer dissertation year fellowship for research related to education, 1989-90; Grants from Inter-American Foundation (for the West Indies), 1983-84, and Canadian Education Association, 1993-95.

WRITINGS:

Hard Work, Hard Choices: A Survey of Women in St. Lucia's Export-Oriented Electronics Factories, Institute for Social and Economic Research, University of the West Indies, 1986.
Last Chance High: How Girls and Boys Drop in and out of Alternative Schools, Yale University Press (New Haven, CT), 1993.

Work represented in anthologies, including *Education in Urban Areas: Cross-National Dimensions,* edited by Nelly P. Stromquist, Praeger, 1994; and *Poverty: Feminist Perspectives,* Centre for Research in Women's Studies and Gender Relations (Vancouver), 1994. Contributor to periodicals.

*   *   *

KENNEDY, Pagan
     See KENNEDY, Pamela

*   *   *

KENNEDY, Pamela   1962-
     (Pagan Kennedy)

PERSONAL: Born September 7, 1962, in Washington, DC; daughter of Gordon (an economist) and Joan (a homemaker; maiden name, Burke) Kennedy. *Education:* Wesleyan University, B.A., 1984; Johns Hopkins University, M.A., 1988.

ADDRESSES: Agent—Kim Witherspoon, 157 West 57th St., New York, NY 10019.

CAREER: Voice Literary Supplement, "zine" columnist, 1991—; freelance writer. Host of Boston-based cable television show. Recycling and antiwar activist.

AWARDS, HONORS: National Endowment for the Arts fiction grant, 1993.

WRITINGS:

UNDER PSEUDONYM PAGAN KENNEDY

Stripping and Other Stories, Serpent's Tail, 1994.
Platforms: A Microwaved Cultural Chronicle of the 1970s, St. Martin's, 1994.
Spinsters (novel), Serpent's Tail, 1995.

Contributor to periodicals, including *Interview, Nation, Mademoiselle, Women's Review of Books, Mirabella,* and *Voice Literary Supplement.* Publisher of the fanzine *Pagan's Head.*

WORK IN PROGRESS: Pagan's Head, a compilation of articles from the fanzine *Pagan's Head,* to be published by St. Martin's.

SIDELIGHTS: Columns and articles about pop culture by Pagan Kennedy have been printed frequently in large-circulation periodicals like the *Voice Literary Supplement,* as well as in Kennedy's self-published fanzine, *Pagan's Head.* Considered an "insightful" chronicler of popular trends and fashions by a reviewer in *Publishers Weekly,* Kennedy interprets deeper meanings behind fads of the 1970s in the book *Platforms: A Microwaved Cultural Chronicle of the 1970s.* In addition, Kennedy's short fiction, which can be found in such literary journals as *The Quarterly,* is collected in the book *Stripping and Other Stories.*

Suggesting that clever marketing strategies were responsible for selling "hipness" to the American public, Kennedy cites in *Platforms* the example of "Earth shoes"—consumers, guided through advertising and promotion, formed the impression that Earth shoes "had something to do with nature." Other aspects of the 1970s are discussed in *Platforms* as well, such as the social and political forces which influenced trends in television and film. In *Publishers Weekly,* a reviewer applauded *Platforms* as a "hilarious, highly personalized history of what may be the goofiest of modern decades."

Many of the short stories in *Stripping* describe epiphanies in the lives of various females. In the story "The Tunnel," Kennedy tells of a young girl's new-found feeling of satisfaction after she lies to her father. "Most of Kennedy's stories, regardless of time or place, record the loss of innocence by young women and girls who don't necessarily regret their passage into adulthood," commented a critic in *Kirkus Reviews,* who termed *Stripping* "a winning collection." Other stories, such as "The Black Forest"—in which a university student studies German philosopher Friedrich Nietzsche for the first time—lead a female character to a moment of transformation. *Los Angeles Times Book Review* critic Chris Goodrich wrote that, in Kennedy's fiction, "smart young women [attempt] to make sense of a perplexing world, one not so much hostile as unpredictable and indifferent." In the *New York Times Book Review,* Katherine Ramsland pointed out that certain stories in *Stripping*—such as "The Black Forest"— "reveal a rare talent for tussling with life's disquieting problems."

Kennedy told *CA:* "For years, I had several parallel careers; I wrote fiction, I published my own fanzine, and I covered underground culture for various magazines. At first, the game for me was to fit myself into whatever form seemed most handy—if an idea seemed most like a short story, I'd turn it into that; or if the idea seemed kind of dopey, I'd turn it into a piece for my self-published fanzine. Nowadays, I'm trying to bridge genres—my nonfiction book about the 1970s has a lot of short story-like memoirs stuck in it. And I'm turning the collected issues of my fanzine into a novel, a fictional story about my real life."

BIOGRAPHICAL/CRITICAL SOURCES:

BOOKS

Kennedy, Pagan, *Platforms: A Microwaved Cultural Chronicle of the 1970s,* St. Martin's, 1994.

PERIODICALS

Kirkus Reviews, December 1, 1993, p. 1481.
Los Angeles Times Book Review, June 26, 1994.
New York Times Book Review, April 24, 1994, p. 16.
Publishers Weekly, March 14, 1994.

*　　*　　*

KEOHANE, Dan 1941-

PERSONAL: Born July 14, 1941, in Cork, Ireland; son of Dan (a farmer) and Mary (Lynch) Keohane. *Education:* Ruskin College, Oxford, Special Diploma, 1972; University of Sussex, B.A. (with first class honors), 1975; University of Warwick, M.A., 1976.

ADDRESSES: *Home*—74 Marina Dr., Newcastle, Staffordshire ST5 0RS, England. *Office*—Department of International Relations, University of Keele, Keele, Staffordshire ST5 5BC, England.

CAREER: University of Keele, Keele, England, lecturer in international relations, 1977—.

WRITINGS:

Labour Party Defence Policy since 1945, St. Martin's (New York, NY), 1993.
(Editor with A. Danchev) *International Perspectives on the Gulf Conflict, 1990-1991,* St. Martin's, 1994.

WORK IN PROGRESS: Research on the security policy of British political parties.

*　　*　　*

KESSLER, Judy 1947-

PERSONAL: Born February 21, 1947, in Seattle, WA; daughter of Harry A. (in business) and Charlette (a homemaker) Kessler; married Harold T. P. Hayes (a writer and editor; now deceased) March 4, 1983. *Education:* Stanford University, B.A., 1969.

ADDRESSES: *Office*—Time Inc. Ventures, 11100 Santa Monica Blvd., Suite 1950, Los Angeles, CA 90025. *Agent*—Esther Newberg, International Creative Management, 40 West 57th St., New York, NY.

CAREER: *People* magazine, New York City, writer, 1974-80; *The Today Show,* New York City, producer, 1980-84; *Entertainment Tonight,* Los Angeles, CA, producer, 1984-86; *Gorillas in the Mist* (film), coproducer, 1987-88; Creative Affairs, Time Inc. Ventures, Los Angeles, vice president. Wake Forest University, member of board of visitors.

MEMBER: Authors Guild.

AWARDS, HONORS: *Reader's Digest* award for best nonfiction, 1992, for *Inside Today: The Battle for the Morning.*

WRITINGS:

Inside Today: The Battle for the Morning, Villard/Random, 1992.
Inside People: The Stories behind the Stories, Villard/Random, 1994.

WORK IN PROGRESS: *Meet Me Where We Used to Be,* an autobiography.

SIDELIGHTS: Judy Kessler told *CA:* "I became deeply involved in Africa with my late husband, Harold T. P. Hayes, the legendary editor of *Esquire,* who wrote extensively on Africa.

"I completed his book, *The Dark Romance of Dian Fossey*, after his death in 1989. That inspired my interest in writing my own books."

* * *

KIRBY, John R. 1951-

PERSONAL: Born September 4, 1951, in Montreal, Quebec, Canada; son of Tom Robert (an accountant) and Ida May (LaFerme) Kirby; married Margaret L. Whitehead (a statistician); children: Robert John. *Education:* McGill University, B.A. (with honors), 1972; University of Alberta, Ph.D., 1976. *Politics:* "Confused." *Religion:* "Likewise."

ADDRESSES: Home—Kingston, Ontario, Canada. *Office*—Faculty of Education, Queen's University, Kingston, Ontario, Canada K7L 3N6.

CAREER: University of Newcastle, Newcastle, Australia, began as lecturer, became associate professor, 1976-87; Queen's University, Kingston, Ontario, Canada, began as associate professor, became professor of education, 1987—.

MEMBER: Canadian Psychological Association, Canadian Association for Educational Psychology (president, 1994-96), CSSE, American Psychological Association, American Educational Research Association.

WRITINGS:

(With Das and Jarman) *Simultaneous and Successive Cognitive Processing,* Academic Press, 1979.
(Editor with Biggs) *Cognition, Development, and Instruction,* Academic Press, 1980.
(Editor) *Cognitive Strategies and Educational Performance,* Academic Press, 1984.
(With Williams) *Learning Problems: A Cognitive Approach,* Kagan & Woo, 1991.

Co-author of the book *Assessment of Cognitive Processes,* Allyn & Bacon. Contributor to scientific journals.

WORK IN PROGRESS: Research on educational psychology, intelligence, learning disability, and spatial cognition.

* * *

KIRK, Janice E(mily) 1935-

PERSONAL: Born September 16, 1935; daughter of Claude Ellis (in real estate) and Angeletta Ruth (a teacher; maiden name, Skidmore) Milton; married Donald Robert Kirk (a college teacher, writer, and photographer), December 29, 1956; children: Ned, Amy. *Education:* University of Oregon, B.Mus., 1958; University of Colorado, M.Mus., 1994. *Religion:* Christian. *Avocational interests:* Camping, watercolor painting, ping pong, gardening, sewing.

ADDRESSES: Home—Palo Cedro, CA.

CAREER: Music teacher at schools in Springfield, OR, 1957-61; Shasta County Language, Art, and Music Project, writer and art coordinator, 1974-77; teacher of art, music, language, and gifted education at a public school in Palo Cedro, CA, 1978-88; Simpson College, Redding, CA, adjunct professor of voice, 1989—. Operated a private music studio for twelve years; performs as a soprano soloist for churches and community programs; choir director. Artist and illustrator.

MEMBER: National Association of Teachers of Singing, Shasta County Arts Council, Redding Writers Forum.

WRITINGS:

(With husband, Donald R. Kirk; also illustrator) *Cherish the Earth,* Herald Press (Scottdale, PA), 1993.

ILLUSTRATOR

Wild Edible Plants of Western North America, Naturegraph, 1970.
Kathy Hansen, *Egypt Handbook,* Moon Publications, 1990.

WORK IN PROGRESS: A singing manual; research on the appreciation and understanding of the natural world and on Christian earth stewardship.

SIDELIGHTS: Janice E. Kirk told *CA:* "I took up writing because of growing environmental abuse. I did not want to become involved in this issue. I am a singer, artist, and teacher, not a naturalist, scientist, or city planner. I thought I was too old and busy, but I could not ignore the fact that the world I sing about is becoming a mess. The landscapes I enjoy painting are disappearing. Camping and hiking areas we love are being overrun by people. Our local countryside is invaded by developers.

"I felt the problems were partly spiritual, but found few resources in the church for lay people. My husband and I wrote *Cherish the Earth* to highlight biblical support for earth care. We hope this motivates Christians to care for the Earth. Extraordinary renewal is still possible."

KITT, Sandra (E.) 1947-

PERSONAL: Born June 11, 1947, in New York, NY; daughter of Archie B. and Ann (Wright) Kitt. *Education:* Received A.A. from Bronx Community College of the City University of New York; City College of the City University of New York, B.A., 1969, M.F.A., 1975; also attended School of Visual Arts, New School, and University of Guadalajara. *Religion:* Methodist.

ADDRESSES: Home—New York City. *Agent*—Ling Lucas, Nine Muses and Apollo Agency, 2 Charlton Street, New York, NY 10014.

CAREER: Philip Gips Studios, Inc., art assistant, 1970-72; New York City Board of Education, New York City, teacher in Cloisters Workshop Program, 1972-73; *Information Specialist,* New York City, librarian, 1974-92; American Museum of Natural History, New York City, manager of library services at Richard S. Perkin Library, Hayden Planetarium, 1992—. Museum of Contemporary Arts, assistant to the registrar and assistant coordinator at Children's Art Center, 1972-73; New York City Office of Cultural Affairs, teacher at Printmaking Workshop, 1974-80. Freelance graphic artist and illustrator, with work exhibited throughout the United States and represented in corporate collections, including American Institute of Graphic Arts and African-American Art Museum of Los Angeles; greeting card designer for UNICEF; printmaker. Recording for the Blind, reader and monitor; New York City Mayor's Volunteer Corps, member. Guest on television programs, including *Geraldo, Donohue, NBC Today,* and on Black Entertainment Television.

MEMBER: Special Libraries Association, Published Authors Network, Romance Writers of America, Novelists INK, American Library Association (Black Caucus).

AWARDS, HONORS: NIA Woman of Excellence Award from the mayor of New York City, 1993.

WRITINGS:

ROMANCE NOVELS

Rites of Spring, Harlequin American, 1984.
Adam and Eva, Harlequin American, 1984.
All Good Things, Doubleday, 1984.
Perfect Combination, Harlequin American, 1985.
Only with the Heart, Harlequin American, 1985.
With Open Arms, Harlequin American, 1987.
An Innocent Man, Harlequin American, 1989.
The Way Home, Harlequin American, 1990.
Someone's Baby, Harlequin American, 1991.
Love Everlasting, Odyssey Books, 1993.
Love Is Thanks Enough (also known as *Friends, Fami-lies, and Lovers*), Harlequin, 1993.
Serenade, Pinnacle Books, 1994.
Sincerely, Pinnacle Books, 1995.

OTHER

(Illustrator) Isaac Asimov, *Asimov's Guide to Halley's Comet,* Walker and Co. (New York, NY), 1985.
(Illustrator) Asimov, *Beginnings: The Story of Origins. . . ,* Walker and Co., 1986.
The Color of Love (novel), Dutton (New York, NY), 1995.

Author of unreleased screenplays *Forgiving,* 1988, and *Snatched!* 1992. Contributor of articles and reviews to museum and library journals.

WORK IN PROGRESS: Significant Others, for Signet.

* * *

KLEIN, Donald F. 1928-

PERSONAL: Born September 4, 1928, in New York, NY; married; children: five. *Education:* Colby College, B.A. (magna cum laude), 1947; New York University, graduate study, 1947-48; State University of New York College of Medicine, M.D., 1952.

ADDRESSES: Office—New York State Psychiatric Institute, College of Physicians and Surgeons, Columbia University, 722 West 168th St., New York, NY 10032.

CAREER: U.S. Public Health Service Hospital, Staten Island, NY, rotating intern, 1952-53; Creedmoor State Hospital, resident in psychiatry, 1953-54 and 1956-58; Creedmoor Institute for Psychobiologic Studies, research associate, 1957-59; Hillside Hospital, research associate, 1959-64, senior staff psychiatrist, 1965, director of research, 1965-70, medical director for evaluation, 1970-71; State University of New York at Stony Brook, professor of psychiatry, 1972-76; Columbia University, New York City, lecturer, 1976-78, professor of psychiatry, 1978—, director of Department of Therapeutics, 1976—, director of New York State Psychiatric Institute, 1976—. Qualified psychiatrist, State of New York; diplomate, National Board of Medical Examiners, American Board of Psychiatry and Neurology, and American Board of Clinical Pharmacology. Queens Hospital Center, psychiatrist in chief, 1970-71, full attending psychiatrist, 1972-85; Presbyterian Hospital, attending psychiatrist, 1977—. Long Island Jewish-Hillside Medical Center, director of research and evaluation in psychiatry, 1972-76; New York State Psychiatric Mental Health Clinical Research Center, director, 1978—.

Queens College of the City University of New York, adjunct professor, 1969-92; visiting professor at University of Auckland, 1975, Albert Einstein College of Medicine, Yeshiva University, 1976-77, and University of Hawaii at Manoa, 1977, 1985, and 1986. National Foundation for Depressive Illness, president, 1983—; Information Exchange on Young Adult Chronic Patients, member of national advisory board, 1983—; National Depressive and Manic Depressive Association, member of scientific advisory board, 1986—; Lyme Research Foundation, member of scientific advisory council, 1993—; Foundation of Thanatology, member of professional board of advisers; consultant to Medical Research Council of New Zealand, National Institute of Mental Health, and U.S. Office of Technology Assessment. *Military service:* U.S. Public Health Service, senior assistant surgeon and staff psychiatrist at U.S. Public Health Service Hospital, Lexington, KY, 1954-56.

MEMBER: International Neuropsychology Society (member of executive committee, 1967), Collegium Internationale Neuro-Psychopharmacologicam, International Brain Research Organization, European Brain and Behavior Society, American Society of Clinical Psychopharmacology (president, 1992—), American Association for the Advancement of Science, American College of Neuropsychopharmacology (life fellow; president, 1981; chairperson of Committee on Public Concern, 1983, 1987, and 1988; chairperson of Task Force for the Development of a Non-Profit Foundation to Investigate Issues of Scientific Misconduct, 1989-92), American Psychiatric Association (life fellow; chairperson of Task Force on Guidelines for the Protection of Human Subjects in Psychiatric Research, 1977-79 and 1982-84), American Psychopathological Association (president, 1979-80), Psychiatric Research Society, Society of Life History Research in Psychopathology, Society of Neuroscience, Society for Psychophysiological Research, Society for the Study of Social Biology, Association for Clinical Psychosocial Research (fellow), American Society for Clinical Pharmacology and Therapeutics, Society for Research in Child and Adolescent Psychopathology, Society for Light Treatment and Biological Rhythms, Royal College of Psychiatrists (founding member; fellow), Phi Beta Kappa.

AWARDS, HONORS: Grants from National Association of Private Psychiatric Hospitals, 1965 and 1971; Samuel W. Hamilton Award, American Psychopathological Association, 1980; Psychiatric Award, Taylor Manor Hospital, 1985; William R. McAlpin Award for Research Achievement, 1988; Gold Medal, Society of Biological Psychiatry, 1990; Heinz E. Lehman Research Award, State of New York, 1991; Paul Hoch Distinguished Service Award, American College of Neuropsychopharmacology, 1991; William A. Console, M.D., Award in Psychiatry, State University of New York Alumni Society, 1992; Thomas W. Salmon Medal for Distinguished Service in Psychiatry, New York Academy of Medicine, 1993; grants from National Institute of Mental Health and Dreyfus Charitable Fund.

WRITINGS:

(With J. M. Davis) *Diagnosis and Drug Treatment of Psychiatric Disorders,* Williams and Wilkins, 1969, second edition (with R. Gittelman, F. Quitkin, and A. Rifkin) published as *Diagnosis and Drug Treatment of Psychiatric Disorders: Adults and Children,* 1980.

Psychiatric Case Studies: Treatment, Drugs, and Outcome, Williams and Wilkins, 1972.

(Editor with R. Gittelman-Klein, and contributor) *Progress in Psychiatric Drug Treatment,* Brunner, Volume I, 1975, Volume II, 1976.

(Editor with R. L. Spitzer, and contributor) *Evaluation of Psychological Therapies: Psychotherapies, Behavior Therapies, Drug Therapies, and Their Interactions,* Johns Hopkins University Press, 1976.

The Physicians Handbook on Depression, Pfizer, 1977.

(Editor with Spitzer, and contributor) *Critical Issues in Psychiatric Diagnosis,* Raven Press, 1978.

(Editor with J. G. Rabkin, and contributor) *Anxiety: New Research and Changing Concepts,* Raven Press, 1981.

(With P. H. Wender) *Mind, Mood, and Medicine: A Guide to the New Biopsychiatry,* Farrar, Straus, 1981.

(Editor with M. R. Liebowitz, A. J. Fyer, and J. M. Gorman) *Modern Problems of Pharmacopsychiatry,* Volume XXII: *Anxiety,* S. Karger (Basel), 1987.

(With Wender) *Do You Have a Depressive Illness?,* New American Library, 1988.

(With Wender) *Understanding Depression,* Oxford University Press, 1993.

Work represented in books, including *Psychopharmacology of Anxiety,* edited by P. J. Tyrer, Oxford University Press, 1989; *Anxiety: Psychobiological and Clinical Perspectives,* edited by N. Sartorius, Hemisphere Publishing, 1990; and *Panic Disorder and Agoraphobia: A Guide for the Practitioner,* edited by J. R. Walker, R. Norton, and C. Ross, Brooks/Cole, 1991. Contributor of more than five-hundred articles and reviews to medical journals. Associate editor and editor of reviews and commentaries section, *Neuropsychopharmacology: Journal of the American College of Neuropsychopharmacology,* 1986—; member of editorial board, *Archives of General Psychiatry,* 1975—, *Journal of Abnormal Child Psychology,* 1976—, *Comprehensive Psychiatry,* 1977—, *Journal of Clinical Psychopharmacology,* 1979—, *Journal of Psychiatric Research,* 1983—, *Journal of Clinical Psychiatry,* 1987—, *International Journal of Methods in Psychiatric Research,* 1991—, *European Psychiatry,* 1992—, and *Anxiety,* 1993—.

*   *   *

KNAUFT, Bruce M.   1954-

PERSONAL: Born January 25, 1954, in Hartford, CT; son of Edwin B. (an executive) and Ruth (McNeill) Knauft; married Eileen M. Cantrell (an anthropologist), December 7, 1979; children: Eric. *Education:* Yale University, B.A. (magna cum laude), 1976; University of Michigan, Ph.D., 1983.

ADDRESSES: Home—1976 Silvastone Dr., Atlanta, GA 30345. *Office*—Department of Anthropology, Emory University, Atlanta, GA 30322.

CAREER: University of California, San Diego, La Jolla, postdoctoral research fellow, 1983-85; Emory University, Atlanta, GA, assistant professor, 1985-90, associate professor of anthropology, 1990—. Conducted field research in Papua New Guinea.

AWARDS, HONORS: Fellow, National Institutes of Health, 1983-85; Guggenheim fellow, 1990-94; fellow at Center for Advanced Studies in the Behavioral Sciences, Stanford, CA, 1991-92; fellow at Ecole des Hautes Etudes en Sciences Sociales, Paris, 1994.

WRITINGS:

Good Company and Violence: Sorcery and Social Action in a Lowland New Guinea Society, University of California Press, 1985.
South Coast New Guinea Cultures: History, Comparison, Dialectic, Cambridge University Press, 1993.

Work represented in anthologies, including *Fragments for a History of the Human Body,* Part III, edited by Michel Feher, Ramona Haddaff, and Nadia Tazi, Urzone, 1989; and *The Anthropology of Peace and Nonviolence,* edited by Leslie Sponsel and Thomas Gregor, Lynne Rienner, 1994. Coeditor of "Melanesian Studies Series," University of California Press. Contributor to anthropology journals.

*   *   *

KOERNER, Joseph Leo   1958-

PERSONAL: Born June 17, 1958, in Pittsburgh, PA; son of Henry (an artist) and Joan Koerner; married Lisbet Rausing (a science historian), June 3, 1988; children: Benjamin Henry Anders. *Education:* Yale University, B.A. attended University of Heidelberg, 1982-83; University of California, Berkeley, M.A., 1984, Ph.D., 1988.

ADDRESSES: Office—Department of Fine Arts, Harvard University, Cambridge, MA 02138.

CAREER: Harvard University, Cambridge, MA, assistant professor of fine art, 1989-91, professor of fine art, 1991—. University of Constance, guest professor of literature, 1992. Seminar on Visual Representation and Cultural History, Harvard University, chair, 1994.

MEMBER: Council of the Associates of the Frick Art Reference Library, Phi Beta Kappa.

AWARDS, HONORS: Mellon Fellowship, 1980-82, for study at Clare College, Cambridge University; fellowships from Deutsche Akademischer Austauschdienst (DAAD), 1982-83, University of California, Berkeley, 1983-86, Society of Fellows, Harvard University, 1986-89, and Alexander von Humboldt Foundation, 1991-92; Greene Cup for general learning, Clare College, Cambridge, 1982; Newnes English Prize, Clare College, 1982; Honorary Master of Arts, Harvard University, 1992; Jan Mitchell Prize for the History of Art, 1992 for *Caspar David Friedrich and the Subject of Landscape.*

WRITINGS:

Die Suche nach dem Labyrinth: Der Mythos von Daedalus und Ikarus, Suhrkamp Verlag (Frankfurt), 1983.
Caspar David Friedrich and the Subject of Landscape, Yale University Press (New Haven, CT), 1990.
(With Rainer Crone) *Paul Klee: Legends of the Sign,* Columbia University Press (New York), 1991.
The Moment of Self-Portraiture in German Renaissance Art, University of Chicago Press (Chicago), 1993.

Contributor of articles, reviews, and essays to periodicals and professional journals, including *New Republic, Art Bulletin, RES: Anthropology and Aesthetics,* and *Frankfurter Allgemeine Zeitung.*

Reaktion Books, advisory editor, 1987—; *RES: Anthropology and Aesthetics,* editorial adviser, 1990—; *Art Bulletin,* book review editor, 1992—; *Arachne: An Interdisciplinary Journal of Languages and Literature,* adviser, 1993—; *Word & Image,* editor, 1993—.

WORK IN PROGRESS: The Image in Quotations, a book on the visual culture of the Reformation; *The*

Family Portrait, a book on art history, biography, and autobiography; "The Image of the Black in Northern Art, 1500-1600" (tentative title) for *The Image of the Black in Western Art,* Volume 3: *The Sixteenth through Eighteenth Centuries,* for the Menil Foundation and Harvard University Press.

SIDELIGHTS: Joseph Leo Koerner told *CA:* "I believe that the things we call images and collect as art *should* once again become as different from one another, and motivate as distinct readings as: a butter-cream sculpture melting in the window of a Viennese cake shop, a jewel studded *joyeux* in the Duke of Berry's collection of gifts, a sketch my late father did of me hanging here by my desk, a pair of Air Jordans in a Spike Lee film, and a canvas decorated in oil and signed 'Cezanne.'"

*   *   *

KOHN, Alan J(acobs)   1931-

PERSONAL: Born July 15, 1931, in New Haven, CT; son of Curtis I. and Harriet J. Kohn; married Marian S. Adachi, August 28, 1959; children: Lizabeth Sawyer, Nancy, Diane Neil, Stephen. *Education:* Princeton University, A.B., 1953; Yale University, Ph.D., 1957.

ADDRESSES: Home—18300 Ridgefield Rd. N.W., Seattle, WA 98177. *Office*—Department of Zoology, University of Washington, Seattle, WA 98195.

CAREER: Hopkins Marine Station, laboratory assistant, 1951; Narragansett Marine Laboratory, junior assistant in marine biology, 1952; Marine Biological Laboratory, Woods Hole, MA, technician, 1953; Hawaii Marine Laboratory, associate in research, 1954, visiting collaborator, 1955-56; Yale University, New Haven, CT, W. W. Anderson fellow at Bingham Oceanographic Laboratory, 1958; Florida State University, Tallahassee, assistant professor of zoology, 1958-61; University of Washington, Seattle, assistant professor, 1961-63, associate professor, 1963-67, professor of zoology, 1967—, adjunct professor of environmental studies, 1978—, adjunct professor at Quaternary Research Center, 1986—. Thomas Burke Memorial Washington State Museum, affiliate curator of malacology, 1965-70, adjunct curator, 1971—. Smithsonian Institution, National Research Council senior postdoctoral research associate, 1967, research associate at National Museum of Natural History, 1985—, senior fellow of the museum, 1990; University of Hawaii at Manoa, visiting professor, 1968. Visiting investigator at Mid-Pacific Marine Laboratory, Enewetak, 1957 and 1971-73, Bernice P. Bishop Museum, 1961, and University of the Ryukyus, 1982-83; participant in Yale Seychelles Expedition

to the Indian Ocean, 1957-58, and U.S. Biology Program of the International Indian Ocean Expedition, 1963. Council for the International Exchange of Scholars, member, 1986-90, chairperson of Australasia Area Committee, 1986-90, member of executive committee, 1988-89.

MEMBER: International Society for Reef Studies, American Association for the Advancement of Science (fellow), American Society of Zoologists (president-elect, 1995-96), American Society of Limnology and Oceanography, American Society of Naturalists, Society of Systematic Biologists, Ecological Society of America, American Malacological Union (president, 1982-83), British Ecological Society, Marine Biological Association of the United Kingdom, Marine Biological Association of India (fellow), Malacological Society of Japan, Australian Coral Reef Society, Pacific Science Association, Hawaiian Academy of Sciences, Linnean Society of London (fellow), Malacological Society of London, Sigma Xi (president of University of Washington chapter, 1971-72).

AWARDS, HONORS: Guggenheim fellow, 1975-76.

WRITINGS:

A Chronological Taxonomy of Conus, 1758-1840, Smithsonian Institution Press, 1992.
(Editor with F. W. Harrison) *Microscopic Anatomy of Invertebrates, Volume 5: Mollusca I,* Wiley, 1994.
(With F. E. Perron) *Life History and Biogeography: Patterns in Conus,* Oxford University Press, 1994.

Contributor of about ninety articles to scientific journals. Member of editorial board, *American Zoologist,* 1973-77, *Malacologia,* 1974—, *American Naturalist,* 1976-78, *Journal of Experimental Marine Biology and Ecology,* 1981-84, *Coral Reefs,* 1981-87, *American Malacological Bulletin,* 1983—, and *Marine Research,* 1993—.

*   *   *

KORMAN, Bernice   1937-

PERSONAL: Born July 23, 1937, in Montreal, Quebec, Canada; daughter of George (a manufacturer) and Claire (Schwartz) Silverman; married Charles Isaac Korman (an accountant), June 26, 1960; children: Gordon. *Education:* Concordia University, Montreal, B.A., 1958. *Avocational interests:* Swimming, music, baseball.

ADDRESSES: Home—20 Dersingham Crescent, Thornhill, Ontario L3T 4E7, Canada. *Agent*—Curtis Brown Ltd., Ten Astor Place, New York, NY 10003.

CAREER: Columnist for the *Suburban* (English-language weekly newspaper), 1964-81; Teleterm, Inc., Markham, Ontario, executive assistant, 1980—.

MEMBER: Canadian Society of Children's Authors, Illustrators, and Performers.

WRITINGS:

(With son, Gordon Korman) *The D-Poems of Jeremy Bloom,* Scholastic Inc., 1992.

WORK IN PROGRESS: A sequel to *The D-Poems of Jeremy Bloom;* several Regency romances.

SIDELIGHTS: Although *The D-Poems of Jeremy Bloom* has done well, Bernice Korman considers her personal claim to fame to be the fact that she is the mother of young-adult novelist Gordon Korman. "To collaborate with him on a book was a delight," she remarked, "but it was merely an extension of the years I spent typing and editing his grammar—he started writing at age twelve!"

Korman is currently at work on more poems, and a sequel to *The D-Poems of Jeremy Bloom* is in the works. "And I'm hard at work writing Regency romances, a genre I enjoy," she commented. She continues to find the writing process as rewarding as seeing her finished work in print: "For those who believe that the act of creating a book is at least half of the art, you ought to see Gordon and Bernice Korman collaborating! If laughter and sheer enjoyment count for anything, we've found the system!"

*   *   *

KOTLER, Neil G. 1941-

PERSONAL: Born April 17, 1941, in Chicago, IL; son of Maurice (in business) and Betty (a homemaker; maiden name, Bubar) Kotler; married Wendy I. Abrams (a teacher), December 19, 1971; children: Jena J. *Education:* Brandeis University, A.B., 1962; University of Wisconsin—Madison, M.S., 1963; University of Chicago, Ph.D., 1974. *Politics:* Independent. *Religion:* Jewish. *Avocational interests:* Drawing, art, piano.

ADDRESSES: Home—200 South Abingdon St., Arlington, VA 22204. *Office*—Office of External Affairs, Smithsonian Institution, Washington, DC 20560.

CAREER: U.S. Peace Corps, Washington, DC, volunteer teacher of Ethiopian history in Asmara, Ethiopia, 1964-66; De Paul University, Chicago, IL, instructor in American government and political science, 1967-71; Dartmouth College, Hanover, NH, instructor in

American government and political science, 1971-73; University of Texas at Austin, instructor, 1974-75; U.S. House of Representatives, Washington, DC, began as legislative assistant, became legislative director, 1975-84; Smithsonian Institution, Washington, DC, special assistant and program officer, 1986—. Georgetown University, instructor, 1979. Smithsonian Institution, co-producer of the documentary videotapes *Democracy and Rights: One Citizen's Challenge* (also see below), 1989, and *Citizen Stories: Democracy and Responsibility in American Life* (also see below), 1991.

MEMBER: Phi Beta Kappa.

WRITINGS:

(With Eduardo L. Roberto) *Social Marketing: Strategies for Changing Public Behavior,* Free Press, 1989.
(Editor) *Completing the Food Chain: Strategies for Combating Hunger and Malnutrition,* Smithsonian Institution Press (Washington, D.C.), 1989.
Democracy and Rights: One Citizen's Challenge (documentary videotape), Smithsonian Institution and Close Up Foundation, 1989.
(Editor) *Sharing Innovation: Global Perspectives on Food, Agriculture, and Rural Development,* Smithsonian Institution Press, 1990.
Citizen Stories: Democracy and Responsibility in American Life (documentary videotape), Smithsonian Institution and Close Up Foundation, 1991.
(Editor) *Frontiers of Nutrition and Food Security in Asia, Africa, and Latin America,* Smithsonian Institution Press, 1992.
(Co-editor) *The Statue of Liberty Revisited: Making a Universal Symbol,* Smithsonian Institution Press, 1994.

WORK IN PROGRESS: A book on museums and marketing, with Philip Kotler; research on the vocations and roles of politicians.

SIDELIGHTS: Neil G. Kotler told *CA:* "My books and other writings reflect my lifelong concern for teaching and public service. As a Peace Corps volunteer in Ethiopia, I wrote articles and monographs on Ethiopian and Eritrean history that I hope were of value to my students; this I did, through articles, as a university instructor in political science and American politics. Opportunities at the Smithsonian allowed me to edit a series of books on world food and agriculture and on innovations adopted in non-industrialized nations of the world to feed their peoples. I want to devote the next several years as a writer to advancing museums as centers for enlightenment, education, and historical and cultural understanding. As a political science instructor, I want to help rehabilitate the standing of politics and politicians in the United States and other democratic societies."

* * *

KRAMER, Edward (E.) 1961-
(Nathan Eliot)

PERSONAL: Born March 20, 1961, in Brooklyn, NY; son of Leon Abraham and Helen Miriam (Scheinman) Kramer. *Education:* Emory University, B.S., 1983, M.P.H., 1984. *Religion:* Jewish. *Avocational interests:* Collecting art, caving, exotic snakes.

ADDRESSES: Home—P.O. Box 148, Clarkston, GA 30021-0148.

CAREER: Georgia Mental Health Institute, Briarcliff Adolescent Center, Atlanta, behavior management therapist, 1984-85; Metropolitan Atlanta Council on Alcohol and Drugs, Atlanta, program coordinator for Substance Use Prevention and Education Resource, 1985-87; quality assurance consultant, Atlanta, 1987-88; Anchor Hospital, Atlanta, associate director of standards compliance and director of research for Talbott Recovery System, 1988-90; Psychiatric Healthcare Consultants, Atlanta, medical management consultant for addictive and psychiatric programs, 1990-91; Metropolitan Regional Educational Service Agency, Atlanta, educational grants consultant and conference training coordinator, 1991-93; Resource Network International, Atlanta, project manager, 1993—. Dragon Con, Inc., president; Mithril Publishing, Inc., founder, president, and publisher, 1993—; Titan Games and Comics, Inc., vice president. Truckstop Youth Lodge, group leader and intake counselor, 1979-80; American Red Cross, multimedia standard first aid instructor and basic life support instructor, 1980-87, member of DeKalb/Rockdale Disaster Action Team, 1982-88; DeKalb County Youth Assistance Program, counselor, 1980-83; Atlanta Mayor's Task Force on Domestic Violence, member, 1983-85; DeKalb County Juvenile Court, volunteer probation officer, 1983-91; Big Brothers/Big Sisters of Metropolitan Atlanta, member of Gwinnett County Outreach Office, 1988-90; Council of Juvenile Court Judges, cochairperson of Foster Care Review Panel, 1991—. Writer and photographer for the music industry.

MEMBER: National Association of Alcoholism and Drug Abuse Counselors, National Association of Health Care Quality, American Public Health Association, Horror Writers of America, Science Fiction Writers of America, Georgia Addiction Counselors Association, Georgia Public Health Association.

WRITINGS:

(Editor with Philip Jose Farmer, Richard Gilliam, and Martin H. Greenberg) *Tales of Riverworld,* Warner Books, 1992.

(Editor with Gilliam and Greenberg) *Grails: Quests, Visitations, and Other Occurrences,* Unnameable Press, 1992.

(Editor with Farmer, Gilliam, and Greenberg) *Quest to Riverworld,* Warner Books, 1993.

(Editor with Gilliam and Greenberg) *Confederacy of the Dead,* New American Library, 1993.

(Editor with Gilliam, Greenberg, and Wendy Webb) *Phobias: Stories of Your Deepest Fears,* Pocket Books, 1994.

(Editor with Gilliam and Greenberg) *Grails: Quests of the Morning,* New American Library, 1994.

(Editor with Gilliam and Greenberg, and contributor) *Grails: Visitations of the Night,* New American Library, 1994.

(Editor) *Elric: Tales of the White Wolf,* White Wolf, 1994.

(Editor) *Dark Destiny: Unseen Architects of the World,* White Wolf, 1994.

(Editor with Webb, Gilliam, and Greenberg, and contributor, under pseudonym Nathan Eliot) *Phobias II,* Pocket Books, 1995.

(Editor with Gilliam and Greenberg) *Excalibur,* Warner Books, 1995.

(Editor with Greenberg and Neil Gaiman) *Sandman: The Anthology,* HarperCollins, 1995.

(Editor with Nancy A. Collins) *Forbidden Acts: The Darker Side of Human Attraction,* Avon, 1995.

(Editor with Collins) *Dark Love,* New American Library, 1995.

(Editor with Peter Crowther) *Tombs: Tales beyond the Crypt,* White Wolf, 1995.

(Editor) *Dark Destiny II: Darker Forces from the Past,* White Wolf, 1995.

Work represented in anthologies, including *Journeys to the Twilight Zone III,* edited by Carol Serling, DAW Books, 1994; and *Phantoms of the Night,* edited by Gilliam and Greenberg, DAW Books, 1995. Contributor of hundreds of articles and photographs to periodicals.

* * *

KRAMER, Helen 1946-

PERSONAL: Born August 13, 1946; daughter of

Hyman (an antiques dealer) and Miriam (an educator; maiden name, Yeager) Kramer; married Paul Kramer (a film producer), March 31, 1985. *Education:* Attended Cornell University, New York University, and New School for Social Research. *Politics:* Liberal. *Religion:* Jewish.

ADDRESSES: Home and office—222 Park Ave. S., No. 29, New York, NY 10003; and 38 Nidzyn Ave., Box 121, Remsenburg, NY 11960. *Agent*—Jane Dystel.

CAREER: Gestalt Associates, New York City, founder, 1975, supervisor, 1975-85; REAL Solutions, New York City, founder, 1990, director, 1990—.

WRITINGS:

Liberating the Adult Within, Simon & Schuster (New York), 1994.

*   *   *

KRAMER, Linda Konheim   1939-

PERSONAL: Born November 8, 1939, in New York, NY; daughter of Clarence Jack and May (Sternberg) Konheim; married Samuel Robert Kramer (a housing administrator), April 27, 1977; children: Nicholas Clarence. *Education:* Smith College, B.A., 1961; Yale University, B.F.A., 1963; New York University, M.A., 1968, and doctoral study.

ADDRESSES: Home—372 Central Park W., No. 15P, New York, NY 10025.

CAREER: Solomon R. Guggenheim Museum, New York City, curator and administrator, 1963-79; Sotheby Parke-Bernet, New York City, part-time cataloger of modern drawings, 1980-81; Sotheby's, New York City, expert in modern drawings, 1981-85; Brooklyn Museum, Brooklyn, NY, curator of prints and drawings, 1985-94; independent curator and freelance writer, 1994—. Western Washington University, member of advisory board, College of Fine Arts, 1987.

MEMBER: American Association of Museums, College Art Association, Print Council of America, ArtTable.

WRITINGS:

Selected Sculpture and Works on Paper, Solomon R. Guggenheim Museum, 1969.
Prints from the Guggenheim Museum Collection, Solomon R. Guggenheim Museum, 1978.

(With Sarah Faunce and Karyn Zieve) *French Nineteenth-Century Drawings and Watercolors at the Brooklyn Museum,* Hudson Hills Press (New York, NY), 1993.

Author of exhibition catalogs. Contributor to periodicals, including *Curator, Drawing,* and *American Ceramics.*

WORK IN PROGRESS: A catalogue raisonne of the prints of Janet Fish; research on the sculpture of Aristide Maillol.

*   *   *

KRANTZ, Grover S.   1931-

PERSONAL: Born November 5, 1931, in Salt Lake City, UT; son of Victor E. and Esther S. Krantz; married Patricia Howland, 1953 (marriage ended, 1957); married Joan Brandson, 1958 (marriage ended, 1962); married Evelyn Einstein, 1965 (marriage ended, 1974); married Diane C. Horton (an English teacher), November 5, 1982. *Education:* University of Minnesota—Twin Cities, Ph.D., 1971. *Politics:* "Left wing." *Religion:* Atheist.

ADDRESSES: Home—Pullman, WA. *Office*—Department of Anthropology, Washington State University, Pullman, WA 99164.

CAREER: Washington State University, Pullman, professor of anthropology.

WRITINGS:

Climactic Races and Descent Groups, Christopher Publishing House (Hanover, MA), 1980.
Geographical Development of European Languages, Peter Lang Publishing (New York), 1988.
Big Footprints: A Scientific Inquiry into the Reality of Sasquatch, Johnson Books (Boulder, CO), 1992.

SIDELIGHTS: Grover S. Krantz told *CA:* "I am a professor of anthropology, specializing in human evolution. Sasquatch is a sideline, pursued on my own time and with my own money."

*   *   *

KRIEGER, Michael J.   1940-

PERSONAL: Born May 13, 1940, in San Francisco, CA; son of Alfred and Nancy Krieger; married, wife's name, Susan. *Education:* University of California, Berkeley, B.A.

ADDRESSES: Home—Washington state. *Agent*—Tom Wallace, The Wallace Agency, 177 East 70th St., New York, NY 10021.

CAREER: International Building Products, Inc., San Francisco, CA, owner, 1964-69; Consolidated Foods Corporation, Geneva, Switzerland, European manager, 1969-74. Journalist and travel writer, 1974—.

WRITINGS:

Tramp: Sagas of High Adventure in the Vanishing World of the Old Tramp Freighters, Chronicle Books, 1986.
Conversations with the Cannibals: The End of the Old South Pacific, Ecco Press, 1994.

Contributor of articles to periodicals; author of travel essays syndicated to newspapers by Universal Press Syndicate.

SIDELIGHTS: Michael J. Krieger told *CA:* "From 1964 to 1969, I owned and operated International Building Products, Inc., a shipping and import-export company, with offices in Singapore and San Francisco. I chartered and accompanied freighters carrying cargoes from ·Indonesia and Malaysia to Taiwan, Singapore, and Hong Kong. Then from 1969 to 1974 I was European manager for companies of the Consolidated Foods Corporation—headquartered near Geneva, Switzerland—and was responsible for the movement of all the companies' exports to Europe and Africa.

"I began writing in 1974. My work, which is on a broad range of subjects, appears in both American and European periodicals and has been syndicated in the travel sections of over two hundred newspapers by Universal Press Syndicate. I was the first Western journalist to be allowed by the People's Republic of China to do stories on that country's entire maritime transportation system."

*　　*　　*

KRITZER, Amelia Howe   1947-

PERSONAL: Born January 7, 1947, in Cambridge, MA; daughter of Bennie W. and Iris T. Howe; married Herbert Kritzer; children: three. *Education:* Attended Wittenberg University, 1965-68; Temple University,

B.S., 1969; University of Wisconsin—Madison, Ph.D., 1988.

ADDRESSES: Home—1343 Headlee Ave., No. 13, Morgantown, WV 26505. *Office*—Division of Theater, West Virginia University, P.O. Box 6111, Morgantown, WV 26506-6111.

CAREER: University of Wisconsin—Madison, research and editorial assistant for *Theatre Journal,* 1984-85; University of Wisconsin—Milwaukee, lecturer in theater and dance, 1989; University of Wisconsin—Madison, lecturer in English, 1989-90; Indiana University—Bloomington, visiting assistant professor of theater and drama, 1990-91; West Virginia University, Morgantown, assistant professor of theater, 1991—, and director of plays. University of Wisconsin Center, Rock County, guest director, 1992.

MEMBER: Association for Theatre in Higher Education, American Society for Theatre Research, American Theatre and Drama Society, Women's Theatre Program.

AWARDS, HONORS: Fellow of Radiological Consultants Associates, 1994.

WRITINGS:

The Plays of Caryl Churchill: Theatre of Empowerment, St. Martin's, 1991.
Plays by Early American Women, 1775-1850, University of Michigan Press, 1994.

Work represented in anthologies. Contributor of articles and reviews to academic journals.

WORK IN PROGRESS: Research on theater history and dramatic literature, performance theory and dramatic criticism, and feminist studies.

*　　*　　*

KROEGER, Brooke   1949-

PERSONAL: Born February 18, 1949, in Kansas City, MO; daughter of David (a retailer) and Helen (a real estate agent; maiden name, Bratt) Weinstein; married John C. Kroeger (a sales manager; divorced, 1983); married Alexander M. Goren (an investor), June 24, 1984; children: (first marriage) Brett (daughter); (second marriage) Andrea (stepson), Elisabeth Selina (stepdaughter). *Education:* Boston University, B.S., 1971; Columbia University, M.S., 1972.

ADDRESSES: Home and office—1175 Park Ave., New York, NY 10128. *Agent*—Philippa Brophy, Sterling Lord Literistic, 1 Madison Ave., New York, NY 10010.

CAREER: United Press International, reporter in Chicago, IL, 1973-76, correspondent from Brussels, Belgium, 1977, London, England, 1978-79, and Tel Aviv, Israel, 1979-80, bureau chief in Tel Aviv, 1981-83, and editor for Europe, the Middle East, and Africa, 1983-84; *Newsday-New York Newsday,* New York City, United Nations correspondent and deputy metropolitan editor, 1984-87; writer.

WRITINGS:

Nellie Bly: Daredevil, Reporter, Feminist, Times Books, 1994.

Contributor to magazines and newspapers.

WORK IN PROGRESS: A biography of Fannie Hurst, completion expected in 1997.

*   *   *

KROHN, Claus-Dieter   1941-

PERSONAL: Born July 30, 1941, in Hamburg, Germany; son of Willy (a merchant) and Gudrun (Kunther) Krohn; married Elisabeth Grundmann (a city planner), April 28, 1985. *Education:* Attended Universities of Hamburg and Zurich, 1964-66, and Free University of Berlin, 1966-69; earned D.Phil., 1973, and Habilitation, 1979. *Politics:* Liberal.

ADDRESSES: Home—Mansteinstrasse 41, 20253 Hamburg, Germany. *Office*—University of Luneburg, 21332 Luneberg, Germany.

CAREER: Free University of Berlin, Berlin, Germany, assistant professor, 1973-76; University of Luneburg, Luneburg, Germany, professor of modern history, 1977—.

WRITINGS:

Wissenschaft im Exil, Campus, 1987, translation by Robert and Rita Kimber published as *Intellectuals in Exile: Refugee Scholars and the New School for Social Research,* University of Massachusetts Press, 1993.

IN GERMAN

Stabilisierung und oekonomische Juteressen, Bertelsmann, 1974.

Wirtschaftstheorien als politische Juteressen, Campus, 1981.

WORK IN PROGRESS: Research on German refugee economists after 1933.

*   *   *

KRONENFELD, Jennie J(acobs)   1949-

PERSONAL: Born August 11, 1949, in Hampton, VA; daughter of Harry (a realtor) and Bessie (a teacher; maiden name, Pear) Jacobs; married Michael Reed Kronenfeld (a librarian), September 6, 1970; children: Shaun Jacobs, Jeffrey Brian, Aaron Benjamin. *Education:* University of North Carolina at Chapel Hill, B.A., 1971; Brown University, M.A., 1973, Ph.D., 1976. *Politics:* Democrat. *Religion:* Jewish.

ADDRESSES: Home—8808 North 86th Pl., Scottsdale, AZ 85287. *Office*—School of Health Administration and Policy, Arizona State University, Box 874506, Tempe, AZ 85287-4506.

CAREER: University of Alabama, Birmingham, began as assistant professor, became associate professor, 1975-80; University of South Carolina—Columbia, began as associate professor, became professor of public health, 1980-90; Arizona State University, Tempe, professor of health administration and policy, 1990—.

MEMBER: American Sociological Association (past chairperson of Medical Sociology Section), American Public Health Association, Society for Women in Society (past vice president), Southern Sociological Society (past vice president).

WRITINGS:

(Editor with E. D. Charles, Jr.) *The Social and Economic Impact of Coronary Artery Disease,* Lexington Books, 1980.
(With Marcia Lynn Whicker) *U.S. Health Policy: An Analysis of the Federal Role,* Praeger, 1984.
(With Whicker) *Sex Role Changes: Technology, Politics, and Policy,* Praeger, 1986.
(With Whicker) *Captive Populations: Caring for the Young, the Sick, the Imprisoned, and the Elderly,* Praeger, 1990.
Controversial Issues in Health Care Policy, Sage Publications, 1993.
(With Whicker and R. A. Strickland) *Getting Tenure,* Sage Publications, 1993.
(With Whicker) *Confronting Ethical Dilemmas in Research and Technology,* Sage Publications, 1994.

Work represented in anthologies, including *Monitoring Health Status and Medical Care,* edited by Lois Montero, Ballinger, 1976. Contributor to sociology and health care journals. *Research Annual: Research in the Sociology of Health Care,* JAI Press, coeditor, 1993-94, editor, 1994—.

* * *

KROOTH, Dick
See KROOTH, Richard

* * *

KROOTH, Richard 1935-
(Dick Krooth; Mark Able, a pseudonym)

PERSONAL: Born May 8, 1935, in Chicago, IL; son of Arthur Louis (a merchant) and Helen Dolly (a teacher; maiden name, Feldman) Krooth; married Ann Baxandall (a teacher and writer), August 30, 1963; children: Karl William. *Education:* De Paul University, B.S., 1958; University of Wisconsin—Madison, J.D., 1962; attended Atlanta University, 1963-64; University of California, Santa Barbara, Ph.D., 1980. *Politics:* "Progressive." *Religion:* "Global."

ADDRESSES: Home and office—Berkeley, CA. *Agent*—c/o Harvest Publishers, P.O. Box 9515, Berkeley, CA 94709.

CAREER: Constitutional attorney, 1962-77; Law and Labor Research Group of Santa Barbara, CA, director, 1978-79; Riverside County Criminal Youth Division, Riverside, CA, academic director of Diversion Team, 1980-82; Madison Area Technical College, Madison, visiting professor of American socio-economic institutions, judicial systems, and political science, 1983-84; California Institute, Berkeley, professor of political science and comparative socio-economic development, 1985-89; San Francisco State University, San Francisco, CA, lecturer in interdisciplinary social sciences, 1990; Sonoma State University, Rohnert Park, CA, lecturer in criminal justice, 1991-92; Golden Gate University, San Francisco, adjunct professor of international studies, 1993—. Americas Research Group, director, 1983-84; American Arbitration Association, arbitrator, 1983—; Scientific Legal Services, Inc., jury consultant, 1987—. Anti-Defamation League of B'nai B'rith, member of civil liberties staff in New York City and Atlanta, GA, 1962-64; Wisconsin Alliance Research Center, research director, 1968-72; Isla Vista Community Research Group, coordinator, 1980-81; American/Russian Friendship Association, economic analyst. University of Wisconsin—Madison, special research as-

sistant in economics and sociology, 1966-72; Omega School, associate in political science and legal institutions, 1969-72; University of California, Berkeley, visiting scholar, 1985-86, research associate, 1989, 1993—; California Institute of Management, research associate, 1987-89; speaker at colleges and universities, including University of Colorado, Universities of California in Davis and Riverside, and University of Winnipeg.

MEMBER: American Sociological Association, American Economic Association, Association of Borderlands Scholars, Pacific Sociological Association, Western Social Science Association, Georgia Bar Association, Phi Gamma Mu, De Paul Alumni Association, University of California Alumni Association, Smithsonian Institution (associate).

AWARDS, HONORS: Grants from University of California, Riverside, 1979-93, Texas A & M University, 1989-91, and Louis M. Rabinowitz Foundation.

WRITINGS:

Empire: A Bicentennial Appraisal, Harvest Publishers, 1975.

Japan: Five Stages of Development and the Nation's Future, Harvest Publishers, 1976.

The Great Social Struggle and the Foundations of Social Theory, Harvest Publishers, Volume I, 1978, Volume II, 1979, Volume III, 1980.

Arms and Empire: Imperial Patterns before World War II, Harvest Publishers, 1981.

The Struggle for Grenada: A Question of Authority, the Executive, the Congress, and the Invasion, Wisconsin Peace Press, 1984.

The Dynamics of Enterprise in the American Milieu, CIM Press, Volume I: *Socio-Economic Contours,* 1985, Volume II: *Legal Dimensions,* 1988.

Common Destiny: Japan and America in the Global Age, McFarland, 1990.

(With Hiroshi Fukurai and Edgar W. Butler) *Race and the Jury: Racial Inequality and the Search for Justice,* Plenum, 1993.

(With Boris Vladimirovitz) *The Quest for Freedom: The Transformation of Europe in the 1990s,* McFarland, 1993.

(With Minoo Moallem) *The Middle East: A Geopolitical Study of the Region in the New Global Era,* McFarland, 1994.

(With Fukurai and Butler) *Anatomy of a Jury: The McMartin Trial,* Rutgers University Press, 1994.

Mexico in the Twenty-First Century: Free Trade, Dollar Diplomacy, and Social Justice, McFarland, in press.

The Great Homestead Struggle, Ramparts/Harvest Publishers, in press.

Contributor to books, including *The 1992 Los Angeles Riots and the Rebellion,* edited by Mark Baldassare, Westview, 1994. United States sociology correspondent, *Economic and Political Weekly* (Bombay), 1979-84. Member of research and editorial staff, *Harvest Quarterly,* 1975-78. Contributor to academic journals. Some writings appear under the name Dick Krooth and under the pseudonym Mark Able.

WORK IN PROGRESS: The Center of the World: China in the Throes of a New World Order, with Chen Tong-Chou, for the United Nations, publication expected in 1996; *Voices from the Heartland: Protest and Social Disorder,* with wife Ann Baxandall; *Japan on the Global Assembly Line,* with Fukurai; *Global Ecology: Crisis and the "New World Order."*

SIDELIGHTS: Richard Krooth told *CA:* "For clarity of thought, writing is a necessity that helps me focus on the logic of expression. Almost all my 'knowledge' comes from sight and the printed word. The inflows from sound, touch, smell, taste, as well as the inexplicable intuitive rush, I reproduce with words on paper, or mediate by type, again on paper. I practice writing, too, building up secret files, stowing away the wordsmith's failures and successes. The writing craft appears in innumerable drafts, helping to guide and direct my future script."

*   *   *

KUEHL, Stefan   1966-

PERSONAL: Born August 26, 1966, in Hamburg, Germany; son of Otto (a manager) and Eva (a teacher; maiden name, Pabel) Kuehl. *Education:* Johns Hopkins University, M.A., 1992; University of Bielefeld, Germany, M.A., 1993; attended Oxford University, 1994. *Politics:* Social Democrats. *Religion:* Atheist.

ADDRESSES: Home—Amselweg 24, 25451 Quickborn, Germany.

CAREER: Civil service, 1986-88; independent consultant, 1990-94.

AWARDS, HONORS: Ernst Fraenkel Prize for Contemporary History, 1993; Capital Prize, 1993.

WRITINGS:

The Nazi Connection: Eugenics, American Racism, and German National Socialism, Oxford University Press (New York, NY), 1994.

WORK IN PROGRESS: A work on international racism and research into complexity in organizations.

*   *   *

KUHL, Stefan
See KUEHL, Stefan

*   *   *

KUVSHINOFF, Boris W.   1922-

PERSONAL: Born June 26, 1922, in Monticello, MN; son of Vasiliy Semyonovich (an Eastern Orthodox priest) and Anastacia Ioanovna (Kapanyova) Kuvshinoff; married Hrisa Kazara (a counseling psychologist), September, 1958; children: Boris W. II, Nicolai B., Anastacia Maria. *Education:* University of Kentucky, Civil Engineering Certificate, 1944; University of Washington, B.A., 1952, graduate study, 1953-54; further graduate study at American University, 1965-69; attended Antioch College. *Religion:* Eastern Orthodox.

ADDRESSES: Home—1103 Starway Ct., Baltimore, MD 21228.

CAREER: Johns Hopkins University, Applied Physics Laboratory, Laurel, MD, translator of foreign scientific and technical literature, 1958-60, supervisor of document library, 1960-70, information section supervisor of Fire Problems Program, 1971-79, technical documentation analyst, 1980-85, program manager for U.S. Air Force Logistics Command Automated Warehouse Acquisition, 1986-87, manager of APL Business Systems Documentation, 1988-93, Stewart Janney fellow, 1990; writer, 1993—. National Bureau of Standards, member of U.S. team for U.S./U.S.S.R. Cooperative Agreement on Housing and Other Construction, 1977-82; co-developer of an indexing system for the U.S. budget. *Military service:* U.S. Army, member of U.S. delegation to Allied Control Commission for Bulgaria, 1944-46.

WRITINGS:

(Translator) K. I. Shchelkin and Y. K. Troshin, *Gas Dynamics of Combustion,* Mono Book Corp., 1965.
(Editor and translator) R. I. Soloukhin, *Shock Waves and Detonations in Gases,* Mono Book Corp., 1965.
(Compiler and editor) *Fire Sciences Dictionary,* Wiley, 1977.
(With R. A. Henle) *Desktop Computers: In Perspective,* Oxford University Press (New York), 1992.

Work represented in anthologies, including *Fire Technology,* National Fire Protection Association, 1983; and *The Book of Days: 1987,* Pieran Press, 1986. Managing editor, *Fire Technology Abstracts,* U.S. Government Printing Office, 1977-79; managing editor, *McClure Center,* 1989-91. Contributor to professional journals.

WORK IN PROGRESS: Revising *Fire Sciences Dictionary; Tales of the Firebird's Feather,* an adventure story in rhyme, based on the 1861 Russian fantasy "The Humpbacked Pony," by P. Yershov.

*   *   *

KYLE, Molly M.   1959-

PERSONAL: Born June 4, 1959, in Pontiac, MI; children: Hannah, Jay. *Education:* Swarthmore College, B.A. (with distinction), 1980; Massachusetts Institute of Technology, M.S., 1983; Cornell University, Ph.D., 1988.

ADDRESSES: Office—Department of Plant Breeding and Biometry, 312 Bradfield Hall, Cornell University, Ithaca, NY 14853.

CAREER: University of California, Berkeley, postdoctoral fellow in plant pathology, 1988-89; Boyce Thompson Institute, Ithaca, NY, visiting scientist and research associate in Plant Molecular Biology Program, 1989-90; Cornell University, Ithaca, assistant professor of plant genetics, 1991—. Woods Hole Children's School of Science, teacher, 1980; consultant to Winrock International Institute for Agricultural Development.

AWARDS, HONORS: Award from American Women in Science Foundation, 1986; postgraduate fellowships from National Science Foundation, 1988, and Life Sciences Research Foundation, 1988-91.

WRITINGS:

(Editor and contributor) *Resistance to Viral Diseases of Vegetables: Genetics and Breeding,* Timber Press (Beaverton, OR), 1993.

Work represented in anthologies. Contributor to scientific journals.

L

LAMM, Leonard Jonathan 1945-

PERSONAL: Born September 8, 1945, in New York, NY. *Education:* Amherst College, A.B., 1966; London School of Economics and Political Science, London, M.Sc., 1967; Princeton University, M.A., 1971; New School for Social Research, Ph.D., 1990.

ADDRESSES: Office—Spunk Fund, Inc., 780 Third Ave., 24th Floor, New York, NY 10017.

CAREER: Clinical psychologist and psychotherapist in private practice, New York City. Associated with Spunk Fund, Inc.

WRITINGS:

The Idea of the Past, New York University Press, 1993.

WORK IN PROGRESS: I Saw Five Lies: Narratives of Psychotherapy; and *End of Story: Life and Death of a Community Mental Health Clinic.*

* * *

LANGDON, E(sther) Jean Matteson 1944-

PERSONAL: Born September 1, 1944; daughter of Erdley Stone and Esther Kate (Charles) Matteson; married Thomas A. Langdon, 1966 (divorced, 1982); children: Elena May, Alan Stone. *Education:* Carleton College, Northfield, MN, B.A. (cum laude), 1966; University of Washington, Seattle, M.A., 1968; Tulane University, Ph.D., 1974. *Politics:* "Yes." *Religion:* "Yes."

ADDRESSES: Home—C.P. 5114, Florianopolis, Santa Catarina, Brazil. *Office*—Pos-Graduacao em Antropologia, Universidade Federal de Santa Catarina, Florianopolis, Santa Catarina, Brazil.

CAREER: Universidad del Cauca, Popayan, Colombia, part-time professor, 1973; John Jay College of Criminal Justice of the City University of New York, New York City, adjunct professor of anthropology, 1974-76; Cedar Crest College, Allentown, PA, associate professor, 1976-84; Universidade Federal de Santa Catarina, Santa Catarina, Brazil, professor of social anthropology, 1983—, vice coordinator of Pos-Graduacao de Ciencias Sociais, 1986-88. Indiana University—Bloomington, research associate; field research includes a study of land reform in Costa Rica, 1964-65, research among migrant workers in the Yakima Valley, WA, 1967, work among urban workers in the village of Citlaltepec, Mexico, under the auspices of the University of Pittsburgh, 1968, and interdisciplinary research in ethnomedicine of the Sibundoy Indians of Colombia, 1970-74; consultant to Brazil's National Foundation of Health.

MEMBER: American Anthropological Association, Associacao Brasileira de Antropologia, Mortar Board.

AWARDS, HONORS: Grant for Costa Rica, National Science Foundation, 1964-65; grant for Colombia, U.S. Public Health Service, 1970; travel grant for England, American Council of Learned Societies, 1982; travel grants for Brazil, Conselho Nacional de Pesquises, 1988, 1991, research grant, 1988—; fellow of CAPES, 1993-94.

WRITINGS:

(Editor with Gerhard Baer, and contributor) *Portals of Power: South American Shamanism,* University of New Mexico Press, 1992.

(Editor with Maria Cipoletti, and contributor) *Concepciones de la Muerte y el mas alla,* Abya-Yaloa, 1992.

Author of the book *Novas perspectivas de xamanismo no Brasil,* 1994. Work represented in anthologies, including *Understanding Religion and Culture: Anthropological and Theological Perspectives,* edited by John Morgan, University Press of America, 1979; *Political Anthropology: Perspectives from Indigenous Cultures of Ecuador,* edited by Jeffrey Ehrenreich, Society for Latin American Anthropology, 1985; and *Shamanism: Past and Present,* edited by Mihaly Hoppal and Otto von Sadovszky, International Society for Trans-Oceanic Research, 1989. Contributor of more than thirty articles to sociology and anthropology journals.

WORK IN PROGRESS: Research on oral literature and shamanic narratives.

*   *   *

LASKIN, David   1953-

PERSONAL: Born October 25, 1953, in New York, NY; son of Meyer (in business) and Leona (a physician; maiden name, Cohen) Laskin; married Kathleen O'Neill (a law professor), April 17, 1982; children: Sarah and Alice (twins), Emily. *Education:* Harvard College, B.A., 1975; New College, Oxford University, M.A., 1977. *Politics:* "Dubious Democrat."

ADDRESSES: Home—18757 Ridgefield Rd. Northwest, Seattle, WA 98177. *Agent*—Diane Cleaver, Diane Cleaver Inc., 55 Fifth Ave., New York, NY 10003.

CAREER: Freelance writer, 1979—.

WRITINGS:

Getting into Advertising, Ballantine, 1986.
The Parents Book for New Fathers, Ballantine, 1988.
Eastern Islands, Facts on File, 1990.
(With wife, Kathleen O'Neill) *The Little Girl Book,* Ballantine, 1992.
A Common Life: Four Generations of American Literary Friendship and Influence, Simon & Schuster, 1994.
A History of Weather, Doubleday (New York), 1995.

WORK IN PROGRESS: Research on American literary marriages.

SIDELIGHTS: David Laskin told *CA:* "*A Common Life: Four Generations of American Literary Friendship and Influence* is the book I was born to write. It is a group portrait of the friendships between some of the writers I have loved best for as long as I can remember—Herman Melville and Nathaniel Hawthorne, Henry James and Edith Wharton, Robert Lowell and Elizabeth Bishop. Katherine Anne Porter and Eudora Welty, 'my' fourth pair of friends, were wonderful new discoveries for me, especially Porter's *Noon Wine* and Welty's *One Writer's Beginnings.*

"Literary biography has come under considerable attack recently, some of it fashionable twaddle, some of it richly deserved. The massive, formless, crushingly detailed authors' lives that burden bookshop shelves these days are the 'loose baggy monsters' of contemporary letters. But the worst flaw of many of these thousand-pagers is, I believe, not their volume but their tone: revulsion masquerading as critical analysis.

"And yet the form itself is by no means doomed to failure or pettiness. The better biographies and memoirs are among the best books being written today. These books begin and end with respect, even reverence, for their subjects. Reverence tempered by deep knowledge and even deeper humility. The four friendships that I was lucky enough to write about were also grounded in reverence: in each case, literary admiration was the source of the personal relationship, and this shared love of the work endured the turmoil and combat of ordinary life. I have tried to keep this love of the work to the fore in *A Common Life.*"

BIOGRAPHICAL/CRITICAL SOURCES:

PERIODICALS

Globe & Mail, June 15, 1991, p. C8.

*   *   *

LAUTERBORN, Robert F.   1936-

PERSONAL: Born April 3, 1936, in Albany, NY; son of Ferdinand R. and Julia M. (O'Brien) Lauterborn; married Sylvia A. Stebbings, September 28, 1963; children: Michael Alan, David Ian. *Education:* Columbia University, A.B., 1956. *Politics:* Conservative Republican. *Religion:* Roman Catholic. *Avocational interests:* Competitive running, bridge.

ADDRESSES: Home—1403 Gray Bluff Trail, Chapel

Hill, NC 27514. *Office*—CB 3365, University of North Carolina at Chapel Hill, Chapel Hill, NC 27599.

CAREER: Syracuse Herald Journal, Syracuse, NY, advertising sales representative, 1957-60; General Electric Co., worked in marketing and corporate communications, 1960-76; International Paper, New York City, director of marketing communications and corporate advertising, 1976-86; University of North Carolina at Chapel Hill, J. L. Knight Professor of Advertising, 1986—. Morgan, Anderson and Co., principal; Sawyer, Riley, Compton, member of board of directors.

MEMBER: Business Marketing Association International (chairperson), American Academy of Finance, Advertising Research Foundation, Association for Education in Journalism and Mass Communication, American Academy of Advertising, National Advertising Review Board.

WRITINGS:

(Coauthor) *Integrated Marketing Communications,* NTC Business Books, 1992.

SIDELIGHTS: Robert F. Lauterborn told *CA:* "I've always been fascinated by process—how things work. I always looked for better ways to do things, for the *real* objectives, for what truly matters. I have been turned on by start-ups; I'm not much interested in maintenance. I have also always been a writer.

"I love teaching, partly because it drives my own learning curve, and partly because I love to see the lights go on when somebody 'gets it.' Somebody once called me a 'compulsive sharer,' which is probably why I also love to make presentations."

* * *

LAWSON, Philip 1949-

PERSONAL: Born July 9, 1949, in Morecambe, England; son of Wilfred (a librarian) and Maureen (a homemaker) Lawson; married Eileen Hunter (a librarian), March 8, 1969; children: Elizabeth, Caroline. *Education:* Victoria University of Manchester, B.A. (with honors), 1971, M.A., 1975; University of Wales, University College of Wales, Aberystwyth, Ph.D., 1980. *Politics:* None. *Religion:* Anglican.

ADDRESSES: Home—Edmonton, Alberta, Canada. *Office*—Department of History, University of Alberta, Edmonton, Alberta, Canada T6G 2H4.

CAREER: University of St. Andrews, St. Andrews, Scotland, lecturer, 1980-81; Dalhousie University, Halifax, Nova Scotia, postdoctoral fellow, 1981-83; University of Alberta, Edmonton, McTaggart fellow, 1983-86, professor of history, 1986—.

MEMBER: North American Conference of British Studies.

AWARDS, HONORS: Killam fellow, 1981-83.

WRITINGS:

George Grenville: A Political Life, Clarendon Press, 1984.
Imperial Challenge: Quebec and Britain in the Age of the American Revolution, McGill-Queen's University Press, 1989.
The East India Company: A History, Longman, 1993.

Member of editorial board, *Parliamentary History.*

WORK IN PROGRESS: A study of the impact of British imperial expansion (c. 1688-1833) on British society, politics, and culture; editing a special issue of *Parliamentary History* dedicated to Atlantic legislatures in the colonial period.

SIDELIGHTS: Philip Lawson told *CA:* "In the normal scholarly way, I began writing books and doing research to further my academic career. This career was supposed to take place in Britain, but thanks to the savaging of the universities by the Thatcher government in the early 1980s, I was obliged to look elsewhere for employment. It was with great good fortune that I found work in Canada. It is a wonderful place to do British history, and the successes I've had in the publishing world are due, almost entirely, to the excellent environment and working conditions offered by the universities here. Working here has also allowed me to stand back and see British history in a new light, and to write about imperial expansion with a fresh perspective.

"I still recommend to all my students that reading the greats is essential, T. B. Macaulay and G. M. Trevelyan in particular. Also, I cannot go long without dipping into Jane Austen and E. M. Forster. The best history writing is still literary and imaginative, and it is imperative to keep it that way. In my own work, I hope to achieve some steps toward this goal and illustrate how empire affected Britain in the pre-Victorian period."

LEACH, William   1944-

PERSONAL: Born February 12, 1944, in New Brunswick, NJ; son of Thomas and Esther Matilda (Lee) Leach. *Education:* Rutgers University, B.A., 1965; Cornell University, M.A., 1968; University of Rochester, Ph.D., 1976. *Politics:* Independent. *Religion:* None. *Avocational interests:* Piano, horticulture, and lepidopterology.

ADDRESSES: Home—225 West Shore Dr., Carmel, NY 10512.

CAREER: Teacher at New York University, Columbia University, and the University of the South; freelance writer.

AWARDS, HONORS: Herbert Hoover Book Prize, Hoover Presidential Library, and National Book Awards finalist for best nonfiction book, both 1993, both for *Land of Desire: Merchants, Power, and the Rise of a New American Culture.*

WRITINGS:

True Love and Perfect Union: The Feminist Reform of Sex and Society, Basic Books (New York), 1981, second edition with new introduction, Wesleyan University Press (Middletown, CT), 1989.
Edith Wharton (biography), introduction by Martina S. Horner, Chelsea House (New York), 1987.
(Author of commentary) L. Frank Baum, *The Wonderful Wizard of Oz,* Wadsworth Publishing (Belmont, CA), 1991.
Land of Desire: Merchants, Power, and the Rise of a New American Culture, Pantheon (New York), 1993.

WORK IN PROGRESS: A book on citizenship and place in modern America.

SIDELIGHTS: William Leach has written in various genres, including commentary, biography, and two works concerning American culture, *True Love and Perfect Union: The Feminist Reform of Sex and Society* and *Land of Desire: Merchants, Power, and the Rise of a New American Culture.* The latter book garnered significant attention, earned a nomination for the National Book Award for nonfiction in 1993, and won the 1993 Herbert Hoover Book Prize.

A study of the feminist movement in the nineteenth century, *True Love and Perfect Union* examines, in particular, the relationship of feminism to other reform movements of the period. Including in his book excerpts from letters and diary entries of nineteenth-century feminists, Leach documents the efforts of feminists to create an ideology of equality between the sexes based on a growing body of sociological evidence as well as democratic political ideals. Critic Nancy F. Cott, writing in *New York Review of Books,* found Leach's volume "especially valuable in its exploration of the links between feminist beliefs and the rational, positivist ideology of nineteenth-century science. . . . His attempt to integrate feminist thought with that of other reform movements, and his identification of little-known male and female feminists, will help other scholars to explore the reform networks of the post-bellum period. Indeed, Leach adds more substance to an era in which feminism is little known." Thomas DePietro told *Nation* readers: "Perhaps some feminists will be offended by Leach's questioning of past reformers' motives and his implicit directives for future radical behavior. This would be unfortunate, since William Leach . . . writes from a deep concern for the success of future radical movements."

In Leach's 1993 book, *Land of Desire,* readers learn how and why America became the first nation to develop a mass consumer culture and the mass consumption economy that went along with it. The book focuses on the growth of the big department stores and advertising agencies usually associated with the rise of consumerism. But it also deals with the roles of other agencies that have been largely neglected in studies of this kind, especially museums, banks, hotels, universities, business schools, government promoters, writers, and even clerics. Overall, *Land of Desire* shows how diverse power structures interacted to give birth to modern American consumer society. Reviewing the book in the *Nation,* Paul Levine commented that "Leach brings to the job talents that make his work indispensable, including a prose style uncluttered by academic jargon and a narrative talent augmented by a sharp eye for crucial detail." Similarly, Margo Jefferson in the *New York Times* praised the book's "scholarly exactness and writerly elegance." "Before wistfully recalling a simpler, austere America," declared Joel Drucker in the *Los Angeles Times Book Review,* "read *Land of Desire.*"

BIOGRAPHICAL/CRITICAL SOURCES:

PERIODICALS

Harper's, November, 1993, p. 10.
Los Angeles Times Book Review, December 26, 1993, p. 2.
Nation, April 4, 1981, pp. 409, 411; January 3-10, 1994, pp. 26-27.

New Yorker, September 6, 1993, p. 117.
New York Review of Books, March 17, 1983, pp. 36-40.
New York Times, December 1, 1993, p. C24.
New York Times Book Review, November 7, 1993, p. 20.
Washington Post Book World, August 1, 1993, p. 3.

*   *   *

LEATHERWOOD, (James) Stephen   1943-

PERSONAL: Born October 12, 1943, in Ozark, AL; son of Aubrey Leon (an insurance executive) and Lillian Kathleen (a real estate broker; maiden name, Judah) Leatherwood; married Melinda Weishaar, March 20, 1965 (divorced, 1974); children: Stephen Keith, Shannon Kathleen. *Education:* California State University, Northridge, B.S., 1966; graduate study at San Diego State University, 1969-76; Texas A&M University, Ph.D., 1994. *Politics:* Democrat. *Religion:* Protestant.

ADDRESSES: Home—San Diego, CA. *Office*—Ocean Park Conservation Foundation, Staff Quarters, Flat C, Ocean Park, Aberdeen, Hong Kong.

CAREER: Teacher of mathematics and English and coach of football, soccer, and track at a military academy in Miami, FL, 1967; U.S. Navy marine mammal research unit, San Diego, CA, began as administrative assistant, became administrative officer in San Diego and at Point Mugu, 1968-70; Naval Oceans Systems Center, San Diego, research biologist in biomedical division, 1970-78; National Marine Fisheries Service, National Marine Mammal Laboratory, Seattle, WA, coordinator of Arctic Whale Research Task, 1978; Hubbs Sea World Research Institute, San Diego, research scientist in San Diego and institute manager in Orlando, FL, 1979-81; Hubbs Marine Research Center, San Diego, senior staff scientist at Sea World Research Institute, 1982-88; United Nations Environment Program, Nairobi, Kenya, acting secretary of Marine Mammal Action Plan, 1989; International Union for the Conservation of Nature, cetacean specialist group, La Jolla, CA, deputy chairperson, 1990, chairperson in Hong Kong, 1991—. Oceans Unlimited, director, 1989; Ocean Park Conservation Foundation, director, 1993—; Ocean Park Corp., director of veterinary and education department, 1994—; Center for Research on Indian Ocean Marine Mammals (Colombo, Sri Lanka), director of cetacean research group; Whale Center (Oakland, CA), member of board of advisers; Terra Marine Research and Education, Inc., member of scientific advisory council;

Marine Mammal Center (Sausalito, CA), member of scientific advisory board; Kid Lab, honorary member of board of directors; Mirage Dolphin Program, member of scientific advisory board for marine operations. Lecturer in oceanography and marine biology for expeditions aboard the ships *World Discoverer* and *Society Explorer,* in South America, the South Pacific, the Indian Ocean, IndoAustralia, and Antarctica; Oceanic Society, field instructor in the Bahamas, Baja California, Sri Lanka, Argentina, Brazil, Peru, the Seychelles, and East Africa; instructor at Laverne College and University of California extension. Consultant for the production of films and television documentaries, including *A Whale Called Sunshine,* Disney, 1972; *The Great Whales,* National Geographic Society, 1978; *A Whale for the Killing,* American Broadcasting Company, 1982; *Where Have All the Dolphins Gone?,* Public Broadcasting Service, 1989; and *Dolphins, Whales, and Us,* Columbia Broadcasting System, 1990; consultant to U.S. Marine Mammal Commission, National Fish and Wildlife Service, and International Whaling Commission. San Diego Natural History Museum, research associate.

MEMBER: Cetacean Society International (member of scientific advisory board), Society for Marine Mammalogy (charter member), American Society of Mammalogists, Alliance of Marine Mammal Parks and Aquariums (institutional member), American Association of Zoological Parks and Aquariums, American Cetacean Society, San Diego Society of Natural History (fellow), Southeast Association of Zoos and Aquariums (chair, membership and standards committee).

WRITINGS:

(With R. R. Reeves) *The Sierra Club Handbook of Whales and Dolphins,* Sierra Books (San Francisco), 1983.
(Editor with M. L. Jones and S. L. Swartz) *The Gray Whale, Eschrichtius robustus,* Academic Press (Orlando), 1983.
(With Reeves) *The Sea World Book of Dolphins,* Harcourt (San Diego), 1987.
(Editor with Reeves) *The Bottlenose Dolphin: Recent Progress in Research,* Academic Press (San Diego), 1990.
(With Reeves and B. S. Stewart) *The Sierra Club Handbook of Seals and Sirenians,* Sierra Books, 1992.
(With T. A. Jefferson and M. Webber) *Marine Mammals of the World,* United Nations Food and Agriculture Organization, 1994.

Work represented in anthologies, including *Marine Mammals of Eastern North Pacific and Arctic Waters,* edited by D. Haley, Pacific Search Press, 1986; *Research on Dolphins,* edited by M. M. Bryden and R. Harrison, Oxford University Press, 1986; and *Handbook of Marine Mammals,* Volume V: *The First Book of Dolphins,* edited by S. H. Ridgway and R. J. Harrison, Academic Press (London), 1994. Contributor of more than a hundred articles to scientific journals and popular magazines.

* * *

LEBRETON, J(ean) D(ominique) 1950-

PERSONAL: Born February 19, 1950, in Saint-Etienne, Loire, France; son of Philippe P. and Suzanne (Prevot) Lebreton; married Claire Berton (divorced, 1993); children: Marien, Julie, Florent. *Education:* Diplome Universitaire d'Etudes Scientifiques, 1969; University of Grenoble, Maitrise d'informatique, 1971, Certificat de la Maitrise de Mathematiques et Applications Fondamentales, 1971; University of Lyon, Diplome d'Etudes Approfondies, 1972; Doctorat de specialite, 1974, Doctorat es-sciences, 1981.

ADDRESSES: Office—CEFE/CNRS, BP 5051, Montpellier Cedex II 34033, France.

CAREER: Centre d'Ecologie Fonctionnelle et Evolutive, Montpellier, France, director of research, 1985—. *Military service:* 1974-75.

MEMBER: Biometric Society (president, 1990-92).

AWARDS, HONORS: Silver medal, CNRS, 1990.

WRITINGS:

(With others) *Mathematiques pour biologistes: Exercices et problemes commentes* (title means "Mathematics for Biologists: Exercises and Commentary on Problems"), Masson (Paris), 1981.
(Editor, with C. Millier) *Modeles dynamiques deterministes en biologie* (title means "Dynamic Determinist Models in Biology"), Masson, 1982.
(Editor, with others) *Population Biology of Passerine Birds: An Integrated Approach,* Springer (Berlin), 1990.
(Editor, with P. M. North) *Marked Individuals in the Study of Bird Population,* Birkhauser (Basel), 1992.
(Editor, with B. Asselain) *Biometrie et Envi-*

ronnement (title means "Biometrics and Environment"), Masson, 1993.
(Editor, with C. M. Perrins and G. J. M. Hirons) *Bird Population Studies: Their Relevance to Conservation and Management,* Oxford University Press, 1993.

SIDELIGHTS: J. D. Lebreton describes his career as a "hybrid between population biology (birds mostly) and applied mathematics (statistics and modelling)." The author told *CA* that he "often thinks of the saying by Michel Serres: 'The Earth, formerly our mother, has become our daughter.'" Lebreton is also concerned with "the responsibility of scientists."

* * *

LECKIE, Shirley A(nne) 1937-

PERSONAL: Born June 15, 1937, in Claremont, NH; daughter of Edward (a farmer) and Hazel (maiden name, Rahlston; present surname, Casillo) Howard; married Matthew J. Swora, 1956 (marriage ended, 1972); married William H. Leckie (a university administrator), December 26, 1975; children: (first marriage) Matthew, Kimberly Swora Beck, Maria Gabrielle. *Education:* University of Missouri—Kansas City, B.A., 1967, M.A., 1969; University of Toledo, Ph.D., 1981. *Politics:* Democrat. *Avocational interests:* Swimming, movies, concerts.

ADDRESSES: Home—1137 Dappled Elm Ln., Winter Springs, FL 32708. *Office*—Department of History, University of Central Florida, Orlando, FL 32816.

CAREER: University of Toledo, Toledo, OH, academic adviser, 1972-77, coordinator of adult liberal studies, 1974-77, director of external affairs and adult liberal studies, 1977-80, assistant dean of continuing education for business and professional seminars, 1980-81; Millsaps College, Jackson, MS, assistant professor of history and associate dean of continuing education, 1981-82; University of North Carolina at Asheville, director of continuing education and special programs, 1983-85; University of Central Florida, Orlando, assistant professor, 1985-88, associate professor of history, 1988—. Orlando Metropolitan Women's Political Caucus, member, 1987—.

MEMBER: Organization of American Historians, Western History Association, Southern Historical Association, Coalition for Western Women's History, Phi Alpha Theta.

AWARDS, HONORS: David Woolley and Beatrice

Cannon Evans Biography Award, 1993, for *Elizabeth Bacon Custer and the Making of a Myth.*

WRITINGS:

(With husband, William H. Leckie) *Unlikely Warriors: General Benjamin H. Grierson and His Family,* University of Oklahoma Press, 1984.

(Editor) *The Colonel's Lady on the Western Frontier: The Correspondence of Alice Kirk Grierson,* University of Nebraska Press, 1989.

Elizabeth Bacon Custer and the Making of a Myth, University of Oklahoma Press, 1993.

Work represented in anthologies. Contributor of articles and reviews to history and education journals. Member of editorial board, *Northwest Ohio Quarterly.*

WORK IN PROGRESS: A biography of Angie Debo, completion expected in 1997.

SIDELIGHTS: Shirley A. Leckie told *CA:* "Writing is the most difficult task I undertake. While I pick a topic because it interests me initially, I do not love it until I have spent long hours of drudgery, forcing myself to write and rewrite. The research, by contrast, is much easier. If I am not careful, I will do too much, as a way of postponing the hard work of actually sitting down and trying to decide what it is I really think and want to say. I never know, myself, until I have rewritten my work many times.

"One day, after many tedious hours, the work takes on a life of its own. From then on, although it is still hard, writing is no longer drudgery. It becomes what I love to do as I discover more about who my subjects are and what their world was like. When I am finished, I have said goodbye to a beloved friend, and I feel a sense of bereavement.

"Eventually I undertake another biography. Living with a person from the past is essential to me, for it helps me overcome my neurosis. It enables me to put my present world into perspective as I live from day to day, wondering what mysteries will be solved at the computer, what new discoveries will be made, and what new understandings will be achieved. I am grateful to my subjects for leaving enough of themselves behind so that I have been able to enter into their lost worlds and gain, however briefly and imperfectly, some sense of who they were. Whatever the sales or reviews of my work, the process of writing—the work itself—is my best reward."

LeCOMPTE, Mary Lou   1935-

PERSONAL: Born September 28, 1935, in Houston, TX; daughter of Ruben Thomas (a farmer) and Frances (a teacher; maiden name, Hanly) Anselin; married Melville L. LeCompte, August 2, 1976. *Education:* Texas Woman's University, B.S., 1957, M.A., 1958; University of Southern California, Ph.D., 1966.

ADDRESSES: Home—12609 Dessau, No. A-143, Austin, TX 78754.

CAREER: St. Mary's College of Maryland, St. Mary's City, head of health, physical education, and recreation department, 1958-60; University of Texas at Austin, began as instructor, became assistant professor, 1960-93, associate professor of physical education, 1993—.

MEMBER: North American Society for Sport History, National Association for Sport and Physical Education (president of History Academy, 1992-93), American Alliance for Health, Physical Education, Recreation, and Dance, Organization of American Historians, American Historical Association, Western History Association, Rodeo Historical Society, Texas State Historical Association, Texas Oral History Association, Texas American Studies Association, Southwest/Texas Popular Culture Association, West Texas Historical Association.

AWARDS, HONORS: National Association for Sport and Physical Education, Distinguished Service Award, 1993; Presidential Certificate of Appreciation, 1994.

WRITINGS:

(With Mary Buice Alderson) *Step Right In: Making Dance Fun for Boys and Girls,* Kendall/Hunt, 1973.

Cowgirls of the Rodeo: Pioneer Professional Athletes, University of Illinois Press, 1993.

Work represented in anthologies. Contributor of about ninety articles and reviews to physical education and history journals. Reviewing editor, *Physical Educator,* 1982-87; newsletter editor, American Alliance for Health, Physical Education, Recreation, and Dance, 1992.

*   *   *

LEE, Robert E(dwin)   1918-1994

OBITUARY NOTICE—See index for *CA* sketch: Born October 15, 1918, in Elyria, OH; died of cancer,

July 8, 1994, in Los Angeles, CA. Playwright and educator. With longtime collaborator Jerome Lawrence, Lee wrote many successful plays, including the Broadway hit *Auntie Mame* and its musical adaptation, *Mame,* both of which were later adapted as popular feature films. The partnership began in 1942 when Lee, who was overseeing radio ads for a New York City advertising agency, met Lawrence, a writer for CBS radio. During the next five decades the duo wrote thirty-nine plays, including fourteen Broadway productions. Two of their most enduring plays are *Inherit the Wind,* based on the Scopes "Monkey" trial of 1929, and *The Night Thoreau Spent in Jail,* which focuses on civil disobedience; these works, as well as their 1978 play *First Monday in October*—about the first woman member of the United States Supreme Court—were also adapted for film. Becoming an adjunct professor at the University of California, Los Angeles, in 1967, Lee taught aspiring actors, playwrights, and screenwriters. It was his conviction that the role of a theater artist is to explore political, psychological, and philosophical issues through drama; the ensuing product should then enlighten audiences while also entertaining them. The honors Lee received during his career include a 1948 Peabody award for radio programming, the *Variety* New York Drama Critics Poll in 1955 and the British Drama Critics award for best foreign play in 1960, both for *Inherit the Wind,* and Tony awards in 1955 and 1966. In 1988 Lee received the Best Comedy/Drama Special award by the National Television Academy for the television adaptation of *Inherit the Wind,* and was recognized with a Lifetime Achievement Award at the William Inge Festival. Lee was named to the American Theatre Hall of Fame in 1990. Among his later works is the 1990 play *Whisper in the Mind,* written with Lawrence and Norman Cousins.

OBITUARIES AND OTHER SOURCES:

BOOKS

Who's Who in America, 47th edition, Marquis, 1992.

PERIODICALS

Los Angeles Times, July 10, 1994, p. A24.
Times (London), July 20, 1994, p. 19.

*   *   *

LENTZ, John C(layton) Jr.   1957-

PERSONAL: Born August 1, 1957, in Alexandria, VA; son of John Clayton Sr. (an agent of the Central Intelligence Agency) and Roberta E. (a homemaker) Lentz; married Deanne M. (a hospice worker), September 27, 1986; children: John Clayton III, Margaret M. *Education:* Kenyon College, B.A. (with honors), 1979; Yale University, M.Div., 1983; University of Edinburgh, M.Th., 1984, Ph.D., 1989. *Avocational interests:* Sports.

ADDRESSES: Home—1619 Compton Rd., Cleveland Heights, OH 44118. *Office*—3031 Monticello Blvd., Cleveland Heights, OH 44118.

CAREER: Associate pastor of a Presbyterian church in Winchester, VA, 1989-94; pastor and head of staff at a Presbyterian church in Cleveland Heights, OH, 1994—. Free Medical Clinic of Winchester, member of board of directors.

AWARDS, HONORS: North American Theological Award; award from Rotary International.

WRITINGS:

Luke's Portrait of Paul, Cambridge University Press, 1993.

*   *   *

LERMAN, Leo   1914-1994

OBITUARY NOTICE—See index for *CA* sketch: Born May 23, 1914, in New York, NY; died of pulmonary failure, August 22, 1994, in Manhattan, NY. Editor, literary critic, and author. Associated with Conde Nast magazines for more than fifty years, Lerman began his career as an actor, manager, and designer for stage shows in the Catskills and on Broadway. In 1942, Lerman started his long affiliation with Conde Nast, contributing articles to *Vogue, Harper's Bazaar, Saturday Review of Literature,* and *House and Garden.* Over the years he went on to assume the positions of contributing editor of *Mademoiselle,* consulting feature editor of *Vogue,* and editor in chief of *Vanity Fair,* and was named editorial adviser at Conde Nast in 1983. Lerman also reviewed books for the *New York Times Book Review.* According to William Grimes in the *New York Times,* Lerman "achieved something close to legendary status at Conde Nast for his ability to spot trends and topical subjects" for the magazine. The author of *Leonardo da Vinci: Artist and Scientist* (1940) and *Michelangelo: A Renaissance Profile* (1942), Lerman received the Lotus Club Award for his third book, *The Museum: One Hundred Years and the Metropolitan Museum of Art* (1969). He was working on a memoir, *Call It Friendship, Call It Love,* at the time of his death.

OBITUARIES AND OTHER SOURCES:

BOOKS

Who's Who in the East, 24th edition, Marquis, 1992.

PERIODICALS

New York Times, August 23, 1994, p. B6.
Washington Post, August 24, 1994, p. D5.

* * *

LERUDE, Warren (Leslie) 1937-

PERSONAL: Born October 29, 1937, in Reno, NV; son of Leslie R. (a restauranteur) and Ione (a homemaker; maiden name, Lundy) Lerude; married Janet Lagomarsino, August 24, 1961; children: Eric Warren, Christopher Mario, Leslie Ann. *Education:* University of Nevada—Reno, B.A., 1961. *Avocational interests:* Traveling, skiing, reading, fly fishing, sailing, jogging.

ADDRESSES: Home—3825 North Folsom Dr., Reno, NV 89509. *Office*—Reynolds School of Journalism, University of Nevada—Reno, Reno, NV 89557.

CAREER: Fallon Eagle-Standard, Fallon, NV, managing editor, 1959; Associated Press, reporter and editor in Nevada and California, 1960-63; *Nevada State Journal* and *Reno Evening Gazette,* reporter, 1963-65, news editor, 1965-68, managing editor, 1968-72, executive editor, 1972-77, publisher, 1977-81; University of Nevada—Reno, professor of journalism, 1981—; consultant and lecturer.

Pulitzer Prize juror, 1973, 1974, 1976, 1980, and 1981; *USA Today,* member of editorial board, 1982—; member of board of directors for Oakland *Tribune* and KNPB-TV, Reno; national chair of Associated Press Managing Editors Association and Freedom of Information Committee; director of Greater Reno Chamber of Commerce and United Way of Northern Nevada; University of Nevada—Reno Foundation, trustee; Biggest Little City Commission, member of executive board; Nevada State Fair Board, member. *Military service:* U.S. Navy Reserve, 1957-59.

MEMBER: American Society of Newspaper Editors, American Newspaper Publishers Association, Nevada State Press Association (president, beginning in 1979), California-Nevada News Executives Council of the Associated Press, California Newspaper Publishers Association (chair), Press Club of San Francisco, Sigma Delta Chi (president), Reno Rotary Club.

AWARDS, HONORS: Pulitzer Prize in journalism for editorial writing (with Foster Church and Norman F. Cardoza), Columbia University School of Journalism, 1977.

WRITINGS:

(With Marion Merriman) *American Commander in Spain: Robert Hale Merriman and the Lincoln Brigade* (biography; part of "Nevada Studies in History and Political Science" series), University of Nevada Press, 1986.

Contributor of numerous articles to periodicals, including *New York Times, Sunset, Nevada Magazine,* and *Newsday.*

SIDELIGHTS: Warren Lerude's career as a journalist spans more than three decades, highlighted by a Pulitzer Prize for editorial writing in 1977. Since 1981, he has been a professor of journalism at the University of Nevada. He collaborated with Marion Merriman to write *American Commander in Spain: Robert Hale Merriman and the Lincoln Brigade,* the biography of her husband, who was killed in the Spanish Civil War in 1938. Literary legend holds that the charismatic Robert Hale Merriman was Ernest Hemingway's model for Robert Jordan, the hero of *For Whom the Bell Tolls.*

In *American Commander in Spain,* the authors note that Robert Hale Merriman was an economics student and teacher at the University of California, Berkeley. He was in Moscow studying the Soviet economic system with Marion when civil war erupted in Spain in 1936. Lerude and Merriman point out that their subject joined a volunteer force called the International Brigade and was appointed commander of the Abraham Lincoln Battalion. Merriman, who distinguished himself in combat, was killed in battle in 1938.

American Commander in Spain, published on the fiftieth anniversary of the start of the Spanish Civil War, is based on Marion Merriman's diaries and on her husband's battle diaries, which he entrusted to her the last time she saw him. The book tells Marion Merriman's story as well, as she also volunteered to take on administrative tasks for the Fifteenth Brigade in Spain. *Chicago Tribune* contributor John Blades praised *American Commander in Spain,* noting that the story is told "with great economy and skill" and is "as dramatically constructed as a novel or film." In the *New York Times Book Review,* David D. Gilmore also commended the book: "As a firsthand account of the confusion and fear and hope of the Spanish battles, it is unsurpassed; but it also reveals a poignant awareness of the impact of the war on families and children and on the love between men and women. . . . [T]he book is a priceless addition to Spanish Civil War literature."

Lerude told *CA:* "The motivations I've found in thirty years of writing and journalism include sharing insights, gathering those of others, thinking about them, writing facts, interpreting them, and attempting to get at that which is essential, humorous, or poignant. Digging deeper and taking time to write with fullness in the medium of a book gives even greater joy and fulfillment. The basic rule of getting the story and getting it right is essential in all of the work."

BIOGRAPHICAL/CRITICAL SOURCES:

PERIODICALS

Chicago Tribune, June 24, 1986.
New York Times Book Review, June 8, 1986.
Washington Post Book World, June 29, 1986, p. 6.

* * *

LEV, Peter 1948-

PERSONAL: Born June 15, 1948, in Cleveland, OH; son of Herbert S. (a wholesaler) and Yola (a reading teacher; maiden name, Shapiro) Lev; married Yvonne Tuchalski (a librarian), June 27, 1976; children: Sara Larissa. *Education:* Wesleyan University, Middletown, CT, B.A., 1970; University of California, Los Angeles, M.A., Ph.D., 1980. *Religion:* Jewish. *Avocational interests:* Travel, sports, jazz.

ADDRESSES: Office—Department of Mass Communication, Towson State University, Towson, MD 21204.

CAREER: University of Texas at Dallas, visiting assistant professor, 1980-82; Towson State University, Towson, MD, began as assistant professor, became professor of mass communication, 1983—. Towson Recreational Council, coach of girls' basketball and soccer teams.

MEMBER: Literature/Film Association (vice president, 1991-93; president, 1993-94), University Film and Video Association, Society for Cinema Studies.

WRITINGS:

Claude Lelouch, Film Director, Fairleigh Dickinson University Press (East Brunswick, NJ), 1983.
The Euro-American Cinema, University of Texas Press (Austin, TX), 1993.

Contributor to periodicals, including *Journal of Film and Video, New Orleans Review, Canadian Review of American Studies,* and *Post Script.* Member of editorial board, *Literature/Film Quarterly.*

WORK IN PROGRESS: A book on American films of the 1970s; *The Zone,* a screenplay, with Steve Weiss.

SIDELIGHTS: Peter Lev told *CA:* "I became interested in cinema in 1968 during a semester abroad in Paris. Returning to the United States, I completed my humanities degree and went to graduate film school. At the University of California, Los Angeles, I studied film production, as well as history, theory, and criticism. As a technician, I was all thumbs, so film production became a less important part of my goals.

"I have been fortunate to make a living as a university teacher of film. Everyone has complaints about academic life, but I enjoy both the teaching and the chance to write. My research has centered on American and European film history. Sometimes these major topics are distinct in my work, and at other times they tend to merge. My current book focuses on American films of the 1970s, but even here European films will appear as points of comparison.

"Perspectives change. As a young man, I had at least a notion to change the world. Now, a lot of energy goes into more modest concerns: figuring out the hows and whys and whats of film history and, through that history, social life."

* * *

LEVINE, Nancy D. 1955-
(Faith Henry)

PERSONAL: Born February 16, 1955, in Kansas City, MO; daughter of Thomas U. (an auditor) and Margaret (a schoolteacher; maiden name, Leonard) Derr; married Gary E. Levine (a business owner), May 29, 1977; children: Jessica, Evan, Amy. *Education:* University of Missouri—Kansas City, B.A. (with distinction), 1984, M.A., 1990. *Religion:* Christian.

ADDRESSES: Home—Kansas City, MO.

CAREER: University of Missouri—Kansas City, part-time teacher of sociology, 1992—, and member of Women's Council. Part-time teacher at Penn Valley Community College, 1992—, and Maple Woods Community College, 1993. Talent Group of Kansas City, voice-over artist, 1989—.

MEMBER: Midwest Sociological Society, Phi Kappa Phi, Alpha Kappa Delta (president, 1985).

AWARDS, HONORS: Family Study Award, Womens' Council, University of Missouri—Kansas City, 1989.

WRITINGS:

(With C. Neil Bull) *The Older Volunteer: An Annotated Bibliography,* Greenwood Press (Westport, CT), 1993.

Some writings appear under the pseudonym Faith Henry.

WORK IN PROGRESS: Children's books.

*   *   *

LIDE, David R. 1928-

PERSONAL: Born May 25, 1928, in Gainesville, GA; son of David Reynolds (an accountant) and Kate (a homemaker; maiden name, Simmons) Lide; married Mary Lomer, November 5, 1955 (marriage ended December 12, 1988); married Bettijoyce Breen (a government program manager), December 17, 1988; children: David Alston, Vanessa Lide Whitcomb, James Hugh, Quention Robert. *Education:* Carnegie-Mellon University, B.S., 1949; Harvard University, M.A., 1951, Ph.D., 1952.

ADDRESSES: Home and office—13901 Riding Loop Dr., North Potomac, MD 20878.

CAREER: National Bureau of Standards, physicist, 1954-63, chief of Molecular Spectroscopy Section, 1963-69, director of Office of Standard Reference Data, 1969-88.

AWARDS, HONORS: Fulbright Scholar and Ramsay Memorial fellow, 1952-53; research fellow at Harvard, 1953-54; National Science Foundation senior postdoctoral fellow, 1959-60 and 1967-68; Department of Commerce, Silver Medal, 1965, and Gold Medal, 1968; Samuel Wesley Stratton Award, 1968;

Presidential Rank Award, Meritorious Executive, 1986; Herman Skolnik Award in Chemical Information, American Chemical Society, 1988.

WRITINGS:

Basic Laboratory and Industrial Chemicals, CRC Press (Boca Raton, FL), 1993.
(With G. W. A. Milne) *Handbook of Data on Organic Compounds,* 3rd edition, CRC Press, 1993.
(With Henry V. Kehiaian) *CRC Handbook of Thermophysical and Thermochemical Data,* CRC Press, 1994.
(Editor in chief) *CRC Handbook of Chemistry and Physics,* 75th edition, CRC Press, 1994.
Handbook of Organic Solvents, CRC Press, 1994.

Also contributor to books, including *Encyclopedia of Physics,* Addison-Wesley; *Encyclopedia of Physical Science and Technology,* Academic Press; *Encyclopedia of Physics,* Van Nostrand; and *World Book.* Author of numerous research papers, scientific reviews, and articles. Editor, *Journal of Physical and Chemical Reference Data,* 1972—; associate editor, *CODATA Bulletin,* 1974-83; and member of editorial boards, *Applied Spectroscopy Reviews,* 1968-76, *Journal of Chemical Information and Computer Science,* 1986-89, and *Journal of Engineering Data,* 1987—.

*   *   *

LINDGREN, James M. 1950-

PERSONAL: Born September 3, 1950, in Elmhurst, IL; son of Raymond L. (an accountant) and Lorraine (in business; maiden name, Connelly) Lindgren; married Mary Ann Weiglhofer (a researcher), September 2, 1978; children: Brian K., Charles A. *Education:* University of Dayton, B.A., 1972, M.A., 1977; College of William and Mary, Ph.D., 1984. *Politics:* Independent. *Religion:* Independent.

ADDRESSES: Home—12 Grace Ave., Plattsburgh, NY 12901. *Office*—Department of History, State University of New York College at Plattsburgh, Plattsburgh, NY 12901.

CAREER: Shelby County River Corridor Project, Shelby County, OH, historic inventory supervisor, 1978; Old Dominion University, Norfolk, VA, instructor in history, 1978-79, 1980; State University of New York at Plattsburgh, assistant professor, 1984-91, associate professor, 1991-94, professor of history, 1994—. Consultant to Colonial Williamsburg Foundation.

MEMBER: American Studies Association, Organization of American Historians, Phi Beta Kappa, Phi Alpha Theta.

AWARDS, HONORS: G. Wesley Johnson Prize, National Council on Public History, 1991, for the article "'Virginia Needs Living Heroes': Historic Preservation in the Progressive Era"; grant from National Endowment for the Humanities, 1992.

WRITINGS:

Preserving the Old Dominion: Historic Preservation and Virginia Traditionalism, University Press of Virginia (Charlottesville), 1993.
Preserving New England: Preservation, Progressivism, and the Remaking of Memory, Oxford University Press (New York City), 1995.

Contributor to history journals.

WORK IN PROGRESS: Preserving Maritime America: Marine Museums and Popular Culture in the United States, completion expected in 1997.

*   *   *

LINDVALL, Michael L(loyd) 1947-

PERSONAL: Born June 24, 1947, in Minneapolis, MN; son of Lloyd Calvin and Jeanne Elizabeth Lindvall; married Terri Vaun Smith; children: Madeline, Benjamin, Grace. Education: University of Wisconsin, B.A., 1970; Princeton Theological Seminary, M.Div., 1974. Politics: Independent. Religion: Presbyterian.

ADDRESSES: Home—1747 Cypress Pt., Ann Arbor, MI 48108. Office—First Presbyterian Church of Ann Arbor, 1432 Washtenaw Ave., Ann Arbor, MI 48104.

CAREER: Drayton Avenue Presbyterian Church, Ferndale, MI, associate pastor, 1974-79; First Presbyterian Church of Northport, Long Island, NY, pastor, 1979-92; First Presbyterian Church of Ann Arbor, Ann Arbor, MI, senior pastor, 1992—.

WRITINGS:

The Good News from North Haven: A Year in the Life of a Small Town, Doubleday (New York, NY), 1991.

Contributor of short stories to periodicals, including Good Housekeeping.

WORK IN PROGRESS: A sequel to The Good News from North Haven: A Year in the Life of a Small Town and a spiritual murder mystery.

SIDELIGHTS: Michael L. Lindvall is a Presbyterian minister whose experiences with small-town life in Minnesota and Michigan are reflected in his novel, The Good News from North Haven: A Year in the Life of a Small Town. The volume contains eighteen interwoven stories that span a year in the life of a rural parish, told by the pastor of a fictional Protestant church in a declining farm-town in southwestern Minnesota. Through the eyes of the narrator and his wife, Lindvall explores timeless truths and the ways in which they reveal themselves through the most routine events of life.

Lindvall told CA: "Years ago I heard American humorist Garrison Keillor read a 'letter' on his radio program, A Prairie Home Companion. The letter was a long, rambling fiction, ostensibly addressed to Keillor from some long-lost friend who explained—evocatively and poignantly, to all of us as we listened to Keillor read it—why he had not succumbed to a recently presented temptation to fall into adultery. The conceit of a letter written to oneself by a nonexistent friend struck me as an intriguing way to tell a story from a distance. It also occurred to me that it might offer an occasional counterpoint to the rhythm of more traditional preaching.

"Over the next few years, I wrote several stories imbedded in 'letters,' and read them to the congregation I was pastoring on the North Shore of Long Island. I presented them as though they were real correspondence from an old classmate now pastoring a tiny church in the Midwest. These 'letters from Dave' arrived once or twice a year and always— 'providentially,' as I told the Sunday congregation— during an especially busy week when I was unable to find the time to put a sermon together. I never publicly owned the fact that there was no Dave, the existence or nonexistence of whom became a matter of much local speculation. Even when everyone knew that there was no Dave Battles and no North Haven, Minnesota, the congregation faithfully continued to play at the ruse. 'Had any letters from Dave lately, Pastor?' they asked."

The idea of "weaving" these tales into a book came from an editor at Good Housekeeping magazine, where some of Lindvall's letter-stories were published in 1987 and 1990. Reflecting on the setting of the book, Lindvall explained: "Many of the stories in Good News from North Haven are loosely based on my memories of small town life, or on remembrances told to me by friends and family over the years. At first I had set the stories in central Illinois, a part of the world I have only seen from Interstate 70. My editor asked me if I knew much about the area. I admitted that I really didn't, so he asked what part of the world I knew best. I told him Minnesota, but said that I thought Garrison Keillor owned it. 'No, he doesn't,' he answered. North Haven moved to Minnesota. The world of the small town, now largely foreign in experience to most American readers, is nevertheless an evocative, symbolically powerful, almost mythic world. In a sense, it is where we are all from, or, more accurately, where we imagine ourselves to be from. In such places abide little churches, most of which function as large, extended families full of character and characters, a community in which all the complexities and dramas of human life are played out. They are played in a slightly different key in small towns and little churches, but the melody seems familiar to suburbanites and urbanites alike. In fact, the tune often sounds fresher in another key."

Lindvall added: "Most of the stories in this book are 'religious,' but without the deadly earnestness of much religious fiction. My goal was to make a book that might be read both by people who recognize God's presence in their lives and by those who long to sense that presence but have found it elusive, perhaps because they have not disciplined themselves to look closely.

"Perhaps the most rewarding aspect of the experience of having written this book has been receiving letters and calls from readers who have found some of their own story in one of these tales. I don't know that a writer (or a preacher) can ask for much more than the occasional assurance that you have expressed what you have come to know as true in such a way that others recognize the experience as their own, as well."

*   *   *

LINNELL, David   1928-

PERSONAL: Born October 31, 1928, in Bulawayo, Southern Rhodesia (now Zimbabwe); son of Michael Gerald (a bank official) and Marjorie Desailly (Hadfield) Linnell; married, wife's name Rosemary (a lecturer and writer), January 17, 1951; children: Juliet Desailly, Kate. *Education:* Attended Central School of Speech and Drama, London, 1946, 1949-50.

ADDRESSES: Home—6 Godstalls Lane, Steyning, West Sussex BN44 3NE, England.

CAREER: Actor in repertory and co-director of Minsler Theatre Guild, 1950-54; Elmira Little Theatre, Elmira, NY, co-director, 1954-55; advertising copywriter, 1956-67; Curtain Theatre, London, manager and administrator, 1967-89. *Military service:* British Army, Royal Artillery, 1947-49.

WRITINGS:

Blake, Palmer, Linnell & Co., Book Guild (Lewes), 1994.

SIDELIGHTS: David Linnell told *CA:* "My venture into authorship was the result of waiting in vain for those experts who said they were writing a life of my great-grandfather John Linnell. Then in 1989, on taking early retirement, I suddenly found myself with time on my hands and decided that I had better write my ancestor's life myself. There was a wealth of material in the family archives, and I enjoyed the research and the routine of writing regularly every day. I decided early on that I wanted the book to appeal to as wide a readership as possible, and not just to the art historian. As a result, I included as much background as I could about the family life of an artist in Victorian times. If I can now find another subject that fires my imagination, then another biography is very likely."

*   *   *

LITTLEJOHN, Duffy   1953-

PERSONAL: Born Douglas C. Littlejohn, August 8, 1953, in Pacific Palisades, CA; son of Fred G. (a manufacturer's representative) and Dorothy K. (a homemaker; maiden name, Kihm) Littlejohn. *Education:* Attended University of California at Los Angeles, 1970-71; New Mexico Highlands University, 1972-73; University of California at Santa Barbara, B.A., 1979; University of California at Davis, J.D., 1983; attended French School for Political Refugees (Paris, France), 1990-91. *Politics:* Liberal/Democratic. *Religion:* "Non-specific theist." *Avocational interests:* Acting, debate, writing, history, bass guitar.

ADDRESSES: Office—c/o Zephyr Rhoades Press, 1940 Loomis St., San Luis Obispo, CA 93405-2052.

CAREER: McCarthy, Flowers, and Roberts (law firm), San Francisco, CA, attorney, 1983-84; Meadows and Doris (law firm), San Francisco, attorney, 1984-85; San Francisco District Attorney's Office, assistant district attorney, 1985-87; Alameda County District Attorney's Office, Oakland, CA, senior deputy district attorney, 1987-89; self-employed criminal defense attorney, 1989-90, 1992—; semi-retired in Paris, France, from 1990-92; author.

WRITINGS:

Hopping Freight Trains in America, Sand River Press (Los Osos, CA), 1993.
Cindertrail Tales, Zephyr Rhoades Press (San Luis Obispo, CA), 1994.
The Anomaly, Zephyr Rhoades Press, 1995.
Flight from Paradise, Zephyr Rhoades Press, 1995.
Drifting, Zephyr Rhoades Press, in press.

WORK IN PROGRESS: Southbound, to be published by Zephyr Rhoades Press in 1997.

SIDELIGHTS: Attorney Duffy Littlejohn has spent much of his adult life riding freight trains illegally. In this way he has travelled throughout the continental United States, the western provinces and territories of Canada, between Mexico and Bolivia, and through sixteen European countries. His 1993 book, *Hopping Freight Trains in America,* divulges some of the information he gleaned concerning when and how to catch freight trains, how to dress when travelling the rails, how to behave toward other illegal travellers and toward railroad employees, and how to negotiate the train safely. Although the author emphasizes the book's usefulness in teaching others how to travel free via freight trains, a reviewer for *Rail Reading* concluded that the book lets the reader share: "some of the excitement [of hopping trains] without the risk of actually doing it."

A railway spokesperson denied several of the claims Littlejohn makes in *Hopping Freight Trains* in an article by Danna Dykstra Coy in the *County Telegram-Tribune.* Regarding Littlejohn's claim that the typical railroad looks the other way when faced with those who ride the rails for free, a Southern Pacific Railroad spokesperson countered: "By and large this is extremely dangerous stuff he's saying. You won't find a railroad anywhere that won't treat a trespasser as a danger to themselves and to the train itself, when you consider such things as a person falling off and possibly causing an accident." Although Coy quoted the author in defense: "You have a greater chance of killing yourself slipping on a wet floor in your bathroom than riding a train," Littlejohn was also reported, however, as saying, "If you're not on top of the situation, you can become railroad pizza real quick." Nonetheless, *Booklist* reviewer John Mort praised *Hopping Freight Trains in America* as "a colorful history of railroads,"

adding, "There is no other book on this subject."

Duffy Littlejohn told *CA:* "*Hopping Freight Trains in America* is a how-to book. It's the definitive piece on when, where, what to wear, and what to expect when riding the rails. I've traveled over 400,000 miles by freight train and still do it whenever the weather suits my clothes. I know railroad lore and railroad history hands-down, even though I spend the majority of my time practicing criminal law.

"Not only does my book include railroad history, detailed instructions on every aspect of the sport of freight train hopping, and information on how railroads work and how we can capitalize on it, the book also includes the '100 Commandments of Riding the Rails,' an appendix, glossary of terms, bibliography, and index. I take particular care to emphasize the safety hazards of the sport, which should be of high interest to anyone contemplating riding the rails.

"*Hopping Freight Trains in America* is selling well with people who are just now discovering this sport (e.g. 'yuppie hobos'—of which there are thousands), and with other folks who like (or like to think about) rocking and rolling free and wild on the railroad with the wind screaming through their hair. The book is also selling particularly well with armchair railroad buffs, the avant garde, adventurers, hobby shop aficionados, and their friends and family."

BIOGRAPHICAL/CRITICAL SOURCES:

PERIODICALS

Booklist, December 15, 1993.
County Telegram-Tribune (San Luis Obispo, CA), May 29, 1992, pp. A1, A14.
Rail Reading, January-February, 1994.
Santa Maria Times (Santa Maria, CA), August 15, 1994, p. B1.

*   *   *

LIU, Eric 1968-

PERSONAL: Born November 1, 1968, in Poughkeepsie, NY; son of Chao-Hua and Julia Liu. *Education:* Yale University, B.A. (summa cum laude), 1990; doctoral study at Harvard University.

ADDRESSES: Home—24 Inman St., No. 8, Cambridge, MA 02139. *Office—Next Progressive,* P.O. Box 391017, Cambridge, MA 02139. *Agent*—Raphael Sagalyn, The Sagalyn Literary Agency,

4825 Bethesda Ave., Suite 302, Bethesda, MD.

CAREER: Next Progressive, Cambridge, MA, founder, 1991, editor, 1991—. Speechwriter for the White House and National Security Council, 1993-94.

WRITINGS:

(Editor) *Next: Young American Writers on the New Generation,* Norton (New York, NY), 1994.

*   *   *

LOCK, C. J. S.
See LOCK, Charles (John Somerset)

*   *   *

LOCK, Charles (John Somerset) 1955-
(C. J. S. Lock)

PERSONAL: Born April 15, 1955, in Dorchester, Dorset, England; son of Henry Ensor Fossett (a lawyer) and Helen Jane Boscawen (Somerset) Lock; married Nicoletta Isar (an art historian), July 31, 1993. *Education:* Keble College, Oxford, B.A., 1977, D.Phil., 1982. *Religion:* Orthodox Christian.

ADDRESSES: Office—Department of English, Erindale College, University of Toronto, Mis-sissauga, Ontario, Canada L5L 1S6.

CAREER: Hoegskolan i Karlstad, Karlstad, Sweden, lecturer, 1980-82; University of Toronto, Toronto, Ontario, Canada, assistant professor, 1983-88, associate professor, 1988-93, professor of English, 1993—.

WRITINGS:

Thomas Hardy, St. Martin's (New York, NY), 1992.

Contributor to periodicals. Contributing editor, *Powys Journal;* associate editor, *Semiotic Review of Books.* Some writings appear under the name C. J. S. Lock.

WORK IN PROGRESS: A biography of English novelist John Cowper Powys.

*   *   *

LOEN, Raymond O(rdell) 1924-

PERSONAL: Born July 15, 1924, in Howard, SD; son of Lauris and Selina Edith (Langorgen) Loen; married Omeline Janelle, June 17, 1950; children:

Kurtis, Jon, Philip, Pamela, Brock. *Education:* Columbia University, B.S., 1948, M.S., 1949. *Politics:* Republican. *Avocational interests:* Tennis, fishing, golf.

ADDRESSES: Home and office—R. O. Loen Co., 16 Becket St., Lake Oswego, OR 97035-1034.

CAREER: Uarco, Inc., New York City and Philadelphia, PA, sales representative, sales trainer, and city sales manager, 1949-53; H. B. Maynard and Co., Inc., Pittsburgh, PA, staff consultant and senior consultant, 1953-59; Fibreboard Corp., San Francisco, CA, sales training manager and director of management services, 1959-63; R. O. Loen Co., Lake Oswego, OR, principal, 1963—. Loen, Brandt, Inc., founder and director, 1965-70; Swift Energy Co., founder and member of board of directors; United Medical Laboratories, Inc., past chairperson of board of directors; Lancet Medical Industries, Inc., founder and past member of board of directors; Graphic Software Systems, Inc., past member of board of directors; management consultant to large and small businesses throughout the United States. *Military service:* U.S. Naval Reserve, active duty, 1943-46; served in Pacific theater; became lieutenant junior grade.

MEMBER: Sons of Norway, Columbia University School of Business Alumni Association, Mountain Park Racquet Club, Clackamas Fly Fishers, Alpha Kappa Psi.

WRITINGS:

Manage More by Doing Less, McGraw-Hill, 1971.
Supervising by Objectives, Addison-Wesley, 1971.
Superior Supervision: The Ten Percent Solution, Lexington Books, 1994.

Contributor to professional journals.

SIDELIGHTS: Raymond O. Loen told *CA:* "My career thrust has been to help individuals, groups, and organizations to realize their potential through better management."

*   *   *

LONDON, Lawrence Steven 1950-
(Lawrence L. Stevens)

PERSONAL: Born June 14, 1950, in Brooklyn, NY; son of Jack and Elsie (a comptroller) London; married; wife's name, Helen F. (an executive), June 20, 1976; children: Joseph Brian, Ellie Faith, Abbey

Ruth. *Education:* Brooklyn College of the City University of New York, B.A., 1972; University of Baltimore, J.D., 1975. *Politics:* Republican.

ADDRESSES: Home—2404 Diana Rd., Baltimore, MD 21209.

CAREER: Attorney, 1975—. Lecturer for Baltimore County adult education program.

WRITINGS:

(Under pseudonym Lawrence L. Stevens) *Landlording as a Second Income,* Scarborough House, 1994.

WORK IN PROGRESS: Revising *Landlording as a Second Income.*

SIDELIGHTS: Lawrence Steven London told *CA:* "*Landlording as a Second Income* was written because there were too few books on the subject. Sure, the libraries were full of 'get rich by real estate' books, but these were pie-in-the-sky books for acquiring property (always with no money down) and immediately thereafter selling it for profit. Practical, day-to-day landlording questions were left unanswered.

"My book was prepared literally on the run. I am a runner whose running partners are fellow landlords. I used my daily runs, discussing landlording principles and techniques, to produce a 'Heloise/Ann Landers' book for landlords.

"Philosophically I am from the *Reader's Digest*/Dale Carnegie, 'everyone-can-succeed-but-they-must-try' school. My greatest satisfactions are the 'no vacancy' signs and the Christmas cards I receive from my tenants—signs that my philosophy and approach work."

*   *   *

LOWE, Rodney   1946-

PERSONAL: Born January 26, 1946, in Epson, England; married Susan Lesley Warman (a language teacher), 1972; children: Virginia, Alexander. *Education:* University of Bristol, B.A., 1967; London School of Economics and Political Science, London, Ph.D., 1976.

ADDRESSES: Home—Southbank, 109 High St., Upper Weston, Bath BA1 4DG, England. *Office*—Department of Historical Studies, University of Bristol, Bristol BS8 1TB, England.

CAREER: Heriot-Watt University, Edinburgh, Scotland, lecturer in history, 1972-78; University of Bristol, Bristol, England, reader in history, 1979—. Australian National University, visiting research fellow, 1994.

AWARDS, HONORS: ESRC senior research fellow, 1994-95.

WRITINGS:

Adjusting to Democracy, Oxford University Press, 1986.
Economic Planning in Britain, 1943-51, H.M.S.O., 1992.
The Development of the Welfare State, 1939-51, H.M.S.O., 1992.
The Welfare State in Britain since 1945, St. Martin's, 1993.

WORK IN PROGRESS: The Watershed Years: Replanning the Welfare State in Britain, 1957-64, completion expected in 1997; research on welfare policy under the British Conservative Party and on comparative welfare states.

SIDELIGHTS: Rodney Lowe told *CA:* "I am committed to using my university posts and writing to encourage students and the general public to appreciate the excitement of studying recent history; to acknowledge the similarities and differences in the way advanced industrial countries respond to economic and social problems; and to acquire the information to make good, independent decisions about the sort of society they want to live in. Civil servants and politicians, via the media, are also targets for my work."

*   *   *

LOWENBERG, Carlton   1919-

PERSONAL: Born January 9, 1919, in Boston, MA; son of Hyman (an owner of a confectionery company) and Daisy Thurston (Church) Lowenberg; married Territa A. Aldred (an art teacher), 1945 (died, 1990); children: Carla (deceased). *Education:* Brown University, B.A. (cum laude), 1949; attended University of Connecticut, 1947. *Avocational interests:* Wood sculpture, birding, book collecting.

ADDRESSES: Home—3136 Tice Creek Dr., No. 1, Walnut Creek, CA 94595.

CAREER: Lincoln Bookshop, Providence, RI, part-time employee, 1948-49; Palindrome Bookstore, Berkeley, CA, manager and specialist in books on art, psychology, and psychiatry, 1949-50; May Co., San Francisco, CA, business analyst, 1950; Asia Foundation, San Francisco, director of Books for Asia Program, 1951-81. Charles M. Tanner Productions, script writer, 1953-56. Emily Dickinson Private Collection, developer, 1981-91. *Military service:* American Maritime Commission, 1941-46; served in European, Pacific, and Asian theaters; became chief mate.

MEMBER: Emily Dickinson International Society, Emily Dickinson Music Society (founder; past president), Audubon Society, Friends of the Town Library of Lafayette, CA, Phi Beta Kappa.

WRITINGS:

Emily Dickinson's Textbooks, West Coast Print Center, 1986.
Musicians Wrestle Everywhere: Emily Dickinson and Music, Fallen Leaf Press, 1991.

Author of the unpublished book *Textbooks of Hampshire County.* Contributor of articles and reviews to periodicals.

*   *   *

LOWENBERG, Susan   1957-

PERSONAL: Born November 21, 1957, in Bismarck, ND; daughter of Arthur Lee (a meteorologist) and Mildred Louise (a homemaker; maiden name, Schroeder) Eichelberger; married Anton David Lowenberg (a professor), May 21, 1988; children: Derek Arthur, Marissa Emily. *Education:* California State University, B.A., 1979; University of California, Los Angeles, M.L.S., 1981; Bradley University, M.B.A., 1986. *Politics:* Democrat. *Religion:* Lutheran. *Avocational interests:* Cross-stitching, reading.

ADDRESSES: Office—California Institute of the Arts, 24700 McBean Parkway, Santa Clarita, CA 91355.

CAREER: Bradley University, Peoria, IL, librarian, 1981-86; California State University Library, Northridge, chair of circulation department, 1986-89; University of Colorado, Boulder, head of access services department, 1989-90, science librarian and curator of Map Library, 1991-92; California Institute of the Arts, Santa Clarita, librarian of information resources and theatre/dance, 1993—.

MEMBER: American Library Association, Association of College and Research Libraries, California

Academic and Research Librarians, California Library Association.

AWARDS, HONORS: Meritorious Performance and Professional Promise Award, California State University, Northridge, 1989.

WRITINGS:

C. S. Lewis: A Reference Guide, 1972-1988, G. K. Hall (New York), 1993.

*   *   *

LUMPKIN, Betty S(tewart)   1934-

PERSONAL: Born April 10, 1934, in Anniston, AL; daughter of Dave T. and Mable (maiden name, Stephens; present surname, Ogburn) Stewart; stepdaughter of David Leon Ogburn; married Pete Lumpkin, March 20, 1954; children: John. *Education:* Attended Auburn University; University of Tennessee at Chattanooga, B.S. (with honors), 1959, Certificate in Administration and Supervision, 1982; Middle Tennessee State University, M.Ed. (summa cum laude), 1972; further graduate study at University of Tennessee at Knoxville, Chattanooga State Technical Community College, and Indiana University—Bloomington; Southern College, Certificate in Library Science. *Religion:* Christian. *Avocational interests:* Private pilot, travel, Auburn University football games, the Atlanta Braves.

ADDRESSES: Home—7718 Mahan Gap Rd., Ooltewah, TN 37363; and P.O. Box 659, Harrison, TN 37341.

CAREER: Elementary schoolteacher in Chattanooga, TN, 1966-67; junior high school English teacher and curriculum coordinator in Chattanooga, 1967-74; middle school librarian in Ooltewah, TN, 1974-75; substitute teacher at public schools in Simsbury, CT, 1975-79; Ooltewah High School, Ooltewah, head librarian and head of library department, 1979—. Freedoms Foundation, vice-president of education for Chattanooga chapter; James County Depot Restoration Committee, member; workshop presenter.

MEMBER: International Reading Association, American Business Women's Association (chapter president and vice-president of Chattanooga Area Council), Southeast Library Association, Tennessee Library Association (member of board of directors), Chattanooga Area Library Association (past president), Phi Delta Kappa, Alpha Society.

AWARDS, HONORS: Named woman of the year, American Business Women's Association; Louise Meredith Award, Tennessee Library Association, 1992.

WRITINGS:

(With Barbara Head Sorrow) *CD-ROM for Librarians and Educators,* McFarland and Co., 1993.

*   *   *

LYNN, John A(lbert)   1943-

PERSONAL: Born March 18, 1943, in Glenview, IL; son of Judd Benjamin (an electrical contractor) and Adelle (an academic administrator; maiden name, Savage) Lynn; married Andrea Ellen Kramer (a writer), June 13, 1965; children: Daniel Morgan, Nathanael Greene. *Education:* University of Illinois at Urbana-Champaign, A.B., 1964; University of California, Davis, M.A., 1967; University of California, Los Angeles, Ph.D., 1973. *Politics:* Democrat. *Religion:* Agnostic. *Avocational interests:* Miniature sculpture, bagpiping.

ADDRESSES: Home—910 West Hill, Champaign, IL 61821. *Office*—Department of History, University of Illinois at Urbana-Champaign, 309 Gregory Hall, 810 South Wright, Urbana, IL 61801.

CAREER: Indiana University, visiting assistant professor of history, 1972-73; University of Maine at Orono, assistant professor of history, 1973-77; University of Illinois at Urbana-Champaign, assistant professor of history, 1978-83, associate professor of history, 1983-91, professor of history, 1991—. Midwest Consortium on Military History, chair, 1987—; Society for Military History, midwest regional coordinator, 1989—; Marine Corps University, Oppenheimer Chair of Warfighting Strategy, 1994-95.

MEMBER: American Historical Association, Society for French Historical Studies, Western Society for French History.

AWARDS, HONORS: Phi Alpha Theta prize for the best first book by a member, 1985.

WRITINGS:

The Bayonets of the Republic: Motivation and Tactics in the Army of Revolutionary France, 1791-94, University of Illinois Press (Urbana), 1984.
(Editor) *The Tools of War: Ideas, Instruments, and Institutions of Warfare, 1445-1871,* University of Illinois Press (Urbana), 1990.
(Editor) *Feeding Mars: Logistics in Western Warfare from the Middle Ages to the Present,* Westview Press (Boulder, CO), 1993.

WORK IN PROGRESS: Soldiers of Glory: The French Army of the Grand Siecle, 1610-1715, expected completion, 1995; research into the evolution of Western armies, 800-2000 A.D.

M

MACAULAY, Ronald K. S. 1927-

PERSONAL: Born November 3, 1927, in West Kilbride, Ayrshire, Scotland; son of Robert Wilson and Mary Robb (McDermid) Macauley; married Janet Grey, July 25, 1956; children: Harvey Steven, Anna Virginia Robb. *Education:* University of St. Andrews, M.A., 1955; University College of North Wales, diploma in linguistics, 1965; University of California, Los Angeles, Ph.D., 1971.

ADDRESSES: *Office*—Department of Linguistics, Pitzer College, 1050 North Mills Ave., Claremont, CA 91711-6110.

CAREER: British Institute, Lisbon, Portugal, lecturer, 1955-60; British Council, Buenos Aires, Argentina, lecturer, 1960-64; Pitzer College, Claremont, CA, assistant professor, 1965-67, associate professor, 1967-73, professor of linguistics, 1973—, dean of faculty, 1980-86, vice president for academic affairs, 1984-86. Visiting lecturer, International Summer School for English Language teachers, Santiago, Chile, 1961, Buenos Aires, Argentina, 1961, and ICANA Summer School for English teachers, Buenos Aires, 1962, 1964; visiting instructor, University of California, Los Angeles, summer quarter, 1968; visiting scholar, The Scottish Council for Research in Education, Edinburgh, 1973.

AWARDS, HONORS: Grant from the Social Science Research Council, London, 1979; National Endowment for the Humanities Summer Fellowship for College teachers, 1979; Scholar-in-Residence, Pitzer College, fall, 1989; National Endowment for the Humanities Fellowship, spring, 1990; John Randolph and Mary Haynes Fellowship, summer, 1991.

WRITINGS:

(Editor with R. P. Stockwell) *Linguistic Change and Generative Theory,* Indiana University Press (Bloomington), 1972.

Language, Social Class, and Education: A Glasgow Study, Edinburgh University Press, 1977.

(With M. Ramirez, A. Gonzalez, B. Cox, and M. Perez) *Spanish-English Bilingual Education in the United States,* Center for Applied Linguistics (Arlington, VA), 1977.

Generally Speaking: How Children Learn Language, Newbury House (Rowley, MA), 1980.

Locating Dialect in Discourse: The Language of Honest Men and Bonnie Lassies in Ayr, Oxford University Press (New York), 1991.

The Social Art: Language and Its Uses, Oxford University Press (New York), 1994.

Contributor to *The Major Syntactic Structures of English,* edited by Stockwell, P. Schachter, and B. H. Partee, Holt, 1973; *The Scots Language in Education,* edited by J. D. McClure, Aberdeen College of Education, 1975; *On Language: Rhetorica, Phonologica, Syntactica: Festschrift for Robert P. Stockwell,* edited by C. Duncan-Rose and T. Venneman, Routledge, 1988. Contributor of articles to periodicals, including *English Language Teaching, American Anthropologist, Lingua, American Ethnologist, Language, International Journal of the Sociology of Language,* and *Language in Society.*

WORK IN PROGRESS: (With D. Brenneis) *Reader in Linguistic Anthropology,* to be published by Westview Press.

SIDELIGHTS: Ronald K. S. Macaulay told *CA:* "I have done most of my research in Scotland, and I am constantly amazed by the eloquence of ordinary people I have recorded over the years. Many of them left school at the age of fifteen and had little in the way of formal schooling since then, but they have a remarkable ability to express themselves effectively. I am working on various ways in which I hope to make this eloquence known to others."

*   *   *

MacFADDEN, Bruce J.   1949-

PERSONAL: Born September 3, 1949, in Albany, NY; married Jeannette D. (a registered nurse), December 7, 1991. *Education:* Cornell University, B.S. (with honors), 1971; Columbia University, M.Phil., 1974, Ph.D., 1976.

ADDRESSES: Home—1024 Northwest 17th St., Gainesville, FL 32605. *Office*—Florida Museum of Natural History, University of Florida, Gainesville, FL 32611-2035.

CAREER: Associated with the Florida Museum of Natural History, University of Florida, Gainesville.

AWARDS, HONORS: Senior Fulbright fellow in Bolivia, 1994.

WRITINGS:

Fossil Horses: Systematics, Paleobiology, and Evolution of the Family Equidae, Cambridge University Press, 1992.

*   *   *

MacGILL-CALLAHAN, Sheila   1926-

PERSONAL: Born July 20, 1926, in London, England; daughter of Patrick (a writer) and Margaret (a writer; maiden name, Gibbons) MacGill; married Leo P. Callahan (a teacher), 1956; children: Patrick, Mary Messite, Deborah Knowlton, Justin. *Politics:* Socialist-Democrat. *Religion:* Roman Catholic. *Avocational interests:* Neighborhood activist, politics, interior decorating, collecting old toys.

ADDRESSES: Home—401 Beach 47 St., Far Rockaway, NY 11691. *Agent*—Susan Cohen, Writers House Inc., 21 West 26th St., New York, NY 10010.

CAREER: CWA-CIO (labor union), New York City, organizer, steward, and educational council chair, 1947-57; Radio Free Europe, New York City, 1958-60; Writer's House Inc., New York City, reader, factotum, 1987-93; full-time writer, 1993—.

MEMBER: Society of Children's Book Writers and Illustrators, Jewish Arts Center, Authors Guild, Authors League of America, Mystery Writers of America, Smithsonian.

AWARDS, HONORS: Notable book citation, National Council of Social Studies, and Outstanding Science Trade Book designation, National Science Teachers Association, both 1991, both for *And Still the Turtle Watched.*

WRITINGS:

Death in a Far Country (fiction), St. Martin's, 1993.

JUVENILE

And Still the Turtle Watched, illustrated by Barry Moser, Dial, 1991.
The Children of Lir, illustrated by Genady Spirin, Dial, 1993.

WORK IN PROGRESS: Sequel to *Death in a Far Country;* a children's version of Gilgamesh; and *Children of the Dead End,* an adaptation of a children's book published by Patrick MacGill.

SIDELIGHTS: "I come from a writing family," Sheila MacGill-Callahan commented. "My father, Patrick MacGill, who died in 1963, was known as 'the Navy Poet.' His two most famous books, *Children of the Dead End* and *The Rat Pit,* are still in print from Caliban Books in London. My mother, Margaret Gibbons MacGill, wrote romance novels of the type that are published today by Harlequin and Silhouette. Unfortunately, they are no longer available.

"My two sisters are both editors, one retired and one active. They each have a hardcover book to their credit. One niece is well known as a regular contributor to Catholic magazines; my daughter Deborah is an aspiring writer as is my son, Justin. One might say that it is in the genes.

"My first love was the ballet. I grew too tall (5'10") so I switched to acting, but I found that my ambition was bigger than my talent. When I stayed at home with the children I tried to write but was not successful. I kept trying off and on without success for the next twenty-five years.

"Finally, when I retired from one of my brainless jobs, I decided to give it one more try. I saw a job advertised in the *New York Times* for a receptionist at a literary agency, Writers House Inc. I applied, was hired, and (after a decent interval) sneaked one of my manuscripts into a pile going to an agent. The rest is my personal history. Dial Books bought *And Still the Turtle Watched*. Then, in quick succession, they contracted for five more books and St. Martin's Press bought my adult mystery, *Death in a Far Country* and gave me a two-book contract because they wanted a sequel. The moral of this story is: IF YOU CAN'T LICK THEM, JOIN THEM!"

* * *

Mac NAMARA, Desmond 1918-

PERSONAL: Born May 10, 1918, in Dublin, Ireland; son of Patrick and Teresa (a couturier; maiden name, Owens-MacBride) Mac Namara; married Priscilla Feare (a script reader), June 28, 1952; children: Oengus, Oisin. *Education:* Attended National College of Art, Dublin, and Trinity College, Dublin, 1938-41. *Politics:* "A socialist since the age of reason." *Religion:* "Born Catholic."

ADDRESSES: Home—1 Woodchurch Rd., London NW6 3PL, England.

CAREER: Stage designer, sculptor, and film animator. Also arts tutor for adult education programs.

AWARDS, HONORS: Purser traveling scholar, 1944.

WRITINGS:

A New Art of Papier Mache, Arco, 1963.
Puppetry, Arco, 1965.
Picture Framing: From Basic to Baroque, David & Charles, 1986.
De Valera, Chelsea House, 1988.
The Book of Intrusions, Dalkey Archive Press, 1994.

Literary critic, *New Statesman*.

WORK IN PROGRESS: A book on the history of picture framing.

SIDELIGHTS: Desmond Mac Namara told *CA:* "My lifelong concern is with the splendid and monumental absurdities squeezed out between layers of common sense, bigotry, science, and other forms of human endeavor.

"I am contemplating a comic novel on the gigantic Victorian academic dispute over ritual and/or gourmet cannibalism among the ancestors of the Breton, Welsh, Scottish, and Irish Celts. The research would be difficult; are the classical scholars trustworthy?"

MADENSKI, Melissa (Ann) 1949-

PERSONAL: Born August 31, 1949 in Portland, OR; daughter of Harold M. (in sales) and Florence (a homemaker; maiden name, Stavseth) Hegge; married Mark Madenski (a cabinetmaker), June 9, 1979 (died, 1987); children: Dylan, Hallie. *Education:* Portland State University, B.A., 1971; attended Breadloaf School of English M.A. Program, Middlebury College, 1990 and 1992. *Avocational interests:* Gardening, bicycling, hiking.

ADDRESSES: Home—9990 Slab Creek Rd., Neskowin, OR 97149.

CAREER: Clackamas and Oceanlake Elementary Schools, Lincoln City, OR, teacher, 1972-77; Neskowin Valley School, Neskowin, OR, language arts instructor, 1984-85; free-lance writer/editor. Teacher of writing workshops; teacher of English as a Second Language. Comanager in Bowsprit and Allegory bookshops, Lincoln City, and affiliated with Canyon Way Bookstore, Newport, OR, and Cafe Roma Books, Lincoln City, 1972-85. Intern at Northwest Writing Institute, Lewis and Clark College, Portland, OR, 1994—.

MEMBER: Society of Children's Book Writers.

AWARDS, HONORS: American Library Association Notable Book Award in social studies, 1991, for *Some of the Pieces*.

WRITINGS:

Some of the Pieces, illustrated by Deborah Kogan Ray, Little, Brown, 1991.

Contributor of non-fiction articles and essays to periodicals, including *Oregon Coast, Oregonian Daily, Practical Homeowner, Christian Science Monitor,* and *National Geographic Traveller.*

WORK IN PROGRESS: In My Mother's Garden, illustrated by Sandra Speidel, Little, Brown, publication expected 1995. Continued work on essays, collection of essays on travel; researching non-fiction for periodicals, including the effect of "natural" areas in urban settings and "restoration" projects in natural areas.

SIDELIGHTS: Melissa Madenski commented: "I didn't 'always want to be a writer.' When I was in grade school, I had to write at least ten versions of 'What I Did This Summer,' but beyond that I kept only a diary with the briefest of entries. I did, however, love to read above all else. I read when I was and wasn't supposed to. I read sitting in a chair, in bed, and while walking to school—until my mother, afraid I might get hit by a car, threatened to take my books away. Then I hid my book under my coat and began to read as soon as I was out of her sight. I was the only student in class to have my Scholastic book order delivered in a box or sack because of the number of titles. There was nothing I liked more than the cover of a new book that held the promise of taking me on some new adventure.

"Real life doesn't often fit into the confines of a book, thank heavens. But I think a story is a little like clay. You get to mold the details into something that makes a reader keep turning the pages to 'see what happens.' Some of those details really happened and some things may be made up, but what is important is that you put things together in a way that serves the story you're telling. So when people ask me if a story is true, I always feel slightly dishonest saying yes or no, because so much of truth is in fiction and so much of fiction can be in a true story that the division isn't always clear to me.

"Some people say it is important to write what you know. I know one author who says that's rubbish, that it's important to explore what you don't know. But I think the only rule to follow is to write what you're compelled to tell. Even if it's a story that's been told before, your view of the world will make it unique. I've never been good at giving advice. I think what has most often worked for me in pursuing anything is to do it, even when I'm tired, discouraged, and feeling like a failure. I get up every morning before my children, before the sun—and sometimes before the birds—because I'm compelled to tell stories, even if those words never reach anyone but my own family.

"The measure of a good story is that it can be read or told again and again and again. It simply becomes richer and more loved with each retelling."

BIOGRAPHICAL/CRITICAL SOURCES:

PERIODICALS

Booklist, October 15, 1991.
Kirkus Review, October 1, 1991.
Philadelphia Inquirer, February 9, 1992.

* * *

MAFHAM, Rod(ney Arthur) Preston
See PRESTON-MAFHAM, Rod(ney Arthur)

MAGEE, Doug 1947-

PERSONAL: Born January 24, 1947, in Rome, NY; son of Robert (in sales) and Ruth (a teacher; maiden name, Coe); married Mary Hedahl (an actor), March 17, 1991; children: Timothy Maxwell, Joseph Neilon. *Education:* Amherst College, B.A., 1969; Union Theological Seminary, M.Div., 1973. *Politics:* "Very far to the left." *Religion:* "Hmmm."

ADDRESSES: Home—309 East 108th St., No. 5A, New York, NY 10029. *Office*—1659 Lexington Ave., New York, NY 10029.

CAREER: Writer.

WRITINGS:

FOR CHILDREN

(And photographer) *Trucks You Can Count On,* Dodd, Mead, 1985.
(Author and photographer with Robert Newman) *All Aboard ABC,* Dutton, 1991.
(Author and photographer with Newman) *Let's Fly from A to Z,* Dutton, 1992.

NONFICTION

Slow Coming Dark: Interviews from Death Row, Pilgrim Press, 1980.
What Murder Leaves Behind: The Victim's Family, Dodd, Mead, 1983.

TELEPLAYS

Somebody Has to Shoot the Picture, HBO, 1990.
Conviction: The Kitty Dodds Story, CBS, 1993.

BIOGRAPHICAL/CRITICAL SOURCES:

PERIODICALS

Booklist, October 15, 1980, p. 289; April 1, 1985, p. 1121; October 1, 1990, p. 336; October 15, 1992, p. 435.
Bulletin of the Center for Children's Books, July-August, 1985; September, 1990, p. 12.
Choice, April, 1981, p. 1167.
Christian Science Monitor, March 30, 1981, p. 19.
Library Journal, October, 1980, p. 2100; June 1, 1983, p. 1152.
New York Review of Books, March 5, 1981, p. 6.
Publishers Weekly, May 13, 1983, p. 46; September 28, 1990, p. 100.
School Library Journal, May, 1985, p. 79; November, 1990, p. 96; November, 1992, p. 85.
Village Voice, March 1, 1981, p. 37; August 30, 1983, p. 40.

MAHOWALD, Mary Briody   1935-

PERSONAL: Born March 24, 1935, in Jamaica, NY; daughter of Thomas M. and Mae A. (Allen) Briody; married Anthony P. Mahowald (a professor), April 11, 1971; children: Maureen, Lisa, Michael. *Education:* St. Francis College, Brooklyn, NY, B.A. (magna cum laude), 1965; Marquette University, M.A., 1967, Ph.D., 1969. *Politics:* Democrat. *Religion:* Roman Catholic.

ADDRESSES: Home—5650 South Dorchester Ave., Chicago, IL 60637. *Office*—MC 2050, University of Chicago, 5841 South Maryland Ave., Chicago, IL 60037-1470.

CAREER: Schoolteacher in New York City, 1955-65; St. Joseph's College, Brooklyn, NY, instructor in philosophy, 1969-70; Villanova University, Villanova, PA, assistant professor of philosophy, 1970-72; Indiana University-Purdue University, Indianapolis, assistant professor, beginning in 1972, associate professor of philosophy, ending in 1982; Case Western Reserve University, Cleveland, OH, associate professor, 1982-89, professor of philosophy and biomedical ethics, 1989-90, Mather Visiting Professor, 1984-85, co-director of Center for Biomedical Ethics, 1985-88; University of Chicago, Chicago, IL, professor of medical ethics, 1990—, senior scholar at MacLean Center for Clinical Medical Ethics, 1990-92, assistant director of the center, 1992—. Philosophy Documentation Center, assistant editor, 1977-80; University Hospitals of Cleveland, director of Ethics Program, 1987-89; Oberlin College, visiting professor, 1988. Indiana Committee for the Humanities, member of executive subcommittee, 1979-82; U.S. Office of Technology Assessment, member of Advisory Panel on New Developments in Neuroscience, 1988-90; U.S. Department of Defense, member of Breast Cancer Integration Panel, 1993-94.

MEMBER: North American Society for Social Philosophy (division co-chairperson, 1981-94, copresident, 1995-97), American Philosophical Association, Indiana Philosophical Association (president, 1981-82).

AWARDS, HONORS: Grants from National Endowment for the Humanities, 1976 and 1978, American Philosophical Association, 1976, Armington Foundation for Values and Children, 1984 and 1988, and National Institutes of Health, 1992-95.

WRITINGS:

An Idealistic Pragmatism, Nijhoff (The Hague), 1972.
(Editor) *Philosophy of Woman: Classical to Current Concepts,* Hackett, 1978, 3rd edition, 1994.
Women and Children in Health Care: An Unequal Majority, Oxford University Press, 1993.

Contributor to books, including *New Directions in Ethics,* edited by J. P. DeMarco and R. M. Fox, Routedge and Kegan Paul, 1986; *Human Values in Critical Care Medicine,* edited by S. J. Youngner, Praeger, 1986; *Bioethics and the Fetus,* edited by J. M. Humber and R. A. Almeder, Humana Press, 1991; *Obstetrics: Psychological and Psychiatric Syndromes,* edited by P. J. O'Grady and M. Rosenthal, Elsevier Science Publishing, 1992; *Debates over Medical Authority: New Challenges in Biomedical Experimentation,* edited by R. Blank and A. Bonnicksen, Columbia University Press, 1992; *Dental Ethics,* edited by B. D. Weinstein, Lea & Febiger, 1993; and *Women and Prenatal Testing,* edited by K. H. Rothenberg and E. J. Thomson, Ohio State University Press, 1994. Contributor of more than a hundred articles and reviews to professional journals. Member of editorial board, "Social Philosophy Research Institute Book Series," 1990—. Assistant editor, *Philosopher's Index Retrospective Edition,* 1976-77; guest editor, *Journal of Social Philosophy,* 1986; special editor, *Clinical Research,* 1988; member of editorial board, *Philosophy in Context* and *Journal for Peace and Justice,* both 1988—, and *Hypatia,* 1991—.

WORK IN PROGRESS: Research on the impact of the human genome project on women.

SIDELIGHTS: Mary Briody Mahowald told *CA:* "I feel that the subtitle of my last book, *Women and Children in Health Care: An Unequal Majority,* expresses the motivation for much of my teaching, research, writing, and clinical work. It is a remedial emphasis that was triggered by experience and nurtured early, when I decided to gather together in one text, and in a course I was teaching, the views of well-known philosophers on women. What I found was that the majority of these views were inconsistent with the authors' concepts of (supposedly generic) 'man.' In health care, too, I find that women's experience and perspective are often ignored, and that children are often unacknowledged as developing moral agents in their own right."

*   *   *

MALZAHN, Manfred   1955-

PERSONAL: Born April 21, 1955, in Iserlohn, Germany; son of Eugen (in business) and Maria Herrmann (a homemaker) Malzahn; married Gabriele Gertrud

Leichtle (a singer), January 24, 1991; children: Philip, Patrick. *Education:* Attended University of the Ruhr, Bochum, Germany; University of Wuppertal, Germany, Ph.D., 1983. *Politics:* "Socialist skeptic." *Religion:* "None."

ADDRESSES: Home—Wuermtalstrasse 14 A, D-81375 Munich, Germany. *Office*—Department of Foreign Language and Literature, Chung Cheng University, Chiayi 62107, Taiwan, R.O.C.

CAREER: University of Edinburgh, Edinburgh, Scotland, foreign language assistant, 1985-88; University of Monastir, Kairouan, Tunisia, senior lecturer, 1988-89; University of Setif, Setif, Algeria, senior lecturer, 1990; University of Malawi, Zomba, senior lecturer, 1991-92; National Chung Cheng University, Chiayi, Taiwan, professor, 1993—.

MEMBER: Association for Scottish Literary Studies.

WRITINGS:

Aspects of Identity: The Contemporary Scottish Novel (1978-1981) As National Self-Expression, Peter Lang (Frankfurt am Main), 1984.
(Coauthor) *Instant Lessons: Materialien fuer den Konversationsunterricht,* Deutscher Akademischer Austanschdienst (Bonn, Germany), 1987.
Germany 1945-1949: A Source Book, Routledge (New York), 1991.
(Editor) *Chancellor College First Year Literature Anthology,* University of Malawi (Zomba), 1992.
(Translator) Albrecht Dihle, *Greek and Latin Literature of the Roman Empire,* Routledge, 1994.
Scots: Das Englisch der Schotten, Peter Rump (Bielefeld), 1994.

Contributor to books, including *The History of Scottish Literature: Volume 4, Twentieth Century,* University Press of Aberdeen, 1987; *Studies in Scottish Fiction: 1900-1950,* edited by Joachim Schwend, Peter Lang, 1990; and *A Break in the Clouds,* edited by Cynthia A. Stevens, National Library of Poetry (Owings Mills), 1993. Contributor of articles, reviews, and poetry in English, German, and Scots dialect to various literary publications, including *Southern Literary Journal, ScotLit,* and *Journal of Humanities.*

WORK IN PROGRESS: Intensivstation. Musikalisches Drama in sechzehn Szenen von Manfred Malzahn (Text) und Stefan Karpati (Musik), first performance planned in Munich, Germany.

SIDELIGHTS: Manfred Malzahn told *CA:* "I write in two languages—three, if you count Scots as separate from English. Teaching literature, I feel that I need to be able to practice what I preach, at least as a dabbler in all kinds of writing from poetry to fiction to history to songs. Main subject in all of them: what it means to be human, and to make the best of it."

BIOGRAPHICAL/CRITICAL SOURCES:

PERIODICALS

Books in Scotland, volume 15, 1984.
Scottish Literary Journal, supplement 23, 1985.
Studies in Scottish Literature, volume 20, 1985.
Times Literary Supplement, July 15, 1994.

*   *   *

MANFRED, Frederick (Feikema)   1912-1994
(Feike Feikema)

OBITUARY NOTICE—See index for *CA* sketch: Surname originally Feikema; legally changed to Manfred in 1952; born January 6, 1912, in Rock Township, Doon, IA; died of lymphoma, September 9, 1994, in Luverne, MN. Journalist and novelist. Perhaps best known for the five volume epic *The Buckskin Man Tales,* set in the nineteenth-century American West, Manfred's writing style has been described by critics as a mixture of history and "first-rate" fiction. After graduating from Calvin College in Grand Rapids, Michigan, Manfred began writing for the *Minneapolis Journal* in the late 1930s and *Modern Medicine* in 1942, before serving as writer-in-residence at colleges later in his career. His first novel, *The Golden Bowl* (1944), established Manfred's reputation as a storyteller and earned him a grant from the American Academy of Arts and Letters in 1945. It was soon after changing his name from Feikema to Manfred in 1952 that the author began his popular series *The Buckskin Man Tales.* The first book, *Lord Grizzly* (1954), focused on life in the American frontier, in a fictional land Manfred called Siouxland. Manfred is also the author of *Green Earth* (1977) and *Sons of Adam* (1980), and he had just finished an autobiographical novel, *The Wrath of Love,* at the time of his death.

OBITUARIES AND OTHER SOURCES:

BOOKS

Who's Who in America, 47th edition, Marquis, 1992.

PERIODICALS

Chicago Tribune, September 11, 1994, sec. 2, p. 6.

New York Times, September 9, 1994, p. D16.
Washington Post, September 13, 1994, p. B7.

* * *

MANKILLER, Wilma (Pearl) 1945-

PERSONAL: Born November 18, 1945, in Stilwell, OK; daughter of Charley and Clara Irene (Sitton) Mankiller; married Hector H. Olaya, November 13, 1963 (divorced, 1975); married Charlie Soap, October 13, 1986; children: (first marriage) Felicia Marie Olaya, Gina Irene Olaya. *Education:* Attended Skyline College, 1973, and San Francisco State College, 1973-75; Union for Experimenting Colleges and Universities, B.A., 1977; postgraduate study at University of Arkansas, 1979. *Politics:* Democrat. *Religion:* "Personal." *Avocational interests:* Reading.

ADDRESSES: Office—P.O. Box 948, Tahlequah, OK 74465-0948.

CAREER: Cherokee Nation, Tahlequah, OK, community development director, 1977-83, deputy chief, 1983-85, principal chief, 1985-95; writer. President of Inter-Tribal Council of Oklahoma; Oklahoma Academy for State Goals, 1985-90; Ms. Foundation for Women, member of board, 1987-94; Ford Foundation trustee, 1994. Member of National Congress of American Indians, 1994.

MEMBER: Cherokee County Democratic Women's Club, National Tribal Chairmen's Association, National Congress of American Indians.

AWARDS, HONORS: Donna Nigh First Lady Award, Oklahoma Commission for the Status of Women, 1985; American Leadership Award, Harvard University, 1986; inducted into the Oklahoma Women's Hall of Fame, 1986; John W. Gardner Leadership Award, 1988; honorary degree, Yale University, 1990; named to the Oklahoma Hall of Fame, 1994.

WRITINGS:

(With Michael Wallis) *Mankiller: A Chief and Her People* (autobiography), St. Martin's, 1993.
(Author of foreword) Marilou Awiakta, *Selu: Seeking the Corn-Mother's Wisdom,* Fulcrum, 1993.

Contributor of fiction to periodicals, including the story "Keeping Pace with the Rest of the World," in *Southern Exposure.*

WORK IN PROGRESS: Coediting *Readers Guide to History of Women in the United States,* to be published by Houghton-Mifflin.

SIDELIGHTS: In her book, *Mankiller: A Chief and Her People,* Wilma Mankiller relates her experiences as Principal Chief of the Cherokee Nation and provides a concise history of the Cherokee people. Written with Michael Wallis, author of *Route 66* and other books, *Mankiller* was published in 1993. *Publishers Weekly* contributor Phyllis Tickle termed the book a "spiritual biography," observing that it is "more concerned on its surface with the political than the spiritual; yet beneath its events and meetings and crises there runs a sense of rootedness and reverence we can recognize as Native American."

Mankiller begins with accounts from the Cherokee leader's childhood, the early part of which was spent in rural Oklahoma. Mankiller's family consisted of her Cherokee father, her mother, who was of Irish descent, and her ten brothers and sisters. When two continuous seasons of drought left her family's farm barren, Mankiller and her family were relocated to San Franciso with aid from the U.S. government. As Mankiller explained to Michele Wallace in *Ms.,* "We are a people with many, many social indicators of decline and an awful lot of problems, so in the fifties they decided to mainstream us, to try to take us away from the tribal landbase and the tribal culture, get us into the cities. It was supposed to be a better life."

Upon moving to California at age eleven, however, Mankiller experienced culture shock, exacerbated by poverty and racism. Her experiences led her to become active in the Native American rights movement in the 1960s. At the age of eighteen, Mankiller married Hector Olaya, and the couple had two daughters before their divorce in 1975. Mankiller had begun attending college in the early 1970s, and after her divorce she returned to Oklahoma to finish her degree at the Union for Experimenting Colleges and Universities.

In 1977, Mankiller secured a position as community development director of the Cherokee Nation. She then spearheaded various programs, including the creation of water systems and the rehabilitation of houses. Mankiller was elected Deputy Chief in 1983, and when Principal Chief Ross Swimmer resigned in 1985 to become director of the U.S. Bureau of Indian Affairs, Mankiller filled the vacancy. The leader did not feel that she had a mandate from her people, however, until she was elected Principal Chief in 1987.

Although her gender was at first an issue among male members of the tribe, Mankiller proved herself to be a capable leader. Historically, as Mankiller pointed out in *Ms.,* female leadership was common among Native Americans. "In fact . . . early historians referred to our tribal government as a petticoat government because of the strong role of women in the tribe. Then we adopted a lot of ugly things that were part of the non-Indian world and one of those things was sexism. . . . So in 1687 women enjoyed a prominent role, but in 1987 we found people questioning whether women should be in leadership positions anywhere in the tribe."

Neither a reservation nor a completely sovereign goverment, the Cherokee Nation is a unique entity. As chief, Mankiller oversaw a government representing approximately 70,000 people and controlling more than 45,000 acres of land in Oklahoma. As Mankiller recounts, the Cherokee originally inhabited the southeastern United States but were forced off their land by the federal government in 1848. In what became known as the Trail of Tears, more than four thousand Cherokee died as the tribe marched west.

In her book, Mankiller also addresses the more modern problems of the Cherokee Nation and describes how she worked to improve access to education, jobs, and heath care. "I'd like to see whole, healthy communities again," Mankiller told Wallace in *Ms,* "communities in which tribe members would have access to adequate health care, higher education if they want it, a decent place to live and a decent place to work, and a strong commitment to tribal language and culture."

In addition to her political accomplishments, Mankiller describes her personal triumphs as well. She has survived a kidney transplant, a car accident that left her in need of seventeen operations, and myasthenia gravis, which causes weakening of the muscles. The accounts of Mankiller's personal struggles and those of her people, critics have noted, combine to make *Mankiller* an inspiring work.

One reviewer, writing in *Library Journal,* stated that "as more Native American women are celebrated, it is hoped that many high-quality books like this one will appear." *Publishers Weekly* contributor Genevieve Stuttaford observed, "In this inspiring story, Mankiller offers herself as a valuable role model—for women as well as for Native Americans." Mankiller relinquished her role as Principal Chief in August of 1995 to concentrate on local issues in Oklahoma.

BIOGRAPHICAL/CRITICAL SOURCES:

BOOKS

Contemporary Newsmakers, Gale, 1986, p. 250.

Jackson, Guida M., *Women Who Ruled,* ABC-CLIO, 1990.
Mankiller, Wilma, and Michael Wallis, *Mankiller: A Chief and Her People,* St. Martin's, 1993.

PERIODICALS

Library Journal, November 15, 1993, p. 84.
Ms., January, 1988, p. 68; July/August, 1994, p. 59.
Publishers Weekly, October 18, 1993, p. 60; December 13, 1993, p. 30.*

—Sketch by Michelle Motowski

* * *

MANN, Judy 1943-

PERSONAL: Born December 24, 1943, in Washington, DC; daughter of Charles B. (a U.S. foreign aid official) and Margaretta W. (a teacher and artist) Warden; married Jack Mann (divorced, 1986); married Richard T. Starnes (a writer), September 24, 1989; children: (first marriage) Devin, Jeffrey, Katherine. *Education:* Attended Barnard College, 1960-64.

ADDRESSES: Home—1812 Susquehannock Dr., McLean, VA 22101. *Office—Washington Post,* 1150 15th St. NW, Washington, DC. *Agent*—Suzanne Gluck, International Creative Management, 40 West 57th St., New York, NY 10019.

CAREER: Washington Post, Washington, DC, columnist, 1972—. Gender Gap Farm (cattle farm), co-owner. Guest on radio and television talk shows, including *Good Morning America, Prime Time Live,* and *Inside Edition;* public speaker.

AWARDS, HONORS: Global Media Award, Population Institute, 1994; awards from National Women's Political Caucus, National Abortion Rights Action League, American Association of University Women, and Washington-Baltimore Newspaper Guild; D.Letters, Grinnell College.

WRITINGS:

Mann for All Seasons (columns), Mastermedia, 1990.
The Difference: Growing up Female in America, Warner Books, 1994.

Contributor to periodicals, including *Ms., Working Woman,* and *Reader's Digest.*

SIDELIGHTS: Judy Mann told *CA:* "I have been writing about women, families, politics, and gender conflicts for seventeen years. I have covered the women's movement as a journalist and lived it as a working mother. I have two sons and a daughter. It was my daughter's approaching adolescence four years ago that sparked my interest in doing a very personal investigation of the difference between boys and girls, how they are brought up and educated, and what parents can do to prevent girls from feeling like they are second best."

*   *   *

MANSFIELD, Howard   1957-

PERSONAL: Born June 14, 1957, in Huntington, NY; son of Pincus (an engineer) and Bernice (a homemaker; maiden name, Feldstein) Mansfield; married Sy Montgomery (a writer), September 26, 1987. *Education:* Syracuse University, B.A. (with honors), 1979. *Politics:* "Town Meetin' Time." *Religion:* Jewish. *Avocational interests:* "Rot. The great challenge of arresting rot and decay in an older New Hampshire house and a too-old car; the moral implications; the many lessons rot teaches: Nature goes her own way. Hang on."

ADDRESSES: Home and office—P.O. Box 127, Hancock, NH 03449. *Agent*—Christina Ward, P.O. Box 515, North Scituate, MA 02060.

CAREER: Full-time writer. Board member, *Monadnock Perspectives,* 1986—. Chair of Hancock Town Library board of trustees, 1994—.

MEMBER: Society for Commercial Archaeology.

AWARDS, HONORS: Gold Medal for Commentary, City and Regional Magazine Competition, William Allen White School of Journalism, 1985.

WRITINGS:

Cosmopolis: Yesterday's Cities of the Future, Rutgers Center for Urban Policy Research (New Brunswick, NJ), 1990.
In the Memory House, Fulcrum Publishing (Golden, CO), 1993.

Contributor of commentary and articles on history, architecture, and design to periodicals, including *New York Times, Washington Post, Boston Globe, Chicago Tribune, Los Angeles Times, Philadelphia Inquirer, Christian Science Monitor, American Heritage, Walking,* and *New England Monthly.*

WORK IN PROGRESS: Skylark: Three Inventors on the Wing from the Gold Rush to the Moon Landing.

SIDELIGHTS: Howard Mansfield is the author of two books that examine the landscape of American culture. The first, 1990's *Cosmopolis: Yesterday's Cities of the Future,* looks at the utopias depicted in World's Fairs, the cities envisioned by Italian Futurists, the City Beautiful, and the city of tomorrow. In addition to writing the text, Mansfield designed and conducted the photo research for *Cosmopolis,* which contains 143 illustrations.

Mansfield's next publication, 1993's *In the Memory House,* is a series of nonfiction essays that reflect on the voids left in the landscape as a result of America's progress and examines, according to the author, "how each generation reinvents history and chooses its own ancestors." In a world where highways and condominiums are commonplace, Mansfield writes, many people have forgotten, or never known, the joys of a simpler life and time. In his essay, "A Lost Spring," for example, Mansfield tells of an old man living in the two-hundred-year-old home of his childhood. Mansfield used to visit the man and listen to his stories of life in the house, which stands in the shadow of a maple tree. "The tree is what you look at first," Mansfield writes. "The house seems to be keeping the tree company."

Summers in the old house, the man told Mansfield, were very hot, but a plunge in the swimming hole, fed by a spring, brought cool relief. The author imagines the children "swimming there in summer twilight," as he passes the house and the tree, but laments that the spring was stopped up by engineers years ago, when the road was widened and a new bridge installed. Mansfield concludes: "And when I am away from this corner of New Hampshire, down among the landscape of haste—parking lot and highway, mall and condo—I look into the faces of my countrymen and I think of the plugged spring."

In the Memory House has garnered praise from many critics, among them Paul Gruchow, who wrote in *Hungry Mind Review:* "Now and then an idea suddenly bursts into flame, as if by spontaneous combustion. One instance is the recent explosion of American books about the idea of place. . . . But the best of them, the deepest, the widest-ranging, the most provocative and eloquent, is Howard Mansfield's *In the Memory House." New York Times Book Review* contributor Philip M. Isaacson also applauded Mansfield's essays, noting that "through the intensity of [Mansfield's] language, his pace and wit, the predisposed reader can take the leap into collective memory and even catch, with Mr. Mansfield, that damp sweet scent of the past. . . . Although we have yet to learn to face the true past, banking what we can of it in memory houses such as this wise and beautiful book may preserve it until a time in which the smell of wet hay, a restorative sense of our shared past, will replace lamentation, elegy or indifference."

Mansfield told *CA:* "Visitors to New England usually arrive with a lot of baggage. They are weighed down by a lifetime of Norman Rockwell and Currier and Ives. They want nostalgia and quaintness. *In the Memory House* is an attempt to see New England plain. I was looking for the contours of historical memory itself.

"Memory is a defining characteristic of New England—this great desire to mark the landscape with historical monuments, to crowd little museums full of small acts of homage, and to tell certain stories.

"Each essay in the book is about a moment of commemoration—or the failure to commemorate. At such moments, our aspirations are on full view. When we seek to honor something, we are staking a claim: This is us. In history, unlike heredity, we choose our ancestors.

"We have journeyed a long way, once ever so optimistically, and find ourselves far removed from the one-room schoolhouse and the swimming hole, from the horse car and elm-lined Main Street. We try nostalgia, elegy, jeremiad. All our efforts at recollection, and somewhere the past itself, are in the memory house."

BIOGRAPHICAL/CRITICAL SOURCES:

BOOKS

In the Memory House, Fulcrum Publishing, 1993.

PERIODICALS

Hungry Mind Review, winter, 1993-94, p. 20.
New York Times Book Review, November 21, 1993, p. 21.

*   *   *

MARCUS, Millicent   1946-

PERSONAL: Born September 23, 1946, in Baltimore, MD; daughter of Sydney and Marion (a laboratory technician; maiden name, Tunick) Marcus; married Robert Hill (a professor of French), June, 1976; children: Jacob, Lucy. *Education:* Cornell University, B.A. (magna cum laude), 1968; Yale University, Ph.D., 1974. *Politics:* "Democrat, yellow dog variety." *Religion:* Jewish.

ADDRESSES: Home—3815 Avenue G, Austin, TX 78751. *Office*—Department of French and Italian, MUS 2.114, University of Texas at Austin, Austin, TX 78712-1197.

CAREER: University of Texas at Austin, instructor, 1973-74, assistant professor, 1974-80, associate professor, 1980-87, professor of Italian, 1987—. University of Colorado, assistant director of Study Abroad Program, Siena, Italy, 1979; Syracuse University, visiting professor in Syracuse in Italy Program, 1986-87; University of Pennsylvania and Bryn Mawr College, visiting professor at Italian Studies Summer Institute in Florence, 1987-89, 1991, 1993.

MEMBER: Modern Language Association of America, American Boccaccio Association (regional representative), Phi Beta Kappa.

AWARDS, HONORS: Grants from Rockefeller Foundation, 1978, and American Council of Learned Societies, 1981-82; Howard R. Marraro Prize from Modern Language Association of America, 1988; Guggenheim fellow, 1989-90; Getty senior research grant, 1993-94.

WRITINGS:

Italian Film in the Light of Neorealism, Princeton University Press, 1986.
Filmmaking by the Book: Italian Cinema and Literary Adaptation, Johns Hopkins University Press, 1993.

Work represented in anthologies, including *Perspectives on Fellini,* edited by Peter Bondanella and Cristina Degli Esposti, Macmillan, 1993; and *Cinema Voices: Francesco Rosi,* Flicks Books, 1994. Contributor of about forty articles and reviews to scholarly journals. Member of editorial board, *Italica, Forum Italicum,* and *Texas Studies in Language and Literature.*

WORK IN PROGRESS: Research for the film section of *Italy 1919.*

*   *   *

MARSELLA, Anne (Francesca)   1964-

PERSONAL: Born August 12, 1964, in Fresno, CA; daughter of Gary (a stockbroker) and Barbara (an artist; maiden name, Erro) Marsella. *Education:* Mills College, B.A., 1986; University of Paris VIII, M.A., 1990. *Religion:* "Ex-Catholic."

ADDRESSES: Home—44 rue Mathis, 75019 Paris,

France. *Agent*—Kim Witherspoon, 157 West 57th St., New York, NY 10019.

CAREER: University of Paris, Dauphine, professor of English, 1992-93; University of Paris II, Assas, professor of English, 1993-94; University of Cergy, Pontoise, lecturer in English, 1994—.

AWARDS, HONORS: Elmer Holmes Bobst Award for Emerging Writers, New York University, 1994, for *The Lost and Found and Other Stories.*

WRITINGS:

The Lost and Found and Other Stories (short stories), New York University Press (New York), 1994.

Editor for Organization for Economic Cooperation and Development, Paris, 1992—.

WORK IN PROGRESS: An epistolary novel; translating *The Lost and Found and Other Stories* into French.

SIDELIGHTS: After earning her master's degree in French literature from the University of Paris, Anne Marsella decided to make her home in the city, deeming Paris the perfect backdrop for her career as a writer. Her stories, some of which form the 1994 collection *The Lost and Found and Other Stories,* often feature strangers in foreign lands, and Marsella, as an American in Paris, knows firsthand the feelings of displacement. Paris, in fact, is often the setting for her stories. The Paris she describes, however, is not the city commonly portrayed in travelogues; instead, Marsella told *CA,* she writes of "a Paris unknown to most. I set out to explore the lives of the city's immigrants, the displaced souls who inhabit its penurious quarters."

Many of the characters Marsella created for *The Lost and Found* are from Third World countries or impoverished backgrounds. According to *New York Times Book Review* critic Daniel Woodrell, Marsella's characters "live on one of those streets not pointed out to tourists, and lead the sort of lives most of us don't know much about." The main character in the title story, for instance, is a Mexican woman working in Paris as a clapper for a television game show, *The Lost and Found Show.* Her life, too, is a journey through the lost and found, as she prays to St. Jude, the patron saint of lost causes, to help her find her long-lost father, a jewel thief.

Another of the stories, "Miss Carmen," portrays a Chilean woman and her awe over the vast wealth she observes as a housekeeper in California's San Joaquin Valley. Carmen enjoys her luxurious surroundings until she falls in love with a ranch foreman, who reminds her of the men back home. Her love is unrequited, and, for the despondent Carmen, the valley suddenly seems barren. Other stories in Marsella's collection feature men and women from countries such as Istanbul, Nigeria, and Morocco, all of whom are displaced to another land.

Marsella earned the Elmer Holmes Bobst Award for Emerging Writers for *The Lost and Found* and has been praised by critics for her adept handling of dialect and character. Woodrell, in his *New York Times Book Review* assessment of the collection opined: "Marsella's writing is precise and has the rare ability to be both oratorical and intimate. . . . The range and diversity Anne Marsella displays, stunning for a first collection, give convincing proof of a fresh talent emerging with full, and impressive, power."

Marsella told *CA:* "Writing from the position of a foreigner allows me a great amount of psychological as well as linguistic freedom. I write with at least two languages, sometimes three or four. The English I hear everyday is colored with accent and unusual syntax. This is often what I hear when I write. I hear the voices of foreigners. It seems to me that in living outside a society that defines you, you are freer to discover other identities, to get into the heads of others. This obviously can be done at home as well; however, the experience of living abroad has been very enriching for me and my writing. I enjoy being a foreigner; it changes not only how I view the world but how I hear."

BIOGRAPHICAL/CRITICAL SOURCES:

PERIODICALS

New York Times Book Review, June 5, 1994, p. 44.

*   *   *

MARSHALL, Charles F(rancis)   1915-

PERSONAL: Born October 28, 1915, in Hoboken, NJ; son of Karl (a knitwear manufacturer) and Barbara (a homemaker; maiden name, Kromer) Marshall; married Marian Margaretta Schmidt (died July 21, 1976); married Mary E. Carmody Strathman (a registered nurse), December 28, 1984; children: Charles Francis, Jr., John F., Karla F. Marshall Waid, James F., Richard F., Thomas F., Marian Marshall Larson, William F.; (stepchildren) Robert G. Strathman, John D. Strathman, Carol A. Greene. *Education:*

Columbia University, B.A., 1937; attended U.S. Army Military Intelligence School. *Politics:* Conservative independent. *Religion:* Roman Catholic. *Avocational interests:* Politics and history.

ADDRESSES: Home—42-13 243rd St., Douglaston, NY 11363.

CAREER: Partner in a knitwear manufacturing business, Ridgewood, NY. *Military service:* U.S. Army, 1942-46; served in Italy, France, Germany, and Austria.

WRITINGS:

Discovering the Rommel Murder, Stackpole, 1994.

Columnist, *Beachhead News,* during World War II.

SIDELIGHTS: Charles F. Marshall told *CA:* "I have been fascinated by Field Marshal Erwin Rommel since my basic training days, when Rommel was engaged with the British in North Africa. In the course of my intelligence work, I interrogated Mrs. Rommel. I was intrigued by her and her son, and we developed a fine rapport. This led to months of research in the course of which I interviewed, among others, the field marshal's aide, his friends, his doctor, and the historian he had appointed to be his official biographer. The greatest help to me was a friendship with General Hans Speidel, Rommel's chief of staff in Normandy.

"*Discovering the Rommel Murder* is a composite of these sources, plus Rommel's letters to his wife from the battlefield and my own war journals. The original manuscript for this book was written in 1946. Although publisher after publisher professed a fascination with the story, I could find no publisher at that time because, in the words of one, they could not publish a 'piece which is essentially a glorification of a German military leader, even though his reputation for tactical ability and chivalry in the field did spread through the ranks of his own enemies.'"

*　　　*　　　*

MARTEL, Yann 1963-

PERSONAL: Born June 25, 1963, in Salamanca, Spain; son of Emile (a civil servant) and Nicole (a civil servant; maiden name, Perron) Martel. *Education:* Attended Trent University, 1981-84 and 1986-87; Concordia University, B.A., 1985. *Politics:* "Social politics: left wing. Economic politics: con-

fused. Overall politics: moderately nationalist—don't want to be an American." *Religion:* Atheist.

ADDRESSES: Agent—Jan Whitford, Lucinda Vardey Agency, 10 St. Mary St., Suite 510, Toronto, Ontario M4Y 1P9, Canada.

CAREER: "Odd jobs at odd places at odd times." Has worked as library worker, tree planter, dishwasher, security guard, and parking lot attendant.

MEMBER: PEN Canada.

AWARDS, HONORS: Journey Prize for the best short story in Canada, 1991, for "The Facts behind the Helsinki Roccamatios"; National Magazine Award for best short story, 1992, for "The Time I Heard the Private Donald J. Rankin String Concerto with One Discordant Violin, by the American Composer John Morton"; Air Canada Award, 1993, for "Bright Young New Thing."

WRITINGS:

The Facts behind the Helsinki Roccamatios and Other Stories, Knopf, 1993.

WORK IN PROGRESS: Life of Imilac (tentative title), a novel, completion expected in 1995.

SIDELIGHTS: Yann Martel told *CA:* "I write because it's the only way I know how to create, and to create is to live. I am thirty-one years old. I am in the infancy of my art."

*　　　*　　　*

MARTIN, Harold Harber 1910-1994

OBITUARY NOTICE—See index for *CA* sketch: Born September 17, 1910, in Commerce, GA; died of respiratory failure, July 10, 1994, in Atlanta, GA. Journalist. A columnist for the *Atlanta Constitution* for thirty-five years, Martin was best known for his in-depth war reporting for the *Saturday Evening Post,* where he covered three wars as a correspondent during the period from 1946 through 1969 (Martin had joined the United States Marine Corps during World War II, and was awarded the Bronze Star for his service in the Pacific theatre). In 1956, Martin was coauthor, with General Matthew Ridgway, of *Soldier: The Memoirs of Matthew B. Ridgway.* Martin also penned 1973's *Ralph McGill, Reporter,* which earned the Lillian Smith Award. His other books include *Cats, Dogs, Children, and Other Small Creatures* (1980), *A Good Man, A Great*

Dream: D. W. Brooks of Gold Kist (1982), and *Atlanta and Environs: A Chronicle of Its People and Events, Years of Change and Challenge, 1940-1976,* (1987).

OBITUARIES AND OTHER SOURCES:

BOOKS

Who's Who in America, 46th edition, Marquis, 1990.

PERIODICALS

Washington Post, July 12, 1994, p. B6.

* * *

MASON, James (Neville) 1909-1984

PERSONAL: Born May 15, 1909, in Huddersfield, Yorkshire, England; died of a heart attack, July 27, 1984, in Lausanne, Switzerland; buried in Vevey, Switzerland; son of John (a textile merchant) and Mabel Hattersley (Gaunt) Mason; married Pamela Kellino (an actress and television personality), February, 1941 (marriage dissolved, 1965); married Clarissa Kaye (an actress), August 13, 1971; children: (first marriage) Portland Allen, Alexander Morgan. *Education:* Attended Marlborough College, 1923-28; Peterhouse College, Cambridge University, B.A., 1931, M.A., 1943. *Avocational interests:* Art, politics, trends, travel, and gardening.

CAREER: Actor in theater, films, and television, 1931-84. First stage appearance in *The Rascal,* 1931; other plays include *Gallows Glorious,* 1933, *Twelfth Night,* 1933, *The Cherry Orchard,* 1933, *Henry VIII,* 1933, *Measure for Measure,* 1933 and 1954, *Love for Love,* 1933, *Queen of Scots,* 1934, *Parnell,* 1936, *The Road to Rome,* 1937, *A Man Who Has Nothing,* 1937, *Bonnet over the Windmill,* 1937, *The Heart Was Not Burned,* 1938, *Sixth Floor,* 1939, *Divorce for Chrystabel,* 1940, *Jupiter Laughs,* 1941, *Bathsheba,* 1947, *Oedipus Rex,* 1954, *Paul and Constantine,* 1957, *Mid-Summer,* 1958, and *Faith Healer,* 1979.

First film appearance in *Late Extra,* 1935; other films include *Prison Breaker,* 1936, *Fire over England,* 1936, *High Command,* 1937, *Catch as Catch Can,* 1937, *The Return of the Scarlet Pimpernel,* 1938, (and producer with Pamela Kellino and Roy Kellino) *I Met a Murderer,* 1939, *This Man Is Dangerous,* 1939, *Mill on the Floss,* 1939, *Hatter's Castle,* 1941, *Secret Mission,* 1942, *The Night Has Eyes,* 1942, *The Bells Go Down,* 1942, *Thunder*

Rock, 1942, *The Man in Grey,* 1943, *They Met in the Dark,* 1943, *Candlelight in Algeria,* 1944, *Fanny by Gaslight,* 1944, *Hotel Reserve,* 1944, *A Place of One's Own,* 1944, *They Were Sisters,* 1945, *The Wicked Lady,* 1945, *The Seventh Veil,* 1945, *Odd Man Out,* 1947, *The Upturned Glass,* 1947, *Caught,* 1948, *Madame Bovary,* 1949, *East Side, West Side,* 1949, *One-Way Street,* 1950, *A Lady Possessed,* 1951, *Pandora and the Flying Dutchman,* 1951, *The Desert Fox,* 1951, *Five Fingers,* 1952, *Botany Bay,* 1952, *The Prisoner of Zenda,* 1952, *Desert Rats,* 1953, *The Story of Three Loves,* 1953, *Julius Caesar,* 1953, *Prince Valiant,* 1954, *A Star Is Born,* 1954, *Twenty Thousand Leagues under the Sea,* 1954, *Forever Darling,* 1955, *The Man Between,* 1955, (and producer) *Bigger Than Life,* 1956, *Island in the Sun,* 1956, *Cry Terror,* 1958, *The Decks Ran Red,* 1958, *North by Northwest,* 1959, *Journey to the Center of the Earth,* 1959, *The Marriage Go Round,* 1961, *Lolita,* 1962, *The Fall of the Roman Empire,* 1964, *The Pumpkin Eater,* 1964, *Lord Jim,* 1965, *Genghis Khan,* 1965, *The Blue Max,* 1966, *Georgy Girl,* 1966, *The Deadly Affair,* 1967, *Stranger in the House,* 1967, *Duffy,* 1968, *The Seagull,* 1968, *Mayerling,* 1969, *Spring and Port Wine,* 1969, *Cold Sweat,* 1970, *Age of Consent,* 1970, *Kill,* 1971, *Bad Man's River,* 1971, *Child's Play,* 1972, *The Last of Sheila,* 1973, *The Mackintosh Man,* 1973, *Frankenstein: The True Story,* 1973, *The Autobiography of a Princess,* 1973, *11 Harrowhouse,* 1973, *Mandingo,* 1975, *Great Expectations,* 1975, *Heaven Can Wait,* 1978, *Bloodline,* 1979, *The Passage,* 1979, *Ffolkes,* 1980, *A Burning Man,* 1981, *Evil under the Sun,* 1981, *The Verdict,* 1982, *Yellowbeard,* 1983, and *The Shooting Party,* 1984.

AWARDS, HONORS: Voted Britain's top box-office star, 1944-47; won Great Britain's first National Motion Picture Award, 1946; Academy Award nomination, best actor, 1954, for *A Star Is Born;* Academy Award nominations, best supporting actor, 1966, for *Georgy Girl,* and 1982, for *The Verdict.*

WRITINGS:

(With Pamela Kellino) *I Met a Murderer* (screenplay; based on a story by Kellino), Grand National, 1939.

(With first wife, Pamela Mason; and illustrator) *The Cats in Our Lives,* Current Books, 1949.

(Editor with P. Mason; and illustrator) *Favorite Cat Stories of Pamela and James Mason,* J. Messner, 1956.

(And illustrator) *Before I Forget* (autobiography), Hamish Hamilton, 1981.

SIDELIGHTS: British-born actor James Mason's career on stage and screen spanned over fifty years. During that time he gifted film audiences in particular with several distinguished performances, garnering Academy Award nominations for his roles in *A Star Is Born, Georgy Girl,* and *The Verdict.* He was adept at playing either villains or tragically flawed heroes, and while he also found himself in some lesser quality films, the London *Times* in 1984 eulogized him upon his death as being able to "lift the poorest material just as he could enrich the best." Motion picture fans might also remember Mason from such productions as *The Man in Grey, The Seventh Veil, Odd Man Out, Julius Caesar, Twenty Thousand Leagues under the Sea, North by Northwest, Lolita,* and *Heaven Can Wait.*

Mason's interest in acting began while attending Cambridge University, where he performed in a few school productions while pursuing a degree in architecture. His graduation coincided with the early years of the Great Depression, and he found it easier to get acting jobs than architectural assignments. His stage debut was in a 1931 production of *The Rascal;* he received rave reviews and went on to do several of William Shakespeare's plays during the early 1930s. Though Mason continued with occasional stage work during much of his career, 1935 marked his entrance into motion pictures. His first was *Late Extra,* in which he portrayed a reporter. Mason next starred in some low-budget British films of the type that have acquired the name "quota quickies." The vehicle which really brought him to popularity with British movie viewers was 1939's *I Met a Murderer;* international stardom came with 1943's *The Man in Grey.*

In the late 1940s Mason and his first wife, the former Pamela Kellino, moved from Great Britain to Hollywood, California. There he became a part of the American film industry, starring in motion pictures such as *The Desert Fox* and *Bigger Than Life.* Also while in the United States, he and Pamela co-authored two books on the subject of their shared interest in cats, *The Cats in Our Lives* and *Favorite Cat Stories of Pamela and James Mason.* The actor also illustrated both books, with what John Beecroft in the *New York Herald Tribune Weekly Book Review* hailed as "remarkably fine cat pictures." *The Cats in Our Lives* was praised as "most engaging" by Carl Van Vechten in the *New York Times,* who went on to note that the chapters, which alternated between husband and wife, "harmonize agreeably."

Toward the end of his life, Mason penned an autobiography, *Before I Forget,* published in 1981.

Like his cat books, he illustrated this as well. *British Book News* contributor Roger Manvell particularly praised Mason's "entertaining sketches of film personalities." Philip French, writing in the London *Observer,* asserted that while the book is not particularly revealing about his marriages, "the real interest" of *Before I Forget* "resides in the account of his acting career."

BIOGRAPHICAL/CRITICAL SOURCES:

BOOKS

Mason, James, *Before I Forget,* Hamish Hamilton, 1981.

PERIODICALS

British Book News, January, 1982, p. 48.
New York Herald Tribune Weekly Book Review, April 17, 1949, p. 4.
New York Times, April 10, 1949, p. 6.
Observer (London), September 6, 1981, p. 28.

OBITUARIES:

PERIODICALS

Chicago Tribune, July 28, 1984.
Los Angeles Times, July 28, 1984.
New York Times, July 28, 1984.
Times (London), July 28, 1984.
Washington Post, July 28, 1984.*

*   *   *

MASUD
See CHOUDHURY, Masudul Alam

*   *   *

MATRANGA, Frances Carfi   1922-

PERSONAL: Born May 18, 1922, in North Tarrytown, NY; daughter of Joseph (a contractor) and Nellie (Corallo) Carfi; married Philip Matranga, Sr. (a driver for Anchor Motors), November 2, 1941; children: Philip, Jr., Paul, Peter, Francine. *Education:* Voice lessons for light opera with Maestro Leon Ardin at Carnegie Hall, New York City, 1941-42. *Politics:* Republican. *Religion:* Christian. *Avocational interests:* "Reading! (And not just fiction. I LOVE to read.)"

ADDRESSES: Home and office—1600 Harmony Dr., Port Charlotte, FL 33952-2703.

CAREER: Freelance writer. Co-founder, writers' workshops, Port Charlotte, FL, 1975-83.

MEMBER: Society of Children's Book Writers and Illustrators.

AWARDS, HONORS: Runner-up, CBS-TV Scriptwriting Competition, 1959; first prize, New York Writers Guild Fiction Contest, 1960, for "Death Trap"; honorable mention, National Writers Club fiction contest, 1975, for "Fourthborn"; honorable mention, National Writers Club fiction contest, 1976, for "That's My Mama!"; second place for fiction, Evangelical Press Association Convention, 1980, for "The Dare"; also recipient of two prizes and four honor certificates from the annual *Writer's Digest* international competitions.

WRITINGS:

Land of Shadows, Manor Books, 1977.
Summer Magic, Dell, 1979.
Destiny in Rome, Dell, 1979.
Angel Face, Barbour Books, 1994.

Land of Shadows, Summer Magic, and *Destiny in Rome* have been translated into six different languages.

"NINA CRISTINA MYSTERY" SERIES

The Secret behind the Blue Door, Baker Books, 1981.
The Mysterious Prowler, Victor Books, 1984.
The Forgotten Treasure, Victor Books, 1986.
The Mystery of the Missing Will, Victor Books, 1986.
The Big Top Mystery, Victor Books, 1987.

FOR CHILDREN

Follow the Leader, Concordia, 1982.
The Perfect Friend, Concordia, 1985.
The Contest, Concordia, 1986.
One Step at a Time, Concordia, 1987.

PICTURE BOOKS

My Book of Prayers, illustrated by Vic Mitchell, Standard Publishing, 1985.
I'm Glad I'm Me, illustrated by Joanne (Jodi) McCallum, Standard Publishing, 1991.

OTHER

Author/illustrator of two activity books, Standard Publishing, 1983. Contributor of stories and poems to anthologies for children. Also contributor to more than three hundred periodicals, including *Mystery Digest, Cricket, Junior Scholastic, Christian Life, Popular Psychology,* and *Woman's World.*

WORK IN PROGRESS: "Sammy's Visit to Heaven," an article about a sixteen-year-old's extraordinary spiritual experience; two children's books: *Pixie Dinkerdoo and the Lollipop Kitten* and *Marjorie's Revenge.*

SIDELIGHTS: "Ever since I was little," Frances Carfi Matranga commented, "I loved hearing stories, and books fascinated me. My mother was a terrific storyteller, and I pestered her constantly. By the time I was eight, I was devouring book after book. I would take out ten books at a time from my hometown Warner Library, using my mother's card as well as my own. How I loved that beautiful library! It became my second home. I would read my borrowed books one after another, and even sat by my bedroom window reading in the moonlight when I was supposed to be sleeping. I wore eyeglasses at the time and ever since, and one day my mom told me I was born with the marks of glasses on my nose. Hmm . . . interesting.

"My first literary acceptance came in 1952, fifteen dollars from *True Story Magazine* for a humorous but embarrassing incident that happened when I was a teenager. I got conked on the nose while singing on stage before an audience. The other performer— a girl dressed as a boy—had a small basket of fruit hanging by its handle on the curved end of the cane held over her shoulder. She misjudged the distance between us as she turned away from me, and *bingo*— my poor nose! With scarlet face, I managed to finish my song.

"I have worked hard as a freelance writer and it has been uphill all the way. You really have to love your work to stick to it, for the money as a freelancer is nothing to brag about and you're alone so much of the time. The good Lord gave me several talents, and although writing and designing greeting cards was more profitable for me, writing fiction suits me best. You don't wear eyeglasses singing on stage, but writers and spectacles go together. Born with the marks of eyeglasses on my nose? Hmm. . . .

"My advice to aspiring writers is to read read read, especially the kind of literature you would like to write, whether fiction or nonfiction. If reading isn't important to you, I doubt you have what it takes to be a writer. But if you enjoy reading and are set on writing, study the monthly *Writer's Digest* and/or *The Writer.* Join a writer's critique group, if possible. Don't get discouraged. Remember, it took me ten years to make my first sale and only because I persevered. Why did I persevere? My whole heart was in it, that's why, and I believed in myself. Don't give up your dream too easily."

MAURER, Warren R(ichard) 1929-

PERSONAL: Born May 13, 1929, in Hegins, PA; son of William R. (a coal miner) and Edna S. (a homemaker; maiden name, Schmeltz) Maurer; married Jadwiga Graubard (a university professor), July 7, 1956; children: Stephen M., Elizabeth T. Maurer Powers. Education: Franklin and Marshall College, B.A., 1951; attended University of Munich, 1953-54; University of Chicago, M.A., 1957; University of California, Berkeley, Ph.D., 1966.

ADDRESSES: Home—2202 Westdale Rd., Lawrence, KS 66049. Office—Department of Germanic Languages and Literatures, 2080 Wescoe Hall, University of Kansas, Lawrence, KS 66045-2127.

CAREER: University of California, Berkeley, acting instructor, 1964-65; Indiana University—Bloomington, assistant professor, 1965-68; University of Kansas, Lawrence, associate professor, 1968-73, professor of Germanic languages and literature, 1973—, department chair, 1969-72. Lecturer at colleges and universities. Radio Free Europe, employee in Germany. Military service: U.S. Army, Military Intelligence; served in Germany.

WRITINGS:

The Naturalist Image of German Literature: A Study of the German Naturalists' Appraisal of Their Literary Heritage, Fink Verlag (Munich), 1972.
(Coeditor) Rilke: The Alchemy of Alienation, Regents Press of Kansas (Lawrence), 1980.
Gerhart Hauptmann, G. K. Hall (Boston), 1982.
Understanding Gerhart Hauptmann, University of South Carolina Press (Columbia), 1992.
Gerhart Hauptmann: A Century of Criticism (monograph), Camden Press, 1994.

Work represented in anthologies, including The Fortunes of German Writers in America, edited by Wolfgang Elfe, James Hardin, and Gunther Holst, University of South Carolina Press, 1992. Contributor of articles and reviews to German studies journals.

* * *

McCALL, Nathan 1955(?)-

PERSONAL: Born c. 1955; son of a factory worker; divorced twice; children: Monroe, Ian, Maya. Education: Norfolk State University, B.A.

ADDRESSES: Office—Washington Post, 1150 15th St. NW, Washington, DC 20017.

CAREER: Virginia Pilot/Ledger Star, reporter; Atlanta Constitution, Atlanta, GA, reporter, until 1989; Washington Post, Washington DC, reporter, 1989—.

WRITINGS:

Makes Me Wanna Holler: A Young Black Man in America (autobiography), Random House, 1994.

ADAPTATIONS: The film rights to Makes Me Wanna Holler have been purchased by Columbia Pictures, to be filmed by John Singleton.

SIDELIGHTS: "Sooner or later, every generation must find its voice," wrote Henry Louis Gates, Jr., in the New Yorker. "It may be that ours belongs to Nathan McCall." Gates was one of the many reviewers who praised McCall's 1994 autobiography, Makes Me Wanna Holler: A Young Black Man in America. In it, McCall describes his transformation from an angry and self-destructive criminal to a successful Washington Post writer. He tells of his upbringing in a middle-class section of Portsmouth, Virginia, the son of strict but caring working-class parents. Though he is a good student, McCall is picked on and beaten by white classmates at his mostly white junior high school; searching for protection in numbers, he falls in with a group of tough black boys. "Alone I was afraid of the world and insecure," he writes in Makes Me Wanna Holler. "But I felt cockier and surer of myself when hanging with my boys. . . . There was no fear of standing out, feeling vulnerable, exiled and exposed. That was a comfort even my family couldn't provide."

Throughout high school, McCall and his "boys" regularly engage in gang fights, burglaries, and "training" girls—that is, gang raping them. In 1975 he receives a sentence of four weekends in jail for the attempted murder of another black youth; while on probation for that crime, however, he holds up a McDonalds—an act that earns him a sentence of twelve years in jail. It is there that, working as the inmate librarian, McCall discovers a book about another angry black man who ends up in jail: Richard Wright's Native Son. "I identified strongly with Bigger [Thomas, Native Son's protagonist]," he recalled in Makes Me Wanna Holler. "The book's portrait of Bigger captured all those conflicting feelings—restless anger, hopelessness, a tough facade among blacks and a deep-seated fear of whites—that I'd sensed in myself but was unable to express."

That an author could describe so clearly the things McCall himself had been feeling amazes him and leads him to other books, including The Autobiography of Malcolm X. Slowly, he begins to see himself not as a "bad nigger" but as "an intelligent-thinking human being." When released on parole after just three years, McCall enters the journalism program at Norfolk State University; after graduation, he obtains positions with first the *Virginian Pilot/Ledger Star* and then the *Atlanta Journal-Constitution* before being approached by the *Washington Post*. Though he has established an impressive record, McCall lies on his application where it asks, "Have you ever been convicted of a felony?" Though the *Post* initially rejects him, he is finally hired in 1989.

One of the first things to strike critics was the power of McCall's narrative voice. "He is a mesmerizing storyteller," praised Gates, "whose prose is richly inflected with the vernacular of his time and place. In fact, his colloquial style is so unshowy and unforced that his mastery is easy to overlook." *Washington Post Book World* reviewer Paul Ruffins concurred: "Without indulging in exhibitionism, McCall here strips himself naked in an honest confession. He may have a past he regrets, but *Holler* is a strong downpayment on his redemption."

Many reviewers drew a comparison between McCall and such authors as Malcolm X, Eldridge Cleaver, and Richard Wright—and, more directly, between McCall and the character of Bigger Thomas from Wright's *Native Son*. "In some respects," Gates wrote, "I'd venture that the young McCall was closer to Bigger Thomas than Wright was." In fact, contended Ruffins, "McCall's evolution from angry thug to edgy black professional is much more relevant to most people's lives" than those previous authors. "Malcolm X, Eldridge Cleaver and George Jackson all discovered religion or revolution, extraordinary truths that transformed their lives. In prison McCall finds his salvation in smaller ideas like, 'Work hard,' and 'Think before you act.'"

Still, some critics found *Makes Me Wanna Holler* to contain its share of flaws. Adam Hochschild, writing in the *New York Times Book Review,* felt "mounting exasperation at the way Mr. McCall blames the white world for almost everything he suffers. . . . At the three newspapers Mr. McCall has worked at, in the endless clashes with white colleagues or bosses that he describes, he is always in the right, and the problem is always the other person's racism." However, according to Hochschild, "Mr. McCall's anger goes far beyond race, for he seldom gives a shred of credence to the point of view of anyone else, white or black." He concluded: "This fury becomes a substitute for any real analysis of why his early life

turned out as it did, and of what can be done to save a generation of young black men from the same fate."

Hochschild was not the only reviewer to point out McCall's inability to explain the reason for his errancy; other critics, though, found it one of the book's strengths rather than weaknesses. "What sets [*Makes Me Wanna Holler*] apart from similar works by less talented writers is [its] refusal to oversimplify or offer easy prescriptions for the underclass dilemma," commented Jack E. White in *Time*. Gates, too, found McCall's ambiguity "a sign of the fierce honesty that infuses the entire book; he's willing to address the question without pretending to have an answer to it."

In the end, McCall maintains he does not feel a part of mainstream society. "At times I feel suspended in a kind of netherworld, belonging fully neither to the streets nor to the establishment," he wrote in *Makes Me Wanna Holler*. Such dislocation applies to his position at the *Post* as well, according to *Detroit News* reviewer Ruth Coughlin: "He says it's a place where he doesn't feel comfortable, even though a good thing about being in the mainstream is that it brought him into contact 'with a lot of good whites who made it a lot more complicated for me to just dismiss all white people. I'm there on the rolls, I'm signed up in the personnel office . . . but I don't feel that I belong.'"

BIOGRAPHICAL/CRITICAL SOURCES:

BOOKS

McCall, Nathan, *Makes Me Wanna Holler: A Young Black Man in America,* Random House, 1994.

PERIODICALS

At Random, winter, 1994, pp. 45-51.
Detroit News, February 16, 1994, p. C1.
New Yorker, March 7, 1994, pp. 94-99.
New York Times Book Review, February 27, 1994, p. 11-12.
Publishers Weekly, January 3, 1994, p. 64.
Time, March 7, 1994, p. 68.
Washington Post Book World, February 6, 1994, p. 2.*

—*Sketch by Brandon Trenz*

*　　*　　*

McCARTNEY, (James) Paul 1942-

PERSONAL: Born June 18, 1942, in Liverpool, England; son of James (a musician and in cotton sales) and Mary (a nurse and midwife) McCartney; married Linda Eastman (a photographer and musician), 1969; children: Heather (stepdaughter), Mary, Stella, James. *Education:* Attended the Liverpool Institute. *Avocational interests:* Sailing, painting, carpentry, organic farming.

ADDRESSES: Home—Sussex, England; and Scotland. *Office*—MPL Communications Ltd., 1 Soho Sq., London W1V 6BQ, England.

CAREER: Member of musical group, the Quarrymen, 1957-59; toured Scotland with them as the Silver Beetles, 1960; played with group in Hamburg, Germany, beginning 1960; group made first major appearance as the Beatles near Liverpool, England, 1960; performed with Beatles in countries including the United Kingdom, the Netherlands, Sweden, France, Denmark, Hong Kong, Australia, New Zealand, Canada, Germany, Italy, Japan, the Philippines, and the United States, 1963-66, continued to record with the Beatles until they disbanded in 1970; solo performer, 1970—; formed MPL group of companies, London, England, 1970—; performer with group, Wings, 1971-81, toured United Kingdom, Europe, Australia, United States, and Canada; also toured United Kingdom, Europe, Japan, Brazil, Canada, and the United States during 1989-90.

Appeared in films, including *A Hard Day's Night,* United Artists (UA), 1964; *Help!,* UA, 1965; *Yellow Submarine,* UA, 1968; *Let It Be,* UA, 1970; *Rockshow,* 1981; *Give My Regards to Broad Street,* 20th Century-Fox, 1984; and *Get Back,* Seven Arts, 1991. Has also appeared on television programs, including the *Ed Sullivan Show,* CBS, 1964, *Magical Mystery Tour,* 1967, and *Paul McCartney up Close,* MTV, 1993.

AWARDS, HONORS: Member of the Order of the British Empire, 1965; several Ivor Novello awards, including International Achievement, 1980, International Hit of the Year Award (with Stevie Wonder), for "Ebony and Ivory," 1982, and for outstanding contribution to music, 1989; named Freeman of the City of Liverpool, 1984; British Academy of Film and Television Award for best animated film, 1984, for *Rupert and the Frog Song;* numerous Grammy awards, from the National Academy of Recording Arts and Sciences, including Lifetime Achievement Award, 1990; P.R.S. special award for unique achievement in popular music, 1990.

WRITINGS:

SONGBOOKS; WITH JOHN LENNON

(With George Harrison) *Golden Beatles,* Campbell Connelly, 1966.

The Music of Lennon and McCartney: Second Omnibus of Popular Songs, Hansen Publications, 1969.
Great Songs of Lennon and McCartney, edited by Milton Okun, Quadrangle, 1973.
Fifty Great Songs, P. J. Foss, 1973.
Fifty Hit Songs, P. J. Foss, 1974.
The Beatles for Classical Guitar, Music Sales Corp., 1974.
The Beatles Lyrics, introduction by Jimmy Savile, Futura, 1975.
The Beatles Lyrics Illustrated, introduction by Richard Brautigan, Dell, 1975.

SCREENPLAYS; AND COMPOSER

Give My Regards to Broad Street, Twentieth Century-Fox, 1984.

Also author of screenplay and composer for the animated film *Rupert and the Frog Song,* 1984.

RECORD ALBUMS; LYRICS AND MUSIC WITH JOHN LENNON, RECORDED WITH THE BEATLES

Please Please Me, Capitol, 1963.
With the Beatles, Capitol, 1963.
A Hard Day's Night (soundtrack), Capitol, 1964.
Beatles for Sale, Capitol, 1964.
Help! (soundtrack), Capitol, 1965.
Rubber Soul, Capitol, 1965.
Revolver, Capitol, 1966.
Sergeant Pepper's Lonely Hearts Club Band, Capitol, 1967.
Magical Mystery Tour (soundtrack), Capitol, 1967.
The Beatles (also known as *The White Album*), Capitol, 1968.
Yellow Submarine (soundtrack), Capitol, 1969.
Abbey Road, Capitol, 1969.
Let It Be (soundtrack), Capitol, 1970.

RECORD ALBUMS; LYRICS AND MUSIC; RECORDED WITH WINGS

Ram, Capitol, 1971.
Wild Life, Capitol, 1971.
Red Rose Speedway, Capitol, 1973.
Band on the Run, Capitol, 1973.
Venus and Mars, Capitol, 1975.
Wings at the Speed of Sound, Capitol, 1976.
Wings over America, Capitol, 1976.
London Town, Capitol, 1978.
Wings Greatest, Capitol, 1978.
Back to the Egg, Capitol, 1979.

RECORD ALBUMS; LYRICS AND MUSIC AS A SOLO ARTIST, EXCEPT AS NOTED

McCartney, Capitol, 1970.

McCartney II, Capitol, 1980.

(Two songs, including "Ebony and Ivory," composed and recorded with Stevie Wonder) *Tug of War,* Capitol, 1982.

("Say, Say, Say" and "The Man" composed and recorded with Michael Jackson) *Pipes of Peace,* Capitol, 1983.

Give My Regards to Broad Street (soundtrack), Capitol, 1984.

Press to Play, Capitol, 1986.

All the Best (greatest hits), Capitol, 1987.

CHOBA B CCCP, Capitol, 1988.

(Some songs composed with Elvis Costello) *Flowers in the Dirt,* Capitol, 1989.

Tripping the Live Fantastic, Capitol, 1990.

Unplugged: The Official Bootleg, Capitol, 1991.

(Composed with Carl Davis) *Paul McCartney's Liverpool Oratorio,* Capitol, 1991.

(Some songs composed with Costello) *Off the Ground,* Capitol, 1993.

Paul Is Live, Capitol, 1993.

Also composer and performer (together with Youth, as the group "The Fireman") of *Strawberries Oceans Ships Forest,* 1994. Also composer or co-composer of songs recorded by other artists, including Elvis Costello's "Veronica" and "Playboy into a Man."

FILM AND TELEVISION SCORES

The Family Way (film), Warner Bros., 1966.

(With others) *Live and Let Die* (film), United Artists, 1973.

The Zoo Gang (television series), ATV, 1974.

Give My Regards to Broad Street (film), Twentieth Century-Fox, 1984.

(With others) *Spies Like Us* (film), Warner Bros., 1985.

Also composer of scores for the television series *Thingumybob,* 1968, and the animated film *Rupert and the Frog Song,* 1984; co-composer of the film *Twice in a Lifetime,* 1984; composer of soundtracks for other animated shorts.

SIDELIGHTS: Paul McCartney's contributions to the development of popular music in the latter part of the twentieth century are considered monumental by many popular music critics. As one of four members and virtually half of the songwriting talent behind the Beatles, he helped revolutionize rock music during the 1960s. With the late John Lennon, McCartney is responsible for such pop standards as "She Loves You," "I Want to Hold Your Hand," "Help!," "Yesterday," and "Eleanor Rigby." The pair—as part of the famed group—also produced classic albums such as *Sergeant Pepper's Lonely Hearts Club Band* and *Abbey Road.* After the Beatles broke up in 1970, McCartney continued his hit-making ways. Either as a solo artist or with his subsequent band Wings, he climbed the charts with songs such as "Maybe I'm Amazed," "My Love," "Band on the Run," "Jet," "My Brave Face," and 1993's "Hope of Deliverance." McCartney has also composed music for other recording artists. He has created film scores and has even written two screenplays—the best known of these being 1984's *Give My Regards to Broad Street.*

In 1991 McCartney tried his hand at classical music, collaborating with Carl Davis to create *The Liverpool Oratorio.* His critical acclaim as a solo artist has not always lived up to that during his Beatles heyday, but as Cathy Booth reported in *Time,* "McCartney is the most successful songwriter in the history of the U.S. record industry, having penned thirty-two No. 1 hits. . . . McCartney has racked up more gold and platinum disks (seventy-five) than any other performer in history. His song *Yesterday* is the most recorded ever, with more than two thousand versions." Guy Garcia, reviewing a 1993 television concert performance in the same periodical, concluded that "McCartney has never rocked harder."

McCartney was born June 18, 1942, in Liverpool, England. He inherited his aptitude for music from his father, who, though he made his living in cotton sales, also played the piano and the trumpet. Like many young English boys of his generation, McCartney was influenced by the rock and roll sounds coming from America during the 1950s. As an adolescent, McCartney attended the Liverpool Institute, where he was acquainted with fellow student and future Beatle George Harrison. While he was still a teenager, he met John Lennon at a camp, and the two struck up a fast friendship, quickly beginning the musical collaboration that would later become legendary. During the late 1950s, McCartney and Lennon founded a group; they invited Harrison to join as well. One of the first of many names this band would carry was the Quarrymen. Another title they tried out was the Silver Beetles, a tribute to rock pioneer Buddy Holly's group, the Crickets. This name soon evolved into the Beatles.

During the early 1960s McCartney, Lennon, Harrison—and other band members Stu Sutcliffe and Pete Best—played a series of successful club dates in Hamburg, Germany. They had returned to Liverpool and were fairly popular on the club scene there when they were discovered by Brian Epstein, who became their manager. Sutcliffe had already left the band, and Epstein suggested the replacement of Best by another drummer, Ringo Starr. By 1963 the Beatles were the most popular rock and roll group in England. The following year they began to win over U.S. listeners; by the time McCartney and his colleagues made their first celebrated appearance on Ed Sullivan's television variety show, the Beatles were monopolizing the top spots on the American pop charts.

McCartney and the Beatles were not just a case of phenomenal musical success, however. They were a cultural phenomenon as well, a part of the change in sensibilities that took place during the 1960s. Russel Nye explained in his book *The Unembarrassed Muse: The Popular Arts in America:* "While the Beatles' audience might be preponderantly pubescent, at the same time their musical ideas attracted and influenced serious, sophisticated, professional musicians. A substantial part of their popularity among the young was perhaps more sociological than musical. . . . Their exuberant vitality, their delicate handling of sentimentality, and their real lyrical gifts offered something new and fresh to popular music. At the same time, their topical, carefully-coded lyrics, with concealed references to sex, drugs, and rebellion, captivated restless and uncertain youth everywhere." The Beatles continued in their popularity, generally increasing the musical and lyrical complexity of their songs, until the group broke up in 1970.

During the course of the Beatles' existence, they also made some successful and critically acclaimed films. Their first, *A Hard Day's Night,* was released in 1964. Though put together quickly and relatively inexpensively, audiences loved it and critics were for the most part pleasantly surprised by the film's quality. Many lauded the comedic acting talent of the four musicians, but Jonathan Cott in *Ramparts* found deeper meaning in the motion picture: "*A Hard Day's Night* combines radical innocence and religious revelation, inviting ecstasy and salvation to that soul [poet William Butler] Yeats wrote about: 'self-delighting, self-appeasing, self-affrighting'; whose 'own sweet will is Heaven's will.'" In 1969 McCartney and the other Beatles lent their voices and music to an animated film, *The Yellow Submarine.* Writing about the film in *Icons of Popular Culture,* Spencer C. Bennett declared that the Beatles were "creating a revolution in the format of the cartoon." He opined further that "the band explores the sense of celebration through fantasy without attempting to paraphrase the soap opera atmosphere of Walt Disney."

The main importance of the Beatles, however, lay in their music. And, though George Harrison contrib-

uted a few of his own compositions to the group's catalogue, the major part of the band's repertoire came from the songwriting team of Lennon and McCartney. The personality differences between these two men made their music special. Most analysts of their work feel that Lennon brought in a hard-edged radicalism that on its own was too strange for most fans to enjoy, while McCartney was responsible for the more sentimental and professionally polished aspect of the pair's product. It was these same personality differences, however, that were a major factor in the break-up of the Beatles in 1970. As a solo artist, McCartney has, of course, penned his own songs. He has also collaborated with other musicians, including Stevie Wonder and Elvis Costello. But as he confessed to Booth: "It would be mad to think I'd written with anyone better since John. He was a one-off, very special guy."

After the Beatles broke up, McCartney quickly released an eponymous album. It was a popular and critical success, spawning the hit song, "Maybe I'm Amazed." Hubert Saal, reviewing *McCartney* in *Newsweek,* observed that "what's extra special about the record is the incredible richness of melody, the tastefulness and wit of the lyrics and the expressive range of McCartney's voice." T. E. Kalem in *Time* was not as enthralled as Saal, but conceded that "the new album is good McCartney—clever, varied, full of humor."

Despite the triumph of his first solo effort, however, McCartney quickly formed a new band, Wings, which lasted approximately ten years. He also performed and recorded with his wife, Linda, who was a member of Wings and whose musical collaboration with McCartney has long outlasted that group. McCartney's luck with Wings was uneven; one of the high points of his work with the band was the album *Band on the Run,* which included both the title hit and the popular single, "Jet." This release was hailed as a "triumph" in *Melody Maker* and prompted Noel Coppage in *Stereo Review* to remark that McCartney "seems the ex-Beatle most likely to become an *ex*-ex-Beatle, to surmount the aftermath. Paul not only has much greater vocal range . . . than the others but is turning out to have rangier vision about arrangements also—and he has the gift of ambiguity."

A few years after Wings disbanded McCartney tried his hand at screenwriting. He wrote, composed the score, and acted in the 1984 film, *Give My Regards to Broad Street.* Although McCartney plays himself in the film and some of the scenes are based on reality, the story is fictional. It revolves around a missing master tape for a new McCartney album; suspects in the theft include an ex-convict McCartney has recently hired to work for him. Ringo Starr appears in *Give My Regards to Broad Street,* as does Linda McCartney. Though the movie was neither a commercial nor critical success, *Rolling Stone* contributor Christopher Connelly stated that some scenes, particularly McCartney's musical performances, "are quite likable. . . . *Tug of War's* 'Ballroom Dancing' gets a first-class raveup treatment." In the same year that *Give My Regards to Broad Street* was released, another McCartney screenwriting effort was available as well. He wrote and composed the score for *Rupert and the Frog Song,* which, though not well known, garnered an award for best animated film in 1984.

After a well-received concert tour in 1989 and 1990, McCartney took his career in yet another new direction. His native Liverpool's Royal Philharmonic asked him to help commemorate its one hundred and fiftieth year. The result was his collaboration with Carl Davis on what Booth described as "a ninety-minute choral epic called *Paul McCartney's Liverpool Oratorio.*" The work met with somewhat lukewarm critical response, but Andrew Porter in the *New Yorker* observed that "McCartney . . . can write tunes—he wrote 'Yesterday' and 'Eleanor Rigby'—and he sets words well. Davis in theatre, film, and dance scores has shown himself an able composer. . . . I rather enjoyed their honestly communicative oratorio." Porter went on to relate that the motto of McCartney's alma mater, the Liverpool Institute—"Not for ourselves alone but for the whole world are we born"—"set to strong, memorable chorale-like phrases, opens the work and recurs as an ennobling refrain." McCartney continues to be involved with the Liverpool Institute as well, and is helping to raise money for the school's performing arts curriculum.

McCartney's latter-day efforts in the realm of popular music have drawn an increasingly friendlier response from critics. *Flowers in the Dirt,* the album McCartney released in 1989, included a hit single, "My Brave Face," that he wrote with new-wave rocker Elvis Costello. David Fricke, discussing *Flowers in the Dirt* in *Rolling Stone,* called it McCartney's "most critically acclaimed" effort "in years." Parke Puterbaugh, reviewing McCartney's 1993 album *Off the Ground* in the same periodical, asserted that it "contains some fine songs and sustains a guardedly optimistic mood that conveys a faith in the future." Regarding *Off the Ground*'s first single, "Hope of Deliverance," Puterbaugh added that it "is one of those perfect little tunes McCartney

plucks from his songwriter's subconscious like a pearl from a shell." For his part, as McCartney told Booth, "I'd rather be remembered as a musician than a celebrity."

BIOGRAPHICAL/CRITICAL SOURCES:

BOOKS

Contemporary Literary Criticism, Gale, Volume 12, 1980, pp. 353-85; Volume 35, 1985, pp. 277-94.
Fishwick, Marshall, and Ray B. Browne, editors, *Icons of Popular Culture,* Bowling Green University Press, 1970.
Gambaccini, Paul, *Paul McCartney in His Own Words,* Flash, 1976.
Nye, Russel, *The Unembarrassed Muse: The Popular Arts in America,* Dial, 1970.
Tremlett, George, *The Paul McCartney Story,* White Lion, 1976.

PERIODICALS

Chicago Tribune, October 26, 1984.
Entertainment Weekly, March 4, 1994, p. 14.
Los Angeles Times, October 26, 1984.
Melody Maker, May 31, 1975, p. 22.
Newsweek, April 20, 1970, p. 95.
New Yorker, December 23, 1991, p. 98.
New York Times, October 26, 1984.
Ramparts, October, 1965.
Rolling Stone, December 6, 1984, p. 57; June 15, 1989, p. 40; February 8, 1990, p. 42; February 18, 1993, p. 56.
Stereo Review, March, 1974, pp. 88-89.
Time, April 20, 1970, p. 57; June 8, 1992, pp. 84-86; February 8, 1993, pp. 72, 74, 78.*

—*Sketch by Elizabeth Wenning*

*   *   *

McCLENDON, Lise (Webb) 1952-

PERSONAL: Born February 8, 1952, in Carmel, CA; daughter of John H. (a college professor) and Betty M. McClendon; married Kipp B. Webb (a cardiologist). *Education:* University of Nebraska, Lincoln, B.A., 1974; University of Missouri—Kansas City, M.A., 1981.

ADDRESSES: Home—Billings, MT. *Agent*—Kimberley Cameron, Reece Halsey Agency, 8733 Sunset Blvd., Suite 101, Los Angeles, CA 90069.

CAREER: Writer.

MEMBER: Mystery Writers of America, Sisters in Crime, Montana Authors Coalition.

WRITINGS:

The Bluejay Shaman, Walker and Co., 1994.

WORK IN PROGRESS: Another "Alix Thorssen" mystery; *Ticker* (tentative title), a medical thriller.

*   *   *

McCLINTICK, David   1940-

PERSONAL: Born April 29, 1940, in Hays, KS; son of Jay Dean (an executive) and Dorothy (Sturges) McClintick; married Judith Ludlam (a music educator), June 30, 1968; children: Joanna Katherine. *Education:* Harvard University, B.A. (cum laude), 1962. *Avocational interests:* Music.

ADDRESSES: Agent—Amanda Urban, International Creative Management, 40 West 57th St., New York, NY 10019.

CAREER: Wall Street Journal, New York City, staff writer and investigative reporter, 1968-79; freelance writer, 1979—. *Military service:* U.S. Army, Intelligence Branch, 1964-68; became first lieutenant.

MEMBER: Authors Guild, Authors League of America, National Academy of Recording Arts and Sciences, Harvard Club of New York City.

AWARDS, HONORS: Grammy Award, best album text, Academy of Recording Arts and Sciences, 1980; National Book Award finalist, and *Los Angeles Times* Book Prize, both 1982, for *Indecent Exposure; Indecent Exposure* was named one of ten "indispensable" books on the subject of business; Edgar Allan Poe special award, Mystery Writers of America; distinguished alumni award, Columbia University graduate school of journalism; three Pulitzer Prize nominations.

WRITINGS:

Stealing from the Rich: The Home-Stake Oil Swindle, M. Evans, 1977, Morrow/Quill, 1983.
Indecent Exposure: A True Story of Hollywood and Wall Street, Morrow (New York), 1982.
Swordfish: A True Story of Ambition, Savagery, and Betrayal, Pantheon (New York), 1993.

Contributor to periodicals, including *Esquire, Vanity Fair,* the *New York Times,* and the *Washington Post.*

WORK IN PROGRESS: A biography of Frank Sinatra.

SIDELIGHTS: David McClintick honed his writing skills with eleven years of investigative reporting at the *Wall Street Journal.* He then used his investigative and writing abilities to create three nonfiction books. McClintick's first book, *Stealing from the Rich: The Home-Stake Oil Swindle,* revolves around the Robert Trippet investment scandal. Trippet developed a company that was supposed to pull oil from abandoned wells. He enticed investors with high interest rates, then paid off the initial investors with money received from newer investors. As Rudy Maxa wrote in the *Washington Post,* "McClintick walks us through the company's history chronologically, describing the fine net Trippet wove." *Stealing from the Rich,* Maxa concluded, is an "important" book.

McClintick's second book, *Indecent Exposure: A True Story of Hollywood and Wall Street,* became a national bestseller. In it the author details the story of Columbia Studios president David Begelman, who was discovered to have forged signatures on checks. Begelman eventually pled no contest to a grand theft charge. Because of the many corporate notables named in the book, *Indecent Exposure* received a good deal of pre-publication publicity. In a *Washington Post* article, Curt Suplee interviewed McClintick about the storm surrounding his book. McClintick explained his motivation for writing the story: "If there had been *only* a Begelman scandal, there would have been no book. . . . It suddenly came to me—the crucial insight—that what I had on my hands was not just a scandal, but well beyond, [a tale of] corporate blood-spilling, family alliances that go back five decades split asunder, psychological warfare, brutality and violence in the board room."

A National Book Award finalist and recipient of a *Los Angeles Times* Book Prize in 1982, *Indecent Exposure* was popular with readers and critics alike. In his *New York Times* review, Christopher Lehmann-Haupt commented that McClintick "manages to make us care about it all. He makes us care by means of the detail that he lavishes on the drama. . . . We care because of the sharpness with which the heroes and villains are drawn." Writing in the *Times Literary Supplement,* Philip French remarked that "this book offers revealing, and often startling, insights into the operations of Hollywood today, into the way studios are affected by their position within conglomerates, how the news media (many of them owned by the same conglomerates) cover show business, and how, after that brief heady period of artistic independence which filmmakers enjoyed in the 1960s, the hard-faced businessmen with an undefined flair and little interest in anything but money, power and influence, are in charge again."

In a *Publishers Weekly* interview with Charles Trueheart, McClintick commented about *Indecent Exposure:* "It's amazing . . . how many people have asked me, 'Is it fiction or nonfiction?' When a book is about Hollywood there's a tendency to think that it has to be a novel. People don't think of Hollywood as attached to the real world, and in many ways, of course, it's not."

In 1993, McClintick published *Swordfish: A True Story of Ambition, Savagery and Betrayal,* detailing an early 1980s U.S. Drug Enforcement Agency (DEA) sting operation in Miami, Florida, nicknamed Operation Swordfish. The operation's principle player was Robert Darias, the frontman for a DEA-run money laundering organization, Dean International. Darias began a professional relationship with Marlene Navarro, a beautiful, French-educated woman who worked as the director of Columbian drug lord Carlos Jader Alvarez's North American business. Aware of the danger he would be in if things went sour, Darias tape recorded every conversation with both criminals and DEA agents; when the operation was eventually aborted, Darias used the tapes to protect himself from both entities.

Though they found Darias's tapes to be the centerpiece of the book, most critics felt McClintick hadn't edited his material very judiciously. "Readers should be prepared to absorb page after page of transcribed dialogue," warned *New York Times Book Review* contributor Robert Stone. "Eventually the ratio of detail to significance becomes unsatisfying." Elson was more blunt: "McClintick . . . uses the transcripts of those conversations in such numbing detail that he seemingly ran out of pages to conclude the narrative properly." Jones concluded, however, that "'Swordfish' is still a chilling yarn."

Newsweek's Malcolm Jones, Jr., wrote: "Thanks to Darias's paranoid foresight . . . [McClintick] is able to spin a wonderfully seedy, double-edged variation on the old saw about no honor among thieves," adding "McClintick is a born storyteller, and his book is a great spy saga." *Time*'s John Elson also praised McClintick's subject matter: "The chronicle of the federal drug bust known as Operation Swordfish . . . reads like an episode of *Miami Vice* scripted by John le Carre."

BIOGRAPHICAL/CRITICAL SOURCES:

PERIODICALS

Los Angeles Times Book Review, August 15, 1982, p. 4; October 31, 1982.
Nation, September 18, 1982, pp. 245-47.
Newsweek, May 24, 1993, pp. 62-63.
New York Review of Books, September 23, 1982, p. 6.
New York Times, July 3, 1982; August 3, 1982, p. 23; August 9, 1982.
New York Times Book Review, August 22, 1982, p. 7; May 30, 1993, p. 3.
Publishers Weekly, August 27, 1982; June 3, 1988.
Time, September 27, 1982; May 17, 1993.
Times Literary Supplement, April 29, 1983, p. 429.
Washington Post, December 30, 1977; July 27, 1982, p. C1; August 24, 1982.

*　　*　　*

McCORMICK, Anita Louise　1957-

PERSONAL: Born November 22, 1957, in Huntington, WV; daughter of Robert Miller (an electronics technician) and Wanda Elouise (a homemaker; maiden name, Humphrey) McCormick. *Politics:* Independent. *Religion:* Christian. *Avocational interests:* Shortwave and ham radio, painting, drawing, gardening, cats.

ADDRESSES: Home—1332 Tenth Ave., Huntington, WV 25701.

CAREER: Writer. Freelance copy editor for TAB/McGraw-Hill, 1992—.

MEMBER: International Dark-Sky Association, Radio New York International, A*C*E* Radio Club.

WRITINGS:

Shortwave Radio Listening for Beginners, TAB/McGraw-Hill, 1993.
Space Exploration, Lucent Books, 1993.
Vanishing Wetlands, Lucent Books, 1994.
The Shortwave Listener's Q & A Book, TAB/McGraw-Hill, 1994.

Contributor to periodicals, including *Buzzworm, Country Woman, Grit, Listen, Mature Living,* and *Moose.*

SIDELIGHTS: A shortwave radio listener for over twenty years, Anita Louise McCormick drew on her expertise while writing the instructional book *Short-*

wave Radio Listening for Beginners. The volume discusses many aspects connected to shortwave listening, including tips on purchasing equipment, and also profiles some of the popular stations that broadcast from countries around the world. A reviewer in *Popular Communications* found *Shortwave Radio Listening for Beginners* "a highly useful reference book for any shortwave monitor." In *Booklist,* John Mort described the volume as an "excellent primer." McCormick is also the author of *Space Exploration,* which addresses the various concerns of America's space program.

McCormick told *CA:* "Even as a small child I was always interested in writing. When I was about five years old, I started making up stories. When I was about fifteen years old, I tried submitting my work to various general-interest magazines but had no luck. When I was in my mid-twenties I decided to give writing another try. I subscribed to *Writer's Digest,* joined their book club, and made use of all the 'how-to' books on writing for publication that the local library had to offer. In 1987 I sold my first short article. The pay wasn't much, but at least I could finally say that I was a published writer. From that point, I submitted short pieces about whatever I thought would stand a chance of getting published.

"I'd been an avid radio hobbyist ever since I was twelve years old, so I cranked out quite a few articles on how easy it is for the average non-technical person to get involved in long-distance AM and shortwave (international) listening. While I was writing these articles I hoped to eventually write a book that would show how easy it is to get involved in shortwave listening. In 1992, my dream came true. I was given a contract at TAB/McGraw-Hill, which released *Shortwave Radio Listening for Beginners* in 1993.

"My advice to new writers: Write about something you're interested in, let your enthusiasm show through in your writing, and DON'T GIVE UP!"

BIOGRAPHICAL/CRITICAL SOURCES:

PERIODICALS

Booklist, May 15, 1993.
Monitoring Times, June, 1993.
Popular Communications, December, 1993, October, 1994.

*   *   *

McDONOUGH, James R(ichard)   1946-

PERSONAL: Born August 4, 1946, in New York, NY; son of Eugene Patrick (in the U.S. Army) and Lucy (a homemaker; maiden name, Buonomano) McDonough; married Patricia Diane McKenzie (a homemaker), June 8, 1969; children: James, Michael, Matthew. *Education:* Attended Brooklyn Polytechnic Institute, 1964-65; U.S. Military Academy, West Point, B.S. (distinguished graduate), 1969; Massachusetts Institute of Technology, M.S., 1974; U.S. Army Advanced Studies Fellow, 1986-88.

ADDRESSES: Office—HHC, 2nd Battalion, 41st Infantry, 2nd Armored Division, Ft. Hood, TX 76546.

CAREER: U.S. Army, lieutenant colonel and battalion commander, has served as ranger, combat infantryman, platoon leader, company commander; served in Vietnam; intelligence assignments in Korea and Europe; has worked for U.S. State Department and Defense Nuclear Agency. U.S. Military Academy at West Point, professor of political science, 1975-78; writer.

MEMBER: U.S. Army War College (fellow), Association of the United States Army, Phi Kappa Phi.

AWARDS, HONORS: Purple Heart; three Bronze Star Medals for Valor; Combat Infantryman's Badge; four Army Commendation medals; three Meritorious Service medals; four Army Achievement medals; Ranger Tab; Paratrooper Wings; U.S.M.A. welterweight boxing champion, 1968 and 1969; Mickey Marius Award for outstanding boxer in U.S.M.A. class of 1969.

WRITINGS:

National Compulsory Service, U.S. Military Academy (West Point, NY), 1977.
Text on International Relations, U.S. Military Academy, 1977.
Platoon Leader, Presidio (Novato, CA), 1985.
The Defense of Hill 781: An Allegory of Modern Mechanized Combat, Presidio, 1988.
The Limits of Glory: A Novel of Waterloo, Presidio, 1991.

Author, "Reflections on Being a Platoon Leader" in *Marine Corps Gazette.*

SIDELIGHTS: James R. McDonough is a highly decorated U.S. Army officer who has focused his literary efforts on tales of the battlefield. After graduating from the U.S. Military Academy (U.S.M.A.) at West Point, McDonough served in combat in Vietnam, then returned to the United States and enrolled at the Massachusetts Institute of

Technology. He earned his master's degree in political science in 1974 and soon began teaching at the U.S. Military Academy. In 1977 the U.S.M.A. published his first books, *National Compulsory Service* and *Text on International Relations.*

Since then, McDonough, a lieutenant colonel at Fort Hood, Texas, has written three books. *Platoon Leader* recounts his days leading troops in the Vietnam war zone. "Given the author's strong military background," wrote Frank McAdams in the *Los Angeles Times,* "much of the book is steeped in tactics, strategy and the usual 'Nam jargon." In a *Washington Post Book World* review, Josiah Bunting called McDonough's work "taut, pokerfaced, unadorned." Bunting assessed McDonough's primary focus in *Platoon Leader* as "here is the war, here we are, assigned to fight in it. Let me describe how we made the best of what we were ordered to do." Bunting contended: "No book by a professional American soldier has done it so well."

McDonough followed *Platoon Leader* with *The Defense of Hill 781: An Allegory of Modern Mechanized Combat,* an instructional tale pitting a dead Army officer and his phantom troops against Soviet-armed opponents. Following this work, McDonough wrote *The Limits of Glory: A Novel of Waterloo,* which focuses on the great nineteenth century battle between Napoleon's forces and the British. Although some critics pointed to flaws in *The Limits of Glory,* *Library Journal* contributor C. Christopher Pavek acknowledged McDonough's "obvious knowledge of the battle and his understanding of its political and personal ramifications."

BIOGRAPHICAL/CRITICAL SOURCES:

PERIODICALS

Library Journal, September 1, 1991, p. 231.
Los Angeles Times, July 31, 1985.
Publishers Weekly, May 6, 1988, p. 100; August 9, 1991, p. 45.
Washington Post Book World, August 4, 1985, pp. 1-2.

* * *

McLOUGHLIN, Leslie J.   1935-

PERSONAL: Born February 24, 1935, in Ormskirk, Lancashire, England; son of Peter and Elizabeth McLoughlin; married, wife's name Christine, July 27, 1963; children: one son, one daughter. *Education:* Attended Victoria University of Manchester, University of Leeds, and University of London.

Avocational interests: Travel, reading, European languages, tennis.

ADDRESSES: Agent—c/o St. Martin's Press, 175 Fifth Ave., New York, NY 10010.

CAREER: Teacher of Arabic in Aden, Lebanon, the United Kingdom, and the United States, 1964-75; McLoughlin Associates, London, England, consultant on the Arab world, 1993—. *Military service:* British Army, 1955-65.

WRITINGS:

Ibn Saud: Founder of a Kingdom, St. Martin's, 1993.
A Nest of Spies? A History of M.E.C.A.S., Alhani, 1994.

Also translator of Ghazi Algosaibi's *Apartment Freedom,* 1994.

WORK IN PROGRESS: Editing P. K. Hitti's *History of Arabs.*

* * *

McNEER, May (Yonge)   1902-1994

OBITUARY NOTICE—See index for *CA* sketch: Born in 1902, in Tampa, FL; died of complications after a stroke, July 11, 1994, in Reston, VA. Author. A prolific writer of children's books, McNeer often worked with her illustrator husband, Lynd Ward, until his death in 1985. McNeer's 1958 publication *Armed with Courage* won the Thomas Alva Edison Award for special excellence in contributing to character development of children. Among McNeer's literary subjects are historical fiction, biographies, and regional studies, in addition to fictional works. Other books by McNeer include *Martin Luther* (1953), *America's Abraham Lincoln* (1957), *The Alaska Gold Rush* (1960), *America's Mark Twain* (1962), and *Give Me Freedom* (1964).

OBITUARIES AND OTHER SOURCES:

BOOKS

Authors of Books for Young People, 3rd edition, Scarecrow, 1990.

PERIODICALS

Washington Post, July 13, 1994, p. C6.

* * *

MEIKLE, Clive
See BROOKS, Jeremy

MELLAN, Olivia 1946-

PERSONAL: Born October 14, 1946, in Brooklyn, NY; daughter of Eli (an attorney and judge) and Sara (a homemaker; maiden name Tepper) Mellan; married Anand Mundra, October 21, 1976 (divorced May, 1984); married Michael Shapiro (a law professor), May 17, 1987; children: Aniel Michael Mundra. *Education:* Mt. Holyoke College, B.A. (magna cum laude), 1968; Georgetown University, M.S., 1971. *Religion:* Jewish. *Avocational interests:* Writing spoof songs, jewelry-making, travel, theater, dance concerts, ballroom dancing.

ADDRESSES: Home—Washington, DC. *Office*—Olivia Mellan and Associates, Inc., 2607 Connecticut Ave., N.W., Washington, DC 20008.

CAREER: Psychotherapist in private practice, Washington, DC, 1974—; affiliated with Washington Therapy Guild. Consultant to businesses and organizations in communications, stress management, money psychology. Volunteer for Psychologists for Social Responsibility and D.C. Statehood Party. Guest on television shows, including *The Oprah Winfrey Show, Today,* and *20-20.*

MEMBER: American Association for Counseling and Development, American Society for Training and Development, Phi Beta Kappa.

WRITINGS:

Ten Days to Money Harmony: A Guide for Individuals and Couples (workbook), self-published, 1989.
Money Harmony: Resolving Money Conflicts in Your Life and Relationships, Walker and Co. (New York), 1994.

Contributor to periodicals and professional journals, including *Personal Financial Planning* and *Family Therapy Networker.*

WORK IN PROGRESS: A book about overcoming overspending as a couple or family unit to be published by Walker and Co. in 1995.

SIDELIGHTS: Olivia Mellan told *CA:* "I am a psychotherapist whose central mission in my twenty-year career can be summed up by the phrase 'therapy education.' I am inspired by the notion of helping people learn some tools and processes of growth and change to transform their lives from being centered on survival to becoming centered on thriving and giving their gifts to the world. In the next three years, I would like to have a TV talk show in which I would interview healers of every kind—physical, mental, spiritual. I want to destigmatize the idea of getting help, and to point the way toward a variety of valuable modes of helping and healing in many different fields.

"In my work I have helped individuals and couples balance their difficult and emotionally charged relationships to money—and to each other. My money harmony work resulted in my self-publishing a workbook, an audiocassette for the general public, one for financial planners and other money professionals, and articles which later appeared in various publications. I have also enjoyed doing 'business therapy' with organizations and offices, helping people at work learn to value each other's contributions, to resolve differences, and to learn to brainstorm creatively in a group. One of my greatest passions is working with couples. Giving them techniques to resolve angers and hurts, learn to listen empathetically, learn to negotiate clearly—that gives me great satisfaction."

*   *   *

MELNYCZUK, Askold 1954-

PERSONAL: Born December 12, 1954, in Irvington, NJ; son of Edward (an employee of a beer manufacturer) and Olena (a homemaker; maiden name, Zahajkewycz) Melnyczuk. *Education:* Attended Antioch College, 1972-73; Rutgers University, Newark Campus, B.A., 1976; Boston University, M.A., 1978. *Politics:* Independent. *Religion:* "Lapsed Catholic, lazy Buddhist."

ADDRESSES: Home—11 Chestnut St., Medford, MA 02155. *Office*—Boston University, 236 Bay State Rd., Boston, MA 02215.

CAREER: Boston University, Boston, MA, preceptor and editor, 1982—.

WRITINGS:

What Is Told, Faber (Winchester, MA), 1994.

Editor of *Agni.*

WORK IN PROGRESS: Necessity, a novel, completion expected in 1996; *The Criminal Element,* stories.

*   *   *

MEYEROWITZ, Joanne 1954-

PERSONAL: Born April 8, 1954, in Washington,

DC; daughter of Irving and Freda (Goldberg) Meyerowitz. *Education:* University of Chicago, B.A., 1976; Stanford University, M.A., 1978, Ph.D., 1983.

ADDRESSES: Home—4332 Dane Ave., Cincinnati, OH 45223. *Office*—Department of History, University of Cincinnati, Cincinnati, OH 45221.

CAREER: University of Cincinnati, Cincinnati, OH, assistant professor, 1985-90, associate professor of history, 1990—.

WRITINGS:

Women Adrift: Independent Wage Earners in Chicago, 1880-1930, University of Chicago Press, 1988.
(Editor) *Not June Cleaver: Women and Gender in Postwar America, 1945-1960,* Temple University Press, 1994.

*   *   *

MEYERS, Maan
See MEYERS, Martin

*   *   *

MEYERS, Martin   1934-
(Maan Meyers, a joint pseudonym)

PERSONAL: Born December 26, 1934, in New York, NY; son of Joseph (a waiter) and Sara (a cook; maiden name, Goldberg) Meyers; married Annette Brafman (a writer), August 19, 1963. *Education:* Attended Performing Arts High School, 1948-49, Seward Park High School, 1950-52, and American Theatre Wing, 1957-59.

ADDRESSES: Agent—Ms. Chris Tomasino, RLR 7, West 51st St., New York, NY 10019.

CAREER: Actor and writer. Has appeared in Broadway plays, including *Zorba;* appeared in such feature films as *The Incident;* portrayed the character Stan Perlo on the television daytime drama *One Life to Live. Military service:* U.S. Army, 1953-55; became corporal.

MEMBER: Mystery Writers of America, Sisters in Crime, Private Eye Writers of America, Screen Actors Guild.

WRITINGS:

"PATRICK HARDY" SERIES

Kiss and Kill, Popular Library, 1975.

Hung up to Die, Popular Library, 1976.
Red Is for Murder, Popular Library, 1976.
Reunion for Death, Popular Library, 1976.
Spy and Die, Popular Library, 1976.

"DUTCHMAN" SERIES; WITH WIFE, ANNETTE MEYERS, UNDER JOINT PSEUDONYM MAAN MEYERS

The Dutchman, Doubleday (New York), 1992.
The Kingsbridge Plot, Doubleday, 1993.
The High Constable, Doubleday, 1994.

Author of *A Federal Case,* Scholastic Publications, 1978; and *Suspect* (novel based on the 1987 film of same name), Bantam (New York), 1987. Wrote lyrics for the television show *Captain Kangaroo,* broadcast by Columbia Broadcasting System (CBS-TV).

WORK IN PROGRESS: (With wife, Annette, as Maan Meyers) *The Dutchman's Dilemma,* "the further adventures of Pieter Tonneman and Racqel Mendoza."

SIDELIGHTS: The "Dutchman" series began with Annette Meyers's idea of the character of the Dutchman: a large blond lawman in a black hat, leather jacket, loose-fitting shirt, and boots who lived during the time when New Amsterdam became New York. Martin Meyers conducted preliminary research on New Amsterdam and discovered Pieter Tonneman, who was a Schout (sheriff) in New Amsterdam in 1664, and who fit Annette's description. The Meyers thoroughly researched the history of the region of modern-day Manhattan that was once New Amsterdam, as well as the history of the people who lived there, in order to create a narrative that accurately portrayed life during the period.

Martin Meyers told *CA:* "In the years it took us to research and write *The Dutchman,* we spent hours at the New York Historical Society and in the New York Public Library, reading as much as we could about the Dutch, English, Jews, Africans, and Native Americans who walked the five hundred yards of lower Manhattan that was New Amsterdam.

"We pored over maps and read about food and clothing, weapons, the flora and fauna, and the furniture. We wandered those five hundred yards at the tip of Manhattan, once bordered on three sides by water and on the fourth by a wooden wall that is now Wall Street.

"The most amazing thing we discovered was that New Amsterdam then, and New York City now, in terms of its people and what moves them, are strikingly similar."

MICKELBURY, Penny   1948-

PERSONAL: Born May 31, 1948, in Atlanta, GA; daughter of Arthur Jennings (a painting contractor) and Mexico (a college librarian; maiden name, Hembree) Mickelbury. *Education:* Attended University of Georgia, 1966-71. *Politics:* "Not if I can avoid it." *Religion:* Native American Spirituality.

ADDRESSES: Home—Washington, DC. *Office*—c/o Lisa A. Jones, 1200 G Street N.W., Suite 370, Washington, DC 20005.

CAREER: Worked for the newspaper *Atlanta Voice,* Atlanta, GA, 1968-69 (summers); *Banner-Herald,* Athens, GA, reporter, 1970-71; *Washington Post,* Washington, DC, reporter, 1971-72; National Center on Black Aged, Washington, DC, public relations director, 1972-75; WHUR-FM, Washington, DC, news reporter, 1975-78; WJLA-TV (ABC), Washington, DC, news reporter, 1978-84, assistant news director, 1984-87. Worked as a teacher at City Kids Repertory Company, New York City, 1988-89; Alchemy: Theatre of Change, New York City, cofounder and managing director, 1990-93; teacher of writing in Washington, DC, and Baltimore, MD, 1994—.

MEMBER: Writers Guild of America (East).

WRITINGS:

PLAYS

Time Out, produced as a staged reading at the Susan Charlotte Studios, New York City, 1989.
Waiting for Gabriel, produced as a staged reading at the Tribeca Film Center, New York City, 1991.

Also author of the play *Warm Robes of Remembrance,* 1993.

MYSTERY NOVELS

Keeping Secrets, Naiad Press, 1994.
Night Songs, Naiad Press, 1995.

Contributor of short stories to anthologies, including *Naiad Press Collection,* Naiad Press, 1994, and *Spooks, Spies, and Private Eyes: Black Mystery and Suspense Fiction,* edited by Paula Woods, Doubleday, 1995.

Keeping Secrets has been translated into German.

WORK IN PROGRESS: Dark Water Running, a historical novel, completion expected in 1996; *When*

We All Wanted to Look Like Angela Davis, a collection of short stories about growing up black, female, and Southern; a mystery novel, to be published by Naiad Press in 1996; research on the relationship between runaway slaves and Indians, on the life of Harriet Tubman, and on the life of Sojourner Truth.

SIDELIGHTS: Penny Mickelbury told *CA:* "Every word I write originates in the reality of having been born female, black, and southern; of having been dipped in the waters that proclaim the sanctity of clan and land, and in the belief in the eventual and ultimate triumph of good over evil. These themes permeate the body of my work, including the murder-mystery series, in which the protagonists are an investigative newspaper reporter and a police lieutenant who heads the hate crimes unit. Equally intrinsic to my writing is the goal of telling the truth about who black Americans really are and historically have been, contrary to the myths, misconceptions, and lies that prevail in the American consciousness.

"For most of my fifteen years as a journalist, I wrote about government and politics. As a playwright and novelist, I write about people and their relationship with each other and with the land; about their spiritual beliefs and how those beliefs often conflict with the reality of a larger society; about what happens to people's spirits when they collide one time too often with that thing called reality. I write overwhelmingly about African Americans, more and more about Native Americans, equally about men and women, and often about children. I often write about spirituality as it was practiced by our ancestors, and about efforts to regain and reclaim that lost connection.

"I have been, and continue to be, most influenced by the writings of Toni Morrison, Paule Marshall, and James Baldwin. Each conveys a powerful lyricism that transforms the ordinary and makes it holy. Each writer succeeds in finding and blending the mundane and the mystical in both language and character that frequently results in the magical. Each writer possesses a reverence for language and the craft of writing that is worthy of emulation."

*   *   *

MILHORN, H(oward) Thomas, Jr.   1936-

PERSONAL: Born October 30, 1936, in Kingsport, TN; son of Howard Thomas and Fay (Dillow) Milhorn; married Katrina Harris (a nurse), September 14, 1968; children: Toby. *Education:* Lincoln Memorial University, B.S. (magna cum laude),

1960; University of Mississippi, Ph.D., 1964, M.D., 1975. *Politics:* Republican. *Religion:* Baptist.

ADDRESSES: Home—1900 45th Ct., Meridian, MS 39305. *Office*—Chemical Dependency Services, Laurel Wood Center, 5000 Highway 39 N., Meridian, MS 39303.

CAREER: Pressure Vessel Manufacturing Co., Los Angeles, CA, mechanical drafter, 1956-57; Sandford Process Co., Los Angeles, junior engineer, summers, 1958-59; Eastman Kodak Co., Tennessee Division, Kingsport, mechanical drafter, summer, 1964; University of Mississippi, School of Medicine, Jackson, faculty member, 1964-92, retiring as associate professor of psychiatry and human behavior and professor of family medicine, physiology, and biophysics, also resident in family practice, 1977-80; Laurel Wood Center, Meridian, MS, medical director for Chemical Dependency Services, 1992—. Private practice of addiction medicine and general medicine.

MEMBER: American Medical Association, American Academy of Family Physicians, American Society of Addiction Medicine, Mississippi Academy of Family Physicians, Lauderdale County Medical Society.

AWARDS, HONORS: National Institutes of Health, fellow, 1964-65, grant, 1968-72; selected for Mead-Johnson national visiting faculty program, 1992-93.

WRITINGS:

The Application of Control Theory to Physiological Systems, Saunders, 1966.
Fluid and Electrolyte Balance, American Academy of Family Physicians, 1982.
Chemical Dependence: Diagnosis, Treatment, and Prevention, Springer-Verlag, 1990.
Drug and Alcohol Abuse: The Authoritative Guide for Parents, Teachers, and Counselors, Plenum, 1994.

Contributor of about one hundred-seventy articles to scientific journals.

Writings have been translated into Japanese.

WORK IN PROGRESS: Caduceus Awry, a medical suspense novel.

SIDELIGHTS: H. Thomas Milhorn, Jr., told *CA:* "I began my writing career as a graduate student in physiology and biophysics. Soon after receiving my Ph.D., I published my first book, a biomedical engineering textbook that was later translated into Japanese. Since then, I have published articles in scientific journals and written a monograph on fluid and electrolyte balance and two books on substance abuse. I have just completed my first novel, a medical thriller. I write for the enjoyment of writing and the thrill of seeing my work in print. I look forward to pursuing future literary works, with an emphasis on fiction."

*   *   *

MILLER, Jane 1949-

PERSONAL: Born April 27, 1949, in New York, NY. *Education:* Pennsylvania State University, B.A.; Humboldt State University, M.A.; University of Iowa, M.F.A.

ADDRESSES: Office—Modern Languages Building, University of Arizona, Tucson, AZ 85721.

CAREER: University of Arizona, Tucson, professor of English.

MEMBER: Associated Writing Programs (member of board of directors).

AWARDS, HONORS: Lila Wallace-*Reader's Digest* Award; Guggenheim fellow; grant from National Endowment for the Arts; award from Vermont Council of the Arts; Jerome Shestack Prize, *American Poetry Review;* Western States Book Award in Poetry, 1993; Pushcart Prize, 1994.

WRITINGS:

Many Junipers, Heartbeats, Copper Beech Press, 1980.
(With Olga Broumas) *Black Holes, Black Holes, Black Stockings,* Wesleyan University Press, 1983.
American Odalisque, Copper Canyon Press (Port Townsend, WA), 1987.
Working Time: Essays on Poetry, Culture, and Travel, University of Michigan Press, 1990.
August Zero, Copper Canyon Press, 1993.

*   *   *

MILLER, Richard B. 1927-

PERSONAL: Born June 10, 1927, in Scotia, NY; son of Bradford and Mary Elizabeth Miller; married Ruth Johnson, November 17, 1951; children: Brad, Katherine, Vance, Margaret. *Education:* Syracuse University, B.A., 1950; graduate study at Syracuse University and Columbia University.

ADDRESSES: Home—205 Madison Ave., Box 503, Cresskill, NJ 07626.

CAREER: Writer and editor.

WRITINGS:

Investment and Plant Location in Europe, Noyes Data, 1965.
Financial Opportunities for Closely-Held Corporations, Executive Enterprises, 1979.
(With Paul Nadler) *The Banking Jungle,* Wiley, 1985.
Tax Haven Investing, Probus Publishing, 1988.
The Banker's Desk Book, Prentice-Hall, 1988.
Super Banking, Dow Jones-Irwin, 1989.
The Banking Yearbook, Prentice-Hall, 1990.
American Banking in Crisis, Dow Jones-Irwin, 1990.
Ghost Towns of California, Renaissance House, 1991.
Citicorp: Story of a Banking Crisis, McGraw, 1993.

Editor of *Sugar y Azucar, Bankers Monthly,* and *The Bankers Magazine;* co-editor of a newspaper for civil service employees; author and editor of business newsletters.

*   *   *

MILLING, Michael C. Crowley
See CROWLEY-MILLING, Michael C.

*   *   *

MIN, Anchee   1957-

PERSONAL: Born January 14, 1957, in Shanghai, China; immigrated to the United States, 1984; daughter of Naishi (an astronomy instructor) and Dinyun (a teacher; maiden name, Dai) Min; married Qigu Jiang (a painter), 1991 (divorced, 1994); children: Lauryan (daughter). *Education:* Attended the School of the Art Institute of Chicago, 1985-91, received B.F.A., M.F.A. *Avocational interests:* Promoting education in China.

ADDRESSES: Home—Chicago, IL. *Agent*—Sandra Dijkstra Literary Agency, 1155 Camino del Mar, Suite 515-C, Del Mar, CA 92014.

CAREER: Artist and writer. Worked in China at Red Fire communal farm, near East China Sea, 1974-76; Shanghai Film Studio, Shanghai, actress, 1976-77, set clerk, 1977-84; worked in the United States as a waitress, messenger, gallery attendant, and babysitter.

AWARDS, HONORS: Carl Sandburg Literary Award, 1993, for *Red Azalea.*

WRITINGS:

Red Azalea (memoir), Pantheon (New York City), 1994.
Katherine (novel), Putnam (New York City), 1995.

SIDELIGHTS: Anchee Min, who grew up in China during the Cultural Revolution, describes her experiences in the memoir *Red Azalea.* The Cultural Revolution, initiated by Chinese Communist Party Chairman Mao Tse-Tung and lasting from 1966 until Mao's death in 1976, was a radical movement intended to revitalize devotion to the original Chinese Revolution; during this time, China's urban youths were organized into cadres of Red Guards and empowered to attack citizens, including party officials, who did not uphold the strict tenets of the Revolution. Recounting her participation in Little Red Guards, a group of students selected for their fidelity to the Communist Party, Min tells of an attempt to prove her own loyalty to the Party by denouncing Autumn Leaves, a favorite teacher, and accusing her of imperialist activities. Before an assembly of two thousand people, Autumn Leaves was beaten and humiliated and pressured to confess that she is "an American spy." Min then writes, "Autumn Leaves called my name and asked if I really believed that she was an enemy of the country. . . . She asked me with the same exact tone she used when she helped me with my homework. . . . I could not bear looking at her eyes. They had looked at me when the magic of mathematics was explained. . . . When I was ill, they had looked at me with sympathy and love. I had not realized the true value of what all this meant to me until I lost it forever that day at the meeting."

At age seventeen, Min was sent to Red Fire Farm, a collective of some 13,000 workers near the East China Sea. She lived there for three years, enduring hardship, laboring to grow cotton in unyielding soil. Seeking solace from the deprivations, Min engaged in a love affair with a female platoon leader, although both could have easily been betrayed and condemned by other workers. Min eventually escaped Red Fire Farm when picked as a finalist—from a pool of twenty thousand candidates—for a film version of a political opera by Madame Mao, *Red Azalea.* But Min's success was short-lived: In September, 1976, Mao died, Madame Mao fell into disfavor, the political system was thrown into chaos, and the film was abandoned in mid-production. Min worked at the film studio as a set clerk for six years.

With the assistance of actress Joan Chen, a friend from acting school, Min came to the United States in 1984 as a student at the School of the Art Institute of Chicago. She knew virtually no English when she arrived in the United States, and immersed herself in English studies. Min told Penelope Mesic of *Chicago* magazine that she forbade herself to speak any Chinese, "so I would learn the language." In a writing course at the institute, Min wrote about Red Fire Farm. She sent the story to the literary magazine *Granta,* where it was published in the spring of 1992. Based on this story, an agent sold Pantheon the rights to Min's autobiography for a large advance. Min finished writing *Red Azalea* on Christmas Day, 1992. "I was vomiting, my whole body was shaking after a year of living my past life and having to face myself," Min recounted to Mesic. "I was so driven and so glad to be given the opportunity."

Min tells *Red Azalea* in uncomplicated declarative sentences, a style that reviewers noted for its effective rendering of the subject matter. According to a *New York* contributor, the writing "suits the brutality of Min's story as well as her own childlike frankness and ferocity." Min told *CA,* "I write what I know. I write about what I can't escape from. I don't love writing, but I enjoy the mind battle. I fight with myself to be a winner."

Reviewers also appreciated Min's account of the Cultural Revolution, finding it a significant contribution to Chinese studies. In *Publishers Weekly,* a critic stated that *Red Azalea* "is earthy, frank, filled with stunning beauty and of enormous literary and historical interest." Describing the book as a "roller-coaster ride through Chinese art and politics," *New York Times Book Review* contributor Judith Shapiro remarked that *Red Azalea,* a "memoir of sexual freedom," exists as "a powerful political as well as literary statement."

BIOGRAPHICAL/CRITICAL SOURCES:

BOOKS

Min, Anchee, *Red Azalea,* Pantheon (New York), 1994.

PERIODICALS

Chicago, January, 1994, pp. 55-57, 13-14.
Entertainment Weekly, March 25, 1994, p. 50.
New York, January 31, 1994, p. 63.
New Yorker, February 21, 1994, p. 119.
New York Times, January 26, 1994, p. C19.
New York Times Book Review, February 27, 1994, p. 11.

Publishers Weekly, December 13, 1993, p. 21; December 20, 1993, p. 57.

*   *   *

MINC, Alain J. R.   1949-

PERSONAL: Born April 15, 1949, in Paris, France; son of Joseph Minc and Leja Bogacz; married Sophie Boisrond, September 6, 1975; children: Edouard, Constance, Thomas. *Education:* Attended Ecole des Miner de Paris, Institute d'Etudes Politiques, and Ecole Nationale d'Administration.

ADDRESSES: Home—225 Rue de l'Universite, Paris 75007, France. *Office*—7 Avenue George V, Paris 75008, France.

CAREER: City of Paris, France, inspector of finances, 1975-79; St. Gobain, Paris, director of finance, 1979-86; Cerus, Paris, vice president and director general, 1986-91; President of A. M. Council, 1991—. Member of Supervisory Boards of Sarl le Monde, Pinault-Printemps, and Yves St. Laurent; member of the European Board of Westinghouse.

MEMBER: Society of Teachers of the World (served as president).

AWARDS, HONORS: Legion of Honor.

WRITINGS:

(With M. Simon Nora) *Rapport sur l'informatisation de la societe* (title means "Report on the Informatization of Society"), Le Seuil, 1978.
L'apres-crise est comence (title means "The After-Crisis Has Begun"), Gallimard, 1982.
L'avenir en face (title means "Facing the Future"), Seuil, 1984.
Le syndrome finlandais (title means "The Finland Syndrome"), Seuil, 1986.
La machine egalitaire (title means "The Equality Machine"), Grasset, 1987.
La grande illusion, Grasset, 1989, published in English as *The Great European Illusion,* Blackwell, 1992.
L'argent fou (title means "Mad Money"), Grasset, 1990.
La vengeance des nations (title means "The Vengeance of Nations"), Grasset, 1991.
Francais, si vous osiez (title means "French, If You Dare"), Grasset, 1991.
Le media choc (title means "The Media Shock"), Grasset, 1993.
Le nouveau moyen-age (title means "The New Middle Age"), Gallimard, 1993.

Also author of numerous articles published in *Le Monde,* French weeklies, and a number of foreign journals.

*   *   *

MIRACLE, Andrew W. (Jr.)   1945-

PERSONAL: Born April 26, 1945, in Avon Park, FL; son of Andrew W. (an educator) and Theda (a teacher; maiden name, Dunavent) Miracle; married Christine (Tina) Satz (a psychotherapist); children: Rebekah Laurel, Jedidiah Andrew. *Education:* Princeton University, A.B., 1967; University of Florida, M.A., 1973, Ph.D., 1976.

ADDRESSES: Office—Department of Sociology, Texas Christian University, Fort Worth, TX 76129. *Agent*—Linda Allen, 1949 Green St., No. 5, San Francisco, CA 94123.

CAREER: Texas Christian University, Fort Worth, assistant professor of anthropology, 1976-82, associate professor of anthropology and director of master of liberal arts program, 1982-88, professor of anthropology and executive director of Tandy Technology Scholars, 1988—. Boys & Girls Clubs of Greater Fort Worth, on board of directors, 1979-93, secretary, 1982-83, president, 1984-86, chairman of the board, 1986-87; Association for the Study of Play, member-at-large of executive council, 1979-81, head of local arrangements committee, 1981, member of nominating committee, 1986, president, 1988; Aymara Foundation, member of board of directors, 1973—, president, 1973-79, chair of the William E. Carter Scholarship Fund, 1986—, treasurer, 1990—; Southern Anthropological Society, head of local arrangements committee, 1981, chair of program committee, 1981, member of nominating committee, 1981, councilor of executive board, 1982-83, president, 1988-89, chair of nominating committee, 1990, member of Mooney Book Award committee, 1990-92, endowment campaign committee, 1992—; O'Hara Center for Youth Development, Boys & Girls Clubs of America, executive director, 1984-93; SocNet Project, member of advisory board, 1985-91; American Anthropological Association, fellow and member of nominating committee (general anthropology section), 1988; Society for Applied Anthropology, fellow and member of program committee, 1992-93.

MEMBER: North American Society for the Sociology of Sport (member of program committee, 1981), Council on Anthropology and Education, Society for Cross-Cultural Research.

AWARDS, HONORS: Has received grants from organizations, including National Science Foundation and National Institute of Education.

WRITINGS:

(Editor, with Aidan O. Dunleavy and C. Roger Rees) *Studies in the Sociology of Sport,* Texas Christian University Press (Fort Worth, TX), 1982.

(Editor) *Bilingualism: Social Issues and Policy Implications,* University of Georgia Press (Athens), 1983.

(Editor, with Rees) *Sport and Social Theory,* Human Kinetics Press (Champaign, IL), 1986.

(Editor, with David N. Suggs, and contributor) *Culture and Human Sexuality,* Brooks/Cole (Pacific Grove, CA), 1993.

(Editor with Rees) *Lessons of the Locker Room: The Myth of School Sports,* Prometheus Books (Amherst, NY), 1994.

(With Tina S. Miracle) *Human Sexuality: Understanding Your Basic Needs,* Brooks/Cole (Pacific Grove, CA), 1995.

Has served as editor of *Newsletter of the Aymara Foundation,* 1978-83; associate editor of *Western Sociological Review,* 1979-80, *Newsletter of the Association for the Anthropological Study of Play,* 1981-82, *Research Quarterly for Exercise and Sport,* 1983-87, and *The Social Science Journal,* 1983-88; series editor of *North American Society for the Sociology of Sport,* 1982-84; and member of editorial board for *Sociology of Sport Journal,* 1983-86, *Play & Culture,* 1991-93, and *Play Research and Theory,* 1993-94.

Contributor to anthologies, including *Encyclopedia of Cultural Anthropology,* Henry Holt (New York), in press. Contributor to professional journals and publications.

Author's work has been translated into Japanese.

WORK IN PROGRESS: Anthropology and Sports: An Holistic Assessment, a book; (with Frederick T. Miller) *Solving Intergenerational Conflict and Increasing Organizational Productivity: Leadership into the 21st Century,* a book; *Sociocultural Anthropology: What It Means to Be Human,* a book; (with John Loy and Garry Chick) research on war, sports, and sexual aggression.

SIDELIGHTS: Andrew W. Miracle told *CA:* "When I was young I read incessantly. It never occurred to me, even at the age of ten, that I too couldn't write books. However, it was only in conjunction with my academic career that I began writing in earnest.

"Writing provides a sense of personal accomplishment—during the process and at completion—but primarily I write as an extension of my career as an anthropologist and educator. I want to share some of the knowledge I have acquired, as well as my enthusiasm for anthropology, and my excitement and appetite for learning.

"One of my mentors in graduate school once related an Irish saying to help me through dissertation difficulties: 'Tis dogged is as dogged does.' Since that time I have submitted to the bucket of glue approach in order to complete a project.

"I am a highly organized, meticulous procrastinator. I outline everything endlessly, while hoping for eurekas of insight and creativity. One of my priority lists calculates the time required to finish a project on schedule. I never procrastinate past that point. At that moment, out comes the bucket of glue, and insight or no, I write until the manuscript is complete.

"I prefer to work in large blocks of time, but if I only have time for a paragraph, that is what I write. After the glue comes out I frequently write from fourteen to eighteen hours each day, sometimes for weeks at a time.

"Writing for a general audience is never easy for an academician. All disciplines have been built on foundations of technical terms and jargon, and it is difficult to shed the language and assumptions it took so long to learn during the professionalization process. However, I try to write in a way that enhances comprehension of my subject without requiring the reader to have a degree in anthropology.

"My advice to aspiring writers: stop thinking about it and get a bucket of glue."

*   *   *

MISBIN, Robert I. 1947-

PERSONAL: Born March 20, 1947, in Brooklyn, NY; son of Miriam and Bernard Misbin; married Eloise Hanman, October 20, 1974; children: Rachel, Leah. *Education:* Brooklyn College of the City University of New York, B.S. (magna cum laude), 1967; Johns Hopkins University, M.D., 1971; University of Washington, Certificate in Clinical Ethics, 1991.

ADDRESSES: Home—Gainesville, FL.

CAREER: Boston University, Boston, MA, began as intern, became resident in internal medicine, 1971-73; Brandeis Unviersity, Waltham, MA, fellow in biochemistry, 1973-74; Ciba-Geigy Corp., Summit, NJ, senior clinical pharmacology associate, 1974-76; Rutgers University, clinical instructor, 1974-76; University of Florida, Gainesville, assistant professor, 1976-81, associate professor of medicine, 1981—. Shands Teaching Hospital, associate director of Clinical Research Center, 1979-88, and member of Ethics Advisory Committee and Quality Assurance Committee; Hospice at Alachua General Hospital, member of Ethics Committee and Quality Assurance Committee; Internal Medicine Ethics Group, chairperson.

MEMBER: European Association for the Study of Diabetes, American Board of Internal Medicine (fellow), Society for Bioethics Consultation, American College of Physicians, American Diabetes Association, Endocrine Society, American Association for the Advancement of Science, Society of Clinical Endocrinologists (charter member), Delaware Valley Ethics Committee Network, Phi Beta Kappa, Sigma Xi.

AWARDS, HONORS: Mead Johnson Award for Presentation, 1970; grants from National Institutes of Health, 1978-83, 1985-88, American Diabetes Association, 1978-79, Juvenile Diabetes Association, 1978-80, 1980-82, Kroc Foundation, 1983-84, and Diabetes Research and Education Foundation, 1986; American Cancer Society fellow in medical ethics, Memorial Sloan-Kettering Cancer Center, 1991-92.

WRITINGS:

(Editor) *Euthanasia: The Good of the Patient, the Good of Society,* University Publishing Group, 1992.

*   *   *

MISHLER, Clayton (R.) 1908-1992

PERSONAL: Born February 17, 1908, in Johnstown, PA; died February 2, 1992; son of Frank (a bricklayer) and Anna (Doell) Mishler; married Audrey Groves (a dietitian), May 28, 1941; children: Craig. *Education:* Attended high school.

ADDRESSES: Agent—Craig Mishler, 3910 McMahon Ave., Anchorage, AK 99516.

CAREER: Veterans Administration, Washington, DC, medical administrator in Detroit, MI, Minneapolis, MN, and Washington, DC, 1947-71. *Military service:* U.S. Navy, storekeeper, 1943-46; served in China; received Bronze Star.

WRITINGS:

Sampan Sailor: A Navy Man's Adventures in World War II China, Brassey's, 1994.*

* * *

MITCHELL, Stephen   1948-

PERSONAL: Born May 26, 1948, in Oxford, England; son of David and Barbara Marion (Davies) Mitchell; married Matina Warren Weinstein, 1974; children: Lawrence, Daniel, Sam. *Education:* Oxford University, B.A., 1970, M.A., D.Phil., 1975.

ADDRESSES: Home—39 Sketty Rd., Uplands, Swansea SA2 0EU, Wales. *Office*—University College of Swansea, University of Wales, Swansea SA2 8PP, Wales.

CAREER: University of Wales, University College of Swansea, began as lecturer, became professor, 1976—.

WRITINGS:

Anatolia: Land, Men, and Gods in Asia Minor, two volumes, Clarendon Press, 1994.

Author of monographs.

* * *

MITCHELL, William J.   1944-

PERSONAL: Born December 15, 1944, in Australia. *Education:* University of Melbourne, B.Arch., 1967; Yale University, M.E.D., 1969; Cambridge University, M.A., 1977.

ADDRESSES: Office—School of Architecture and Planning, Room 7-231, Massachusetts Institute of Technology, 77 Massachusetts Ave., Cambridge, MA 02139.

CAREER: Yuncken-Freeman Architects, Melbourne, Australia, architect, 1967-68; University of California, Los Angeles, assistant professor, 1970-74, associate professor, 1974-80, professor of architecture and urban design, 1980-86, head of architecture and urban design program, 1973-77, 1980-86; Harvard University, Cambridge, MA, visiting professor, 1985, professor, 1986-89, G. Ware and Edythe M.

Travelstead Professor of Architecture, 1989-92; Massachusetts Institute of Technology, Cambridge, professor of architecture and media arts and sciences, and dean of School of Architecture and Planning, 1992—. Urban Innovations Group, Los Angeles, CA, president, 1973-74; Computer-Aided Design Group, Marina del Rey, CA, founding partner, 1978-91. Cambridge University, lecturer, 1978-80.

MEMBER: Royal Australian Institute of Architects (fellow).

AWARDS, HONORS: D.H.L. from New Jersey Institute of Technology, 1992.

WRITINGS:

Computer-Aided Architectural Design, Van Nostrand, 1977.
(With R. Liggett and T. Kvan) *The Art of Computer Graphics Programming,* Van Nostrand, 1987.
(With Charles W. Moore and William Turnbull, Jr.) *The Poetics of Gardens,* MIT Press, 1988.
(Editor with M. McCullough and P. Purcell) *The Electronic Design Studio,* MIT Press, 1990.
The Logic of Architecture, MIT Press, 1990.
(With McCullough) *Digital Design Media,* Van Nostrand, 1991.
The Reconfigured Eye, MIT Press, 1992.
City of Bits: Space, Place, and the Infobahn, MIT Press, in press.

* * *

MOGHADAM, Valentine M.   1952-

PERSONAL: Born September 17, 1952, in Iran; daughter of Victor Mirza-Moghadam (an engineer) and Germaine Malik Mirzaoff (a homemaker). *Education:* University of Waterloo, B.A., 1974; American University, Washington, DC, M.A., 1982, Ph.D., 1986. *Politics:* "Left Wing/Socialist." *Religion:* Catholic.

ADDRESSES: Office—United Nations University/ WIDER Institute, Katajanokanlaituri 6B, 00160 Helsinki, Finland.

CAREER: United Nations University, WIDER Institute, senior research fellow, 1990—. United Nations staff member employed to undertake research on gender-and-development issues. Association for Middle East Women's Studies, member of board of directors, 1993-95.

MEMBER: International Sociological Association, American Sociological Association, Association for

Women in Development, British Society for Middle Eastern Studies, Center for Iranian Research and Analysis, Middle East Studies Association, Society for International Development, Society for Iranian Studies, Sociologists for Women in Society, U.S. Council for INSTRAW.

AWARDS, HONORS: ACLS Travel Grant, 1988; Pembroke Center for Research on Women, Brown University, fellowship, 1988-89; *Choice* Outstanding Academic Book, 1993-94, for *Modernizing Women.*

WRITINGS:

(Editor and contributor) *Democratic Reform and the Position of Women in Transitional Economies,* Clarendon Press (Oxford), 1993.

Modernizing Women: Gender and Social Change in the Middle East, Lynne Rienner (Boulder, CO), 1993.

(Editor and contributor) *Gender and National Identity: Women and Politics in Muslim Societies,* Zed Books, (London), 1994.

(Editor and contributor) *Identity Politics and Women: Cultural Reassertions and Feminisms in International Perspective,* Westview Press (Boulder, CO), 1994.

Contributor of reviews to professional journals, including *World Development, International Sociology, Contemporary Sociology, American Political Science Review, Sociological Focus, International Journal of Middle East Studies, MESA Bulletin, New Left Review,* and *Iranian Studies.*

WORK IN PROGRESS: Editing, with Nabil Khoury, and contributing to *Women's Economic Activities in the Arab World: Patterns, Determinants, Policies*; editing and contributing to *Trajectories of Patriarchy and Development: Theoretical, Historical, and Comparative Perspectives*; researching global economic restructuring and women workers in industrializing and transition economies; researching gender and social transformation.

SIDELIGHTS: Valentine M. Moghadam told *CA:* "Born in Iran, I have lived in the United States, Canada, Mexico, and Finland, and have travelled in professional and personal capacities to many countries including Afghanistan, Malaysia, Vietnam, Russia, Algeria, Morocco, Tunisia, Hungary, Turkey, and the former Yugoslavia. Although I am attached to the country of my birth, I feel that I am a 'citizen of the world' and a woman of different cultures, and this motivates some of my writings.

My book *Modernizing Women: Gender and Social Change in the Middle East* was not only an academic exercise in the study of social change and its gender dimension in the region, but an endeavor towards cross-cultural understanding. I wrote the book primarily for non-experts, in an attempt to clarify what appears to be mystifying, to explain what many regard as inexplicable, and to dispel myths and stereotypes concerning women's positions in countries of the Middle East and North Africa. In examining economic development, state policies, revolutions, demographic changes, and Islamic movements—and through a focus on how women of different social classes have been affected by and have responded to these processes—I was able to argue that educated and employed middle-class women are the main agents of social transformation and modernization in the region. Far from being passive and subordinate, they are *modernizing women.*

"Other writings have sought to extend feminist and gender analysis to transformations in Eastern Europe and the former Soviet Union, and economic policies in developing countries. Here I have tried to show that economic developments and political changes have gender dynamics that need to be anticipated or addressed in policy and integrated into economic, political, and social theory.

"I have also tried to theorize gender in cultural reassertions and 'fundamentalist' movements around the world, but here there is more of a personal and political involvement. My essays on Afghanistan have tried to show that gender issues were central to the conflict between the Marxist governments and the Islamist opposition, and that women were pawns in male-directed power struggles, but that they were better off under the Marxist modernizers than under a tribal-Islamist Mujahideen regime. The immediate outcome of the Iranian revolution was a bitter disappointment to feminists and leftists, and some of my writings have reflected this. Nonetheless, it is important to examine all angles, identify winners and losers, and acknowledge positive developments for women. These positive developments, incidentally, have come about as a result of agitation by women within Iran.

"In recent years I have published a lot, mainly because I live in a city with relatively few distractions! And because I live alone, I can spend long days at my office, pounding away at my computer or poring over manuscripts and documents with no one around and no interruptions. I love music—classical Western and Persian, blues, jazz, and classic rock—but I can't work with it on, and I admire and envy people who can.

"Someday I would like to write a historical novel—similar in genre to Roy Mottahedeh's *The Mantle of the Prophet*—which would take place in Iran and revolve around my rather colorful family. But that story will have to wait."

*　　*　　*

MOORE, Allan F.　1954-

PERSONAL: Born September 13, 1954, in Carshalton, England; son of Ronald F. (a railway auditor) and Jean E. (Griffin) Moore; married Sarah Ann (a clarinetist), October 28, 1978; children: Eleanor. *Education:* University of Southampton, B.A., 1976, Ph.D., 1990; attended University of Surrey, 1978. *Politics:* "Christian environmental socialist."

ADDRESSES: Office—Department of Music, Thames Valley University, St. Mary's Rd., Ealing, London W5 5RF, England.

CAREER: Thames Valley University, London, England, senior lecturer in music, 1985—.

AWARDS, HONORS: Prizes for musical composition.

WRITINGS:

Rock: The Primary Text, Open University Press, 1993.

Contributor to music journals.

WORK IN PROGRESS: The Cultural/Philosophical Milieu of Twentieth-Century Western Music, completion expected c. 2000; research on musicology of popular music, serial and post-serial theory and analysis, and conceptions of musical style and genre.

SIDELIGHTS: Allan F. Moore told *CA:* "My approach to writing seems to veer constantly between various sets of extremes: treating musicology as simply a game (tracing the relationships of sound patterns) and as a serious contribution to our self-understanding; a concern with the particular (without descending into anecdote) within an obsession for the meta-narrative; avowing a seriousness which betokens a near-utilitarian positivism and yet pays heed to the perils of reductionism. I think I write in order to enable readers to plunder my thoughts in

constructing their own understanding, rather than to convince them of anything. I also write in order to understand what I think, recognizing that any result is only temporary, including probably all the foregoing."

*　　*　　*

MORAN, James P.　1958-

PERSONAL: Born December 29, 1958, in Chicago, IL; son of James F. (a salesperson) and Elayne (a homemaker; maiden name, Cusack) Moran. *Education:* Purdue University, B.A., 1981; Suffolk University Law School, J.D., 1984.

ADDRESSES: Home—466 St. Paul St., Denver, CO 80206. *Office*—Federal Public Defender, 1099 18th St., Suite 300, Denver, CO 80202. *Agent*— Nicholas Ellison, 55 5th Ave., New York, NY 10003.

CAREER: Judicial law clerk, Denver, CO, 1987-88; assistant U.S. attorney, Denver, 1988-93; assistant federal public defender, Denver, 1993—.

MEMBER: Colorado State Bar Association.

WRITINGS:

Public Garden, Crown (New York, NY), 1994.

Contributor to periodicals, including *High Plains Literary Review* and *Seattle Review.*

WORK IN PROGRESS: Sullivan's Loop, a novel.

*　　*　　*

MORROW, E(verett) Frederic　1909-1994

OBITUARY NOTICE—See index for *CA* sketch: Born April 20, 1909, in Hackensack, NJ; died of a stroke, July 19, 1994, in New York. Governmental consultant, banker, and author. Beginning in 1952 Morrow worked with President Dwight D. Eisenhower, first as a personal adviser, and later as administrative assistant appointed by Eisenhower to the Special Projects Group. Morrow's experience as one of the first blacks to serve in a high-ranking position at the White House resulted in his book *Black Man in the White House,* published in 1963. He also authored two other books, 1975's *Way Down South up North,* and 1980's *Forty Years a Guinea Pig.* In 1964, Morrow began an eleven year career in the banking industry as vice president of Bank of America, International, in New York City. Beginning in 1975, he was an executive in the Educational Testing Service, located in Princeton, New Jersey.

OBITUARIES AND OTHER SOURCES:

BOOKS

Who's Who in America, 47th edition, Marquis, 1992.

PERIODICALS

Washington Post, July 22, 1994, p. B4.

*　　*　　*

MOSKOWITZ, Faye (Stollman)　1930-

PERSONAL: Born July 31, 1930, in Detroit, MI; daughter of Aaron (a builder) and Sophie (a homemaker; maiden name, Eisenberg) Stollman; married Jack Moskowitz (a lawyer), August 29, 1948; children: Shoshana M. Grove, Frank, Seth, Elizabeth. *Education:* George Washington University, B.A., 1970, M.A., 1979. *Politics:* Democrat. *Religion:* Jewish.

ADDRESSES: Home—3306 Highland Pl. N.W., Washington, DC 20008. *Office*—George Washington University, Department of English, Washington, DC 20052. *Agent*—Tim Seldes, Russell and Volkenning, 50 West Twenty-ninth St., New York, NY 10001.

CAREER: George Washington University, Washington, DC, lecturer, 1972, 1973, 1979, and 1982, associate professor, 1989—; Edmund Burke College Preparatory School, Washington, DC, middle school director, 1975-86; writer. Worked in various teaching positions during the 1970s; has appeared as a commentator on National Public Radio's *All Things Considered* and on television; member of Washington Area Poetry Advisory Board and Jenny McKean Moore Fund for Writers (president, 1975-85).

MEMBER: PEN, Poets and Writers, Associated Writing Programs, Pioneer Women.

AWARDS, HONORS: Alice Goddard Douglas Award for American Literature, George Washington University, 1970; first prize, George Mason University Literary Contest, 1974, for "Original and Echo"; honorable mention, George Mason University Literary Contest, 1975, for "A Leak in the Heart," and 1976, for "Every Little Movement Has a Meaning All Its Own"; Residency in Vence, France, Karolyi Memorial Foundation, 1980; Bread Loaf Scholar, Bread Loaf Writer's Conference, 1983; PEN Syndi-

cated Fiction awards, 1991 and 1993; Washington DC Mayor's Award for Literary Excellence, 1993.

WRITINGS:

A Leak in the Heart: Tales from a Woman's Life (essays), David Godine, 1985.
Whoever Finds This: I Love You (stories), David Godine, 1988.
And the Bridge Is Love: Life Stories (essays), Beacon Press, 1991.
Her Face in the Mirror: Jewish Women Writing on Mothers and Daughters, Beacon Press, 1994.

Also author of *Wigwag Mag* and the pieces "Original and Echo" and "Every Little Movement Has a Meaning All Its Own." Work represented in anthologies, including *New York Times HERS Columns.* Contributor of short stories, poetry, and essays to periodicals, including *Chronicle of Higher Education, New York Times, U.S.A. Today,* and *Washington Post.*

SIDELIGHTS: Author Faye Moskowitz draws heavily on her life experiences in the essays, anecdotes, and works of short fiction for which she is known. Her childhood in a small Michigan town during the Great Depression, her Jewishness in a largely Christian society, the discovery that she had an older sister who died of heart valve complications—all of these experiences figure in her work. Since her first short stories, poems, and essays began appearing in journals in the 1970s, Moskowitz has written for national newspapers and magazines, has appeared on radio and television, and has published three collections of her work: *A Leak in the Heart: Tales from a Woman's Life, Whoever Finds This: I Love You,* and *And the Bridge Is Love: Life Stories.* About *A Leak in the Heart,* a collection of personal essays, Elaine Kendall of the *Los Angeles Times* commented: "Though the essays are brief, the prose direct and unpretentious, the result is a lyrical drama of Americanization, a literary genre particularly our own, still being re-enacted and renewed all over this country."

In her next book, *Whoever Finds This: I Love You,* Moskowitz presents the reader with ten fictional stories that relate a number of themes, including the death of a baby from a heart defect and a teenage girl who has saved for cosmetic surgery since childhood. "Ms. Moskowitz writes with refreshing grace, astringent humor and an occasional haunting sorrow that carries its own cloud," remarked Mark Childress in the *New York Times Book Review.* "Her voice is engaging, her sadness not too overwhelming, and serious ambition is evident on every page." Of Moskowitz's third collection of short pieces, *New York Times Book Review* contributor Miriam Rinn wrote that the tone of *And the Bridge Is Love* "is that of a warmhearted, nurturing sensibility, the proverbial Jewish mother without the sarcasm."

BIOGRAPHICAL/CRITICAL SOURCES:

PERIODICALS

Los Angeles Times, August 14, 1985, pp. 10, 12.
New York Times Book Review, August 21, 1988, p. 12; December 22, 1991, p. 11.
Washington Post Book World, May 12, 1985, p. 5.

* * *

MOSS, Robert (John) 1946-

PERSONAL: Born in 1946, in Australia.

ADDRESSES: Office—Economist, 25 St. James's St., London SW1, England.

CAREER: Canberra Times, Canberra, Australia, leader writer, 1967-69; *Economist,* London, England, leader writer, 1970-74, editor of "Foreign Report," 1974-80; syndicated columnist with the *London Daily Telegraph.* Australian National University, Canberra, lecturer in history, 1968-69.

MEMBER: National Association for Freedom (director, 1975—), Foreign Affairs Research Institute (council member, 1976—).

WRITINGS:

NOVELS

(With Arnaud de Borchgrave) *The Spike,* Crown (New York), 1980.
Death Beam, Crown, 1981.
(With de Borchgrave) *Monimbo,* Simon & Schuster (New York), 1983.
Moscow Rules, Villard (New York), 1985.
Carnival of Spies, Villard, 1987.
Fire Along the Sky, St. Martin's (New York), 1990.
Mexico Way, Simon & Schuster, 1991.

NONFICTION

Urban Guerrillas: The New Face of Political Violence, Temple Smith (London), 1972.
Chile's Marxist Experiment, David & Charles (Newton Abbot, England), 1973, Wiley (New York), 1974, Spanish translation published by Editoria National Gabriela Mistral (Santiago, Chile), 1974.

The War for the Cities, Coward, McCann & Geoghehan (New York), 1972.
The Collapse of Democracy, Temple Smith, 1975, new edition, Abacus (London), 1977.

OTHER

(Editor) *The Stability of the Caribbean,* Center for the Study of Conflict, Georgetown University (Washington, DC), 1973.

Also author of numerous studies for Institute for the Study of Conflict (London), including *Uruguay: Terrorism versus Democracy,* 1971, *The Santiago Model-1: Revolution within Democracy?* and *The Santiago Model-2; Polarisation of Politics,* 1973, *Revolutionary Challenges in Spain,* 1974, and *The Campaign to Destabilize Iran,* 1978. Editor of *The Ulster Debate,* 1973. Contributor of articles to *Economist.*

SIDELIGHTS: Before emerging as a best-selling novelist with the publication of *The Spike* in 1980, Robert Moss established himself as an authority on political and military upheaval. He edited "Foreign Report," an intelligence bulletin published weekly by the influential periodical *Economist,* from 1974 to 1980. In 1981, Moss was the first journalist to reveal that Bulgarians were involved in an attempt to assassinate Pope John Paul II.

Moss's nonfiction studies of revolutionary struggles earned him a reputation as an outspoken conservative analyst of ideological confrontation. A reviewer for *Economist* praised *Chile's Marxist Experiment* for its exposition of "the facts the mythologizers of [Chile's Leftist president] Allende ignore." But others took issue with the book for being too one-sided. *Choice* described it as "a conservative and by many standards reactionary analysis of Allende's thirty-four months in power." *Chile's Marxist Experiment,* and Moss's other early books, indicate to critics that he is a champion of capitalist democracy.

This perspective reappears in Moss's novels of international intrigue. *The Spike* and *Monimbo* (both co-authored with Belgian-born journalist Arnaud de Borchgrave), as well as Moss's first novel written on his own, *Death Beam,* share similar concepts. In *The Spike,* Soviet intelligence operatives use "disinformation" to manipulate the weak-willed and gullible American media. In *Death Beam,* the Soviet Union develops a new super-weapon; the CIA is tipped off, but American intelligence is too deeply mired in its inaccurate estimates of Soviet military capabilities to believe reports of the weapon.

Monimbo tells of a plot by Cuban officials to overthrow the U.S. government by inciting racial hatred and committing acts of terrorism, subversion, and assassination.

Moss's critics generally agreed that his books share two strengths: they weave an entertaining web of political intrigue, and they are founded upon Moss's expertise in ideological conflict and state intelligence. However, many reviewers also recognized some weaknesses: Les Whitten, for example, wrote in the *Washington Post* that Moss and coauthor de Borchgrave rely too much on name-dropping. Whitten also opined that the authors have crafted an unlikely plot with "serious credibility problems." However, he added, the book is worth reading because "sometimes clumsily, sometimes with finesse and steely humor, de Borchgrave and . . . Moss tell us something compellingly that we should start believing. It amounts to this: 'The United States is a good country, and as countries go a moral one.'"

BIOGRAPHICAL/CRITICAL SOURCES:

PERIODICALS

Economist, February 12, 1972, p. 55; December 1, 1973, p. 131; December 6, 1975, p. 117.
Globe and Mail (Toronto), February 2, 1985.
Observer (London), February 3, 1974, p. 30; May 12, 1985, p. 21; July 21, 1985, p.2288.
National Review, October 1, 1976, p. 1073; July 22, 1977, p. 842; May 12, 1978, p. 607.
New Statesman, March 17, 1972, p. 358; January 30, 1976, p. 135.
New York Times, June 22, 1980.
New York Times Book Review, June 29, 1980, p. 14; November 1, 1981, p. 15, 22; February 17, 1985, p. 20; August 2, 1987, p. 16; July 28, 1991, p. 15.
Publishers Weekly, June 7, 1976, p. 69; August 21, 1981, p. 43; February 25, 1983, p. 79; November 23, 1984, p. 68; April 24, 1987, p. 62; May 17, 1991, p. 53; December 20, 1991, p. 65.
Spectator, January 6, 1974, p. 109; January 3, 1976, p. 9.
Times (London), August 18, 1983.
Times Literary Supplement, March 17, 1972, p. 293; February 8, 1974, p. 124; August 22, 1980, p. 943.
Washington Post, May 13, 1980, pp. B1, B11; May 21, 1981; November 12, 1981.*

*   *   *

MOTCHENBACHER, C(urt) D.   1931-

PERSONAL: Born November 19, 1931, in Canby, MN; son of Chris (a train dispatcher) and Loretta (a homemaker; maiden name, Parsons) Motchenbacher; married first wife, Gretchen, 1953 (divorced, June, 1991); married second wife, Mary Jo (a homemaker), January 10, 1993; children: Ellen Motchenbacher Sherry, Janet Motchenbacher Haviland, Charles. *Education:* South Dakota State College (now University), B.S.E.E., 1953; graduate study at University of Minnesota—Twin Cities. *Religion:* Congregationalist.

ADDRESSES: Home—P.O. Box 111778, No. 1099, Hialeah, FL 33011.

CAREER: Honeywell, Inc., Minneapolis, MN, engineer, 1956, research engineer at Corporate Research Center, Hopkins, MN, 1957-67, engineering fellow and meteorology instructor at Defense Systems Division, 1967-82, senior engineering fellow in torpedo development at Underseas Systems Division, 1983-87. Georgia Institute of Technology, visiting scholar, 1992-93. Deacon, Mizpah Congregational Church. *Military service:* U.S. Air Force, 1954-55; became first lieutenant.

MEMBER: Minnesota Academy of Science (president, 1965), Minnesota Society of Professional Engineers (vice-president, 1966).

AWARDS, HONORS: Named Young Engineer of the Year, Minnesota Society of Professional Engineers, 1965.

WRITINGS:

(With F. Fitchen) *Low-Noise Electronic Design,* Wiley, 1972.
(With Alvin Connelly) *Low-Noise Electronic System Design,* Wiley, 1993.

SIDELIGHTS: C. D. Motchenbacher told *CA:* "While working at the Honeywell Corporate Research Center as an electronic engineering consultant in the 1960s, I had the opportunity to develop a new low-noise design methodology. To help other Honeywell engineers with their design and analysis, I wrote an extensive design manual. This was expanded into my first book, which, to my surprise, remained in print for twenty years. During 1992 and 1993 I worked with Dr. Alvin Connelly to update the technology and expand the book for academic use.

"In 1987 I retired from Honeywell. Since then I have been living on a thirty-eight-foot sailboat in Florida and the Caribbean."

MOTION, Andrew (Peter) 1952-

PERSONAL: Born October 26, 1952, in London, England; son of Andrew Richard (a brewer) and Catherine Gillian (Bakewell) Motion; married Joanna Jane Powell, 1973 (divorced, 1983); married Janet Elisabeth Dalley, 1985; children: two sons, one daughter. *Education:* Oxford University, B.A. (first class honors), 1974, M.Litt., 1978. *Avocational interests:* Cooking.

ADDRESSES: Home—124 Becklow Rd., London W12, England. *Office*—Chatto & Windus, 40 William IV St., London WC2, England. *Agent*—Pat Kavanagh, 10 Buckinghamshire St., London WC2, England.

CAREER: Poet, biographer, novelist, editor, and critic. University of Hull, Hull, England, lecturer in English, 1977-81; *Poetry Review,* London, England, editor, 1981-83; Chatto & Windus, London, poetry editor, 1983-89, editorial director, 1985-87.

MEMBER: Royal Society of Literature.

AWARDS, HONORS: Newdigate Prize, 1975, for *Inland;* Arvon/*Observer* Poetry Prize, 1981, for *The Letter;* Rhys Memorial Prize, 1984, for *Dangerous Play;* fellow of the Royal Society of Literature, 1982; Dylan Thomas Award, 1987, for *Natural Causes;* Somerset Maugham Award, 1987, for *The Lamberts;* also recipient of the Gregory Award, the Cholmondeley Award, and the Cheltenham Prize.

WRITINGS:

Inland (single poem), Cygnet Press (Oxfordshire), 1976.
The Pleasure Steamers (single poem), Sycamore Press, 1978.
The Pleasure Steamers (poems; includes "Inland" and "The Pleasure Steamers"), Sycamore Press, 1978, 3rd edition, 1983.
The Poetry of Edward Thomas, Routledge & Kegan Paul, 1980.
Independence (single poem), Salamander Press, 1981.
Philip Larkin, Methuen, 1982.
(Editor with Blake Morrison) *The New Penguin Book of Contemporary British Poetry,* Penguin, 1982.
Secret Narratives, Salamander Press, 1983.
Dangerous Play: Poems, 1974-1984, Salamander Press, 1984.
The Lamberts: George, Constant and Kit (biography), Chatto & Windus, 1986.
Natural Causes (poems), Chatto & Windus, 1987.

The Pale Companion (novel), Viking, 1989.
Famous for the Creatures (novel), Viking, 1991.
Love in a Life (poems), Faber, 1991.
Philip Larkin: A Writer's Life (biography), Farrar, Straus, 1993.

Also author of *The Letter.* Some of Motion's manuscripts are housed at the University of Hull.

SIDELIGHTS: Andrew Motion is considered one of the late twentieth century's most gifted English poets, winning several major literary prizes and issuing critically acclaimed collections of poetry. Widely recognized for his narrative poetry, Motion fashions fictional characters or portraits of actual figures to give voices to his own feelings on life, love, and loss.

His first collection, *The Pleasure Steamers,* is largely made up of Motion's award-winning poem, "Inland," which depicts its seventeenth-century narrator's forced move to a new village after a flood. Feelings of fear, insecurity, and helplessness are explored as the narrator and other villagers are cast out of their homeland. *Inland,* according to *Times Literary Supplement* critic John Mole, "is a considerable achievement in itself, but it becomes increasingly interesting as one reads and rereads the poems grouped around it in the collection's first and third sections. It can be seen as an historical paradigm of Andrew Motion's own acute sense of isolation. He too seems to be a stranger in his own land, and poem after poem finds him becoming the ghost of himself."

The other sections of *The Pleasure Steamers* include poems penned after Motion's mother was injured in an accident while horseback riding and left comatose for several years. The accident parallels with "Inland"'s flood; Motion was suddenly thrust into a strange and unsure place with the loss of his mother's vitality and presence. Using the voices of an English family, Motion writes of his "horsey" childhood on an estate, of storing away his mother's clothes, of years of visiting his mother's bedside, and, finally, of dealing with her death. Commenting on Motion's connecting of historical events with present feelings, Mole wrote: "It is the tension between his sense of belonging to, and being refined out of, the world he describes which gives Mr. Motion's work its distinctive strength." Mole concluded that "*Pleasure Steamers* is an impressive book."

Motion further explores the process of grieving a lost love in his lengthy poem "Independence." Set in India, the work is narrated by a man who married in 1947, the year of his country's independence, but lost his young wife and unborn baby after his wife suffered a miscarriage. The poem focuses on public and private independence as the narrator's political freedom is overshadowed by the prison of grief now built around him, but also offers a poignant study of bereavement. "'Independence,'" wrote Mole in a *Times Literary Supplement* review, "is a work of vivid surfaces and considerable depth." Claude Rawson, in *London Review of Books,* noted that "Motion is very strong at rendering the particularities of grief," and found the poem "a bold as well as a delicately orchestrated success."

As in "Independence," Motion looks through the eyes of others to create storytelling verses in *Secret Narratives,* a collection inspired by secrets: wartime codes, letters, diaries, and whispers. Historical figures, among them Anne Frank and Albert Schweitzer, appear in the poems, which often contain mystical messages. One of the poems inspired *Times Literary Supplement* reviewer Tim Dooley to remark: "'Wooding,' a poem of no special intellectual ambition, shows most clearly the strength of feeling Motion can wring from a minimum of technical effects and explains why it is no insult to his predecessors to see this poet as a natural heir to the traditions of Edward Thomas and Ivor Gurney." Dooley found that the poems in *Secret Narratives* "also underline how persistently the subject of mourning has enabled Motion to produce writing of the finest quality."

In addition to his widely read narratives, Motion has edited poetry collections and issued two critical studies, the first being *The Poetry of Edward Thomas.* Motion's look at Thomas has been praised for its thorough examination of Thomas's work and life. *Times Literary Supplement* reviewer C. H. Sisson commended Motion's work on the popularly read Thomas, writing: "One cannot be entirely convinced of the necessity for so much expatiation but, given the existence of the genre, one must say that Andrew Motion has done his work well and that there should be no call for such another study for some time to come."

The second of Motion's critical studies focuses on the work of England's much-loved poet Philip Larkin, about whom Motion also published a biography, *Philip Larkin: A Writer's Life.* Motion's insight on Larkin, who died in 1985, was gained by his friendship with the colorful poet, a rotund, balding character who, in his last years, wrote and spoke prolifically about his unsuccessful attempts at love,

his obsession with pornography, and his personal prejudices. In a lengthy *New Yorker* critique of *Philip Larkin: A Writer's Life,* Martin Amis found the biography "confidently managed, and chasteningly thorough; it is also an anthology of the contemporary tendencies toward the literal, the conformist, and the amnesiac. Future historians of taste wishing to study the Larkin fluctuation will not have to look very much further."

Motion earned yet another literary prize with the publication of his biography *The Lamberts: George, Constant and Kit,* which delves into the destructive ways of a talented family. George Lambert, who died in 1930 at the age of fifty-seven, was Australia's leading painter early in the twentieth century. With his wife, Amy, he moved to Paris, where he took a mistress and subjected his wife and children to abuse. One of his sons, Constant, was a gifted musician and composer of *The Rio Grande* for orchestra and chorus. An alcoholic, Constant died in his forties, as did his son, Kit, manager of the rock group The Who and producer of the rock-opera *Tommy.* At his death, Kit was feeding a twelve-year addiction to heroin.

Infidelity and abuse abound in Motion's portrait of the Lamberts, which London *Times* critic James Wood deemed "a deeply moving chronicle of sheer human waste, balanced by the composed obliquity of Motion's prose." Wood also noted: "Most biographies merely sift the top-soil of history, confirming the already known. Andrew Motion's *The Lamberts* is a biography that mines much deeper, retrieving old truths and creating new realities." A *New York Times* review of *The Lamberts* by Michiko Kakutani also commended Motion's work for being "sympathetic rather than voyeuristic in tone. In fact, in telling this story of talent and loss and missed connections, this story of wayward fathers and damaged sons, Mr. Motion has succeeded in producing both an exemplary family biography and an absorbing social history."

BIOGRAPHICAL/CRITICAL SOURCES:

BOOKS

Contemporary Literary Criticism, Volume 47, Gale, 1988.
Dictionary of Literary Biography, Volume 40: *Poets of Great Britain and Ireland since 1960,* Gale, 1985.
Jones, Peter, and Michael Schmidt, editors, *British Poetry since 1970: A Critical Survey,* Carcanet Press, 1980.

PERIODICALS

London Review of Books, June 17-30, 1982, pp. 20-21.
New Republic, July 19-26, 1993, pp. 30-37.
New Yorker, July 12, 1993, pp. 74-80.
New York Times, April 29, 1987.
Times (London), October 31, 1987.
Times Literary Supplement, August 11, 1978, p. 906; January 23, 1981, p. 80; April 2, 1982, p. 392; August 19, 1993, p. 886.*

*   *   *

MOY, James S.   1948-

PERSONAL: Born September 12, 1948, in Chicago, IL; son of Robert Fook Shew Moy and Ann Ngan Kwan Chin Moy. Education: University of Illinois, Chicago, A.B., 1971, A.M., 1973; attended California Institute of the Arts, 1971-72, Goodman School of Drama, 1973, and University of Chicago, 1976; University of Illinois, Urbana, Ph.D., 1977; attended School of Criticism and Theory, Northwestern University, 1983.

ADDRESSES: Home—3121 Oxford Rd., Madison, WI 53705. Office--Department of Theater and Drama, University of Wisconsin, 821 University Ave., Madison, WI 53706.

CAREER: University of Texas, Austin, instructor in theater history, 1977-79; University of Oregon, Eugene, assistant professor of theater, 1979-81; University of Wisconsin, Madison, assistant professor, 1981-84, associate professor, 1984-94, professor of theater and drama, 1994—; theatrical performer and director. Member of editorial board, Empirical Research in Theater, 1982-83; adjudicator for Chicago International Film Festival, 1985—, and Illinois Film Festival, 1988-90; manuscript reader, Routledge Press, 1990-92; reader, PMLA, 1991-92; juror, ATHE Best Essay Award (theory & criticism), 1992-93; judge, San Francisco Ethnic Dance Festival, 1994.

MEMBER: American Drama Society, American Society for Theatre Research, American Studies Association, Association for Asian American Studies, Association for Theater in Higher Education, Modern Language Association, National Asian American Telecommunications Association, Speech Communication Association, Amnesty International, Urgent Action Group.

AWARDS, HONORS: Grants from the National Endowment for the Humanities, 1976, the University of Wisconsin, 1982-83 and 1987-88, the American Council of Learned Societies, 1986, the Newberry Library—Center for Renaissance Studies Consortium, 1990, and Ford Foundation, 1991-92.

WRITINGS:

Marginal Sights: Staging the Chinese in America, University of Iowa Press (Iowa City), 1993.
(Contributor) Asian American Encyclopedia, Salem Press (Los Angeles, CA), 1993.
(Editor, with Soo-Young Chin, Wendy L. Ng, and Gary Okihiro) Re-Visioning Asian America: Locating Diversity (essays), Washington State University Press (Pullman), 1994.

Contributor to books, including Encyclopedia Britannica; Reading the Literatures of Asian American, edited by Amy Ling and Shirley Geok-lin Lim, Temple University Press (Philadelphia, PA); Asian Americans in the United States, edited by Alexander Yamato, Soo-Young Chin, Wendy L. Ng, and Joel Franks, Kendall-Hunt (Dubuque, IA), 1993; and Staging Difference: Cultural Pluralism in American Theatre and Drama, edited by Marc Maufort, Peter Lang (New York), in press. Contributor to periodicals, including Modern Drama, Redneck Review of Literature, High Performance, Theatre Research International, and Comparative Drama. Theater Journal, coeditor, 1982-83, editor, 1984-85, associate editor, 1986-90.

WORK IN PROGRESS: Books about Asian American self-representations; postmodern structural characteristics in nineteenth-century American popular entertainments; and the history of theatrical entertainments in Chicago, 1833-1871.

*   *   *

MURPHY, James Bernard   1958-

PERSONAL: Born August 23, 1958, in New York, NY; son of Donald (an attorney) and Jane (a homemaker) Murphy; married Kirsten Cronin (a homemaker), June 6, 1987; children: Leo, Joshua. Education: Yale University, B.A., 1980, M.C.P., 1983, Ph.D., 1990. Politics: Democrat. Religion: Roman Catholic.

ADDRESSES: Home—4 Morrison Rd., Hanover, NH 03755. Office—Department of Government, Dartmouth College, Hanover, NH, 03755.

CAREER: Dartmouth College, Hanover, NH, assistant professor of government, 1990—. Parish Council of St. Denis, member, 1994—.

MEMBER: American Political Science Association, American Catholic Philosophical Association.

WRITINGS:

The Moral Economy of Labor, Yale University Press (New Haven, CT), 1993.

WORK IN PROGRESS: Natural Law and the Laws of Nature; research on semiotics and jurisprudence.

*   *   *

MURRAY, Paul T(hom, Jr.) 1944-

PERSONAL: Born July 3, 1944, in Alexandria, LA; married Suzanne Adams (a nurse manager); children: Rebecca, Jessica, Matthew. *Education:* University of Detroit, A.B., 1966; Ohio State University, M.A., 1967; Florida State University, Ph.D., 1972. *Politics:* Liberal Democrat. *Religion:* Roman Catholic. *Avocational interests:* Long distance running, skiing, reading.

ADDRESSES: Home—116 North Pine Ave., Albany, NY 12203. *Office*—Department of Sociology, Siena College, Loudonville, NY 12211.

CAREER: Meharry Medical College, Nashville, TN, research associate at Center for Health Care Research, 1970-72; Millsaps College, Jackson, MS, assistant professor of sociology, 1972-78; University of Montevallo, Montevallo, AL, assistant professor of sociology, 1978-79; Siena College, Loudonville, NY, professor of sociology, 1979—. Albany Board of Education, vice-president, 1992-94, president, 1994; Hudson Mohawk Road Runners Club, president, 1982-83. Consultant to U.S. Department of Justice and Lawyers Committee for Civil Rights Under Law; expert witness in civil rights cases.

MEMBER: American Sociological Association, Eastern Sociological Society, New York State School Boards Association (delegate, 1992-93), Capital District School Boards Association (delegate, 1991—), Pine Hills Neighborhood Association.

AWARDS, HONORS: Distinguished Service Award, Hudson Mohawk Road Runners Club, 1984; grant from Lyndon B. Johnson Foundation, 1988.

WRITINGS:

The Civil Rights Movement: References and Resources, G. K. Hall (Thorndike, ME), 1993.

Contributor to books, including *Global Voices, Global Visions,* edited by Lynn Miller-Lachmann, Bowker, 1994. Contributor to periodicals, including *Journal of Black Studies, Social Problems, Humanity and Society,* and *Voices.*

WORK IN PROGRESS: Research on racial violence and race riots in America.

SIDELIGHTS: Paul T. Murray told *CA:* "The origins of *The Civil Rights Movement* can be traced to my involvement in the movement as a student in the 1960s. During the summer of 1966, I volunteered to work in rural Madison County, Mississippi, with the American Friends Service Committee. I returned to Mississippi for the next two summers to complete research for my master's thesis.

"From 1972 to 1978 I was on the faculty of Millsaps College in Jackson, Mississippi. While there, I worked with the Lawyers Committee for Civil Rights Under Law on voting rights litigation. Subsequently, I was a consultant and expert witness for the Civil Rights Division of the U.S. Department of Justice.

"Since moving to New York in 1979, I have continued my study of the civil rights movement. In recent years I have taught courses on the movement and on the 1960s. I am especially fond of the freedom songs from the movement, and I seek to integrate them into my teaching."

N-O

NAFF, Clay
See NAFF, Clayton

*   *   *

NAFF, Clayton 1956-
(Clay Naff, Clayton Faris Naff, Clay Faris)

PERSONAL: Born April 3, 1956, in Berkeley, CA; son of Thomas (a historian) and Joan Adele (Rice) Naff; married Lorene Cary (a writer), 1980 (divorced, 1983); married Rumiko Handa (an assistant professor of architecture), June 19, 1987; children: Maya Handa. *Education:* University of Pennsylvania, B.A. (magna cum laude), 1978; attended Temple University School of Law, 1978-80, Annenberg School of Communications, 1983, and Wharton School, 1985. *Politics:* Democrat. *Religion:* Unitarian. *Avocational interests:* "Meals on Wheels" volunteer driver.

ADDRESSES: Home—5505 Amherst St., Lubbock, TX 79416. *Agent*—Jonathan Dolger, Jonathan Dolger Agency, 49 East 96th St., No. 9B, New York, NY 10128.

CAREER: University of Pennsylvania News Bureau, Philadelphia, 1985-87, began as reporter, became associate editor; *American Banker,* Tokyo, Japan, correspondent, 1987-88; *Japan Times,* Tokyo, editor and reporter, 1988-89; Associated Press, Tokyo, reporter, 1989-90; United Press International, Tokyo, correspondent, 1990-91; *Bloomberg Business News,* Tokyo, contributing editor, 1993-94. University of Michigan, Center for Japanese Studies, adjunct research fellow, 1991-92; Texas Tech University, Asian Pacific Rim Area Studies, adjunct research associate, 1992—. "All Things Considered," National Public Radio (NPR), contributing reporter, 1990-93; "Marketplace" program, American Public Radio (APR), commentator, 1991—.

MEMBER: American Civil Liberties Union (board member for Lubbock, TX, branch), Democratic Party, Doctors without Borders, Japan Policy Research Institute, People for the American Way.

WRITINGS:

(With Tsukasa Matsui) *Understanding American Humor* (nonfiction), Nan'un-do (Tokyo), 1987.
(With Matsui) *American Life from A to Z* (nonfiction), Kenkyusha (Tokyo), 1988.
About Face: How I Stumbled onto Japan's Social Revolution (nonfiction), Kodansha International (New York), 1994.
Barbarians Invade Tokyo (short stories), Kenkyusha (Tokyo), 1994.

Contributor to books, including *Navigating the Japanese Market: Business and Socio-Economic Perspectives,* edited by Samia El-Badry, Heidi Lopez-Cepero, and Travis Hope, University of Texas (Austin, TX), 1994. *Jiji Eigo Kenkyu,* columnist, 1988-91. Also writes as Clay Naff, Clayton Faris Naff, and Clay Faris.

WORK IN PROGRESS: "*The Red Medusa,* a historical suspense novel about the United States-led occupation of Japan and how its ideals were corrupted by Cold War fears of communism."

SIDELIGHTS: Clayton Naff told *CA:* "An incurable traveler, I first hit the road shortly after my birth in 1956 in Berkeley, California. At the age of one, my parents took me on a trans-Atlantic voyage by ship to England. My family thereupon resided in London for three years, while my father pursued a doctorate in history at the University of London. After those studies were complete, my family lived in Paris, Istanbul, and, for six years, in Cairo, Egypt, where my father taught at the American University. Returning to the United States in 1966, my family eventually settled in Philadelphia, when I was eleven.

"At that time, I decided to become a writer, hoping the avocation would permit me to get back out on the road. For a sixth grade project, I produced a short book about a group of boys in Boise, Idaho. This was the most exotic place I could imagine at that time, having actually spent much of my life in reputedly exotic locales. The book was crudely written, badly illustrated, and bound in plain cardboard, but it would be twenty years before I produced another.

"All the same, I did resume my travels. As a college student, I returned to Egypt and then sojourned throughout Europe while attempting to make a start as a writer. A few short stories and poems were all I produced, to no great acclaim. Feeling the time was not quite right to embark on a career as a writer, on graduation from the University of Pennsylvania I enrolled in law school at Temple University. However, the desire to be a writer continued to gnaw at me, and after a semester of law, I returned to England, to the seaside town of Brighton, where I produced a novella, still unpublished. Back in the United States, I cut short my law studies and moved to New York to become a journalist.

"This too proved difficult at first, and I moved back to Philadelphia and took a job at my alma mater in the Office of International Programs. Through that job, I met a Japanese architect who would eventually become my wife, and through her discovered what would become an enduring interest in Japan.

"While employed in international programs, I continued to work at freelance journalism, and by 1985 I had secured a full-time job as a reporter and editor with an academic news service. Two years later, shortly after marrying Rumiko Handa, the Japanese architect, I moved to Tokyo on the strength of a job as correspondent for the *American Banker* newspaper.

"Over the course of the next four years, I ascended rapidly through a series of journalistic jobs, including stints at the *Japan Times* and the Associated Press and culminating in a year as Tokyo correspondent for United Press International. In that position, I covered such momentous events as the Cambodian peace talks, Soviet leader Mikhail Gorbachev's historic visit to Tokyo, and Japan's querulous response to the Persian Gulf crisis. I also produced an investigative piece on allegations that Japan was attempt-

ing to suppress criticism of it in the United States. While serving at UPI, I reported frequently for National Public Radio, and continued for several years afterward to produce feature pieces for its respected 'All Things Considered' program, as well as becoming a commentator for American Public Radio's 'Marketplace.'

"During my four years of residence in Japan, I returned to writing fiction in my spare moments. Much of it was published in Japan, and later a collection of my humorous stories about encounters between Japanese and foreigners was published in paperback under the title, *Barbarians Invade Tokyo*.

"Also during that period, my wife and I had our first child, a daughter named Maya, born May 2, 1989. Two years later, my wife received an offer from the University of Michigan to teach architecture. Together we decided to move back to the United States, and so I left UPI and set off to write a book I'd been contemplating about grassroots social change in Japan.

"With the launch of my wife's academic career, I embarked on a career of full-time writing, punctuated by bouts of summertime journalism in Japan. In this I was aided by offers of research positions, first at the Center for Japanese Studies of the University of Michigan, and later, when my wife changed jobs, at the Asian studies program at Texas Tech University. My first major book, *About Face*, was published in 1994 to considerable praise from Japan experts, and I immediately set about writing another, this time a historical novel about the U.S. occupation of Japan.

"I hope to continue writing and lecturing during the academic year and reporting in the off-season."

*   *   *

NAFF, Clayton Faris
See NAFF, Clayton

*   *   *

NAPLEY, David   1915-1994
(Sir David Napley)

OBITUARY NOTICE—See index for *CA* sketch: Born July 25, 1915, in London, England; died September 24, 1994. Lawyer and writer. Noted for his successful career as a trial lawyer, Napley was an expert in criminal defense. After graduating from the Law Society's School of Law in 1935, Napley joined the legal firm of Kingsley, Napley, as a senior partner. His flamboyant style, strong oral presentations, and his tendency to champion seemingly defenseless cases (even while commanding exorbitant fees) led to a reputation as "a kind of legalistic Robin Hood," according to the London *Times.* Among Napley's highly publicized cases were the murder trails of Jeremy Thorpe, Michael Luvaglio, and Jeremy Bamber. Napley was active on the council of the Law Society and was created Knight Bachelor in 1977 for his efforts. Along with the book *Not without Prejudice,* which highlights the author's career to the year 1982, Napley wrote several works in his field, including *Crime and Criminal Procedure* (1963) and *The Technique of Persuasion* (1970), as well as fictional works, including *The Camden Town Murder* (1987) and *Rasputin in Hollywood* (1990).

OBITUARIES AND OTHER SOURCES:

BOOKS

Who's Who, 144th edition, St. Martin's, 1992.

PERIODICALS

Times (London), September 27, 1994, p. 23.

* * *

NAPLEY, Sir David
   See NAPLEY, David

* * *

NATTIEZ, Jean-Jacques   1945-

PERSONAL: Born December 30, 1945, in Amiens, France; son of Jean (a teacher) and Jacqueline (a teacher; maiden name, Lancelle) Nattiez; married (separated); children: Florence, Muriel. *Education:* Universite de Paris VIII, doctorate. *Religion:* None.

ADDRESSES: Home—4845 Rosedale, Montreal, Quebec, Canada H4V 2H3. *Office*—Faculte de musi-que, Universite de Montreal, CP 61-28, Succursale A, Montreal, Quebec, Canada H3C 3J7.

CAREER: Universite de Montreal, Montreal, Quebec, Canada, professor of music.

MEMBER: International Musicological Society, American Musicological Society, Society for Ethnomusicology, Societe francaise de musicologie, Societe francaise d'ethnomusicologie, Societe francaise d'analyse musicale.

WRITINGS:

Proust As Musician, Cambridge University Press, 1989.

Music and Discourse, Princeton University Press, 1990.
Wagner Androgyne, Princeton University Press, 1993.
The Boulez-Cage Correspondence, Cambridge University Press, 1994.

WORK IN PROGRESS: Opera, a novel; research for a book of musical semiology.

SIDELIGHTS: Jean-Jacques Nattiez told *CA:* "I began to write at the age of sixteen, overtrained by my father (a French literature teacher) through American advertising. Writing about music is a very big challenge for me. Yes, things must be said about music, but what and how? All of my work in musicology turns around the nature of writing *about* music. I have been deeply influenced by Jean Mo-lino, an unknown professor of literature at the University of Lausanne, by musicologist Leonard B. Mayer, and by composer and conductor Pierre Boulez."

* * *

NECHAS, Eileen (T.)   1944-

PERSONAL: Born June 24, 1944, in Philadelphia, PA; daughter of Louis (in sales) and Freda (a homemaker; maiden name, Neidorf) Tucker; married Marshall R. Mazer, June 21, 1964 (divorced, December, 1981); married James W. Nechas (a professor of English), October 15, 1982; children: (first marriage) Dale M., Julie R.; (second marriage) Jonathan, Alexander. *Education:* Kutztown University of Pennsylvania, B.S. (summa cum laude), 1978. *Avocational interests:* Cooking, films, reading, travel.

ADDRESSES: Home and office—326 North 30th St., Allentown, PA 18104. *Agent*—Connie Clausen, Connie Clausen Associates, 250 East 87th St., New York, NY 10128.

CAREER: Prevention, Emmaus, PA, research associate and writer, 1980, associate editor, 1980-81, senior editor, 1981-86; Rodale Press, Emmaus, executive editor, 1986-89; freelance writer, 1989—. Lecturer at colleges and universities, including Hunter College of the City University of New York, Temple University, and Lehigh University; workshop leader; media spokesperson, including appearances on *Good Morning America, Regis and Kathie Lee,* and *People Are Talking.*

AWARDS, HONORS: Silver Award, Health Information Resource Center, 1994, for the article "It's Not All in Your Head."

WRITINGS:

(With Denise Foley) *What Do I Do Now?: Parent-Tested, Expert-Approved Solutions to 100 Common and Uncommon Parenting Problems,* Fireside Press, 1992.

(With Foley) *The Women's Encyclopedia of Health and Emotional Healing,* Rodale Press, 1992.

(With Foley) *Unequal Treatment: What You Don't Know about How Women Are Mistreated by the Medical Community,* Simon & Schuster, 1994.

(Coauthor) *The Doctor's Book of Home Remedies for Children,* Rodale Press, 1994.

Coauthor of "Children's Health Bulletin," a syndicated column. Contributor to popular magazines, including *Woman's Day, McCall's, Working Mother, Heart and Soul,* and *Teacher.* Executive editor, *Children,* 1986-89; contributing editor, *Healthy Woman.*

*   *   *

NELSON, Mariah Burton   1956-

PERSONAL: Born April 14, 1956, in Springfield, PA; daughter of Arthur D. (a hospital president) and Sarah B. (a psychiatrist) Nelson. *Education:* Stanford University, B.A., 1978; San Jose State University, M.P.H., 1983. *Avocational interests:* Reading, bicycling, golf, hiking, swimming, advocate and coach for women's basketball.

ADDRESSES: Home—Arlington, VA. *Agent*—Felicia Eth Literary Representation, 555 Bryant St., Suite 350, Palo Alto, CA 94301.

CAREER: Freelance writer, 1980—; public speaker for colleges and professional organizations, 1988—. College basketball player at Stanford University, 1974-78; professional basketball player, 1979-80; associate editor, *Women's Sports and Fitness Magazine,* 1984-87; member of task force on women's sports, Feminist Majority Foundation, 1993—; member of task force on sexual harassment, Women's Sports International, 1994—; participant on task forces on sexual harassment and homophobia, Women's Sports Foundation, 1994—. Has discussed issues relating to sports and feminism on National Public Radio and on television programs such as *Today, Good Morning America, Crossfire, Larry King Live,* and *Sonya Live.*

MEMBER: Washington Independent Writers (board member, 1990-92); Washington Women's Sports Network (founding member), 1993.

AWARDS, HONORS: Miller Lite/Women's Sports Foundation magazine journalism award, 1988, finalist, 1990, 1991, and 1994; Amateur Athletic Foundation's Book Award, 1992, for *Are We Winning Yet? How Women Are Changing Sports and Sports Are Changing Women;* Run Jane, Run's Nancy Rehm Memorial Award for excellence in sports writing, 1994; National Organization for Women Sportswriting Award, 1995.

WRITINGS:

Are We Winning Yet? How Women Are Changing Sports and Sports Are Changing Women, Random House (New York City), 1991.

The Stronger Women Get, the More Men Love Football: Sexism and the American Culture of Sports, Harcourt (New York), 1994.

Out of Bounds (one-act play), published in *Places Please: The First Anthology of Lesbian Plays,* edited by Kate McDermott, Aunt Lute (Iowa City), 1985. Founding writer of "Daylife," a weekly column for the *Washington Post* weekend section, 1987. Contributor to periodicals, including *New York Times, USA Today, Washington Post, Women's Sports and Fitness, Ms. Magazine, Glamour, Fitness, Cosmopolitan, New Woman, Golf Illustrated, Chicago Tribune,* and *Los Angeles Times.*

SIDELIGHTS: Mariah Burton Nelson told *CA:* "After I wrote *Are We Winning Yet?,* I went on an eleven-city book tour and granted hundreds of radio and television interviews. I talked about women's athletic achievements and women's efforts to create a humanitarian sports model. I was shocked by the virulence of male anger and resistance to my message. I kept hearing: 'Yeah, but women will never play pro football.' The odd thing was, I wasn't talking about football. I was talking about women's growing strength and competence in a variety of sports. I was suggesting that often, on a recreational level, women and men can compete together on an equal basis. In some sports, such as horse or auto racing, they can and do compete together on a professional basis. But some men kept desperately—hysterically, even—bringing the discussion back to football, pointing to football as an arena that proved male athletic superiority. It interested me: why do men love football so much? What does it have to do with masculinity and femininity? Why, when discussing women's strength, do men insist on talking about football? In my second book, *The Stronger Women Get, the More Men Love Football,* I answer these questions. The book explores sexism and sexual abuse as enacted through sport, a tenacious bastion of male supremacy.

"I see my books as a beginning. Feminists have examined virtually all aspects of American culture: language, religion, science, education, child care, parenting, sex, the military, the arts, and more. We haven't looked at sports, perhaps turned off by the combat mentality there, or fooled into thinking it's only a game. I write nonfiction because I've never been good at making things up. I write about my own experiences—being molested by a swimming coach, playing professional basketball overseas, competing in the Gay Games, coaching girls' basketball—because stories like these have not been told. I think my strength is in being willing to say what others aren't saying—telling the truth as I see it."

*   *   *

NELSON, Robert M(cDowell, Jr.)   1945-

PERSONAL: Born August 23, 1945, in Philadelphia, PA; son of Robert McDowell (a naval officer and area representative for a tree company) and Jane (a homemaker; maiden name, Strite) Nelson; married Elizabeth H. McDade (a health educator), May 6, 1989; children: Erin Carlisle. *Education:* University of Virginia, B.A. (with high honors), 1967; Stanford University, M.A., 1972, Ph.D., 1975. *Politics:* "Apolitical." *Religion:* Agnostic.

ADDRESSES: Home—Richmond, VA. *Office*—Department of English, University of Richmond, Richmond, VA 23173.

CAREER: University of Richmond, Richmond, VA, instructor, 1968-71, assistant professor, 1975-85, professor of English, 1985—.

MEMBER: Association for the Study of American Indian Literatures, American Literature Association, Western Literature Association, Phi Beta Kappa, Pi Delta Epsilon.

AWARDS, HONORS: Woodrow Wilson fellow, 1967; grants from National Endowment for the Humanities, 1987, and National Endowment for the Arts, 1992.

WRITINGS:

Place and Vision: The Function of Landscape in Native American Fiction, Peter Lang Publishing, 1993.

Work represented in anthologies, including *Dictionary of Literary Biography,* Volume 6: *American Novelists Since World War II,* Second Series, Gale, 1980; and *The Concise Dictionary of American Lit-*

erary Biography: Broadening Views, 1968-1988, Gale, 1989. Contributor of articles and reviews to academic journals and literary magazines, including *Leviathan.* Coeditor, *Studies in American Indian Literatures,* 1989—.

WORK IN PROGRESS: A study of oral and ethnographic pretexts of the "embedded texts" in Leslie Silka's *Ceremony.*

*   *   *

NESTER, William R.   1956-

PERSONAL: Born December 18, 1956, in Cincinnati, OH. *Education:* Miami University, Oxford, OH, B.A. (history) and B.A. (international studies), both 1979; University of California, Santa Barbara, M.A., 1984, Ph.D., 1987. *Avocational interests:* Travel, literature, art, music, film, all wilderness activities.

ADDRESSES: Office—Department of Government and Politics, St. John's University, Jamaica, NY 11439.

CAREER: Amvic Language School, Okayama, Japan, teacher of English and French, 1980-81; Berkeley Language School, Tokyo, Japan, teacher of English and French, 1983; ABC Language School, Tokyo, teacher of English and French, 1983-84; University of London, London School of Oriental and African Studies, London, England, lecturer in Far East politics, 1987-89; St. John's University, Jamaica, NY, assistant professor of government and politics, 1989—.

MEMBER: Phi Alpha Theta.

WRITINGS:

Japan's Growing Power over East Asia and the World Economy: Ends and Means, St. Martin's (New York), 1990.
The Foundations of Japanese Power: Continuities, Changes, Challenges, M. E. Sharpe (Armonk, NY), 1990.
Japanese Industrial Targeting: The Neomercantilist Path to Economic Superpower, St. Martin's (New York), 1991.
Japan and the Third World: Patterns, Power, Prospects, Macmillan (London), 1991, St. Martin's (New York), 1992.
American Power, the New World Order, and the Japanese Challenge, Macmillan (London), 1992, New York University Press (New York), 1993.

European Power and the Japanese Challenge, New York University Press (New York), 1993.

International Relations: Geopolitical and Geoeconomic Conflict and Cooperation, HarperCollins (New York), 1994.

Contributor to books, including *Handbooks to the Modern World: Asia and the Pacific,* edited by Robert Taylor, Facts on File (New York), 1990; and *The International Relations of Japan,* edited by Kathleen Newland, Macmillan (London), 1990. Contributor of articles and reviews to magazines and newspapers, including *Asian Profile, Journal of Developing Societies, Africa Today, Millenium,* and *Women's Studies.*

*   *   *

NEWSHOLME, Christopher (Mansford) 1920-

PERSONAL: Born February 13, 1920, in Ripon, Yorkshire, England; son of Henry Pratt (a chief medical officer of health) and Kathleen Dennis (a homemaker; maiden name, Cooper) Newsholme; married Eunice Mary Ford (a librarian), August 5, 1947; children: Stephen John, Timothy. *Education:* Royal Veterinary College (London), July, 1943. *Politics:* Conservative. *Religion:* Church of England. *Avocational interests:* Gardening, plant photography, drawing, painting, fishing, beekeeping.

ADDRESSES: Home and office—Longwood, Beaford, Winkleigh, Devon EX19 8AD, England.

CAREER: Veterinary surgeon in Warwickshire, Gloucestershire, Essex, and Suffolk, England, 1947-72. *Military service:* Royal Army Veterinary Corps, affiliated with Military Farms Department in India, 1943-47.

MEMBER: Royal College of Veterinary Surgeons.

WRITINGS:

Willows: The Genus Salix, Timber Press (Beaverton, OR), 1992.

(Contributor) Tony Lowe, editor, *National Plant Collections Directory,* edited by Tony Lowe, National Council for the Conservation of Plants and Gardens, 1993.

WORK IN PROGRESS: Botanical research concentrating on dwarf willows.

SIDELIGHTS: A veterinary surgeon, Christopher Newsholme retired in 1972 to North Devon, England, to an area overlooking the Torridge river, where he set about clearing an overgrown region that revealed a rich growth of willows. Eventually this area became an Official National Collection of willows collected worldwide, which Newsholme maintains while growing and studying more than four hundred species and varieties of the genus. The members comprising this genus are diverse, ranging from tiny plants only a few inches high to stately trees up to one hundred feet in height. Although most varieties thrive in moist ground and cold climates, a few types prefer dry soil.

Newsholme's twenty years of experience with willows is documented in his 1992 book, *Willows: The Genus Salix,* in which he describes the many plants in the family *Salicaceae* and discusses their origin, management, and cultivation. He concentrates, however, on the selection of willows for specific sites, from ornamental trees for large or small gardens to tiny plants suitable for sink gardens. Newsholme also offers detailed instructions for caring for willows; facts concerning the hardiness and growth rate of various types; and unique, distinguishing features of willow varieties. Sixty-five color photographs and numerous botanical line drawings accompany his text.

The many different varieties of willows makes cataloging and discussing them a painstaking task, but according to critics, Newsholme successfully does so in *Willows. Garden Journal* reviewer John White, curator of the Westonbirt Arboretum, found that *Willows* "clearly reflects the author's years of willow growing as well as his considerable knowledge of the literature. . . . This high-quality book is clearly written with great authority." Botanist Roy Lancaster, in a review in *The Horticulturalist,* similarly praised Newsholme's book, noting the author "has done an excellent job of what must at times have seemed a daunting task." Reviewer Richard Schulhof, writing in the Arnold Arboretum journal *Arnoldia,* credits Newsholme's work as "a long-needed treatise" and "the best available reference for. . .gardeners willing to experiment with the unusual forms of a familiar genus."

Newsholme told *CA:* "The writing of the book was the result of my consuming passion for this genus—remarkable for its infinite variety and beauty. I feel very strongly that the ornamental and environmental value of the willow has not received the attention that it deserves. My National Collection now comprises 228 *Salix* species and 207 cultivars, collected from numerous sources worldwide. The study of the vegetative reproduction of plants from cuttings is very absorbing and essential to the establishment and maintenance of a specialist collection. I have always found that the exchanges of plant material and botanical information have no international boundaries, yielding great satisfaction."

BIOGRAPHICAL/CRITICAL SOURCES:

PERIODICALS

The Garden Journal of the Royal Horticultural Society, May, 1993, p. 225.
The Horticulturalist, January, 1993.
Arnoldia, Volume 53, number 3, 1993, pp. 31-32.
The Plantsman, December 1993.

*   *   *

NEWTON, Roger G(erhard)   1924-

PERSONAL: Born November 30, 1924, in Landsberg/Warthe, Germany; son of Arthur (a dentist) and Margarete Minna Blanca; maiden name, Blume) Neuweg Newton; married Ruth Gordon (a writer), June 18, 1953; children: Julie Newton Cucchi, Rachel Newton Bellow, Paul. Education: Harvard University, A.B. (summa cum laude), 1949, M.A., 1950, Ph.D., 1953. Religion: Jewish. Avo-cational interests: Reading, music, gardening.

ADDRESSES: Home—1023 South Ballantine Rd., Bloomington, IN 47401. Office—Department of Physics, Indiana University—Bloomington, Bloomington, IN 47405.

CAREER: Worked at Institute for Advanced Study, Princeton, NJ, 1953-55; Indiana University—Bloomington, assistant professor, 1955-58, associate professor, 1958-60, professor of physics, 1960—, distinguished professor, 1978—, department head, 1973-80, director of Institute for Advanced Study, 1982-86. Military service: U.S. Army, 1946-47; served in Japan.

MEMBER: American Physical Society (fellow; chairperson of Dannie Heineman Prize Committee, 1991), American Association for the Advancement of Science (fellow; council delegate, 1986-88), Bloomington Civil Liberties Union (president, 1968; member of board of directors, 1969-72).

AWARDS, HONORS: Jewett fellow, 1953-55; senior fellow of National Science Foundation, 1962-63.

WRITINGS:

(Translator with J. Bernstein) R. von Mises, Positivism, Harvard University Press, 1951.
The Complex J-Plane, Benjamin, 1964.
Scattering Theory of Waves and Particles, McGraw, 1966, 2nd edition, Springer-Verlag, 1982.
Inverse Schroedinger Scattering, Springer-Verlag, 1989.
What Makes Nature Tick?, Harvard University Press (Cambridge, MA), 1993.

Editor, Journal of Mathematical Physics, 1992—; associate editor of Inverse Problems, 1985—, and American Journal of Physics, 1986-88.

*   *   *

NG, Fae Myenne   1957(?)-

PERSONAL: Surname is pronounced "Ing"; born c. 1957, in the United States; daughter of a seamstress and a laborer; married Mark Coovelis (a writer). Education: Attended University of California—Berkeley; Columbia University, M.F.A.

ADDRESSES: Home—Brooklyn, NY. Agent—c/o Eric Ashworth, Candida Donadio & Associates, 231 West 22nd St., New York, NY 10011.

CAREER: Writer. Worked as a waitress and at temporary jobs for ten years.

AWARDS, HONORS: National Endowment for the Arts grant.

WRITINGS:

Bone, Hyperion (New York), 1993.

Contributor to American Voice, Crescent Review, City Lights Review, Calyx, and Harper's.

SIDELIGHTS: Fae Myenne Ng's first novel, Bone, is a story about a Chinese-American family and its struggle to define and understand itself. The narrator, Leila, is the eldest daughter of the family, and the only one her mother, Mah, had with her first husband, Lyman Fu. Her sisters, Ona and Nina, were born to Mah and her second husband Leon Leong, an itinerant seaman. The central event of the novel, even though it does not occur within the narrative, is middle daughter Ona's suicide—she jumped from the thirteenth story of a tenement building in San Francisco. "All of the Leongs blame themselves for Ona's death," declares Michiko Kakutani in the New York Times. "Leon thinks he's brought bad luck on the family by failing to honor a promise he made to his adoptive father to return his bones to China. Mah . . . worries that her own sins—having an affair with her boss, Tommy Hon—have doomed the family to unhappiness. And Leila berates herself for not having paid more attention to Ona's problems, for not figuring out that something was wrong." "*Bone,*" states Diane Yen-Mei Wong in *Belles Lettres,* "is a book about survival and the price it exacts on immigrants and their children."

Although *Bone* has no real resolution—Ona's suicide is never explained or even understood—it does have several uniting themes. One of these is the sense of separation and alienation the Leong girls have as the children of immigrants. Their status as Chinese-Americans accentuates the situation, because for many years Chinese workers did not settle in America. Many of these men "saw America as a place to work and China as home," explains Nancy Stetson in the *Chicago Tribune.* "They always intended to return home, but couldn't, due to the Chinese revolution and American laws." Since these old men were prevented from returning to China alive, many hoped that their remains might be taken back to China after their deaths. This attachment to China also represents the traditional view that the whole Leong family has discarded by choosing to become Americans. "It is Mah and Leon, in fact, who are the real rebels," writes Richard Eder in the *Los Angeles Times.* "Immigrating to America was a leap into peril; it meant two lifetimes of punishing labor and social humiliation. It meant settling for the 'bone' of the title. It meant that their children could live with more choices—and with burdens of guilt and cultural confusion." The Leong girls, Kakutani states, feel "at once resentful of their parents' enslavement to the past and wistful about the history that eludes them here in the United States."

Critics welcomed Ng as a promising new talent. *Washington Post* contributor Cristina Garcia says that *Bone* "leaves a bittersweet wake in the heart," while Kakutani declares that Ng "writes with grace, authority and grit." Bill Mahin, writing in the *Chicago Tribune,* calls *Bone* "a hopeful, charming and surprisingly joyous work." *Voice Literary Supplement* contributor James Marcus asserts Leila's narration "make[s] *Bone* a particularly attractive debut, and [it] should also give the book a long shelf life, since this theme—the wondrous, inevitable, sorrow-inflicting powers with which one's family is always endowed—won't go out of style for at least another millennium."

BIOGRAPHICAL/CRITICAL SOURCES:

BOOKS

Contemporary Literary Criticism, Volume 81, Gale, 1993.

PERIODICALS

Belles Lettres, spring, 1993, p. 21.
Chicago Tribune, February 25, 1993, sec. 5, p. 3; April 4, 1993, p. 3.
Library Journal, January, 1993, p. 166.
Los Angeles Times, January 14, 1993, p. E5.
Ms., May/June, 1993, p. 75.
New Yorker, February 8, 1993, p. 113.
New York Times, January 29, 1993, p. C26.
New York Times Book Review, February 7, 1993, pp. 7, 9.
People, March 15, 1993, p. 34.
Publishers Weekly, November 9, 1992, pp. 71-72.
USA Today, March 10, 1993, p. D6.
Voice Literary Supplement, February, 1993, p. 5.
Washington Post, January 10, 1993, p. 8.*

*　　　*　　　*

NGUYEN huong
　　See NGUYEN-VO, Thu-huong

*　　　*　　　*

NGUYEN-VO, Thu-huong　　1962-
　　(Nguyen huong)

PERSONAL: Born October 19, 1962, in Vietnam; married; children: Huy, The-an. *Education:* California State University, Long Beach, B.A., 1984, M.A., 1990; doctoral study at University of California, Irvine. *Politics:* "I don't know whether it's to be labeled left or right, but I'm for the further expansion of democracy and the necessary rights into all spheres of life." *Avocational interests:* Reading, gardening, "and of course driving the kids around."

ADDRESSES: Home—Garden Grove, CA.

CAREER: Instructional aide for public schools in Long Beach and Westminster, CA, 1981-84; Anaheim Public Library, Anaheim, CA, part-time librarian, 1985-92.

WRITINGS:

Khmer-Viet Relations and the Third Indochina Conflict, McFarland and Co., 1992.

Contributor to Vietnamese-language periodicals.

Some writing appears under the name Nguyen huong.

WORK IN PROGRESS: Vietnamese discourses on social welfare and a framework for cultural change.

SIDELIGHTS: Thu-huong Nguyen-vo told *CA:* "I was born in Vietnam and left it when I was twelve. I never understood how I could just leave a place. My awareness of its absence was so acute that it acquired a presence. I sought to understand the tumultuous events that brought so much destruction to the people of Indochina. I thought knowledge is the same as understanding. I thought knowledge can change the future as an act of redemption for the past. So I studied political science.

"My master's thesis became the basis of my book *Khmer-Viet Relations and the Third Indochina Conflict.* The two years of research for that book took me to hell and back several times. I began to realize then that you can study and 'know' a subject and still not understand. How can a person 'understand' a row of children (seen through the eyes of M. Szymusiak in *The Stones Cry Out*) weeping, running and falling, following their parents to the site of their execution?

"I continue to study social science as if knowledge in the abstract, knowledge of social and political events in general, can make me understand that event in particular which filled my childhood with the sounds of shelling and brought me to this country. I continue to do this as if, somehow, understanding it would reassemble the pieces, and allow the past to become continuous with the present and future. 'There' would become continuous with 'here,' and Vietnam could be continuous with me.

"After visiting Vietnam nineteen years after I left, I realize the place I thought about all these years is not discoverable, and its presence is not recoverable. I wonder if the arts, as purer manifestations of culture, would not be better at constructing meaning than social science is."

*   *   *

NIEBUHR, Gary Warren   1954-

PERSONAL: Born March 11, 1954, in Milwaukee, WI; son of Warren Leonard and Joyce Marie Niebuhr; married Denice Gawlik (a teacher). *Education:* University of Wisconsin—Milwaukee, M.A.L.S., 1976.

ADDRESSES: Home—P.O. Box 341218, Milwaukee, WI 53234.

CAREER: Village of Greendale, WI, library director. Private Investigator Entertainment Service (PIES; a mail order business specializing in private eye fiction), operator. Coordinator of conferences, including Bouchercon, 1981, and Eyecon '95; public speaker.

AWARDS, HONORS: Anthony Award nomination from the conference Bouchercon, 1994, for *A Reader's Guide to the Private Eye Novel.*

WRITINGS:

(Editor with Orietta A. Hardy-Sayles, and contributor) *The Big Jacuzzi: A Collection of Shallow Short Stories,* Bootleg Press, 1992.
(Editor with Hardy-Sayles, and contributor) *Farewell, My Lobby: A Collection of Shameless Short Stories,* Private Investigator Entertainment Service, 1993.
A Reader's Guide to the Private Eye Novel, G. K. Hall, 1993.

Contributor of articles, interviews, and reviews to magazines, including *Deadly Pleasures, Mystery and Detective Monthly,* and *Detective News.*

*   *   *

NIEMELA, Pirkko   1939-

PERSONAL: Born January 21, 1939, in Helsinki, Finland; daughter of Gunnar Emil (a civil servant) and Aira Inkeri (a college teacher; maiden name, Karjalainen) Saaren-Seppala; married Pekka Niemela (a film director), June 24, 1964. *Education:* University of Turku, M.A., 1965; University of Uppsala, Ph.D., 1968; University of Stockholm, Phil.D., 1973. *Religion:* Lutheran. *Avocational interests:* Paddling in the Turku archipelago.

ADDRESSES: Home—Bramenk 2 D 72, 20110 Turku, Finland. *Office*—Department of Psychology, University of Turku, 20500 Turku, Finland.

CAREER: University of Turku, Turku, Finland, assistant teacher of psychology, 1976; Finnish Academy of Science, researcher, 1976-83; University of Turku, professor of psychology, 1983—. Family therapist, 1984—; psychoanalyst, 1989—.

MEMBER: Finnish Professors Union, Finnish Psychologists Union, American Psychological Association.

WRITINGS:

(Editor with Kaj Bjorkqvist) *Of Mice and Women: Aspects of Female Aggression,* Academic Press, 1992.

Author of books in Finnish. Contributor to books and psychology journals.

WORK IN PROGRESS: Books on the decision to become a mother and on women's individualization; a longitudinal study of the idealization of motherhood; a longitudinal study of couples attempting to decide about parenthood; research on early interactions between mothers and babies.

SIDELIGHTS: Pirkko Niemela told *CA:* "I study the conflicts and psychodynamics of parenthood. What do women and men do about their ambivalent feelings regarding parenthood and children? How do they decide about becoming parents? How do they cope with their ambivalence when they are becoming and being parents?

"I see the idealization of motherhood (that is, denying the ambivalence and only emphasizing the positive sides of parenthood) as a defense against the ambivalence of parenthood. Along with this idealization, I also find the acceptance of the impossible demands: that a mother should always love her children, never get irritated about child care, sacrifice herself, be perfect as a mother, and get one's life contents through motherhood. My research shows that it is, in many ways, better to accept the ambivalence and work through the conflicts about parenthood than to deny the ambivalence. Denied ambivalence and anger find their expression through the body and worsen the relationships with the spouse, one's children, and with other mothers."

*   *   *

NISSENSON, Marilyn 1939-

PERSONAL: Born January 19, 1939, in Bellefonte, PA; daughter of M. I. (in business) and Beatrice (a homemaker; maiden name, Berman) Claster; married Hugh Nissenson (a writer), November 10, 1962; children: Katherine, Kore Johanna. *Education:* Wellesley College, B.A., 1960; Columbia University, M.A., 1961.

ADDRESSES: Agent—Wendy Weil Agency, 222 Madison Ave., New York, NY 10016.

CAREER: Television writer, 1964-90.

WRITINGS:

WITH SUSAN JONAS

Cuff Links, Abrams, 1991.
The Ubiquitous Pig, Abrams, 1992.
Going, Going, Gone, Chronicle Books, 1994.
Snake Charm, Abrams, 1995.

*   *   *

NOBISSO, Josephine 1953-
(Nuria Wood, Nadja Bride)

PERSONAL: Born February 9, 1953, in Bronx, NY; daughter of Ralph (a mason contractor) and Maria (a homemaker; maiden name, Zamboli) Nobisso; married Victor Jude (an antiques restorer), July 26, 1981; children: one daughter. *Education:* State University of New York—New Paltz, B.S. (cum laude), 1974; attended Universita di Urbino, Italy, 1971-74. *Religion:* Roman Catholic. *Avocational interests:* Hiking, reading, collecting children's books, yoga, family days, vegetarianism, contemplative walks.

ADDRESSES: Home and office—P.O. Box 1396, Quoque, NY 11959.

CAREER: Self-employed writer and lecturer, 1971—. New York State certified teacher with a specialization in early childhood. Writing instructor and creator of copyrighted writing program: "The Nobisso Recommendations—Guiding Students to Write in Their Authentic Voices."

MEMBER: Society of Children's Book Writers and Illustrators, Writers Guild, Authors League of America, Westhampton Writers Festival.

AWARDS, HONORS: "Best Kids' Book of the Year," *Parents* magazine, 1989, for *Grandpa Loved;* "Friend of Education Award," Delta Kappa Gamma Beta Pi, 1991.

WRITINGS:

FOR YOUNG READERS

Grandpa Loved, illustrated by Maureen Hyde, Green Tiger Press, 1989.
Grandma's Scrapbook, illustrated by Hyde, Simon & Schuster, 1991.
Shh! The Whale Is Smiling, illustrated by Hyde, Simon & Schuster, 1992.
For the Sake of a Cake, illustrated by Anton Krajnc, Rizzoli International, 1993.
Hot Cha Cha, Candlewick Press, in press.

NOVELS

(Under pseudonym Nuria Wood) *With No Regrets,* Berkley, 1983.
(Under pseudonym Nuria Wood) *The Family Plan,* Berkley, 1984.
(Under pseudonym Nadja Bride) *Hide and Seek,* Quest, 1985.

WORK IN PROGRESS: Time Travels Well (a novel for young adults); screenplay and novelization titled, *The Psychic Life of Esther Cane* (for adults); numerous picture books.

SIDELIGHTS: Josephine Nobisso commented: "The incidents in my family are the stuff of legend. There was the grandfather who appeared to his ten children even though he was hundreds of miles away, the grandmother who unearthed an ancient urn that toppled every dish in the farmhouse in its fury to be re-buried, and the perfectly healthy grandfather whose prediction to die upon seeing the birth of a certain grandchild (me, I'm afraid to say), came true.

"My books find their source in the densely atmospheric and passionately happy world that was my childhood. If an author's voice is a function of her personality, then I can hope that mine is 'sharply original' for that's what my work is often called.

"It has taken some of my stories up to twenty years to see the light of day as published books. But I persevere, believing, as a playwright once said, that 'hope is an orientation of the heart. It is not the conviction that something will turn out well, but the certainty that something makes sense, regardless of how it turns out.'

"My years of bungling through writing helped me eventually to develop a most innovative writing method, full of surprising strategies. What's next? My writing life constitutes a full-time commitment, and my life is all of a piece. I'm writing all the time (even in my dreams!), planning workshops, running my office and home, and waking up very early to accomplish it all."

* * *

NOBLE, Kathleen 1950-

PERSONAL: Born June 16, 1950, in New York, NY. *Education:* Attended Regis College, 1968-70, University of Massachusetts, 1971-72, Cambridge University, University of London, and Oxford University, all 1975; University of Washington, B.A., 1976, M.Ed., 1978, Ph.D., 1984.

ADDRESSES: Office—University of Washington, Guthrie Annex II, NI-20, Seattle, WA 98195. *Agent*—Felicia Eth, 555 Bryant St., Ste. 350, Palo Alto, CA 94301.

CAREER: Child Development and Mental Retardation Center, University of Washington, research assistant, 1976-77; Highline-West Seattle Mental Health Center, Seattle, emergency services therapist and intern, 1978; Kitsap Mental Health Center, Bremerton, WA, coordinator of Primary Prevention/ Natural Helpers Project, 1979-81; Central Washington University, Ellensburg, lecturer, 1980-86; Kent Valley Youth Services, Kent, WA, specialist in drug/alcohol education and prevention, 1982; University of Washington, Seattle, teaching associate and project coordinator, 1985-87; independent practice, Seattle, psychologist, 1986-94; Center for the Study of Capable Youth, University of Washington, assistant director and psychologist, 1989—; University of Washington, research assistant professor of educational psychology, 1990-93, research assistant professor of women's studies, 1993—.

MEMBER: American Educational Research Association.

WRITINGS:

The Sound of a Silver Horn: Reclaiming the Heroism in Contemporary Women's Lives, Ballantine Books (New York), 1994.
(With K. D. Arnold and R. F. Subotnik) *Remarkable Women: Perspectives on Female Talent Development,* Hampton Press, 1995.
Riding the Windhorse: Psychological Health and the Experience of Transcendence, Ballantine Books, in press.

Contributor to books, including *Girls, Women, and Giftedness,* Trillium Press (Toronto), 1990; *Studies in Human Development and Professional Helping,* University of South Carolina Press (Columbia), 1991; *Handbook of Special Education: Research and Practice, Volume 2,* Pergamon Press (New York), 1992; and *Talent Development: Proceedings from the 1991 Henry B. and Jocelyn Wallace National Research Symposium on Talent Development,* Trillium Press, 1992. Contributor of articles to periodicals, including *Roeper Review, Gifted Child Quarterly, Gifted Child Today, Women and Therapy, Journal for the Education of the Gifted, Advanced Development Journal, Satorion: Nebraska Associa-*

tion for the Gifted Journal, Psychology of Women Quarterly, and *The Counseling Psychologist.*

SIDELIGHTS: Kathleen Noble told *CA:* "I took a circuitous route to writing and my current career. Having come of age during the late 1960s, I felt driven by a need to be actively involved in movements for social justice, particularly women's rights. I entered Regis College in 1968, majoring in political science, but I dropped out in 1970 because I wanted to be more involved in political activities. Two years later, after having spent a year in the Boston branch of VISTA (Volunteers in Service to America), I hitchhiked across the United States and decided to resettle myself in Seattle. I returned to the University of Washington as an undergraduate and earned a bachelor's degree in an interdisciplinary, pre-law program, preparatory to entering law school. Unexpectedly, however, I suffered a cardiac arrest and near death experience at the age of twenty-five, which completely altered my vocational plans. As I recovered from and absorbed the impact of this experience, my desire to understand what I had experienced while 'dead' made my previous career goal pale by comparison. Thus, I gave up the goal of a legal career and some months later was accepted into graduate school in counseling psychology. This field had not been remotely interesting to me prior to my near death experience, but now it seemed the perfect place to begin to decipher and integrate that extraordinary event.

"After completing my doctorate I was at a complete loss as to where my career might go. I had felt from the age of four that I would, could, and should write, but never knew what that would entail. I left graduate school with two principal areas of interest: the psychological impact of giftedness in the lives of women and girls; and the relationship between psychological health and spiritual experience, the subject of my doctoral dissertation. Neither area was (or is) considered academically 'mainstream,' so my prospects for an academic career were slim to say the least. Still, I was determined to pursue the subjects about which I felt most passionate and committed. In January, 1985, in order to keep body and soul together while I figured out what to do with my life, I accepted a three-year post-doctoral appointment at the University of Washington to develop and manage a school-to-work transition program for disabled secondary students. However, because this was neither my area of expertise nor interest, I was determined to do something to keep my spirit and interests alive.

"Very little research attention had been paid to the issue of giftedness in women when I began to write about that subject in 1985. To argue the case for more research and training, I organized three annual, international conferences at the University of Washington (1986, 1987, and 1988) to help highly capable women recognize talent in themselves and others and contribute their abilities more fully to the world. I also wrote my first scholarly paper entitled 'The Dilemma of the Gifted Woman,' which was published in *Psychology of Women Quarterly* in September, 1987, and which initiated a remarkable chain of events that culminated in my first book, *The Sound of a Silver Horn.* 'The Dilemma' was cited and discussed in the February, 1988, issue of *Vogue* magazine, after which I was contacted by Felicia Eth, a literary agent who encouraged me to write a book about gifted women. My thoughts about the subject were continuing to evolve, however. I was becoming far less interested in identifying the 'problems' of women than I was in generating solutions. Having been aware since childhood of the power of mythology to change the way people think about themselves and their lives, I decided to explore real women's lives using the metaphor of the heroic quest. This idea began its life as a theoretical article entitled 'The Female Hero: The Quest for Healing and Wholeness,' which was published in *Women and Therapy* in winter, 1990. It then evolved into a book proposal, and became *The Sound of a Silver Horn.*

"I have not lived exclusively as a writer, nor do I think I would like to. My work at the university, albeit part-time, provides me with a sense of community and variety that I find critical to my creativity and productivity. While I crave a fair amount of solitude in order to write, I find too much solitude to be isolating and oppressive. During the process of writing *Silver Horn,* I was very fortunate in receiving a five-week residency at Hedgebrook Farm, a retreat for women writers on Whidbey Island, Washington, which I found to be the perfect blend between solitude and community.

"Although I have a natural feel for the written word, unlike some writers I do not live to write; I only write about subjects that I care about. Because I have always been impatient with scholarly or professional writing that is pedantic and boring, I try to make my writing lively, readable, and accessible to a wide audience. I hope to achieve several goals through my books, articles, and chapters. Principally I hope to raise individual and community consciousness. I hope that my writing helps women of all ages to realize that each of us is capable of living heroic and authentic lives, and that we must do so if we are to begin to reverse the damage created by millennia of misogyny. I also hope to encourage other writers, artists, and scholars to create new images of women that validate and reflect our strength, courage, initiative, and authenticity in everyday life, and thereby encourage more women to confront the escalating social, political, ecological, and economic crises that abound on planet earth. Finally, I hope to create models of psychological and spiritual resilience for both women and men which encourage us to resist the inertia of the status quo and take responsibility for the larger community of which we are members.

"This final theme figures significantly into my new project. I have recently begun work on a book entitled *Riding the Windhorse: Psychological Health and the Experience of Transcendence.* As the name suggests, I am returning to an earlier interest to explore, through interviews with a variety of women and men, the ways in which spiritual experiences enhance our resilience, promote psychological maturity, and affect the course of our lives. The title comes from the Buddhist teacher Chongyam Trungpa, and is a metaphor for the energy of basic goodness. My hope is to show that these experiences, though long ignored or denigrated by the larger psychiatric community, are in fact quite common and crucial to our psychological and planetary health.

"I don't feel that I have much advice to offer fledgling writers, since I still am one myself. What I have learned about writing, so far, is that it's the hardest and most satisfying work I've ever done. It requires a high tolerance for solitude and uncertainty and demands that we pay close attention to the inner self because that is the source from which our words come. We have to have a strong sense of where we're going when we begin a project so that we don't get lost, while simultaneously recognizing that books have a life of their own and will always surprise us if we allow them to. And we have to carefully cultivate the craft of writing so that we will have confidence, during those inevitable dry and difficult times, in our ability to write well even if we feel we have nothing to say!"

*   *   *

NYE, Naomi Shihab   1952-

PERSONAL: Born March 12, 1952, in St. Louis, MO; daughter of Aziz and Miriam Naomi (Allwardt) Shihab; married Michael Nye (a lawyer and photographer), September 2, 1978; children: Madison Cloudfeather (son). *Education:* Trinity University, B.A., 1974. *Politics:* Independent. *Religion:* Ecumenical. *Avocational interests:* Traveling, reading, cooking.

ADDRESSES: Home—806 South Main, San Antonio, TX 78204.

CAREER: Freelance visiting writer at all levels, 1974—; University of Texas at Austin, visiting writer, spring, 1995.

MEMBER: Poets and Writers, Texas Institute of Letters, RAWI (Association of Arab American writers).

AWARDS, HONORS: Voertman Poetry Prize, Texas Institute of Letters, 1980, for *Different Ways to Pray,* and 1982, for *Hugging the Jukebox; Hugging the Jukebox* was named a notable book of 1982 by the American Library Association (ALA); winner of three Pushcart Prizes; I. B. Lavan Award, Academy of American Poets, 1988, for younger American poets; Charity Randall Prize for Spoken Poetry, with Galway Kinnell, International Poetry Forum, 1988; *This Same Sky* was selected as a notable book of 1992 by the ALA; *Sitti's Secrets* was named a best book of 1994 by *School Library Journal.*

WRITINGS:

POETRY

Tattooed Feet (chapbook), Texas Portfolio (Texas City), 1977.
Eye-to-Eye (chapbook), Texas Portfolio, 1978.
Different Ways to Pray, Breitenbush (Portland, OR), 1980.
On the Edge of the Sky (chapbook), Iguana (Madison, WI), 1981.
Hugging the Jukebox, Dutton (New York), 1982.
Yellow Glove, Breitenbush, 1986.
Invisible, Trilobite (Denton, TX), 1987.
Mint, State Street Press (Brockport, NY), 1991.
Travel Alarm (chapbook), Wings Press, 1993.
Red Suitcase, BOA Editions, 1994.
Words under the Words: Selected Poems, Far Corner Books, 1995.

Contributor of "Twenty Other Worlds" to *Texas Poets in Concert: A Quartet,* edited by Richard B. Sale, University of North Texas Press, 1990. Essay chosen for inclusion in *Best American Essays 1991,* edited by Joyce Carol Oates. Contributor of poems to periodicals, including *Atlantic Monthly, The Georgia Review,* and *New Virginia Reader.*

FICTION; FOR CHILDREN

Sitti's Secrets, illustrated by Nancy Carpenter, Four Winds/Macmillan, 1994.

Benito's Dream Bottle, illustrated by Yu Cha Pak, Simon and Schuster (New York, NY), 1995.

RECORDINGS

Rutabaga-Roo (songs), Flying Cat (San Antonio), 1979.

Lullaby Raft (songs), Flying Cat, 1981.

The Spoken Page (poetry reading), International Poetry Forum (Pittsburgh), 1988.

OTHER

(Modifying editor for poetry translations with Salma Khadra Jayyusi) Fadwa Tuqan, *A Mountainous Journey: An Autobiography,* text translated by Olive Kenny, Graywolf, 1990.

(Modifying editor with translator May Jayyusi) Muhammad al-Maghut, *The Fan of Swords: Poems,* edited by Salma Khadra Jayyusi, Three Continents (Washington, DC), 1991.

(Editor) *This Same Sky: A Collection of Poems from around the World* (for children), Four Winds, 1992.

Contributor of stories and essays to periodicals, including *Virginia Quarterly Review, Southwest Review, Georgia Review, Ploughshares, Manoa, Houston Chronicle,* and *Austin Chronicle.*

WORK IN PROGRESS: Editing a poetry anthology with Paul Janeczko; preparing *Lullaby Raft* (picture book) to be illustrated by Vivienne Flesher for Simon and Schuster.

SIDELIGHTS: Naomi Shihab Nye is known for award-winning poetry that lends a fresh perspective to ordinary events, people, and objects. "For me the primary source of poetry has always been local life, random characters met on the streets, our own ancestry sifting down to us through small essential daily tasks," Nye was quoted as saying by Jane L. Tanner in *Dictionary of Literary Biography (DLB).* Nye's poetry is also informed by her Palestinian American background as well as other cultures. In her work, according to Tanner, "Nye observes the business of living and the continuity among all the world's inhabitants. . . . She is international in scope and internal in focus."

Nye was born in St. Louis, Missouri, to a Palestinian father and an American mother of German descent. After spending much of her childhood in St.

Louis, Nye moved with her family to Jerusalem, which was then part of Jordan. Nye attended a year of high school in Jordan before her family moved to San Antonio, Texas, where the poet continues to live with her husband and son. "My poems and stories often begin with the voices of our neighbors, mostly Mexican-American, always inventive and surprising," Nye wrote in a press release for Four Winds Press. "I never get tired of mixtures."

Nye's first collection, a chapbook entitled *Tattooed Feet,* was published in 1977, and *Eye-to-Eye* followed in 1978. The poet's early work, written in free verse, often reflects the theme of a journey or quest. The opening poem of *Tattooed Feet,* "Pilgrimage," describes Via Dolorosa street in Jerusalem; another verse is entitled "Home." According to Tanner, "Nye finds grandeur in the mundane, even in minutiae, from the West Bank to Mexico to a car wash in Paris, Texas, 'perfectly ordered images / sophisticated enough to be called poetry.'" Tanner continued, "What is remarkable is Nye's ability to draw clear parallels between the ordinary and the sublime."

In her first full-length collection, *Different Ways to Pray,* Nye explores the differences as well as the shared experiences of cultures as varied as those in California, Texas, South America, and Mexico. The poem "Madison Street" is set in America, where Nye comments, "I was not here when all this started / still there is some larger belonging." In another verse the poet focuses on cultural unity: "My grandmother's eyes say Allah is everywhere." And in "Grandfather's Heaven" a child declares: "Grandma liked me even though my daddy was a Moslem." As Tanner observed in *DLB,* "with her acceptance of different 'ways to pray' is also Nye's growing awareness that living in the world can sometimes be difficult." The quality of *Different Ways to Pray* was recognized by the Texas Institute of Letters, which awarded Nye the Voertman Poetry Prize in 1980.

Nye followed *Different Ways to Pray* with *On the Edge of the Sky,* a slim volume printed on handmade paper, and *Hugging the Jukebox,* a full-length collection that also won the Voertman Poetry Prize. In *Hugging the Jukebox* Nye continues to focus on the ordinary, on connections between diverse peoples, and on the perspectives of those in other lands. She writes: "we move forward, / confident we were born into a large family, / our brothers cover the earth." Nye creates poetry from everyday scenes in "The Trashpickers of San Antonio," where the trashpickers are "murmuring in a language soft as rags." Other poems in *Hugging the Jukebox* include the lullaby "Martita y Luisa," "Nelle," and the title verse, which is about a young boy who lives in the Caribbean with his grandparents. The boy in "Hugging the Jukebox" is enthusiastic about the jukebox he adopts, singing its songs in a way that "strings a hundred passionate sentences in a single line."

Reviewers generally praised *Hugging the Jukebox,* noting Nye's warmth and celebratory tone. Writing in the *Village Voice,* Mary Logue commented that in Nye's poems concerning "daily tasks," "sometimes the fabric is thin and the mundaneness of the action shows through. But, in an alchemical process of purification, Nye often pulls gold from the ordinary." Logue also observed that "when Nye chooses to push herself and write dramatically, she creates powerful poems." And according to *Library Journal* contributor David Kirby, the poet "seems to be in good, easy relation with the earth and its peoples."

Nye's next collection, *Yellow Glove,* was published in 1986. Unlike her earlier work, the poems in *Yellow Glove* are tempered by tragedy and sorrow. In this collection Nye considers the Palestinian-Israeli conflict in "Blood," describes a cafe in combat-weary Beirut, bemoans "a world where no one saves anyone," and observes in "The Gardener" that "everything she planted gave up under the ground." As Tanner commented in *DLB,* "Still there arises out of these tragic phrases a message of hope, a realization that strength comes from facing adversity and that joy won from sorrow is priceless." *Georgia Review* contributor Philip Booth declared that Nye "knows more than most of us how many people(s) live; and she does justice to them, and to the need for change, by bringing home to readers both how variously and how similarly all people live."

In addition to her poetry collections, Nye has produced fiction for children, poetry and song recordings, and poetry translations. She has also edited *This Same Sky: A Collection of Poems from around the World,* a book for young people that was published in 1992. An anthology of poetry in translation, *This Same Sky* represents the work of 129 poets from sixty-eight countries. In her introduction, Nye writes, "Whenever someone suggests 'how much is lost in translation!' I want to say, 'Perhaps—but how much is gained!'"

Reviewers praised *This Same Sky,* which also includes a country and poet index, a map, and suggestions for further reading. These extras, according to a *Horn Book* reviewer, give "additional luster to a book which should prove invaluable for intercultural education as well as for pure pleasure." Although Lauralyn Persson noted in *School Library Journal* that some of the poems in the collection would be better appreciated by adults, she observed that the book is "brimming with much lovely material." And *Booklist* contributor Hazel Rochman called *This Same Sky* "an extraordinary anthology, not only in its global range . . . but also in the quality of the selections and the immediacy of their appeal."

Sitti's Secrets, an illustrated narrative for children, was published in 1994, and concerns an Arab American child's relationship with her *sitti* (Arabic for grandmother) who lives in a Palestinian village. The child, Mona, recalls visiting Sitti in Palestine: the surroundings, the culture, and how the two of them invented their own "sign" language to overcome the English-Arabic language barrier. And when Mona returns to the United States, she sustains the bond with her sitti through her active imagination. Mona also writes a letter to the president of the United States asking him for peace, and informing him that she knows he would like her sitti a great deal if he were to meet her. A reviewer for *Booklist* praised Nye for capturing the emotions of the "child who longs for a distant grandparent" as well as for writing a narrative that deals personally with Arabs and Arab Americans. A contributor to *Kirkus Reviews* asserted that Nye "deftly assembles particulars" of the relationship between grandmother and granddaughter, and "[recounts] the incidents with quiet eloquence," while a critic in the *Bulletin of the Center for Children's Books* described *Sitti's Secrets* as "lyrically reflective."

Naomi Shihab Nye told *CA:* "I believe everything poet William Stafford ever said. (He would tip his head and look skeptical to hear that.) I believe poetry is as basic to our lives (as in 'getting back to basics') and to education as anything else there could possibly be. I salute all the writers workshops for teachers and the writers-in-the-schools projects around the United States which have blossomed in the last twenty years. Student writing shows the positive effects. This is a particularly *American* phenomenon, and we should support and champion it whenever possible!"

BIOGRAPHICAL/CRITICAL SOURCES:

BOOKS

Dictionary of Literary Biography, Volume 120: *American Poets since World War II,* Gale, 1992.
Nye, Naomi Shihab, *Different Ways to Pray,* Breitenbush, 1980.
Nye, *Hugging the Jukebox,* Dutton, 1982.

Nye, *Yellow Glove,* Breitenbush, 1986.

PERIODICALS

Booklist, October 15, 1992, p. 425, March 15, 1994, p. 1374.
Bulletin of the Center for Children's Books, March, 1994, p. 228.
Georgia Review, spring, 1989.
Horn Book, March/April, 1993, p. 215.
Kirkus Reviews, February 15, 1994, p. 231.
Library Journal, August, 1982.
School Library Journal, December, 1992, p. 139.
Village Voice, January 18, 1983, p. 37.

OTHER

Press release from Four Winds Press, 1993.

—*Sketch by Michelle Motowski*

* * *

O CUILLEANAIN, Cormac 1950-

PERSONAL: Born November 14, 1950, in Cork, Ireland; son of Cormac (a university professor) and Eilis (a writer; maiden name, Dillon) O Cuilleanain; married Phyllis Gaffney (a university lecturer), January 4, 1974; children: Lean and Orla (daughters), Eoin (son). *Education:* National University of Ireland, University College, Dublin, B.A., 1970, M.A., 1972; Cambridge University, Ph.D., 1982; Dublin Institute of Technology, Diploma in Applied Linguistics, 1982. *Politics:* "Supporter of Irish Labour Party." *Religion:* Agnostic.

ADDRESSES: Home—16 Prince Edward Terr., Blackrock, County Dublin, Ireland. *Office*—Department of Italian, Trinity College, Dublin 2, Ireland.

CAREER: Institute of Public Administration, Dublin, Ireland, editor, 1977-78; Trinity College, Dublin, lecturer in Italian, 1978-79; Ward River Press, Dublin, editor, 1979-83; National University of Ireland, University College, Dublin, lecturer in Italian, 1983-86; Trinity College, lecturer in Italian, 1986—. Irish Writers' Centre, chairperson, 1991-93; Foundation for Italian Studies, member of board of directors, 1986—.

MEMBER: Irish Translators' Association (chairperson, 1986-91), Irish Writers' Union, Society for Italian Studies, Dublin Medieval Society.

AWARDS, HONORS: John Florio Translation Prize, 1974, for *Cagliostro.*

WRITINGS:

(Translator) Roberto Gervaso, *Cagliostro,* Gollancz (London), 1974.
(Translator) Pietro Valpreda, *The Valpreda Papers,* Gollancz, 1975.
Religion and the Clergy in Boaccacio's "Decameron", Edizione di Storia e Letteratura (Rome), 1984.
(Editor with Eric G. Haywood, and contributor) *Italian Storytellers: Essays on Italian Narrative Literature,* Irish Academic Press (Dublin), 1989.
(Translator) Eva Cantarella, *Bisexuality in the Ancient World,* Yale University Press (New Haven), 1992.
(Editor with John C. Barnes) *Dante and the Middle Ages,* Irish Academic Press, in press.

Work represented in anthologies, including *Language Across Cultures,* edited by Liam MacMathuna and David Singleton, IRAAL, 1984; and *Word and Drama in Dante: Essays on the "Divina Commedia",* edited by John C. Barnes and Jennifer Petrie, Irish Academic Press, 1993. Contributor of articles, translations, and reviews to language and Italian studies journals.

WORK IN PROGRESS: Research on literary translation, Boccaccio, Dante, and on the practical joke in Italian literature.

SIDELIGHTS: Cormac O Cuilleanain told *CA:* "Translators are hybrids. I am the son of a fiction writer, Eilis Dillon, and a professor of Irish literature, Cormac O Cuilleanain. I am the younger brother of a poet and academic, Eilean Ni Chuilleanain, and a violinist, Maire Ni Chuilleanain. Translators are also unoriginal (at least the good ones are), so my life can be construed as a set of variations on familiar themes.

"I trained as a violinist and played (briefly) in three professional orchestras. Part of my schooling was in Rome, which opened up Italy and its language and literature for me. I studied Italian at university, took postgraduate degrees, and now teach Italian at Ireland's oldest university. I also worked for five years in book publishing and have been active in cultural, political, and professional organizations. Out of all this comes the bridge-building activity of translation.

"In 1972 my mother's literary agent, David Bolt, found me a commission to translate an Italian biography of the eighteenth-century Sicilian con-man Count Cagliostro. My version won a prize for the best modern Italian translation published in Britain in 1974. Naively, I assumed that this would lead to glittering commissions and win me respect as an Italian scholar. In fact, commissions from publishers were few enough, while the status of translation as a literary and academic activity has only begun to rise in recent years. However, my personal enjoyment of translation, as an ego-free form of writing, has been enormous. In addition, since we set up the Irish Translators' Association in the mid-1980s, I have come to realize how essential my fellow-hybrids are in bringing new life to the world's writing."

* * *

OLAFSSON, Olafur Johann   1962-

PERSONAL: Born September 26, 1962, in Reykjavik, Iceland; son of Olafur Johann (a writer) and Anna (Jonsdottir) Sigurdsson; married Anna Olafsdottir (a homemaker), September 12, 1986; children: Olafur Johann, Jr. *Education:* Brandeis University, graduated (summa cum laude), 1985.

ADDRESSES: Home—New York, NY. *Office*—Sony Electronic Publishing Co., 9 West 57th St., New York, NY 10019. *Agent*—Morton Janklow, Janklow & Nesbit Associates, 598 Madison Ave., New York, NY 10022.

CAREER: Sony Electronic Publishing Co., New York City, president, 1991—.

MEMBER: Phi Beta Kappa.

WRITINGS:

Absolution, Pantheon, 1994.

* * *

OLDERR, Steven   1943-

PERSONAL: Born September 28, 1943, in Topeka, KS; married Patricia Pingatore (a teacher of French), February 22, 1968; children: William. *Education:* Northern Illinois University, B.A., 1968; DePaul University, M.A., 1970; Rosary College, M.A.L.S., 1972. *Politics:* Independent. *Religion:* Episcopalian. *Avocational interests:* Bicycling, scouting, soccer.

ADDRESSES: Home—1165 South Wenonah, Oak Park, IL 60304.

CAREER: Substitute teacher at public schools in Chicago, IL, 1970-71; Eisenhower Public Library, Harwood Heights, IL, assistant director, 1972-74;

Riverside Public Library, Riverside, IL, director, 1974-88; Naperville Public Libraries, Naperville, IL, assistant director, 1992—. *Military service:* U.S. Army, nuclear weapons assembler, 1961-63.

MEMBER: American Library Association, League of American Bicyclists, Just for Kicks Soccer Team, Boy Scouts of America.

AWARDS, HONORS: Olderr's Young Adult Fiction Index was named an Outstanding Reference Book of the Year by *School Library Journal,* 1992.

WRITINGS:

Symbolism: A Comprehensive Dictionary, McFarland and Co., 1986.
Mystery Index, American Library Association, 1987.
Olderr's Fiction Subject Headings, American Library Association, 1991.
(Compiler) *Reverse Symbolism Dictionary,* McFarland and Co., 1991.

Compiler of the annuals *Olderr's Fiction Index,* St. James Press, 1987-91, and *Olderr's Young Adult Fiction Index,* St. James Press, 1988-91. Columnist, *Forest Park Review,* 1973-75.

WORK IN PROGRESS: Use-Based Materials Budgeting for Libraries; Olderr's Bicyclopedia, completion expected in 1995.

SIDELIGHTS: Steven Olderr told *CA:* "My writing stems from my personal and professional interests. If I can't find a book that does what I need, I write my own. While studying for a degree in English, I wrote a number of papers dealing with symbolism in literature, even though basic information was hard to find. After I established myself in my library career, I addressed this need in my first book, *Symbolism: A Comprehensive Dictionary.* Its success led to the companion volume, *Reverse Symbolism Dictionary,* five years later.

"When I became the director of the Riverside Public Library, I inherited a clientele mad for mysteries and set about building up the collection. With the knowledge I gained in the process, I wrote *Mystery Index.* The success of that book led to a full-time job writing the *Fiction Index* and *Young Adult Fiction Index* series. Curiously, these books did not enjoy the same success as *Mystery Index.* Perhaps readers of general fiction lack the zeal of mystery fans. *Fiction Subject Headings* was a spinoff of the fiction index series. I wanted to use the Library of Congress subject headings, but had to adapt them for fiction. It wasn't my intention to write another book in the process; it just turned out that way.

"As the assistant director of the Naperville Public Libraries, my efforts to bring traditional library statistics to bear on materials funding prompted the development of some simple, but unique, funding formulas, which will result in the book *Use-Based Materials Budgeting for Libraries*.

"My volunteer work as a Boy Scout bicycling merit badge counselor was the genesis of another work in progress, *Olderr's Bicyclepedia*. That started life as a short glossary to explain bicycling terms to my young charges, but it grew into a seven-hundred-page manuscript. The problem begins when one learns that an ordinary ten-speed bicycle has more than ten-thousand parts. The manuscript grew so large and continues to change so fast that I am considering publishing the work on the Internet as shareware, which will cost less than a book and can be updated easily.

"As a professional librarian, I find a great satisfaction in making knowledge more accessible to others. I view each book as a building block that future researchers can use to advance the store of human knowledge. Although I have worked as an administrator during most of my library career, it is my early work as a reference librarian that I feel is most important in my writing. It taught me how to do research and how to design a work that is understandable and accessible.

"When not working at the library, I play soccer, ride my mountain bike, and go camping with my scout troop, all winter and summer. While these activities give me energy and help me keep my creative edge, they also cut into my writing time, so I keep a list of books that I want to write after I retire from active library service or wear out my knees."

*   *   *

O'NAN, Stewart 1961-

PERSONAL: Born February 4, 1961, in Pittsburgh, PA; son of John Lee (an engineer) and Mary Ann (an economist; maiden name, Smith); married Trudy Anne Southwick (a social worker), October 27, 1984; children: Caitlin Elizabeth, Stephen James. *Education:* Boston University, B.S., 1983; Cornell University, M.F.A., 1992. *Politics:* "Hopeful." *Religion:* "See Flannery O'Connor, John Cheever."

ADDRESSES: Home—407 Utica St., Ithaca, NY 14850. *Agent*—Georges Borchardt, Inc., 136 East 57th St., New York, NY 10022.

CAREER: Grumman Aerospace Corporation, Bethpage, NY, test engineer, 1984-88; writer.

MEMBER: Cornell Book and Bowl.

AWARDS, HONORS: Ascent Fiction Prize (for short story "Econoline"), 1988; Columbia Fiction Award (for short story "The Third of July"), 1989; Drue Heinz for Literature, 1993 for *In the Walled City;* William Faulkner Prize, 1993, for *Snow Angels*.

WRITINGS:

NOVELS

Snow Angels, Doubleday (New York, NY), 1994.

Also author of the novels *End of Memory,* and *Sentimental Journey,* both 1994, and *Kissing the Dead,* in press.

OTHER

In the Walled City (short stories), University of Pittsburgh Press, 1993.
(Editor) John Gardner, *On Writers and Writing,* introduction by Charles Johnson, Addison-Wesley, 1994.

Also author of screenplays for *Angels* (based on the novel by Denis Johnson), and *The Violent Bear It Away* (based on the novel by Flannery O'Connor), both 1994.

WORK IN PROGRESS: On the 101st Airborne Division in Vietnam, 1968-1969.

SIDELIGHTS: Stewart O'Nan told *CA:* "In my fiction and in the screenwriting projects I take on, I seem to have a strange and absolute religious vision of America as it is. I am primarily a realist and hope to show great empathy for my people without softening the difficult situations they find themselves in—yet my work inevitably veers into the cruel and the sentimental. My characters are lonely people who have a real need to believe; the struggle between faith and doubt produces either heartening victories (as in Cheever) or horrifying defeats (Flannery O'Connor, Robert Stone). The work is often ugly and unsettling due to this extreme split between hope and despair. It is extreme fiction masquerading behind the guise of mainstream realism. I hope it is generous, or, as Cheever said, 'humane.'"

*   *   *

ORR, Robert T.   1908-1994

OBITUARY NOTICE—See index for CA sketch: Born August 17, 1908, in San Francisco, CA; died after a long illness, June 23, 1994, in Larkspur, CA. Biologist, educator, and writer. Orr was an authority on animal behavior and biology. He earned his doctorate from the University of California at Berkeley in 1937 and began a distinguished career as curator at the California Academy of Sciences in 1936, becoming senior scientist in 1975, and curator emeritus in 1989. Throughout his career Orr also taught at such institutions as Stanford University, the University of California, Berkeley, and the University of San Francisco. He was a contributor to various journals and zoological publications, as well as the author of many books which include Vertebrate Biology (1961), The Animal Kingdom (1965), and Marine Mammals of California (1972).

OBITUARIES AND OTHER SOURCES:

BOOKS

Who's Who in America, 46th edition, Marquis, 1990.

PERIODICALS

New York Times, July 3, 1994, p. 28.

*   *   *

O'SHAUGHNESSY, Ellen Cassels   1937-

PERSONAL: Born October 1, 1937, in Columbia, SC; daughter of Melvin O. (a professional golfer) and Grace Ellen (a writer; maiden name, Cassels) Hemphill; married John F. O'Shaughnessy (a teacher), December, 1979 (divorced, March, 1990); children: John H., Anne H. Sloan. Education: Attended University of South Carolina, 1955-57, and Golden Gate University, 1974; International University, B.A., 1977; Fielding Institute, M.A., 1979. Politics: Republican. Religion: Protestant. Avo-cational interests: Painting acrylics for children (carousel horses).

ADDRESSES: Home—P.O. Box 51063, Pacific Grove, CA 93950.

CAREER: Monterey Peninsula Unified School District, Monterey, CA, teacher's aide and art instructor, 1968-74; Pacific Grove Unified School District, Pacific Grove, credentialed adult school teacher and teacher's aide, 1974-82, special education consultant, 1984-85; Psychological Services, Fort Ord, CA, intern, 1976; substitute teacher for special education classes, 1983-84; Synthesis (publishing company), Pacific Grove, CA, owner, writer, and publisher, 1984—.

WRITINGS:

Teaching Art to Children, privately printed, 1974.
Synthesis (symbolic-language series for developmentally disabled and non-reading adults), Synthesis, 1981.
You Love to Cook Book (symbolic-language cookbook), Synthesis, 1983.
I Could Ride on the Carousel Longer, Synthesis, 1989.
Somebody Called Me a Retard Today . . . And My Heart Felt Sad, Walker, 1992.

WORK IN PROGRESS: "A very easy-to-understand method for learning to play piano . . . ideal for developmentally disabled adults."

SIDELIGHTS: Ellen O'Shaughnessy's career as a writer and publisher grew out of her years of experience as a teacher of developmentally disabled adults. She developed a symbolic language called Synthesis and created a series of books and a cookbook for her students, incorporating her work into a project for her M.A. degree in psychology. "This project took three years of research, and it works!" O'Shaughnessy commented.

"I feel the most comfortable with my students and friends who are disabled because of their strengths and love. We laugh a lot and genuinely care about one another. I wrote Somebody Called Me a Retard Today . . . And My Heart Felt Sad for them because we get teased a lot. It seems that many people are critical or pull back when the handicap is on the outside and are far less critical when the handicap is on the inside.

"When I get an idea for a book, I become compulsive and preoccupied," O'Shaughnessy noted. "When the project is finished, I come back to reality and find that colors are much brighter than I remembered. I sometimes wonder just where this 'place' is that I go to and how I know when to come back."

O'Shaughnessy, who was described as "one very special woman" by Susan Cantrell in the *The Californian,* explained her motivation for writing: "What I hope to achieve through the books I write is not always clear to me. I want to do more than entertain. I think that I want children (or adults) to be moved or changed in attitude or understanding after reading one of my books. When I developed a language and books for developmentally disabled adults and they could 'read' for the first time in [their lives], we all wept with excitement. That's what I'm trying to say . . . I hope that my books have impact."

O'Shaughnessy has this advice for aspiring writers: "Since I wrote a very simple little book with what I consider as a message for children—to *be kind*—I suggest that any young authors forget about the competition and send your manuscript to a publisher! Your message may be just what is needed at the time. Just mail it in and be patient. If it is rejected, just mail it out again. Keep your spirits up. Remember how many great writers have been rejected over and over and then found success!"

BIOGRAPHICAL/CRITICAL SOURCES:

PERIODICALS

Californian, June 11, 1990.
Kirkus Reviews, October 15, 1992.

*   *   *

OSMOND, Jonathan   1953-

PERSONAL: Born October 6, 1953, in Coventry, England; son of Eric and Mary (Morris) Osmond; married Maria Magdalena Sztajerwald, 1987; children: Alexander, Laurence, Conrad. *Education:* Attended Queen's College, Oxford, 1971-75; University of Hamburg, 1973-74; University of Munich, 1975-76; and St. Antony's College, Oxford, 1976-79.

ADDRESSES: Office—School of History and Archaeology, University College, University of Wales, Cardiff, P.O. Box 909, Cardiff CF1 3XU, Wales.

CAREER: Theodor Heuss research fellow, Institute of Bavarian History, Munich, 1977-78; University of Leicester, Leicester, England, lecturer in history, 1979-93; Humboldt University, Berlin, Humboldt research fellow, 1993; Central European University, Budapest, visiting professor, 1993; University of Wales, Cardiff, professor of modern European history, 1994—.

WRITINGS:

German Reunification: A Reference Guide and Commentary, Longman (New York), 1992.
Rural Protest in the Weimar Republic, St. Martin's (New York), 1993.

WORK IN PROGRESS: Research for a social history of East German agriculture, 1945-1961.

*   *   *

OUT TO LUNCH
See WATSON, Ben

P

PAE, Sung Moon 1939-

PERSONAL: Born December 6, 1939, in Taegu, South Korea; son of John (a physician) and Pearl (a homemaker) Pae; married August 15, 1968; wife's name, Sook J. (a registered nurse and social worker); children: William, Suzan, Jeanne. *Education:* Kansas State University, M.A., 1971; University of Kansas, Ph.D., 1975. *Politics:* Democrat. *Religion:* Presbyterian.

ADDRESSES: Home—608 Louisiane Circle, Bellevue, NE 68005. *Office*—Division of Social Sciences, Bellevue University, Bellevue, NE 68005.

CAREER: Bellevue University, Bellevue, NE, professor of social sciences and chairperson of division, 1975—, and Con Agra Distinguished Professor of Political Science.

MEMBER: American Political Science Association, Korean Association of Nebraska (member of board of directors).

WRITINGS:

Testing Democratic Theories in Korea, University Press of America, 1986.
Korea Leading Developing Nations: Economy, Democracy, and Welfare, University Press of America, 1992.

WORK IN PROGRESS: The Fire of My Soul, an autobiography, completion expected in 1996.

SIDELIGHTS: Sung Moon Pae told *CA:* "Life, liberty, and the pursuit of happiness have been fascinating topics throughout human civilizations of both the East and the West. They can be directly related and attributed to economic development, democratization, and social welfare services. I wanted to pursue a longitudinal, comparative study of more than one hundred-fifty countries in the world, concerning the reasons why some countries had successfully enhanced these human endeavors, and why other countries had lagged far behind, which resulted in poverty, deprivation of human rights and freedoms, and disease.

"Amidst despair and frustration, the Republic of Korea has shown spectacular accomplishments in the improvement of the economy, democracy, and welfare services. I decided to explore the Korean model. It may provide other countries, both advanced and developing, with reference for examination, critical review, and possible emulation."

*   *   *

PAINE, Sheila 1929-

PERSONAL: Born September 29, 1929; married Leslie Paine, December 23, 1953 (died, 1974); children: Denzil, Rosamund, Morwenna, Imogen. *Education:* Attended Hammersmith College of Art and Oxford Polytechnic. *Politics:* None. *Religion:* Church of England.

ADDRESSES: Agent—c/o St. Martin's Press, 175 Fifth Ave., New York, NY 10010.

CAREER: Writer and lecturer on international embroidery traditions. Has conducted research on embroidery in Western Europe, Russia, East Africa, Egypt, Israel, India, Mexico, United States, and other countries. Royal Geographical Society, fellow.

MEMBER: Institute of Linguists, Embroiders Guild,

British-Yemeni Society, Oxford Italian Association.

AWARDS, HONORS: Sunday Times travel writing contest, 1989; *Independent* travel writing award, 1991.

WRITINGS:

Chikan Embroidery: The Floral Whitework of India, Shire Ethnography, 1989.
Embroidered Textiles: Traditional Patterns from Five Continents, Rizzoli, 1990.
The Afghan Amulet: Travels from the Hindu Kush to Razgrad, St. Martin's, 1994.

Contributor of articles and reviews to periodicals, including *Embroidery, Country Living,* and *Times Literary Supplement.*

SIDELIGHTS: Sheila Paine told *CA:* "It was a rug in the souk of Fez in Morocco that launched me on my writing career. I hadn't the slightest intention of buying it but succumbed to the blandishments of traders with generations of dealers' blood coursing through their veins. I was so cross with myself that I stopped at a cafe in the next town and wrote step by step exactly how it had happened. This piece of writing was runner-up in the *Sunday Times* travel writing contest. Preferring to be a winner, I tried for the *Independent*'s travel writing award the following year and won it. I was then approached by Penguin and asked to write a travel book, but refused.

"I had been travelling for many years recording embroidery traditions and had written two books on the subject, but my travel jottings on people and places I had always thrown away, thinking they were of interest only to myself. Now I began to keep them, but still refused a contract as I feel strongly that travel writing must record the truth and can only be submitted for publication once the journeys are complete and have proved interesting enough for readers to enjoy.

"The aim of my travelling is always to search for the social context, traditions and patterns of embroidery and to record them in my embroidery books. The aim of my travel writing is to lead my readers with me, observing and describing the people and places, the hilarious moments, the dangerous moments. I am very careful never to make judgements but to leave my readers to form their own. I spare them the pedestrian details, the personal problems, the tedium of the road. I refrain from navel-fluffism. I steer clear of library references. I hope to be only thought-provoking and entertaining."

PAPER, Lewis Jay 1946-

PERSONAL: Born October 13, 1946, in Newark, NJ; son of Sidney and Dorothy (Neiman) Paper; married Jan Clachko, September 4, 1972; children: Lindsay, Brett. *Education:* University of Michigan, B.A., 1968; Harvard University, J.D., 1971; Georgetown University, LL.M., 1972.

ADDRESSES: Office—Grove, Engelberg, and Gross, 2033 M St. NW, Suite 404, Washington, D.C. 20036. *Agent*—Scott Meredith Literary Agency Inc, 845 Third Ave., New York, NY 10022.

CAREER: Admitted to the Bar of the District of Columbia, 1971, New Jersey Bar, 1975, and Maryland Bar, 1984; Citizens Communications Center, Washington, DC, attorney, 1972-73; Lowenstein, Sandler, Brochin, Kohl, and Fisher, Newark, NJ, associate attorney, 1975-78; Federal Communications Commission, Washington, DC, assistant general counsel, 1978-79, associate general counsel, 1979-81; Grove, Engelberg, and Gross, Washington, DC, partner, 1981—. Harvard University, teaching fellow in government, 1969-71; legislative counsel to Senator Gaylord Nelson, Washington, DC, 1973-75.

MEMBER: Washington Council of Lawyers.

WRITINGS:

The Promise and the Performance: The Leadership of John F. Kennedy, Crown (New York), 1975, revised edition published with an introduction by Senator Bill Bradley as *John F. Kennedy: The Promise and the Performance,* Da Capo (New York), 1980.
Brandeis, Prentice-Hall (Englewood Cliffs, NJ), 1983.
Empire: William S. Paley and the Making of CBS, St. Martin's (New York), 1987.

Contributor of articles to periodicals and professional journals.

SIDELIGHTS: A lawyer who has been active in legal circles for more than twenty years, Lewis Paper is also the author of several well-recieved books concerning politics, law, and business. In his 1975 volume *The Promise and the Performance: The Leadership of John F. Kennedy,* Lewis Paper provides an analysis of the presidency of John F. Kennedy, comparing it to other administrations from Theodore Roosevelt's to Richard Nixon's. Examining Kennedy's personality, programs, and political failures and successes, Paper focuses on "the President's concept of the office; the methods by which he intends to make decisions; the manner in which he intends to serve that concept and execute those decisions to lead the public; and the images he will cast among his many constituencies," noted William V. Shannon in the *New York Times Book Review.* Paper concludes in *The Promise and the Performance* that Kennedy's most notable achievement was his ability to inspire the confidence and ideals of the American public.

During the writing of *The Promise and the Performance* Paper conducted numerous interviews with political insiders in addition to studying various biographical sources, and his exhaustive research has been noted by critics. Although Shannon pointed out in the *New York Times Book Review* that the work "is sadly slowed by . . . excessive caution," the critic commented that "Paper writes clean, sober prose, is intellectually honest and careful, has done primary research in the Kennedy papers, and has some valid insights." In the *National Review,* Alan L. Miller stated that *The Promise and the Performance* is "a balanced study of a pragmatist who seldom allowed his political progress to be burdened by the excess baggage of ideology."

Brandeis, published in 1983, is Paper's biography of Louis D. Brandeis, the U.S. Supreme Court justice who served from 1916 to 1939 and established a reputation as a vigorous defender of First Amendment rights. Maintaining a generally liberal position on the Supreme Court, Brandeis was known for his dissents on such issues as the constitutionality of president Franklin D. Roosevelt's "New Deal"; the justice was also noted for his pioneering efforts in the American Zionist movement. Critics generally praised Paper's portrait of Brandeis for being detailed and objective. Edwin M. Yoder, in the *Washington Post Book World*, maintained that "a judicious objectivity is the principal strength of this sober, factual, informative but rather unadventurous portrait." In the *Los Angeles Times Book Review,* Eliot Janeway asserted that the author "has made a landmark contribution to the oral history of this century; he has conducted painstaking personal interviews, invaluable for the annals, of more former clerks to Supreme Court justices than any previous scholar. In the process, he has brought not only Brandeis but Associate Justice Oliver Wendell Holmes down from the rarefied atmosphere of Olympus; his research has added a dimension of humility and humanity to each of these extremely different great men."

Paper's next book, *Empire: William S. Paley and the*

Making of CBS, is a biography of the Columbia Broadcasting System (CBS) "empire builder." Paley's career is traced from the beginning of network television, when he contracted such popular entertainers as Lucille Ball, Arthur Godfrey, Amos 'n' Andy, Jack Benny, Red Skelton, and Bing Crosby, to the late 1980s, when the he was widely perceived as a "guru" in the television industry. While some critics faulted, what they perceived as *Empire*'s awkward chronological structure and lack of discussion of its subject's dynamic personality, others applauded Paper's objective depiction of Paley and his career. In the *Washington Post Book World* Kenneth Bilby stated, "In his pursuit of an often elusive quarry, Paper has succeeded in achieving a rare degree of editorial balance. He has also provided the most penetrating biographical look thus far." Steve Daley, writing in *Tribune Books,* remarked that "Lewis Paper's estimable biography goes a long way toward clarifying the image. William Paley is an American original, and Paper's mix of broadcast history and anecdotal style serves to flesh out a story of power, ambition, and influence."

BIOGRAPHICAL/CRITICAL SOURCES:

PERIODICALS

Los Angeles Times Book Review, September 25, 1983, p. 2.
National Review, June 11, 1976, p. 634.
New York Times Book Review, December 28, 1975, pp. 2, 22; April 13, 1980, p. 43; November 20, 1983, pp. 11, 35; August 30, 1987, p. 26.
Publishers Weekly, September 29, 1975, p. 48.
Tribune Books (Chicago), September 20, 1987, pp. 9, 11.
Washington Post Book World, October 23, 1983, pp. 4, 14; August 30, 1987, p. 5.*

*   *   *

PATZERT, Rudolph W.   1911-

PERSONAL: Born October 15, 1911, in New York, NY; son of Rudolph J. (worked in a confectionery shop) and Mary Ellen (Mundy) Patzert; married Theresa J. Levin (a social worker), January 24, 1938; children: William, Andrew. *Education:* Attended City College (now the City University of New York), U.S. Coast Guard Academy, and Maritime Commission Training Schools. *Religion:* Protestant.

ADDRESSES: Home—1756 Belle Meade Rd., Encinitas, CA 92024.

CAREER: U.S. Merchant Marine, 1928-82, beginning as merchant seaman, retiring as captain. Also worked for a newspaper printer.

MEMBER: National Maritime Union; Masters, Mates, and Pilots.

AWARDS, HONORS: Military—Combat awards for the North Atlantic, Mediterranean, Caribbean, and Vietnam, British award for service in North Atlantic combat, and award from the government of Israel.

WRITINGS:

Running the Palestine Blockade, Naval Institute Press (Annapolis, MD), 1994.

WORK IN PROGRESS: The Trembling Ship, on offshore oil exploration.

*   *   *

PAULING, Linus (Carl) 1901-1994

OBITUARY NOTICE—See index for *CA* sketch: Born February 28, 1901, in Portland, OR; died of prostate cancer, August 19, 1994, in Big Sur, CA. Scientist, political activist, and author. The only person in history to win two unshared Nobel Prizes, Pauling was awarded his first Nobel Prize in 1954 for his research on the chemical bond which holds molecules together and the subsequent understanding of complex chemical structures; his second Nobel was in 1962 for his efforts toward peace. In addition, Pauling's work was acknowledged as instrumental in laying the groundwork for James Watson's and Francis Crick's discovery of the structure of DNA (deoxyribonucleic acid). After receiving his doctorate from California Institute of Technology in 1925, Pauling began a long career at that establishment, rising from a research associate in 1927 to professor of chemistry in 1964. During this period Pauling's chemistry textbooks were widely used, and his 1939 volume, *The Nature of the Chemical Bond and the Structure of Molecules and Crystals: An Introduction to Modern Structural Chemistry,* was considered a landmark work. Pauling's research into molecular structure paved the way for the scientific understanding of the structure of antibodies and proteins, the development of new drugs, and the formation of plastics and synthetic fibers. It was for these pioneering contributions that Pauling was awarded the Nobel Prize for chemistry in 1954. Also during the 1950s, Pauling became a leading voice against the international nuclear arms race. At risk during the McCarthy era—when such activity was considered potentially

"communist"—Pauling persevered in gathering the signatures of 11,021 scientists on a petition entreating the United Nations to ban the testing of nuclear weapons. Further, he gathered his arguments together in an influential book entitled *No More War!,* published in 1958. In the 1970s, citing what some scientists considered dubious evidence, Pauling began advocating consumption of large doses of vitamin C to increase the body's immune systems against infectious diseases. His book on the subject, *Vitamin C and the Common Cold* (1970), became a best-seller. Other publications by Pauling include *Science and World Peace* (1967), *Structural Chemistry and Molecular Biology* (1968), and *How to Live Longer and Feel Better* (1986).

OBITUARIES AND OTHER SOURCES:

BOOKS

Who's Who in the World, 11th edition, Marquis, 1992.

PERIODICALS

Chicago Tribune, August 21, 1994, sec. 2, p. 8; August 28, 1994, sec. 2, p. 6.
Los Angeles Times, August 20, 1994, pp. A1, A24; August 21, 1994, p. A3.
New York Times, August 21, 1994, pp. A1, B51.
Times (London), August 22, 1994, p. 17.

*   *   *

PEARCE, David W(illiam) 1941-

PERSONAL: Born October 11, 1941, in Harrow, England; son of William Henry (a glassblower) and Gladys Muriel (a shop assistant; maiden name, Webb) Pearce; married Susan Mary Reynolds; children: Daniel Benjamin, Corin Gareth. *Education:* Lincoln College, Oxford, B.A. (with first class honors), 1963, M.A., 1967; attended London School of Economics and Political Science, London, 1963-64. *Religion:* None.

ADDRESSES: Home—90 Kimbolton Rd., Bedford MK40 2PE, England. *Office*—Centre for Social and Economic Research on the Global Environment, University College, University of London, Gower St., London WC1E 6BT, England.

CAREER: Worked for Kodak Ltd., 1959-60; University of Lancaster, Bailrigg, England, began as assistant lecturer, became lecturer in economics, 1964-67; University of Southampton, Southampton, England, began as lecturer, became senior lecturer in economics, 1967-74; University of Leicester, Leicester, England, director of Public Sector Economics Research Centre, 1974-77; University of Aberdeen, Aberdeen, Scotland, professor of political economy, 1977-83, head of department, 1981-83; University of London, London, England, professor of economics, 1983—, and political economy, 1985—, head of department, 1984-88, director of London Environmental Economics Centre, 1988-90, associate director of the center, 1990-92, director of Centre for Social and Economic Research on the Global Environment, a joint venture with University of East Anglia, 1991—. University of Adelaide, professor, 1982; Cambridge University, Denman Lecturer, 1988, Henry Sidgwick Memorial Lecturer, 1990; University of Liverpool, Annual Economic Lecturer, 1990; University of Southampton, Fawley Foundation Lecturer, 1990; University of Lancaster, Esmee Fairbairn Lecturer, 1990; University of Newcastle, Proctor & Gamble Lecturer, 1991; University of Bath, Koy Boey Lin Lecturer, 1991; Oregon State University, visiting lecturer, 1993. World Energy Council, member of board of directors, 1991—; United Nations Global Environment Facility, member of scientific and technical advisory panel, 1991—; United Nations Economic Commission, chairperson of Long-Range Transport of Air Pollutants Economic Task Force, 1992—; World Resources Institute, member of council, 1992—; World Bank, member of advisory group to the vice-president for environmentally sustainable development, 1993—; International Union for the Conservation of Nature, member of Species Survival Commission for ethnozoology; European Economics and Financial Centre, member of board of directors, 1991—. British Social Science Research Council, vice-chairperson of Economic Affairs Committee, 1984-85; member of Public Finance Consortium, 1983-85, National Radiological Protection Board, 1980-86, and Institute of Petroleum Energy Economics Group, 1984—; National Institute of Economic and Social Research, member of board of governors, 1985—. Coopers, Lybrand, Deloitte, senior adviser, 1990-91; London Economics, senior environmental adviser, 1990-92; National Grid Co., member of environment advisory committee, 1991—; environment adviser to Dow Chemical Co., 1991—, and Vauxhall Motors, 1992—.

MEMBER: Royal Society of Arts (fellow), Royal Society for the Protection of Birds (member of council, 1990-92).

AWARDS, HONORS: Named to Global Five Hundred Roll of Honor, United Nations Environment Program, 1989; Gambrinus-Giuseppe Mazzotti Prize for Literature, 1991, for *Blueprint for a Green Economy.*

WRITINGS:

(With S. G. Sturmey) *Economic Analysis,* McGraw, 1966.

Cost Benefit Analysis, Macmillan, 1971, 2nd edition, 1983.

(With C. J. Hawkins) *Capital Investment Appraisal,* Macmillan, 1971.

(With A. K. Dasgupta) *Cost Benefit Analysis: Theory and Practice,* Macmillan, 1972.

(Editor) *The Economics of Natural Resource Depletion,* Macmillan, 1975.

Environmental Economics, Longman, 1976.

(With W. J. L. Ryan) *Price Theory,* Macmillan, 1977.

(With I. Walter) *Resource Conservation: The Social and Economic Dimensions of Recycling,* New York University Press, 1977.

(Editor) *The Valuation of Social Cost,* Allen & Unwin, 1978.

(With L. Edwards and G. Beuret) *Decision Making for Energy Futures: A Case Study of the Windscale Inquiry,* Macmillan, 1979.

Waste Paper Recovery, Organization for Economic Cooperation and Development (Paris), 1979.

(With C. A. Nash) *Social Projects Appraisal,* Halstead, 1981.

(General editor) *The Macmillan Dictionary of Economics,* MIT Press, 1981, 4th edition, 1992.

(With J. Schmedtje, M. Mitchell, and others) *Portugal: Issues and Options in the Energy Sector,* World Bank, 1984.

(With M. Webb) *The Economic Benefits of Power Supply,* World Bank, 1985.

(Editor with D. Collard and D. Ulph) *Economics, Growth, and Sustainable Environments: Essays in Honour of Richard Lecomber,* Macmillan, 1987.

(With C. Perrings, J. B. Opschoor, and others) *Economics and the Environment: A Contribution to the National Conservation Strategy for Botswana,* International Union for the Conservation of Nature, 1988.

(With A. Markandya) *Environmental Policy Benefits: Monetary Valuation,* Organization for Economic Cooperation and Development (Paris), 1989.

(With R. Kerry Turner) *The Economics of Natural Resources and the Environment,* Johns Hopkins University Press, 1989.

(With Markandya and E. Barbier) *Sustainable Development: Economics and the Environment in the Third World,* Edward Elgar, 1990.

(Editor and contributor) *Renewable Natural Resources: Economic Incentives for Improved Management,* Organization for Economic Cooperation and Development (Paris), 1989.

(With Markandya and Barbier) *Blueprint for a Green Economy,* Earthscan, 1989.

(With Barbier, J. Burgess, and T. Swanson) *Elephants, Economics, and Ivory,* Earthscan, 1990.

(With J-Ph. Barde) *Valuing the Environment: Six Case Studies,* Earthscan, 1991.

(Editor with Opschoor, and contributor) *Persistent Micropollutants: Economics, Ecotoxicology, Decision-Making,* Kluwer (Dordrecht), 1991.

(With Markandya, Barbier, Swanson, and others) *Blueprint 2: Greening the World Economy,* Earthscan, 1991.

(With Turner) *Benefits Estimates and Environmental Decision Making,* Organization for Economic Cooperation and Development (Paris), 1992.

(With C. Bann and S. Georgiou) *The Social Costs of Energy,* H.M.S.O., 1992.

(With J. Warford) *World Without End: Economics, Environment, and Sustainable Development,* Oxford University Press, 1993.

Economic Values and the Natural World, MIT Press, 1993.

(With Turner and I. Bateman) *Environmental Economics: An Elementary Introduction,* Johns Hopkins University Press, 1993.

Blueprint 3: Measuring Sustainable Development, Earthscan, 1993.

(With I. Brisson, J. Barton, and others) *Externalities From Landfill and Incineration,* H.M.S.O., 1993.

(With D. Whittington and Georgiou) *A Technical Manual for the Appraisal of Environmental Projects and Policies,* Organization for Economic Cooperation and Development (Paris), 1994.

(With Katrina Brown) *The Causes of Tropical Deforestation,* UCL Press, 1994.

(With D. Moran) *The Economic Value of Biological Diversity,* Earthscan, 1994.

(With Swanson and R. Cervigni) *The Valuation and Appropriation of the Global Benefits of Plant Genetic Resources for Agriculture,* United Nations Food and Agriculture Organization (Rome), 1994.

(With Whittington and Georgiou) *The Economic Value of Environmental Benefits in Developing Countries,* United Nations Environment Program (Nairobi), 1994.

Other books include (with I. Walter and H. Siebert) *Risk and the Political Economy of Resource Development,* Macmillan. Work represented in anthologies, including *Pricing the European Environment,* edited by S. Navrud, Oxford University Press, 1992; *Economics and Ecology: Contributions to Sustainable Development,* edited by E. Barbier, Chapman & Hall, 1993; and *Intellectual Property Rights and Biodiversity Conservation,* edited by T. Swanson, Cambridge University Press, 1994. Executive editor of the series "Macmillan Studies in Economics," Macmillan, 1971-80; editor, "Longman Series in Modern Economics," Longman, 1975—; joint editor, "Macmillan Studies in Finance," Macmillan, 1975-81. Contributor of about two hundred articles to scholarly journals. Coeditor, *Ecological Economics;* member of editorial board, *International Journal of Social Economics, Resources Policy, Energy Economics, International Journal of Environmental Studies, Resources and Conservation, Journal of Economic Studies, Energy Policy, Environment and Planning, Environmental and Resource Economics, World Economy, European Environment, Integrated Environmental Management, Ecodecision, Journal of Environmental Planning and Management, Bio-diversity Letters,* and *Resource and Energy Economics;* past member of editorial board, *Futures* and *Journal of Environmental Economics and Management.*

WORK IN PROGRESS: Ecological Economics: Essays in the Theory and Practice of Environmental Economics, for Edward Elgar; *Blueprint 4: Capturing Global Value,* Earthscan; *Macroeconomy and the Environment,* with G. Atkinson, R. Dubourg, and others.

*   *   *

PECK, Dale   1967-

PERSONAL: Born July 13, 1967, in Bay Shore, NY; son of Dale (a plumber) and Eileen (Staplin) Peck. *Education:* Drew University, B.A., 1989.

ADDRESSES: Agent—Irene Skolnick, 121 West 27th St., Suite 601, New York, NY 10001.

CAREER: Novelist.

MEMBER: Former member of AIDS Coalition to Unleash Power (ACT UP).

AWARDS, HONORS: Guggenheim fellow, 1994.

WRITINGS:

Martin and John: A Novel, Farrar, Straus (New York; published in England as *Fucking Martin,* Chatto & Windus), 1993.

WORK IN PROGRESS: The Law of Enclosures, a novel based in part on characters in *Martin and John,* to be the second "of a planned seven-book series which are linked only in a minor way by characters but are strongly linked by common themes."

SIDELIGHTS: The 1993 appearance of *Martin and John: A Novel* catapulted writer Dale Peck to the forefront of contemporary American gay fiction. Before the publication of his first novel, Peck was a member of ACT UP in New York City, an AIDS activist group known for their controversial tactics—Peck was the man who disrupted an on-air CBS newscast in 1990. *Martin and John* developed in part out of Peck's own experiences and relationships, and many reviews of the book discussed its intensely confessional tone, part autobiography, part anti-autobiography. *Los Angeles Times Book Review* critic Richard Eder termed it "a dazzling explosion of voices and stories that hide behind and emerge out of each other. It is a book of theatrical quick changes."

Because of its layers, its hidden corners, its repetitiveness, *Martin and John* resists an easy description of plot. It is narrated by John, a young man who has fled an abusive household. His lover is Martin, who eventually becomes ill with AIDS, and the sequence of events between them takes place primarily in New York City and Kansas. Interspersed into the sparse narrative action are a legion of smaller stories, each one also involving characters named Martin and John. Sometimes Martin is a rich man who showers young John with love, jewelry, and affection; in other instances he is a fellow security guard in Kansas, a teenage runaway found in a barn, or a sadistic New York pimp. John changes character as well as he recounts an upbringing fraught with conflict and abuse. Most of his recollections involve a widowed father with a drinking problem who savagely beats John when the teenager admits his homosexuality; other vignettes recount his father dressing up in his dead wife's clothes. In some stories the death of John's mother occurred when he was still young, in other instances she lingers in a nursing home for years or is perfectly healthy, happy, and divorced—but then one of her boyfriends is a man named Martin who seduces the teenage John. "It can be hard to make out, and I had to go back over it a second time," wrote Eder of *Martin and John*'s complicated structure; "and it changed color and shape somewhat when I did. But the darkness, glitteringly backlit or spotlit . . . prevails almost entirely."

In an interview published in *Contemporary Literary Criticism Yearbook,* Peck explained the genesis of *Martin and John:* "There are autobiographical themes in the book but no autobiography. The only 'real life' aspects of the novel are the settings based on places I've lived. . . . There are similarities in the character of the father to my father, there are similarities in the character of John to my own character, and there are similarities in the female characters to my stepmothers. . . . None of them, however, are actually based on real people." Later in the interview, Peck explained how the structure developed: "The novel originally began with a short story—the story 'Transformations' was the first Martin and John story I wrote. Then, when I wrote another story dealing with the same issues, I couldn't think of character names and so I used the [names Martin and John again]. After writing those two stories, I conceived of the whole project of *Martin and John.* I worked on the book for about four years, and when it was finished I had five hundred pages of manuscript from which I cut 300 pages of stories."

Voice Literary Supplement writer Vince Aletti discussed the novel's spiraling effect between Martin and John's real relationship in the traditional narrative and the fantasy episodes that John writes of in the parallel text, comparing it to a puzzle. "Attempting to transform his history into fiction—something healing, revealing, and 'true'—John can only shuffle things around. And no matter how many times he reinvents his story, he keeps coming back to a few ugly, sad facts: abuse, abandonment, lost love, death." Aletti faulted this approach that Peck undertook, opining that by "teasing his story every which way—whipping up raw tragedy, offhand comedy, and lots of hallucinated melodrama with a very small constellation of characters—he's playing author in a showy, postmodern way." In the end Martin dies of AIDS, cared for by John until a terrible demise in a bathtub. The reader next finds the surviving John in his room, writing, and waiting for his own illness to develop.

Many critics praised the first-time novelist and his tour-de-force work. *New York Times* reviewer Michiko Kakutani noted that "if this fiercely written novel offers an indelible portrait of gay life during the plague years, it also opens out to become a universal story about love and loss and the redemptive powers of fiction. It is a story about the cycles of pain and grief that spiral through people's lives, and the efforts an artist makes to reorder and transcend that hurt." Kakutani commended the young author's level of compassion and insight, concluding that "his wisdom about human feelings, his talent for translating those feelings into prose and his sophisticated mastery of literary form all speak to a maturity that belies his 25 years. In short, a stunning debut." *Times Literary Supplement* reviewer Gregory Woods faulted Peck for "at times sounding as if he had just been given a thesaurus," yet termed the instances "minor faults in a fascinating first novel." In the *Los Angeles Times Book Review* piece, Eder asserted that "Peck's first novel has a dark brilliance and moments of real beauty, but it is a book that is shocking, hard to accept fully, and hard to ignore. It is impassioned in its identification with the gay condition, yet it rides fiercely athwart any common notion of political correctness."

BIOGRAPHICAL/CRITICAL SOURCES:

BOOKS

Contemporary Literary Criticism Yearbook, Volume 81, Gale, 1993.

PERIODICALS

Los Angeles Times Book Review, January 24, 1993, pp. 3, 7.
New York Times, February 9, 1993, p. C15.
New Yorker, February 1, 1993, p. 107.
Observer, May 23, 1993, p. 71.
Times Literary Supplement, March 26, 1993, p. 20.
Tribune Books (Chicago), January 16, 1994, p. 8.
Voice Literary Supplement, February, 1993, pp. 5-6.

—*Sketch by Carol Brennan*

*   *   *

PELLETIER, Cathie 1953(?)-

PERSONAL: Born in c. 1953, in Allagash, ME; daughter of a lumber contractor; companion of Jim Glaser (a country music singer and songwriter). *Education:* University of Maine, B.A.

ADDRESSES: Home—Nashville, TN. *Agent*—c/o Crown Publishing, 201 East 50th St., New York, NY 10022.

CAREER: Writer.

WRITINGS:

The Funeral Makers, Macmillan, 1986.
Once upon a Time on the Banks, Viking, 1989.
The Weight of Winter, Viking, 1991.
The Bubble Reputation, Crown, 1993.
A Marriage Made at Woodstock, Crown, 1994.

Also the author of a book of poetry, published in 1976.

SIDELIGHTS: Born and raised in rural Allagash, Maine, Cathie Pelletier is the youngest of six children born to a French-Canadian father and an Irish mother, descendants of the town's first settlers. Pelletier was always advanced for her age and by age seventeen was attending the University of Maine. After she was expelled for campus hijinks, she hitch-hiked across America, returned to finish her degree, and then decided to move to Nashville to become a songwriter. There she lived first with a family of undertakers who were "crazy as loons" as she related to *People* magazine, and then moved in with country-music singer Jim Glaser.

Pelletier's first three novels, *The Funeral Makers, Once upon a Time on the Banks,* and *The Weight of Winter,* are set in the fictional town of Mattagash, Maine, and draw heavily on the author's own experiences growing up in a small New England town. Critics have described Pelletier's characters as mean, undereducated, bored, gossipy, and oversexed. Several remarked on a similarity between the author's low-class characters and those depicted in the southern gothic novels of Flannery O'Connor and Erskine Caldwell. Many critics praised the humor with which the author saves her unpleasant characters from complete degradation. At the center of the trilogy is the McKinnon family, headed by Marge McKinnon, an elderly spinster; Marge's sister Pearl, who lives in Portland with her husband, a mortician; and Sicily McKinnon, the youngest sister, who tricked the elementary school principal into marriage years before, and now is cursed with an oversexed teenage daughter, Amy Joy. *Los Angeles Times* critic Wanda Urbanska wrote: "Pelletier has created a droll yet detailed, mean but magical kingdom out of an inbred, isolated cast of characters grimly united by geography."

Set in 1959, *The Funeral Makers* finds the McKinnon family gathering to prepare for the death of Marge, who is suffering from a grave case of beri-beri caused by her thirty-year diet of tea and rice. The funeral is somewhat overshadowed by revelations of the affair between fourteen-year-old Amy Joy and thirty-two-year-old Chester Lee, a low-class thief. While many critics praised the comedic bent of Pelletier's depiction of the occurrences surrounding Marge McKinnon's death, a reviewer for *People* magazine remarked: "When the author stops playing solely for laughs, however, the characters become more believable and appealing." *New York Times*

Book Review contributor Susan Kenney commented: "The author describes with impressive sympathy as well as irony the various ways her characters' lives and expectations are constrained, warped and in some cases ultimately destroyed by generations of living in a place so remote that indoor plumbing is still a novelty."

The second novel in the trilogy, *Once upon a Time on the Banks,* takes place in 1969 and centers on the marriage between Amy Joy and Jean-Claude Cloutier, a Roman Catholic French Canadian who has trouble with the English language. The wedding will be the event of the season and Mattagash quickly fills up with guests, invited and uninvited, offering Pelletier the opportunity to portray a large variety of New England eccentrics. In the *New York Times Book Review* novelist Fannie Flagg called *Once upon a Time on the Banks* "another bawdy, poetic crazy quilt of a book," and along with Elaine Kendall writing in the *Los Angeles Times,* drew comparisons between Pelletier's second novel and Erskine Caldwell's classic, *Tobacco Road.* Flagg concluded: "Pelletier accomplishes what every great novelist should. She creates a place, invites you in, walks you around, talks to you, lets you see and feel and hear it, allows you to get to know the people."

The Weight of Winter, Pelletier's third novel set in Mattagash, portrays the town's beleaguered inhabitants under the added pressure of a deep, six-month winter that brings out the worst in each of them. According to Tim Sandlin of the *New York Times Book Review, The Weight of Winter* features snow as a major character: "Pelletier uses weather like a pro. She sets the tone with snow, develops metaphors with snow, advances plot with snow; snow becomes an entity as complex and cruel as any alcoholic family." From a doomed twelve-year-old to the town's oldest inhabitant, 107-year-old Mathilda Fennelson, the snow beats them down until the promise of spring offers them some little hope. Sandlin concluded: "Cathie Pelletier has a strong voice. She writes powerful scenes, creates people we ache for and a world we believe in."

With her 1993 novel, *The Bubble Reputation,* Pelletier leaves the McKinnon family behind, but in relating the story of Rosemary O'Neal, grieving for her husband, a suicide, critics noted her continued use of humor to lighten what is at heart a sad story. Through letters she writes in her head to her dead husband, Rosemary examines her life, frequently interrupted by the appearance of friends and relatives ostensibly offering support but really there to be ministered to in their own troubles. Elizabeth

Lenhard remarked in the *Atlanta Constitution:* "Cathie Pelletier's bewitching novel is as much life-embracing comedy as real-life tragedy."

In *A Marriage Made at Woodstock,* Pelletier again examines human life and expectations, this time through the eyes of a couple. Chandra and Frederick met at Woodstock in 1969, fell in love, and married. By the 1990s, they have grown so apart that they divorce. Chandra still retains the reforming zeal of her youth, while Frederick has traded in his dream of becoming a poet for the steady paycheck of an accountant. *A Marriage Made at Woodstock* is about life choices and growing up at any age. Stephen McCauley, writing in the *New York Times Book Review,* noted that although the "central characters are not terribly compelling . . . the smart vitality of Ms. Pelletier's prose and of her keen observations carries the book."

BIOGRAPHICAL/CRITICAL SOURCES:

PERIODICALS

Atlanta Constitution, June 20, 1993, p. N11.
Los Angeles Times, July 16, 1986; November 3, 1989.
New York Times Book Review, June 1, 1986, pp. 7, 19; October 22, 1989, p. 21; November 24, 1991, p. 3; August 7, 1994, p. 11.
People, July 14, 1986, p. 13, pp. 76-77.*

*   *   *

PENSON, Mary E.   1917-

PERSONAL: Born September 14, 1917, in Riverside, IL; daughter of William F. and Estelle (Auslander) Schramm; married John B. Penson (a commercial artist), April, 1940 (deceased); children: John B., Bonnie Blanton, Marge Anderson, James W. *Education:* Northern Illinois University, B.S., 1960, M.S., 1963. *Politics:* "I vote my conscience." *Religion:* Unitarian. *Avocational interests:* Traveling.

ADDRESSES: Home—2608 Fallcreek St., Arlington, TX 76014.

CAREER: DeKalb High School, DeKalb, IL, English teacher, 1963-80. Served in various offices of the Arlington, TX, branch of the American Association of University Women (AAUW), and as a docent at Fielder Museum, Arlington.

MEMBER: Society of Children's Book Writers and Illustrators.

WRITINGS:

You're an Orphan, Mollie Brown!, Texas Christian University Press, 1993.

WORK IN PROGRESS: Two more "Mollie" books and several novels for young adults.

SIDELIGHTS: "Ever since I can remember I have been writing," Mary E. Penson commented. "One of my prized possessions is a beautiful copy of *Heidi* given to me as a writing award by the Elmhurst Public Library and the local PTA when I was in the fifth grade. In high school I wrote for the newspaper. In college I wrote for *Towers,* the literary magazine, and as a high school English teacher I sponsored *New Pennies,* the literary magazine, and taught creative writing."

Penson taught creative writing at the secondary level for seventeen years; her students consistently won prizes for their works in competitions held by *Atlantic Monthly* and *Scholastic Magazine.* She has been a guest speaker on creative writing at the University of Illinois Articulation Conference, the Illinois Teachers of English Association Conference, and the National Scholastic Press Association Convention. Penson noted that she has demonstrated the teaching of creative writing to the gifted under a grant from the State of Illinois, served as a judge of literary magazines for the National Scholastic Press, and judged the Annual Excellence in Writing program sponsored by the National Council of Teachers of English.

Penson continued: "In retirement I finally had time to practice what I preached and started writing children's stories and novels. Six years later, with a drawer full of rejected material, I sold my first short story. Now I write regularly for the Christian press and have just had my first novel, *You're an Orphan, Mollie Brown!,* published by Texas Christian University Press. A second Mollie Brown book is in the works as are several contemporary novels for the junior high crowd."

*   *   *

PERLOFF, Richard M. 1951-

PERSONAL: Born July 28, 1951, in Columbus, OH; son of Robert (a professor) and Evelyn (a professor) Perloff; married Julie Krevans (a professor); children: Michael. *Education:* Received A.B. from University of Michigan, M.S. from University of Pittsburgh, and Ph.D. from University of Wisconsin—

Madison. *Politics:* "Radical-liberal." *Religion:* Jewish.

ADDRESSES: Home—University Heights, OH. *Office*—Department of Communication, Cleveland State University, Cleveland, OH 44115.

CAREER: Ohio State University, Columbus, post-doctoral fellow in psychology, journalism, and communication, 1978-79; Cleveland State University, Cleveland, OH, assistant professor, 1980-85, associate professor, 1985-94, professor of communication, 1994—.

WRITINGS:

(Editor with S. Kraus) *Mass Media and Political Thought: An Information Processing Approach,* Sage Publications, 1985.
The Dynamics of Persuasion, Lawrence Erlbaum (Hillsdale, NJ), 1993.

Contributor to communication journals.

SIDELIGHTS: Richard M. Perloff told *CA:* "I have always liked to write but, like most of those who end up writing, my topics, focus, and orientation are far different than I ever imagined. I thought I would write fiction or, failing that, go into journalism. Instead, I seem to have found my element in scholarly writing on the topics of persuasion and communication.

"Persuasion has always fascinated me, though I am not sure why or how this interest developed. I began my book thinking that persuasion was bad, was negative. I even wrote a whole section on brain-washing and how it began. By the end of the book, however, I had decided that persuasion was a skill, that it is one of the things that defines people. In some way, the research had persuaded me to take a more positive, optimistic view of people and persuasive communications.

"I am a doer when it comes to writing. I don't outline much or mull over which way to go. I read as much as I can about every possible facet of the issue, and then I write. I feel that putting the words on paper is an act of excitement, sometimes even courage, and it also provides a sense of satisfaction and accomplishment. Later I compose, revise, reexamine, and rewrite. This is the active, engaging part of the job, and I like it, frustrating as it is. It is the conquering of the frustrations and development of clear conclusions that makes the effort worthwhile."

PETERS, Russell M.   1929-

PERSONAL: Born January 5, 1929, in Mashpee, MA; son of Steven Amos (a selectman) and Clara (an activist; maiden name, Miles) Peters; married Ann M. Gilmore (a lawyer), 1950; children: Amanda. *Education:* Morgan State University, B.S., 1956; Harvard Graduate School of Education, Ed.M., 1980. *Politics:* Democrat. *Religion:* Indian Spiritualist. *Avocational interests:* Research on Indian history, golf.

ADDRESSES: Home—128 Williams St., Jamaica Plain, MA 02130.

CAREER: Honeywell Information Systems, Wellesley Hills, MA, marketing representative, 1961-74; Federal Energy Management Agency, Boston, MA, technical hazards specialist, 1987—. Mashpee Wampanoag Tribal Council, president, 1974-80, 1992—. Northeast American Indian Center, board of directors, 1993. Member of Repatriation Committee of Peabody Museum, Harvard; board member of Massachusetts Foundation for the Humanities. *Military service:* U.S. Army, 1946-53; served in infantry; became captain.

MEMBER: Indian Spiritual and Cultural Council, Inc.

AWARDS, HONORS: Massachusetts Institute of Technology fellowship, 1978-79.

WRITINGS:

Wampanoags of Mashpee, Russell M. Peters, 1987.
Clambake, Lerner Publications Co., 1991.
Regalia, Sundance, 1993.

WORK IN PROGRESS: Research on significant Indian leaders.

SIDELIGHTS: "My primary topic is 'The Wampanoags of Mashpee,'" Russell M. Peters commented. "This tribe met the English when they landed in Plymouth in 1620, yet little is known about this tribe of Indians who have maintained a distinct Indian community. I am dedicated to write about, create visual material [about], and promote the native people who survived the settlement of America. I want to make Wampanoag a word that Americans will associate with the Pilgrims, Thanksgiving, and Indian pride.

"I am president of the Mashpee Wampanoag Indian Tribal Council and work to achieve federal recognition for our tribe. Our biggest struggle is to main-tain our identity as Indian people in a society that constantly attempts to extinguish native customs and traditions. Writing and research is a way to make our presence felt, and to continue the spirit of the Wampanoag."

*   *   *

PETTIFER, James   1949-

PERSONAL: Born June 4, 1949, in Hereford, England; son of John (a company director) and Jeanne Mary (a homemaker) Pettifer; married Susan Ann Comely (an administrator), June 6, 1974; children: Julia, Alexander. *Education:* Hertford College, Oxford, M.A. (with honors), 1971. *Politics:* Social Democrat. *Religion:* Church of England. *Avocational interests:* Gardening, travel in the Balkan countries.

ADDRESSES: Office—St. Antony's College, Oxford OX2, England. *Agent*—Curtis Brown, 28/9 Haymarket, London SW1Y 4SP, England.

CAREER: Writer and researcher specializing in Greece, Albania, the former Yugoslav republic of Macedonia, Serbia, Bulgaria, and Turkey. St. Antony's College, Oxford, senior associate member.

MEMBER: Royal Institute for International Affairs.

WRITINGS:

The Greeks: The Land and the People since the War, Viking, 1993.
Blue Guide to Albania, Norton, 1994.

Contributor to periodicals, including *International Affairs, The World Today,* and *The Economist.*

WORK IN PROGRESS: Blue Guide to Bulgaria; a book about contemporary Turkey; and a book with Miranda Vickers about the end of communism in Albania.

*   *   *

PFEFFER, Wendy   1929-

PERSONAL: Surname is pronounced *Pef*-er; born August 27, 1929, in Upper Darby, PA; daughter of Wendell (a high school principal and college professor) and Margaret (a homemaker; maiden name, Nelson) Sooy; married Thomas Pfeffer (an engineer), March 17, 1951; children: Steven T., Diane Kianka. *Education:* Glassboro State College, B.S., 1950.

Avocational interests: Sailing, playing bridge, traveling, reading, collecting antiques, cross country skiing, walking.

ADDRESSES: Home—3 Timberlane Dr., Pennington, NJ 08534. *Agent*—Renee Cho, McIntosh and Otis, 310 Madison Ave., New York, NY 10017.

CAREER: First grade teacher in Pitman, NJ, 1950-53; Pennington Presbyterian Nursery School, cofounder, director, and early childhood specialist, 1961-91; free-lance writer, 1981—. Jointure for Community Adult Education, writer's workshop teacher, 1986; member of focus group for Mercer County libraries, 1993; speaker and instructor for creative writing workshops.

MEMBER: Society of Children's Book Writers and Illustrators, Association for Supervision and Curriculum Development, Popcorn Park Wildlife Club, Patti Lee Gauch Writer's Workshop.

WRITINGS:

Writing Children's Books: Getting Started: A Home Study Course, Fruition Publications, 1985.
Starting a Day Care Business, a Rewarding Career: A Home Study Course, Fruition Publications, 1989.
The Gooney War, illustrated by Mari Goering, Betterway Publications, 1990.
All About Me: Developing Self Image and Self-Esteem with Hands-On Learning Activities, edited by Mary B. Minucci and Mary L. Johansen, First Teacher, 1990.
The World of Nature, edited by Margery Kranyik and Mary L. Johansen, First Teacher, 1990.
(Coauthor) *The Sandbox,* Child's Play, 1991.
Popcorn Park Zoo: A Haven with a Heart, photographs by J. Gerard Smith, Messner, 1992.
From Tadpole to Frog, HarperCollins, 1994.
Goldfish, HarperCollins, in press.

Contributor to *Past and Promise: Lives of New Jersey Women,* 1990. Also author of numerous stories and articles for publications, including *The Grade Teacher, The Friend, Children's Digest, The Instructor, National Association of Young Writers News,* and *First Teacher.*

WORK IN PROGRESS: Baby Wolves Live in Loving Families; Spiderlings; Sea Turtles; writing for Silver Burdette Ginn's new elementary science program.

SIDELIGHTS: Wendy Pfeffer commented: "I grew up in a household of mathematics and language. My father, a professor of mathematics, was in demand as a speaker on 'Magical Mathematics' as well as 'The Origin of Words and Phrases.' Two brief examples of his thousands are: 'COP' being short for 'Constabulary of Police,' and 'TIP' which stood for 'To Insure Promptness.' I was also introduced to the Latin derivatives of words at a very early age.

"From the time I was very young I wanted to write. When I learned to print, the first thing I did was to compose a story like *Hansel and Gretel.* In fact, it *was Hansel and Gretel.* When I was a little older, I kept a diary, then was editor of both the high school newspaper and yearbook. Years later, as I read and dramatized books while teaching young children, I felt that gnawing urge to write again. In fact, I knew I had to write.

"The majority of my work is nonfiction, which, in order to be successful, must be as compelling as fiction. Research is basic to nonfiction and interests me because I learn so much from it. Besides, as I research one topic I always have a file going to add ideas for other topics.

"I enjoy working with children of all ages, leading creative writing workshops, and speaking to school groups on writing. My presentations vary depending on the ages and interests of the children. Even though I stopped teaching to have more time to write, now I feel I have the best of both worlds, working with children and writing. As I said before, I must write—so I do. For me, writing is a challenge and a joy."

BIOGRAPHICAL/CRITICAL SOURCES:

PERIODICALS

Asbury Park Press, July 1, 1992.
Booklist, September 1, 1990, p. 62; June 1, 1992, p. 1760.
NJEA Review, October 1992, p. 50.
Kirkus Reviews, June 15, 1992, p. 783.
Library Talk, September/October, 1992.
Retirement Life, May, 1992, p. 38.
School Library Journal, November, 1990, p. 98; July, 1992, p. 87.
Science Books and Films, October, 1992.

*   *   *

PHILIPSON, Susan Sacher   1934-1994

OBITUARY NOTICE—See index for *CA* sketch: Born December 12, 1934, in New York, NY; died July 18, 1994, in Chicago, IL. Copyeditor and author. Philipson graduated from the University of Michigan in 1956 and became a free-lance editor for such publishing concerns as Random House, Alfred A. Knopf, and Doubleday and Company. She was the author of *A Lion for Niccolby,* published in 1963, and was a regular contributor of articles to *Library Journal.*

OBITUARIES AND OTHER SOURCES:

PERIODICALS

Chicago Tribune, September 1, 1994, pp. 3, 11.

* * *

PIATT, Bill
   See PIATT, Robert William, Jr.

* * *

PIATT, Robert William, Jr. 1950-
   (Bill Piatt)

PERSONAL: Born October 10, 1950, in Santa Fe, NM; son of Robert William and Betty Piatt; married Rosanne Gordon (an attorney), 1970; children: three. *Education:* Eastern New Mexico University, B.A., 1972; University of New Mexico, J.D., 1975.

ADDRESSES: Office—School of Law, Texas Tech University, Lubbock, TX 79409.

CAREER: General Services Administration, Washington, DC, law clerk, 1974; State of New Mexico, assistant attorney general, 1975-76, assistant public defender, 1976; New Mexico State University, Las Cruces, visiting assistant professor of law, 1976-78; University of Oklahoma, Norman, assistant professor of law, 1978-79; private practice of law in Santa Fe, NM, 1979-83; Washburn University of Topeka, Topeka, KS, associate professor of law, 1983-87; Southern Illinois University, Carbondale, visiting professor of law, 1987-88; Texas Tech University, Lubbock, associate professor, 1988-90, professor of law, 1990—. University of New Mexico, faculty member, summers, 1990 and 1993; Universidad de Guanajuato, professor, summers, 1992 and 1994; lecturer at colleges and universities, including University of Washington, Seattle, University of Iowa, Tulane University, and Harvard University; workshop coordinator; guest on television and radio programs; consultant on immigration and language rights.

MEMBER: American Bar Association, Association of American Law Schools, Lubbock County Bar Association (member of board of directors), Lubbock

County Mexican-American Bar Association (president, 1994).

WRITINGS:

UNDER NAME BILL PIATT

A Layperson's Guide to New Mexico Law, Center for Business Services, New Mexico State University, 1977.
Only English? Law and Language Policy in the United States, University of New Mexico Press, 1990.
Language on the Job: Balancing Business Needs and Employee Rights, University of New Mexico Press, 1993.
Immigration Law: Cases and Materials, Michie Co., 1994.

Contributor to books, including *Language Loyalties: A Source Book on the Official English Controversy,* edited by James Crawford, University of Chicago Press, 1992. Contributor to law journals.

BIOGRAPHICAL/CRITICAL SOURCES:

PERIODICALS

American West Chronicle, fall, 1990.
Choice, February, 1994, p. 898.
National Law Journal, July 9, 1990.
Texas Bar Journal, February, 1990.

* * *

PINKNEY, David H(enry) 1914-1993

OBITUARY NOTICE—See index for *CA* sketch: Born July 2, 1914, in Elyria, OH; died May 26, 1993, in Seattle, WA. Historian, educator, and writer. A long-time professor of history at the University of Missouri and the University of Washington, Pinkney is also remembered for his work with the American Historical Association (for which he was elected president in 1980) and for editing the journal *French Historical Studies.* In 1956 Pinkney helped found the Society for French Historical Studies, a group which fostered the historical study of France on an international level. Pinkney is the author of *Napoleon III and the Rebuilding of Paris* (1958), *The French Revolution of 1830* (1972), and *Decisive Years in France, 1840-1847* (1986).

OBITUARIES AND OTHER SOURCES:

PERIODICALS

Perspectives (American Historical Association), October, 1993, p. 19.

PITTS, Michael R. 1947-

PERSONAL: Born July 31, 1947, in Rush County, IN; son of Roy Madison and Gertrude Aileen (Powers) Pitts; married Carolyn Sue Mudd, 1976; children: Angela, Yvonne (deceased). *Education:* Ball State University, B.S., 1969, M.A., 1970. *Avocational interests:* Reading, collecting records and videotapes, gardening.

ADDRESSES: Home—512 North St., Chesterfield, IN 46017.

CAREER: Ball State University, Muncie, IN, member of periodicals library staff, 1968-70; high school history teacher in New Castle, IN, 1970-72; *Anderson Daily Bulletin,* Anderson, IN, city government reporter and entertainment editor, 1972-74; Madison County Council of Governments, Anderson, IN, public relations director, 1974-77; *Anderson Herald,* copy editor, reporter, and entertainment editor, 1977-78; Franklin Life Insurance Co., insurance agent, 1978-79; Metropolitan Life Insurance Co., insurance agent, 1979-80; H & R Block, Anderson, tax preparer, 1981; free-lance writer, 1981—; Anderson Public Library, Anderson, genealogy librarian, 1991—. General Electric Cablevision, film reviewer, 1974-78; lecturer on film history and entertainment.

MEMBER: National Genealogical Society, Indiana Historical Society, Friends of the Henry Henley Public Library.

WRITINGS:

(With James R. Parish) *The Great Spy Pictures,* Scarecrow, 1974.
(With Parish) *Film Directors: A Guide to Their American Films,* Scarecrow, 1974.
(With Parish) *Great Gangster Pictures,* Scarecrow, 1976.
Radio Soundtracks: A Reference Guide, Scarecrow, 1976, 2nd edition, 1986.
(With Parish) *The Great Western Pictures,* Scarecrow, 1976.
(With Parish and Don E. Stanke) *The All-Americans,* Arlington House, 1977.
(With Parish) *The Great Science Fiction Pictures,* Scarecrow, 1977, 2nd edition published as *The Great Science Fiction Pictures II,* 1990.
(With Louis H. Harrison) *Hollywood on Record: The Film Stars' Discography,* Scarecrow, 1978.
(With Parish) *Hollywood on Hollywood,* Scarecrow, 1978.
Famous Movie Detectives, Scarecrow, 1979.

Horror Film Stars, McFarland and Co., 1981, 2nd edition, 1991.
(With Richard H. Campbell) *The Bible on Film: A Checklist 1897-1980,* Scarecrow, 1981.
Hollywood and American History: A Filmography of over 250 Motion Pictures Depicting U.S. History, McFarland and Co., 1984.
(With Parish) *The Great Spy Pictures II,* Scarecrow, 1986.
Western Movies: TV and Video Guide to 4,200 Genre Films, McFarland and Co., 1986.
(With Parish) *The Great Gangster Pictures II,* Scarecrow, 1987.
Kate Smith: A Bio-Bibliography, Greenwood Press, 1988.
(With Parish) *The Great Western Pictures II,* Scarecrow, 1988.
(With Parish) *The Great Detective Pictures,* Scarecrow, 1990.
(With Parish) *Hollywood Songsters: A Biographical Dictionary,* Garland Publishing, 1990.
Famous Movie Detectives II, Scarecrow, 1991.
Kate Smith on the Radio: A Log, 1919-47, Kate Smith/God Bless America Foundation, 1992.
(With Parish) *The Great Hollywood Musical Pictures,* Scarecrow, 1992.
Poverty Row Productions: The Films and the Studios, 1929-1940, McFarland and Co., in press.

Columnist, *Big Reel,* 1978—, and *Classic Images,* 1987-91. Contributor to film journals and history magazines. Author of liner notes for sound recordings.

SIDELIGHTS: Michael R. Pitts told *CA:* "I began writing at age twelve and had my first article published in 1969. Growing up on a farm in central Indiana, I got most of my entertainment from television. I particularly enjoyed vintage films, especially those hosted on local television from Indianapolis by Frances Farmer and Gene Allison. I have an affinity for horror films (my favorite stars were Lon Chaney, Jr. and Bela Lugosi) and 'B' westerns (Bob Steele was my favorite cowboy hero). Mainly I prefer films from the 1930s or low-budget or obscure films in general. D. W. Griffith is my favorite director, and Charles Bronson and Yvonne De Carlo are my favorite stars. I believe movies are to be enjoyed, and not necessarily to be picked apart for political or psychological connotations.

"Besides writing about movies, an avocation which became my profession, I enjoy music and have been collecting records for more than thirty years. I like vocalists and have been privileged to meet and know Nick Lucas and Rudy Vallee. Among the other performers I collect are Frankie Laine, Tony Martin, Kate Smith, Skeeter Davis, Margaret Whiting, Bob Braun, Slim Whitman, Hank Snow, Vaughn Monroe, Patsy Montana, Eddie Dean, Red River Dave, Gene Austin, Tex Ritter, John Gary, and Marty Robbins."

* * *

POLLARD, Helen Perlstein   1946-

PERSONAL: Born September 4, 1946, in Manhattan, NY; daughter of Bernard L. (an optometrist) and Eva (a biologist; maiden name, Chatzinoff) Perlstein; married Gordon C. Pollard, June 11, 1967 (divorced, January, 1986); children: Jason C., Riva Adele. *Education:* Barnard College, A.B. (magna cum laude), 1967; Columbia University, Ph.D., 1972. *Religion:* Unitarian-Universalist.

ADDRESSES: Home—1408 Roxburgh Ave., East Lansing, MI 48823. *Office*—Department of Anthropology, 354 Baker Hall, Michigan State University, East Lansing, MI 48824.

CAREER: State of California, staff archaeologist for a highway salvage program, 1965; State University of New York College at Plattsburgh, instructor, 1972-73, assistant professor of environmental science, 1973-77, adjunct assistant professor of anthropology, 1975-85; State University of New York at Oswego, visiting assistant professor of anthropology, 1985-86; Michigan State University, East Lansing, assistant professor, 1986-91, associate professor of anthropology, 1991—. Lerma River Basin Survey, field director and ceramic consultant, 1972; member of excavations at Urichu, Tarascan State. New York Archaeological Council, member, 1976-86. Hickory Hill Condominium Association, member of board of directors, 1992-95.

MEMBER: American Anthropological Association (fellow), Latin American Anthropology Group, Society for American Archaeology (fellow), Current Anthropology (associate), Archaeological Institute of America, Association for Field Archaeology, Michigan Archaeological Society, Phi Beta Kappa.

AWARDS, HONORS: Woodrow Wilson fellow, 1967-68, 1970-71; Ford Foundation fellow, 1972; grants from National Endowment for the Humanities, 1976-80, 1994-97, National Science Foundation, 1976-80, American Council of Learned Societies, 1982, and National Geographic Society and Wenner-Gren Foundation for Anthropological Research (for Urichu), 1989.

WRITINGS:

Tariacuri's Legacy: The Prehispanic Tarascan State, University of Oklahoma Press, 1993.

Work represented in anthologies, including *Ancient Road Networks and Settlement Hierarchies in the New World,* edited by C. Trombold, Cambridge University Press, 1991; and *Economies and Polities in the Aztec Realm,* edited by M. Smith and M. Hodge, University of Texas Press, 1994. Contributor of articles and reviews to anthropology and other scholarly journals. Contributing editor, *Anthropology Newsletter,* 1990-92.

* * *

POPPER, Karl R(aimund)   1902-1994

OBITUARY NOTICE—See index for *CA* sketch: Born July 28, 1902, in Vienna, Austria; died of pneumonia, cancer, and kidney failure, September 17, 1994, in Croydon, England. Philosopher, teacher, and writer. Educated at the universities of Vienna, New Zealand, and London, Popper began his career as a lecturer in philosophy at the University of Canterbury in 1937. In 1945 he transferred to the London School of Economics and Political Science, where he was professor of logic and scientific method from 1949 to 1969. He was variously affiliated with such institutions of higher learning as Harvard, Massachusetts Institute of Technology, Oxford, Cambridge, and others. Knighted in 1965 by Queen Elizabeth, Popper was known to be highly influential in establishing the "intellectual framework" of England's Conservative Party, especially under the leadership of Margaret Thatcher. He began his publishing career in 1935 with his first book *Logic der Forschung: Zur Erkenntnistheorie der modernen Naturwissenschaft,* which became an international best-seller and established Popper's importance as an "eloquent philosopher." Popper later translated the book into English in 1959 as *The Logic of Scientific Discovery.* The author's anti-Marxist viewpoint was evident in the two-volume *The Open Society and Its Enemies* (1945). Other works by Popper include *Die Zukunft ist Offen* (1984), *Popper Selections* (1985), and *A World of Propensities* (1990). Popper's works have been translated into twenty-six languages.

OBITUARIES AND OTHER SOURCES:

BOOKS

Who's Who, 144th edition, St. Martin's, 1992.

PERIODICALS

Washington Post, September 19, 1994, p. B4.

* * *

POVOD, Reinaldo   1959-1994

OBITUARY NOTICE—See index for *CA* sketch: Born September 18, 1959, in New York, NY; died of tuberculosis, July 30, 1994. Playwright. Povod was the author of several critically acclaimed and commercially successful plays set in the harsh, crime-ridden milieu of New York's lower east side Hispanic community. His best known work, the award-winning *Cuba and His Teddy Bear,* was produced on Broadway in 1986 with Robert Deniro in the role of a tough drug dealer and Ralph Macchio as his son, a compassionate teenager with literary aspirations. A second dramatic work, *La Puta Vida Trilogy* (title means "This Bitch of a Life"), is comprised of three one-act plays which, like *Cuba and His Teddy Bear,* are grimly realistic depictions of urban Hispanic life. Povod's plays have been highly praised for their lively dialogue and forceful expression of his lurid and often tragic subjects. At the time of his death Povod was collaborating with Richard Barbour on a play entitled *Super Fishbowl Sunday.*

OBITUARIES AND OTHER SOURCES:

PERIODICALS

New York Times, August 2, 1994, p. D18.

* * *

POWELL, David A.   1952-

PERSONAL: Born May 1, 1952, in West Virginia. *Education:* West Virginia University, B.A. (cum laude), 1973; Pennsylvania State University, M.A., 1978; University of Pennsylvania, M.A., 1980, Ph.D., 1985.

ADDRESSES: Home—33 Stringham Ave., Valley Stream, NY 11580. *Office*—Department of French, Hofstra University, 1000 Fulton, Hempstead, NY 11550-1090.

CAREER: Universite de Strasbourg, Strasbourg, France, lecturer, 1978-79; Universite de Paris X, Nanterre, France, lecturer, 1981-83; University of Pennsylvania, Philadelphia, lecturer in French, 1983-84; Barnard College, New York City, instructor in French, 1984-86; Hofstra University, Hempstead, NY, assistant professor of French, 1986—, associate dean for student academic affairs, 1990-94, director of summer programs in Nice, 1988, 1990, 1994. Columbia University, assistant professor, summer, 1985, instructor, summer, 1986; Tulane University, guest lecturer, 1986.

MEMBER: Centre International George Sand et le Romantisme, Modern Language Association of America, Friends of George Sand (copresident), Les Amis de George Sand.

WRITINGS:

George Sand, Twayne, 1990.
(Editor) *George Sand Today: Proceedings of the Eighth International George Sand Conference,* University Press of America, 1991.
(Coeditor) *The World of George Sand,* Greenwood Press, 1991.

Work represented in books, including *Correspondences: Studies in Literature, History, and the Arts in Nineteenth-Century France,* edited by Keith Busby, Rodopi (Amsterdam), 1993; *A Critical Bibliography of French Literature,* Volume V: *The Nineteenth Century,* Part I, edited by David Baguley, Syracuse University Press, 1994; and *Autobiography, Historiography, Rhetoric: A Festschrift for Frank Paul Bowman,* Rodopi (Amsterdam), 1994. Contributor of articles and reviews to scholarly journals. Coeditor in chief, *George Sand Studies,* 1989—.

WORK IN PROGRESS: While the Music Lasts: The Representation of Music in the Writings of George Sand.

SIDELIGHTS: David A. Powell told *CA:* "I decided in junior high school that I wanted to become a French teacher. In high school, where I played the oboe, I saw that music might also be an enjoyable career, but less stable; this reaction bespeaks my Protestant, working-class upbringing. I manage to bring together these two fields of intense interest in my research, where I investigate how nineteenth-century French authors, and authors from different language groups and time periods, treat music in their fiction.

"I continue to play piano, flute, and recorders as a rank amateur, but I enjoy it. I've often wondered whether my chosen profession was not just a pretext for getting away from home to travel abroad. This remains one of my most pleasurable pastimes, along with concert-going and eating."

POWELL, Pamela 1960-

PERSONAL: Born March 5, 1960, in Boston, MA; daughter of George L. and Doris (a secretary at the Museum of Fine Arts; maiden name, Cox) Powell. Education: Attended Wesleyan University, 1979-80; Goddard College, B.A., 1983. Politics: Democrat (liberal). Religion: Non-denominational Christian. Avocational interests: Ice skating, swimming, cross-country skiing, sailing/boats.

ADDRESSES: Home—1320 8th St., Anacortes, WA 98221.

CAREER: Writer, 1984—. Operation Crossroads Africa, West Indies, group leader (summers), 1984-85; Outward Bound School, Boston, MA, Rockland, ME, Maryland, and Florida, instructor, 1988-92; World Horizons, Minto, AK, group leader (summer), 1992; Pacific Crest Outward Bound School, Anacortes, WA, instructor, 1993—. English as a Second Language teacher, Prague, Czechoslovakia, 1990-91; author in residence, Cambridge, MA, 1993. Worked on boats as a deckhand, mate, first mate, and captain, in waters off North and South America, 1978—. Instructor in writing; teaches writing workshops for children and adults.

MEMBER: Society of Children's Book Writers and Illustrators.

AWARDS, HONORS: Edna St. Vincent Millay Fellowship, Austerlitz, NY, 1990; Arlington Arts Council Grant, Arlington, MA, 1992; third prize for "Write Now" short story contest in the Ottawa Citizen, 1992; Walden Fellowship (residency), Gold Hill, OR, 1993.

WRITINGS:

The Turtle Watchers, Viking/Penguin, 1992.

Contributor to books, including Filtered Images: Women Remembering Their Grandmothers (anthology), edited by Susan Aglietti, Vintage '45 Press, 1991. Contributor to Kennebec: A Portfolio of Maine Writing (literary journal); and to magazines and newspapers, including Sail, Cruising World, Annapolis Capital, and Ottawa Citizen.

WORK IN PROGRESS: Research on Czech village life and diseases caused by environmental pollution for a second novel for children (set in Czechoslovakia), tentatively titled The Village Cure; Cellar Boats, a picture book; and a screenplay.

SIDELIGHTS: "I've always loved to read. I guess around sixth grade was when I first loved writing stories," Pamela Powell commented. "My favorite teacher, Mr. Seldin, encouraged us to fill our notebooks with stories, poems, or whatever we wanted to write. He used to read to us out loud too, as did my mother and my English godmother, Pamela, whom I was named after.

"I am a firm believer in following your heart. Often I don't know what I will be doing for the coming months, but something always seems to work out. It's that way with writing too. I don't usually follow a plan for my writing, but rather see what emerges. I have traveled a great deal, in the Caribbean where I lived for three years and found the inspiration for my first novel, The Turtle Watchers, and in Europe, the setting for my next book.

"I am fortunate to have found support for my writing early on. A recent gift—a writer's residency in southern Oregon—six weeks to write without any other responsibilities! It came as a real blessing, as I hadn't had a steady home of my own in about ten years! Now I am settling down in the watery area of Puget Sound, and am very glad to be here.

"Among my very favorite writers and books are those for children: Madeline L'Engle, E. B. White, C. S. Lewis, Louisa May Alcott. Their books are among the ones that made me who I am. I am very grateful to them for that. Reading books for kids is still one of my greatest pleasures! And if I can give a child joy and maybe tears through my writing, and in that way change their lives a little, then I feel I have succeeded."

*   *   *

POWER, Patrick C(arthage) 1928-

PERSONAL: Born May 14, 1928, in Dungarvan, Waterford, Ireland; son of John and Ellen (O' Shea) Power; married Pauline McGrath, December 29, 1954; children: Geraldine, Vera, Ann, Helen, Paul. Education: Department of Education (Dublin, Ireland), teacher's training certificate and diploma, 1955; University College of Galway, B.A., 1964, M.A., 1965; National University of Ireland, Ph.D., 1971.

ADDRESSES: Home—Ballyneale, Carrick-on-Suir, County Tipperary, Ireland. Agent—Helen Walsh, 93 Willow Park, Clonmel, County Tipperary, Ireland.

CAREER: Writer. Member of Roman Catholic religious order; teacher at school in Ballyneale, Ireland. Collector for the Irish Folklore Commission; lecturer on local history.

WRITINGS:

The Story of Anglo-Irish Poetry, 1800-1922, Mercier Press (Cork, Ireland), 1967.
A Literary History of Ireland, Mercier Press, 1969.
The Book of Irish Curses, Mercier Press, 1974, Templegate (Springfield, IL), 1975.
Carrick-on-Suir and Its People, Anna Livia Books (Dun Laoghaire, Ireland), 1976.
Sex and Marriage in Ancient Ireland, Mercier Press, 1976.
Heritage Trails in South Tipperary, South Tipperary County Council (Clonmel), 1987.
History of South Tipperary, Mercier Press, 1989.
History of Waterford: City and County, Mercier Press, 1990.
St. Mary's Parochial School Clonmel, School Committee (Clonmel), 1993.

Translator of *The Poor Mouth = An Beal Bocht: A Bad Story about the Hard Life,* by Flann O'Brien, Viking (New York), 1974, and of *Cuirt an Mhean-Niche—The Midnight Court,* by Brian Merriman, Mercier Press, 1978.

WORK IN PROGRESS: A first novel, based on events in a small Irish village from 1914 to 1923.

SIDELIGHTS: Patrick C. Power told *CA:* "I first decided that I should be a writer in 1939 but had to wait until twenty-eight years later for the first publication of a book. I always wished to introduce my fellow Irish and others to ourselves. I belong to the purely English culture and also to the Gaelic one, with its distinctive literature—very ancient and also modern.

"My greatest wish is to have the historical novel which I am writing accepted. I seem to be making it a compendium, not just of the national experience during a dramatic period of Irish history but also of the stories and the life-ways of a time when Ireland was dragging herself through blood into the modern world. Little Irish villages are dying. I wish to set one village's ethos in the mouths of its characters."

*   *   *

PRESTON-MAFHAM, Rod(ney Arthur) 1942-

PERSONAL: Born June 14, 1942, in London, England; married Jean Brown (a manager of a picture library), July 31, 1969; children: Mark, Juliet, Lauren. *Education:* University of London, B.Sc., 1963; Wye College, London, M.Sc., 1965, Ph.D., 1968. *Avocational interests:* Steam railway locomotives, classical music.

ADDRESSES: Home and office—Premaphotos Wildlife, Amberstone, 1 Kirland Rd., Bodmin, Cornwall PL30 5JQ, England.

CAREER: Premaphotos Wildlife (picture library), Bodmin, England, partner and photographer, 1976—. Biology teacher and department head at a grammar school in Alcester, England, 1974-88.

WRITINGS:

(With brother Ken Preston-Mafham) *Spiders of the World,* Blandford Press, 1984.
(With K. Preston-Mafham) *Butterflies of the World,* Blandford Press, 1988.
The Book of Spiders and Scorpions, Crescent Books, 1991.
(With K. Preston-Mafham) *Cacti: The Illustrated Dictionary,* Blandford Press, 1991.
(With K. Preston-Mafham) *Primates of the World,* Blandford Press, 1992.
(With K. Preston-Mafham) *The Encyclopedia of Land Invertebrate Behaviour,* MIT Press, 1993.

SIDELIGHTS: Rod Preston-Mafham told *CA:* "My writing career arose by chance. A friend had been asked to write a book on spiders, but lacked both the time and the photographs to produce it. My brother Ken and I had both, so we collaborated on *Spiders of the World.* This has proved, for its subject, a very popular book. My brother and I aim to provide the person on the street with scientific information about the living world in such a manner that they can both read and understand it."

*   *   *

PUCCI, Pietro 1927-

PERSONAL: Born November 12, 1927, in Modena, Italy; naturalized U.S. citizen; son of Emilio and Linda (Gualdi) Pucci; married, wife's name Jeannine. *Education:* Liceo Muratori, B.A., 1945; University of Pisa, Ph.D., 1949; University of Florence, Libera Docenza, 1962.

ADDRESSES: Home—512 East Seneca St., Ithaca, NY 14850. *Office*—Department of Classics, 125 Goldwin Smith Hall, Cornell University, Ithaca, NY 14853.

CAREER: University of Florence, Florence, Italy, assistant professor of classics, 1951-52; University of Ottawa, Ottawa, Ontario, Canada, assistant professor of classics, 1959-61; University of Kansas, Lawrence, assistant professor of classics, 1961-62; Cornell University, Ithaca, NY, assistant professor, 1962-67, associate professor, 1967-72, professor of classics, 1972—, head of department, 1983-87 and 1990-91. University of California, Santa Cruz, visiting professor, 1969; University of Florence, visiting professor, 1970; Ecole des Hautes Etudes (Paris), director of studies, 1984 and 1989.

AWARDS, HONORS: Fellow of the French government, 1955-57, and the German government, 1957-58; junior fellow at Center for Hellenic Studies, Washington, DC, 1970; fellow of American Council of Learned Societies, 1972; Guggenheim fellow, 1980-81; fellow of National Endowment for the Humanities, 1989.

WRITINGS:

Aristofane e Euripide: Studi Stilistici e Metrici, Accademia Nazionale de Lincei (Rome), 1961.
(Translator and author of commentary) *Platone: Simposio, Fedro, Alcibiade I, Alcibiade II, Teage, Ipparco, Carmide, Lachete, Liside,* Bari, 1966.
Hesiod and the Language of Poetry, Johns Hopkins University Press (Baltimore, MD), 1977.
The Violence of Pity: Euripides' Medea, Cornell University Press, 1980.
Odysseus Polytropos: Intertextual Studies on the Odyssey and the Iliad, Cornell University Press, 1987.
Oedipus and the Fabrication of Man, Johns Hopkins University Press, 1992.

Work represented in anthologies, including *Poetry and Poetics from Ancient Greece to the Renaissance: Studies in Honor of James Hutton,* Cornell University Press, 1975; *Post-Structuralist Classics,* edited by Andrew Benjamin, Routledge & Kegan Paul, 1988; and *Innovations in Antiquity,* edited by Ralph Hexter and Daniel Selden, Routledge & Kegan Paul, 1992. Contributor of about forty articles to scholarly journals.

*   *   *

PYENSON, Lewis (Robert) 1947-

PERSONAL: Born September 26, 1947, in Point Pleasant Beach, NJ; son of Jacob I. (a professor) and Regina (Podolsky) Pyenson; married Susan Sheets (a professor), August, 1973; children: Nicholas, Cath-

arine, Benjamin. *Education:* Swarthmore College, B.A. (with honors), 1969; University of Wyoming, M.S., 1970; Johns Hopkins University, Ph.D., 1974.

ADDRESSES: Office—Department of History, University of Montreal, C.P. 6128 Succursale A, Montreal, Quebec, Canada H3C 3J7.

CAREER: University of Montreal, Montreal, Quebec, began as lecturer, became professor, 1973-86, professor of the history of science, 1986—. David M. Stewart Museum, honorary curator of scientific instruments, 1991—. Universite Louis Pasteur, visiting lecturer, 1975; Johns Hopkins University, visiting professor, 1978; University of Pennsylvania, senior fellow in history and sociology of science, 1979-80; McGill University, member of board of curators, Osler Library for the History of Medicine, 1982—; University of Leiden, associate of Center for the History of European Expansion, 1984—; Princeton University, visiting fellow in history of science, 1986-87. Joint Atlantic Seminar in the History of Physics, founder, 1974. Bibliopolis Press (Naples), member of scientific advisory board, 1982—; consultant to Guggenheim Foundation, American Institute of Physics, and Smithsonian Institution.

MEMBER: Royal Society of Canada (fellow), Sociedad de Historia de la Medicina Hispanoamericana (Spain; honorary member), Asociacion Biblioteca Jose Babini (Buenos Aires; external member), Sociedad Latinoamericana de la Historia de las Ciencias (Mexico City; founding member), Sigma Xi.

AWARDS, HONORS: Fellow of Social Sciences and Humanities Research Council of Canada, 1979-80, 1983, and 1986-87; Herbert C. Pollock Award, Dudley Observatory, Schenectady, NY, 1986-87; Killam senior fellow, Canada Council of Arts, 1989-91.

WRITINGS:

(Editor and author of introduction and notes) Leopold Infeld, *Why I Left Canada: Reflections on Science and Politics* (translated from Polish by Helen Infeld), McGill-Queen's University Press, 1978.
Neohumanism and the Persistence of Pure Mathematics in Wilhelmian Germany, American Philosophical Society (Philadelphia, PA), 1983.
The Young Einstein: The Advent of Relativity, Adam Hilger, 1985.
Cultural Imperialism and Exact Sciences: German Expansion Overseas, 1900-1930, Verlag Peter Lang, 1985.

Empire of Reason: Exact Sciences in Indonesia, 1840-1940, E. J. Brill, 1989.

Civilizing Mission: Exact Sciences and French Overseas Expansion, 1830-1940, Johns Hopkins University Press, 1993.

Contributor to books, including *Scientific Colonialism: A Cross-Cultural Comparison,* edited by Nathan Reingold and Marc Rothenberg, Smithsonian Institution Press, 1987; *New Trends in the History of Science,* edited by R. P. W. Visser, H. J. M. Bos, and others, Rodopi (Amsterdam), 1989; and *Companion to the History of Modern Science,* edited by R. C. Olby, G. N. Cantor, and others, Routledge & Kegan Paul, 1989. Contributor of more than sixty articles and reviews to history and science journals. Associate editor, *Historical Studies in the Physical Sciences,* 1980—; advisory editor, *Isis,* 1978-81, and *History of Science,* 1991—.

WORK IN PROGRESS: Science in Society, with wife Susan Sheets-Pyenson, for Fontana; *True Jacob,* a novel; editing *Society and Celebrity: Nollet's Courtly Physics,* an exhibition catalog.

Q-R

QUIGLEY, Declan   1956-

PERSONAL: Born December 12, 1956, in Belfast, Northern Ireland; son of Edmond Gerard (a union official) and Kathleen Theresa (Murphy) Quigley. *Education:* London School of Economics and Political Science, London, B.Sc., 1978, Ph.D., 1984; Cambridge University, M.Phil., 1979.

ADDRESSES: Home—Belfast, Northern Ireland. *Office*—Department of Social Anthropology, Queen's University of Belfast, Belfast BT7 1NN, Northern Ireland.

CAREER: Cambridge University, Cambridge, England, postdoctoral research fellow, 1986-89, lecturer in social anthropology, 1990-92; Queen's University of Belfast, Belfast, Northern Ireland, lecturer in social anthropology, 1992—.

MEMBER: European Association of Social Anthropologists, Anthropology Association of Ireland, British Association of Social Anthropologists.

AWARDS, HONORS: British Academy fellow, 1986-89.

WRITINGS:

The Interpretation of Caste, Clarendon Press, 1993.
(With Vinay Skivastava) *L'Inde des tribus oubliees,* Chene (Paris), 1993.
(Editor with David N. Gellner) *Contested Hierarchies: A Collaborative Ethnography of Caste among the Newars of the Kathmandu Valley, Nepal,* Clarendon Press, 1995.

WORK IN PROGRESS: Comparative research on monarchies, ritual, and power; research for a general theory of social anthropology.

RAPHAEL, Chaim   1908-1994
(Jocelyn Davey)

OBITUARY NOTICE—See index for *CA* sketch: Born July 14, 1908, in Middlesborough, England; died October 10, 1994, in London, England. Educator, government official, and writer. Raphael taught Hebrew at Oxford University in the 1930s after earning a degree there. During World War II Raphael served as a liaison officer for internment camps in both Britain and Canada and later headed the information departments of the British treasury and civil service. In the early 1970s he returned to academic life with a position at the University of Sussex. He wrote a number of works on Jewish history and traditions, including *The Walls of Jerusalem: An Excursion into Jewish History, Encounters with the Jewish People, The Road from Babylon, A Jewish Book of Common Prayer,* and *The Festivals.* Raphael also wrote a series of mystery novels under the pseudonym Jocelyn Davey. The tales, which began with 1956's *A Capitol Offence: An Entertainment,* featured the sleuthing of scholarly and urbane philosophy professor Ambrose Usher. The novel was followed by several others, including *A Touch of Stagefright, Murder in Paradise,* and *A Dangerous Liaison.*

OBITUARIES AND OTHER SOURCES:

BOOKS

The Writers Directory: 1992-1994, St. James Press, 1991, p. 808.

PERIODICALS

New York Times, October 13, 1994, p. B15.

RATEY, John J(oseph)   1948-

PERSONAL: Born April 7, 1948, in Rochester, PA; married; children: two. *Education:* Colgate University, A.B., 1970; attended Northeastern University, Harvard University, Boston University, and Boston College, 1970-72; University of Pittsburgh, M.D., 1976.

ADDRESSES: Home—11 Benton St., Wellesley, MA 02181. *Office*—NEPC, Medfield State Hospital, 45 Hospital Rd., Medfield, MA 02052. *Agent*—Jill Kneerim, 1 Beacon St., Boston, MA 02108.

CAREER: Massachusetts Mental Health Center, Boston, psychiatric attendant, 1970-71; DARE, Inc., Boston, halfway house parent, 1971-72; St. Francis General Hospital, Pittsburgh, PA, rotating intern in neurology, 1976-77; Massachusetts Mental Health Center, psychiatric resident, 1977-80, chief resident in Inpatient Service, 1979-80, supervisor of residents, 1980—, assistant director of residency training, 1982-88. Harvard Medical School, clinical fellow in Chronic Care Program, 1978-79; instructor, 1980-86, assistant professor, 1986—; Tufts University, assistant clinical professor, 1980-81; Colloquium Internationale Neuro-Psychopharmacologicum (Munich), guest lecturer, 1988. Clinton Child and Family Center, chief psychiatrist, 1978-82; New England Pyschiatric Consultants, director, 1978—; Medfield State Hospital, clinical director of Developmental Disabilities Unit, 1986-89, director of research, 1986—, acting executive medical director, 1989-91. Boston Center for the Study of Autism, founder and member of steering committee, 1986; Clinical Aggression Research Group, founder and developer, 1990; Children with Attention-Deficit Disorder, member of advisory board, 1992—; consultant to City of Boston, CAMARY Corp., and Wheat Ridge Developmental Center.

MEMBER: American Psychiatric Association.

AWARDS, HONORS: Falk fellow, American Psychiatric Association, 1978-80; grants from National Institute of Mental Health, 1984-86, and E. R. Squibb and Co., 1984-88; Harry C. Solomon Award, 1985; grants from Sandoz Pharmaceuticals, 1987-88, State of California, 1988, Mead Johnson Pharmaceuticals, 1988, Solvay-Duphar Pharmaceuticals, 1990-92, Abbott Laboratories, 1993—, and Lilly Research Laboratories, 1993—.

WRITINGS:

(Editor and contributor) *Mental Retardation: Developing Pharmacotherapies,* American Psychiatric Association Press, 1991.
(With E. Hallowell) *Driven to Distraction: The Emotional Experience of ADD,* Pantheon (New York, NY), 1994.
(Editor and contributor) *The Neuropsychiatry of Behavior Disorders,* Blackwell Scientific, 1994.

Work represented in books, including *Manual of Psychiatric Emergencies,* edited by S. E. Hyman and G. E. Tesar, Little, Brown, 1994; *Neuropsychiatry: A Comprehensive Textbook,* edited by B. Fogel and R. Schiffer, Williams & Wilkins; and *Attention Deficit Disorder in Adults,* edited by K. Nadeau, Chesapeake Press. Contributor of more than forty articles and reviews to medical journals.

WORK IN PROGRESS: Answers to Distractions, with E. Hallowell; *The Grey Ceiling: Overcoming the Subtle Differences in the Brain That Hold Us Back,* with C. Johnson; research on the clinical effectiveness of beta blockers and serotonin active agents; research on the theoretical aspects of aggression and affect tolerance; research on the neuropsychiatry of developmental disabilities; research on the identification and treatment of adult attention deficit disorder.

*   *   *

RAYMOND, Derek
See COOK, Robert William Arthur

*   *   *

REES, C. Roger   1946-

PERSONAL: Born November 23, 1946, in Burton-on-Trent, England; son of Leslie (a teacher) and Enid (a teacher; maiden name, Smith) Rees; married Marlen Baege, 1973; children: Eleanor, Allyson. *Education:* University of London, B.Ed., 1970; University of Maryland at College Park, M.A., 1972, Ph.D., 1977.

ADDRESSES: Home—Madison, NJ. *Office*—Department of Health Studies, Physical Education, and Human Performance Science, Adelphi University, Garden City, NY 11530. *Agent*—Linda Allen Agency, 1949 Green St., San Francisco, CA 94123.

CAREER: Texas Christian University, Fort Worth, assistant professor, 1980-83; Adelphi University, Garden City, NY, associate professor, 1983-92, professor of sociology and the social psychology of sport and physical education, 1992—. Lecturer at institutions of higher education in Germany, England, Israel, and South Africa; guest on television programs.

AWARDS, HONORS: Grant from Quantum Corp.

WRITINGS:

(Editor with Aidan O. Dunleavy and Andrew W. Miracle) *Studies in the Sociology of Sport,* Texas Christian University Press, 1982.

(Editor with Miracle) *Sport and Social Theory,* Human Kinetics, 1986.

(Editor with Gary T. Barrette and Ronald S. Feingold) *Sport Pedagogy: Myths, Models, and Methods,* Human Kinetics, 1987.

(With Miracle) *Lessons of the Locker Room: The Myth of School Sports,* Prometheus Books, 1994.

Work represented in anthologies. Contributor of about fifty articles to scholarly journals.

WORK IN PROGRESS: Research on sport and self-identity among German and American adolescents.

SIDELIGHTS: C. Roger Rees told *CA:* "I have been involved in sports for most of my life, as an athlete and as a sociologist. My book *Lessons of the Locker Room* is a controversial review of the evidence for and against the claim that high school sports 'build character,' and is the first comprehensive examination of the effects that school sports have on students, schools, and communities across America.

"I have also been active in the field of applied sport sociology. The question of how sport can make a more positive contribution to society not only provided the motivation for my book, but also led to a seventeen-year relationship with the South Queens Little League Association, where my colleagues and I developed workshops for volunteer coaches."

BIOGRAPHICAL/CRITICAL SOURCES:

PERIODICALS

Sports Illustrated, August 22, 1988.

*   *   *

REIN, Raanan 1960-

PERSONAL: Born June 17, 1960, in Tel Aviv, Israel; married; children: two. *Education:* University of Tel Aviv, B.A. (with distinction), 1986, M.A., 1988, Ph.D. (with distinction), 1991.

ADDRESSES: Office—Department of History, Tel Aviv University, Ramat Aviv 69978, Israel.

CAREER: IDF radio station, foreign news editor, 1979-82; *Al Hamishmar* newspaper, writer of commentaries on foreign affairs, 1982-84; *Hadashot* newspaper (Hebrew), Tel Aviv, foreign news editor, 1984-87; *Estudios Interdisciplinarios de America Latina y el Caribe* (Spanish), Tel Aviv, associate editor, 1992—; Tel Aviv University, lecturer, 1992—.

AWARDS, HONORS: The Aranne School of History scholarship for excellent students, University of Tel Aviv, 1987-88; Raul Valenberg Foundation award, 1988, 1992; Maurice Pulver Foundation grant, 1988; Spanish Foreign Ministry scholarship for Ph.D. candidates, 1989-90; Higher Education Council, Jerusalem, research grant, 1989-91; Wolf Foundation postdoctoral fellowship, University of Tel Aviv, 1992-94; University Research Foundation, Tel Aviv University, research grant, 1994-95; Yad Hanadiv Humanities fellowship, Rothschild Foundation, Jerusalem, 1994-95.

WRITINGS:

The Franco-Peron Alliance: Relations between Spain and Argentina, 1946-1955, translation by Martha Grenzeback, University of Pittsburgh Press, 1993.

Contributor to *La politica argentina, 1930-1955* (Spanish), edited by C. Malamud, Instituto Universitario Ortega y Gasset, 1992; contributor of articles and reviews in English, Spanish, and Hebrew to periodicals, including *Hispania, Gesher, Zmanim, Cuadernos Americanos, International Problems, Society, & Politics, Anuario del Instituto de Estudios Historico-Sociales, State, Government, & International Relations, Journal of Latin American Studies,* and *Mediterranean Historical Review.*

WORK IN PROGRESS: Research in progress on Spanish-Israeli relations during the Francoist dictatorship, populism and education: the case of Peronist Argentina, and Argentine nationalism after World War II.

SIDELIGHTS: In his 1993 book, *The Franco-Peron Alliance: Relations between Spain and Argentina, 1946-1955,* Raanan Rein examines the political relationship between General Juan Peron of Argentina and Generalissimo Francisco Franco of Spain, leaders of the only two fascist states following World War II. When the Allies imposed an economic and political embargo on Franco following their victory in World War II, Peron helped the Spanish regime to survive by selling them large amounts of wheat.

Rein presents a thorough study of both regimes as well as of their alliance, which deteriorated in the early 1950s, when Franco became an official ally of the United States. After a long, tumultuous, and complex rule, Peron was eventually deposed in 1955 and then was allowed to settle in Spain. In a review in the *Times Literary Supplement,* Mark Falcoff asserted: "Based on exhaustive work in Spanish, Argentine, American and British diplomatic archives, it is a significant contribution to the history of both Spain and Argentina, and also to our knowledge of Cold War politics."

BIOGRAPHICAL/CRITICAL SOURCES:

PERIODICALS

Times Literary Supplement, February 25, 1994.

*   *   *

REINHARDT, Gottfried   1913-1994

OBITUARY NOTICE—See index for *CA* sketch: Born March 20, 1913 (one source cites 1911), in Berlin, Germany; died of pancreatic cancer, July 19, 1994, in Los Angeles, CA. Writer, producer, and director of films and stage plays. A veteran figure in the American film industry, Reinhardt made his most notable films during the 1940s and 1950s. These include *Two-Faced Woman,* the last film in which Greta Garbo appeared, and *Situation Hopeless—But Not Serious,* the first film to feature Robert Redford, which Reinhardt both produced and directed. Reinhardt was born in Berlin, the son of the Austrian theatrical actor/director Max Reinhardt, and in 1932 came to the United States to work as an assistant to the director Ernst Lubitsch. He later wrote screenplays and librettos, and produced such films for Metro-Goldwyn-Mayer as *The Red Badge of Courage,* directed by John Huston. During the 1960s Reinhardt directed plays in Salzburg, Austria. In 1979 he released *The Genius,* a biography of his father, and he also finished a memoir of his life in the theater and film industry, entitled *Proscenium Loge.*

OBITUARIES AND OTHER SOURCES:

BOOKS

International Motion Picture Almanac, Quigley, 1994.

PERIODICALS

Chicago Tribune, July 7, 1994, sec. 2, p. 6.

REISS, Edward   1964-

PERSONAL: Born May 18, 1964, in Igtham, England; son of R. W. (a commuter and "leg spin bowler") and Frances (a homemaker and "renaissance woman"; maiden name, Clemence) Reiss. *Education:* Clare College, Cambridge, scholar, 1984; University of Bradford, Ph.D., 1990. *Religion:* "Muggletonian."

ADDRESSES: Home—Flat 3, 24 Sherborne Rd., Bradford, West Yorkshire BD7 1RB, England.

CAREER: Writer, lecturer, and shiatsu therapist.

WRITINGS:

The Strategic Defense Initiative, Cambridge University Press, 1992.
An Original Introduction to Marx, Pluto Press, 1995.

Also author of various creative and academic papers on "Star Wars," Marxism, alternative medicine, and related subjects.

SIDELIGHTS: Edward Reiss told *CA: The Strategic Defense Initiative* analyzes the SDI as a case study of the dynamics of the arms race. I used the Pentagon's SDI contract data base to show how those who recommended the program also benefited from it. I was motivated by a conviction that the funds spent on 'Star Wars' would be better given to more humane and constructive projects.

"The book was described by R. H. Baker in *Defense Analysis* as 'the best book I have read this year, a clear, cogent and coherent account of the evolution of the Strategic Defense Initiative (SDI) . . . invaluable for the detailed and documented analysis of the politics of influence.' Baker also called it 'irresistible.'

"Whilst writing this book, my interest in alternative medicine developed. I believed I had found a cure for insomnia, particularly in chapters 9 and 10. I therefore set about studying shiatsu and traditional Chinese Medicine. I am interested in how Oriental medicine, with its holistic model of human being, challenges conventional academic assumptions in the social sciences.

"My book on Marx aims to be precise, fresh, and jargon-free. It provides an up-to-date account of Marx, with original ideas about the imaginative and emotional aspects of his work."

BIOGRAPHICAL/CRITICAL SOURCES:

PERIODICALS

Defense Analysis, August, 1993, pp. 252-53.

*   *   *

REXINE, John E(fstratios)   1929-1993

OBITUARY NOTICE—See index for *CA* sketch: Born June 6, 1929, in Boston, MA; died October 23, 1993. Classical scholar, professor, and author. Rexine was the author of such studies as *Solon and His Political Theory, Religion in Plato and Cicero,* and *The Hellenic Spirit: Byzantine and Post-Byzantine.* He received his doctorate from Harvard University in 1964 and taught at Brandeis University and later Colgate University, where in 1977 he was appointed as Charles A. Dana Professor of the Classics. A prolific author of scholarly books and articles, Rexine once stated that writing "is a form of catharsis. . . . [It] is a vehicle for the expression of ideas but also for the expression of the self."

OBITUARIES AND OTHER SOURCES:

Date of death provided by Rexine's widow, Elaine L. Levine, September 20, 1994.

BOOKS

Who's Who in America, 48th edition, Marquis, 1994.

*   *   *

RHEA, Gordon Campbell   1945-

PERSONAL: Born March 10, 1945, in Arlington, VA; son of Booth Buford and Mildred Gazave (a homemaker) Rhea; married Catherine B. Rhea (a homemaker), June, 1986; children: Campbell, Carter. *Education:* Indiana University, A.B. (summa cum laude), 1967; Harvard University, M.A., 1968; Stanford University, J.D., 1974.

ADDRESSES: Home—11104 Elmview Pl., Great Falls, VA 22066. *Office*—2115 Queen St., Christianstel, St. Croix, VI 00820.

CAREER: Admitted to Bars of California, Washington, DC, Virgin Islands, and the U.S. Supreme Court. Law Offices of Barry Tarlow, Los Angeles, CA, associate, 1974-75; Senate Select Committee on Intelligence Activities, Washington, DC, special assistant to the Chief Counsel, 1975-76; assistant U.S. attorney, Washington, DC, 1976-81; assistant U.S.

attorney, U.S. Virgin Islands, 1981-82; Law Offices of Alkon, Rhea, and Hart, St. Croix, U.S. Virgin Islands, partner, 1982—. U.S. Peace Corps, volunteer in Ethiopia, 1968-70; Thales Marine, woodcrafter, 1970-71.

MEMBER: American Bar Association.

AWARDS, HONORS: Jules and Frances Landry Award, Louisiana State University Press, 1994, for *The Battle of the Wilderness: May 5-6, 1864.*

WRITINGS:

The Battle of the Wilderness: May 5-6, 1864, Louisiana State University Press (Baton Rouge), 1994.

*   *   *

RIBOWSKY, Mark   1951-

PERSONAL: Born February 2, 1951, in New York, NY; son of Solomon and Frances (Moskowitz) Ribowsky; married Sondra Goldstein (a marketing director). *Education:* New York University, B.A., 1973.

ADDRESSES: Home—New York City. *Agent*—Edward J. Acton, 928 Broadway, New York, NY 10010.

CAREER: Journalist and author. Worked as a staff writer at *TV Guide.*

WRITINGS:

He's a Rebel: The Truth about Phil Spector—Rock and Roll's Legendary Madman, Dutton (New York), 1989.
Slick: The Silver and Black Life of Al Davis, Macmillan (New York), 1991.
Don't Look Back: Satchel Paige on the Shadows of Baseball, Simon & Schuster (New York), 1994.
The History of the Negro Leagues, Birch Lane Press (New York), 1995.

Contributor to periodicals, including *Inside Sports.*

SIDELIGHTS: Mark Ribowsky, a journalist by profession, is also a biographer of famous (and sometime notorious) sports and music figures. His 1989 book, *He's a Rebel: The Truth about Phil Spector—Rock and Roll's Legendary Madman,* received widespread attention for its controversial revelations about producer and songwriter Phil Spector, one of the most influential figures in 1960s pop music. The publication of the book coincided with Spector's induction into the Rock and Roll Hall of Fame. *Slick: The Silver and Black Life of Al Davis,* was Ribowsky's next foray into the field of contemporary biography and appeared in 1991. The volume draws upon Ribowsky's background as a sportswriter to portray the life and career of one of professional football's more infamous coaches, Al Davis of the Los Angeles Raiders. In 1994, Ribowsky portrayed baseball great Satchel Paige in his book *Don't Look Back.*

He's a Rebel exposes the personal and creative life of Phil Spector, a musician, songwriter, and record producer of humble origins who rose to celebrity status in the early 1960s as the mastermind behind such tunes as "Be My Baby" and "Da Doo Ron Ron." The now-reclusive and eccentric Spector did not contribute to the volume and later disputed some of its claims, but Ribowsky interviewed many former associates and friends of Spector in compiling the profile. *He's a Rebel* chronicles Spector's early years that were shaken by his father's suicide. As a southern California seventeen-year-old, Spector cut a record with a group called the Teddy Bears that quickly climbed the charts. Ribowsky reveals the origins of the hit song's title—"To Know Him Is to Love Him"—as the epitaph on the tombstone of Spector's father. At his peak the producer crafted enormously popular songs for such "girl" groups as the Ronettes and the Crystals. The songs came to define a new musical direction for American pop music, combining the influences of African American rhythm and blues with innovative studio technology.

He's a Rebel details the methods of production utilized by Spector in building his "Wall of Sound"— a cacophonous amalgam of numerous guitars, basses, pianos, and drums topped with reverberating strings, choruses, and keening lead vocals. Recorded in mono to forge the multifarious elements into a single, monstrous emanation, Spector's Wall of Sound was unlike anything previously heard by the pop music world.

By 1966 Spector's innovations, in light of new studio technology, had become dated. His reign as a hitmaker over, Spector continued his career as a record producer, working with established performers such as the Beatles (providing final, reconstructive production on the group's abandoned "Let It Be" album that was primarily produced by George Martin), as well as the Righteous Brothers, Tina Turner, and the Ramones.

He's a Rebel also details the more unsavory aspects of Spector's personal life, including his abusive marriage to Ronette lead vocalist Ronnie Spector, drug and alcohol dependency, and his obsession with extreme security. These paranoid measures, which have intensified with his increasing reclusiveness, include a phalanx of armed bodyguards and electric fences that surround his California mansion. In addition to arming his guards, Spector also fortified himself, indulging a fascination for guns and frequently carrying and/or brandishing one. Ribowsky narrates one incident in which Spector, dissatisfied with a recording session at which John Lennon was present, took out a gun and fired it overhead. Eccentricities aside, the volume also relates the enigmatic producer's lasting influence on American pop music, noting even the fictional film and literary characters that have been mirrored on Spector's well-known persona.

Critical reaction to *He's a Rebel* was mixed. Reviewing the book for the *New York Times Book Review,* Abe Peck faulted the author for erecting "a wall of hype" in his numerous instances of hyperbolic assertion, and remarked that "this book, like some of Mr. Spector's work, is just plain overproduced." Conversely, noted rock critic and historian Greil Marcus, writing in *California,* lauded the author's restraint in presentation: "The virtue of Ribowsky's book is that he brings the story down to earth without sacrificing its drama." *Chicago Tribune* writer Lynn Van Matre remarked that "Ribowsky tells Spector's story in straightforwardly readable, workmanlike fashion." In a review of the volume for *Vanity Fair,* writer James Wolcott praised the author's skill in eliciting pithy details from former friends and colleagues. Wolcott stated that the "book has sprinkled powder on Spector's trail to retrace his shifty footsteps. And by doing so it inadvertently maps the wayward path of pop music and its pretensions."

In his next work, *Slick: The Silver and Black Life of Al Davis,* Ribowsky assembled an expose of another controversial figure, long-time Los Angeles Raiders coach and team owner Al Davis. At the time of the book's publication in 1991, Davis had led his team to four Super Bowls, racking up an outstanding winning record over three decades. Yet Davis's career has long been fraught with controversy, and Ribowsky chronicles the behind-the-scenes machinations that have made many in the sport avowed enemies of the owner/coach. The biography begins with details of Davis's Brooklyn, New York, upbringing and continues with his failures as a college athlete. *Slick* reveals the duplicitous manner by which Davis landed his first coaching jobs at Adelphi University and with the United States Army football team, each of which he unexpectedly commanded with great success. Moving into professional football, he soon secured a position with the Oakland Raiders, then a part of the American Football League. Assuming the mantle of league commissioner, he played a key role in the merger of that body with the National Football League in 1970. Ensconced in the Raider's organization, Davis expanded his influence by gaining ownership of the team through unsavory arm-twisting—he threatened to expose one of the team's silent partners, a rival football coach. By pitting shareholders against the team's general partner, Wayne Valley, Davis was able to wrestle control of the organization. The caustic interview that Valley's widow contributed to the book provides an example of the low opinion of Davis held by many in the world of professional football.

Slick received generally favorable reviews upon publication. Mark Goodman of the *New York Times Book Review* praised Ribowsky's revelations about the more underhanded actions of Davis's career, but faulted the tone of the writing, comparing it to that of television sportscasters. "Such hyperventilated blather is at best fitfully amusing even when you are just flicking the dial," Goodman wrote. A reviewer for the *Buffalo News* observed that "the strength of this book [is that] Ribowsky doesn't opt for simple character assassination. His Al Davis is a more complex man, not easy to like, but full of admirable qualities." *Daily Review* writer Carl Steward commented that "Ribowsky paints a remarkably accurate portrayal of Davis's unrelenting and unscrupulous rise to power," calling the volume "as close as you're going to get to an insightful, incisive portrayal."

In 1994, Ribowsky published *Don't Look Back: Satchel Paige on the Shadows of Baseball,* a biography chronicling the life and career of one of the sport's seminal players. Paige was a standout pitcher in the negro leagues, an entity that existed before Jackie Robinson crossed the color line to play professional ball for the Brooklyn Dodgers in 1947. Renowned for his pitching talent, Paige was equally recognized as a showman and frequently walked hitters to load the bases so that he could dramatically strike out the last batter. He was also regarded as something of a baseball philosopher who created such proverbs as "Don't look back, something may be gaining on you"—from which Ribowsky's book

takes its title. Despite his great athletic ability and appeal to sports fans, it was not until 1948 (after nearly twenty years in the negro leagues) that Paige was asked to join the Cleveland Indians, finally making it to the majors at the age of 42. In his four seasons with the Indians, he defined himself as a formidable pitcher. In his first season alone he pitched two shutouts (allowing the opposing team no runs) and only lost one game. Paige's contributions to baseball were recognized in 1971, when he was inducted into the Baseball Hall of Fame.

In numerous reviews, *Don't Look Back* was praised as an accurate and unsentimental account of the ballplayer's life. Murray Polner wrote in the *Nation* that "Ribowsky's thoughtful portrait captures the audacious Paige, warts and all." Calling the work a "well-researched biography," *New York Times Book Review* contributor Warren Goldstein found that, while the book was informative and entertaining, there were "so many details about Paige's complicated wanderings that the reader is occasionally lost in the profusion of leagues, all-star combinations and barnstorming enterprises." While he acknowledges that many facts surrounding Paige's playing feats are unreliable (some blatantly apocryphal), *Wall Street Journal* reviewer Frederick C. Klein appraised that, compared to other Paige biographies, Ribowsky has delivered "a better look than anyone so far." Also comparing *Don't Look Back* to other accounts of Paige's life, Polner termed the book "far more searching," favoring it over Paige's autobiography (which was reportedly ghost-written). Polner concluded that "Ribowsky's Paige is remarkably durable."

Ribowsky told *CA:* "My specialty is letting the sanctified air out of over-mythologized figures in American popular culture. In this way, they can be seen in human terms essential to understanding their motivations and impulses. Usually, dark obsession is at the heart of artistic and business success, and the much-abused unauthorized biography format is only useful if it explains this."

BIOGRAPHICAL/CRITICAL SOURCES:

PERIODICALS

Buffalo News (Buffalo, NY), September 15, 1991, p. H6.
California, February, 1989, pp. 104-05.
Chicago Tribune, April 17, 1989.
Daily Review (Hayward, CA), September 4, 1991.
Nation, April 4, 1994.
New York Times Book Review, May 14, 1989, p. 23;

November 17, 1991, p. 22; April 10, 1994, p. 22.
Simi Valley Enterprise, September 4, 1991, pp. 9-10.
Vanity Fair, January, 1989, pp. 24-30.
Wall Street Journal, April 22, 1994.

*   *   *

RICHTER, Gregory C. 1955-

PERSONAL: Born July 2, 1955, in Lynwood, CA; son of Ernest M. (an electrical engineer) and Alison (Gambier-Bousfield) Richter; married Liyan Liao (a translator), May 13, 1988; children: Evan Liao. *Education:* Attended University of Goettingen, 1975-76; University of California, Santa Cruz, B.A. (with honors), 1977; University of California, San Diego, M.A., 1979, Ph.D., 1982; University of Uppsala, Certificate in Advanced Swedish, 1986. *Avocational interests:* Chamber music performance (piano).

ADDRESSES: Home—Kirksville, MO. *Office*—Division of Language and Literature, Northeast Missouri State University, Kirksville, MO 63501.

CAREER: World Translation, Inc., La Jolla, CA, programmer for computer-based Russian-English and German-English translation systems, 1982-83; Northeast Missouri State University, Kirksville, assistant professor, 1983-87, associate professor of linguistics, Russian, and German, 1987—. Lecturer at colleges and universities, including U.S./U.S.S.R. Educator Encounter, 1987, and Guangzhou Institute of Foreign Languages, Guangzhou, China, 1990-92. University of Iceland, visiting scholar, 1981.

MEMBER: American Association of Teachers of German, Midwest Modern Language Association, Linguistic Association of the Southwest, Foreign Language Association of Missouri.

WRITINGS:

(Translator from German) Otto Rank, *The Incest Theme in Literature and Legend: Fundamentals of a Psychology of Literary Creation,* Johns Hopkins University Press (Baltimore, MD), 1992.
(Translator from German) Rank, *Psychology and Soul-Belief,* Johns Hopkins University Press, 1994.

Translator (from French) of Antoine Meillet's *Introduction to the Comparative Study of the Indo-European Languages,* 1994. Contributor of articles and translations to periodicals.

SIDELIGHTS: Gregory C. Richter discussed his translation of Otto Rank's *Inzestmotiv:* "I was led to undertaking the project through my interest in linguistics (work from Saussure to Chomsky), translation theory (works of George Steiner), and drama. I am passionately interested in drama, given its powerful capacity to convey the experiences of the human psyche."

Richter's languages include German, Russian, French, Spanish, Swedish, and Chinese. He also has extensive knowledge of Dutch, Icelandic, Finnish, Latin, Italian, Old Icelandic, and Old English.

*   *   *

RICOSTRANZA, Tom
See ELLIS, Trey

*   *   *

RINGQUIST, Evan J. 1962-

PERSONAL: Born August 6, 1962, in Minneapolis, MN; married, wife's name Laurie (an analyst). *Education:* Moorhead State University, B.A., 1984; University of Wisconsin, M.S., 1985, M.A., 1986, Ph.D., 1990. *Politics:* Lutheran. *Avocational interests:* Fishing, hiking, canoeing, gardening.

ADDRESSES: Office—Department of Political Science, Florida State University, Tallahassee, FL 32306.

CAREER: Texas Tech University, Lubbock, assistant professor, 1990-93; Florida State University, Tallahassee, assistant professor of political science, 1993—. Legal Environmental Assistance Foundation, member of advisory board.

MEMBER: American Political Science Association, Policy Studies Organization, Midwestern Political Science Association, Southern Political Science Association, Southwest Political Science Association, Western Political Science Association, Sierra Club (member of national research advisory board).

WRITINGS:

Author of the book *Environmental Protection at the State Level: Politics and Progress in Controlling Pollution,* M. E. Sharpe (Armonk, NY), 1993. Contributor to books and political science journals.

WORK IN PROGRESS: Green Justice for All? The Effects of Race and Class in Environmental Protection; Politicians, Pavements, and the Environment:

Re-Casting Theories of Agency Behavior, completion expected in 1996.

* * *

ROBIE, Bill
  See ROBIE, William A., Jr.

* * *

ROBIE, William A., Jr.   1947-
  (Bill Robie)

PERSONAL: Born November 6, 1947, in Philadelphia, PA; son of William A. (a physician and naval officer) and Jessie (a registered nurse; maiden name, Parker) Robie; married Amy Ann Arthur (a researcher), July 31, 1992; children: John William. *Education:* Received B.A. and M.A. from East Carolina University; conducted doctoral study at University of Maryland, Baltimore County. *Avocational interests:* Flying, collecting antique radios, aircraft restoration.

ADDRESSES: Home—1023 Courtney Rd., Arbutus, MD 21227; and Route 5, Box 527, Greenville, NC 27834. *Office*—709 Administration Building, University of Maryland, Baltimore County, Baltimore, MD.

CAREER: Professional actor, 1972-90; University of Maryland, Baltimore County, Baltimore, adjunct teacher of U.S. history, 1990—. Member of selection boards for aviation awards, including Collier Trophy, Elder Statesmen of Aviation Award, and Brewer Trophy. *Military service:* U.S. Navy, Submarine Service, until 1969.

MEMBER: National Aeronautic Association, Pi Kappa Phi, Gamma Theta Upsilon, Phi Alpha Theta, Gamma Beta Phi.

WRITINGS:

(Under name Bill Robie) *For the Greatest Achievement: A History of the Aero Club of America and the National Aeronautic Association,* Smithsonian Institution Press (Washington, D.C.), 1993.

WORK IN PROGRESS: An Aero Mechanician's Logbook, a novel about flying in the United States before World War I; research on pioneering aviators and related events.

SIDELIGHTS: William A. Robie, Jr. told *CA* that one of his hobbies is aircraft restoration. In 1989 he restored the 1931 *Sky Ghost* for the National Soaring Museum in Elmira, New York.

* * *

ROBINSON, Andrew   1957-

PERSONAL: Born March 14, 1957, in Oxford, England; son of Frank Neville H. (a physicist) and Daphne Isobel (Coulthard) Robinson. *Education:* Oxford University, degree (with honors), 1979; London School of Oriental and African Studies, London, M.A., 1986.

ADDRESSES: Home—13 Lonsdale Sq., London N1 1EN, England. *Office*—*Times Higher Education Supplement,* Admiral House, 66-68 East Smithfield, London E1 9XY, England.

CAREER: Worked for Macmillan Publishers, 1979-82, and Granada Television, 1983-89; freelance writer, 1990-94; *Times Higher Education Supplement,* London, England, literary editor, 1994—.

WRITINGS:

Satyajit Ray: The Inner Eye, Deutsch, 1989, University of California Press, 1990.
The Art of Rabindranath Tagore, Deutsch, 1989.
(With Simon Berthow) *The Shape of the World: The Mapping and Discovery of the Earth,* Rand McNally, 1990.
(Editor and translator, with Krishna Dutta) *Noon in Calcutta: Short Stories from Bengal,* Bloomsbury Publishing, 1992.
Earth Shock: Hurricanes, Volcanoes, Earthquakes, Tornados, and Other Forces of Nature, Thames & Hudson (London, England), 1993, also published in England as *Earthshock: Climate, Complexity, and the Forces of Nature.*
(With Dutta) *Rabindranath Tagore: The Myriad-Minded Man,* Bloomsbury Publishing, 1995.
Writing and Its Origins (tentative title), Thames & Hudson, 1995.

SIDELIGHTS: Andrew Robinson told *CA:* "Following a long visit to India in 1975, when I was eighteen years old, I became deeply interested in Indian culture, the culture of Bengal in particular. In 1982 I met Satyajit Ray and began to research his biography, which was published in 1989. Ray is, in my view, among the greatest artists of the twentieth century. This is not widely appreciated either in the West or in India, a situation I am trying gradually to change.

"Much more famous in his time, but now even less

well understood, is another great Indian, Rabindranath Tagore, who won the Nobel Prize for literature in 1913. I was drawn to him by my work on Ray, who adapted Tagore's stories and a novel to make some wonderful films. During the 1980s I began to grasp the range of Tagore's achievements, which led me to write another biography.

"Both Ray and Tagore were sensitive to both Indian and western culture in the widest sense, and both were able to create out of their sensitivity. Consequently, at its best, their work has a dimension that is missing from the work of most of their contemporaries, whether western or Indian. I am deeply attracted to this broadness and sophistication of outlook. It has, I feel, broadened my understanding in the books I have written on relatively 'mainstream' subjects, including the history of mapping and exploration, the history and science of great natural forces, and the origins and development of writing systems. All these books involved the study of many cultures.

"I do not write for an academic audience as such, but, in my more serious books, I consciously try to satisfy academics, both those in the humanities and in the sciences. My first university degree, in chemistry, has helped me to bring an analytical approach to my writing and to avoid the pitfalls that beset writers whose training is purely in the humanities or purely literary. (Most writers on Ray have been film critics; most writers on Tagore, literary people.) In some cases, such as the book on writing systems, I have collaborated actively with scholars at the forefront of their subjects. The challenge of popularizing a subject without misrepresenting or trivializing it, excites me—and the response has generally been a gratifying one.

"I view my work as a literary editor in the same way. For the *Times Higher Education Supplement,* I try to commission book reviews from authorities who are able to communicate to readers in many disciplines. Ray, Tagore, and Michael Ventris, the decipherer of Linear B, are my guides here; none of them were interested in scholarship for the sake of scholarship."

*   *   *

ROGOW, Zack   1952-

PERSONAL: Born May 8, 1952, in New York, NY; son of Lee (a writer) and Mildred (a civil service worker and homemaker; maiden name, Weisfeld) Rogow; married Anne D. Sachs (a teacher and

writer), July 6, 1986; children: Miranda, Lena. *Education:* Yale University, B.A. (cum laude), 1975; City College of the City University of New York, M.A., 1977. *Avocational interests:* Art, architecture, baseball.

ADDRESSES: Home—San Francisco, CA. *Office*—Graduate School of Education, University of California, Berkeley, CA.

CAREER: Sweet Ch'i Press, managing editor, 1983-87; substitute teacher, 1986-89; Benemann Translation Center, production coordinator, 1989-92; San Francisco State University, San Francisco, CA, managing director of Poetry Center, 1992; University of California, Berkeley, editor for Graduate School of Education, 1993—. Gives workshops for children and adults on literature, theater, and art history.

MEMBER: American Literary Translators Association, P.E.N. American Center.

AWARDS, HONORS: Fellow of California Arts Council, 1993-94; Translation Prize from International P.E.N. and Book-of-the-Month Club, 1994, for *Earthlight.*

WRITINGS:

Glimmerings (poems), More Than Coincidence Press, 1979.
Make It Last (poems), Slow Motion Press, 1983.
A Preview of the Dream (poems), Gull Books, 1985.
Oranges (juvenile), illustrated by Mary Szilagyi, Orchard Books, 1988.

Work represented in anthologies, including *The Epistolary Form and the Letter as Artifact,* Pig Iron Press, 1991; and *Time Is the Longest Distance,* edited by Ruth I. Gordon, HarperCollins, 1991. Contributor of poems, fiction, and reviews to magazines, including *American Poetry Review, Home Planet News, Yomimono, New Delta Review, Calliope,* and *Galley Sail Review.*

TRANSLATOR

(With others) Maryam Sachs, *The Kiss,* HarperCollins, 1992.
(With Bill Zavatsky) Andre Breton, *Earthlight,* Sun and Moon (Los Angeles, CA), 1993.
Andre Breton, *Arcanum 17,* Sun and Moon, 1994.

Translator of *The Dice Cup* by Max Jacob, Sun Press. Work represented in anthologies. Contributor of translations to periodicals.

WORK IN PROGRESS: Two books of poems, *Monologues* and *Eager for Each Detail;* translating George Sand's *Horace.*

SIDELIGHTS: Zack Rogow told *CA:* "My father was a promising short story writer who had just sold his first screenplay to Hollywood when he died in a plane crash at the age of thirty-six. I suppose I became a writer partly to finish the work he started. To be honest, I have to admit I *also* tried my hand at every other art form, from modern dance to macrame, but had no talent for those disciplines. Writers have always been on my personal list of heroes, so they were the ones I finally decided to try and copy.

"I grew up in polyglot Manhattan. I loved to imitate people's speech, from the Hyannisport vowels of the Kennedys to the curses of the tough guys hanging out on the corner.

"I enjoy writing poetry, both for the intellectual pinball it stimulates and for the feeling. Poetry shakes up the matter that's settled at the bottom of my thoughts, at the same time that it swirls my emotions. I like writing in the voices of characters who are extremely different from me, as a way to understand how the world looks through their irises.

"I became interested in literary translation as a way of reading certain French texts. In college I stumbled on poems of Andre Breton that so faithfully created the hallucinatory/romantic mindframe I was searching for then that I realized it was actually possible to describe the indescribable. I began translating those texts to prove to myself that much less was beyond words than most people assume. Percy Shelley said, 'Poets are the unacknowledged legislators of the world.' If that is so, translators are their campaign managers.

"Children's books are a more recent form for me. I am intrigued by the possibilities of using poetic speech in writing for children. Can it be done, still sell books, and not bore kids? I aim to find out."

*   *   *

ROLAND, Charles G.   1933-

PERSONAL: Born January 25, 1933, in Winnipeg, Manitoba, Canada; son of John Sanford (an accountant) and Ethel Leona (maiden name, McLaughlin; later surname, Steel) Roland; married Marjorie Kyles, October 16, 1953 (marriage ended, June, 1973); married Connie Lynn Rankin (an actress), September 22, 1979; children: John K., Christopher F., David C., Kathleen C. Roland Ruben. *Education:* University of Manitoba, M.D., 1958.

ADDRESSES: Home—1201 North Shore Blvd. E., Suite 1106, Burlington, Ontario, Canada L7S 1Z5. *Office*—HSC-3N10, McMaster University, Hamilton, Ontario, Canada L8N 3Z5.

CAREER: Practiced medicine in Ontario, 1959-64; American Medical Association, senior editor, 1964-69; Mayo Clinic, Rochester, MN, professor of the history of medicine, 1969-77; McMaster University, Hamilton, Ontario, Canada, Jason A Hannah Professor of the History of Medicine, 1977—. McGill University, member of board of curators, Osler Library; Hannah Institute for the History of Medicine, coordinator of Osleriana Literature Project, 1978, and Microfiche Collection of Canadian Medical Periodicals, 1982.

MEMBER: Canadian Society for the History of Medicine (president, 1993-95), American Medical Writers Association (fellow; president, 1968-69), American Osler Society (president, 1986-87).

AWARDS, HONORS: Jason A. Hannah Medal, Royal Society of Canada, 1994, for *Courage under Siege.*

WRITINGS:

(Editor with J. P. McGovern) *William Osler: The Continuing Education,* C.C Thomas, 1969.
(With L. S. King) *Scientific Writing,* American Medical Association, 1971.
Good Scientific Writing: An Anthology, American Medical Association, 1971.
William Osler's "The Master Word in Medicine": A Study in Rhetoric, C.C Thomas, 1972.
(Editor) E. P. Scarlett, *In Sickness and in Health: Reflections on the Medical Profession,* McClelland & Stewart, 1972.
(With E. F. Nation and McGovern) *An Annotated Checklist of Osleriana,* Kent State University Press, 1976.
(Editor with J. D. Key) *The Origin of Vaccine Inoculation by Edward Jenner, M.D., F.R.S.,* Majors Scientific Books, 1977.
(With L. S. Baker and G. S. Gilchrist) *You and Leukemia: A Day at a Time,* Mayo Comprehensive Cancer Center, 1976.
(With P. Potter) *An Annotated Bibliography of Canadian Medical Periodicals, 1826-1975,* Hannah Institute for the History of Medicine, 1979.

(Editor and contributor) *Health, Disease, and Medicine: Essays in Canadian History,* Clarke Irwin, 1983.

Secondary Sources in the History of Canadian Medicine: A Bibliography, Wilfrid Laurier University Press, 1985.

(Editor with J. A. Barondess and McGovern) *The Persisting Osler: Selected Transactions of the First Ten Years of the American Osler Society,* University Park Press, 1985.

(Editor with McGovern) *The Collected Essays of Sir William Osler,* Volume I: *The Philosophical Essays,* Volume II: *The Educational Essays,* Volume III: *The Historical and Biographical Essays,* Classics of Medicine Library, 1985.

(With Richard L. Golden) *Sir William Osler, 1849-1919: An Annotated Bibliography with Illustrations,* Norman Publications, 1988.

Clarence Hincks: Mental Health Crusader, Dundurn Press, 1990.

Courage under Siege: Disease, Starvation, and Death in the Warsaw Ghetto, Oxford University Press, 1992.

Harold N. Segall: Pioneer of Canadian Cardiology, Fitzhenry and Whiteside, 1994.

(Editor with Barondess) *The Persisting Osler 2: Selected Transactions of the Second Ten Years of the American Osler Society,* Krieger, 1994.

Also author of *Long Night's Journey into Day: Details of POW Life in the Camps at Hong Kong,* in press, and *The Gray, Dismal Experience: Allied Prisoners of War in World War II,* in press. Work represented in anthologies, including *Books, Manuscripts, and the History of Medicine,* edited by P. M. Teigen, Science History Publications, 1982; *Life in Niagara in the Capital Period, 1792-1796;* and *British Trials of Japanese War Criminals, 1946-1948,* edited by John R. Pritchard. Author of "Thoughts about Medical Writing," a bi-monthly column in *Anesthesia and Analgesia,* 1970-76, and "Ontario Archives," a biweekly column in *Ontario Medicine,* beginning in 1982. Contributor of more than seventy articles and reviews to medical and history journals.

*   *   *

ROSS, Bill D.   1921-1994

OBITUARY NOTICE—See index for *CA* sketch: Born May 25, 1921, in Sioux City, IA; died of cancer, August 30, 1994, in New Brunswick (one source cites Trenton), NJ. Writer and journalist. A U.S. Marine combat correspondent during World War II, Ross was among the fighting forces that landed at the Pacific island of Iwo Jima, where one of the most decisive and casualty-ridden battles of the war took place. In 1985 he published *Iwo Jima: Legacy of Valor,* which many commentators consider the definitive account of this famous battle; Ross's book was praised for its authenticity, objectivity, and comprehensiveness. Before joining the Marines, Ross was a reporter in his home state of Iowa. After the war he returned to journalism, working for United Press International and Associated Press. He also worked in public relations, and in 1953 began a full-time career as a free-lance writer. In addition to *Iwo Jima,* Ross also published *Trenchcoat Brigade* and *Perleliu: Tragic Triumph,* which chronicles another casualty-heavy war campaign.

OBITUARIES AND OTHER SOURCES:

PERIODICALS

New York Times, September 16, 1994, p. B3.
Washington Post, September 9, 1994, p. B7.

*   *   *

ROSS, Diana   1944-

PERSONAL: Born Diane Ross, March 26, 1944, in Detroit, MI; daughter of Fred (a factory worker) and Ernestine Ross; companion of Berry Gordy (a record producer and executive); married Robert Ellis Silberstein (a rock music promoter), January, 1971 (divorced, 1976); married Arne Naess (in shipping), October 23, 1985; children: (with Gordy) Rhonda; (first marriage) Tracee, Chudney; (second marriage) Ross Arne, Evan. *Education:* Graduated Cass Technical High School, Detroit, MI, 1962.

ADDRESSES: Office—RTC Management, P.O. Box 1683, New York, NY 10185-1683. *Agent*—c/o Shelly Berger, 6255 Sunset Blvd., Los Angeles, CA 90028.

CAREER: Singer and actress. Singer with the Supremes, 1962-64, lead singer, 1964-69 (group renamed Diana Ross and the Supremes, 1967); solo performer, 1969—. Album recordings with the Supremes (Ross, Florence Ballard, and Mary Wilson; in 1967 Cindy Birdsong replaced Ballard) include *Meet the Supremes; At the Copa; Bit of Liverpool; Country Western and Pop; Supremes A-Go-Go; Greatest Hits, Vols. 1-3,* all released by Motown, 1964-70. Top-ten singles recorded with the Supremes include, "Where Did Our Love Go," "Baby Love," and "Come See about Me," all 1964; "Stop! In the Name of Love," "Back in My Arms Again," and "I Hear a Symphony," all 1965; "My

World Is Empty without You," "Love Is Like an Itching in My Heart," "You Can't Hurry Love," and "You Keep Me Hanging On," all 1966; "Love Is Here and Now You're Gone," "The Happening," "Reflections," and "In and out of Love," all 1967; "Love Child," 1968; "I'm Livin' in Shame" and "Someday We'll Be Together," both 1969.

Solo albums include: *Baby It's Me, Touch Me in the Morning, Lady Sings the Blues, Live at Caesar's Palace,* and *The Boss,* all released by Motown; *Eaten Alive, Ross, Swept Away, Why Do Fools Fall in Love,* and *Red Hot Rhythm and Blues,* all released by RCA. Top-ten singles as a solo artist include "Ain't No Mountain High Enough," 1970; "Touch Me in the Morning," 1973; "Theme from Mahogany (Do You Know Where You're Going To)," 1975; "Love Hangover," 1976; "Upside Down," "I'm Coming Out," and "It's My Turn," all 1980; "Why Do Fools Fall in Love," 1981; "Mirror, Mirror" and "Muscles," both 1982; "Missing You," 1985; "Chain Reaction," 1986. Other albums include *Christmas in Vienna,* recorded with Placido Domingo and Jose Carreras. Also represented in many Motown compilation albums.

Actress in motion pictures, including *Lady Sings the Blues,* Paramount, 1972; *Mahogany,* 1975; and *The Wiz,* Universal, 1978; and in made-for-television movie, *Out of Darkness,* ABC, 1994. Performer in television specials, including *Diana,* 1971, and *An Evening with Diana Ross,* NBC, 1977. Performer on stage in *An Evening with Diana Ross,* Palace Theatre, New York City, 1976.

Also president of Diana Ross Enterprises, Inc., which includes Anaid Film Productions, Inc., Diana Ross Foundation, RTC Management Corporation, Chondee, Inc., Rosstown, Inc., and Rossville, Inc. Co-owner of Motown Records, 1989—.

MEMBER: Screen Actors Guild, American Federation of Television and Radio Artists.

AWARDS, HONORS: Vice President Hubert H. Humphrey Citation Award for work with Youth Opportunity Program; Mrs. Martin Luther King, Jr., and Reverend Abernathy Citation Award; named Female Entertainer of the Century by *Billboard* magazine; named World's Outstanding Singer by *Cashbox* and *Record World;* Grammy Award, female entertainer of the year, 1970; National Association for the Advancement of Colored People (NAACP) Award, 1970; Entertainer of the Year Award, *Cue* magazine, 1972; Golden Apple Award, 1972; Gold Medal Award, *Photoplay,* 1972; Academy Award

nomination, best actress, and Golden Globe Award, both 1972, for *Lady Sings the Blues;* Cesar Award (French), best actress, 1975, for *Mahogany;* Antoinette Perry Award, 1977, for *An Evening with Diana Ross;* inducted into Rock and Roll Hall of Fame, 1988.

WRITINGS:

Secrets of a Sparrow: Memoirs (autobiography), Villard Books (New York), 1993.

SIDELIGHTS: In her autobiography, *Secrets of a Sparrow: Memoirs,* singer Diana Ross remembers growing up poor in Detroit, singing in the Baptist church choir, performing for her parents' guests, and harmonizing with her neighbors on the street corners of the Brewster-Douglass housing project. Among her peers were many future Motown music legends, including Smokey Robinson, Eddie Kendricks, Florence Ballard, and Mary Wilson. As a student in Detroit public schools, Ross excelled academically, athletically, and musically, participating in numerous sports and musical groups while working in a department store part-time. She also became a member of a singing group with several other girls, including Ballard and Wilson, who called themselves the Primettes, a "sister act," to the Primes, who would later become the hit singing group the Temptations.

Ross, Ballard, and Wilson got their big break into show business when Berry Gordy, president of the record company Hitsville (later Motown), signed them in 1962 to sing backup vocals for artists such as Marvin Gaye and Martha Reeves and the Vandellas. Within two years the Supremes, as they came to be known, released "Where Did Our Love Go?," which sold more than a million singles and topped the chart for months. A string of hits followed, and the Supremes were one of only a handful of groups to challenge the Beatles on 1960s music charts. Ross, groomed by Gordy, emerged as the brightest star of the three singers, inspiring Gordy to change the group's name to "Diana Ross and the Supremes" in 1967. Gordy also took an intimate interest in Ross, fathering her first daughter, Rhonda, a fact which Ross acknowledged in an interview on the *Oprah Winfrey Show* in 1994.

With Gordy's encouragement, and because she was increasingly asked to perform without the Supremes, Ross decided to break away from the trio and launch a solo career, resulting in further hit recordings and several acting roles, including her portrayal of blues legend Billie Holiday in *Lady Sings the Blues,* and an ambitious model in

Mahogany. In 1981 Ross made another break, this time from Motown and Gordy's direction, and founded RTC Management, naming it after the first initials of her daughters, Rhonda, Tracee, and Chudney. RTC includes fashion, publishing, and film production divisions, giving Ross many ways to exhibit her talents in clothing design, acting, and producing.

Although many words have been written about Ross, not all of them flattering, Ross issued *Secrets of a Sparrow* to illustrate how her success has been largely due to talent, hard work, and personal goals. She desired to contribute what she felt was an accurate portrayal of her life, highlighting both her successes and failures, so that her own story would stand amongst the unauthorized Ross biographies. Explaining her motive for writing her story to James T. Jones IV in *USA Today,* Ross said: "What's given me my success in my life is my beliefs, but people don't get that. They're looking for some real dirty secrets. The secret is there are no secrets."

BIOGRAPHICAL/CRITICAL SOURCES:

BOOKS

Contemporary Theatre, Film, and Television, Volume 5, Gale, 1988.
Haskins, James, *Diana Ross: Star Supreme,* Viking, 1985.
Notable Black American Women, Gale, 1992.
Ross, Diana, *Secrets of a Sparrow: Memoirs,* Villard Books, 1993.
Taraborelli, J. Randy, *Diana,* Doubleday, 1985.

PERIODICALS

Los Angeles Times, November 6, 1993, Calendar section, p. 1.
USA Today, November 11, 1993, p. D1.*

*   *   *

ROTUNDO, Louis C.   1949-

PERSONAL: Born October 28, 1949, in Sanford, FL; son of Louis F. and Doris E. Rotundo; married Sherrye C. Parr (a consultant), March 17, 1973. *Education:* University of Central Florida, B.A. (history) and B.A. (political science), 1972, M.A., 1975; attended University of Florida.

ADDRESSES: Office—4948 Courtland Loop, Winter Springs, FL 32708.

CAREER: Valencia Community College, instructor in federal government, 1977; U.S. Senator Lawton

Chiles, Washington, DC, staff assistant, 1977-80; Florida Ocean Thermal Energy Consortium, deputy director, 1980-82; Florida Solar Energy Center, special assistant to director, 1980-84; University of Central Florida, special assistant to president, 1984-87; Rotundo and Associates, Winter Springs, FL, private consultant specializing in business and governmental legislation, procedures, and fundraising activities, 1987—. Visiting lecturer in Soviet studies at Combat Studies Institute (Ft. Leavenworth, KS); consultant on active deceptive measures, Central Intelligence Agency, 1985; member of editorial board, *Journal of Soviet Military Studies;* advanced research fellow, U.S. Army War College Foundation.

WRITINGS:

(Editor) *Battle for Stalingrad: The Soviet General Staff Analysis of the Battle on the Volga,* Pergamon-Brassey, 1989.
Forgotten Dawn: The X-1 at Pinecastle, Greater Orlando Aviation Authority, 1990.
Into the Unknown: The X-1 Story, Smithsonian Institution Press (Washington, D.C.), 1994.

Contributor to various newspapers and political science publications, including *Journal of Contemporary History, Journal of Strategic Studies,* and *Military Affairs Journal.*

WORK IN PROGRESS: Soviet Strategy in the Great Patriotic War and *Supersonic Flight* (tentative title).

SIDELIGHTS: Louis C. Rotundo told *CA:* "As a boy growing up in Sanford, Florida, I bordered on the shy side. Today, I have established myself as a consultant and writer. I call myself a 'private consultant and lobbyist, but the other half of me is an historian.' When asked what advice I might give to aspiring writers, I respond 'Write what you know.'"

BIOGRAPHICAL/CRITICAL SOURCES:

PERIODICALS

Sanford Herald, November 5, 1989, p. 2C; June 21, 1994, p. 3B.

*   *   *

RUDD, Anthony   1963-

PERSONAL: Born March 6, 1963, in Winchester, England; son of Julian (a cleric) and Shelia Strannack Rudd. *Education:* Cambridge University, B.A. (with honors), 1985; St. Andrews University, M.Phil., 1986; attended Oxford University, 1986-

88. *Politics:* "Mostly left of centre." *Religion:* "Post-modernist Calvinism." *Avocational interests:* Travel, walking, literature, history.

ADDRESSES: Home—40 Belmont Rd., Bristol B56 5AS, England. *Office*—Department of Philosophy, University of Bristol, 9 Woodland Road, Bristol, England.

CAREER: Wilde Sapke (solicitors), London, England, trainee solicitor, 1990-92; qualified as solicitor, 1992; University of Bristol, teaching assistant in department of philosophy, 1993—.

MEMBER: Cogito Society (treasurer, 1994).

WRITINGS:

Kierkegaard and the Limits of the Ethical, Oxford University Press (New York, NY), 1993.

WORK IN PROGRESS: A book about skepticism and responses to skepticism by Wittgenstein and Heidegger.

SIDELIGHTS: Anthony Rudd told *CA:* "My book on Kierkegaard was the eventual outcome of research done at Oxford. It is an attempt to use Kierkegaard's writings as a resource for understanding the position of ethics and religion in modern society, where the growth of individualism has done much to undermine the social context in which they have traditionally flourished. Kierkegaard's concept of 'Subjective Truth' seems to me to offer a fruitful alternative to both relativism, with its denial that there is any absolute truth, and dogmatic objectivism, which fails to recognize the importance of the individual's personal appropriation of the truth.

"By the time the book was published, I had been to law school and was working for a firm of solicitors in London, having decided that there would be little opportunity to pursue an academic career in the then-economic situation. However, the recession caught up with the legal profession as well, and after a period of unemployment I was able to return to academic philosophy—in any case, a more congenial occupation for me than law. I am currently attempting to develop my ideas further in the field of the theory of knowledge.

"My way of writing is fairly unsystematic; it involves reading around an issue for some time before sitting down to write, without any plan—I find I can only develop and articulate my ideas in the course of writing. The resulting, rather stream-of-consciousness typescript has then to be re-worked in a more formal and hopefully comprehensible fashion."

*   *   *

RUEMMLER, John D(avid) 1948-
(Courtney Bishop)

PERSONAL: Surname is pronounced Rum-ler; born June 8, 1948, in Granite City, IL; son of Adam L. (a press operator) and Rose C. (Kowalinski) Ruemmler; married Patricia Anne Spencer (an educator), July 2, 1982; children: Jessica Caitlin, Adam Dylan. *Education:* University of Illinois, B.A., 1970. *Politics:* Liberal Democrat. *Religion:* Lean Buddhist. *Avocational interests:* Hiking, travel, reading.

ADDRESSES: Home—1611 Jamestown Dr., Charlottesville, VA 22901. *Office*—c/o Studio 500, 815 West Main St., Charlottesville, VA 22903.

CAREER: Writer, 1980—; Iron Crown Enterprises, Charlottesville, VA, writer and editor, 1983-90; Writer's Digest School and Institute of Children's Literature, Charlottesville, writing instructor, 1990—. Volunteers in Service to America (VISTA), Corning, NY, teen crisis counselor, 1972, supervisor, Teen Center, Corning, 1972-73; has also worked as a public school teacher, a billing clerk, and a steelworker.

MEMBER: Society of Children's Book Writers and Illustrators, National Writer's Club, National Writer's Union, Phi Beta Kappa.

AWARDS, HONORS: Eaton Literary Award, 1988, for *Hitler Does Hollywood.*

WRITINGS:

Mirkwood, Iron Crown Enterprises, 1981.
Rangers of the North, Iron Crown Enterprises, 1982.
Night of the Nazgul, Iron Crown Enterprises, 1984.
(Under pseudonym Courtney Bishop) *Brothers in Arms,* Lynx Publications, 1988.
Smoke on the Water, Shoe Tree Press, 1992.

Also author of the comic novel *Hitler Does Hollywood.*

WORK IN PROGRESS: Waterfall, a middle-grade novel; *Prisoner in the White House,* a biography of Louisa Adams; research for a biographical novel about Edgar Allan Poe.

SIDELIGHTS: John Ruemmler's first six published

works of fiction have sold more than four hundred thousand copies around the world. He credits this success in part to his "travels here and abroad—like my anti-poverty work and my job with big business in Manhattan—[which] have broadened my understanding of people from all walks of life," he commented. In addition, Ruemmler has worked as a steel mill laborer, a billing clerk, an instructor of adult basic education, a teen crisis counselor, an editor, and an instructor for a writing school. "Writing is an attitude, a way of looking at life," Ruemmler further remarked. "The key is to develop that attitude into something productive, and to do that most new writers need instruction as well as imagination."

Ruemmler's novel for young adults, *Smoke on the Water,* tells of the relationship between an English colonist, Thomas Spencer, and a Powhatan Native American, Eagle Owl, who are at first enemies but eventually come to understand each other. Although these two boys inhabit different cultures, their lives and interests are similar, and the troubles they face, such as racism and parent-child relationships, are similar to the concerns of contemporary young adults. A critic for the *Bulletin of the Center for Children's Books* pointed out that "the boys live almost parallel lives . . . complete with enemy rivals for the attention of the girl each boy loves." As a *Publishers Weekly* reviewer noted, "despite a profound language barrier—they communicate a wish to be friends and serve as a 'bridge of understanding between their peoples.'"

This bridge, however, crumbles with the massacre of 1622 in which the Powhatans killed three hundred Jamestown settlers. Although he had earlier defied the wishes of the elders and helped Thomas escape from the Powhatans, Eagle Owl finally joins the warriors of his tribe, and Thomas similarly must unite with the colonists. The boys' very similarity necessitates the destruction of their fragile friendship; such alliances cannot survive social conflict. Gerry Larson concluded in the *School Library Journal* that *Smoke on the Water* is "a beautifully written, well researched, and valuable source of information on early America."

BIOGRAPHICAL/CRITICAL SOURCES:

PERIODICALS

Bulletin of the Center for Children's Books, January, 1993, p. 156.
Publishers Weekly, June 22, 1992, p. 64.
School Library Journal, November, 1992, p. 124.

RUESCHEMEYER, Dietrich   1930-

PERSONAL: Born August 28, 1930, in Berlin, Germany; son of Philipp (a physician) and Eufemia (a physician; maiden name, Ross) Rueschemeyer; married Marilyn Schattner (a professor), June 14, 1962; children: Julia Yael, Simone Margalit. *Education:* Attended University of Munich, 1950-51; University of Cologne, Diploma in Economics, 1953, Dr.Rer.Pol., 1958; postdoctoral study at Columbia University, University of Chicago, and University of California, Berkeley, 1960-61. *Politics:* "European-style social democrat."

ADDRESSES: Home—60 Oriole Ave., Providence, RI 02906. *Office*—Department of Sociology, Brown University, Box 1916, Providence, RI 02912.

CAREER: University of Cologne, Cologne, Germany, research assistant at Sociological Research Institute, 1953-55, and Seminar for Sociology, 1956-62; Dartmouth College, Hanover, NH, assistant professor of sociology, 1962-63; University of Toronto, Toronto, Ontario, assistant professor, 1963-65, associate professor of sociology, 1965-66; Brown University, Providence, RI, associate professor, 1966-71, professor of sociology, 1971—, department head, 1975-79, director of Center for the Comparative Study of Development, 1989—. Hebrew University of Jerusalem, visiting associate professor, 1969, visiting fellow, 1990; Oxford University, academic visitor at Nuffield College, 1979, and Wolfson College, 1982; Free University of Brussels, Foreign Franqui Professor, 1987.

MEMBER: International Sociological Association, American Sociological Association, American Political Science Association.

AWARDS, HONORS: Fellow of Rockefeller Foundation, 1960-61, Canada Council, 1966, Ford Foundation, 1968-69, Berlin's Institute of Advanced Study, 1987-88, and Swedish Collegium for Advanced Study in the Social Sciences, 1992; named Torgny T. Segerstedt Professor, Swedish Council for Studies in Higher Education, 1992; Outstanding Book Award, Political Sociology Section, American Sociological Association, 1992, for *Capitalist Development and Democracy.*

WRITINGS:

Lawyers and Their Society: A Comparative Study of the Legal Profession in Germany and in the United States, Harvard University Press, 1973.
(Editor with Peter Evans and Theda Skocpol) *Bring-*

ing the State Back In, Cambridge University Press, 1985.

(Editor with Peter Evans and Evelyne H. Stephens) *States versus Markets in the World System,* Sage Publications, 1985.

Power and the Division of Labor, Stanford University Press, 1986.

(With Evelyne Huber Stephens and John Stephens) *Capitalist Development and Democracy,* University of Chicago Press, 1992.

(Editor with Louis Putterman) *State and Market in Development: Synergy or Rivalry?,* Lynne Rienner, 1992.

IN GERMAN

(Editor with R. Koenig and E. K. Scheuch) *Das Interview: Formen, Technik, Auswertung,* 2nd edition, [Cologne], 1957.

(Editor and translator, with Brigitta Heister) Talcott Parsons, *Beitraege zur soziologischen Theorie,* Neuwied, 1964.

Anwaltschaft und Gesellschaft, Enke (Stuttgart), 1976.

WORK IN PROGRESS: Editing *State, Social Knowledge, and the Origins of Modern Social Policies,* with Theda Skocpol, for Princeton University Press; editing *Participation and Democracy: An East-West Comparison;* research on democratization and on rational choice theory.

SIDELIGHTS: Dietrich Rueschemeyer told *CA:* "My interest in social science developed from my growing up in Germany during and after the Nazi time. Participating in the political reconstruction of Germany after 1945 through youth and adult education led me to sociology. My interests widened to include social theory, but focused in substance on the sociology of knowledge, the study of the professions, political sociology, and the study of international development."

*   *   *

RUOKANEN, Miikka   1953-

PERSONAL: Born April 11, 1953, in Rovaniemi, Finland; son of Osmo (a shopkeeper) and Elisa (a teacher) Ruokanen; married in 1973; wife's name, Katariina (marriage ended, 1985); children: Juho (son). *Education:* University of Helsinki, M.Th., 1977, D.Th., 1982; attended University of Zurich, 1978, and Yale University, 1992.

ADDRESSES: *Home*—Saaterinportti 2 C 41, 00720 Helsinki, Finland. *Office*—Faculty of Theology,

P.O. Box 33, Aleksanterinkatu 7, University of Helsinki, 00014 Helsinki, Finland.

CAREER: Minister of the (Lutheran) Church of Finland, 1977—. University of Helsinki, docent, 1983-93, professor of dogmatics, 1993—. Missionary in Russia, 1993—.

MEMBER: International Association for Mission Studies, International Congress for Luther Research, Luther-Gesellschaft (Germany).

AWARDS, HONORS: Scholar of World Council of Churches in Zurich, 1978; Fulbright scholar in the United States, 1992.

WRITINGS:

Hermeneutics as an Ecumenical Method in the Theology of Gerhard Ebeling, Luther-Agricola Society (Helsinki), 1982.

Doctrina divinitus inspirata: Luther's Position in the Ecumenical Problem of Biblical Inspiration, Luther-Agricola Society (Helsinki), 1985.

The Catholic Doctrine of Non-Christian Religions According to the Second Vatican Council, E. J. Brill, 1992.

Theology of Social Life in Augustine's "De civitate Dei", Vandenhoeck & Ruprecht (Goettingen), 1993.

Author of books in Finnish, including an introduction to Christianity.

WORK IN PROGRESS: *Truth and Context: Models of Christianity in Asia and Africa; The Pneumatological Concept of Grace in Luther's "De servo arbitrio".*

*   *   *

RYAN, Margaret   1950-

PERSONAL: Born June 23, 1950, in Trenton, NJ; daughter of Thomas Michael (an accountant) and Anne (a secretary; maiden name, Jansen) Ryan; married Steven Lerner (a computer salesperson), August 29, 1974; children: Emily Ryan. *Education:* University of Pennsylvania, B.A., 1972; Syracuse University, M.A., 1974; attended Columbia University, 1976.

ADDRESSES: *Home*—250 West 104th St., No. 63, New York, NY 10025.

CAREER: Ryan Business Writing, speechwriter and owner, 1976—. New York State Poets in Public Service, teacher, 1987-91.

MEMBER: Poetry Society of America, National Association of Female Executives.

AWARDS, HONORS: College poetry prize, *Mademoiselle* magazine, 1972; Davidson Prize for Sonnets, Poetry Society of America, 1986; New York Foundation for the Arts fellowship, 1987.

WRITINGS:

So, You Have to Give a Speech!, F. Watts, 1987.
Figure Skating, F. Watts, 1987.
How to Read and Write Poems, F. Watts, 1992.

POETRY

Filling out a Life, Front Street Press, 1981.
Black Raspberries, Parsonage Press, 1988.

WORK IN PROGRESS: Revised edition of *So, You Have to Give a Speech!;* poetry manuscript.

SIDELIGHTS: Margaret Ryan commented: "I knew I wanted to be a writer from the time I was seven years old. We were asked to write a composition about spring during class; it was second grade. All my classmates struggled and chewed their pencils and thought and wrote and scratched out. I closed my eyes, and could see spring: a deep green lawn dotted with dandelions; lilacs in bloom at the edge of the lawn; a robin foraging for worms. I wrote down what I saw. My teacher read it out loud to the class . . . I liked the recognition of my talent; I was a shy child who rarely spoke in class, so it was nice to have a voice, finally, even if it was the teacher's voice reading my words. I knew then that I would be a writer.

"I began to write poems when I was in high school. I liked reading poems: Shakespeare's sonnets, e. e. cummings, Edna St. Vincent Millay, Ernest Downson, Edgar Allan Poe. So I began trying to write poems of my own when I was about fifteen. At that time, folk music was very popular, and there was an emphasis on the lyrics of popular songs. So writing poems seemed like a very natural thing to do. Again, I learned that I was good at it: I submitted works to my high school literary magazine, and they were published. It was a great pleasure to see my poems in print.

"In college, I was lucky to have a wonderful Latin teacher who taught Catullus and Ovid and Horace as poems, real living poems, not as artifacts of a dead language. Through him I learned much about the form of poetry, its structure and subtlety. For a time I thought I, too, would like to be a Latin teacher.

But then when I was a senior in college, I won the *Mademoiselle* magazine poetry contest and I knew I only wanted to be a poet. So I went to graduate school in creative writing, in Syracuse.

"I met my husband there. We were married in 1974 and moved to New York City. Guess what? There were no jobs for poets! In fact, it was the middle of a recession, and there were very few jobs at all. I got work in an advertising agency that did ads and catalogs for art galleries in New York. I was chosen because I knew how to spell the word 'Renaissance,' and no one else applying for the job could spell it!

"Eventually, I found work as a speechwriter. It is in many ways like writing poetry: you are writing for the voice; it must be rhythmical and interesting to the ear; it has to tell a story and be convincing. You also have to learn a lot of interesting facts, which can then be used in poems.

"Here's how I came to write a book about writing poetry: from a poetry workshop I was in, I knew an editor at Franklin Watts. He knew I was also a speechwriter, and asked me to do a book about it for high school students. So I wrote *So, You Have to Give a Speech!*

"Later, they asked me if I would like to write a book about something else, and I suggested *Figure Skating.* I have loved skating since I was a child, and it's always nice to write about something you love. Then a new editor came to Franklin Watts, and wanted to do a book about poetry. He called me because on the jacket of the speech book it said I was also a poet.

"I had then been teaching children how to read and write poems for several years, through a program called Poets in Public Service. I taught in schools all around New York City: kindergartens and high schools, middle schools and grade schools, in the city and in the suburbs, and everywhere I saw how much children liked poetry if they could just read it without too much emphasis on 'what it meant.' I had my own daughter by then, too, and I knew that making things—poems, pictures, puppets, cookies, anything creative—made kids feel better about themselves. So I agreed to write the book.

"It was hard to do, because I love poetry so much and know so much about it. I had trouble deciding what was most important to say in five thousand words—which is hardly anything. I wanted to make sure I communicated some of the conventions of poetry, and the excitement of poetry, and answered the kinds of questions I had about poems when I was a child. Finding the pictures was fun. It was great to think up visual ways of representing ideas like repetition or metaphor.

"I still write poems and meet with a group of poets once a month or so to discuss what we've written. And I still write speeches for business executives. And I'm working on revising the first book I did for Franklin Watts, on giving speeches, to include some information on recent speeches, such as those given by Bill Clinton and George Bush during the election [in 1992].

"But poetry is my first love, and I am assembling a third collection of poems. They are mostly about love, but some are about growing up with my brother, others are about my daughter, and some are even about my work. But even in those poems, they are about how I love the things of this world, and love to name them, too."

BIOGRAPHICAL/CRITICAL SOURCES:

PERIODICALS

Booklist, April 15, 1987, p. 1270; February 1, 1988, p. 936.
Book Report, May, 1987, p. 56; March, 1988, p. 49.
Library Talk, May, 1993, p. 11.
School Library Journal, August, 1987, p. 98; March, 1988, p. 209; January, 1992, p. 132.
Voice of Youth Advocates, August, 1987, p. 139.
Wilson Library Journal, June, 1987, p. 65.

S

SAGER, Carole Bayer 1947-

PERSONAL: Born March 8, 1947, in New York, NY; daughter of Elias and Anita (Nathan) Bayer; married Burt Bacharach (a composer), 1982 (divorced); children: Cristopher Elton Bacharach. *Education:* New York University, B.S. (speech and dramatic art), 1967.

ADDRESSES: Office—c/o Guttman and Pam Ltd., 8500 Wilshire Blvd., Suite 801, Beverly Hills, CA 90211.

CAREER: Lyricist, singer, and novelist, 1965—.

AWARDS, HONORS: Voted best new artist in France and Germany, German Record Academy, 1977; Grammy Award nomination (with Marvin Hamlisch), song of the year, and Academy Award nomination (with Hamlisch), for best song, both 1977, both for "Nobody Does It Better," from *The Spy Who Loved Me;* Academy Award nomination (with Hamlisch), best song, 1979, for "Looking through the Eyes of Love," from *Ice Castles;* Grammy Award nomination (with Hamlisch, Alan Parsons, and Eric Woolfson), best original score for a motion picture or television special, 1979, for *Ice Castles;* Grammy Award nomination (with Burt Bacharach), song of the year, and Academy Award (with Bacharach), best song, both 1981, both for "Arthur's Theme (Best That You Can Do)," from *Arthur;* Grammy Award (with Bacharach), song of the year, and Grammy Award nomination (with Bacharach and others), record of the year, both 1986, both for *That's What Friends Are For.*

WRITINGS:

Extravagant Gestures (novel), Arbor House (New York), 1985.

LYRICIST FOR STAGE AND MOTION PICTURES

(With Marvin Hamlisch) *The Spy Who Loved Me* (including "Nobody Does It Better"), United Artists, 1977.

(With Hamlisch) Neil Simon, *They're Playing Our Song* (musical stage play; first produced in Los Angeles, CA, at Ahmanson Theatre, Center Theatre Group, 1978), Random House (New York), 1980.

(With Hamlisch) *Ice Castles,* Columbia, 1979

(With Michael Small) *Continental Divide,* Universal, 1981.

(With Hamlisch) *The Devil and Max Devlin,* Buena Vista, 1981.

(With Hamlisch) *I Ought to Be in Pictures,* Twentieth Century-Fox, 1982.

(With Burt Bacharach) *Night Shift,* Warner Bros., 1982.

(With Bacharach and Bill Conti) *Baby Boom,* United Artists/Metro-Goldwyn-Mayer, 1987.

Contributor of lyrics to songs in motion pictures, including (with Bacharach) "Arthur's Theme (Best That You Can Do), *Arthur,* 1981; *Making Love,* 1983; *Tough Guys,* 1986; *Three Men and a Baby,* 1987; and *Arthur 2: On the Rocks,* 1988. Also lyricist of songs for stage plays, including *Dancin',* 1978; *Up in One,* 1979; and *The Madwoman of Central Park West,* 1979.

OTHER

Lyricist for pop music songs, including (with Bacharach) "That's What Friends Are For," "On My Own," "Heartlight," "A Groovy Kind of Love," "Don't Cry out Loud," "When I Need You," "Come in from the Rain," "Heartbreaker," "If You Remember Me," "It's My Turn," and "Love Is My Decision."

Sager has recorded and released her some of her own work, including *Carole Bayer Sager,* 1977, *Carole Bayer Sager, Too,* 1979, and *Carole Bayer Sager/Sometimes Late at Night,* 1981.

SIDELIGHTS: Lyricist Carole Bayer Sager has collaborated not only with her former husband, Burt Bacharach, but with such notable artists as Marvin Hamlisch, Neil Sedaka, Melissa Manchester, Bette Midler, Peter Allen, Quincy Jones, and Michael McDonald to produce many hit songs, most of which speak of the cynicism, hope, joys, and sorrows of love and relationships. Numbering among the impressive list of singers who have recorded her songs are Frank Sinatra, Michael Jackson, Barbara Streisand, Aretha Franklin, Elton John, and Stevie Wonder. Sager herself has also issued three albums of her original compositions.

A long-running musical comedy, *They're Playing Our Song,* was written by playwright Neil Simon and inspired by Sager and composer Marvin Hamlisch's romantic relationship of several years. Featuring songs Sager wrote with Hamlisch, *They're Playing Our Song* enjoyed a lengthy Broadway run and has become a summer stock favorite.

To Sager's credit, several of her songs and collaborations have won major awards, including a Grammy Award, and an Academy Award shared with Bacharach for "Arthur's Theme (Best That You Can Do)" from the movie *Arthur.* Some of Sager's most successful ventures have been in collaboration with Bacharach. The songwriting duo also garnered a Grammy for Song of the Year in 1986 with their composition *That's What Friends Are For.* Recorded by Dionne Warwick, Stevie Wonder, Elton John, and Gladys Knight, *That's What Friends Are For* not only made its home at the top of the music charts but donated all of its profits to the American Foundation for AIDS Research.

Familiar with storytelling through her many songs, Sager made her debut as a novelist in 1985 with *Extravagant Gestures.* The main character in the book is Katie Fielding, an expert on mother-daughter relationships, despite having an unusual relationship with her own estranged, eccentric mother. When she learns her mother is terminally ill, Katie determines to make peace with her. In the process, Katie marries, bears a child, and begins to understand her mother and herself in a new light.

Throughout *Extravagant Gestures* Sager sprinkles references to modern culture; the characters, for example, discuss their books on Phil Donahue's talkshow, share secrets concerning their eating disorders, exercise with Jane Fonda, travel by limousine, and consider shopping a cure for nearly every ailment. Although *Globe and Mail* contributor Sherie Posesorski criticized *Extravagant Gestures* as being "a cheap knock-off of Erica Jong," she nevertheless commended Sager for her characterization. A *Publishers Weekly* critic also enjoyed Sager's "cast of well-drawn characters," and deemed *Extravagant Gestures* "an engaging read."

Sager told *Washington Post* interviewer Megan Rosenfeld that her goal as a novelist was "to write something from me, that turned me on, that told a story. And I didn't even know what that story was until I was well into writing it." Describing the year she spent crafting *Extravagant Gestures* as a "growth experience," Sager added: "As a collaborative being, a person who has spent 20 years writing lyrics for composers, this was the first time I felt I could do something alone."

BIOGRAPHICAL/CRITICAL SOURCES:

PERIODICALS

Globe and Mail (Toronto), March 1, 1986, p. C8.
New York Times, January 13, 1986.
Publishers Weekly, July 26, 1985, p. 155.
Washington Post, September 30, 1985.*

*   *   *

St. GEORGE, Andrew   1962-

PERSONAL: Born April 17, 1962. *Education:* Cambridge University, B.A. (with double first class honors); also studied at Harvard University and Oxford University.

ADDRESSES: Agent—c/o Chatto & Windus/The Hogarth Press, 30 Bedford Square, London WC1B 3RP, England.

CAREER: Edelman PR (public relations firm), New York City, 1985-86; Columbia University, New York City, professor of literature and film, 1986-90; Oxford University, Oxford, England, 1987-93. Media consultant to Landmark Film Corporation and McLuham-McLuhan First Media Group; founder and director of Oxford Writing Ltd and Wenham-St George Media Group.

MEMBER: PEN International, Architectural Association.

WRITINGS:

The Sosnow Travel Essays, Cambridge University Press, 1988.

JOH: Jocelyn Hambro of Hambros Bank, Cambridge University Press, 1992.

Browning and Conversation, Macmillan, 1993.

The Descent of Manners, Random House, 1993.

WORK IN PROGRESS: (Editor) *Browning: Dramatis Personae,* for Oxford University Press; a history of Norton Rose, one of the United Kingdom's largest and oldest law firms.

* * *

St. JOHN, Bob J. 1937-

PERSONAL: Born January 10, 1937, in Canton, OK; son of Edwin H. (a mechanic) and Verna (Wheeler) St. John; married Katherine Scott (a teacher), May, 1963; children: Scott, Todd. *Education:* North Texas State University, B.A., 1960. *Politics:* "Liberal democrat." *Religion:* "Liberal protestant." *Avocational interests:* Reading, movies, theater, visiting South Padre Island, TX.

ADDRESSES: Home—800 Sherbrook, Richardson, TX 75080. *Office—Dallas Morning News* Communications Center, Dallas, TX 75265.

CAREER: Dallas Morning News, Dallas, TX, sports columnist and writer, 1960-77, general columnist, 1977—. Creative writing instructor at El Centro College, Dallas. Guest lecturer on creative writing at numerous colleges and high schools. Semi-professional baseball player; former YMCA boys' baseball coach.

AWARDS, HONORS: Spur Award nomination for best nonfiction book, Western Writers Association, 1977, for *On Down the Road: The World of the Rodeo Cowboy;* named Coach of the Year, Richardson Sports Association League, 1980; two-time winner of Schick Pro Football Writers of America award; named outstanding pro football writer, *Women's Sport* magazine; winner of more than 30 journalism awards.

WRITINGS:

We Love You Cowboys, Sport Magazine Press, 1972.

(With Sam Blair and Roger Staubach) *Staubach: First Down, Lifetime to Go* (biography), Word Publishing (Waco, TX), 1974.

The Dallas Cowboys (picture book), photographs by Malcolm Emmons, Prentice-Hall (Englewood Cliffs, NJ), 1974.

On Down the Road: The World of the Rodeo Cowboy, forewords by Larry Mahan and Walt Garrison, photographs by Lewis Portnoy, Prentice-Hall, 1977.

Landry: The Man Inside (biography), Word Publishing, 1979.

Sketches in His Own Key (collected columns), Shoal Creek Publishers (Bryan, TX), 1981.

Tex! The Man Who Built the Dallas Cowboys (biography), Prentice-Hall, 1988.

While the Music Lasts (collected columns), Taylor Publishing (Dallas), 1988.

The Landry Legend: Grace under Pressure (biography), Word Publishing, 1989.

South Padre: The Island and Its People, foreword by Ann Richards, Taylor Publishing (Dallas), 1991.

Heart of a Lion: The Wild and Woolly Life of Bobby Layne (biography), introduction by George Plimpton, Taylor Publishing, 1991.

Also author of *The End of Autumn* (novel), 1985. Contributor of articles to periodicals, including *Argosy, D, Pro Quarterback, Real West, Sport,* and *Scene.*

SIDELIGHTS: Prize-winning journalist Bob St. John is noted for displaying a keen perception in his profiles of people and events. Starting as a sports columnist (and later becoming a general columnist) at the *Dallas Morning News,* St. John writes on a variety of subjects and offers his observations on numerous aspects of life. He has also employed his writing skills in producing several books on sports and sports figures; two collections of his newspaper columns; a portrait of Texas's South Padre Island; and a novel.

With his background in sports writing and living in a city where football is of great importance and influence, it comes as no surprise that St. John would produce several volumes on the Dallas Cowboys football team, players, and managers. Among his publications focusing on the Cowboys' organization are *Staubach: First Down, Lifetime to Go,* a portrait of former quarterback Roger Staubach; *Tex! The Man Who Built the Dallas Cowboys,* a colorful biography of former organization president Tex Schramm; and *Landry: The Man Inside* and *The Landry Legend: Grace under Pressure,* two biographies of longtime Cowboys coach Tom Landry.

Cowboys of a different sort are featured in St. John's *On Down the Road: The World of the Rodeo Cowboy,* a sociological look at rodeo culture. In preparing the book, St. John followed the rodeo circuit for one season, from its Fourth of July beginning until the National Finals. *On Down the Road* chronicles St. John's experiences on the circuit, profiles rodeo veterans and newcomers and their devotion to the grueling sport, and explains rodeo events and terms. Nominated for the Spur Award by the Western Writers Association, *On Down the Road* is considered one of the definitive books written on the subject of rodeo. In a *Los Angeles Times* review of the book, critic Robert Kirsch praised St. John's effort, suggesting: "You don't have to be a rodeo fan like me to appreciate this handsome, beautifully illustrated book, no mere celebration of the sport or entertainment or madness but a solid piece of reporting and evocation. It's full of fun as well."

Although his books have generally fared well with critics, St. John has received the most accolades for his *Dallas Morning News* columns, some of which are thematically arranged in the collection *Sketches in His Own Key.* According to a *Dallas Morning News* review by Gene Shuford, *Sketches in His Own Key* "validates all the kudos [St. John] has already received from distinguished literary critics and his equally impressive list of awards for his writing." In reviewing St. John's collection, Shuford judged St. John's style "simple and clean, moving with the subtle prose rhythms of repetition and balance, echo and re-echo, that would do credit to a Hemingway," and determined "the most impressive quality of this book . . . is the author's poetic sensitivity to the pathos, the irony and the tragedy in the lives of all sorts of people."

Sketches in His Own Key was also praised by James Hoggard in a *Dallas Times-Herald* review. "So much of this work is thrilling," Hoggard exclaimed, "that we're stunned to remember that most items in this collection first appeared in a throwaway publication. Last year's newspapers are ashes and mulch in the town dumps. That's fine. Our interest in the gossip is fickle; but St. John's columns, worthy of endurance, remain. Wonderful, short pieces, they're even better in this book whose sensitive and intelligent organization intensifies our pleasure in them. . . . Bob St. John exhibits a continuing excellence that regular columnists rarely attain."

BIOGRAPHICAL/CRITICAL SOURCES:

PERIODICALS

Dallas Morning News, December 20, 1981.
Dallas Times-Herald, January 10, 1982.
Los Angeles Times, May 2, 1977, section IV, p. 10.
Publishers Weekly, June 17, 1988; September 6, 1991.

SALAMAN, Nicholas 1936-

PERSONAL: Born February 4, 1936, in Minehead, Somerset, England; son of Sebastian Max Clement (a veterinarian) and Joan Elisabeth (a naturalist; maiden name, Patterson) Salaman; married Elisabeth Cecily Selater, October 1, 1960 (divorced, 1974); married Lyndsay Margaret Meiklejohn (a film producer), September 15, 1983; children: Sophia, Charlotte, Rose, Phoebe. *Education:* Attended Radley College, 1949-54; Trinity College, Oxford, M.A. (with honors), 1959. *Politics:* "Some degrees south of center." *Religion:* Church of England. *Avocational interests:* Baroque music, nineteenth-century printing.

ADDRESSES: Home—London, England. *Office*—Salaman Mallet Ltd., 40-42 Lexington St., London W1, England. *Agent*—Blake Friedmann, 37-41 Gower St., London WC1, England.

CAREER: Advertising copywriter, London, England, beginning 1959; has served as creative director of advertising agencies; director and partner of London Herb & Spice Co., Ltd., South Croydon, Surrey, England, 1978—, My First Books, London, 1984—, and Salaman Mallet Ltd., London, 1994—; free-lance author, 1981—. *Military service:* British Army, 1954-56; became lieutenant.

MEMBER: Chelsea Arts Club, Beefsteak Club.

WRITINGS:

The Frights, Secker & Warburg (London), 1981.
Dangerous Pursuits, Secker & Warburg, 1983.
Cleanaway! (juvenile), illustrated by Oscar Grillo, My First Books (London), 1984.
Quick on the Draw (juvenile), illustrated by Alan Adler, My First Books, 1984.
A Pocketful of Beams (juvenile), illustrated by Martin Chatterton, My First Books, 1984.
Writeaway! (juvenile), illustrated by Peter Till, My First Books, 1984.
Falling Apart, Secker & Warburg, 1986.
Forces of Nature, Secker & Warburg, 1989.
The Grimace, HarperCollins, 1991.
The Garden of Earthly Delights, HarperCollins, 1993.
Rogue Female, HarperCollins, 1995.

Also author of television play *The Walls Came Tumbling Down* for the "Armchair Theatre" series; also author of stage play, *Mad Dog,* performed at Hampstead Theatre.

SIDELIGHTS: Nicholas Salaman has written advertising copy for many years, and is a partner in two businesses—one of which, My First Books, is a publishing company which has printed his titles for children, including *Cleanaway!* and *A Pocketful of Beams.* He has also written plays for television and the stage. Salaman is perhaps best known in his native England for his successful, satirical novels for adults, which include *The Frights, Dangerous Pursuits,* and *Falling Apart.*

The Frights takes its title from the myriad kinds of terrors which Salaman's characters face daily—from imaginary creatures who hold one child captive with fear to the constant dread of capture by the Germans which terrifies a one-quarter Jewish woman. And, while the novel also focuses on the characters' efforts to survive World War II with their customs and traditions intact, the tone of the work remains humorous throughout. According to Paul Taylor in the *Times Literary Supplement,* "guilt, anxiety and terror keep bursting in," but do not "wipe away one's grin of pleasure at the lunatic proceedings." Polite British society is constantly satirized in the novel, and Taylor concluded that *"The Frights* is a debut to rejoice at. Exuberant, high-spirited and deftly plotted, it is notable for its author's inventively comic turns of phrase."

Dangerous Pursuits, Salaman's second novel, focuses on Britisher Ray Croucher, a prudish war veteran who crusades to protect his country against both modernity and foreign influences, and Chloe, the woman he competes for against a slick American adversary. The book was well received by critics. Andrew Gimson in the London *Times* declared that "Salaman is as readable as twenty years spent as an advertising copywriter ought to have made him, and achieves the trick without glibness." J. K. L. Walker in the *Times Literary Supplement* labeled *Dangerous Pursuits* "a gleefully unrealistic comedy of pursuit and bloodless revenge," and further noted that it was "crisply written." John Mellors admired the novel's male protagonist, and wrote in the *Listener* that "Croucher's character and conduct enable Salaman to satirize Britain past (for which Croucher yearns) and Britain present (in which Croucher feels betrayed and baffled)."

Salaman's 1986 novel, *Falling Apart,* features Charlet, a thirty-four-year-old woman who uses sex as a way to climb to the top levels of a fast food corporation. As Andrew Hislop announced in the *Times Literary Supplement,* "the ingredients seem familiar enough for contemporary fiction: Yuppy adultery and alienation, role reversal in the modern couple, satire on imported American consumer culture," but the book is also "well peppered with *piquant* wit." In 1989's *Forces of Nature* Salaman turns to a juvenile protagonist, 1950s adolescent Freddie, who fears he is homosexual despite a fulfilling sexual encounter with his landlady. Mick Imlah lauded the work in the *Times Literary Supplement,* asserting that "the painful slapstick is executed with relish, but also with some refinement. Apart from the amusing recreation of archetypal boyhood experience . . . Freddie is convincingly individuated by such details as the hymn tunes he plays solemnly on the piano."

Salaman told *CA:* "To paraphrase Belloc, I'm tired of prose, I'm still more tired of rhyme/But money gives me pleasure all the time."

BIOGRAPHICAL/CRITICAL SOURCES:

PERIODICALS

Listener, June 30, 1983.
Observer (London), June 26, 1983, p. 31.
Times (London), June 30, 1983.
Times Literary Supplement, September 4, 1981, p. 1018; July 1, 1983, p. 696; May 23, 1986, p. 554; June 30, 1989, p. 714.

*   *   *

SALAMON, Sonya   1939-

PERSONAL: Born November 1, 1939, in Pittsburgh, PA; daughter of Marcus (an undertaker and sales person) and Ethel Snider (Strasser) Blank; married Myron Salamon (a professor of physics), June 12, 1960; children: David, Aaron. *Education:* Carnegie Institute of Technology (now Carnegie-Mellon University), B.F.A., 1957; University of California, Berkeley, M.A., 1965; University of Illinois at Urbana-Champaign, Ph.D., 1974. *Politics:* Democrat. *Religion:* Jewish. *Avocational interests:* Walking, art, reading.

ADDRESSES: Home—715 West Pennsylvania, Urbana, IL 61801. *Office*—University of Illinois at Urbana-Champaign, 1105 West Nevada, Urbana, IL 61801.

CAREER: University of Illinois at Urbana-Champaign, Urbana, assistant professor, 1974-80, associate professor, 1980-87, professor of family studies, 1987—, affiliate in anthropology, 1984—, and agricultural economics, 1986—, associate of Center for Advanced Study, 1981-82, coordinator of graduate program in human development and family studies, 1981-88, 1991-93. W. K. Kellogg National Rural Studies Committee, member, 1988—; U.S. Department of Agriculture, Economic Research Service, visiting scholar of Agriculture and Rural Economics Division, 1988-89.

MEMBER: American Anthropological Association, National Council on Family Relations, Rural Sociological Society (member of council, 1988-90), Society for Applied Anthropology (fellow), Society for Economic Anthropology.

AWARDS, HONORS: Fellow, German Academic Exchange Program, 1975; senior policy fellow, Rural Sociological Society, 1988-89.

WRITINGS:

Prairie Patrimony: Family, Farming, and Community in the Midwest, University of North Carolina Press, 1992.

Member of editorial board, "Rural Studies Series," Westview, 1983-85. Contributor to sociology journals. Co-editor, *Rural Sociology,* Volume LVIII, number 4, 1993; member of editorial board, *Family Relations,* 1989-94.

SIDELIGHTS: Sonya Salamon told *CA:* "I am the author of a book and approximately thirty publications that describe holistically the lives of family farmers and people from small communities in rural Illinois. My research has called attention to the cultural variation of the rural Midwest, embodied in ethnic groups, that accounts for divergence in farm persistence, land tenure, and the vitality of rural communities. My book drew on a decade of ethnographic studies of seven Illinois farming communities. I demonstrate how family land transfers serve as a mechanism for recreating the social relations fundamental to Midwestern ethnic identities. Half the communities I describe are dominated by families of German descent and half by what I call 'Yankees,' or people with British Protestant ancestry. These two groups are dominant in the rural Midwest, and the ethnic identity they manifest is a powerful force shaping the social fabric of the region. The Yankees treat farming as a business and land as a commodity; it is profit, rather than persistence of the farm, that motivates their actions. Farmers of German descent, however, see farming as a way of life and land as a sacred family possession, and they hold the continuity of farm ownership as the highest priority. The commitment of ethnic Germans to act on their beliefs in this regard, I argue, explains why this group now makes up more than half of the Midwestern farm population.

"My current research focuses on the changes taking place in rural communities and the impact of these changes on families. Such communities are small in size and geographically distinct, making them ideal laboratories for studying ordinary family interactions in the clearly bounded contexts of neighborhood, social network, church, or schools. Due to population decline, school consolidations, and loss of local industries, rural communities are experiencing rapid change. An issue that currently interests me is the social outcome of increasing cultural diversity in previously homogenous small towns, as minority or economically disadvantaged families move into surplus housing. After a series of rural community studies, I am learning to identify what family factors and what community factors combine to affect whether oldtimers are either supportive or harmful toward newcomer families.

"My other research focus is the real impact of families on the environment. Farm families share an occupation that involves direct manipulation of the land; indirectly they determine our water quality and the abundance of wildlife. Because their work is inextricably tied to the land, farmers present a unique opportunity for studying how family actions can shape the local physical environment and the social consequences of these choices. I am presently involved in a study to discover the social and cultural factors behind why some families aggressively adopt sustainable agricultural systems and other families, in the same community, maintain conventional farming systems."

*   *   *

SALITAN, Laurie P.

PERSONAL: Born in Englewood, NJ. *Education:* University of Pennsylvania, B.A., 1983; Oxford University, D.Phil., 1986.

ADDRESSES: Office—Department of Political Science, Johns Hopkins University, Baltimore, MD 21218.

CAREER: Johns Hopkins University, Baltimore, MD, assistant professor of political science, 1987—.

WRITINGS:

Politics and Nationality in Contemporary Soviet-Jewish Emigration, 1968-89, St. Martin's (New York, NY), 1992.

WORK IN PROGRESS: Research on "comparative ethnopolitics."

SALWOLKE, Scott 1964-

PERSONAL: Born January 18, 1964, in Dubuque, IA; son of Burnett and Carilee (O'Neill) Salwolke; married Monica M. Manning (a teacher), September 2, 1989; children: Mitcheel Lee. *Education:* Attended Loras College, 1982-84; Creighton University, B.A., 1986.

ADDRESSES: Home—1435 Mount Pleasant, Dubuque, IA 52001-4234.

CAREER: Area Residential Care, Dubuque, IA, vocational instructor, 1989—.

WRITINGS:

Nicholas Roeg: Film by Film, McFarland and Co. (Jefferson, NC), 1993.
All This Filming Isn't Healthy: The Films of Michael Powell and the Archers, Scarecrow, 1995.

Author of one film script and two short plays.

SIDELIGHTS: Scott Salwolke told *CA:* "My main interest is film. Ultimately I want to write films, and until then I will be content with writing about film. I began my writing career in junior high school and received an award for my writing. I worked on my college newspaper and as a freelance writer for local newspapers and magazines. While this helped me to hone my writing skills, I found little enjoyment in the reporting of events. I find film criticism more challenging; it is a field which is constantly undergoing change. I hope I can contribute to the debate."

*   *   *

SALZMAN, Marian 1959-

PERSONAL: Born February 15, 1959, in New York, NY; daughter of Norman (a business executive) and Ruby (a consultant; maiden name, Freeman) Salzman; *Education:* Brown University, B.A., 1980; attended Harvard University Graduate School of Arts and Sciences.

ADDRESSES: Home—666 Greenwich Street, Apartment 1103, New York, NY 10014. *Office*—BKG Youth, 79 Fifth Ave., New York, NY 10003.

CAREER: Career Insights Magazine, Providence, RI, editor, 1981-83; freelance writer, 1983-86; *Management Review Magazine,* New York City, editor, 1984-85; Kehoe, White, Savage, & Company, New York City, director of media relations, 1986-88;

CV: The College Magazine, editor-in-chief, 1988-89; BKG Youth Inc., New York City, president and creative director, 1989—. Brown University Club, director, 1986-89.

AWARDS, HONORS: Susan Colver Rosenberger Prize in sociology, Brown University, 1980; Dorot Foundation fellowship, 1980; New York Public Library "Best Book for the Teenage" Award, 1992.

WRITINGS:

(With Deidre Sullivan) *Inside Management Training,* NAL/Plum, 1985.
(With Nancy Marx) *MBA Jobs!,* AMACOM, 1986.
(With Nancy Marx Better) *Wanted: Liberal Arts Graduates,* Doubleday/Anchor, 1987.
(With Ann O'Reilly) *War and Peace in the Persian Gulf: What Teenagers Want to Know,* Peterson's Guides, 1991.
(With Teresa Reisgies) *Greetings from High School,* Peterson's Guides, 1991.
(With Reisgies) *150 Ways Teens Can Make a Difference,* Peterson's Guides, 1991.
(With Sullivan) *Kids Can Do,* William Morrow/Avon, 1994.

Contributor to *Beauty Handbook, The Brown University Family Therapy Letter, Forbes,* and *Self.*

WORK IN PROGRESS: Generation Rap, a book for parents about the generation gap between them and their teens. Conducting broad-based research on twenty-somethings; on teen culture, especially a day in the lives of teens; and on family life in America.

SIDELIGHTS: Marian Salzman commented: "About my life: It's probably not all that surprising that I have made my professional career an extension of high school and college—both times were remarkably happy for me. I have always been over-committed. By day I work in an office and fly around the country. By night I am a book addict, reading, writing, and thinking about book ideas. I have also been both sociable and something of a loner. When I was in junior high, I clearly remember deciding to write a book documenting the perils of growing up in suburbia, of growing up as the oldest of three sisters who are all born within thirty-two months, and of fighting the stereotype of being a giggly blonde. Recently I found some of my notes and, while they are funny, they never would have cut it as a book. But, not surprisingly, I did author a book for teenagers about making the transition from junior high to high school, and I did get the opportunity to rag on things like zits, the long wait for a driver's license, and the anticlimactic prom.

"I spent a very happy, stimulating three years at Brown University just as it was emerging as the hot school. This dramatically altered my thinking: what college taught me was that, provided you could maintain the stamina to last through the all-nighters, everything is possible. You just have to dream and persevere. After Brown I floated for a while, tried graduate school, and then helped found a career magazine for college students. For three years I was an editor, a typist, an advertising salesperson, and a work junkie. That experience helped to shape my future professional expectations since I learned how to stay enthusiastic and interested for fifty, sixty, seventy hours a week.

"Now, more that ten years later, life is simpler. The good news is that I can still roam the country, looking for the next story or trend, counseling clients that want to touch young markets; the bad news is that no one asks me for identification when I sit down at a bar or cocktail lounge. Thus, for me, the last rite of passage is behind me: I am truly an adult whose professional role model is 'Harriet the Spy.' That's what I expected to be at fifteen and what I am at thirty-three."

One of Salzman's many books, *150 Ways Teens Can Make a Difference* (for grades eight to twelve), offers quick and easy information for young adults who want to know the practical aspects of volunteer work. One important concept reported in the book is how to match one's personality and talents to a job. Pat Braun in *Booklist* said "it clearly demonstrates that teen volunteers feel good about themselves and the jobs they accomplish." At the end of the book is a list of groups, organized state by state, that teens can contact. About Salzman's *Greetings from High School,* written with the help of Teresa Reisgies and several thousand teenage contributors, a *Booklist* reviewer summarized the book as "an upbeat catchall geared to the college-bound teen [that] contains advice on everything from getting along in school to dating and stress." *School Library Journal* contributor Dona Weisman noted that the book is "well organized and . . . easy-to-read" and commented that *Greetings from High School* should be a "popular and useful book."

BIOGRAPHICAL/CRITICAL SOURCES:

PERIODICALS

Booklist, February 1, 1992, p. 1019; June 1, 1992, p. 1727.
New York Post, March 12, 1992.
School Library Journal, November, 1991, pp. 143-44; April, 1992, p. 161.
Wilson Library Bulletin, June, 1991, pp. 113-14.

SAMS, Ferrol (Jr.) 1922-

PERSONAL: Born September 26, 1922, in Fayetteville, GA; son of Ferrol (a school superintendent) and Mildred (Matthews) Sams; married Helen Fletcher (a physician), July 18, 1948; children: Ferrol III, Ellen, James, Fletcher. *Education:* Attended Mercer University; Emory University, M.D., 1949. *Politics:* Democrat. *Religion:* Protestant. *Avocational interests:* Horticulture.

ADDRESSES: Office—101 Yorktown Drive, Fayetteville, GA 30214. *Agent*—c/o Longstreet Press, 2140 Newmarket Pkwy., Suite 118, Marietta, GA 30067.

CAREER: Physician in private practice, Fayetteville, GA, 1951—; Emory University, Atlanta, GA, instructor in creative writing, 1991—. *Military service:* 1943-47.

AWARDS, HONORS: D.Lit. from Mercer University, 1987, Emory University, 1992, Medical University of South Carolina, 1993, and Rhodes College, 1994; Townsend Prize for Fiction, 1991, for *When All the World Was Young.*

WRITINGS:

Run with the Horsemen (novel), Peachtree Publishers (Atlanta, GA), 1982.
The Whisper of the River (novel), Peachtree Publishers, 1984.
The Widow's Mite and Other Stories (short stories), Peachtree Publishers, 1987.
The Passing: Perspectives of Rural America (nonfiction), paintings by Jim Harrison, Longstreet Press (Marietta, GA), 1988.
Christmas Gift! (nonfiction), Longstreet Press, 1989.
When All the World Was Young (novel), Longstreet Press, 1991.
Epiphany (short stories), Longstreet Press, 1994.

ADAPTATIONS: Sams's short stories "The Widow's Mite" and "Judgment" were adapted as one-act plays for the stage by Betty Cooper Hirt and presented at A.R.T. Station Theatre in Stone Mountain, GA, 1993. *The Whisper of the River* was adapted as a drama by Dr. Linda Welden and presented at Appalachian State University in Boone, NC, 1994.

WORK IN PROGRESS: Short stories.

SIDELIGHTS: Ferrol Sams, who regards himself as "a country doctor" according to *Publishers Weekly,* gained widespread recognition with the publication of his first book, *Run with the Horsemen.* Sams began writing after attending Emory University as a medical student. Rising each morning at five a.m. to study for his medical board examinations, he maintained this early morning routine after becoming certified, and filled the early hours by recording his memories of life in rural Fayette County, Georgia, where his family roots can be traced back 150 years. Eventually, as Sams told Steve Walburn of *Atlanta Magazine,* "I could again feel and hear and smell the earth. And I thought the scene would make others feel, hear and smell it. . . . Then I found out I could embroider the truth here, invent some characters there, and before long I was into it."

Sams's notes, handwritten in a spiral notebook, became the manuscript for his first novel, *Run with the Horsemen,* a national bestseller, and the first of three books about Porter Osborne, a prank-playing farmboy and aspiring doctor, who, like his creator, grew up between World Wars in rural Georgia. Sams told Bob Summer of *Publishers Weekly* that his novels are "autobiographical, although people who read them as straight autobiography and believe everything in them actually happened are mistaken."

Run with the Horsemen was warmly received by many critics, among them Alice Digilio, who in a *Washington Post* review asserted that Sams "has fashioned a first novel remarkable both for its humor and its sustained and detailed picture of a mischievous southern farmboy's life during the Great Depression." And *New York Times Book Review* commentator Robert Miner deemed Sams's writing "elegant, reflective and amused. Mr. Sams is a storyteller sure of his audience, in no particular hurry, and gifted with perfect timing."

The second of the Porter Osborne books, *The Whisper of the River,* takes Porter to a Baptist college in Middle Georgia during the late 1930s. Despite the religious structure of the school, Porter indulges in pranks and re-examines his own beliefs. "It's a rollicking tale, a regional story of growing up," wrote a *Washington Post Book World* critic. In another review for the same periodical, George Core opined: "*The Whisper of the River* is not merely a collection of humorous anecdotes and tall tales by a masterly yarnspinner, for it has a wider scope and a deeper significance that embraces college life in most of its manifestations—generational conflict, race relations, the coming of war, and other themes of enduring value."

Between his second and final books of the Porter trilogy, Sams encountered writer's block and was unable to continue writing Porter's story. Sams's

editor suggested he turn his attention to a book of short stories; thus, *The Widow's Mite and Other Stories* was born. The title story, based on the Biblical parable about the woman who gave what little she could despite her great need, is a story about giving and tells of the plight of a tithing woman who receives $125,000 in inheritance money when her husband is decapitated. Other stories in the collection also provide moral lessons as Sams writes of subjects ranging from the evils of sex and alcohol, to the misconduct of the clergy. Shelby Hearon, writing in the *New York Times Book Review,* judged *The Widow's Mite* "a fine assemblage of tales about the charities and malices of gospel-heeding, neighbor-loving Southerners, which read as if they'd been recounted firsthand on the deepest porch in town."

Sams also issued two volumes of nonfiction during his hiatus from the Porter Osborne saga: *The Passing: Perspectives of Rural America,* which includes paintings by Jim Harrison, and *Christmas Gift!,* a volume of Sams's memories of old-fashioned, southern Christmases. In the latter book, Sams writes of his family's historic homestead, of Christmas cakes and ambrosia, and of the time-worn ornaments that are ceremoniously hung on the tree year after year. Considered by a *Publishers Weekly* critic to be a "charming account of the celebration of Christmas," *Christmas Gift!* inspired Linton Weeks of the *Atlanta Constitution* to write: "The doctor-writer possesses considerable wit and skill. And, though he sometimes uses too much treacle and lard, no one writing today is better at serving up helping after helping of home-cooked, Old South-style prose."

After his *Christmas Gift!* break, Sams continued Porter's story in *When All the World Was Young,* in which the main character enters medical school. Although Porter is still a practical joker and obsessed with sex and dating, his serious side emerges when, riddled with guilt at his lack of involvement in the war effort, he purposely flunks out so he can join the army and become a surgeon's assistant. "This spirited coming-of-age novel," judged Genevieve Stuttaford in *Publishers Weekly,* "is also ruefully funny, tinged with the wisdom of hindsight." *Atlanta Constitution* contributor and World War II veteran Benjamin Griffith also enjoyed the third installment of Porter's life, although he warned that "some will tire of the fumbling obscenities, the anal-stage allusions and the gratuitous profanities that endlessly lace the conversations of citizen-soldiers trying to appear seasoned. Alas, the author's ear is accurate; it is much as I remember it from my World War II days. The sides of most readers will also tire from constant laughter."

Despite his success as a writer, Sams is first a physician, maintaining a busy clinic in Fayetteville with his wife and two of his sons. "I'm really fortunate as a writer," Sams told Walburn in *Atlanta Magazine*. "I don't have to write for money or critics. The only thing I have to write for are people who like to read, and I've been very blessed that a lot of people like to read what I write."

Sams told *CA:* "Writing is hard work and a difficult discipline but, next to medicine, is the most fulfilling thing a person can do."

BIOGRAPHICAL/CRITICAL SOURCES:

PERIODICALS

Atlanta Constitution, October 22, 1989, p. L10; October 20, 1991, p. N9; December 6, 1991, p. J2; February 4, 1993, p. A3.
Atlanta Magazine, June, 1992, pp. 46-9, 122-25.
Los Angeles Times, December 16, 1982.
New York Times Book Review, November 28, 1982, p. 27; July 8, 1984, p. 30; December 13, 1987, p. 7.
Publishers Weekly, February 12, 1988, p. 61; August 25, 1989, p. 54; October 11, 1991, p. 48; November 22, 1991, pp. 35-6.
Washington Post, October 4, 1982, p. C8.
Washington Post Book World, August 12, 1984, p. 12; January 13, 1985, p. 4; February 23, 1986, p. 12.

　　　　　　　　　—*Sketch by Nancy Gearhart Godinez*

*　　*　　*

SCHEINDLIN, Raymond P.　1940-

PERSONAL: Born May 13, 1940, in Philadelphia, PA; son of Irving and Betty Scheindlin; children: Dor Baer Scheindlin, Dahlia Scheindlin. *Education:* Gratz College, Teacher's Certificate, 1959; attended Hebrew University of Jerusalem, 1959-60; University of Pennsylvania, B.A. (with honors), 1961; Jewish Theological Seminary of America, M.H.L., 1963, Rabbi, 1965; Columbia University, Ph.D. (with distinction), 1971.

ADDRESSES: Home—420 Riverside Dr., Apt. GC, New York, NY 10025. *Office*—Jewish Theological Seminary of America, 3080 Broadway, New York, NY 10027.

CAREER: McGill University, Montreal, Quebec, assistant professor of Jewish studies, 1969-72; Cornell University, Ithaca, NY, assistant professor of Hebrew language, 1972-74; Jewish Theological Semi-

nary of America, New York City, associate professor, 1974-85, professor of medieval Hebrew literature, 1985—, head of Department of Jewish Literature, 1977-79, 1981-83, 1990-93, provost, 1984-89, leader of Genesis Seminar, 1992—. Rabbi of Kane St. Synagogue, Brooklyn, NY, 1979-82. New York University, visiting associate professor, 1975-76; Columbia University, member of instructional staff, 1979, member of Seminar in Islamic Studies, c. 1980—; Oxford University, senior associate fellow of Centre for Postgraduate Hebrew Studies, 1989—. Heritage Chamber Orchestra, member of advisory committee, 1986-88; Catalan Museum of Jewish Culture, member of board of advisers, 1993—.

MEMBER: World Union of Jewish Studies, American Academy for Jewish Research, Association for Jewish Studies (member of board of directors, 1974-75), National Association of Professors of Hebrew, Society of Judeo-Arabic Studies (member of executive committee, 1991—), Jewish Publication Society of America (member of board of directors, 1987-93).

AWARDS, HONORS: Guggenheim fellow, 1988; travel grant, Comite Conjunto Hispano-Norteamericano para la Cooperacion, Cultural y Educativa, 1991; fellow, Center for Judaic Studies, University of Pennsylvania, 1993.

WRITINGS:

Form and Structure in the Poetry of al-Mu'tamid Ibn 'Abbad, E. J. Brill, 1974.
201 Arabic Verbs, Barron's, 1978.
Miriam and the Angel of Death (opera libretto; story by Y. L. Peretz; music by Lee Goldstein), Jewish Theological Seminary of America, 1984.
Wine, Women, and Death: Medieval Hebrew Poems on the Good Life, Jewish Publication Society, 1986.
The Gazelle: Medieval Hebrew Poetry on God, Israel, and the Soul, Jewish Publication Society, 1991.
The Psalm of the Distant Dove (cantata; music by Hugo Weisgall), Theodore Presser, 1992.
(Translator) Ismar Elbogen, *Jewish Liturgy in Its Historical Development,* Jewish Publication Society, 1993.

Work represented in anthologies, including *Rabbinic Fantasy,* edited by David Stern and Mark Mirsky, Jewish Publication Society, 1990; *The Legacy of Islamic Spain,* edited by Salma Khadra Jayyusi, E. J. Brill, 1992; and *Convivencia: Jews, Muslims, and Christians in Medieval Spain,* Braziller, 1992. Contributor of more than thirty articles, translations, and reviews to scholarly journals. Member of editorial committee, *Prooftexts,*

1981, 1988—; member of editorial advisory board, *Edebiyat,* 1992—.

WORK IN PROGRESS: Editing *The Cambridge History of Arabic Literature: Al-Andalus,* with Maria Rosa Menocal and Michael Sells, publication by Cambridge University Press expected in 1996; a verse translation, *Anthology of Golden Age Hebrew Poetry;* research on the poetry of Solomon Ibn Gabirol in the light of Arabic parallels; a comparative study of Arabic religious poetry and Hebrew liturgical poetry of medieval Spain.

*   *   *

SCHIAVONE, Giuseppe   1938-

PERSONAL: Born August 29, 1938, in Rome, Italy. *Education:* University of Rome, Laurea, 1961, Libera Docenza, 1967.

ADDRESSES: Home—Via Etruria 12, 00183 Rome, Italy. *Office*—Faculty of Political Science, University of Catania, Catania, Italy.

CAREER: General Confederation of Italian Industry, Rome, officer of Department of Economic and Statistical Studies, 1962-73; University of Catania, Catania, Italy, professor of international organization, 1973—. Institute of European Studies, Alcide de Gasperi, president and director of scientific research at School of Postgraduate Studies; Institut Robert Schuman pour l'Europe, president. Italian Ministry of Foreign Affairs, expert; lecturer at public and private institutions; consultant to United Nations Development Program.

WRITINGS:

The Institutions of Comecon, Macmillan, 1981.
(Editor) *East-West Relations: Prospects for the 1980s,* Macmillan, 1982.
(Editor) *Western Europe and South-East Asia: Cooperation or Competition?,* Macmillan, 1989.
International Organizations: A Dictionary and Directory, 3rd edition, Macmillan, 1992.

Work represented in anthologies. Contributor of more than forty articles to academic journals.

SIDELIGHTS: Giuseppe Schiavone told *CA:* "My main area of interest is the analysis of the structure and activities of international (intergovernmental) organizations, with particular focus on multilateral economic cooperation and development policy issues at both the global and the regional levels. Special interests include the institutional framework of pan-European cooperation in the economic and security fields, the relations of the European Union with European economies in transition and with developing countries and their regional organizations, the policies of international financial and trade institutions, and blueprints for reform of the United Nations system. Current research is devoted to the international law of the environment and to the newly-created regional and sub-regional cooperation and integration groupings in Europe, Latin America and the Caribbean, and the Asia-Pacific."

*   *   *

SCHLICKE, Priscilla   1945-

PERSONAL: Born October 10, 1945, in Everett, WA; daughter of Laurence and Adelaide Smith; married Paul Schlicke (an author); children: Edward, Alexander. *Education:* Attended University of Washington, Seattle, University of California, San Diego, and Robert Gordon University.

ADDRESSES: Home—26 B Bradford Rd., Guiseley, Leeds, England.

CAREER: Robert Gordon University, Aberdeen, Scotland, senior lecturer, 1983-94; writer. National Preservation Advisory Committee, member of Education Panel.

MEMBER: Library Association.

WRITINGS:

(With husband, Paul Schlicke) *The Old Curiosity Shop: An Annotated Bibliography,* Garland Publishing, 1988.
(Editor) *Walford's Guide to Reference Material,* Volume I: *Science and Technology,* Library Association Publishing (London), 1993.

WORK IN PROGRESS: A study of biography; research on multimedia and electronic publishing.

SIDELIGHTS: Priscilla Schlicke told *CA:* "My writing reflects my profession: teaching, publishing, and information science in higher education. I wish that my writing reflected my interests: gardens, travel, France, and mid-brow novels about middle-aged, middle-class women. Perhaps someday?"

*   *   *

SCHOENBROD, David   1942-

PERSONAL: Born August 18, 1942, in Chicago, IL;

son of Robert D. and Charlotte (Marschak) Schoenbrod (both advertising executives). *Education:* Yale College, B.A. (magna cum laude), 1963; Oxford University, B.Phil., 1965; Yale Law School, LL.B., 1968.

ADDRESSES: Office—New York Law School, 57 Worth St., New York, NY 10013.

CAREER: Lawyer; admitted to practice in New York State, United States Supreme Court, Court of Appeals for the First, Second, and District of Columbia Circuits, and Federal District Court of the Southern and Eastern Districts of New York. Judge Spottswood Robinson, III, U.S. Court of Appeals, D.C. Circuit, law clerk, 1968-69; Bedford-Stuyvesant Restoration/D&S Corp., director of program development, 1969-71; Association of the Bar of the City of New York, staff attorney, special committee on electric power and the environment, 1971-72; Natural Resources Defense Council, Inc., senior staff attorney, 1972-79; Yale Law School, visiting lecturer, 1977; New York University School of Law, associate professor, 1979-83; New York Law School, associate professor, 1984-85, professor, 1985—.

MEMBER: National Environmental Task Force and Panel of Arbitrators, American Arbitration Association.

WRITINGS:

(With others) *Electricity and the Environment: A Report of the Special Committee on Electric Power and the Environment,* West Publishing, 1972.
(With others) *A New Direction in Transit,* New York City Department of City Planning, 1978.
(With others) *Remedies: Public and Private,* West Publishing, 1990.
Power without Responsibility: How Congress Abuses the People through Delegation, Yale University Press, 1993.

Contributor of articles on energy and natural resources regulation, environmental law, and administrative law to professional journals, including *Minnesota Law Review, American Economic Review,* and *California Law Review.* Contributor of columns to newspapers, including *New York Times* and *Wall Street Journal.*

SCHRAMM, Laurier L. 1954-

PERSONAL: Born October 27, 1954, in Saskatoon, Saskatchewan, Canada; married Ann Marie Schramm (a biologist), 1978; children: Katherine M., Victoria L. *Education:* Carleton University, B.Sc. (with honors), 1976; Dalhousie University, Ph.D., 1980.

ADDRESSES: Office—Petroleum Recovery Institute, 3512 33rd St. NW., Calgary, Alberta, T2L 2A6 Canada.

CAREER: Syncrude Canada Ltd., Edmonton, Alberta, Canada, research chemist, 1980-84, senior research scientist, 1984-88; Petroleum Recovery Institute, Calgary, Alberta, staff research scientist, 1988-90, senior staff research scientist and leader of chemical enhanced oil recovery group, 1990-92, senior staff research scientist and leader of process sweep improvement group, 1992—. University of Calgary, Calgary, adjunct associate professor of chemistry, 1991-94, adjunct professor of chemistry, 1994—. Chemical Institute of Canada, served on Calgary Section Executive, 1989—; Association of the Chemical Profession of Alberta, registrar and director, 1994—.

MEMBER: American Chemical Society, International Association of Colloid and Interface Scientists.

AWARDS, HONORS: Chemical Institute of Canada, fellowship, 1993.

WRITINGS:

(Editor and contributor) *Emulsions: Fundamentals and Applications in the Petroleum Industry,* American Chemical Society (Washington, D.C.), 1992.
The Language of Colloid and Interface Science, American Chemical Society, 1993.
(Editor and contributor) *Foams: Fundamentals and Applications in the Petroleum Industry,* American Chemical Society, 1994.
(Editor) *Suspensions: Fundamentals and Applications in the Petroleum Industry,* American Chemical Society, 1995.

Contributor of articles to professional journals.

WORK IN PROGRESS: Suspensions: Fundamentals and Applications in the Petroleum Industry, a book to be published by the American Chemical Society.

SCHULMAN, Audrey   1963-

PERSONAL: Born May 9, 1963, in Montreal, Quebec, Canada; daughter of Henry Evan (in computer trade and stockbroking) and Ingrid (an artist; maiden name, Style) Schulman. *Education:* Attended Sarah Lawrence College, 1981-83; Barnard College, B.A., 1985. *Religion:* Pantheist.

ADDRESSES: Agent—Richard Parks, 138 East 16th St., New York, NY 10003.

CAREER: Writer. Computer consultant in multi-media, 1986—.

WRITINGS:

The Cage (novel), Algonquin, 1994.

The Cage has been translated into German and Dutch.

WORK IN PROGRESS: Quieting the Child and *In Control.*

SIDELIGHTS: Audrey Schulman is the author of *The Cage,* a novel about Beryl, a young female photographer employed to study polar bears in the Canadian tundra. Beryl is the lone woman among three men who make up the rest of the expedition team. As a critic in *Kirkus Reviews* points out, Beryl was "hired not for her talent or experience, but because she's the only applicant small enough to fit inside the cage." The cage itself represents an enclosure of "helplessness and inferiority from which women are emerging to challenge men," according to Barbara Love in *Library Journal.* With the expedition proving to be arduous, Beryl must contend with both brutal weather conditions and difficult social circumstances in stifling living quarters. When she actually encounters the polar bears, Beryl experiences an intense exhileration; as Schulman writes, "The large female stuck the front of her paw in between the bars. . . . She fanned her long white claws at Beryl, like fingers gesturing her forward. . . . Beryl wanted to kiss each individual claw." In the *Village Voice,* Carol Anshaw noted that after the encounter, *The Cage* resorts to devices commonly found in "wilderness adventure" novels, such as "animals will turn out to be nobler than humans."

Nonetheless, Anshaw praised Schulman's talent, one of "unusual elegance," and stated that "there is something winning in the way she co-opts the power in what is traditionally a male literary genre, parallelling the way her protagonist siphons off power from the bears she's photographing." A reviewer in *Publishers Weekly* was impressed by the depth of Schulman's characters which, combined "with detailed observation of the natural world and crisply described action," results in a "startling and memorable" work.

Schulman told *CA:* "The most striking themes in my novels are of extreme wilderness settings (such as the arctic or steaming Indonesian islands), and of wild animals. I live in the city, in an apartment building with an over-pruned garden. The novel offers me escape. Perhaps if I lived in the Amazon, I'd write about Harlem."

BIOGRAPHICAL/CRITICAL SOURCES:

BOOKS

Schulman, Audrey, *The Cage,* Algonquin, 1994.

PERIODICALS

Kirkus Reviews, February 15, 1994.
New York Times Book Review, April 20, 1994.
Publishers Weekly, February 14, 1994.
Village Voice, October 6, 1994.

*   *   *

SCOFIELD, Sandra (Jean)   1943-

PERSONAL: Born August 5, 1943, in Wichita Falls, TX; daughter of Edith Hambleton; married Allen Scofield (a carpenter; died, 1975); married Bill Ferguson (a teacher), July 10, 1975; children: (first marriage) Jessica. *Education:* University of Texas, B.A., 1964; University of Oregon, M.A., 1978, Ph.D., 1979. *Politics:* "Skeptical Democrat." *Religion:* "Raised Catholic." *Avocational interests:* Reading, visiting museums and galleries.

ADDRESSES: Home and office—P.O. Box 3329, Ashland, OR 97520. *Agent*—Emma Sweeney, 280 Riverside Dr., New York, NY 10025.

CAREER: Taught elementary and high school in Texas, Illinois, California and Oregon for six years; Southern Oregon State College, assitant professor of education, 1979-80, adjunct professor of English, 1991—; writer.

MEMBER: PEN, Authors Guild, Oregon Insitute of Literary Arts, Austin Writers League.

AWARDS, HONORS: Second place, Katherine Anne Porter Fiction Prize, 1985, for the story "Private Rights"; New American Writing Award, 1989, for *Gringa,* and 1992, for *Beyond Deserving;* American

Academy and Institute of Arts and Letters First Fiction Award nomination, 1989, for *Gringa;* creative writing fellowship, National Endowment of the Arts, 1989; National Book Award nomination, 1991, and American Book Award, 1992, for *Beyond Deserving; Beyond Deserving* was named one of the *New York Times Book Review*'s "Notable Books of the Year," 1992; Oregon Book Award nomination, 1994, for *More Than Allies.*

WRITINGS:

NOVELS

Gringa, Permanent Press, 1989.
Beyond Deserving, Permanent Press, 1991.
Walking Dunes, Permanent Press, 1992.
More Than Allies, Permanent Press, 1993.
Opal on Dry Ground, Villard, 1994.

OTHER

Contributor to anthology *Common Bonds,* Southern Methodist University Press, 1990; also contributor of stories to periodicals, including *Redbook, Calyx, Missouri Review,* and *Ploughshares Reader;* contributor of book reviews to periodicals, including the *New York Times Book Review, Dallas Morning News,* and *Washington Post Book World.*

WORK IN PROGRESS: A Chance to See Egypt, about a midwestern widower who travels to a village in Mexico.

SIDELIGHTS: Sandra Scofield first began writing short stories for publication in the 1970s, and in 1985 she took second place in the Katherine Anne Porter Fiction contest for an effort entitled "Private Rights." Her first novel, *Gringa,* published in 1989, garnered her even more critical acclaim. *Gringa* won a New American Fiction Award that year, was nominated for the American Academy and Institute of Arts and Letters First Fiction Award, and brought Scofield to the attention of the National Endowment of the Arts, who awarded her a creative writing fellowship. Since *Gringa,* Scofield has published four other novels, including *Beyond Deserving,* which brought her a 1992 American Book Award.

Scofield is known for her detailed characterizations; as Frances Stead Sellers observed in the *Washington Post Book World,* "Scofield has a keen eye for the details of human interactions and an appealing sympathy for her characters." In a *Publishers Weekly* interview with Doug Marx, Scofield commented: "I think the difficulties and complexities of people are explained by accretion. There are little things that

have added up to this moment when you really have to choose—and looking for that moment is what interests me."

Scofield was born in 1943 in Wichita Falls, Texas. She had a difficult childhood, with a chronically ill mother who died in 1958. She was cared for by nuns in a convent and by her grandmother and aunt. "Which shows there are many ways to be mothered," Scofield told *CA.* Scofield wrote poetry while pursuing a degree in speech and theater at the University of Texas; afterwards, she spent years she described to *CA* as "nomadic and aimless," living in New York City, Mexico, Chicago and Berkeley. Along the way she "accrued education, like pounds," and wrote steadily. Yet she did not begin submitting her work for possible publication until much later. She explained to Marx: "Not taking myself 'seriously' as a writer, I wasn't trying to figure out what anybody was buying. I was trying to figure out what I had to say."

In the meantime, Scofield married Allen Scofield, a carpenter, and gave birth to a daughter, Jessica. Giving birth proved to be a pivotal experience; as she recalled to Marx, she came home from the hospital and began to write a play that she had thought about during labor. "I still had to have a life, a job, and so forth, but I never stopped writing after that. Plays, short novels, short stories poured out of me." Scofield's first husband died in 1975. In that same year, she married Bill Ferguson, an English teacher. She credits Ferguson with the "stability and nurturance" it took for her to commit herself fully to writing.

Eventually, though, Scofield began reading fiction by women authors—such as Margaret Atwood and Toni Morrison—in *Redbook* magazine. She told Marx that she "began to realize that I didn't have to write like Saul Bellow or Norman Mailer, that I could be a writer even though I hadn't been to war or developed an existential stance. Reading women gave me permission to start thinking about writing for myself." She submitted some of her own work to *Redbook,* which promptly accepted it. After this initial success, however, Scofield went through a dry period of ten years before she was inspired to write for publication again. One story, "Trespass," was printed in the *Ploughshares Reader;* it would later become the first section of her second novel, *Beyond Deserving.*

In Scofield's first novel, *Gringa,* she chronicles the life story of Abilene Painter, a Texan woman who was gang raped as a teenager and who eventually becomes the mistress of a Mexican bullfighter. While living with the bullfighter, Tonio, in Mexico City, she becomes involved in the student protests which took place there during the 1968 Summer Olympics, incidents that the author had observed firsthand. Writing in the *New York Times Book Review,* Michele Wolf called *Gringa* "a richly sensory portrait of a world of exile—not only in a foreign land but within one woman's own skin."

Scofield followed *Gringa* with 1991's *Beyond Deserving,* a chronicle of an Oregon family. The main characters are "Fish" Fisher and his estranged wife Katie; Fish has just been released from prison and is trying to regain Katie's love. Despite having taken another lover and despite Fish's past physical abuse, Katie is receptive. The novel also concerns Fish's twin brother Michael—perceived by their parents as the "good" twin—and his wife Ursula, who are discontented despite their seemingly perfect middle-class lifestyle.

As *New York Times Book Review* contributor Rand Richards Cooper explained, "the narrative of *Beyond Deserving* is discursive, taking us unhurriedly forward through the life of the Fisher clan while backtracking frequently to fill us in on their pasts. . . . The pleasures . . . are discoveries of character." The reviewer concluded by calling *Beyond Deserving* an "intelligent and observant novel." A *Los Angeles Times Book Review* critic was also enthusiastic, asserting that Scofield's "patient accumulation of thousands of details about the Fishers reminds us that most family novels, in comparison, are cartoons."

In another of Scofield's novels, *Walking Dunes,* the protagonist is an eighteen-year old boy, David Puckett, who is finishing high school and dealing with the return of his long-absent father. The story is set in the late 1950s, and Scofield describes the period's high school social scene in great detail. Though this aspect of the novel caused Jane Vandenburgh to remark in the *New York Times Book Review* that "the true horror of high schools is their terrible sameness," *Los Angeles Times Book Review* contributor Joanna Kavanagh praised Scofield's "finely tuned ear and eye for all the cadences and nuances" of that particular social setting. "Never missing a beat," Kavanagh continued, "she fetchingly recaptures all the flotsam and jetsam minutiae. It's as though she had just walked out the door 15 minutes ago."

Scofield's most recent novels, 1993's *More Than Allies* and 1994's *Opal on Dry Ground,* each examine the importance of motherhood, and the roles mothers play in families. "I didn't realize how imbued our culture is with negative views of mothering," she told *Houston Chronicle* contributor Melissa Fletcher Stoeltje. "I found there were basically three kinds of mothers—the smothering mother, the mother who abandons, and the perfect mother. From what I could figure out, the only way to be the last mother was to have a perfect child." *Opal on Dry Ground,* in particular, describes the relationship between a mother and her daughters. "I wanted to write a book about an older mother," she told Stoeltje. "In writing *Opal,* I was kind of celebrating that role—the baffled mother who has no idea how she's arrived at the place she is. She's sent her kids off in leaky boats, but she's doing the best she can."

Opal on Dry Ground concerns the two grown daughters of Opal Duffy who move back in with their mother when their own lives begin to fall apart. Though *Boston Globe* reviewer Elizabeth Shostak found the novel coming "close, at times, to seeming trite," in the end "Scofield's comic but compassionate vision saves the book from banality." Abby Frucht, writing in the *New York Times Book Review,* also found the story occasionally problematic. "The people in 'Opal on Dry Ground' are awash in . . . contradictions, but their ambivalence never tries our patience. Not all writers could render sympathetically Opal's and her daughters' conflicted feelings toward men and one another, but Ms. Scofield does so with a style as subtle and understated as family loyalty itself." Frucht heralded *Opal* as "a novel whose plot, like a vast open sky, is enlivened with a fireworks display of colorful, twisting, brilliantly rendered emotions."

BIOGRAPHICAL/CRITICAL SOURCES:

PERIODICALS

Boston Globe, July 5, 1994.
Houston Chronicle, June 1, 1994, 1E.
Los Angeles Times Book Review, December 15, 1991, p. 6; October 18, 1992, p. 9.
New York Times Book Review, April 23, 1989, p. 20; October 13, 1991, p. 14; September 15, 1992, p. 27; July 24, 1994.
Publishers Weekly, November 9, 1992, pp. 63-64.
Washington Post Book World, November 24, 1991, p. 10.

—Sketch by Elizabeth Wenning

SCOTT, Franklin D(aniel)　　1901-1994

OBITUARY NOTICE—See index for *CA* sketch: Born July 4, 1901, in Cambridge, MA; died August 30, 1994, in Claremont, CA. Professor and writer. A professor of history for over three decades, Scott was an authority on modern Swedish political history and Scandinavian immigration to the United States. His books on these subjects include *The United States and Scandinavia, Sweden: The Nation's History,* and *Trans-Atlantica: Essays on Scandinavian Migration and Culture.* In 1966 Scott's research established that the Vinland Map of 1440, which illustrated that Vikings possessed extensive knowledge about the New World, was a reprint of a thirteenth century document. A graduate of the University of Chicago, Scott received a master's degree and a Ph.D. from Harvard University, as well as pursuing graduate studies at the University of Stockholm. He retired as a professor of history from Northwestern University, where he had taught since 1935.

OBITUARIES AND OTHER SOURCES:

BOOKS

Who's Who in America, 47th edition, Marquis, 1992, pp. 3023-24.

PERIODICALS

Chicago Tribune, September 7, 1994, sec. 3, p. 11.

*　　*　　*

SCOTT, Nina M.　　1937-

PERSONAL: Born September 4, 1937, in Hamburg, Germany; daughter of John B. (a spice importer) and Hildegard (a homemaker; maiden name, Kuppermann) Budde; married James E. Scott (an instructor in chemistry), August 26, 1961; children: Catherine, Christopher, Samuel. *Education:* Wellesley College, B.A., 1959; Stanford University, M.A., 1961, Ph.D., 1968. *Politics:* Democrat. *Religion:* Episcopal.

ADDRESSES: Home—Amherst, MA. *Office*—Box 33945, University of Massachusetts at Amherst, Amherst, MA 01003-3945.

CAREER: University of Massachusetts at Amherst, professor of Spanish, 1968—. University of Buenos Aires, senior lecturer, 1987.

MEMBER: International Institute in Spain, Modern Language Association of America, Latin American Studies Association, American Association of Teachers of Spanish and Portuguese, Feministas Unidas, Letras Femeninas, Northeast Modern Language Association, New England Council of Latin American Studies (vice president, 1993-94, president, 1994-95).

AWARDS, HONORS: Fulbright grants for Germany, 1983-84, South America, 1985, and Argentina, 1987; Prize from New England Council of Latin American Studies, 1985, for the article "Sor Juana Ines de la Cruz: 'Let Your Women Keep Silence in the Churches. . .'"

WRITINGS:

(Editor with A. Horno-Delgado, Eliana Ortega, and N. Saporta Sternbach) *Breaking Boundaries: Latina Writing and Critical Readings,* University of Massachusetts Press, 1989.
(Editor with F. J. Cevallos-Candau, Jeffrey A. Cole, and N. Suarez-Arauz) *Coded Encounters: Writing, Gender, and Ethnicity in Colonial Latin America,* University of Massachusetts Press, 1994.

Translator of *Sab; and, Autobiography,* by Gertrudis Gomez de Avellaneda, University of Texas Press. Member of editorial board, *Latin American Research Review,* 1994-97.

WORK IN PROGRESS: A bilingual anthology of early Spanish-American women writers, for University of New Mexico Press.

SIDELIGHTS: Nina M. Scott told *CA:* "My special focus in research and writing is the work of Spanish-American women writers, from very early colonial figures to contemporary Latina writers. My three books reflect this interest. *Breaking Boundaries* was one of the first critical volumes to deal with the wide spectrum of Latina writers in the United States. My belief that the entire book should be accessible to English-speaking readers led me to translate *Sab* and the autobiography of Gertrudis Gomez de Avellaneda. *Sab* is a feminist and antislavery text, originally published in 1841, eleven years before *Uncle Tom's Cabin.* In both works, Avellaneda is attentive to the parallels between bonded slavery and the female condition. *Coded Encounters* deals with cross-disciplinary issues in colonial Latin America, with a large section of women's roles and writings during this era. My latest project, the bilingual anthology, continues my desire to make accessible to English-speaking readers the exciting and little-known texts of early Spanish-American women writers: companions of the conquistadores, nuns, and nineteenth-century feminists."

SEEFELDT, Carol 1935-

PERSONAL: Born May 3, 1935, in St. Louis, MO; daughter of George and Mary Wohanka; married Eugene Seefeldt (a counselor); children: Paul, Andrea. *Education:* University of Wisconsin—Madison, B.A., 1956; University of South Florida, M.A., 1968; Florida State University, Ph.D., 1971.

ADDRESSES: Home—881 Mount Airy, Davidsonville, MD 21035.

CAREER: University of Maryland at College Park, professor, 1971—.

WRITINGS:

Continuing Issues in Early Childhood, Macmillan, 1988.
Young and Old Together, National Association for the Education of Young Children, 1990.
Developmental Continuity, Association for Childhood Education International, 1990.
Social Structures for the Preschool/Primary Child, Macmillan, 1990.
Early Childhood Education, Macmillan, 1993.

Author of nearly a dozen other books. Editor of the book *The Early Childhood Curriculum,* Teachers College Press. Contributor of nearly two hundred articles to education journals.

SIDELIGHTS: Carol Seefeldt told *CA:* "Being able to write has always been important to me. As a part of my undergraduate degree in early childhood education, I selected journalism courses as electives. When I had completed all journalism courses that could be taken by non-majors, I asked the head of the journalism department if I could declare journalism as a major. I was told that, although I was an accomplished writer, it would not be possible to enter the journalism department. I was, after all, a woman, who would need to continue in the field of education in order to be home when my children arrived home from school!

"As a result, I completed my degree in early childhood education, not journalism, and have enjoyed more than thirty-seven years in the field. The ability to write, quickly and in a way that was accessible to the reader, developed while I was taking journalism courses, has served me well as an early childhood educator. Over the years I have published seventeen books, received more than one million dollars in research grants, and published about two hundred research and scholarly publications. As I near retirement, my goal is to publish a 'real' book, one for the general market, instead of a book for educators."

*   *   *

SEIGEL, Catharine F. 1933-

PERSONAL: Born June 7, 1933, in Yonkers, NY; daughter of John and Julia (Flynn) Fressie; married Jules Seigel; children: Julia Anne, Sean, Jessica. *Education:* Marietta College, B.A. (magna cum laude), 1955; Syracuse University, M.A. (European history), 1957; doctoral study at Cornell University; University of Rhode Island, M.A. (English), Ph.D., 1976.

ADDRESSES: Home—1117 Saugatucket Rd., Peace Dale, RI 02879.

CAREER: State University of New York, assistant professor of English, 1957-59; Catholic University of America Press, Washington, DC, assistant editor, 1959-60; Catholic University of America, Washington, DC, instructor in English, 1960-65; University of Rhode Island, Kingston, lecturer, 1966-75; Rhode Island School of Design, Providence, professor of English, 1975—, department head, 1983-90.

MEMBER: Modern Language Association of America, Association of Departments of English, Northeast Modern Language Association, Phi Beta Kappa.

AWARDS, HONORS: Grant from National Endowment for the Humanities, 1986; humanities scholar, Rhode Island Council on the Humanities, 1987; John R. Frazier Teaching Award, 1988.

WRITINGS:

The Fictive World of Conrad Aiken: A Celebration of Consciousness, Northern Illinois University Press (DeKalb, IL), 1992.

Contributor to books, including *Conrad Aiken: A Priest of Consciousness,* edited by Ted Spivey and Arthur Waterman, AMS Press, 1990. Contributor to periodicals, including *Malcolm Lowry Review, Journal of School Health, Literature and Psychology, Journal of Popular Culture,* and *Modern Language Review.*

*   *   *

SELVON, Sam
See SELVON, Samuel (Dickson)

SELVON, Samuel (Dickson)   1923-1994
(Sam Selvon)

OBITUARY NOTICE—See index for *CA* sketch: Born May 20, 1923, in Trinidad, West Indies; died April 16, 1994, in Trinidad, West Indies. Novelist and short story writer. A West Indian writer, Selvon captured the spirit of a changing culture in his short stories and novels, exploring the ramifications of British colonial influence on Trinidad as well as the racial tensions existing between black Africans and Indians living in the West Indies. Judged by critics to be impassioned, charming, and sometimes ribald, Selvon's works are noted for their vibrant local color, faithfulness to the Trinidadian dialect, and conversational tone. After emigrating from Trinidad to England in 1950, Selvon published his first novel, *A Brighter Sun,* which garnered considerable acclaim in both England and the United States. He broke new ground with his 1962 novel *I Hear Thunder,* which centers on the educated native bourgeoisie living in the West Indies. Selvon's later novels, including *The Plains of Caroni* and *Moses Ascending,* were praised for their beautifully evocative scenes and authentic language.

OBITUARIES AND OTHER SOURCES:

BOOKS

Contemporary Novelists, 5th edition, St. Martin's, 1991.
Reference Guide to English Literature, St. James Press, 1991.
Who's Who, 146th edition, St. Martin's, 1994, p. 1713.

PERIODICALS

Times (London), May 14, 1994, p. 21.

*   *   *

SENIE, Harriet F.   1943-

PERSONAL: Born September 23, 1943, in New York, NY; daughter of Ernest and Gerda (Goetz) Freitag; married Stephen R. Senie, 1965 (divorced, 1973); children: Laura. *Education:* Brandeis University, B.A., 1964; Hunter College, M.A., 1971; Institute of Fine Arts, Ph.D., 1981. *Politics:* Liberal. *Avocational interests:* Travel.

ADDRESSES: Home and office—215 Sackett St., Brooklyn, NY 11231-3604.

CAREER: Moore College of Art, instructor, 1974-

75; Hunter College, New York City, adjunct professor, 1974-78; Adelphi University, Garden City, NY, instructor, 1976-79; *New York Post,* New York City, art critic, 1978-79; State University of New York, Amelie A. Wallace Gallery, Old Westbury, NY, gallery director and assistant professor, 1979-82; Princeton University, Art Museum, associate director, 1982-86; *Artnews,* art critic, 1986-87; City College of New York, New York City, director of museum studies program, professor, 1986—. Consultant for Lever Brothers, Equitable, and the City of New York, 1965-69 and 1972-73; Department of Higher Education, Channel 13, art consultant, 1979-85.

MEMBER: College Art Association, American Studies Association, American Association of Museums, Art Table, Council of State University of New York Gallery and Exhibition Directors (vice president, 1979-82).

AWARDS, HONORS: Kress Foundation research grant, 1978-79; Princeton University Spears Fund research grant, 1983; President's Grant for Innovative Teaching, City College of New York, 1986; National Education Association Museum Studies grant, 1987; PSC City University of New York research grant, 1988, 1991; Eisner Scholars Award, City College of New York, 1989; Rifkind Scholars Award, City College of New York, 1993.

WRITINGS:

Contemporary Public Sculpture: Tradition, Transformation, and Controversy, Oxford University Press (New York), 1992.
(Editor with Sally Webster, and contributor) *Critical Issues in Public Art: Content, Context, and Controversy,* HarperCollins (New York), 1992.
Dangerous Precedent: Richard Serra's "Tilted Arc" in Context, University of California Press (Berkeley), in press.

Contributor of introduction to *Projects and Proposals: The New York City Percent for Art Program,* New York City Department of Cultural Affairs, 1988; contributor to *The Memorial Redefined,* edited by Linda Cunningham, College Art Association, 1989; *Encyclopedia of New York City,* Yale University Press, 1995. Curator of art exhibits and author of catalogs, including *William King: Sculpture in Vinyl, Wood, and Aluminum* and *Fabric into Art,* Wallace Gallery, SUNY, 1980; and *Sculptures for Public Places: Maquettes, Models, and Proposals,* Marisa del Re Gallery, New York, 1986; contributor of articles and reviews to periodicals, including *Art Journal, Artnews, Orte, Arts, New York Post, Art*

Bulletin, and *Villager.*

WORK IN PROGRESS: Modern Art in America: New Perspectives, with Sally Webster.

BIOGRAPHICAL/CRITICAL SOURCES:

PERIODICALS

Journal of American History, December, 1993, p. 1154.
Philadelphia City Paper, September 24-October 1, 1993, p. 26.
Public Art Review, winter/spring, 1993, p. 25.
Sculpture, September-October, 1993, p. 50.

*   *   *

SERET, Roberta 1945-

PERSONAL: Born July 7, 1945, in New York, NY; daughter of Sam and Shirley Seret; married Michael Bayer (a doctor), June 30, 1968; children: Gregory Bayer, Clifford Bayer. *Education:* Queens College of the City University of New York, B.A., 1968; New York University, M.A., 1970, Ph.D., 1974. *Avocational interests:* Gardening and writing fiction.

ADDRESSES: Home: New York, NY, and Connecticut. *Office*—American Welcome Services, New York, NY 10128.

CAREER: Ladycliff College, Highland Falls, NY, instructor in French, 1970-71; Briarcliff College, Pleasantville, NY, instructor in English, 1972-73; Bergen Community College, Paramus, NJ, adjunct instructor in English, 1975-76; Marymount Manhattan College, New York City, adjunct instructor in English, 1976-78, affiliated with department of continuing education, 1977-78; Hunter College of the City University of New York, New York City, adjunct instructor of English, 1976-79; Pace University, White Plains, NY, adjunct associate professor in English, 1979-83; American Welcome Services (a relocation consulting firm specializing in international and intercultural corporate transfers), New York City, founder and president, 1982—; New York City Chamber of Commerce, director of relocation, 1986-90; Marymount Manhattan College, New York City, affiliated with department of courses for adults, 1990. Member of board of directors, New York University Alumni Association, 1982, Auxiliary of the New York Medical Society, 1984-86 (president-elect, 1985-86), Doctors' Hospital Gifts Committee, 1985-86, and American-Italian Cancer Research Foundation, 1986-88.

MEMBER: British-American Chamber of Commerce, Swiss Society, Rotary International Club of New York.

AWARDS, HONORS: Carnegie-Mellon teaching fellowship, Hunter College, 1977-78.

WRITINGS:

Welcome to New York, self-published, 1983, second edition, Harper (New York City), 1985, third edition, self-published, 1989, fourth edition, self-published, 1993.
Voyage into Creativity: The Modern Kunstlerroman, Peter Lang (New York City), 1992.

Contributor to periodicals, including *Changing Homes* and *Mobility.*

SIDELIGHTS: Roberta Seret was born and raised in New York City. Earning a master's degree in French and a doctorate in comparative literature, she taught at the college level for a number of years. Her career then took a business turn in 1982 when she began providing relocation services to corporations and individuals moving into the New York City region. Over the next decade, Seret began writing journal articles focused on intercultural business issues and the personal concerns of individuals living in New York City for the first time. This work culminated in the publication of four editions of *Welcome to New York,* in which she offers newcomers practical advice, short cuts, and secrets—the kind of information usually acquired only after years of living in New York City. Seret is also the author of *Voyage into Creativity: The Modern Kunstlerroman,* a study of the novels of D. H. Lawrence, James Joyce, Hermann Hesse, and Theodore Dreiser. The volume reflects her academic background and lifelong interest in literature.

Seret told *CA:* "In 1982 I started a relocation consulting firm, American Welcome Services, to assist newcomers to the United States and New York. Over the years I have given workshops, seminars, and orientation sessions throughout the United States and in Paris, Geneva, London, and Tokyo, focusing on cross-cultural affairs, American culture, and comparative international business practices.

"I believe that if newcomers can understand the mentality and customs of Americans as well as the mechanism of their new city, their acclimation will be easier."

SERVER, Lee

PERSONAL: Born in Springfield, MA; son of Robert and Elizabeth (Hill) Server. *Education:* Attended New York University Film School.

ADDRESSES: Home—Brooklyn, NY. *Agent*—Roslyn Targ, 105 West Thirteenth St., New York, NY 10011.

CAREER: Writer.

WRITINGS:

Screenwriter: Words Become Pictures, Main Street Press, 1987.
Sharks, P. R. Books, 1989.
Tigers, Portland House, 1991.
Danger Is My Business: An Illustrated History of the Fabulous Pulp Magazines, Chronicle Books, 1993.
Over My Dead Body: The Sensational Age of the American Paperback: 1945-1955, Chronicle Books, 1994.
Sam Fuller: Film Is a Battleground, McFarland, 1994.

Contributor of "The Story of the Big Love" in *The Fine Art of Murder,* Carroll & Graf, 1993; author of "Interview with John Bright" in *El Enemigo Publico* (a Spanish translation of the screenplay to *Public Enemy*), Viridiana; contributor to periodicals, including *Film Comment, Films in Review,* and *Mystery Scene.*

WORK IN PROGRESS: Crete, a travel book, for Sun Tree Publishing; *The Fast One,* a screenplay for Licht-Mueller Productions; the introduction to *Hard-Boiled,* for Chronicle Books.

SIDELIGHTS: Lee Server is a versatile writer whose subjects include literary history, film criticism, travel, and animals. He is the author of *Screenwriter: Words Become Pictures,* which features interviews with twelve Hollywood screenwriters from the 1930s to the 1950s, the animal books *Sharks* and *Tigers,* and *Sam Fuller: Film Is a Battleground,* a critical study of the director of the motion pictures *Shock Corridor, The Naked Kiss,* and *The Big Red One.* Among Server's most widely reviewed publications are *Over My Dead Body: The Sensational Age of the American Paperback: 1945-1955* and *Danger Is My Business: An Illustrated History of the Fabulous Pulp Magazines,* a chronicle of the rise and decline of the pulp, a type of periodical popular during the early- to mid-twentieth century and

named after the rough paper it was printed on. Precursor to paperback novels as well as comic books, the pulp was a popular medium for stories in many genres (including romance, adventure, horror, and science fiction) and Server presents nearly one hundred full-color pictures of the often bizarre and gruesome covers. In *Newsday,* April Bernard found *Danger Is My Business* "exceptionally well-designed," with "lurid cover illustrations reproduced in their full glory, along with priceless samples of the storytelling art."

"Top [pulp] writers could pound out two million to three million words a year, coming up with titles like 'The Priestess of Shame' and 'When the Death Bat Flies,'" according to Kenneth Turan in the *Los Angeles Times Book Review.* Although many of these short stories and novellas were formulaic and forgettable, authors such as Tennessee Williams and Ray Bradbury published their first work in pulp magazines. The supernatural fiction of H. P. Lovecraft—who is considered by contemporary critics to be foremost among twentieth-century gothic horror writers—frequently appeared in the pulp *Weird Tales* and is excerpted along with representative passages from other genres in *Danger Is My Business.* Appraising the volume, *New York Times Book Review* contributor Daniel Harris concluded that the world of pulps—"with temptresses slipping stilettos from their garter belts" and "nefarious aviators dodging the tracers of ace pilots"—had been "a world frozen in midscream, and Mr. Server is to be congratulated for preserving these gloriously kitschy tableaux."

In the years following World War II, the market for "pop fiction" turned toward paperback books. The boom in inexpensive paperbacks, initially aimed at returning servicemen, is covered by Server in *Over My Dead Body.* Besides providing a history of the postwar paperback phenomenon, Server presents nearly one hundred full-color reproductions of paperback covers, many of which are characterized by lurid sex and violence and are "delightfully disgusting," in the words of Rebecca Ascher-Walsh in *Entertainment Weekly.*

Server informs in *Over My Dead Body* that paperbacks "catered to the former soldiers' supposed preference for sexy, violent stories, plainly written and not too long. The grim sordid tone of so many postwar paperbacks could also be ascribed to the veterans' tastes—readers who had been trained to kill were understandably inclined to have a darker than average viewpoint." Crime novelist Mickey Spillane—who, according to Server, penned "blood-

and-sex-drenched mysteries of an unprecedented ferocity"—was the most popular and influential paperback writer during this era. Novels by two noted Beat authors, Williams S. Burroughs and Jack Kerouac, were published as paperback originals in the 1950s. Science-fiction visionary Philip K. Dick saw his first works published as paperbacks.

Critics who reviewed *Over My Dead Body* appreciated Server's efforts to preserve the sensational era of early paperback fiction. "Server is best when describing the early subgenres which, then as now, blossomed from the seed of a single bestseller," stated a reviewer in *Publishers Weekly,* using as an example the "hillbilly fiction" that resulted from the popular novel by Erskine Caldwell set in the rural South, *God's Little Acre.* "If you remember when paperbacks cost only twenty-five cents and were known as pocket books because they really fit inside a pocket," commented Robert Armstrong in the Minneapolis *Star Tribune,* "Lee Server's illustrated history of the medium is sure to bring a smile and a nod of recognition."

Server told *CA:* "After attending New York University, I spent a number of years traveling in Europe, Asia, and elsewhere, with lengthy residences in Thailand, India, and Greece. I lived a beachcomber existence on a modest income from writing travel articles and dozens of 'erotic' novels for low-end paperback houses. I eventually returned to the United States. Years of hack writing followed, during which I turned out reams of anything that would sell, from record reviews to recipes.

"Beginning with *Screenwriter: Words Become Pictures,* I began to concentrate on more personal projects, reflecting my longtime interest in film and literature and various aspects of pop culture. Although the books involve much historical research—a great deal of it first-hand—I consider each one a creative project, the material shaped and the illustrations chosen for intended dramatic effects. It would be fair to say that the choice of subjects shows a certain predilection for art on the fringes of the culture. One review of *Danger Is My Business* called it 'wrong-side-of-the-tracks Americana' and I would go along with that."

BIOGRAPHICAL/CRITICAL SOURCES:

BOOKS

Server, Lee, *Over My Dead Body: The Sensational Age of the Paperback: 1945-1955,* Chronicle Books, 1994.

PERIODICALS

Cedar Rapids Gazette, May 9, 1993.
Chicago Tribune Books, March 7, 1993, p. 8.
Entertainment Weekly, March 19, 1993, p. 57; June 3, 1994, p. 52.
Los Angeles Times Book Review, June 13, 1993.
New York Times Book Review, July 25, 1993, p. 16.
Newsday, April 4, 1993, p. 36.
Publishers Weekly, April 11, 1994, p. 61.
Star Tribune (Minneapolis), May 29, 1994.

*   *   *

SETTANNI, Harry   1945-

PERSONAL: Born March 8, 1945, in Chicago, IL; son of Eugene (a violinist) and Grace (an insurance broker; maiden name, Gengenbach) Settanni. *Education:* St. Joseph's University, B.S., 1967; Villanova University, M.A., 1972; St. John's University, Ph.D., 1976. *Avocational interests:* Reading and astronomy.

ADDRESSES: Office—Humanities Department, Holy Family College, 9701 Frankford Ave., Philadelphia, PA 19114; St. Joseph's University, 54th and City Line Aves., Philadelphia, PA.

CAREER: St. Joseph's University, Philadelphia, PA, instructor, 1976-78; St. John's University, Jamaica, NY, assistant professor, 1978-82; Holy Family College, Philadelphia, PA, instructor, 1987—; St. Joseph's University, instructor, 1990—.

MEMBER: American Philosophical Association, Greater Philadelphia Philosophical Association.

WRITINGS:

Holism, A Philosophy for Today: Anticipating the Twenty-First Century, Peter Lang (New York), 1990.
The Probabilist Theism of John Stuart Mill, Peter Lang, 1991.
What Is Man?, Peter Lang, 1991.
Five Philosophers: How Their Lives Influenced Their Thought, University Press of America (Lanham, MD), 1992.
The Philosophical Foundations of Paranormal Phenomena, University Press of America, 1992.
Scientific Knowledge: Discovery of Nature or Mental Construction?, University Press of America, 1992.
What Is Freedom of Choice?, University Press of America, 1992.
What Is Morality?, University Press of America, 1992.

Logic Workbook, Saint Joseph's University Press (Philadelphia), 1993.

Controversial Issues in Philosophy, University Press of America, 1994.

Five Primers in the Social Sciences and Assorted Writings, University Press of America, 1995.

SIDELIGHTS: Harry Settanni told *CA:* "My first book, *Holism, A Philosophy for Today: Anticipating the Twenty-First Century,* is the key to many of my later writings, even though the later writings can easily be read independently of *Holism.* In this first work, I describe a view of the world which combines science, religion, art, and politics into one unified whole. I describe reality as an interconnected, interdependent, organic whole.

"Today, it may be extremely useful to view the world in this manner even if this explanation of the world is not ultimately true. For even as a mental construction of reality, a holistic view of the world may provide motivation to solve such problems as the environment and the threat of global warfare. The environment is an interconnected, interdependent system and so is the globe itself. Man must begin to see himself as an integral part of this whole rather than as separate and isolated from it. In other words, he must now see himself as a steward of the earth and its resources rather than the way he has often conceived of himself in the past, as lord and ruler of the earth who is somehow separate and isolated from it because of his special dignity. The book points out that there is also dignity in the role of steward, a dignity we must believe in if we are to have a future. The holistic world-view, I claim, can solve problems in the future by viewing man as an integral part of the world and the environment much better than the view of man as an isolated individual in the past ever could. As an isolated individual, man over-specializes in everything and so cannot see problems as organically interconnected and interdependent.

"Several of my lifelong interests came together in my first book, *Holism.* Around this time, after several years of teaching, I began to think that science, art, religion, and politics were essentially one field, not four separate fields, despite being more often than not and at various times in history, in open conflict with one another. Reality could be viewed as interconnected and interdependent—and so were all four fields of reality. Is it not the central role of myths and symbols to make man a part of the social and physical world—to make him a part of the interconnected, interdependent whole?

"There were and are many studies, cited in *Holism,* which essentially claim that each of the four fields relates to an interconnected, interdependent organic whole. In art, we must relate the work of art to the artist and his times. They are interconnected and interdependent, organically. The artwork would be radically different without knowing the artist and his times. In science, one must approach the environment as interconnected and interdependent; the electron is interconnected with its surrounding field, radically so. In politics (interpreted very broadly so as to include the social sciences), man should be connected with and interdependent upon a real community and should do however much or however little he or she can to extend this community to the globe as a whole. In religion, one should attempt to interconnect and interrelate God and the individual and human society and nature as much as possible.

"My second book, *What Is Man?,* poses four perennial questions about human nature and then shows how all four questions are interrelated. An affirmative answer to these questions places one squarely within the context of a holistic (the word means *whole* in Greek) view of man; a negative answer to all four places one squarely within the realm of a non-holistic view of man; essentially an isolated view of man as totally separate from nature and society, conquering both as a 'rugged individualist.' But has man really conquered both nature and human society? Has not the possibility of war and the present condition of the environment proven this earlier picture of man erroneous? Why not try the holistic picture or mental construction of man as a part of his surrounding society and subject to the laws of that global society?

"Is not man subject to a global, natural law like that of the Stoics? This author believes he is, and I attempt to elaborate that vision of man as subject to an objective, universal morality at least in the broad outlines of his behavior in *What Is Morality?.* Science also must be conceived of holistically and take into account the personal and social background of the scientist in formulating theories. I elaborate this point of view in *Scientific Knowledge: Discovery of Nature or Mental Construction?.*

"To adopt a holistic view of the world is not to adopt a closed world view or mental construction in which one may seem to some to know everything and in which no future discoveries are possible. In the space exploration of the future, man may well attempt to find increasingly broader interconnections, both physical and social (with other life forms?!) and this process may never end. The process certainly will not finish with the earth itself—so no one can accuse *Holism* of being a stagnant philosophy which has all the answers or even all the important answers. But it does have a sound method. I employed this sound method in a somewhat humorous science fiction novelette, *Concentric Circles,* which extends the method into the future.

"I have now written over ten books and most of them are at least loosely related to the philosophy of holism. I have touched on many different areas and fields within this philosophy, and there is still much to be learned. Some of my life-long interests, along with several outstanding professors I knew, stimulated this work, in which I have attempted to unify as much as I had learned of different fields of inquiry. And this approach, rather than mere specialization, in which the experts can't talk to one another, may be more relevant to an organically interdependent and interconnected world with the twin threats of environmental holocaust and nuclear war than any other approach at the present time (and into the near future).

"As for myself, I hope to keep on learning and writing and teaching."

*   *   *

SHANE, Scott   1954-

PERSONAL: Born May 22, 1954, in Augusta, GA; son of Presson S. (a chemical engineer and professor) and Emily (a naturalist and homemaker; maiden name, Baker) Shane; married Frances P. Weeks (a teacher of English as a foreign language), September 18, 1976; children: Martha, Laura, Nathan. *Education:* Williams College, B.A., 1976; attended Leningrad State University, 1976; Oxford University, B.A., 1978. *Avocational interests:* Hiking, woodworking, Russia and the Russian language.

ADDRESSES: Home—705 Kingston Rd., Baltimore, MD 21212. *Office*—*Baltimore Sun,* 501 North Calvert St., Baltimore, MD 21278.

CAREER: Washington Star, Washington, DC, clerk and reporter, 1979-80; *Greensboro News and Record,* Greensboro, NC, reporter, 1980-83; *Baltimore Sun,* Baltimore, MD, reporter, 1983—, Moscow correspondent, 1988-91, project reporter, 1992—. Johns Hopkins University, teacher, 1991.

AWARDS, HONORS: Regional and national journalism awards.

WRITINGS:

Dismantling Utopia: How Information Ended the Soviet Union, Ivan R. Dee (Chicago, IL), 1994.

WORK IN PROGRESS: Research on U.S. urban problems, such as poverty, drugs, and crime, on the rise of suburbs and decline of cities, and on U.S. intelligence agencies.

SIDELIGHTS: Scott Shane told *CA:* "Having studied Russian literature and language at college and at Leningrad State University, I was fortunate enough to be posted to Moscow by the *Baltimore Sun* in 1988. I filed about a thousand stories from ten Soviet republics and watched the decline and fall of the old regime. When I returned to the United States with my family in late 1991, I took a few months to teach and to draft a book exploring the impact of information on the collapse of Communist rule. I argue in *Dismantling Utopia* that the information revolution in the rest of the world forced the Soviet leadership to begin tinkering with reform, and that the subsequent easing of controls on the media proved fatal to the system and to the empire. Since finishing the book, I have been reporting on the decline of the American city, which I hope eventually to explore in my next book."

*   *   *

SHAPIRO, Barry M.   1944-

PERSONAL: Born November 30, 1944, in New York, NY; son of Gustav (a payroll supervisor) and Helen (a municipal secretary; maiden name, Futenman) Shapiro. *Education:* State University of New York at Binghamton, B.A., 1965; University of Chicago, M.A., 1968; University of California, Los Angeles, Ph.D., 1988.

ADDRESSES: Office—Box 154, Allegheny College, Meadville, PA 16335.

CAREER: Allegheny College, Meadville, PA, associate professor of history, 1988—.

WRITINGS:

Revolutionary Justice in Paris, 1789-1790, Cambridge University Press (New York, NY), 1993.

Contributor to *French Historical Studies* and *Psychohistory Review.*

WORK IN PROGRESS: Guizot and the Politics of Centrism, completion expected in 1996.

SHARKEY, Joe 1946-

PERSONAL: Born October 15, 1946, in Philadelphia, PA; son of Joseph C. (an engineer) and Marcella (Welch) Sharkey; married Lynne White (a nurse), 1970 (marriage ended); married Nancy Albaugh (an editor), 1984; children: Lisa, Caroline, Christopher. *Education:* Attended Pennsylvania State University.

ADDRESSES: Home—Glen Ridge, NJ.

CAREER: Philadelphia Inquirer, Philadelphia, PA, columnist, 1970-76; *Philadelphia Bulletin,* Philadelphia, assistant city editor, 1976-81; *Albany Times-Union,* Albany, NY, executive city editor, 1981-84; *Wall Street Journal,* New York City, assistant national editor, 1984-89; freelance writer, 1989—.

WRITINGS:

Death Sentence, Signet, 1990.
Deadly Greed, Simon & Schuster (New York, NY), 1991.
Above Suspicion, Simon & Schuster, 1993.
Bedlam, St. Martin's, 1994.
Gina, Simon & Schuster, 1995.
Eagle Scout: Ross Perot and the New American Myth, St. Martin's, in press.

*   *   *

SHATNER, William 1931-

PERSONAL: Born March 22, 1931, in Montreal, Quebec, Canada; son of Joseph and Anne Shatner; married Gloria Rand, August 12, 1956 (divorced, 1969), married Marcy Lafferty (an actor), October 20, 1973; children: (second marriage) three daughters. *Education:* McGill University, B.A., 1952. *Avocational interests:* Breeding American saddle horses.

ADDRESSES: Agent—c/o Larry Thompson Organization, 345 North Maple Dr., Suite 183, Beverly Hills, CA 90210.

CAREER: Film, stage, and television actor. Made stage acting debut in 1952; performed at Montreal Playhouse, summers, 1952-52, Canadian Repertory Theatre, Ottawa, 1952-54, and Stratford Shakespeare Festival, Stratford, Ontario, 1954-56; appeared on Broadway in plays, including *Tamburlaine the Great,* 1956, *The World of Suzie Wong,* 1958, and *A Shot in the Dark,* 1961. Appeared in films, including *The Brothers Karamazov,* 1958, *Judgment at Nuremburg,* 1961, *Dead of Night,* 1974, *The Devil's Rain,* 1975, *Star Trek: The Motion Picture,* 1979,

Star Trek II: The Wrath of Khan, 1982, *Star Trek III: The Search for Spock,* 1984, *Star Trek IV: The Voyage Home,* 1986, *Star Trek V: The Final Frontier,* 1989, *Bill and Ted's Bogus Journey,* 1991, *Star Trek VI: The Undiscovered Country,* 1991, and *Star Trek: Generations,* 1994. Appeared in television series, including *Star Trek,* 1966-69, animated *Star Trek* series, 1973-75, *Barbary Coast,* 1975-76, *T.J. Hooker,* 1982-87, and *Rescue 911,* 1993—. Appeared in television movies, including *Go Ask Alice,* 1972, *Crash,* 1978, and *Secrets of a Married Man,* 1984. Actor, director, and executive producer of *Tekwar* television movies and series based on his novels, USA network, 1994—. Recording artist, albums include *The Transformed Man.*

MEMBER: Actors Equity Association, American Federation of Television and Radio Artists, Screen Actors Guild, Directors Guild.

AWARDS, HONORS: Tyrone Guthrie Award, 1956; Theatre World Award, 1958, for performance in *The World of Suzie Wong.*

WRITINGS:

"TEK" SERIES OF SCIENCE FICTION NOVELS

TekWar, Putnam (New York), 1989.
TekLab, Putnam, 1991.
TekLords, Putnam, 1991.
Tek Secret, Putnam, 1993.
Tek Vengeance, Putnam, 1993.
Tek Power, Putnam, 1994.

NONFICTION

(With Lisabeth Shatner) *Captain's Log: William Shatner's Personal Account of the Making of Star Trek V: The Final Frontier,* Pocket Books (New York), 1989.
(With Michael Tobias) *Believe,* Berkley Publishing (New York), 1992.
(With Chris Kreski) *Star Trek Memories* (autobiography), HarperCollins (New York), 1993.
(With Kreski) *Star Trek Movie Memories* (autobiography), HarperCollins, 1994.

ADAPTATIONS: Shatner's successful "Tek" novel series has been adapted to a television series titled *Tekwar* on the USA network, 1994—.

SIDELIGHTS: William Shatner is an actor who has worked prolifically over four decades in films, television, and on stage. It is for his portrayal of Captain James T. Kirk on the short-lived television series *Star Trek,* however, that he is best known. Shatner's appearances as Kirk in the series, which ran from 1966 to 1969, and the subsequent films elevated him to the role of pop culture hero to millions of viewers. In addition to his acting, Shatner is also the author of the popular "Tek" series of science fiction novels and a number of nonfiction books, including two memoirs dealing with his *Star Trek* experiences.

Nineteen ninety-three's *Star Trek Memories* was cowritten with Chris Kreski (an editor at MTV and a scriptwriter for the animated series *Beavis and Butthead*) and includes interviews with members of the original cast. The book offers a behind-the-scenes portrait of the original series. Shatner tells of *Star Trek* creator Gene Roddenberry's dispute with certain producers who urged him to eliminate from the script the characters of Mr. Spock, the pointy-eared Vulcan portrayed by actor Leonard Nimoy, and Uhura, played by African American actress Nichelle Nichols. Both characters proved to be cornerstones of the show's popularity. Shatner recalls racial tension on the set and interviews Nichols at length; the actress credits civil rights activist Martin Luther King, Jr., with inspiring her to remain in the cast despite the producers' pressure on her to quit. Learning from Nichols that others in the cast of *Star Trek* often resented him, Shatner also spoke with actors Walter Koenig and George Takei, who remember their indignation at Shatner's attempts to change the scripts by cutting their lines. A reviewer in *Publishers Weekly* described *Star Trek Memories* as "a candid, captivating reminiscence, packed with stellar anecdotes and backstage lore." Rosemary L. Bray, writing in the *New York Times Book Review,* reported that she found "wonderful bits of gossip and a record of happy accidents that led to some of the show's signature moments." In *People,* Michael A. Lipton termed the book a "breezy, entertaining memoir."

Although *Star Trek* aired as a television series for only three seasons, the show produced a legion of devoted fans who refer to themselves as "Trekkers" or "Trekkies." With the advent of his own science fiction creation, the "Tek" series of novels, Shatner has developed another loyal following, the "Tekkies." Despite mixed reviews, such as *Entertainment Weekly*'s Benjamin Svetkey's assessment that Shatner "probably won't win any Pulitzers," the "Tek" series has sold nearly a million copies. Set in the 22nd century, the novels pit Jake Cardigan, former cop turned private investigator, against various killer robots, diabolic computers, and other futuristic evils in the fight to control Tek, an addictive, mind-controlling substance.

The first novel of the series, *TekWar,* received a positive critique by *Locus* reviewer Carolyn Cushman, who considered the novel "an entertaining romp thanks to the author's understanding of plot elements and timing." While London *Times* critic Tom Hutchinson did not believe *TekWar* broke any new ground in the hybrid genre of hard-boiled detective/science fiction, he stated that the story was told "quite entertainingly." By the publication of the fifth "Tek" novel, *Tek Secret,* Shatner's writing style is noticeably "more sober, serious, and realistic," according to Roland Green in *Booklist.* The critic added that the series "is certainly moving in the right direction."

Shatner told *Entertainment Weekly*'s Svetkey that the "Tek" novels came about during a lull in the filming of *Star Trek V: The Final Frontier,* when the actor developed his ideas about Jake Cardigan and his war on Tek. "I'd doodle with a paragraph," he told Svetkey, "and it would grow into two pages. . . . Eventually the book sort of evolved by itself." Apparently surprised by his success as a novelist, Shatner revealed that he had conceived the "Tek" series "as the sort of books you could read on airplanes and throw away afterwards. . . . But they've become this *phenomenon.*" Also an avid horse breeder and rider, Shatner commented on the creative process, saying it would "be as difficult for me to give up ideas as it would to give up horses. That's why publishing a novel is so wondrous to me. That *I* could have a book in print."

In 1994 Shatner added the volume *Star Trek Movie Memories* to his nonfiction writings, which also includes 1989's *Captain's Log: William Shatner's Personal Account of the Making of Star Trek V: The Final Frontier.* A companion piece to *Star Trek Memories,* the 1994 book recounts Shatner's experiences working on the seven feature films that were inspired by the original series (Shatner's final appearance was in *Star Trek Generations,* which was released just prior to his book). The actor/author, again collaborating with Kreski, relates the ego and power struggles that were common during filming. As with his first *Star Trek* book, Shatner utilizes interviews with his fellow cast and crew to flesh out the details. In addition to the personal dynamics of the films, the book also contains trivia tidbits about the films themselves (one passage reveals that *Star Trek IV: The Voyage Home* was originally intended as a vehicle for comedian Eddie Murphy). Despite viewing Shatner's discussion of his "efforts to hog the spotlight" as being "frighteningly nonchalant," *Entertainment Weekly* contributor Albert Kim found *Star Trek Movie Memories* to be an "entertaining, well-drawn, and fairly balanced look" at some of the ingredients that have made the *Star Trek* films so phenomenally popular.

BIOGRAPHICAL/CRITICAL SOURCES:

BOOKS

Shatner, William, and Chris Kreski, *Star Trek Memories,* HarperCollins (New York), 1993.
Shatner and Kreski, *Star Trek Movie Memories,* HarperCollins, 1994.

PERIODICALS

Booklist, June 15, 1992, p. 1811; September 1, 1993, p. 6.
Entertainment Weekly, January 15, 1993, pp. 30-33; October 8, 1993, pp. 46-47; November 25, 1994, pp. 64-65.
Library Journal, April 15, 1991, p. 129.
Locus, August, 1989, p. 55.
New York Times Book Review, December 26, 1993, p. 15.
People, November 27, 1989, p. 40; November 1, 1993, p. 27; February 18, 1994, p. 40.
Publishers Weekly, November 8, 1991, pp. 53-54; October 12, 1992, p. 62; October 19, 1992, p. 62; September 13, 1993, pp. 108-109; October 17, 1994, p. 67.
Times (London), March 17, 1990.
USA Today, November 9, 1993, sec. D, p. 3.*

* * *

SHAW, Christine 1952-

PERSONAL: Born June 24, 1952. *Education:* Lady Margaret Hall, Oxford, II-class honours degree, 1974, D.Phil., 1983.

ADDRESSES: Home—Ely, England. *Office*—European Humanities Research Centre, University of Warwick, Coventry CV4 7AL, England. *Agent*—John McLaughlin, Campbell, Thomson & McLaughlin Ltd., 1 King's Mews, London WC1N 2JA, England.

CAREER: European University Institute, Florence, Italy, *chercheur,* 1976-77; University of London, England, deputy editor at London School of Economics and Political Science, 1980-85, tutor at Westfield College, 1983-89, co-chairperson of Seminar on Italian History since c. 1550, Institute of Historical Research, 1988—, research officer in Business History Unit, London School of Economics and Political Science, 1989-91. University of Warwick, visiting fellow at European Humanities Research Centre, 1991, senior research fellow, 1991—.

MEMBER: Royal Historical Society (fellow).

AWARDS, HONORS: British Council scholar in Rome, 1975-76.

WRITINGS:

(Deputy editor) *Dictionary of Business Biography,* five volumes, Butterworth & Co. (London), 1983-86.
Julius II: The Warrior Pope, Basil Blackwell (London), 1993.

Work represented in anthologies, including *Florence and Italy: Renaissance Studies in Honour of Nicolai Rubinstein,* edited by Peter Denley and Caroline Elam, Westfield, 1988; *Business History: Concepts and Measurement,* edited by Charles Harvey, Frank Cass, 1989; and *Business in the Age of War and Aggression,* edited by Richard Davenport-Hines, Frank Cass, 1990. Contributor of articles and reviews to business and history journals.

WORK IN PROGRESS: British Businessmen As a European Species (tentative title), comparing the backgrounds and career patterns of British business people of the nineteenth and twentieth centuries with those of French, German, and Italian business people; a book on Italian political exiles in the fifteenth century; research for a biography of Rodrigo Borgia, who became Pope Alexander VI.

SIDELIGHTS: Christine Shaw told *CA:* "I believe strongly that history is too important a subject to be left to shrink into a merely academic discipline, and that it should certainly not be allowed to become a victim of intellectual fashions. The general reader with an interest in history should not be left with a choice between concoctions from secondary sources and forbiddingly abstruse academic history. I aim to write thoroughly researched books that can be of geniune interest to the non-specialist, as well as to students, teachers, and professional historians.

"My original research interest as a doctoral student was Italian Renaissance political history, and I have always continued to work in that field. My fascination for it has never flagged. Research in Italian archives has been one of my greatest pleasures since I first set foot in one during my second year as a graduate student.

"My interest in business history began when I was asked by Professor Charles Wilson (author of the classic company history of Unilever) to be his research assistant for a history of the British newspaper, magazine, and book distributors W. H. Smith and Son. Since joining the editorial team of the *Dictionary of Business Biography* in 1980, I have specialized, within business history, in the study of nineteenth- and twentieth-century business people. Currently, I am concentrating on Italian Renaissance history, but I intend to work on business history again in the future."

* * *

SHEEHAN, Helen E(lizabeth) 1944-

PERSONAL: Born May 16, 1944, in New Jersey; daughter of Thomas J. and Alice (Holland) Sheehan. *Education:* Syracuse University, B.A. (cum laude), 1966; University of Pennsylvania, M.A., 1975, Ph.D., 1983. *Religion:* Roman Catholic.

ADDRESSES: Home—Jersey City, NJ. *Office*—Department of Sociology and Anthropology, St. John's University, 8000 Utopia Parkway, Jamaica, NY 11439.

CAREER: U.S. Peace Corps, Washington, D.C., volunteer in Hyderabad, India, 1966-68; Department of Social Services of the City of New York, Brooklyn, NY, social caseworker, 1968-69; American Red Cross, Newark, NJ, social caseworker, 1970-71; St. Mary Hospital, Hoboken, NJ, medical social worker, 1971-73; Chestnut Hill College, Philadelphia, PA, instructor in sociology, 1980; University of Pennsylvania, Philadelphia, instructor in sociology, 1980-81; St. Joseph's University, Philadelphia, lecturer in sociology, 1981-82; Villanova University, Villanova, PA, lecturer in sociology, 1983; University of Pennsylvania, lecturer in sociology and research assistant at Philadelphia Geriatric Center, 1983-84; Thomas Jefferson University, Philadelphia, lecturer in general studies in health sciences, 1984; State University of New York College at Purchase, visiting assistant professor of sociology, 1984-86; American Cancer Society, New York City, director of professional education programs in medical affairs, 1986-88; Department of Veterans Affairs, Medical Center, East Orange, NJ, program coordinator of Cancer Center, 1988-90, research sociologist, 1990-91; University of Medicine and Dentistry of New Jersey, New Jersey Medical School, Newark, adjunct assistant professor and research coordinator of environmental health and occupational medicine, 1991-92; St. John's University, Jamaica, NY, assistant professor of sociology and anthropology, 1992—. College of St. Elizabeth, adjunct assistant professor, 1991-92; Ramapo College, adjunct assistant professor, 1992; University of Medicine and Dentistry of New Jer-

sey, adjunct associate professor, 1992—.

MEMBER: International Association for the Study of Traditional Asian Medicine, American Sociological Association, American Anthropological Association, Society for Medical Anthropology, Society for Cultural Anthropology, Association for Asian Studies, Independent Scholars of South Asia, National Forum of Women Health Care Leaders, National Association of Returned Peace Corps Volunteers, Mid-Atlantic Association for Asian Studies, Medical History Society of New Jersey, New Jersey Association of Returned Peace Corps Veterans, Theta Chi Beta.

AWARDS, HONORS: Fellow of Berkeley Urdu Language Program in Pakistan, 1976; Superior Performance Award, Department of Veterans Affairs, 1990; grants from New Jersey Historical Commission, 1991, 1992.

WRITINGS:

(Editor with Richard P. Wedeen, and contributor) *Toxic Circles: Environmental Hazards from the Workplace into the Community,* Rutgers University Press, 1993.

Contributor of articles and reviews to professional journals.

WORK IN PROGRESS: Revising a dissertation on traditional medicine in India, including materials on alternative medicine in the United States; a demographic analysis of the New Jersey Home for Disabled Soldiers, 1866-1976, an analysis of original patient records of the first home for soldiers disabled in the Civil War.

SIDELIGHTS: Helen E. Sheehan told *CA:* "My experience as an American Peace Corps volunteer in a health and nutrition program in India established my interests in sociology, anthropology, and health. I pursued advanced degrees in South Asian studies and sociology, prompted by these earlier experiences. My research and teaching are in the areas of health and medicine, with special interests in the impact on people's lives as evidenced in the book *Toxic Circles* and my dissertation research on the continued use of India's traditional medical systems in modern India."

* * *

SHELDON, John
See Bloch, Robert (Albert)

SHEPHERD, Donna Walsh
  See WALSH SHEPHERD, Donna

* * *

SHERWOOD, Frances 1940-

PERSONAL: Born June 4, 1940, in Washington, DC; daughter of William (a lawyer, biochemist, and linguist) and Barbara Sherwood; married twice; first marriage lasted two years; second marriage lasted twenty-five years; children: (second marriage) Lark and Leander (twin sons), Ceres Madoo (daughter). *Education:* Attended Howard University, c. 1960; Brooklyn College, B.A., 1967; graduate study at New York University, 1968; Johns Hopkins University, M.A., 1975. *Politics:* Liberal. *Religion:* None. *Avocational interests:* Flute playing, folk and country western dancing, baking, gardening, travel.

ADDRESSES: Home—424 Manitou Place, South Bend, IN 46616. *Office*—Northside Hall, Room 420, Indiana University, South Bend, P.O. Box 7111, South Bend, IN 46634.

CAREER: Indiana University, South Bend, creative writing and journalism instructor, 1986-94, full professor, 1994—; writer.

MEMBER: PEN.

AWARDS, HONORS: Teaching fellow at Johns Hopkins Writing Seminars, 1973-74; Stegner fellow in fiction, Stanford University, 1976; visiting fellow at Yaddo, 1986; O. Henry Awards, 1989, for the short story "History," and 1992, for the short story "Demiurges"; National Endowment for the Arts fellowship, 1990.

WRITINGS:

Everything You've Heard Is True (short stories), Johns Hopkins University Press (Baltimore, MD), 1989.
Vindication (novel), Farrar, Straus (New York), 1993.
Green (novel), Farrar, Straus, 1995.

Contributor of short stories to anthologies; contributor of short stories to periodicals, including the *Greensboro Review, Sonora Review, Playgirl, Seattle Review, Kansas Quarterly, California Quarterly, Sequoia,* and *Cream City Review.*

WORK IN PROGRESS: A third novel, *Firebird.*

SIDELIGHTS: Frances Sherwood garnered critical acclaim for her first novel, *Vindication,* a fictionalized biography of the eighteenth-century feminist writer Mary Wollstonecraft; at the same time, she became the center of a literary controversy. *Vindication* closely follows the historical details of Wollstonecraft's life, although at certain points Sherwood creates situations and a psychology for the character which prompted objections from some reviewers. Ironically, the very inventiveness Sherwood displays in *Vindication*—a novel which caused Margaret Forster to "worry" in the *New York Time Book Review* that readers will mistake the fiction for biographical truth—was also perceived as a compositional strength. Forster admitted, "If I had known nothing about Mary Wollstonecraft I would have loved this novel."

The Wollstonecraft of *Vindication* is first portrayed as an abused child. Her vicious father regularly beats his wife and children, while the family's nurse sexually molests young Mary. Tragedy occurs frequently throughout Wollstonecraft's relatively short life: she is cheated out of her inheritance by her indifferent brother, her most meaningful relationship (with childhood friend Fanny Blood) ends abruptly in death, her romantic entanglements (with painter Henry Fuseli and adventurer Gilbert Imlay) result in her own obsessive behavior and psychological breakdown. When Fuseli breaks off their affair to remain with his wife, Wollstonecraft goes mad and is committed to the London asylum for the insane known as Bedlam; this ironic fictional event is particularly offensive to critics who view Wollstonecraft as an early pioneer for women's independence. "There are instances where Ms. Sherwood is not simply filling in gaps but inventing events that never happened and that are alien to the spirit of Wollstonecraft," stated Forster in the *New York Times Book Review.* On the other hand, Richard Eder noted in the *Los Angeles Times Book Review* that "Sherwood's accomplishment is to give her Mary, with whom she takes various historical liberties, a voice and a mind that dart erratically as if released from a dark room into the light. . . . Her growing notion of what women should be comes in dizzying flashes, like stars from a blow to the head."

As Wollstonecraft matures, she fails at several different attempts to live independently of a husband—including a stint as a governess in Ireland, a position from which she is dismissed for refusing to beat the children—and ends up sick and desperate on the doorstep of her publisher, Joseph Johnson, who takes her in, employs her on his journal, and encourages her writing talent. Through his efforts

Wollstonecraft publishes her best-known work, *A Vindication of the Rights of Women,* a manifesto demanding equal rights for women. In Johnson's house she also meets such important nineteenth-century luminaries as Thomas Paine, William Blake, and William Godwin (she will eventually marry Godwin, by whom she will give birth to Mary, the future wife of poet Percy Bysshe Shelley and author of the gothic novel *Frankenstein*). While Wollstonecraft flourishes as a writer, she is witness to certain defining details of the era. "The excesses of the French Revolution are acutely observed through Wollstonecraft's eyes," noted a reviewer for *Publishers Weekly,* who commended Sherwood's "meticulously rendered background detail."

The research that Sherwood gathered on the life of Wollstonecraft persuaded her that she should write a novel, rather than the straight biography she had initially conceived. "I was fascinated by the history of underwear, plumbing, food," the author told Gayle Feldman in *Publishers Weekly.* In researching various aspects of the late eighteenth century, Sherwood uncovered elements that, while not directly related to the historical Wollstonecraft, enhance the spirit of her fictional counterpart. "In the novel, Mary's first love is gay, but in reality she didn't fall in love with him. But that gives me the opportunity to talk about discrimination against gays. The book is full of fabrications, but I also hope it is authentic," Sherwood commented in *Publishers Weekly.* In *Newsweek,* Laura Shapiro observed that "Sherwood doesn't try to outdo the facts; she plunges into them, discovering (or creating—it hardly matters) a horribly mistreated child, a tormented woman, an angry feminist, a passionate writer."

Numerous critics applauded *Vindication.* The book, stated Shapiro in *Newsweek,* "is startling, depressing, enlightening and unforgettable, and that doesn't begin to do it justice. . . . This astonishing first novel exerts a grip on the imagination that can't be shaken off." Eder commented in the *Los Angeles Times Book Review* that "*Vindication* makes the feminist as real as the woman; something that Camille Paglia also aims at, in a way, except that Paglia is a polemicist, not an artist. Sherwood, the artist, yokes two battling souls in a personage as bright and unstable as the blue light and red shift of a quasar." In response to the controversy surrounding Sherwood's fictionalization of Wollstonecraft's life, Catherine Texier remarked in *Harper's Bazaar* that "after reading *Vindication,* I plunged into a couple of Wollstonecraft biographies, trying to find out what Sherwood had made up. Less than I ex-

pected, it turns out. . . . Sherwood's major twist is her characters' eroticism. Mary's infatuations are turned into full-fledged sexual liaisons, and her love affair with Imlay becomes a kinky fantasy of S&M games and cross-dressing." Texier concluded that the novel "reads like a fast-paced, literary bodice-ripper." Such was the intention of Sherwood, who told interviewer Jennifer Brostrom in *Contemporary Literary Criticism,* "I wanted to create an authentic sense of what life was like during this time, and I also wanted to write a really juicy book that people would want to read—a real page-turner."

BIOGRAPHICAL/CRITICAL SOURCES:

BOOKS

Sherwood, Frances, *Vindication,* Farrar, Straus, 1993.
Contemporary Literary Criticism, Volume 81, Gale, 1994.

PERIODICALS

Harper's Bazaar, May, 1993, pp. 70, 72.
Los Angeles Times Book Review, May 9, 1993, pp. 3, 9.
New Statesman and Society, June 4, 1993, p. 40.
New York Times Book Review, July 11, 1993, p. 21.
Newsweek, June 7, 1993, p. 64.
Publishers Weekly, October 12, 1992, p. 20; March 1, 1993, p. 36.
Times Literary Supplement, May 21, 1993, p. 23.
Voice Literary Supplement, June, 1993, pp. 14-15.
Washington Post Book World, June 27, 1993, p. 9.

—*Sketch by Scot Peacock*

*   *   *

SHIELDS, Nancy E. 1928-

PERSONAL: Born April 17, 1928, in Wheeling, WV; daughter of George Harrison and Nelle (Oates) Abrams; married Thomas C. Shields, Jr. (divorced, 1971); children: Erin Shields Everett, Thomas C. III. *Education:* Marymount College, B.A. (cum laude), 1971; Long Island University, M.S. (library science), 1972; Western Connecticut State University, M.S. (education), 1977; State University of New York at Albany, Certificate of Advanced Study in Information Science, 1986. *Religion:* Episcopalian. *Avocational interests:* Reading, travel, needlework, decorating, politics.

ADDRESSES: Home—La Jolla, CA.

CAREER: Library media specialist in New York, 1971-93.

MEMBER: American Association of University Women, New York State United Teachers, Delta Kappa Gamma (legislative chairperson of Alpha Omicron chapter), Beta Phi Mu.

AWARDS, HONORS: Named Teacher of the Year by Western Connecticut Superintendents Association and Union Carbide Corp., 1986.

WRITINGS:

(With Mary E. Uhle) *Where Credit Is Due: A Guide to Proper Citing of Sources—Print and Nonprint,* Scarecrow, 1985, revised edition, 1995.
Index to Literary Criticism for Young Adults, Scarecrow, 1988.
Dictionary of Occupational Terms: A Guide to the Special Language and Jargon of Hundreds of Careers, JIST Works, 1994.

WORK IN PROGRESS: Research for two books.

SIDELIGHTS: Nancy E. Shields told *CA:* "The Latin proverb about necessity being the mother of invention was the genesis for my writing career. As a library media specialist, I encouraged high school students to use filmstrips, videos, and other types of non-print materials for their research. When footnote and bibliography time came, however, the standard style manuals provided little help. My plain-English, on-their-level booklet proved so helpful that I started the search for a publisher, and *Where Credit Is Due: A Guide to Proper Citing of Sources—Print and Nonprint* resulted.

"For a librarian (to use the old and not politically correct term) there are few thrills that surpass seeing your name on the cover of a book. Recalling the Latin proverb again, I prepared an index to more than four-thousand authors who were listed in reference sources such as Gale's multi-volume *Contemporary Literary Criticism.* The index included their works of literary criticism for different time periods, as well as reference sources for other prominent publishers. Thanks to the computer, complete information could be provided, instead of the usually alphabetic gobbledegook that forces the user to flip back and forth throughout the book, trying to find the information. As one reviewer noted, however, the title *Index to Literary Criticism for Young Adults* was a poor choice; the book is useful to all ages.

"After a few years I forgot that I had sworn I was through with writing and would never again spend hours researching or sitting at a computer, instead of enjoying life and my children. That old Latin proverb would not be denied, since students were now coming to me with vocabulary assignments that dealt with occupations. Many of the words, especially newer words and recent laws affecting jobs, were not included in the usual sources and, although there were specialized dictionaries on almost everything imaginable, there was no specialized dictionary for terms dealing with occupations. The result was *Dictionary of Occupational Terms: A Guide to the Special Language and Jargon of Hundreds of Careers,* which includes, for the first time, information on military and civilian occupations in the same volume; nonsexist terms; new words such as roadie, fast tracker, and glass ceiling; laws such as OSHA and COBRA; and the specialized terms used in the federal civil service.

"In addition to a revision of *Where Credit Is Due,* I have been gathering research material for two new books. Maybe my nonwriting vow is really dead. My recent move to laid-back southern California may, however, have an opposite effect."

*   *   *

SICKER, Martin   1931-

PERSONAL: Born November 27, 1931, in New York, NY; son of Hyman (a cantor) and Lillian (a homemaker; maiden name, Handelman) Sicker; married Ahouva Fixman (a teacher), September 15, 1959; children: Yoav, H. Adam. *Education:* Received B.A. (magna cum laude) from C. W. Post College of Long Island University, and M.A. and Ph.D. from New School for Social Research. *Religion:* Jewish.

ADDRESSES: Home—2224 Richland St., Silver Spring, MD 20910.

CAREER: Senior executive of the U.S. government, 1957-82; American Association of Retired Persons, director of work force programs, 1990—.

WRITINGS:

The Making of a Pariah State, Praeger, 1987.
The Judaic State, Praeger, 1988.
The Strategy of Soviet Imperialism, Praeger, 1988.
The Bear and the Lion, Praeger, 1988.
Between Hashemites and Zionists, Holmes & Meier, 1989.
Israel's Quest for Security, Praeger, 1989.
The Genesis of the State, Praeger, 1991.
Judaism, Nationalism, and the Land of Israel, Westview (Boulder, CO), 1992.
What Judaism Says about Politics, J. Aronson, 1994.

SIKES, Melvin P.   1917-

PERSONAL: Born December 24, 1917, in Sikesville, MO. *Education:* Illinois Institute of Technology, Diploma in Metallurgy; University of Chicago, Ph.D., 1950, postdoctoral study, 1950; further postdoctoral study at University of Texas at Austin, 1959.

ADDRESSES: Home—8703 West Point Dr., Austin, TX 78759.

CAREER: Veterans Counseling Service, Tuskegee Institute, AL, director, 1945-47; Wilberforce University, Wilberforce, OH, dean of College of Liberal Arts and Sciences, 1950-52; Bishop College, Marshall, TX, administrative dean, 1952-55; Veterans Administration Hospital, Houston, TX, trainee in clinical and counseling psychology, 1959; Baylor University of Medicine, Houston, TX, clinical assistant professor of psychiatry, 1961-68; University of Texas at Austin, professor of educational psychology, 1969-83, program director of Research and Development for Teacher Education, 1978-81; author. Wiley College, visiting professor; National Drug Education Center, Norman, OK, faculty member; Lutheran School of Theology at Chicago, member of board of directors. Veterans Administration Hospital, Houston, clinical and counseling psychologist, 1960-68; U.S. Department of Justice, community relations specialist, 1968-69. Texas State Plan for the Prevention, Treatment, and Control of Alcohol Abuse and Alcoholism, regional chairperson; Living Bank of Houston, member of board of directors; consultant to International Harvester and Central Intelligence Agency. Summer work as shearman, steel inspector, and labor relations committee representative, Carnegie-Illinois Steel Corp. *Military service:* U.S. Army Air Forces, bombardier and navigator, 1941-43, member of Tuskegee Airmen, 1943-45; became second lieutenant.

MEMBER: American Psychological Association, National Council on Alcoholism (affiliate board member), Society of Afro-American Policemen, Texas Peace Officers Association (associate member), Houston Psychological Association (past member of executive committee).

AWARDS, HONORS: Community Service Award, Dallas Council on Alcoholism, 1967; Meritorious Service Award, Veterans Administration, 1968; Honorary Badge, Fort Worth Police Department, 1968; Zeta Phi Beta Community Service Award, 1972; Danforth associate, 1974; grants from Hogg Foundation for Mental Health, 1972, 1977-79, 1980, U.S. Department of Health, Education, and Welfare, 1973, and National Institute of Education, 1978-79, 1979-82.

WRITINGS:

(With P. Meacham) *Directory of Black Professionals in Predominantly White Institutions of Higher Education,* Hogg Foundation for Mental Health, 1972.
World of the Alcoholic (tape recordings), Behavioral Sciences Library of New York, 1974.
The Administration of Injustice, Harper, 1975.
(With Joe Feagin) *Living with Racism: The Black Middle-Class Experience,* Beacon Press, 1994.

Contributor to books, including *Discipline and Learning: An Inquiry into Student-Teacher Relationships,* National Education Association, 1975. Contributor to professional journals.

BIOGRAPHICAL/CRITICAL SOURCES:

PERIODICALS

Ebony, October, 1968.
Time, April 16, 1968, p. 57.

*   *   *

SIRE, H. J. A.   1949-

PERSONAL: Born October 22, 1949, in Barcelona, Spain; son of Alfred William and Isabel (Monegal-Deas) Sire. *Education:* Exeter College, Oxford, M.A., 1972. *Politics:* "Jacobite." *Religion:* Roman Catholic.

ADDRESSES: Office—c/o Travellers Club, 106 Pall Mall, London SW1Y 5EP, England. *Agent*—Curtis Brown and John Farquharson, 162-168 Regent St., London W1R 5TB, England.

CAREER: Schoolmaster, 1973-85; head of an English language school in Barcelona, Spain, 1986-87; representative of Aston University in Barcelona, 1988-93.

MEMBER: Society of Authors, Travellers Club.

WRITINGS:

Gentlemen Philosophers (history), Churchman Publishing, 1988.
The Knights of Malta (history), Yale University Press, 1994.

WORK IN PROGRESS: A biography of Father Martin D'Arcy of the Society of Jesus.

SIZER, Mona Young 1934-
(Deana James)

PERSONAL: Born October 22, 1934, in Booneville, AR; daughter of Fred Ransom (an accountant) and Hona Helene (a telephone operator; maiden name, Bevens) Young; married James Henry Sizer (a certified public accountant), January 27, 1962; children: Rachel Andrea. *Education:* Texas State College for Women (now Texas Woman's University), B.A. and M.A., 1955; attended Southern Methodist University, University of Texas at Dallas, Brookhaven College, and Central State University (Edmond, OK). *Politics:* Independent. *Religion:* Methodist.

ADDRESSES: Home and office—13229 Meandering Way, Dallas, TX 75240. *Agent*—Maria Carvainis, Maria Carvainis Agency, Inc., 235 West End Ave., New York, NY 10023.

CAREER: Novelist. Worked for thirty-five years as a high school English teacher; Brookhaven College, creative writing teacher.

MEMBER: Romance Writers of America, Western Writers of America, Greater Dallas Writers Association.

AWARDS, HONORS: Awards from *Romantic Times* include best Victorian novel award, 1988, for *Crimson Obsession,* and Reviewers' Choice Award, 1991, for *Speak Only Love;* Lifetime Achievement Award for New Age Fiction, 1989, for *Angel's Caress.*

WRITINGS:

ROMANCE NOVELS, UNDER PSEUDONYM DEANA JAMES

Lovestone, Zebra Books, 1983.
Lovespell, Zebra Books, 1984.
Lovefire, Zebra Books, 1985.
Texas Storm, Zebra Books, 1986.
Texas Tempest, Zebra Books, 1986.
Texas Star, Zebra Books, 1987.
Crimson Obsession, Zebra Books, 1988.
Hot December, Bantam, 1988.
Captive Angel, Zebra Books, 1988.
Angel's Caress, Zebra Books, 1989.
Masque of Sapphire, Zebra Books, 1990.
Texas Heart, Zebra Books, 1990.
Speak Only Love, Zebra Books, 1991.
Acts of Passion, Zebra Books, 1992.
Acts of Love, Zebra Books, 1992.
Seek Only Passion, Zebra Books, 1993.
Beloved Rogue, Zebra Books, 1994.

WORK IN PROGRESS: Rhinestone, a novel set in Hollywood in 1913; *The Countess and the Copper,* a Victorian romantic suspense novel.

SIDELIGHTS: Mona Young Sizer told *CA:* "I took my Bachelor of Arts and Master of Arts from Texas Woman's University in 1955. Over the past forty years, I have taken advanced and non-credit studies from time to time at Southern Methodist University, the University of Texas at Dallas, Brookhaven College, and Central State University in Edmond, Oklahoma. In 1979, when a colleague suggested that I take a Ph.D., I decided to write novels instead. Within two years I had sold my first one.

"Books and the love of books have been my life. I believe that fiction should be for pleasure and enlightenment. Therefore, I give short shrift to critics who condemn a popular novel or worse, a popular novelist, because his readers enjoy his works. As for those who condemn the love scenes in romance as pornographic, I note that the same people frequently laud scenes of squalor, sadism, and random violence as being evocative of the true human condition. My response is, 'Not my condition.'

"Likewise, a critic may condemn the author's characterization as shallow when the character finds love and engages in sexual acts to express her love. In the next review, the same critic will extol another author's characterization of a serial killer who degrades and murders other human beings. In response to this, I mock the critics who believe that romance writers must live their scenes. I ask, 'How do other authors know what serial killers are like?'"

*   *   *

SKORUPSKI, John 1946-

PERSONAL: Born September 19, 1946; married; children: two daughters. *Education:* Cambridge University, D.Phil., 1973. *Avocational interests:* The arts, skiing, hill walking.

ADDRESSES: Office—Department of Moral Philosophy, University of St. Andrews, St. Andrews KY16 9AL, Scotland.

CAREER: Worked as teacher in Nigeria and Belgium; worked as teacher at University of Glasgow, Glasgow, Scotland; University of Sheffield, Sheffield, England, professor of philosophy, 1984-90; University of St. Andrews, St. Andrews, Scotland, professor of moral philosophy, 1990—.

MEMBER: Aristotelian Society (president, 1990-91),

Royal Society of Edinburgh (fellow).

WRITINGS:

John Stuart Mill, Routledge, 1989.
English-Language Philosophy, 1750-1945, Oxford University Press, 1993.

Also author of *Symbol and Theory,* 1976.

* * *

SKOWRONEK, Stephen   1951-

PERSONAL: Born March 8, 1951, in Somerville, NJ; married; children: two. *Education:* Oberlin College, A.B. (with highest honors), 1973; Cornell University, M.A. (with distinction), 1976, Ph.D., 1979.

ADDRESSES: Home—168 Rimmon Rd., Woodbridge, CT 06525. *Office*—Department of Political Science, Yale University, New Haven, CT 06520.

CAREER: Cornell University, Ithaca, NY, instructor in American government, 1977; University of California, Los Angeles, assistant professor, 1978-82, associate professor of American government, 1982-85; Yale University, New Haven, CT, professor of American government and American studies, 1986—, director of undergraduate studies in political science, 1989-94. Brookings Institution, guest scholar, 1986 and 1987; University of Notre Dame, Exxon Education Foundation Lecturer, 1986; Reed College, Ducey Lecturer, 1990; guest lecturer at colleges and universities, including Columbia University and University of Maryland at College Park, 1987, Harvard University, 1988, and University of Oregon, 1990. Yale University Press, founder and managing editor of *Studies in American Political Development: An Annual,* 1986—.

MEMBER: American Political Science Association (president of Politics and History Section, 1994-95), Social Science History Association, American Historical Association, Society for History in the Federal Government, Phi Beta Kappa, Phi Kappa Phi.

AWARDS, HONORS: Fellow of Woodrow Wilson International Center for Scholars, 1985-86; Richard E. Neustadt Prize, best book on the presidency, and J. David Greenstone Prize, best book in politics and history, both American Political Science Association, 1994, for *The Politics Presidents Make.*

WRITINGS:

Building a New American State: The Expansion of National Administrative Capacities, 1877-1920, Cambridge University Press, 1982.
The Politics Presidents Make: Leadership from John Adams to George Bush, Harvard University Press (Cambridge, MA), 1993.

Contributor to books, including *The Presidency and the Political System,* edited by Michael Nelson, Congressional Quarterly, 1984, 4th edition, 1994; *Studies in American Political Development: An Annual,* Volume I, Yale University Press, 1986; and *The Dynamics of American Politics,* edited by Larry Dodd and Calvin Jillson, Westview, 1993. Contributor of articles and reviews to political science journals. Member of editorial board, *Presidential Studies Quarterly,* 1986—, *Polity,* 1987-93, and *Yale Journal of Law and the Humanities,* 1987.

* * *

SLAVIN, Robert E(dward)   1950-

PERSONAL: Born September 17, 1950, in Bethesda, MD; son of Joseph G. (a psychologist) and Miriam (a homemaker; maiden name, Crohn) Slavin; married Nancy A. Madden (an educational researcher), July 22, 1973; children: Jacob, Benjamin, Rebecca. *Education:* Reed College, B.A., 1972; Johns Hopkins University, Ph.D., 1975.

ADDRESSES: Home—Baltimore, MD. *Office*—Center for Research on Effective Schooling for Disadvantaged Students, Johns Hopkins University, 3505 North Charles St., Baltimore, MD 21218.

CAREER: Johns Hopkins University, Baltimore, MD, director of elementary program at Center for Research on Effective Schooling for Disadvantaged Students, 1975—.

MEMBER: International Association for the Study of Cooperation in Education (president, 1987-90), American Educational Research Association.

AWARDS, HONORS: American Educational Research Association, Raymond Cattell Early Career Award, 1985, Palmer O. Johnson Award, 1988.

WRITINGS:

Using Student Team Learning, Team Learning Project, Johns Hopkins University (Baltimore, MD), 1978, 3rd edition, 1986.
(With D. L. DeVries, G. M. Fennessey, and others) *Teams-Games-Tournament: The Team Learning Approach,* Educational Technology Publications, 1980.

Cooperative Learning in Student Teams: What Research Says to the Teacher, National Education Association, 1982, revised edition, 1987.

Student Team Learning: An Overview and Practical Guide, National Education Association, 1983, 2nd edition, 1988.

Cooperative Learning, Longman, 1983.

Research Methods in Education: A Practical Guide, Prentice-Hall, 1984, 2nd edition, 1992.

(Editor with S. Sharan, S. Kagan, C. Webb, and others) *Learning to Cooperate, Cooperating to Learn,* Plenum, 1985.

(With wife, Nancy A. Madden, and M. B. Leavey) *Team-Accelerated Instruction: Mathematics,* Charlesbridge, 1986.

Educational Psychology: Theory into Practice, Prentice-Hall, 1986, 4th edition, 1994.

(Editor) *School and Classroom Organization,* Lawrence Erlbaum, 1989.

(Editor with N. L. Karweit and Madden) *Effective Programs for Students at Risk,* Allyn & Bacon, 1989.

Cooperative Learning: Theory, Research, and Practice, Prentice-Hall, 1990.

(With Madden, Karweit, and others) *Success for All: A Relentless Approach to Prevention and Early Intervention in Elementary Schools,* Educational Research Service, 1992.

(Editor with Karweit, B. A. Wasik, and Madden) *Preventing Early School Failure: Research, Policy, and Practice,* Allyn & Bacon, 1994.

WORK IN PROGRESS: Research on comprehensive reform of elementary schools, especially those serving students at risk of school failure.

*   *   *

SLEE, Debora A.   1949-

PERSONAL: Born July 12, 1949, in Grand Rapids, MI; daughter of Vergil N. (a doctor and writer) and Beth E. (an artist; maiden name, Stoke) Slee; married H. Joachim Schmidt (a computer consultant and lawyer), June 14, 1980; children: Peter J. Schmidt. *Education:* University of Michigan, B.A., 1971; William Mitchell College of Law, J.D. (cum laude), 1979.

ADDRESSES: Home—2074 Highland Parkway, St. Paul, MN 55116. *Office*—P.O. Box 8181, St. Paul, MN 55108.

CAREER: Admitted to the Bar of the State of Michigan, 1979, New Hampshire, 1988, and Minnesota, 1990. Schmidt & Slee, Ann Arbor, MI, attorney, 1979-84; Mid-America Research Institute, Ann Ar-

bor, senior staff attorney, 1984-85; Tringa Press, Chelmsford, MA, managing editor, 1985-87; Health NorthEast, Inc., Manchester, NH, director of quality management, 1987-90; The Tringa Group (a consulting firm), St. Paul, MN, partner, 1985—. American Institute for Paralegal Studies, Ann Arbor, instructor, 1982-84; Downtown Development Authority, Ann Arbor, member, 1983-85; Washtenaw County Bar Association, MI, vice president of Young Lawyers Section, 1984-85; Oratorio Society of Minnesota, St. Paul, operations manager and singer, 1991—.

MEMBER: Minnesota State Bar Association Health Law Section and Arts and Entertainment Law Section, Minnesota Society of Hospital Attorneys.

WRITINGS:

(With father, Vergil N. Slee) *Health Care Terms,* Tringa Press (St. Paul, MN), 2nd edition, 1991.

(With V. N. Slee) *Health Care Reform Terms: An Explanatory Glossary of Words, Phrases, and Acronyms Used in Today's U.S. "Health Care Reform" Movement,* Tringa Press, 1993, 2nd edition, 1994.

Contributor to *The Law of Hospital and Health Care Administration,* by A. F. Southwick, Health Administration Press, 1988; and *Selected Criminal Defenses,* Minnesota County Attorneys Council, 1978.

WORK IN PROGRESS: A third edition of *Health Care Terms,* for Tringa Press, publication expected in 1995.

SIDELIGHTS: With her father, Vergil N. Slee, a medical doctor, attorney Debora A. Slee has compiled *Health Care Reform Terms: An Explanatory Glossary of Words, Phrases, and Acronyms Used in Today's U.S. "Health Care Reform" Movement,* a resource for deciphering jargon related to the United States health care reform initiative undertaken by U.S. President Bill Clinton's administration and led by First Lady Hillary Rodham Clinton. *Health Care Reform Terms* attempts to offer assistance to health care providers and consumers alike by providing clear, concise definitions of words, phrases, and acronyms used in discussions of health care reform. Often several terms have been used to refer to a single concept or action, and when these new terms are used, their meaning, if it is not lost, becomes confused and distorted. For instance, what was first known as the "Health Insurance Purchasing Cooperative (HIPC)" has been subsequently referred to as "Health Plan Purchasing Cooperative (HPPC)" and "health alliance." *Health Care Reform Terms* sorts through such bewildering terminology so its users can spend more time considering the issues involved in health care reform and less time trying to decipher the language of the proposal.

Debora A. Slee told *CA:* "*Health Care Reform Terms* went to a second edition within six months of the original book. All the 'players' in health care reform tend to introduce their own terminology to distinguish their plan from all the others. For intelligent debate on health care to take place, each party must understand what the other is talking about. Our books aim to contribute to this necessary understanding. We are currently working on the third edition of our 'big book,' *Health Care Terms,* which will bring together the 'reform' terminology along with terms which have been proliferating in all areas of health care during the recent past."

For further information on Vergil N. Slee, see his entry in this volume.

BIOGRAPHICAL/CRITICAL SOURCES:

OTHER

Press release from Tringa Press, 1994.

*   *   *

SLEE, Vergil N(elson)   1917-

PERSONAL: Born September 24, 1917, in Eaton, Rapids, MI; son of William Willey (a Methodist minister) and Matilda Elizabeth (a teacher; maiden name, Nelson) Slee; married Beth Ellen Stoke (a painter), June 10, 1941; children: Dan, Sara, David, Debora A. *Education:* Albion College, B.A. (with highest honors), 1937; Washington University, M.D. (cum laude), 1941; University of Michigan, M.P.H., 1947.

ADDRESSES: Home—16 Udoque Ct., Brevard, NC 28712.

CAREER: Barry County Health Department (became Barry County Health Center), Barry County, MI, director, 1947-48 and 1949-56; Southwestern Michigan Hospital Council, Professional Activity Study (PAS), founding director, 1953-55; Commission on Professional and Hospital Activities, Ann Arbor, MI, founding director, 1956-71, president, 1971-80, president emeritus, 1980—; Tringa Group, Brevard, NC, chief executive officer, 1982—; Health Commons Institute, Portland, ME, chairperson of the board, 1993—; writer. Lecturer at University of Michigan, 1947-78; president, Council on Clinical

Classifications. Member of World Health Organization's Expert Advisory Panel on Health Statistics, 1959-79, and U.S. National Committee on Vital and Health Statistics's International Classification of Diseases Subcommittee, 1970-75. Member of board of directors of Estes Park Institute, 1981—, and Helena Health Institute, 1991-93; member of board of trustees of Transylvania Community Hospital, 1990—. *Military service:* U.S. Army Air Force, 1942-46; flight surgeon.

MEMBER: American Public Health Association (fellow), American College of Physicians (fellow), Phi Gamma, Alpha Omega Alpha, Phi Kappa Phi, Delta Omega.

AWARDS, HONORS: Jackson Johnson scholarship, Washington University, 1937-41; Key Award, Michigan Hospital Association, 1968; honorary fellowship, American College of Healthcare Executives, 1969; Resolution of Commendation, Southwestern Michigan Hospital Council, 1978; special citation, Michigan Hospital Association, 1980; Resolution of Commendation, American Hospital Association Board of Trustees, 1980; Edwin L. Crosby fellowship, Nuffield Provincial Hospitals Trust, 1981; Richard and Hinda Rosenthal Award, American College of Physicians, 1982; Award of Merit, American Association of Healthcare Consultants, 1988.

WRITINGS:

Health Care Terms, Tringa Press (St. Paul), 1991, (with daughter, Debora A. Slee) 2nd edition, 1991.
(With D. A. Slee) *Health Care Reform Terms: An Explanatory Glossary of Words, Phrases, and Acronyms Used in Today's U.S. "Health Care Reform" Movement,* Tringa Press, 1993, 2nd edition, 1994.
Coding and Classification in Health Care, Tringa Press, 1995.

Creator, with U.S. National Center for Health Statistics, of the *International Classification of Diseases,* 9th revision: *Clinical Modification,* 1978. Also contributor to periodicals, including *Annals of Internal Medicine, Bulletin of the American College of Surgeons, Hospital Progress, Medical Record News,* and *Modern Hospital.* Member of editorial board of *Medizinische Dokumentation,* 1961-81.

WORK IN PROGRESS: A third edition of *Health Care Terms,* for Tringa Press, publication expected in 1995; *Health Care Terms—Community Health Care Reform Edition,* also 1995.

SIDELIGHTS: Vergil N. Slee is a doctor and medical administrator whose publications include *Health Care Terms, Coding and Classification in Health Care,* and *Health Care Reform Terms: An Explanatory Glossary of Words, Phrases, and Acronyms Used in Today's U.S. "Health Care Reform" Movement.*

For further information on Debora A. Slee, including her work with her father, see her entry in this volume.

BIOGRAPHICAL/CRITICAL SOURCES:

PERIODICALS

Press release from Tringa Press, 1994.

* * *

SMITH, Dale L.   1953-

PERSONAL: Born May 23, 1953, in Lake Charles, LA; married Karen Farkas, May 22, 1984. *Education:* Massachusetts Institute of Technology, Ph.D., 1987.

ADDRESSES: Office—Department of Political Science, Florida State University, Tallahassee, FL 32306.

CAREER: Florida State University, Tallahassee, professor of political science.

WRITINGS:

(Editor with James L. Ray) *The Nineteen Ninety-Two Project and the Future of Integration in Europe,* M. E. Sharpe, 1992.

* * *

SMITH, Marya 1945-

PERSONAL: Born November 12, 1945, in Youngstown, OH; daughter of Cameron Reynolds (an attorney) and Jean (a community volunteer; maiden name, Sause) Argetsinger; married Arthur B. Smith, Jr. (an attorney), December 30, 1968; children: Arthur Cameron, Sarah Reynolds. *Education:* Cornell University, B.A. (English literature), 1967. *Politics:* Democrat. *Religion:* Roman Catholic. *Avocational interests:* Horseback riding, running, tennis, reading.

ADDRESSES: Home and office—714 Gunderson Ave., Oak Park, IL 60304. *Agent*—Perry Browne, Pema Browne Ltd., Pine Rd., HCR 104-B, Neversink, NY 12765.

CAREER: Seventeen magazine, New York City, editorial assistant, 1967-68; University of Chicago Press, Chicago, IL, copywriter, 1968-70; Drucilla Handy Co., Chicago, publicity writer, 1970-72; freelance writer, Chicago, 1972-74; Cornell University, Ithaca, NY, Department of Communications, lecturer in magazine writing, 1976-77; freelance writer, Chicago, 1978—. Reading tutor, Oak Park Public Library.

MEMBER: Society of Children's Book Writers and Illustrators, Authors Guild, Authors League of America, National Writers Union, Children's Reading Round Table, Chicago Women in Publishing.

AWARDS, HONORS: Finalist, Prix de Paris writing contest for college seniors, *Vogue* magazine, 1967; second prize, George A. McCalmon playwrighting competition, Cornell University, 1967; Associated Church Press news writing award, 1986, for article "What to Expect When You Shelter an Unwed Mother," published in *Salt* magazine; poetry awards from Triton College's Salute to the Arts and Poets and Patrons' annual poetry contests, 1986, 1987, and 1989.

WRITINGS:

Across the Creek, Arcade, 1989.
Winter-Broken, Arcade, 1990.

Also author of three one-act comedies produced at Playwrights' Center Theatre, Chicago, IL. Contributor to various periodicals, including *Chicago, Ingenue, Sphere, Chicago Tribune Magazine,* and *Salt.*

WORK IN PROGRESS: Hire Power, a two-act play.

SIDELIGHTS: Marya Smith's first novel, *Across the Creek,* follows twelve-year-old Ryerson, who is sent to his grandmother's farm after his mother's death. Rye is uncomfortable in this unfamiliar rural setting, removed from the possessions and friends that defined the happy life he led before his mother's death. Rye simultaneously discovers a creek on the property and a younger girl, with whom he develops a relationship through the construction of a stone altar on the creek-bank. In this nameless girl, Rye perceives a striking resemblance to childhood pictures of his mother, and he eventually convinces himself that she actually is his mother, returned in her youth to guard over him. When school begins, however, Rye finds that the girl attends classes for the developmentally disabled, and the subsequent dissipation of his fantasy provides Rye with both a crisis and the opportunity for personal growth.

In a *Horn Book* review, Martha V. Parravano noted that the book ran into some difficulty in its depiction of peer pressure and developmental disability, but maintained that "as a portrait of an unusual friendship and a young boy's response to loss, *Across the Creek* is sure-footed and strong." A reviewer for *Publishers Weekly* similarly commended the portrayal of "grief and longing that give rise to the protagonist's romantic fantasy."

Smith's second book, *Winter-Broken,* broaches another highly emotional topic. Twelve-year-old Dawn prides herself on her ability to remain silent in the face of, and in avoidance of, her alcoholic father's physical abuse. Dawn escapes the traumas of her home life by making regular visits to a nearby farm, where she develops an attachment to a horse she names Wildfire. Eventually the man in charge of the farm notices Dawn's interest, and she is invited to tend to the horse. When the owner has a heart attack and Wildfire is sold, Dawn finds the resolve to seek help for the problems brought on by her family.

In a review for the *Bulletin of the Center for Children's Books,* Kathryn Pierson likened *Winter-Broken* to *Across the Creek,* finding both "powerful but slow-moving." Nancy Vasilakis noted in a *Horn Book* review that the novel "reveals many of the grim facts of child abuse," but considered the ending "optimistic," yet "not unrealistic."

BIOGRAPHICAL/CRITICAL SOURCES:

PERIODICALS

Booktalker, March, 1991, p. 16.
Bulletin of the Center for Children's Books, January, 1990, p. 121; November, 1990, p. 71.
Horn Book, March/April, 1990, p. 204; November/December, 1990, p. 744.
Publishers Weekly, December 22, 1989.

* * *

SOLBRIG, Dorothy J. 1945-

PERSONAL: Born March 14, 1945, in Baltimore, MD; daughter of Henry Milton, Jr. (a physicist) and Hannah G. (a physicist; maiden name, McKee) Crosswhite; married Otto T. Solbrig (a professor), June 21, 1969. *Education:* Goucher College, A.B., 1966; University of Michigan, M.A., 1969; Simmons College, M.S., 1972.

ADDRESSES: Office—Biological Laboratories Library, Harvard University, 16 Divinity Ave., Cambridge, MA 02138.

CAREER: Harvard University, Cambridge, MA, librarian, 1971—.

MEMBER: American Library Association.

WRITINGS:

Introduction to Population Biology and Evolution, Addison-Wesley, 1979.
(Co-author) *So Shall You Reap,* Island Press (Washington, DC), 1994.

* * *

SOLOMON, Marion F. 1935-

PERSONAL: Born August 19, 1935, in Brooklyn, NY; daughter of Samuel and Clara (Sax) Fried; married Matthew R. Solomon, June 10, 1956; children: Bonnie Solomon Mark, Glenn. *Education:* University of Southern California, M.S.W., 1965.

ADDRESSES: Home—1023 Westholme Ave., Los Angeles, CA 90024. *Agent*—Linda Chester, 666 Fifth Ave., 37th Floor, New York, NY 10103.

CAREER: Psychologist in Los Angeles, CA, 1964—. Department of Humanities, Sciences, and Social Sciences, coordinator of mental health series; associate of City of Hope and Streissand Center for Jewish Cultural Arts.

MEMBER: American Academy of Psychoanalysis, American Family Therapy Association (scientific affiliate), American Association of Marriage and Family Therapy, American Group Psychotherapy Association, American Orthopsychiatric Association, National Association of Social Workers, Society for Clinical Social Work, California Association of Marriage and the Family.

WRITINGS:

(Co-editor) *The Borderline Patient: Emerging Concepts in Diagnosis, Etiology, Psychodynamics, and Treatment,* Analytic Press (Hillsdale, NJ), 1987.
Narcissism and Intimacy: Love and Marriage in an Age of Confusion, Norton (New York, NY), 1989.
Lean on Me: The Power of Positive Dependency in Relationships, Simon & Schuster (New York, NY), 1994.

WORK IN PROGRESS: Men, Women, and Relationships in the Twenty-First Century; research on "the borderline couple."

SIDELIGHTS: Marion F. Solomon told *CA:* "I have long been concerned about the messages psychology has given about the need to be strong and independent in order to achieve maturity and be able to love another. Many people who do what psychologists suggest wonder why they feel so lonely and isolated. I watched colleagues and friends take what seemed to be the road away from unhappiness—divorce—only to discover that the problem is not resolved by searching for the right partner, but by being the right partner.

"After thirty years of marriage and twenty-five years of treating marital problems, I began to write about what I live and teach—how to make relationships work. The response has been enormously gratifying, and I continue to write about what I know best—loving, interdependent relationships."

*   *   *

SPARKE, Penny   1948-

PERSONAL: Born June 11, 1948, in London, England; daughter of Kenneth Stanley (an accountant) and Jacqueline Anne (a homemaker; maiden name, Castell) Sparke; married John William Small (a designer), November 25, 1987; children: Molly Anne, Nancy Louise, Celia Jane. *Education:* Attended University of Sussex, 1967-71, and Brighton Polytechnic, 1971-75. *Politics:* Labour.

ADDRESSES: Home—Galveston Lodge, Galveston Rd., East Putney, London SW1S 2SA, England. *Office*—School of Humanities, Royal College of Art, Kensington Gore, London SW7 2EU, England. *Agent*—Jane Bradish-Ellames, Curtis Brown, Haymarket House, 4th Floor, 28/29 Haymarket, London SW1Y 4SP, England.

CAREER: Brighton Polytechnic, Brighton, England, principal lecturer in the history of design, 1975—. Royal College of Art, senior lecturer, 1981—, head of School of Humanities, 1994—. Organizer of exhibitions.

MEMBER: Design History Society (secretary, 1977-80).

WRITINGS:

(Editor) *Design by Choice,* Academy, 1981.
Ettore Sottsass, Junior, Design Council, 1982.

Consultant Design, Pembridge Press, 1983.
Design and Culture, Allen & Unwin, 1986.
Modern Furniture, Bell & Hyman, 1986.
(Editor) *Did Britain Make It?,* Design Council, 1986.
Design in Context, Bloomsbury, 1987.
Electrical Appliances, Bell & Hyman, 1987.
Japanese Design, M. Joseph, 1987.
Italian Design, Thames & Hudson, 1988.
(Editor) *The Plastics Age,* Victoria and Albert Museum, 1989, and Overlook Press.
(Editor) *The Cutting Edge,* Swarovski, 1992.

WORK IN PROGRESS: "As Long as It's Pink": The Sexual Politics of Taste; research on women, taste, and design.

SIDELIGHTS: Penny Sparke told *CA:* "I write about design in a cultural context. I am interested in the meaning of things and their history. At present I am fascinated by the idea of gender and design."

*   *   *

SPRAGUE, Marshall   1909-1994

OBITUARY NOTICE—See index for *CA* sketch: Born March 14, 1909, in Newark, OH; died September 9, 1994, in Colorado Springs, CO. Writer and journalist. Sprague wrote numerous books about the American West, including *Money Mountain: The Story of Cripple Creek Gold, Massacre: The Tragedy of White River, Great Pioneer Heroes,* and his highly praised historical account *Newport in the Rockies: The Life and Good Times of Colorado Springs.* After graduating from Princeton University in 1930, Sprague worked as a journalist in New York, China, and Paris. In 1936 he became a feature writer and book reviewer for the *New York Times,* as well as a contributor to magazines. From the early 1950s into his later years, Ross produced studies that chronicle and celebrate the American West from the frontier period to the present.

OBITUARIES AND OTHER SOURCES:

BOOKS

Directory of American Scholars, Volume 1: *History,* 8th edition, Bowker, 1982.

PERIODICALS

Chicago Tribune, September 18, 1994, sec. 2, p. 7.
New York Times, September 17, 1994, p. 12.

SPRINGER, Margaret 1941-

PERSONAL: Born January 9, 1941, in England; emigrated to Canada, 1952, naturalized Canadian citizen; married Christopher Springer, May, 1966; children: Colin, Alison. *Education:* McGill University, B.A., 1961; B.L.S., 1964.

ADDRESSES: Home and office—91 Blythwood Rd., Waterloo, Ontario, Canada N2L 4A1. *Agent*—David Bennett, Transatlantic Literary Agency, 72 Glengowan Rd., Toronto, Ontario, Canada M4N 1G4.

CAREER: McGill School of Library Science, librarian, 1964-66; St. Paul's United College, librarian, 1966-74 and 1977-80; freelance writer, 1982—. Faculty member for the Institute of Children's Literature, 1988—, *Highlights for Children* Writer's Workshop, 1988 and 1993, and Conestoga College Continuing Education Department, 1993—; Boyds Mills Press, consulting editor, 1990—; judge for fiction contests.

MEMBER: Canadian Authors Association, Canadian Society of Children's Authors, Illustrators, and Performers, Society of Children's Book Writers and Illustrators, Writer's Union of Canada.

AWARDS, HONORS: Winner of two Pewter Plate Awards, *Highlights for Children* magazine, both 1990, for Author of the Month (September), and for Arts Feature of the Year.

WRITINGS:

A Royal Ball (children's story), illustrated by Tom O'Sullivan, Bell Books, 1992.

Contributor of children's fiction, nonfiction, and poetry to periodicals, including *Highlights for Children, Turtle, Pennywhistle Press,* and *Clubhouse.* Contributor of articles on writing for children to *Canadian Author, SCBWI Bulletin,* and *Children's Writer.*

WORK IN PROGRESS: Stories and articles for children's magazines; articles on writing for adults; junior novel and picture book texts.

SIDELIGHTS: A Royal Ball may be Margaret Springer's first children's book, but it is not her first venture into children's literature. Since 1982, her poetry, fiction, and nonfiction have appeared in such magazines as *Highlights for Children, Turtle, Pennywhistle Press,* and *Clubhouse.* To date, she has seen publication of more than seventy of her stories and articles.

A Royal Ball is the story of Queen Zygoma and King Mervin. Although their realms are right next to each other, the queen and king, for reasons no one can remember, have long been enemies. However, Queen Zygoma's seven daughters and King Mervin's seven sons conspire to bring peace between their parents.

The inspiration for Springer's stories come in various ways. She often keeps newspaper clippings that interest her and uses them as the basis for her stories. She also keeps a jar filled with words written on scraps of paper, and picks them out for story ideas. For instance, "Dishpan Ducks," published in *Highlights for Children* in 1990, was inspired by newspaper clippings about oil spills. Another story, "Elephant Yoga," came about when she reached into her jar and drew the words "jungle," "waterfall," and "mouse." Springer even keeps a file of names for her characters. She collects names from birth notices in the paper, concert programs, and lists of contest winners. She even collects names when she travels so that she has a diversity of names to choose from. She once came upon the name Ryoji in a school program and decided to use it in a story. It took her a long time to find out whether it was a boy's name or a girl's, though she eventually learned that it was a boy's.

When it comes to the actual writing, Springer works in a number of different ways. She explained, "I write on a computer or laptop, but sometimes I still use scrap paper and pencil at the picnic table." Whatever tools she uses for her writing, Springer enjoys the imaginative thinking that goes into creating stories for children. "I love the sense of wonder and fun that is natural to all young children," she stated in an interview published in *Institute of Children's Literature Anthology,* "and I try to recapture that in myself."

BIOGRAPHICAL/CRITICAL SOURCES:

BOOKS

Institute of Children's Literature Anthology, 1986.

PERIODICALS

Inside Highlights for Children, July-August, 1987. *Kitchener-Waterloo Record,* March 30, 1990, p. C1. *Quill & Quire,* January, 1993, p. 30.

* * *

STALEY, Allen (Percival Green) 1935-

PERSONAL: Born June 4, 1935, in St. Louis, MO; son of Walter Goodwin and Martha (Green) Staley; married Etheleen Lichtenstein, July 26, 1968; children:

Oliver, Peter. *Education:* Princeton University, B.A., 1957; Yale University, M.A., 1960, Ph.D., 1965.

ADDRESSES: Home—151 Central Park West, New York, NY 10023. *Office*—Department of Art History, Columbia University, Broadway and West 116th, New York, NY 10027.

CAREER: Frick Collection, New York City, lecturer, 1962-65; Philadelphia Museum of Art, Philadelphia, PA, assistant curator, 1965-69; Columbia University, New York City, assistant professor, 1969-71, associate professor, 1971-76, professor of art history, 1976—.

WRITINGS:

(With Frederick J. Cummings) *Romantic Art in Britain: Paintings and Drawings, 1760-1860,* Praeger (New York), 1968.
The Pre-Raphaelite Landscape, Oxford University Press (New York), 1973.
(With Helmut von Erffa) *The Paintings of Benjamin West,* Yale University Press (New Haven, CT), 1986.

Contributor to anthologies, including *Whistler Lithographs: An Illustrated Catalogue Raisonne,* edited by Mervyn Levy, Jupiter Books, 1975, *American Paintings in the Detroit Institute of Arts, Volume 1: Works by Artists Born before 1816,* edited by Mary Black, Hudson Hills Press, 1991, and *Impossible Picturesqueness: Edward Lear's Indian Watercolors, 1873-1875,* edited by Vidya Dehejia, Columbia University Press, 1990. Author of introduction to *Unfaded Pageant: Edwin Austin Abbey's Shakespearean Subjects* by Lucy Oakley, Columbia University Press, 1994.

SIDELIGHTS: Art historian and professor Allen Staley earned high praise for his book *The Pre-Raphaelite Landscape,* a study of the nineteenth-century artistic discipline which called for an abandonment of Raphael's ideal realism, the classic Renaissance method that altered its subject to reflect the ideals of the time. The Pre-Raphaelites returned to a more immediate and realistic representation of the world, reminiscent of the work by fourteenth- and fifteenth-century Italian artists. Although not a complete history of the Pre-Raphaelite movement, Staley's book studies various schools of the movement and highlights numerous Pre-Raphaelite painters, such as William Holman Hunt and Dante Rossetti.

Among the critics applauding Staley's book is a

Times Literary Supplement reviewer who wrote: "The literature of Pre-Raphaelitism is extensive. . . . but Allen Staley's *The Pre-Raphaelite Landscape* is the first complete study of the landscape. It is a comprehensive book, and likely to remain the standard work for some time to come." And John Canaday, writing in *New York Times Book Review,* deemed *The Pre-Raphaelite Landscape* a "a constant delight" as well as a "book to give thanks for."

Another of Staley's critically acclaimed books is *The Paintings of Benjamin West,* which Helmut von Erffa, a teacher at Swarthmore College, began writing in the 1940s. Staley joined von Erffa's effort in 1976, with the book being published after von Erffa's death. Judged "a monumental achievement" by John Russell in the *New York Times Book Review,* *The Paintings of Benjamin West* is a lengthy tome chronicling the life and work of the American painter and courtier who, for more than twenty-five years, figured prominently among British artists and royals, even serving as president of the Royal Academy in London.

Reviewer John Hayes, writing in the *Times Literary Supplement,* paid tribute to Staley's book on West, proclaiming: "Allen Staley charts West's career as a painter in an introductory essay of just the right length which tells us, without a word wasted, everything we need to know. Few art historians have a more comprehensive grasp of the interrelationships in this period."

BIOGRAPHICAL/CRITICAL SOURCES:

PERIODICALS

New York Times Book Review, December 2, 1973, p. 89; June 1, 1986, p. 12.
Time Literary Supplement, August 10, 1973, p. 924; October 24, 1986, p. 1179.*

* * *

**STANGOS, Nicolas   1936-
(Nikos Stangos)**

PERSONAL: Born November 21, 1936, in Athens, Greece; son of Constantine (an architect) and Natalia (a teacher; maiden name, Syvrides) Stangos. *Education:* Attended Wesleyan University, Middletown, CT, 1955-56; Denison University, B.A. (with honors), 1958; graduate study at Harvard University, 1958-60. *Politics:* Socialist. *Religion:* Greek Orthodox. *Avocational interests:* Music.

ADDRESSES: Home—38 Montagu Sq., London W1H

1TL, England. *Office*—Thames & Hudson Ltd., 30-34 Bloomsbury St., London WC1B 3QP, England.

CAREER: Ekistics Doxiadis Associates, Athens, Greece, education director, 1962-65; press attache at Greek embassy in London, England, 1965-67; Penguin Books Ltd., London, senior commissioning editor, 1967-74; Thames & Hudson Ltd., London, editorial director, 1974—. Consultant to Institute of Contemporary Arts, London, and Arts Council of Great Britain.

MEMBER: Cranium Club, Groucho Club.

AWARDS, HONORS: Fulbright scholar, 1955-56.

WRITINGS:

(Editor under name Nikos Stangos) David Hockney, *That's the Way I See It,* Chronicle Books, 1993.

Also editor of *John Berger Sel Essays,* 1972; *Concepts of Modern Art,* 1974; and *Hockney by Hockney,* by David Hockney, 1976. Also author of *Selected Poems,* 1975, 3rd edition, 1994. Translator.

*　　*　　*

STANGOS, Nikos
    See STANGOS, Nicolas

*　　*　　*

STARGELL, Willie
    See STARGELL, Wilver Dornel

*　　*　　*

STARGELL, Wilver Dornel   1941-
    (Willie Stargell)

PERSONAL: Born March 6, 1941, in Earlsboro, OK; married first wife (divorced); married second wife, Dolores (marriage ended); children: Wendy, Precious, Dawn, Wilver Jr., Kelli. *Education:* Attended Santa Rosa Junior College.

ADDRESSES: Home—813 Tarpin Dr., Wilmington, NC 28409. *Office*—c/o Atlanta Braves, 521 Capitol Ave. S.W., Atlanta, GA 30312-2803.

CAREER: National League baseball player with the Pittsburgh Pirates, 1962-83; national league coach with the Atlanta Braves, 1989—. Member of the National Advisory Council on Sickle Cell Anemia.

MEMBER: Black Athletes Foundation (president).

AWARDS, HONORS: Named to National League All-Star Team, 1964-66, 1971-73, and 1978; *Sporting News* and United Press International Comeback Player of the Year, 1978; *Sports Illustrated* Sportsman of the Year, 1979; *Sporting News* Major League Player of the Year, 1979; inducted into National Baseball Hall of Fame, 1988.

WRITINGS:

(With Tom Bird; as Willie Stargell) *Willie Stargell* (autobiography), HarperCollins (New York), 1984.

SIDELIGHTS: In his book, *Willie Stargell,* Hall-of-Famer Willie Stargell and coauthor Tom Bird chronicle Stargell's glorious career as a member of the Pittsburgh Pirates baseball team. During his 21 seasons with the team, Stargell hit 475 home runs, batted in more than 1,500 runs, and, as team captain, led the Pirates to a World Series championship in 1979. He was also the only player of his day to hit a baseball several times into the lofty upper deck of Pittsburgh's Three Rivers Stadium.

Stargell's eventual success on the playing field is even more remarkable in light of his difficult upbringing. The son of teenaged parents, Stargell was abandoned by his father when a baby and at age five by his mother, who left him with an abusive aunt in the projects of Oakland, California. In his book, Stargell recalls his aunt's harshness but writes that her strict approach to raising him taught him discipline. His positive thinking also helped him survive injustices during his stint with a minor league farm team in the early days of his career. For example, while the white players were lodged in hotels, the black players were put up in separate boardinghouses.

Even after achieving success, Stargell had numerous opportunities to feel life had let him down: he was divorced from his first wife, his second wife was left paralyzed by a stroke before their marriage was dissolved, and one of Stargell's daughters was diagnosed with sickle-cell anemia. Nevertheless, Stargell notes positive aspects to all of these setbacks, including his participation in the development of a foundation to fight his daughter's illness.

Some reviewers of Stargell's book complained that he is too optimistic and forgiving, but Genevieve Stuttaford in a *Publishers Weekly* review asserts, "What renders the autobiography noteworthy . . . is the portrait of the man himself: no Pollyanna,

Stargell nonetheless sees the best in everyone." He even doles out little gold "Stargell Stars" to those he feels are also winning in the game of life.

Perhaps one of the greatest honors Stargell has known is his being asked to recite the words of Martin Luther King Jr. in composer Joseph Schwantner's "New Morning for the World: Daybreak of Freedom," with the Eastman Philharmonia orchestra. Robert Freeman, director of the University of Rochester's Eastman School of Music, commissioned Schwantner to write the tribute to King with Stargell in mind. According to Freeman, Stargell exemplifies characteristics that bring people together. Writing in the *New York Times,* George Vecsey quoted Stargell: "'I feel very honored and flattered to be part of this. Dr. King has meant everything to me. He was a great inspiration, standing for everything that is good in living.'" Vecsey judged Stargell's Carnegie Hall debut performance a success, writing: "Stargell's voice is a musical instrument. The retired slugger never went for the home run of impersonation, but rather stroked the ball where it was pitched, allowing the composition to work on its own. . . . Later the professionals backstage talked of a new career for Willie Stargell." After his performance, Stargell gave little gold stars to the musicians and stagehands. "Even in Carnegie Hall," Vecsey wrote, "he was still Captain Willie."

BIOGRAPHICAL/CRITICAL SOURCES:

BOOKS

Hall, Susan, editor, *Out of Left Field: Willie Stargell and the Pittsburgh Pirates,* Two Continents, 1976.
Stargell, Willie and Tom Bird, *Willie Stargell,* HarperCollins, 1984.

PERIODICALS

Los Angeles Times, April 12, 1984.
New York Times, January 19, 1983.
New York Times Book Review, June 3, 1984, p. 11.
Publishers Weekly, January 20, 1984, p. 81.*

* * *

STARK, Evan 1942-

PERSONAL: Born March 10, 1942, in New York, NY; son of Irwin (a writer) and Alice (a teacher) Stark; married Anne Flitcraft (a physician); children: Aaron, Sam, Daniel, Rachel. *Education:* Attended Brandeis University, 1963; University of

Wisconsin, M.S., 1967; State University of New York—Binghamton, Ph.D., 1984; Fordham University, M.S.W., 1990. *Avocational interests:* Democratic town committee, coaching soccer.

ADDRESSES: Home—201 West Park Ave., New Haven, CT 06511.

CAREER: Rutgers University, Newark, NJ, professor of public administration, 1986—; Shoreline Clinic, Madison, CT, psychotherapist; Domestic Violence Training Project, New Haven, CT, co-director. Consultant to Centers for Disease Control.

MEMBER: National Association of Social Workers.

AWARDS, HONORS: Governor's Victim Service Award, 1990; Trend Setter Award, National Health Council, 1993; Sanctity of Life Award, Brandeis University, 1993.

WRITINGS:

Everything You Need to Know about Family Violence, Rosen Publishers, 1989, revised edition, 1991.
Everything You Need to Know about Sexual Abuse, Rosen Publishers, 1990, 2nd edition, 1992.
Everything You Need to Know about Boys, Rosen Publishers, 1992.
Everything You Need to Know about Gangs, Rosen Publishers, 1992.

Also editor of *Everything You Need to Know* series, Rosen Publishers, 1989-92. Author of more than fifty scholarly articles.

WORK IN PROGRESS: Research on poverty, domestic violence, child abuse, youth violence.

SIDELIGHTS: "Most writing about social issues is moralistic, theoretically naive and one-dimensional, whether directed at children or adults," Evan Stark commented. "My purpose in writing for children is to make fairly sophisticated issues—like violence and sexual abuse—accessible through real-life stories and case histories. I am a feminist who has worked for many years as an activist and researcher in the battered women's movement."

* * *

STEFFENS, Bradley 1955-

PERSONAL: Born February 10, 1955, in Waterloo, IA; son of Henry Wallace (a machinist) and Marcella Rose (a switchboard operator; maiden name,

Krueger) Steffens; married Bonnie Rose Szumski (an editor), July 5, 1980 (marriage ended); children: Ezekiel, Tessa Rose. *Education:* Attended Macalester College, St. Paul, MN, 1973-74. *Religion:* Lutheran. *Avocational interests:* Racquetball, golf, aerobics.

ADDRESSES: Home—13628 Pomerado Rd., No. 36, Poway, CA 92064-3539. *Office*—c/o Mitchell International, 9889 Willow Creek Rd., San Diego, CA 92131-1119.

CAREER: Deluxe Check Printers, Inc., St. Paul, MN, copywriter, 1982-87; Gelbach Lee, St. Paul, copywriter, 1987-88; Mitchell International, San Diego, CA, copywriter, 1989-94.

MEMBER: Society of Children's Book Writers and Illustrators.

AWARDS, HONORS: Contemporary Writers Series awards, Depot Arts Center, Duluth, MN, 1985 and 1987; winner of Emerging Voices Competition, The Loft, Minneapolis, MN, 1987; recipient of poetry prizes from *Artemis, New Worlds Unlimited,* the St. Paul Chapter of the American Association of University Women, and the White Bears Arts Council.

WRITINGS:

NONFICTION

(With Harry Nickelson) *Vietnam,* Lucent Books, 1989.
(With James House) *The San Francisco Earthquake,* Lucent Books, 1989.
Working Mothers, Greenhaven Press, 1989.
Animal Rights, Greenhaven Press, 1989.
Printing Press: Ideas into Type, Lucent Books, 1990.
The Children's Crusade, Lucent Books, 1991.
Photography: Preserving the Past, Lucent Books, 1991.
Free Speech: Identifying Propaganda Techniques, Greenhaven Press, 1992.
Phonograph: Sound on Disk, Lucent Books, 1992.
The Fall of the Roman Empire, Greenhaven Press, 1994.
Addiction: Distinguishing between Fact and Opinion, Greenhaven Press, 1994.
Censorship, Lucent Books, 1994.
Loch Ness Monster, Greenhaven Press, in press.

PLAYS

Pageant of the Masters, produced in Minneapolis, MN, by KFAI Radio Players, 1979.

Last Stand, produced in Minneapolis, at Playwrights' Center, 1979.
Virodha-Bhakti: A Sequence of Pageants, produced in Minneapolis, by Olympia Arts Ensemble, 1980.
The Cursing of the Fig Tree, produced in Minneapolis, at Augsburg College Chapel, 1982.

OTHER

Contributor of poetry to periodicals, including *Crosscurrents, Bellingham Review, Stone Country, Bellowing Ark,* and *Loonfeather.* Contributor of commentaries and opinion pieces to periodicals, including *Los Angeles Times, Minnesota Literature,* and *San Diego Writer's Monthly.*

WORK IN PROGRESS: Auriga and Other Poems; The Right of the State (adult), an examination of First Amendment controversies.

SIDELIGHTS: Bradley Steffens commented: "I first thought about being a writer in eleventh grade. My creative writing teacher, James Malone, told our class to write something about the automobile culture of Los Angeles, where we lived. It could be anything, Malone said—an essay, a poem, a short story, the first chapter of a novel. Wanting to avoid homework, I dashed off a twenty-line poem in class and turned it in. The next day, Malone sat on the corner of his desk with a piece of paper in his hand. 'Someone has turned in the first assignment,' he said, 'and I want to share it with you.' He began to read my poem aloud. A trained actor, he read with sensitivity and passion. When he finished, the room was silent. He looked up from the page. 'That, boys and girls, is poetry,' he said. He walked over to my desk and laid the paper in front of me. 'Publish it this semester, and I'll give you an "A" in the course,' he promised. 'You won't have to do another thing.' That morning changed my life. I changed my high school major. I changed the college I planned to attend. I began to write in earnest. I sent the poem out, and kept sending it out after it was rejected. Two years later, that poem, 'Automobile,' was accepted by the editor of *River Bottom,* a small literary journal published in Eau Claire, Wisconsin. After that, I never considered doing anything but writing."

BIOGRAPHICAL/CRITICAL SOURCES:

PERIODICALS

School Library Journal, May, 1992, p. 128; May, 1993, p. 135.

STEINBERG, Laurence 1952-

PERSONAL: Born July 8, 1952, in New Jersey; son of Irwin (a consultant) and Mollie (a homemaker) Steinberg; married Wendy Brodhead (a writer), August 27, 1982; children: Benjamin James. *Education:* Vassar College, A.B., 1974; Cornell University, Ph.D., 1977.

ADDRESSES: Office—Department of Psychology, Temple University, Philadelphia, PA 19122. *Agent*—Barbara Lowenstein, New York, NY.

CAREER: University of California, Irvine, professor, 1977-83; University of Wisconsin, Madison, professor, 1983-88; Temple University, Philadelphia, PA, professor, 1988—.

MEMBER: Phi Beta Kappa, American Psychology Association (fellow).

WRITINGS:

Adolescence, McGraw-Hill, 1985, revised, 1989 and 1993.
When Teenagers Work, Basic Books, 1986.
You and Your Adolescent, Harper, 1990.
(With wife, Wendy Steinberg) *Crossing Paths,* Simon and Schuster (New York, NY), 1994.
Childhood, McGraw-Hill, 1995.

* * *

STEINBERG, Wendy 1952-

PERSONAL: Born April 8, 1952, in Pasadena, CA; daughter of James Austen (an architect) and Monica Sennett (a secretary) Brodhead; married Laurence Steinberg (a professor), August 27, 1982; children: Benjamin James. *Education:* Mills College, B.A., 1974; Temple University, M.A., 1991. *Politics:* Democrat. *Religion:* Episcopalian.

ADDRESSES: Home—132 Valley Rd., Ardmore, PA 19003. *Office*—Institute of Contemporary Art, 118 S. 36th St., Philadelphia, PA 19104. *Agent*—Barbara Lowenstein, New York, NY.

CAREER: Institute of Contemporary Art (ICA), Philadelphia, PA, public relations director; writer.

MEMBER: AAM.

WRITINGS:

(With husband, Laurence Steinberg) *Crossing Paths,* Simon and Schuster (New York, NY), 1994.

STEPHENS, Andy 1956-

PERSONAL: Born April 27, 1956, in London, England; son of Kenneth and Patricia (South) Stephens; married Jane King (an information scientist), June 26, 1982; children: Jesse, Rosie. *Education:* Loughborough University, B.Sc., 1977.

ADDRESSES: Home—40 Woodgrange Ave., London N12 0PS, England. *Office*—British Library, 96 Euston Rd., London NW1 2DB, England.

CAREER: Affiliated with British Library, London, England, 1977—, became head of chief executive's office in 1992.

WRITINGS:

The History of the British National Bibliography: 1950-1973, British Library Bibliographic Services Division (London, England), 1994.

Contributor to professional and academic journals.

* * *

STERN, Howard 1954-

PERSONAL: Born January 12, 1954, in Roosevelt, Long Island, NY; son of Ben (a radio engineer and manager of a recording studio) and Rae Stern; married; wife's name, Alison (a social worker); children: Emily, Debra, and a third daughter. *Education:* Boston University, B.A., 1976. *Religion:* Jewish. *Politics:* Libertarian. *Avocational interests:* Transcendental meditation.

ADDRESSES: Home—Long Island, NY. *Agent*—Don Buchwald, 10 East 44th St., New York, NY 10017.

CAREER: Worked briefly in advertising in the mid-1970s; WRNW-radio, Westchester County, NY, disk jockey, production director, and program director, 1976; WCCC-radio, Hartford, CT, disk jockey, in the late 1970s; WWWW-radio, Detroit, MI, disk jockey, 1980-81; also worked for WWDC-radio, Washington, D.C., and WNBC-radio, New York City, between 1981-85; K-Rock, New York City, nationally syndicated radio talk-show host, 1985—. Host of syndicated television show on WWOR, New Jersey, 1990-92; host of the *Howard Stern Interviews* television program on the E! network, beginning in 1993; host of numerous pay-per-view cable events. Libertarian candidate for governor of the state of New York, 1994.

WRITINGS:

Private Parts (autobiography), Simon & Schuster (New York), 1993.

Author of numerous radio transcripts, song parodies, and unproduced film scripts, including *The Adventures of Fartman.*

SIDELIGHTS: Howard Stern is one of the best-known radio personalities of the late twentieth century. In a talk show format with topics ranging from politically incorrect rants to his own masturbatory fantasies, Stern has defined himself to listeners as a volatile humorist who freely speaks his mind. While such behavior has earned him enormous popularity and wealth, it has also incurred the wrath of both conservatives and liberals who are offended by a show they deem crude and tasteless. Rather than curb his antics in the face of such strong disapproval, Stern has, much to the delight of his loyal fans, increased his exposure by expanding into mediums outside of radio. To that end he has hosted television talk shows (and pay-per-view cable events) and pursued several film deals. In 1993 he published his first book, *Private Parts,* a work that is part autobiography and part unexpurgated extension of Stern's radio personality.

Stern grew up on Long Island, New York, watching his father, who was a radio engineer and ran a successful recording studio in Manhattan, work with comedians such as Don Adams and Larry Storch. "I thought they had the coolest job in the world," Stern told *Rolling Stone.* By age ten he had his own tape recorder with which he recorded routines. While attending Boston University, he became active in student radio, partaking in a spoof of the popular syndicated radio show *The King Biscuit Flour Hour.* After graduation, Stern worked for a time in advertising, but his exposure to radio in college lured him toward that field. He took a job with a small radio station in Westchester County, New York. Working as both a disk jockey and production director, Stern was restricted in his on-air comedy, but, as he told *Rolling Stone,* "snuck in whatever creativity I could during the commercials."

Frustrated by his inability to work original material into his radio job, Stern moved on to succession of positions, hoping to find creative freedom and a receptive audience. By the early 1980s his brand of radio was catching on and each successive job brought him higher ratings and more listeners. Along the way he assembled a group of sidekicks, including Robin Quivers, Fred Norris, and Jackie

"The Joke Man" Martling, who acted as on-air foils. In the mid-1980s Stern fulfilled his wish to work in New York City by signing on with WNBC. A combination of his controversial material and feuds with various staff members, however, resulted in his termination. Despite being fired, Stern was one of the hottest, if not *the* hottest, radio personality in the city. The job offers were numerous, and, unlike previous instances, Stern was able to negotiate a contract on his own terms. He settled on K-Rock, a station that gave him the coveted morning spot and assured him control over the content of his show. In addition, Stern's show would be syndicated nationally, exponentially increasing the size of his audience.

With this new prominence, Stern quickly established himself as a personality to whom no subject was taboo. His mischief-making included a lesbian dial-a-date prank, the beration of such celebrities as Oprah Winfrey and Roseanne, and a spontaneous debate over rock musician Kurt Cobain's suicide with Ted Nugent, another musician who was guest hosting at a rival New York City station. Despite presenting extreme examples of such, Stern has said that it is the element of truth in what he says that makes his jokes funny. "The truth is funny because we lie all day long," he told *Rolling Stone.* "We have to smile at the right time. We have to act like we care what other people say. . . . I lie too, but on the radio I say what I want."

By the end of the 1980s, Stern's morning show was the highest rated radio program in New York, the country's largest market, and with his syndication deal, his audience was estimated in the millions. *Time* magazine dubbed him "radio's most notorious 'shock jock,'" and by the 1990s, when Stern was expanding his ambitions to include television and film, his fiercest competitors were his imitators. According to *Rolling Stone,* Stern's daily show is "a four-hour black-comedy schmooze-fest, punctuated by song parodies, prerecorded comedy bits, sleazy studio antics and live commercials that stray freely from the copy." The most controversial element to the show, Stern's ad-lib remarks on sensitive topics, has won him both enemies and defenders. *Rolling Stone* wrote: "Stern claims to be an equal-opportunity offender—though gays, blacks, women and the disabled tend to get targeted more often than straight white males." Hence, Stern's critics display a spectrum of political attitudes, from conservative, religious-based groups to gay-and-lesbian and feminist groups generally considered liberal. For all the criticism, however, Stern's legions of fans have continued to grow, and their hunger for all things Howard has, in short concentrated bursts, matched the popularity of such superstars as Madonna.

When it was published in 1993, *Private Parts* broke Simon and Schuster's 70-year record for reprint figures within the first week of its release. A book signing at a New York Barnes and Noble store eclipsed an earlier signing by Madonna for her book *Sex.* Giving Stern's fans what they want, the book offers the reader access to many of the thoughts that course through its author's head, while also serving up a healthy dose of his rapid-fire humor. While its popular status was indisputable, critical reaction to *Private Parts* was often more uneven. "*Private Parts* proves that in America today, anything can be a 'book' and anyone can be an 'author,'" wrote *Boston Globe* contributor Scott Shuger. Noting that the book is a meaner, more explicit version of Stern's show, *People* magazine contributor Joe Queenan called *Private Parts* "a reasonably funny book" that boasts "some really good jokes" while calling its author "the poet laureate of urban American white trash." Wendy Warren Keebler of the *Detroit Free Press* noted that "the book succeeds brilliantly in translating Stern's personality, spontaneity and audacity from the radio waves onto the printed page."

Both those who praised and those who panned Stern's work remarked that readers would have to take their analyses at face value or buy the book themselves because the author's reliance on expletives prevented them from quoting *Private Parts* at any significant length. Walter Goodman of the *New York Times Book Review* remarked that Stern's sense of humor is reminiscent of noted counterculture comedian Lenny Bruce's but Bruce "was driven by a passion against hypocrisy; he was on a mission. Mr. Stern, powered by the pleasures of exhibition, is just on a kick." Or, as *Time* contributor Elizabeth L. Bland appraised, Stern's brand of humor "is every pubescent male's sex fantasy given voice; a one-man obscene gesture to the politically correct and socially discreet; the national id run wild."

BIOGRAPHICAL/CRITICAL SOURCES:

BOOKS

Stern, Howard, *Private Parts,* Simon & Schuster, 1993.

PERIODICALS

Boston Globe, November 12, 1993, p. 54.
Detroit Free Press, November 3, 1993, sec. D, p. 3.
Newsweek, October 25, 1993, pp. 75-76.
New York Times Book Review, November 14, 1994, p. 7.
People, November 22, 1993, pp. 32-33.
Publishers Weekly, October 18, 1993, p. 12.

Rolling Stone, June 14, 1990, pp. 83-89.
Time, November 30, 1992, pp. 72-73.*

*   *   *

STEVENS, Lawrence L.
  See LONDON, Lawrence Steven

*   *   *

STEWART, David W.   1929-

PERSONAL: Born December 12, 1929, in Holland, MI; son of S. Glenn (a paper mill executive) and Esther (a homemaker; maiden name, Wood) Stewart; married Billie Ackerman (a consultant), December 30, 1988; children: Miriam, Mark Irwin. *Education:* College of Wooster, B.A., 1951; University of Wisconsin—Madison, M.S., 1976, Ph.D., 1979. *Politics:* Democrat. *Religion:* Episcopalian. *Avocational interests:* Wilderness canoeing, collecting presidential biographies.

ADDRESSES: Home—6801 32nd St. N.W., Washington, DC 20015. *Office*—American Council on Education, 1 Dupont Circle, Suite 250, Washington, DC 20036.

CAREER: Electrical Information Publications, Madison, WI, editor, 1960-66; University of Wisconsin System, Madison, assistant to the chancellor of the Extension, 1967-72, senior academic planner, 1972-80; American Council on Education, Washington, DC, director of program development, 1985—. Coalition of Adult Education Organizations, president, 1988-89.

MEMBER: American Association for Adult and Continuing Education (member of board of directors, 1991-93), Politics of Education Association, Teachers of English to Speakers of Other Languages, Common Cause, Sierra Club, Zero Population Growth.

AWARDS, HONORS: Imogene Okes Award, American Association for Adult and Continuing Education, 1987; Philip Frandson Award for Literature, National University Continuing Education Association, 1988.

WRITINGS:

Adult Learning in America: Edvard Lindeman and His Agenda for Lifelong Education, Robert E. Krieger, 1987.
(With Henry A. Spike) *Diploma Mills: Degrees of Fraud,* Macmillan, 1988.

Immigration and Education: The Crises and the Opportunities, Lexington Books (New York, NY), 1993.

Contributor to professional journals.

SIDELIGHTS: David W. Stewart told *CA:* "The core of my professional interest is adult education. My books and journal articles reflect this. I hope that my work has, in some small way, advanced the cause of a true learning society."

*   *   *

STEWART, James B.   1957(?)-

PERSONAL: Born c. 1957, in Quincy, IL. *Education:* Attended DePauw University; Harvard Law School, LLB.

ADDRESSES: *Agent*—c/o Simon & Schuster, 1230 Avenue of the Americas, New York, NY 10020.

CAREER: Cravath, Swaine, & Moore (law firm), New York City, attorney; *Wall Street Journal,* senior writer and front page editor, 1983-92; writer.

AWARDS, HONORS: George Polk Award, Long Island University (journalism department), 1987, Gerald Loeb Award, University of California, Los Angeles (John E. Anderson Graduate School of Management), and Pulitzer Prize, Columbia University (graduate school of journalism), all 1988, all with Daniel Hertzberg, all for *Wall Street Journal* coverage of the October, 1987, stock market crash and Wall Street insider trading.

WRITINGS:

The Partners: Inside America's Most Powerful Law Firms, Simon and Schuster, 1983.
The Prosecutors: Inside the Offices of the Government's Most Powerful Lawyers, Simon and Schuster, 1987.
Den of Thieves, Simon and Schuster, 1991.

Served as executive editor of *American Lawyer.* Contributor to periodicals, including the *New Yorker.*

SIDELIGHTS: James B. Stewart, a former attorney and editor for the *Wall Street Journal,* is the author of three critically acclaimed books on law and financial investment. The first two volumes, *The Partners: Inside America's Most Powerful Law Firms,*

published in 1983, and *The Prosecutors: Inside the Offices of the Government's Most Powerful Lawyers,* published in 1987, offer insights into some of the most powerful operators in the American legal system. Stewart's third book, 1991's *Den of Thieves,* probes insider trading as well as other illegal activities which have scandalized the investment world in the 1980s.

The Partners profiles eight of the largest and most powerful law firms in the United States, with the focus on each firm being a major legal battle it has been involved with. The book opens with the story of clandestine negotiations between two large firms—under the direction of their American banking clients—for the release of fifty-two American hostages held in Iran by Islamic extremists. Stewart also tells of the ten-year defense of the IBM Corporation against a barrage of private and governmental anti-trust suits; the restructuring of Chrysler Corporation's enormous debt; and the settling of American millionaire Nelson Rockefeller's large estate following his sudden death. As Stewart relates in *The Partners,* the attorneys in these firms stopped at nothing in their quest to win, a devotion which prompted them to work seven days a week, employ questionable tactics, and bill exorbitant amounts. One lawyer, who worked an entire day and billed the client for twenty-four hours, was soon topped by a colleague who also worked an entire day, but then took a transcontinental flight which enabled him to bill twenty-seven hours in a one-day period.

The Partners was well-received by critics, with many reviewers praising the volume's insights and strong narrative qualities. In the *New Republic,* James J. Cramer admired Stewart's research and presentation of detail while offering minor criticism regarding the emphasis on attorneys over the clients who employ them. In summation, Cramer proclaimed the book a useful text: "Considering how little the public, including many noncorporate lawyers, knows about the crucial roles these corporate lawyers can play, Stewart's efforts can only be saluted." Calling *The Partners*'s collection of legal dramas "first rate," *Newsweek* contributor Aric Press praised Stewart's ability to tell a story, but expressed a desire for more analysis and editorial commentary from the author. John Jay Osborn, Jr., writing in the *Washington Post Book World,* stated that "Stewart has written a fascinating, fast moving narrative study of a vital American institution." In the *New York Times Book Review,* Neal Johnston commented that the author "has done an effective job of illuminating the realities of those institutions which continue to shape America."

Stewart's follow-up, *The Prosecutors,* examines several complicated cases brought by federal prosecutors during the 1980s, including the McDonnell Douglas Corporation's bribes to Pakistani officials and charges of impropriety leveled against former Reagan administration Attorney General Edwin Meese. Employing a format similar to *The Partners,* Stewart presents each case as a separate story, relating the key players and events. As Walter Walker wrote in the *Washington Post Book World:* "Stewart has written a highly entertaining account of several of the more notorious prosecutions conducted in this country over the past ten years." *New York Times Book Review* contributor Seymour Wishman found the historical content of *The Prosecutors* important, yet also highly readable: "Each of the stories unfolds with the suspense of a terrific detective novel, but the book is even better than that because the stories are true."

For his next book, *Den of Thieves,* Stewart shifted focus from the legal community to America's financial system, taking account of the greed and dirty-dealing that marred the stock market landscape during the 1980s. The volume examines numerous scandals which erupted during the decade, with special attention paid to insider trading scams (the practice of using secret information regarding impending business transactions as an advantage in buying and selling). At the height of the decade's avarice, players such as Ivan Boesky and Michael Milken were reaping tremendous profits at the expense of nearly all stock market investors, a majority of whom were unsuspecting middle- and lower-income Americans.

Boesky, who specialized in insider trading, was able to "predict" which mergers, buyouts, and takeovers would actually occur and thus invest and profit from the most lucrative outcome. Working out of the investment firm Drexel Burnham Lambert, Milken came to be Boesky's closest ally in the world of merger-making, earning the moniker of junk bond king (junk bonds are securities that advertise high yield but are better described as high risk; they are often sold as quick financing for takeover maneuvers). In Milken's case, junk bonds rarely rewarded their buyers with anything; they suffered the downside of "high risk" while Milken and Boesky profited from their sale by way of a skilled cycle of duplicity. Artificially reducing the value of certain securities, Milken would buy up the holdings of his clients (who had no way of knowing the actual values) and then sell them to Boesky for a small profit. Boesky would then sell the securities back to Drexel Burnham Lambert at a higher price and profit. The firm would then resell the same securities to their clients for even higher prices. As Stewart recounts in *Den of Thieves,* Boesky and Milken's reign ended with a string of indictments that rocked the very foundations of the investment world and resulted in lengthy prison terms for both men—and a large clean-up bill that fell on the shoulders of the American taxpayers.

Reviewers praised *Den of Thieves* as a historically significant record of Wall Street plundering; the account, some noted shed new light on the complicity of the financial news media and government regulators in these financial misdealings. A reviewer for the *New Yorker* termed the book a "fascinating account," while *New Republic* contributor Cramer stated that Stewart's work "stand[s] as the definitive history of the financial depredations of the decade. *Den of Thieves* provides details of manipulations that will jolt even the most knowing observers of the period." Investment banker and financial columnist Michael M. Thomas observed in the *New York Times Book Review* that *Den of Thieves* "is an absolutely splendid book and a tremendously important book, as good a book on Wall Street as I have ever read." Appraising its informational content, Thomas wrote that "the genius of this book is that it lets the larger questions emerge entirely from the narrative."

Den of Thieves embroiled Stewart in several controversies. In October, 1991, Alan Dershowitz, Michael Milken's defense lawyer, launched a public campaign accusing Stewart of anti-Semitism, bias, and factual inaccuracy. Following Dershowitz's publication of a full-page advertisement in the *New York Times,* Stewart and his defenders waged a war of words, exchanging volleys with Milken's sympathizers through articles and letters to the editor in the *New York Times* and the *Wall Street Journal.* In the *Nation,* Cramer defended Stewart's identification of the religious backgrounds of various players as presentation of fact and specifically termed Dershowitz's charges as "thoroughly shabby allegations." In September, 1992, Michael F. Armstrong, a prominent New York lawyer, sued Stewart for libel, claiming to have been wrongly accused in the book of preparing a false affidavit for a client. Despite these troubles *Den of Thieves* earned the respect of numerous critics and financial insiders, and went on to become a bestseller.

BIOGRAPHICAL/CRITICAL SOURCES:

PERIODICALS

Business Week, October 28, 1991, p. 16; December 9, 1991, p. 12.

Commentary, March, 1992, p. 54.

Financial World, November 12, 1991, p. 104.

Fortune, October 21, 1991, p. 195.

Gentlemen's Quarterly, August, 1992, p. 66.

Management Today, April, 1992, p. 106.

Nation, December 16, 1991, p. 783-785.

New Republic, Match 21, 1983, pp. 38-39; December 16, 1991, p. 50-53.

Newsweek, February 14, 1983, p. 77; October 14, 1991, p. 48.

New Yorker, November 18, 1991, p. 135.

New York Times, February 3, 1983; September 27, 1987, section 7, p. 20; April 1, 1988, section B, p. 4.

New York Times Book Review, March 6, 1983, pp. 13, 20; September 27, 1987, p. 20; October 13, 1991, pp. 1, 36-37.

People Weekly, December 16, 1991, p. 45.

USA Today, December 8, 1987, section B, p. 7; September 13, 1988, section B, p. 2.

Wall Street Journal, May 1, 1987, p. 26; February 29, 1988, p. 26; April 1, 1988, p. 2; May 11, 1988, p. 26; September 13, 1988, p. 42.

Washington Post Book World, February 20, 1983, pp. 5, 15; September 20, 1987, pp. 5,9.

Washington Monthly, January/February, 1992, p. 48.*

* * *

STEWART, Melville Y.   1935-

PERSONAL: Born June 19, 1935, in Boston, MA; son of Charles Norris (a chef) and Nellie Yorke (a soloist; maiden name, Consuello) Stewart. *Education:* Gordon College, B.A., 1958; Westminster Theological Seminary, M.Div., 1961; Andover Newton Theological School, S.T.M., 1968; University of Connecticut, M.A., 1972; University of Minnesota—Twin Cities, Ph.D., 1983; postdoctoral study at Oxford University, 1986. *Avocational interests:* Guitar, drawing, travel, old books.

ADDRESSES: Home—1490 Lincoln Terr., Columbia Heights, MN 55421. *Office*—Department of Philosophy, Bethel College, St. Paul, MN 55112.

CAREER: Pastor of Baptist churches in Hazardville, CT, 1961-64, Jamaica Plain, MA, 1964-67, and New Bedford, MA, 1967-71; Bethel College, St. Paul, MN, professor of philosophy, 1972—. St. Petersburg State University (Russia), visiting professor, 1992-93; St. Petersburg Christian College, adjunct professor, 1993.

WRITINGS:

The Greater-Good Defence: An Essay on the Rationality of Faith, St. Martin's, 1992.

(General editor) *Sovremen'iy Problev'i Filosofii Religii* (title means "Contemporary Issues in Philosophy of Religion"), Progress Press (Moscow), 1994.

WORK IN PROGRESS: Editing *Contemporary Philosophy of Religion,* with Paul Reasoner; editing *Contemporary Epistemology and Metaphysics,* with Alan Padgett; editing *The Symposium of Chinese-American Philosophy and Religious Studies,* with Zhang Zhigang.

SIDELIGHTS: Melville Y. Stewart told *CA:* "My year in Russia, and a visit to China to teach and lecture at various universities, made it clear to me that anthologies in philosophy were needed in both Russian and Chinese. This led me to the companion-translation concept, and I am presently working on several volumes in philosophy, which will appear in English, Russian, and Chinese."

* * *

STOKES, Gale   1933-

PERSONAL: Born September 5, 1933, in Orange, NJ; son of Howard Gale (in advertising) and Ida Jane (a homemaker; maiden name, Bassett) Stokes; married Roberta Black (an artist), April 5, 1958; children: John Gale, Karen Elizabeth. *Education:* Colgate University, B.A., 1954; Indiana University, M.A., 1965, Ph.D., 1970. *Politics:* Liberal Democrat. *Religion:* Unitarian. *Avocational interests:* Folkdancing, vintage dancing.

ADDRESSES: Home—3746 Georgetown, Houston, TX 77005. *Office*—History Dept., MS42, Rice University, Houston, TX 77251. *Agent*—Keppler Associates, 4350 North Fairfax Dr., Suite 700, Arlington, VA 22203.

CAREER: Rice University, Houston, TX, began as instructor, became professor of history of Eastern Europe, 1968—, chair of department, 1980-82. Public lecturer on Yugoslavia and Eastern Europe, 1990—. American Council of Learned Societies and the Social Science Research Council (joint committee on Eastern Europe), chair, 1986-89; Woodrow Wilson Center, fellow, 1990-91; George Washington University, fellow, 1991. *Military service:* U.S. Air Force, 1954-63, attained rank of captain.

MEMBER: Institute for Sino Soviet Studies.

AWARDS, HONORS: George R. Brown Award for superior teaching, Rice University, 1989, 1990, and 1993; Vucinich Prize for the best book in the field of Russian, Eurasian, and East European Studies, American Association for the Advancement of Slavic Studies, 1993; numerous academic awards and grants.

WRITINGS:

Legitimacy through Liberalism: Vladimir Jovanovic and the Transformation of Serbian Politics, University of Washington Press (Seattle), 1975.

(Editor) *Nationalism in the Balkans: An Annotated Bibliography,* Garland (New York), 1984.

(Co-editor, with Bela Kiraly) *War, Insurrection, and the Eastern Crisis, 1875-78,* East European Monographs (Boulder, CO), 1985.

Politics as Development: The Emergence of Political Parties in Nineteenth-Century Serbia, Duke University Press (Durham, NC), 1990.

From Stalinism to Pluralism: A Documentary History of Eastern Europe since 1945, Oxford University Press (New York), 1991.

The Walls Came Tumbling Down: The Collapse of Communism in Eastern Europe, Oxford University Press (New York), 1993.

Contributor to journals, including *American Historical Review, Eastern European Politics and Societies, Journal of Modern History, Journal of Interdisciplinary History, Slavic Review,* and *Social Research.* Member of editorial boards for *Eastern European Politics and Societies, Slavic Review,* and *Problems in Post-Communism.*

WORK IN PROGRESS: A European history textbook for D.C. Heath; research into post-1989 Eastern Europe, the Yugoslav crisis, and nationalism.

SIDELIGHTS: Stokes told *CA:* "I am a specialist in the history of Eastern Europe. When I graduated from college my mother gave me a present of a trip to Europe on the condition I go with The Experiment in International Living (now World Learning), which provided for home stays. I chose to go to Yugoslavia, staying in Ljubljana (now Slovenia). Entering the United States Air Force to fly B-52s as a navigator, I kept up my interest in the Balkans, so that when I finally decided to resign to attend graduate school, I chose to pursue that interest. At first I wished to avoid any contact with policy issues and took a real delight in the obscurity of my specialized subject: nineteenth century Serbian politics, on which I wrote two books. In the mid-1980s,

however, when I joined a national committee that promoted scholarship on Eastern Europe I met a number of people in other fields and became intrigued by what seemed to be basic changes taking place in the region, particularly in Poland and Hungary. Early in 1989 I signed a contract with Oxford University Press to produce a documentary history of the region after 1945, and while working on that book it occurred to me that a monograph on what I called at that time 'The New Pluralism' in Eastern Europe would be useful. In September, 1989, I proposed such a book and initiated several grant proposals. With the collapse of the Berlin Wall, not only did Oxford offer me a contract, but I received several grants that permitted me to take two years of leave to write *The Walls Came Tumbling Down: The Collapse of Communism in Eastern Europe.*

"For me the most enjoyable part of the writing process is research. As a historian I greatly enjoy coming in visceral, palpable contact with the documents that living human beings touched and cared about in the past. To puzzle out their concerns, their passions, and their satisfactions, as well as their failures, their foibles, and their bullheadedness, gives me the sensation of being an integral part of the great human adventure. The most satisfying aspect of being a historian is the sudden sense of enlightenment you get when you realize how things fit together, or at least how you intend to project meaning by putting things together in your own way. And then the hardest part: transmitting this sensation to the reader.

"I am still in contact with the friend I made in Ljubljana in 1954. The interests that contact generated—made possible by my mother's thoughtfulness—continues to shape my professional life."

*   *   *

STOLTENBERG, John (Vincent)   1944-

PERSONAL: Born June 7, 1944, in Minneapolis, MN; son of Vincent G. (a tool engineer) and Margaret D. (a secretary; maiden name, Horstmann) Stoltenberg; life partner of Andrea Dworkin (a writer). *Education:* St. Olaf College, B.A., 1966; Union Theological Seminary, M.Div., 1969; Columbia University, M.F.A., 1972. *Politics:* "Radical feminist."

ADDRESSES: Agent—Elaine Markson Literary Agency, 44 Greenwich Ave., New York, NY 10011; (lecture) Program Corporation of America, 599 West Hartsdale Ave., White Plains, NY 10607.

CAREER: Writer. The Open Theatre, New York City, administrative director and writer-in-residence, 1971-74; *Essence,* New York City, managing editor, 1980-85; *Working Woman,* New York City, consulting and project development editor, 1985-87; *Lear's,* New York City, managing editor, 1988-91; *On the Issues* magazine, New York City, special projects advisor, 1993-94, executive editor, 1994—. New School of Social Research, New York City, instructor, 1991. Speaker and leader of workshops at universities and conferences across the U.S.; has made numerous appearances on television talk shows, including *Donahue* and *Geraldo,* and on radio programs. Cofounder of *Men against Pornography,* 1983.

MEMBER: PEN, Authors Guild.

AWARDS, HONORS: Danforth graduate fellowship, 1966; Rockefeller theological fellowship, 1966; New York State creative arts public service fellowship in playwriting, 1974.

WRITINGS:

Refusing to Be a Man: Essays on Sex and Justice, Breitenbush (Portland, OR), 1989, reprinted, Meridian (Utica, NY), 1990.
The End of Manhood: A Book for Men of Conscience, Dutton (New York), 1993.
What Makes Pornography "Sexy?", Milkweed Editions, 1994.

Author of several plays. Contributor to anthologies, including *For Men against Sexism: A Book of Readings,* edited by Jon Snodgrass, Times Change Press, 1977; *Against Sadomasochism: A Radical Feminist Analysis,* edited by Robin Ruth Linden, et al., Frog in the Well, 1982; *Men Confront Pornography,* edited by Michael S. Kimmel, Crown, 1990; *Pornography: Women, Violence, and Civil Liberties,* edited by Catherine Itzin, Oxford, 1992; *Against the Tide: A Documentary History of Profeminist Men in the United States,* edited by Michael S. Kimmel and Thomas E. Mosmiller, Beacon, 1992; *Transforming a Rape Culture,* edited by Emilie Buchwald, et al., Milkweed Editions, 1993; *Making Violence Sexy: Feminist Views on Pornography,* edited by Diana E. H. Russell, Teachers College Press, 1993. Contributor to periodicals, including *Changing Man* and *On the Issues.*

WORK IN PROGRESS: Goners, a novel; a sequel to *Goners;* "a rock/rap opera."

SIDELIGHTS: John Stoltenberg is a former playwright who has devoted himself increasingly to radi-

cal feminism. Stoltenberg summarizes his "central philosophical project" in both *Refusing to Be a Man* and *The End of Manhood* as being "to clarify that gender is an ethical category, not a metaphysical one." In *Refusing to Be a Man,* which appeared in 1989, Stoltenberg argues that "male sexual identity is entirely a political and ethical construction . . . and masculinity has personal meaning only because certain acts, choices, and policies create it—with devastating consequences for human society," including rape, homophobia, pornography, battery, and men's control of women's reproduction. Also in *Refusing to Be a Man,* Stoltenberg goes on to contend that "precisely because that personal and social identity is constructed, we can refuse it, we can act against it, we can change. The core of our being can choose allegiance to justice instead." While a reviewer in *Publishers Weekly* stated that Stoltenberg "sometimes pushes his rhetoric to extremes"—seeking laws to allow women to sue makers of pornography, for example—Rita Mae Brown, writing in the *Los Angeles Times Book Review,* proclaimed *Refusing to Be a Man* "remarkable," and she added, "Stoltenberg has made a brave foray into the future."

Stoltenberg followed *Refusing to Be a Man* with the 1993 volume *The End of Manhood: A Book for Men of Conscience,* wherein he continued his criticism of conventional masculinity as destructive, even self-destructive, and, ultimately, inconsistent with notions of fairness and equality. Stoltenberg stresses the practical value of recognizing the difference between manhood and selfhood in one's everyday personal relationships—in love, sex, family, and friendships.

Stoltenberg told *CA:* "What brought me into a radical-feminist way of looking at things most profoundly was having felt different from men all my life. It was radical feminism that said to me, 'The whole gender-identity trap is a construct, and it's a setup that has to do with the power of men over women.' I felt then that I could relax, that I could honor the difference between myself and this fictitious sex class. And I found a new kind of personal strength.

"Over many years that strength grew as I found a form for my anger against what men were doing to women. I knew that those men were doing something to me too, because their hatred of everything feminine was killing off something in me that I valued. In a sense my personal connection to feminism came through a struggle for a selfhood that wasn't measured against a standard of masculinity, a selfhood that wasn't scared of the parts of myself that were too 'unmanly,' a self that could own those parts and at the same time confront the things men had done in the world that were damaging to women and that were also leaving no safe space for the self I wanted to be. Through radical feminism, I understood this had to mean challenging men's power over women.

"The kind of sexual connection that I wanted with people was always about fairness and justice. I always thought that was the sexiest part of sex—the deepest possible feeling between two people. When I began to see how pornography is the sexualization of dominance and submission, that resonated in a very personal way for me too, because I had always thought that dominance was the way men had sex; I had always thought that dominance was what I was supposed to *do* in sex. Men *had* to be dominant, the all-powerful sexual conquerer. Well, I never got very good at that, and I always felt like sort of a failure.

"When I started hearing from woman friends who had been battered, from women who had been raped, it was very upsetting—and it still is. And I started paying attention to what a lot of men were doing in sex, and through sex. A lot of men's sexuality gets twisted into a very hostile shape, such that animosity is a precondition for sexual feelings—for example, a man who can beat his wife or girlfriend and then want to have sex with her right after, for whom violence is like foreplay.

"I feel I become a better self to the extent that I actively work to end the setup of men's sexual domination over women. When I'm really centered in that self, it's as if my selfhood doesn't have a gender. I know that in the world I'm a man, but I feel that my life course is really a refusal to be a man. I'm in opposition to the very existence of manhood because the only way to belong to it is by putting down women. And I'm on a life course to take apart the sex-class system so that no one would want to belong to the phoney category 'real men' anymore."

BIOGRAPHICAL/CRITICAL SOURCES:

BOOKS

Stoltenberg, John, *Refusing to Be a Man: Essays on Sex and Justice,* Breitenbush (Portland, OR), 1989, reprinted, Meridian (Utica, NY), 1990.

PERIODICALS

Los Angeles Times Book Review, October 22, 1989, p. 4.

Publishers Weekly, April 7, 1989, p. 122; September 6, 1993, p. 78.

*   *   *

STOOPS, Erik D. 1966-

PERSONAL: Born November 18, 1966, in Cleveland, OH; son of Sherrie L. Stoops (an author). *Education:* Attended Scottsdale College and Phoenix College; Arizona State University, B.S., 1991, master's degree candidate. *Politics:* Republican. *Religion:* Jewish.

ADDRESSES: Home—c/o 7123 North 11th Dr., Phoenix, AZ 85023.

CAREER: Metro Discovery Center, Phoenix, AZ, Living Treasures zoological center, vice-president of education center, 1989-93, museum director and curator of reptiles, 1990-92. Public speaker at schools for Outreach programs.

MEMBER: American Zoological Parks and Aquariums, Society of Children's Book Writers and Illustrators.

WRITINGS:

JUVENILE

(With Annette T. Wright) *Snakes,* Sterling, 1992.
(With mother, Sherrie L. Stoops) *Sharks,* illustrated by Jeffrey L. Martin, Sterling, 1994.
(With Jeffrey L. Martin and Debbie Lynne Stone) *Dolphins,* Sterling, 1994.
(With Martin and Stone) *Whales,* Sterling, 1994.
Penguins & Seals (CD-ROM), Emerging Technology Consultants, 1994.

OTHER

(With Wright) *Snakes and Other Reptiles of the Southwest,* Golden West, 1991.
(With Wright) *Breeding Boas/Pythons,* TFH, 1992.
Poisonous Animals of the Desert, Golden West, 1993.
(With Martin) *Poisonous Insects of the Desert,* Golden West, 1994.

WORK IN PROGRESS: Continuing a nature series for Sterling, to include forthcoming book *Alligators and Crocodiles.*

SIDELIGHTS: Erik D. Stoops is a specialist in herpetology, the study of reptiles and amphibians. In addition to writing articles and books on snakes, he is an expert in the care of boas and pythons in captivity, and he has bred and raised them and many other species of reptiles. His book *Snakes* is the first in a series of nature books dealing with many animal species.

Stoops works closely with registered nurse Annette T. Wright, coauthor of *Snakes,* in propagating certain reptiles that may be challenging to breed, especially endangered species. Together, they strive to protect wildlife, working with zoological agencies nationwide and even volunteering their own facilities as a holding or rehabilitation center.

Stoops's primary goal is to educate children about reptiles and their significance to the wildlife community. For two years, he worked at the Metro Discovery Center Children's Museum, where he curated the "Discover Living Treasures" exhibit about reptiles and wrote articles for the museum's educational programs. In addition, he is involved with the Phoenix chapter of the Boy Scouts, helping them earn merit badges by teaching them about wildlife conservation and proper care of neonates (newly born reptiles). With Wright, he conducts seminars that include hands-on contact with live animals.

*　　*　　*

STOREY, Dee
See STOREY, Denise Carol

*　　*　　*

STOREY, Denise Carol 1950-
(Dee Storey)

PERSONAL: Born July 1, 1950, in Grand Haven, MI; daughter of Richard W. (a veterinarian and sculptor) and Dolores (a psychologist) Storey. *Education:* Attended Albion College, 1968-70; Michigan State University, B.A., 1972, M.A., 1974, Ph.D., 1977. *Religion:* Jewish. *Avocational interests:* Quilting, reading.

ADDRESSES: Home—1945 Harry St., Saginaw, MI 48602. *Office*—College of Education, 238 Wickes Hall, Saginaw Valley State University, University Center, MI 48602.

CAREER: Teacher at an elementary school in Fruitport, MI, 1973; Michigan State University, East Lansing, instructor in continuing education, 1975-78; University of Nebraska—Lincoln, assistant professor at Center for Curriculum and Instruction, 1978-85; Marycrest College, Davenport, IA, assis-

tant professor of education, 1986-87; Saginaw Valley State University, University Center, MI, associate professor of children's literature, language arts, and reading, 1987—, coordinator of elementary education curriculum, 1989—. Substitute teacher at public schools in Lincoln, NE, and Muskegon, MI; Ticawa Reading Camp, reading instructor, summers, 1972-73. Storyteller and workshop presenter; Nebraska Golden Sower Award, co-initiator, 1980, director, 1981-85; Nebraska Children's Book Award, cofounder.

MEMBER: International Reading Association, National Council of Teachers of English, National Council for Social Studies.

WRITINGS:

UNDER NAME DEE STOREY

Twins in Children's and Adolescent Literature: An Annotated Bibliography, Scarecrow, 1993.

Contributor of articles and reviews to academic journals and a quilting magazine. Editor of the newsletter *Dragonlode,* 1981-84.

WORK IN PROGRESS: Adolescent Literature Presented in Diverse Formats, a reference book for teachers; research on censorship.

SIDELIGHTS: Dee Storey told *CA:* "When I was a child, I read books about girls who attended boarding school (I desperately wanted to live with them) and devoured mysteries. I am embarrassed to say that I read every Nancy Drew book that I could find. I was impressed that she had chums, drove a roadster, went to luncheon; she was brighter and braver than her father. My favorite books when I was a child were *The Secret Garden* and *Jane Eyre.* As an adult, I still prefer mysteries.

"When I was a second-grade teacher in Fruitport, Michigan, I needed to take graduate courses in order to keep my teaching certificate up to date. I was re-introduced to the wonderful world of children's literature. I had originally intended to be a reading teacher; however, I changed my major and received a doctorate in children's and adolescent literature. I must own over a thousand children's books. One room in my house is wall-to-wall books!

"I started writing my reference books on twins in literature because everyone thought my sister, who was pregnant with her second child, would have twins. Although she did not, I continued to read about twins. I located about three-hundred-fifty books about twins, and books about characters who wanted to be twins. I wrote to many of their authors, asking if they were twins and why they wrote about twins. Many took time to write and explain their motives. I am indebted to their input, because these comments personalized my reference book.

"I am now working on another annotated bibliography, this time about books written in diary, journal, letter, or alternating-narrator style. I have always been intensely interested in *The Diary of Anne Frank,* and I wondered if there were fictional counterparts. I have found that some authors are so convincing when they write fictional diaries that the characters seem real.

"Aside from teaching children's literature, I make several storytelling presentations at local schools during the school year. I love the imagination that it takes to be a teller of and listener to stories.

"I am very interested in problems related to censorship. As an author and a reader, I feel enraged when people are denied the right to read. I was brought up to believe that no one can take away your thoughts, and reading is an open window to the world. I have written articles and given speeches about issues related to censorship.

"I am also a cat lover! My cat Meg is named after a character in *Little Women.* She is not a patient reader, and will frequently crawl under or over a book I am reading in order to distract me. She loves climbing the bookshelves. When I am finished with a manuscript, I put it in a box to keep it in order; Meg frequently naps on the freshly printed manuscript! She is a wonderful companion, even if she doesn't like reading!"

*   *   *

STOWE, Cynthia   1944-

PERSONAL: Born September 7, 1944, in New Britain, CT; married Robert Stowe (a minister and director of a senior center), February 22, 1980. *Education:* University of Connecticut, B.A., 1966; University of Hartford, M.Ed., 1970. *Avocational interests:* Swimming and quiltmaking.

ADDRESSES: Agent—Liza Voges, Kirchoff Wohlberg, Inc., 866 United Nations Plaza, New York, NY 10017.

CAREER: Board of Education, New Britain, CT, school psychologist, 1969-74; Rescue, Litchfield, CT, school psychologist, 1974-78; Northwest Regional Center, Torrington, CT, psychologist, 1979; Project Aware, Bath, ME, coordinator/teacher, 1980-81; Linden Hill, Northfield, MA, special education teacher, 1982-88; board of education psychologist, Greenfield, MA, 1988-89; board of education special education teacher, Shutesbury, MA, 1989-91; writer, 1991—.

MEMBER: Society of Children's Book Writers and Illustrators.

WRITINGS:

Home Sweet Home, Good-bye, Scholastic, 1990.
Dear Mom, in Ohio for a Year, Scholastic, 1992.
Not So Normal, Norman, A. Whitman, 1994.

WORK IN PROGRESS: Continuing work on realistic, contemporary middle grade novels; fantasy and historical fiction; early chapter books, books for third and fourth graders, picture books, and adaptations of folk tales.

SIDELIGHTS: Cynthia Stowe commented: "I discovered my fascination with writing after I was forced to rest following surgery. Not able to work for a time, I took an oil painting class. My teacher told me to just keep painting, to let my creative self emerge. One day, when I was expressing dissatisfaction with my work, my teacher said, 'Take a week off from painting. Go home and write.' 'Write?' I asked. 'Why would I want to write?'

"I did, however, follow his advice. I remember the place where I first took up pencil and pad. On that day, I discovered that my creative self was a writer, and I have been seriously working every since.

"In my 'other' professional life, I have worked as a school psychologist and a special education teacher. Mostly, I've worked with people who have challenges in their lives. They've come in all ages and sizes, from preschoolers to adults. These people are represented in my books. I try to present them with the courage and honesty and, often, great senses of humor that so many of them possess.

"Many of my books deal with regular people in contemporary life. Humor is a big part of my work, because I feel that we can look at issues with humor that we might shy away from otherwise. I hope that kids who are dealing with major issues, such as the divorce of their parents, will read my books and feel a little less alone. I hope that all kids will gain understanding of others."

BIOGRAPHICAL/CRITICAL SOURCES:

PERIODICALS

Booklist, April 1, 1990, p. 1560; November 15, 1992, p. 599.
Bulletin of the Center for Children's Books, January, 1993, p. 158.
Childhood Education, winter, 1990, p. 119.
Children's Book Review Service, April, 1990, p. 107; winter, 1993, p. 72.
Children's Book Watch, October, 1992, p. 5.
Horn Book, January, 1990, p. 246.
Journal of Reading, October, 1990, p. 154.
Kirkus Reviews, February 15, 1990, p. 271.
Library Talk, September, 1990, p. 34.
Publishers Weekly, September 21, 1992, p. 95.
School Library Journal, April, 1990, p. 126; March, 1993, p. 202.
Voice of Youth Advocates, June, 1990, p. 100; April, 1993, p. 30.
Wilson Library Bulletin, September, 1990, p. 12.

*   *   *

STRAHINICH, H. C.
See STRAHINICH, Helen C.

*   *   *

STRAHINICH, Helen C. 1949-
(H. C. Strahinich)

PERSONAL: Surname is pronounced "Stra-nich"; born March 11, 1949, in Columbus, OH; daughter of Herbert (in business and a teacher) and Helene (in sales; maiden name, Goodman) Cummins; married John James Strahinich (a journalist), April 20, 1979; children: Nichola Montana. *Education:* Brandeis University, B.A. (cum laude), 1972; Harvard University, M.Ed., 1976.

ADDRESSES: Home and office—32 Southbourne Rd., Jamaica Plain, MA 02130.

CAREER: Jamaica Plain High School, Boston, MA, special needs teacher, 1974-76; Belmont High School, Belmont, MA, learning disabilities specialist, 1976-77; Boston Center for Adult Education, Boston, teacher, 1977; University of Lowell, Lowell, MA, instructor, summer, 1977; The Reading Institute, Boston, supervisor and reading specialist, 1977-79; Holt, Rinehart, and Winston, New York City, textbook editor, 1979-80; freelance writer, 1980—.

WRITINGS:

Guns in America, Walker & Co., 1992.

Selector and adaptor of stories for *Sounds of Our Heritage* series, Holt, 1979-80; author of teacher's manual and skills component for *Scope English Anthology* series, Scholastic, 1982. Author, editor, and revisionist of materials for teachers and students, grades kindergarten through adult education courses, for numerous companies, including Economy Company, D.C. Heath, Houghton Mifflin, Silver Burdette and Ginn, First Teacher, Harcourt, Psych Corp., Scott Foresman, Macmillan, and Charles Merrill. Contributor to periodicals, including *Boston Herald* and *Middlesex News.*

WORK IN PROGRESS: A murder mystery (adult); an historical novel (young adult); a coming-of-age novel (young adult); and numerous short stories and picture books.

SIDELIGHTS: "I guess I'm a late bloomer," Helen C. Strahinich commented. "Nobody ever told me I was born to write, and it took me thirty years to find out.

"Through my twenties, I taught different subjects in different schools in Boston. I usually got bored with a job after a few years. One thing I never tired of, however, was writing materials to help my students become better readers and writers. When I moved to New York City, I stopped teaching and took a job as a textbook editor at Holt, Rinehart, and Winston.

"At this time, I was also learning what it takes to become a writer by watching my husband. He was struggling to start a career in journalism. I discovered that it takes more than raw talent to make a writer. It also takes determination and sweat—lots of sweat.

"On my first project at Holt, I worked on a new folklore series for elementary schools—*Sounds of Our Heritage.* I collected and edited folk tales, poems, stories, articles, and photographs from different regions of the United States. I also got to write short articles for a few of these books, my first shot at professional writing.

"When I returned to Boston (where my husband landed his first job as a reporter), I became a freelancer—a self-employed writer and editor, mostly for different textbook publishers—which is what I've been doing ever since. Two great things about freelancing are freedom and variety. A third great thing is getting paid to write. I've written everything from video scripts to biology articles to science fiction stories. I've carved out time to write a book of nonfiction (*Guns in America*), to have a baby (my daughter Nicky), and to buy and remodel a house (in Jamaica Plain, Massachusetts). I've also done a stint as a journalist writing about family issues, children's entertainment, and children's books.

"Every morning I get up at 5:45 to work on special projects, such as *Guns in America*. I like early mornings when the house is quiet and my mind is fresh and uncluttered. During this time I also write fiction: novels, short stories, and children's books.

"I joined a writers group four years ago. We read and critique one another's stories and poetry. I find it helpful to give and get feedback about writing that may not be published right away. When I rewrite and revise this work I have my friends' ideas as well as my own to think about."

*   *   *

STRONACH, Bruce   1950-

PERSONAL: Born August 24, 1950; son of Walter Thomas (a farmer and federal agricultural inspector) and Virginia Kathleen (an artist and homemaker; maiden name, LeVarn) Stronach; children: Tomoko, Mariko, Eriko. *Education:* Attended Boston University, 1968-69; Keene State College, B.A. (cum laude), 1974; Tufts University, Fletcher School of Law and Diplomacy, M.A., M.A.L.D., 1976, Ph.D., 1980. *Politics:* Independent. *Religion:* Independent. *Avocational interests:* Golf, rugby, climbing, skiing, piano.

ADDRESSES: Home and office—Graduate School of International Relations, International University of Japan, Yamato-machi, Niigata-ken 949-72, Japan.

CAREER: Keio University, Tokyo, Japan, visiting lecturer and visiting scholar at International Center and Center for Communications Research, 1976-85; Merrimack College, North Andover, MA, assistant professor, 1985-90, associate professor and associate dean, 1990-94; International University of Japan, professor and dean of Graduate School of International Relations, 1994—. Ward mayor of Yamato-machi, Niigata-ken.

MEMBER: Association for Asian Studies.

WRITINGS:

Japan and America: Opposites That Attract, Seibido (Tokyo), 1988.

(Editor with Richard Powers and Hidetoshi Kato) *The Handbook of Japanese Popular Culture,* Greenwood Press, 1989.
Popular Culture in Japan and America, Seibido, 1991.
(With Curtis H. Martin) *Politics East and West: A Comparison of Japanese and British Political Culture,* M. E. Sharpe, 1993.
Beyond the Rising Sun: Nationalism in Contemporary Japan, Praeger, 1994.

WORK IN PROGRESS: Giving It Up, a novel; research on Japanese political attitudes and U.S.-Japanese relations, especially the interdependencies of these relations.

SIDELIGHTS: Bruce Stronach told *CA:* "I was raised in rural Maine and have lived most of the past eighteen years of my life in Japan. The combination of my experiences in these two most dissimilar cultures has affected both my outlook on life and the subject matter about which I write. My main motivation for writing is to inform the American public about Japan and its relationship with the United States. Having been an academic and university administrator for many years, much of my writing has been for an academic audience, but I strive in both my academic and journalistic writing to reach a much broader and general audience. There is a large gap between what is known by academics about Japan and the way in which Japan is portrayed in the mass media. It is important that academics reach the general public in order to keep people better informed. An academic who writes only for other academics soon loses touch with reality."

*   *   *

STRONGE, James H.   1945-

PERSONAL: Born October 14, 1945, in Birmingham, AL; son of Harold and Birdie Stronge; married Teresa Sellers, May 28, 1971; two children. *Education:* University of Alabama, Birmingham, B.S., 1974, M.A., 1976; University of Alabama, Tuscaloosa, Ph.D., 1983.

ADDRESSES: Office—School of Education, College of William and Mary, P.O. Box 8795, Williamsburg, VA 23187-8795.

CAREER: High school history teacher in Fairfield, AL, 1974-77, guidance counselor, 1976-77, special education coordinator, 1977-78, central office administrator, 1978-83; Bradley University, Peoria, IL, assistant professor, 1983-87, associate professor of educational administration, 1987-89, director of Institute for Gifted and Talented Youth, 1986-88, director of Center for Research and Service, 1986-89; College of William and Mary, Williamsburg, VA, associate professor of educational administration, 1989—.

MEMBER: American Educational Research Association, National Council of Professors of Educational Administration, Phi Delta Kappa.

AWARDS, HONORS: Fellow of Lilly Endowment, 1987-89; Book of the Year Award from American Library Association, 1994, for *Educating Homeless Children and Adolescents.*

WRITINGS:

Evaluation of Ancillary School Personnel Training Manual, Illinois State Board of Education, 1988.
Ancillary School Personnel: An Evaluation Model (monograph), Illinois State Board of Education, 1988.
(With V. Helm) *Evaluation of Professional Support Personnel in Education,* Sage Publications, 1991.
(With C. Tenhouse) *Educating Homeless Children and Youth: Issues and Answers* (monograph), Phi Delta Kappa, 1990.
(Editor and contributor) *Educating Homeless Children and Adolescents: Evaluating Policy and Practice,* Sage Publications, 1992.

Contributor of more than thirty articles to education journals. Guest editor, *Education and Urban Society,* 1993, and *Journal of Personnel Evaluation in Education,* 1995.

BIOGRAPHICAL/CRITICAL SOURCES:

PERIODICALS

USA Today, March 9, 1993, p. 1D.

*   *   *

SUM, Ngai-Ling   1952-

PERSONAL: Born December 7, 1952; daughter of Chai Cheong (a civil servant) and Mo Kwan (a homemaker; maiden name, Lo) Sum; married Bob Jessop (a professor), February 17, 1992. *Education:* University of Birmingham, B.S.S., 1975; University of Hong Kong, M.A., 1979, M.Ed., 1985, M.S.S., 1989; University of Lancaster, Ph.D., 1994.

ADDRESSES: Home—7A Castle Hill, Lancaster LA1 4YS, England. *Office*—Department of Sociology, University of Lancaster, Bailrigg, Lancaster LA1 4YL, England.

CAREER: Panel chairperson for a girls' school in Hong Kong, 1976-89; City Polytechnic of Hong Kong, Hong Kong, part-time lecturer, 1988-92; University of Sheffield, Sheffield, England, research fellow, 1994-97.

AWARDS, HONORS: Wingate scholar in London, 1994.

WRITINGS:

(Co-author) *Historical Dictionary of Hong Kong and Macau,* Scarecrow, 1991.

WORK IN PROGRESS: Research on the political economy of Hong Kong and East Asia; research on "greater China" as a regional unit.

*   *   *

SUNDAHL, Daniel James   1947-

PERSONAL: Born February 14, 1947; son of Jesse C. and Eileen A. Sundahl; married Ellen F. Donohoe (an executive assistant), August 8, 1975. *Education:* Gustavus Adolphus College, B.A., 1972; Northern Arizona University, B.A., 1973; University of Utah, M.A., 1977, Ph.D., 1982. *Politics:* "Traditional conservative." *Religion:* Lutheran. *Avocational interests:* Fly fishing.

ADDRESSES: Home—2220 North Lake Wilson Rd., Hillsdale, MI 49242. *Office*—Hillsdale College, Hillsdale, MI 49242.

CAREER: Hillsdale College, Hillsdale, MI, Russell Amos Kirk Professor of English and American Studies and director of American studies program, 1983—.

MEMBER: Modern Language Association of America, American Studies Association, National Association of Scholars, Michigan Association of Scholars.

AWARDS, HONORS: Gwendolyn Brooks Prize, 1992.

WRITINGS:

Loss of Habitat, Edwin Mellen, 1993.
Hiroshima Maidens: Imaginary Translations From the Japanese, Edwin Mellen, 1994.

WORK IN PROGRESS: The Small Logics, poems; *The Art of Figuring Synthetically,* a study of Henry James.

SIDELIGHTS: Daniel James Sundahl told *CA:* "I'm from a small town in southwestern Minnesota. I grew up in farming country, grass roots, Scandinavian. My grandfather was a Norwegian homesteader; my other grandfather owned a print shop. I enjoy open spaces, independence, some solitude, but not too much. I learned early that there is nothing in nature that can't be taken as a sign of both mortality and invigoration.

"When I was still at an early age, my Norwegian homesteader grandfather would read me passages from Norwegian sagas; my other grandfather would let me help him set type. I learned to read backwards, as it were.

"My own father, many years ago, advised me to keep life simple. That's not easy when one's outlook is saga-like and epic. Still, I believe in the unbought grace of life, as Edmund Burke said, and find it all around me. Writing is its spiritual equivalent.

"I am now in my forties; it is ripeness, I tell my wife. I work daily on my teaching, book reviews, some essays, some poems. I've foundered into a good life, with good friends, a good bit of work, good students, a home in the country. I've fished the Big Two-Heart in northern Michigan, and will do so again in summers yet to come. It is, as Hemingway knew, a good place."

* * *

SWANSON, David 1935-

PERSONAL: Born July 26, 1935, in Chicago, IL; son of Carl Paul and Evelyn Frances (Berg) Swanson. *Education:* Northwestern University, B.S., 1957. *Politics:* Independent. *Religion:* Congregationalist. *Avocational interests:* Travel (Asia, Europe, Australia, New Zealand).

ADDRESSES: Home and office—7235 West Wells St., Wauwatosa, WI 53213-3607.

CAREER: Manpower, Inc., Milwaukee, WI, director of corporate personnel, 1965-71; Jim Weller and Partners (advertising agency), Milwaukee, vice-president and account supervisor, 1971-73; Waukesha County Technical College, Pewaukee, WI, director of Career Center, 1973-82; Career Seminars, Milwaukee, owner and president, 1982—.

Advertising Ltd. (Milwaukee), owner and president, 1973-82. *Military service:* U.S. Navy, 1957-60.

MEMBER: National Speakers Association.

WRITINGS:

The Resume Solution: How to Write (and Use) a Resume That Gets Results, JIST Works, 1991.

SIDELIGHTS: David Swanson told *CA:* "I am a performer, and an assistant—a speaker first, by profession, but underneath, a performer; and I assist people in finding themselves. As a speaker, it is my intent to move people, from where they are, or from being stuck to where they either want to be, or should be, or can be. This is not motivation. Motivation is an interior, self-generated function. I can only seek to move people so that they might become self-motivated.

"It is my mission in life to do this and, especially, to move people who did not expect to be moved. I enjoy it thoroughly, and I confess to enjoying the gratitude directed my way from those who have been positively affected.

"I discovered this personal mission in 1977, and I have focused on working to that end ever since. Each summer, I am chief of staff for the international 'What Color Is Your Parachute?' workshop, offered by author Richard Nelson Bolles. I also speak annually at more than fifty colleges and universities in the United States, Canada, Europe, Asia, and Australia.

"I like movies, talk radio, news shows, haven't seen a sitcom in years other than *Mary Tyler Moore* or *All in the Family,* and read more than a hundred magazines each month, plus a pile of books."

* * *

SZYMANSKI, Leszek 1933-

PERSONAL: Surname is pronounced "Shi-*man*-ski"; born April 5, 1933, in Warsaw, Poland; son of Kazimierz (a telecommunications engineer) and Halina (Podgorska) Szymanski; married; wife's name, Marivick (a clerk), 1986; children: Jose (Jozef). *Education:* Polish University Abroad, Ph.D., 1975; University of London, B.A., 1978; California State University, M.A., 1986. *Politics:* "Progressive Conservatist." *Religion:* Unitarian-Universalist. *Avocational interests:* Sociology, politics, anthropology, travel, languages.

ADDRESSES: Agent—c/o Publicity Director, Hippocrene Books, Inc., 171 Madison Ave., New York, NY 10016.

CAREER: Writer. *Wspotczesnosc,* chief editor, 1956. Worked as security guard, doorman, and laborer.

AWARDS, HONORS: Short story award, Union of Polish Writers, 1956; award from Towanystwo Knewienie Noitrioji, 1978.

WRITINGS:

Escape to the Tropics, Parnasus (Sydney), 1960.
On the Wallaby Track, [London], 1965.
Naneczona, Kronika & Gwiazde Polarne, 1965.
Living with the Weird Mob, Trident, 1970.
Warsaw Aflame, Polpress, 1973.
Putaski Bohetar Niozmany, Wici, 1980.
Casimir Pulski: A Hero of the American Revolution, Hippocrene (New York), 1994.

T

TALLMOUNTAIN, Mary 1918-

PERSONAL: Born Mary Demoski, 1918, in Nulato, Alaskan Territory (now Alaska).

ADDRESSES: Home—241 Jones St., No. 7E, San Francisco, CA 94102.

CAREER: Writer. Worked as a legal secretary in San Francisco, CA.

WRITINGS:

There Is No Word for Goodbye, Blue Cloud Quarterly, 1981.
Continuum, Blue Cloud Quarterly, 1988.
A Light on the Tent Wall: A Bridging (poetry), introduction by Paula Gunn Allen, Native American Series No. 8, University of California-Los Angeles American Indian Studies Center, 1990.

Also author of the poetry collection *A Quick Brush of Wings,* 1991. Work represented in numerous anthologies, including *Earth Power Coming, The Remembered Earth,* and *That's What She Said: Contemporary Poetry and Fiction by Native American Women,* edited by Rayna Green, Indiana University Press, 1984.

SIDELIGHTS: The poetry of Mary TallMountain is rife with imagery and symbols drawn from her Athapascan heritage and childhood in rural Alaska. Collections of her work include 1981's *There Is No Word for Goodbye* and *Continuum,* published in 1988. TallMountain became a poet when she was in her fifties after working for many years as a legal secretary. The impetus to write came after striking up a friendship with Native American scholar and poet Paula Gunn Allen; for a year-and-a-half TallMountain wrote for sixteen hours a day and met with Allen weekly for tutoring. The result was a body of lyrical work that draws heavily upon her early years in an Alaskan village during the 1920s. Born of Athapascan, Russian, and Irish ancestry, TallMountain lived within view of Siberia and in her poetry often evokes her memories of the Yukon River. Yet the idyllic village existence was shattered when she was six; her mother contracted tuberculosis and the little girl was adopted by a non-Native family. In this new world TallMountain's schooling in the traditions of her Athapascan culture came to an end. The rest of her years were marked by tragedy: both her brothers died of tuberculosis, her natural father was unknown to her for six decades, her adoptive father died during the Depression after financial setbacks, and her adoptive mother committed suicide shortly after that. TallMountain herself suffered from bouts of depression for many years, compounded by a problem with alcoholism. When she began writing, she managed to reach back through all of those difficult years and recapture the magic of her childhood. In the introduction to TallMountain's work in *A Light on the Tent Wall: A Bridging,* Allen said of her: "If you know the land of her origins and the cadences of the People, if you recall the rhythm of Roman liturgy, the solemnity of the Mass, if you read this collection with care, hearing the eerie, powerful silences that surround the words, you will know who she is, what extinction is, and what survival engenders." TallMountain's other published works include 1991's *A Quick Brush of Wings* and a contribution to the 1984 anthology *That's What She Said: Contemporary Poetry and Fiction by Native American Women.*

BIOGRAPHICAL/CRITICAL SOURCES:

BOOKS

TallMountain, Mary, *A Light on the Tent Wall: A*

Bridging, introduction by Paula Gunn Allen, Native American Series No. 8, University of California-Los Angeles American Indian Studies Center, 1990.*

*   *   *

TARGETTI, Ferdinando   1945-

PERSONAL: Born July 1, 1945, in Como, Italy; son of Lodovico (an industrialist) and Anita (Cattania) Targetti; married Boguslawa Kinda (a bank employee), November 15, 1982. *Education:* Graduate of Bocconi University; also attended London School of Economics, London, Pembroke College, Cambridge, and New York University.

ADDRESSES: Home—Via Vigevano, 20144 Milan, Italy. *Office*—Department of Economics, University of Trento, Via Imama 1, 38100 Trento, Italy.

CAREER: Bocconi University, Milan, Italy, assistant, 1970-74, lecturer in economics, 1974-90; University of Trento, Trento, Italy, professor of economic policy, 1987—. Visiting professor at New York University, 1984, University of Paris XIII, 1991 and 1994, University of Brescia, University of Pavia, and Free University Institute of Castellanza; lecturer at universities in France, England, the United States, Spain, Poland, and Hungary. Credito Lombardo, vice-chairperson; Banca Agricola Milanese, past member of board of directors. Province of Milan, member of board of directors of Comercati 2000; Region of Lombardy, member of board of directors of Fiera Milano; Council House of Sesto San Giovanni, vice-chairperson of board of directors of Parco Scientifico per le Tecnologie Ambientali; Gramsci Foundation, member. *Military service:* Italian Air Force, 1968-69. Italian Air Force Reserve; present rank, lieutenant.

MEMBER: European Association of Comparative Economic Systems, AISSEC.

AWARDS, HONORS: St. Vincent Prize, best book in economics, 1989.

WRITINGS:

(Editor with A. P. Thirlwall) *The Essential Kaldor,* Duckworth, 1989.
(Editor with Thirlwall) *Further Essays on Economic Theory and Policy,* Duckworth, 1989.
Nicholas Kaldor: The Economics and Politics of Capitalism as a Dynamic System, Oxford University Press, 1992.

Privatization in Europe: West and East Experiences, Dartmouth Gower House, 1992.

UNTRANSLATED WORKS

Valore e accumulazione, Etas Libri (Milan), 1978.
(Editor and contributor) *Lezioni di economia: L'inflazione,* Feltrinelli, 1979.
L'intervento dello Stato per le maggiori scuole di pensiero economico, Unicopli-Universitaria (Milan), 1979.
(Editor) Nicholas Kaldor, *Occupazione, moneta e tassazione,* Einaudi (Turin), 1987.
(Editor with L. Marcolungo and M. Pugno) *L'economia mondiale in trasformazione,* F. Angeli, 1988.
(Editor) Kaldor, *Economia e politica di un capitalismo in mutamento,* Mulino (Bologna), 1988.

Work represented in anthologies. Contributor of more than a hundred articles and reviews to economic journals.

*   *   *

TAYLOR, Carl S.   1949-

PERSONAL: Born October 18, 1949. *Education:* Michigan State University, B.S. (with honors), 1971, M.A., 1976, Ph.D., 1980.

ADDRESSES: Office—Institute for Children, Youth, and Families, Michigan State University, 27 Kellogg Center, East Lansing, MI 48824.

CAREER: Centrax Diversified Services, Inc., Detroit, MI, manager, 1977-89; Jackson Community College, Jackson, MI, director of Department of Criminal Justice and Public Safety, 1989-90; Grand Valley State University, Allendale, MI, professor of criminal justice and director of Youth Culture Studies Center, 1991-94, clinical professor, 1994—. Michigan State University, assistant professor and adjunct assistant professor, 1984-90, professor and director of community youth development programs at Institute for Children, Youth, and Families, 1994—; University of Michigan, Ann Arbor, member of Public Health Think Tank on Substance Abuse, 1990; National Institute for Corrections, instructor, 1990-93; Federal Bureau of Investigation (FBI), guest lecturer at FBI academy, 1991, 1993. Starr Commonwealth Schools, Albion, MI, member of board of trustees, 1991—; Children's Defense Fund, member of Black Community Crusade for Children's Task Force on Violence, 1992—; Michigan Governor's Committee on Juvenile Justice, member, 1994—; consultant to National Institute of Justice.

MEMBER: American Society of Criminology, National Association of Police Chiefs, American Corrections Association, American Society for Industrial Security, Academy of Criminal Justice Sciences, Michigan Association of Police Chiefs, Michigan Law Enforcement Training Directors Association.

AWARDS, HONORS: Guggenheim grant, 1991.

WRITINGS:

Rock Concerts: A Parents' Guide, Centrax Diversified Services (Detroit), 1984.
Private Security Training Manual, Centrax Diversified Services, 1985.
Urban Gangs and Public Schools, National School Safety Program (Pepperdine, CA), 1987.
The Sociology and Distribution of Gangs, Pacific Research and Evaluation Institute (Rockford, MD), 1989.
Dangerous Society, Michigan State University Press (East Lansing), 1990.
Girls, Gangs, Women, and Drugs, Michigan State University Press, 1993.

Work represented in anthologies, including *Gangs in America,* edited by R. Huff, Sage Publications, 1990. Contributor to professional journals.

*   *   *

TAYLOR, Dave 1948-
(J. David Taylor, David Taylor)

PERSONAL: Born July 6, 1948, in Ottawa, Ontario, Canada; son of Wesley (a creator of greeting cards) and Edna (a homemaker; maiden name, McMartin) Taylor; married Anne MacPherson (a teacher), 1973; children: Liza, Ashley. *Education:* Received B.A., 1972; received teaching certification, 1972; received M.Ed., 1982.

ADDRESSES: Agent—Crabtree Publishing Co. Ltd., 350 5th Ave., Suite 3308, New York, NY 10118.

CAREER: Peel Board of Education, Mississauga, Ontario, Canada, teacher, 1972—.

WRITINGS:

SELF-ILLUSTRATED WITH PHOTOGRAPHS

(As David Taylor) *Sharks (Nature's Children),* Grolier, 1987.

(As J. David Taylor) *Game Animals of North America,* Discovery Books, 1988.
Ontario's Wildlife, Boston Mills Press, 1988.
(With McClung, Caldwell, and Maplesden) *Cycles I & II,* Prentice Hall, 1990.
(With McClung, Caldwell, and Maplesden) *Cycles I & II Teacher's Guide,* Prentice Hall, 1990.
(With Kettle) *The Fishing Book,* Boston Mills Press, 1990.
Safari: Journey to the End, Boston Mills Press, 1990.
The Alligator and the Everglades, Crabtree (New York), 1990.
The Bison and the Great Plains, Crabtree, 1990.
The Elephant and the Scrub Forest, Crabtree, 1990.
The Lion and the Savannah, Crabtree, 1990.
Endangered Forest Animals, Crabtree, 1992.
Endangered Grassland Animals, Crabtree, 1992.
Endangered Wetland Animals, Crabtree, 1992.
Endangered Mountain Animals, Crabtree, 1992.
Endangered Island Animals, Crabtree, 1993.
Endangered Ocean Animals, Crabtree, 1993.
Endangered Savannah Animals, Crabtree, 1993.
Endangered Desert Animals, Crabtree, 1993.

WORK IN PROGRESS: Books on bears and Algonquin Provincial Park, Ontario.

SIDELIGHTS: "I am a teacher first and foremost," Dave Taylor explained. "This desire on my part to help children and adults learn about their natural world is one of the main reasons why I write and illustrate books. I am also a classroom teacher and not surprisingly my subjects all include some aspect of science and outdoor education. My last teaching assignment was at the Britannia School Farm where I helped develop and implement a new program combining agriculture and environmental education. I have also worked as a science/social science consultant for my board of education. I began my teaching career in 1972 and have taught grades three through eight.

"I like to experience the things I write about and photography helps me to do this. Whether it is sitting in a blind watching ducks or following the wildebeest migration in Africa in a landcruiser, being there and seeing it helps me understand nature's complexity. While it is hard work it is also great fun.

"One of the questions I am often asked is 'Isn't it dangerous work?' Most of the time it is quite safe. After years of working with animals you get to a point where you can 'read' their behavior. However, I never take an animal for granted and always show them respect. Even so, I have been charged by moose, grizzlies, elephants, elk, and black bears. Fortunately, I did not panic and run and was literally able to talk my way out of it by speaking softly and backing slowly away to a point where the animal no longer considered me a danger.

"My family travels with me as often as we can afford it. Although I travel the world to do research, my favorite locations are the Southern and Western United States, Canada, and Alaska."

*   *   *

TAYLOR, David
See TAYLOR, Dave

*   *   *

TAYLOR, J. David
See TAYLOR, Dave

*   *   *

TAYLOR, Nick   1945-

PERSONAL: Born November 21, 1945, in Asheville, NC; son of John Puleston Wotton (a surveyor and draftsman) and Clare Eleanor (a newspaper reporter; maiden name, Unger) Taylor; married Charlotte Wise, 1969 (divorced, 1974); married Barbara Nevins (a television reporter), August 26, 1983. *Education:* Western Carolina University, B.A., 1967. *Politics:* Democrat. *Religion:* Episcopalian. *Avocational interests:* Sailing, tennis, travel, reading, listening.

ADDRESSES: Agent—Lynn Nesbit, Janklow and Nesbit Associates, 598 Madison Ave., New York, NY 10022.

CAREER: Newspaper and television reporter in Shelby, NC, Charlotte, NC, Dayton, OH, and Atlanta, GA, 1967-76; campaign worker for Jimmy Carter and for John Lewis, state of Georgia, 1976-80; writer, 1981—.

MEMBER: Authors Guild, PEN American Center.

WRITINGS:

Bass Wars: A Story of Fishing Fame and Fortune, McGraw (New York), 1987.
Sins of the Father: The True Story of a Family Running from the Mob, Simon & Schuster (New York), 1989.
Ordinary Miracles: Life in a Small Church, Simon & Schuster, 1993.

A Necessary End, Nan A. Talese/Doubleday (New York), 1994.
(With Yaron Svoray) *In Hitler's Shadow,* Nan A. Talese/Doubleday, 1994.

WORK IN PROGRESS: Raising Richie, the story of a foster child.

SIDELIGHTS: "Listening is what a nonfiction writer does," Nick Taylor told *CA.* The author of several nonfiction books, including *Bass Wars: A Story of Fishing Fame and Fortune, Sins of the Father: The True Story of a Family Running from the Mob,* and *A Necessary End,* Taylor went on to explain that a writer "has to listen well, not only for the information that's necessary to the book, but for what lies underneath it, the hope and ambition, sorrow and disappointment, pain and joy that make characters human and bring them alive." In composing *Sins of the Father,* Taylor called upon this ability to deliver the story of Salvatore Polisi, a drug dealer who entered a federal witness-protection program to avoid a prison sentence. Polisi, a career criminal, is described by A. M. Pyle in the *Chicago Tribune* as "a horrible little man" who nonetheless harbors a "passionate pride" for his athletic sons. It was Polisi's commitment to his family which compelled him to attempt an honest life—buying a go-kart course in upstate New York—but he eventually succumbed to the lucrative temptation of drug-dealing. Polisi's entry into the witness-protection program is the major underpinning of *Sins of the Father.* Pyle commented in the *Chicago Tribune* that "it is Taylor's depiction of the effect of that decision that is the book's great strength. For Polisi's choice, beyond making him a marked man among his old criminal associates, placed his entire family in a ghastly limbo."

Taylor's own commitment to family is reflected in his writing. He told *CA* that "the hardest listening I have done was when my parents were confined to nursing homes during the final months of their lives. It's a time recounted in *A Necessary End,* a memoir of my parents in their last years, of their deaths, and of my relationship with them during this time. This required patience and compassion, for which I was rewarded with far richer memories of my parents than I could have imagined. As I try to find in nonfiction an essence beyond reportage, the business of listening seems ever more essential."

BIOGRAPHICAL/CRITICAL SOURCES:

PERIODICALS

Chicago Tribune, October 2, 1989.

TAYLOR, Paul F. 1927-

PERSONAL: Born July 14, 1927, in Warm Springs, GA; son of V. F. W. (an attorney) and Clara (a social worker and homemaker; maiden name, Miller) Taylor; married Sue Ann Sutton (a homemaker), June 4, 1961; children: Larry F. *Education:* Attended Berea College; Eastern Kentucky State College, B.A., 1953; University of Kentucky, M.A., 1955, Ph.D., 1969. *Politics:* Republican. *Religion:* Protestant. *Avocational interests:* Sports, travel, hiking.

ADDRESSES: Home—925 Stonecase Ct., Lexington, KY 40509.

CAREER: Harlan County Board of Education, Harlan County, KY, teacher, 1946-47; Bell County Board of Education, Bell County, KY, teacher, 1949-51; De Kalb County Board of Education, De Kalb County, GA, teacher, 1955-59; Georgia Military Academy, College Park, GA, 1959-63; Augusta College, Augusta, GA, professor, 1967-94. Westminster School (Augusta, GA), board of directors, 1972-79. *Military service:* U.S. Army, private first class, 1951-53.

WRITINGS:

Bloody Harlan: The United Mine Workers of America in Harlan County, Kentucky, 1931-1941, University Press of America (Lanham, MD), 1990.
ABC-CLIO Companion to the American Labor Movement, ABC-CLIO (Santa Barbara, CA), 1993.

WORK IN PROGRESS: Manuscript on experiences as a one-room school teacher in Kentucky.

SIDELIGHTS: Paul F. Taylor told *CA:* "While at Augusta College I revised my Ph.D. dissertation which, in 1990, was published as *Bloody Harlan: The United Mine Workers of America in Harlan County, Kentucky, 1931-1941* by the University Press of America. Then ABC-CLIO, upon learning of *Bloody Harlan,* invited me to compile the *ABC-CLIO Companion to the American Labor Movement,* which was published in 1993."

Taylor added: "While I thoroughly enjoyed my teaching career, it became natural for me to study and write about American labor, especially since I grew up in the coal fields. Harlan County, Kentucky, was the last major coal-producing county in Appalachia to be unionized by the United Mine Workers of America. A decade-long struggle caused the county to become nationally known as 'bloody Harlan.' Because I lived in the area, I had a deep interest in the miners and their efforts to organize the union. Thus my two books on labor."

* * *

TAYLOR, William 1938-

PERSONAL: Born October 11, 1938, in Lower Hutt, Wellington, New Zealand; son of Alexander Ivan and Rosa Dorothea (Went) Taylor; married Delia Wellington, 1965 (divorced, 1976); children: Robin Alexander, Julian Alexander. *Education:* Attended Christchurch Teachers' College, New Zealand, 1957-58. *Avocational interests:* Reading, music, gardening, skiing, hunting.

ADDRESSES: Home—Kaitieke Rd., R.D. 2, Owhango, King Country, New Zealand.

CAREER: Primary school teacher in New Zealand, 1959-85; Ohakune School, Ohakune, New Zealand, principal, 1979-85; writer, 1985—. Mayor of Borough of Ohakune, New Zealand, 1981-88.

AWARDS, HONORS: Choysa Bursary for Children's Writers, 1984; Esther Glen Medal, New Zealand Library Association, 1991, for *Agnes the Sheep;* Inaugural Children's Writing Fellowship, Palmerston North College of Education, New Zealand, 1992; *Agnes the Sheep* and *Knitwits* were cited by the American Library Association (ALA) and the New York Public Library.

WRITINGS:

Pack up, Pick up, and Off, Price Milburn, 1981.
My Summer of the Lions, Reed Methuen, 1986.
Possum Perkins, Ashton Scholastic, 1986, published in the United States as *Paradise Lane,* Scholastic, 1987.
Shooting Through, Reed Methuen, 1986.
Break a Leg!, Reed Methuen, 1987.
Making Big Bucks, Reed Methuen, 1987.
The Worst Soccer Team Ever, Reed Methuen, 1987.
I Hate My Brother Maxwell Potter, Heinemann Reed, 1990.
The Kidnap of Jessie Parker, Heinemann Reed, 1990.
Agnes the Sheep, Ashton Scholastic, 1991.
The Porter Brothers, HarperCollins, 1991.
Beth and Bruno, Ashton Scholastic, 1992.
Fast Times at Greenhill High, Puffin, 1992.
Knitwits, Scholastic, 1992.
Supermum and Spike the Dog, HarperCollins, 1992.
S.W.A.T., HarperCollins, 1993.
The Blue Lawn, HarperCollins, 1994.

Some of Taylor's works have been translated into Danish and French.

WORK IN PROGRESS: Dimwits (tentative title), a sequel to *Knitwits,* for Scholastic; a humorous work for older readers.

SIDELIGHTS: "I grew up in rural New Zealand in the years immediately following World War II," William Taylor commented. "My family moved around a lot, and I was probably a fairly introverted child and adolescent. I have since made up for this! I am the eldest of four children, and we were blessed with loving, if somewhat feckless, parents. There was never much money. My father served for five years during the war in North Africa, the Middle East, and Europe. I didn't know him until I was seven years old. Our parents had wide interests in music, books, theater, and sports. As I get older I increasingly realize what a great debt I owe to them both. While it is true that I am what I have made of myself, the seeds of just whatever it is I have made, the beginnings, are right back there in my childhood and easily traceable to my mother and father."

After his rich and varied childhood, Taylor left home and school at age sixteen and began work in a bank. By the age of twenty-one he had become a teacher, a profession he continued for more than twenty-five years. When he retired from teaching to pursue a full-time career as a writer, Taylor reflected on his time spent in education and found that he had "loved every year." He also found plenty of inspiration. "In practical terms," he noted, "the immediate genesis of my writing is likely to be found in the hundreds of children I have taught and in my own two sons whom I brought up as a single parent from 1975."

Taylor's first published work is titled *Pack up, Pick up, and Off,* but he first became known to American audiences as the author of *Paradise Lane,* originally released in New Zealand under the title *Possum Perkins.* Because of her intelligence, her alcoholic mother, and her overbearing, potentially abusive father, Rosie Perkins—Taylor's adolescent protagonist in the book—is isolated in the school community of her small town. Her only neighbor on Paradise Lane is Michael, a boisterous young man who seems her complete opposite. A grudging friendship develops between the two and is strengthened when Rosie finds an orphaned baby possum which she decides to keep and raise. Michael teases Rosie for her nurturing compassion, which he secretly admires, and he begins to feel a greater affection for her. The death of the possum and the support she eventually receives from Michael and his family are incentive for Rosie to confront her own family and seek help.

Ethel R. Twichell praised the convincing characters, "their psychological interaction, and the gentle flowering of Rosie and Michael's love" in a *Horn Book* review of *Paradise Lane.* A *Publishers Weekly* reviewer similarly praised the dramatic climax of the novel, and the tension that builds "as Rosie's independence begins to threaten her parents' status quo." A *Kirkus Reviews* contributor called the relationship between Rosie and Michael, and their subsequent emotional growth, "riveting—and unforgettable."

In 1991 Taylor won New Zealand's Esther Glen Medal for *Agnes the Sheep.* In this tale, Agnes is inherited by a pair of teenagers, Belinda and Joe, following the death of her previous owner, an ill-tempered old woman. A series of comic adventures ensues, during which the pair fight a constant battle to keep Agnes from friends and neighbors who think that she belongs on the dinner table. Agnes's tendency to misbehave reaches its peak in a wild chase through a supermarket. In the end, however, there is a note of sadness as Agnes dies and Belinda and Joe begin to lose interest in each other.

Critics generally praised the humor of *Agnes the Sheep.* In particular, Betsy Hearne claimed in a *Bulletin of the Center for Children's Books* review that the novel would serve as an introduction and means to "studying satirical literature." Taylor's satire spares no one, observed Connie Tyrell Burns in a *School Library Journal* review; he makes light of "teachers, education, priests, and the church in this zany and merry romp."

Among Taylor's more recent novels, *Knitwits* has also received approval for its quirky sense of humor. Chas bets his next-door-neighbor, Alice, that he can knit a sweater by the time his expectant mother has her baby. This results in a series of misadventures, including the discovery of his knitting by some male friends, who then become avid knitters themselves. "This blithe look at an expectant family has no dropped stitches," quipped a *Kirkus Reviews* contributor.

It was at the time of his grandson's birth that Taylor wrote *Knitwits.* "The whole notion behind that book rests very much on his small shoulders," the author recalled. "I watched the video of James's pre-natal scan. I understand how very well that valiant knitter, Chas, in *Knitwits* must have felt when, halfway through the uphill garment-creating battle, he watched a strangely similar video of his yet-to-be-born sibling!"

BIOGRAPHICAL/CRITICAL SOURCES:

PERIODICALS

Booklist, May 15, 1991, p. 1794.
Bulletin of the Center for Children's Books, March, 1991, p. 179; January, 1993, p. 158.
Horn Book, March, 1988, p. 212.
Kirkus Reviews, November 1, 1987, p. 1580; September 1, 1992, p. 1135.
Publishers Weekly, September 11, 1987, p. 96.
School Library Journal, December, 1987, p. 105; March, 1991, p. 196.

*   *   *

TECHINE, Andre   1943-

PERSONAL: Born in 1943.

ADDRESSES: Office—c/o French Film Office, 745 Fifth Ave., New York, NY 10151.

CAREER: Screenwriter and director of motion pictures.

AWARDS, HONORS: Award for best director from Cannes Film Festival, 1985, for *Rendezvous.*

WRITINGS:

SCREENPLAYS; AND DIRECTOR

(With Marilyn Goldin) *Barocco,* Films La Boetie, 1976.
(With Pascal Bonitzer and Jean Gruault) *Les Soeurs Bronte,* Gaumont, 1979; published as *Les Soeurs Bronte: Un film de Andie Techine,* Editions Albatros, 1979.
(With Olivier Assayas) *Rendez-Vous,* Spectrafilm, 1987, released in the United States as *Rendezvous,* 1987.
(With Bonitzer and Assayas) *Le Lieu du crime,* Kino International, 1986, released in the United States as *Scene of the Crime,* 1987.
(With Bonitzer) *The Innocent,* Union Generale Cinematographique, 1988.

Also author and director of *Souvenirs d'en France,* released in the United States as *French Provincial;* and of the films *Hotel des Ameriques;* and *La Matiouette.*

OTHER

Contributor to periodicals, including *Cahiers du Cinema.*

SIDELIGHTS: Andre Techine is a prominent French filmmaker whose films are, at once, both conventional and rather idiosyncratic. A longtime reviewer for the influential film periodical *Cahiers du Cinema*—which counts Francois Truffaut and Jean-Luc Godard among its many contributors who became celebrated artists—Techine turned to filmmaking in the 1970s. Among his early works is *French Provincial,* an abbreviated epic recalling Orson Welles's more violently truncated *The Magnificent Ambersons.* With *French Provincial,* which charts the decline of a wealthy French family, Techine appropriated a slightly jarring editing style—rushing scenes and even entire spans of time—also found in Welles's epic. *Nation* reviewer Terrence Rafferty acknowledged this similarity, and he even indicated that *French Provincial* "pays homage" to Welles's film.

With *Barocco,* which Techine completed in the 1970s, he gave unique shape and drive to the thriller genre. *Barocco,* featuring such prominent performers as Isabelle Adjani and, in dual roles, Gerard Depardieu, sets a romance within a crime story. As is often the case with Techine's films, *Barocco* depicts emotionally charged characters and situations. He also makes use of dizzying camera-work and melodramatic characterizations.

Les Soeurs Bronte, another of Techine's films from the 1970s, is a characteristically objectified representation of the literary family whose members included Charlotte Bronte, author of the romantic novel *Jane Eyre,* and Emily Bronte, author of the dramatic tale *Wuthering Heights.* Like previous Techine productions, *Le Soeurs Bronte* boasted an impressive cast—Isabelle Adjani, for instance, played Emily Bronte, and Isabelle Huppert played the lesser known Anne Bronte. But as with previous Techine productions, *Le Soeurs Bronte,* showed only briefly in American cinemas, but it later played on cable television.

In 1985 Techine completed *Rendezvous,* a haunting drama about a mediocre actress's involvement with a deranged, self-destructive actor, his disturbingly-shy roommate, and his emotionally-empty director. The romance between the heroine, Nina, and the manic actor, Quentin, ends abruptly when he is struck and killed by an automobile. The roommate, Paulot, then comes increasingly to bear on Nina, who is desperate for stability and security. She eventually lands the role of Juliet in a Shakespearean production being prepared by Quentin's former director, Scrutzler. Through her involvement with Scrutzler, Nina uncovers the secret of Quentin's self-destructive bent. But she becomes haunted, even humiliated, by his memory, as she contends with both the unsettling Paulot and the aloof Scrutzler. For *Rendezvous,* Techine won the prize for best director at the 1985 Cannes Film Festival.

In Europe, *Rendezvous* established Techine as an accomplished filmmaker. But it was his next film, *Scene of the Crime,* that won him his greatest acclaim in the United States. Set in the French countryside, *Scene of the Crime* is a drama in which mood is foremost. The film, simply described, concerns a middle-aged mother's romance with a fugitive from justice. But the true mood of the work is one of ominous tension, as the mother and the escaped prisoner both risk, however briefly, personal wellbeing for the sake of their mutual attraction. Among the film's American supporters was *New York*'s David Denby, who described *Scene of the Crime* as "the kind of old-fashioned 'story' movie in which the atmosphere binds you to the characters, emotions." He deemed the film "completely absorbing." And Janet Maslin wrote in the *New York Times* that Techine's film "is alive wth danger and sexual possibility," and called it an "elegant thriller."

Techine followed *Scene of the Crime* with the lesser-known *The Innocent,* about a young woman who becomes embroiled in romantic intrigue while searching for her runaway brother on the Mediterranean French coast. *The Innocent,* like Techine's previous productions, is marked by sweeping camerawork and a lush soundtrack.

Although Techine has enjoyed great acclaim in Europe, he remains a somewhat obscure artist to American filmgoers. *Nation* reviewer Terrence Rafferty ranked Techine among "the very few directors who seem capable of a great film" and added that he needs only to uncover "a form and subject elegant and suggestive enough to make coherent all he knows about the way the world looks and the way it works."

BIOGRAPHICAL/CRITICAL SOURCES:

PERIODICALS

Cahiers du Cinema, May, 1986, pp. 96-98.
Maclean's, April 20, 1987, p. 53.
Nation, February 7, 1987, pp. 154-56.
New York, February 2, 1987, pp. 87-88.
New York Times, January 23, 1987, pp. C14.*

TENENBAUM, Shelly 1955-

PERSONAL: Born December 11, 1955, in New York, NY; daughter of Henry (in business) and Lola (a homemaker; maiden name, Geizhals) Tenenbaum; married Glenn Stevens (a professor); children: Jonathan. *Education:* Antioch College, B.A., 1977; Brandeis University, M.A., 1983, Ph.D., 1986. *Religion:* Jewish.

ADDRESSES: Home—Cambridge, MA. *Office*—Department of Sociology, Clark University, Worcester, MA 01610.

CAREER: Clark University, Worcester, MA, assistant professor, 1986-93, associate professor of sociology and Jewish studies, 1993—.

WRITINGS:

A Credit to Their Community: Jewish Loan Societies in the United States, 1880-1945, Wayne State University Press (Detroit, MI), 1993.
(Editor with Lynn Davidman) *Feminist Perspectives on Jewish Studies,* Yale University Press (New Haven, CT), in press.

SIDELIGHTS: Shelly Tenenbaum told *CA:* "In graduate school I read Ivan Light's book *Ethnic Enterprise in America,* a study that analyzes Japanese, Chinese, and Caribbean credit networks in the United States. That book jarred my memory of twin brothers who attended high school with me in New York City and used to meet with our grandfather weekly at a place called the Hebrew Free Loan Society. That recollection made me wonder about the existence of Jewish loan facilities. My initial investigation convinced me that ethnic credit organizations were not only common in immigrant Jewish communities, but also supplied entrepreneurs with capital; this made the organizations important for the rapid rise of East European Jews up the economic ladder. As a result, I wrote my book *A Credit to Their Community: Jewish Loan Societies in the United States, 1880-1945,* about these ethnic institutions."

*   *   *

THACKERAY, Frank W. 1943-

PERSONAL: Born March 16, 1943, in Pittsburgh, PA; son of Frank E. (in sales) and Lucille (a homemaker; maiden name, Schneider) Thackeray; married Katherine Lukacs (a teacher), November 27, 1991; children: Alex, Max. *Education:* Dickinson College, B.A., 1965; Defense Language Institute of the West

Coast, Certificate in Polish, 1968; Temple University, M.A., 1970, Ph.D., 1977.

ADDRESSES: Home—1884 Douglass Blvd., Louisville, KY 40205. Office—Division of Social Sciences, Indiana University Southeast, 4201 Grant Line Rd., New Albany, NY 47150-2158.

CAREER: Anne Arundel Community College, Arnold, MD, visiting lecturer, 1976; Rutgers University, Camden Campus, Camden, NJ, visiting lecturer, 1977; Indiana University Southeast, New Albany, assistant professor, 1977-82, associate professor, 1982-88, professor of history and Slavic studies, 1988—. U.S. State Department, member of Scholar-Diplomat Seminar, 1980.

MEMBER: North American Association of Sport Historians, American Historical Association, American Association for the Advancement of Slavic Studies, Polish American Historical Association, Fulbright Alumni Association.

AWARDS, HONORS: Fulbright grants for Poland, 1972-73 and 1973-74.

WRITINGS:

Antecedents of Revolution: Alexander I and the Polish Congress Kingdom, 1815-1825, East European Monographs, 1980.
(Editor with John E. Findling) Statesmen Who Changed the World: A Bio-Bibliographical Dictionary of Diplomacy, Greenwood Press, 1993.
Events That Changed the World: Twentieth Century, Greenwood Press, 1994.

Contributor to books, including Imperial Power and Development: Papers on Pre-Revolutionary Russian History, edited by Don K. Rowney, Slavica, 1990; and Eastern Europe and the West, edited by John Morison, St. Martin's, 1992. Contributor to scholarly journals.

*   *   *

t'HART, Marjolein C.   1955-

PERSONAL: Born March 30, 1955, in Voorburg, Netherlands; daughter of Bastiaan Burgert (a geologist) and Cornelia Maria (a teacher; maiden name, Rientsma) t'Hart. Education: University of Groningen, M.A., 1981. Politics: "Leftist." Religion: None.

ADDRESSES: Home—Helmholtzstraat 71 II, 1098 LG Amsterdam, Netherlands. Office—Department of History, University of Amsterdam, Spuistraat 134, 1012 VB Amsterdam, Netherlands.

CAREER: University of Groningen, Groningen, Netherlands, research assistant in sociology, 1981-85; University of Leiden, Leiden, Netherlands, research assistant in political science, 1985-86; Free University of Amsterdam, Amsterdam, Netherlands, assistant professor of history, 1988-89; Erasmas University, Rotterdam, Netherlands, assistant professor of history, 1989; University of Amsterdam, Amsterdam, senior lecturer in history, 1990—.

AWARDS, HONORS: Vera List fellow at New School for Social Research, New York City, 1986-87; fellow of Netherlands Institute for Advanced Studies in Humanities and Social Sciences, 1992-93.

WRITINGS:

The Making of a Bourgeois State: War and Finance during the Dutch Revolt, Manchester University Press, 1993.

WORK IN PROGRESS: Editing A Financial History of the Netherlands, with others; editing Achieving Cities: A Comparison of Antwerp, London, and Amsterdam, with others, completion expected in 1997; research on the history of energy.

*   *   *

THOMAS, R. George   1914-

PERSONAL: Born August 13, 1914, in Pontloltyn, Wales; son of Joseph (a master grocer) and Nellie (a homemaker; maiden name, Williams) Thomas; married Jessie Clotidle Moseley (a lecturer), September 11, 1943; children: Richard Wyn, Philip Anthony. Education: University College, Cardiff, B.A., 1936, M.A., 1938, Ph.D., 1943. Politics: Liberal Democrat. Religion: Church of England. Avocational interests: Singing with the Beach Choral Society.

ADDRESSES: Home—10 Towy Rd., Llanishen, Cardiff, Wales, CF4 4NJ.

CAREER: University College, Cardiff, lecturer in English (became senior lecturer), 1946-67, chair in English, 1968, professor of medieval English, 1974-80; professor emeritus, University of Wales, 1980—. Military service: British Army, 1940-46; served in Iceland, India, Burma, and the Far East; became Lieutenant Colonel.

MEMBER: English Association, The Welsh Academy, Philological Society, The Viking Society (trustee), Yr Academi Gymraeg.

WRITINGS:

EDITOR

Letters from Edward Thomas to Gordon Bottomley, Oxford University Press, 1968.

The Collected Poems of Edward Thomas, Clarendon Press, 1978.

Thomas, Edward, *Letters to America, 1914-1917,* Tragara Press, 1989.

Thomas, *The Pilgrim and Other Tales,* Dent, 1991.

Selected Letters of Edward Thomas, Oxford University Press, 1995.

Familiar Letters: Edward and Helen Thomas, Whittington Press, 1995.

OTHER

(Translator and author of introduction) Nordal, Sigurdur Johannssen, *Hrafnkels saga Freysgodi: A Study,* University of Wales Press (Cardiff), 1958.

Dickens' Great Expectations, Edward Arnold, 1964; revised, 1972.

(Author of introduction) I. Jenkins, editor, *The Collected Poems of Idris Davies,* Gwasgomer, 1972.

Edward Thomas, University of Wales Press, 1972, revised, 1993.

(Translator) *Sturlunga Saga,* 2 volumes, Twayne, 1972-74.

Edward Thomas: A Portrait, Oxford University Press, 1985.

Work represented in anthologies, including *Critical Writings on R. S. Thomas,* edited by Sandra Ansley, Poetry & Wales Press, 1982; and *Dylan Thomas Remembers,* 1978. Contributor of numerous articles to periodicals, including *Anglo-Welsh Review, Humanus Sum, Poetry Wales, Review of English Studies, Modern Language Quarterly, Modern Language Review,* and *Times Literary Supplement.*

WORK IN PROGRESS: A comparison of the poetry of Edward Thomas, W. H. Davies, Dylan Thomas, and R. S. Thomas.

SIDELIGHTS: After translating both Sigurdur Nordal's landmark study of the Icelandic saga *Hrafnkels saga freysgodi* and the *Sturlunga saga,* Professor R. George Thomas turned his attention to editing, collecting, and commenting on the work of English poet and nature writer Edward Thomas. Professor Thomas told *CA:* "My interest in the three Thomases

(Edward, Dylan, R. S.) stems from my own poems; over twenty poems published over thirty years; and a desire still unfulfilled to explain/interpret the special nature of Welsh writers in English."

Thomas's first published work on Edward Thomas was a collection of letters written by the poet; Thomas was also asked by the poet's widow to edit her husband's manuscripts, including his poetry, letters, and wartime diary. The resulting volume, *The Collected Poems of Edward Thomas,* was judged a "rigorous, masterly overhaul" by *Washington Post* reviewer Robert W. Smith. Likewise, Donald Davie of the *Times Literary Supplement* described the edition as "magnificently meticulous."

In a subsequent biography, *Edward Thomas: A Portrait,* Professor Thomas describes the poet's artistic and personal struggles as well as his frustrated literary aspirations. For much of his career, Edward Thomas wrote literary criticism and articles for London journals, believing that his creative talents were being wasted as he worked to support his family. Late in his life, with the encouragement of Robert Frost, Thomas turned to poetry, publishing his first volume in 1916. He died a year later on a World War I battlefield.

While some commentators have maintained that only under the stressful conditions of war could Thomas have turned to poetry, George Thomas asserts that he would have become a poet regardless. Reviewing the biography for the London *Times,* Fiona MacCarthy described Professor Thomas's prose style as "far from searing" but found that the subject matter "is still a story of enormous fascination, very moving in most basic human terms." She concluded: "This is an old-fashioned book in a good sense, gaining more from acumen than it loses from prolixity." Robert Wells, writing for the *Times Literary Supplement,* seconded MacCarthy's opinion, adding that Thomas's depiction of Victorian England was a most successful part of the work.

BIOGRAPHICAL/CRITICAL SOURCES:

PERIODICALS

Globe and Mail (Toronto), October 24, 1987.
London Magazine, June, 1969.
Times (London), October 3, 1985.
Times Literary Supplement, November 23, 1979, p. 21; October 4, 1985, p. 1090.
Washington Post Book World, February 21, 1979, p. D4.

THOMPSON, Joel A. 1950-

PERSONAL: Born September 22, 1950, in Leaksville (now Eden), NC; son of Calvin C. (a welder) and Jane (a teacher; maiden name, Simmons) Thompson; married Gloria Matthews, August 17, 1974; children: Zachary, Samuel, Leah. *Education:* North Carolina State University, B.S.E.E. (with honors), 1972; Appalachian State University, M.A., 1975; University of Kentucky, Ph.D., 1979.

ADDRESSES: Home—P.O. Box 2096, Boone, NC 28607. *Office*—Graduate Studies and Research, Appalachian State University, Boone, NC 28608.

CAREER: Appalachian State University, Boone, NC, professor of political science, 1978—, chair of political science department, 1987-93, associate dean, 1993—.

MEMBER: American Political Science Association, Council of Graduate Schools in the United States, Southern Political Science Association.

WRITINGS:

(Editor with G. Larry Mays) *American Jails,* Nelson-Hall, 1988.
(Editor with Gary F. Moncrief) *Changing Patterns in State Legislative Careers,* University of Michigan Press (Ann Arbor), 1994.

WORK IN PROGRESS: A book on state legislative campaign finance, coedited by Moncrief, for Congressional Quarterly Press in 1996.

*   *   *

THOMPSON, Thomas L. 1939-

PERSONAL: Born January 7, 1939, in Detroit, MI; son of Howard Matthew (a housepainter) and Marion (a store clerk; maiden name, MacDonald) Thompson; married Dorothy E. Irvin, December 17, 1963 (divorced, 1980); married Shirley E. Vanke (an artist and author), August 5, 1985; children: (adopted) Samir Said Hanef, Claudia Hilary. *Education:* Duquesne University, B.A., 1962; attended Blackfriar's College, Oxford, 1962-63; attended Tubingen University, 1963-71; Temple University, Ph.D., 1976. *Politics:* Social democrat. *Religion:* Roman Catholic.

ADDRESSES: Home—Gurrevej 161A, DK-3000, Elsinore, Denmark. *Office*—University of Copenhagen, Kobmagergade 46, DK 1150, Copenhagen, Denmark.

CAREER: University of Dayton, instructor of theology, 1964-65; University of Detroit, assistant professor of theology, 1967-69; University of Tubingen, research associate, 1969-77; Brady High School, St. Paul, MN, teacher, 1980-82; Ecole Biblique, Jerusalem, Israel, annual professor of Old Testament, 1985; Lawrence University, Appleton, WI, associate professor of religion, 1988-89; Marquette University, Milwaukee, WI, associate professor of theology, 1989-93; University of Copenhagen, Copenhagen, Denmark, professor and chair of Old Testament, 1993—. Handyman and housepainter in North Carolina and Minneapolis, MN, 1977-87.

MEMBER: Deutsche Palastina Verein, European Association of Ancient Near Eastern Archeology, Danish Bible Society, British Society of Old Testament Studies, European Society of Biblical Studies, Catholic Biblical Association, Chicago Society of Biblical Research.

AWARDS, HONORS: Gressmann fellowship, 1974, for *The Historicity of the Patriarchal Narratives;* National Endowment for the Humanities, fellow, 1987.

WRITINGS:

The Historicity of the Patriarchal Narratives: The Quest for the Historical Abraham, De Gruyter (Berlin), 1974.
The Settlement of Sinai and the Negev in the Bronze Age, Dr. Reichert Verlag (Weisbaden), 1975.
The Settlement of Palestine in the Bronze Age, Dr. Reichert Verlag, 1979.
The Origin Tradition of Ancient Israel, Sheffield Academic Press (Sheffield), 1987.
Toponomie Palestinienne, Peeters (Louvaine, Belgium), 1988.
Early History of the Israelite People, Brill (Leiden, Netherlands), 1992.

Also the author of more than one hundred articles, maps, and reviews published since 1962.

WORK IN PROGRESS: The Bible and History?, coauthored with Shirley E. Vanke, due in 1996; *Tradition: The Bible for a Secular Age,* due in 1999; *Prolegomena to the Bible's Composition,* due in 1999; research on the historical geography of ancient Palestine, the composition of Exodus-Numbers, and the Old Testament and theology.

SIDELIGHTS: Thomas L. Thompson told *CA:* "In 1967, I began my Ph.D. dissertation with the idea that I might be able to identify which of the stories about Abraham, Isaac, and Jacob in Genesis were earliest and had originated in the patriarchal period itself. I then thought that scholars had proven that the period between the 19th and 17th centuries BCE (Before the Common Era) was the time in which the stories of Abraham, Isaac, and Jacob referred. Whether the patriarchs were to be understood as individuals or as personifications of peoples, I had no doubts whatever that these stories were historical. I was fully convinced that biblical archaeology had long since proven this. My conviction did not reflect any religious commitment or personal piety so much as it simply reflected what was taken within the academic discipline internationally as obvious and true. Working within this understanding of the field, I hoped to understand better the origins and development of the oldest historical accounts in Genesis. According to the Bible, the patriarchs of Genesis had come from Northern Mesopotamia, from the city of Haran—a major trading center in the region of the upper Euphrates.

"The dissertation was finished in late 1971 and published early in 1974. It set out to offer not only a new understanding of the patriarchal narratives and the early history of Palestine but to give comparative ancient Near Eastern studies more critical methods. To my great surprise, it has been successful in all of these goals. The folktale motif of 'the success of the unpromising' had to be played out first, however, and I became something of a Salman Rushdie in biblical studies, unemployed and unemployable for ten years.

"This changed, unexpectedly, in 1985 when I was appointed by the Catholic Biblical Association as their annual professor to the Ecole Biblique in Jerusalem. I was quick to discover that by 1985 I had somehow become one of the establishment in the international field of Old Testament studies. My work of 1974 was not only now nearly universally accepted outside of the United States, but it was being taught as a matter of course in most graduate programs—even in those few ivy league schools still dominated by the ultra-conservative remnants of the Albright school. It had become a keystone of what was now established opinion.

"In very recent biblical studies, I am really no longer a rare bird in my field: one who asks questions of the data—without wanting to defend or prove anything in particular—but just looking for answers to questions unanswered. We haven't had such queer birds in theology for a very long time. The flight back to the sources for so many of my contemporaries in the sixties and seventies ended in

little crashes and collapses of personal fancy that unfortunately decimated the church's intellectuals in favor of the security of that long grey line of insurance brokers who today populate our seminaries and universities everywhere. What I have been writing and trying to do in biblical studies is, I believe, what the best of my generation would have done if they had survived the intellectual collapse of every major thought in the field. Their audience still exists, however. They are listening and hungry for discussion. This audience did not grow up with the mind-numbing brutality of communism's and fascism's social system's creation that my father's generation did. They have, however, suffered the intellectual disorientations that the collapse of that totalitarian world has brought. That I have survived and still write and teach has been accidental. My work reflects the changes in biblical archaeology that have come about over the last two decades as that of few others does."

*   *   *

THOMPSON, W. Grant 1935-

PERSONAL: Born January 26, 1935, in Windsor, Ontario, Canada; married Susan Elizabeth James, September 7, 1963; children: Julie Elizabeth, Jennifer Kyra, Eric James Adam. *Education:* University of Toronto, M.D., 1960.

ADDRESSES: Office—Division of Gastroenterology, A1, Ottawa Civic Hospital, 1053 Carling Ave., Ottawa, Ontario, Canada K1Y 4E9.

CAREER: Toronto General Hospital, Toronto, Ontario, Canada, junior intern, 1960-61; general practice of medicine in Tavistock, Ontario, 1961-62; Montreal General Hospital, Montreal, Quebec, Canada, began as junior assistant resident, became senior assistant resident in medicine, 1962-64; Vancouver General Hospital, Vancouver, British Columbia, Canada, assistant resident in pathology, 1964-65; Montreal General Hospital, resident in medicine, 1965-66, resident in gastroenterology, 1966-67; Royal Postgraduate Medical School, London, England, research fellow at Hammersmith Hospital, 1967-68; University of Ottawa, Ottawa, Ontario, lecturer, 1968-71, assistant professor, 1971-74, associate professor, 1974-79, professor of medicine, 1979—, chairperson of Division of Gastroenterology, 1979—. Ottawa Civic Hospital, physician, 1969—, chief of Division of Gastroenterology, 1979—. University of Bristol, fellow at Bristol Royal Infirmary, 1977-78, visiting professor, 1994-95; Victoria University of Manchester, visiting professor, 1994-95; lecturer at colleges and universities in Canada, the United States, and abroad; guest on television and radio programs. Member of advisory board, Canadian Foundation for Ileitis and Colitis, 1980—, and International Foundation for Bowel Dysfunction, 1992—; consultant to Proctor & Gamble, Roche Pharmaceuticals, and U.S. National Institutes of Health. Coeliac Ottawa, honorary adviser, 1980-86; Ottawa-Carleton Regional Health Council, member, 1985-90. *Military service:* Royal Canadian Navy Reserve, 1954-59; became lieutenant.

MEMBER: Royal College of Physicians and Surgeons of Canada (fellow; member of examining boards for internal medicine, 1974-76, and for gastoenterology, 1981-86, chairperson of board, 1983-86), Canadian Medical Association, Canadian Association of Gastroenterology (member of council, 1974-77; member of executive committee, 1992-94), American College of Physicians (fellow), American College of Gastroenterology (fellow), American Gastrointestinal Association (member of Council on Nerve-Gut Interactions, 1981-86), American Medical Writers Association (honorary member), Ontario Medical Association.

AWARDS, HONORS: McLaughlin Foundation research fellow, 1967-68; Nuffield Foundation fellow in England, 1977-78; book award, allied health category, American Medical Writers Association, 1980, for *The Irritable Gut.*

WRITINGS:

The Irritable Gut, University Park Press, 1979.
Gut Reactions, Plenum, 1989.
The Angry Gut: Coping with Colitis and Crohn's Disease, Plenum, 1993.
(With D. A. Drossman, J. E. Richter, N. J. Talley, and others) *Functional Gastrointestinal Disorders,* Little, Brown, 1994.
The Upper Gut, Plenum, in press.

Creator of educational films, videotapes, audiotapes, and pamphlets. Contributor to books. Contributor of more than one hundred and seventy articles and reviews to medical journals. Editor, *Update Medicine: Annals of the Royal College of Physicians and Surgeons of Canada,* 1980-86.

*   *   *

THOMPSON, William J.   1939-

PERSONAL: Born in 1939, in Invercargill, New Zealand; son of Eric A. and M. Anne Thompson. *Education:* University of Auckland, New Zealand, B.Sc., 1961, M.Sc., 1962, D.Sc., 1982; Florida State University, Ph.D., 1967. *Avocational interests:* Landscaping, architecture, etymology, international penfriends, swimming, cycling, hiking.

ADDRESSES: Office—Department of Physics and Astronomy, University of North Carolina, Chapel Hill, NC 27599-3255. *Agent*—Gregory Franklin, Wiley-Interscience, 605 Third Ave., New York, NY 10158-0012.

CAREER: University of North Carolina, Chapel Hill, faculty member, 1969—, became professor of physics, 1978—.

WRITINGS:

Computing in Applied Science, Wiley (New York), 1984.
Computing for Scientists and Engineers, Wiley-Interscience (New York), 1992.
Angular Momentum, Wiley-Interscience, 1994.
Atlas for Computing Mathematical Functions, Wiley-Interscience, in press.

Contributing and associate editor of *Computers in Physics* journal.

SIDELIGHTS: William J. Thompson told *CA:* "I have spent thirty-five years probing the inner mysteries of the atom, learning more and more about less and less, while publishing more than one hundred research papers in nuclear physics. I am now using my expository skills to write what I understand about mathematics and its applications to science and engineering.

"My current interest is combining text and formulas with graphics, so that readers and learners can visualize abstract formulas. Thus, by envisioning information, readers understand and remember easily what they see, just as it is easier for travelers to use an atlas rather than only a travel guide. Such a mix of words, formulas and graphics needs to be prepared by the author, since publishers have not moved quickly enough into such publishing styles.

"Another of my interests is in publishing as a cottage industry. As an associate and contributing editor for the magazine *Computers in Physics,* I bring together in print the work of physicists, applied mathematicians, and computer scientists, so that each discipline learns from the other. One of my main involvements is using computers to do graphics and symbolic computing as well as number crunching. Longer term, I plan to use my experience in desktop publishing with graphics to write about two of my avocations—landscaping and the relation of etymology to culture. My garden catalogue and plant locations are already entered in a hypertext data base that allows easy retrieval of information. Whether the roots of words can be described interestingly in such a multimedia format remains to be explored."

* * *

THOMSON, Pat 1939-

PERSONAL: Born April 28, 1939, in Norwich, England; married Roy Thomson (a leather chemist), June 6, 1961; children: Susanna, Alexander. *Education:* University of Leeds, B.A. (honors), 1960, postgraduate certificate in education, 1961; University of Loughborough, M.L.S., 1982, Diploma in Librarianship, 1982. *Avocational interests:* Opera and collecting baby rattles. ("I make sure that the baby has finished with them, of course.")

ADDRESSES: Home—The Long House, Behind 43 West St., Oundle PE8 4EJ, England. *Office*—Nene College, Boughton Green Rd., Northampton NN2 7AL, England. *Agent*—Laura Cecil, 17 Alwyne Villas, London N1 2HG, England.

CAREER: Nene College, Northampton, England, education librarian, 1975—. Has also taught French.

MEMBER: Federation of Children's Book Groups (honorary vice president), Society of Authors, Children's Book History Society.

WRITINGS:

(Compiler) *Rhymes around the Day,* illustrated by Jan Ormerod, Lothrop, 1983.
Trouble in the Cupboard, Yearling, 1987.
Family Gathering: A Collection of Family Stories, illustrated by Toni Goffe, Dent, 1988.
Strange Exchange, Gollancz, 1991.
Beware of the Aunts!, illustrated by Emma Chichester Clark, McElderry Books, 1992.
Tales Told after Lights Out (short stories), Harper-Collins, 1993.

"SHARE-A-STORY" SERIES

The Treasure Sock, illustrated by Tony Ross, Gollancz, 1986, Delacorte, 1987.
One of Those Days, illustrated by Bob Wilson, Delacorte, 1986.
Can You Hear Me, Grandad?, illustrated by Jez Alborough, Delacorte, 1986.

My Friend Mr. Morris, illustrated by Satoshi Kitamura, Delacorte, 1987.
Thank You for the Tadpole, illustrated by Mary Rayner, Delacorte, 1987.
Good Girl Granny, illustrated by Faith Jaques, Delacorte, 1987.
Dial D for Disaster, illustrated by Paul Demeyer, Trafalgar Square, 1990.
No Trouble at All, illustrated by Jocelyn Wild, Trafalgar Square, 1990.
Best Pest, illustrated by Peter Firmin, Trafalgar Square, 1990.
The Best Thing of All, illustrated by Margaret Chamberlain, Trafalgar Square, 1990.

"JETS" SERIES

Jacko, illustrated by Caroline Crossland, Black, 1989.
Rhyming Russell, illustrated by Crossland, Black, 1991.
Messages, illustrated by Crossland, Black, 1992.

EDITOR OF ANTHOLOGIES

A Basket of Stories for Seven Year Olds, illustrated by Rachel Birkett, Doubleday, 1990.
A Sackful of Stories for Eight Year Olds, illustrated by Paddy Mounter, Doubleday, 1990.
A Bucketful of Stories for Six Year Olds, illustrated by Mark Southgate, Doubleday, 1991.
A Chest of Stories for Nine Year Olds, illustrated by Peter Bailey, Doubleday, 1991.
A Pocketful of Stories for Five Year Olds, illustrated by P. Dann, Doubleday, 1992.
A Satchel of Stories, illustrated by Doffy Weir, Doubleday, 1992.
A Stocking Full of Christmas Stories, illustrated by Bailey, Doubleday, 1992.

OTHER

Nonfiction editor of *Books for Your Children.* Contributor to *Books for Keeps, School Librarian, Bookmark,* and *International Review of Children's Literature and Librarianship.*

Jacko has been published in Welsh, Finnish, and Catalan.

SIDELIGHTS: "I began writing rather late," Pat Thomson commented. "I was the typical, avid child reader; but it was not until I returned to work when my children were growing up that I decided to work with books in a teacher training college. I became particularly concerned with the quality and nature of early reading material, wondering if boring, ba-nal 'readers' actually made children not want to read. Consequently, my first books had in mind children who were only just getting to grips with print, but who surely needed the pleasures of lively language and challenging imaginings."

Thomson created the unique "Share-a-Story" series so that young children and their parents could enjoy reading together. In the "Share-a-Story" books, the text on the right is written in a simpler style than the text on the left. The parent reads on the left side, while the child reads on the right; the goal is for the parent to teach the child to read the text on the left, and hence to be able to read the book on his or her own.

Thomson's books feature an assortment of what many readers have found to be lovably eccentric characters. In *Beware of the Aunts,* a young girl describes her nine aunts' unusual habits: one wears strange clothes, one overeats, and one might be a witch. All, however, are very generous, as a Christmas get-together proves. The title character of *My Friend Mr. Morris* interprets everything he hears literally; for example, he believes that a hat band is a band which performs on a hat.

"I draw a great deal on family life for my stories," Thomson explained. "*Beware of the Aunts!* celebrates the funny, strong-minded, and highly individual women in my extended family. *Good Girl Granny* is based on episodes in my grandmother's childhood. School life is also a rich source of amusement and inspiration."

In addition to writing books, Thomson has compiled several anthologies of stories for children, including anthologies for Doubleday, a collection of books anthologized by age that includes *A Pocketful of Stories for Five Year Olds* and *A Bucketful of Stories for Six Year Olds.* She has also written articles about children's books and library studies for several magazines, including *Books for Keeps, School Librarian,* and *Bookmark.*

Thomson commented: "I believe I have a strong sense of the audience I am writing for, but I suppose one always ends up 'writing for oneself' to some degree, especially when the characters seize the imagination. That is the greatest pleasure—to live richly in one's head and to share that with young readers."

BIOGRAPHICAL/CRITICAL SOURCES:

PERIODICALS

Publishers Weekly, December 25, 1987, p. 73;

March 9, 1992, p. 57.
School Library Journal, February, 1987, p. 35; September, 1988, p. 66; January, 1989, p. 67; February, 1991, p. 21; July, 1992, p. 65.
Times Educational Supplement, November 14, 1986, p. 40; July 11, 1988, p. 30; March 24, 1989, p. 25; September 21, 1990, p. R4.

*   *   *

THORNE-FINCH, Ron(ald Barry)   1958-

PERSONAL: Born April 11, 1958, in Winnipeg, Manitoba, Canada. *Education:* University of Manitoba, B.A., 1980, M.A., 1984, M.S.W., 1990.

ADDRESSES: Home—Winnipeg, Manitoba, Canada. *Office*—Klinic Community Health Center, University of Manitoba, Winnipeg, Manitoba, Canada.

CAREER: Klinic Community Health Centre, Winnipeg, Manitoba, public educator, counseling instructor and supervisor, group facilitator, and individual clinician, 1982—. University of Manitoba, instructor, 1988—. Suicide Prevention and Intervention Network, founding member, 1987—; private consultant and workshop facilitator, 1989—; research consultant to Environment Canada.

AWARDS, HONORS: Clara Kemila Anderson Memorial Award for Social Work, 1990.

WRITINGS:

Exporting Danger: A History of the Canadian Nuclear Energy Export Programme, Black Rose Books (Montreal), 1986.
Ending the Silence: The Origins and Treatment of Male Violence Against Women, University of Toronto Press, 1992.

*   *   *

THURLEY, Simon   1962-

PERSONAL: Born August 29, 1962, in Huntingdon, England; son of T. M. (a veterinarian) and R. Thurley. *Education:* Attended Bedford College, London, 1982-85, and Courtauld Institute of Art, London, 1985-89. *Politics:* None. *Religion:* Christian.

ADDRESSES: Home—London, England. *Office*—Hampton Court Palace, Surrey KT8 9AU, England.

CAREER: English Heritage, London, England, inspector, 1988-90; Historical Royal Palaces Agency, chief curator, 1990—.

WRITINGS:

(With Christopher Lloyd) *Henry VIII: Images of a Tudor King,* Phaidon, 1990.
The Royal Palaces of Tudor England, Yale University Press, 1993.

WORK IN PROGRESS: The Royal Palaces of Stuart England, 1604-1714.

SIDELIGHTS: Simon Thurley told *CA:* "The aim of my work is to blend architectural and social history, in order to interpret the royal buildings of England. This approach, which has been increasingly dominant in architectural writing since the late seventies, is partially aimed at bringing architectural history to a wider audience. The methodological approach to my writing I translate into three dimensions as the chief curator of six English royal palaces."

*　　*　　*

THYBONY, Scott   1948-

PERSONAL: Born October 17, 1948, in Virginia; son of William W. and Elizabeth H. Thybony; married June 8, 1974; wife's name, Sandy; children: Erik. *Education:* Received B.A. from University of Arizona.

ADDRESSES: Office—P.O. Box 1381, Flagstaff, AZ 86002.

CAREER: Writer, river guide, archaeologist, and teacher.

AWARDS, HONORS: Lowell Thomas Award for travel journalism, 1987; first place journalism award, National Association of Black Journalists, 1992, for "The Black Seminole: A Tradition of Courage," published in *Smithsonian,* August, 1991.

WRITINGS:

A Guide to Hiking the Inner Canyon, Grand Canyon Natural History Association, 1981.
(With Robert and Elizabeth Rosenberg) *The Medicine Bows,* Caxton Printers, 1985.
Fire and Stone: A Guide to Wupatki and Sunset Crater, Southwest Parks and Monuments Association, 1987.
Walnut Canyon, Southwest Parks and Monuments Association, 1988.
Grand Canyon Trail Guide: Hermit, Grand Canyon

Natural History Association, 1989.
Grand Canyon Trail Guide: Havasu, Grand Canyon Natural History Association, 1989.
Arizona, Graphic Arts Center, 1990.
Fort Davis: The Men of Troop H, Southwest Parks and Monuments Association, 1990.
(With Jim Babbitt) *Grand Canyon Trail Guide: South and North Bass,* Grand Canyon Natural History Association, 1991.
Aztec Ruins National Monument, Southwest Parks and Monuments Association, 1992.
Canyon Country Parklands, National Geographic Society, 1993.
Rock Art of the American Southwest, Graphic Arts Center (Portland, OR), 1994.
The Official Guide to Hiking the Grand Canyon, Grand Canyon Natural History Association, 1995.
Burntwater, University of Arizona Press, 1995.

Work represented in books, including *Pathways to Discovery,* National Geographic Society, 1991; *America's Hidden Treasures,* National Geographic Society, 1992; and *On Nature's Terms: Contemporary Voices,* edited by Thomas Lyon and Peter Stine, Texas A & M University Press, 1992. Columnist for *National Geographic Traveler.* Contributor to magazines and newspapers, including *Outside, Whole Earth Review, Men's Journal, Smithsonian,* and *National Wildlife.*

*　　*　　*

TODD, Alexander (Robertus)   1907-

PERSONAL: Born October 2, 1907, in Glasgow, Scotland; son of Alexander (a justice of the peace) and Jane (Lowrie) Todd; married Alison Sarah Dale, January 30, 1937; children: Alexander Henry, Helen Todd Brown, Hilary Alison. *Education:* University of Glasgow, B.Sc., 1928, Carnegie research scholar, 1928-29, D.Sc., 1938; University of Frankfurt am Main, Dr.phil.nat., 1931; Oxford University, D.Phil., 1933; Cambridge University, M.A., 1944. *Avocational interests:* Fishing, golf.

ADDRESSES: Office—9 Parker St., Cambridge CB2 2RU, England.

CAREER: University of Edinburgh, Edinburgh, Scotland, assistant in medical chemistry, 1934, Beit Memorial research fellow, 1935-36; Lister Institute of Preventive Medicine, London, England, staff member, 1936-38; University of London, London, England, reader in biochemistry, 1937-38; University of Manchester, Manchester, England, Sir

Samuel Hall professor of chemistry and director of chemical laboratories, 1938-44; Cambridge University, Cambridge, England, professor of organic chemistry and director of chemical laboratories, 1944-71; author. Advisory Council on Scientific Policy, chair, 1952-64; Royal Committee on Medical Education, chair, 1965-68; Christ's College fellow, 1944—, master, 1963-78; University of Strathclyde, chancellor, 1963-91; Fisons Ltd., director, 1963-78; National Research Development Corp., director, 1968-76; held visiting professorships at California Institute of Technology, 1938, University of Chicago, 1948, University of Sydney, 1950, Massachusetts Institute of Technology, 1954, Cambridge University, 1954, University of California, 1957, and Texas Christian University, 1980.

MEMBER: International Union of Pure and Applied Chemistry, (president, 1963-65), Royal Society (president, 1975-80), Chemical Society (president, 1960-62), Society of Chemical Industry (president, 1981-82), Parliamentary and Scientific Committee (president, 1983—), American Academy of Arts and Sciences, American Philosophical Society, BAAS (president, 1969-70), NAS, Nuffield Foundation (trustee, 1950-79, chair of managing trustees, 1973-79), Governors of United Cambridge Hospitals (chair, 1969-74), Croucher Foundation (trustee chair, 1980-87, president, 1987—), member of the Australian, Austrian, Ghana, Indian, Iranian, Japanese, Polish, and Soviet Academies of Science, Academy of Natural Philosophy (Halle, Germany), New York Academy of Sciences.

AWARDS, HONORS: Meldola Medal, Chemical Society, 1936; Lavoisier medallist, French Chemical Society, 1948; Royal Copley medal, Royal Society, 1949 and 1955; Knight of the British Empire, 1954, for distinguished service to the Empire; Nobel Prize for Chemistry, Nobel Prize Foundation, 1957, for research on nucleotides, nucleotide coenzymes, and the chemical structure of nucleic acid; Cannizzaro Medal, Italian Chemical Society, 1958; Paul Karrer Medal, University of Zurich, 1962; Stas Medal, Belgian Chemical Society, 1962; Longstaff Medal, Chemical Society, 1963; named Baron Todd of Trumpington in the County of Cambridge, 1962; Order pour le Merite (Germany), 1966; Lomonosov medal, Union of Soviet Socialist Republics Academy of Sciences, 1978; Copernicus Medal, Polish Academy of Science, 1979; honorary fellow of the Australian Chemical Institute, the Manchester College of Technology, Royal Society of Glasgow, Royal Society of Edinburgh, Royal College of Physicians; honorary member of the French, German, Spanish, Belgian, Swiss, and Japanese Chemical Societies;

honorary fellow of Oriel College, Oxford, 1955, Churchill College, 1971, Cambridge, 1971, and Darwin College, Cambridge, 1981; received honorary LL.D. degrees from the universities of Glasgow, Melbourne, Edinburgh, California, Manchester, and Hokkaido, an honorary Dr.rer.nat. from the University of Kiel, an honorary D.Litt. from the University of Sydney, and honorary D.Sc. degrees from the universities of London, Exeter, Warwick, Sheffield, Liverpool, Oxford, Leicester, Durham, Wales, Madrid, Aligarh, Strasbourg, Harvard, Yale, Michigan, Paris, Adelaide, Strathclyde, Cambridge, Phillippines, Tufts, Hong Kong, and Australian National University; also received Order of Merit and Second Class Order of the Rising Sun (Japan).

WRITINGS:

(Editor) Robinson, Robert, *Perspectives in Organic Chemistry,* Interscience Publishers (New York), 1956.
Problems of the Technological Society, University of Ghana/Ghana Publishing Corp., 1973.
A Time to Remember: The Autobiography of a Chemist (memoir), Cambridge University Press (New York), 1984.

Author of "Organic Chemistry: A View and a Prospect," first published in the *Times Science Review,* winter, 1961, and later in the 1961 annual report of the Smithsonian Institution. Contributor of articles to numerous professional journals.

SIDELIGHTS: Alexander Todd chronicles an illustrious scientific career in his 1984 memoir *A Time to Remember: The Autobiography of a Chemist.* Todd's life spans the twentieth century and its major scientific achievements, and the chemist's work was an integral part of those groundbreaking deeds. Born in Scotland in 1907, Todd received degrees from the universities of Glasgow, Frankfurt, Oxford, and Cambridge before embarking on his career as a researcher in organic chemistry. As he recounts in his memoirs, it was almost by accident that he became involved in the field of vitamin research while studying in Edinburgh. His explorations into this area centered around the role and structure of coenzymes, and an important part of this research involved synthesizing a substance called ATP, or adenosine triphosphate. This chemical compound provides the energy for muscular activity in animals. This subject was also related to Todd's subsequent field of study in nucleic acids, nucleotides, and nucleotide coenzymes, all of which are essential components of every living cell. By unlocking the secrets of them, Todd helped pave the way for other scientists to learn more about DNA, the chain of enzymes also found in living cells that determine the organism's genetic make-up. Such discoveries after World War II ushered in the modern age of genetics, and in 1957 Todd was awarded the Nobel Prize for his work on the coenzymes.

As he chronicles in *A Time to Remember,* Todd spent much of his career at Cambridge University, where he taught organic chemistry, chaired the department, and was instrumental in the development of the University Chemical Laboratory. Later he played a key role in the formation of Churchill College at Cambridge, an institution which provides a haven for scientific research and higher education and is modeled on the Massachusetts Institute of Technology. Another interesting facet of Todd's research is his work with the plant *Cannabis sativa* and its active ingredient, delta-9-tetrahydrocannabinol, or THC. This plant is commonly known as marijuana, and due to its illegal status in England, Todd was forced to submit twenty-five copies of each research paper he authored on the subject to the Bureau of Drugs and Indecent Publications. His work in the field established that THC had pharmacological properties that could be separated from its narcotic attributes. Over the years Todd was awarded countless accolades for his work; in addition to the Nobel Prize, the scientist received medals and honors from nearly every academic body within the international scientific community and was made a knight of the British Empire in 1957 and a baron in 1962. Although he acknowledged Todd's achievements as a scientist, *Times Literary Supplement* reviewer Jorge Calado judged the contents of *A Time to Remember* too technical to appeal to general readers and too broad to be helpful to researchers, and lamented that it provides "precious little insight into the workings of a great mind."

BIOGRAPHICAL/CRITICAL SOURCES:

BOOKS

Current Biography, H. W. Wilson, 1958.
Todd, Alexander, *A Time to Remember: The Autobiography of a Chemist,* Cambridge University Press, 1984.

PERIODICALS

Times Literary Supplement, August 3, 1984, p. 867.*

*   *   *

TOFFLER, Heidi   1929-

PERSONAL: Born August 1, 1929, in New York; daughter of William and Elizbeth Farrell; married Alvin Toffler (a writer), April 29, 1950; children: Karen. *Education:* Long Island University, B.A.; graduate study at New York University and American University.

ADDRESSES: Agent—Curtis Brown Ltd., 10 Astor Pl., New York, NY 10003.

CAREER: Writer. United Nations Development Fund for Women (UNIFEM), member of board of directors.

AWARDS, HONORS: Medal of the President of Italian Republic; honorary degrees from Manhattan College and Dowling College.

WRITINGS:

WITH HUSBAND, ALVIN TOFFLER

Future Shock, Random House, 1970.
Eco-Spasm, Bantam, 1975.
The Third Wave, Morrow, 1980.
Powershift, Bantam, 1990.
War and Anti-War, Little, Brown, 1993.

*   *   *

TOLL, Nelly S.   1935-

PERSONAL: Born 1935, in Lwow, Poland; daughter of Zygmunt and Rose Mieses; married Erv Toll; children: Sharon, Jefferey. *Education:* Rowan College, B.A.; Rutgers University, M.A.; also attended Hahnaman University. *Religion:* Jewish.

ADDRESSES: Agent—Cindy Kane, Dial Books, 2 Park Ave., New York, NY 10016.

CAREER: Worked as a tour guide for the Philadelphia Museum of Art. Creative writing instructor, Rowan College, Glassboro, NJ. Frequent lecturer at public schools, colleges, and universities.

AWARDS, HONORS: Children's Book Award, International Reading Association, 1994, for *Behind the Secret Window.*

WRITINGS:

(With W. Keedoner) *Behind the Closed Window* (play), produced at Princeton McCarther Theatre, Princeton, NJ, 1978.
(And contributor of illustrations) *Without Surrender: Art of the Holocaust,* Running Press, 1982.
(And illustrator) *Behind the Secret Window: Memories of a Hidden Childhood,* Dial Books, 1993.

Also contributor of articles and short stories to publications, including *Stone Soup.* Some of Toll's illustrations have been released as postcards, and are sold by the U.S. Holocaust Museum in Washington, DC.

SIDELIGHTS: In her 1993 book *Behind the Secret Window: Memories of a Hidden Childhood,* Nelly S. Toll describes the German Nazi invasion of Lwow, Poland in 1941, and how it sent her Jewish family into hiding. Toll, who was six years old at the time of the invasion, recalls vividly her mother's attempts to hide them—first in the home of a Christian family and later in a cramped, bricked-up room in a gentile section of the city. During their thirteen months of hiding, Toll's father and younger brother were caught and murdered. Still, she and her mother persevered. Toll spent much of her time writing in her diary, which served as inspiration for *Behind the Secret Window.* "Nelly Toll is a riveting companion to Anne Frank," Judy Silverman writes in *Voice of Youth Advocates,* going on to describe Toll's book as "a very important story that needed to be told."

Behind the Secret Window stands out from other Holocaust tales in that it includes twenty-nine full-color watercolor illustrations that the six-year-old Toll had painted while in hiding. Though some indirectly portray the loneliness and fear she and her mother felt, most of these illustrations depict the young girl's normal daily activities, void of war and violence, while others display the child's hopeful longings for her family's happy reunion after the war. (Eight of Toll's paintings are displayed in Israel's Yad Vashem Holocaust Museum.) Ellen Fader, reviewing *Behind the Secret Window* for *School Library Journal,* claims that readers "will gain a new perspective on growing up during wartime." "Without emphasizing horror and loss," a *Publishers Weekly* critic concludes, "Toll conveys the effects of human evil and human folly, summoning up the forces of tragedy and courage."

Toll commented: "We must not forget how low human beings can stoop, so that this catastrophe will not happen again."

BIOGRAPHICAL/CRITICAL SOURCES:

PERIODICALS

Bulletin of the Center for Children's Books, March, 1993, p. 227.
Kirkus Reviews, March 15, 1993.
Publishers Weekly, April 19, 1993, p. 63.
School Library Journal, March, 1993, p. 232.
Voice of Youth Advocates, February, 1993.

TOPEK, Susan Remick 1955-

PERSONAL: Born February 13, 1955, in Dayton, OH; daughter of Russell L. and Betty K. Remick; married Joseph S. Topek (a rabbi), May 22, 1977; children: Leah Elsa, Sara Gila, Chana Malka. *Education:* Attended Young Judaea Year Course, 1973-74; University of Texas at Austin, B.A., 1977; attended Hebrew College, 1978. *Religion:* Jewish.

ADDRESSES: Home—75 Sheep Pasture Rd., Setauket, NY 11733.

CAREER: Jewish Community Center, Boston, MA, group social worker, 1977-79; Temple Isaiah, Stony Brook, NY, Sunday and after school Hebrew teacher, 1985—; North Shore Jewish Center Pre-School, Pt. Jeff, NY, camp director and teacher, 1986—.

MEMBER: Jewish Early Childhood Association, NAEC, Hadassah.

WRITINGS:

(And illustrator) *Israel Is,* Kar-Ben Copies, 1988.
A Holiday for Noah, Kar-Ben Copies, 1990.
Ten Good Rules, Kar-Ben Copies, 1991.
A Turn for Noah, Kar-Ben Copies, 1992.
A Taste for Noah, Kar-Ben Copies, 1993.

SIDELIGHTS: Susan Topek commented: "Finding interesting and appropriate Jewish books for two- and three-year-olds is always a problem. I wrote my first book after I went looking for a book on Israel. When I couldn't find one, I wrote it and illustrated it myself. From that one, stories from my toddler or pre-kindergarten classes came to me. Sometimes ideas would come from things the children said—as in *A Holiday for Noah*—and sometimes I'd design a book because I could not find one I liked. I write stories that I like to read and hear. I try to listen as a child would, so that my stories make children smile, think, and feel good. I feel that I am very lucky and that writing books for children is a gift. Writing Jewish books makes me feel proud and hopefully the children feel that also."

*   *   *

TRIPP, Valerie 1951-

PERSONAL: Born September 12, 1951, in Mount Kisco, NY; daughter of Granger (an advertising executive) and Kathleen (a teacher; maiden name, Martin) Tripp; married Michael Petty (a teacher), June 25, 1983; children: Katherine. *Education:* Yale

University, B.A. (with honors), 1973; Harvard University, M.Ed., 1981. *Avocational interests:* Reading, hiking, conversation.

ADDRESSES: Home—1007 McCeney Ave., Silver Spring, MD 20901. *Office*—c/o Pleasant Co., 8400 Fairway Pl., Middleton, WI 53562.

CAREER: Worked at Little, Brown, and Co., Boston, MA, 1973; Addison-Wesley, Menlo Park, CA, writer in language arts program, 1974-80; freelance writer, 1981—.

AWARDS, HONORS: Children's Choice Award, International Reading Association, 1987, for *Meet Molly: An American Girl.*

WRITINGS:

"AMERICAN GIRLS COLLECTION" SERIES

Meet Molly: An American Girl, illustrated by C. F. Payne, vignettes by Keith Skeen and Renee Graef, Pleasant Co., 1986.
Molly Learns a Lesson: A School Story, illustrated by Payne, vignettes by Skeen and Graef, Pleasant Co., 1986.
Molly's Surprise: A Christmas Story, illustrated by Payne, vignettes by Skeen, Pleasant Co., 1986.
Happy Birthday, Molly!: A Springtime Story, illustrated by Nick Backes, vignettes by Skeen, Pleasant Co., 1987.
Happy Birthday Samantha!: A Springtime Story, illustrated by Robert Grace and Nancy Niles, vignettes by Jana Fothergill, Pleasant Co., 1987.
Changes for Samantha: A Winter Story, illustrated by Luann Roberts, Pleasant Co., 1988.
Changes for Molly: A Winter Story, illustrated by Backes, vignettes by Skeen, Pleasant Co., 1988.
Molly Saves the Day: A Summer Story, illustrated by Backes, vignettes by Skeen, Pleasant Co., 1988.
Samantha Saves the Day: A Summer Story, illustrated by Grace and Niles, vignettes by Roberts, Pleasant Co., 1988.
Felicity's Surprise: A Christmas Story, illustrated by Dan Andreasen, vignettes by Roberts and Skeen, Pleasant Co., 1991.
Felicity Learns a Lesson: A School Story, illustrated by Andreasen, vignettes by Roberts and Skeen, Pleasant Co., 1991.
Meet Felicity: An American Girl, illustrated by Andreasen, vignettes by Roberts and Skeen, Pleasant Co., 1991.
Changes for Felicity: A Winter Story, illustrated by Andreasen, vignettes by Roberts and Skeen, Pleasant Co., 1992.

Felicity Saves the Day: A Summer Story, illustrations by Andreasen, vignettes by Roberts and Skeen, Pleasant Co., 1992.
Happy Birthday Felicity!: A Springtime Story, illustrated by Andreasen, vignettes by Roberts and Skeen, Pleasant Co., 1992.

"JUST ONE MORE STORIES" SERIES

The Singing Dog, illustrated by Sandra Kalthoff Martin, Children's Press, 1986.
Baby Koala Finds a Home, illustrated by Martin, Children's Press, 1987.
The Penguins Paint, illustrated by Martin, Children's Press, 1987.
Squirrel's Thanksgiving Surprise, illustrated by Martin, Children's Press, 1988.
Sillyhen's Big Surprise, illustrated by Martin, Children's Press, 1989.
Happy, Happy Mother's Day!, illustrated by Martin, Children's Press, 1989.

OTHER

An Introduction to Williamsburg (nonfiction), Pleasant Co., 1985.
Home Is Where the Heart Is (play), Pleasant Co., 1990.
Actions Speak Louder Than Words (play), Pleasant Co., 1990.
War on the Homefront (play), Pleasant Co., 1990.

Baby Koala Finds a Home has been translated into Spanish.

WORK IN PROGRESS: "Ten books about girls in the fourth grade today."

SIDELIGHTS: Valerie Tripp grew up in a large family, sandwiched between two older sisters and one younger sister and brother. The Tripp children were a close-knit group, spending their free time playing games, riding bikes, and, when winter came, sledding and ice skating. "We were a noisy, rambunctious, rag-taggle bunch," she explains in a publicity brochure issued by one of her publishers, the Pleasant Company. But their favorite activity was reading. Tripp learned to read while playing school with her older sisters, and she, in turn, taught her younger siblings. Tripp's parents encouraged the family's love of books.

Tripp has vivid and mostly fond memories of school: "I liked school, especially reading. I was like [my character] Molly in that I loved the teachers and always wanted to be the star of the school play. . . . Also, unfortunately, just like Molly, I was terrible at multiplication."

Tripp was one of the first women to be admitted to Yale University; she graduated with honors in 1973. After college, she worked in publishing, first at Little, Brown, and Co., and later at Addison-Wesley, where she wrote educational materials, such as songs, stories, and skills exercises for the language arts division.

In 1981, she received her Masters of Education degree from Harvard University. Since then, she has developed educational programs for such companies as Houghton Mifflin, Macmillan, and Harcourt Brace Jovanovich. Her children's books provide her with the greatest opportunity to combine her background in education with her love of writing. She has written six books of verse for the "Just One More Stories" series, which is aimed at beginning readers. She is best known, however, for her "American Girls Collection."

The "American Girls" books focus on young women growing up during different periods in American History. Tripp has thus far written about three girls: Molly, a nine-year-old whose father serves in England during World War II; Samantha, an orphan who lives with her aunt and uncle in turn-of-the-century New York City; and Felicity, who lives in Williamsburg, Virginia, and whose life changes drastically during the outbreak of the American Revolution.

Tripp draws on events from her own childhood experiences when writing. Samantha's adventures in New York City are based on Tripp's own visits to the city. "Sometimes my whole family would go into the city to see a Broadway show, or go to a museum or a concert or the ballet," she remarked. "When I was writing *Happy Birthday Samantha!,* I remembered the feeling of exhilaration of being in the busy, fast-moving, enormous city. I knew just how Samantha felt."

Felicity's adventures reflect Tripp's fascination with colonial history. When the author was ten, she visited Williamsburg with her family. She uses her experience of attending a concert at the Governor's Palace as the basis for Felicity's night of dance at the same facility. For both writer and character, their respective evenings are among their most memorable ones.

BIOGRAPHICAL/CRITICAL SOURCES:

PERIODICALS

Booklist, November 1, 1991, p. 523; May 1, 1992, p. 1603.

Bulletin of the Center for Children's Books, October, 1991, p. 51.
School Library Journal, January, 1992, p. 116; February, 1992, p. 90.

OTHER

Pleasant Company Introduces an American Girls Author: Valerie Tripp (publicity brochure), Pleasant Co., 1992.

* * *

TUBB, Jonathan N. 1951-

PERSONAL: Born in 1951; married; children: three.

ADDRESSES: Home—3 Leighton Gardens, London NW10 3PX, England. *Office*—Western Asiatic Department, British Museum, London WC1B 3DG, England.

CAREER: British Museum, London, England, curator of Syria-Palestine section, and director of Museum's excavations at Tell es-Sa'idiyeh (ancient Zarethan) in Jordan.

MEMBER: Society of Antiquaries (fellow).

WRITINGS:

(Editor) *Palestine in the Bronze and Iron Ages: Papers in Honour of Olga Tufnell,* University of London, Institute of Archaeology, 1985.
Archeology and the Bible, British Museum Publications, 1990.
Excavations at the Early Bronze Age Cemetery of Tiwal esh-Sharqi, British Museum Publications, 1990.
Bible Lands, Knopf, 1991.

Contributor of scholarly articles to journals.

BIOGRAPHICAL/CRITICAL SOURCES:

PERIODICALS

Times Literary Supplement, September 12, 1986, p. 1010.
Voice of Youth Advocates, April, 1992, p. 60.*

* * *

TUCKER, Spencer C. 1937-

PERSONAL: Born September 20, 1937, in Buffalo, NY; son of Cary S. (an army officer) and Elizabeth B. (a homemaker) Tucker; married Barbara Worcester, 1967 (divorced, 1974); married Beverly Blaunt (a psychotherapist), January 30, 1993. *Education:* Virginia Military Institute, B.A., 1959; attended University of Bordeaux, 1959-60; University of North Carolina at Chapel Hill, M.A., 1962, Ph.D., 1966. *Politics:* Democrat. *Religion:* Episcopalian. *Avocational interests:* Collecting original prints.

ADDRESSES: Home—3200 Wabash Ave., Fort Worth, TX 76109. *Office*—Department of History, P.O. Box 32888, Texas Christian University, Fort Worth, TX 76129.

CAREER: University of North Carolina at Chapel Hill, instructor in history, 1962-65; Wake Forest University, Winston-Salem, NC, instructor in history, 1965; University of Maryland at College Park, assistant professorial lecturer in history, 1966-67; Texas Christian University, Fort Worth, began as assistant professor, became associate professor, 1967-90, professor of history, 1990—, department head, 1992—. University of Maryland at College Park, assistant professorial lecturer, 1969-70. Smithsonian Institution, visiting research associate, 1969-70. Texas Christian University Press, member of board of directors, 1991-94. Sycamore Hill Library, member of board of trustees. Military analyst for television and radio programs. *Military service:* U.S. Army, Military Intelligence, 1965-67; became captain.

MEMBER: North American Society for Oceanic History, Society for Military History, U.S. Naval Institute, Nautical Research Guild, American Association of University Professors, Southwestern Social Science Association, Southern Historical Association (European Section), Addison and Randolph Clark Society (member of board of directors, 1993-95), Phi Beta Delta.

AWARDS, HONORS: Fulbright fellow in France, 1959-60; Vice Admiral Edwin B. Hooper grant, Division of Naval History, Department of the Navy, 1988-89; John Lyman Book Award, North American Society for Oceanic History, 1989, for *Arming the Fleet.*

WRITINGS:

Arming the Fleet: U.S. Naval Ordnance in the Muzzle-Loading Era, Naval Institute Press, 1989.
The Jeffersonian Gunboat Navy, University of South Carolina Press, 1993.
(Editor and contributor) *An Encyclopedia of the First World War,* Garland Publishing, 1994.

(With Frank Reuter) *The Chesapeake-Leopard Affair,* Naval Institute Press, in press.

Work represented in anthologies. Contributor of more than fifty articles and reviews to history and military studies journals.

WORK IN PROGRESS: The Great War, 1914-18, publication by University College of London Press expected in 1996; editing *An Encyclopedia of the Vietnam War,* Garland Publishing, 1997; a book on heavy Civil War ordnance, with Edwin Olmstead and Wayne Stark, Museum Restoration Service; research for a book on eighteenth- and nineteenth-century American naval technological innovation, with Tyrone Martin.

*   *   *

TURNBULL, Colin M(acmillan)   1924-1994

OBITUARY NOTICE—See index for *CA* sketch: Born November 23, 1924, in Harrow, England; died of pneumonia, July 28, 1994, in Kilmarnock, VA. Anthropologist and writer. Turnbull was an anthropologist renowned for his studies of the cultures of eastern and central Africa. His best known work, *The Forest People,* focuses on a tribe of Congo pygmies and has been praised for its insightful portrait of a flourishing society unstained by injustice and cruelty. A later study, *The Mountain People,* provides a complementary perspective in its examination of the northern Ugandan tribe of the Ik, whose lives are models of selfishness, desolation, and evil. Turnbull received his doctorate in social anthropology from Oxford University in 1964, and his academic career included professorships at Columbia University and at Vassar and Hunter Colleges. In 1976 he joined the faculty of George Washington University, from which he retired as a professor of anthropology in 1985. An important later work by Turnbull is *The Human Cycle,* which studies how various cultures determine significant stages in the lives of their individual members.

OBITUARIES AND OTHER SOURCES:

BOOKS

Who's Who in America, 45th edition, Marquis, 1988.
Writers Directory: 1994-1996, St. James Press, 1994.

PERIODICALS

New York Times, August 1, 1994, p. B8.
Washington Post, July 31, 1994, p. B7.

TYRE, Peg 1960-

PERSONAL: Born April 26, 1960, in Washington, DC; married Peter Blauner (a novelist), June 24, 1989; children: one son. *Education:* Brown University, B.A.

ADDRESSES: Agent—Richard Pine, Arthur Pine Associates, Inc., 250 West 57th St., New York, NY 10019.

CAREER: Newsday, New York City, law enforcement journalist, 1989—.

WRITINGS:

Strangers in the Night, Crown, 1994.

Coauthor of the book *Two Seconds Under the World,* 1994; author of *In the Midnight Hour,* a sequel to *Strangers in the Night,* 1995.

U-V

UBELAKER, Douglas H.   1946-

PERSONAL: Born August 23, 1946, in Horton, KS; son of Henry Edward (a barber and jeweler) and Wilma Ann (an elementary schoolteacher; maiden name, Stasler) Ubelaker; married Maruja Andrade Heymann (an elementary schoolteacher), April 12, 1975; children: Max Henry, Lisa Ann. *Education:* University of Kansas, B.A. (with honors), 1968, Ph.D., 1973. *Religion:* Roman Catholic.

ADDRESSES: Office—Department of Anthropology, National Museum of Natural History, Smithsonian Institution, Washington, DC 20560. *Agent*—Russell & Volkening, 50 West 29th St., New York, NY 10001.

CAREER: National Museum of Natural History, Washington, DC, head of anthropology department, 1980-85, assistant director, 1988, became curator of anthropology. Smithsonian Institution, chairperson of Museum of Man Planning Group, 1980-85, head of Division of Physical Anthropology, 1989-92. George Washington University, professorial lecturer in anatomy and anthropology, 1986—. Conducted anthropological field work in South Dakota, 1965-69, Maryland, 1971, 1972, and 1980, coastal Ecuador, 1973, 1974, and 1978—, and the Dominican Republic, 1974. American Board of Forensic Anthropology, diplomate, 1979; expert witness on the identification of human skeletal remains; consultant in forensic anthropology to Federal Bureau of Investigation and District of Columbia. *Military service:* U.S. Army, 1969-71.

MEMBER: American Academy of Forensic Sciences (fellow; head of physical anthropology section, 1990-91; member of American Board of Forensic Anthropology, 1992—), American Association of Physical Anthropology (member of editorial board, 1985-92), Paleopathology Association (co-chairperson of Preservation Committee, 1986-91), American Association for the Advancement of Science, Plains Anthropological Society, Anthropological Society of Washington, Washington Academy of Sciences, Sigma Xi.

WRITINGS:

(With William M. Bass) *A Review of Human Origins,* Lawrence-Journal World Press, 1969, 6th edition (with Bass, Richard L. Jantz, and Fred H. Smith), University of Tennessee Press, 1990.

Human Skeletal Remains: Excavation, Analysis, Interpretation, Aldine, 1978, 2nd edition, Taraxacum, 1989.

(With Henry Scammell) *Bones: A Forensic Detective's Casebook,* HarperCollins, 1992.

(Editor with John W. Verano, and contributor) *Disease and Demography in the Americas,* Smithsonian Institution Press, 1992.

Author of *The Ayalan Cemetery: A Late Integration Period Burial Site on the South Coast of Ecuador,* 1981; co-editor of *Plains Indian Studies: A Collection of Essays in Honor of John C. Ewers and Waldo R. Wedel,* 1982. Contributor to books, including *Diet, Demography, and Disease: Changing Perspectives on Anemia,* edited by P. Stuart-Macadam and S. Kent, Aldine de Gruyter, 1992; *The Native Population of the Americas in 1492,* 2nd edition, edited by W. M. Denevan, University of Wisconsin Press, 1992; and *Powhatan Foreign Relations, 1500-1722,* edited by Helen C. Rountree, University Press of Virginia, 1993. Contributor of about one hundred-fifty articles and reviews to anthropology, archaeology, and forensic journals. Member of editorial board, *Journal of Forensic Sci-*

ences, 1990—, and *Homo: Journal of Comparative Human Biology,* 1994—.

*   *   *

VALLBONA, Rima-Gretel Rothe   1931-
   (Rima de Vallbona)

PERSONAL: Born March 15, 1931, in San Jose, Costa Rica; daughter of Ferdinand Hermann and Emilia (Strassburger) Rothe; married Carlos Vallbona (a physician), December 26, 1956; children: Nuri Vallbona Kaufhold, Carlos-Fernando, Maite, Marisa Vallbona Rayner. *Education:* Sorbonne, University of Paris, Diploma in Teaching French, 1953; University of Salamanca, Diploma in Hispanic Philology, 1954; University of Costa Rica, M.A., 1962; Middlebury College, D.M.L., 1981. *Politics:* "Moderate Democrat." *Religion:* Roman Catholic.

ADDRESSES: Home—3706 Lake St., Houston, TX 77098. *Office*—Department of Modern Languages, University of St. Thomas, Houston, TX 77006.

CAREER: Liceo J. J. Vargas Calvo, San Pedro Montes de Oca, Costa Rica, professor of Spanish and French, 1955-56; University of St. Thomas, Houston, TX, professor, 1964—, head of department, 1966-71, head of modern languages department, 1978-80, and Cullen Foundation Professor of Spanish, 1989—. Institute of Hispanic Culture of Houston, member of board of directors, 1970-71, 1974-76, 1988, director of cultural committee, 1973; Rice University, professor for summer programs in Buenos Aires, 1972, and Madrid, 1974, visiting professor, 1980-83; University of Houston, visiting professor, 1975-76; Casa de Argentina de Houston, member of board of directors and vice-president, both 1978-79, and head of scholarship committee. Cultural Arts Council of Houston, member of literary panel, 1984-86, member of board of directors, 1990; Houston Public Library, member of board of directors, 1984-86; City of Houston, member of Task Force and Arts Education Committee, 1989-91.

MEMBER: Instituto Internacional de Literatura Iberoamericana, American Association of Teachers of Spanish and Portuguese (vice-president, 1973-75), National Writers Association, Instituto Literario y Cultural Hispanico (secretary of culture, 1985—), Texas Freelance Writers Association.

AWARDS, HONORS: Fifth prize, Nadal Novel Prize contest, 1964, for *Noche en vela;* Aquileo J. Echeverria Novel Prize, 1968; Jorge Luis Borges Short Story Prize, Fundacion Givre, Argentina, 1977; Agripina Montes de Valle Novel Prize, 1978; SCOLAS Literary Award, Southwest Conference of Latin American Studies, 1982; Ancora Award, best book in Costa Rica, 1983-84; Medal of Civil Service, King Juan Carlos of Spain, 1989.

WRITINGS:

UNDER NAME RIMA DE VALLBONA

Los infiernos de la mujer y algo mas (stories), Ediciones Torremozas, 1992, translation by Lillian L. de Tagle published as *Flowering Inferno: Tales of Sinking Hearts,* Latin American Review Press (Pittsburgh), 1993.

IN SPANISH; UNDER NAME RIMA DE VALLBONA

Noche en vela (novel; title means "Night of the Wake"), Editorial Costa Rica, 1968, 4th ed., 1984.
Yolanda Oreamuno (nonfiction), Editorial del Ministerio de Cultura de Costa Rica, 1971.
Polvo del camino (stories), Editorial Escritores Unidos de Costa Rica, 1973.
La salamandra rosada (stories), Editorial Geminis (Montevideo), 1979.
La obra en prosa de Eunice Odio (critical anthology), Editorial Costa Rica, 1981.
Mujeres y agonias (stories), Arte Publico (Houston), 1982, 2nd edition, 1989.
Las sombras que perseguimos (novel), Editorial Costa Rica, 1983, 2nd edition, 1990.
Baraja de soledades (stories), Ediciones Rondas (Barcelona), 1983.
Cosecha de pecadores (stories), Editorial Costa Rica, 1988.
El arcangel del perdon (stories), Editorial Palacios (Buenos Aires), 1990.
Mundo, demonio y mujer (novel), Arte Publico (Houston), 1991.
Vida i ducesos de la Monja Alferez (critical edition), Arizona State University Press, 1992.
La narrative de Yolanda Oreamuno (nonfiction), Editorial Costa Rica, in press.

Member of editorial board, *Letras Femeninas,* 1970—; co-chairperson of editorial board, *Foro Literario,* 1984-89.

WORK IN PROGRESS: Outstanding Hispanic Women, a bilingual collection of the lives of historical women, for children, completion expected in 1996; *Life in Colonial Times in Latin America,* based on autobiographical manuscripts written by nuns in the New World during the seventeenth and eighteenth centuries.

SIDELIGHTS: Rima-Gretel Rothe Vallbona told *CA:* "Writing is like breathing for me. Imagination, creativity, the rich, poetic language of dreams, together with a heavy dose of reality, constitute my daily literary task.

"I was only a child when my enjoyment of telling fantastic stories to others began. I wrote some of them in tiny notebooks that my sisters quickly threw away without respect to my emerging talents. In my teens I told my stories with drawings, using the techniques of the comics that I enjoyed so much. These stories were romantic novels for friends who came to my house, day after day, to read the continuing plots. Thus my first audience was born, composed of two or three friends—but one has to start from scratch, don't you think?

"Years passed and, while attending university, I wrote only diary entries and long letters to my sweetheart Carlos, a Spaniard who later became my husband. During the first years of our marriage, following the Hispanic tradition, I stayed home to fulfill the duties of a housewife. Extremely frustrated because I could not put my professional capabilities and knowledge to use, I secretly started to write my first novel, *Noche en vela.*

"I wrote this novel without any doubts, as if I were a real expert in the art of narration. I guess the miracle happened because I performed the task without ambitions. I so much enjoyed escaping from my routine chores through my creativity that I realized my true vocation was to become a writer. This was confirmed when I earned fifth place in the Nadal Novel Prize Contest in 1964. With that first recognition, I could prove to my mother that I was right: my fate was not to work and earn the meager salary of a secretary or spend the rest of my life performing the monotonous work of a housewife.

"My critics consider my narrative to be essentially existentialist, and I agree with them. From an early age, I have been obsessed with nothingness, the absurdity of life, the problem of free choice, the anguish and pains we confront throughout life. These obsessions were later nourished by my readings of Sartre, Nietzsche, Dostoevsky, Unamuno, and others. The poorly romantic literary attitude of my youth ended when I encountered writers like Cervantes, Gide, Colette, Saint Exupery, Hemingway, and Faulkner.

"My main objective has not been to tell a story or develop a plot, but to pinpoint many serious social problems and expose devious human behavior. I also want to depict relevant aspects of my Hispanic world, especially those relating to women. The truth is that I am tormented by questions that feed my inspiration and make me deal even with metaphysics.

"Now that I am on the verge of retiring from my career as a university professor, I have committed myself to several important projects and will be able to dedicate myself solely to my writing career. I now know that it pays to be part of this privileged age called seniority."

*   *   *

van BELLE, Gerald

PERSONAL: Born July 23, in Enschede, The Netherlands; married, wife's name, Johanna (a physician); children: Loeske Ritter, William John, Gerard, Christine, Louis. *Education:* University of Toronto, B.A., 1962, M.A., 1964, Ph.D., 1967.

ADDRESSES: Home—17210 25th Ave. N.E., Seattle, WA 98155. *Office*—Department of Environmental Health, SC-34, School of Public Health and Community Medicine, University of Washington, Seattle, WA 98195.

CAREER: Florida State University, Tallahassee, assistant professor of statistics, 1967-72; University of Washington, Seattle, associate professor, 1975-76, professor of biostatistics, 1976-90, professor of environmental health and head of department, 1991—.

WRITINGS:

The Control of Infections in Hospitals, University of Toronto Presxs, 1966.
(Co-author) *Biostatistics: A Methodology for the Health Sciences,* Wiley, 1993.

WORK IN PROGRESS: Research on Alzheimer's Disease and Sudden Infant Death Syndrome.

*   *   *

van der LINDE, Laurel   1952-

PERSONAL: Born March 7, 1952, in Cleveland, OH; daughter of Donald (a Navy pilot) and Shirley (an opera singer; maiden name, Handel) van der Linde; children: Gower. *Education:* University of California at Los Angeles, B.A. (cum laude), 1974; studied ballet with Mia Slavenska, Michael Pancrieff, Rosemary Valeve, and Irina Kosmouska, 1966-70.

ADDRESSES: Home—30841 Gilmour Rd., Castaic, CA 91384.

CAREER: Actress and dancer in Broadway plays, including *Annie, Seven Brides for Seven Brothers,* and *A Chorus Line,* 1976-82; cofounder of Landmark Entertainment Group (multimedia entertainment), North Hollywood, CA, 1982-86; author, 1991—; founder of Carousel Classics (audio books), 1992—. Trainer and breeder of Arabian and Lipizzan horses, 1984—.

MEMBER: American Book Association, Society of Children's Book Writers and Illustrators.

WRITINGS:

The Devil in Salem Village, Millbrook Press, 1992.
The Pony Express, Macmillan, 1993.
The White Stallions: The Story of the Dancing Horses of Lipizza, Macmillan, 1994.
Legends in Their Own Time, Millbrook Press, 1994.

Contributor to periodicals, including *California Arabian, Arabian Horse Times,* and *Equus.*

SIDELIGHTS: Horses, which play a significant role in Laurel van der Linde's life, are also the subject of several of her books for children; when she isn't writing, she trains and breeds Arabian and Lipizzan horses at her California ranch. Nevertheless, horses are but one aspect of van der Linde's background. Trained as a ballet dancer, she later had a successful career on the Broadway stage, appearing in such musicals as *Annie, A Chorus Line, Seven Brides for Seven Brothers, Annie Get Your Gun,* and a revival of *My Fair Lady.* Later, van der Linde became involved in other aspects of the entertainment industry and cofounded the multimedia entertainment company Landmark Entertainment Group. In addition, she formed a children's audio book company, Carousel Classics. The company's first release was *The Juicy Truth about Johnny Appleseed,* with the titles *The Legend of Sleepy Hollow* and *The New Adventures of Paul Bunyan* following soon after.

In 1992 van der Linde finished her own children's book, *The Devil in Salem Village,* which is a recounting of the witch trials that took place in Salem, Massachusetts, in 1692. These trials occurred after members of the Salem community accused a group of young women with consorting with the devil. As a result several young women were convicted as witches and subsequently burned at the stake. In *Voice of Youth Advocates,* Victoria Yablonsky called the book "an excellent introduction" to this episode of American colonial life.

Following *The Devil in Salem Village,* van der Linde focused her writing on horses. One of the resulting books is 1993's *The Pony Express,* a chronicle of the early western American service that employed horsemen to carry letters. Covering such topics as the diet of the horses and skirmishes with hostile Indians, van der Linde provides a chronology of the famous mail carriers and their mounts. She also provides photographs from the time, samples of the mail the Pony Express carried, and locations of the various stations that were scattered throughout the frontier. A reviewer for the *Bulletin of the Center for Children's Books* remarked that *The Pony Express* makes for "lively reading," and stands as a "thoroughly enjoyable account" of that part of American history. Van der Linde also wrote *The White Stallions: The Story of the Dancing Horses of Lipizza* and *Legends in Their Own Time,* a biography about famous horses, both in 1994.

BIOGRAPHICAL/CRITICAL SOURCES:

BOOKS

Willis, John, editor, *Theatre World,* Volume 39: *1982-1983,* Crown, 1984, pp. 11, 223, 225.

PERIODICALS

Bulletin of the Center for Children's Books, July/ August, 1993.
Horse Illustrated, July, 1990.
Voice of Youth Advocates, August, 1992.

* * *

van der ZEE, Barbara (Blanche) 1932- (Barbara Griggs)

PERSONAL: Born September 14, 1932, in Chipping, Camden, England; daughter of Frederick Landseer (an artist) and Nina (a homemaker; maiden name, Muir) Griggs; married Henri van der Zee (an author and journalist), June 5, 1970; children: Bibi, Ninka. *Education:* University of Birmingham, B.A., 1952. *Religion:* Roman Catholic.

ADDRESSES: Home—6A Wedderburn Rd., London NW3, England. *Agent*—Richard Simon, 32 College Cross, London N1 1PR, England.

CAREER: Writer. Journalist for *Vogue,* 1955-57, *Daily Express,* 1957-58, and *Evening Standard,* 1958-68, became fashion editor, 1961-69; *Daily Mail,* fashion editor, 1972-79; freelance author and journalist, 1979—. Research Council for Complementary Medicine, trustee, 1984-87.

MEMBER: National Institute of Medical Herbalists (honorary member), Soil Society, McCarrison Society.

WRITINGS:

WITH HUSBAND, HENRI van der ZEE

William and Mary, Knopf (New York), 1973.

New Amsterdam, Viking, 1977, published in the United States as *A Sweet and Alien Land: The Story of the Dutch in New York,* Viking (New York), 1978.

1688: Revolution in the Family, Viking, 1988.

AS BARBARA GRIGGS

Bibi's Cook Book, illustrated by Don Roberts, Allen & Unwin (London), 1976.

(With Shirley Lowe) *Nouveau Poor, or, How to Live Better on Less,* illustrated by Tom Barling, Hodder & Stoughton (London), 1976.

Green Pharmacy: A History of Herbal Medicine, Viking, 1982.

The Home Herbal, Norman & Hobhouse, 1982.

The Food Factor, Viking, 1986.

Zest for Life, Ebury Press, 1989.

(With Michael van Straten) *Superfoods,* Dorling Kindersley, 1990.

(With van Straten) *The Superfoods Diet Book,* Dorling Kindersley, 1992.

(With van Straten) *Superfast Foods,* Dorling Kindersley, 1994.

The Green Witch Herbal: Restoring Nature's Magic in Home, Health, and Beauty Care, Healing Arts Press (Rochester, VT), 1994.

OTHER

Contributor to periodicals, including *New Health, Daily Mail, Cosmopolitan, Tatler,* and *Vogue.*

WORK IN PROGRESS: A revised and updated edition of *The Home Herbal,* for Pan Books.

SIDELIGHTS: Journalist Barbara van der Zee is the author of books on varied subjects, including history, biography, herbal medicine, and food. Van der Zee coauthored several historical and biographical volumes with her husband, Henri van der Zee. Their first collaboration produced the dual biography *William and Mary,* which details the lives and times of the seventeenth-century British monarchs. As outlined in the book, the pair was invited by the British Parliament in 1688 to rule the island nation in place of the ousted James II. William—a Dutch prince—and Mary (William's wife and the daughter of James II) came into step with the ascending En-glish middle class, a force which would be instrumental in the burgeoning industrialization of England. Such growth, according to Alden Whitman in the *New York Times,* "required, among other things, a fairly stable social order, which William and Mary, in their sober-sided fashion, helped to institute."

William and Mary was warmly received by critics; Whitman, in the *New York Times,* described the book as "a readable and enlightening portrayal of two people, their monarchy and their age." Whitman also stated that the van der Zees "have skilfully created two living, breathing, pulsating human beings." A *Times Literary Supplement* reviewer called the biography "sensitive and honest," indicating that it was written "with zest and sympathy."

The van der Zees next wrote *New Amsterdam,* which was released in the United States as *A Sweet and Alien Land: The Story of the Dutch in New York.* The book chronicles the settling of the Dutch colony in North America, which began with six farms in what is now Manhattan. The Dutch called their land claim New Netherland, and began building Fort Amsterdam in the Manhattan area in 1625. *A Sweet and Alien Land* details the politics and history behind New Netherland, including the Dutch-British rivalry, the Native American resistance to the European presence, and the eventual Dutch surrender of New Netherland to the British in the 1670s. Determining the book "by far the most detailed I know" about New Netherland, *New York Times Book Review* contributor Bruce Bliven, Jr., gave *A Sweet and Alien Land* an enthusiastic review. Bliven observed that the van der Zees's "joint style, however they achieve it, is a delight" and concluded that the authors "have managed a storytelling feat of great distinction."

The van der Zees also collaborated on *1688: Revolution in the Family,* which focuses on the 1688 Glorious Revolution in England and the split it engendered within the royal family (it was this rift in the Stuart family that enabled William and Mary to ascend to the English throne). *Times Literary Supplement* reviewer Conrad Russell remarked that the authors bring to their book "a journalist's highly trained ear for the innuendo behind apparently innocuous statements, which gives them insights into the working both of high politics and of family jealousies." Although Russell noted that the van der Zees do not cast the story of 1688 in a new light, the critic commended the authors for creating "a book well enough written to be hard to put down."

Barbara van der Zee has also written books on food and herbs, beginning with *Bibi's Cook Book,* under the name Barbara Griggs. Van der Zee began *Bibi's Cook Book,* which describes how to make infant food at home, soon after her first child was born. As van der Zee told *CA:* "I didn't want her first introduction to real food to be stuff out of tins and jars. There didn't seem to be a book around telling me what she ought to be getting, why, and how much; so I adopted the usual journalist's approach to a problem: research it and turn the answer into a book. It was my introduction to a fascinating new subject world—human health and nutrition."

As *Bibi's Cook Book* was being published in 1976, van der Zee began work on *Green Pharmacy: A History of Herbal Medicine,* which explores the gulf between modern medicine, with its emphasis on aggressive intervention, and herbal medicine, which favors slower, plant-based cures. Van der Zee has also written *The Home Herbal* and 1994's *Green Witch Herbal: Restoring Nature's Magic in Home, Health, and Beauty Care.* The author told *CA* that she finds the uses of herbs "deeply fascinating—partly because, perhaps, as a former fashion editor, I'm very tuned to the wavelengths of contemporary awareness, and there has never been a deeper or more widespread interest in this subject than now. I see this, optimistically, as an indication that mankind is slowly getting back to a consciousness of his own grassroots, and of his need to live in harmony with the biosphere of which he is an integral part. Our time for living any other way is running out fast."

BIOGRAPHICAL/CRITICAL SOURCES:

PERIODICALS

New York Times, July 24, 1973, p. 33.
New York Times Book Review, March 19, 1978, p. 11.
Times Literary Supplement, October 19, 1973, p. 1279; August 12, 1988, p. 879.
Village Voice, November 23, 1982, p. 52.

* * *

VENTURA, Michael 1945-

PERSONAL: Born October 31, 1945, in Bronx, NY; son of Michael Luciano (a cab driver) and Clelia (a clerical worker; maiden name, Scandurra) Ventura. *Politics:* "Radical." *Religion:* "Complex."

ADDRESSES: Home—8033 Sunset Blvd., No. 97, Los Angeles, CA 90046. *Agent*—Melanie Jackson, 250 West 57th St., No. 1119, New York, NY 10107.

CAREER: Austin Sun, Austin, TX, arts editor, 1974-77; *Los Angeles Weekly,* Los Angeles, CA, co-founder, 1978, senior editor, 1978-93; freelance writer, 1993—.

MEMBER: Writers Guild of America West, P.E.N. West, Authors Guild.

WRITINGS:

The Mollyhawk Poems, Wings Press, 1977.
Shadow-Dancing in the U.S., J. P. Tarcher, 1985.
Night Time, Losing Time, Simon & Schuster, 1989.
(With James Hillman) *We've Had One Hundred Years of Psychotherapy and the World's Getting Worse,* Harper, 1992.
Sitting on Moving Steel, Wings Press, 1993.
Letters at Three A.M.: Reports on Endarkenment, Spring Publications, 1993.
The Zoo Where You're Fed to God, Simon & Schuster, 1994.

Author of "Letters at Three A.M.," a column in *Austin Chronicle* and *Los Angeles Village View.*

WORK IN PROGRESS: Two trilogies, "The Tiger, the Rock, and the Rose" and "From Vegas to Nowhere."

SIDELIGHTS: Michael Ventura told *CA:* "I write for a country called America, a country that doesn't exist now, a country that never existed. Yet, at certain times and through certain souls, America gave (and gives) humanity a dream of the people, for the people, by the people, and this dream will haunt the world from now on. I write in the name of that haunting. I write for the living and the dead, the unborn and the young. I write for the stone people, the rose people, and the tiger people. I write for Randolph Bourne, Sherwood Anderson, Emma Goldman, Walt Whitman, James Baldwin, Henry Miller, Nelson Algren, Willa Cather, Charlie Parker, Billie Holiday, John Cassavetes, Stevie Ray Vaughan—to pass on what they, and many others, have given me. I write for my family, my friends, my gods. I write in answer to the spirit in me that has said, since I was a boy: *write.*

"I write the way a tiger hunts, the way a leaf grows, the way a stone shines underwater in a river, not because it is anything special, but because this is how it was created, and it can do nothing else. I write, not to save or attack anything (though there are things I've tried to save through writing and things I've attacked) but as a way of honoring *everything,* both what I've tried to preserve and what I've attacked.

"I write because it is my way of being a man, and the woman in me speaks through that man. I write because it is my way of being a citizen, and the rebel in me speaks through that citizen. I write because it is my way of being a friend, a lover, a worker. I write in the faith that those who read are as complex, as desperate, as hopeful, afraid, courageous, tired, haunted, and as full of dreams as I am, and in the faith that, when they read, they complete what I write, taking what I write into territories I do not know. I write in trust of that unknowing. I write to pray, to laugh, to leave home and come home, and to find a home, and to make a home. I write to move from here to there. I write to go the distance.

"I write to be remembered, but I also write to be forgotten—not only because every word and every language will be forgotten, but forgotten because to enter into the memory of another is to become a changeling, a creature hardly recognizable to oneself, so to be remembered is at once to be forgotten. I write to lose myself and to find that which is more than myself—that which connects me to my ancestors, to eternity, to the unknown that is to come, to the unknown that is right here, to you. I write because my life is at stake. I write to sit long in the silence that rises when writing is done."

*   *   *

VERBA, Joan Marie   1953-

PERSONAL: Born December 12, 1953, in Waltham, MA; daughter of Bennie Arthur (a computer marketer) and Mildred Maurine (Whetstine) Verba. *Education:* University of Minnesota, B.S., 1975; graduate study at Indiana University, 1975-77. *Politics:* Democrat. *Religion:* United Methodist.

ADDRESSES: Office—P.O. Box 1363, Minnetonka, MN 55345.

CAREER: Control Data Corporation and Unisys, computer programmer, 1978-87; Lerner Publications, word processor, 1989—.

MEMBER: Society of Children's Book Writers and Illustrators, Minnesota Science Fiction Society (past member of board of directors), SF Minnesota, Mythopoeic Society (member of board of directors).

WRITINGS:

Voyager: Exploring the Outer Planets, Lerner Publications, 1991.
North Dakota, Lerner Publications, 1992.

WORK IN PROGRESS: A history of "Star Trek" fanzines, covering the years 1967-87, and a biography of C. S. Lewis, tentatively titled *Myth Made Real.*

SIDELIGHTS: Joan Marie Verba commented: "My interest in science and science fiction began when I was in second grade. The teacher placed a map of the solar system on a bulletin board, which led me to read everything I could find on space and space travel. In junior high and high school, J. R. R. Tolkien's *The Hobbit* and C. S. Lewis's *Out of the Silent Planet* were required reading, and that expanded my interest in fantasy studies as well, though I had been reading fantasy on my own much earlier.

"I had an interest in writing stories before I graduated from high school, and began having my stories published in amateur publications starting in 1973, but did not have any professional ambitions until 1978 when I attended the World Science Fiction Convention. I started my first novel in 1982, saw my first magazine article published in 1984, and published my first professional short story in 1985. When the opportunity came to write a book about Voyager, I was more than happy to put my knowledge and love of science to work. My current writing projects also relate to my interests in fantasy and science fiction, which I believe help society to understand its past and anticipate its future."

*   *   *

VERNEREY, Denise   1947-

PERSONAL: Born July 30, 1947; daughter of Claude and Jacqueline (Deneri) Laplace; married Patrick Vernerey (a dentist), December 17, 1970; children: Laurent, Julien, Benoit. *Education:* Attended University of Paris, 1966-69, University of Munich, 1967-68, and Ecole du Louvre, 1981-85. *Religion:* Roman Catholic.

ADDRESSES: Home—45 blvd. Gouvion, St. Cyr, Paris 75017, France.

CAREER: Teacher of German, English, and French, 1970-83; Le Louvre, Paris, France, researcher, 1986-89; Kairos Vision (multimedia editor), manager and founder, beginning in 1989.

MEMBER: Association Francaise de l'Edition Electronique.

WRITINGS:

Les antiques du musee de Laon, Reunion des Musees Nationaux, 1988.

Le Parthenon, Reunion des Musees Nationaux, 1989.

Au pays des dieux, les Grecs, Nathan, 1989.

Decovvertes junior, Gallimard, 1990.

(With Sophie Descamps-Lequime) *The Ancient Greeks: In the Land of the Gods* (translated by Mary K. LaRose; illustrated by Annie-Claude Martin), Millbrook Press, 1992.

WORK IN PROGRESS: Co-producing compact disc editions of *Gothic Cathedrals of Europe, Romanesque Art and Civilization,* and *Painted Caves of Europe.*

SIDELIGHTS: Denise Vernerey told *CA:* "I founded Kairos Vision in 1989, after completing an interactive kiosk about the Parthenon at the Louvre. Kairos Vision is a multimedia society devoted to cultural exploration. In 1991 Kairos was selected by the French Culture Ministerium to collaborate on the production of a laser disc on the Gothic cathedrals of Europe. We were then selected by the European Union to develop this presentation for compact disc interactive (CDi) and CDROM versions. Two other titles are now in production, and further titles will cover Chronos, the Eiffel Tower, and museum programs."

*   *   *

VERNON, Betty D(esiree)   1917-

PERSONAL: Born December 27, 1917, in London, England; married James William (a civil servant and barrister); children: Antony Martin, Angela Gail. *Education:* Bedford College, London, B.A. (honors), 1938. *Politics:* Socialist. *Religion:* Jewish.

ADDRESSES: Home—20 Grove Hill, Topham, Exeter, Devon, England.

CAREER: Author, 1982—. Freelance writer, specializing in political, educational, and feminist issues; held positions, including Justice of the Peace, Alderman, and councillor, 1950-78. Active in local government organizations, including the London County Council; member of numerous committees.

MEMBER: Fabian Society, Labour Party.

AWARDS, HONORS: Honorary research fellow, University of Exeter, 1956.

WRITINGS:

Ellen Wilkinson, 1891-1947, Croom Helm, 1982.

Margaret Cole, 1893-1980: A Political Biography, Croom Helm, 1986.

Contributor to *Commodity Control,* Cape, 1943; contributor of a chapter on education to *Social Welfare and the Citizen,* Penguin, 1957. Also contributor of articles and reviews to numerous periodicals, including the *Guardian, Books and Bookmen, Teacher, Education Municipal Review,* and *Times Educational Supplement.*

SIDELIGHTS: British writer Betty D. Vernon is the author of biographies chronicling the lives of two noted English political activists of the twentieth century. In both *Ellen Wilkinson, 1891-1947* and *Margaret Cole, 1893-1980: A Political Biography,* Vernon has examined the personal lives and political contributions made by the socialist-minded women, as well as depicting the reformist era in which they lived. The author, herself a socialist active in local politics, has been a writer on economic and social issues since the 1940s.

The first of Vernon's two biographies, *Ellen Wilkinson,* reveals the long career of the former minister of education, a career that officially began in 1915 when she was appointed women's organizer for an association of cooperative employees. This post, which came when she was only twenty-four, led to many other activities and positions. Wilkinson won her first election in 1924, and went on to a long career in the British parliament as a Labour Party representative. As Vernon's biography points out, Wilkinson played key roles in many of the ideological struggles within the Labour Party over the decades, and was friend and confidant to some of Britain's most illustrious political activists. During World War II she became an organizer for civil defense programs. The war and its outcome also served to change Wilkinson's mind about her previous support of communism. After the war was over, she served as minister of education under prime minister Clement Attlee.

Kenneth O. Morgan of the *Times Literary Supplement* noted some of the biography's omissions, but acknowledged the difficulties that Vernon faced in researching into Wilkinson, who left almost no personal papers behind upon her death in 1947. He praised the book's final outcome as a "modest, unpretentious, clearly-written study [that] contains much illuminating information, while its fair-minded, unhectoring tone carries conviction."

In her next book, *Margaret Cole,* Vernon again chronicles the life of an important activist in the leftist political climate of pre-World War II Britain. As the biography recounts, Cole was born into a privileged and intellectual family where the children were encouraged to speak Latin. After receiving a university degree and teaching for a short while, she became a full-time political worker during World War I, a decision due in part to her brother's imprisonment as a conscientious objector. Cole began working for the Fabian Society, a British group formed in 1884 to promote socialism. There she came into contact with other noted personalities of the day, including G. D. H. Cole, whom she later married. Together they produced an enormous amount of work over the decades—they were editors of a socialist journal, wrote countless pamphlets for both the Labour Party and the Fabian Society, and in their spare time wrote detective stories. Cole herself raised three children, chaired numerous committees (she was especially active in educational reform) and sat on the London County Council for twenty-five years. After her husband died in 1959, she penned his biography. She continued to be politically active well into her senior years.

Yet Vernon also sheds light on the more human side of the crusader: the Cole who sought solace from her husband's aloofness and chronic infirmity in an extramarital affair, and the elderly woman, now a Dame of the British Empire, who was unswervingly rude to those who nursed her in her final years. In this biography, Vernon had much more success with portraying her subject through personal archival materials. Unlike Ellen Wilkinson, Cole left behind an enormous amount of published works and correspondence, and Vernon also incorporated interviews with Cole's surviving contemporaries. *Times Literary Supplement* critic Phyllis Willmott faulted the book for its failure to integrate some important political events into the narrative, but commended Vernon's skill in letting Cole's own "very personable and particular voice" impart itself to the reader. Critiquing *Margaret Cole* for the *Observer,* Peter Clarke remarked that the subject "emerges from it as a woman of remarkable spirit."

BIOGRAPHICAL/CRITICAL SOURCES:

PERIODICALS

Observer, April 13, 1986, p. 24.
Times (London), March 27, 1986.
Times Literary Supplement, February 5, 1982, p. 125; June 13, 1986, p. 642.*

VERNON, James 1965-

PERSONAL: Born February 3, 1965, in Widdbridge, Suffolk, England; son of Terence John and Stella Margaret (maiden name, Cross; present surname, Chadwick) Vernon; married Ros Xanthe Wyatt, July 20, 1991; children: Jack Dillon. *Education:* Victoria University of Manchester, B.A. (with first class honors), 1987, Ph.D., 1991. *Politics:* "Radical." *Avocational interests:* Ipswich Town Football Club, walking the dog.

ADDRESSES: Home—Old Glossop, England. *Office*—Department of History, Victoria University of Manchester, Manchester M13 9PL, England.

CAREER: Victoria University of Manchester, Manchester, England, British Academy fellow, 1991-94, lecturer in modern history, 1994—.

WRITINGS:

Politics and the People, Cambridge University Press, 1993.
Re-Reading the Constitution, Cambridge University Press, 1995.

WORK IN PROGRESS: Imagining Cornwall, completion expected in 1996; research on citizenship and national identity in twentieth-century England.

*   *   *

VIEIRA, Sergio 1941-

PERSONAL: Born May 4, 1941, in Tete, Mozambique; son of Francisco and Ines Vieira; married; wife's name, Benilde; children: two sons, one daughter. *Education:* Attended University of Lisbon, 1959-61, College d'Europe, Brussels, Belgium, 1962, and Institut d'Etudes Politiques, Universite de Paris, 1962-64; Universite d'Algier, Licence en Sciences Politiques (with distinction), 1967.

ADDRESSES: Home—Maputo, Mozambique. *Office*—CEA UEM, C.P. 1993, Maputo, Mozambique. *Agent*—c/o Africa World Press, Inc., P.O. Box 1892, Trenton, NJ 08607.

CAREER: FRELIMO (Mozambique's independence party), founding member, 1962, representative in Algiers, 1964-67, and Cairo, 1969-70, secretary of the presidency, 1967-75; Cabinet of the President of Mozambique, director, 1975-77; Banco de Mozambique, governor, 1978-81; political positions in Mozambique include minister of agriculture,

1981-83, governor for the Niassa Province and deputy minister of defense, 1983-84, and minister of security and co-chairperson of Mozambican/South African Joint Security Commission, 1984-87; University Eduardo Mondlane, Maputo, Mozambique, professor, 1987—, director of Centre for African Studies, 1987-92. Economic Commission of the Non-Aligned Summit, chairperson, 1979; SAGE, general manager, 1992-93; Assembly of the Republic of Mozambique, chairperson of Social Affairs Commission; consultant to BPD, 1994. *Estudos Mocambicanos,* publisher, 1987-92. *Military service:* Reserve Army of Mozambique; present rank, colonel (retired).

MEMBER: International PEN, International Association of Sociology, Council for the Social Sciences Research Development in Africa, African Academy of Sciences, African Association of Political Sciences, Associacao dos Escritores Mocambicanos (founder; fellow; chairperson of council), Organizacao Nacional dos Professores, Organizacao da Juventude Mocambicana, Fauna (founder and chairperson of council).

AWARDS, HONORS: Book Award from Leipzig Book Fair, 1984, for *Tambem Memoria do Povo;* Order of Eduardo Mondlane.

WRITINGS:

Disarmament and Development: A Mozambican View, Varna, 1988.
Southern Africa, Mozambique: From Rivalries to Global Convergence, Council for Foreign Relations (New York), 1988.
War and Peace in Southern Africa: The Mozambican Reply to Pretoria's Undeclared War, Edicesa (Harare), 1989.
(Editor with I. Wallerstein, W. Martin, and others) *How Fast the Wind? Southern Africa, 1975-2000,* Africa World Press, 1992.
The Possible Changes and Transformations, Western Cape University, 1992.
The History of the National Liberation Struggles: On the Relationship Between the Struggle and the Content and Direction of the Post-Colonial Society; The Case of Mozambique, SAPES (Harare), 1993.
Governing During Transition, Centre for Policy Studies (Johannesburg), 1993.

Author of books published only in Portuguese, including *Tambem Memoria do Povo,* 1983. Work represented in anthologies. Contributor to periodicals, in English and Portuguese.

WORK IN PROGRESS: Research on international relationships, strategic studies, prevention and resolution of conflicts, confidence-building in the regional and international arena, and consolidation of civil, pluralist, and democratic societies.

*   *   *

VILLAFANE, Eldin   1940-

PERSONAL: Born December 27, 1940, in Santa Isabel, PR; married Margarita Lopez (a public schoolteacher); children: Karen Ann, Eldin Lynn, Dwight Louis. *Education:* Attended Hartwick College, 1959-61; Central Bible College, Springfield, MO, B.A., 1969; Wheaton College, Wheaton, IL, M.A., 1970; Boston University, Ph.D., 1988.

ADDRESSES: Home—36-C Burroughs St., Boston, MA 02130. *Office*—Center for Urban Ministerial Education, Gordon-Conwell Theological Seminary, 363 South Huntington Ave., Boston, MA 02130.

CAREER: Yabucoa Baseball Club, Yabucoa, PR, semi-professional baseball player, 1961-62; worked for banks in New York City and San Juan, PR, 1962-66; General Council of the Assemblies of God, Springfield, MO, editorial assistant, 1968-69; teacher of mathematics and English as a second language, and dean of students and community relations for public schools in New York City, 1970-73; Gordon-Conwell Theological Seminary, South Hamilton, MA, assistant professor, 1976-82, associate professor, 1982-90, professor of Christian social ethics, 1990—, founding director of Center for Urban Ministerial Education, Boston, 1976-90, associate dean for urban and multicultural affairs, 1990-93, executive director of Contextualized Urban Theological Education Enablement Program, 1990—. Ordained minister of Assemblies of God; minister of education at a Christian church in Bronx, NY, 1970-73; WHDH-Radio, moderator of the radio ministry *Algo Nuevo,* 1976-79; interim pastor at Christian center in Cambridge, MA, 1984; preacher at churches, retreats, and conventions. Spanish American Bible Institute, professor, 1971-72; North Central Bible College, visiting professor, 1991; guest lecturer at colleges and universities, including Harvard University, Hartford Seminary, and Azusa Pacific University. Fund for Theological Education, faculty member in Hispanic Summer Program, 1989; Latin America Mission of the United States of America, member of general council. Poder de la Palabra de Dios en la Ciudad, president; Greater Boston Development Coalition, co-chairperson; member of board of directors, Emmanuel Gospel Center and Organizing and Leadership Training Center; member of advisory board, Tapestry (women's leadership development ministry) and Massachusetts Adolescent Violence Prevention Project. Past member of board of directors, U.S. Lausanne Committee, World Vision for U.S. Ministry, Academia para la Historia de la Iglesia Latina, Massachusetts Council of Churches, Christians for Urban Justice, Boston's Latino Housing Task Force, Puerto Rican Tenants in Action, Villa Victoria Community Housing Development, Shelter, Inc., Roxbury's Yes We Can Movement, and Boston's Christian Schools, Inc.; past member of Jewish-Hispanic Dialogue of the Jewish Community Relations Council of Greater Boston, Greater Boston Coalition for Religion and the Economy, Boston mayor's Hispanic Task Force, and City Mission Society.

MEMBER: Society for Pentecostal Studies (first vice president), Hispanic Association for Bilingual Bicultural Ministries (member of national board of directors), Association for Hispanic Theological Education (past member of national board of directors), Evangelicals for Social Action (member of national advisory board), American Academy of Religion, Society of Biblical Literature, Society for the Scientific Study of Religion, La Comunidad of Hispanic American Scholars of Theology and Religion (past president; past member of national board of directors), Evangelistic Association of New England, New England Sunday School Association (past member of board of directors), Association of Hispanic Evangelical Ministers of Massachusetts (past member of board of directors), Encuentro Ministerial.

AWARDS, HONORS: Recognition Award, Confraternidad de Jovenes, Poder de la Palabra de Dios, 1989; named one of the nation's ten most influential Hispanic religious leaders and scholars, *National Catholic Reporter,* 1992.

WRITINGS:

(With Ramon Sanchez and Roberto Dominguez) *Ricardo Tanon: El Poder y la Gloria de Dios,* Cooperativa de Artes Graficas Romualdo Real (San Juan), 1980.

The Liberating Spirit: Toward an Hispanic American Pentecostal Social Ethic, University Press of America, 1992.

(Translator and author of preface) Stephen Mott, *Biblical Ethics and Social Change,* Eeerdmans, 1994.

Also author of *An Evangelical Call to a Social Spirituality: Reflections on Urban Theology and Ministry,* 1994. Work represented in anthologies, including *Led by the Spirit: The Story of New York Theological Seminary,* edited by George W. Webber, Pilgrim Press, 1990; and *Barrios and Borderlands: Cultures of Latinos and Latinas in the United States,* edited by Denis L. Heyck, Routledge Press, 1994. Contributor to periodicals, including *Transformation, Urban Mission,* and *Christianity and Crisis.* Contributing editor, *Journal of Hispanic/Latino Theology;* associate editor, *Pneuma: Journal of the Society for Pentecostal Studies;* theological editor, *Alpha and Omega;* member of editorial board, *PRISM* and *Asociacion para la Educacion Teologica Hispana;* member of editorial advisory board, *Journal of Pentecostal Theology.*

WORK IN PROGRESS: Manda Fuego Senor: Historia del Movimiento Pentecostal Hispano, Asambleas de Dios, for Berean College of the Assemblies of God, completion expected in 1996; "The Crucified God: The Christ of Latino Popular Religiosity," to be included in *The Global God: Multicultural Evangelical Views of God,* edited by William Spencer and Aida Spencer, publication by Scripture Press Publications expected in 1996.

W

WALDREP, Christopher (Reef) 1951-

PERSONAL: Born November 19, 1951, in Oak Ridge, TN; son of Reef Vuin (an educator) and Ella Christine (a homemaker; maiden name, Yates) Waldrep; married Pamela Jean Heiney (a librarian); children: Janelle Christine, Andrea Jean. *Education:* Eastern Illinois University, B.S., 1973; Purdue University, M.A., 1974; Ohio State University, Ph.D., 1990. *Politics:* Democrat. *Religion:* Methodist.

ADDRESSES: *Home*—R.R.1, Box 181A, Charleston, IL 61920. *Office*—Department of History, Eastern Illinois University, Charleston, IL 61920.

CAREER: Art teacher at public schools in Washington Court House, OH, 1974-90; Eastern Illinois University, Charleston, assistant professor, 1990-94, associate professor of history, 1994—.

MEMBER: American Historical Association, Organization of American Historians, American Society for Legal History, Southern Historical Association, Kentucky Historical Association, Filson Club.

WRITINGS:

Night Riders: Defending Community in the Black Patch, Duke University Press, 1993.

Contributor to history journals.

WORK IN PROGRESS: Research on race and the law in the nineteenth-century American South.

SIDELIGHTS: Christopher Waldrep told *CA:* "I was born in Tennessee and lived in Mississippi for a time. Although I have lived in the North for many years, I have retained an interest in the South. Be-tween 1974 and 1990 I taught art to high school and middle school students in Washington Court House, Ohio. I started traveling to Kentucky on weekends to conduct small research projects. As time passed, I went to Kentucky more and more, and began publishing historical articles in the *Register of the Kentucky Historical Society.* I still taught art, but I came to think of myself as more historian than artist.

"As I traveled in Kentucky, collecting information for articles, people urged me to write about the Night Riders, a vigilante movement active early in the twentieth century. These night-riding tobacco farmers used violence to resist encroaching industrialization. At first, I thought them too recent to be interesting; I wanted to go back into history as far as I could. While visiting the Filson Club Historical Society, however, I discovered the Willson Papers, an extensive collection of correspondence by the governor of Kentucky during the Night Rider crisis. Willson's day-to-day communications with state militia officers, local judges, and detectives formed a narrative more exciting than any novel I'd ever read. I decided to write a book.

"Now I am a professor of history at Eastern Illinois University, the same place where I earned my undergraduate degree more than twenty years ago. I teach constitutional and social history, and I am researching race and the criminal justice system in the American South. I will soon complete a book on criminal justice in Vicksburg, Mississippi, and, ultimately, a book on the entire South, synthesizing my own research with that of other historians.

"I tell my students that historians can be categorized according to what they identify as the engine that makes things happen. I belong to that school of scholarship that identifies law as an important force in history. The heart of the problem with the Night Riders, I found, was that local courts stepped aside, allowing vigilantism free reign. In Mississippi, my research is revealing that whites sought to deny blacks access to the courts."

*   *   *

WALKER, Martin   1949-

PERSONAL: Born January 23, 1949, in Durham, England; son of Thomas Martin and Dorothy (a homemaker; maiden name, McNeil) Walker; married Julia Watson (a novelist), 1978; children: Kate, Fanny. *Education:* Balliol College, Oxford, B.A., M.A. (with first class honors), 1969. *Religion:* "Agnostically inclined Church of England."

ADDRESSES: Home—3462 Macomb St. N.W., Washington, DC 20016. *Office—Guardian,* 1730 Rhode Island Ave. N.W., No. 502, Washington, DC 20036. *Agent*—Ellen Levine, 15 East 26th St., No. 1801, New York, NY 10010-1505.

CAREER: Guardian, London, England, reporter, columnist, and foreign correspondent, 1972—, Moscow bureau chief, 1983-88, U.S. bureau chief in Washington, DC, 1989—. European Policy Institute, associate director in London and Geneva, Switzerland; European Institute, Washington, DC, vice-chairperson. Regular broadcaster for BBC-TV and BBC-Radio, including presenter of the documentary *Perestroika: Soviet Popular Culture,* BBC-TV, 1987, and the series *Martin Walker's Russia,* BBC-Radio, 1990; Washington commentator for Radio Telefeis Eiran, Radio and TV New Zealand, and for Australia's ABC-TV and ABC-Radio; regular commentator for CNN, CBC, C-Span, CBS-TV, and National Public Radio. Harvard University, Harkness fellow and resident tutor at Kirkland House, 1969-70; New School for Social Research, senior fellow of World Policy Institute; Loyola College, Baltimore, MD, H. L. Mencken Lecturer, 1994; lecturer at colleges and universities in Moscow, Pittsburgh, Toronto, Chicago, and New York City, and at National War College. *Military service:* Royal Air Force, Cadet Corps, 1962-66.

MEMBER: International Institute of Strategic Studies.

AWARDS, HONORS: Congressional fellow, American Political Science Association, 1970; named British Reporter of the Year, What the Papers Say Awards, 1987; named Foreign Correspondent of the Year by the Soviet magazine *Krokodil,* 1988.

WRITINGS:

The Happy Unicorns: Anthology of Young British Poets, Sidgwick & Jackson, 1972.
The National Front: Right-Wing Politics in Berlin, Fontana, 1977.
The Infiltrator (novel), Granada, 1978, Dial, 1979.
Daily Sketches: A History of Political Cartoons, Muller, 1978.
A Mercenary Calling (novel), Doubleday, 1981.
Powers of the Press: A Comparative Study of the World's Leading Newspapers, Quartet, 1981, Pilgrim Press (New York City), 1982.
The Eastern Question (novel), Granada, 1983.
The Waking Giant: Gorbachev and Perestroika, Pantheon, 1987.
Perestroika: Soviet Popular Culture (television documentary), BBC-TV, 1987.
Martin Walker's Russia, M. Joseph, 1989.
Martin Walker's Russia (radio series), BBC-Radio, 1990.
The Independent Traveller's Guide to the Soviet Union, Harper, 1990.
(With wife Julia Watson) *The Insight Guide to Washington, DC,* Insight Guides, 1992.
The Cold War: A History, Fourth Estate, 1993, Henry Holt, 1994.

Contributor to periodicals in the United States and abroad. Associate editor, *Demokratizatsiya;* member of editorial board, *World Policy Journal.*

WORK IN PROGRESS: The President We Deserve, a study of the Clinton presidency, publication by Crown expected in 1996.

SIDELIGHTS: Martin Walker told *CA:* "My original plan to become an academic did not survive the tedium of Harvard's graduate school of arts and sciences. Journalism seemed like more fun, with lots more travel and the chance to talk to interesting people, and just as much opportunity to work on subjects that interested me and to produce books. So it proved to be.

"Journalism has provided endless inspirations and opportunities to write, not just articles, but essays and books, too. My first book, *The National Front,* a study of the neo-fascist New Right in Britain, emerged from my domestic reporting for the *Guardian.* Covering the Portuguese revolution of 1974 inspired my first novel, *The Infiltrator,* as my coverage of the Angolan war inspired *A Mercenary Calling,* and the pre-coup atmosphere of Turkey in 1979 and 1980 led to *The Eastern Question.* Most of my journalistic career became raw material for my history *The Cold War.*

"In 1979, newly married and on an extended working honeymoon, my wife and I found ourselves in Iran as the Ayatollah's rule consolidated, and then in Afghanistan. We drove from Pakistan through the Quetta pass to Herat, which had just been re-taken after a burst of liberation that had seen a hundred Soviet military advisers and their families slaughtered, and their heads paraded through the town on pikes. In Kabul, the night sky was electric with the tracers of the gunships. The Khalq and Parcham factions of the Afghan Communist Party were at war, the Soviet advisers were joining in, and I had to defy the curfew to chase down some bottled water for my wife, who was stricken with dysentery. We left through the Khyber Pass on the last civilian convoy.

"Not for the first or the last time, I confronted the terrifying irony that, while my press card and passport paraded my neutrality, my skin made me indistinguishable from a hated Russian invader or, in other places at other times, from an equally loathed American imperialist. At a roadblock in southern Ethiopia in 1975, just after the fall of Haile Selassie, my harmless library card for the British Museum reading room almost got me shot as an American spy. Dodging Moroccan armored columns with the Polisario guerrillas of the western Sahara in 1977, or being held at gunpoint by Colonel Gadafy's troops in Libya in 1981, the role of the Cold War proxies of the Third World was brought sharply home. We were all white outsiders, trying to impose our will, or our order, on places where the locals found our presence unwelcome.

"I doubt that I could function happily without the daily adrenaline rush of journalism, the constant thrill of news and the challenge of deadlines. But equally, I could not be content if that were the sum of my work. I need the sense of detachment, of considering the deeper and more enduring currents that flow beneath the news, that writing books and essays provides. Journalism may be 'the first rough draft of history,' but books let me take that process a tentative step further. I can hardly believe my luck; it's better than working, and they pay me for it."

*　　*　　*

WALLER, Douglas C.　1949-

PERSONAL: Born June 30, 1949, in Norfolk, VA; son of Thomas C. (a naval officer) and Barbara A. (a homemaker) Waller; married, November 11, 1972; wife's name, Judith B. (a teacher); children: Drew, Colby, David. *Education:* Wake Forest Uni-

versity, B.A.; University of North Carolina at Charlotte, M.A.

ADDRESSES: Home—5001 Dodson Dr., Annandale, VA 22003. *Office*—Washington Bureau, *Time,* Washington, DC. *Agent*—Kris Dahl, International Creative Management, 40 West 57th St., New York, NY 10019.

CAREER: U.S. Congress, Washington, DC, legislative assistant, 1980-88; *Newsweek,* New York City, correspondent from Washington, DC, 1988-94; *Time,* New York City, correspondent from Washington, DC, 1994—. *Military service:* U.S. Army Reserve, discharged, 1980.

MEMBER: National Press Club.

WRITINGS:

(With Ed Markey) *Nuclear Peril: The Politics of Proliferation,* Ballinger, 1980.
Congress and the Nuclear Freeze: An Inside Look at the Politics of a Mass Movement, University of Massachusetts Press, 1987.
The Commandos, Simon & Schuster, 1994.

WORK IN PROGRESS: Research on naval aviation and on "the making of a top gun."

*　　*　　*

WALSH SHEPHERD, Donna　1948-

PERSONAL: Born October 29, 1948, in Centralia, WA; daughter of Maurice R. (an educator) and Bernice Olivia (an artist; maiden name, Swearingen) Walsh; married Morris W. Shepherd (a certified public accountant), June 10, 1972; children: Chadney, Shane, Aaron. *Education:* Olympic College, A.A.; Central Washington University, B.A.; University of Alaska, Anchorage, M.F.A. *Avocational interests:* Traveling, hiking, gardening.

ADDRESSES: Office—Department of English, University of Alaska, Anchorage, 3211 Providence Dr., Anchorage, AK 99504.

CAREER: University of Alaska, Anchorage, instructor in literature and writing, 1988—; technical writing consultant; children's book author.

MEMBER: Society of Children's Book Writers and Illustrators, Alaska Press Women.

AWARDS, HONORS: Best children's book, National Press Women, 1993, for *The Aztecs;* Excellence in

Journalism Award—Pacific Northwest division, 1993; awards from Alaska Press Women; award for University of Alaska, Anchorage and *Anchorage Daily News* writing contest.

WRITINGS:

Trixie Belden and the Mystery at Mead's Mountain, Western, 1978.
The Aztecs, F. Watts, 1992.
Uranus, F. Watts, 1994.
Auroras, F. Watts, in press.

Also contributor to periodicals.

WORK IN PROGRESS: Tundra, for F. Watts, 1996.

SIDELIGHTS: Donna Walsh Shepherd commented: "So often children consider nonfiction boring. Really, all the adventures and possibilities of the world live in nonfiction. I want my subject, whatever it is, to come alive and connect to the rest of the world. To do this, I try to experience as much of my subject as possible, whether it's walking where the ancient Aztecs walked and were killed, or looking through a telescope at Uranus and talking with *Voyager* scientists, or sleeping outside at thirty degrees below zero to watch the auroras catch fire to the sky. I believe in adventure, and the best of life's adventures begin in books.

"My writing career began with a book. One Christmas I took my children to visit my parents. Late one night I pulled an old Trixie Belden mystery off the shelf and read it with the same devouring delight I had as a child. As I put the book back on the shelf at three in the morning, I thought, 'That really was a good book. I could never write anything like that.' But my mind answered back, 'Well of course I could.' By morning I had plotted a whole new Trixie Belden mystery. Although very little of that ended up in print, I did get to write a Trixie Belden book. Later I began writing for magazines and newspapers and am now returning to children's books, which are so much fun and lead to so many wonderful adventures."

*   *   *

WARD, May McNeer
  See McNEER, May (Yonge)

*   *   *

WARD, W. R. 1925-

PERSONAL: Born March 23, 1925, in Chesterfield, Derbyshire, England; son of William Cromwell Gilmour (a civil servant) and Clarice (a homemaker; maiden name, Bowmer) Ward; married Barbara Elizabeth Uridge (a lecturer), October 9, 1949; children: Faith Ward Fraser, William Aidan, James Neil. *Education:* Oxford University, B.A., 1946, M.A., D.Phil., 1951. *Politics:* "Floating." *Religion:* Methodist.

ADDRESSES: Home—21 Grenehurst Way, Petersfield, Hampshire SU31 4AZ, England.

CAREER: Oxford University, Oxford, England, lecturer at Ruskin College, 1946-49; Victoria University of Manchester, Manchester, England, began as assistant lecturer, became senior lecturer in modern history, 1949-65; University of Durham, Durham, England, professor of modern history, 1965-86.

MEMBER: Royal Historical Society (vice-president, 1987-91), Ecclesiastical History Society (president, 1970-71), Chetham Society (secretary, 1963-84; president, 1984-93).

AWARDS, HONORS: D.Th., University of Basel, 1992.

WRITINGS:

English Land T . . . in the Eighteenth Century, Oxford University Press, 1953.
Georgian Oxford, Oxford University Press, 1958.
Victorian Oxford, Frank Cass, 1965.
Religion and Society in England, 1790-1850, Batsford, 1972.
The Early Correspondence of Jabez Bunting, Camden Society, 1972.
Early Victorian Methodism: The Correspondence of Jabez Bunting, Oxford University Press, 1976.
Theology, Sociology and Politics: The German Protestant Social Conscience, 1890-1933, P. Lang, 1979.
(With R. P. Heitzenrater) *Works of John Wesley, 18-25: Journals and Diaries,* Nashville, 1988—.
The Protestant Evangelical Awakening, Cambridge University Press, 1992.
Faith and Faction, Epworth, 1993.
(Editor) *Pol . . . Studies by W. H. Chaloner,* Chetham Society, 1993.
Pars . . . Parish: An Eighteenth Century Survey, Surrey Records Society, 1994.
Parson and Parish in Eighteenth Century Hampshire, Hampshire Record Series, 1994.

WORK IN PROGRESS: A survey of twentieth-century German church history; research on religion in Europe in the eighteenth century; research on the German Protestant reception of Dostoevsky and

Tolstoy; a church history of modern Britain.

* * *

WARNER, Margaret
See HUMPHREYS, Margaret

* * *

WARREN, James Francis 1942-

PERSONAL: Born April 1, 1942, in New York, NY; son of James F. and Elsie (Copeland) Warren; married Carol Ann Schug (a university teacher); children: Kristin. Education: State University of New York College at Cortland, B.A., 1964; Ohio University, M.A., 1971; Australian National University, Ph.D., 1975.

ADDRESSES: Home—6 Tintal Pl., Kardinya, Perth, Western Australia 6150. Office—Asian Studies Programme, Murdoch University, Murdoch, Perth, Western Australia 6150.

CAREER: U.S. Peace Corps, Washington, DC, volunteer in Sabah, Malaysia, 1967-68; Murdoch University, Perth, Australia, associate professor of modern Southeast Asian history, 1976—, head of Asian studies program, 1977, 1981, 1987, director of Asia Research Centre, 1988-89. Yale University, visiting teaching fellow, 1983; Kyoto University, visiting professorial research fellow, 1993.

MEMBER: Asian Studies Association of Australia, Philippine Studies Association of Australia, Malaysian Studies Association of Australia, Asian Studies Association (United States).

AWARDS, HONORS: Fellow of Social Science Research Council, 1982, and Australia Research Council, 1991.

WRITINGS:

The North Borneo Chartered Company's Administration of the Bajauy, 1878-1909, Ohio University, 1971.
The Sulu Zone, 1768-1898: The Dynamics of External Trade, Slavery, and Ethnicity in the Transformation of a Southeast Asian Maritime State, University of Singapore Press, 1981.
Rickshaw Coolie: A People's History of Singapore, 1880-1940, Oxford University Press, 1986.
At the Edge of Southeast Asian History: Essays by James Francis Warren, New Day Press, 1987.
Ah Ku and Karayuki-san: Prostitution in Singapore, 1870-1940, Oxford University Press, 1993.

WORK IN PROGRESS: Suicide in Singapore Chinese Society, 1880-1940, a book; Typhoon: Climate, History, and Society in the Philippines (tentative title), a book; research on aspects of Singapore Chinese working-class history and society since 1880.

SIDELIGHTS: James Francis Warren told CA: "A passion for a forgotten past of people who have stood outside history and recovery of a whole set of social relations have been a central preoccupation running through my work. The lessons in anthropology for the study of history suggest how to create a total set of social relations, a cultural system, in a historical past. This approach, involving the relationship between anthropology and history, is something I have stressed in my teaching over the past fourteen years, and I have tried to make it work in my writing.

"Rickshaw Coolie: A People's History of Singapore, 1880-1940, is the initial volume in a trilogy on the urban and social history of Singapore and the Chinese laboring classes. It is about the life and circumstances of the rickshawmen of Singapore. The book examines the origin and development of the rickshaw trade in Singapore, its control and regulation from the standpoint of the Chinese and British, the method of earning a livelihood in rickshaw pulling, and the character of a rickshaw coolie's life.

"Ah Ku and Karayuki-san: Prostitution in Singapore, 1870-1940, the second volume of the trilogy, aims to reconstitute the world of Chinese and Japanese prostitutes, examine the nature of their interaction with Singapore, and the causes and effects of immigration and colonialism on their lives. I hope that this study of prostitution and the regulation of prostitution in Southeast Asia will illuminate the complex mechanisms through which race, gender, and sexualities were refracted and shaped by migration, colonialism, and the city. I envisage the volume making a major contribution to women's history, working-class history, and the social history of sexuality, colonialism, and urbanism.

"The third volume of the trilogy, Suicide in Singapore Chinese Society, 1880-1940, concerns a way of dying. There is a lack of theoretical background for understanding suicide in comparative terms, and historically. The empirical evidence that will be presented in the third volume, along with a particular history of the Chinese laboring classes and the city, will be of concern to all those interested in the development of cross-cultural understanding and explanations of suicide.

"I have also been working on an environmental history of the Philippines. I hope to examine a wide variety of factors in the sweep, subject, and approach of this history of cyclonic storms, including economics, politics, institutions, population, culture, and the environment. I also have ongoing research interests in slavery, bondage, and dependency in Southeast Asia, and I am interested in the application of prosopography (collective biography) as the central method for researching and writing about the social history of the region."

* * *

WARREN, Richard (Andrew)   1961-

PERSONAL: Born April 7, 1961, in New York, NY; son of George and Florence (Brock) Warren. *Education:* Harvard University, A.B. (cum laude), 1983; University of Chicago, M.A., 1986, Ph.D., 1994.

ADDRESSES: Home—1680 University Dr., No. 11, Charleston, IL 61920. *Office*—History Department, Eastern Illinois University, Charleston, IL 61920.

CAREER: Departamento de Estudios Internacionales, Universidad de las Americas, Mexico City, Mexico, professor, 1993-94; Eastern Illinois University, Charleston, IL, assistant professor of history, 1994—; lecturer and workshop presenter.

MEMBER: American Historical Association, Conference on Latin American History, Latin American Studies Association.

AWARDS, HONORS: Leopold Schepp Foundation Scholarship, Harvard University, 1982-83; Graduate Fellowship, University of Chicago, 1984-88; Herschel G. Shaw Scholarship, University of Chicago, 1985-86; Tinker Foundation Summer Research Travel Grant, 1986; Fulbright/IIE Dissertation Research Grant, Mexico, 1988-90; University of Chicago Latin American Studies Travel Grant, 1993.

WRITINGS:

(Translator) Enrique Tandeter, *Coercion and Market: Silver Mining in Colonial Potosi, 1692-1826,* University of New Mexico Press (Albuquerque), 1993.

Contributor to *Encyclopedia of Latin American History,* Scribner's (New York, NY), forthcoming.

WORK IN PROGRESS: Studies on vagrancy and political order in Mexico, political ritual in Mexico during the nineteenth century, and Mexican nation-state formation during the nineteenth century.

* * *

WASHBURN, Stan   1943-

PERSONAL: Born January 2, 1943, in New York; son of Sherwood L. (an anthropologist) and Henrietta (Pease) Washburn; children: Anne, John. *Education:* California College of Arts & Crafts, B.F.A., 1967, M.F.A., 1968.

ADDRESSES: Office—2010 Virginia St., Berkeley, CA 94709. *Agent*—Frederick Hill Associates, 1842 Union St., San Francisco, CA 94123.

CAREER: North Point Gallery, San Francisco, CA, artist. College Preparatory School, Oakland, CA, trustee, 1986—.

WRITINGS:

George's Dragon, Godine, 1974.
Moral Alphabet of Vice & Folly, Arbor House, 1986.
Intent to Harm, Pocket Books (New York, NY), 1994.

* * *

WATERSTON, Alisse   1951-

PERSONAL: Born in 1951. *Education:* New York University, B.A., 1973; Columbia University, M.A., 1980; Graduate Center of the City University of New York, Ph.D., 1990.

ADDRESSES: Home—New Rochelle, NY. *Office*—HIV Center for Clinical and Behavioral Studies, Columbia University, 722 West 168th St., New York, NY 10032; and Surveys Unlimited, Horowitz Associates, Inc., 1971 Palmer Ave., Larchmont, NY 10538.

CAREER: Pace University, White Plains, NY, adjunct instructor in anthropology and sociology in White Plains and Pleasantville, NY, 1981-85; Narcotic and Drug Research, Inc. (now National Development and Research Institutes, Inc.), New York City, research fellow, 1986-91; State University of New York College at Purchase, adjunct assistant professor of social sciences, 1991-92; Fordham University, Bronx, NY, adjunct assistant professor of anthropology and sociology, 1992-93; Columbia University, New York City, postdoctoral research fellow at HIV Center for Clinical and Behavioral

Studies, 1994—. Horowitz Associates, Inc., senior analyst and project director, 1991-92, president of Surveys Unlimited, Ethnic Marketing Research Division, 1992—. Westchester County Youth Bureau, public policy and needs assessment researcher, 1982-85; New York Task Force on Immigrant Health, member of committee on medical ethnography, 1992—. Tuckahoe After School Care, Inc., president and founding vice president; City of New Rochelle, member of Neighborhoods and Affordable Housing Group, Future Visions Citizens Advisory Committee, 1994. American Marketing Association, chairperson of public relations for Ethnic Marketing Leadership Council, 1993—.

MEMBER: Society for the Anthropology of North America, American Anthropological Association, American Ethnological Association, American Public Health Association, American Sociological Society, Society for Applied Anthropology, Society for Medical Anthropology, Society for Urban Anthropology.

WRITINGS:

Street Addicts in the Political Economy, Temple University Press (Philadelphia), 1993.

Work represented in anthologies, including *Drug Use in America: Social, Political, and Cultural Perspectives,* edited by Peter Venturelli, Jones & Bartlett, 1994. Contributor to academic journals.

SIDELIGHTS: Alisse Waterston told *CA:* "My major career goal is to work as an applied anthropologist on urban social issues and thereby contribute solutions to some of our most pressing social problems. I am particularly interested in issues related to HIV/AIDS and substance abuse as these affect society's most vulnerable populations (for example, low-income, minority women). Toward this end, I apply my skills, energy, and talent in research, writing, and teaching, and in forging new alliances between academic research and community-based organizations that serve these populations.

"My early experiences informed my anthropological perspective on social issues. As a child, I was introduced to a mixture of cultures by the composition of my own family and by many years of living and traveling between New York, Cuba, and, later, Puerto Rico. After graduating from high school in San Juan, I moved to New York to continue my studies and work as a teacher in a Latino community in Brooklyn.

"My first research effort on urban social issues be-

gan during this time. As a participant-observer, I conducted research on the interplay between the cultural construction of gender and decision-making processes among heterosexual couples in an ethnically mixed, working-class neighborhood (primarily Puerto Rican and African American). This project led me to graduate school and to public policy and needs assessment research, which I conducted for the Westchester County Youth Bureau.

"I continued to develop my interest in the social context of social problems through my book *Street Addicts in the Political Economy.* In this study, I use an anthropological approach to analyze the relationship between social issues and the broader economic, political, and ideological context within which social problems are situated. My interested in AIDS developed from this work on street addicts, who are particularly vulnerable to HIV infection. I am currently conducting HIV prevention research among women who have a history of homelessness and diagnosis of mental illness."

*   *   *

WATKINSON, Sandra
See HAARSAGER, Sandra

*   *   *

WATSON, Ben 1956-
(Out To Lunch)

PERSONAL: Born October 18, 1956, in Kingston, London, England; son of William (an Orientalist) and Katherine (a translator; maiden name, Armfield) Watson. *Education:* Gonville and Caius College, Cambridge, B.A., 1977. *Politics:* "Revolutionary socialist." *Religion:* None. *Avocational interests:* Free jazz, classical new complexity composers, funk (gangtsa and go-go), cyberpunk fiction, language poetry.

ADDRESSES: Office—c/o Quartet Books Ltd., 27 Goodge St., London W1P 1FD, England.

CAREER: Trade Union and Community Resource and Information Centre, Leeds, England, publications officer, 1981-85; MFT Computers, Leeds, programmer, 1986-88; Kernel (now F1) Training, Leeds, relational database trainer, 1988-91; music journalist, 1991—.

WRITINGS:

Frank Zappa: The Negative Dialectics of Poodle Play, Quartet Books, 1994, St. Martin's, 1995.

POETRY COLLECTIONS; UNDER PSEUDONYM OUT TO LUNCH

1-2-3-4, Leeds SWP Roneo, 1980.
28 Sliverfish Macronix, Equipage, 1992.
Untrue Plonker Dunkin', Involution, 1994.
Turnpike Ruler, Equipage, 1994.

Writer for BBC-Radio. Contributor to periodicals, including *Wire, Hi Fi News, Resonance, Rubberneck,* and *Musical Times.*

WORK IN PROGRESS: Johnny "Guitar" Watson and the Story of West Coast R&B.

SIDELIGHTS: Ben Watson told *CA:* "I studied history at Gonville and Caius College, Cambridge, then changed to English literature in order to be supervised by the poet Jeremy Prynne. A follower of Charles Olson, Prynne presented lectures full of American radical thought—the Black Mountain school, questions about geographical space, the movement of peoples, imperialism, sixties 'happenings' and the relationship of art to life—in a deceptively conservative format. To my amazement, much of what he said appeared to be treated (in a very different way) by the rock musician Frank Zappa. This instigated a dissatisfaction with class-bound culture and social stratification that has informed my politics and poetics ever since. Punk was also a significant moment (my pseudonym Out to Lunch originated because I used to wear a raincoat with that slogan on the back). Currently I am still involved with music, especially with composer Simon Fell, who has set passages of my Zappa book to music in *Four Slices of Zappa,* released in 1992, and composed a jazz concerto around poems I wrote about record shops in Leeds, released as *Music for 10(0)* by Leo in 1995. I was the last person to interview Frank Zappa before he died, and his interest in my writing surprised and pleased me. Maybe the intellect and the body can get it together after all."

*   *   *

WATSON, Carol 1949-
(Harriet Hains)

PERSONAL: Born in 1949.

ADDRESSES: Home—3 Geraldine Rd., Strand-on-the-Green, Chiswick, London W4 3PA, England.

CAREER: Freelance writer and editor.

WRITINGS:

The House, illustrated by Colin King, Usborne, 1980.

The Shop, illustrated by King, Usborne, 1980.
The Town, illustrated by King, Usborne, 1980.
(With D. Bareijo) *Round the World in Spanish,* Usborne, 1980.
(With Katherine Folliot) *Round the World in French,* Usborne, 1980.
(With Mariolina Freeth) *Round the World in Italian,* Usborne, 1980.
(With Cornelie Tucking) *Round the World in German,* Usborne, 1980.
Robbers, illustrated by Stephen Cartwright, Usborne, 1981.
(Reteller) *Aesop's Fables,* illustrated by Nick Price, Usborne/Hayes, 1982.
(Reteller) *Animal Legends,* illustrated by Price, Usborne/Hayes, 1982.
(Reteller) *Magical Animals,* illustrated by Price, Usborne/Hayes, 1982.
(Editor) *The Usborne Book of Animal Stories,* Usborne, 1982.
Opposites, illustrated by David Higham, Usborne, 1983.
Shapes, illustrated by Higham, Usborne, 1983.
Sizes, illustrated by Higham, Usborne, 1983.
(With Robyn Gee) *Better English* (contains *English Grammar, English Spelling,* and *English Punctuation*), illustrated by Kim Blundell, Usborne, 1983.
1 2 3, illustrated by Higham, Usborne, 1984.
(With Heather Amery) *Colours,* illustrated by Higham, Usborne, 1984.
Telling the Time, illustrated by Higham, Usborne, 1984.
Simple Sums, illustrated by Higham, Usborne, 1984.
Shire Horse, illustrated by Sally Fear, A & C Black, c. 1988.
If You Were a Guinea Pig, Collins, 1988.
If You Were a Rabbit, Collins, 1988.
If You Were a Hamster, Collins, 1988.
(Editor) *Please God . . . .: B.B.C. Radio Leicester's Book of Children's Prayers,* Fount Publications, 1989.
(Author and compiler) *365 Children's Prayers,* Lion Publishing, 1989.
If You Were a Kitten, illustrated by Sue Cony, Dinosaur, 1989.
If You Were a Puppy, illustrated by Valerie Petrone, Dinosaur, 1989.
My Little Christmas Box, Lion Publishing, 1990.
Write-a-Story: At the Seaside, CollinsEducational, 1990.
Write-a-Story: Charlie's Chickenpox, Collins-Educational, 1990.
Write-a-Story: It's Snowing, CollinsEducational, 1990.
Write-a-Story: Moving Day, CollinsEducational, 1990.

Write-a-Story: The Invitation, CollinsEducational, 1990.

Read French: A Bilingual Picture Wordbook, French translations by M. L. Sharp, Usborne, 1991.

(Author and compiler) *Prayers for a Fragile World,* illustrated by Rhian Nest James, Lion Publishing, 1991.

If You Were a Photographer, illustrated by Petrone, Belitha, 1992.

If You Were a Pilot, illustrated by Petrone, Belitha, 1992.

(With Brian Jones) *Space Activity Book,* Gollancz, 1992.

(Under pseudonym Harriet Hains) *My Baby Brother,* photography by Steve Shott, illustrations by Conny Jude, Dorling Kindersley, 1992.

(Under pseudonym Harriet Hains) *My New Puppy,* photography by Shott, illustrations by Jude, Dorling Kindersley, 1992.

(Under pseudonym Harriet Hains) *My New School,* Dorling Kindersley, 1992.

(Under pseudonym Harriet Hains) *Our New Kitten,* Dorling Kindersley, 1992.

Also author of *English Grammar, English Spelling,* and *English Punctuation,* all for Usborne; *Mouse House,* Octopus Books; and *Write Your Own Storybooks* (four books), *First Facts, First Skills, Glue, Water, Paint,* and *Scissors,* all for Collins. Reteller for *Giants,* Collins. Reteller of fairy tales for *Storyteller* magazine.

Some of Watson's books have been translated into Gaelic or Welsh.

SIDELIGHTS: Carol Watson has collected and retold ancient legends and moral tales for young children. Presented in a comic-book style, they include *Aesop's Fables, Animal Legends,* and *Magical Animals.* The use of nonlinear storytelling and the simplification required by the comic format have led some reviewers to express doubts about the treatments, but others have noted that the less formal style might make the books appealing to readers not yet old enough for standard versions. Watson's *Robbers* is presented in a similar format, which *School Librarian* reviewer Cliff Moon commented achieves "the perfect balance" between text and illustration.

Watson has also written the text for a number of books through which the youngest of children can learn simple concepts and vocabulary. Her concept books for preschoolers include *Opposites, Shapes, Sizes,* and *Simple Sums. Opposites* introduces children to its basic concept through a comparison of two friends, one fat and one thin. In *Sizes* Watson uses the animals on Farmer Jo's farm to compare big, bigger, small, and smaller. *Simple Sums* is a "first-rate" introduction to mathematics, asserted a reviewer for the *Junior Bookshelf,* and Watson's vocabulary books *The Shop, The House,* and *The Town* are "definitely the best of their type," according to Moon.

For *If You Were a Kitten* and *If You Were a Puppy,* factual books in which Watson teaches how to care for pets, reviewers have recommended that adults supervise their children due to the difficulty of some of the vocabulary. *School Librarian* contributor Irene Babsky praised the books for their "imaginative insight into the world and needs of the animals" and the "wealth of information" they convey. Both books were praised for their charming illustrations and for the inclusion of a resource section in the back with advice, details of common health problems, and addresses for further information.

Watson's *Shire Horse* describes the life of a cart horse named Gilbert, and, like *If You Were a Kitten* and *If You Were a Puppy,* is intended for slightly older children. The stages of Gilbert's life are described in a manner which has been praised for both its simplicity and its clarity, including the training and grooming needed to prepare for showing the horse. A reviewer for *Books for Your Children* concluded that *Shire Horse* is "a very pleasing book both to look at and to think about."

BIOGRAPHICAL/CRITICAL SOURCES:

PERIODICALS

Booklist, March, 1981, p. 24; November 1, 1982, p. 364.

Books for Your Children, February, 1985, p. 32; summer, 1988, p. 16.

Junior Bookshelf, October, 1989, p. 233.

School Librarian, June, 1982, p. 127; December, 1982, p. 328; November, 1989, p. 146.

School Library Journal, February, 1983, pp. 63-64, p. 86; March, 1984, p. 167; April, 1984, pp. 109-110.

*   *   *

WAYLAND, April Halprin 1954-

PERSONAL: Born April 20, 1954, in Los Angeles, CA; daughter of Leahn J. (a farmer) and Saralee (a concert pianist; maiden name, Konigsberg) Halprin; married Gary Carlton Wayland (a certified public accountant), October 17, 1981; children: Jeffrey.

Education: University of California, Davis, B.S. (cum laude), 1976. *Religion:* Jewish.

ADDRESSES: Home—143 South Kenter Ave., Los Angeles, CA 90049. *Agent*—Curtis Brown, Ltd., 10 Astor Place, New York, NY 10003.

CAREER: Children's book writer and speaker. Has worked variously as a farmer, a government housing study worker for the Rand Corporation, a governess for comedian and talk show host Joan River's daughter, and a marketing manager for Pacific Bell. Cofounded Positive Education Inc., a nonprofit tutorial agency.

MEMBER: Authors Guild, Authors League of America, PEN, Society of Children's Book Writers and Illustrators, Association of Booksellers for Children, Southern California Children's Booksellers Association, Southern California Council on Literature for Children and Young People, Santa Monica Traditional Folk Music Club (founder, 1978).

AWARDS, HONORS: To Rabbittown was named a Junior Literary Guild selection, 1989, and was selected as a "Book of the Year" by Mommycare.

WRITINGS:

To Rabbittown, illustrated by Robin Spowart, Scholastic, 1989.
The Night Horse, illustrated by Vera Rosenberry, Scholastic, 1991.
It's Not My Turn to Look for Grandma!, illustrated by George Booth, Knopf, in press.

Contributor to anthologies, including *Poems for Mothers,* edited by Myra Cohn Livingston, McElderry Books, 1990; *If the Owl Calls Again,* edited by Livingston, McElderry Books, 1990; *Poems for Brothers, Poems for Sisters,* edited by Livingston, Holiday House, 1991; and *Roll Along: Poems on Wheels,* edited by Livingston, McElderry Books, 1993. Wayland's stories for children are also presented on the *Halfway Down the Stairs* radio program for KPFK-FM.

WORK IN PROGRESS: "A billion books."

SIDELIGHTS: "To rebel in my family, you had to join management in a Fortune 500 company and wear a suit every day," April Halprin Wayland commented. The daughter of a farmer and a concert pianist, Wayland grew up in Santa Monica, California, and spent her holidays and vacations at the family farm in Yuba City, five hundred miles north. Wayland began writing when she was thirteen years

old. "I learned to type and I was bitten by the writing bug," she confessed. "My bedroom was downstairs, so after everyone was asleep, I would type poems and stories late into the night and then hide them away in my desk drawer." Music was another of Wayland's interests. She began playing the violin at age ten, became interested in folk music in college, and founded the Santa Monica Traditional Folk Music Club in her late twenties. "Between fifty and one hundred of us still meet once a month with banjos, dulcimers, harmonicas, guitars, fiddles, mandolins, spoons, and bones—to play and sing and learn new tunes," she said.

After she graduated from college, Wayland held an assortment of jobs. She helped run the family farm after her father's death, worked as a governess for the daughter of comedian Joan Rivers, and cofounded a nonprofit tutorial organization called Positive Education, Inc. Finally, however, she settled into the corporate workforce. She went to work for Pacific Bell, eventually being promoted to marketing manager. Wayland's mother was skeptical about this career choice. "As I moved up in the corporate world," Wayland recalls, "my mother would stand in the doorway and sigh, 'You should quit and become a children's book writer—you'd be much happier.' Why are mothers always right?"

One of Wayland's first ventures into children's writing was a picturebook for her nephew, Joshua. "It wasn't brilliant literature, but I illustrated, xeroxed, laminated, and bound it," she noted. "The night I finished it, I was so jazzed, I couldn't sleep."

Wayland decided to become a full-time writer. She has issued three picture books, *To Rabbittown, The Night Horse,* and *It's Not My Turn to Look for Grandma!* In each volume she explores children's relation to animals using humor and whimsy. "I see my books as mixtures of colors," she explained. "I want each to be as clear and as strong and as beautiful as it can be. I love the picture book format."

Wayland remarked, "I can't say enough about the community of children's book writers in Southern California. Teachers have become mentors and friends—everyone generously shares his/her knowledge. I thrive in groups, and this community (in addition to my husband) has had much to do with the joy I find in my career." She added, "I once decided that I wanted to publish 133 children's books by my ninetieth birthday. Then I re-read *Charlotte's Web* by E. B. White and I realized that *one* wonderful book was enough. So my new goal is to write each book as brilliantly as I can."

BIOGRAPHICAL/CRITICAL SOURCES:

PERIODICALS

Publishers Weekly, January 13, 1989, p. 87.
School Library Journal, April, 1989, p. 92; April, 1991, p. 104.

*   *   *

WEAVER, Pat
  See WEAVER, Sylvester L(aflin), Jr.

*   *   *

WEAVER, Sylvester L(aflin), Jr.   1908-
  (Pat Weaver)

PERSONAL: Born December 21, 1908, in Los Angeles, CA; son of Sylvester L. and Isabel (Dixon) Weaver; married Elizabeth Inglis (an actress), January 23, 1941; children: Trajan Victor Charles, Susan Sigourney. Education: Dartmouth College, B.A. (magna cum laude), 1930. Politics: Republican. Religion: Episcopalian.

ADDRESSES: Home—818 Deerpath Rd., Santa Barbara, CA 93108. Agent—Frank Cooper, Los Angeles, CA.

CAREER: Originator of the magazine-style television show. Columbia Broadcasting System (CBS), Los Angeles, CA, writer and producer, 1932; CBS, San Francisco, CA, program director, 1933-35; Young & Rubicam, New York City, manager, 1935-38, vice president and member of executive committee, 1946-49; American Tobacco Co., advertising manager, 1938-46; National Broadcasting Co. (NBC), New York City, vice president, became vice chair, president, then chair, 1949-56; McCann Erickson, New York City, chair, 1958-63; Subscription TV, Los Angeles, president, 1963-66; worked as consultant in Santa Barbara, CA, 1967—. American Heart Association, chair, 1959-63; Muscular Dystrophy Association, on board of directors, 1967—, president, 1975—. Military service: Served in U.S. Navy, 1942-45.

MEMBER: Phi Beta Kappa.

AWARDS, HONORS: Peabody award, 1956; Emmy award, 1967; recipient of Sylvania, Look, and Variety awards; named to TV Hall of Fame, 1985.

WRITINGS:

(Under name Pat Weaver) The Best Seat in the House: The Golden Years in Radio and Television, Knopf, 1994.

WORK IN PROGRESS: Books and plays.

*   *   *

WEDEEN, Richard Peter   1934-

PERSONAL: Born January 19, 1934, in Brooklyn, NY; son of Sydney and Dorothy (Mason) Wedeen; married June 27, 1957; children: Timothy. Education: Attended Oberlin College, 1951-52; Harvard University, A.B., 1955; New York University, M.D., 1959.

ADDRESSES: Home—574 South Forest Dr., Teaneck, NJ 07666. Office—Veterans Administration Medical Center, East Orange, NJ 07018-1095.

CAREER: Beth Israel Hospital, New York City, intern, 1959-60, medical resident, 1960-61; Mount Sinai Hospital, New York City, research fellow in medicine and National Institutes of Health trainee in renal diseases, 1961-63, research assistant, 1961-65, medical resident, 1963-64, research associate, 1965-66; Mount Sinai School of Medicine of the City University of New York, New York City, instructor, 1966-68, assistant professor of medicine, 1968-72; University of Medicine and Dentistry of New Jersey, Newark, associate professor, 1972-76, professor of medicine, 1976—, clinical professor of interdisciplinary studies and professor of preventive medicine, both 1990—, director of Division of Occupational and Environmental Medicine, 1990—. Jersey City Medical Center, chief of renal section, 1971-75, director of Department of Medicine, 1976-78; Veterans Administration Medical Center (East Orange, NJ), associate chief of staff for research and development, 1978—, acting chief of staff, 1988-89; Veterans Biomedical Research Institute, president, 1989—; University Hospital (Newark), staff physician, 1990—. Harvard Medical School, visiting lecturer, 1968-69; University of Antwerp, visiting professor, 1985; lecturer at colleges and universities, including Johns Hopkins University, Oregon Health Sciences University, Yale University, Rutgers University, University of Maryland at College Park, and University of Washington, Seattle. Operation Crossroads Africa, medical program adviser, 1964-76; Legal Services of New Jersey, member of Lead Paint Working Group, 1989—; New Jersey Department of Health, member of Occupational Health Surveillance Advisory Committee, 1990. Performer with "A Cautionary Medicine Show" a "Medical Folk Musical," traveling shows about the history of industrial health.

MEMBER: International Society of Nephrology, American Society of Nephrology, American Society for Clinical Investigation, American College of Physicians (fellow), American Physiological Society, American Federation for Clinical Research, Society for Experimental Biology and Medicine, American Public Health Association, American Association for the History of Medicine, American Heart Association (member of board of directors of Hudson County Division, 1972-77), Collegium Ramazzini (fellow), Nephrology Society of New Jersey (president, 1974), Medical History Society of New Jersey (vice-president, 1986-87; president, 1988-89), New York Society of Nephrology.

AWARDS, HONORS: Grants from National Institutes of Health, 1964-77, American Heart Association, 1972-82, Veterans Administration, 1978-88, U.S. Department of Veterans Affairs, 1990-91, New Jersey Historical Commission, 1990-91 and 1992, and National Institute of Environmental Health Sciences, 1993-98; Polechek Foundation fellow, Mt. Sinai School of Medicine of the City University of New York, 1967-68; Outstanding Speaker Award from American Association for Clinical Chemistry, 1991.

WRITINGS:

Poison in the Pot: The Legacy of Lead, Southern Illinois University Press (Carbondale), 1984.
(Editor with H. E. Sheehan, and contributor) *Toxic Circles: Environmental Hazards from the Workplace into the Community,* Rutgers University Press (New Brunswick, NJ), 1993.

Work represented in anthologies, including *Diseases of the Kidney,* edited by R. Schrier and C. Gottschalk, Little, Brown, 4th edition, 1988, 5th edition, 1992; and *Human Lead Exposure,* edited by H. Needleman, CRC Press, 1992. Contributing editor, *American Journal of Industrial Medicine, 1987-92;* assistant editor, *Mount Sinai Journal of Medicine,* 1990—. Contributor of more than seventy articles to medical journals.

*   *   *

WEGMANN, Peter   1957-

PERSONAL: Born March 27, 1957, in Winterthur, Switzerland; son of Hans Wegmann (a merchant) and Emmy Wegmann-Steiner. *Education:* Attended University of Munich, 1980; University of Zurich, lic. phil, 1982, Ph.D., 1985. *Religion:* Protestant.

ADDRESSES: Home—Feldstrasse 45, Winterthur, Switzerland, CH-8400. *Office*—Stiftung Oskar Reinhart, Stadthausstrasse 6, Winterthur, Switzerland, CH-8400.

CAREER: Museum of the Oskar Reinhart Foundation, Winterthur, Switzerland, curator, 1983—.

WRITINGS:

Gottfried Semper's Art Theory, Stadtbibliothek (Winterthur), 1985.
(Coeditor) *Grenzbereiche der Architektur,* Wiese Verlag (Basel), 1985.
C. D. Friedrich to F. Holder, Insel Verlag (Frankfurt am Main), 1993, published in the United States as *Caspar David Friedrich to Ferdinand Hodler,* Metropolitan Museum of Art (New York, NY).

Also author of other publications in art history.

WORK IN PROGRESS: Research in the field of European painting.

*   *   *

WEINER, Marc A.   1955-

PERSONAL: Born February 7, 1955, in Seattle, WA; son of Seymour S. and Bobbie (West) Weiner; married Autje Petersen, August 21, 1982. *Education:* University of Massachusetts at Amherst, B.A. (summa cum laude), 1978; Stanford University, M.A., 1979, Ph.D., 1984.

ADDRESSES: Home—810 South Henderson, Bloomington, IN 47401. *Office*—Department of Germanic Studies, 644 Ballantine Hall, Indiana University—Bloomington, Bloomington, IN 47405.

CAREER: Indiana University at Bloomington, assistant professor, 1985-92, associate professor of Germanic studies, 1992—, associate professor of film studies, 1994—. Harvard University, Andrew W. Mellon faculty fellow at Center for Cultural and Literary Studies, 1987-88.

MEMBER: Modern Language Association of America (member of executive committee, division on nineteenth- and early twentieth-century German literature, 1994), American Association of Teachers of German, German Studies Association.

AWARDS, HONORS: Fulbright grants, 1980; scholarship from Richard Wagner Gedenkstaette, 1980; fellow of German Academic Exchange Service, 1991; Alexander von Humboldt fellow in Cambridge, England, 1992, and Heidelberg, Germany, 1992-93.

WRITINGS:

Arthur Schnitzler and the Crisis of Musical Culture, Carl Winter (Heidelberg), 1986.

(Editor) Vera Stegmann, *Igor Strawinsky und Bertold Brecht: Zur Poetik eines epischen Musiktheaters* (monograph), Peter Lang (New York), 1991.

Undertones of Insurrection: Music, Politics, and the Social Sphere in the Modern German Narrative, University of Nebraska Press (Lincoln), 1993.

Richard Wagner and the Anti-Semitic Imagination, University of Nebraska Press, in press.

Work represented in anthologies, including *Music and German Literature,* edited by James M. McGlathery, Camden House, 1992; *Re-Reading Wagner,* edited by Reinhold Grimm and Jost Hermand, University of Wisconsin Press, 1993; and *A History of Jewish Writing in Germany,* edited by Sander L. Gilman and Jack Zipes, Yale University Press, in press. Editor, *German Quarterly,* 1994—. Contributor to academic journals.

*   *   *

WEISS, Timothy F.   1949-

PERSONAL: Born December 17, 1949, in Omaha, NE; son of Francis (an engineer) and Margaret (a nurse; maiden name, Ort) Weiss; married Charlotte Thompson (an instructor in French), May 4, 1985. *Education:* University of Colorado, B.A. (with distinction), 1971; University of Wisconsin—Madison, M.A., 1974; University of New Mexico, Ph.D., 1981.

ADDRESSES: Home—1 Colburn Dr., 14 Whispering Pines, Orono, ME 04473. *Office*—Department of English, University of Maine at Orono, Orono, ME 04469.

CAREER: University of Illinois at Urbana-Champaign, Urbana, assistant professor of English, 1985-91; University of Maine at Orono, director of professional writing, 1991—.

MEMBER: Modern Language Association of America, Fulbright Association, National Council of Returned Peace Corps Volunteers.

AWARDS, HONORS: Senior Fulbright scholar, 1988-89, 1993-94.

WRITINGS:

Fairy Tale and Romance in the Works of Ford

Madox Ford, University Press of America, 1984.
On the Margins: The Art of Exile in V. S. Naipaul, University of Massachusetts Press, 1992.

WORK IN PROGRESS: Intercultural Space, on literary criticism and post-colonial literature.

*   *   *

WELLS, Susan (Mary)   1951-

PERSONAL: Born December 12, 1951, in Bath, England. *Education:* New Hall College, Cambridge University, B.A. (with honors), 1973; M.S., 1977. *Avocational interests:* Scuba diving.

ADDRESSES: Home—56 Oxford Rd., Cambridge CB4 3PW, England.

CAREER: Natural History Museum, London, England, scientific officer, 1974; Station Biologique de la Tour du Valat, Camargue, France, researcher, 1974-77; International Union for Conservation of Nature and Natural Resources (IUCN) SSC Traffic Group, London, researcher, 1978-80; IUCN Conservation Monitoring Centre, Cambridge, England, research officer, 1980-83; senior research officer and senior editor of IUCN/United Nations Environment Programme (UNEP) Directory of Coral Reefs of International Importance, 1983-87. International Council for Bird Preservation (ICBP), Cambridge, assistant director of information and editor of *World Birdwatch,* 1988; independent environmental consultant, 1989-91; University of Newcastle-upon-Tyne, Newcastle-upon-Tyne, England, research associate, 1991-92; International Center for Living Aquatic Resources Management (ICLARM), Manila, Philippines, consultant, 1992. Scientific advisor for television programs on coral reefs, invertebrates, and birds; speaker on conservation issues on radio programs and at professional conferences.

MEMBER: International Society for Reef Studies, IUCN/SSC Mollusc Specialist Group (co-chair), IUCN Coral Reef Fish Group, IUCN/SSC Invertebrate Task Force, Unitas Malacologia, Marine Conservation Society Coral Reef Team, NGO Forum for U.K. Dependent Territories Forum.

AWARDS, HONORS: Second place award, Sir Peter Kent Conservation Book Prize, 1992, for *The Greenpeace Book of Coral Reefs.*

WRITINGS:

(With R. M. Pyle and N. M. Collins) *The IUCN Invertebrate Red Data Book,* IUCN (England

and Switzerland), 1983.

(With M. Haywood) *Manual of Marine Invertebrates,* Salamander Books, 1989.

(Editor and contributor) *Coral Reefs of the World,* Volume 1: *Atlantic and Eastern Pacific,* Volume 2: *Indian Ocean, Red Sea and Gulf,* Volume 3: *Central and Western Pacific,* United Nations Environment Programme, 1989.

The Illustrated World of Oceans, Simon and Schuster, 1991.

Explore the World of Mighty Oceans, Western, 1992.

(With N. Hanna) *The Greenpeace Book of Coral Reefs,* Sterling, 1992.

Coral Reef (pop-up book), HarperCollins Children's Books, in press.

Contributor to *Encyclopaedia of the Animal Kingdom,* edited by R. Burton, Optimum Books, 1982, and *The Atlas of Endangered Species,* edited by J. Burton, Macmillan, 1991. Also editor of newsletters, including *Reef Encounter* and *Tentacle.* Contributor to scientific journals and periodicals, including *New Science, Scientific Approaches to Management of Shellfish Resources,* and *Biology and Conservation of Sea Turtles.*

WORK IN PROGRESS: Researching coral reef conservation.

*   *   *

WESLAGER, C(linton) A(lfred)   1909-1994

OBITUARY NOTICE—See index for *CA* sketch: Born April 30, 1909, in Pittsburgh, PA; died August 5, 1994, in North Star, DE. Historian, archaeologist, educator, and writer. Weslager wrote numerous books and scholarly articles focusing on the state of Delaware and its people, including the Native Americans and early European settlers in that region. After retiring from the DuPont Company, where he worked in various capacities for thirty years, Weslager joined the faculty at Wesley College, and later the University of Delaware, as a professor of Delaware history. Subsequently he taught at Widener University, from which he retired in 1983. Publications by Weslager include *Delaware's Forgotten Folk, Dutch Explorers, Traders and Settlers in the Delaware Valley, History of the Delaware Indians,* and *The Nanticoke Indians, Past and Present.*

OBITUARIES AND OTHER SOURCES:

BOOKS

Who's Who in America, 47th edition, Marquis, 1992.

Who's Who in the World, 11th edition, Marquis, 1993.

PERIODICALS

Washington Post, August 9, 1994, p. B6.

*   *   *

WEXLER, Alan   1947-

PERSONAL: Born August 11, 1947; son of Nathan and Minnie (Idoff) Wexler. *Education:* State University College at Oneonta, B.A., 1969, M.A., 1972.

ADDRESSES: Home—26 Van Dam St., New York, NY 10013.

CAREER: The Maverick Group, New York City, senior copywriter, 1993—; author. Worked variously as a bike messenger, short-order cook, waiter, cashier, computer operator, advertising salesperson, and dude ranch cowboy.

AWARDS, HONORS: Who Was Who in World Exploration was named *Library Journal*'s Best Reference Source of 1992.

WRITINGS:

The Scandal Annual, Paper Jacks, 1986.

(With Carl Waldman) *Who Was Who in World Exploration,* Facts on File, 1992.

The Atlas of Westward Expansion, Facts on File, 1994.

Encarta, Microsoft, 1995.

SIDELIGHTS: Alan Wexler told *CA:* "My writing career began as a writer for a Milton Bradley trivia game called *Stage Two.* The jump to writing history isn't too hard to understand if you think of trivia as simply history all broken up. In between, I wrote a few mass-market paperback humor books, including an annual retrospective on the year's best scandals called *The Scandal Annual* (1986).

"Writing history requires a sense of humor. The facts are often sobering enough. When writers and teachers impose their own moral imperatives on history, it makes for a top-heavy product that may be 'politically correct' but is so lacking in fun that it turns off more people than it attracts.

"What is really alarming is that book publishers are now kow-towing to the demands of special interest groups in academia and are going out of their way to make their books more 'politically correct'—even at the expense of distorting historical facts to inflate the significance of women, Native Americans, and African Americans in American history.

"These days, writers should look to the needs of the burgeoning electronic publishing industry as an outlet for their talent. CD-ROMs are now in the same marketing phase as books were when Gutenberg perfected the printing press five hundred years ago. Technology has created a new demand for written material that far outstrips the supply. Writers who are intimidated by computers and for whom the very thought of writing for computers is abhorrent, consider this: there were probably many who would not give up the feather for the fountain pen, and later a few diehards were loathe to adapt to the typewriter. Likewise, some today still eschew the word processor for their Smith Coronas. There was also a time not long ago when many writers would never 'stoop' to writing for the movies or television. The more things change, the more they stay the same."

*   *   *

WHEATON, Barbara Ketcham   1931-

PERSONAL: Born July 18, 1931, in Philadelphia, PA; daughter of George Walker (a lumber merchant) and Ruth (Van Sciver) Ketcham; married Robert Wheaton (a historian), October 6, 1956; children: Catherine, Joseph, Henry. *Education:* Mount Holyoke College, B.A. (cum laude), 1953; Harvard University, Radcliffe College, M.A., 1954; Ecole des Trois Gourmandes, diplome (*avec mention*), 1965.

ADDRESSES: Home and office—268 Elm St., Concord, MA 01742.

CAREER: Writer.

MEMBER: Women's Culinary Guild (charter member), American Institute of Wine and Food (board of advisors), Women's Culinary Guild of New England, Culinary Historians of Boston (cofounder, cochair).

AWARDS, HONORS: Louise Fitzrandolph Fellowship, Mount Holyoke College, 1953, for graduate work in art history; Helen Dupree Bullock Research Award, Societe des Dames d'Escoffier, 1981.

WRITINGS:

Savoring the Past: The French Kitchen and Table from 1300 to 1789, University of Pennsylvania Press, 1983.

(Editor, and author of introduction) Agnes B.

Marshall, *Victorian Ices and Ice Cream: 117 Delicious and Unusual Recipes Updated for the Modern Kitchen,* Metropolitan Museum of Art/Scribner, 1984 (originally published as *Book of Ices,* Marshall's School of Cookery, 1885; appeared as *Ices Plain and Fancy,* Metropolitan Museum of Art, 1976).

(With Patricia Kelly) *Bibliography of Culinary History: Food Resources in Eastern Massachusetts,* G. K. Hall, 1987.

Contributor of reviews and articles to *Harvard Magazine* and *The Papers of the Bibliographical Society of America.*

WORK IN PROGRESS: "I'm making a computerized database of selected European recipes before 1800. I hope to expand it into an analysis of recipes. Then I'll get back to writing about them."

SIDELIGHTS: When Barbara Ketcham Wheaton began studying culinary history, she quickly found gaps in the existing literature and began what eventually became a twenty-year investigation into the subject. Wheaton's extensive research in this little-studied topic garnered praise for her first book, *Savoring the Past: The French Kitchen and Table from 1300 to 1789.* The work explores representative meals for each era of this period in French history, including the medieval feast, the sixteenth-century collation, the fete in the seventeenth century, and the intimate supper of the eighteenth. Though the recipes of the time are an important part of the work, Wheaton focuses on the social, cultural, and political signals in the cooking of the day. In the *New York Times Book Review,* critic Gloria Levitas commented: "Combining historical imagination with a sturdy sense of reality, this delightful book shows how food was used to display status, assert privilege and maintain group solidarity in medieval, Renaissance and pre-Revolutionary France."

Some critics noted Wheaton's remarks concerning, such topics as the nursery rhyme about blackbirds being baked in a pie and whether Catherine de Medici did indeed usher in a new era in French cooking during her reign in the sixteenth century. Calling the book "lively," Jane Grigson of the *Times Literary Supplement* asserted that Wheaton's account could have more fully discussed the less pleasant aspects of culinary history, such as the pervasive stench of spoiled food caused by lack of modern sanitation and refrigeration. Nonetheless, many reviewers found much to praise in Wheaton's history. Peter Quennell remarked in the *Spectator* that

"Savouring the Past, despite its rather meretricious title, is a scholarly, amusing and highly informative treatise. I have learned much from it."

Wheaton told *CA:* "Culinary history has been insufficiently studied; eating is a crucial part of human behavior and it is time that we found out about it. I like to travel, especially in Europe. Museums and architecture interest me most. I speak French, and read (haltingly) Dutch, German, and Italian cookbooks."

BIOGRAPHICAL/CRITICAL SOURCES:

PERIODICALS

Boston Globe Magazine, May 1, 1983, pp. 14, 75-77.
New York Times Book Review, July 24, 1983, pp. 7, 17.
Spectator, October 22, 1983, pp. 23-24.
Times Literary Supplement, December 23, 1983, p. 1442.

*　　*　　*

WHELDON, David　1950-

PERSONAL: Born January 13, 1950, in Leicestershire, England; son of Wilfrid and Florence (Sturgeon) Wheldon; married Sarah Longlands (an artist), December 31, 1993. *Education:* Bristol University, M.B.Ch.B., 1973. *Avocational interests:* Writing novels, poetry, caving, carpentry.

ADDRESSES: Home—Swift Villa, 72 Kimbolton Road, Bedford, MK40 2NZ, England. *Office*—c/o The Bodley Head, 9 Bow St., London, England, WC2. *Agent*—Mr. B. Coward, Lloyd-George & Coward, Fairfax Pl., Dartmouth, Devon, England.

CAREER: Yeovil General Hospital, house surgeon, 1973-74; Frenchay Hospital, Bristol, England, house physician, 1974; Radcliffe Infirmary, Oxford, England, resident pathologist, 1974-75, registrar in pathology, 1975-77, senior registrar in microbiology, 1977-79; Bedford General Hospital, consultant microbiologist, 1980-92; consulting microbiologist in various hospitals throughout England; writer.

MEMBER: Royal College of Pathologists (fellow); Cerberus Spelaeological Society.

AWARDS, HONORS: Triple First Award, 1983, for *The Viaduct.*

WRITINGS:

The Viaduct (novel), Bodley Head, 1982, Penguin, 1983.
The Course of Instruction (novel), Bodley Head, 1984.
A Vocation, Bodley Head, 1986.
At the Quay, Barrie & Jenkins (London, England), 1990.

WORK IN PROGRESS: "Two manuscripts which intensify and give direction to the questions encountered in the earlier work; their form is changing, too; from my beginnings as a writer in prose form I am finding a poetic voice which widens expression. This writing makes difficult demands on its readers, and is not publishable. I am unsure how important this is. I would in the end prefer to follow an inner lucidity rather than an outward convention."

SIDELIGHTS: Physician David Wheldon wrote his award-winning first novel, *The Viaduct,* in the evenings after a full day's work at a hospital. *The Viaduct* and its successors, *The Course of Instruction* and *A Vocation,* are extended metaphors that invite the reader to meditate on numerous philosophical questions.

The Viaduct follows the random travels of a man named Alexander, who has left his native city after serving a prison sentence for sedition in order to escape further persecution by the authorities. His aimless travels serve as a metaphor for the uncertainty and spiritual questioning inherent in human existence. However, according to *Los Angeles Times* book editor Art Seidenbaum, Wheldon "is not doctrinaire. He is barely descriptive. . . . The setting is almost as austere as an empty stage and the language is almost as plain as a public school primer. The beauty of this first novel is in the mind of the beholder because the reader must also question and look for answers and make complicated choices." In the *Times Literary Supplement,* Linda Taylor wrote, "He is good . . . at conveying the way in which the apparent freedom and honesty of the transient life ultimately lead to lack of communication and dullness." London *Times* reviewer Gay Firth called Wheldon's novel "full of vivid characterization and event" and "strange, original, gentle to read." Miranda Seymour, writing in the *Spectator,* noted: "This is a subtle and intriguing novel, responding to many interpretations. . . . There are moments when Mr. Wheldon becomes so Kafkaesque that I wondered if he had set out to write a pastiche, or even if the novel was a translation of some undiscovered work by a Czech writer."

Wheldon's second novel, *The Course of Instruction,* also features a protagonist named Alexander. He is invited through an official-looking letter to attend "a course of instruction," but when he arrives at the designated location he encounters a bizarre and somewhat sinister environment where no mention is made of any such class. Calling *The Course of Instruction* more powerful than *The Viaduct,* London *Times* critic Nicholas Shakespeare remarked that characters "are described in prose that is meticulously precise. Meticulous too is the way David Wheldon sustains his allegory and mystery." "Wheldon's writing is precise and chilly," commented Grace Ingoldby in the *New Statesman.* "Resisting melodrama, Wheldon's mix of the familiar and the strange made *The Course of Instruction* a convincing, disturbing read."

In Wheldon's third novel, *A Vocation,* a transient named Colver arrives in a strange village where the minimal activity is directed by the tolling of a monastery bell. According to John Melmoth in the *Times Literary Supplement,* "*A Vocation* is a more sonorous and extended exercise than its predecessors." Melmoth concluded that Wheldon's "allegory secretes a protective covering that is capable of concealing a multitude of sins. It is resistant to analysis—one either enjoys it or one doesn't."

BIOGRAPHICAL/CRITICAL SOURCES:

PERIODICALS

Los Angeles Times, October 12, 1983.
New Statesman, March 23, 1984, p. 27.
Spectator, April 30, 1983, p. 25.
Times (London), March 24, 1983; March 29, 1984.
Times Literary Supplement, April 1, 1983, p. 324; April 13, 1984, p. 396; May 23, 1986, p. 552.

*　　*　　*

WHITE, Jonathan　1956-

PERSONAL: Born May 9, 1956, in Los Angeles, CA; son of William Robert (an engineer) and Jayne (Perry) White. *Education:* Lewis and Clark College, B.A. (cum laude), 1978. *Politics:* Democrat. *Avocational interests:* Scuba diving, surfing, skiing, hiking, sailing.

ADDRESSES: Home and office—P.O. Box 299, Orcas, WA 98280.

CAREER: Director of a nonprofit educational organization, sponsoring seminars aboard a wooden schooner along the Pacific Northwest coast, 1983-93; general contractor on Orcas Island, WA, 1994—. Orcas Island Public Library, member of book selection committee; Resource Institute, member of board of directors.

WRITINGS:

Talking on the Water, Sierra Books, 1994.

Contributor to periodicals, including *Orion* and *Whole Earth Review.*

WORK IN PROGRESS: Research on the relationship between tides, people, and the moon, with a book expected to result.

SIDELIGHTS: Jonathan White told *CA:* "I live on a small island in northwestern Washington. Writing is the most difficult and, by far, the most satisfying thing I do. It's like wrestling with an angry dog at the level of the sentence. I call my studio, which I built this winter out among the madronas, an infirmary and, as Annie Dillard suggests, when I go out there, I don't so much write essays or books as I sit up with them, as one does with a dying friend. It is a good way to explore, for I often find myself saying or thinking things I never would have, if I had not sat down in the first place."

*　　*　　*

WHITE, Stephen K.　1949-

PERSONAL: Born January 18, 1949, in Richmond, VA; married; children: two. *Education:* University of Virginia, B.A. (with high distinction), 1970; attended University of Konstanz, 1978-79; Graduate School of the City University of New York, Ph.D., 1980.

ADDRESSES: Office—Department of Political Science, Virginia Polytechnic Institute and State University, P.O. Box 0130, Blacksburg, VA 24063-0130.

CAREER: University of Hartford, Hartford, CT, assistant professor of political science, 1980-81; Virginia Polytechnic Institute and State University, Blacksburg, assistant professor, 1981-87, associate professor, 1987-91, professor of political science, 1991—, director of graduate studies, 1988-89, 1991—. University of Frankfurt, research fellow, 1987-88. Conference for the Study of Political Thought, member of planning committee, 1990—.

MEMBER: American Political Science Association, Phi Beta Kappa.

AWARDS, HONORS: Fulbright fellow in Germany, 1978-79; grants from National Endowment for the Humanities, 1981, 1991, fellowship, 1984; fellow of American Council of Learned Societies, 1981-82, and German Academic Exchange, 1982; Alexander von Humboldt fellow in Germany, 1987-88.

WRITINGS:

The Recent Work of Jurgen Habermas: Reason, Justice, and Modernity, Cambridge University Press, 1988.
(Editor and contributor) *Lifeworld and Politics: Between Modernity and Post-Modernity,* University of Notre Dame Press, 1989.
Political Theory and Postmodernism, Cambridge University Press, 1991.
Edmund Burke: Modernity, Politics, and Aesthetics, Sage Publications, 1994.
(Editor and contributor) *The Cambridge Companion to Habermas,* Cambridge University Press, 1995.

Work represented in anthologies, including *Idioms of Inquiry: Critique and Renewal in Political Science,* edited by Terence Ball, State University of New York Press, 1987; *The Aesthetics of the Critical Theorists,* edited by Ronald Roblin, Edwin Mellen Press, 1990; and *Politics at the End of History,* edited by Dasilva and Kanjirathinkal, Peter Lang, 1993. Contributor of articles and reviews to political science journals. Member of editorial board, *Philosophy and Social Criticism.*

*   *   *

WHITE, William D.   1945-

PERSONAL: Born July 13, 1945, in Philadelphia, PA; son of Gilbert F. (a professor) and Anne (a geographer; maiden name, Underwood) White; married Olivia Peabody Murray, August 24, 1985; children: Lydia Bayard, Gilbert Edward Livingston. *Education:* Haverford College, B.A., 1967; Harvard University, Ph.D., 1975. *Politics:* Democrat. *Religion:* Society of Friends (Quakers).

ADDRESSES: Home—5607 Dorchester Ave., Chicago, IL 60637. *Office*—Institute of Government and Public Affairs, University of Illinois at Chicago Circle, 921 West Van Buren, Suite 230, Chicago, IL 60637.

CAREER: University of Illinois at Chicago Circle, Chicago, assistant professor, 1975-82, associate professor, 1982-94, professor of economics, 1994—, associate professor of government and public affairs,

1989-94, professor, 1994—, associate director of Institute of Government and Public Affairs, 1991-94.

AWARDS, HONORS: Woodrow Wilson fellow, 1967-68.

WRITINGS:

Public Health and Private Gain: The Economics of Occupational Licensure of Clinical Laboratory Personnel, Routledge & Kegan Paul, 1979.

Co-editor of the book *Competitive Approaches to Health Care Reform,* Urban Institute (Washington, DC).

WORK IN PROGRESS: Editing *Health Care Reform and the Role of the States,* with Robert Rich.

*   *   *

WHITEMAN, Roberta J. Hill   1947-

PERSONAL: Born in 1947; daughter of a musician/teacher; married Ernest Whiteman (an artist), 1980; children: Jacob, Heather, Melissa. *Education:* University of Wisconsin, B.A.; University of Montana, M.F.A., 1973; University of Minnesota, Ph.D.

ADDRESSES: Home—3354 Runway F, Eau Claire, WI 54601.

CAREER: Instructor for Poets-in-the-Schools Program at various locales, including Minnesota, Arizona, and Oklahoma; University of Wisconsin, Eau Claire, instructor of American literature.

WRITINGS:

Star Quilt (poetry), illustrated by Ernest Whiteman, Holy Cow! Press, 1984.

Work represented in *Carriers of the Dream Wheel: Contemporary Native American Poetry,* edited by Duane Niatum, Harper, 1975; *The Third Woman: Minority Women Writers of the United States,* edited by Dexter Fisher, Houghton, 1980; and *Harper's Anthology of Twentieth Century Native American Poetry,* edited by Niatum, Harper, 1988.

WORK IN PROGRESS: Researching a history of the Oneida migrations.

SIDELIGHTS: Roberta J. Hill Whiteman, a poet of Wisconsin Oneida heritage, is the author of *Star Quilt,* a poetry collection which integrates her ancestral culture with European-based approaches to verse. Whiteman grew up in Wisconsin among the Oneida community and also in Green Bay; the family moved between the two locales several times. In previous centuries the Oneida were forced to make a series of moves that displaced them from their ancestral lands in New York State. By the twentieth century the tribe was scattered throughout various parcels of land in the United States and Canada.

A sense of dispossession engendered by forced migration has long been a part of Oneida culture, and this attitude is evident in Whiteman's poetry. The selections in *Star Quilt* are centered around the concepts of six basic directions—north, south, east, west, the sky, and the earth. The works are written in the iambic form, a rhythmic structure common to the poetry of western civilization. One poem, "Women Seed Player," is based on a modernist painting by Dakota artist Oscar Howe. Other works speak to Whiteman's children and future generations of Oneida.

Whiteman credits the influence of other contemporary Native American writers as well as her musician father and well-read grandmother for instilling her work with its own rhythms and confidence. Commenting on both historical displacement as well as her family's own transient nature in *Survival This Way: Interviews with American Indian Poets,* Whiteman stated: "For most of my life I felt this sense of exile and alienation and a fear. . . . But there is this sense of home and of completeness that I also feel. Somehow I think that part of the writing is to set the record straight—for myself, to explain things for myself as if I were still a child inside."

BIOGRAPHICAL/CRITICAL SOURCES:

BOOKS

Bruchac, Joseph, *Survival This Way: Interviews with American Indian Poets,* Sun Tracks/University of Arizona Press, 1987.*

*   *   *

WHITESELL, Faris Daniel 1895-1984

OBITUARY NOTICE—See index for *CA* sketch: Born August 11, 1895, in Vigo County, IN; died November 24, 1984. Baptist minister and writer. Whitesell was the author of numerous handbooks and study manuals in the field of homiletics and evangelism, including *Sixty-five Ways to Give an Evangelistic Invitation, The Art of Bible Preaching,* and *Preach-*

ing on Bible Characters. After working as a civilian clerk with the U.S. Navy Department in Washington, D.C., he moved to Chicago, where he attended Moody Bible Institute and became a Baptist. Whitesell subsequently entered William Jewell College, from which he graduated in 1921, having been ordained the previous year by Tabernacle Baptist Church in Kansas City, Missouri. He also received advanced degrees from Loyola University and Northern Baptist Theological Seminary. At the latter school he served on the faculty for forty years, retiring in 1965. Whitesell held pastorates in the Chicago area and was active as a preacher at evangelistic campaigns and conferences throughout the United States and Canada.

OBITUARIES AND OTHER SOURCES:

PERIODICALS

Northern, winter, 1985, p. 1.

*   *   *

WILLIAMS, Philip F. (C.) 1956-

PERSONAL: Born April 5, 1956, in Little Rock, AR; son of Franklin S. (a university professor) and Elizabeth B. (a public schoolteacher) Williams; married Yenna Wu (a university teacher), November, 1990; children: Nigel S. W. *Education:* University of Arkansas, B.A., 1978; graduate study at Cornell University, 1978-79; University of California, Los Angeles, M.A., 1981, Ph.D., 1985; attended Peking University, 1982-83. *Religion:* "Secular humanist." *Avocational interests:* Classical music, gardening, tennis.

ADDRESSES: Home—Riverside, CA. *Office*—Department of Languages and Literatures, Arizona State University, Tempe, AZ 85287-0202.

CAREER: Occidental College, Los Angeles, CA, instructor, 1984; University of California, Los Angeles, instructor, 1984, visiting assistant professor of Chinese, 1986; Arizona State University, Tempe, assistant professor of Chinese, 1986-90; Harvard University, Cambridge, MA, postdoctoral research fellow at Fairbank Center, 1990-91; University of Vermont, Burlington, assistant professor of Chinese, 1991-92; Arizona State University, associate professor of Chinese, 1993—. U.S. Department of State, escort and interpreter, 1986—. University of California, Los Angeles, member of executive committee, Contemporary Chinese Film Festival, 1982; public speaker; guest on television programs.

MEMBER: American Association of University Professors, Association for Asian Studies, American Association for Chinese Comparative Literature, Chinese Language Teachers Association, Southwest Conference of Asian Studies (member of executive board, 1994—), Phi Beta Kappa.

AWARDS, HONORS: Grant for China from U.S. National Academy of Sciences, 1982-83; grants from National Endowment for the Humanities, 1989, and Pacific Cultural Foundation, 1990-91.

WRITINGS:

Village Echoes: The Fiction of Wu Zuxuang, Westview, 1993.

Work represented in anthologies, including *Great Events From History II: Arts and Culture,* Salem Press (Pasadena, CA), 1993. Editor of "Center for Asian Studies Monograph Series," Arizona State University, 1990. Contributor of more than twenty-five articles, translations, and reviews to Asian studies and literature journals, including Chinese periodicals. Member of editorial board, *Journal of Asian Culture,* 1979-82, 1985-86.

WORK IN PROGRESS: A monograph, *Infinitely Malleable? Fiction and Essays From the Chinese Gulag.*

SIDELIGHTS: Philip F. Williams told *CA:* "Whatever influence a literary work may exert occurs one mind at a time. Even if the work is being recited aloud to a large audience, each member of the audience will interpret the work with a slightly different set of emphases. To say this is not the same thing as professing a free-wheeling cognitive relativism, because the literary work establishes interpretive constraints at the same time that it allows individual variations of interpretation. Yet this view of a literary work's impact on the reader disqualifies some of the more extravagant academic literary theorists from meriting more than a passing interest to serious scholars of literature, for these theorists' ejection of the human subject from the picture or ceding of decision-making power to a reified 'interpretive community' falsifies the experience of reading. While many literary theories aid plausible literary interpretation, many others are only theoretical in the sense that a conspiracy theory is theoretical. Laroche Foucauld would warn us against 'altogether believing' in any theory, and I would add

that broad reading in imaginative literature may well be the best antidote to the blandishments of academic interpretive wisdom."

*   *   *

WILLIAMS, (Robert Paul) Tad   1957-

PERSONAL: Born in 1957; married; wife's name, Nancy.

*ADDRESSES: Home—*California.

CAREER: Writer. Apple Computers, Knowledge Engineering Department, technical writer; host of *One Step Beyond* (talk show), on KFKC Radio. Author and co-producer of *Valleyvision* (a television series); musician; illustrator; teaches seminars.

AWARDS, HONORS: John W. Campbell Award nomination for Best Newcomer in Science Fiction and Fantasy, 1986, for *Tailchaser's Song.*

WRITINGS:

Tailchaser's Song, DAW, 1985.
The Dragonbone Chair: Book One of Memory, Sorrow, and Thorn, DAW, 1988.
Stone of Farewell: Book Two of Memory, Sorrow, and Thorn, DAW, 1990.
(With Nina Kiriki Hoffman) *Child of an Ancient City,* illustrated by Greg Hildebrandt, Atheneum, 1992.
To Green Angel Tower: Book Three of Memory, Sorrow, and Thorn, DAW, 1993.
Caliban's Hour, illustrated by the author, HarperPrism, 1994.

WORK IN PROGRESS: OTHERLAND, a science fiction novel.

SIDELIGHTS: Fantasy writer Tad Williams's first novel, *Tailchaser's Song,* tells the story of Fritti Tailchaser, a cat whose prospective mate, Hushpad, vanishes. When Tailchaser tries to locate her, he finds himself on a quest against an evil cat god. Along the way, he meets many cats, including the Queen of the entire species, and learns much of the lore of his kind. A *Publishers Weekly* critic lauded *Tailchaser's Song,* which was nominated for a John W. Campbell Award, as an "extravagantly detailed fantasy" that "should engage the fancy of cat lovers."

Williams followed *Tailchaser's Song* with the first book in his "Memory, Sorrow, and Thorn" trilogy, *The Dragonbone Chair.* The novel's protagonist, Simon, is a young scullion in the evil King Elias's castle who is taken under the wing of Morgenes, a doctor and magician. After Simon and Morgenes aide Elias's younger brother Josua, Simon sets off on a quest for three magic swords, one of which is discovered by the story's end. Simon's companions on the journey include a wolf named Qantaqa and a troll called Binabik; in the background are also the elfin Sithi, an ancient immortal race. Though a *Publishers Weekly* reviewer labeled the book "derivative," the critic did concede that the book is "richly detailed, sweeping" and "colorfully characterized."

In *Stone of Farewell,* Williams continues the story of Simon, who becomes the first mortal to enter the realm of the Sithi. He enlists their aid against Elias and the Storm King, Ineluki. *Library Journal* applauded the second book's "vivid, likable characters and exotic cultures"; *Publishers Weekly* called *Stone of Farewell* "panoramic, vigorous," and "often moving."

Williams brought the "Memory, Sorrow, and Thorn" trilogy to a conclusion with *To Green Angel Tower,* in which the enemies of Elias and Ineluki come together, along with all three swords needed to defeat them. The action is "suitably apocalyptic," according to *Publishers Weekly,* which also praised "the extraordinary tension built up in the book's closing pages."

Before the publication of *To Green Angel Tower,* Williams collaborated with Nina Kiriki Hoffman on *Child of an Ancient City.* In this work, which includes pictures by the illustrator Greg Hildebrandt, travelers pursued by a "vampyr" challenge the being to a story contest. If the travelers win, they may continue their journey unmolested, but if the vampyr wins he will devour them. Sally Estes, writing in *Booklist,* hailed *Child of an Ancient City* as "a haunting fantasy in which the ill-fated 'monster' is as sad to behold as Dr. Frankenstein's creation."

The novel *Caliban's Hour,* which appeared in 1994, is Williams's narrative extension of Shakespeare's play *The Tempest.* Twenty years after the events of the play, the slave Caliban arrives in Italy to confront Miranda, the daughter of Prospero. Having left the island on which she and her father were exiled to, Miranda is now a mature woman and Caliban intends to enact revenge for the bad treat-

ment he received from her and her father. "*The Tempest* has always been one of my favorite plays," Williams commented in *Locus,* noting that the ill effects of imperialism, which Shakespeare hinted at in his work, are currently responsible for global bloodshed. "What got me going on that in the first place was that in the play, Caliban says in effect, 'This was my island first. I was here first, and you came along and basically tricked me. . . . You treated me well for a while, and then you turned me into a servant,'" Williams explained in *Locus.* "Of course by the end of the play, not only have they turned him into a servant, they've chastised him for wanting his independence back again." According to a reviewer in *Publishers Weekly,* Williams's "prose is lucid and smooth" and "puts a very different spin on events."

BIOGRAPHICAL/CRITICAL SOURCES:

PERIODICALS

Booklist, December 1, 1992, p. 662.
Kirkus Reviews, September 15, 1985, p. 980.
Library Journal, June 15, 1990, p. 139.
Locus, January, 1995, pp. 4-5, 73.
Publishers Weekly, September 27, 1985, p. 84; August 19, 1988, p. 58; June 1, 1990, p. 51; January 11, 1993, p. 56; November 28, 1994.*

*   *   *

WILLUMSON, Glenn G(ardner)   1949-

PERSONAL: Born June 22, 1949, in Glendale, CA; son of Donald (an engineer) and Aileen (Gardner) Willumson; married Margaret Moore, June 20, 1970; children: Erik Ryan, Ashley Aileen. *Education:* St. Mary's College, Moraga, CA, B.A., 1971; University of California, Davis, M.A., 1984; University of California, Santa Barbara, Ph.D., 1988.

ADDRESSES: Office—Palmer Museum of Art, Pennsylvania State University, University Park, PA 16802.

CAREER: Mentor teacher for public high schools in Concord, CA, 1977-81; University of California, Davis, associate curator of Nelson Art Gallery, 1982-83; Getty Center for the History of Art and the Humanities, Santa Monica, CA, worked in collection development, 1988-92; Pennsylvania State University, University Park, curator of Palmer Museum of Art, 1992—, adjunct professor of art history, 1994—. University of California, Irvine, visiting professor, 1990. Cambridge University Press, member of editorial board for photography.

MEMBER: College Art Association, American Studies Association, Association of Historians of American Art, Society for Photographic Education (member of governing board for mid-Atlantic region).

AWARDS, HONORS: Grant from J. Paul Getty Trust, 1991.

WRITINGS:

W. Eugene Smith and the Photographic Essay, Cambridge University Press, 1992.
Collecting with a Passion, Palmer Museum of Art, Pennsylvania State University, 1993.

WORK IN PROGRESS: Research on the visual culture of the transcontinental railroad.

SIDELIGHTS: Glenn G. Willumson told *CA:* "I am a historian of American culture who is particularly interested in the ways in which objects provide insight into both the age of their creation and the time of our interpretation. I am a specialist in the history of photography, but my research interests are interdisciplinary and span a variety of media."

*   *   *

WILSON, David M(ackenzie)   1931-

PERSONAL: Born October 30, 1931, in Dacre Banks, Yorkshire, England; son of Joseph (a minister) and Nora (a lecturer; maiden name, Smith) Wilson; married Eva Sjoegren (an author and artist), 1955; children: Simon, Kate. *Education:* St. John's College, Cambridge, M.A., 1954; University of Lund, Sweden, graduate degree, 1954, Litt.D., 1976.

ADDRESSES: Home—The Lifeboat House, Castletown, Isle of Man IM9 14D, England.

CAREER: British Museum, London, England, assistant keeper, 1955-64, director, 1977-92; University of London, London, England, reader, 1964-71, professor of medieval archaeology, 1971-76; University College London, joint head of department of Scandinavian studies, 1973-76; Cambridge University, Cambridge, Slade Professor, 1985-86. Crabtree Orator, 1966; Ancient Monuments Board for England, member, 1976-84; Museum of London, governor, 1976-81; trustee of National Museums of Scotland, 1985-87, and National Museums of Merseyside, 1986—; member of Nottingham University Council, 1988-94, and Historic Buildings and Monuments Commission, 1990—. Fellow of Society of Antiquaries, 1959, and British Academy, 1981.

MEMBER: Royal Irish Academy, Royal Swedish Academy of Science, Royal Academy of Letters, History, and Antiquities (Sweden), Norwegian Academy of Science and Letters, German Archaeological Institute, Royal Gustav Aldof's Academy of Sweden, Royal Society of Letters of Lund, Vetenskapssocieteten (Sweden), Royal Society of Science and Letters (Gothenburg, Sweden), Royal Society of Science (Uppsala, Sweden), Royal Norwegian Society of Science and Letters, Polish Archaeological and Numismatic Society (honorary member), Society for Medieval Archaeology (secretary, 1957-77), British Archaeological Association (president, 1962-68), Viking Society (president, 1968-70).

AWARDS, HONORS: Order of Polar Star (Sweden), 1977; Felix Neuburgh Prize, Gothenburg University, 1978; knighted, 1984; honorary degrees include Fil.Dr. from University of Stockholm, Dr.Phil. from universities of Aarhus and Oslo, D.Litt. from universities of Liverpool, Birmingham, Nottingham, and Leicester, and L.L.D. from University of Pennsylvania.

WRITINGS:

Anglo-Saxon Ornamental Metalwork 700-1100 in the British Museum, British Museum, 1960.
The Anglo-Saxons, Thames & Hudson, 1960, 3rd edition, 1980.
(With Ole Klindt-Jensen) *Viking Art,* Allen & Unwin, 1966, 2nd edition, 1980.
(With G. Bersu) *Three Viking Graves in the Isle of Man,* Society for Medieval Archeology, 1969.
(With Peter Foote) *The Viking Achievement,* Sidgwick & Jackson, 1970, reprinted, St. Martin's, 1990.
(With A. Small and A. C. Thomas) *St. Ninian's Isle and Its Treasure,* Aberdeen University Press, 1973.
The Viking Age in the Isle of Man, Odeunse University Press, 1974.
(Editor) *The Archaeology of the Anglo-Saxons,* Methuen, 1976.
Civil and Military Engineering in Viking Age Scandinavia, National Maritime Museum, 1978.
(Editor) *The Northern World: The History and Heritage of Northern Europe,* Thames & Hudson, 1980.
The Vikings and Their Origins, Thames & Hudson, 1980.
Anglo-Saxon Art: From the Seventh Century to the Norman Conquest, Thames & Hudson, 1984.
The Forgotten Collector: Augustus Wollaston Franks of the British Museum, Thames & Hudson, 1984.
The Bayeux Tapestry, Knopf, 1985.

(Editor) *The Collections of the British Museum,* Cambridge University Press, 1989.

The British Museum: Purpose and Politics, British Museum, 1989.

(Editor with Else Roesdahl) *From Viking to Crusader: The Scandinavians and Europe, 800-1200,* Rizzoli, 1992.

Awful Ends, British Museum Press, 1992.

Showing the Flag, Museum and Galleries Commission, 1992.

WORK IN PROGRESS: A book (in Swedish) on Viking art in Sweden.

SIDELIGHTS: A former director of the British Museum with a background in archaeology, David M. Wilson has also distinguished himself as author and editor of books on Viking and Anglo-Saxon life, history, and art. Since the 1960s, Wilson has produced works such as *The Anglo-Saxons, Viking Art, The Bayeux Tapestry,* and *British Museum: Purpose and Politics.* Wilson received critical attention with *The Viking Achievement,* written with Peter Foote, and *The Vikings and Their Origins. The Viking Achievement* focuses on Scandinavian societies during the years 800 to 1200, describing daily life, art, social customs, trade, religion, law, and poetry, among other subjects. The book was praised by a *Times Literary Supplement* reviewer, who called it "a workmanlike and informative survey" that is "well illustrated."

The Vikings and Their Origins, like *The Viking Achievement,* surveys a period of Scandinavian history. Wilson organizes the book into four sections: "The Unveiling of Scandinavia," "The Era of the Great Migrations," "The Viking Attack," and "The Vikings at Home." The volume's brevity, critics noted, makes it a good choice for college libraries or for those who desire an introduction to the material. A *Times Literary Supplement* reviewer called *The Vikings and Their Origins* "a neatly sketched part-outline of a huge and complicated subject." Reviewing the book in 1980, *Times Literary Supplement* contributor Gwyn Jones noted that "the text provides a balanced introduction to its many-sided subject."

In 1984, Wilson issued *Anglo-Saxon Art: From the Seventh Century to the Norman Conquest,* which surveys media such as manuscript painting, metalwork, ivory carving, and stone sculpture. "Sir David intends the book to serve as an introduction, a synthesis of the present state of study, and this it does admirably," wrote George Zarnecki in the *Times Literary Supplement.* According to Zarnecki, *Anglo-Saxon Art* "is beautifully produced and generously illustrated and is meant for the layman and student alike." A *Washington Post Book World* contributor observed that Wilson brings to his book "a scholar's passion for his material, and a prose style of enviable grace and clarity."

Wilson is also author of *The Bayeux Tapestry,* which was published in 1985. The book describes the Bayeux Tapestry, which is a 230-foot-long strip of embroidered linen that, in pictures and words, narrates the story of the Norman conquest of England in 1066. Made in England in the eleventh century, the Tapestry is now housed in a museum in Bayeux, France. In addition to Wilson's text, the book contains 146 pages of color photographs. Writing in the *Times Literary Supplement,* George Zarnecki praised Wilson's "short, lively, and eminently sensible text," and commented that "this book can be warmly recommended for both its beauty and its sound scholarship." *New York Times Book Review* contributor D. J. R. Bruckner observed that Wilson's "appendixes on society, customs, and buildings of the era convey his enormous learning with engaging good humor." *The Bayeux Tapestry,* Bruckner concluded, "is a grand and exciting book."

Wilson's other works include *The Collections of the British Museum,* which he edited, and *British Museum: Purpose and Politics.* Both books were published in 1989, while Wilson served as director of the celebrated institution. *British Museum,* according to *Times Literary Supplement* reviewer Martin Kemp, is "skilfully and effectively" written.

BIOGRAPHICAL/CRITICAL SOURCES:

PERIODICALS

Contemporary Review, May, 1980, p. 280.

Los Angeles Times Book Review, December 8, 1985, p. 12.

New York Times Book Review, December 15, 1985, p. 22.

Spectator, March 8, 1980.

Times Literary Supplement, June 11, 1970, p. 632; February 8, 1980, p. 135; December 14, 1984, p. 1448; March 21, 1986, p. 301; December 29, 1989, p. 1435.

Washington Post Book World, December 2, 1984, p. 7; December 8, 1985, p. 12.

*   *   *

WILSON, Eva 1925-

PERSONAL: Born July 1, 1925, in Stockholm, Sweden; daughter of Gunnar (a writer) and Dichte (an author) Sjogren; married David Wilson (an archaeologist), April 23, 1955; children: one son, one daughter. *Education:* Four years at art school in Stockholm as a potter and sculptor.

ADDRESSES: Home—The Lifeboat House, Castletown, Isle of Man, Great Britain.

CAREER: Potter in Denmark, 1945-50; Lund University, illustrator and photographer in department of archaeology, 1950-55; freelance archaeological illustrator and writer, 1955—.

MEMBER: Association of Archaeological Illustrators and Surveyors.

AWARDS, HONORS: Fellow of the Society of Antiquaries, London, 1991.

WRITINGS:

"BRITISH MUSEUM PATTERN BOOK" SERIES

Early Medieval Designs, Dover Publications (New York), 1983.
North American Indian Designs, Dover Publications, 1984.
Ancient Egyptian Designs, Dover Publications, 1986.
Islamic Designs, Dover Publications, 1987.

OTHER

8,000 Years of Ornament: An Illustrated Handbook of Motifs, British Museum Publications (London, England), 1994, published in the United States as *Ornament—8,000 Years: An Illustrated Handbook of Motifs,* Harry N. Abrams (New York), 1994.

SIDELIGHTS: Eva Wilson told *CA:* "My books on patterns and ornament are the result of my experiences as an archaeological illustrator—and my close association with the British Museum during the years when my husband was its director. My approach to the study of patterns and motifs is based on a practical knowledge of human artistic expression in different media ranging from many cultures, gained during many years of patient work at the drawing board. The professional discipline of detailed accuracy, rather than interpretation and reconstruction, has allowed me to approach the study of the history and development of motifs from a rather different angle than the art historian. I sometimes feel that the drawings, which illustrate my books, are more eloquent in expressing what I want to say than the words I write."

WOJCIECHOWSKI, Susan (Susan Albertson)

PERSONAL: Born in Rochester, NY; daughter of Michael and Regina (Stenclik) Osinski; married Paul Wojciechowski, November 26, 1966; children: Joel, Christian, Mary. *Education:* Nazareth College, B.A.

ADDRESSES: Home—56 Reitz Pkwy., Pittsford, NY 14534.

CAREER: Elementary school teacher; free-lance writer, 1981—; school librarian, 1986—.

MEMBER: Society of Children's Book Writers and Illustrators, Rochester Area Children's Authors and Illustrators.

AWARDS, HONORS: And the Other, Gold was named one of the best books of the year, Child Study Association, and was chosen as a recommended Book for the Teen Age by the New York City library, both 1988; *Patty Dillman of Hot Dog Fame* was nominated for the Florida Sunshine State Young Readers' Award, 1992.

WRITINGS:

And the Other, Gold, Orchard Books, 1987.
Patty Dillman of Hot Dog Fame, Orchard Books, 1989.
Promises to Keep, Crown, 1991.
The Best Halloween of All (picture book), illustrated by Susan Meddaugh, Crown, 1992.

Contributor to periodicals and professional journals, including *Baby Talk, Times Union, National Catholic Education Association,* and *Upstate Magazine.* Has published writings in England under the name Susan Albertson.

WORK IN PROGRESS: Don't Call Me Beanhead and *The Christmas Miracle of Jonathan Toomey,* both to be published by Candlewick Press.

SIDELIGHTS: With her humorous, true-to-life portrayals of young adults, Susan Wojciechowski has been compared to such authors as Judy Blume and Paula Danziger. The best-known of all Wojciechowski's characters is thirteen-year-old Patty Dillman, a student at St. Ignatius Junior High. Wojciechowski's first three books follow Patty's adventures as she discovers boys, learns to value her friends, and becomes involved with social problems. Peer pressure is an issue of importance to Wojciechowski, who explained in a publicity brochure issued by her publisher: "When I was in school, fitting in, belonging, wearing the right clothes—these problems did not exist to the extent that they do today. Kids feel they have to grow up so fast today. I try to tell them that it's okay not to have a boyfriend at twelve or thirteen, that it's OK to be a kid."

In *And the Other, Gold* Patty is best friends with Tracy until Patty meets Tim, a school football star. Suddenly, the thrill of having a boyfriend overwhelms her, and she finds herself too busy to continue her friendship with Tracy. In the end Tracy realizes the truth of an old Girl Scout song, "Make new friends, but keep the old; one is silver and the other, gold." A reviewer for *Publishers Weekly* praised the book's "sweet blend of goofiness and grownup concerns," and Marcia Hupp in the *School Library Journal* called it "a likable and breezy novel."

The sequel *Patty Dillman of Hot Dog Fame* finds Patty taking ski lessons in order to be with Tim and continuing to engage in lighthearted mischief-making with Tracy. Patty's outlook on life changes drastically, however, when she goes to work in a soup kitchen for a school project. Patty isn't too thrilled about serving food to homeless people, but her apprehension is soon replaced by compassion as she begins to care about the people she serves. What's more, she meets a boy named Alex, who seems to share some of her social interests. A *Publishers Weekly* reviewer concluded that Patty has "honest concerns and humorous, realistic solutions" to her problems.

Wojciechowski commented: "Through my writing, I try to reach children in a special way, by portraying them as real people—warts and all—and showing them that they are more or less alike, despite their differences."

BIOGRAPHICAL/CRITICAL SOURCES:

PERIODICALS

Horn Book, March/April, 1988, p. 205.
Kirkus Reviews, October 1, 1987, p. 1469.
Publishers Weekly, November 13, 1987, pp. 71-72; May 19, 1989, p. 85; September 7, 1992, p. 59.
School Library Journal, November 1987, pp. 107-108; September, 1992, p. 214.

OTHER

Wojciechowski, Susan, publicity release, Crown/Random House, c. 1993.

WOLFF, Milton   1915-

PERSONAL: Born October 8, 1915, in Brooklyn, NY; son of John Max and Celia (a homemaker; maiden name, Meyer) Wolff; married second wife, Frieda (died, 1984); children: Susan Wolff Wallis, Peter. *Education:* Attended Whitman Art School, New Haven, CT, and Art Students League. *Politics:* "Independent left-activist." *Religion:* None.

ADDRESSES: Home—414 Kearney, No. 5, El Cerrito, CA 94530-3626.

CAREER: Writer. *Military service:* Served in the Spanish Civil War, 1937-38. U.S. Army, served during World War II in Burma and European theater; became major; received two Bronze Stars.

MEMBER: Veterans of the Abraham Lincoln Brigade and Associates.

WRITINGS:

Another Hill (novel), University of Illinois Press (Champaign, IL), 1994.

Author of *Thursday's Child,* Glen Press. Work represented in anthologies of short fiction. Contributor to periodicals.

WORK IN PROGRESS: A sequel to *Another Hill; Member of the Working Class,* the first volume of the trilogy "Sand Castles," in which *Another Hill* is the second volume.

SIDELIGHTS: Milton Wolff told *CA:* "I was born in New York in 1915. After high school, I spent ten months in Franklin Delano Roosevelt's Civilian Conservation Corps in 1933. Then, abandoning a job in New York's garment district, I volunteered for the International Brigades fighting in Spain in 1937. *Another Hill* is that story, more or less.

"After Poland was invaded by the Nazis, I was recruited for British intelligence work by General William (Wild Bill) Donovan. After Pearl Harbor, I joined the U.S. Army infantry serving in Burma. That was followed by service in Italy with the Office of Strategic Services (the subject of a book in progress).

"After the war I went to art school. I participated in the Civil Rights Congress, traveling the South to solicit support for framed blacks, Willie McGee, the Martinsville Seven, and others. I also worked briefly against the Smith Act, and appeared before the Subversive Activities Control Board and the House Un-American Activities Committee as a hostile witness.

"When I came out to California in 1968, retired at the age of fifty-three, and married my second wife Frieda, I thought I might as well try putting my military experiences down on paper. I always had this yen to write. Fortified by [Russian novelist] Tolstoy's wise observation that 'history would be an excellent thing if only it were true,' I decided to write a novel, something as nearly true as one could make it. After all, I reasoned, people, places, and events are all viewed subjectively, but there is an ineffable impression of a great event that remains immutable over time. The Spanish Civil War has been called the 'good fight,' and those who fought it were, for the most part, 'pure in heart.' Now, more than twenty years later, the combined forces of a movie option (since dropped) and an editor have helped me get the book published so I can get on with my other projects.

"In recent years I served as commander, later spokesperson, for the San Francisco Bay Area post of the Veterans of the Abraham Lincoln Brigade and Associates. I led many campaigns in that role, including humanitarian aid projects for Central American countries, such as centers for independent living in Managua and Havana. My latest action was joining the Travel Challenge to Cuba, and linking our post to the Lift the Embargo on Cuba movement."

*   *   *

WONG, Baoswan Dzung
See DZUNG WONG, Baoswan

*   *   *

WOOD, Nuria
See NOBISSO, Josephine

*   *   *

WOODHULL, Winifred   1950-

PERSONAL: Born August 18, 1950, in Washington, DC. *Education:* Pennsylvania State University, B.A.; University of Wisconsin—Madison, M.A., Ph.D., 1979.

ADDRESSES: Office—Department of Literature 0410, University of California, San Diego, La Jolla, CA 92093.

CAREER: University of Virginia, instructor, 1980-81; Dickinson College, instructor, 1981-86; University of Minnesota, instructor, 1986-87, 1988-89; Carleton College, instructor, 1987-88; University of California, San Diego, La Jolla, associate professor of French and cultural studies, 1989—.

WRITINGS:

Transfigurations of the Maghreb: Feminism, Decolonization, and Literatures, University of Minnesota Press (Minneapolis), 1993.

WORK IN PROGRESS: Research on gender, colonialism, and national identity in 1930s France.

*   *   *

WOODS, Paula L.   1953-

PERSONAL: Born June 22, 1953, in Los Angeles, CA; daughter of Isaac M. and Florence H. Woods; married Felix H. Liddell (a writer and consultant), 1986. *Education:* University of Southern California, B.A., 1973; University of California, Los Angeles, M.P.H., 1976.

ADDRESSES: Office—P.O. Box 241650, Los Angeles, CA 90024. *Agent*—Faith Childs, Faith Childs Literary Agency, 275 West 96th St., New York, NY 10025.

CAREER: Woods/Liddell Group (consulting firm), Los Angeles, CA, president, 1988—. Livre Noir (book packaging company), collector, 1994—; National Medical Enterprises, vice-president. Watts Health Foundation, member of board of directors, 1989-94.

AWARDS, HONORS: Mary McLeod Bethune Award from National Council of Negro Women.

WRITINGS:

(With husband, Felix H. Liddell) *I, Too, Sing America: The African American Book of Days,* Workman Publishing (New York, NY), 1992.
(Editor with Liddell) *I Hear a Symphony: African Americans Celebrate Love* (Literary Guild selection), Anchor Press (New York, NY), 1994.
Spooks, Spies, and Private Eyes: Black Mystery and Suspense Fiction, Doubleday (New York, NY), 1995.

SIDELIGHTS: Paula L. Woods told *CA:* "My goal is to bridge the gap between literature and art, on one hand, and black popular culture on the other, through the development of books that are accessible to the broadest spectrum of African American and general readers. I left corporate America six years ago, with the goal of doing what makes me happy. With the publications of our books and others that my husband/partner and I are planning, I've more than met that goal."

* * *

WOODWARD, C. Hendrika
See WOODWARD, Caroline (Hendrika)

* * *

WOODWARD, Caroline (Hendrika) 1952-
(C. Hendrika Woodward)

PERSONAL: Born March 14, 1952, in Fort St. John, British Columbia, Canada; daughter of David Morgan (a homesteader) and Dina (a homesteader; maiden name, Hoogenboom) Woodward; partner of Jeff George (a bookstore owner and writer), since July 1, 1986; children: Seamus Thomas. *Education:* University of British Columbia, B.A., 1974, Teacher's Certificate, 1976; David Thompson University Centre, Diploma, 1984. *Politics:* "Socialist with anarchist tendencies." *Religion:* "Non-practicing Druid."

ADDRESSES: Home—New Denver, British Columbia, Canada. *Office*—P.O. Box 249, New Denver, British Columbia, Canada V0G 1S0.

CAREER: Writer. Worked as greenhouse worker, file clerk, social worker, creative writing teacher, and in overseas youth exchange programs.

MEMBER: Federation of British Columbia Writers.

WRITINGS:

A Blue Fable, privately printed, 1981.
Disturbing the Peace, Polestar Press (Vancouver, British Columbia, Canada), 1990.
Alaska Highway Two-Step (novel), Polestar Press, 1993.

Playwright. Work represented in anthologies. Contributor to literary magazines. Some writings appear under the name C. Hendrika Woodward.

WORK IN PROGRESS: The So-So Workers, a collection of stories; *Publish and Perish,* a mystery novel.

SIDELIGHTS: Caroline Woodward told *CA:* "Writing is the only work I've ever done that allows me to synthesize my life experiences and those of others—my daydreams, my nightmares, and every piece of

grit that has ever stuck in my sensitive craw! Writing frees me to imagine times and people and places, to live again in a world over which part of me hovers, wings whirring, waiting to see what will happen next. I find this act of creating to be the most liberating, joyous, healing, and useful work I've ever done, and I am truly grateful to be doing it. Readers are a delightful bonus!"

* * *

WOOLLEY, Paul 1948-

PERSONAL: Born April 23, 1948, in St. Andrews, Scotland. *Education:* Cambridge University, M.A., Ph.D.; also attended Free University of Berlin. *Avocational interests:* Performing and listening to music, languages.

ADDRESSES: Home—Troejborguej 24 st tv, DK-8200 Aarhus N, Denmark. *Office*—Kemish Institut, University of Aarhus, DK-8000 Aarhus C, Denmark.

CAREER: Cambridge University, Cambridge, England, research fellow in chemistry and biophysics at Magdalen College; Max Planck Institut, Goettingen, Germany, began as research fellow in chemistry and biophysics, became scientific researcher and teacher; University of Aarhus, Aarhus, Denmark, scientific researcher and teacher. Freelance translator.

WRITINGS:

(Translator) *Steps Towards Life,* Oxford University Press, 1992.

Contributor of about seventy articles and reviews to scientific journals.

* * *

WORRELL, Rupert DeLisle 1945-

PERSONAL: Born January 12, 1945, in Barbados. *Education:* University of the West Indies, B.Sc., 1967; McGill University, Ph.D., 1975.

ADDRESSES: Home—Glenisla, Fisherpond, St. Joseph, Barbados.

CAREER: Central Bank of Barbados, director of research, 1973-84, director of research and information, 1985-89, deputy governor, 1990—. Consultant to Inter-American Development Bank, United Nations Economic and Social Council, and U.S. Agency for International Development.

MEMBER: International Economic Association, International Institute of Forecasters, International Institute of Public Finance, Barbados Economics Society (past president), American Economic Association, U.S. National Tax Association, Caribbean Studies Association, Western Economic Association.

AWARDS, HONORS: Fellow of U.S. Federal Reserve Board and the Federal Reserve Bank of St. Louis, MO, 1977, Woodrow Wilson School, Princeton University, 1980-81, and Economic Growth Center, Yale University, 1985; Fulbright fellow at Institute for International Economics, Washington, DC, 1989; guest scholar, Woodrow Wilson Center for International Scholars, Smithsonian Institution, 1993.

WRITINGS:

(Editor and contributor) *The Economy of Barbados, 1946-80,* Central Bank of Barbados, 1982.
Small Island Economies: Structure and Performance in the English-Speaking Caribbean Since 1970, Praeger, 1987.
(Editor with Compton Bourne) *Economic Adjustment Policies for Small Nations: Theory and Experience in the English-Speaking Caribbean,* Praeger, 1989.
(Editor with Bourne and Dinesh Dodhia) *Financing Development in the Commonwealth Caribbean,* Macmillan, 1991.
Economic Policies in Small Open Economies: Prospects for the Caribbean, Commonwealth Secretariat (London), 1992.
(Editor with Jorge Dominguez and Robert Pastor) *Democracy in the Caribbean: Political, Economic, and Social Perspectives,* Johns Hopkins University Press, 1993.

Contributor to books, including *The Premise and the Promise: Free Trade in the Americas,* Overseas Development Council (Washington, DC), 1992; *Tax Reform in the Caribbean,* edited by Karl Theodore, University of the West Indies, 1992; and *Open-Economy Macroeconomics,* edited by Helmut Frisch and Andreas Wortgotter, Macmillan, 1993. Contributor of more than thirty articles to economic and Caribbean studies journals. Past newsletter editor, Barbados Economics Society.

*   *   *

WORTH, Valerie
See BAHLKE, Valerie Worth

*   *   *

WRIGHT, David (John Murray) 1920-1994

OBITUARY NOTICE—See index for *CA* sketch: Born February 23, 1920, in Johannesburg, South Africa; died of cancer, August 28, 1994, in Waldron, England. Poet, journalist, translator, editor, and biographer. Wright was a South African-born English poet whose poetry collection inspired by the country of his birth, *To the Gods the Shades,* was highly praised for its lyrical expression of the attractive as well as the troubling aspects of South Africa. When he was seven years old Wright was rendered completely deaf by scarlet fever. He was sent to England when he was fourteen to attend the Northhampton School for the Deaf, and in his most popular book, *Deafness: A Personal Account,* he recalls his experiences as a deaf child. After graduating from Oxford University in 1942, Wright moved to London and joined the editorial staff of the *Sunday Times.* His first collection of poems was published in 1947. In addition to his work as a poet, Wright also produced a translation of *Beowulf* and a prose rendering of Chaucer's *Canterbury Tales,* coedited the celebrated literary and arts journal *X,* and published a biography of the South African poet Roy Campbell. Among Wright's later books are *Elegies* and *Poems and Versions,* which appeared in 1990 and 1991, respectively.

OBITUARIES AND OTHER SOURCES:

BOOKS

Contemporary Poets, St. Martin's, 1990.
Writers Directory: 1994-1996, St. James Press, 1994.

PERIODICALS

New York Times, September 5, 1994, p. 37.
Times (London), August 29, 1994, p. 15.
Washington Post, September 6, 1994, p. B4.

*   *   *

WYMAN, Bill 1936-

PERSONAL: Original name, William George Perks; born October 24, 1936, in London, England; son of William (a bricklayer) and Kathleen (Jeffrey) Perks; married Diane Maureen Cory, October 24, 1959 (divorced October 10, 1969); companion of Astrid Margareta Lundstrom, 1967-83; married Mandy Smith (a model), June 2, 1989 (divorced); children: (first marriage) Stephen Paul.

ADDRESSES: Ripple Records Ltd., c/o Panacea Entertainment Management, 2705 Glendower Ave., Los Angeles, CA 90027.

CAREER: Musician, singer, and songwriter. Guitar and bass player for the Cliftons pop music band in

London, England, 1961-62; bassist for the Rolling Stones (originally Rollin' Stones) rock 'n' roll band, 1962-93; songwriter, singer, and musician on solo pop music projects, 1974—. Founded Ripple Records, in 1981; opened restaurant, Sticky Fingers, in 1989. *Military service:* Royal Air Force, 1955-57; served in West Germany as an air craftsman.

WRITINGS:

(With Ray Coleman) *Stone Alone: The Story of a Rock 'n' Roll Band* (autobiography), Viking (New York), 1990.

Wyman's solo albums include *Monkey Grip,* 1974, *Stone Alone,* 1976, *Bill Wyman,* 1981, and *Willie and the Poor Boys,* 1985. He also composed the soundtrack for the film *Green Ice,* 1980.

SIDELIGHTS: In December of 1962, William ("Bill") George Perks was invited to play bass with a trio of struggling young rock musicians who called themselves the Rollin' Stones. The group's members—Brian Jones, Keith Richards, and Mick Jagger—had a vision of bringing American rhythm and blues to the London music scene. Before the end of January, 1963, Bill Perks had become Bill Wyman and the band had become the Rolling Stones. Before the end of the decade, the band had become what many consider the finest rock 'n' roll band in the world.

In *Stone Alone: The Story of a Rock 'n' Roll Band,* Wyman recounts his humble beginnings as the eldest of six children in a working-class family in London, telling of his attraction to the pop music of the late 1950s and his early efforts as a musician. Wyman explores the origins of the Rolling Stones, the group in which he and his "mates" eventually earned world-wide acclaim. He also illustrates how the Stones came to represent the great cultural revolution of the 1960s. "Wyman presents a lively and detailed reminiscence of the Stones' ascent," writes Janet Maslin in the *New York Times Book Review.* "He methodically catalogues the riots, the groupies, the souvenirs, the bad press . . . and the good." According to *Washington Post Book World* contributor Richard Harrington, "Wyman's documentary approach does work well in conveying the mob hysteria that swept the Stones ever further into the media spotlight, and often the dispatches seem to come right from the heart of a cultural war zone."

Wyman's history of the Rolling Stones also highlights the characters that made up the original band. "Wyman makes a concerted effort to downplay Jagger's and Richards's roles as architects of the group's success," comments David Sinclair in the *Times,* "and to elevate instead the contribution of the doomed Brian Jones, whom he describes as the true founder and guiding light of the original Rolling Stones." As for Wyman himself, writes Sinclair, he "emerges as a resilient personality, out of tune with his group's social instincts, yet committed to its music, and prepared, with reservations, to act as a stabilising influence at the foot of a fairly rigid hierarchy."

In *Stone Alone,* Wyman provides numerous facts, figures, dates, and details about the Rolling Stones, information sought out by the group's fans. Yet, in Harrington's opinion, "while *Stone Alone* has a wealth of detail, it has little depth. It reads like what it is: a combination of Wyman's meticulously kept diaries and clips of the day (evenly drawn in that pre-rock magazine era from disapproving adult newspapers and fawning teen journals)." Gene Santoro offers a slightly different perspective in his review in the *Nation.* He writes, "The myriad details . . . are what makes *Stone Alone* both slow going and hard to put down." He adds, "It does fill in nuances that could come only from an insider, even as distanced an insider as Wyman." And, as Sinclair comments, "It is the candid evocation of a life lived in fascinating times, the opening of a window on another world, that makes this a story worth reading."

BIOGRAPHICAL/CRITICAL SOURCES:

BOOKS

Wyman, Bill, and Ray Coleman, *Stone Alone: The Story of a Rock 'n' Roll Band,* Viking, 1990.

PERIODICALS

Nation, February 4, 1991, p. 139.
New York Times Book Review, November 18, 1990, p. 12.
Times (London), November 10, 1990.
Washington Post Book Review, November 18, 1990, p. 11.*

Y-Z

YASHIMA, Taro
See IWAMATSU, Jun Atsushi

* * *

YEGUL, Fikret K.   1942-

PERSONAL: Born October 27, 1942, in Terme, Turkey. *Education:* Middle East Technical University, B.Arch., 1964; Yale University, B.Arch., 1965; University of Pennsylvania, M.Arch., 1966; Harvard University, Ph.D., 1975.

ADDRESSES: Home—Santa Barbara, CA. *Office*—Department of the History of Art, University of California, Santa Barbara, CA 93106.

CAREER: University of California, Santa Barbara, professor of the history of architecture, 1976—. *Military service:* Turkish Air Force, 1968-70; became lieutenant.

MEMBER: American Institute of Archaeology, Society of Architectural Historians, College Art Association.

AWARDS, HONORS: Fulbright fellow, 1964-66; Hitchcock Award, Society of Architectural Historians, 1994, for *Baths and Bathing in Classical Antiquity.*

WRITINGS:

The Bath-Gymnasium Complex at Sardis, Harvard University Press, 1986.
Gentlemen of Instinct and Breeding, Oxford University Press, 1991.
Baths and Bathing in Classical Antiquity, MIT Press, 1992.

Contributor to learned journals.

WORK IN PROGRESS: Research on Roman and Greek architecture.

* * *

YEO, Wilma (Lethem)   1918-1994

OBITUARY NOTICE—See index for *CA* sketch: Born December 23, 1918 (one source cites 1917), in Republican City, NE; died July 27, 1994, in Kansas City, MO. Writer and teacher. Yeo was an author of books for children and novels for young adults. Her works include *Mrs. Neverbody's Recipes, Stranger at Winfield House,* and *Gypsy Summer.* Acknowledging the influence of Mary Roberts Rinehart's novel *Tish,* Yeo once remarked that "as I look back through the stories I have written, I see that almost every one of them has a 'kooky,' adventurous, little old lady much like Tish lurking about. I have called her Mrs. Neverbody, Mrs. Witherspoon, and many other names, but I am sure she is really Tish in disguise." Yeo attended Kansas City Junior College and the University of Kansas City (now University of Missouri at Kansas City). In 1960 she began working as a volunteer school librarian, and in 1966 became the fiction editor for *Fine Arts Discovery* magazine. Beginning in 1967 Yeo taught creative writing classes for adults. She later taught at the University of Missouri at Kansas City.

OBITUARIES AND OTHER SOURCES:

BOOKS

Who's Who of American Women, 8th edition, Marquis, 1974.

PERIODICALS

Society of Childrens' Book Writers and Illustrators Bulletin, October-November, 1994, p. 5.

* * *

YOCKEY, Hubert P(almer)   1916-

PERSONAL: Born April 15, 1916, in Alexandria, MN; son of Frederick Milton (a public school principal) and Mae (an English teacher; maiden name, Palmer) Yockey; married Mary Ann Leach (a realtor), June 9, 1946; children: Franklin Wayne, Cynthia Ann, Eric Milton (deceased). *Education:* University of California, Berkeley, A.B., 1938, Ph.D., 1942. *Politics:* Democrat. *Religion:* Protestant.

ADDRESSES: Home and office—1507 Balmoral Dr., Bel Air, MD 21014-5638.

CAREER: Affiliated with University of California Radiation Laboratory, Berkeley, CA, 1942-44, Tennessee Eastman Corporation, Oak Ridge, TN, 1944-46, North American Aviation, Inc., Downey, CA, 1946-52, and Convair, Fort Worth, TX, 1952-53; Oak Ridge National Laboratory, Oak Ridge, TN, assistant director of Health Physics Division, 1953-59; affiliated with Aerojet-General Nucleonics, San Ramon, CA, 1959-62; Hughes Research Laboratories, Malibu, CA, principal scientist, 1962-64; U.S. Army, Aberdeen Proving Ground, MD, supervisory nuclear engineer, GM-15, 1964-87; writer, 1987—. Boy Scouts of America, cubmaster, 1962-64, scoutmaster, 1965-68, explorer post advisor, 1968-75.

MEMBER: American Physical Society (fellow), American Nuclear Society, American Association for the Advancement of Science, Health Physics Society, Sierra Club, Phi Beta Kappa, Explorers Club of New York (fellow), Greater Washington Canoe Cruisers, Greater Baltimore Canoe Club (president, 1983-84).

WRITINGS:

(Editor with Robert P. Platzman and Henry Quastler, and contributor) *Symposium on Information Theory in Biology,* Pergamon Press (New York), 1958.
Information Theory and Molecular Biology, Cambridge University Press (United Kingdom), 1992.

Contributor to *The Biology of Aging,* American Institute of Biological Sciences Symposium No. 6, 1960; contributor of articles to *Explorers Journal, CANOE, Journal of Theoretical Biology, Radiation Research, Physical Review, Journal of Applied Sciences, Review of Scientific Instruments, Journal of Applied Physics,* and *Health Physics.*

WORK IN PROGRESS: The Life Message, "explains how information theory overturns all popularly held theories on the origin of life and shows why molecular biology must take the origin of life as one of its axioms;" *Tales of the Missinaibi,* "weaves together the story of [Yockey's] canoeing expeditions on the Missinaibi River with the history of the river;" and *What Does Not Kill Me (Makes Me Stronger),* "tells the history of Quebec's wild rivers from the Ice Age through their exploration by the Paleoninuit and Paleoindians, their exploitation for fur and trade by Europeans to the threat of their modern destruction by the dams of the James Bay Company;" research on the application of information theory and coding theory to molecular biology and the analysis of protein and DNA sequences in addition to the origin of life.

SIDELIGHTS: Hubert P. Yockey told *CA:* "My book *Information Theory and Molecular Biology* is the first book to demonstrate that information theory and coding theory are the mathematical foundation of molecular biology. I show why the standard model of the origin of life, as well as scenarios based on chance and self-organization, can never describe how non-living matter became living matter and must be discarded. As Niels Bohr said in 1933, the origin of life must be accepted as an axiom. I also explain how the application of information theory and coding theory to such problems as gene sequence analysis will produce accurate results much quicker than current ad hoc methods.

"My recreational time is spent hiking or paddling in the wilderness and these experiences provide the basis for my outdoors writing. I led the first descent of the Whale River (La Riviere de la Baleine), in the wilderness of northern Quebec, to Ungava Bay and up the Koksoak to the Inuit village of Kuujjuaq (see my article, 'First Down Quebec's Whale River,' *Explorers Journal,* vol. 62, 1984, pp. 98-105). The only previous exploration of this wilderness wild river was done by Hudson's Bay Company explorer Erland Elandson in 1838.

"In addition, I led the last descent of the Kaniapiscau River in northern Quebec as a wild river before it was dammed by the James Bay Society, a large electrical utility in Quebec. This expedition is described in my work in progress on the wild rivers of northern Quebec, *What Does Not Kill Me (Makes Me Stronger)."*

* * *

YOUNG, Collier
See Bloch, Robert (Albert)

* * *

YOUNG BEAR, Ray A.   1950-

PERSONAL: Born November 12, 1950, in Tama, IA; married; wife's name, Stella.

ADDRESSES: Home—1623 310th St., Tama, IA 52339.

CAREER: Cofounder with Stella Young Bear of the Black Eagle Child Dance Troupe of Arts Midwest; Eastern Washington University, Cheney, WA, visiting writer and lecturer, 1987; University of Iowa, Iowa City, instructor in Native American literature, 1989; Iowa State University, Ames, IA, visiting writer and lecturer, 1993; poet and author.

MEMBER: Iowa Arts Council, Artists in Schools Program.

AWARDS, HONORS: Received grants from the National Endowment for the Arts, 1976, for creative writing.

WRITINGS:

Waiting to Be Fed (poem), Graywolf Press (Port Townsend, WA), 1975.
Winter of the Salamander: The Keeper of Importance, Harper & Row (New York), 1980.
The Invisible Musician: Poems, Holy Cow! Press (Minneapolis), 1990.
Black Eagle Child: The Facepaint Narratives, foreword by Albert E. Stone, University of Iowa Press (Iowa City), 1992.

WORK IN PROGRESS: Remnants of the First Earth (fiction); *The Rock Island Hiking Club* (poetry); *The Red Earth Journal* (nonfiction).

SIDELIGHTS: Ray A. Young Bear has issued a number of acclaimed volumes of poetry and prose whose content is heavily influenced by his Native American Meskwaki (the "Red Earth People") ancestry and childhood in central Iowa. In his work Young Bear has explored the dilemmas inherent in the genre of contemporary Native American literature and criticized the usurpation of certain stylistic devices by non-Native American writers. His poems have also examined the fragmented state of the Meskwaki in the twentieth century and how important it is to maintain traditions for future generations, especially language. Young Bear is one among a handful of tribal-affiliated writers who speaks, writes, and thinks in his first language, Meskwaki.

Young Bear's first verse publication, *Waiting to Be Fed,* appeared in 1975. It was followed in 1980 by *Winter of the Salamander: The Keeper of Importance,* in which he writes on a diverse number of topics ranging from tribal culture of centuries past to the Vietnam War. In "grandmother," the volume's opening poem, Young Bear portrays his beloved relative, a woman who moves casually between two worlds, two places in time. The volume's title poem addresses certain plights encountered by the Meskwaki Nation, while others in the collection condemn modern environmental abuses ravaging both the land and the Native Americans who live close to it. The publication of *Winter of the Salamander* catapulted Young Bear to the forefront of an emerging Native American literary movement, and it soon appeared on required reading lists for university courses in the field. In a review for *World Literature Today,* Norma Wilson described Young Bear's second volume as "impressive, his imagery precise."

In *The Invisible Musician: Poems,* published in 1990, Young Bear often focuses on the contrast between the values of mainstream American society and those of the poet's Meskwaki tribe in Iowa. In one selection, "The King Cobra As Political Assassin," two snakes (through a dream) engage in a fatal duel, symbolizing a meeting between an assassin and a major political figure. Other pieces are meant to provoke thought on environmental and political issues. Young Bear also incorporates six songs in the Meskwaki language into the volume. Because of the numerous references to tribal customs and culture, as well as to more personal events in the author's life, *The Invisible Musician* includes a set of notes explaining many of the allusions. Marilyn Kallett of the *American Book Review* deemed Young Bear's effort "powerful . . . stamped with the integrity of his craftsmanship and with his people's struggle for existence." Robert F. Gish in the *Bloomsbury Review* was also appreciative of *The Invisible Musician,* noting that Young Bear "is generally acknowledged by poets, critics, and students of American Indian literature as the nation's foremost contemporary Native American poet."

Black Eagle Child: The Facepaint Narratives is the title of Young Bear's 1992 work that took over twenty years to complete, a combination of prose, poetry, and native language that forms a quasi-auto-biographical account of the author's life. The story is set in a Native American community that closely parallels the Meskwaki Settlement in Iowa where Young Bear was raised and presently resides. The narrative recounts the life of Edgar Bearchild, a boy coming of age in both his own extended family on the reservation and in the contemporary world outside. It begins as he and a friend, Ted Facepaint, undergo a rite of passage that involves ingesting an unappetizing hallucinogenic drug. Later, Ted, who represents the more traditional aspects of Native American culture, visits Edgar while they are away at college. Together they partake of a related but synthetic hallucinogenic drug popular among college students at the time, but this "trip" proves less satisfying. As *Black Eagle Child* progresses and Edgar moves farther away from tribal homeland expectations, it becomes apparent that Ted is the person that Edgar would have been had he remained on the inside and not undertaken his vocation as a writer. Becoming a poet, he realizes, has saved him from journeying down other paths, such as alcoholism, that are difficult to avoid. After a two-year academic stint, Edgar returns to his childhood home, as the author himself did, and lives there as a quasi-famous writer. Young Bear's tale incorporates numerous mystical elements that have counterparts in traditional Native American culture, including animalistic figures and an act of resurrection.

In an article for the journal *Poetry,* Bruce Murphy reflected that *"Black Eagle Child* is about modern life, but reminds one of the origins of poetry in naming and the preservation of collective memory." *Los Angeles Times Book Review* writer Douglas Glover asserted that the author's "narrative bears all the indications of a sophisticated and cunning literary intelligence. Young Bear has a novelist's eye for precise social and atmospheric detail." In a *New York Times Book Review* article reprinted in *Contemporary Literary Criticism,* James R. Kincaid maintained that the work "mixes voices, landscapes, and tones in such a way as to move us deeply without letting us settle into any sense of tragic participation." And Carl L. Bankston III in *Bloomsbury Review* stated that "this is a magnificent piece of literature. Its multileveled design and the richness of its language enable it to bear continual rereading, and each reading offers new rewards."

BIOGRAPHICAL/CRITICAL SOURCES:

BOOKS

Contemporary Literary Criticism, Volume 76, Gale, 1992.

PERIODICALS

American Book Review, January, 1982, p. 16; April, 1991, p. 10.
Bloomsbury Review, May/June, 1990, p. 9; September, 1992, p. 7.
Choice, June, 1986, p. 1509; October, 1992, p. 303.
Kliatt, September, 1990, p. 29.
Library Journal, September 15, 1980, p. 1865.
Los Angeles Times Book Review, April 12, 1992, p. 10.
Poetry, March, 1993, pp. 339-55.
World Literature Today, summer, 1981, p. 515.

—*Sketch by Carol Brennan*

* * *

YOUNT, Steven 1948-

PERSONAL: Born April 15, 1948; son of Wallace Evan (an owner of a grocery and sporting goods store) and Jennie (a newspaper editor; maiden name, Adams) Yount; married Susanne Proudlove (a computer systems analyst), May 24, 1985; children: James Adams. *Education:* Appalachian State University, B.A., 1973; University of Texas at Austin, M.A., 1981.

ADDRESSES: Home—7612 Mine Valley Rd., Raleigh, NC 27615. *Agent*—Peter Miller, Peter Miller Agency, Inc., 220 West 19th St., Suite 501, New York, NY 10011.

CAREER: Writer in Austin, TX, 1982-87, and Raleigh, NC, 1991—; University of Texas at Austin, film historian at Humanities Research Center, 1987-88; Lyndon B. Johnson Presidential Library, Austin, archivist, 1989-90. *Military service:* U.S. Air Force, radio intercept analyst, 1966-70; served in Okinawa and Vietnam.

WRITINGS:

Wandering Star (novel), Ballantine, 1994.
Blue Suede Shoes (novel), Ballantine, in press.

Author of the stage play *New Year's Eve—Cactus Bar—1966,* 1980, and the screenplays *Interesting Times,* 1981, *Tramp Star,* 1983, and *Blue Suede Shoes,* 1986.

SIDELIGHTS: Steven Yount told *CA:* "*Wandering Star* was originally a commissioned screenplay, but after reading several rewrites by 'top Hollywood screenwriters,' rewrites that transformed my work into a tiresome regurgitation of every cliche ever uttered on horseback during prime time, I decided to turn my screenplay into a novel. The experience has been so gratifying that I have foresworn screenplays and look forward to a life of historical research and narrative writing.

"*Blue Suede Shoes* is a novel set in 1956, recounting the subversive effects of the invasion of rock 'n' roll music on the population of a small southern town."

*   *   *

ZELIZER, Barbie 1954-

PERSONAL: Born January 1, 1954, in Columbus, OH; daughter of Cody and Dorothy (a homemaker) Zelizer; married Michael Glick (a director of an infectious disease clinic); children: Noa, Jonathan, Gideon. *Education:* Hebrew University of Jerusalem, B.A. (English literature) and B.A. (political science), both 1976, M.A. (summa cum laude), 1981; University of Pennsylvania, Ph.D., 1990.

ADDRESSES: Home—Bala Cynwyd, PA. *Office*—Department of Rhetoric and Communication, Weiss Hall, Temple University, Philadelphia, PA 19122.

CAREER: Jerusalem Post, Jerusalem, Israel, section editor, 1973-76; project assistant and materials coordinator for an educational program on the Holocaust sponsored by Van Leer Institute, Jerusalem, and Ben-Gurion University of the Negev, Beersheba, Israel, 1976-78; Israel Television, participant observer in news department, 1979-80; Hebrew University of Jerusalem, Jerusalem, Israel, course coordinator at Communications Institute, 1981-83; University of Pennsylvania, Philadelphia, instructor in communication and urban studies, 1988-90; Temple University, assistant professor of rhetoric and communication, 1990—. University of Delaware, instructor, 1988-89; Columbia University, research fellow at Freedom Forum Center for Media Studies, 1994-95; lecturer at educational institutions, including Ecoles des Hautes Etudes en Sciences Sociales, Vassar College, University of Maryland at College Park, Princeton University, and Haverford College. Reporter and feature writer for Jewish Telegraphic Agency, 1978-80, and Reuters News Agency, 1980-83; editor and translator for Israel Foreign Ministry, Ruder & Finn Public Relations, Israel Department of Immigrant Absorption, and Jewish Agency.

MEMBER: International Communication Association, Speech Communication Association, Association for Education in Journalism and Mass Communication, Union for Democratic Communications.

AWARDS, HONORS: Top Paper Award, Popular Communication Interest Group, International Communication Association, 1988; Nichols-Ehninger Award for Communication and Rhetorical Theory, Speech Communication Association, 1990; Guggenheim fellow, 1994-95.

WRITINGS:

(With Itzhak Roeh, Elihu Katz, and others) *Almost Midnight: Reforming the Late-Night News,* Sage Publications, 1980.
Covering the Body: The Kennedy Assassination, the Media, and the Shaping of Collective Memory, University of Chicago Press, 1992.

Work represented in books, including *American Heroes in a Media Age,* edited by Robert Cathcart and Susan Drucker, Hampton Press; *Bodylore,* edited by Katharine Young, University of Tennessee Press, 1993; and *Narrative and Social Control: Critical Perspectives,* edited by Dennis K. Mumby, Sage Publications, 1993. Reporter and features writer for *London Financial Times,* 1981-83, and *Israel Today,* 1982-83. Contributor of articles and reviews to communication journals and newspapers. Editor, *PopComm Newsletter,* 1993—; member of editorial board, *Critical Studies in Mass Communication,* 1991-93, and *Journal of Communication,* 1991—.

WORK IN PROGRESS: "Words against Images: Positioning Newswork in the Age of Photography," to be included in *Media Workers: Toward a History of the Rank and File,* edited by Hanno Hardt; "Every Once in a While: 'Schindler's List' and the Shaping of History," to be included in *Spielberg's Holocaust: Critical Perspectives on "Schindler's List,"* edited by Yosefa Loshitzky; "The Politics of 'Having Been There': World War II and the Eyewitness Report," to be included in *Perspectives on Political Reporting,* edited by Robert DeMaria and Michael Schudson.

*   *   *

ZENANI, Nongenile Masithathu 1905(?)-

PERSONAL: Born c. 1905.

ADDRESSES: Home—Transkei, South Africa.

CAREER: Medical doctor.

WRITINGS:

The World and the Word: Tales and Observations from the Xhosa Oral Tradition, University of Wisconsin Press (Madison, WI), 1992.

*   *   *

ZINSSER, Judith P.   1943-

PERSONAL: Born July 24, 1943, in New York, NY; daughter of Hans H. (a doctor) and Anne S. (a doctor; maiden name, Drinker) Zinsser; married John E. Lippmann (an advertising executive), December 31, 1969 (divorced, 1983); children: Sarah K. Lippmann. *Education:* Bryn Mawr College, B.A. (magna cum laude), 1964; Columbia University, M.A., 1969; Rutgers University, Ph.D., 1993.

ADDRESSES: Home—210 North College Ave., Oxford, OH 45056. *Office*—254 Upham Hall, Miami University, Oxford, OH 45056.

CAREER: Brearley School, New York City, history teacher, 1964-68; United Nations International School, New York City, humanities teacher, 1969-93; Rutgers University, New Brunswick, NJ, instructor in history, 1991-93; Miami University, Oxford, OH, assistant professor of history, 1993—. Bryn Mawr College, trustee, 1971-77; Columbia University Teacher's College, part-time instructor and advisor, 1989-90. Active in the International Schools Association and International Baccalaureate Office (IBO), Geneva, Switzerland; has worked as a delegate to United Nations conferences for the IBO and also as an assistant examiner, 1983-93. Served as an educational consultant to various organizations, including the World Law Fund, Center for Global Perspectives, and the National Women's History Project. Organizer of numerous panels and academic seminars on women's and world history.

MEMBER: World History Association (vice president and president-elect, 1992-98, member of executive council, 1991-94), American Historical Association (member, committee on women historians, 1980-82, James Harvey Robinson Prize committee, 1982-84, program committee, 1990), Berkshire Conference of Women Historians.

AWARDS, HONORS: Research grant from the American Association of University Women, 1992; graduate fellow, Rutgers Center for Historical Analysis, 1992-94; UNESCO representative to Ad Hoc Working Group on Indigenous Populations, 1993; Alumni

Teaching Scholar award, Miami University, 1994-95.

WRITINGS:

Understanding the Universal Declaration of Human Rights, International Schools Association (Geneva, Switzerland), 1978.
Approaches to the Comparative History of the Americas, International Baccalaureate Office (Geneva), 1982.
(With Bonnie S. Anderson) *A History of Their Own: Women in Europe from Prehistory to the Present,* two volumes, Harper (New York), 1988.
History and Feminism: A Glass Half Full (for the series "The Feminist Impact on the Arts and Sciences"), Twayne/Macmillan (New York), 1993.
A New Partnership: Indigenous Peoples and the United Nations, Unesco, 1994.

Associate editor, with Mort and Peter Bergman, of *The Chronological History of the Negro in America,* New American Library, 1969; contributor to numerous academic journals, including *History Teacher* and *Journal of World History;* member of editorial board of *Journal of World History,* 1989—.

A History of Their Own: Women in Europe from Prehistory to the Present has been translated into Spanish, German, Italian, and Chinese.

WORK IN PROGRESS: The Gendering of Intellectual Authority, a study of the history establishment in the United States during the first half of the twentieth century; research on demonologies of seventeenth-century France; research on Emilie du Chatelet, an eighteenth-century French philosopher.

SIDELIGHTS: Judith P. Zinsser contributed to the field of women's studies in 1988 with the publication of the two-volume *A History of Their Own: Women in Europe from Prehistory to the Present,* which she wrote with fellow historian Bonnie S. Anderson. *A History of Their Own* examines European history over the centuries from a female perspective. Together the authors explore how changing social, political, and economic dynamics affected the lives of everyday women. Zinsser and Anderson argue that gender—rather than national origin, economic, religious, or social status—was the uniting factor in shaping the lives of women in Europe through the ages.

The first volume of *A History of Their Own* chronicles women's lives from prehistoric Europe to the end of the Middle Ages. Zinsser and Anderson analyze the lives of their subjects by dividing them into four separate groups: women of the fields, churches, castles, and walled towns. The section on peasant women, whose lives, they argue, remained largely unchanged until the twentieth century, chronicles the backbreaking work that a farm woman endured for the better part of her life—she functioned as a field hand, animal caretaker, cook, weaver, and seamstress, in addition to the usual duties of wife and mother.

The segment in *A History of Their Own* on women in the church describes the changing status of women in Christianity over the centuries, and depicts the lives of nuns and abbesses who gained a measure of control over their lives and their communities. As a member of a religious community, a woman chose some harsh living conditions, but ones that often seemed preferable to a life on the outside. This section also examines the veneration of the Virgin Mary.

Next, Zinsser and Anderson examine the lives of women nobles who lived in the castles and manors of Europe, and reveal how little power they really held—despite popular opinion—compared to women of less affluent footing. Last, *A History of Their Own* reveals the varying layers of social and economic status for women who lived inside the great walled towns. The authors uncover the ways in which women gained a modicum of status as skilled craftspeople, but were later forced out of the professions when fortunes and political climates changed.

The second volume of *A History of Their Own* recounts the changes wrought by developments in European history during the periods of the Renaissance, Enlightenment, Industrial Revolution, and finally the modern age. Like the initial volume, this second part analyzes the everyday life for women in all walks of life, and weaves into the narrative little-known examples of women who managed to break from social constraints and forge a more radical identity for themselves. The work also pays heed to the numerous revolutionary political movements that swept through Europe in the nineteenth and early twentieth centuries, and explores women's contributions to, and exclusions from, them. This second volume concludes with an overview of the development of modern feminism; Zinsser and Anderson provide insight into the work of crusaders like the Pankhurst sisters of England and the implications of women entering the workforce in ever-increasing numbers.

Critical reaction to the two-volume *A History of Their Own* was laudatory if cautious. In a review of the first volume, G. W. Bowersock of the *New York Times Book Review* termed it "a noble undertaking," but opined that "it would be a pity if it became the standard work on the subject." Bowersock was critical of the authors' omission of more detailed information concerning women in ancient Greece and Rome, especially as the critic felt that these issues later made important contributions to the Middle Ages. Anne K. Mellor of the *Los Angeles Times Book Review* maintained Zinsser and Anderson treated the divergent regional cultures too generically in the first volume, but deemed it "a richly textured account of what women did in Europe before 1800, an account that leaves me overwhelmed with admiration for our foremothers' ability to survive." Reviewing the second volume for the *New York Times Book Review,* Lynn Hunt noted the repeated appearance in the text of misogyny as an integral force denigrating women's status throughout the centuries; the critic claimed that if conditions were really as abominable as the authors describe, then the development of feminism would have been nearly impossible. Yet Hunt noted that "the emphasis here on the detail of women's lives and on uncovering women's own words about their struggles and successes makes this an exciting and moving book," and concluded by praising *A History of Their Own*'s contribution to the field of historiography. "It may only be one possible history among many," Hunt remarked, "but in the form given it here, it is a compelling one."

BIOGRAPHICAL/CRITICAL SOURCES:

PERIODICALS

Los Angeles Times Book Review, May 1, 1988, p. 2.
New York Times Book Review, August 14, 1988, p. 15; December 18, 1988, p. 24.

—*Sketch by Carol Brennan*

ZUNIGA, Jose M.   1969-

PERSONAL: Born May 8, 1969, in Cincinnati, OH; son of Salvador Salazar (in U.S. Army) and Raquel (a clothing designer; maiden name, Vaca) Zuniga. *Education:* Attended Texas A & M University, University of Texas at Austin, San Antonio College, Department of Defense Information School, and U.S. Army Academy of Health Sciences. *Politics:* "Political difference is good for democracy. It's political indifference that's harmful." *Religion:* "Religion is a journey, not a destination." *Avocational interests:* Politics, history.

ADDRESSES: Home—San Francisco, CA. *Agent*—George M. Greenfield, Lecture Literary Management, Inc., 817 East 82nd St., New York, NY 10028.

CAREER: San Antonio Express-News, San Antonio, TX, general assignments reporter; *Dallas Latino Reporter,* Dallas, TX, staff writer; *Fourth Write,* San Antonio, editor; *Ranger,* San Antonio, managing editor; *San Francisco Frontiers,* San Francisco, CA, associate editor. Public speaker on the U.S. military and homosexuals; volunteer for organizations supporting gay and lesbian rights. *Military service:* U.S. Army, editor of *Cav Country* and *Star Presidian,* 1989-93; served in Southwest Asia and Kuwait; became sergeant; named Sixth U.S. Army Soldier of the Year, 1992, and U.S. Army Journalist of the Year, 1993; received five Commendation Medals and Combat Medical Badge.

MEMBER: National Lesbian and Gay Journalists Association, National Gay and Lesbian Task Force, Gay and Lesbian Alliance Against Defamation, Authors Guild, Veterans of Foreign Wars, American Legion.

AWARDS, HONORS: Member of Edith Fox King College Journalism Hall of Fame; Proud Gay American Award from Gay and Lesbian Alliance Against Defamation, 1993.

WRITINGS:

Soldier of the Year, Pocket Books (New York, NY), 1994.

Contributor to periodicals, including *Advocate.*

WORK IN PROGRESS: Johannes, a novella; *Tweaked,* nonfiction about the gay drug subculture in the 1990s.